Special Edition

USING

MICROSOFT®

OFFICE 97

PROFESSIONAL

Special Edition

USING MICROSOFT® OFFICE 97 PROFESSIONAL

Written by Rick Winter and Patty Winter

Lisa A. Bucki • Conrad Carlberg • Gordon Padwick
Patrice-Anne Rutledge • Paul Sanna • Jan Snyder
Nancy Stevenson • Rob Tidrow • Julie Vigil

Special Edition Using Microsoft Office 97 Professional

Library of Congress Catalog No.: 96-70764

ISBN: 0-7897-0896-5

99 98 97   6 5 4 3 2 1

Interpretation of the printing code: the rightmost double-digit number is the year of the book's printing; the rightmost single-digit number, the number of the book's printing. For example, a printing code of 97-1 shows that the first printing of the book occurred in 1997.

Credits

PRESIDENT
Roland Elgey

PUBLISHING DIRECTOR
David W. Solomon

TITLE MANAGER
Kathie-Jo Arnoff

EDITORIAL SERVICES DIRECTOR
Elizabeth Keaffaber

MANAGING EDITOR
Michael Cunningham

DIRECTOR OF MARKETING
Lynn E. Zingraf

ACQUISITIONS MANAGER
Elizabeth South

SENIOR PRODUCT DIRECTOR
Lisa D. Wagner

PRODUCT DIRECTOR
Robert Bogue

PRODUCTION EDITOR
Lori A. Lyons

EDITORS
Geneil Breeze
Lisa Gebken
Kate Givens
Christine Prakel
Brian Sweany
Nick Zafran

TECHNICAL EDITORS
Jeff Hall
Troy Holwerda
John W. Nelsen
Gabrielle Nemes
Tony Schafer
Timothy J. Schubach

TECHNICAL SPECIALIST
Nadeem Muhammed

MEDIA DEVELOPMENT SPECIALIST
David Garratt

ACQUISITIONS COORDINATOR
Tracy Williams

SOFTWARE RELATIONS COORDINATORS
Patty Brooks
Susan Gallagher

PRODUCT MARKETING MANAGER
Kris Ankney

STRATEGIC MARKETING MANAGER
Barry Pruett

ASSISTANT PRODUCT MARKETING MANAGERS
Karen Hagen
Christy Miller

EDITORIAL ASSISTANT
Ginny Stoller

BOOK DESIGNER
Ruth Harvey

COVER DESIGNER
Dan Armstrong

PRODUCTION TEAM
Debra Bolhuis
Marcia Brizendine
Kevin Cliburn
Wil Cruz
Trey Frank
Tammy Graham
Jason Hand
Daniel Harris
Oliver Jackson
Dan Julian
Bob LaRoche
Erich Richter
Donna Wright

INDEXER
Ginny Bess

Composed in *Century Old Style* and *Franklin Gothic* by Que Corporation.

To Jerry and Dick Winter (also known as Mom and Dad). Without you, we may have never learned the value of understanding, commitment, perseverance, and of course, spelling.

About the Authors

Patty Winter is a senior partner at PRW Computer Training and Services. She has worked with computers since 1982, training adults, testing programs, developing course material, and creating solutions for user productivity. She has trained over 3,000 adults. Her emphasis has been on peopleware. She is lead author of *Special Edition Using Microsoft Office 97 Professional* and *Special Edition Using Microsoft Office Professional for Windows 95*; author of *Excel 5 for Windows Essentials*; contributing author of *Special Edition Using Microsoft Office,* and coauthor of *Excel for Windows Sure Steps, Look Your Best with Excel,* and *Q&A QueCards*. In 1959, Patty acquired a preexisting brother Rick (see below), and has been directing him since.

Rick Winter is a senior partner at PRW Computer Training and Services. Rick is a Microsoft Certified Trainer and Certified Professional for Access and has trained over 3,000 adults on personal computers. He is lead author of *Special Edition Using Microsoft Office 97 Professional* and *Special Edition Using Microsoft Office Professional for Windows 95;* coauthor of Que's *Excel for Windows SureSteps, Look Your Best with Excel*, and *Q&A QueCards*. He has also contributed to over 20 books for Que. Rick is the revision script writer for *Video Professor Lotus 1-2-3 Version 2.2 and 3.0 Level I* and *Lotus 1-2-3 Version 2.2 and 3.0 Level II* and scriptwriter for *Video Professor Lotus 1-2-3 Version 2.2 and 3.0 Level III*. In 1994, Rick was president and is currently a director of Information Systems Trainers, a professional training organization based in Denver, Colorado. Rick has a B.A. from Colorado College and an M.A. from the University of Colorado at Denver.

PRW Computer Training and Services, based in Idaho Springs, Colorado, is a recognized leader in training, training materials, and consulting. This is the fourth *Special Edition Using Microsoft Office* book that Patty and Rick have worked on and third edition where they have been the lead authors. PRW won the prestigious Rocky Mountain Chapter Society for Technical Communication's Distinguished Award for their work on Que's *Excel for Windows SureSteps* in 1994. If your company needs training or programming on any of the Microsoft Office applications, you should contact PRW regarding on-site courses.

For information on course content, on-site corporate classes, or consulting, contact PRW at the following address:

PRW Computer Training and Services
491 Highway 103
Idaho Springs, CO 80452

(303) 567-4943 or (303) 567-2987 Voice (8-5 MST)
CompuServe: **71702,1462**
Internet: **71702.1462@compuserve.com**

Lisa Bucki has been involved in the computer book business for more than 5 years. In addition to *Que's Guide to WordPerfect Presentations 3.0 for Windows*, she wrote the *10 Minute Guide to Harvard Graphics*, the *10 Minute Guide to Harvard Graphics for Windows*, and the *One Minute Reference to Windows 3.1*. She coauthored Que's *The Big Basics Book of PCs* and *The Big Basics Book of Excel for Windows 95*. She has contributed chapters dealing with presentation graphics and multimedia for other books, as well as spearheading or developing more than 100 titles during her association with Macmillan.

Conrad Carlberg is president of Network Control Systems, Inc., a software development and consulting firm that specializes in the statistical forecasting of data network usage. He holds a Ph.D. in statistics from the University of Colorado, and is a three-time recipient of Microsoft Excel's Most Valuable Professional award.

Gordon Padwick is a senior programmer analyst who is responsible for developing integrated applications based on Microsoft's Office suite. He has worked with computers for more years than he cares to remember, and has experience as an engineer and a manager in many hardware and software design projects. He has worked with Windows and Windows applications since Microsoft introduced the first version of Windows in 1987.

Previously, Padwick was an independent consultant who specialized in Windows applications. He has authored and contributed to many books about word processing, spreadsheets, databases, graphics, desktop publishing, and presentation software; his most recent publication is Que's *Building Integrated Office Applications*. In addition, he has presented training classes, provided computer applications support, and developed custom database applications.

Padwick is a graduate of London University, and has completed postgraduate studies in computer science and communications. He currently lives in southern California.

Patrice-Anne Rutledge is a computer trainer and database developer and systems analyst who works for an international high-tech company in the San Francisco Bay area. She writes frequently on a variety of topics, including technology, business, and travel. She is a coauthor of *Using Paradox 5 for Windows* and *Using PerfectOffice*, both published by Que. Patrice discovered computers while pursuing her original career as a translator and was quickly hooked. She holds a degree from the University of California and has been using FoxPro for the past four years.

Paul Sanna has been using PCs for almost 10 years and Windows NT since its first Beta program. Paul is a Project Manager in the development department of Hyperion Software, Stamford, CT, where he works on the company's line of client/server financial accounting software. He has coauthored three books on Windows 95: *Understanding Windows 95*, *Inside Windows 95* (New Riders), and *The Windows Installation and Configuration Handbook* (Que). Paul has a degree in English from Boston University. He lives in Bethel, CT, with his wife Andrea, and his twin daughters, Rachel and Allison, and their new sister, Victoria. He can be reached on the Internet at **psanna@ix.netcom.com**.

Janice A. Snyder is an independent consultant, specializing in microcomputer desktop applications and Web page authoring. She has worked with 1-2-3 spreadsheets for 12 years, since the days of Release 1A. She is the revision author of Que's *Easy 1-2-3 Release 5 for Windows* and *1-2-3 Release 5 for Windows Quick Reference*; development editor for *Using 1-2-3 Release 5 for Windows, Special Edition* and *I Hate 1-2-3 for Windows*; and technical editor for Que Education and Training's *Lotus 1-2-3 SmartStart*. Snyder also has co-authored or edited many other books for Que Corporation, including books on MS Office, Word, Excel, PowerPoint, Access, dBASE, Quicken, Quickbooks, WinFax Pro, Word-Perfect, Quattro Pro, and Internet applications.

Nancy Stevenson is a freelance writer, teacher, and consultant. Her most recently completed book, *Using Word for Windows,* was published by Que in the spring of 1995. Ms. Stevenson teaches technical writing at Purdue University in Indianapolis. Prior to going freelance, she was a Publishing Manager at Que, and before that worked as a trainer, consultant, and product manager at Symantec Corporation in California.

Rob Tidrow has been using computers for the past six years and has used Windows for the past four years. Mr. Tidrow is a technical writer and recently was the Manager of Product Development for New Riders Publishing, a division of Macmillan Computer Publishing. Rob is coauthor of the best-selling *Windows for Non-Nerds*, and has coauthored several other books including *Inside the World Wide Web*, *New Riders' Official CompuServe Yellow Pages*, *Inside Microsoft Office Professional*, *Inside WordPerfect 6 for Windows*, *Riding the Internet Highway, Deluxe Edition*, and the *AutoCAD Student Workbook*. In the past, Mr. Tidrow created technical documentation and instructional programs for use in a variety of industrial settings. He has a degree in English from Indiana University. He resides in Indianapolis with his wife, Tammy, and two boys, Adam and Wesley. You can reach him on the Internet at **rtidrow@iquest.net**.

Julie Vigil lives in Denver, Colorado with her husband, Jeff, and her family of two ferrets and a dog. Julie has been working with networks for over 12 years and is a Certified NetWare Engineer. She has been teaching classroom and customized classes on Microsoft and Novell products for 10 years in the Rocky Mountain Region. She is currently the Senior Network Engineer for NetResults Network Solution Providers, Inc. She enjoys sewing, golfing, and woodworking and plans to pursue a professional golfing career in her next life.

We'd Like to Hear from You!

As part of our continuing effort to produce books of the highest possible quality, Que would like to hear your comments. To stay competitive, we *really* want you, as a computer book reader and user, to let us know what you like or dislike most about this book or other Que products.

You can mail comments, ideas, or suggestions for improving future editions to the address below, or send us a fax at (317) 581-4663. For the online inclined, Macmillan Computer Publishing has a forum on CompuServe (type **GO MACMILLAN** at any prompt) through which our staff and authors are available for questions and comments. The address of our Internet site, the Macmillan Information SuperLibrary is **http://www.mcp.com** (World Wide Web). Our Web site has received critical acclaim from many reviewers—be sure to check it out.

In addition to exploring our forums, please feel free to contact me personally to discuss your opinions of this book. My e-mail address is **lwagner@que.mcp.com**.

Thanks in advance—your comments will help us to continue publishing the best books available on computer topics in today's market.

Lisa D. Wagner
Senior Product Director
Que Corporation
201 W. 103rd Street
Indianapolis, Indiana 46290 USA

N O T E Although we cannot provide general technical support, we're happy to help you resolve problems you encounter related to our books, disks, or other products. If you need such assistance, please contact our Tech Support department at 317-581-3833.

To order other Que or Macmillan Computer Publishing books or products, please call our Customer Service department at 800-428-5331.

Contents at a Glance

Table of Contents

VI | Using Access

31 Creating a Database 703

VII | Integrating Microsoft Office Applications

37 Working with Wizards, Multiple Documents, and Cut, Copy, and Paste   849

38 Sharing Data Between Applications with Linking and Embedding   877

VIII | Internets, Intranets, and Workgroups

43 Hyperlinks Between Documents   1005

Introduction

by Rick Winter

So much to learn, so little time. Corporations continue doing more with less (meaning *you* have to do more in less time). Computer software packages continue to add more and more features and come out faster with new releases. The job you have today looks nothing like the one you had five years ago. The information age accelerates and you are expected to keep up.

Special Edition Using Microsoft Office 97 Professional packs as much information in as little space as possible. In the space that it takes to describe one application, this book packs in information about many applications. *Special Edition Using Microsoft Office 97 Professional* discusses Microsoft Word, Excel, PowerPoint, Access, Outlook, Binder, Bookshelf, the various applets such as Microsoft Graph, WordArt, ClipArt Gallery, Map, Organization Chart, and tells how to tie them together.

Special Edition Using Microsoft Office 97 Professional pools the talents of a diverse collection of software experts. Que chose the members of this team for their proven ability to write clear, instructional text as well as their expertise with Microsoft Office and the individual applications that make up the suite. The authors have corporate, nonprofit, small business, consulting, and training experience. This varied experience provides a well-rounded foundation to help answer your questions about Microsoft Office.

This collaborative approach gives you the best information about the individual suite applications as well as expert advice on how to get the most out of integrating them. ▪

Who Should Use This Book?

Special Edition Using Microsoft Office 97 Professional is the right choice for home-office workers, corporate personnel, workers in small business and nonprofits, students, instructors, consultants, computer support staff—anyone using any of the Office suite applications and wanting to get up to speed quickly on the Office applications.

This book is especially for you if:

- ▪ You know one application, such as Microsoft Word. Leverage your knowledge and spend a fraction of the time learning your second application.
- ▪ You don't know any of the applications in Microsoft Office. Start off on a fast pace by learning the common features of all the applications and then branch to the application that interests you the most.
- ▪ You know Microsoft Office 4 or Office 95 and want a quick reference of the new features available in all the applications of Office 97.
- ▪ You want to learn how to use the tremendous amount of tools presented through the Microsoft Office suite in whatever document you are creating.
- ▪ You are sharing data across a workgroup or the Internet. This book shows you how Office helps you and others collaborate effectively on a project.

This book assumes that you are familiar with Microsoft Windows 95 or Windows NT but not familiar with all the applications in the Office suite.

This book covers Microsoft Office 97 on both Windows 95 and Windows NT 3.51 or higher. If you have Microsoft Office 95, most features are the same; however, you may notice slight differences in screens and menu options, and you will not be able to use new items such as Outlook and Web features. Most screen shots were created with Windows 95 or Windows NT 4, so your screen may look slightly different if you use Windows NT 3.51. There are notes when the Office 95 and Office 97 differ significantly. For your information, other references and Microsoft sometimes refer to individual applications in Office 95 as version 7, (Word version 7, for example) and version 8 in Office 97 applications.

Special Edition Using Microsoft Office 97 Professional is the ideal companion volume *to Special Edition Using Microsoft Word 97, Special Edition Using Microsoft Excel 97, Special*

Edition Using Microsoft PowerPoint 97, Special Edition Using Microsoft Access 97, and *Special Edition Using Windows 95*—all from Que.

How This Book Is Organized

The authors designed *Special Edition Using Microsoft Office 97 Professional* to complement the documentation that comes with Microsoft Office. Less experienced users will find the step-by-step information in this book helpful; experienced users will appreciate the comprehensive coverage and expert advice. After you become proficient with one or more of the applications within Office, you can use this book as a desktop reference.

Special Edition Using Microsoft Office 97 Professional is divided into eight parts:

- Part I: Features You'll Only Need to Learn Once
- Part II: Using Word
- Part III: Using Excel
- Part IV: Using Multimedia in Microsoft Office
- Part V: Using PowerPoint
- Part VI: Using Access
- Part VII: Integrating Microsoft Office Applications
- Part VIII: Internets, Intranets, and Workgroups

Part I introduces you to Microsoft Office and creates the foundation you need for working with all the Office applications. In Chapters 1–3, you learn about the features shared by the Office applications that enable you to move from program to program without starting all over every time you begin learning a new application. Chapter 4 deals with managing files and work areas across applications. Chapter 5 shows you how to use Office Assistant and the online help feature that is similar for all the Office applications. Part I helps prepare you for Part VII, which deals with using the Office applications together to create a range of documents. If you are unfamiliar with Office and need to work with one or more of the applications, you should read Part I.

Parts II, III, V, and VI cover the essentials of Word 97, Excel 97, PowerPoint 97, and Access 97. Chapters 6–11 cover the essentials of Word, Chapters 12–18 cover the essentials of Excel, Chapters 25–30 cover the essentials of PowerPoint, and Chapters 31–36 cover the essentials of Access. If you know one of the Office applications and need to get up to speed quickly on one or more of the other suite applications, you should work through these focused presentations. Even if you haven't used any of the Office applications, you can get up to speed quickly by working through this part of the book.

Part IV covers the appealing opportunities multimedia presents for your Microsoft Office documents. In all the applications, you can visually enhance your documents and even include sound and motion pictures. Chapters 19 and 20 show you how to create charts from your data by using Microsoft Graph or Excel and place them in any Microsoft Office application. Chapter 21 shows you how to add pictures and ClipArt to your documents. Chapter 22 shows you how to add voice, sound, movie, and video clips to your documents. Chapter 23 shows you how to manipulate pictures by adding shapes, curves, and lines. Chapter 24 shows you how to use Microsoft Bookshelf, a complete reference library you can integrate with other Office 97 applications.

Part VII presents one of the strongest reasons for using Microsoft Office, dealing as it does with how these suite applications work in concert. Chapter 37 shows you how to cut, copy, and paste to bring information from various sources into a letter and memo. Chapter 38 allows you to link information between different applications, which means that when you change information in the source document, the target document will change. The target document in this chapter is a business report.

In Chapter 39, you learn how to create a presentation and switch between windows; look up information; cut, copy, and paste text and data; and link and embed information. You create an outline in Word, grab data and create charts from Excel, and pull all this together into a PowerPoint and Word presentation. Chapter 40 shows you how to use Microsoft Binder to combine files from different programs into a single file for editing, storage, and printing. Chapter 41 shows you how to customize the desktop, toolbars, and menus in the Office applications. In Chapter 42, you learn how to use Visual Basic for Applications (VBA) to automate tasks across applications in the suite.

Part VIII shows you how you use the Internet, an intranet, and a network to communicate effectively with people throughout your company, the nation, and the world. Chapter 43 shows how you can use hyperlinks to attach to another document or a document on the Internet. You learn how to transform your office documents to Web documents in Chapter 44. Chapter 45 is an introduction to Outlook, Microsoft's new e-mail, faxing, and scheduling application. Chapter 46 is for those of you who want to continue using Exchange and Schedule+ for your communications needs. Finally, Chapter 47 shows you how you can increase your workgroup's productivity by using Microsoft Office features.

In Chapters 18, 42, and 44 are special sections by expert users of Microsoft Office. These sections are indicated as "Techniques from the Pros" and provide you with lots of tips, tricks, traps, and advice on how to design and develop successful, professional Microsoft Office applications.

Conventions Used in This Book

Office enables you to use both the keyboard and the mouse to select menu and dialog items: you can press a letter or you can select an item by clicking it with the mouse. Underlined letters such as <u>F</u>ile, <u>O</u>pen identify letters you press or click to activate menus, choose commands in menus, and select options in dialog boxes.

This book assumes that your mouse is set for right-handed operation. You use the left mouse button for clicking on toolbar buttons, menus, and dialog box choices. You use the right mouse button for bringing up shortcut menus. Unless otherwise indicated, a mouse click means clicking the left mouse button. If you switch the mouse to left-handed operation through the Control Panel in Windows, you use the right button for choosing toolbars, menus, and dialog box choices and the left button for shortcut menus.

Your screen may appear slightly different from the examples in this book because of your installation and hardware setup. The screen items and functionality may change due to what applications and portions of applications are installed as well as your hardware and network options. You may see slight changes for menus, dialog box options, and toolbars. If you installed Microsoft Office through the default installation choices, the Microsoft Office Shortcut Bar will be placed in your Taskbar's Programs Startup location. This means that every time you turn on Windows, the Shortcut Bar will appear on the top of your screen (unless you customize the Shortcut Bar). Most of the figures in the book do not include the Shortcut Bar. You can turn off the Shortcut Bar temporarily by clicking the Control menu button and choosing Exit on the menu. Chapter 41 shows you how you can customize the Microsoft Office Shortcut Bar.

Names of dialog boxes (such as Open) and dialog box options (such as File <u>N</u>ame) have initial capital letters. Messages that appear on-screen display in a special font: `Document1`. New terms are introduced with *italic* type. Text that you type appears in **boldface**. Uppercase letters distinguish file and folder names.

The following example shows typical command sequences:

Choose <u>F</u>ile, <u>O</u>pen, or press Ctrl+O.

The programs included with Office provide toolbars for your convenience. By clicking a button in the toolbar, you can execute a command or access a dialog box. Chapters in this book often contain button icons in the margins, indicating which button you can click to perform a task.

So that you can quickly see the new items added since Microsoft Office 95, there is a new icon in the margin.

N O T E This paragraph format indicates additional information that may help you avoid problems, or that you should consider when you use the described features.

 T I P This paragraph format suggests easier or alternative methods of executing a procedure.

CAUTION

This paragraph format warns the reader of hazardous procedures (for example, activities that delete files).

TROUBLESHOOTING

Troubleshooting sections anticipate common problems...and then provide you with practical suggestions for solving those problems.

This book uses margin cross-references to help you access related information in other parts of the book.

▶ **See** "Section title," **p. xx**

Features You'll Only Need to Learn Once

CHAPTER 1

New Ways of Working

by Lisa A. Bucki and Rick Winter

Combining a vendor's software products to sell them as one unit is not new. Software bundles have been around for years. However, what is new is the full integration of these software products. Integration no longer means just switching between applications or one application that attempts but fails to do the work of four applications.

In what is termed the *office suite*, leading software vendors provide core office applications such as word processing, spreadsheet, database, and presentation graphics. The core products are the award-winning applications in their categories. Vendors add to this core some auxiliary applications such as electronic mail, graphing, personal information management, and organization charting, offering the entire suite of products for an extremely competitive purchase price. In fact, entire suites cost about as much as a word processor alone cost a few years ago.

What's included in Office 97

Several different applications work together to form the full Office 97 suite, and this section introduces them.

What's new with Office 97

Later chapters detail the new features in individual Office 97 applications, but this section describes the best of the best.

The design goals of Office 97

Learn more about how Office 97 improves ease-of-use, helping you get more done with fewer headaches.

How to determine which application to use

Look here for a review of which Office 97 application to use to handle common business computing tasks.

With Microsoft Office 97, Microsoft takes its suite vision to the next level. Improving on Office 95, the applications in Office 97 look and work even more alike—thus reducing the learning curve, improving user productivity, and helping the suite's tools work together more rapidly. Office 97 offers new features for sharing data and documents, better-than-ever communications tools, and Internet and intranet access and publishing capabilities. ■

What's Included in Office 97

As with previous versions of Office, you can choose which components to install on your system based on your needs and the amount of available hard disk space on your system. Microsoft Office 97 includes the following components, from which you can choose:

- ■ Microsoft Office 97 Shared Features, including the Microsoft Office Shortcut bar, Office Assistant, Office Binder, and more
- ■ Microsoft Word 97
- ■ Microsoft Excel 97
- ■ Microsoft PowerPoint 97
- ■ Microsoft Access 97
- ■ Microsoft Outlook 97
- ■ Microsoft Bookshelf Basics

What's New with Office 97

Microsoft Outlook is a major new application bundled with Office 97. Additionally, you get a number of new features in all the products, as well as in the interoperability between products.

Familiar Windows 95 Features

The new version of Office runs under Windows 95 or Windows NT and takes advantage of its features that make your computer easier to use.

The Windows taskbar (see Figure 1.1) allows you to start applications as well as open minimized applications with a single click. The close button (x) in the upper-right corner of a window makes closing documents and applications much easier. When you minimize an application by using the Minimize (underscore) button, the application appears minimized as a rectangle on the taskbar. You also can add shortcuts to launch Office 97 applications to the Windows 95 desktop.

FIG. 1.1

Click once on a minimized application to open the application's window.

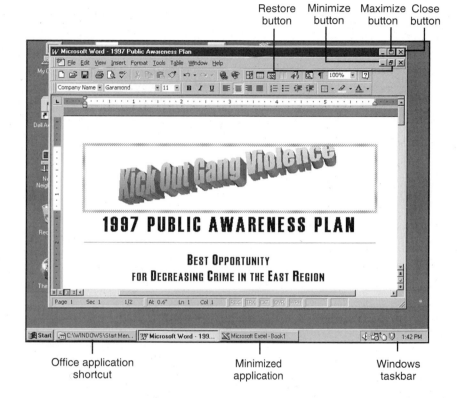

After you've installed Office 97, the Windows 95 or Windows NT Start menu will offer the New Office Document and Open Office Document commands so that you can easily start and open documents from all the Office applications.

Windows 95 and Windows NT allow you to use file names of up to 255 characters including spaces. This greatly increases flexibility, finding, and understanding of what you have saved. Windows 95 also has added a number of file properties that Office 97 expands. Now you can quickly look up statistics on your document such as the creation date and number of words, plus you can save author and document information with your file. Enhanced search capabilities are built in directly to standard file dialog boxes to help you find your file based on the contents, time, or other properties of your file (see Figure 1.2).

FIG. 1.2

Long file names and file dialog box features help you remember and find your documents.

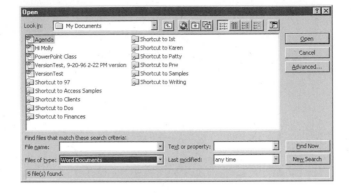

In addition, Windows 95 ships with Microsoft Exchange, a communications program that enables your system to connect with other users via e-mail (which you also can accomplish using Office's new Outlook 97 application, described next), fax, and more. Additionally, Windows 95 offers Dial-Up Networking, which you can use to connect directly to an Internet service provider via modem if your computer isn't already connected to the Internet via a network. Office and its applications exploit these Windows communications capabilities, providing you many opportunities to send your Word document, Excel spreadsheet, PowerPoint presentation, or Access report to people inside and outside your office (see Figure 1.3).

FIG. 1.3

Send your files as e-mail message attachments from within Office applications when Microsoft Exchange, a Windows 95 feature, is installed.

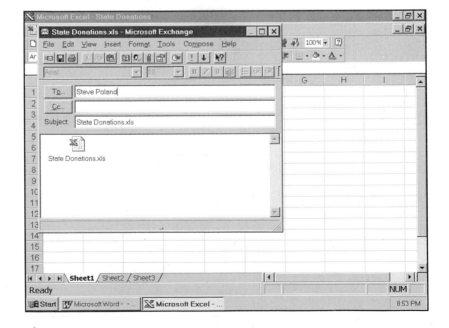

Introducing Outlook: A New Office Application

Office 95 offered Schedule+, an application that allowed you to create appointments, write to-do lists, and set meetings with colleagues. In place of Schedule+, Microsoft Office 97 offers Outlook 97, a new application that provides a unified e-mail address list (which can include fax numbers for quick faxing), message management, calendar planning and meeting scheduling, to-do list management (see Figure 1.4), journal and note taking, and more. Chapter 45, "Using Outlook Desktop Information Manager," covers how to use this new personal management tool.

▶ **See** "Getting Started with Outlook," **p. 1079**

FIG. 1.4
Use Outlook 97 to make mail messages, assignments, appointments, and tasks easier to manage.

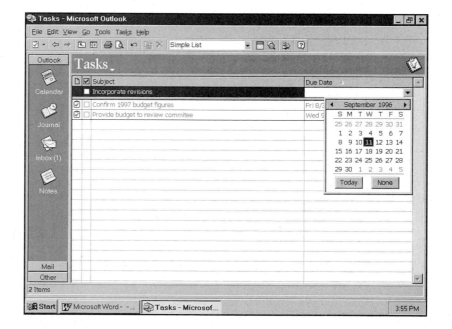

Improvements in All Office Products

In Office 97, there are improved consistencies between applications as well as new features. One of the most obvious changes is to the look and feel of toolbars and menus. The menu bar and toolbars have a more "flat" appearance, so you see a raised 3-D highlight when you point to a command or button. When a menu command has a corresponding toolbar button, that button appears with the command name on the menu, for consistency. You can even customize shortcut menus (which pop up when you right-click an item on-screen) in this version of Office. The following table lists additional major changes, new features, and what you need to do to get started with the feature.

Table 1.1   Features New or Changed in Office 97

Feature	Get Started	
The Web toolbar enables you to access the Internet or an intranet from within an Office 97 application, via the Web toolbar. The Web features work in concert with a Web browser like Internet Explorer 3.0, which also must be installed on your system.	View, Toolbars, Web, p. 1029	
Hyperlinking enables you to insert a highlighted link point to another document on your hard disk or a network drive, or to a URL address for an Internet or intranet Web page. Clicking the link takes you to the document referenced by the link.	Insert, Hyperlink or click the Insert Hyperlink button, p. 1007, 1040	
With its Web publishing capabilities, you can publish your Office documents as attractively formatted Internet or intranet Web pages.	File, Save As HTML (in most applications), p. 1036, 1075; also choose to use a Web template when starting a new document, p. 256	
Microsoft on the Web enables you to jump to several specific links on Microsoft's Web site.	Help, Microsoft on the Web, p. 136	
The *Office Assistant* replaces the Answer Wizard, and appears in a small window on-screen (see Figure 1.5) to give you advice specific to the task you're currently performing.	Help, Microsoft (application) Help, or click the Office Assistant button, p. 129	
The Office-shared drawing feature called *Office Art* replaces the separate drawing tools in Word, Excel, and PowerPoint, offering more consistency and enhanced capabilities, such as gradations in lines and fills, and a selection of fill patterns and backgrounds. Office Art includes Word Art, 3-D effects, AutoShapes, and more.	View, Toolbars, Drawing, or click the Drawing button, p. 558 also, Insert, Picture p. 631	

Feature	Get Started
ClipArt Collection online allows you to get additional clip art from Microsoft's web site.	Insert, Picture, Connect to Web for Additional Clips Button, p. 528
Visual Basic for Applications has been updated, and is now available in Word (replaces WordBasic), Excel, PowerPoint, and Access. This improvement makes it even easier to create custom business "applications."	Tools, Macro, Visual Basic Editor (except in Access), p. 961
Office Binder 97 (Figure 1.6) offers new features, including previewing Binder file printouts, adding headers and footers, creating blank sections based on document templates, and more.	Start, Programs, Microsoft Binder, p. 921
Comments enable each editor to add special notes within a document.	Insert, Comments p. 272, 449-450, 693
Multiple level undo has now expanded to include Excel and PowerPoint (in addition to Word).	Edit, Undo, p. 74
With *Track Changes*, edits made by you and other users will be highlighted, and you can later review and accept or remove changes. This resembles the revision marking feature in the previous version of Word.	Tools, Track Changes (in Word and Excel) p. 629, 1166
IntelliMouse is a new type of pointing device from Microsoft that offers traditional scrolling as well as panning, AutoScrolling, zooming, and DataZoom (automatic outlining).	When IntelliMouse is installed, Office applications automatically support its various features where they apply, p. 303

ON THE WEB

Microsoft devotes part of its Web site to Office, offering tips, tricks, and more:

http://www.microsoft.com/msoffice/

FIG. 1.5

The Office Assistant not only lets you select help about specific topics, it also offers tips and enables you to type questions the way you want to ask them.

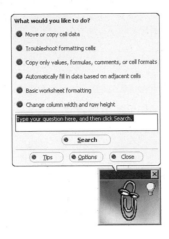

FIG. 1.6

The Office Binder 97 now lets you apply a header and footer to all or selected sections in the Binder file.

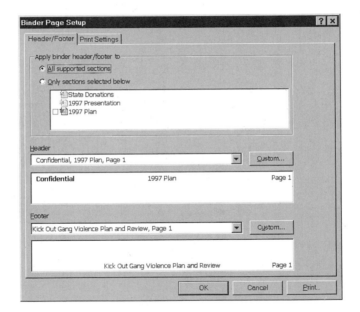

Individual Software Improvements

In addition to the general improvements throughout Office 97, each of the products in the suite has enhancements.

 TIP For an online summary of new features in each individual application, open the application and the Office Assistant and type **What's New**. When you initially see the new Office Assistant help feature, it may display a topic called "Key information for upgraders and new users." Click that topic for a preview of new features. (For more about the Office Assistant, see Chapter 5, "Using Help and Office Assistant.")

Microsoft Word 97   Microsoft Word 97 offers numerous small and large improvements over its predecessor. For example, you can add a background or a watermark (a graphic that repeats on every page) to a Word document, summarize the document, and use the Tables and Borders toolbar to have more control over table and border formatting. The following table lists some of the major enhancements to Word 97 and notes how to get started with each feature.

Table 1.2   Features New or Changed in Word 97

Feature	Get Started
AutoSummarize generates an Abstract or executive briefing for a file, and places it in the current document or a new one. You can control the length of the summary compared to the full document length.	Tools, AutoSummarize, p. 250
The *Select Browse Object* button on the vertical scroll bar gives you a fast method for navigating to key areas in a document.	Click Select Browse Object button, p. 76
Draw a table with the mouse.	Choose Tables and Borders button and drag mouse to draw table. Use Tables and Borders toolbar to format table, p. 281
Add a border to a page.	Format, Borders and Shading, Page Border tab, p. 289
The *Letter Wizard* (Figure 1.7) helps you format and enter key information for your letters, to ensure they always look consistent and professional and include appropriate details like enclosure notes.	Tools, Letter Wizard p. 165, 850

continues

Table 1.2 Continued

Feature	Get Started	
Display the *Document Map* in a pane at the left side of the screen to see an overview of the structure (headings) of your document.	View, Document Map, or click Document Map icon, p. 153	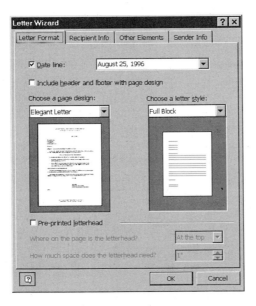
AutoComplete is an improved AutoText capability that allows you to type common entries more quickly.	Type start of entry and press Enter when screen tip displays your entry, p. 150	
Automatic Grammar Checking marks incorrect grammar with a green wavy line as you type.	Tools, Options, Spelling & Grammar tab, Check Grammar As You Type, p. 197	
Save multiple versions of the document in the same file.	File, Versions, p. 277	

FIG. 1.7
Use the Letter Wizard to create great-looking letters in a snap.

Microsoft Excel 97   As for Word 97, Excel 97 offers numerous enhancements to the features offered in its previous version. The following table covers some of the more significant enhancements to Excel 97 and how to get started with each feature.

Table 1.3   Features New or Changed in Excel 97

Feature	Get Started
Conditional Formatting helps you make your workbooks more dynamic and informative. You can specify that a cell will display one type of formatting based on a formula result that doesn't meet your criteria, and another type of formatting when the formula result does meet your criteria.	Format, Conditional Formatting, p. 371
The new *Share Workbook* feature lets multiple users open a workbook on a network and edit the document simultaneously.	Tools, Share Workbook, p. 1165
The worksheet has expanded to include 65,536 rows and you can type up to 32,000 characters in a cell.	In an empty worksheet, press End then Down Arrow to see size of worksheet, p. 300
Natural language formulas allow you to create formulas that use row and column headers instead of range references.	Type formulas with headers such as **=Sum(January)** or **=Average(Personnel)**, p. 374
Use the *Formula Palette* to enter worksheet functions and the new Range finder buttons to select ranges.	Click the Paste Function button and choose function from the Paste Function dialog box and fill in the Formula Palette to complete the function, p. 394 *f*ₓ
Data Validation lets you provide clues to help other users make the correct value entries. You can set criteria to use to double-check cell entries, display a message when a cell is selected (Figure 1.8), and specify an error message to display when an entry doesn't match the criteria.	Data, Validation, p. 418

continues

Table 1.3   Continued

Feature	Get Started	
Circle invalid data allows you to see at a glance all entries that don't meet your validation rules.	Tools, Auditing, Show Auditing Toolbar and click on Circle Invalid Data button, p. 383, 385	
The enhanced *Get External Data* features enable you to both query Access and other databases on your system or a network, and to query an Internet or intranet resource.	Data, Get External Data, Create New Query, p. 431	
Page Break Preview allows you to move page breaks by dragging them.	View, Page Break Preview, p. 401	
Rotate text in cells.	Format, Cells, Alignment tab, p. 357	
Indent text in cells.	Click on Increase button on Formatting toolbar, p. 354	
Chart enhancements include up to 32,000 points per series, chart tips, data tables in charts, more formatting options for charts, and new chart types including bubble, pie of pie, bar of pie, pyramid, cone, and cylinder.	Choose Chart Wizard button and follow Chart Wizard, p. 492	
You can create an Excel form to compile data from Web users.	Tools, Wizard, Web Form, p. 1051	

Microsoft PowerPoint 97   PowerPoint 97 has been revised with two goals in mind: making its features more easy and intuitive to use in creating presentations, and better integrating it with the other Office applications. In addition to the extensive fine-tuning you'll see in PowerPoint 97, look for the major enhancements outlined in the following table.

FIG. 1.8
You can now have Excel validate cell entries to ensure another user that your worksheet doesn't make a mistake.

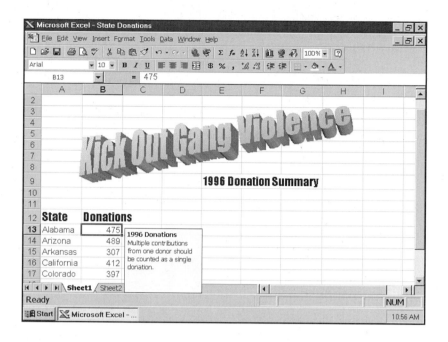

Table 1.4   Features New or Changed in PowerPoint 97

Feature	Get Started
The *Common Tasks* toolbar appears automatically to help you access frequently used features more readily.	View, Toolbars, Common Tasks
If you create a slide and want to insert slides after it to elaborate on its key points, use the *Expand Slide* feature.	Tools, Expand Slide, p. 629
If you want to include a "voice over" explanation for your slides when the presentation runs, record your own *Narration* automatically, slide by slide.	Slide Show, Record Narration, p. 697
You can now play CD Audio tracks during your presentation.	Insert, Movies and Sounds, Play CD Audio Track, p. 698

continues

Table 1.4   Continued

Feature	Get Started
To add more ways to navigate through your on-screen slide slow, such as jumping to the first or last slide, add *Action Buttons* (see Figure 1.9) to any slide you want.	Slide Show, Action Buttons, p. 699
Create a *Custom Show* to print a particular combination of slides.	Slide Show, Custom Shows, p. 684
PowerPoint Central connects you with resources such as templates, sounds, and animation clips on the CD-ROM ValuPack and sites on the Internet.	Tools, PowerPoint Central, p. 593
Slide Finder allows you to preview and insert slides from another presentation.	Insert, Slides from Files, p. 613
You can now type *Speakers Notes* in Notes Pages View.	View, Speaker Notes, p. 614, 620
Animated charts and enhanced custom animation allow you to create moving effects on your presentation.	Slide Show, Custom Animation, p. 694
Control a presentation from one computer and show it on another.	Slide Show, View on Two Screens, p. 689
Run a presentation from a kiosk.	Slide Show, Set Up Show, Browsed at a Kiosk (Full Screen), p. 688

Microsoft Access 97   Microsoft Access 97 also sports numerous enhancements that will be highlighted in later chapters of this book. The following table describes the most major changes to Access 97 and clarifies how to get started with each feature.

FIG. 1.9
Easily add buttons to presentation slides to make the presentation easier to navigate.

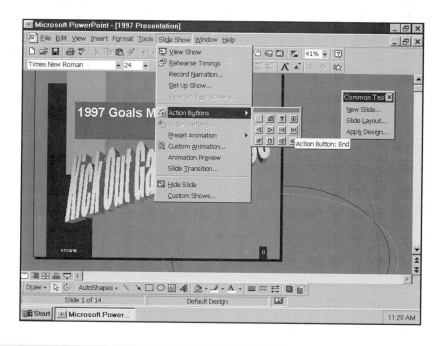

Table 1.5   Features New or Changed in Access 97

Feature	Get Started
The *Publish to the Web Wizard* converts your Access information to a dynamic Internet or intranet site including query pages, a home page unifying the other pages, and more. You can apply a consistent HTML template to all the pages, and automatically post the pages to your Web server.	File, Save As HTML, p.1056
A new *Hyperlink data type* is supported to allow insertion of links to other objects, documents or Internet sites.	In table design, choose Hyperlink data type. To add hyperlink, choose Insert, Hyperlink, p. 764
Year 2000 support improved.	Type 1/1/00 to 12/31/29 for dates in the 21st century, p. 761
Filter list with typed entry.	Right-click on cell in column and enter value in Filter For, p. 777

continues

Table 1.5   Continued

Feature	Get Started	
Improved design features include the ability to create forms with multiple tabs.	Click the Tab Control button on the Toolbox toolbar, p. 810	
Lightweight Forms and Reports load without loading Visual Basic for Applications, leading to faster performance.	By default, all forms and reports are lightweight until you add code or controls.	
Use *ActiveX Controls* to enhance your forms and reports, and help them offer more interactivity than ever.	Tools, ActiveX Controls p. 811	
Run database utilities (compact and repair) on an open database.	Tools, Database Utilities, Compact Database or Repair Database, p. 715	
User-Level Security Wizard creates a secured copy of the database.	Tools, Security, User-Level Security Wizard, p. 1173	

Design Goals of Microsoft Office

The goal of Microsoft Office 97 is to provide users with the following:

- A common user interface (standardized operation of menus, toolbars, and dialog boxes)
- Quick access from one office suite application to another
- Data shared across applications
- Resources shared across applications
- Information shared across workgroups and Web sites
- A common task automation language

Microsoft strives to meet these goals. Many of the core applications continue to undergo revisions to meet these goals. The resulting menu or toolbar changes may slow you down at first, but in the long run you'll be pleased with how the common user interface across applications increases efficient and effective use of all applications.

Providing a Common User Interface

A clear benefit of a common user interface across applications is that by learning one application in the suite, you know the operational basics of the other applications. Figure 1.10 illustrates the similarity between Excel and Word menu bars and toolbars. Notice that Word has a Table menu option, but Excel has a Data menu option. Although the goal is to provide one common user interface, some degree of uniqueness will remain in each application. However, key common features such as the File, Open and Edit, Find commands can be found in exactly the same place in each application.

▶ **See** "Using Online Help," **p. 133**

▶ **See** "Using Wizards," **p. 141**

▶ **See** "Displaying ScreenTips," **p. 139**

Microsoft Office applications provide consistency in more than just similar toolbars and menus. Dialog boxes, customizable features, and operational features are similar, too.

Word menu bar
and toolbars

Word document
window

FIG. 1.10
Menus and toolbars
are consistent across
applications.

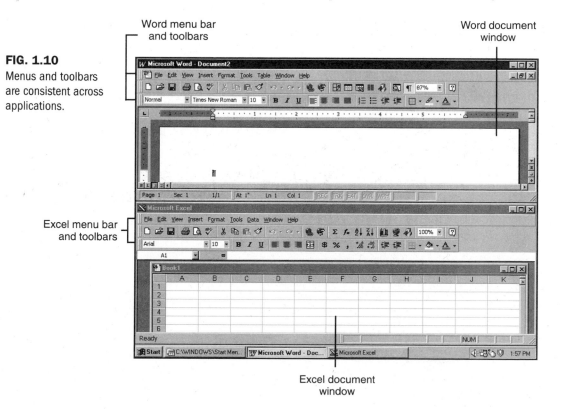

Excel menu bar
and toolbars

Excel document
window

Quick Access to Other Applications

Microsoft Office provides the Microsoft Office Shortcut Bar. By default, this toolbar appears along the top of the Windows 95 desktop (see Figure 1.11).

FIG. 1.11

The Microsoft Office Shortcut Bar provides easy access to opening and creating documents and Office Manager features.

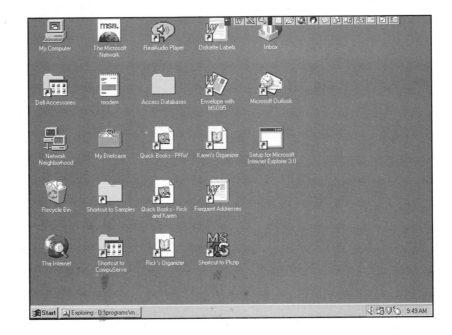

You can use the Shortcut Bar to do the following:

- Start new files based on templates and wizards.
- Open existing files and automatically launch the related application.
- Add tasks, make appointments, record tasks, and add contacts and journal entries.
- Create a new Outlook message.
- Switch between and launch Microsoft Office applications.

The Shortcut Bar is just one way that Microsoft Office provides quick access to applications. In Office 97, you can also create hyperlinks between documents. Additionally, in each Microsoft Office application, there are OfficeLinks, which are toolbar buttons or menu choices that provide direct access to pertinent features of other applications. For example, in Word you can insert an Excel Worksheet into a document by simply clicking a toolbar button. Doing so launches Excel and provides the full features of Excel for that embedded worksheet (see Figure 1.12). Note that, without having to leave Word, the menus and toolbars change to Excel's when you edit the worksheet. Table 1.1 gives a summary of some of the methods to convert documents between applications.

FIG. 1.12

Connectivity between applications allows you to insert an Excel worksheet into a Word document and edit the worksheet using Excel menus and toolbars without leaving Word.

Word document name

Word title bar

Excel menu bar, toolbars, and formula bar

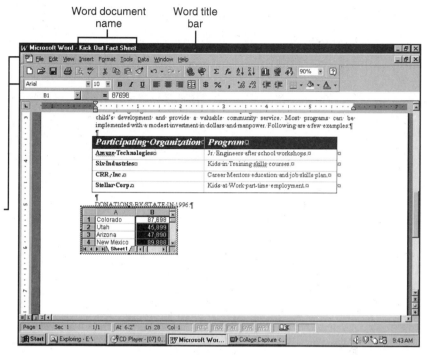

Table 1.6   Toolbar Buttons and Menu Choices for Sharing Information Between Microsoft Office Applications

Description	Toolbar Button	Menu Choice
Insert a hyperlink that will open other Office documents		Insert, Hyperlink
Inserts an Excel Worksheet into a Word document		Insert, Object, Microsoft Excel Worksheet
Converts a Word outline into a PowerPoint presentation		File, Send To, Microsoft PowerPoint
Translates Word or Excel outline into a PowerPoint presentation		From PowerPoint, choose Insert, Slides from Outline

continues

Table 1.6   Continued

Description	Toolbar Button	Menu Choice
Queries Access from Excel		Data, Get External Data, Create New Query
Uses an Access table or query for a Word merge		Tools, OfficeLinks, Merge It with MS Word
Converts an Access table, query, form, or report to a Word document		Tools, OfficeLinks, Publish It with MS Word
Copies an Access table or query to an Excel worksheet		Tools, OfficeLinks, Analyze It with MS Excel

Sharing Data Across Applications

Microsoft Office products provide several methods of sharing data between applications:

Method	Description
Copying	Copies the data from the source application to the target application using the Clipboard.
Linking	Links a copy of the data from the source document to the target document (and saves data with the source document).
Embedding	Embeds data from the source document into the target document (saves data with the target document).

The Microsoft Office applications share data effortlessly. When you copy a table from Excel or Access to Word, for example, you get a Word table that retains all the fonts and formats from Excel or Access. You do not need to reformat your table, as you might with some other products.

▶ **See** "Switching Between Documents," **p. 124**

▶ **See** "Copying Spreadsheet Information," **p. 864**

▶ **See** "Using Common Steps to Link Documents," **p. 880**

Linking and embedding features take advantage of Microsoft Windows OLE specifications. Linked documents automatically update when a source document changes.

Embedded documents provide access to the source application while storing the data in the target application. Each feature has its pros and cons and serves a specific purpose.

Microsoft Office 97 extends the data sharing beyond application integration by providing workgroup integration with Microsoft Outlook 97 (which works with Microsoft Exchange). Users can mail documents, spreadsheets, presentations, and data files from within the source application. Routing slips can be attached to files that Outlook then broadcasts to the group or routes to each person, in sequence, one at a time.

Sharing Resources Across Applications

A key element in Microsoft Office is the recognition that certain resources are needed by more than one application. Clip art is needed to perform word processing tasks, spreadsheet tasks, and presentation graphic tasks, for example. Rather than duplicating program overhead, Microsoft Office provides an auxiliary application, Microsoft Clip Gallery 3.0 (see Figure 1.13), for use with all applications. The same is true of the need for a query engine (to ask questions of your data), a graphing tool, and an organization chart drawing tool.

▶ **See** "Using Microsoft Clip Gallery 3.0," **p. 528**

Providing a Common Language

Providing a common language across applications is the most challenging goal of Microsoft Office. In the past, each product had a different programming and/or macro language. Office 97 now provides a common macro programming language for all the applications: Visual Basic for Applications (VBA). VBA uses OLE and can send keystrokes to other applications (making it possible for VBA to run a cross-application process).

FIG. 1.13
Microsoft Clip Gallery, one of the auxiliary applications that ships with Microsoft Office, is used by all applications to insert predrawn graphics.

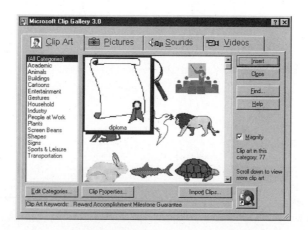

▶ **See** "Understanding VBA," **p. xx** (Ch42)

Determining Which Application to Use

Table 1.7 lists some common office tasks and suggested application tools to accomplish each task:

Table 1.7 Application Suggestions for Common Tasks

Task	Application	Comments
Create letters, memos, reports, term papers	Word	Use Word for projects that are word intensive.
Create budgets, invoices, income tracking, statistics	Excel Access	Use Excel for projects that are heavy on numbers with lots of calculations. Alternatively use Access for large lists when you'll be searching for a lot of information and making many reports off the same set of data.
Create slides, overheads, presentations	PowerPoint	Use PowerPoint for presentations when you want to produce 35mm slides, transparencies, audience handouts, or computer-run presentations.
Maintain mailing lists, including e-mail addresses and fax numbers	Word, Access, Excel, or Outlook	Maintain data in Word, Access, Excel, or Outlook.
Create mailouts or personalized documents	Word	Merge mailing list data into Word to print personalized cover letters, brochures, and labels.
Create a table of financial data to be used in a Presentation	Excel PowerPoint	Create a table in Excel. Embed a table into a PowerPoint slide.
Send a document to a group of people for feedback, and receive a response	Word, Excel Access, PowerPoint Outlook	Create the document, spreadsheet, report, or presentation in the desired application(s). Send the file(s) using the routing feature.
Track client contacts, log phone support, and follow up with a form	Access	Create a contact database in Access with related tables for clients, phone calls, projects, letters, and correspondence. Create forms for data entry. Optionally print letters directly from Access.

Task	Application	Comments
	Outlook	Use Outlook's contact management and other features to build your contact list, schedule follow-up calls, and more.
	Word	Optionally merge client contact data into Word and print follow-up form letters from Word.
Provide audit trail between supporting	Excel	Create the supporting schedules needed in Excel.
Spreadsheet data and annual report document	Word	Create the annual report in Word. Use OLE to link the data from Excel to the Word document. Whenever the spreadsheet data changes, the annual report document is updated automatically.
Create, print, and distribute a department newsletter	Word	Create a newsletter in Word.
	Exchange	Distribute a newsletter electronically using Exchange's Send feature.
Schedule work with members of your group, others	Outlook	Create a to-do list, then assign the tasks to and automatically send messages about appointments.

With four or five new software applications so tightly integrated, deciding on which product to use for which task could be difficult. Experience with each application is the best guide on how to combine the powers of each application to meet your needs.

The rest of this book is dedicated to helping you in this endeavor. The next few chapters in Part I review the common features found in all Microsoft suite applications and point out any digressions.

Parts II, III, V, and VI guide you through the features and capabilities of each product. Part IV shows you how to use multimedia objects such as charts, pictures, sound, and motion pictures. Part VII provides business scenarios to illustrate how Microsoft Office products work together. Part VIII shows you how to take advantage of Office 97's Web publishing, Web navigation, communications, and Outlook personal information management features.

Sit back and enjoy the new way of working that Microsoft Office provides.

 Use the Office Shortcut Bar's Start a New Document button, and let Office decide which application you need to use.

CHAPTER 2

Getting Started and Identifying Screen Parts

by Lisa A. Bucki

One of the benefits of Microsoft Office applications is that after you know one application, each new application is easier to learn than the previous program; each program uses the Windows 95 structure and has been fine-tuned to maintain consistency with the other applications in the suite. In Office 97, Microsoft slightly reorganized menus, toolbars, and dialog boxes so that the products are now even more similar. In some cases, such as with drawing tools, features that were significantly different from application to application have been revamped to be more similar—or even identical.

For experienced users, these changes will be welcome improvements. If you haven't used previous versions of Office but need to get up to speed quickly, you'll be pleased with the fact that what you learn in one application will apply in all the others. This chapter introduces you to the key screen elements in the Office applications, and teaches you some of the basic skills you'll need to get started using Office. ■

Start and exit programs and files

Learn how to open any Office application to begin working in it, and how to close it when you've finished.

Move between programs

Most computer users have many tasks to perform in the same day—or hour. See how you can leave the programs you need open, and select the one you need.

Move around the screen

Take a look at the various on-screen elements and what functions they perform.

Manipulate parts of the screen

Learn how to make some adjustments to the screen appearance to suit your working style.

Compare work areas of different applications

Review the differences between the areas where you build documents.

Launching Programs

Windows applications are designed to accommodate users coming from different plat-
forms and possessing different skills. For example, you can launch an application in
several different ways. You can use the keyboard, the mouse, or both devices together.
You can use the Windows taskbar, the Office Shortcut Bar 97, or Windows Explorer.

Starting a Program from the Taskbar

To start a program in Windows 95, you begin by clicking the Start button on the bottom-
left corner of the desktop (screen). The Start menu appears. Simply point to the Programs
choice, and a submenu appears listing the program groups, as well as programs not in
groups. (When you move the mouse, Windows displays a highlight to track the position
of the mouse pointer, so you don't need to click the commands that display submenus.)
Move the mouse to a program name or first to a program group and then to a program
name on the program group submenu. Once you find the program you want, such as
Microsoft Word, click the left mouse button to open the program. See Figure 2.1 to see
how easily you can open a program using the taskbar at the bottom of the desktop.
This method enables you to open a program with two single clicks.

FIG. 2.1
Use the Start button
on the taskbar to
launch any program.

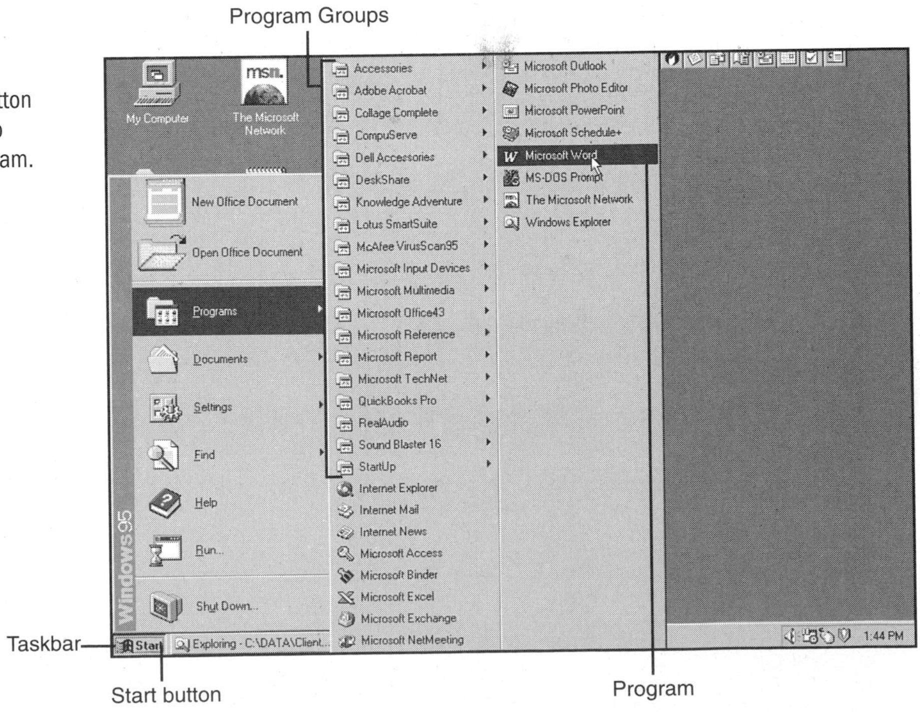

Program Groups

Taskbar

Start button

Program

Opening a Document from the Taskbar

Opening a document from the desktop using the taskbar is as easy as starting a program from the taskbar—maybe even easier. You perform the same actions as you do when you launch programs. Click the Start button, point to the Documents folder (rather than the Programs folder), point to the document you want to open, and click the left mouse button. The Document folder stores the names of the last 15 files you opened, regardless of what program you used to create them. This technique makes it easy to find documents you use over and over again, even if you use more than one program to create your favorite documents (see Figure 2.2).

Part
I
Ch
2

FIG. 2.2
Use the taskbar to open existing documents from any program you have been using.

Documents folder⎯

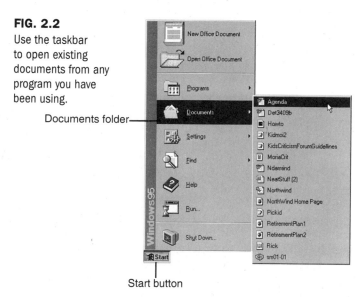

Start button

N O T E When you use the taskbar to open documents, Windows first looks to see whether the associated program is currently running. If it is, Windows switches to the current session of the associated program and then opens the document you requested. Windows does not start a new session of the program for each document you open. ■

Opening a Document from Windows Explorer

If you prefer using a tree structure to access your files, you can use Windows Explorer to open specific documents from folders. You launch Windows Explorer the same way you launch any program. Click the Start button on the taskbar, point to the Programs folder, point to Windows Explorer at the bottom of the Programs submenu, and click your left mouse button. After you have opened Windows Explorer, you can use the tree to move to the subfolder or folder that stores the document file you want to open (see Figure 2.3).

FIG. 2.3

Use Windows Explorer to launch files from subfolders or folders in a tree structure.

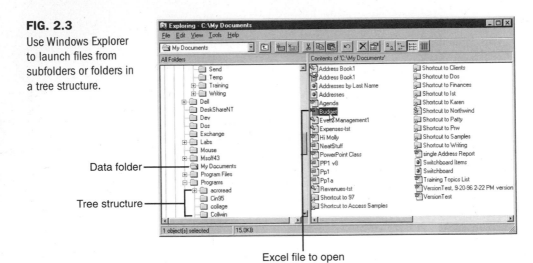

Data folder

Tree structure

Excel file to open

 TIP   You can also click your right mouse button on the Start button and choose <u>E</u>xplore from the shortcut menu to launch Explorer.

The left side of the Explorer window shows a list of folders. If there is a + (plus sign) next to a yellow folder icon, the folder has subfolders. Click the + to see subfolders under the folder. After you expand the folder, a minus sign (–) appears next to the subfolder indicating you can collapse that particular branch of folders. Click the minus sign to shrink the list back so the subfolders no longer appear. When you reach the folder you want, click the folder to show the contents in the right side of the window.

Find the document you want to open in the right side of the Explorer window and double-click the file name to switch to or open the program and open the document at the same time.

Opening a Document from the Shortcut Bar

If you were used to using the Microsoft Office Manager toolbar in Microsoft Office Version 4.0 or the Office 95 Shortcut Bar, you may want to use the Microsoft Office Shortcut Bar 97 to start a document. If the Shortcut Bar is not displayed, you can turn it on the same way you launch programs. Click the Start button on the taskbar, point to the <u>P</u>rograms folder, point to the StartUp folder, point to and click the Microsoft Office Shortcut Bar icon. The Shortcut Bar is displayed as a row of buttons at the top of the desktop.

N O T E   You can also start a new document or open an existing document from the Windows taskbar. When you click the Start button, you see the New Office Document and Open Office Document commands at the top of the menu. ▪

After you have the Shortcut Bar displayed, you can use any of the tools to perform common actions. One of these buttons is New Office Document; click this button to start a new document. Microsoft Office displays the New dialog box, as shown in Figure 2.4. From this dialog box you first determine what type of document you want to create and click the appropriate tab to display the built-in templates and wizards.

FIG. 2.4
Choose the type of document you want to create from the New Office Document dialog box.

Tabs for groups of document types

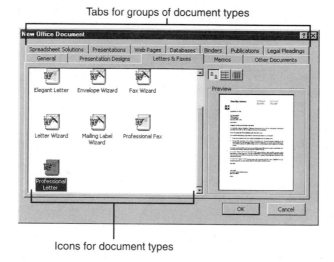

Icons for document types

To start a new document using the Microsoft Office Shortcut Bar 97, follow these steps:

1. If necessary, display the shortcut bar by clicking Start on the taskbar and choosing Programs, StartUp, Microsoft Office Shortcut Bar.

2. Click the Start a New Document button on the Microsoft Office 97 Shortcut Bar. The New dialog box appears.

3. Click the appropriate tab for the type of document you want. Figure 2.4 shows the Letters & Faxes tab selected.

4. Click to select the appropriate icon on the tab you want to use. Figure 2.4 shows the Professional Letter icon selected.

5. Click OK or press Enter. (You can skip this step if you simply double-click the icon representing the type of document you'd like to create.)

You don't even need to know which program to use; you just determine the type of document you need to create, and Microsoft Office starts the program. The wizard or template you choose is also opened. Figure 2.5 shows the Microsoft Word program with the Professional Letter template open for you to type a letter. You follow the prompts to type information into the letter. The section in Chapter 3 titled "Typing and Editing" explains how to get started with entering text into a document.

FIG. 2.5
The Professional Letter template is open and ready for you to type a letter.

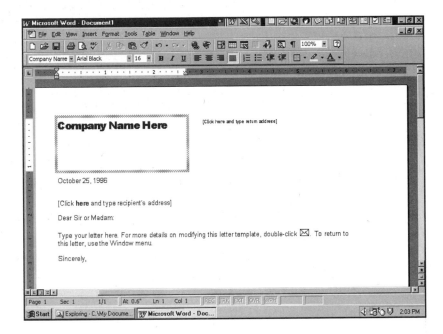

TROUBLESHOOTING

When I double-click a file name in the Explorer, the file does not open and I get a box around the file name. If you do not double-click quickly enough, Windows interprets your action as two single clicks. The first click selects the file name and the second click puts you into edit mode, allowing you to edit the file name. You can rename the file when you have this rectangle surrounding the file name (just type in a new file name). If you want to open the file, double-click faster or make sure you position the mouse pointer on the icon to the left of the file name when you double-click. You can also click your right mouse button once and choose Open on the shortcut menu.

I cannot find the Microsoft Office Shortcut Bar in the Startup group. Your setup may not have installed the Shortcut Bar. On the Office installation options, change the option for Office Tools and then check Microsoft Office Shortcut Bar.

Looking at the Microsoft Office Shortcut Bar

The Microsoft Office Shortcut Bar 97 on the Windows 95 desktop enables you not only to start a program, but to launch Office programs, start a new document, open an existing document, make an appointment, add a task, add a contact, or launch the Microsoft Book-shelf Basics application (see Chapter 3). You can customize the Microsoft Office Shortcut Bar by adding your own buttons. You can even use multiple toolbars.

Using the Microsoft Office Shortcut Bar 97

To display the Shortcut Bar, click the Start button on the taskbar and choose Programs, StartUp, Microsoft Office Shortcut Bar. Now just click the button on the Shortcut Bar that represents the task you want to accomplish, and Microsoft takes you to the program associated with that task. For example, if you choose New Contact, Microsoft opens your Microsoft Outlook file in the Outlook program and takes you to the Contact dialog box for you to add your contact (see Figure 2.6). See Chapter 45, "Using Outlook Desktop Information Manager," to learn how to use the features in Microsoft Outlook.

FIG. 2.6

Type the first name of the contact you want to add and move through the window using the Tab key.

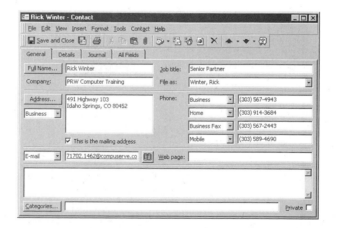

There are 15 default buttons on the Shortcut Bar 97 (you can change, add, and remove the buttons) as shown in Table 2.1.

Table 2.1   Office 97 Shortcut Bar Buttons

Click This Button	To Do This
▣	Displays a menu that gives choices on modifying the Shortcut Bar, bringing up Help, and Exiting (removing the Shortcut Bar from the screen).

continues

Table 2.1 Continued

Click This Button	To Do This
	Launches Microsoft Word so you can create or update a word processing document.
	Launches Microsoft Excel so you can create or update a spread-sheet.
	Launches Microsoft Access so you can create or update a database.
	Displays the New dialog box so you can choose the type of document you want to create.
	Displays the Open dialog box—choose the location and existing file you want to edit.
	Launches Internet Explorer (if loaded), allowing you to surf the Internet.
	Launches Bookshelf Basics, an auxiliary program that offers reference information such as a dictionary, quotations reference, and more.
	Launches Microsoft Outlook and displays its Notes feature to create a note.
	Launches Microsoft Outlook to create a new e-mail message.
	Launches Outlook and creates a new entry for your journal.
	Launches Outlook to allow you to look at your messages or do any other Outlook task.
	Launches Outlook and goes to the Appointment dialog box of the Calendar feature, allowing you to create a new appointment.
	Launches Outlook and goes to the Task dialog box, allowing you to create a new task.
	Launches Outlook and goes to the Contact dialog box, allowing you to add a new person.

Moving Between Programs

You can use the Microsoft Office Shortcut Bar 97 to move between programs in two different ways. You can also use the taskbar to move between programs. You can click a button on the Office Shortcut Bar 97 to start or switch to a program and open a specific document window. If you have more than one toolbar selected under the Customize Toolbars tab (see Chapter 41, "Customizing the Desktop, Toolbars, and Menus," to learn more about customizing the toolbar), you can click one of the toolbar buttons at the end of the Shortcut bar to display different Shortcut Bars.

If you need to show more than one toolbar, click the first button on the Shortcut Bar (which displays the Shortcut Bar menu), choose Customize, and click the Toolbars tab.

Select the toolbars in the Show These Folders As Toolbars box (see Figure 2.7) and choose OK. The Microsoft Office Shortcut Bar will show a new set of buttons for one of the toolbars you selected. It does not show all the buttons for all the toolbars simultaneously. The toolbar also will offer a "master" button for each toolbar, which you click to redisplay the buttons for that toolbar. These "master" buttons appear toward the left or right ends of the Shortcut Bar.

FIG. 2.7
The Toolbars tab allows you to display one or more different toolbars.

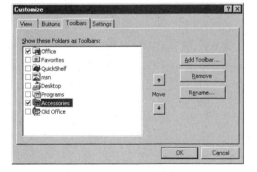

To return to the Office toolbar, for example, click the Office tools button that now appears beside the button that displays the Shortcut Bar menu, as shown in Figure 2.8.

Closing the Microsoft Office Shortcut Bar

If you no longer want to see the Shortcut Bar, double-click the menu button on the far left end of the Shortcut Bar. This method is the fastest way to close the Shortcut Bar. You also can choose the Exit command from the Shortcut Bar menu (see Figure 2.9).

Office tools button   Accessories tools buttons

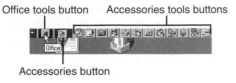

FIG. 2.8

The Microsoft Office
Shortcut Bar shows
the Office ScreenTip
and the Accessories
toolbar and program
icons.

Accessories button

FIG. 2.9

Double-clicking the
Control-menu icon is
the fastest way to
close the Shortcut bar.

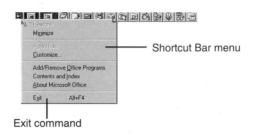

Shortcut Bar menu

Exit command

TROUBLESHOOTING

I can't find the Shortcut Bar to launch it. Depending on your setup and how the programs may
be customized, the program may be in different locations. Popular places to look for the Microsoft
Office Shortcut Bar 97 after you choose the Start button on the taskbar is on the Programs
menu, the Microsoft Office submenu (off the Programs menu), or the StartUp submenu (off the
Programs menu). You may also need to rerun the Office Install disk.

I would like to add Microsoft Office programs to the Microsoft Office Shortcut Bar. From the
Microsoft Office Shortcut Bar, click the Shortcut Bar button and choose Customize. Click the
Buttons tab and select the applications you want to add and choose OK.

I can't see ScreenTips for the buttons on the Microsoft Office Shortcut Bar. Make sure you
pause your mouse pointer over the button. You may need to turn ScreenTips on by clicking the
Shortcut Bar button, clicking Customize, choosing the View tab, and checking Show ScreenTips.

I see a different toolbar than the one shown in the book. You can have a number of different
toolbars for the Microsoft Office Shortcut Bar 97 or change the tools on the bar. Click the
Shortcut Bar button, choose Customize, choose the Toolbars tab, and check which toolbars you
want to use. To return to the toolbar shown in this book, deselect all options except the Office
toolbar.

Closing Programs

After you have finished working in an application, you probably want to close it—especially if your computer has limited memory. All Windows programs, whether they are Microsoft Office applications or not, close the same way. Do one of the following:

- Click the Close button (the x) in the upper-right corner of the application window.
- Double-click the program Control-menu icon in the upper-left corner of the application window.
- On the menu bar, choose File, Exit.
- Press Alt+F4.

 TIP You can close an application by clicking the right mouse button on the application icon on the taskbar and choosing Close.

▶ **See** "Saving, Opening, and Closing Files," **p. 97**

If you have not saved changes to your documents, you will see a dialog box asking whether you want to save changes to each of your open documents. You probably want to save your documents. If prompted, type the name of the file and the location in the File Save As dialog box.

Viewing Parts of the Window

One of the best parts of learning Windows and Microsoft Office 97 is the similarity between different applications. After you learn one program, the next and subsequent programs are easier to learn. This point is especially true because parts of the window are similar.

Understanding Common Window Elements

Figure 2.10 shows a review of the elements on a screen. Each application usually displays the application window itself and at least one document window. Table 2.2 describes the common elements on the application window and the document window.

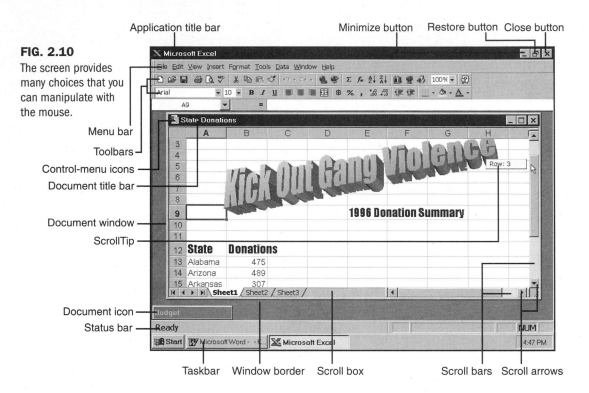

FIG. 2.10

The screen provides many choices that you can manipulate with the mouse.

Table 2.2   Window Features Common to Application and Document Windows

Feature	Description/Use
Control-menu icon	Microsoft Program icon in upper-left corner of window.
Title bar	Title bar is dark if window is active, grayed if other window is active. The color may be different if you have changed colors in the Display Properties of the Control Panel.
Minimize button	Click to shrink window to icon.
Maximize button	Click button to change window to largest possible size.
Restore button	Click this button to change window to last smaller size window.
Close button	An X appears on this button. Click this button to close the window.
Menu bar	Click one of the words to select a menu or press Alt and then type underlined letter on menus.
Window border	Thin gray line surrounding a window that is not maximized.
Window corner	Textured box in bottom-right corner of window.

T I P You can minimize all open programs by clicking the right mouse button in an empty spot on the taskbar and choosing Minimize All Windows.

Using Toolbars in Microsoft Office Applications

One of the ongoing improvements Microsoft made with the 97 upgrades of Word, Excel, and PowerPoint was to improve the toolbars so that the tools are more consistent across the Microsoft Office 97 applications. Although some buttons are unique to each application, many buttons are common to all or some of the applications. You now can choose from more than one toolbar in all the applications. You also can customize the toolbars by adding or removing buttons.

▶ **See** "Customizing Application Toolbars," **p. 949**

To turn a toolbar on or off, follow these steps:

1. Click the right mouse button on an active toolbar.

   A pop-up menu shows a list of the potential toolbars. Microsoft displays those toolbars with a check mark to the left of the name. Figure 2.11 shows a list of the toolbars for each application.

FIG. 2.11
When you click the right mouse button on a toolbar, a menu appears, showing the active and available toolbars.

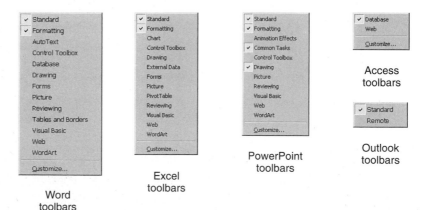

Word toolbars

Excel toolbars

PowerPoint toolbars

Access toolbars

Outlook toolbars

2. Click the toolbar you want to turn on or off. If the toolbar is floating, you can also click the toolbar's Control-menu icon to close the toolbar.

N O T E If the program doesn't presently show any toolbars, choose View, Toolbars and select the toolbar(s) you want to display. ■

Part
I
Ch
2

N O T E Microsoft Access and Microsoft Outlook menus and toolbars change, depending on what portion of the program you are in. For example, if you just enter Access and show the database window, the Database toolbar displays. If you are designing a form, the Form Design toolbar displays; if you view the form, the Form View toolbar displays. You can tell the name of the toolbar(s) displayed by clicking the right mouse button in the toolbar and seeing the name(s) shown with check marks. In Figure 2.11, only the Database and Web toolbars are available for Access and only the Standard and Remote toolbars for Outlook. ▣

Some toolbars display automatically or display other buttons when you change the view. For example, Word adds an Outline toolbar when you change to Outline view. Excel adds a Charting toolbar when you use the Chart Wizard.

If a toolbar button is dimmed, that means that the button is not currently available. If you want to see what a toolbar button does, simply point to it with the mouse until a yellow ScreenTip describing it appears.

CAUTION

Although you can turn on any Access toolbar at any time by clicking the right mouse button on a toolbar, selecting Customize, and selecting which toolbars you want in the Toolbars tab of the Customize dialog box, it is not a good idea. Because the toolbars are changing all the time anyway, it is confusing to have extra tools displayed when you don't need them. If you have too many toolbars displayed, choose View, Toolbars, Customize. Choose the unneeded toolbar from the list and then click Reset.

Using Menus

In addition to common toolbars, Microsoft also has reworked the menus in the Microsoft Office applications to come up with similar placement for commands.

Directly below the title bar in all applications is the *menu bar*. In most Microsoft Office and Windows applications, the menu bar begins with the File, Edit, and View menus and ends with the Window and Help menus. When the mouse pointer is on a menu, the pointer changes to a white arrow. To pull down a menu, click the menu name. If you want to use the keyboard, press Alt and the underlined letter on the menu. When you open a menu, a list of commands appears. Click the command or type the letter of the underlined character. As you point to menu choices, the status bar on the bottom of the screen shows a description of the menu or command.

If you accidentally go into the wrong menu, you can take one of these steps:

- Click another menu.

- Click in the document to turn off the menu.

- Press Alt or click the menu again to get out of the menu.

- Press Esc to keep the menu word highlighted. Press Esc a second time to get out of the menu.

Common Menu Symbols   Menus throughout Windows applications have common symbols that help you know what will happen when you select the command. The symbols include ellipses, arrows, check marks, option bullets, toolbar buttons, and shortcut keys.

Each menu is divided into sections by horizontal lines. The sections generally group similar commands together (such as <u>S</u>ave, Save <u>A</u>s, and Save As <u>H</u>TML) or group commands that are mutually exclusive. The following list describes common menu symbols:

- Three dots, or an *ellipsis*, after a command indicates that a dialog box appears after you choose the command. For example, the command <u>F</u>ile, <u>P</u>rint occurs in all five applications, and an ellipsis indicates that the Print dialog box follows the selection of this command. For more information on dialog boxes, see "Using Dialog Boxes" later in this chapter.

- Microsoft Office applications have arrows on the right side of some menus indicating that another drop-down menu will appear. After you point to the command with an arrow, you choose another command on the resulting menu. Figure 2.12 shows that in Excel, if you choose F<u>o</u>rmat, <u>R</u>ow, you get another menu that begins with H<u>e</u>ight.

 T I P   Look for shortcut key combinations to your most used commands on the right side of a menu and toolbar buttons on the left side of a menu.

FIG. 2.12
An arrow on the right side of a command indicates another menu follows.

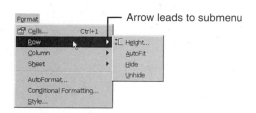

Arrow leads to submenu

■ Another character on some menus is a *check mark* to the left of the menu choice. A check mark indicates that the choice is selected and that the choice can be on or off. For example, the Window menu of all Microsoft Office 97 applications shows a list of open documents on the bottom of each menu. The active open document is indicated by a check mark. Figure 2.13 shows a check mark next to Ruler, indicating that the ruler is turned on. You click Ruler to turn the ruler off.

FIG. 2.13
The Ruler choice
is checked, or
toggled on.

■ To the right of some commands are *keyboard shortcuts*. Instead of using the menu, you can press the shortcut key or key combination to choose the command. Most shortcuts begin with holding the Ctrl key down in combination with a letter. For example, to undo your latest action, press Ctrl+Z in all applications. Shortcut keys also include function keys (for example, F7 for Spelling) and editing keys (for example, Delete to erase the selection). Refer to Figure 2.12, which shows that the shortcut key for Format, Cells is Ctrl+1.

■ Finally, some submenus are actually "floating" menus that you can drag to any location and leave on-screen. If you see a title bar at the top of a submenu, as shown in Figure 2.14, you can tear off that submenu and drag it to any location you prefer on-screen, so that its choices remain available.

In addition to maintaining common symbols on menus, Microsoft has repositioned menu commands to appear on the same menus within each application as much as possible.

Shortcut Menus Microsoft has shortcut menus for Word, Excel, PowerPoint, Access, and Outlook. To access a shortcut menu, select the item you want to change and click the right mouse button in the selected area. The menu that appears gives you options for only the selection. You don't have to wade through the menu bar to figure out what menu items go with what you are doing.

FIG. 2.14
You can "tear off" this menu and drag it to its own floating window on-screen.

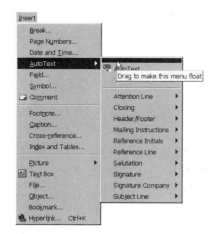

In addition to shortcut menus for toolbars, Microsoft has shortcut menus for selected text, drawing and graphics objects, rows, columns, and others depending on your application. Figure 2.15 shows an example of the shortcut menus for selected text in each of the applications. Notice that most of the shortcut menus have Cut, Copy, and Paste, but each menu also has items specific to the application.

FIG. 2.15
The shortcut menus for selected text contain similar and different menu items for each application.

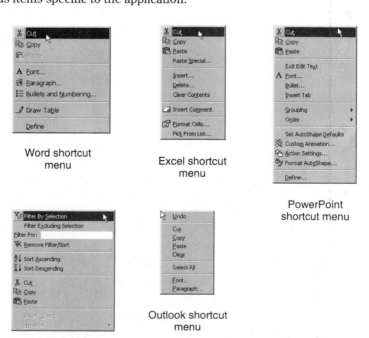

Word shortcut menu

Excel shortcut menu

PowerPoint shortcut menu

Access shortcut menu

Outlook shortcut menu

Like the menu bar menus in Office 97 applications, shortcut menus also now offer buttons corresponding to toolbar buttons for commands that have a toolbar button.

Using Dialog Boxes

When you choose a command with an ellipsis, a dialog box appears. The dialog box can be very simple with only one button (such as OK), or the dialog box can have many choices. Just as the menus have common symbols, so do the dialog boxes. Figure 2.16 shows examples of two dialog boxes.

FIG. 2.16
The Print dialog box of Word and Format Cells dialog box of Excel show features of all dialog boxes.

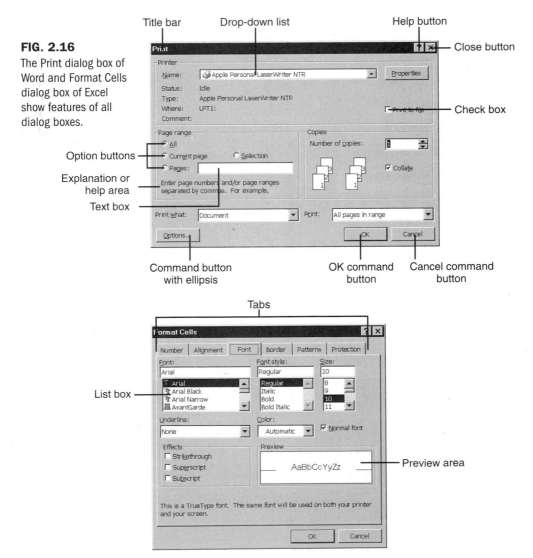

Dialog boxes enable you to see all the current settings for a command as well as change them. As features have become richer in options, Microsoft added tabs (for example, the Font tab is selected and displayed in the Format Cells dialog box shown in Figure 2.16). Click a tab to go to that area of the dialog box. Sometimes, you may need to see your underlying document to make a choice in the dialog box. Drag the title bar of the dialog box to move the dialog box out of the way. Within a dialog box you click an object to select or change the value. For example, in the Font Style list box, click Italic to select italic. Within a dialog box you generally click an object, type a value, or select from a list.

Microsoft includes the ? button on the top right corner of almost every dialog box window. If you need help on a specific part of the dialog box, you can click the ? button and then point to the part of the dialog box where you need help and click again. Microsoft displays a pop-up help window for that area of the dialog box. This method is called *context-sensitive help*.

In addition to using the mouse to make selections in a dialog box, you also can use several keyboard methods:

- ■ Press Tab to move to each section of a dialog box.
- ■ Press Shift+Tab to move backward through the dialog box.
- ■ Press Alt+ any underlined letter on a choice in the dialog box to move to that choice.
- ■ Press the up or down arrow to make a selection in a list.
- ■ Press the space bar to select or deselect a choice in a check box.

To get out of a dialog box without selecting any of the settings, choose Cancel or press Esc. To use the settings, choose OK. In some cases, click the Close button to finish your selections. Notice that some command buttons have ellipses (Options button in Figure 2.16). An ellipsis indicates that another dialog box will appear when you choose this button.

TROUBLESHOOTING

I accidentally chose a menu or a toolbar. If you are still in a menu, click another menu or press Alt to turn off the menu. If you are in a dialog box, click the Close (X) button or press Esc. If you changed the text or a graphic, click Undo or press Ctrl+Z. If you launched another program, click the Close (X) button.

A menu or dialog box choice doesn't work or it is dimmed. The choice may not be available, depending on what you're doing. One of the most common things you need to do is select your item first before you can change it. For example, you can't choose Edit, Copy unless something is selected.

Manipulating Parts of the Screen

When you're working in an application with all the new features of Microsoft Office for Windows 95, you may find that your screen gets cluttered. When this happens, you can choose to hide elements in the program window, the Microsoft Office Shortcut Bar, or even the taskbar on the desktop.

TIP To see what an item is on-screen, press Shift+F1 or click <u>H</u>elp and choose What's <u>T</u>his?; then click the screen item you want help about. A pop-up explanation appears.

Hiding Screen Elements

Most applications that come with the Microsoft Office suite have a <u>V</u>iew and <u>T</u>ools menu. You begin with these menus if you want to change the way the screen looks.

Using the View, Toolbars Command   If you decide you want to change the view of your screen, the best place to start is with the <u>V</u>iew menu. For instance, in any of the programs, you can choose to turn the toolbars off or display other toolbars. You simply choose <u>V</u>iew, Toolbar(s). A submenu appears (see the example from Excel in Figure 2.17), listing the toolbars available in that application. A check beside a toolbar indicates that it's toggled on. Click to remove the check to hide a toolbar. To redisplay any toolbar, choose <u>V</u>iew, Toolbars, then click the toolbar name to place a check beside it and redisplay it.

FIG. 2.17
The <u>T</u>oolbars choice on the <u>V</u>iew menu for the applications in the Microsoft Office suite turn on or off toolbars.

TIP In Word and Excel, you can also use View, Full Screen to temporarily conceal all toolbars, status bar, and other screen items for maximum editing space. To return to normal view, click the Close Full Screen button on the small remaining toolbar.

Part

I

Ch

2

CAUTION

Because there are so many toolbars in Access and because they are supposed to automatically display as you move to different parts of the program, use caution when choosing View, Toolbars to manually change the toolbars that display.

Using the Tools, Options Command   You can choose Tools, Options (and then, generally, the View tab) to change the view of window elements such as the status bar, scroll bars, and in Excel the formula bar, row and column headings, and sheet tabs as well as others. When you choose Tools, Options, the Options dialog box opens. You then turn on or off specific options by clicking the option you want to change. Figure 2.18 shows the View tabs of the Word and Excel Options dialog boxes.

FIG. 2.18
Change options by turning them on or off with a click of the mouse.

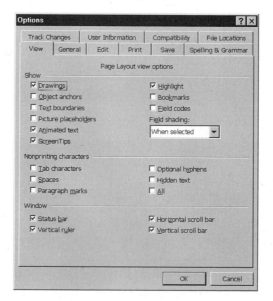

View tab, Options dialog
box in Word

FIG. 2.18
(Continued)

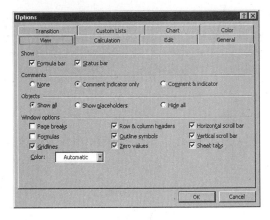

View tab, Options dialog
box in Excel

Magnifying the View

You may determine that you need to change the view of your document for editing purposes. With most Microsoft Office applications, you have an option on the Standard toolbar called Zoom Control. You also can use the Zoom command on the View menu. If your document doesn't fit on the screen, you may need to make it smaller to see how it lays out on the page. In some instances, you may want to make the document bigger to see detail better. In either case, you can change the view using the Zoom Control button or the Zoom command on the View menu. Figure 2.19 shows a document in Word, with the Page Width zoom control being selected.

TIP In Excel, you can select a row (or range) of columns and then click the Zoom button and choose Selection to force the zoom to display all columns from your selection.

Using Auto Hide on the Shortcut Bar

You may turn on the Microsoft Office Shortcut Bar and become frustrated with all the clutter Microsoft adds to the screen. Using the Shortcut Bar is nice, but being able to see more of your workspace may take priority. One of the added features with the Shortcut Bar is the Auto Hide command. If you want the Shortcut Bar visible when you are working in another part of the screen, but hidden while you are working in an application, you need to turn on Auto Hide. To turn on the Auto Hide command for the Shortcut Bar, use the following steps:

1. Point to an open spot on the Shortcut Bar (where a button is not) and click your right mouse button.

2. Click Customize, click to clear the check mark beside the Auto Fit into Title Bar area choice, and then click OK.

3. Right-click an open spot on the Shortcut Bar, and then click the Auto Hide command.

FIG. 2.19
Zoom in to see more
of the page at a time.

Zoom Control button   Zoom choices

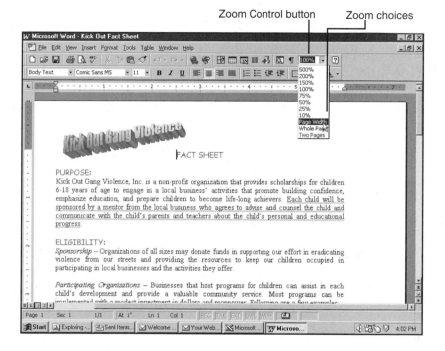

Part
I
Ch
2

 TIP Similarly, you can right-click the Windows taskbar, click Properties, then click the Auto Hide command and click OK to hide the taskbar.

To see how this method works, move into your workspace and click to make the application window active. Move the pointer back over the Shortcut Bar and back into the workspace. When you get into the workspace, the Shortcut Bar disappears. If you move the pointer to the edge of the screen where the Shortcut Bar is located, it reappears. See Figures 2.20 and 2.21 to compare the screens.

TROUBLESHOOTING

I lost my toolbars. How do I get them back? You could have accidentally clicked a right mouse button on a toolbar and unmarked the toolbar on the shortcut menu. To bring back toolbars, use the View, Toolbars command and choose the toolbar you want.

continues

continued

If you accidentally choose <u>V</u>iew, F<u>u</u>ll Screen in Word or Excel, you lost all toolbars and the status bar. Click the <u>C</u>lose Full Screen button, or press Esc to return the screen to normal. You can also type Alt+V to bring up the View menu (hidden in Word) and type U to choose the F<u>u</u>ll Screen command.

I can't find other parts of the screen. Use the following table to get your screen back to normal:

Screen Item	How to Get It Back
Typing	Check the scroll bars to see whether you moved outside the typing area. You may also have selected typing and pressed a key replacing the typing. Click the Undo button to see whether you deleted the text.
The whole document	Check the <u>W</u>indow menu and choose the document name. If you haven't saved the document yet, you may need to choose each of the generic document names (Document3, Book1, Presentation).
The whole application	Check taskbar to see if the program is minimized. Otherwise, you will need to open the application again by choosing Start on the taskbar and choosing <u>P</u>rograms and the application name.
Any edge or edge item (title bar, maximize button, restore button, minimize button) of document window	Drag title bar or choose <u>W</u>indow <u>A</u>rrange.
Any specific button on a toolbar	<u>V</u>iew, <u>T</u>oolbars, select the toolbar and choose <u>R</u>eset.
Status Bar	<u>T</u>ools, <u>O</u>ptions, View Tab, Status <u>B</u>ar check box
Scroll Bars	<u>T</u>ools, <u>O</u>ptions, View Tab, Horizontal Scroll Bar and Vertical Scroll Bar check boxes
Ruler (Word)	<u>V</u>iew, <u>R</u>uler
Formula Bar (Excel)	<u>V</u>iew, <u>F</u>ormula Bar
Row and Column Headers (Excel)	<u>T</u>ools, <u>O</u>ptions, View Tab, Row & Column He<u>a</u>ders. To turn on or off printing of row and column headers, choose <u>F</u>ile, Page Set<u>u</u>p, Sheet tab and use Row and Col<u>u</u>mn Headings.
Sheet Tabs (Excel)	<u>T</u>ools, <u>O</u>ptions, View Tab, Sheet Ta<u>b</u>s
Paragraph and tab symbols (Word)	To turn on or off, click the Show/Hide ¶ button on the Standard toolbar.
Pictures (Word)	Uncheck <u>T</u>ools, <u>O</u>ptions, View Tab, <u>P</u>icture Placeholders.

Shortcut Bar

FIG. 2.20
Both the Shortcut Bar and the status bar are visible.

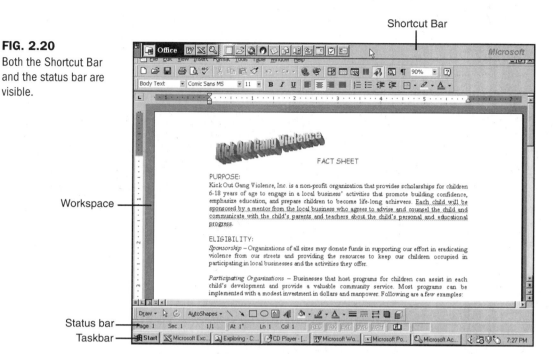

Workspace

Status bar
Taskbar

Part

I

Ch

2

FIG. 2.21
Both the Shortcut Bar and the status bar are hidden.

Workspace

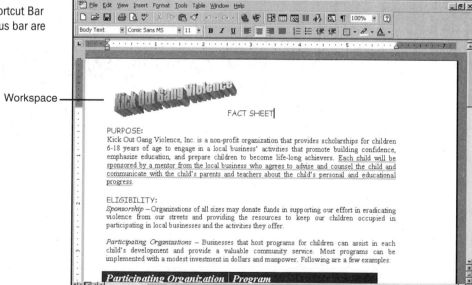

Looking at the Work Areas of Office Applications

The Microsoft Office applications have many similarities; for example, all applications have at least one document window, a menu bar, toolbars, and status bars. However, each Microsoft Office application has a different focus and a different kind of work area.

Word 97 Document

The work area of Word 97 is the document (see Figure 2.22). The document window is like a blank sheet of paper on which you can type. When your typing reaches the margin, the text automatically wraps to the next line. The focus of Word is text. Although you can place numbers and data in Word documents, the strength of Word is its capability to format text documents, such as letters, memos, and reports. The length of your document is virtually unlimited.

FIG. 2.22

Text automatically wraps in a Word document.

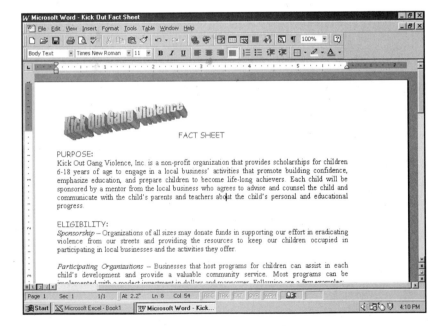

Excel 97 Worksheet

The work area of Excel 97 is a grid of columns and rows called a *worksheet* and is similar to a table (see Figure 2.23). The Excel document is called a workbook and is a collection of worksheets and/or charts. The focus of Excel is a cell, which is the intersection of a row and column. All data must go into cells. Although you can place text boxes across a range of cells, long sections of text are better left to Word. Excel's strength is its capability to summarize and analyze numbers. Excel also has significant charting capabilities that enable you to create many types of pie, bar, column, and line charts.

FIG. 2.23
One of Excel's strengths is the ability to work with numbers and create formulas.

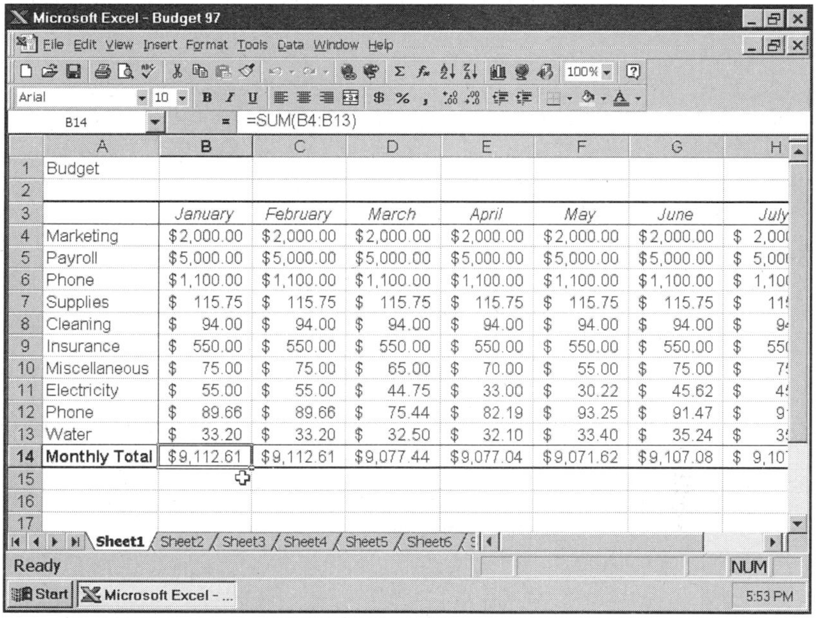

An Excel worksheet has 256 columns (indicated by letters A to IV) and 65,536 numbered rows. Each cell is indicated by the column letter and the row number. E6, for example, is the cell in the fifth column and sixth row. An Excel workbook can have several sheets. Each sheet has 256 columns and 65,536 rows.

PowerPoint 97 Slide

The focus of PowerPoint 97 is the slide (see Figure 2.24). PowerPoint is used primarily to make presentations. You can create slides for uses such as overhead transparencies, 35mm slides, or on-screen presentations.

Each slide has attached objects, which may include a title, bulleted items, other text, and graphics. To edit an object, you first need to select the object.

You can view PowerPoint slides in different ways. Outline view shows the titles of all slides in list format with their attached bulleted items. Slide view (the normal view) shows one slide at a time. Slide Sorter view shows more than one slide at a time. Notes Pages view enables you to type notes for each slide.

FIG. 2.24

PowerPoint is strong on creating bulleted slides to support your ideas.

Access 97 Table

The focus of Access is the database table (see Figure 2.25). The table is a row-and-column format similar to that of an Excel worksheet; the number of rows and columns changes, however, depending on the table.

Each row in the table is a *record* of information about one person, place, or thing. Each column in the table is a *field* that shows an item of information about the record—for example, last name, phone number, quantity, or price. Because Access is a relational database, you can connect multiple tables through a related field.

As you do in Excel, you enter information in the intersection of a row and column or in a specific field within a record.

Queries enable you to see a portion of a table or related tables (see Figure 2.26). Queries are organized in rows and columns and include the same information as a table (or summaries and calculations based on data in a table). You could use a query to find the name and phone number of all clients in California, to link a customer table with an order table, or to find the total sales for each salesperson.

Forms enable you to enter information into a table or view information from a table or query (see Figure 2.27). A form usually is organized one record to a page, although for convenience, you may want to display more than one record, but display only some of the available fields for each record. The fields from the table or query appear throughout the page. Forms can include more than one table or query and can be organized in row and column format.

FIG. 2.25
A major feature of Access is the table.

Each row is a record —

Each column is a field —

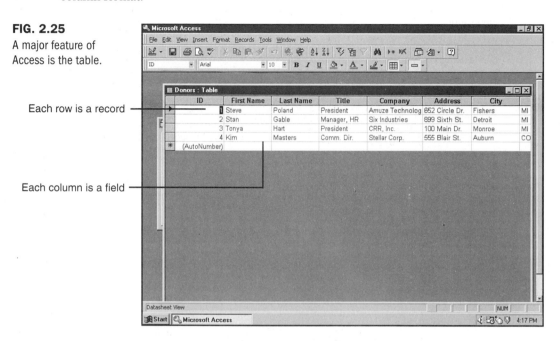

FIG. 2.26
The Design view of an Access query allows you to show only the fields and records you want to see, or it can link different database tables.

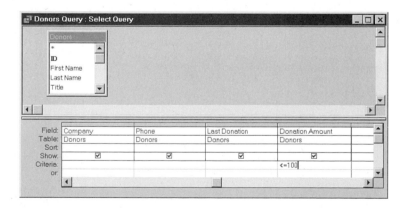

Reports are used to print a list or summary of information from tables and queries. Access makes it easy to create a report using the Report Wizard (see Figure 2.28), which walks you through the process. Reports usually are in table form, but can include subtotal and total lines. In some cases, reports can be output as labels.

Part
I
Ch
2

All related tables, queries, forms, and reports are organized into one file called a *database*. Access to the different parts of the database is provided through the database window, which displays tabs for tables, queries, forms, reports, macros, and modules (see Figure 2.29). When you click a tab, the list of that type of object in the database appears. When you click the Forms tab, for example, a list of forms appears. To edit information in the database, go to the appropriate table, query, or form and then edit or add information in a field.

FIG. 2.27

An Access form makes data entry easy.

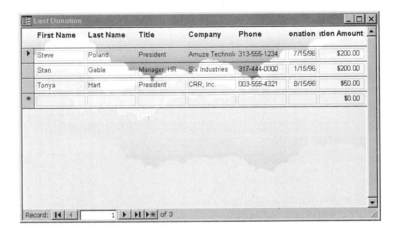

FIG. 2.28

You can design reports with the Report Wizard.

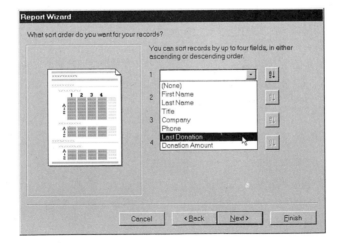

FIG. 2.29

The Database window is the "control center" of the database, enabling you to go to any object.

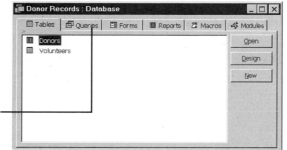

Click one of these tabs to display a list of database objects

The strength of Access is its capability to find, input, output, and link information. The amount and kinds of information that you can manage in Access are significantly greater than Excel, which has its own database feature. ●

Part
I

Ch
2

Typing and Formatting Basics

by Lisa A. Bucki and Rick Winter

With the 97 versions of applications in the Microsoft Office suite, typing and formatting information is even easier than it was before. Not only do the screens look and act similar in the Microsoft Office suite of programs, but the basics for typing and formatting information across the applications also are similar. After you learn one application, learning the next one is easier. So many of the functions work the same way throughout the applications that your learning curve should be small. For example, if you want to enhance text with bold, italic, or underline characteristics, you choose the same command using the menu, the buttons on the toolbars, or the keyboard shortcuts regardless of which application you are using. ■

Enter information in Office applications

Learn the basics for typing, editing, and selecting text, no matter which application you're working in. Also learn to undo mistakes when you make them.

Move around the document

Review the mouse and keyboard techniques you can use to navigate in Office.

Change how your document looks

See how to format documents using the toolbars, keyboard shortcuts, and menus.

Find and fix errors

Learn to use the Spelling Checker and AutoCorrect features to create documents that are accurate as well as attractive.

Find and replace text

When you need to jump to a location where a particular word or value appears, or would like to use one term in place of another, you can use the techniques described here.

Typing and Editing

Typing and editing within different Windows 95 applications is similar. When you're working in an application, you are in one of three modes—text, cell, or object. In text mode, a vertical blinking line called the insertion point is visible. As you type, the insertion point moves to the right; when you come to the end of the line, text automatically wraps to the next line. In cell mode, the cell is selected, and when you type whatever was in the cell is replaced. In object mode, you first need to select the object and then single- or double-click to edit the object. Each of the Microsoft Office 97 applications can include any of these modes. The way you edit items differs depending on the mode. The following sections explain these three different modes in greater detail.

Working in Text Mode

The normal Word 97 screen is an example of *text mode*. When you move the mouse across an area in text mode, the mouse pointer becomes an I-beam. Click the I-beam mouse pointer to position the insertion point. As you type, the insertion point pushes existing text after the insertion point to the right. If you want to replace text, drag the I-beam mouse pointer to select the text to replace. When you begin typing, the new text replaces any selected text.

▶ **See** "Editing Text in a Word Document," **p. 156**

▶ **See** "Editing Worksheet Data," **p. 322**

When you move the mouse pointer into any text box within a Microsoft Office 97 application dialog box, the I-beam replaces the arrow, as shown in the File Name text box in the Save As dialog box (see Figure 3.1). Drag the mouse pointer across text in the text box to select the text, and then type the new entry. In this example, text was selected and the name **Kick Out Fact Sheet** was typed. Kick Out Fact Sheet replaced the selected text.

FIG. 3.1
Typing in a text box of a dialog box is similar to typing in a Word document.

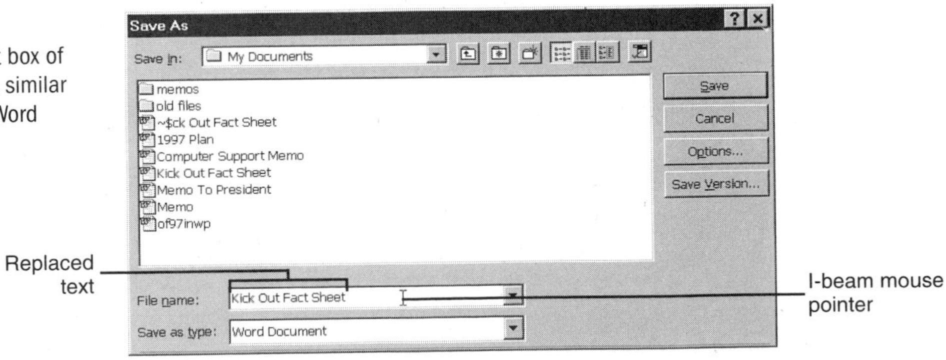

Replaced text

I-beam mouse pointer

▶ **See** "Selecting Cells and Ranges," **p. 308**
▶ **See** "Editing Worksheet Data," **p. 322**

In Excel 97, the mouse pointer is normally a thick white plus sign as you move the mouse pointer across the screen. When the mouse pointer is on a menu or on a toolbar for any application, the pointer is an arrow. When your mouse pointer enters the formula bar at the top of the screen, however, it changes to an I-beam that you can drag across to select text or click to position the insertion point (see Figure 3.2). You also can accomplish in-cell editing if you move the thick white plus sign to the cell and double-click. The mouse pointer changes to an I-beam while you are in the cell, and the blinking insertion point appears. This mode is called *edit mode* in Excel.

FIG. 3.2
When the mouse pointer is in the formula bar, it changes to an I-beam mouse pointer.

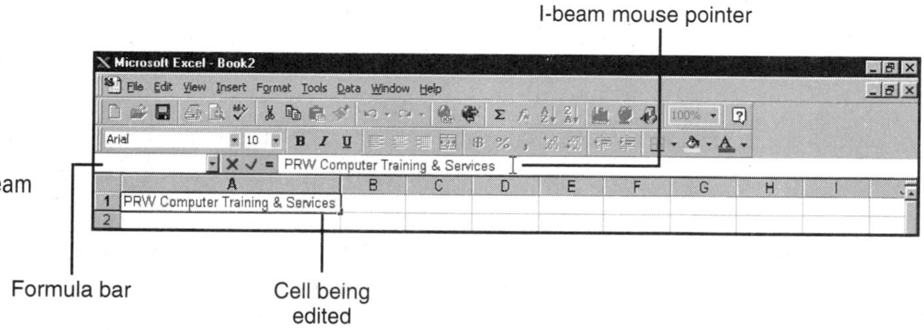

I-beam mouse pointer

Formula bar

Cell being edited

▶ **See** "Entering and Editing Text," **p. 625**

In PowerPoint 97, when you move the mouse pointer across most text items, the mouse pointer becomes an I-beam. While you are in Outline view, you can click and drag on any text to select the text as if you were in a Word document. However, editing a slide works slightly differently. When you click, you position the insertion point within the text and select the text object at the same time. When the text object is selected, a hatched outline (selection box) appears around the object (see Figure 3.3).

Access 97 works like a combination of Word and PowerPoint. When you are in a datasheet (a row and column-grid similar to an Excel worksheet) for a query, table, or a form (see Figure 3.4), the mouse pointer is an I-beam. Click the I-beam at the location you want to edit or drag the mouse to select existing text, and type the new text or delete the old text.

When you are in design mode in a form or report, you edit text slightly differently, as shown in Figure 3.5. Instead of an I-beam, the mouse pointer is an arrow. You first need to click the arrow on the text object to select it. Then the mouse pointer changes to an I-beam, and with your second click you can position the insertion point to edit text.

FIG. 3.3

You can edit text within a selected text object in PowerPoint.

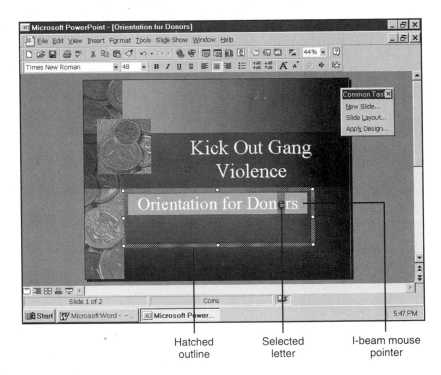

Hatched outline

Selected letter

I-beam mouse pointer

FIG. 3.4

Click the I-beam mouse pointer to position the insertion point in the area to edit.

ID	First Name	Last Name	Title	Company	Addr
1 Steve	Poland	President	Amuze Technologi	652 Circl
2 Stan	Gable	Manager, HR	Six Industries	899 Sixth
3 Tonya	Hart	President	CRR, Inc.	100 Main
4 Kim	Masters	Comm Dir.	Stellar Corp.	555 Blair
(AutoNumber)				

Record: 4 of 4

I-beam mouse pointer

FIG. 3.5
Click the arrow mouse
pointer to select the
text to edit and then
click a second time to
position the insertion
point for editing.

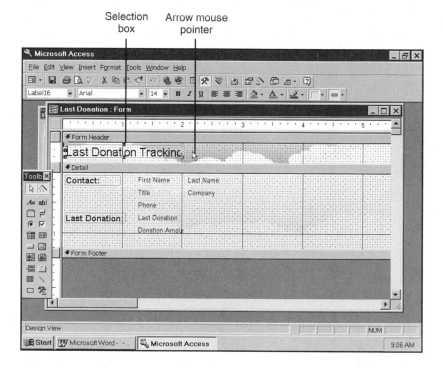

Working with Cells, Text Boxes, and Fields

Excel worksheets, Word tables, and Access tables and queries are organized in rows and
columns. The intersection of a row and column is called a cell. When you press Tab, you
move to the next cell. If you press Shift+Tab, you move to the previous cell. When you
move to a cell with Tab or Shift+Tab in Word or Access, the text within the cell is selected.
When you type, new text replaces the existing text. In Excel, when you press Tab or
Shift+Tab, the text is not selected. Type the new entry for the cell and press Enter or Tab
to replace the entry.

▶ **See** "Moving Around in a Worksheet," **p. 301**
▶ **See** "Navigating in Datasheet View," **p. 754**
▶ **See** "Working with Tables," **p. 280**
▶ **See** "Navigating Form View," **p. 811**

Forms and dialog boxes work similarly to tables. In a dialog box, if you press Tab
or Shift+Tab until you come to a text box, the current item in the text box is selected.

As soon as you type the first character, the old entry is erased. If you want to edit an entry rather than replace it, click the I-beam mouse pointer to position the insertion point. Access forms (see Figure 3.6), Word data-entry forms, Excel data forms, and the upper part of an Exchange mail message contain fields for entering or editing information. Fields are placeholders for information that you fill in on a form.

FIG. 3.6
You can click in or press Tab to go to the field in an Access form for data input.

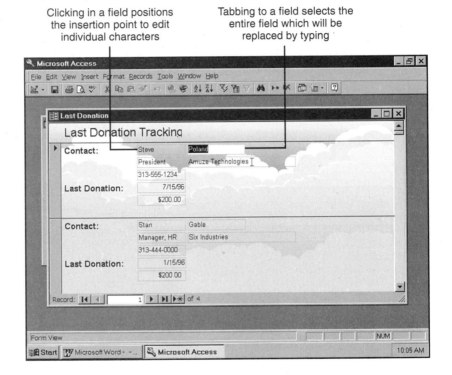

Clicking in a field positions the insertion point to edit individual characters

Tabbing to a field selects the entire field which will be replaced by typing

Working with Objects

In some cases, you may have objects attached to your document. Objects can include charts, pictures, clip art, WordArt, AutoShapes, drawing objects, and other documents. If you click an object, small, square resizing handles appear around the object at each corner and in the middle of each side. In some cases, the selection handles are open boxes. In other instances, such as in form design view in Access, the selection handles are black boxes, and an outline appears around the selected object.

▶ **See** "Creating and Printing Excel Charts," **p. 491**
▶ **See** "Selecting and Grouping Objects," **p. 642**
▶ **See** "Editing an Embedded Object," **p. 905**

You can perform any of the following actions on a selected object:

- To delete the object, press Delete.

- To move the object, move the mouse pointer onto the object (or on the transparent "border" surrounding the object) until the pointer changes to a four-headed arrow (or a hand in Access). Drag the object to the new position on the document.

- To change the size, stretch, or flatten the object, move the mouse pointer on top of one of the resizing handles until the pointer changes to a small, black double arrow (see Figure 3.7). Drag the double arrow to make the object smaller or larger.

Black double arrow

FIG. 3.7
Resize this selected object (clip art) by dragging the black double arrow.

- If positioned inside a selected text object as shown in Figure 3.8, the mouse pointer will be an I-beam. Click to position the insertion point. Then press Backspace to delete characters before the insertion point or Delete to delete characters after the insertion point.

- To edit non-text objects, you can double-click the object. One of two things happens: you enter the program that created the object, or the menu and toolbar of your current program change to the menu and toolbar of the source object. Figure 3.9 shows an example of an Excel worksheet object within a Word document.

FIG. 3.8

In design view for an Access form, you click on a text label to select it and then the mouse pointer changes to an I-beam allowing you to position the insertion point.

Resizing handles   Selection box   I-beam mouse pointer

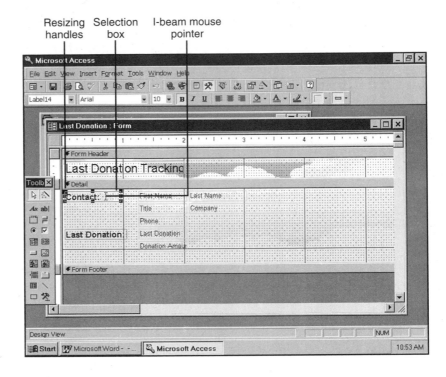

Word Title bar   Excel Toolbars

FIG. 3.9

When you insert an Excel worksheet into Word, you can select the object and then double-click to edit the worksheet in Excel.

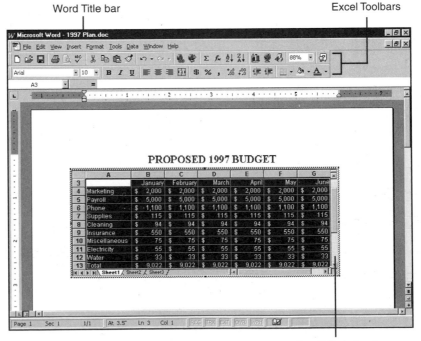

Excel Worksheet

TIP After you see the selection handles around an object, you can right-click to display a shortcut menu of options for working with the object, including such choices as formatting the object or opening its source application for editing.

Selecting Text

As mentioned in the preceding section, you select an object by clicking it. However, you have much more flexibility when you select text rather than the object. You can edit, change the appearance, copy, or move text by first selecting the text and then performing the procedure to make the change. Some text selection techniques are similar in all applications. For example, you can always drag across a text area with the I-beam mouse pointer to select text. You also can hold down the Shift key and use your direction keys to expand the selection or click the mouse at the end of the selection.

Some applications have different text selection techniques, as shown in Table 3.1. For example, to select a row in Word and Excel, position the mouse pointer at the far left end of the row and click. In Word, you move the mouse pointer to the far left margin, and the mouse pointer changes to a right-pointing arrow, indicating you can select the whole line; in Excel, you point to the row heading number, and the pointer changes to a white plus sign.

 TIP To select a range of text, click at the beginning, hold down Shift, and click at the end of the range. You can also extend or contract a selected range by holding down Shift and clicking at the new end of the range.

Table 3.1   Text Selection Techniques Using the Mouse

Application	Selection Area	Mouse Pointer Appearance	Perform This Function
All	Text	I-beam	Drag
All	Word	I-beam	Double-click word
Word	Line(s)	White arrow	Click or drag before text in left margin
Excel	Row(s)	White plus sign	Click or drag on row selector(s) before text

continues

Table 3.1 Continued

Application	Selection Area	Mouse Pointer Appearance	Perform This Function
Access	Row(s)	Black right arrow	Click or drag on record selector of datasheet or on vertical ruler of form and report design
Word	Table column(s)	Black down arrow	Click or drag above first row of table
Excel	Column(s)	White plus sign	Click or drag on column letter(s) in worksheet frame
Access	Column(s)	Black down arrow	Click or drag on field name(s) in table or grid or in horizontal ruler in design view
Word	Entire document	White arrow	Hold down Ctrl and click in left margin
Excel	Entire worksheet	White plus sign	Click Select All button above row numbers and to the left of column letters
Access	Entire table	White arrow	Click button above row selectors and to left of field names
Excel	Multiple ranges	White arrow	Select first range and hold Ctrl and select next ranges
Access and PowerPoint	Multiple objects	White arrow	Select first item, hold Shift, and select other items

No matter what application you're working in, click outside a selection to cancel the selection.

Using Undo

Keep in mind that after you select text, anything you type will replace the selected text. If you replace text by mistake, you can undo your last action by immediately choosing Edit, Undo or pressing Ctrl+Z.

Word, Excel, and PowerPoint have a multiple-level Undo feature that enables you to undo more than just the last procedure. Multiple-level undo is new to the latest versions of Excel and PowerPoint. To use this Undo feature, click the Undo button to undo the last procedure. Click the drop-down arrow portion of the button to show a list of procedures, and select the procedure you want to undo, as shown in Figure 3.10.

FIG. 3.10
You can reverse typing and formatting mistakes in Word using the Undo and Redo buttons.

Undo   Redo

 Word, Excel, and PowerPoint also have a Redo button that enables you to redo any of the actions you have undone. The Redo button reverses an undo. If you want to undo your undo, use redo. The Redo button also has a drop-down arrow that shows a list of procedures you can redo.

In certain views, Access and Outlook also offer an undo button, so you can undo a change. However, redo isn't available in either of these applications.

Moving Around the Document

To move throughout the document, you can use the mouse and the keyboard. Moving around a document is similar in each application. To position the insertion point or cell pointer, click a visible area on-screen.

▶ **See** "Moving Around in a Worksheet," **p. 301**

Using Scroll Bars

Scroll bars enable you to scroll the view of the document. They are located on the right side and the bottom of the workspace. Be careful when using the scroll bar, the insertion point remains in the location before the scroll took place and may not be visible on-screen. You may start typing in the wrong place. Make sure that the insertion point is visible by clicking where you want to begin typing.

Part

I

Ch

3

NOTE   The horizontal scroll bar in Excel and some views of Access take up only the bottom right side of the window. In Excel, you use tabs to the left side of the scroll bar to move to different sheets (or pages) of the workbook. In Access, you use the buttons on the left side of the scroll bar to move to different records. ◼

▶ **See** "Navigating in Datasheet View," **p. 754**

The scroll bars are divided into three parts: the scroll arrows, the scroll box, and the scroll bar (see Figure 3.11). Use each part as follows:

- ◼ *Down or up scroll arrow.* Click an arrow to move one line at a time. (This technique is true except in PowerPoint.) Although clicking an arrow moves just one line in Outline view, clicking a scroll arrow in Slide view moves one slide at a time.

- ◼ *Vertical scroll box.* Drag the scroll box in the scroll bar. When you drag the box all the way to the bottom, you are at the bottom of the document, no matter how many pages the document has. Scroll tips show you where you will be moving to as you drag the scroll box.

- ◼ *Vertical scroll bar.* Click between the scroll box and a scroll arrow to move one full screen at a time.

- ◼ *Horizontal scroll bar.* Drag the box in the scroll bar, click an arrow, or click in the scroll bar to move left and right on wide documents.

- ◼ *Next and Previous arrows.* In Word and PowerPoint Slide view, you have two double arrows at the bottom of the vertical scroll bar. Click the double arrows to move to the Next or Previous page or slide.

- ◼ *Select Browse Object.* The Word vertical scroll bar now offers this button that works in concert with the Next and Previous arrows. Clicking the Select Browse Object button displays a pop-up palette of different types of objects you can browse for, such as comment notes, edits you've been tracking, and fields. When you point to one of the choices on the palette, a description for the choice appears at the top of the palette, as in Figure 3.12. Click one of the choices, such as Browse by Edits, to close the palette. The Previous and Next scroll bar buttons become highlighted, to indicate they're in a new mode. Clicking one of these buttons then moves to the previous or next object of the type you selected, such as the next or previous edit in the document. Two of the choices on the Browse by Object palette are Go To and Find, which display the Go To and Find dialog boxes, respectively, rather than altering the operation of the Previous and Next buttons.

TIP   To return Word's Next and Previous buttons on the vertical scroll bar to their normal mode of moving you to the previous or next page, click the Select Browse Object button, then click the Browse by Page choice.

FIG. 3.11
The scroll bar elements allow you to view different parts of the document window.

Scroll arrows   Scroll box   Scroll bar

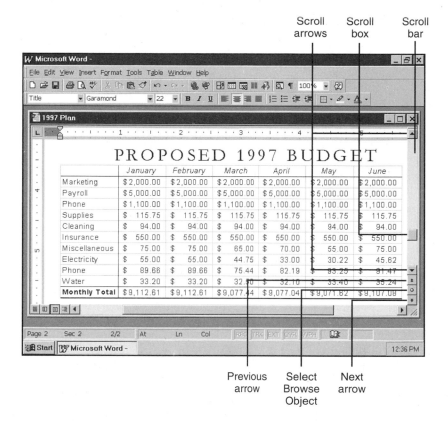

Previous arrow   Select Browse Object   Next arrow

FIG. 3.12
The Select Browse Object button enables you to browse for a variety of objects, and select the Go To and Find features.

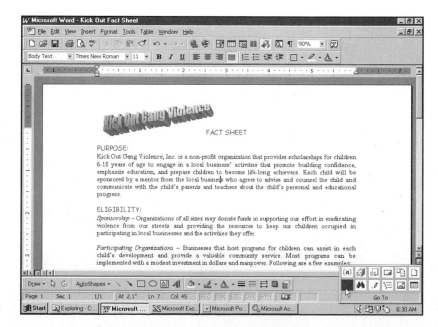

Part

I

Ch

3

Using Direction Keys

The direction keys on the keyboard work similarly in all Office applications, but the result may be different depending on the mode you are in. Direction keys do the following:

- Left- and right-arrow keys move the insertion point one character to the left or right in text mode, or one column to the left or right in cell mode.

- Up- and down-arrow keys move the insertion point one line or row up or down.

- Page Up and Page Down keys move the insertion point one full screen up or down.

- Ctrl+Home moves the insertion point to the top of the document.

- Ctrl+End moves the insertion point to the bottom of the document. In Excel and Access, this key combination moves to the last cell containing data.

- Home moves the insertion point to the beginning of the line in Word and PowerPoint. In Excel and Access, Home moves the active cell pointer to the first column in cell mode or the insertion point to the beginning of an entry in text mode.

- End moves the insertion point to the end of the line in Word and PowerPoint or the end of an entry in Excel and Access text mode. End also works differently in Excel. You press End followed by an arrow key on the keyboard to move to the end of a continuous range of cells.

- Ctrl+↑ and Ctrl+↓ in text mode move the insertion point one paragraph at a time.

- Ctrl+→ and Ctrl+← in text mode move the insertion point one word at a time.

- F5 is the Go To key. Press F5 in Word and then type the page number to go to. Press F5 in Excel and type the cell reference. Press F5 in Access table or form mode and type the record number to move to that record.

Copying and Moving Data

The procedure for copying and moving is generally the same for all Office applications. The procedure works for copying information from one area of a document to a different place on the document, or for copying information from one document to a different document. This same procedure also works for copying information from a document in one application (such as Excel) to a document in another application (such as Word). The item that you are copying can be text, numbers, a chart, a picture, or any other Windows object.

▶ **See** "Copying Worksheet Data," **p. 324**

▶ **See** "Moving and Copying Objects," **p. 645**

Using the Clipboard

The Clipboard is a Windows feature used for copying and moving information in all Office applications. The Clipboard is a temporary storage area that holds a copy of the item when you cut or copy. When you cut, the item is removed from the source application and placed into the Clipboard. When you copy, the item remains in the source application and a copy is placed into the Clipboard. When you paste, a copy of the item you cut or copied goes from the Clipboard into the active application. Because all Windows applications share the Clipboard, you can easily copy information between applications.

▶ **See** "Copying Text Between Word Documents," **p. 860**

Using Cut, Copy, and Paste

The procedure for copying or moving is as follows:

1. Select the item you want to copy or move. If the item is text, drag the I-beam mouse pointer or use some other shortcut. If the item is a picture, chart, or object created in another application, click the object to show the selection box.

2. Do one of the following:

   - To move the selected item, choose Edit, Cut, press Ctrl+X, or choose Cut on the shortcut menu.

   - To copy the selected item, choose Edit, Copy, press Ctrl+C, or choose Copy on the shortcut menu.

3. Use the scroll bars and direction keys to position the insertion point in the document.

4. Choose Edit, Paste, press Crtl+V, or choose Paste on the shortcut menu.

   ▶ **See** "Moving Between Programs," **p. 41**

Moving with Drag-and-Drop

Microsoft Word, Excel, PowerPoint, and Access have a capability that makes moving easier than using the Cut and Paste commands. This feature is called *drag-and-drop*. You first select the text or cells to move, and then drag the selection to the new location. This new location may be in the same document, in a different document, or in a different application.

The mouse pointer changes to a left-pointing arrow when positioned over the selected text, indicating that you can drag-and-drop the selection. In Word and PowerPoint, you position this drag-and-drop mouse pointer anywhere within the selected area. In Excel, you point to the outline surrounding the selected cells. When you click and drag the mouse in Word and PowerPoint, two additional shapes are added to the left-pointing mouse pointer. A small rectangle appears under the mouse pointer, and a dashed vertical line (*ghost insertion point*) appears where the new text will be inserted when you release the mouse button. In Excel, a gray outline appears where the new text will appear when you release the mouse button.

In Excel, you can drag the selection into a document in an open Word or PowerPoint window.

In Access, you can drag and drop a form or report inside another form or report to create a subform or subreport. You can drag and drop a macro on a form to create a command button. You can drag and drop a table or query into a Word or Excel document. You can create a new Access table by dragging an Excel spreadsheet to a database window. You can copy database objects (tables, queries, and more) between two instances of Microsoft Access. When you drag and drop using these options, you copy rather than move the selected object. When you drag an object such as a form to the Windows desktop, you create a shortcut to that object.

Figure 3.13 shows the drag-and-drop feature between Excel and Word. Excel and Word were tiled using the shortcut menu on the taskbar. In Word, you can drag the selection to another place on the same document, to another open document window within the Word program window, or to an Excel worksheet or PowerPoint slide.

FIG. 3.13
The status bar in each application provides help about the task you are performing. This is an example of moving information from Excel to Word.

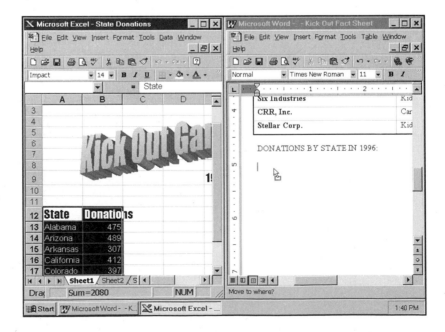

N O T E If you want to copy rather than move the selected item, hold down the Ctrl key, then begin to drag. The mouse pointer adds a small plus sign. To complete the copy, first release the mouse button and then release the Ctrl key.

Alternatively, you can press the right mouse button when dragging a selection. After releasing the mouse button where you want to place the text, a shortcut menu offers the Move Here, Copy Here, Link Here, Create Hyperlink Here, and Cancel commands (see Chapter 43, "Hyperlinks Between Documents," for more about hyperlinks).

TROUBLESHOOTING

I forgot to hold down the Ctrl key when I tried to copy an object. Now my original object is out of place. The operation of the Ctrl key is essential. If you need to restore the source application, return to the source application and click the Undo button or choose Edit, Undo.

When I try to drag from an Excel window to a Word window, I keep deselecting my range in Excel. When you want to drag a range from Excel, make sure you point to the edge of the selected range until the mouse pointer changes to a white arrow, then click and drag.

Part

I

Ch

3

Formatting Documents

Formatting text involves changing the font (typeface), font size, font characteristics (such as bold, italic, and underline), and alignment of text. The general procedure to format text is the same for all the Office applications. First you select the text to format and then you do the formatting. As with other procedures, you can use buttons on toolbars, menu items, shortcut menus, and keyboard shortcuts. Chapters 7, 14, 29, and 34 offer specifics about the formatting tools available in the various Office 97 applications; this section introduces the common formatting features you'll find in most instances.

Using Toolbars and Keyboard Shortcuts to Format

Formatting is usually quicker when you use buttons on the toolbar or keyboard shortcuts than it is when you use the menu. To format text, select the text you want to format, or position the insertion point where you want to begin typing formatted text. Then choose a toolbar button or press a keyboard combination (see Table 3.2).

Table 3.2   Formatting Buttons and Keyboard Shortcuts

Command	Button	Program*	Keyboard	Program*
Bold	**B**	W, E, P, A	Ctrl+B	W, E, P
Italic	*I*	W, E, P, A	Ctrl+I	W, E, P
Underline	U	W, E, P, A	Ctrl+U	W, E, P
Align Left	≣	W, E, P, A	Ctrl+L	W, P
Center	≣	W, E, P, A	Ctrl+E	W, P
Align Right	≣	W, E, A	Ctrl+R	W, P
Justify	≣	W	Ctrl+J	W, P
Font	Arial	W, E, P, A		
Font Size	14	W, E, P, A		
Font Color	A	W, E, A		
Fill Color		E, A		

In the Program columns, W, E, P, and A represent Word, Excel, PowerPoint, and Access. In Access, some buttons are available on the Formatting (Datasheet) toolbar, and others on the Formatting (Form/Report) toolbar. When you use the Bold, Italic, Underline, Font, Font Size, Font Color, and Fill Color buttons on the Access Formatting (Datasheet) toolbar, all characters (and not a selection) in the datasheet will be formatted the same.

 Format Painter allows you to copy the formatting of one section to one or more sections in your document. To use Format Painter, select the text that has the format you want and then click the Format Painter button. Then drag the mouse over the text you want to change. If you double-click the Format Painter button, you can choose multiple selections to apply the format. After a double-click, click the Format Painter button once to turn off the Painter.

▶ **See** "Changing Fonts in Word," **p. 173**

▶ **See** "Enhancing Text," **p. 663**

Using Menus to Format

The formatkting toolbars give you the most-used choices for formatting characters. If you want more detailed choices, use the menu bar. Word, Excel, and PowerPoint have Format menus. Access doesn't show the Format menu at all times, but it is generally available for report and form design and datasheet views. Word, PowerPoint, and Access display different formatting categories on the Format menu itself. Excel displays the formatting categories on tabs of the Format Cells dialog box. Table 3.3 summarizes some of the formatting possible on the Format menus of Word and PowerPoint, and the Format Cells dialog box of Excel. As with the toolbar and shortcut keys, you first need to select the text to format. When you finish with a dialog box, choose OK.

▶ **See** "Using AutoFormat," **p. 250**

Table 3.3	Formatting Commands			
Format	**Word**	**PowerPoint**	**Access**	**Excel**
Font, Font size, Font color, Underline	Font	Font	Add with Formatting toolbar	Font*
Border (lines)	Borders and Shading	Colors and Lines	Add with Toolbox	Border*
Shading (patterns)	Borders and Shading	Colors and Lines	Add with Formatting toolbar	Patterns*
Alignment	Paragraph	Alignment	Align	Alignment*
Line spacing	Paragraph	Line Spacing	Vertical Spacing	Format, Row, Height

These commands are available directly on the Format menu, with the exception of Excel commands marked by an asterisk (*), which are found on the specified tabs of the Format Cells dialog box.

Changing Column Width

Changing the column width of tables in Word, worksheets in Excel, tables in Access, or columns in Outlook is essentially the same. You move above the workspace to the column boundary at the right side of the column you want to change until the mouse pointer changes to a double black arrow, and then drag the column boundary with the mouse until the column is the desired width. Often you can also double-click the double black arrow to have the width automatically fit to the widest entry. In Word, the insertion point must be inside the table. In Excel, the column boundaries appear between the column headings. In an Access datasheet, you point to the column boundary to the right of the field name. In Outlook, you also drag a boundary to the right of a column heading.

▶ **See** "Changing Column Width and Row Height," **p. 351**

 To remove character formatting in Word, press Ctrl+Shift+Z. To remove alignment and other paragraph formatting in Word, press Ctrl+Q.

 TROUBLESHOOTING

When I changed to column width in a Word table, only some of the rows changed width.
Click the Undo button to reset the table. When you change column width, make sure you don't have any cells selected in the table or only those rows will change width. As a precaution, you can also select the entire column before resizing it.

Setting Margins

You can change the margins of your document by using a Page Setup dialog box, similar to the one shown in Figure 3.14.

FIG. 3.14
You can change margins using the Page Setup dialog box in Excel.

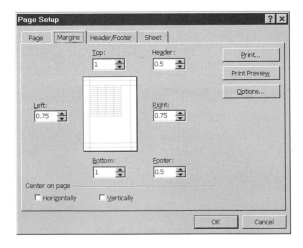

▶ **See** "Working with Large Documents," **p. 237**

To change the margins of your document, follow these steps:

1. Choose File, Page Setup. The Page Setup dialog box appears.

2. Select the Margins tab.

3. Enter measurements in the Top, Bottom, Left, and Right text boxes, or use the up and down arrow buttons beside a text box to change its settings.

4. Choose OK to close the dialog box.

N O T E When you set margins in Word, those measurements apply to all pages in the document, unless you divide your document into sections. ▪

Using Automatic Formatting

Automatic Formatting is a feature that automatically adds fonts, shading, colors, and borders for you to maintain a more consistent look within documents.

▶ **See** "Using Wizards," **p. 141**

▶ **See** "Creating a Presentation Using a Wizard," **p. 608**

To apply automatic formatting to your document, do the following:

▪ For a Word document, choose Format, AutoFormat. In the AutoFormat dialog box choose either AutoFormat Now or AutoFormat and Review Each Change (which enables you to accept or reject the changes or choose the Format Style Gallery command and select from styles in the Template list box). Click OK to continue.

▪ For Excel, position the cell pointer within the area to format and choose Format, AutoFormat. Choose from a list of examples in the Table Format list box (see Figure 3.15).

Part

I

Ch

3

FIG. 3.15
Choose from a list of table formats provided by Excel in the AutoFormat dialog box.

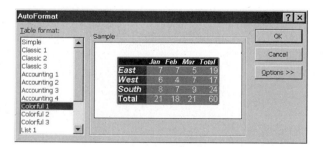

■ For PowerPoint, choose Format, Apply Design and select from the Look In list box of file templates in one of the template folders.

■ For Access, in Report or Form Design view, choose Format, AutoFormat. Choose from a list of examples in the Report or Form AutoFormats list box.

You also can use professionally designed formats through Wizards. Refer to Chapter 5, "Using Help and Office Assistant."

Checking Spelling

Microsoft offers the Spelling command in Word (labeled the Spelling and Grammar command) Excel, PowerPoint, and Access. (Access displays a form, if needed, before proceeding with spelling check.) Most often, you think to check spelling in a word processing document, but now you can check spelling in documents that are worksheets, presentations, and databases. The Tools, Spelling command looks for words that are not in the dictionary. In addition, the Spelling and Grammar command in Word alerts you to punctuation and capitalization problems as well as to repeated words. You can choose to change the spelling or ignore the problem; you even can add the word to the dictionary for later use.

TIP You can check the spelling of the entire document, or you can select text and check spelling only in the selected text.

Using the Spelling Command

 The Spelling command reads text and notifies you when it finds a word that is not in its main dictionary or your custom dictionary. The Spelling dialog box shows you the word in question, suggests a replacement word, and displays a list of other words that are similar in spelling as possible replacements.

To solve a spelling problem, you can use a variety of options. You can change the word, ignore the word, add the word to the dictionary, and delete the word.

To use the Spelling command in Word, Excel, PowerPoint, or Access, choose Tools, Spelling (Spelling and Grammar in Word) or press F7. The Spelling and Grammar dialog box appears in Word (see Figure 3.16), and the Spelling dialog box in other applications.

FIG. 3.16
Word checks spelling
and grammar, and
highlights the
unknown word in
this dialog box.

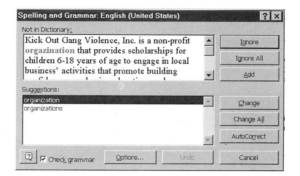

Editing the Document Without Leaving Spelling   If you find you need to edit your document after you have started the spelling check in Word and PowerPoint, follow these steps:

1. Click in your document to make the document window active.

   Notice the Ignore button in the Spelling dialog box changes to Resume in Word.

2. Make the changes needed in the document.

3. Click the Resume button to continue the spell check procedure.

Automatic Spell Checking in Word and PowerPoint   You can instruct both Word and PowerPoint (this feature is new to PowerPoint 97 but was available in Word 95) to check spelling as you type and to highlight words that may be misspelled. Words that may be misspelled are automatically formatted with a wavy red underline to attract your attention. (Word 97 also now places a wavy green underline under words, sentences, and phrases that may contain grammar errors.)

If a word highlighted with a wavy red underline really is misspelled, you can select the word and start the Spelling Checker as usual, or you can simply right-click the word (see Figure 3.17). The shortcut menu that appears offers the option to start the Spelling checker, lets you tell Word or PowerPoint to ignore the word's spelling, and also suggests corrections at the top of the menu. Simply click one of the corrections to use it in place of the selected, misspelled word.

If you don't want Word to highlight misspelled words, open the Tools menu and click Options. In the Options dialog box, click the Spelling & Grammar tab, then clear the check box beside Check Spelling as You Type. (Clearing the Check Grammar as You Type option check box also removes the wavy green automatic grammar checking underlines.)

Part
I

Ch
3

Click OK to close the dialog box. To turn off automatic spell checking in PowerPoint, open the Tools menu and click Options. In the Options dialog box, click the Spelling tab, then clear the check box beside Spelling.

FIG. 3.17

If you right-click a word that may be misspelled and is marked by a wavy red underline, the shortcut menu that appears offers spelling suggestions.

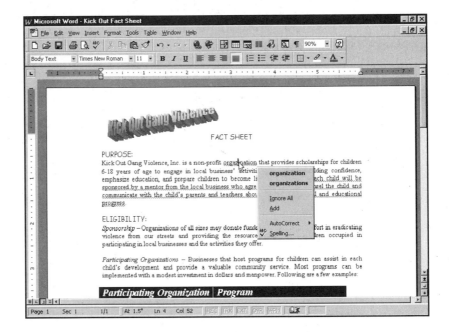

Using Dictionaries

When you use the Spelling command, all four applications look in a default dictionary named CUSTOM.DIC. However, you can create your own custom dictionaries.

Adding Words to a Dictionary   The CUSTOM.DIC dictionary, as well as any other dictionary you create, is stored in either the Program Files\Common Files\Microsoft Shared\Proof folder or the WINDOWS\MSAPPS\PROOF folder normally on your hard drive. If you click the Add button in the Spelling dialog box, any new words you add will automatically become part of the CUSTOM.DIC file. If you add a word in one application, such as Word, you may have to close that application before another program such as Access will recognize the added word. To create a new dictionary (with technical terms for example) from the Spelling dialog box, choose the Options, Dictionaries, New command buttons and pick the file with the dictionary entries. To choose an existing custom dictionary from Word's Spelling dialog box, choose Options, Dictionaries command buttons and select a dictionary name in the Custom Dictionaries list box.

Letting AutoCorrect Do Your Spelling for You

Using AutoCorrect, you can instruct Word, Excel, PowerPoint, or Access to correct spelling mistakes as you make them. If, for example, you often type *teh* rather than *the*, AutoCorrect can fix the error immediately after you make it.

The AutoCorrect feature automatically corrects spelling mistakes and formatting errors, or replaces characters you enter with specific words or phrases. Using this feature saves you time. Suppose that you consistently need to type *Kick Out Gang Violence, Inc.*; rather than typing it out each time, you can add a shortcut *kogv* to your AutoCorrect list and have Word, Excel, PowerPoint, or Access type the name for you. You can enter common mistakes or shortcuts into AutoCorrect, and the next time you make the mistake or type the shortcut, Word, Excel, PowerPoint, or Access corrects it automatically.

Part
I

Ch
3

Adding Words as You Check Spelling

To add words to AutoCorrect while you are checking spelling in Word, Excel, PowerPoint, or Access, make sure the incorrect word is listed in the Not in Dictionary box and the correct word is listed in the Change To box. Then choose the AutoCorrect button rather than the Change or Change All button in the Spelling dialog box.

Adding Words Through the Tools Menu

To set options and make entries for AutoCorrect, choose the Tools, AutoCorrect command. Figure 3.18 shows the AutoCorrect dialog box with a new entry. The AutoCorrect dialog box looks the same for Excel and PowerPoint.

The AutoCorrect dialog box lists five options including converting quote marks and correcting capitalization problems. You can choose to turn these options on or off. The Replace and With text boxes enable you to enter your own items, and the list at the bottom of the AutoCorrect dialog box displays the default list plus any items you add.

TROUBLESHOOTING

I have a lot of words that contain numbers, such as measurements, in my document and I want Word to ignore those words. Choose Tools, Options, and select the Spelling & Grammar tab. Choose Ignore Words with Numbers. Choose OK to close the dialog box.

I want to edit some of the words in a custom dictionary. In Word, choose Tools, Options and select the Spelling & Grammar tab and choose the Dictionaries button. In the Custom Dictionaries area, select the dictionary you want to modify and then click the Edit button.

FIG. 3.18
You can add shortcuts to the AutoCorrect entry list. For example, enter two or three letters to represent a name or company name that you often type.

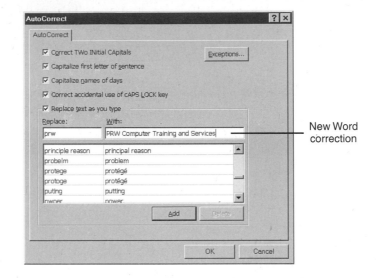

New Word correction

Finding and Replacing Text

Microsoft provides the capability to find and (optionally) replace specific text in your documents, worksheets, or presentations. For example, you can search for all occurrences of the value 1996 and replace it with 1997.

Using the Find Command

You can search the entire document, workbook, or presentation, or you can search only a selected area. To search the entire document or presentation, move the insertion point to the top. To search the entire workbook, select a single cell. To search an entire Access table, select the table by clicking the Select All button (above rows and to the left of fields). To search a specified area or range, select the area or range you want to search. Then follow these steps:

1. Choose <u>E</u>dit, <u>F</u>ind; or press Ctrl+F. The Find dialog box appears (see Figure 3.19).

N O T E In Word 97, the Find, Replace, and Go To features have been combined into a single Find and Replace dialog box. To access the Find features, click the Find tab, or click the Replace tab for a find and replace. Each of these tabs initially appears in a condensed format with fewer options. To view all of a tab's options, click the <u>M</u>ore button. ▪

2. In the Fi<u>n</u>d What text box, type the data you want to find. Then specify the search options in the <u>S</u>earch, <u>L</u>ook in, or check boxes. Some of the options for search include search direction, matching case, find whole words, and whole field or cell.

For a description of any option, click the ? help button and then click the option.

FIG. 3.19
The Find command enables you to locate specific text in your documents, worksheets, or presentations.

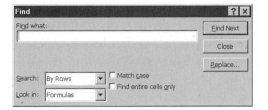

 TIP If the Find dialog box is blocking your view of the document window, click and drag the title bar of the dialog box until you can see the area you are searching.

3. Click Find Next to begin the search. When the application locates the characters, click Find Next to find the next occurrence, or click Replace to access the Replace dialog box (this option is discussed in the next section).

4. Choose Close to end the search and close the dialog box.

NOTE In Excel and Access, if you're not sure of the specific string you are looking for, you can specify wild-card characters in the search string to locate data that contains some or all of the characters. You can use an asterisk (*) to search for any group of characters and a question mark (?) to search for any single character. In Word you can use the same technique if you also select the Use Pattern Matching option on the dialog box. ■

Using the Replace Command

The Replace command (Ctrl+H) is similar to the Find command in that it enables you to locate specific characters in your document (Word, Excel, PowerPoint, or Access). The Replace command then enables you to replace the characters with new data.

To replace data, follow these steps:

1. To search the entire document, move the insertion point anywhere in the document or select a single cell. To search a specified area or range, select the area or range you want to search.

2. Choose Edit, Replace. The Replace dialog box appears. The Replace dialog box is the same as the Find dialog box shown in Figure 3.19 with the addition of a Replace With text box.

3. In the Find What text box, type the data you want to replace. In the Replace With text box, type the data with which you want to replace the current data.

CAUTION

In Excel make sure that you activate Find Entire Cells Only if you are replacing values or formulas. If this option is not selected, Excel replaces characters even if they are inside other strings. For example, replacing 20 with 30 also makes 2000 become 3000.

4. Click Find Next to begin the search. When the application locates the first occurrence of the characters, choose Replace to Replace the highlighted instance, Replace All to replace all occurrences of the text, or Find Next to skip the highlighted instance and move to the next occurrence.

 If you make a mistake when replacing data, close the dialog box and choose Edit, Undo (Ctrl+Z) immediately to reverse the replacement.

5. Choose Close to close the dialog box.

CAUTION

When replacing data in your document, use Replace All with care, because the results may not be what you expect. Whenever you use the Replace command, it's a good idea to first locate the data you want to replace to make sure that the data is correct.

CHAPTER 4

Managing Files and Printing Documents

by Lisa A. Bucki and Rick Winter

One of the most noticeable areas for change in the last version of Microsoft Office was in file management—particularly when you save, open, and search for files. When you work with files, you have more flexibility, more features, and more options.

Office 97 continues to support these file management improvements, including expanded file names, many changes in file dialog boxes, and expanded Summary Info in file properties. The Save and Open dialog boxes have their own toolbars that provide viewing and other options. Find features are now built directly into the file dialog boxes. ■

How to manage document files

Control which documents are open on-screen at any time, save your work, name your files, and choose a location to save a file to.

What to do if you've forgotten where a file is

Learn to use Office 97's sophisticated searching features to find a file by name, contents, or properties.

Tools to differentiate files

Review steps for attaching identification information to a file and viewing other file information (properties).

Creating a hard copy to share with other readers

See the options you have for printing documents, and learn how to preview a printout to double-check it.

How to work with multiple documents

Switch to a different document, when you have more than one document open in an Office application.

Working with Files

For most applications, the work you do on-screen is only in the computer's memory. If the power fails or some other accident happens, you may lose all or part of your work. The process of saving a file copies the information from memory to a file on disk (floppy disk or hard disk). You can manually save the file or set up the program to save the file automatically. When you close a file, you are removing the information from the computer's memory or from your screen. The program prompts you to save the file if you have made any changes since the last save or if you have not yet saved the file. Opening a file involves copying the information from a disk into memory. When you create a new file, a new document window opens. You can either open or create a file within a program, or use the Windows taskbar, as you learned in the sections titled "Opening a Document from Windows Explorer" and "Opening a Document from the Taskbar" in Chapter 2.

N O T E   Access works slightly different from other Microsoft Office applications. When you create a new database, the first thing you do is give the database a name in a File dialog box. When you make changes to a record in a table, query, or form, the changes are saved to disk as soon as you go to the next record; you do not have to use a file-save procedure. You cannot turn this automatic-save feature on or off. However, when you change the design of a form, record, query, or report, you can manually save the changes (or the program will ask whether you want to save the changes when you try to exit that object). The File, Save As/Export command is available only in some cases, and then you give an object (form or report) a name only within the database file itself; you do not go to a file dialog box, as in the other applications. To copy or rename an entire database file, use the Windows Explorer window.

Using File Dialog Boxes

In addition to using the Windows Explorer and the Desktop folders, you can manage files through Microsoft Office programs. When you open, save, or insert a file, a standard file dialog box appears. Many of the features on the file dialog box are the same whether you use Word, Excel, PowerPoint, or Access or whether you are opening, saving, or inserting. Figure 4.1 shows a standard Open dialog box with many of the common features. The toolbar helps you organize your files. The bottom section and Advanced command button help you find your files.

Table 4.1 shows a list of file dialog box features and summarizes their use. The other sections of this chapter discuss these features in more detail.

FIG. 4.1
The Excel Open dialog box has many features common to all standard file dialog boxes.

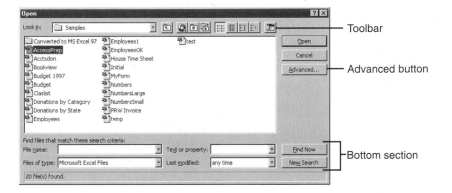

Toolbar

Advanced button

Bottom section

Table 4.1   Common Features on File Dialog Boxes

Button/Element	Description	Use
?	? help button	After you click the question mark, click the part of the dialog box you want explained.
X	Close button	Closes the dialog box without performing any actions. You also can press Esc.
Drop-down list	Save In/Look In drop-down list	Changes location for your files.
List box	Contents List box	Shows the names and optionally other information about the files.
	Up One Level button	Goes to next higher level in hierarchy of file containers.
	Search the Web button	Connects to a World Wide Web search page to search for sites based on a word or phrase.
	Look in Favorites button	Goes to the locations you designate as your "favorites" with the Add Favorites button.
	Add to Favorites button	Adds the file or folder to the location where you have your most-used documents.
	Create New Folder button	Creates a new folder in the location shown in the Look In/Save In drop-down list box.
	List button	Shows names of files only in contents list box.
	Details button	Shows name, size, date of files.
	Properties button	Shows user-entered information about the file.

Part
I

Ch
4

continues

Table 4.1 Continued

Button/Element	Description	Use
	Preview button	Shows the first part of the file.
	Commands and Settings button	Shows menu of options for printing, editing properties, sorting, subfolders, saving searches.
Open	Save/Open/Insert OK buttons	Performs actions requested with all settings from dialog box.
Cancel	Cancel button	Returns to document without doing anything.
Options...	Options button	Displays save options dialog boxes.
Advanced...	Advanced button	Prompts for advanced search capabilities for finding files.
Text box	File Name	Types the name of the file or uses wild cards to display a shortened list of files.
Text box	Files of Type/ Save as Type	Changes the display to show files created by different programs or saves the file so a different program can open the file.
Text box	Text or Property	Searches for text within the document or in property settings.
Text box	Last Modified	Searches for a file based on the date it was last saved.
Check box	Read Only check box	Opens file so you can't overwrite the existing file.
Find Now	Find Now button	Applies the find criteria and looks for the file.
New Search	New Search button	Clears any search criteria.
Check box	Link To File check box	When inserting a file, attaches instructions to read file on disk but does not insert actual file into document.
Check box	Save with Document check box	When linking a file, includes the entire file in the document.

N O T E The Word Save As dialog box offers a Save Version button which enables you to create a version of a document with additional comments, so you can, for example, save a version of a report file each month with specific comments. ■

N O T E Access also has an Exclusive check box on the Open dialog box. When this option is checked, no other users can use the database at the same time. When this option is cleared, users can share the database at the same time. ■

Saving, Opening, and Closing Files

The procedures for saving, opening, and closing files are similar to each other. You choose the necessary commands by using a button, menu item, or shortcut key. In most cases, a standard file dialog box opens, requesting information about the file name, location (drive and folder), and type of file you are using. Sometimes a dialog box does not open. For example, when you save a file after naming it, the program assumes you want to use the default choices in the file dialog box for the name, location, and file type. You can rename the file with the Save As command.

Part

I

Ch

4

Saving a Document

If you want to reuse a document or keep a copy, you need to save the document. If creating a document takes you awhile (say, more than 15 minutes), you also want to save your document to protect against power outages, nasty computer gremlins (problems), and hitting the wrong button.

You can save a document in a number of ways. You can click the Save button on the Standard toolbar, press Ctrl+S, or choose File, Save. When you attempt to close an unsaved document or exit a program with an unsaved document, you can answer Yes to the prompt to save changes. No matter which method you use, the first time you save a document you enter the Save As dialog box as shown in Figure 4.2.

To save the file, type the name in the File Name text box, choose a location in the Save In drop-down list, and choose the Save button.

T I P Always save your work before you leave your computer if you have a document on-screen. Saving your work also wouldn't hurt before you spell-check or start printing.

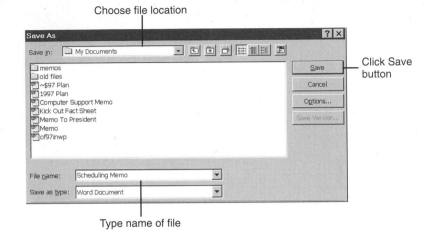

FIG. 4.2

When you save a document for the first time or choose File, Save As, you get the Save As dialog box.

Choose file location

Click Save button

Type name of file

Naming a Document The old rules for naming a file with a maximum of eight characters, a period, and three more characters were very confining. These rules produced cryptic file names such as BUSPLN.DOC, ACCPER.XLS, and GANGPON.PPT. You are free at last of such restrictive rules. You can now have names such as Business Plan, Accounts Breakdown by Percent, and Community Gang Presentation. One of the most useful additions is the ability to use a space in naming files.

Valid file names may now contain the following:

- Spaces
- Up to 255 characters
- All characters except \ / ? : ; [" < > and |

Uppercase and lowercase characters are usually displayed as you type them, but you cannot give a document the same name in different cases (you cannot have one file called *PLAN* and another one called *plan* in the same folder).

N O T E Windows 95 doesn't really alter DOS's 8+3 file-naming system. Windows 95 converts the file name you type to an acceptable name which is usually the first six non-space characters, a tilde (~), and a 1 for the first occurrence of the name (2 for second occurrence, and so on). For example, the Word file name *Business Plan* becomes BUSINE~1.DOC. When you copy or use this file on a DOS computer, the file name is the shortened version. On Windows 95 systems, the long file name is stored with a cross-reference to the short file name. To see the short DOS file name when you are in a file dialog box, click the right mouse button, choose Properties, and look on the General Properties tab. ▪

Part
I

Ch
4

 T I P As long as a file isn't open, you can rename the file from within any Save As or Open dialog box. Simply open the appropriate dialog box, and use the Look In or Save In list to navigate to the folder that holds the file. Right-click the file, then click Rename in the shortcut menu. The file name is highlighted, so you can type the new file name, then press Enter.

Saving Changes to a Named Document After you save a document one time, the name of the document appears in the title bar. When you want to save a document a second time and continue to use the same name, use any of the procedures mentioned earlier (the Save button, Ctrl+S, File, Save, or exiting the document or program and choosing Yes to save changes).

If you want to give the document another name, choose File, Save As. The Save As dialog box appears with the existing name in the File Name text box. Edit the name of the document or change the location in the Save In drop-down list.

Saving All Open Documents If you continue to open documents or create new documents without closing your document, you get more and more documents in memory for the current application. To see a list of documents in memory, choose the Window menu. The open documents appear on the bottom of the menu as shown in Figure 4.3.

FIG. 4.3
Three documents are open. To move to an open document, click the document name.

N O T E Access is unlike Word, Excel, and PowerPoint in that you can have only one database file open at a time but you may have many objects (tables, queries, forms, reports) open at a time in that file. When you choose the Window command, you see these different objects (including the database window) on the bottom of the Window menu. ▪

In Word you can save all open documents by holding Shift and choosing File, Save All. If you have not named one or more of the documents, the Save dialog box appears, prompting you for the file name and location.

Choosing a Location for Your Files

When you save or open a file, the file goes to or comes from a disk somewhere. In the simplest case, a computer may have a hard disk inside the computer (drive C:) and one floppy disk drive (drive A:). However, your personal computer may have additional floppy and hard drives, removable disk cartridges and optical drives, and a CD-ROM. Your computer also may be connected to a network and the Internet, giving you access to computer drives that are not directly attached to your personal computer.

When you first enter a standard file dialog box, you see a drop-down list box. In the Save dialog box you see the Save In list. In the Open dialog box you see the Look In list. A prompt in the list box represents the current location or container where you can save or open files. Underneath the drop-down list is a large open area (the contents list box) showing you the contents of the current container. The contents can be other containers or files.

 When you select the drop-down list as shown in Figure 4.4, you get an overview of the containers available to you for saving or opening files. A cascading list of locations displays. This list represents the hierarchy of locations where you can find or store files. This hierarchy may have many different levels; each level is represented by an indent. Whenever you choose a level through the drop-down list, the new level's contents are shown in the contents list box. If the list has more items than can fit, you see a vertical scroll bar on the right side of the list box. If you want to go back up a level, you can choose the Save In or Look In drop-down list box or click the Up One Level button.

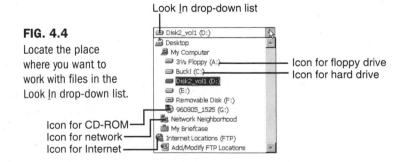

FIG. 4.4
Locate the place where you want to work with files in the Look In drop-down list.

In Figure 4.5, the top level is the Desktop, indicating that all potential locations branch from this location. The two main branches from the Desktop are My Computer and Network Neighborhood, indicating that you work with a file that is physically part of your computer system or other computers that are connected to your computer through a network.

FIG. 4.5
The hierarchy for storing files contains many different levels.

If you select Network Neighborhood from the drop-down list, you see a list of computers on your network in the contents list box as shown in Figure 4.6. You then can double-click any computer besides your own, and a list of shared folders appears in the contents list box. If you double-click a folder, you may see subfolders and files in the contents list box.

FIG. 4.6
Two computers are listed in this computer network.

Part
I

Ch

4

Selecting the My Briefcase choice lists Briefcase files, which enable you to synchronize the contents of multiple copies of a document. (Briefcase comes with Windows 95, and may not be installed on your system.) For example, if you place some Word document files in a Briefcase, you can then copy the Briefcase to your laptop, work on some of the files, then synchronize the files when you copy the Briefcase back to your desktop computer.

Under My Computer in the drop-down list are the different storage devices attached to the computer, such as a 3 1/2" floppy drive (A:) and a removable disk (F:), which happens to be a Syquest drive in this case, shown earlier in Figure 4.4. When you click a floppy drive, you are working with files on a floppy disk. Or, when you click a removable disk choice, you can save your file to a removable disk, such as a Syquest or Iomega Zip or Jaz drive, that's connected to your computer. If you are saving a file, you can optionally type the drive letter (for my machine A: for the floppy disk or F: for the removable disk) before the name of the file in the File Name text box.

The icon for the primary hard disk drive (usually fixed inside your computer) is slightly different in Figure 4.4 and usually is indicated by a C:. The computer shown in Figure 4.4 actually has three hard disks—C:, D:, and E:. Because a hard disk drive has so much more space, files are usually placed inside folders.

To navigate through the hierarchy of computers, drives, and folders, you can do any of the following:

- Use the Save In or Look In drop-down list box.
- Double-click a folder in the contents list box to view the contents of the folder.
- Click the folder one time with the right mouse button and click Open to view the contents of the folder.

- Click the Up One Level button to return to a previous level in the hierarchy.

- Click the Create New Folder button to create a folder underneath the container or folder identified in the Save In drop-down list box of the Save As dialog box.

- Click the Look in Favorites button to jump to the location where the favorites folder is located.
- If you know the location of the file you want to open or save, you can type the hierarchy of drive and folders in the File Name text box such as this example:

C:\Office97\Excel\97Revenue

Working with FTP Files

New to Office 97 is the ability to navigate to files on the Internet (if you are hooked up). FTP stands for File Transfer Protocol. This part of the Internet is different from the Web and is organized in folders and subfolders like your hard drive.

The first step to using FTP is to create a pointer on your computer to a folder on an FTP computer. From the Look In or Save In drop-down in a file dialog box, choose the Add/Modify FTP Locations choice. A dialog box appears as shown in Figure 4.7. Type in the FTP location in the Name of FTP Site text box. This name is called an URL (Uniform Resource Locator). URLs are discussed in more detail in Chapter 44, "Navigating and Publishing on the Web with Office 97." After you type the FTP location, you may need to identify yourself as a user with a password. Click the Add command button to add this site and add another site. Click OK when you finish adding sites.

The next time you go to the Look In or Save In drop-down, the sites you added will appear as shown in Figure 4.8.

You will not be able to save to most FTP sites because they are Read Only. However, you can open a file and then save it to your hard disk.

FIG. 4.7

You can type the full URL such as **ftp://ftp.microsoft.com** or an abbreviated form such as **ftp.microsoft.com**.

FIG. 4.8

You can open documents stored on an Internet FTP site.

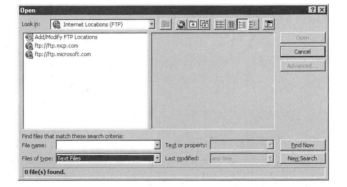

Opening a Document

You have even more options for opening a document than you do for saving a document. Some of these options were discussed in Chapter 2, "Getting Started and Identifying Screen Parts." This section contains a summary of your options to open a document.

To open a document outside a program, take one of the following steps:

■ From the Microsoft Office Shortcut Bar, click the Open Office Document button, select the location, and choose the file. You also can customize the Shortcut Bar to contain files and folders. See Chapter 41, "Customizing the Desktop, Toolbars, and Menus." After you click the Open Office Document button, you enter an Open dialog box.

- From the Windows taskbar, choose Start, <u>D</u>ocuments, then click one of your last 15 documents.

- Click the right mouse button on the Windows taskbar Start button and choose <u>E</u>xplore; then find the file through the Windows Explorer.

- Minimize or close all open programs and double-click a desktop icon such as My Computer, Network Neighborhood, or shortcut folders and navigate through the windows to find your file.

- From the Windows Taskbar, choose Start, and then Open Office Document.

- Press any shortcut keys you attached to a file using the Shortcut tab on the Properties dialog box of a shortcut icon. (See the "Using Advanced File Find Capabilities" section later in this chapter.)

From within a program, take one of the following steps:

- Click the Open button.
- Press Ctrl+O.
- Choose <u>F</u>ile, <u>O</u>pen.

If you choose any of the three preceding items, you enter the Open dialog box. Type the file name in the File <u>N</u>ame text box and choose the location from the Look <u>I</u>n drop-down list.

You can also easily find one of the last files you worked with. At the bottom of the <u>F</u>ile menu is a list of your most recently used files (see Figure 4.9). If no drive and folder display with the file name, the file is from the active folder. Choose the file name to open the file.

◆ TROUBLESHOOTING

When I look for a file, the file name does not appear in the contents list box. The file name may not appear in a contents list box for several reasons. First, you may need to use the scroll bars to display more files in the list. Second, the file may not be the correct type. In the Files of Type list box, select All Files, and see if your file is listed. Third, you may need to change the drive and folder. Finally, if all else fails, search for the file using features discussed in the next section, "Finding Files."

I can't access a file on someone else's computer on the network. On the Windows Desktop, choose Network Neighborhood, then choose the other person's computer name. The other computer needs to have shared folders to enable you to access its files.

I can't read a file from the CD-ROM. Make sure you set up the CD-ROM correctly. If you haven't done so, set up the CD-ROM by choosing Start on the Windows taskbar. Then choose Settings, Control Panel, Add New Hardware, and follow the Hardware Wizard. Additionally, make sure you have the CD-ROM player turned on and the proper CD in the CD drive.

FIG. 4.9
The last few files you opened appear at the bottom of the File menu.

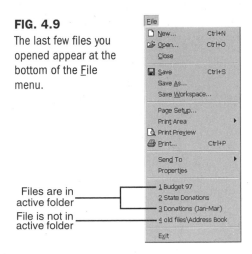

Files are in active folder

File is not in active folder

Finding Files

You can use the Open Office Document button on the Microsoft Office Shortcut Bar to open a document and launch the program that created the document at the same time. After you click the Open Office Document button, the Open dialog box appears. This dialog box is the same one that appears when you are in a program and use File, Open.

When you get to the Open dialog box, you have many options to narrow or expand your search. You can change the display and order of the files, use wild cards in file names, choose a file type, or identify a file by its contents, date, or other properties. These options in the Open dialog box replace the Find File feature from the earlier Windows 3.1-based version of Microsoft Office.

Displaying File Lists

After you have selected a computer, drive, and folder through the Look In drop-down list, you see a list of files (and possibly other folders) in the contents list box. You have four options for viewing this file list. Figure 4.1 showed a file open dialog box with the List button selected. Figure 4.10 shows a file open dialog box with the details button selected. Click the button identified in Figure 4.10 to display the view you want:

Part
I

Ch
4

Click the List button to display file names.

   Click the Details button to display file names, size, type, and date.

   Click the Properties button to display file names and user-supplied infor
mation about the file.

   Click the Preview button to see a picture of the file.

FIG. 4.10

If you click the Details
button you can sort by
file names, size, type,
or date.

List Button

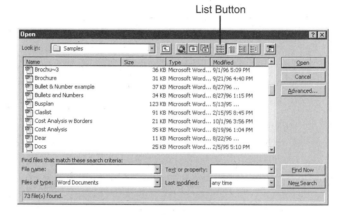

N O T E   Technically, the Access database window (see Figure 4.11) is not a file dialog box.
However, you can picture the database window as a permanently open file dialog box
with the list of all the objects (parts) of the database in this window. To see a list of one type of
object, click the (Tables, Queries, Forms, and so on) tab on the top of the database window.
To open the object, double-click the object name in the list. You can also display the object
names in different views with the four buttons on the toolbars. These buttons are similar to the
file dialog buttons and have the following purposes:

Button	Name	Purpose
	Large Icons	Displays the object names with large icons and names underneath the icons.
	Small Icons	Shows object names with small icons and names to the right of the icons and alphabetizes the list from left to right, then top to bottom.

Button	Name	Purpose
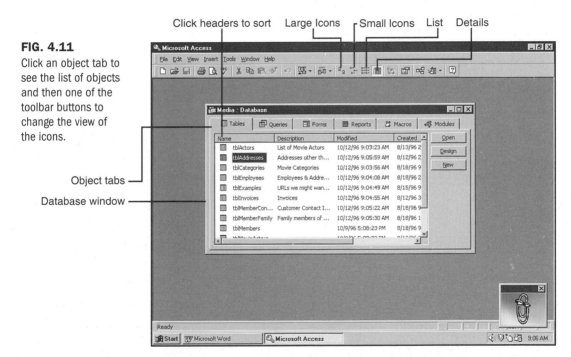 List	List	Shows object names with small icons and alphabetizes the list from top to bottom, then left to right.
Details	Details	Shows a small icon, description of the object (from clicking the right mouse button and filling in properties), and the dates the object was modified and created. Like the details button of the file dialog box, you can also sort the list by clicking the column headers.

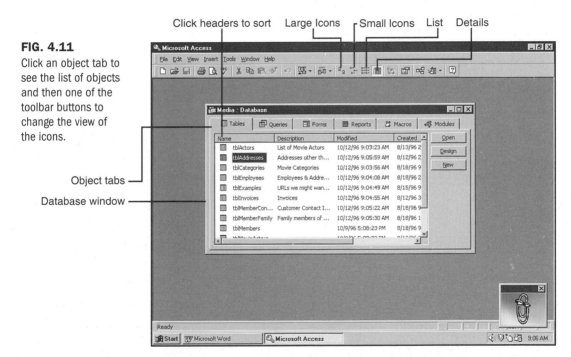

FIG. 4.11
Click an object tab to see the list of objects and then one of the toolbar buttons to change the view of the icons.

Click headers to sort   Large Icons   Small Icons   List   Details

Object tabs

Database window

Sorting the File List

  When you choose the Details button, the list of files displays with the file name, size, type, and modified date and time. The top of the contents list box shows column headers Name, Size, Type, and Modified as shown earlier in Figure 4.10. Click any of these column headers to sort the list ascending by that category. Click the column header again to sort the list descending by that category. For example, to sort the files by date, click the Modified header. Click again to sort the files with the latest date on top of the list.

Using Wild Cards to Shorten the File List

If your file list is particularly long, you may want to limit the list by the file name. Two wild cards can help you limit the list by characters in the name of the file: * (asterisk) and ? (question mark). The asterisk means replace any number of characters. The question mark means replace one character. In the File Name text box of the Open dialog box, you can type the text with wild cards and then choose the Find Now command button. The following list shows some examples.

Type	To Display
B*	All files that begin with B
Rev??	Rev95, Rev96, Rev97
Don	Reasons to Donate, Donations YTD, Orientation to Donors, Don Campbell's Resume

To remove the wild card and all restrictions on the file list, choose the New Search command button.

 Unlike the DOS wild card, you can use multiple asterisks within file names.

Finding a File by Date

When your list is long and you do not remember the exact file name but you do remember the approximate time you last worked on the file, you can limit the file list to just those files modified at a certain time. Use the Last Modified drop-down list and click the Find Now command button to limit the file list by time. Choices from Last Modified include today, yesterday, last week, this week, last month, and this month. To return the file list to show all dates, select any time.

Finding a File by Contents

You may remember where you put a file but don't have any clue what you called it. You can look for a file by the contents inside the file or by the summary information you added to the file. In the Text or Property text box, type some text that you put in the file, such as who you addressed the file to, the subject, or maybe an expense category. After you fill in the Text or Property text box, choose the Find Now button.

Expanding the Search to Include Subfolders

 If the search text isn't found in the current folder, you can expand your search to other folders on the hard drive. Choose the highest level you want to search (for example, the C: drive) in the Look In drop-down list. Then choose the Commands and Settings button. From the drop-down menu choose Search Subfolders as shown in Figure 4.12. Now when you do any of the search procedures, such as using the File Name, Text or Property, Last Modified, Files of Type, or Advanced Searches, subfolders display as well as the files. To group files by their subfolders, check the Group Files by Folder option on the Commands and Settings button. To return to display only the contents of the Look In choice, uncheck the Search Subfolders option.

FIG. 4.12

The contents list box shows folders and files within the folders that meet your criteria.

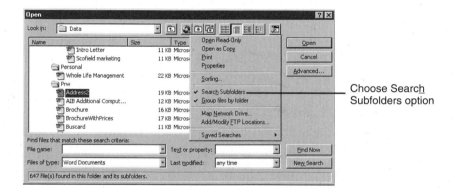

Choose Search
Subfolders option

Part
I

Ch
4

Displaying Types of Files

If you enter the Open dialog box through the Open Office Document button on the Microsoft Office Shortcut Bar, the dialog box shows files of all types. If you enter the Open or Save dialog boxes through a specific program such as Word, Excel, PowerPoint, or Access, the default is to show only those files created by that program. If you want to see a list of all files, choose the File of Type drop-down list and choose All Files. You also can display files from different word processors such as WordPerfect, spreadsheets such as Lotus 1-2-3, or database programs such as dBASE IV. This capability is helpful if you want to open a file created by a different program, or if you want to save a file in a different format for use in a different program.

You usually change the file type when you want to convert a file from one kind of worksheet (Lotus 1-2-3 to Excel), word processing document (WordPerfect to Word), or database (dBASE to Access) to another. In some cases, however, you may want to open a different kind of file. For example, you can open an Excel worksheet file in a Word document. Table 4.2 shows some possibilities for opening different kinds of files.

Table 4.2   File Types You Can Open in a Different Application

Application Opening File	File Type	Result
Word	Excel worksheet	Word table (can be a merge data document)
PowerPoint	Word (outline)	Heading 1 = slide title, Heading 2, 3 = points and subpoints
PowerPoint	Excel worksheet	Each row becomes the title of the slide

If your application can't convert the file type when you try to open a file of a different type, an error message appears, stating that the file format is not valid.

 In Access you don't use File Open to open a different type of file into Access. You can, however, use File, Get External Data, Import to import an Excel worksheet into Access. You will have options indicating the range and whether the first row contains field names or not. You can also export a table, query, form, or report to Word or Excel using the OfficeLinks button on the toolbar.

Using Advanced File Find Capabilities

Although the Text or Property option searches for the contents of the file or any property, you may want to limit your search to one property or use many properties at one time. Follow these steps:

1. Click the Open button on your program's standard toolbar or click the Open Office Document button of the Microsoft Office Shortcut Bar.

2. If you want, fill out the File Name, Text or Property, Files of Type, and Last Modified options as described earlier.

3. Choose the Advanced button. The Advanced Find dialog box appears with any choices you made in the Open dialog box.

4. Choose the Property drop-down list and select the property you want as shown in Figure 4.13.

5. In the Value text box, type the text you are looking for.

6. Choose the Add to List button.

7. If you want to add another condition, choose the And option button (both conditions must be true) or the Or option button (either condition must be true) and complete steps 2–6.

8. When you finish filling in the Advanced Find dialog box, choose the Find Now button on the bottom left of the Advanced Find dialog box.

FIG. 4.13
Choose one of many
properties to search
in the Property drop-
down list.

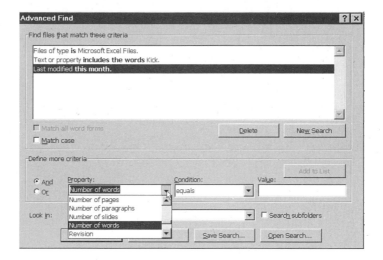

You return to the Open dialog box with the list of files that meet your criteria in the
contents list box.

Some of the other options in the Advanced Find dialog box are listed in Table 4.3.

Table 4.3   Other Options in Advanced Find Dialog Boxes

Option	Description
Match All Word Forms check box	For contents, comments, and other item searches, you can find files that match different forms of the word. For example, if the Value is *to be*, the search looks for *to be, are, is, am.*
Match Case check box	For contents, comments, and other items in the Property choice, you find only those items that match capitalization (uppercase and lowercase) the way you typed the options in the Value text box.
Delete button	Click one of the items in the Find Files That Match These Criteria, and then choose the Delete button to remove that criteria.
New Search button	Clear all search criteria and start over.
Condition drop-down list	This list changes depending on the Property selected and enables you to find matches that contain the entire Value choice, a portion of it, one of the items in the Value choice, items greater or less than a date, and others.

continues

Part
I

Ch
4

Table 4.3   Continued

Option	Description
Look In drop-down list	The same as the Look In on the Open dialog box; it enables you to change the location of your search.
Search Subfolders check box	Same as the menu choice on the Commands and Settings menu in the Open dialog box; it enables you to include files from the current folder and any subfolders you want.
Save Search button	Save any search criteria with a name for later retrieval.
Open Search button	Choose one of the named searches you created with the Save Search command.
Cancel button	Don't do any of the Advanced Find options and return to the Open dialog box the way you left it.

Saving Your Favorite Files and Folders

 If you use the same files or folders over and over, you may want to save them in a special folder called Favorites. In an Open dialog box, move to your favorite file or folder and click the Add to Favorites button.

 When you want to see the Favorites files and folders, click the Look in Favorites button in any file dialog box.

Copying and Moving Files, Printing, and Other Hidden Features

When you are in an Open or Save dialog box, you have other options that are "hidden" and do not display as a choice in the dialog box. Access these options by selecting a file or files and then clicking your right mouse button.

You can select files in one of several ways:

- Click one file name.
- Hold down the Ctrl key and click any files to select more than one file.
- Click the first file, hold down the Shift key and then click the last file to select a group of adjacent files.

After you have selected your file(s), click the right mouse button in part of the selection and choose one of the following:

- Choose Open to open all the selected files.
- Choose Open Read Only to open the files, but you need to give a new name if you want to save the files.

- Choose Open as Copy to have Office create and open a copy of each selected file, so you can save it with a new name, as a new file.

- Choose Print to print the files. (This is not available in Access).

- If a selected file is a PowerPoint presentation file, choose Show to display the slide show on-screen.

- If Windows 95 Quick View is installed on your system, the Quick View choice appears; choosing it displays the contents (text only, no formatting) of each selected file in a Quick View window, so you can decide whether you want to open that particular file in its source application.

- Choose Send To, then choose a floppy or removable drive to copy the file, Fax Recipient to fax the file, Mail Recipient to send a mail version of the file, or My Briefcase.

- Choose Cut to move the files to the Clipboard (and remove the original files).

- Choose Copy to copy the files to the Clipboard (and keep the original files in place).

- Choose Create Shortcut to create another icon in the directory, which is a shortcut to the file (click the right mouse button on the shortcut name and choose Properties to give the shortcut a keyboard shortcut. The shortcut name starts with "Shortcut to.")

- Choose Delete to remove the files to the Recycle Bin.

- Choose Rename to give the file a new name.

- Choose Properties to give a keyboard shortcut to a shortcut file or see file information such as DOS file name, date created, file attributes, summary information, and statistics.

N O T E If you accidentally delete files, you can get them back if you haven't emptied the Recycle Bin. With all programs minimized, double-click the Recycle Bin icon on the Windows Desktop. Choose the file name and choose File, Restore. ■

If you choose Cut or Copy, choose the location (disk or folder) where you want the file to go using the Look in list, and then click the right mouse button and choose Paste from the shortcut menu.

Closing a Document

You can close a document in one of several ways, some of which you learned about in the "Closing Programs" section in Chapter 2:

Part
I
Ch
4

- Click the document Close button (x) in the upper-right corner of the document window (not the application window).

- Double-click the Control menu icon in the upper-left corner of the document window.

- Click one time on the Control menu icon and choose Close from the pull-down menu.

- Choose File, Close.

- Press Ctrl+W.

CAUTION

Make sure you click the document Close button rather than the program Close button. If the document is maximized, the document Close button is on the same row as the menu bar. If the document is not maximized, the Close button is on the right side of the document title bar.

If you saved your last changes to the document, the document closes. If you made changes since your last save or you haven't yet saved, you are prompted to save the document by an on-screen message.

Choose one of the following buttons:

- Choose Yes to save changes. If you have already given the document a name, the document closes. If you haven't given the document a name, the Save As dialog box appears.

- Choose No to not save changes. You lose any changes you have made since your last save, or you lose the entire document if you haven't saved it at all.

- Choose Cancel to return to the document without saving or exiting the document.

TROUBLESHOOTING

I know that a file is in the folder but I don't see it. You may need to use the scroll bar on the bottom or right side of the contents list box. Another possibility is that you have search criteria that excludes your file. Click the New Search button in a file dialog box. Make sure that your file type is correct in the Files of Type drop-down list.

Starting a New Document

In Excel and Word, when you click the New button or press Ctrl+N, a new blank file window opens. In PowerPoint, a new presentation starts by asking you what kind of slide you want.

▶ **See** "Using Template Wizards," **p. 256**

▶ **See** "Understanding Templates and Masters," **p. 601**

▶ **See** "Creating a Presentation Using a Wizard," **p. 608**

In Access, if you use the menu command File, New in a program or click the New Office Document button on the Microsoft Office Shortcut Bar, the New dialog box appears with a series of tabs on the top as shown in Figure 4.14. The tabs show general categories of files you can create. On each tab are files that are templates or wizards. *Templates* are files that may have stored formatting, macros, styles, text, and different menus and toolbars. After you open a template with the File, New command, you still need to give the document a name to save it. *Wizards* are a series of dialog boxes that lead you through the steps of creating a document or performing a function.

Part

I

Ch

4

FIG. 4.14

The New Office Document button displays New dialog box with templates and wizards for Microsoft Office applications.

New Office Document button

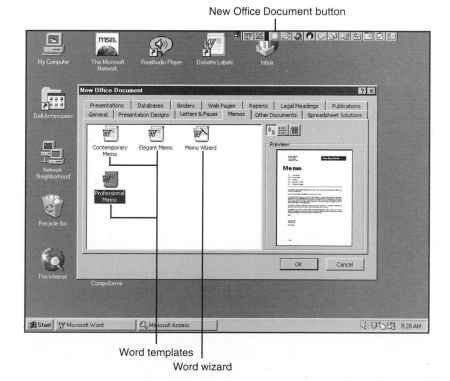

Word templates
Word wizard

Using Save Options

Although most applications require that you save files, Word, PowerPoint, and Excel enable you to set up automatic recovery or automatic saving. You still should use the Save button, the menu command, or the shortcut key to save often, especially after you spend a significant amount of effort to make the document look the way you want or before you perform a major procedure on your file (such as spell checking, sorting, replacing, automatic formatting, or importing). However, if your computer crashes with an unsaved file open and you restart it and reopen Word or Excel, the application will use the data it stored the last time it saved AutoRecover or AutoSave information, and display a copy of the file. In Word and PowerPoint, the AutoRecover file appears on-screen, and you need to resave it. To activate this feature, choose Tools, Options, Save tab, and fill out the AutoRecover options. In Excel, the program prompts you for a file name when it opens the AutoSave file if you had not already saved and named the file. To load AutoSave in Excel, choose Tools, Add-Ins and check AutoSave. To activate this option, choose Tools, AutoSave and check the Automatic Save Every check box and fill in the setting for Minutes.

 TIP You may want to use the Save As feature to save different revisions of the same file until your project is complete.

In addition, Word and Excel enable you to create *backup files*. A backup file has a different icon, and the name begins with *Backup of*. Word creates a backup file after you have saved the original document file at least once. When you save a file the second time and all subsequent times, the backup procedure renames the old file on disk with the same file name, but with a *Backup of* prefix. The document on-screen saves with the original file name. If you need to use your backup file, change the file type to All Files or type **backup*** in the File Name text box. In Word and Excel, to start the backup procedure, choose the File, Save As command and then choose the Options command button, then check the Always Create Backup check box. (In Word, this check box also appears on the Save tab of the Options dialog box.)

NOTE In Access and PowerPoint, there is not a backup procedure as part of the program. To make a backup of the file, first close the file and then go to Windows Explorer by clicking the right mouse button on the Start button and choosing Explore. Go to the file and press Ctrl+C to copy it. Go to the folder in which you want to store the backup copy and press Ctrl+V to paste the copy. ▨

Using File Properties

In Windows 3.1, your file name was limited to eight characters plus a three character extension. Windows 95, Windows NT, and Microsoft Office have greatly expanded the capacity to 255 characters. If you need more than your file name to identify a document, however, you now have many properties you can fill out in the new properties feature.

Viewing and Editing File Properties

You can enter or view properties for a file in many ways. The following lists describe some ways to use file properties.

To view and change file properties, do the following:

- With the file displayed in Word, Excel, or PowerPoint, choose File, Properties. In Access, choose File, Database Properties.
- In a file dialog box, click the right mouse button on the file and choose Properties.

- In a file dialog box, select the file and click the Commands and Settings button. Then choose Properties on the menu.

If you use any of the preceding methods to view file properties, the Office application displays a Properties dialog box for the file. This dialog box enables you to both view and edit the file properties, and it will be discussed in the next subsection titled "Reviewing the File Properties."

To view properties only:

- In a file dialog box, select the file and click the Properties button. The properties of the highlighted file show in a small area you can scroll with a vertical scroll bar as shown in Figure 4.15.

FIG. 4.15
Scroll in the contents list box to see more properties.

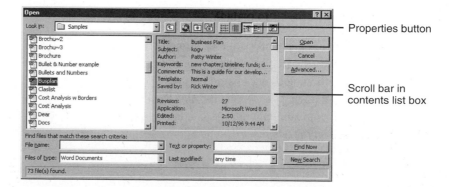

Properties button

Scroll bar in contents list box

You can print your properties for Word files only. Choose File, Print and from the Print What drop-down list choose Summary Info.

Reviewing the File Properties

Depending on how you entered the file properties, when you choose a method that lets you edit and view file properties, you see a dialog box similar to the one shown in Figure 4.16. Up to five tabs appear in the Properties dialog box. The tabs are described in the following sections.

FIG. 4.16
The General page in the Properties sheet shows information about the file.

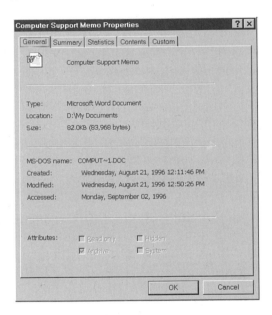

General Tab   Figure 4.16 shows the General page for a Word document. The program has entered the information on this tab for you. The information includes the following:

Item	Description
Name of file	The name also shows an icon representing the program type.
Type:	Type of file. This example shows Microsoft Word Document.
Location:	Name of folder that contains the file.
Size:	The file size shows both in KB (kilobytes) and bytes.
MS-DOS Name:	The converted name based on the first six characters of the file name, a period, and the file type extension. You use this name if you copy to a DOS system.

Item	Description
Created:	The date you first created (or copied) the file.
Modified:	The last time you saved the file.
Accessed:	If you are currently looking at the file, today's date.
Attributes:	You cannot change these attributes from the program's File, Properties command, but you can change them if you enter properties through the Explorer.
Read Only attribute	You can read the file but not save it with the same name.
Archive attribute	The file has been changed since the last backup.
Hidden attribute	The file is normally hidden from file lists.
System attribute	The file is a system file required to run the operating system and should not be modified.

Summary Tab   Figure 4.17 shows the Summary page, where you can enter information about the file to help you organize and later search for the file. Choose any of the text boxes (Title, Subject, Author, Manager, Company, Category, Keywords, or Comments) and enter the text you like. Although you can enter more characters, you can view about 42 characters in each of the fields except Comments. The Comments field has a large view area and you can use the vertical scroll bar to see more text than fits in the text box.

Use the Hyperlink Base text box to enter a base address for document hyperlink locations, so that you don't have to repeat very long addresses in hyperlinks. You can enter an address to a Web site, folder on your computer's hard disk, or folder on a shared network drive. The Save Preview Picture text box saves a picture of the fist page of the document for the Open dialog box.

Statistics Tab   The Statistics page depends on the application. This information tells when your file was created, modified, accessed, and printed; who last saved the file; how many times the file has been revised; and what the total editing time is. Also, Word documents include how long the document is in pages, paragraphs, lines, words, characters, and bytes.

Contents Tab   The information on the Contents page depends on the type of file you have. If the file is an Excel file, the names of the worksheet or module tabs appear. If the file is a PowerPoint file, the names of each of the slides appear as well as information about formatting. An Access database shows a list of all the object types (Tables, Queries, and so forth) and the name of each object. A Word file shows only the Title from the Summary page.

Custom Tab   If you want to create your own properties, you have plenty of flexibility with the Custom page. You can add your own field names and values for whatever properties you want (see Figure 4.18).

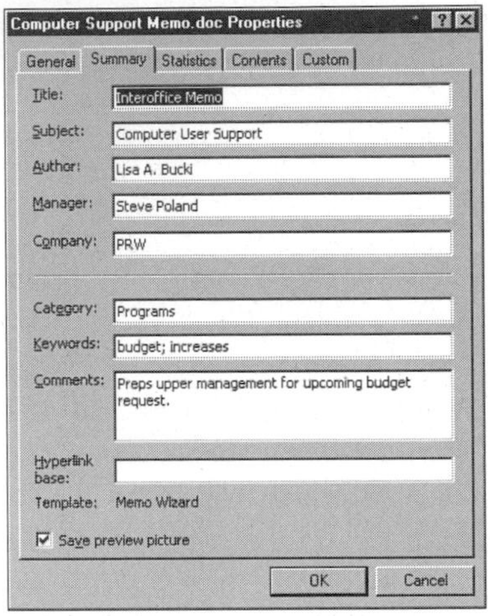

FIG. 4.17

Fill in the Summary page of the Properties sheet to help you find or manage your file.

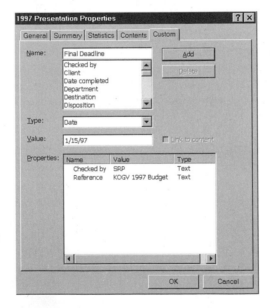

FIG. 4.18

A custom set of properties (in this case, from PowerPoint) may include the additional information you need to manage your documents.

To add your own properties, follow these steps:

1. Choose File, Properties (or Database Properties).

2. Click the Custom tab.

3. Type the name of your field in the <u>N</u>ame text box or choose from one of over 20 field names in the drop-down list box. Included in the drop-down list are items such as Checked By, Department, Source, and Editor.

4. Choose the data type from the <u>T</u>ype drop-down list. Types include Text, Date, Number, and Yes or No.

5. Type a Value in the Value area or choose <u>Y</u>es or N<u>o</u> (if data type is Yes or No, you see Yes, No options only). The value has to match the data type.

N O T E If you check the <u>L</u>ink to Content check box on the Custom page, the <u>V</u>alue box will have a drop-down list where you can choose items within the document to link to, such as a bookmark in Word or a named range in Excel. ▨

6. Choose the <u>A</u>dd command button.

7. Repeat steps 3–6 for any additional fields.

TROUBLESHOOTING

I don't see five tabs on my Properties sheet. Make sure you are using the original file, not a shortcut name when you look at file properties.

I need to associate my documents with account numbers. Open the file and choose <u>F</u>ile Proper<u>t</u>ies and click the Custom tab. Click in the Name text box and type **Account Number**. Choose a <u>T</u>ype and type the number in the <u>V</u>alue field.

Printing Documents

To print or preview the current document, you can use menu commands, toolbar buttons, or shortcut keys. As mentioned in an earlier section, you can print one or more files by clicking the right mouse button on a file name in an Open dialog box, then choosing the <u>P</u>rint command.

Printing All or Part of the Document

 To print the current document, choose the <u>F</u>ile, <u>P</u>rint command, press Ctrl+P, or click the Print button on the Standard toolbar.

N O T E In Access, you select the object in the database window or double-click the item to open it, and then choose one of the methods (Print button; <u>F</u>ile, <u>P</u>rint; or Ctrl+P) to print just that object. ▨

When you use the Print button or shortcut key, the entire document prints. If you use the menu command, a dialog box similar to Figure 4.19 appears, displaying more choices.

FIG. 4.19
The Print dialog box enables you to specify what you want to print in more detail.

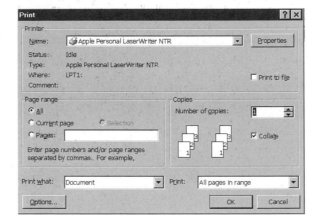

Options in the Print dialog box enable you to print the entire document, the current page, specific pages, or selected text. You also can specify the number of copies to print. In the Pages text box in Word or Slides text box in PowerPoint, you can skip pages (you can type **1-2**, **4-7**, or just **13-** to print page 13 to end of document).

To change the printer, choose the printer from the drop-down list in the Printer section of the Print dialog box.

 TIP If you want to cancel a print job in Word, double-click the print spooler icon in the Word status bar.

Changing Printing Options

If you want to make additional printing choices, choose File, Page Setup and use the Page Setup dialog box (see Figure 4.20). The options in this dialog box enable you to set margins, print headers and footers, specify the print orientation, and change the printer settings.

Using Print Preview

 Although your screen shows what you will see on the printed page, Word, Excel, and Access have a Print Preview option that enables you to see the entire page (or more than one page), including headers and footers, page numbers, and margins. You enter the preview by choosing the File, Print Preview command.

Figure 4.21 shows Print Preview for Access, which provides an example of the key buttons you'll find in the Print Preview for other Office Applications.

FIG. 4.20
You can specify additional printing options in the Excel Page Setup dialog box.

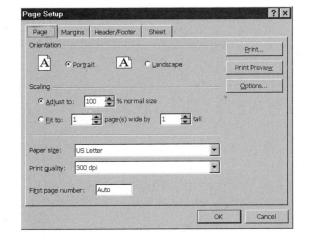

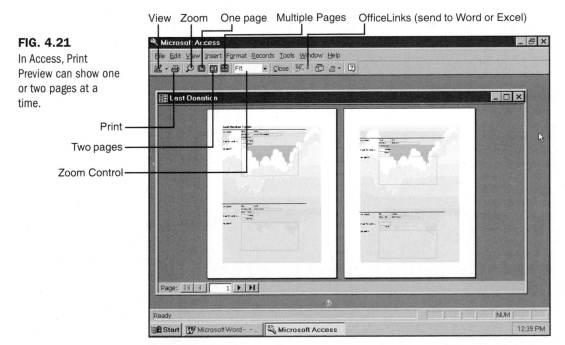

FIG. 4.21
In Access, Print Preview can show one or two pages at a time.

To change margins, click the Margins or View Ruler button, move the mouse pointer to the top or side until the pointer changes to a double-headed black arrow, and drag the margin. To magnify, click the Magnifier (Word) or Zoom (Excel and Access) button and click the document where you want magnification. To turn magnification off, click the document again. In Word, to edit the document, click the Magnifier button to turn magnification off and editing on. In Excel, to use shrink to fit, choose the Setup button, click the Page tab, and choose Fit To and fill in the Page(s) Wide by Tall text boxes. In Word, click the Shrink To Fit button.

Switching Between Documents

When you open more than one file at a time, you have a window for each file. You can switch between open documents (similar to "Switching Between Programs," which you learned about in Chapter 2) using one of the following ways:

- Choose the open document from the bottom of the Window menu.
- Press Ctrl+F6 to cycle through the open documents.
- If parts of documents are visible on-screen, click the one you want to see. If a document is minimized, double-click its icon.

If you want to view or copy information between documents, you may want to display two or more windows. In Word, Excel, and PowerPoint, you can use the drag-and-drop feature to move or copy items between document windows. To move, just click and drag the item to another window; to copy, hold down the Ctrl key while you drag.

- In Word, choose the Window, Arrange All command to display the documents as shown in Figure 4.22.
- In Excel, choose the Window, Arrange command. A dialog box appears, asking how you want to arrange the windows. The Tiled option displays the windows in small rectangles so they fill the screen. Horizontal displays the windows in rows (like Word). Vertical displays the windows in columns. Cascade stacks the windows, with the title bar of each window showing.
- In PowerPoint, choose the Window, Arrange All command to show the documents in tiled form. You also can choose the Window, Cascade command to stack the windows, with the title bar of each window showing.
- In Access, choose the Window menu. You can then choose Tile Horizontally, Tile Vertically, or Cascade to arrange the windows on the screen.

FIG. 4.22
In Word, choose Window, Arrange All to arrange the document windows horizontally.

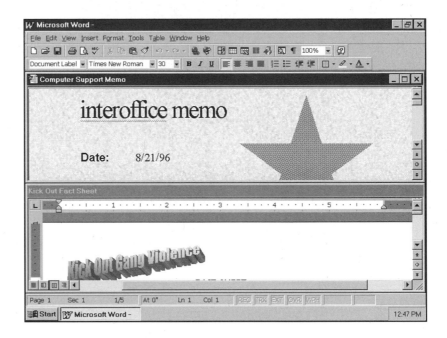

When several documents are visible, a dark title bar indicates which window is active. To make another window active, click that window. To show one of the windows full-screen, click the Maximize button or double-click the title bar. ●

Using Help and Office Assistant

by Lisa A. Bucki

In addition to the screen elements such as toolbars, ScreenTips, and rulers mentioned in Chapter 2, "Getting Started and Identifying Screen Parts," Microsoft has many additional tools to help you become more productive. In particular, the Office applications provide extensive help features to assist you in completing an operation—even if you can't remember the steps. These tools also help you learn more about the capabilities of each Office 97 application. ■

Getting plain English advice

Learn to work effectively with the Office Assistant, which provides context-sensitive help and also displays help topics related to any question you type.

Using online help

Seek out a specific kind of help using the Help Topics dialog box.

Seeking help on the Internet

Learn how selecting a help topic from Microsoft on the Web takes you to more information from Microsoft.

Reviewing screen elements you use for help

See how Microsoft Office applications are specifically designed to provide you with information and tips about the current procedure.

Using wizards to help you create documents and perform other tasks

Wizard automation ensures that you achieve high-quality results. Explore how to use wizards to handle formatting and setup work for you.

Using the Variety of Help Features

Help is available in many different forms. Help includes the traditional online help to many other features that identify parts of the screen or assist you in accomplishing your tasks. The following is a list of help features you can use:

■ *Office Assistant.* Enables you to type a request in plain English and select from a list of possible responses; also displays context-sensitive help about the current operation. Press F1 or choose 1st Help menu item.

■ *Contents and Index.* Enables you to look up help on a topic by searching through a table of contents or index, or searching for a specific term. Choose Help, Contents and Index.

■ *What's This?* Enables you to click any item on-screen to see pop-up help about it. Press Shift+F1 or choose Help, What's This?

■ *Microsoft on the Web.* Enables you to connect directly to useful World Wide Web pages maintained by Microsoft to provide information that may be even more detailed and up-to-date than the help provided with Office. Choose Help, Microsoft on the Web.

■ *Transition help.* Word and Excel give help for users of a competing product (see Help, WordPerfect Help or Help, Lotus 1-2-3 Help), which enables you to change the settings so keys are similar to the old product and helps you look up equivalent procedures in the new product.

■ *About (application).* Displays information about your Office application's version and ID number, and enables you to access the two types of help listed next (from command buttons on the About dialog box). Choose last item on Help menu.

■ *System Info.* A window that shows information about your computer operating system, memory, storage, printing, and so on.

■ *Tech Support.* Takes you to a Help Topics window where you can find phone numbers and procedures for support, downloading files, and asking questions.

■ *Dialog box Help button.* Enables you to click an item in a dialog box for a description of the item.

■ *Tip of the Day.* When you first start the program, a helpful hint appears.

■ *Wizards.* Provide dialog boxes that take you step-by-step through a process. You are prompted for choices throughout the process to build your document. Choose File, New for many wizards but they also appear throughout the Office Applications.

▶ **See** "Using Template Wizards," **p. 256**

N O T E To get information about your computer such as processor type, operating system, memory, and hard drive space, plus information about printing, fonts, and files, choose Help, About then choose the System Info button.

To find telephone numbers for contacting Microsoft, choose Help, About then choose the Tech Support button. You also learn how to log on to the Internet, CompuServe, and other communication services. This information helps you download files and join Microsoft forums to talk to Microsoft support personnel and other users of the product. ■

 T I P To see transitional help about WordPerfect from within Word, double-click the WPH indicator on the status bar.

Working with the Office Assistant

 As you learned in the initial chapters of this book, the Office Assistant is a new feature in Office 97 that appears automatically (until you turn if off by clicking its window's Close button). When the Office Assistant is open, its window moves discreetly out of the way on-screen, even when a dialog box or other item appears. In some cases, such as when the default save format in Word is set to a format other than a Word document, the Assistant opens on its own to make sure you're handling the operation the way you want to. Otherwise, you can display and hide the Office Assistant as needed to ensure that it's not unnecessarily occupying system memory.

Asking the Office Assistant for Help

 Press F1 or choose the first item on the Help menu. Depending on whether you have a selection or are in a dialog box when you open Office Assistant, its contents vary slightly when it appears. If nothing is selected, the Office Assistant simply asks "What would you like to do?" and provides a few buttons plus a text box where you can type a question. In other cases, such as when you open the Office Assistant from a dialog box, Office Assistant prompts you to enter a question and you see a list of other topics, as shown in Figure 5.1.

When you see a list of topics, you can click the round button beside a topic to select it. When you do, the Office Assistant displays the Help window (from normal online help) for that topic. Clicking the See More button displays a listing of additional topics.

Figure 5.1 also shows a yellow light bulb. This indicates that the Assistant has a suggestion on a shortcut or other information that might be useful for the task you are performing. Click the light bulb to see the suggestion.

Part

I

Ch

5

FIG. 5.1
You can choose an existing topic or type a new topic in the Search text box.

Topics ⌐

Type question here —

Command buttons —

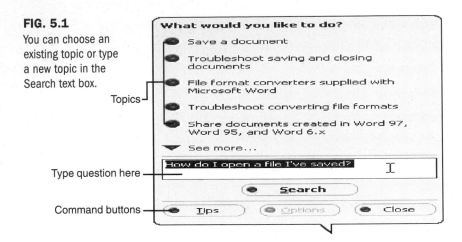

Any time the Office Assistant displays a text box above a Search command button, you can type the question of your choice in the text box, then choose Search. (In some cases, the text box is blank; otherwise, it prompts you with Type your question here, and then click Search.) The Office Assistant displays a list of help topics that may answer your question, in a message that looks much like Figure 5.1. From there, you can click to select a topic or perform another search.

If you don't choose a topic or perform a search when Office Assistant is displaying help, click the Close button to close the message balloon. To close the Office Assistant altogether, right-click the Assistant and choose Hide Assistant from the shortcut menu, or click the Office Assistant window's Close button.

N O T E If you display the Office Assistant in one open Office application and then switch to another Office application, the Office Assistant is open in that application, too. Similarly, if you close the Office Assistant in one application, it is closed in other Office applications as well. ▪

 T I P To redisplay the Office Assistant's previous message to you, click the Office Assistant window's title bar.

When you choose a bulleted item on the Office Assistant, a help window opens (see Figure 5.2). If the window contains more text than displays on-screen at one time, use the scroll bar to see more.

FIG. 5.2
The help window
offers options such
as defining terms or
going to related
topics.

Dotted underline
goes to term

Double arrow
goes to another
topic

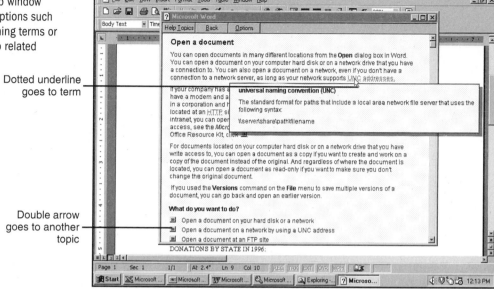

You have a number of help options, depending on what is on the help window:

- Click any dotted underlined text to see the definition of a term. (The mouse pointer is a pointing finger for definition terms).

- Click an icon or a screen item to see the description (when the mouse pointer is a finger).

- Click double arrow buttons to go to a related help topic.

- Click the Back button to go to the last help topic you looked at.

- Click the Options button to add text (Annotate) to your help file or copy, print, or change other help options.

- Click the Help Topics command button to see a dialog box with the following three tabs. (You can also access Help Topics through Help, Contents and Index.)

Contents tab. Enables you to browse topics, similar to a table of contents in a book. Double-click a closed book to see a list of topics (question marks) and related topics (other book icons).

Part

I

Ch

5

Index tab. Enables you to search for text based on the title of each page in help.

Find tab. Enables you to search for any text on a help page.

Customizing the Office Assistant

As with most features in Office 97, the Office Assistant enables you to customize it so that it looks and works as you prefer. You not only can change the actual animated character that appears as the Office Assistant, but you also can control such items as whether pressing F1 displays the Office Assistant, whether you see help about keyboard shortcuts, and whether you see a Tip of the Day when you start an Office application. Follow these steps to customize the Office Assistant:

1. Press F1 to display the Office Assistant.

2. Choose the Options button. The Office Assistant dialog box appears, with the Options tab selected (see Figure 5.3).

FIG. 5.3
The tabs in this dialog box enable you to adjust how the Office Assistant works for you.

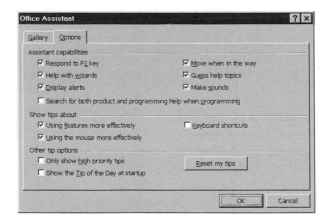

3. To choose an option, click it to place a check mark in the check box beside it. To disable an option, click to clear the check mark. The Options tab offers three categories of options:

   - *Assistant Capabilities.* Enables you to control whether you can press F1 to display Office Assistant, whether Assistant makes sound effects, and similar features.

   - *Show Tips About.* Enables you to select whether Office Assistant displays particular types of tips. If you don't need certain tips, such as keyboard tips, turn those tips off to streamline the Office Assistant.

   - *Other Tip Options.* Control the Tip of the Day and more.

4. If you want to change the animated character in the Office Assistant, choose the Gallery tab to display it.

5. To view the various characters, choose the Next and Back buttons (see Figure 5.4). The characters available depend on how Office 97 was set up on your system. The typical setup installs several characters, but even more are available via a custom setup.

FIG. 5.4
On the Gallery tab, you can choose a new character for the Office Assistant.

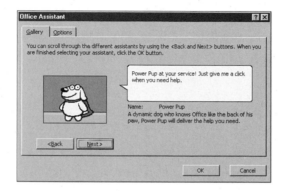

6. When you have displayed the character you want to use, click OK to close the Office Assistant dialog box and begin using the new options.

Using Online Help

You can find help on a topic in a number of ways. Table 5.1 describes some of the ways to enter a help topic.

Table 5.1   Finding Help on a Topic

To Do This	Do This
To find help on options in a dialog box	Press F1 while you're in the dialog box, click the dialog box's ? help button, or right-click the dialog box item.
To find help on a toolbar button	Place the mouse pointer on the button to view its ScreenTip or click the Help button and then click the button.

continues

Table 5.1   Continued

To Do This	Do This
To find help on a menu item	Highlight the item on the menu and press Shift+F1.
To see a ScreenTip about a selection	Make sure the ScreenTips are turned on (choose Tools, Options, click the View tab, and place a check beside the ScreenTips option), make your selection, and point to it with the mouse (see Figure 5.5).
To find help on an item shown on-screen	From the Help menu, choose What's This? or press Shift+F1, then click the item you want help about.
To search for help	From the Help menu, choose Contents and Index. In the Help Topics window, choose the Index or Find tab. Type the text to search, select the topic to display, and choose the Display button.
To display a list of Help topics	From the Help menu, choose Contents and Index. In the Help Topics window, choose the Contents tab.

FIG. 5.5
This ScreenTip gives information about a potential change in the document.

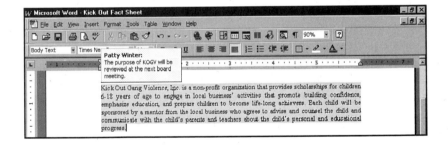

Letting Help Show You What to Do

When someone is helping you learn a process, that person typically shows you what to do, or at least how to start out. Now, online help in Office 97 offers the same capability in some Help windows. Whenever you see a button labeled Show Me, as in Figure 5.6, you can click that button, and Help demonstrates how to find the command or tool you need to use. The mouse pointer moves on its own on-screen and clicks buttons and select commands.

FIG. 5.6
Click a Show Me button for an animated demonstration of how to find a command or option.

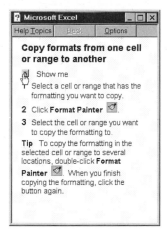

Using Help Options

In addition to the Help Topics button, most topic windows have two other buttons: Back and Options. If you've used buttons to see related topics, you can choose the Back button to retrace your steps. The other button, Options, gives you a number of choices described in Table 5.2.

Table 5.2   Help Window Options

Choose This	To Do This
Annotate	Add your own notes to this page in the help reference. Choose Annotate and then type your note. When finished typing, choose Save. Your note is indicated on the page with a paper clip in the upper-left corner of the topic window. To delete the note, choose Annotate and Delete.
Copy	Place a copy of the entire Help window on the Clipboard. Move to the location where you want the text to go (for example, a Word, Notepad, or WordPad document) and choose Edit, Paste to place the Help text in the document. You can also select a portion of the text to copy with the I-beam mouse pointer before you choose Options and then Copy.
Print Topic	Print the displayed topic.
Font	Change the size of fonts in the Help window. You can choose from Small, Normal (the default), and Large.

continues

Part
I

Ch
5

Table 5.2 Continued	
Choose This	**To Do This**
Keep Help on Top	Some Help windows automatically remain visible when you click back in the document. To change the default, choose On Top to force the Help window to remain visible when you click back to the application. You can also choose Not On Top or Default.
Use System Colors	Change the Help window to the colors defined in the Control Panel.

Accessing Help on the Web

As noted in Chapter 1, one of the primary new features of Office 97 is its Active Web capabilities. Active Web technology enables you to log on to the Internet, via Microsoft's Internet Explorer and your existing Internet connection, from within any Office Application. You can display the World Wide Web page you specify by typing a Web URL (Uniform Resource Locator) address.

N O T E The steps in this section assume that your system is set up to connect automatically to the Internet when you choose any Microsoft on the Web menu choice. If your system is not set up to connect automatically, or you need more help about Active Web capabilities, see Chapter 44, "Navigating and Publishing on the Web with Office 97." ▪

You can take advantage of Office 97's technology to get up-to-date help from a Microsoft Web site using the Help, Microsoft on the Web command in any Office application. This command offers the following choices:

- The first four topics under Microsoft on the Web take you to a Web page that's specific to the application from which you launch the Web help feature. For example, if you choose the Online Support option from within Word, Office displays the Web page providing Microsoft Word online support information.
- The next four choices display Web pages to provide you with help in using the Web and locating other topics or resources on the Web.
- The final choice takes you to the Microsoft home page, so you can review a variety of online information published by Microsoft, or even navigate to help about another Office application.

Using the Microsoft on the Web command saves you the trouble of remembering specific URL addresses; each needed address is specified by the submenu choice. The following steps explain how to access a Microsoft on the Web help topic:

1. Choose the Help, Microsoft on the Web command (see Figure 5.7).

2. Click the submenu choice for the type of help you'd like to see a Web page about.

FIG. 5.7

This command offers choices for connecting to the Internet and viewing helpful World Wide Web pages.

For example, you can click Online Support if you need to access additional help and troubleshooting resources about an application. After you select a submenu choice, Office launches your Internet connection (depending on your configuration, you may need to enter your user name and password when prompted), starts the Internet Explorer, and displays the specified Web page. Figure 5.8 shows an example.

3. You can browse around the Web as needed.

FIG. 5.8

This World Wide Web page gives information about online help for Microsoft Word. The site will look different as Microsoft updates the information.

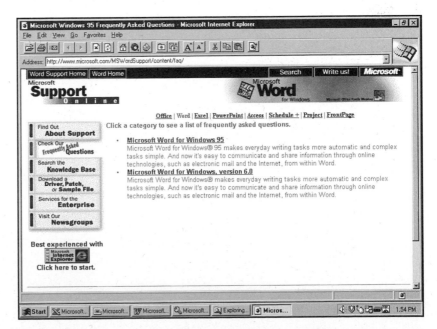

4. When you finish working on the Web, choose Close from the Internet Explorer File menu. Explorer closes, and a message appears, asking if you want to disconnect from the Internet.

5. Click Yes to log off.

Reviewing Screen Elements

In addition to the online help, many help features are built into Microsoft Office products. The most visible are the toolbars, but other screen features that help you are ScreenTips, the status bar, view buttons, and special areas on dialog boxes.

Using Toolbars

Usually one or more toolbars are visible on-screen, as shown in Figure 5.9. The buttons on the toolbars enable you to quickly make a choice. For example, after you highlight a word, you can choose the Bold and Italic buttons to change the font style. An alternative is to choose Format, Font and make choices in the dialog box. The toolbar buttons are quicker, but the menu choices offer more thorough choices. If a toolbar is not visible, choose View, Toolbars, then click its name in the submenu. If you want to add or remove buttons to or from your toolbars, see Chapter 41, "Customizing the Desktop, Toolbars, and Menus."

FIG. 5.9
Click the Bold and Italic buttons for quick formatting.

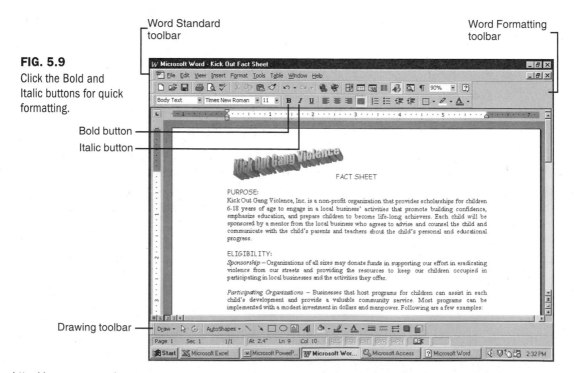

Displaying ScreenTips

ScreenTips assist you in your use of toolbars and other on-screen features. When ScreenTips are on, you can leave your mouse pointer on a button momentarily, and a short description appears at the mouse pointer. If ScreenTips are not visible, choose the Tools menu or right-click a toolbar, then choose Customize. Click the Options tab in the Customize dialog box and select the Show ScreenTips on Toolbars check box.

Microsoft Word and PowerPoint have an added feature with ScreenTips that enables you to see whether a shortcut key exists that duplicates the function of the button. On the Options tab of the Customize dialog box, select Show Shortcut Keys in ScreenTips. When you place your mouse pointer on a toolbar button, the ScreenTip displays the shortcut key if it is available. With the shortcut option, the second button on the standard toolbar becomes *Open (Ctrl+O)* instead of *Open*.

Looking at the Status Bar

The status bar appears at the bottom of the screen. If the status bar is not visible, choose Tools, Options and select Status Bar on the View tab. The status bar shows information about your location in the document, the status of on/off keys (such as Caps Lock, Num Lock, Insert), and program status (such as Macro Record or WordPerfect Help Keys). Figure 5.10 shows the status bar for Microsoft Word.

▶ **See** "Viewing Parts of the Window," **p. 43**

▶ **See** "Viewing Parts of the Window," **p. 43**

FIG. 5.10
Word's status bar shows the location on the document and program status options.

Status bar

Part
I

Ch
5

Using View Buttons

At the bottom of the screen, Word and PowerPoint also have view buttons to help you with your work. The view buttons are similar to toolbar buttons because they also can display ScreenTips. They can change the amount of the document that you can see at one time. They also show additional features (such as an outline, slides, notes, and slide show) for editing and formatting. Figure 5.11 shows the view buttons for Microsoft Word.

FIG. 5.11
The view buttons change the amount of the document displayed and add other features.

Using Help Features in Dialog Boxes

In Microsoft Office 97, toolbar buttons are now included on more dialog boxes. Figure 5.12 shows an Open dialog box for Microsoft Excel with the buttons. ScreenTips are also available so you can see the functions of the buttons.

FIG. 5.12
Microsoft Office 97 adds more toolbar buttons and the ? button to dialog boxes.

In addition to toolbar buttons in dialog boxes, Microsoft Office 97 dialog boxes have a help button. The question mark in the upper-right corner of most dialog boxes enables you to explore the items in a dialog box. When you click the question mark, the mouse pointer changes to a question mark. You can then click an item in the dialog box to get a pop-up description of the feature.

TROUBLESHOOTING

The toolbar button is not visible. The toolbar may not be turned on. Choose View, Toolbars or right-click any toolbar, then click the toolbar you want to see. Another possibility is that the toolbars have been changed. Right-click a toolbar or open the Toolbars menu, then choose Customize. On the Toolbars tab, choose the toolbar where the button should be and click Reset.

The ScreenTip does not appear for a button. Leave the mouse pointer stationary on a button. If you move the mouse, the ScreenTip does not appear. You may also need to turn ScreenTips on. To do so, right-click a toolbar or open the Toolbars menu, then click Customize. Click the Options tab, then click Show ScreenTips on Toolbars.

The status bar or view buttons are not visible on my screen. Choose Tools, Options, and on the View tab check the Status Bar or Horizontal Scroll Bar check boxes.

Using Wizards

One of the greatest help features in the Microsoft Office applications is not really a help feature at all. Wizards do not appear on the Help menu, but they appear throughout the applications. *Wizards* are special dialog boxes that ask you questions about the document you want to create and then use your answers to lay out and format the document.

▶ **See** "Using Template Wizards," **p. 256**

▶ **See** "Creating a Presentation Using a Wizard," **p. 608**

When you start a wizard, as shown in Figure 5.13, and then choose the Next button once, the wizard asks you to enter text in text boxes or choose from a list of options. When you finish filling in one step of the wizard, choose the Next button to go to the next step. You can skip to the last step if you know the default settings for your wizard by choosing Finish. If you want to cancel the wizard, click Cancel or press Esc. On some dialog boxes, you have the capability to return to a previous step by choosing Back.

FIG. 5.13
Word's Fax Wizard prompts you to specify whether you want to send a document and cover sheet, as well as other options.

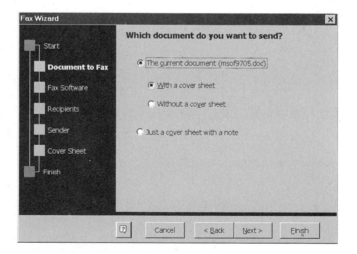

You activate a wizard by different means in the programs. To see a list of some Wizards, click the New Office Document button on the Office Shortcut Bar. There are Wizards for letters, memos, faxes, presentations, Web pages, databases, reports, publications, spreadsheets and others. In addition to creating a new file, you can also use Wizards to create charts, import and convert data, and create Access databases, tables, forms, queries, and reports.

You load wizards by a number of different procedures including the following:

- The original installation of your Office program.
- Any subsequent modifications of your installation (which can be accomplished by clicking the first icon on Office Shortcut bar and choosing Add/Remove Office Programs).
- Copying files from the Office ValuPack directory on the Microsoft Office CD-ROM.
- Going to a Microsoft Web site and downloading templates.
- Purchasing templates from third-party vendors.
- Creating your own templates in the various Office programs.

NOTE Although they are not technically wizards, many of Office's templates work like wizards and are very helpful for starting a document. Instead of answering questions through a wizard dialog box, you replace text on existing documents. These templates are available when you choose File, New from an Office application or click the New Office Document button on the Microsoft Office Shortcut Bar. You can differentiate a Wizard from a template based on a magic wand on the icon. ▨

Using Word

CHAPTER 6

Creating and Editing Documents

by Patty Winter

Of all the applications included with Microsoft Office, Word may be the one you use most. You need a word processor to produce at least letters and envelopes in your everyday work. Using Word, you also can create memos, fax cover sheets, Web pages, reports, newsletters, mailing labels, brochures, tables, and many other business and personal documents.

Not only does Word offer many commands and features that help you complete your work quickly and easily, but you almost don't need to know how to type anymore. Word provides easy graphics handling, outlining, calculations of data in tables, the capability to create a mailing list, list sorting, and efficient file management. In addition, you can perform many desktop publishing tasks, such as publishing Web pages, formatting fonts, creating display type, aligning text, adding graphic borders, and adding shading.

Microsoft Office offers another advantage for using Word as your day-to-day word processor. When you use Word, you have the flexibility to share data and tools with Excel, PowerPoint, Access, Outlook, and other Windows applications. ■

The Word screen and toolbar

To effectively use Word 97, you first need to have an understanding of the Word screen elements and the toolbar basics.

Enter text

Entering text includes not only pressing the keys on the keyboard, but also using the features of Word to view more than letters and numbers, correct mistakes, and move the insertion point.

Insert AutoText entries

The power of using AutoText entries is enhanced in this version of Word.

Select text

You can use your mouse, keyboard, or both when selecting text.

Edit text

Editing text includes undoing mistakes, deleting and moving text, copying text, and changing case.

Save a document

Saving a document includes naming, deciding on the location, and saving changes to the existing document.

Start a new document

Starting a new document can be as effortless as clicking a button or choosing an existing template to base the new document on.

Understanding Word Basics

Word offers many excellent features that help you perform your word processing tasks efficiently. If you are familiar with Windows 3.1 or Windows 95 applications, you probably already know quite a bit about operating Word. You know, for example, how to use such features as the Control menu icon, the Window menu, the Office Assistant, and Help. Additionally, you understand the use of the mouse, scroll bars, dialog boxes, and other features of a Windows application. For more information about Word for Windows, refer to Que's book *Special Edition Using Microsoft Word for Windows 97*.

This section shows you how to use some features and screen elements particular to the Word program, including the toolbars, scroll bars, and the status bar.

▶ **See** "Using Help and Office Assistant," **p. 127**

Using the Word Screen

When you start the program, Word displays specific screen elements as defaults, including the title bar, menu bar, two toolbars, a ruler, scroll bars, and the Office Assistant. Word is so flexible you can, of course, hide these elements or show different components, at any time, by choosing a command from the View menu or the Tools menu. By default, Word is trying to give you the most common tools you need to begin your word processing adventure.

Suppose that you want to hide the ruler. Choose View, Ruler to hide it; choose View, Ruler again to display the ruler. Suppose that you want to turn off the scroll bars. Choose Tools, Options, click the View tab, and click the option you want to turn off in the Window area, then click the OK command button; do the same thing to turn the option back on. A check mark indicates that the option is currently "on" or enabled; a blank check box indicates that the option is off. If you want to turn the Office Assistant off, click the Close button on the top-right corner of the Assistant window.

▶ **See** "Viewing Parts of the Window," **p. 43**
▶ **See** "Using Menus," **p. 46**

Figure 6.1 shows the default Word screen and indicates the components of the screen.

The toolbars are covered in more detail in Chapter 7, "Formatting Documents." The following list describes the screen elements:

- *Title bar*. The title bar contains the name of the program, the name of the document, the Control-menu icon, and the Minimize, Maximize, Restore, and Close buttons. Additionally, the title bar can contain the Microsoft Office shortcut bar.

■ *Menu bar.* The menu bar contains specialized menus containing related commands. Choose commands from the Format menu, for example, to change fonts, set tabs, add a border, and so on.

▶ **See** "Customizing Predefined Toolbars," **p. 949**

■ *Standard toolbar.* This toolbar contains buttons you click to perform common tasks, such as starting a new document, saving a document, checking spelling, and undoing an action. The buttons in the Standard toolbar provide shortcuts for common menu commands.

When you leave the mouse pointer on a button, a ScreenTip appears with the mouse pointer, giving the name of the button. By choosing View, Toolbars, Customize, and the Options tab you can turn these ScreenTips on or off as well as show the ScreenTips shortcut keys (Ctrl+O for Open, and so on). If you're using Office 95, you can access these options by choosing View, Toolbars.

FIG. 6.1
Using Word's screen elements can help you complete tasks quickly and efficiently.

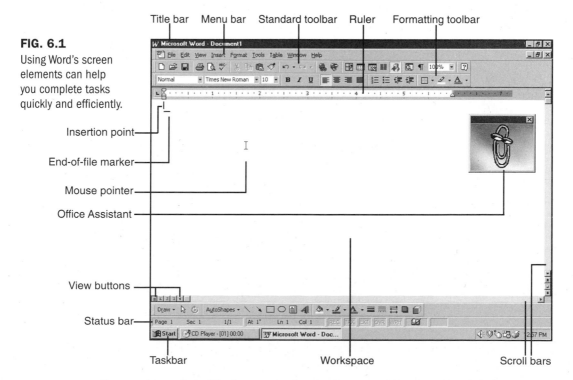

Title bar   Menu bar   Standard toolbar   Ruler   Formatting toolbar

Insertion point
End-of-file marker
Mouse pointer
Office Assistant
View buttons
Status bar

Taskbar   Workspace   Scroll bars

Part
II

Ch
6

■ *Formatting toolbar.* The buttons in the Formatting toolbar provide shortcuts for choosing character or paragraph formatting such as changing fonts, font sizes, styles, alignments, and so on. Use this toolbar to format text quickly as you work.

▶ **See** "Formatting Paragraphs," **p. 178**

- *Ruler*. The ruler provides a quick and easy method of setting tabs and indents in your text. For more information about the ruler, see Chapter 7, "Formatting Documents."

- *Workspace*. The workspace consists of a blank "page" in which you enter or edit text, place pictures and graphics, and work with your document.

- *Insertion point*. The insertion point is showing you where the text, pictures, and graphics will be placed. In other programs it is known as a *cursor*.
  - ▶ **See** "Moving Around the Document," **p. 75**
  - ▶ **See** "Viewing Parts of the Window," **p. 43**

- *Scroll bars*. Use the scroll bars to move quickly to another area of the document.

- *Status bar*. The status bar lists information and displays messages as you work in Word. When you double-click the page, section, or line reference area, the Go To tab on the Find and Replace dialog box is displayed.
  - ▶ **See** "Launching Programs," **p. 34**
  - ▶ **See** "Formatting Paragraphs," **p. 178**

- *Taskbar*. The taskbar is part of Windows 95 and allows you to start applications through the Start button and to switch between applications that have been launched.

- *End-of-file marker*. The short horizontal line indicates the end of the document. You cannot move past this marker.

- *Mouse pointer*. As you move your mouse, the mouse pointer moves on-screen. The mouse pointer may change shape depending on the screen location (I-beam, left-pointing white arrow, right-pointing white arrow, and so on), indicating that you can accomplish different tasks.

- *View buttons*. To the bottom left of the horizontal scroll bar are four View buttons (Normal view, Online Layout view, Page Layout view, Outline view). These buttons allow you to change your view to include margins, headers and footers, or show additional organizing tools.
  - ▶ **See** "Understanding Views," **p. 168**

Entering Text in a Word Document

When you start the Word program, Word supplies you with a new, blank document (named Document1 in the title bar). You can begin to type at the blinking insertion point. When you enter text, that text appears in the workspace at the insertion point.

This section describes the basic techniques of entering text, moving around in a document, and selecting text for editing.

Typing Text

When entering text, you type as you would in any word processor. Word automatically wraps the text at the end of a line—you do not have to press Enter to begin a new line. Press Enter only when you want to start a new paragraph or create a blank line. Word defines a paragraph as any number of letters, words, or sentences ending with a paragraph mark. As you type, Microsoft Word shows you words it does not recognize by underlining them with a red wavy line (see Figure 6.2).

 A *paragraph mark* is a nonprinting character inserted whenever you press Enter. You can view paragraph marks by clicking the Show/Hide ¶ button in the Standard toolbar. To hide paragraph marks, click the Show/Hide ¶ button again. Figure 6.2 shows paragraph marks and the Show/Hide ¶ button in the Standard toolbar. In addition, the right indent marker in the figure is set at 4 1/2 inches so that you can see the automatic word wrap.

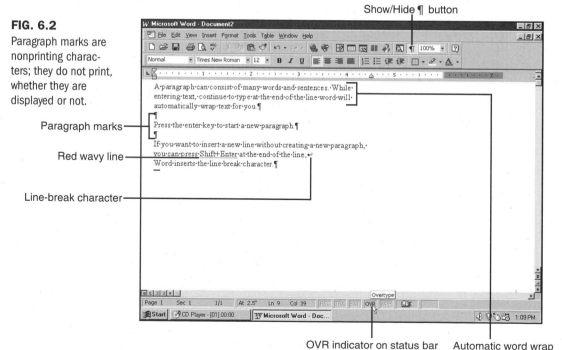

FIG. 6.2
Paragraph marks are nonprinting characters; they do not print, whether they are displayed or not.

The following list contains some useful shortcuts and features you can use when entering text in Word:

- If you make a mistake while typing, press the Backspace key to erase a character to the left of the insertion point.

- Press the Delete key to remove a character to the right of the insertion point.

■ To repeat the text you just typed, choose <u>E</u>dit, <u>R</u>epeat Typing; or press Ctrl+Y.

■ To erase the text you just typed, choose <u>E</u>dit, <u>U</u>ndo Typing; or press Ctrl+Z. You also can click the Undo button in the Standard toolbar.

■ To start a new line without inserting a paragraph mark, press Shift+Enter. Word inserts a line-break character.

▶ **See** "Adjusting Spacing," **p. 178**

▶ **See** "Adding Bullets and Numbering," **p. 186**

■ Double-click the OVR indicator in the status bar to use Overtype mode, in which the text you enter replaces existing text. Double-click the indicator again to turn off Overtype mode.

TROUBLESHOOTING

I have typed quite a bit of my document. What are those funny paragraph marks I see periodically? Those are the nonprinting characters that indicate you pressed Enter to end the line or create a blank line. To turn them off if they are bothersome, click the Show/Hide ¶ button in the Standard toolbar.

Taking Advantage of the AutoText Feature with AutoComplete

One of the new features of Word 97 is the automatic display of AutoText entries and common typing items, such as the current date, the day of the week, the month, and your name. Word versions 6 and 7 introduced AutoText. In Word 97 AutoText is much easier to use. With the AutoText and AutoComplete commands, you can automate entering information that you use frequently. You can create an AutoText entry that includes text only, formatted text, or graphics. When you type something that is in the list of AutoText entries, Word automatically displays the AutoComplete item similar to a ScreenTip. If you want to use the item, press Enter, Tab, or F3, and continue typing after the AutoComplete item is inserted. See Figures 6.3 and 6.4 for a before and after example.

If you have the Office Assistant on, you may see a question to find out if you would like help. You can choose to ignore Assistant and keep typing until you need help, or click one of the option buttons. See Figure 6.3 to see the Assistant. If you choose Cancel, the balloon help goes away, and the assistant waits until you need help later. Click the Close button to turn the Assistant off.

Word 97 comes with many AutoText entries already defined. You can create your own entries or redefine the existing entries.

FIG. 6.3
AutoComplete in
action with the Office
Assistant waiting for a
response from you.

AutoText entry name

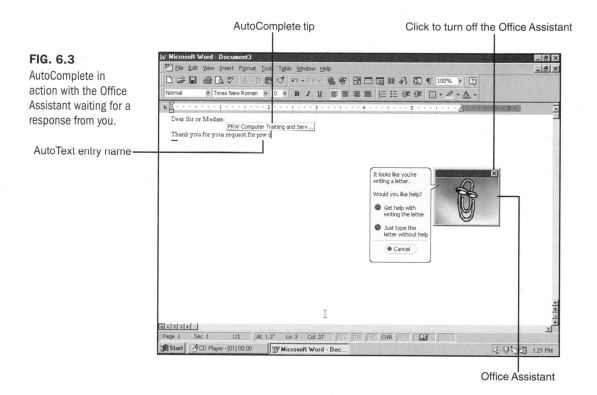

AutoComplete tip

Click to turn off the Office Assistant

Office Assistant

FIG. 6.4
The AutoText entry
is inserted at the
insertion point, now
you can continue
typing your letter.

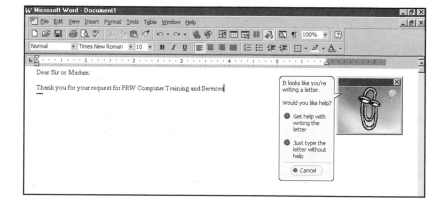

Part
II

Ch
6

To create or change an existing AutoText entry, follow these steps:

1. Create the text or graphics you repeatedly use.

2. Select the text you just created.

3. Choose Insert, AutoText, New, The Create AutoText dialog box appears.

4. Type a name for the AutoText entry in the P̲lease Name Your AutoText Entry box, or leave the default name (see Figure 6.5).

5. Click OK to create or modify the entry. If this is a new entry, you are finished. If the name you typed was an existing entry, you are modifying that entry name; see the following step.

6. If you are modifying an existing entry, a message window is displayed asking if you want to redefine the AutoText entry. Click the Y̲es button to redefine the entry.

After you define the entry, you can use it in your documents by typing the AutoText name and then pressing Enter, Tab, or F3 when you see the tip appear.

FIG. 6.5

Type the name for your AutoText entry or accept the default name.

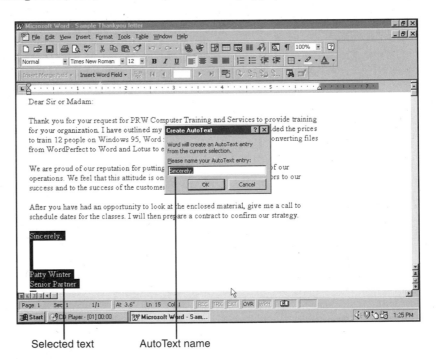

Selected text   AutoText name

Positioning the Insertion Point

To move the insertion point, move the I-beam mouse pointer to the new location and click the left mouse button. You can position the insertion point anywhere in the text area except below the *end marker* (the short horizontal line displayed in the text area). You can move the end marker by inserting paragraph marks (pressing Enter) before the end marker.

If you want to move the insertion point to a location that doesn't appear in the current window, you can use the horizontal or vertical scroll bar to move to the new location.

When the new location appears in the window, place the I-beam pointer where you want to position the insertion point and click the left mouse button.

Office 97 is shipped with an IntelliPoint mouse. This mouse gives you an additional middle mouse button or wheel. With the wheel, you can scroll through your document by rolling the wheel or clicking and holding the wheel down while moving the mouse down or up in the document. The slower you move the mouse, the slower you will scroll in the direction you are moving the mouse. This is a handy feature if you want to be able to read while you are scrolling through the document. For more information on the IntelliPoint mouse, see Chapter 3, "Typing and Formatting Basics."

N O T E The insertion point always stays within the text area. If you click outside the margin boundary, Word places the insertion point in the nearest text.

Additionally, you can press certain keys on the keyboard to move the insertion point quickly to a new location. Using the keyboard to move around in a document is sometimes faster and easier than using the mouse. The following table lists keys you can use to move around in your documents:

Key	Moves Insertion Point
Arrow keys	One character up, down, left, or right
Page Up/Page Down	One screen up or down
Ctrl+ ← /→	One word to the left or right
Home/End	Beginning or end of a line
Ctrl+Home/End	Beginning or end of the document
Ctrl+Page Up/Page Down	Top of the previous or next page
Alt+Ctrl+Page Up/Page Down	Top left or bottom right of screen

Using the Document Map to Move the Insertion Point

 You can click the Document Map button on the Standard toolbar to display the Document Map pane on the left side of the window. In the Doucment Map pane, you can click one of the headings in the document to move to that section of the document. Your insertion point is at the top of the section you clicked. To turn off the Document Map, click the button on the Standard toolbar again.

Selecting Text

After entering text, you may want to delete or move a word, sentence, or paragraph. In addition, you may want to format the text by changing the font or font size, indenting text, and so on. Before you can perform one of these actions on the text in your document, you must select the text. Selecting the text shows Word where to perform the action. After you select text, the selected text temporarily changes to white text on a black background.

If you have changed the text or the background to a different color, the selected text may appear different, for instance, white text with a blue background, or yellow text with a black background. Selected text allows you to perform one or more actions on the selected text.

You can select text by using the mouse, the keyboard, or a combination of methods, depending on how much text you want to select. The following list describes the methods of text selection:

- To select one word when you are changing the font characteristics, you only need to place the insertion point *in the word*, not select the entire word. If you are using an older version of Word, to select one word, position the I-beam pointer anywhere in a word and double-click. The word and the space following the word are selected.

- To select a sentence, hold down the Ctrl key while clicking anywhere in the sentence. Word selects all words in the sentence to the ending punctuation mark, plus the blank space following the punctuation mark.

- To select a paragraph, triple-click the paragraph, or place the mouse pointer in the selection bar, and double-click. The *selection bar* is a vertical white space to the left of the workspace. When you point the mouse in the selection bar, the I-beam pointer changes to a right pointing arrow (see Figure 6.6).

FIG. 6.6

Use the selection bar to select one line quickly; select more than one line by dragging the mouse pointer in the selection bar.

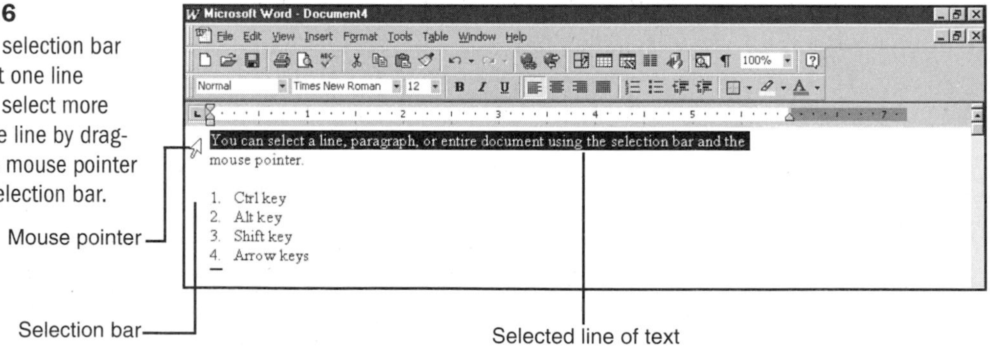

- To select specific text, click and drag the I-beam pointer over one character, one word, or the entire screen.

- To select one line of text, place the mouse pointer in the selection bar to the left of the line and click once.

- To select the entire document, hold down the Ctrl key while clicking the selection bar. Alternatively, press Ctrl+A to select the entire document.

- To select a vertical block of text—the first letters of words in a list, for example— hold down the Alt key while you click and drag the mouse pointer across the text. Figure 6.7 shows a vertical block of selected text.

FIG. 6.7

Select one, two, or more characters vertically by holding down the Alt key while dragging the mouse pointer.

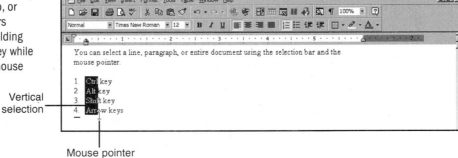

Vertical selection

Mouse pointer

- To select text with the keyboard arrow keys, position the insertion point where you want to start selecting, press and hold down the Shift key, and then press the appropriate arrow key to move up, down, left, or right.

- To select to the end of a line of text with the keyboard, position the insertion point where you want to start selecting and then press Shift+End. Alternatively, select to the beginning of the line of text by pressing Shift+Home.

- To select a block of text, position the insertion point where you want to start selecting, move the mouse pointer to the end of the text you want to select, hold down the Shift key, and click the left mouse button.

- To deselect text, click once anywhere in the workspace of a document or press an arrow key.

CAUTION

If you have text selected and press the space bar or any character key, the selected text is deleted and is replaced by the characters you typed.

TROUBLESHOOTING

I began typing the text, and I messed up my document in a completely different area of the document from where I was looking. There must have been text selected in another area of your document. You must click the mouse to position the insertion point before you begin typing the text. A blinking vertical line indicates the insertion point.

I tried to select text with the mouse, but I had trouble controlling the selection. It takes practice to control the mouse when you select text. Try one of the alternative methods of selecting text described in this section. For example, try positioning the insertion point at the beginning of

continues

Part

II

Ch

6

continued

the selection, holding down the Shift key, and then clicking the mouse at the end of the selection. Another option is to change the mouse properties (choose the Start button on the taskbar, choose Settings Control Panel, and select the Mouse program).

Editing Text in a Word Document

With Word, changes and corrections are easy to make. You can select any text in your document and delete it, copy it, or move it. You also can make other changes easily. How many times have you typed text, only to discover that the Caps Lock feature was on? Don't type the text again; use Word's Change Case command. This section shows you how to edit your document quickly and easily. You can use the Backspace and Delete keys to edit one character at a time, or you can select text first and then edit it. Table 6.1 summarizes the editing commands, buttons, and shortcuts that you can use to edit selected text.

Table 6.1   Procedures for Editing Selected Text

	Delete	Copy	Move	Undo	Redo
Keyboard	Delete or Backspace	Ctrl+C then Ctrl+V	Ctrl+X then Ctrl+V	Ctrl+Z or Alt Backspace	Ctrl+Y or F4
Toolbar buttons	✂	📋	✂	↩ ▾	↪ ▾
		then 📋	then 📋		
Commands	Edit, Clear	Edit, Copy then Edit, Paste	Edit, Cut then Edit, Paste	Edit, Undo	Edit, Redo
Right mouse button	Cut	Copy then Paste	Cut then Paste		
Drag mouse		Ctrl+Drag selection	Drag selection		

▶ **See** "Typing and Editing," **p. 66**

Undoing a Mistake

T I P If you make a mistake while typing text, pressing Backspace or Delete to delete the mistake may be easier than using Undo.

You can reverse many mistakes by using the Undo command. Suppose that you type a sentence and decide you don't like the way it reads. You can delete the sentence by choosing Edit, Undo or by pressing either of the shortcut keys: Ctrl+Z or Alt+Backspace. If you make a correction and change your mind, you can use the Undo command to reverse the action.

Word also provides a Redo command (also on the Edit menu) you can use to reverse the last Undo. The keyboard shortcuts for the Redo command are Ctrl+Y, F4, or Alt+Shift+Backspace. Both the Undo and Redo commands describe the action you just performed, like Undo Typing, Redo Clear, and so on.

The Edit, Undo, or Edit, Redo command works only on the last task you performed. If, for example, you delete a sentence and decide that you want it back, you must choose the Undo command before carrying out another task. However, Word supplies Undo and Redo buttons in the Standard toolbar that enable you to undo or redo other recent actions. Figure 6.8 shows the Undo drop-down list displaying six of the most recent actions.

FIG. 6.8
Use the Undo and Redo drop-down lists to reverse any of the last several actions performed. The Cut, Copy, and Paste buttons allow you to cut, copy, and move text.

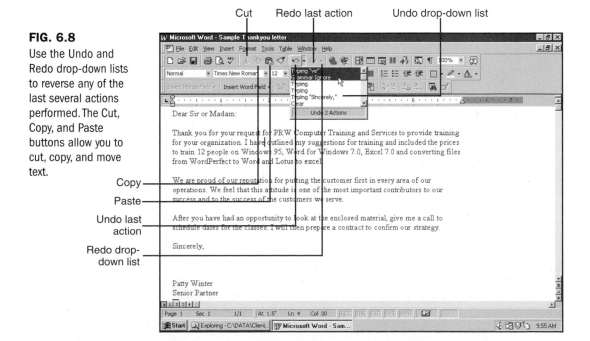

Part

II

Ch

6

Deleting and Moving Text

To delete any amount of text, select the text and press the Delete key. When you press Delete, the text is erased; the only way to recall the text is to choose the Undo command. Alternatively, you can delete text by selecting it and then choosing Edit, Clear. The Edit, Clear command deletes the text just as the Delete key does. You also can delete the previous word by pressing Ctrl+Backspace.

You also can choose Edit, Cut, or press Ctrl+X to remove the text. Edit, Cut moves the selected text from the document to the Windows Clipboard. The text remains on the Clipboard until you use the Edit, Cut or Edit, Copy command again. Figure 6.8 shows the Cut, Copy, and Paste buttons on the Standard toolbar.

> **TIP** You can also click the right mouse button on a selection to cut, copy, and paste.

To move text that you cut to another location in the same document or to another document, position the insertion point where you want the text to appear and choose Edit, Paste; or press Ctrl+V. The cut text reappears at the insertion point. You can paste this text again and again until you cut or copy new text.

Copying Text

To copy text, select the text and then choose Edit, Copy; or press the shortcut key Ctrl+C. Word copies the text to the Clipboard. You then can paste the copied text in a new location or document by positioning the insertion point and then choosing Edit, Paste or pressing Ctrl+V. You can also use the Copy and Paste buttons shown earlier in Figure 6.8.

> **TIP** Use the Cut button on the Standard toolbar, or the Shift+Delete keyboard shortcut to remove text instead of the Delete key. You can bring back the last deletion without undoing any other work by positioning the insertion point and clicking the Paste button.

Copying text or other elements in your documents, such as pictures and charts, is one way to share data between applications. The Windows Clipboard is used by all the Microsoft Office applications. You can, for example, create text in Word, copy it, and paste it in PowerPoint. You also can copy a worksheet from Excel and paste it to a table in Word.

Drag-and-Drop Editing

Another method you can use to move or copy text is called *drag-and-drop editing*. Word supplies this shortcut for moving or copying selected text. You also can use drag-and-drop editing to copy or move graphics or other objects.

To use drag-and-drop editing to move text or graphics, follow these steps:

1. Select the text or graphics you want to move.

 T I P To copy the text or graphic instead of moving it, hold down the Ctrl key as you point to the selected text or graphic, and drag the dotted insertion point to a new location.

2. Point to the selected text or graphic and hold down the left mouse button. The drag-and-drop pointer appears (see Figure 6.9).

FIG. 6.9
By using the drag-and-drop pointer, drag the selected text or graphic to a new location.

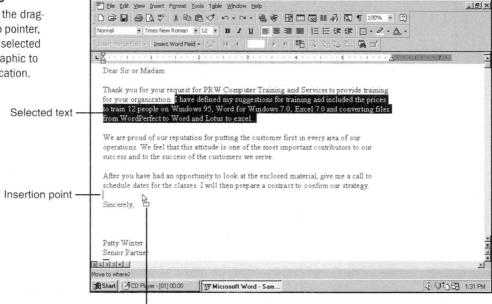

Selected text ——

Insertion point ——

Drag-and-drop pointer

3. Drag the pointer and the dotted insertion point that appears to the new location and release the mouse button.

N O T E The drag-and-drop editing option is activated by default. If you do not want to use drag-and-drop editing, you can turn the feature off by choosing Tools, Options. In the Edit tab, select Drag-and-Drop Text Editing to turn off the option.

Converting Case

Word includes a handy command you can use to convert the case of text you entered earlier. Suppose that you decide you do not want a heading to appear in all caps. You can

Part

II

Ch

6

select the text you want to change and choose Format, Change Case. The Change Case dialog box appears. Select one of the following options:

- *Sentence Case*. Capitalizes only the first letter in selected sentences.
- *Lowercase*. Changes all selected text to lowercase.
- *Uppercase*. Converts all selected text to all capital letters.
- *Title Case*. Capitalizes the first letter of each word of selected text.
- *Toggle Case*. Changes uppercase to lowercase and lowercase to uppercase in all selected text.

NOTE You also can use the shortcut key to change case. Select the text and press Shift+F3. Each time you press the shortcut key, Word cycles through lowercase, uppercase, and initial caps. If a sentence or multiple sentences is selected, initial caps changes the first word of the sentence. If a phrase is selected, initial caps will capitalize the first letter of every word as in book titles. ◼

TROUBLESHOOTING

I accidentally deleted or cleared text that I did not intend to delete. Click the Undo button in the Standard toolbar or use the Ctrl+Z shortcut key to undo the last action.

I pasted selected text in the wrong place. Press Ctrl+Z to undo the paste. Then position the insertion point in the correct location and choose Edit, Paste again.

I accidentally get the drag-and-drop editing pointer when I do not want it. Be careful not to drag a text block after selecting it. If you do drag the mouse and you get the drag-and-drop pointer, press Esc before you release the mouse button. If you do not use the drag-and-drop pointer, consider turning the option off by choosing Tools, Options, selecting the Edit tab, and deselecting the Drag and Drop Text Editing check box.

Saving, Closing, and Opening Word Documents

This section shows you how to save and close a document, open an existing document, and start a new one. The following discussion is specific to Word; for information about basic file management, refer to Chapter 4, "Managing Files and Printing Documents."

▶ **See** "Working with Files," **p. 94**

Saving a Word Document

As in other Microsoft Officeprograms, you save a Word document by assigning it a name and a location in your drive and folder list. After naming the file, you can save changes made in that document without renaming the file by pressing a shortcut key or clicking a button in the Standard toolbar.

> **CAUTION**
>
> Save your documents early in their creation and save often as you work on them. If a power failure occurs while you are working on your document and you have not saved it as a file, you lose the document. By default, Word has an Autosave feature that is automatically turned on. The default is to save your document every 10 minutes. If you leave this option on, you will most likely not lose as much as you would without it. If you would like to Autosave more often that every 10 minutes, you can change the option by choosing Tools, Options. In the Save tab, select the Save AutoRecover Info Every 10 minutes text box and decrease the number of minutes by using the increment buttons or typing a different number in the text box.

Naming a Word Document   The first time you save a document, choose File, Save. Word displays the Save As dialog box, shown in Figure 6.10.

FIG. 6.10
Use the Save As dialog box to identify the document name in the File Name text box or accept Word's default name.

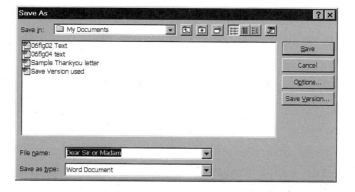

Part

II

Ch

6

When you save a document, Word places the file in the My Documents folder on your hard drive, unless you specified a different folder for Word when you installed Microsoft Office. In addition, Word's default file type is Word Document. Word also suggests a file name for the document; you can accept the suggested name or rename the document to suit yourself by typing a new name in the File Name text box.

Word suggests a name depending on the text in your document. If you have short lines at the top of the document, Word uses the first phrase of text up to a punctuation mark, new line character, or paragraph mark and suggests Word Document for the file type.

You can choose to save a file to a hard drive, floppy drive, network drive, and so on; available drives are in the Save In list. Next, select a folder. Finally, in the Save as Type box, you can select a format other than Word in case you want to use the file in another application, such as Word 6.0/95, HTML Document, DOS Text, WordPerfect 5.1, or WordPerfect 5.x for Windows.

N O T E One of the major additions to Word 97 is the ability to create and save Web pages. You have an option to save your document as an HTML document so that you can use it as a Web page on the Internet. See Chapter 44, the section "Navigating and Publishing on the Web with Office" for a full discussion on developing Web pages. ■

To save a new document, follow these steps:

1. Choose File, Save. The Save As dialog box appears.

2. Type the name of the file in the File Name text box or accept Word's suggested file name. The file name can have as many as 255 characters and can include spaces.

3. Select and change the drive, folder, and file type if you do not want to save with Word's defaults.

4. Choose OK to save the document.

 Saving Changes to a Named Document   After you save your document by assigning it a name and location on the disk, you can continue to work on it. The changes you make are not saved, however, unless you tell Word to save them. You do not need to rename the document file to save changes; you can simply choose File, Save, press Ctrl+S, or click the Save button. Word quickly saves the changes, and you are ready to proceed.

Saving All   The File, Save All command saves all open documents. Additionally, this command saves any open templates, macros, and AutoText entries. When you use the Save All command, Word displays a message box, asking you to confirm that you want to save each open document. If you have not named a document, Word displays the Save As dialog box so that you can name the document. To use the Save All command, hold down the Shift key while you click the File menu. The save command changes to Save All. In Office 95, Save All is on the File menu as a choice.

Opening a Word Document

 To open a saved document in Word, click the Open button, choose File, Open, or press Ctrl+O. Word displays the Open dialog box (see Figure 6.11).

▶ **See** "Opening a Document," **p. 103**

In the Open dialog box, select the file name from the list of files, if you saved it in Word's default folder. Otherwise, you can change the drive and folder, or even the file type, to access the file you want. You can sort, view, and do many options with the Open dialog box. For more information, refer to Chapter 4, "Managing Files and Work Areas."

FIG. 6.11

Select the file from the list of files and choose OK to open the document.

N O T E If you have previously saved an HTML document and choose to open the document, you can use the Document Map to move through the document quickly. Click the Document Map button on the Standard toolbar, and then use the headings in the Document pane to move through the document. ▪

Starting a New Word Document

You can start a new document at any time by clicking the New button, choosing File, New, or by pressing Ctrl+N. When you use the New button or Ctrl+N, a blank document appears using default fonts and other settings from Word's Normal template. When you choose File, New, the New dialog box appears (see Figure 6.12).

▶ **See** "Using Template Wizards," **p. 256**

The New dialog box lists several tabs that are categories for the different templates. A *template* is a basic document design that can include page size and orientation, font sizes, fonts, tab settings, page margins, boilerplate text, tables, and columns. For more information about templates, see Chapter 10, "Working with Large Documents."

T I P Using the shortcut Ctrl+N or the New button in the Standard toolbar skips the New dialog box and bases the new document on the Normal template.

Part

II

Ch

6

Dialog box tabs

FIG. 6.12
In the New dialog box, select the tab for the templates you want to use and then select the template on which you want to base the new document.

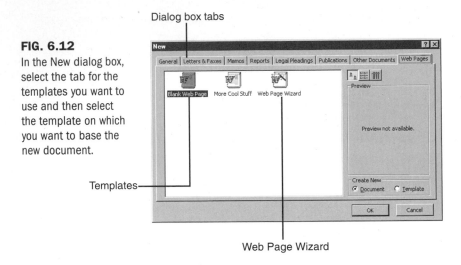

Templates

Web Page Wizard

The Normal template is Word's default. The Normal template has the following characteristics:

- Uses an 8 1/2-by-11-inch portrait-oriented page
- Includes 1-inch top and bottom margins and 1 1/4-inch left and right margins
- Uses Times New Roman 10-point body text
- Supplies three heading styles: Arial 14-point bold, Arial 12-point bold italic, and Arial 12-point. All three heading styles are left-aligned and use single line spacing. They all also add a 12-point space above the heading and a 3-point space below the heading.

To accept the Normal template, choose OK. Word displays a new, blank document. To learn more about the Normal template and customizing options, refer to Que's book *Special Edition Using Microsoft Word for Windows 97*.

One of the new templates is the Blank Web Page and a new Wizard is the Web Page Wizard. The Blank Web Page template has the following characteristics:

- Uses an 8 1/2-by-11-inch portrait-oriented page
- Includes 1-inch top and bottom margins and 1-inch left and right margins
- Uses Times New Roman 12-point body text
- Supplies twenty-six styles common to Web Page formatting
- Changes menus and toolbars to display commands needed for creating Web pages
- Default file type is HTML document

To use the Blank Web Page template, click the Web Page tab, click the Blank Web Page template and choose OK. Word displays a new, blank document with all the tools to create a Web Page.

▶ **See** "Using Template Wizards," **p. 256**

If you need more assistance in creating a Web Page, choose the Web Page Wizard, which will guide you through creating a Web Page with an interactive Wizard.

▶ **See** "Navigating and Publishing on the Web with Office 97," **p. 1025**

N O T E   You can also choose <u>T</u>ools, Letter Wi<u>z</u>ard to create a letter using the Letter Wizard dialog box. By clicking the different tabs, you are presented with a place to enter specific information related to a letter. Your options include the letter format, recipient information, sender information, and other elements such as a reference line, mailing instructions, an attention and subject line, and even an area for courtesy copies (cc). This is an easy way to create a professional-looking letter without knowing how. ▪

TROUBLESHOOTING

I opened a document that was created in another file format, and now I want to save it. Choose <u>F</u>ile, Save <u>A</u>s. In the Save As dialog box, select the format from the Save as <u>T</u>ype drop-down list.

I don't see all the templates mentioned in this chapter. The templates available depend on how Office was installed. You can use the setup program again, get templates off the ValuPack directory on the CD-ROM, or get templates from Microsoft's Web site.

Part

II

Ch

6

Formatting Documents

by Patty Winter

Many of Word's distinctive features and commands pertain to formatting documents. Formatting a document includes assigning fonts and font sizes, adjusting the spacing between lines and paragraphs, aligning text, dividing text into columns, and setting page margins. You may consider many of these tasks to be part of *desktop publishing*—designing and formatting a document so that it is attractive and professional looking. Word provides many desktop publishing features and commands you can use to enhance your business documents as well as your Web pages.

Word not only supplies methods for improving the look of your documents but also makes formatting quick and easy. You can use menu commands and toolbar buttons to transform an ordinary business document into an eye-catching piece.

This chapter shows you how to format text, paragraphs, and pages using the easiest and fastest methods. ■

Document views

Learn the different document views and understand their elements.

Formatting text

Change fonts, font size, font styles, copy formats and add highlight to a document.

Formatting paragraphs

This section covers adjusting line and paragraph spacing, setting tabs, using indents, adjusting alignment, and adding bullets and numbered lists.

Formatting the page

Change page size and orientation, set margins, and create columns.

Understanding Views

Word enables you to view your document in a variety of ways. Each view—Normal, Online Layout, Outline, Page Layout, Master Document, and Print Preview—offers advantages for text editing, formatting, organizing, and similar tasks. You may prefer one view, but you also may want to use other views while formatting documents. This section covers the two most commonly used views: Normal and Page Layout view

 T I P No matter what view or magnification you use, the insertion point remains where it was in the preceding view.

In addition to views, Word provides magnification options for viewing a document. You can magnify the view to 200 percent, for example, or reduce it to fit the entire page (or even the entire document) on-screen. Finally, you can remove or display the various screen elements to produce a better view. This section describes the views and their advantages and disadvantages.

Viewing the Document

The two most common views are Normal and Page Layout. Normal view is mainly for entering and editing text; Page Layout view is perfect for formatting the text and page.

▶ **See** "Previewing a Document," **p. 204**

▶ **See** "Outlining a Document," **p. 238**

The three other views are more specialized:

- Online Layout view optimizes the document layout to make online reading easier mainly for use in creating and editing Web pages. Online Layout view is covered in detail in Chapter 44, "Navigating and Publishing on the Web with Office 97."

- Outline view allows you to collapse documents to heading levels so you can move or copy text easily to reorganize long documents. Outline view is covered in detail in Chapter 10, "Working with Large Documents."

- Master Document view is a method of viewing and organizing several documents at one time; this view is not discussed in this book. For more information, see Que's *Special Edition Using Microsoft Word 97.*

Finally, Print Preview shows how the document is formatted and allows you to make changes from this view without having to go back to an Edit mode. Print Preview is discussed in detail in Chapter 8, "Proofreading and Printing Documents."

Normal View Normal view—the default view in Word—shows the basic document and text. Although you can view various fonts and font sizes, tabs, indents, alignments, and so on, you cannot view formatted columns, page margins, or headers or footers (see Figure 7.1).

FIG. 7.1
The text in columns appears one column per page in Normal view.

Normal View button

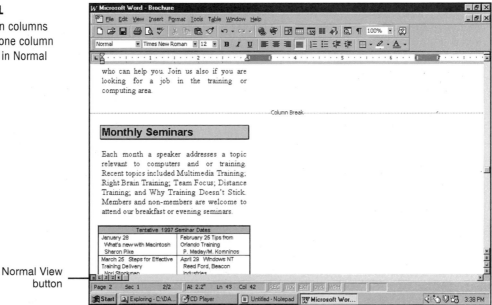

Use Normal view for entering and editing text or for formatting text. Figure 7.1 shows the Normal View button. You learn about the other view buttons in the following sections. You can use the view buttons in the horizontal scroll bar to switch between views quickly.

Page Layout View Page Layout view shows how the text, columns, margins, graphics, and other elements look on the page. Page Layout view provides the *WYSIWYG* (what-you-see-is-what-you-get) view of your document.

Editing and formatting may be slower in Page Layout view, but you can get a better idea of how your document looks as you format and when you finish formatting. Figure 7.2 shows the same document as in Figure 7.1, but in Page Layout view. In both views, the vertical scroll bar has two buttons to move up or down a page at a time.

To change views by using the View menu, use one of these options:

- Choose View, Normal for text editing and entering.
- Choose View, Page Layout to format the text and page.

Part
II

Ch
7

FIG. 7.2

You can view columns and page margins in Page Layout view.

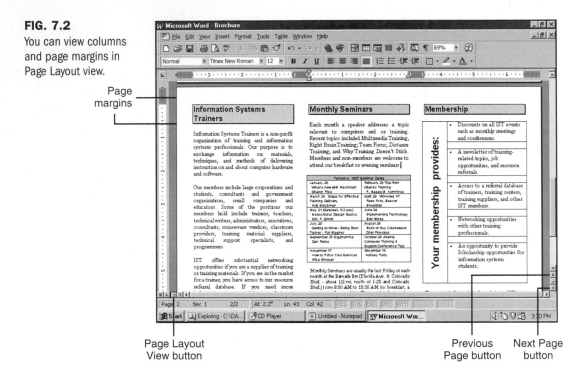

Page margins

Page Layout View button

Previous Page button

Next Page button

Hiding Screen Elements

In addition to changing views, you can display or hide the screen elements so that you can see the document design better. Use the View menu to remove the rulers and toolbars. You also can choose View, Full Screen to view a document with nothing but the Close Full Screen button on-screen with the document.

Figure 7.3 shows the full screen view. You can enter and edit text in this view as well as move pictures and objects. To return to Normal or Page Layout view, press the Esc key or click the Full Screen button.

▶ **See** "Manipulating Parts of the Screen," **p. 52**

Magnifying the View

 To set your own magnification, click the down arrow next to the Zoom Control button, and then select a percentage or enter any number between 10 and 500.

 You can change the magnification of the view to better control how much of your document you see on-screen at any time. Word provides two methods of changing views:

choosing <u>V</u>iew, <u>Z</u>oom or clicking the Zoom Control button in the Standard toolbar. Figure 7.4 shows a document at 69% of magnification. The document also is in page layout view.

FIG. 7.3
Full screen view enables you to see and work with your document with no screen elements or obstructions.

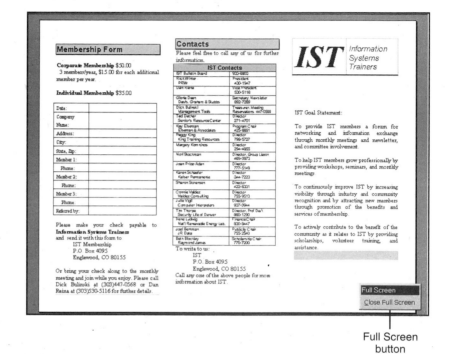

Full Screen button

FIG. 7.4
You can format the text and document at any view magnification.

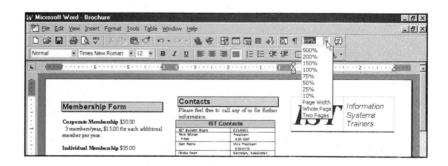

 T I P The Zoom dialog box enables you to view more than two pages at a time in Page Layout view.

To change magnifications by using the Zoom dialog box, follow these steps:

1. Choose <u>V</u>iew, <u>Z</u>oom. The Zoom dialog box appears, as shown in Figure 7.5.

Part
II

Ch

7

FIG. 7.5
Choose Page Width to see an entire line of text in the Zoom dialog box.

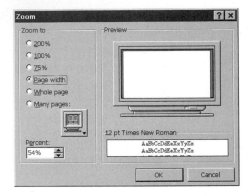

2. In the Zoom To area, select the magnification you want, enter a percentage in the Percent box, or click the monitor button and choose the number of pages you want.

N O T E   The Zoom dialog box and Zoom Control button may appear differently depending on which view (normal or page layout) you are in when you choose the Zoom command. For example, in Page Layout view you have the Whole Page option available in the Zoom dialog box. This option is dimmed if you enter the dialog box while in normal view. ■

3. Choose OK to close the dialog box.

TROUBLESHOOTING

My document is in landscape view, but I cannot see enough of it to edit the text. Use the Zoom Control button in the Standard toolbar to change the view to page width or whole page.

I formatted two columns, but I see only one column on the page. You are in Normal view. Choose View, Page Layout.

My page is formatted with many fonts, font sizes, and graphics; screen redraw is slow. Choose View, Normal to view the less-formatted version of the document and speed screen redraw.

Formatting Text

  To display the Formatting toolbar, choose View, Toolbars, select Formatting, and then choose OK.

Word, like the other programs in Microsoft Office, provides many options for formatting text. You can select a variety of fonts, sizes, and styles to enhance your documents.

In addition, Word provides a Formatting toolbar that makes text formatting easy. Alternatively, you can use the Font dialog box, described later in this section.

You can format text by first selecting the text and then making the formatting changes. Alternatively, you can position the insertion point, make the formatting changes, and then enter the text. All text entered from that point on is formatted according to your specifications until you change the formatting again or move the insertion point to another part of the document.

Changing Fonts in Word

Font is the typeface of the text. A typeface can, for example, be Times New Roman or Helvetica. The font you choose helps create an impression or set the mood for the document. Suppose that you want to create an informal flyer for a sale. You can use a fun font, such as Comic Sans MS, Book Antiqua, or Century Schoolbook. Formal, sophisticated fonts are those like Arial, Matura MT Script Capitals, or Britannic Bold.

N O T E Your computer may have different fonts installed than mentioned here. Fonts are installed both through Windows and Microsoft Office.

 T I P When selecting fonts, choose those with a TT next to the name, indicating TrueType. These fonts look the same on-screen as they do on paper and can be printed on most printers.

Select the font you want to use from the Formatting toolbar's Font drop-down list, shown in Figure 7.6.

When you are looking at the list of available fonts, Microsoft tries to show you where the fonts are coming from. The TT symbol stands for TrueType; this means the font is a scalable font and will print just like it appears. The printer icon next to the font name means the font is generated by the printer definition you have installed. Some fonts don't have anything next to them; those are screen fonts and may or may not print on your printer.

  T I P You can change the direction of your text if the text is in a table. Select the cell to change, click the Change Text Direction button on the Tables and Borders toolbar.

FIG. 7.6

Word lists the most recently used fonts at the top of the list so that you can find them quickly. The rest of the available fonts are listed in alphabetical order.

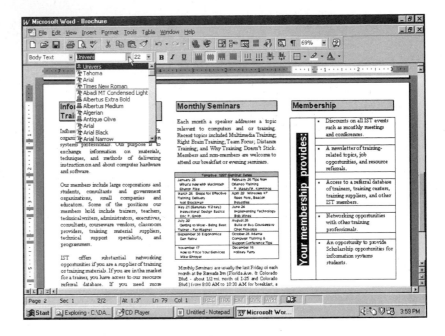

Changing Font Size

Font size is measured in *points*. Points and *picas* are typesetting measurements used for measuring spacing, line thickness, and so on. There are 12 points to a pica and six picas to an inch; therefore, there are 72 points to an inch.

All text you enter in a new, Normal template document is 10-point Times New Roman by default. You can, of course, change the type size. Use the Font Size drop-down list in the Formatting toolbar to select the size you want.

The font sizes available in the Font Size drop-down list depend on your printer. If you know that your printer can print a size that is not listed in the box—15 point, for example—type the number in the Font Size text box and press Enter.

▶ **See** "Using Toolbars and Keyboard Shortcuts to Format," **p. 81**

Choosing Font Styles

Character formats, also called font *styles*, change the appearance of text. The Formatting toolbar supplies buttons for three font styles: bold, italic, and underline. To apply any of these attributes, simply click the B, I, or U button. You can apply one, two, or all three attributes at the same time.

T I P The keyboard shortcuts for bold, italic, and underline are Ctrl+B, Ctrl+I, and Ctrl+U.

Besides these three font styles, Word supplies several effects—including Shadow, Outline, Emboss, Engrave, Strikethrough, Superscript, Subscript, Small Caps, and All Caps—in the Font dialog box.

Using the Font Dialog Box

You can choose Format, Font to display the Font dialog box. Use this dialog box to format the text all at once; for example, you can use the dialog box options to change the font, size, and font style of the selected text. Figure 7.7 shows the Font tab of the Font dialog box.

FIG. 7.7
Use the Font dialog box to perform many changes at one time on the selected text.

Using the Font tab of the Font dialog box, you can select a font and style; look at the results in the Preview box. You also can choose from more attributes than are available in the Formatting toolbar, including single, double, dotted, thick, dash, or wave underlines and colors. After you select the options you want, choose OK to close the dialog box.

Part
II

Ch
7

T I P You can also format text by using Word's styles and your own to format the text the same way over and over. For more information, see Chapter 10.

Copying Formats

Word makes formatting text easy with the Format Painter, which enables you to format an entire document quickly and easily.

When you format text—such as a heading, complicated tabs, or indents—and you need to format other text in the document the same way, you can save time and energy by copying the formatting of the original text. Suppose that you formatted a heading as 18-point Univers, bold and italic, center-aligned, and with five points spacing below the heading. Rather than select and format each heading in your document separately, you can use the Format Painter to copy the format to another heading:

1. Select the formatted text—the text with the format you want to copy.
2. Click the Format Painter button in the Standard toolbar. The pointer changes to a paintbrush and I-beam (see Figure 7.8).
3. Select the text to be formatted, and that text automatically changes to the copied text format.

N O T E You can copy formatting to multiple locations using the Format Painter. Select the formatted text you like, and double-click the Format Painter button to copy the format. For each location you want to apply the format, select the text. Click the Format Painter button again or press Esc when you're finished. ▪

Adding Highlighting to a Document

 Another feature for making text stand out in a document is highlighting. You can highlight the same as you would make text bold, italic, or underlined. First select the text you want to change, and then click the Highlight button on the Formatting toolbar. The background behind the text will change to a different color. If you want to change the highlight color, click the drop-down arrow to the right of the Highlight button and choose a different color. The other option is to choose the highlight color first, then click and drag to select the text you want to highlight. To turn off all highlighting, choose Tools, Options, and on the View tab, deselect Highlight.

N O T E Another form of highlighting is adding Text Borders. With Word 97, you can apply borders to selected text just as you do to paragraphs or tables. First, select the text; then, use the Borders tool on the Formatting toolbar to apply the border. You can also use the Format, Borders and Shading command to see all the new borders you can choose from. For more information on applying borders, see Chapter 11, "Working with Tables and Borders." ▪

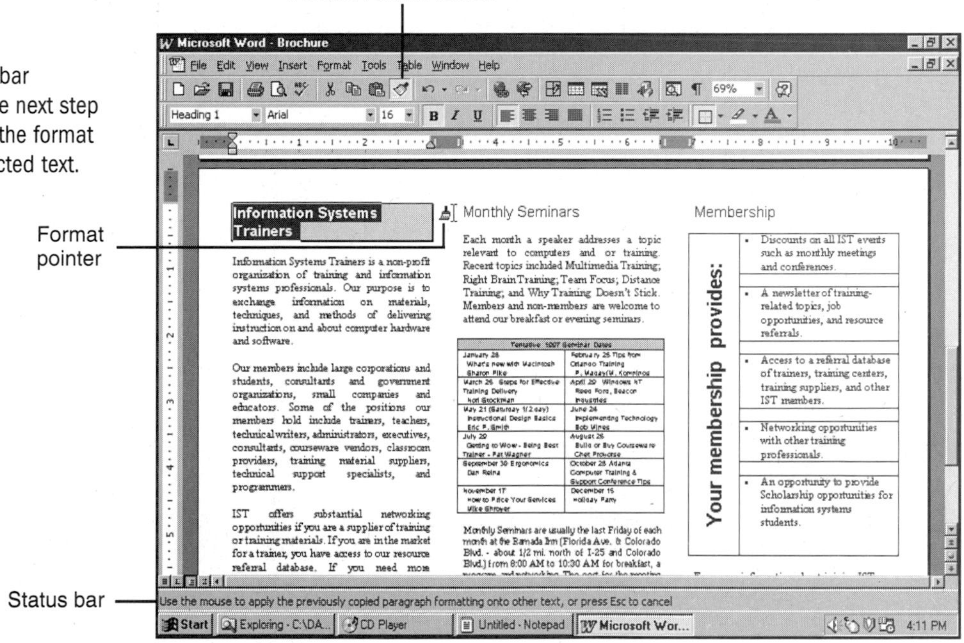

Format Painter button

FIG. 7.8
The status bar explains the next step in copying the format of the selected text.

Format pointer

Status bar

TROUBLESHOOTING

I have changed the font, font size, font style, and alignment of the selected text, and now I want to change the text back to its original formatting. Undo the formatting using the Undo drop-down list in the Standard toolbar. To remove formatting, you also can select the text first and then press Ctrl+Shift+Z.

I just formatted some text by choosing Format, Font, and I want to use the same formatting for text on the next page of my document. Select the new text to format and then choose Edit, Repeat Formatting, or press Ctrl+Y or F4. Word repeats the last formatting command you used. You could also choose to use the Format Painter. Select the text you just formatted, click the Format Painter icon, and select the text you want to change.

Part

II

Ch

7

Formatting Paragraphs

A large part of formatting a page of text occurs when you format the paragraphs of body text, headings, lists, and so on. When producing an attractive, professional-looking document, you want to present a unified arrangement of the text elements. You can accomplish this by specifying line, word, and paragraph spacing; aligning the text; setting tabs and indents; and specifying how the text flows on the page.

N O T E   Word's definition of a paragraph is any amount of text—one character or 10 sentences—ending with a paragraph mark. ▩

  T I P   You can enter text, select it, and then format it, or you can specify the formatting before you enter text.

Word enables you to select a paragraph of text and change its arrangement by choosing commands or clicking buttons in the Formatting toolbar and the Tables and Borders toolbar. This section shows you how to format paragraphs of text.

Adjusting Spacing

You can use spacing to change the design and readability of your text. For the most part, Word's default spacing works quite well for most documents, but you may sometimes want to apply specific spacing. This section shows you how to change line and paragraph spacing, and gives you a few tips on when to adjust spacing.

Line Spacing   Line spacing, also called *leading* (pronounced LED-ing), is the space that separates a line of text from the text above and below it. Without line spacing, uppercase letters, ascenders (the top strokes of t, b, d, and so on), and descenders (the bottom strokes of g, j, y, and so on) in one line would touch those in the next line.

Word's default line spacing is single. Word measures spacing in points or in lines. Text typed in 10-point uses approximately 12-point spacing, or one line (single). Text typed in 12-point uses 14-point spacing, which still is one line. The "line" spacing depends on the size of the type. The larger the type size, the greater the line spacing: 24-point text, for example, uses about 27-point line spacing. Typesetting guidelines generally call for leading to be about 120 percent of the point size of the text.

CAUTION

In most cases, don't use different line spacings in one document (see Figure 7.9). Different spacings confuse the reader and make the text hard to read.

Word enables you to change the line spacing in your text. You can set spacing to single, double, or one and a half lines, or you can set a specific measurement in points. Figure 7.9 shows four paragraphs of text with different line spacings. The top and bottom paragraphs have Word's default: single spacing, or 12-point text on 14-point spacing. The second paragraph is 1.5 lines spacing or 12-point text on 21-point spacing, and the third paragraph is double spaced or 12-point text on 28 point spacing.

FIG. 7.9
Line spacing affects readability and page design.

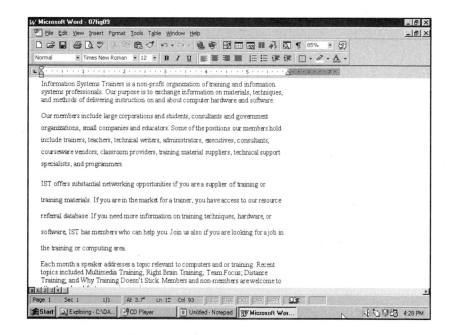

  T I P   Keyboard shortcuts for spacing are Ctrl+2 for double spacing, Ctrl+1 for single spacing, and Ctrl+5 for 1.5 spacing.

To set line spacing, follow these steps:

1. Place the insertion point in the paragraph you want to format or select multiple paragraphs.

2. Choose Format, Paragraph. The Paragraph dialog box appears, as shown in Figure 7.10.

3. Select the Indents and Spacing tab.

4. In the Line Spacing drop-down list, select the option you want; enter a value in the At box, if necessary. These options are described in Table 7.1.

5. Choose OK to close the dialog box.

Part
II

Ch
7

FIG. 7.10

This Paragraph dialog box shows the Indents and Spacing tab displayed. Use the Spacing area to control line spacing.

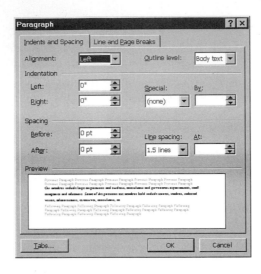

Table 7.1 Line-Spacing Options

Option	Result
Single	Default line spacing (two to five points larger than text size).
1.5 Lines	Spacing that is one and a half times the size of the normal spacing. For 12-point spacing, the spacing is 18 points.
Double	Spacing that is twice the size of the normal spacing. For 12-point spacing, the spacing is 24 points.
At Least	Accommodates larger font sizes within a line of text. In the At box, enter a specific line spacing amount that Word can use as minimum spacing. To allow for a larger font, for example, 12-point text that includes some 18-point characters, the spacing is 20; if you enter **20** in the At box, spacing is adjusted to 20 points.
Exactly	Limits Word to a certain amount of spacing, which you enter in the At box.
Multiple	Decreases or increases line spacing by the percentage you enter in the At box. To increase spacing by 20 percent, for example, enter **1.2**; to decrease spacing by 20 percent, enter **.8**.

Paragraph Spacing   You can add extra space between paragraphs to improve readability in your documents and to add valuable white space. *White space*, or areas of a page that contain no text or graphics, provides rest for the reader's eyes and prevents the page from being too crowded. Readability often is improved when you add space between paragraphs.

Use extra paragraph spacing instead of a first-line indent when you use left-aligned body text, as shown in Figure 7.11. The reader's eyes can find the beginning of a paragraph easily without the indent. You also can add more spacing after headings or subheadings, between items in a list, within tables, and in outlines.

FIG. 7.11
Extra spacing makes the beginning of each paragraph easy to find and provides valuable white space.

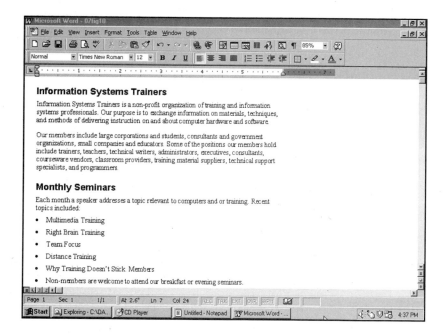

To add extra paragraph spacing, follow these steps:

1. Place the insertion point in the paragraph you want to format or select multiple paragraphs.

2. Choose Format, Paragraph. The Paragraph dialog box appears (refer to Figure 7.10).

3. Select the Indents and Spacing tab.

4. In the Spacing area, enter a value in the Before box, the After box, or in both boxes. You can enter the measurement in lines (li) or points (pt).

5. Choose OK to close the dialog box.

Part
II

Ch
7

TROUBLESHOOTING

I set the line and paragraph spacing in the Paragraph dialog box, and I don't like the results. I want to change the line spacing back to the way it was, but I don't want to change the paragraph spacing. Choose Format, Paragraph, and then select the Indents and Spacing tab. In the Line Spacing drop-down list, select Single. Then choose OK to close the dialog box.

Setting Tabs

You can set tabs in a document by using either the Tabs dialog box or the ruler. This section describes using the ruler to set tabs because it is a quick and easy method for the task. The ruler also is handy for other kinds of paragraph formatting, such as indenting text and changing margins.

 If you want to use leaders with tabs, first choose Format, Tabs; then select tab position, alignment, and leader options in the Tabs dialog box. If you are setting more than one tab, click the Set button after each tab definition.

N O T E   Whether you use the ruler or the Tabs dialog box, you can select the text and then set the tabs, or set the tabs and then enter the text. ■

 When you position the insertion point in any paragraph of text, tab and indent settings for that paragraph appear in the ruler.

To use the ruler to set tab stops in your text, first position the insertion point in the paragraph you want to format or select multiple paragraphs, click the tab alignment button on the horizontal ruler shown in Figure 7.12 until the type of tab you want appears. Then click the place in the ruler where you want to set the tab stop.

FIG. 7.12
Click the ruler to set a tab stop; drag a tab marker in the ruler to reposition the tab stop.

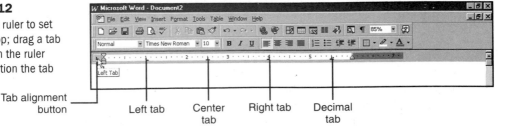

Tab alignment button — Left tab   Center tab   Right tab   Decimal tab

You can reposition any tab stop in the ruler by clicking and dragging the tab marker to a new location. To remove a tab stop, drag the tab marker off the ruler straight down into your document.

Indenting Text

You can use the ruler or the Paragraph dialog box to set indents for text. Using the ruler, you can indent the left side, the right side, or only the first line of a paragraph. Figure 7.13 shows indents for selected text.

FIG. 7.13
Word supplies a dotted guideline to help you align indents and tab stops when using the ruler.

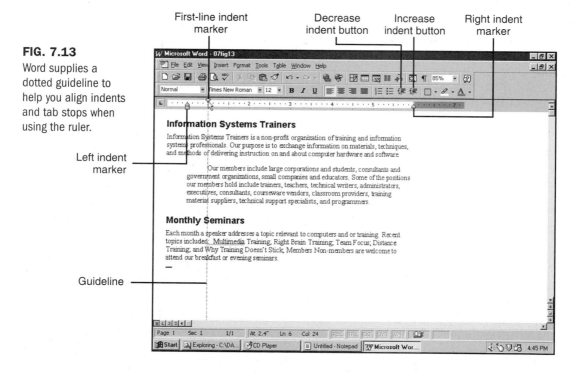

Word also supplies Increase Indent and Decrease Indent buttons, shown in the Formatting toolbar in Figure 7.13. Each time you click one of these buttons, you indent the selected text to the next tab stop or to the preceding tab stop.

 TIP You can set the tab stops or use the default half-inch tab stops.

A *hanging indent* is another type of indent you can create (see Figure 7.14). To create a hanging indent, position the insertion point anywhere in the paragraph and drag the left

Part

II

Ch

7

indent marker (the rectangle and up-pointing triangle on the bottom of the ruler) to the position where you want to indent the paragraph beginning with the second line. Then drag the first-line indent marker (the down-pointing triangle on the top of the ruler) to the position where you want the overhanging line to start.

FIG. 7.14
Create a hanging indent by first dragging the left indent marker and then dragging the first-line marker into position.

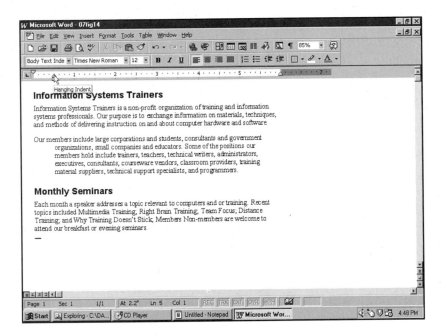

Adjusting Alignment

Alignment is a way of organizing your text. The way you align the text in a document makes the text easy to read, decorative, eye-catching, formal and sophisticated, or casual and flexible. Word enables you to left-align, right-align, center, or justify the text in your documents.

Figure 7.15 shows the four alignments and the corresponding toolbar buttons.

 T I P The keyboard shortcuts for aligning text are: Ctrl+L for Left-aligned, Ctrl+E for Centered, Ctrl+R for Right-aligned, and Ctrl+J for Justified.

N O T E When you use justified text, be sure that you turn on the hyphenation feature. To do so, choose Tools, Language, Hyphenation. In the Hyphenation dialog box, select Automatically Hyphenate Document, and then choose OK. You may have to add this feature by going through the custom installation process. ■

Align Left   Center   Align Right   Justify

FIG. 7.15
Align your text so that the reader can easily follow the message and so that the page is attractive.

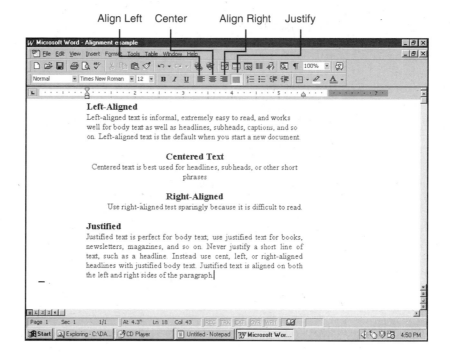

TROUBLESHOOTING

I want to see how the tabs or indents are set in a specific paragraph of text. Position the insertion point in the paragraph and view the indent and tab markers in the horizontal ruler. (To display the ruler, choose View, Ruler.)

I justified the text in a paragraph, and now there are large gaps between the words. Turn on the hyphenation feature by choosing Tools, Language, Hyphenation and then selecting Automatically Hyphenate Document. Choose OK to close the dialog box.

When I tried to change the indent, my left margin appears too far in the middle of the screen and the right margin is off the screen. Drag the left indent marker by the box on the bottom back to the correct position. Then click the mouse to the right of the horizontal scroll box and then to the left of the scroll box to reset the screen view.

I want to align the first part of a line of text on the left side of the screen and the second part of the same line of text on the right side of the screen. Use tabs rather than the align buttons. Create a right tab at the right margin for the right justification.

Part

II

Ch

7

Adding Bullets and Numbering

Bullets and Numbering allow you to pull out information in your documents by making lists easier to read. You can bring emphasis to text by applying either bullets or numbering to lists.

 To create a bulleted list, you simply type the list, select the list after it is typed, and click the Bullet button on the formatting toolbar. Alternatively, you can type the first line with an asterisk (*) and a space at the beginning of the line, and press enter at the end of the line (the asterisk and space convert to a bullet with an indent). You can also choose to turn the bullets on before you type the list. In this case, click the Bullet button on the formatting toolbar and type the list, clicking the bullet button again when you finish to turn bullets off (see Figure 7.16).

FIG. 7.16
A Word document with both a bulleted list and a numbered list.

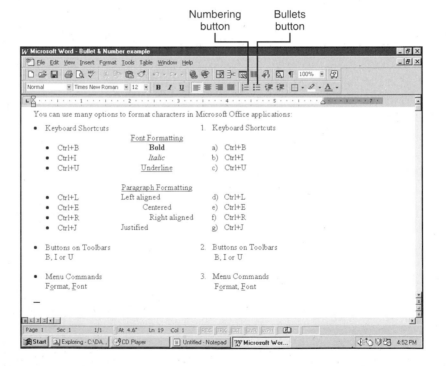

 To create a numbered list, simply type the list, select the list after it is typed, and click the Numbering button on the formatting toolbar. Or, you can type the first line with a number and a space at the beginning of the line, and press enter at the end of the line (the number and space convert to a numbered list with an indent). You could also choose to turn numbering on before you type the list. In this case, you would click the numbering button on the formatting toolbar, type the list, then click the numbering button again when you are finished to turn numbering off (refer to Figure 7.16).

N O T E If you want to insert a blank line or lines without bullets in your list, use Shift+Enter to create manual line breaks. The line following the manual line break does not have a bullet. To add more lines with bullets, press Enter (see Figure 7.17). ■

FIG. 7.17
Bullet and numbered lists with Show/Hide on to see manual line breaks.

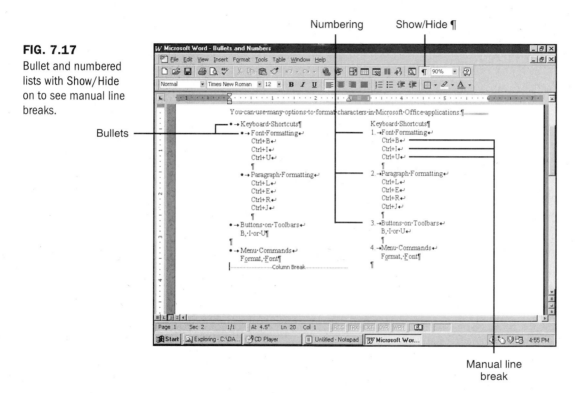

Formatting the Page

Formatting the page includes changing page size and orientation, setting margins, creating columns, and formatting tables. The way you format the page depends on the amount of text, the size and orientation of graphics, the type of document, and so on. Keep in mind that you want to create an attractive, eye-catching page of easy-to-read text.

Suppose that you have several drawings of cars to go into an advertisement with very little text. You can create the ad in *landscape* (wide) orientation with one-inch margins. On the other hand, if your text contains two long lists of items and no graphics, you can use *portrait* (tall) orientation with two columns and half-inch margins.

Part
II

Ch
7

Word's page-formatting commands are flexible and easy to use. You can change the page to fit your text so that you present the most professional-looking document possible. This section describes page formatting.

Changing Size and Page Orientation for Word Documents

The size and orientation of the paper you use depends mostly on your printer. Some printers take 8 1/2-by-11-inch sheets only; others can print sheets ranging from small envelopes to legal-size paper. Most laser and inkjet printers can print in either orientation. Check your printer manual before changing paper size and orientation.

To change page size and orientation, use the Page Setup dialog box. Figure 7.18 shows the Paper Size tab in the Page Setup dialog box.

FIG. 7.18

Choose paper size and orientation, and then view the change in the Preview box.

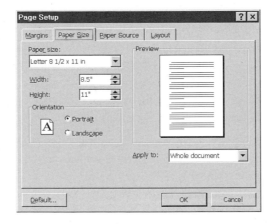

To change paper size and orientation, follow these steps:

1. Choose File, Page Setup. The Page Setup dialog box appears.
2. Select the Paper Size tab.
3. Select a size from the Paper Size drop-down list.
4. In the Orientation area, select Portrait or Landscape.
5. Choose OK to close the dialog box.

Setting Margins

You can change the margins of your document from the default settings to any margin you want. Word's Normal template uses 1-inch top and bottom margins and 1.25-inch left and right margins. You can set the margins by using the Page Setup dialog box, shown in Figure 7.19. Keep in mind that your printer may limit the page margins you can select.

FIG. 7.19
You can change the margins to shorten the line length and add valuable white space.

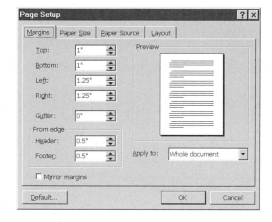

N O T E When you set margins, Word applies those measurements to all pages in a document, unless you have selected text or divided your document into sections. ▪

▶ **See** "Setting Margins," **p. 84**

To change the margins of your document, follow these steps:

1. Choose File, Page Setup. The Page Setup dialog box appears.
2. Select the Margins tab.
3. Enter measurements in the Top, Bottom, Left, and Right boxes.
4. Choose OK to close the dialog box.

N O T E You can now apply page borders by selecting the Format, Borders and Shading command from the menu bar, then selecting the Page Border tab. Select the setting you want for the border, select the Style and Width or select the Art you want to apply to the border around the page. In the Apply To pull-down list, you can choose to apply the page border to the Whole Document, This Section, This Section-First Page Only, or This Section-All Except First Page. When you finish, click OK to apply the page border. ▪

Creating Columns

You can divide the page into one, two, three, or more columns to make the text well-organized and easy to read. Documents such as books, magazines, catalogs, newsletters, brochures, and even advertisements often are divided into columns. Word makes dividing your documents into columns easy. To see your text formatted in columns, you must be in Page Layout view or Print Preview.

N O T E   Normally, divide an 8 1/2-by-11-inch portrait-oriented page into no more than three columns; divide the same-size landscape-oriented page into no more than five columns. When you use too many columns on a page, the lines of text become too short and are hard to read.

T I P   You can create equal-sized columns by holding down the mouse pointer on the Columns button of the Standard toolbar and dragging down to choose the number of columns.

You divide a document into columns by using the Columns dialog box (see Figure 7.20). You can select a preset number of columns and designs or enter a number of columns and each column width, if you prefer. When you enter your own column width, you must specify spacing, called *gutter space,* between the columns.

FIG. 7.20
You can make one column wider than the other for an interesting effect. View the result in the Preview box before choosing OK.

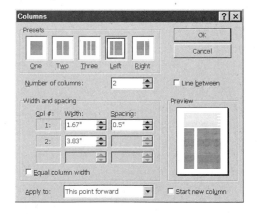

If you like, you can add a line, or rule, between the columns by selecting the Line Between option. Word even enables you to start a new column at the insertion point by selecting the Start New Column option. Preview your column choices in the Preview box before accepting or rejecting the changes in the dialog box.

To format the columns in your document, follow these steps:

1. If you have different numbers of columns throughout your document or if only a portion of your document is to have columns, select the text for which you want to change columns.

2. Choose Format, Columns. The Columns dialog box appears.

3. In the Presets area, select the number or type of columns you want. One, Two or Three will create that number of equal columns. Left or Right will create two unequal columns with the left or right column smaller than the other. You can add additional columns through the Number Of Columns increment box.

4. Use the other options in the dialog box to customize columns. You can adjust the Width of the columns in the Width and Spacing section.

5. Choose OK to accept the changes and close the dialog box.

▶ **See** "Adding Lines, Borders, and Shading," **p. 287**

TROUBLESHOOTING

I created an 8 1/2-by-14-inch document, and now I can't print it. Check your printer manual. You may have changed the page to a size larger than your printer can print.

I made my margins narrower than 1/4 inch, and now some of the edges of the text will not print. Most printers have a required margin—usually 1/4 or 3/8 inch—because they cannot print to the edge of the page. Check your printer manual. Make a habit of allowing at least 3/8-inch margins in all your documents.

Part
II

Ch
7

CHAPTER 8

Proofreading and Printing Documents

by Patty Winter

After you finish entering and editing text, you want to proofread and then print your documents. Word supplies several tools that make proofreading easy. You can use Word's Spelling and Grammar command, plus the Thesaurus command, to proofread your documents and supply suggestions for improvement. You can also use the Find and Replace commands to help you review or change text.

No matter how long or short a document is, using the Spelling and Grammar command is well worth the time it takes. Word quickly reviews the text and alerts you if it finds a misspelled word or any grammatical errors. Additionally, you can use Word's Thesaurus to find alternative words so that your text is not monotonous and repetitive.

After your document is complete, you can print it. Word has a special print preview mode in which you can view the document and make last-minute changes in the design before printing. Finally, you can print your document by using Windows defaults or by setting options in Word. ■

Checking spelling and grammar

Learn about the Automatic Spell Checking feature, the Spelling and Grammar command, and the AutoCorrect feature.

Using Find and Replace

This section explains why and how to use an automated command to find specific information and, if you want, change the information to something else.

Using the Thesaurus

The Thesaurus helps you develop a broader vocabulary and assists you in finding just the right words for your document.

Previewing and printing documents

Learn how to use the Print Preview toolbar and rulers to change the format of a document. This section also explains the options you can use to print documents and envelopes.

Checking Spelling and Grammar

The Spelling and Grammar command reads text and notifies you when it finds a word that is not in its main dictionary; Word also notifies you when you have repeated words and grammatical errors. The Spelling and Grammar dialog box shows you the word or phrase in question, suggests a replacement word or phrase, and displays a list of possible replacement words or grammar corrections.

 TIP You can check the spelling of the entire document or you can select text and check spelling in only the selected text.

▶ **See** "Checking Spelling," **p. 86**

This section briefly reviews the steps to get started with Word's Spelling and Grammar command. You also learn about AutoCorrect, a Word feature that automatically corrects words as you type them.

Using the Spelling and Grammar Command

 To check the spelling and grammar in a document, click the Spelling and Grammar button in the Standard toolbar. The Spelling and Grammar dialog box appears upon finding the first unrecognized word (see Figure 8.1).

TIP You also can check spelling and grammar in a document by choosing Tools, Spelling and Grammar, or by pressing F7.

A new feature in Word 97 is the grammar checker, which is automatically on when you choose to check your spelling. If you want to turn off the grammar option, you can click the Check Grammar option on the bottom of the Spelling and Grammar dialog box (see Figure 8.1). You may want to leave the Check Grammar option on to see what type of grammar problems Word can find for you.

FIG. 8.1

The Spelling and Grammar dialog box highlights unrecognized words and offers suggestions to correct the spelling.

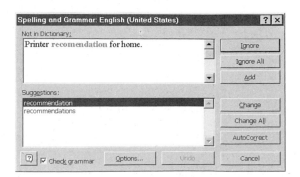

Part

II

Ch

8

Choosing Spelling Options in the Spelling and Grammar Dialog Box   Word highlights a questionable word, displays the sentence with the misspelled word in the Not in
Dictionary: text box, and suggests a change in the Suggestions text box. If you want, you
can choose another word from the Suggestions list box or edit the word in the Not in
Dictionary: box. After you select the proper word, you can choose the Change button to
change this one occurrence or choose Change All to change all occurrences of the
misspelling throughout your document. If you want Word to automatically correct this
misspelled word when you type it in other documents, choose the AutoCorrect button.

If the word is correct and not in the dictionary (such as a person's or company's name),
you can choose to Ignore this one occurrence, Ignore All occurrences in the document, or
Add the word to the dictionary so that the Spelling command will not stop at the word
again.

When you have a repeated word, yox can choose to Delete the second occurrence of the
word or Ignore the repetition.

Choosing Grammar Options in the Spelling and Grammar Dialog Box   If you have
turned the Check Grammar option off, you need to make sure to turn it back on by
clicking the check box on the bottom of the dialog box. Word highlights a questionable
word, phrase, or punctuation mark, then displays the phrase in the problem text box (with
a label defining the grammar problem such as Verb Form:, Possible Question:, and so
on). Word suggests a change in the Suggestions text box (see Figure 8.2).

FIG. 8.2

You can choose to
Ignore or Change
grammar problems
while you check for
spelling errors.

Changing label

Problem text box

Office Assistant

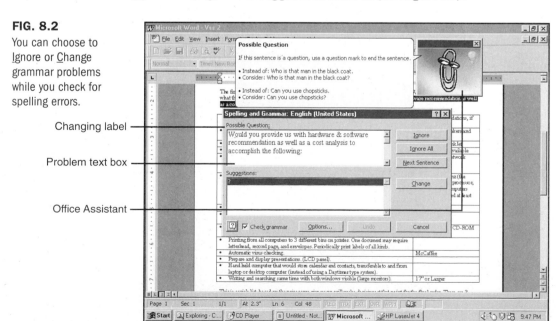

If you want, you can choose another word, phrase, or punctuation mark from the Suggestions list box or edit the item in the problem: text box. After you select the proper correction, you can choose the Change button to change this occurrence.

The following table describes the options in the Grammar dialog box (refer to Figure 8.2):

N O T E   You must read the suggestions carefully. You may find that the suggestion is not valid and that the problem, as the Grammar Checker sees it, is not really a problem. ▪

Option	Explanation
Problem text box	The sentence in question appears in this text box with the problem in green. You can edit the sentence here.
Suggestions	Word defines the problem and may suggest alternative solutions.
Ignore	Choose this button if you want to ignore the problem and move to the next grammar problem, which can be in the current sentence.
Ignore All	Choose this button if you want to ignore the problem throughout the document.
Next Sentence	Choose this button to look for potential problems in the next sentence, ignoring any other problems that may be in the current sentence.
Change	Choose this button to change the sentence if an alternative suggestion was made in the Suggestions box.
Question Mark button	Displays or Hides the Office Assistant, which can provide help for this feature.
Check Grammar	Turns the Grammar checking feature off (no check mark) or on (check mark).
Options	Opens the options for the spelling and grammar checker to enable you to customize rules and styles. Otherwise, access dialog box from Tools, Options and click the Spelling & Grammar tab.
Undo	Reverses the most recent grammar and spelling actions, one at a time.
Cancel/Close	Cancel closes the dialog box without making a change; after you make a change, the Cancel button changes to Close. Click Close to return to your document.

◆

TROUBLESHOOTING

I don't want to check the grammar at the same time I check the spelling. Choose <u>T</u>ools, <u>O</u>ptions, and select the Spelling & Grammar tab. Clear the C<u>h</u>eck Grammar With Spelling option to deactivate it. Then click OK.

I changed my mind about the last change I applied in the Spelling and Grammar dialog box. Click the <u>U</u>ndo button in the dialog box.

Using Automatic Spell and Grammar Checking

One of the best features in Word is Automatic Spell and Grammar Checking. This feature, if turned on, checks your spelling and grammar as you type. When Word encounters a misspelled word, it underlines the word with a red wavy line. When Word encounters a grammatical error, it underlines the word or phrase with a green wavy line. To check the error, point to it and right-click it. The shortcut menu appears. For spelling errors, you see the suggested words in bold at the top of the menu, an <u>I</u>gnore All command, an <u>A</u>dd command, the AutoCorrect command, and the <u>S</u>pelling command (see Figure 8.3). For grammar errors, the shortcut menu shows the suggested fix to the problem in bold at the top of the menu, an Ignore Sentence command, and the <u>G</u>rammar command (see Figure 8.4). You can choose any of the commands by clicking the left mouse button. If you need more information related to these options, see the section "Using the Spelling and Grammar Command" earlier in this chapter.

Using AutoCorrect

The AutoCorrect feature automatically corrects spelling mistakes and formatting errors, or replaces characters you enter with specific words or phrases. Using this feature saves you time. Suppose that you consistently type *anohter* instead of *another* or *WHen* instead of *When*. You can enter these common mistakes into AutoCorrect, and the next time you make the mistake, Word corrects it automatically.

You can use AutoCorrect to expand an abbreviation every time you write one. For example, you could have *adr* expand to include your address. You would type **adr** and press the space bar; *adr* would be replaced with your home or business address, for example, *720 Skyline Drive, Idaho Springs 80452.*

FIG. 8.3
The wavy underline
indicates an
unrecognized word.

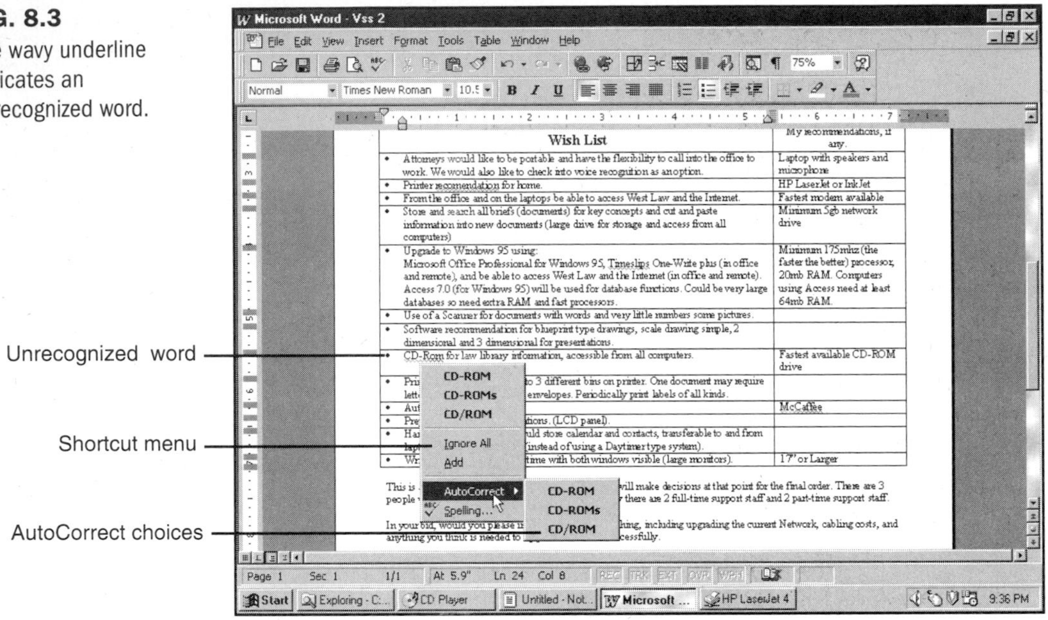

Unrecognized word —

Shortcut menu —

AutoCorrect choices —

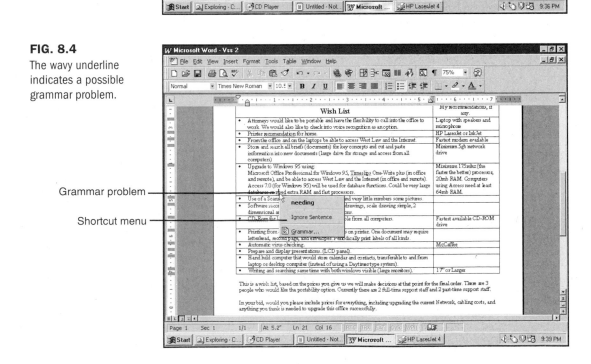

FIG. 8.4
The wavy underline
indicates a possible
grammar problem.

Grammar problem —

Shortcut menu —

N O T E With Word 97, Microsoft has greatly enhanced the automatic spell checking feature by adding Smart spelling. This feature recognizes your name, your organization's name, personal names, commonly used company names from the Fortune 1000 list of companies, all country names, most city names, and even current terminology. Smart spelling also recognizes your typing patterns and does not mark them as errors in the document—for example, words in all uppercase and words with numbers are no longer marked as misspelled words. ■

To set options and make entries for AutoCorrect, choose <u>T</u>ools, <u>A</u>utoCorrect. Figure 8.5 shows the AutoCorrect dialog box with a new entry. Another way to add an entry to AutoCorrect is to choose the AutoCo<u>r</u>rect button in the Spelling and Grammar dialog box, as mentioned in an earlier section.

FIG. 8.5

The AutoCorrect dialog box lists options you can turn on or off, and you can enter words you want automatically corrected.

Click to add new entries to the AutoCorrect list

Click when you are done

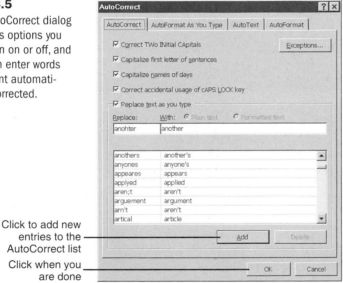

The <u>R</u>eplace and <u>W</u>ith text boxes enable you to enter your own items, and the list at the bottom of the AutoCorrect dialog box displays Word's default list plus any items you add. In the AutoCorrect entry list, type a word that you normally spell incorrectly in the <u>Re</u>place text box and type the correct spelling in the <u>W</u>ith text box. Then choose <u>A</u>dd to add the word to the list. Click OK to close the dialog box.

You can add or delete items from the AutoCorrect dialog box at any time. For more details on AutoCorrect, see "Letting AutoCorrect Do Your Spelling for You" in Chapter 3.

▶ **See** "Checking Spelling," **p. 86**

> **CAUTION**
>
> Don't include words or abbreviations that you never use intentionally in the Replace text box; if you do, every time you type the word, it will change! In this case, you probably want to use the AutoText feature "Taking Advantage of the AutoText Feature" covered in Chapter 6.

Using Find and Replace

 You may find that reviewing a document is easier if you can quickly locate specific text or formatting in different sections of the document. The Find command enables you to search for specifics in your document. If you use the Replace command instead, you not only find what you are looking for, but you can then replace what you found with something else. For instance, you can find the word *that* and replace it with the word *which* (see Figure 8.6).

FIG. 8.6
Click the Replace tab to replace the text in the Find What text box with something new.

Expands dialog box

▶ **See** "Finding and Replacing Text," **p. 90**

To use the Find command, follow these steps:

1. Choose Edit, Find. The Find dialog box appears.

2. In the Find What text box, type the text you need to find. You can choose the More button to choose one or more options in the Find dialog box to enhance your search (see Figure 8.7). These options are described later in Table 8.1.

3. Choose the Find Next button to find the text.

4. When you get to the first occurrence of the item in the Find What text box, you can choose Find Next again, Cancel, or the Replace tab.

5. If you chose the Replace tab, type the text you want to use in the Replace With text box. You can choose one or more options in the Find and Replace dialog box to enhance your search.

FIG. 8.7

The Find and Replace dialog box expands to provide search options.

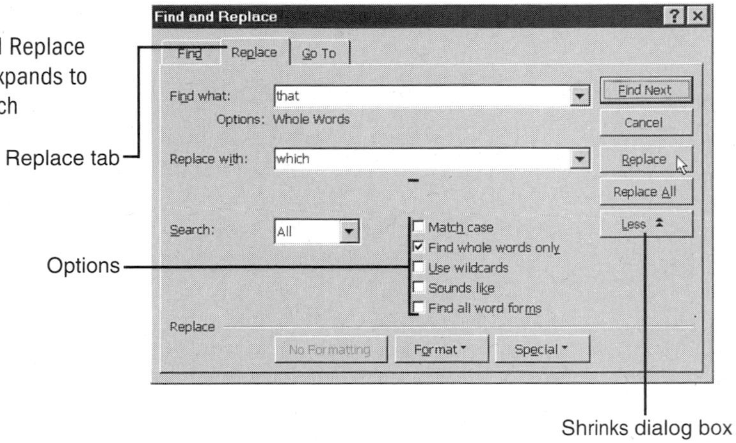

Replace tab —

Options —

Shrinks dialog box

6. To replace the found text, with new text, choose the <u>R</u>eplace button (refer to Figure 8.7).

7. Click the <u>R</u>eplace button again to replace and look for the next occurrence of the found text.

TIP The keyboard shortcut for Find is Ctrl+F; the shortcut for Replace is Ctrl+H; Shift+F4 repeats the last find.

N O T E If you want to use the Replace command without first using the Find command, you can choose <u>E</u>dit, <u>R</u>eplace or use the keyboard shortcut, Ctrl+H to display the Find and Replace dialog box with the Replace tab the active tab. ■

When you are finding or replacing text, you have a number of options for your search. Table 8.1 describes these options on the Find and Replace dialog box.

Table 8.1   Find and Replace Options

Option	Description
<u>S</u>earch	Searches forward (Down), backward (Up), or through the entire document (All).
Mat<u>c</u>h Case	Matches capitalization (uppercase or lowercase) when searching for text.
Find Whole Words Onl<u>y</u>	Finds a match that is an entire word only (if you are looking for *the*, Word doesn't find *other* or *their*).

continues

Table 8.1 Continued

Option	Description
Use Wildcards	Use with special characters (? is a wild card for any one character, * is a wild card for any number of characters). *S?t* will find *Sat, Sit, Set*. *S*t* will find all the preceding items as well as *Soot, Sachet, Saddest,* and others.
Sounds Like	Searches for different spellings of words that sound the same. If you're looking for *There*, Word finds *their, there*, and *they're*.
Find All Word Forms	Searches for all the different grammatical forms of a word. If you type *is* in the Find What text box, Word finds *is, are, be, am*.
No Formatting	Removes formatting from the search criteria if any formatting is added with the Format button.
Format	Searches for item in the Find What text box that includes fonts, styles, and other formatting.
Special	Searches for special characters such as paragraph marks, tabs, line breaks, and others.

For more detailed information on using Find and Replace, see "Finding and Replacing Text" in Chapter 3.

Using the Thesaurus

The Thesaurus supplies a variety of synonyms you can use to replace the word you are looking up. To use the Thesaurus, position the insertion point in the word you want to look up and choose Tools, Language, Thesaurus. Word automatically highlights the word, and the Thesaurus dialog box appears.

 TIP You also can use Shift+F7 to start the Thesaurus.

Suppose that you want to find a synonym for the word *second*. Using the words in the Meanings list box, you can look up either *next* or *moment* (see Figure 8.8). Selecting a word in the Meanings list on the left displays several synonyms in the Replace with Synonym list on the right. Additionally, you can look up new words, related or unrelated to the original word, or go back to a word you looked up earlier. If you want to look up a word that is different from the original word, position the insertion point in the Replace with Synonym text box, type a new word, and then choose Look Up.

FIG. 8.8

Replace the selected word with any of the displayed synonyms, or continue to look up words until you find the meaning you want.

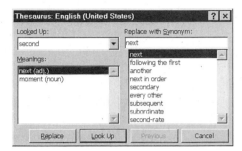

The following table describes the options in the Thesaurus dialog box:

Option	Description
Loo**k**ed Up/**N**ot Found	A drop-down list of all the words you have looked up since you opened the Thesaurus dialog box; the list disappears when you close the dialog box. The text-box name changes to **N**ot Found if the word is not in the Thesaurus.
Meanings/**A**lphabetical List	Definition and part of speech of the selected word. Selecting a different meaning results in a new list of synonyms. **A**lphabetical List appears if the selected word is not in the Thesaurus.
Replace with **S**ynonym	The word in the text box is the selected word you can **L**ook Up or **R**eplace when you choose either of those command buttons. The list of words below the text box is a list of synonyms from which you can select.
Replace with **A**ntonym	If Antonyms is available in the **M**eanings list box, you can highlight it and then select an antonym from this list box.
Replace	Choose this button to substitute the selected word (in the Replace with **S**ynonym text box) for the original word in the text.
Look Up	Displays meanings and synonyms for the selected word (in the Replace with **S**ynonym text box).
Previous	Displays the last word you looked up. Only remembers the words you have looked up during this session of using the Thesaurus.
Cancel	Closes the dialog box.

To use the Thesaurus, follow these steps:

1. Position the insertion point in the word you want to look up.

2. Choose Tools, Language, Thesaurus. Word automatically highlights the word, and the Thesaurus dialog box appears.

3. In the Meanings list, select the meaning you want.

 T I P   Double-click a synonym or meaning to display more synonyms.

4. In the Replace with Synonym list, select the word you want to use as a replacement.

5. Choose Replace to close the dialog box and substitute the new word (the one in the Replace with Synonym text box) for the old one, or click Cancel to close the dialog box without replacing the word.

TROUBLESHOOTING

I looked up several meanings, and now I want to go back to the original word I looked up in the Thesaurus. Choose Looked Up or click the down arrow to the right of that option. A drop-down list of the words you looked up during this session appears. Select the original word.

I want to go back to the last word I looked up. Choose the Previous command button.

Previewing a Document

 After you enter, edit, format, and proofread your text, you are ready to print your document. Sometimes when you format a page of text in normal view, problems are revealed when you print the document. The margins may be too wide, a headline may break in an odd place, a paragraph may be indented by mistake, and so on. You can save time, effort, and paper if you view your document in print preview before you print it. You can either click the Print Preview button on the Standard toolbar, or choose File, Print Preview.

▶ **See** "Printing Documents," **p. 121**

T I P You can edit and format your document in print preview just as you can in page layout or normal view. Use the menus and commands or display any of the toolbars to use as shortcuts. You first need to turn off the magnifier in print preview by clicking the Magnifier button in the Print Preview toolbar.

N O T E You do not have to use print preview before you print a document. If you want to print without first previewing a document, choose File, Print or click the Print button in the Standard toolbar. For more information, see "Printing Word Documents," later in this chapter. ■

Figure 8.9, which shows a document in print preview, reveals a document with too much information being jammed onto one page. You can quickly fix the problems in this view before you print. First thing you may want to fix are the bullets in the first column of the table. Move the mouse pointer to the top of the table above the first column until you see the black down arrow pointer, click to select the entire column. Now you can use the View, Toolbars command to turn on the Formatting toolbar, then click the bullets tool to turn the bullets off. You can make any other changes necessary and see what the document will look like before you print to paper.

FIG. 8.9

Use the tools you are most comfortable with when you are editing (correcting) your documents in print preview.

Formatting Toolbar

Top margin marker

Bottom margin marker

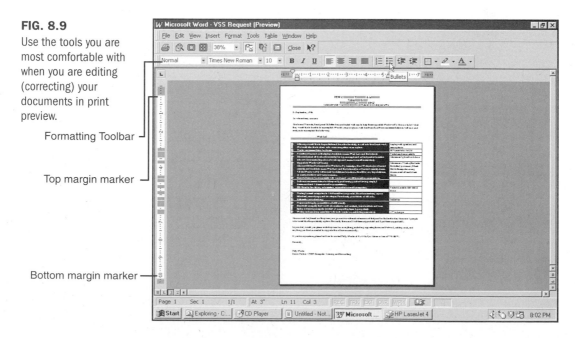

Using the Rulers

 By default, Word does not display the rulers in print preview. You can, however, choose View, Ruler to display both the horizontal and vertical rulers. Use the rulers as you would in any other view: to set tabs, adjust indents, and change the margins.

▶ **See** "Setting Tabs," **p. 182**

▶ **See** "Indenting Text," **p. 183**

 The default view in print preview is whole page view, which is best for adjusting margins.

To adjust the margins, indents, or tabs by using the ruler, click the Magnifier button on the toolbar (to turn the magnifier off), and position the insertion point at the place in the text you want to change. Any changes affect the current section.

To change the margin, move the mouse pointer over the margin marker (the point where the white ruler meets the light gray area) until the mouse pointer changes to a black double-headed arrow (refer to Figure 8.9). If you wait a little bit longer, you see a Screen-Tip telling you the name of the object to which you are pointing. Click and drag the arrow left or right (in the horizontal ruler) or up or down (in the vertical ruler) to change the margin.

To change the indent or tab, point to the indent or tab marker on the ruler until the mouse pointer changes to a white arrow. Then click and drag the arrow left or right in the horizontal ruler to change indent or tab positions.

A dotted guideline appears (see Figure 8.10) across the page as you drag any marker; use the guideline to align elements on the page.

Using the Preview Toolbar

Print preview includes a special toolbar you can use to edit your document. The Preview toolbar works in much the same way as the other toolbars. You can place the mouse pointer on a toolbar button to view the ScreenTip and the description of the button in the status bar.

You can use a toolbar button to print your document, view one page or multiple pages, display or hide the ruler, view the full screen (without screen elements such as the title bar, scroll bars, and so on), exit print preview, and get help on a specific topic. Two toolbar buttons are particularly useful: Shrink to Fit and Magnifier. See Figure 8.11 for a reference to the Print Preview toolbar buttons.

FIG. 8.10

Drag the left and right margin markers (in the horizontal ruler or the top and bottom margin markers (in the vertical ruler) to change the margins.

Left indent marker

Right margin marker

Right indent marker

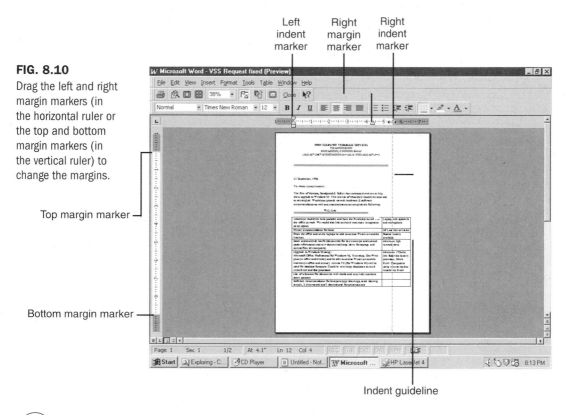

Top margin marker

Bottom margin marker

Indent guideline

T I P Choose Edit, Undo or press Ctrl+Z to reverse the Shrink to Fit operation (the Preview toolbar doesn't include an Undo button).

The Shrink to Fit button adjusts elements in a document, such as line and paragraph spacing and margins, so that you can fit a little bit more on the page. Suppose that your document fills one page, and one or two sentences overflow to a second page as in Figure 8.9 (look at the status bar; on the left it shows you the page you are on and the total number of pages in the document). Try clicking the Shrink to Fit button to squeeze all the text onto the first page (see Figure 8.10).

The magnifier enables you to toggle between the normal mouse pointer and the magnifier pointer. When the magnifier pointer contains a plus sign (+) as shown in Figure 8.11, you can magnify a portion of the document to 100 percent. When the magnifier pointer contains a minus sign (–), clicking the page reduces the view to Whole Page view. To change the magnifier pointer back to the normal pointer, click the Magnifier button again.

Clicking the Print button on the Preview toolbar prints the document using the default options in the Print dialog box. If you want to make changes to any printing options, see the following section, "Printing Word Documents."

TROUBLESHOOTING

I have several lines of text that overflow to the second page of my document, but I would like them to be on the first page. Click the Shrink to Fit button in the Preview toolbar. Magnify the document and look carefully at the changes in the text spacing and sizing. You may prefer to undo the change if the text appears to be too crowded on one page.

I have trouble setting the margins for the document with the ruler in print preview. Choose File, Page Setup, and click the Margins tab. You can type a measurement in the dialog box for the margins you want to change.

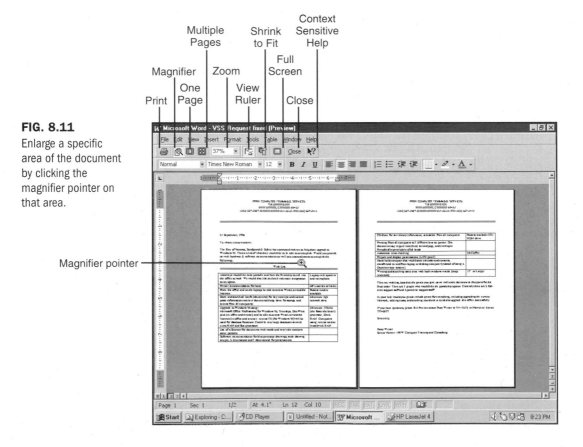

FIG. 8.11
Enlarge a specific area of the document by clicking the magnifier pointer on that area.

Printing Word Documents

When you print from Word, you generally use the defaults set up in Windows. The default options print one copy of all the pages in the document. You can, however, change these defaults in the Print dialog box (see Figure 8.12).

 See "Printing Documents," **p. 121**

FIG. 8.12
To print using the default options in the Print dialog box, click OK.

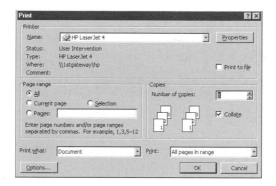

The following table describes the options in the Print dialog box:

Option	Description
Printer Section	
Name	Choose this drop-down button to select another printer on which to print this document.
Properties	Choose this button to change the properties of the selected printer (including paper size, paper orientation, and graphics resolution). The properties are in effect for all documents printed with the printer (not just this document).
Print to File	Choosing this option prints the document to a file on disk so that you can transport the file to another computer or service bureau.
Page Range Section	
All	Prints all pages in the document.
Current Page	Prints only the page in which the insertion point is located.

continues

continued

Option	Description
Pages	Prints the specified pages. Enter a page range in the text box. Separate individual pages with commas (1,4,5); indicate a page range with a hyphen (1-5).
Selection	Select text in the document before choosing to print; click Selection to print only the selected text.
Copies Section	
Number of Copies	Prints specified number of copies. Enter the number of copies to be printed.
Collate	Select this option to print copies in order. If you want two copies of a five-page document, the first copy of pages 1 to 5 will print and then the second copy will print.
Other Options	
Print What	Specify what to print: the document, document properties information, comments, a list of styles, AutoText entries, or key assignments.
Print	Specify which pages to print: all pages, even pages, or odd pages in the page range.
Options	Click this button to customize printing options.
OK	Click this button to send the selected pages to the printer.
Cancel	Click this button to cancel all changes and close the dialog box without printing the document.

▶ **See** "Changing Printing Options," **p. 122**

TROUBLESHOOTING

I tried to print a document and I didn't get an error message but I don't see my document in my printer. Verify that the correct printer is selected in the Name drop-down list of the Print dialog box. Make sure that your printer is turned on and plugged in and that you have paper in the printer.

I want to change to a different printer before printing a document. Choose the Name drop-down list in the Print dialog box. Select a printer from the list of Printers and click OK.

Printing Envelopes

You can print envelopes in Word quickly and easily by choosing Tools, Envelopes and Labels. Word makes it easy to enter the delivery and return addresses, choose an envelope size and method of feed, and then print an envelope. Figure 8.13 shows the Envelopes and Labels dialog box.

 T I P You can merge many addresses at one time with the mail merge feature (see Chapter 9, "Creating Mass Mailings").

FIG. 8.13
Enter the delivery and return addresses, and then choose Print to print the envelope.

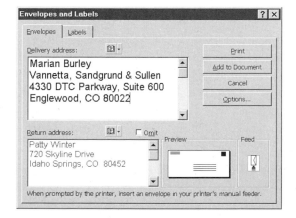

The following table describes the options in the Envelopes and Labels dialog box:

Option	Description
Delivery Address	Enter the name and address to which the envelope will be mailed.
Return Address	Enter your name and address.
Omit	Choose this option to exclude the return address.
Preview	Click the envelope in the Preview box to display the Envelope Options dialog box and the Envelope Options tab. Select the size, bar code, placement, and font for the addresses in this dialog box.
Feed	Click the Feed box to display the Envelope Options dialog box and the Printing Options tab. Select the method of feeding envelopes that best fits your printer.

continues

continued

Option	Description
Print	Choose this button to send the envelope to the printer.
Add to Document	Adds the envelope style and contents to the document so that you can save it for later use.
Cancel	Click this button to cancel your choices and close the dialog box without printing the envelope.
Options	Displays the Envelope Options dialog box.

To print an envelope in Word, follow these steps:

1. Insert an envelope into the printer.

2. Choose Tools, Envelopes and Labels. The Envelopes and Labels dialog box appears.

3. Choose the Envelopes tab.

4. Enter a Delivery Address and Return Address. If you have an address on the document, Word may find the address and place it in the Delivery Address area. You can also click the Insert Address button for either address and choose an address from your Personal Address Book.

5. Select envelope and feed options, if necessary.

6. Choose Print.

TROUBLESHOOTING

I'm trying to print an envelope but I get too much margin for the return address. After typing the name and address of the recipient in the Envelopes and Labels dialog box, choose the Options button. Choose the Envelope Options tab and change the From Left text box in the Return Address section. You also can change the position of the delivery address as well as change the font for both addresses in this dialog box.

I have a problem formatting the text in the Delivery Address area—I frequently get a double-spaced address that doesn't fit on the envelope. How do I adjust formatting? If the Envelope Options tab does not give you enough flexibility to change what you need to on an envelope, return to the Envelopes and Labels dialog box and click the Add to Document option button. Word places a new page at the beginning of your document that contains the information and formatting for your envelope. Change this page as you would any other document. For spacing, select the text you want to change and press Ctrl+1 for single spacing, or choose Format, Paragraph and change the Spacing section of the Paragraph dialog box.

CHAPTER 9

Creating Mass Mailings

by Patty Winter

Using Word's Mail Merge capabilities allows you to automate and personalize letters—such as announcements, change of address notifications, advertisements, personal letters, and many other types of correspondence—by composing the document and including merge fields for information that changes. Each document would have different company names, individuals' names, addresses, and maybe even notes specific to the individual or company. You can place a merge field anywhere in the document; in address lines, salutation, and even the body of the document. See Figure 9.1 for an example of a completed mail merge document. ■

Create main documents

Creating the main document involves use of the Mail Merge toolbar, entering the static information, and deciding what information will change.

Develop the data source

Developing a data source requires planning, deciding on the program for the data source, naming the fields, and adding information to the data source.

Insert merge fields

Using merge fields requires indentifying where to place the variable information in your main document.

Perform the merge

Finally, performing the merge involves sorting records, checking for errors, and determining the merge method.

FIG. 9.1
This document
contains the main
document letter with
the merge fields.

Mail merge toolbar —

Merged fields —

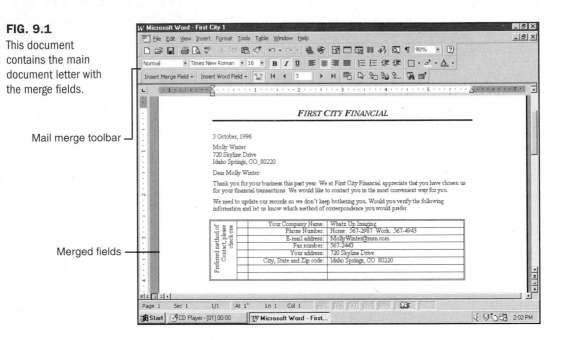

To create a mass mailing you must complete three steps. Word has simplified performing a Mail Merge into steps that are very easy to follow:

1. Create the main document (form letter, envelopes, or mailing labels).

2. Attach the data source (name and address file).

3. Merge the main document with the data source.

When you attach a data source to the form letter, you can use Word to create the data source, or you can use an existing file from another program such as Access, Excel, or your personal address book within Outlook, or even your Schedule+ Contact List.

Creating a Main Document

The first step in creating a mass mailing is to write the letter you want to send. In other words, create a main document.

A *main document* includes the standard text and graphics that are part of each form letter. Word has simplified the process for you with the Mail Merge Helper. The Mail Merge Helper takes you step-by-step through the process of creating a main document and a data source. There is no need to memorize and repeat the steps in creating custom documents—just follow Word's lead.

▶ **See** "Using Wizards," **p. 141**

Creating the Main Document File

To create a main document using Mail Merge Helper, follow these steps:

1. Choose Tools, Mail Merge. The Mail Merge Helper dialog box appears, as shown in Figure 9.2.

FIG. 9.2
Click the Create button to begin the process for creating a mail merge.

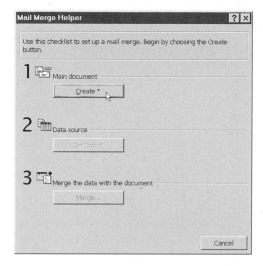

2. Under Step 1 Main Document, click the Create button.

3. From the drop-down list, choose Form Letters. The dialog box shown in Figure 9.3 appears.

FIG. 9.3
Use this dialog box to tell Word if you want to use the Active Window or begin a New Main Document.

4. If the letter you want to use is in the active window, click Active Window.

   Or if you want to create a new document to use as your main document, click New Main Document.

   Notice that the type of document you selected (Form Letters) and the name of your main document are now listed under Step 1, as shown in Figure 9.4.

FIG. 9.4

Under Step 1 in the Mail Merge Helper dialog box, you see the type of document and the name of your main document.

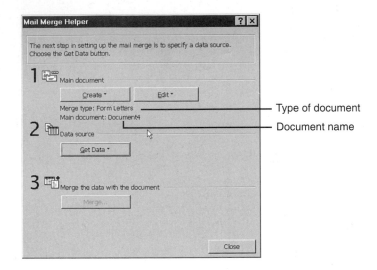

Type of document

Document name

Editing the Main Document

Now you have two choices on the Mail Merge Helper dialog box (see Figure 9.4); under Step 1 you could choose to <u>E</u>dit the main document, or under Step 2, you could <u>G</u>et Data, which allows you to attach the data source to this main document. If you have only created and named a main document, you need to edit the main document to add your body text.

To enter or edit text in the main document, click the <u>E</u>dit button under Step 1. The name of the file appears on the pull-down list. Click the name of your main document to open it.

 Remember that a main document includes the standard text and graphics that will be part of each letter. If you have a letter you have used before, you need to delete the name and address of the last recipient.

If you are creating a letter from scratch, type the paragraphs that will be standard to all letters. Omit items like name, address, city, state, ZIP, and so on. You insert these items as merge fields later.

 So you don't have to type the current date each time you use the same main document, position your cursor on the line where you want the date to appear. Then choose <u>I</u>nsert, Date & <u>T</u>ime. Locate the date format you want and select the <u>U</u>pdate Automatically option located at the bottom of the Date and Time dialog box. Now, each time you open this main document, the current date appears.

Creating a Data Source

A *data source* is a Word table, Excel worksheet, Access database, Address Book, or other file that holds the variable information that you will put into your letter to customize it. The data source holds the names, addresses, phone numbers, and account information of your customers, for example.

Planning Your Data File

The most important step to creating a data source is planning. The most important feature of the data source (database) is flexibility. Take the time to identify all the information that you could ever need about the letter recipients when sending a mass mailing. Then group that information into fields.

▶ **See** "Creating a Database," **p. 703**

A *field* is a category of information. For example, the phone book has fields for last name, first name, suffix (M.D., Sr., III), city (sometimes), and phone number. Your document may include fields such as first name, last name, salutation, address, city, state, ZIP Code, account number, and previous year's sales. All of the fields related to one person or company are called a *record*.

N O T E As you begin creating your data source, having too many fields is better than having too few. Adding one field of information later to thousands of records will be time-consuming and will increase the chance of data entry errors. Deleting or not using an unnecessary field takes just a few simple keystrokes. ▪

When designing your data source, consider how you plan to arrange, or sort, your data. Do not include more than one piece of information in the same field. For example, if you want letters to print alphabetically by last name, you need two fields in your data source: first name and last name. One category, called Name, does not allow you the flexibility to sort by last name.

Entering the Fields in Your Data Source

To create the fields in your data source, follow these steps:

1. Open your main document.
2. Choose Tools, Mail Merge to open the Mail Merge Helper dialog box.
3. Under Step 2, click the Get Data button.

4. To create a new data source, click Create Data Source. A list of common field names appears on the right side of the Create Data Source dialog box, as shown in Figure 9.5.

FIG. 9.5
You can use a mixture of commonly used field names and names you create yourself.

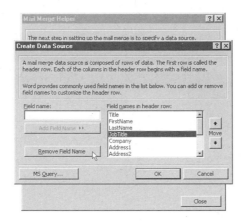

5. Remove the field names you do not want to include by selecting the field name and clicking the Remove Field Name button. Repeat until only the field names you want are listed on the right.

6. Add a field name that is not listed by typing the name in the Field Name box and clicking the Add Field Name button.

N O T E   When adding new fields, do not use spaces in between words, as in **ZipCode**. Field names cannot have spaces.

7. Rearrange fields by selecting a field name and clicking the up-or-down Move arrow to the right of the field names listed.

8. When all of the field names are listed and in the correct order, click OK.

9. When prompted to save your data source, type a file name. Because the data source is separate from the main document, be sure to give it a different name.

10. If you are ready to add data to your data source, click Edit Data Source in the dialog box; if you want to return to your main document, click Edit Main Document.

Adding Information to Your Data Source

To add information to your data source, follow these steps:

1. Open your main document.

2. Click the Edit Data Source button on the Mail Merge toolbar. The Data Form dialog box appears, as shown in Figure 9.6.

FIG. 9.6
Use the Data Form dialog box to enter variable information for your mailing.

3. Type the first field of information. Press Enter or Tab to move to the next field. Repeat until you have completed all applicable fields. You do not need to enter information in every field. If a field does not apply, leave it blank.

4. To add another record, click the Add New button. Repeat data entry until all records are input.

N O T E When you get to the last field in the record, you can press Enter to move to a new record form so you don't have to click the Add New button. ■

5. After you have entered all records, click OK.

Editing a Data Source

After you have entered all your data into the data source document, you'll probably need to edit it. Undoubtedly, you'll need to delete records or change data periodically. Editing a data source is just like editing any Word document. One advantage, however, is that the Mail Merge Helper has a Find feature that eliminates the hassle of scrolling and searching for a specific record.

The first step in editing a data source is to locate the record you want to edit:

1. View any record in the data form by clicking the Edit Data Source button on the Mail Merge toolbar.

2. Click the Find button on the right of the dialog box.

3. Identify a unique piece of information about the record you want, for instance, last name or ZIP Code. Type that information in the Find box.

N O T E   You can type just a part the information to find more records; for instance, type **win** in the last name field to find all the records where win appears in the last name. Be careful to be specific enough to get the results you want.

4. In the In Field drop-down list, select the field in which this information is located.

5. Click Find First to locate the first record that meets the criteria you entered.

6. Click Find Next until the record you want appears. Click the Close button in the Find dialog box.

With the record displayed, make the necessary changes. Then click OK to return to your document.

After locating a record, you may decide to delete it altogether. To delete a record, click the Delete button on the right of the Data Form dialog box.

Inserting Merge Fields

After the standard elements of the letter are complete and you have created your data source, you are ready to identify where to place the variable pieces of information in the main document. This process involves inserting merge fields.

In the example shown in Figure 9.7, First City Financial is using Mail Merge to send letters to clients requesting updated information.

Merge fields are the categories of information that you included in your data source, like first name, city, or state. You use merge fields to tell Word specifically where to put each piece of variable information in the letter.

To insert merge fields into your main document, follow these steps:

1. Open your main document.

2. Place the insertion point where the first variable piece of information should appear.

3. Click the Insert Merge Field button on the Mail Merge toolbar.

Insert Merge Field ▾

4. Select the name of the field you want. The name of the field appears in brackets (<< >>) in your document.

5. Type any words, spaces, or punctuation that may be required between fields.

6. Insert another merge field. Repeat until all fields are entered.

FIG. 9.7
Merge fields are the fields of information that enable you to make a form letter look like a personal letter.

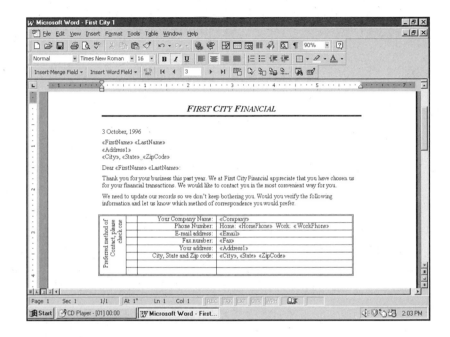

N O T E   When creating a letter, include punctuation in places like the "Dear" line. A standard letter contains this line when all merge fields are included:

Dear <<Title>> <<LastName>>:

Sorting Records in Your Data Source

One of the benefits of using Word to perform a mail merge is being able to sort your records before you print your letters. If the mailing you are doing is important for your business, then making the job easiest for postal workers could be to your advantage. When you print hundreds of letters and take them to the post office to be delivered, if they are sorted in ZIP Code order (even if you don't have a bulk mail permit), they will probably get to the recipients quicker.

Another good reason to sort before you print is if the printer jams, you would be able to begin printing where the problem occurred.

Planning Your Sort

Although planning your sort is not required to perform a merge, it can save you a lot of time in the end. If you do not identify your sort fields ahead of time, you may find yourself sorting and resorting until you get the results you want.

When you are planning to sort, you can select up to three fields for sorting. You can choose only one field if that's all you need.

The first field is the largest grouping. The second field is how you want records sorted within the first group, and the third field is how you want records sorted within the second group.

Suppose that your data source has fields for First Name, Last Name, and Sales Region. If you want records sorted alphabetically in Sales Region, your first field would be Sales Region, your second field would be Last Name, and your third field would be First Name.

Sorting Data According to Certain Fields

To sort your data according to fields you specify, follow these steps:

1. Open your main document.

2. Click the Mail Merge Helper button on the Mail Merge toolbar to open the Mail Merge Helper dialog box.

3. Under Step 3 on the Mail Merge Helper dialog box, click the Query Options button to open the Query Options dialog box shown in Figure 9.8.

FIG. 9.8
Use the Sort Records tab to organize your data source before you merge your document.

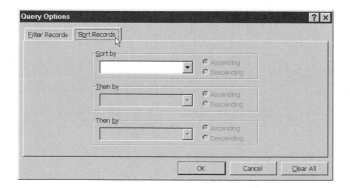

4. In the Query Options dialog box, click the Sort Records tab.

5. Select the first field in the Sort By category. Then press the Tab key.

6. Select the second field in Then By category. Then press the Tab key.

7. Select the third field in the next Then <u>B</u>y field. Then click OK.

8. Click the Close button when you are finished with Mail Merge Helper.

Viewing the Order of the Data

To view your data source to verify that sorting produced the results you want, follow these steps:

Part

II

Ch

9

1. Click the Edit Data Source button on the Mail Merge toolbar.

2. Click the Next Record button on the bottom of the Data Form dialog box to scroll through the records.

3. Click OK to return to your main document.

Merging the Main Document and Data Source

Now that the major components of the project are in place, it's time to merge the two documents into one document—a form letter.

You have two options when merging the files:

- You can merge files directly to the printer.
- You can merge them to a third file of form letters that appear on your screen.

If you are using a new main document that you're merging for the first time, merging to the screen allows you to see the results before you use paper. Your custom documents will not always look as you had anticipated once you get all of the variable information entered. By merging data to the screen, you can save many reams of paper and trips to the printer.

Checking for Errors

Regardless of which option you choose, you should first check to make sure that the merge works properly. You may waste a great deal of time and material if you print hundreds or thousands of letters without checking them first. There are many different errors you may encounter, but Word is very helpful in taking you directly to the problem and helping you determine what the exact problem is. In other words, follow Word's lead.

To check a mail merge for errors prior to merging to the printer or to another document, use these steps:

1. Open the main document.

2. From the Mail Merge toolbar, click the Check for Errors button.

3. In the Checking and Reporting Error dialog box, click the Simulate the Merge and Report Errors in a New Document option. If there are no errors, Word indicates that no errors were found. If errors do exist, Word gives you the option of correcting them now or later. In either case, Word takes you directly to the field or record that has the problem.

Merging Directly to the Printer

If your job shows no errors, you can merge a main document and the data source directly to the printer:

1. Open the main document.

2. On the Mail Merge toolbar, click the Merge to Printer button.

3. Click OK to send the merge directly to your printer.

N O T E   If you want to fax or e-mail a mail merge document, you can use the Merge button on the Mail Merge Helper dialog box to select which electronic means you would like to use. On the pull-down arrow for the Merge To option, select Fax or Electronic Mail, and use the Setup button to define which data field to use for the address. Then merge as normal. For more information on this topic see Que's *Special Edition Using Microsoft Word 97*. ▪

Merging to the Screen Before Printing

If you don't want the letters to go to the printer yet, you can merge the two documents to a third document and view it before printing.

N O T E   If you are working with a main document for the first time, merge to a third document and not directly to the printer. It's not uncommon for merged form letters to look different than expected after all the custom information is included. ▪

To merge a main document and the data source to a third document, follow these steps:

1. Open the main document.

2. On the Mail Merge toolbar, click the Merge to New Document button.

3. View the new document, called Form Letters by default. Scroll through the first several pages to ensure that merge fields went to the right place and page breaks worked.

T I P To see how the merge worked, scroll the document in the window so you can see your merged fields on the screen. Use the Next Page and Previous Page buttons on the vertical scroll bar to scroll down or up to that section of the next page.

4. If everything looks good, choose File, Print to print to your default printer. Then click OK.

N O T E If you merge two documents and do not get the results you expected, don't try to edit each page of the document individually. You can save a lot of time if you simply close the Form Letter document without saving it, edit the main document or data source, and perform the merge again.

Merging Data from an Excel Worksheet

Suppose that you already have data entered into an Excel worksheet. The good news is that you don't have to retype the data. In fact, if you have a lot of names to enter, you can use Excel to create a data source. For large numbers of records, Excel has much greater capability to manage, sort, and edit than a Word table does.

Creating an Excel Database

To create a database in an Excel worksheet (which holds up to 16,384 records), follow these steps:

1. Open or switch to Excel.

 2. Choose File, New, or click the New button on the Standard toolbar.

3. Your field names are the column headings of your worksheet. Type the name of your first field in cell A1. Press the Tab key or the right arrow on your keyboard, or click in cell B1.

4. Type the second field name in cell B1. Press the Tab key or the right arrow on your keyboard. Repeat until all field names are listed as column headings.

 T I P Don't worry about the order of the data. Your goal in this first stage should be accuracy. You can sort the database later.

5. Click in cell A2. Begin typing your data, and save often.

   ▶ **See** "Creating Worksheets," **p. 299**

Using Your Excel Worksheet as a Mail Merge Data Source

Now you can use your Excel database information as your mail merge data source:

1. Return to Word.

2. Open your main document.

3. From the Mail Merge toolbar, click the Mail Merge Helper button.

4. Under Step 2, click Get Data.

5. Choose Open Data Source.

6. In the Files of Type box, select MS Excel Worksheets, as shown in Figure 9.9.

FIG. 9.9
The Open Data Source dialog box looks and works just like the Open File dialog box.

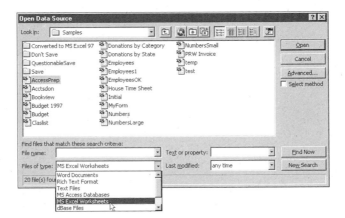

7. Click the Excel file in which you saved your data.

8. Click the Open button.

After you have attached your Excel file as the data source, you can insert merge fields and perform the merge as you do with any other data source. Refer to the sections "Inserting Merge Fields" and "Merging the Main Document and Data Source" earlier in this chapter.

Using Access Data as a Mail Merge Data Source

Another tool for managing your data is Microsoft Access. If you have many fields and records, Access may be more appropriate for your data than a Word table or an Excel worksheet. This is especially true if you need to answer a lot of questions about the data and make many different reports from the data. If you use Access, you can create a query that already sorts and searches your mailing list instead of specifying your data selection rules through Word.

To use Access as your mail merge data source, follow these steps:

1. Open your main document in Word.

2. From the Mail Merge toolbar, click the Mail Merge Helper button.

3. Under Step 2, click Get Data.

4. Choose Open Data Source.

5. In the Files of Type box, select MS Access Databases.

6. Click the Access file where you have mailing information.

7. Click the Open button.

 TIP Use a Microsoft Access query that already has your information selected and sorted for your mail merge.

8. The Microsoft Access dialog box eventually appears as shown in Figure 9.10. Select the Tables or Queries tab; then select the name of the Access object and click OK.

FIG. 9.10
The Microsoft Access dialog box gives you options of choosing existing Access tables or queries for your data source.

After you have attached your Access table or query, you can insert merge fields and perform the merge as you do with any other data source. Refer to the sections "Inserting Merge Fields" and "Merging the Main Document and Data Source" earlier in this chapter.

Using the Address Book for Merging

You can use your Contact List from Schedule+ or your Personal Address Book from Microsoft Outlook as your data source. Microsoft Outlook allows you to create a Personal

Address Book you can use to send e-mail as well as paper mail. One of the pieces of Schedule+ is the Contact List. You can create and maintain a list of names and addresses and use this list to contact business associates, friends, and family. If you have a list of names and addresses in the Contact List of Schedule+ or the Personal Address Book, you can attach this list to your merge document.

You first need to create your Contact List in Schedule+ or your Personal Address Book in Microsoft Outlook; then follow these steps:

1. Open your main document. 
2. From the Mail Merge toolbar, click the Mail Merge Helper button.
3. Under Step 2, click Get Data.
4. Select Use Address Book. The Use Address Book dialog box appears, as shown in Figure 9.11.

FIG. 9.11
Select the Address Book you want to use.

5. In the Choose Address Book list, select the list you want to use and click OK.
6. In the Mail Merge Helper dialog box, click Close.

After you have made your address book the data source, you can insert merge fields and perform the merge as you do with any other data source. See sections "Inserting Merge Fields" and "Merging the Main Document and Data Source" earlier in this chapter.

Specifying Data Selection Rules

If your data source is in Word, Excel, Access, Schedule+, or the Personal Address Book, you can specify the criteria that each record must meet to be included in the Mail Merge. This selection process enables you to maintain information in one location instead of having multiple databases, or worse yet, having the same name in multiple databases.

Deciding Which Fields Have Rules

Creating selection rules can be a bit tricky. When you use more than one rule, you need to connect the rules with an And or an Or. If you use the wrong word or the wrong Compare To condition, you may not have any records merged. Before you explore Word's Query options, write down which records you want and which field holds the information you will be searching. You can specify one rule (all ZIP Codes beginning with 8) or multiple rules (all last names beginning with B with ZIP Codes beginning with 5) up to a total of six rules.

If you want to use multiple rules and you want to merge records that meet all of the rules, use And. If you want to merge records that meet either rule, use Or. The above example would use And to meet both conditions.

The other problem you may encounter is narrowing your search too much. In the preceding example, you get all the records with the last name beginning with B *and* within those records where the ZIP Codes begin with 5.

Identifying Data Criteria

In order that you may use a large database for multiple merge operations, you may want to determine specific rules for the records you will select. To specify rules within your data source, follow these steps:

1. Open your main document.

2. On the Mail Merge toolbar, click the Mail Merge Helper button.

3. Under Step 3 on the Mail Merge dialog box, click Query Options. The Query Options dialog box appears (see Figure 9.12). You see two tabs: Filter Records and Sort Records.

FIG. 9.12
In the Query Options dialog box, enter information to tell Word which records you want to use.

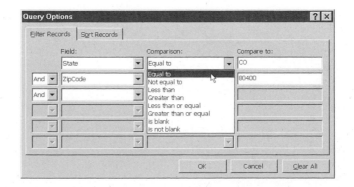

Part
II

Ch
9

4. Click the Filter Records tab.

5. In the Field column, click the down arrow to display the names of your fields. Select the field name for which you want to create a rule.

6. In the Comparison column, click the comparison you want Word to make, such as Not Equal to or Equal to.

7. Click in the Compare To column. Type the value you want Word to check records against. For example, if you want Word to locate all records with a ZIP Code equal to 80000, enter **80000**, as shown in Figure 9.13.

FIG. 9.13
Enter criteria to choose records to merge into form letters.

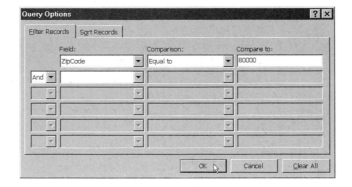

8. Click OK.

9. Click the Close button on the Mail Merge Helper dialog box.

10. Click the View Merged Data button on the Mail Merge toolbar.

By using the View Merged Data button, you can toggle between merged data in your letter and the letter with the merge fields displayed.

Creating Labels Using Mail Merge

After you create your letters, you may want to create labels for mailing purposes. Or you may want to send a preprinted postcard as a follow-up to everyone who received a specific mailing.

Creating labels isn't difficult. All you need to know is the type of label you are using. Then you create a label document and make it your main document. You can reuse the data source you created for your letters.

Creating the Main Document for Mailing Labels

Once letters are printed, you will want to create labels to stick on the outside of envelopes.

To create mailing labels using Mail Merge, follow these steps:

1. Choose Tools, Mail Merge. The Mail Merge Helper dialog box appears.
2. Under Step 1, click Create.
3. From the drop-down list, choose Mailing Labels. A message dialog box from Word appears.
4. Click New Main Document to create the document that will serve as your label template.

Setting Up the Merge

Now you can tell Word where your data is stored, what style of label you are using, and where to place specific merge fields. Word walks you through these steps:

1. From the Mail Merge toolbar, click the Mail Merge Helper button.
2. Under Step 2, click the Get Data button. Then choose Open Data Source.
3. Select the name of the file that holds your data.
4. After you have selected a file, Word prompts you to set up the main document for labels. Click Set Up Main Document to specify the label size and type. The Label Options dialog box appears (see Figure 9.14).

FIG. 9.14
Use the Label Options dialog box to set up your label document.

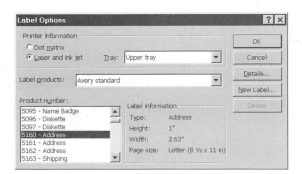

5. Under Printer Information, select the type of printer you have (Dot Matrix or Laser and Ink Jet).
6. Next to Label Products, select the brand of labels you have.

7. Under Product Number, select the style of label you have (the style number is on the outside of the box). Then click OK. The Create Labels dialog box opens (see Figure 9.15).

FIG. 9.15

Use the Create Labels dialog box to insert merge fields for your labels.

NOTE To move quickly to a specific product number, make sure the highlight bar is in the Product Number list box, and type the first number in the product number. The listed product number items scroll to the beginning of the section where those labels should be listed. To find Avery 5160 Address labels, for example, type **5** and then scroll down just a few times. ▪

8. To add merge fields to your label, click Insert Merge Field. Locate and select the name of the first field from your data source. Repeat until all the fields you want on your label are listed.

NOTE When you are adding merge fields to your label, be sure to include all spaces and punctuation that you want to appear on each label. ▪

9. Click OK.
10. Click Close on the Mail Merge Helper dialog box.

Editing the Format of a Label

Once you create the initial format for your label, you may want to make formatting changes. You can go back and edit the format of a label. To return to the label setup process, follow these steps:

1. Open your main document.

 2. From the Mail Merge toolbar, click the Mail Merge Helper button.

3. Under Step 1, click the Edit button and then select the Mailing Label document from the pull-down list.

Printing the Labels

To print the labels, follow the same steps outlined in the section "Merging the Main Document and Data Source" earlier in the chapter. You can use the Merge to New Document or Merge to Printer buttons on the Mail Merge toolbar to print your labels.

Creating Envelopes Using Mail Merge

Envelopes are an alternative to labels when you are deciding how to address your form letters. Creating envelopes is not difficult, but a main consideration is whether your printer tray automatically feeds envelopes. If not, you may find that sticking labels on envelopes is easier than manually feeding hundreds of envelopes.

Creating the Envelopes File

If you want to print envelopes, you need to first create a main document which identifies both the size of the envelope and location of the merge field.

To create envelopes using Mail Merge, follow these steps:

1. Choose Tools, Mail Merge. The Mail Merge Helper dialog box appears.
2. Under Step 1, click Create.
3. From the drop-down list, choose Envelopes. An envelope dialog box appears.
4. Click New Main Document to create the document that will serve as your envelope template.

Setting Up the Merge

Now you can tell Word where your data is stored, what style of envelope you are using, and where to place specific merge fields:

1. From the Mail Merge toolbar, click the Mail Merge Helper button.
2. Under Step 2, click the Get Data button. Then choose Open Data Source.
3. Select the name of the file that holds your data.

4. After you select a file, Word prompts you to format the main document for envelopes. Click Setup Main Document to specify the envelope size and type.

5. Click the Envelope Options tab in the dialog box (see Figure 9.16).

FIG. 9.16
Use the Envelope Options tab in the Envelope Options dialog box to set up your envelope options.

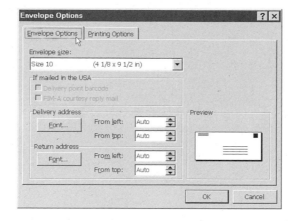

6. Under Envelope Size, select the size of envelope you are using.

7. Under Delivery Address, type specific top and left margins if your requirements are different from a standard envelope.

8. Under Return Address, type specific top and left margins, if your requirements are different from a standard envelope.

9. Click the Printing Options tab (see Figure 9.17).

FIG. 9.17
Use the Printing Options tab in the Envelope Options dialog box to set up your envelope print options.

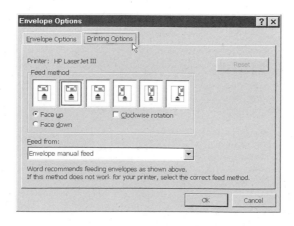

10. Under Feed Method, select the way your envelopes feed.

11. Under Feed From, select whether your printer feeds envelopes from a print tray or requires manual feed. Then click OK.

12. To add merge fields to your envelope, click the Insert Merge Field button on the Mail Merge toolbar. Locate and select the name of the first field from your data source. Repeat until all the fields you want on your label are listed. Click OK after you insert all the fields for your envelope.

13. Click the Close button on the Mail Merge Helper dialog box.

N O T E   When formatting your main envelope document, be sure to include all standard spacing and punctuation in your sample envelope. ▪

Editing the Format of an Envelope

If you want to change the envelope size or the location of merge fields on your envelope, you can edit the format of an envelope later. To return to the envelope setup process, follow these steps:

1. Open your main document.

2. From the Mail Merge toolbar, click the Mail Merge Helper button.

3. Under Step 1, click the Edit button and then select the Envelope document from the pull-down list.

Printing the Envelopes

To print envelopes, follow the same steps outlined in the section "Merging the Main Document and Data Source" earlier in the chapter. You can use the Merge to New Document or Merge to Printer buttons on the Mail Merge toolbar to print your envelopes. ●

Part

II

Ch

9

CHAPTER 10

Working with Large Documents

by Patty Winter

When you are producing a document that contains many pages—from 10 or 15 to hundreds—you need special organizational and managerial techniques. Word provides several features that help you manage long documents. (You can use these features for short documents as well.)

One organizational feature you can use in a large document is *outlining*. Word provides special outlining features, including an outline view that helps you order your text. You can arrange headings and text, move headings to new positions in the outline, and print the outline as you work on it.

Word also provides document-formatting methods that make your work easier. You can use *styles*—preformatted fonts and paragraph attributes—to format your documents quickly and to guarantee consistency within the document.

Word offers a variety of techniques and processes to help you work with large documents. This chapter introduces many of those techniques. ■

Outline a document

Using this feature involves the outline toolbar, promoting and demoting outline levels, collapsing and expanding outline levels, and reorganizing the outline.

AutoFormat

This feature includes many options that perform "as you type" formatting changes as well as using predefined templates from the Style Gallery that contain preset formatting options.

Template wizards

The Web Page Wizard walks you through creating specific types of documents by asking questions and then formatting the document automatically.

Headers and footers

To create headers and footers you need to understand the header and footer pane, the toolbar, automatic fields, and section breaks.

Advanced word processing features

This includes creating a Table of Contents, using footnotes or endnotes, inserting comments, bookmarks, and cross-references, and tracking your changes in a document.

Outlining a Document

 T I P Create an outline first in Word and then use the outline as the basis for a PowerPoint presentation (see Chapter 42, "Using Visual Basic for Applications to Integrate Office").

When creating a large document, use an outline and Outline view to get an overview of how the document is put together. You can also easily rearrange headings and text to better suit the flow of information. Finally, use outlining in long documents to quickly move to a specific location and then view the text.

To outline a document, you assign headings to the text to signify different levels of topic development. You can create up to nine different levels of text, including body text. Word formats and indents each level so that you can organize the text quickly. The headings remain formatted in other views as well, although the indents shown in outline view disappear in Normal and Page Layout views.

Figure 10.1 shows an initial outline for a document. This sample outline contains four levels of headings: *Ethics of Arcs* is Heading 1, *Suppose no more canvas for painting* is Heading 2, *Have to use existing art to create new art* is Heading 3, and *A. Carr - Travels of a Naturalist* is Heading 4. As you enter more headings and body text, you can format the text, arrange the headings, and move text around to better organize the document.

FIG. 10.1

You can plan a document from scratch in Outline view, assigning levels of importance to headings as you write.

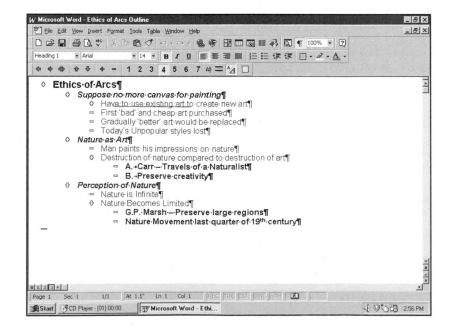

Word provides an outline view in which you can organize your documents. Outline view provides an Outline toolbar (see Figure 10.1) that enables you to assign headings to your text, hide body text or headings, and rearrange your outline. You can outline an existing document or create a new document in Outline view.

The following table gives a brief description of each tool in the Outline toolbar:

Table 10.1   Outline Toolbar Buttons

Button	Button Name	Description
	Promote	Elevates a heading to a higher level
	Demote	Reduces a heading to a lower level
	Demote to Body Text	Reduces the heading to body text
	Move Up	Repositions the selected heading(s) up one heading in the outline
	Move Down	Repositions the selected heading(s) down one heading in the outline
	Expand	Shows subheadings and body text under selected heading
	Collapse	Hides subheadings and body text under selected heading
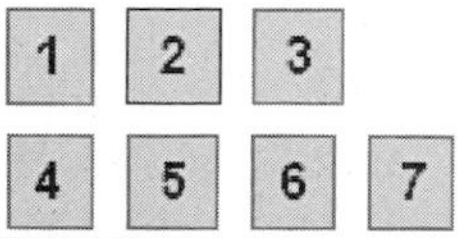	Show Headings	Expands or collapses the 1 through 7 outline to a specific level
	All	Expands or collapses the entire outline or hides all body text
	Show First Line Only	Shows all body text or only the first line of the body text
	Show Formatting	Shows or hides character formatting

continues

Table 10.1   Continued

Button	Button Name	Description
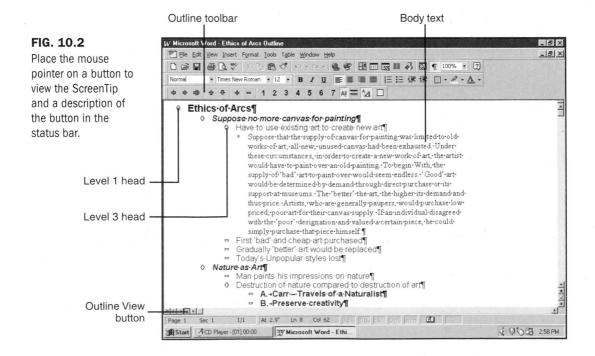	Master Document view	Changes to Master Document view or back to simple outline view. If Master Document view is selected, the Master Document toolbar appears to the right of the Outline toolbar.

Creating an Outline

You create an outline entering, formatting, and assigning headings in Word's Outline view. The view provides helpful features you can use to organize your document. After creating your outline, you easily can change heading levels, add text, and otherwise edit your document by using the Outline toolbar and other features of outline view.

Viewing the Outline   To start creating an outline, choose View, Outline. In Outline view, use the Outline toolbar to specify various levels of headings and body text (see Figure 10.2). Word indents each heading and its text, and formats the text for you.

Outline toolbar   Body text

FIG. 10.2
Place the mouse pointer on a button to view the ScreenTip and a description of the button in the status bar.

Level 1 head

Level 3 head

Outline View button

T I P To change to Outline view, simply click the third view button in the horizontal scroll bar.

N O T E You can reformat any text formats easily by using styles. For more information, see "Formatting with Styles," later in this chapter. ■

Entering Text You can enter text as you normally do by typing paragraphs, heading text, and so on, in Normal, Page Layout, or Outline view. You can assign heading styles to existing text by using the Formatting toolbar.

The Formatting toolbar includes a drop-down list of styles (see Figure 10.3). In the Normal template—the default template for documents—Heading 1 style is used for the broadest topics; Heading 2 is used for the subdivisions of Heading 1 topics; and so on. To view or change the style, click the I-beam mouse pointer anywhere in the paragraph and use the Formatting toolbar.

Part

II

Ch

10

FIG. 10.3

You can assign heading styles by using the Formatting toolbar.

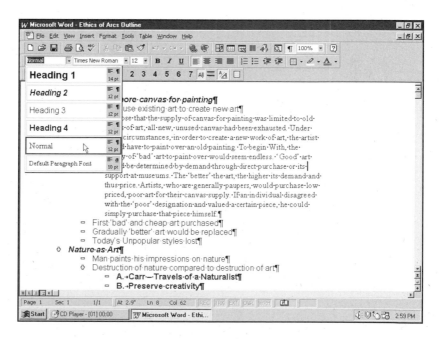

Alternatively, you can designate outline levels as you enter text. Simply select a heading style from the drop-down list in the Formatting toolbar and type the heading. Then change the style, if necessary, and type the next heading or body text (the Normal style is the same as body text style; see the section "Formatting with Styles," later in this chapter).

▶ **See** "Viewing the Document," **p. 168**

▶ **See** "Entering Text in a Word Document," **p. 148**

▶ **See** "Formatting Text," **p. 172**

Selecting Text   Outline view provides a slightly different method of selecting text than do the other views. Each paragraph of text, whether that text is a heading or body text, is preceded by a hollow plus sign (+) or a hollow minus sign (–). If you position the mouse pointer on one of these symbols, the pointer changes to a four-headed arrow. When the pointer changes shape, simply click the plus sign or minus sign to select the associated paragraph and any lower-level headings and body text below it.

> **N O T E** The plus and minus signs also indicate whether more text has been entered under that level of the outline. A hollow plus sign before a Heading 1 entry, for example, means that other headings or body text have been entered under that heading. A hollow minus sign appears when there are no headings or body text associated with this level. A small, hollow box precedes body text.

Suppose that you click the hollow plus sign preceding the *Ethics of Arcs* heading (refer to Figure 10.2). By doing so, you select all text from that point to the next Level 1 heading. (In this case, all the text is selected.) Similarly, if you click the plus sign preceding the Level 2 head, *Suppose no more canvas for painting*, you select all text from that point to the next Level 2 heading, *Nature as Art*. You also can select text by clicking the selection bar (to the left of the text area) or by dragging the I-beam pointer across specific text. After you select the text, you can then choose the level of the heading you want to assign.

 Promoting and Demoting Headings   After assigning various heading levels to your text, you may decide to change those levels. You can do so by using the Promote and Demote buttons in the Outline toolbar. Simply select the text and then click the Promote or Demote button.

The Promote button—the first button from the left in the Outline toolbar—looks like an arrow pointing left. Each time you click the button, the selected text moves up one level (until it reaches Level 1) and displays with less indentation. Similarly, the Demote button—an arrow pointing right—bumps the selected text down one heading level at a time (until it reaches Level 8) and displays with further indentation toward the right. Remember, when you select a heading, you select all text and subheadings within that heading. When you promote or demote the heading, all subheadings follow suit.

 To change a selected heading to body text in a single step, click the Demote to Body Text button—a double arrow pointing right.

Editing an Outline

You can edit an outline by adding, deleting, or rearranging body text and headings. In Outline view, you can add or delete text as you do in any view. But Outline view also provides two features that make it easier for you to rearrange your text: viewing and moving outline levels.

TIP

Double-click the plus sign that precedes a heading to display all the text below that heading. Double-click again to hide all the text.

You can use the Outline toolbar to view specific levels of the outline. In addition, you can rearrange topics easily without cutting and pasting text.

Collapsing and Expanding Outlines You can view various levels of an outline by using the Show Heading buttons—the buttons numbered 1 through 8 in the Outline toolbar. If you click the Show Heading 1 button, for example, only Heading 1 text appears on-screen. If you click the Show Heading 2 button, you see only Heading 1 and Heading 2 text.

If you show only headings with no body text, you are *collapsing* the outline. *Expanding* the outline means just the opposite. If only Heading 2 text is showing, for example, click the Show Heading 3, Show Heading 4, or All button to expand the outline.

Figure 10.4 shows a collapsed outline. The hollow plus sign next to each heading indicates that more text levels exist within that heading. If a hollow minus sign appears next to a heading, the heading contains no further text levels.

Expand   Collapse   Show Heading 1   Show All

FIG. 10.4
Use the Expand and Collapse buttons to reveal text below the selected head.

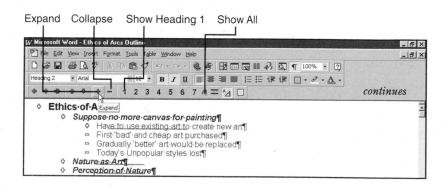

Rearranging Headings and Text You can rearrange topics in your document by selecting and moving headings in Outline view. The easiest method is to collapse the outline to the level to be moved, select the heading you want to move, and drag the heading to its new position. Subheads and body text move with the selected heading.

▶ **See** "Drag-and-Drop Editing," **p. 158**

CAUTION

If you do not collapse the outline before moving the text, you may leave some body text behind. Be sure to select *all* text to be moved.

 T I P   To print the outline at any level, choose File, Print, or click the Print button.

Figure 10.5 shows how the screen looks when you move a heading (and its subheadings and body text) to a new position. The mouse pointer changes to a double-headed arrow, and a guideline moves with the mouse to help you position the heading.

FIG. 10.5

For the most efficient and easiest rearranging of topics, collapse the outline to the heading level to be moved.

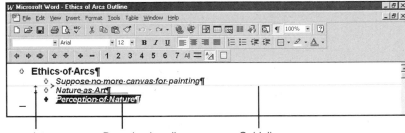

Double-headed mouse pointer   Dragging heading up   Guideline

 TROUBLESHOOTING

 I collapsed the outline so that I could focus on the headings while scrolling through the document, but I want to remind myself about the contents of the body text below each heading. Click the Show First Line Only button in the Outline toolbar to display the first line of body text below each heading.

I want to print only the headings and first lines of body text. Word prints only what is displayed on-screen in Outline view. Display the level of headings you want to print, and then click the Show First Line Only button in the Outline toolbar.

I want to copy only the headings from my document but I get all the subordinate text below the headings. You cannot copy just the headings unless you do it one heading at a time. Instead, create a Table of Contents from the headings (as described in the "Creating a Table of Contents" section later in the chapter). After you create the table of contents, press Ctrl+Shift+F9 to convert the table of contents to regular text.

Formatting with Styles

A style is a collection of formats you can assign to selected text in a document. Each style includes attributes such as font, type size and style, spacing, leading, alignment, indents, and tabs. Styles enable you to format your documents quickly and consistently. Word provides a large number of ready-to-use styles; you also can create your own styles as you work.

▶ **See** "Formatting Text," **p. 172**

▶ **See** "Formatting Paragraphs," **p. 178**

▶ **See** "Changing Fonts, Sizes, and Styles," **p. 358**

There are two types of styles in Word—*paragraph styles* and *character styles*. If you position the insertion point or select any portion of a paragraph and apply a paragraph style, the entire text of the paragraph changes to reflect the new style. Character styles only change text that is selected. In the Style pull-down box on the Formatting toolbar (shown earlier in Figure 10.3), the paragraph symbols before the style name indicate paragraph styles; the (*A*) with an underscore indicates a character style.

One of Word's paragraph styles, for example, is the Heading 1 style used to outline a document. Using the Normal template, heading 1 text initially appears in 14-point Arial, bold, and left-aligned. You can assign this style, or any other style, as often as necessary in your documents.

 Click New on the Standard toolbar to start a new document using the settings from the Normal template.

Word's styles are associated with its *templates*, which are a preset collection of page, paragraph, and character formatting styles you can use to develop a particular type of document. Each time you start a new document, the New dialog box lists many different templates. The Normal template (Word's default) offers three heading formats and a body-text format. Other templates, such as the Letter, Memo, and Resume templates, provide different styles for your use.

Styles are particularly useful when you are working on a large document. Rather than moving from page to page and formatting each heading, list, tab setting, and so on, separately, you can format a style one time and then assign the style to each portion of text you want to format with the style's formats. After you assign styles, you may decide you want to change all occurrences of text formatted with a particular style. Rather than reformatting each occurrence separately, you only need to edit the style.

▶ **See** "Starting a New Word Document," **p. 163**

Part

II

Ch

10

N O T E   Examine some of Word's templates by working with the Style Gallery (see "Using Style Gallery" later in this chapter). From the menu bar choose F̲ormat, Style G̲allery. Choose the template you want to review in the T̲emplate list box. In the Preview section choose S̲tyle Samples. The styles for the template will display with the style name and the formatting associated with the style.

This section shows you how to use Word's styles and how to create and assign your own styles.

Using Word's Styles

To apply a style, first select the text you want to format. Then open the Style drop-down list in the Formatting toolbar and select the style you want to apply (see Figure 10.6).

T I P   To see the style names in the left margin, choose T̲ools, O̲ptions and change the St̲yle Area Width on the View tab to .5. You must be in Normal View to see the style area of the document.

FIG. 10.6
The Normal Template's Heading 2 style is 12-point Arial, bold italic, left-aligned, with spacing set at 12 points before and 3 points after the paragraph.

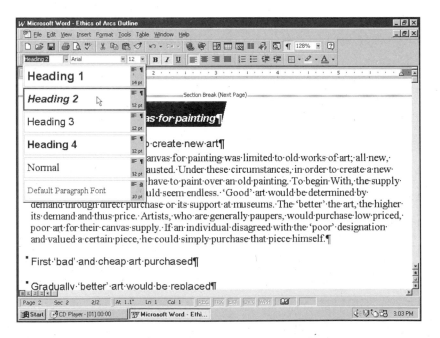

N O T E   The formatting for Heading 2 (and other headings) shown in Figure 10.6 is specific to the Normal template. If the styles have been edited on the Normal template or if you are using a different template, the formatting may be different for each style. If you want to convert styles in your document to take on the formatting characteristics of styles with the same name from another template, you can choose the T̲ools, Templates and Add-I̲ns command. In previous versions the command is F̲ile, T̲emplate.

You can change the format of text after applying a style. You can, for example, change the *Suppose no more canvas for painting* heading in Figure 10.6 to 14 point or center aligned. Changing the format of a particular heading, however, does not change the style itself or other headings to which you apply that style. For more information about changing the attributes of styles, see "Editing a Style," later in this chapter.

Creating a Style

Creating your own styles in Word is easy. Suppose that you want to create a heading style for use throughout your document; you want the style to be 18-point Times New Roman, bold, and center aligned. You can create this style, add it to the Style drop-down list, and use it as you would any other Word style.

To create your own style, follow these steps:

1. Select the text on which you want to base your style, and apply the desired formatting.

2. With the text still selected, click the Style box (not the pull-down arrow) in the Formatting toolbar.

3. Type your own name for the style (see Figure 10.7) and press Enter to add the name to the Styles list.

Times New Roman ⌐ 18 pt. ⌐Bold ⌐ Center

FIG. 10.7
When you enter a new name in the Style box, you do not actually delete the original style; you are just adding a new style to the list.

Type the style name in the Style box

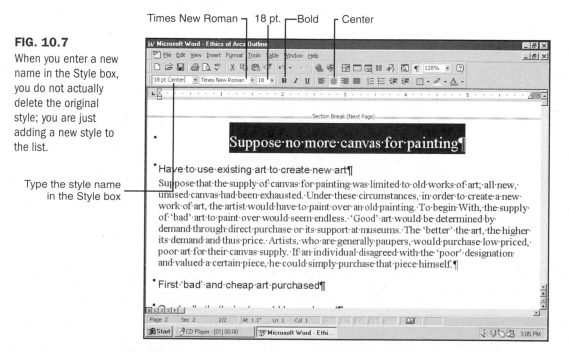

Part
II

Ch
10

Editing a Style

You can edit any style by changing font, size, alignment, tab stops, and so on, whether it is a preset style provided with Word or a style you created. To edit a style, follow these steps:

1. Choose F<u>o</u>rmat, <u>S</u>tyle. The Style dialog box appears (see Figure 10.8).

FIG. 10.8
You can view the attributes of a style in the Description area at the bottom of the dialog box.

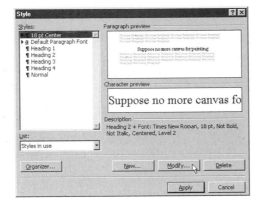

2. In the <u>S</u>tyles list box, select the style you want to modify. Samples of the text as it is now formatted appear in the Paragraph Preview and Character Preview boxes.

3. Choose the <u>M</u>odify button to edit the style. The Modify Style dialog box appears (see Figure 10.9).

FIG. 10.9
Modify a style by selecting an option in the F<u>o</u>rmat drop-down list.

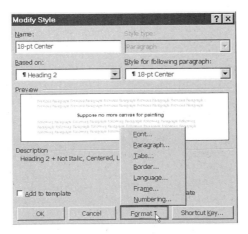

4. Click Format to display a drop-down list of the style attributes you can edit.

 TIP To save the styles you create or edit in a document, save the document so that the styles are always available with that document.

5. Select an attribute—Font, Paragraph, Tabs, and so on—from the list; make the desired changes in the dialog box that appears. (The dialog box that appears is exactly like the one that appears when you choose the corresponding command from the Format menu.) Choose OK to return to the Modify Style dialog box.

6. Repeat step 5 as often as necessary to modify additional style attributes.

7. After making all desired changes, choose OK in the Modify Style dialog box. You return to the Style dialog box.

8. Choose Close to exit the Style dialog box. All text that has been formatted with your style will be changed throughout your document.

CAUTION

After you choose OK from the Modify Style dialog box, the formatting of the style changes throughout your document. If you choose Apply in the Style dialog box, the selected text or text where the insertion point is will now have the changed style, even if this text originally was not formatted with that style. Make sure you choose Close in the Style dialog box at step 8.

 TROUBLESHOOTING

I try to create a style for a few words within a paragraph but after I finish creating the style, the whole paragraph takes on the characteristics of the style. You need to create a character style instead of a paragraph style. To do this, you cannot use the Style pull-down in the Formatting toolbar. Choose Format, Style and choose the New command button. In the Style Type pull-down list of the New Style dialog box, choose Character.

I've applied the same style throughout my document, but it looks different at different places in the document. After you apply a style, you can override the style by manually applying font and paragraph formatting. If you want to remove any manual formatting, select the paragraph—including the paragraph symbol—and press Ctrl+space bar to remove character formatting and Ctrl+Q to remove paragraph formatting.

Using AutoFormat

AutoFormat is a feature of Word that analyzes your document and automatically applies styles (such as headings, subheadings, bulleted lists, and tabs) to your document when you use the AutoFormat command or as you type. When you use the AutoFormat command, you can review AutoFormat's choices and accept or reject them. Using AutoFormat can save you time because Word assigns styles for you. The formatting may not be exactly what you want, but you can still change fonts, styles, sizes, and so on after using AutoFormat.

 Use AutoFormat to remove unnecessary spacing and change asterisk bullets to round bullets and headings to styles.

You can use AutoFormat with unformatted text, or you can begin formatting (by creating and applying a few styles) and then let AutoFormat complete the process. AutoFormat finds similar text and assigns the same styles. If you choose the latter method, you have more control over which styles AutoFormat uses. Experiment with both methods and see which you prefer.

Formatting Text as You Type

If you want to use the AutoFormat feature as you type text, choose Tools, AutoCorrect; click the AutoFormat as You Type tab. You can check as many of the following dialog box options as you want:

Option	How to Make It Work
Headings	Type a short line of text and press Enter twice for Heading 1 style. After two Enters, type **Tab**, type a short line of text and press Enter twice for Heading 2.
Borders	Type three or more hyphens (-) and press Enter for a thin border or equal signs (=) for a double border.
Tables	Type a + (plus sign), a series of - (hyphens) and another + (plus sign). A column is created for each pair of plus signs with the width determined by the number of hyphens. Three hyphens equals enough space for one character, ten equals seven characters.

Option	How to Make It Work
Automatic Bulleted Lists	Start a list with an asterisk (*), lowercase o (o), greater than symbol (>), or a hyphen (-) followed by a space or tab. When you press Enter, each new item will be bulleted with a corresponding bullet. An *, or 0 will produce a ●, a > will produce a ➢ and a - will produce a ■. To end the list press Enter twice.

T I P For those of us who may not like using the mouse to add bullets or numbers, these two options can save lots of time.

Automatic Numbered Lists	Start a list with a number, a letter (uppercase or lowercase), or a lowercase i (i) for roman numerals, followed by a period (.) and a space. When you press Enter, each new item will be numbered accordingly.
Straight Quotes with Smart Quotes	When you type 'single' or "double" quotes, Word automatically changes them to 'smart quotes' or "smart quotes."
Ordinals (1st) with Superscript	Type **1st** or **2nd** to get 1st, 2nd, and so on.
Fractions (1/2) with Fraction Character ($^1/_2$)	Type 1/2 and 3/4 to get $^1/_2$ and $^3/_4$.
Symbol Characters	Type (c) for ©, (r) for ®, (tm) for ™.
Bold and _ Underline_ with Real Formatting	Type words in between the * (asterisks) to make those words bold, and in between the _ (underscore) characters to make those words underlined. For example, *This is Bold* changes to **This is Bold** and _This is underlined_ changes to <u>This is underlined</u>.
Internet and Network Paths with Hyperlinks	When you type an Internet address or network path, Word converts it to a hyperlink field so you go directly to the item by clicking the hyperlink.
Define Styles Based on Your Formatting	When you apply manual formatting to a paragraph, Word will create a new paragraph style based on your formatting so you can apply the style elsewhere for a consistent look.
Format Beginning of List Item Like the One Before It	If you apply character formatting to the beginning of a list, Word will automatically apply the same formatting to the next list item.

▶ **See** "Navigating and Publishing on the Web with Office 97," **p. 1025**

▶ **See** "Navigating in Datasheet View," **p. 754**

TROUBLESHOOTING

I try to automatically apply headings and borders but nothing happens. Return to the AutoFormat As you Type tab by choosing Tools, AutoCorrect, and clicking the AutoFormat As you Type tab. View your selections for the Apply As You Type section. Make sure there is a check mark in the Headings and Borders choices.

N O T E If you are using Microsoft Office 95, the AutoFormat as You Type command is found on the Tools, Options, AutoFormat tab. Make sure to select the AutoFormat as You Type option button. ■

Formatting Text Automatically

To start AutoFormat, choose Format, AutoFormat. A message box—the first AutoFormat dialog box—appears, announcing that formatting is about to begin (see Figure 10.10). To apply formatting without being prompted to review changes, make sure the Option, AutoFormat Now is selected, then choose OK to begin formatting.

FIG. 10.10
Choose OK to begin formatting, Cancel to cancel the command, or Options to customize formatting.

Accepting or Rejecting Changes   If you want to be able to accept or reject AutoFormat changes, select the AutoFormat and Review each Change option. After AutoFormat completes the formatting, another dialog box appears (see Figure 10.11). Choose Accept All to accept all changes. If you choose Accept too hastily, you can reverse your decision by clicking the Undo button in the Standard toolbar. If you do not like the changes you see behind the AutoFormat dialog box, choose Reject All. Alternatively, choose Review Changes or Style Gallery.

FIG. 10.11

You can choose to review changes, reject all changes, or accept all changes.

If you choose to Review **C**hanges, Word shows you each change to the formatting by highlighting the change and displaying a dialog box with a description of the change. You can choose to accept or reject individual changes. If you choose the **S**tyle Gallery button, you can apply different templates and styles to the document to see what they look like.

Reviewing Changes   If you choose to review the changes, Word takes you through the document step-by-step, enabling you to examine each change that AutoFormat made. Figure 10.12 shows the Review AutoFormat Changes dialog box.

FIG. 10.12

Use this dialog box to examine each change and decide whether to keep or reject the change.

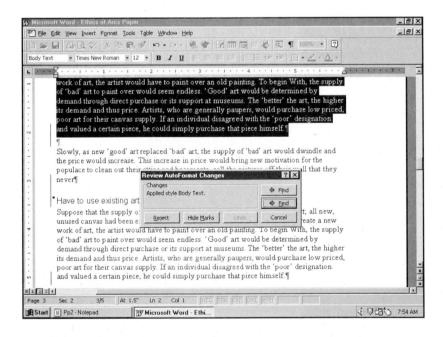

The Review AutoFormat Changes dialog box enables you to accept or reject changes. To accept a change, choose one of the Find buttons. F**i**nd with a left arrow moves to the previous change; **F**ind with a right arrow moves to the next change. If you do not like the formatting, choose the **R**eject button. Word changes the current selection back to its original formatting.

If you don't reject any changes, you'll have a Cancel button that allows you to return to the AutoFormat dialog box. If you reject any changes, the Cancel button changes to Close. Choose Close after reviewing the changes, or at any time, and Word displays the initial AutoFormat dialog box again. You can choose to accept or reject all changes.

As you go through reviewing changes, AutoFormat will show items that have been deleted in red (such as paragraph marks) as well as items that have been added in blue. If you don't want to see the marks where changes have been made, choose the Hide Marks button. If you make a mistake and don't want to reject a change after you choose the Reject button, choose the Undo button.

N O T E   You can click the mouse outside the Review AutoFormat Changes dialog box to work in your document. The dialog box remains on-screen. This way, you can scroll through the document to compare changes, format text, and add or edit text.

Using Style Gallery

Style Gallery is a special dialog box that contains Word's various templates. Each template contains preset page formatting and preset styles. You can use Style Gallery to apply various templates and styles to your document, and view an example in the dialog box before choosing to accept the style.

 You can choose Style Gallery in the AutoFormat dialog box to choose a different template and style for the document.

You can use the Style Gallery with or without AutoFormat. When you use AutoFormat, Word automatically applies a template and style sheet. If you do not like Word's choice, you can choose the Style Gallery command button and choose a different template and style for your document. On the other hand, you can format your document yourself by applying styles to text and paragraphs, and then decide to look at the document with various templates applied. Style Gallery gives a formatted document a different look using various styles of fonts, indents, type sizes, and so on.

To open the Style Gallery from the menu, choose Format, Style Gallery. To open Style Gallery from the AutoFormat dialog box, choose the Style Gallery button. Figure 10.13 shows the Style Gallery dialog box with the Professional Report template displayed.

To use the Style Gallery, follow these steps:

1. From the second AutoFormat dialog box, choose Style Gallery. To use Style Gallery directly, choose Format, Style Gallery. The Style Gallery dialog box appears.

2. Select a template from the Template list.

FIG. 10.13

Apply any of the templates and styles to your document or choose to preview examples of the template.

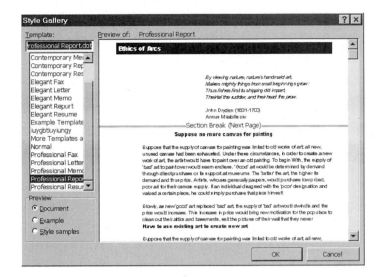

3. To change what displays in the <u>P</u>review Of box, choose one of the options in the Preview section. The default choice, <u>D</u>ocument, shows your document with styles applied from the selected template. To see an example document with many of the styles for the template, choose <u>E</u>xample. To see a list of styles in the template and how they are formatted, choose S<u>t</u>yle Samples in the Preview section.

4. If you find a template and style you like, choose OK. If you do not find a template you like, choose Cancel. Word returns to the AutoFormat dialog box or to your document.

5. If you started from AutoFormat, choose to <u>A</u>ccept or <u>R</u>eject All changes. The dialog box closes, and you return to the document.

TROUBLESHOOTING

I want to use the styles with a particular template, but I can't find the style names. Choose <u>V</u>iew, <u>T</u>oolbars and select the Formatting toolbar; then choose OK. The Style box is the first box at the left end of the toolbar. In addition, change the view from normal or outline to page layout (use the <u>V</u>iew menu to change the view) to display all formatting in the document.

AutoFormat does not seem to change the formatting of my document. By default, AutoFormat assigns styles only to paragraphs formatted in Normal or Body Text style. If you have selected some text and applied a style, or if you used commands in the Format menu to format some text, AutoFormat does not change any of those styles.

I want to format only a section of a document. Select the text you want to format, and then choose F<u>o</u>rmat, <u>A</u>utoFormat.

Using Template Wizards

A *template wizard* is a special template that asks questions and uses your answers to format a document automatically. The available template wizards include Newsletter, Resume, Memo, Letter, Fax, Envelope, Mailing Label, Web Page, and Pleading. Additional wizards can be loaded from the More Templates & Wizards tab. You may also have an Office 95 Templates tab that will include the Agenda, Calendar, Award, and Table wizards.

▶ **See** "Using Wizards," **p. 141**

If you use a template wizard, you must use it before you actually enter text in a document. Choose File, New to display Word's list of templates. Select the type of template wizard you want to use, and then answer the questions as they appear on-screen. This section describes the questions, answers, and formatting associated with the Web Page Wizard.

Choosing a Wizard

To begin a wizard document, choose File, New. The New dialog box appears (see Figure 10.14) with tabs for each type of template and wizard. Select the tab you want and then the template wizard you want to use (for this example, select the Web Page tab and then select the Web Page Wizard); choose OK.

FIG. 10.14
Wizard icons include a magic wand and stars to distinguish them from template icons.

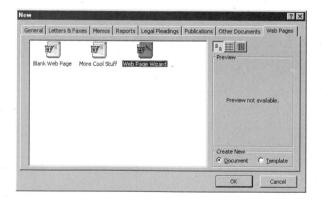

Choosing Wizard Options

Word displays the Web Page Wizard dialog box (see Figure 10.15). The dialog box shows you an example of the Web Page that the wizard will format for you behind the dialog box. The wizard dialog boxes for the Web Page ask you information about the type of page and the formatting of the page. Word applies the formatting related to your answers to the final document when you click the Finish button on the last Wizard dialog box.

▶ **See** "Understanding Common Window Elements," **p. 43**

TIP You can move the Web Page Wizard window by dragging the Title bar to see what's behind it.

Some of the other Wizards, such as the memo and fax wizards, get even more specific and ask you information about who the document is going to and coming from. The most important part of using a Wizard is reading the screen and responding to the questions.

FIG. 10.15

Answer the questions and choose Next to continue creating the Web Page with the Web Page Wizard template.

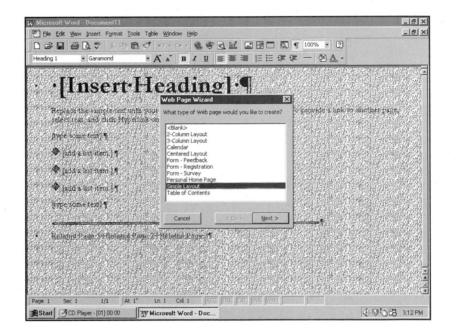

The first dialog box asks what type of Web page you want to create. After making your decision, choose Next to continue formatting the Web Page.

Word displays a second dialog box, asking what visual style you want your page to have (see Figure 10.16). Select the style that appeals to you. Choose Finish to close the Web Page Wizard dialog box.

FIG. 10.16

Answer the question and choose Finish to finish creating the Web Page with the Web Page Wizard template.

▶ **See** "Navigating and Publishing on the Web with Office 97," **p. 1025**

When you are finished using the Wizard, your Web page is displayed with the Office Assistant ready to help you continue with creating your document. When you click the Office Assistant, you can type a specific question to get help with creating your Web page (see Figure 10.17). If you are experienced enough or want to go it alone, you can always choose to close the Assistant.

FIG. 10.17
If this is the first time you have attempted to create a Web page, type your question and let the Assistant help you.

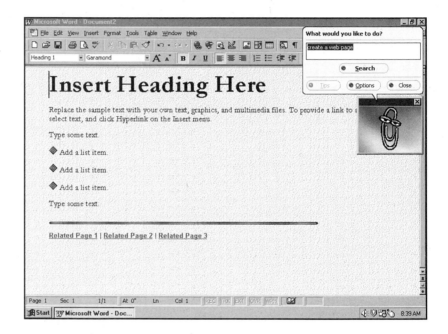

Editing the Web Page

The Web page is displayed with text suggesting what to type in what position. You can select the text and type to replace what's there with your own text (see Figure 10.18). Continue modifying the Web page document by adding your own information.

The text that is formatted in blue and underlined is normally hyperlink text. If you have other pages you want to be able to "jump" to, you would create a hyperlink. To create a hyperlink, select the text and choose Insert, Hyperlink from the menu bar, or click the Insert Hyperlink button in the Standard toolbar (see Figure 10.18).

▶ **See** "Navigating and Publishing on the Web with Office 97," **p. 1025**

FIG. 10.18
Fill in the text to complete your Web page. You can select and format the text, just as you can in any other Word document.

Web toolbar   Insert Hyperlink button

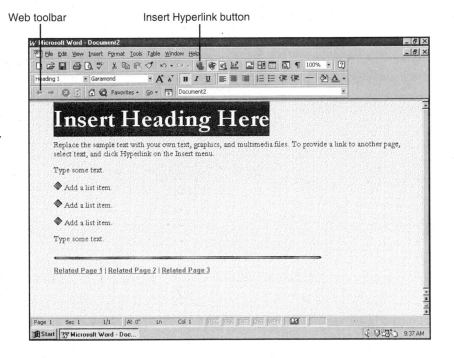

 TIP If the Web toolbar is not displayed, right-click any toolbar and click Web to turn the toolbar on.

You want to keep your Web pages free of clutter, so you may need to create many pages to navigate to and from. After you have the text typed, create your hyperlinks.

To create a hyperlink, follow these steps:

1. Save your document. If you skip this step, Word will prompt you to save before you create a hyperlink.

2. Select the text for the hyperlink.

 3. Click the Insert Hyperlink button on the Standard toolbar. The Insert Hyperlink dialog box is displayed (see Figure 10.19).

▶ **See** "Adding Hyperlinks," **p. 764**

4. Type the path to the document you want to navigate to in the Link to File or URL text box, or use the Browse button to locate the document.

5. Click OK.

After you have created the hyperlink, the text you selected changes to blue text with an underline. If you point to a hyperlink field, you will get a screen tip showing you the location of the file (see Figure 10.20).

FIG. 10.19
Use this dialog box to create hyperlink fields in the Link to File or URL text box, or hypertext fields in the Named Location in File text box.

Use this to type the location of a Web site

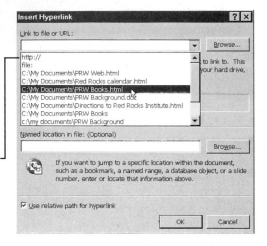

FIG. 10.20
The location of the Web page is displayed in a Screen Tip.

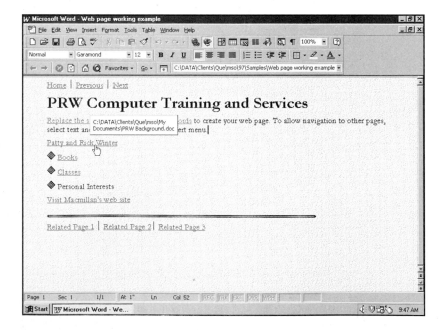

To test your hyperlinks, click one of the hyperlink fields. Word should open the associated Web page as in Figure 10.21.

CAUTION

If you choose to move your Web pages to a new location, make sure you also move the image files associated with them. They have an extension of .gif.

FIG. 10.21
The associated Web page as it appears after clicking on the Hyperlink for books.

Address of document

Another hyperlink field

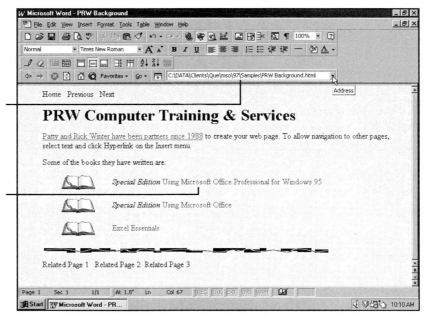

TROUBLESHOOTING

I tried to create a hyperlink to another document but Word says it doesn't exist. To link to other documents, they first have to be created. Create the document you want to link to, make sure to save it as an HTML file. Try the hyperlink command again.

▶ **See** "Saving, Opening, and Closing Files," **p. 97**

Creating a Template

As mentioned previously, Word comes with many built-in templates. You may have instances where you would like to modify an existing template for your office use or start completely from scratch and create a template that you can use over and over. Creating a template is almost as easy as saving a document. However, templates can also be extremely complex because of all the items you can include on them, such as text and formatting, AutoText entries, macros, and styles.

Modifying a Template from the File New Menu   You can modify an existing template and save it as a new template. To create your own template by modifying an existing template, follow these steps:

1. Choose File, New.

2. In the New dialog box, choose the template you want to base your new template on by choosing a Tab and template.

3. On the bottom right of the New dialog box, choose the Template option button.

4. Choose OK to go to the document.

5. Make any changes to the document, including adding styles, adding text, changing formatting, and adding macros.

6. Choose File, Save or click the Save button.

7. In the Save As dialog box, the Templates folder will show in the Save in pull-down list and the Save as Type drop-down will show Document Template. If you want to change the location of the template on the File New dialog box, choose a different folder.

8. Type the name of the template in the File Name text box and choose the Save button.

To use your template, choose File, New and pick your template from the General tab in the File New dialog box.

If you want to create your own template, use the template closest to what you need. In the bottom right of the New dialog box, choose Template and then click the OK button. Make any changes you want to the template. When you save the template, the Save as Type option indicates Document Template.

Saving as a Template File   You can create a template from "scratch" or use an existing Word document and convert it to a template. To save a file as a template, follow these steps:

1. Open your existing document or start with a blank document.

2. Make any changes to the document, including adding styles, adding text, changing formatting, or adding macros.

3. Choose File, Save As.

4. In the Save As dialog box, change the Save as Type drop-down to Document Template.

5. Word will change the location in the Save In pull-down text box to the location where Word templates are located. If you want to change the location of the template on the File New dialog box, choose a different folder.

N O T E   If for some reason Word does not change the location of the templates in the Save in text box, the location is usually in the Templates subfolder of the MSOFFICE folder.

6. Type the name of the template in the File Name text box and choose the Save button.

TROUBLESHOOTING

I want to use a wizard that is not listed in the New dialog box. Make sure that you are in the Template folder in the Word program folder. If you installed the templates in another folder, change to that folder. Alternatively, you may have to run Word Setup and install the templates if you did not install them with Word.

Adding Headers and Footers

Headers and *footers* contain repeated information at the top and bottom of documents. Headers and footers are typically used in long documents and may include one or more of the following: page number, date, company name, author name, or chapter title. You can edit and format headers and footers like any other part of a Word document.

▶ **See** "Creating Headers and Footers," **p. 406**

Inserting a Header or Footer

When you add a header or footer, Word switches to Page Layout view, opens up the Header pane, and displays a Header and Footer toolbar. To add a header or footer, choose View, Header and Footer. The Header and Footer toolbar appears along with a dotted area surrounding the header area (see Figure 10.22). Type in the header pane or use the Switch Between Header and Footer button to go to the footer.

Table 10.2 describes the buttons available on the Header and Footer toolbar:

Table 10.2   Header and Footer Toolbar Buttons

Button	Name	Description
Insert AutoText		Enables you to pick from a list of AutoText entries to insert in the header or footer.
	Insert Page Number	Inserts a page number that automatically updates when you add or delete pages.
	Insert Number of Pages	Inserts the total number of pages in the document and will update automatically.

continues

Table 10.2   Continued

Button	Name	Description
	Format Page Number	Enables you to format the page numbers in the current section of the document.
	Insert Date	Inserts a code for the current date.
	Insert Time	Inserts a code for the current time.
	Page Setup	Opens the Page Setup dialog box to set margins, page orientation, and other layout options.
	Show/Hide Document Text	Displays or hides the document text while you are working in the header or footer.
	Same as Previous	Links or unlinks the connection to the previous header or footer.
	Switch Between Header and Footer	Moves the insertion point between the header or footer editing areas.
	Show Previous	Moves the insertion point to the previous header or footer.
	Show Next	Moves the insertion point to the next header or footer.
Close	Close	Closes the header and footer pane.

In the header or footer pane, you can do any of the following:

■ Type and format text as you can in a normal document.

■ Press Tab to get to the center tab; press Tab again to get to the right-alignment tab. You can also change the tab settings if you want.

T I P   To include the current page number and total pages in your header or footer you could type **Page** (click the Page number button) **of** (click the Number of pages button).

FIG. 10.22

A special dotted area appears, enabling you to write headers and footers.

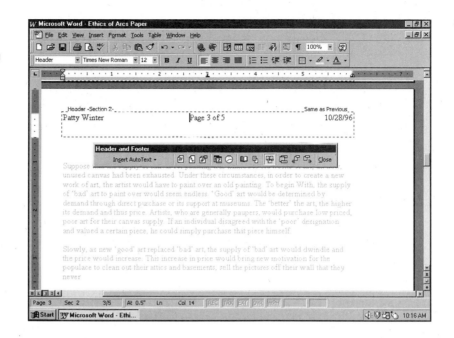

  Click the Page Numbers button to add a page number for each page.

 Click the Number of Pages button to add the total number of pages.

 Click to format the page numbers in the current section.

 Click the Date button to add a field that will show today's date. To have this field updated when printing, make sure that Tools, Options, Print Tab shows Update Fields is checked.

 Click the Time button to add a field that will show the current time.

If you want headers and footers for the first page to appear differently than on other pages, or different headers and footers on odd and even pages, click the Page Setup button. In the Headers and Footers section of the Layout tab, you can check the Different Odd and Even check box to have headers and footers change on facing pages. You can check the Different First Page option to have headers and footers that are different for the first page (this is usually done for report title pages). If you have different sections in your document, you can choose This Section or Whole Document in the Apply To pull-down list. When finished with the Page Setup dialog box, choose OK to return to the Header and Footer pane.

When you finish entering information for the headers and footers, click the Close button to return to the document.

Inserting Fields in the Header or Footer

You can add field codes to the document or in the header or footer—the procedure is the same. To add a code to the header or footer while you are in the header or footer pane, choose Insert, Field. You can choose any of the field codes from the Field dialog box shown in Figure 10.23.

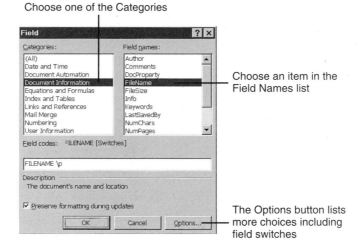

Choose one of the Categories

FIG. 10.23
The FileName code with the \p switch adds a file name with the file location, including the drive and folder.

Choose an item in the Field Names list

The Options button lists more choices including field switches

The following table shows some useful fields for headers and footers:

Result	Categories	Field Names
Document name (include the \p switch for the path name)	Document Information	FileName \p
Name of user who last saved document	Document Information	LastSavedBy
Author Information	Document Information	Author
User Information	User Information	UserName
Section numbering	Numbering	Section

Inserting Section Breaks

You may determine that you need more options for headers and footers than Different First Page or Different Odd and Even Pages. If you need multiple headers and footers in your document, you first need to break your document into different sections. To insert section breaks in your document, follow these steps:

1. Position the insertion point where you want the new section.

2. Choose Insert, Break. The Break dialog box appears, as shown in Figure 10.24.

FIG. 10.24
Use the Break dialog box to add new sections to your document.

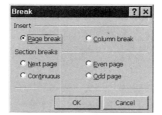

Part
II

Ch
10

3. In the Section Breaks area of the dialog box, select Next Page for a section beginning on a new page.

4. Choose OK to insert the new break and close the dialog box.

5. Repeat steps 1 through 4 for all of the section breaks you need in the document.

6. When you are adding headers and footers, click the Show Next button on the Header and Footer toolbar. You go to the next header or footer pane (see Figure 10.25).

7. To change the header or footer for this section, first click the Same as Previous button on the Header and Footer toolbar to turn this option off.

8. Type the new header of footer information.

9. Repeat steps 6 through 8 for each section of the document.

10. Click Close when you finish adding or editing your headers and footers.

FIG. 10.25
Notice Same as Previous on the top-right corner of the Header or footer pane.

Header pane for Section 2

Status bar shows section and page number

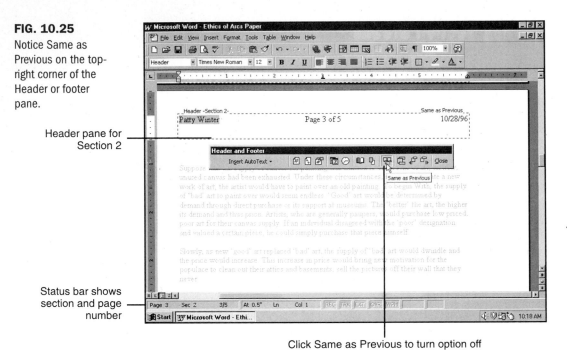

Click Same as Previous to turn option off

Editing or Deleting a Header or Footer

To edit the header or footer, you can double-click the header or footer in page layout view or choose View, Header and Footer. Edit the header or footer as you would regular document text. If you want to delete the header or footer, select the text (press Ctrl+A to select the entire header or footer) and press Delete. Click the Close button on the Header and Footer toolbar to return to the document.

 TIP

Double-click a header or footer in Page Layout view to open the pane for editing.

TROUBLESHOOTING

When I edit a header or footer, it appears in only part of my document. You could have multiple sections in your document or have another option on the page layout dialog box checked. Choose View, Header and Footer and click the Page Setup button on the Header and Footer toolbar. Make sure that both check boxes in the Header and Footer section are deselected. In the Apply To pull-down, make sure that Whole Document is selected.

When I look at my document, the wrong date shows in the header or footer. If you use the Insert Date and Time choice to insert a date, you need to make sure that you choose the Update Automatically check box on the Date and Time dialog box. If you use the Header and Footer toolbar, a field code is inserted in your document. The field code generally will not update until you print or open the document. You can manually update the code if you click the field and press F9.

Creating a Table of Contents

If you use the Heading 1, Heading 2, and Heading 3 styles, you can quickly create a table of contents for your document. To create the table of contents, follow these steps:

1. Press Ctrl+Home to move to the top of the document (or move the insertion point to the location where you want the table of contents to go).

2. If necessary, press Ctrl+Enter to add a page break and press Page Up to move back to the new first page.

3. Choose Insert, Index and Tables. The Index and Tables dialog box appears.

4. Select the Table of Contents tab, as shown in Figure 10.26.

FIG. 10.26

The Index and Tables dialog box enables you to choose from different styles for your table of contents.

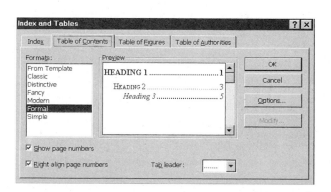

5. Click the Show Levels increment buttons to indicate how many heading levels you want to include.

6. Pick the style for the table of contents from the Formats list box.

7. Choose OK to generate the table of contents.

If you later edit the document, choose Insert, Index and Tables again; when you see the confirm dialog box, indicate that you want to replace the old table of contents.

Part
II

Ch
10

TROUBLESHOOTING

I was able to get some of my heading levels to appear in the table of contents, but not all.
After you choose Insert, Index and Tables and choose the Table of Contents tab, change the Show
Levels increment box to show the number of headings you want.

**I don't really want to see page numbers but would like to see the table of contents to have
an outline of my work.** Choose the Outline View button on the horizontal scroll bar and select the
number of levels you want to view. Alternatively, on the Table of Contents tab of the Index and
Tables dialog box, deselect the Show Page Numbers check box.

I would like to have something else beside dots leading up to the page numbers. On the Table
of Contents tab of the Index and Tables dialog box, you have Tab Leader choices of none, solid
line, and dashes, in addition to dots leading up to the page numbers. You can also deselect the
Right Align Page numbers check box to have the numbers appear directly after the text.

N O T E   If you use captions on your figures (through Insert, Caption), you can generate a table
of figures by choosing Insert, Index and Tables and making choices on the Table of
Figures tab. If you need an index or table of authorities, you first need to mark the text (select the
text and then make the appropriate Mark on the Index and Tables dialog box). When you want to
generate the index or table, choose Insert, Index and Tables, choose the tab on the dialog box you
want, and then choose OK. ▨

Using Footnotes and Endnotes

When you write a report or want to identify the source of your text, you can use *footnotes*
(which go on the bottom of each page) or *endnotes* (which appear at the end of the document). To create an endnote or footnote, first position the insertion point at your reference
in the document and then choose Insert, Footnote. The Footnote and Endnote dialog box
appears, as shown in Figure 10.27.

FIG. 10.27
Choose the Footnote
option to add notes
at the bottom of the
current page. Choose
the Endnote option to
add notes at the end
of the document.

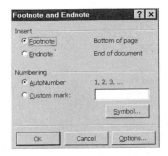

In the Insert section of the dialog box, select Footnote or Endnote; then choose OK. The bottom portion of the screen opens up to enable you to type the reference (see Figure 10.28). When finished, click the document or the Close button. A superscript number appears next to your text in the document referring to the footnote numbers at the bottom of your page or the endnote numbers at the end of your document. To delete a footnote or endnote, highlight the superscript number and press Delete.

FIG. 10.28

If you are in Normal view, a new pane opens up to enable you to add a footnote or endnote. Choose Close to get out of the pane or click your document to continue working.

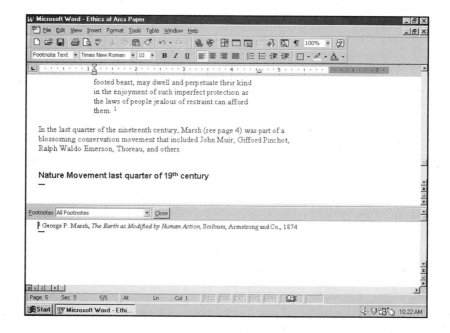

NOTE When creating footnotes or endnotes, you have options on how you want them displayed. After you choose Insert, Footnote to go to the Footnote and Endnote dialog box, AutoNumber is the default choice, which means that each new note will be incremented by one. You can change the mark to appear as a letter, a number, or another character by choosing the Custom Mark option and typing in your choice. The Symbol command button enables you to choose symbols for your custom mark from the Symbol dialog box. The Options command button leads to another dialog box, which enables you to change the location of the footnotes and endnotes, the number format (numbers, letters, symbols), which number to start with, and when to restart numbering. ▪

Inserting Comments in Your Work

Comments are similar to endnotes except that they are usually used when more than one person works on a document (comments help identify the reviewer). To create a comment, choose Insert, Comment. A window opens on the lower part of the document for your comment (see Figure 10.29). When you are finished writing your comment, click Close.

FIG. 10.29

A pane is also created for comments.

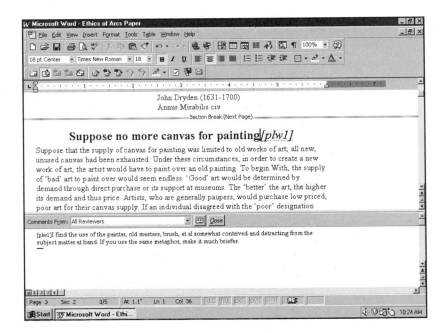

The word to the left of the insertion point is shaded in yellow, indicating a comment (similar to Notes in Excel). When you position the mouse pointer on the shaded word a Screen Tip is displayed, showing you the reviewers name and the comment (see Figure 10.30). This makes it much easier to review the comments.

> **N O T E** If you are using an earlier version of Word, comments are the same as annotations. To insert, you would use the Insert Annotations command. ▪

To edit a comment, right-click the highlighted area and choose Edit Comment from the shortcut menu. To delete the comment, right-click the highlighted area and choose Delete Comment from the shortcut menu. To print comments, choose File, Print and choose Comments from the Print What pull-down list.

FIG. 10.30
Use the ScreenTips to review the comments quickly in your document.

Shaded word —

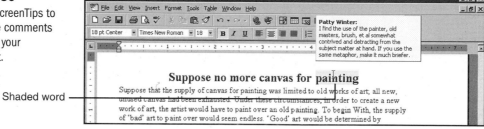

N O T E Use the Reviewing Toolbar to access all the common reviewing tools, including Insert and Review Comments, Save Versions, Track and Review Changes, Highlight text, and Send the document as an e-mail message. ■

TROUBLESHOOTING

 In the Comment pane I have reviewer's initials with no comment and I can't seem to delete them. Close the Comment pane, click the Show/Hide button on the Standard toolbar. Your comment codes will appear on-screen. Double-click a code to edit it. You can either add comment text or click the code again in the document area to select the code, then press delete to delete the code.

Using AutoSummarize

 A new feature in Word 97 is the AutoSummarize command. You can have Word find the key points in your document simply by choosing the Tools, AutoSummarize command. You will then be presented with four options on the type of summary you want to create.

Highlighting Key Points highlights in yellow the major points in your document and leaves the remainder of the text displayed in gray. *Insert an executive summary* inserts the summary at the top of the document. *Create a New Document* inserts the summary into a new doc-ument window that is not linked to the original document. *Hide Everything but the Summary* displays the summary and not the original text.

After you choose the type of summary you want to create, click OK to have Word prepare an automatic summary by picking the sentences most relevant to the main subject of the document.

N O T E If you choose to use the AutoSummarize command, make sure you review the accuracy of the summary. This is based on sentences that Word determines are relevant to the main topic of your document and could be incomplete. ■

Part II
Ch 10

Using Bookmarks and Cross-References

You can use bookmarks to create easy jump-to sections in your document or for cross-references. To create a bookmark, move to or select the text you want to mark as the bookmark. Choose Insert, Bookmark, type the name of the bookmark in the Bookmark dialog box (see Figure 10.31), and choose Add.

TIP Instead of using a bookmark, you can use Shift+F5 to move to your last three revisions.

Once you have a bookmark, you can press Ctrl+G or F5 to display the Go To tab on the Find and Replace dialog box (see Figure 10.32). Choose Bookmark from the Go to What list and type or choose the bookmark name from the Enter Bookmark Name section.

To add a cross-reference to the bookmark in your document (for example, *see page 25* where *25* is the page on which the bookmark appears), first position your insertion point where you want the cross-reference to go, and then choose Insert, Cross-Reference. The Cross-Reference dialog box appears, as shown in Figure 10.33. Choose Bookmark from the Reference Type list. From the Insert Reference To list, choose Page Number; then choose the appropriate bookmark in the For Which Bookmark list box, click the Insert button when you are finished. The reference goes into the document as a field.

FIG. 10.31

To add a bookmark, type the name in the Bookmark Name text box with no spaces and choose Add.

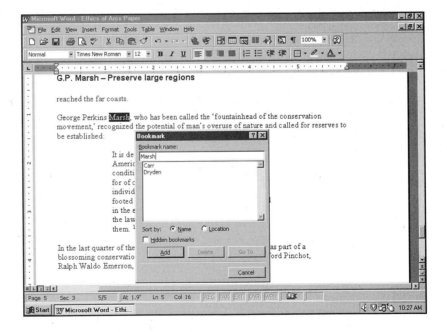

FIG. 10.32
The Go To tab shows a list of all the bookmarks.

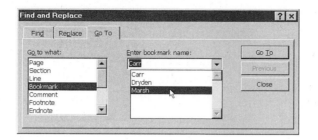

TIP If you want to insert the word "above" or "below" to the cross-reference, click the Include Above/Below check box on the Cross-reference dialog box.

NOTE When you are inserting a cross-reference, Word automatically inserts it as a hyperlink (see Figure 10.32). The hyperlink attached to the cross-reference allows you to click the cross-reference and jump to the related item, in this case the bookmark. If you don't want the cross-reference to have a hyperlink attached, clear the Insert as Hyperlink check box on the Cross-reference dialog box. ■

FIG. 10.33
You can use a cross-reference to refer the reader to the page number on which the bookmark is located.

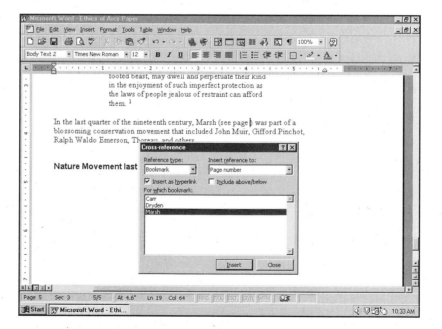

TROUBLESHOOTING

I can't delete my bookmark reference. The cross-reference appears as a code in the document. You can't press Backspace to delete this code with the insertion point only. When your insertion point is on the code, it appears with a gray highlight. Select the entire highlight and press Delete to remove the cross-reference. If you want to delete the bookmark, choose Insert, Bookmark, select the bookmark name, and then choose the Delete command button.

Working with Track Changes

The Track Changes feature allows you to see when changes are made to a document. If multiple people are reviewing a document, each person's revisions can be formatted in a different color. To turn on the Track Changes feature so that changes are visible, choose Tools, Track Changes, Highlight Changes. The Highlight Changes dialog box appears, as shown in Figure 10.33. To add revision marks, check the Track Changes While Editing check box and choose OK. By default, inserted text appears with an underline and deleted text appears with strikethrough formatting; all revisions are marked with a vertical line in the margin.

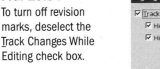

FIG. 10.34
To turn off revision marks, deselect the Track Changes While Editing check box.

N O T E If you are using an earlier version of Word, Track Changes is similar to Revisions. To turn revision marks on or off you would choose, Tools, Revisions and click the Mark Revisions While Editing check box.

If you want to accept revisions and remove the revision marks from the document, choose Tools, Track Changes, Accept or Reject Changes and click the Accept All button. To reject all the revisions entered into the document, click the Reject All button. To review each revision, click the Find button.

In the document the revision appears selected, and the Accept or Reject Changes dialog box in the Changes section displays information related to the change (see Figure 10.35). Choose Accept to make the change or Reject to undo the revision. You can choose the Find button again to go to the next revisions or choose the Find button to go to the previous revision. When you are finished looking at the changes, click the Close button to go back to your document.

FIG. 10.35
Use the Accept or
Reject Changes dialog
box to accept or reject
each revision.

N O T E If more than one person works on the same document, each person could save their
version of the document with a different name (without highlighting their changes). To
see each person's changes, one person opens the original file, then chooses Tools, Track Changes,
Compare Documents, and selects the other files one by one. All the changes will be displayed as
described above. To review the changes follow the instructions above. ■

Saving Multiple Versions of a Document

In earlier versions of Microsoft Word, when you wanted to save different versions of the
same document, you used the Save As command to rename the document. In Word 97,
you can now save different versions of the same document in one file. This enables you to
review earlier versions of the document, or even better, see who made the changes to the
document and when. You can set up Word to automatically save a version of the document
when the file is closed. To save the current version of the document, follow these steps:

1. Choose File, Versions from the menu bar.
2. Click the Save Now button.
3. In the Comments On Version text box, type any applicable comments for this
   version of the document.
4. Click OK to save this version of the document.

After you have saved a document with multiple versions, you may want to save a specific
version as a separate file.

N O T E When you are saving multiple versions of a document, you are archiving the document. You cannot modify a saved version of the document. To make changes to an
earlier version of the document, after you open the version you want to change, you must use the
File, Save As command to save the version as a separate file. ■

If you want to keep a record of who makes changes and when the changes are made,
you can set up versioning to automatically save a version when the document is closed.
Choose the File, Versions command, click the Automatically Save a Version on Close
check box, and click the Close button. Now, every time someone closes this document
after changes have been made, Word will automatically save a version of the document
with Automatic Version displayed in comments.

N O T E When you want to have Word compare versions of this document for you, you must save the versions as separate files and use the Tools, Track Changes, Compare Documents command, as explained earlier in this chapter. ▪

CHAPTER 11

Working with Tables and Borders

by Patty Winter

You can enhance your documents by adding tables to organize information. Using tables instead of aligning data with simple tabs allows you to apply enhancements that liven up the information you're presenting and make it more noticeable.

You can create tables to organize columns of information, produce forms, or add simple spreadsheets to your documents. Word enables you to enter and format text in a table, create calculations in the table, as well as format the table. You can add rows and columns, adjust spacing, perform calculations, add borders, adjust row height, and more.

Word also enables you to add graphics such as lines, borders, and shading to your documents to illustrate them and to add interest. ▪

Insert a table into a document

You learn two ways to insert a table—the Insert Table dialog box and the Draw table tool.

Enter, edit, and format the text in a table

This section covers entering and editing text in cells, making changes to the table by inserting and deleting rows and columns, and formatting the contents of individual cells, rows, and columns.

Modify row height and column width

Changing the default row height and column width can give the information in your table more emphasis.

Add lines, borders, shading, and change the direction of the text in a document

This section allows you to pull the readers attention to the information you want them to notice.

Create sums in a table

Using formulas in Word tables involves understanding basic mathematical functions and where and how to insert formulas in cells.

Working with Tables

A table is a convenient method of organizing text. You can use a table to create forms, reports, simple spreadsheets, and columns of numbers. You even can use tables to produce side-by-side paragraphs, such as those in a resume or an agenda.

Tables consist of columns and rows. Columns are the vertical divisions of the table; rows are the horizontal divisions. The box formed by the intersection of a column and row is called a *cell*. You can fill cells with text and graphics. When you type text into a cell, the text wraps from one line to the next, enlarging the cell as you enter more text.

When you insert a table, you enter the number of columns and rows you want the table to contain. After the table is inserted, you can modify the table and its contents by adding borders and shading, formatting the text, adjusting column width and row height, and so on. This section introduces table basics. For information about adding borders and shading to a table, see "Adding Lines, Borders, and Shading," later in this chapter.

Inserting a Table Using the Menu Command

 You can insert a table by using the Table menu or the Insert Table button on the Standard toolbar. To use the menu, choose T<u>a</u>ble, <u>I</u>nsert Table. The Insert Table dialog box appears (see Figure 11.1).

FIG. 11.1
Enter the number of columns and rows in the Insert Table dialog box.

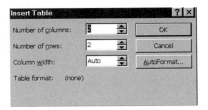

The following list describes the options in the Insert Table dialog box:

- *Number of <u>C</u>olumns.* Enter the number of columns for the table.
- *Number of <u>R</u>ows.* Enter the number of rows for the table.
- *Column <u>W</u>idth.* Set a specific column width for all columns, or leave the option at Auto. Auto column width divides the space between the left and right margins. You can adjust the width of any column at any time.
- *Table Format.* If you use AutoFormat to format the table, this option displays the predefined format.

  ▶ **See** "Using AutoFormat," **p. 250**

■ *AutoFormat.* Displays the Table AutoFormat dialog box, in which you choose styles, borders, fonts, and so on from a list of predefined table formats. AutoFormat is very much like the Style Gallery.

N O T E You always can add rows and columns by choosing Table, Insert Rows, or Table, Insert Columns. You can also delete rows and columns by choosing Table, Delete Rows, or Table, Delete Columns. ▨

T I P As you are entering information into a table, you can press Tab at the end of the last row and Word will automatically create another row in your table.

When you insert a table, Word normally displays the table with a 1/2 pt border. To change the border of the table, see "Adding Lines, Borders, and Shading" later in this chapter.

To insert a table, follow these steps:

1. Position the insertion point where you want to insert the table.
2. Choose Table, Insert Table. The Insert Table dialog box appears.
3. Enter the Number of Columns and the Number of Rows.
4. Optionally, enter a value in the Column Width box.
5. Optionally, choose AutoFormat and answer all the queries in the dialog boxes.
6. Choose OK to insert the table and close the Insert Table dialog box.

Inserting a Table Using the Tables and Borders Button on the Standard Toolbar

If you want to create a more free-form table, you could use the Tables and Borders button on the Standard toolbar to draw your table. To insert a table, simply click the Tables and Borders button on the Standard toolbar, and use the Draw table tool to draw the table's borders (see Figure 11.2).

After you have the outside border for your table, you can continue to use the Draw Table tool to draw the rows and columns for your table (see Figure 11.3). Word will automatically adjust the row height and size of the table to add more rows.

Adding Text to a Table

▶ **See** "Formatting Paragraphs," **p. 178**
▶ **See** "Formatting Text," **p. 172**

Part
II

Ch
11

FIG. 11.2
Using the Draw Table
tool to draw your table.

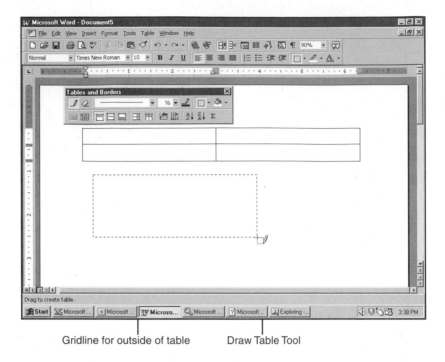

Gridline for outside of table   Draw Table Tool

FIG. 11.3
To draw a partial row,
drag from the right to
the left side of the
table. The dotted line
stops at the vertical
lines for columns.

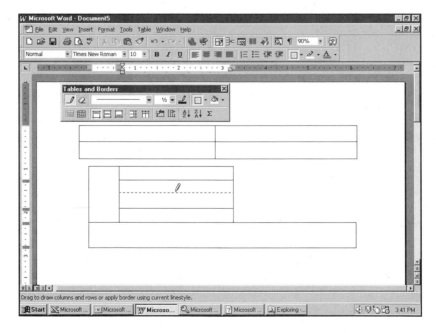

After you insert the table, you can add text. You enter text in a table much the same way
you enter text in any document. Moving around in a table, however, is a bit different.

You can also edit the text in a table as you edit any text. After you enter the text, you can select it to apply various types of formatting, such as type sizes, alignments, and text direction.

Entering Text   To enter text in a table, position the insertion point in a cell and then type the text. To move to another cell in the table, use the arrow keys. The arrow keys move from cell to cell and from row to row. If a cell contains text, an arrow key first moves one character or line at a time and then moves from cell to cell.

Press the Tab key to move the insertion point to the right from one cell to another, highlighting any text in a cell. Press Shift+Tab to move one cell to the left. To actually insert a tab in a cell, press Ctrl+Tab and then set the tab as you normally do.

Selecting Text in a Table   Selecting text in a table is similar to selecting text in any document. You can drag the I-beam pointer over the text to select it, or click the selection bar to select an entire row. In addition, you can use some techniques specific to selecting text in a table. The following is a list of those techniques:

- To select one cell, triple-click that cell or click the left inside edge of the cell.
- To select an entire column, drag the mouse down the column. Alternatively, place the mouse pointer at the top of the column; the pointer changes to a black down arrow. Click to select the column, and click and drag across columns to select more than one column.
- Select an entire row by clicking the selection bar to the left of the table; drag up or down to select more than one row.
- To select the entire table, position the cursor in the table and press Shift+Alt+5 (on the numeric keypad). Alternatively, place the insertion point in the table and choose Table, Select Table.

T I P   Use the ruler to adjust text indents. For more information, see Chapter 7.

After selecting the text, you can format it as you would any other text by applying various fonts, font sizes, alignments, and so on. Figure 11.4 shows vertical text in a column, a selected column, centered and bold headings, right-aligned numbers using a right tab, different font colors, and shaded cells.

Modifying a Table

You use commands in the Table menu to insert or delete rows and columns, change cell height and width, and make other modifications. When you modify a table element, you first must select that element. You select a row, column, or cell the same way you select text in a table; refer to the preceding section for more information.

Part

II

Ch

11

FIG. 11.4
Select text in a table
to format it.

Mouse pointer

New feature,
Vertical text
formatting

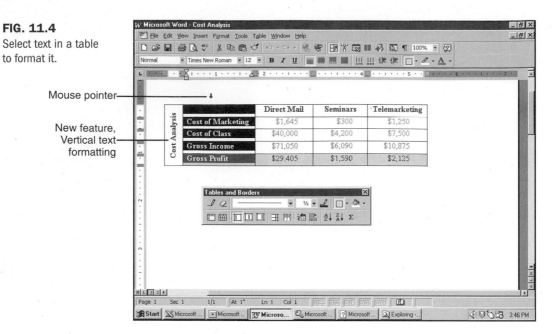

N O T E Depending on what you select, the Table menu commands change. Select a column, and the Table menu has the Insert Columns and Delete Columns commands. Select a cell, and the commands are Insert Cells and Delete Cells. ▪

 T I P To add a row at the bottom of a table, position the insertion point in the bottom right cell and press Tab.

Inserting and Deleting Columns and Rows   Inserting columns and rows is relatively simple, once you understand how Word does it. To insert one row, select a row in the table and choose Table, Insert Rows. Word inserts one row *before*, or above, the selected row. To insert two or more rows, select two or more rows in the table and then choose Table, Insert Rows. Word inserts as many rows as you selected before the selected rows.

Similarly, to insert one column, select one column and then choose Table, Insert Columns. Word inserts one column *to the left of*, or before, the selected column. Select two or more columns to insert two or more columns before the selected columns.

To delete a row or column, select it and then choose Table, Delete Rows or Table, Delete Columns.

To insert or delete a column or row, follow these steps:

1. Select the column or row to be deleted, or select the column or row to the right of or below the place where you want to add a column or row.

2. Point the mouse at the column or row and press the right mouse button to display the shortcut menu.

3. Select Insert Columns/Rows or Delete Columns/Rows.

Adjusting Cell Height   You can change the height of a cell or the height of a row in the Cell Height and Width dialog box. Choose Table, Cell Height and Width. Select the Row or Column tab, depending on which area of the table you want to adjust. Figure 11.5 shows the Cell Height and Width dialog box with the Row tab displayed.

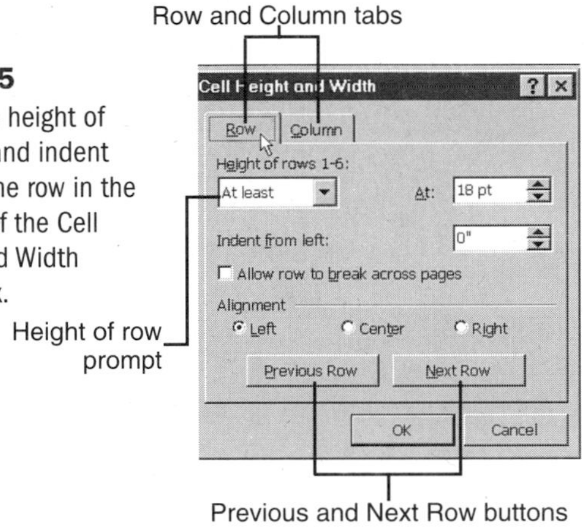

Row and Column tabs

FIG. 11.5
Adjust the height of the rows and indent or align one row in the Row tab of the Cell Height and Width dialog box.

Height of row prompt

Previous and Next Row buttons

To adjust the height of the row, select one of the following options in the Height of Row drop-down list:

- *Auto.* Word adjusts the height of the row to accommodate the tallest font or graphic.
- *At Least.* Enter the minimum row height in the At box. However, Word adjusts the height of the rows to the contents of the cells.

Part
II

Ch
11

■ *Exactly.* Enter a row height in the <u>A</u>t box. If the cell contents exceed the height you entered, Word prints only what fits in the cell.

To indent the selected rows or the entire table from the left margin, type a number in the Indent <u>F</u>rom Left box or use the scroll arrows to select a number.

To allow the text in a row to split across pages, choose the Allow Row to <u>B</u>reak Across Pages option.

To change the horizontal alignment of the selected rows or the entire table, choose Cen<u>t</u>er or <u>R</u>ight in the Alignment options.

By default, when you enter this dialog box, you are changing *all rows* of the table unless you have selected a row first. To adjust one row at a time, first click either the <u>P</u>revious row or the <u>N</u>ext row buttons to display the row number you want to change in the He<u>i</u>ght of Rows prompt, at the top of the dialog box (refer to Figure 11.5). Choose either command button to move from row to row as you adjust the height of the rows. Click OK when you are finished adjusting the rows, or proceed with adjusting columns.

N O T E   If no row is selected when you open the Cell Height and Width dialog box, the He<u>i</u>ght of Row option applies to all rows in the table. When you select a row, the He<u>i</u>ght of Row option applies only to the selected row.   ■

Adjusting Column and Cell Width   You also can adjust column and cell width in the Cell Height and Width dialog box. Choose T<u>a</u>ble, Cell Height and <u>W</u>idth and then select the <u>C</u>olumn tab (see Figure 11.6).

FIG. 11.6
Use the Column tab to specify each column's width and to add space between columns.

To adjust the column width, enter a new width in the <u>W</u>idth of Column text box. The <u>S</u>pace Between Columns option specifies the amount of blank space between column boundaries and the contents of the cell. If you select the <u>A</u>utoFit button, Word automatically resizes all columns in the table to fit the contents of the cells. Click the <u>P</u>revious Column or <u>N</u>ext Column buttons to change other columns in your table.

TROUBLESHOOTING

The Table menu does not show Insert Rows. Your insertion point needs to be in the table with no selections or rows selected before you choose the Table menu to insert or delete rows.

I inserted several rows or columns in the wrong place. Click the Undo button in the Standard toolbar or choose <u>E</u>dit, <u>U</u>ndo. Then select some existing rows or columns, keeping in mind that the new rows or columns are inserted before the selected ones.

I want to add a column to the right of a table. Position the insertion point just outside the last column and choose T<u>a</u>ble, Select <u>C</u>olumn. Then choose the T<u>a</u>ble menu and the <u>I</u>nsert Columns command.

Shift+Alt+5 doesn't select the table. With Num Lock on, use Shift+Alt+5 on the numeric key pad.

Adding Lines, Borders, and Shading

Word includes many graphic elements you can add to your documents, including lines, borders, and shading. Use these elements to attract attention to your document, break the monotony of straight text, emphasize text, and pique the reader's interest.

You can add a line above headings to make them stand out or add lines to a table to help divide the data. Create a shaded border to attract attention to text, or add clip art to a newsletter to make it more interesting.

Word enables you to add graphic lines and borders with the Tables and Borders toolbar or with menu commands. The toolbar method is by far the easier method. You can add borders and shading to text, tables, charts, and other elements by using the Borders toolbar. If you are using an older version of Word, the Borders toolbar is separate from the table commands.

Displaying the Tables and Borders Toolbar

To display the Tables and Borders toolbar, place the mouse pointer on any toolbar that currently appears on-screen and click the right mouse button. The Toolbar shortcut menu appears. Click Tables and Borders, and the Tables and Borders toolbar appears; repeat the process and the toolbar disappears. You can also click the Tables and Borders tool on the Standard toolbar to turn the toolbar on or off. Figure 11.7 shows the Tables and Borders toolbar. Table 11.1 lists the buttons on the Tables and Borders toolbar.

FIG. 11.7
Use the Tables and Borders toolbar for many different formatting functions.

Table 11.1   The Tables and Borders Toolbar

Button	Name	Description
	Draw Table	Draw your table free-form and change existing borders.
	Eraser	Erase or merge cells vertically or horizontally.
	Line Style	Select the type of line you want to use as a border.
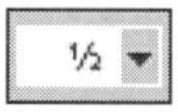	Line Weight	Select the thickness for the line of the border.
	Border Color	Select the color for the border from the color palette.
	Borders	Select the border you want to use from the drop-down list.
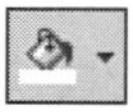	Shading Color	Select the color and type of shading you want to use.
	Merge Cells	First select the cells you want to combine (make as one), then click to merge the selected cells together.
	Split Cells	Click to divide one cell into two or more cells.
	Align Top	Align text on the top of the cell. This is the default alignment.

Button	Name	Description
	Center Vertically	Center text in the cell vertically.
	Align Bottom	Align text on the bottom of the cell.
	Distribute Rows Evenly	First select multiple rows, then click to adjust the row height evenly.
	Distribute Columns Evenly	First select multiple columns , then click to adjust column width evenly.
	Table AutoFormat	Select pre-defined table formats to choose from.
	Change Text Direction	Change the text from horizontal to vertical.
	Sort Ascending	Sort a list in ascending order.
	Sort Descending	Sort a list in descending order.
	AutoSum	Insert the total of a column or row in the cell you are in.

Part
II
Ch
11

The first tool, Draw Table, allows you to draw your table free form instead of using set numbers of rows and columns. The drop-down lists contain options for various line styles and thickness (the Line Style and Line Weight list boxes) and various fills and screens (the Shading Color list box). The Borders button list box lets you specify the border's location. The rest of the buttons allow you to change table and text formatting as well as perform sorts and use the AutoSum formula.

Applying a Border

To apply a border, place the insertion point in the cell where you want the line or border to appear, or select the table, row, column, cell, picture, frame, or text. Choose the Line Style drop-down list from the Tables and Borders toolbar; select a line style. Then, on the Borders drop-down list button, click the border button you want to use. When you click a border button, Word inserts the border. For Office 97, Word now surrounds selected text with a boarder (instead of the whole paragraph). If you click the same border button again, Word removes the border (see Figure 11.8). If you are using Office 95, look at Table 11.1 to see a description of the border types.

Table 11.2 lists the Borders buttons.

FIG. 11.8
Use the Line Style, Line Weight, Borders, and shading tools to assign borders to text, pages, tables, pictures, and other elements.

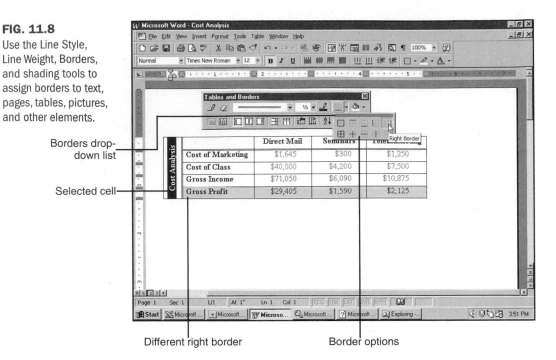

Borders drop-down list

Selected cell

Different right border   Border options

Table 11.2 The Borders Buttons

Button	Name	Description
	Outside Border	Applies a border to the outside of any object or frame or around selected text.
	Top Border	Inserts a border along the top of a table, row, column, cell, frame, or picture, or above a paragraph of text.
	Bottom Border	Inserts a border along the bottom of a table, row, column, cell, frame, or picture, or below a paragraph of text.
	Left Border	Inserts the border along the left side of the object or paragraph.
	Right Border	Inserts the border along the right side of the object or paragraph.
	All Borders	Applies a border to the entire table, inside and outside. Not available in Microsoft Office 95.

Button	Name	Description
	Inside Border	Inserts a border along the inside lines of a table.
	Inside Horizontal Border	Inserts a border on the internal horizontal lines of table. Not available in Microsoft Office 95.
	Inside Vertical Border	Inserts a border on the internal vertical lines of the table. Not available in Microsoft Office 95.
	No Border	Before you use this button to remove a border, select the bordered paragraph, table, or object.

T I P Adjust the length of a border line by selecting it and moving the indent markers in the ruler.

You can apply more than one border to an object or text. For example, you can apply a 3/4-point top border and a 6-point bottom border. To that, you can add 3-point left and right borders, creating a somewhat strange box around the object or text. You can also apply shading to the same text or object to which you have applied one or more borders.

You can apply various shading and colors by selecting the object or the text, or by positioning the insertion point. Choose a shading from the Shading drop-down list in the Tables and Borders toolbar. The list provides shading that is stepped in percentages from 5 percent to 100 percent (or solid). Additionally, Word displays a variety of colors you can apply to text or objects. To apply patterns, use the Format, Borders and Shading command from the menu bar and choose the Shading tab. The pattern list follows the shading list on the Style drop-down list.

Figure 11.9 shows a table with a 2 1/4-point outside border, a double 1/2-point right border on the first cell and on the bottom of the first row, a single 1/2-point inside border, a double 3-point top border above the totals, and a 25-percent shading for the bottom row. This table also shows vertical text direction in the first column, and text centered vertically in the first row.

N O T E There are many new border styles in Word 97. Instead of using the borders you are accustomed to, try some of the new border options. To add or change a border, you can use the Format, Borders and Shading command from the menu bar, and then on the Borders tab, scroll through the Style list to see the additional border styles. In the Setting section of the dialog box, you now have 3-D and Custom as options. ▪

FIG. 11.9
You can choose different borders for the inside and outside of a table, and add shading to specific areas of the table, as well as change the format of the text in the cells.

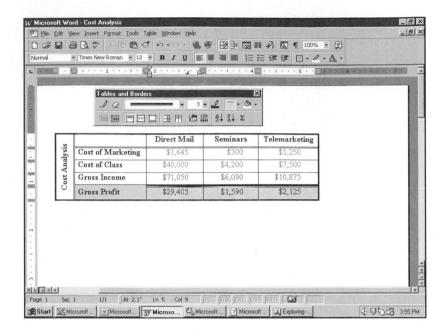

Summing Up in Tables

 TIP To use Excel functions and tables in Word, click the Insert Microsoft Excel Worksheet button.

You may find you have a table that requires numbers in a column or row that need to be calculated. Word provides the access to creating formulas in your Word tables and allows you to perform spreadsheet-type calculations in a table created in Word. If your table has a simple calculation or you don't want to use Excel or a spreadsheet application, or if you want to keep everything in the same application, you can choose Table, Formula to add formulas to your tables.

▶ **See** "Using Formulas," **p. 373**

Inserting a Formula in a Cell

TIP Spreadsheet-type references similar to **=SUM(A2:A9)** are valid in the Word formula field.

Inserting a formula in a cell is similar to performing the same action in a spreadsheet application. If you know how to use spreadsheet programs, you can try what you already know. On the other hand, if you aren't familiar with spreadsheet programs, you can still use formulas in Word. Figure 11.10 shows the Formula dialog box, displayed when you choose Table, Formula.

FIG. 11.10

The formula is used to calculate gross profit in the Direct Mail column.

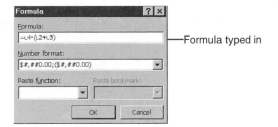
——Formula typed in

N O T E Cell references in Word tables are the same as cell references in spreadsheet applications, with one major difference—you don't have any row or column headings telling you what cell you are using. To determine the cell reference, you need to keep track of the headings yourself. Columns are letters beginning with "A." Rows are numbers beginning with "1." The intersection of the column and row is the cell reference.

In Figure 11.9, the first column is A (Cost Analysis), the second column is B, the Direct Mail column is C, the Seminars column is D, and the Telemarketing column is E. Cost of Marketing is row 2, Cost of Class is row 3, Gross Income is row 4, and Gross Profit is row 5. Therefore, if you are looking at the Gross Income for Direct Mail, the cell reference is C4.

Part II

Ch 11

The following table shows the formulas for the example table shown in Figure 11.9:

To Calculate	Formula
Gross Profit for Direct Mail (cell C5)	= C4-(C2+C3) C4=Direct Mail Gross Income, C2=Cost of Marketing, C3=Cost of Class
Gross Profit for Seminars (cell D5)	= D4-(D2+D3) D4=Seminars Gross Income, D2=Cost of Market-ing, D3=Cost of Class
Gross Profit for Telemarketing (cell E5)	= E4-(E2+E3) E4=Telemarket Gross Income, E2=Cost of Marketing, E3=Cost of Class

 T I P Σ Use the AutoSum tool if you want to sum the column above or the row to the left.

To insert a formula in a cell, follow these steps:

1. Position the insertion point in the cell to receive the formula.

2. Choose Table, Formula.

3. Either accept the default formula to sum the column or row, or delete the default formula and type a formula beginning with = (equal sign) and followed by a mathematical calculation using cell references in place of actual numbers, where needed.

   You could also use the functions that come with Word. Instead of typing a formula in the preceding step, click the Paste Function drop-down list to display the functions within Word's formula field. Some of the common functions include the following:

   - Average(). Calculates the average of the arguments—arguments are cell references inside the parentheses.

   - Count(). Counts the number of items within the arguments, including the beginning and ending reference.

   - MAX(). Finds the highest number within the arguments, including the beginning and ending reference.

   - MIN(). Finds the lowest number within the arguments, including the beginning and ending reference.

4. Choose the Number Format you want to use. You can select from seven number formats:

   - #,##0. Displays the number with commas and no decimal places.

   - #,##0.00. Displays numbers with commas and two decimal places.

   - $#,##0.00;($#,##0.00). Displays numbers with dollar signs, commas, two decimal places, and negative numbers in parentheses.

   - 0. Displays the whole number rounding up, no commas, no decimal places.

   - 0%. Displays the number as a percent rounded up.

   - 0.00. Displays numbers with two decimal places.

   - 0.00%. Displays the number as a percent with two decimal places.

5. Choose OK.

Recalculating a Formula

One of the best reasons to use formulas in your table is the ease with which you can recalculate the formula when one of the values changes. You can enter the new value in the table and have Word perform the recalculation for you. If you have more than one formula to be calculated, you can update all the formulas at one time.

To recalculate formulas in a table, follow these steps:

1. Enter the new value or values in your table.

2. Do one of the following: move to the cell containing the formula, select the row or column containing all the formulas, or select the entire table.

3. Press F9, the calculation key.

TROUBLESHOOTING

I tried to recalculate a formula in my table, but nothing changed. When you move to the field with the formula, you must have the insertion point in the field code or select the entire cell or formula field before you press F9.

Using Excel

CHAPTER 12

Creating Worksheets

by Patrice-Anne Rutledge

In this chapter, you learn the basic techniques for creating worksheets in Excel. The chapter begins with an introduction to fundamental Excel terms and concepts. You then learn how to enter data, move to other areas in the worksheet, and select cells and ranges. Once you've mastered these skills, you'll have the confidence to create nearly any type of worksheet. ■

Worksheet movement

In Excel, you have several options for navigating your worksheets—with the mouse, with the keyboard, and by scrolling.

Data entry

Excel provides easy ways to enter text, numbers, dates, times, and formulas.

Cell and range selection

Select single and multiple cells and ranges with the mouse or keyboard.

Series entries

Excel enables you to automatically enter and format series of data using the AutoFill feature or menu commands.

Saving your work

You can save Excel workbooks in a variety of file formats.

Defining Excel Terms

When you start Excel, a blank workbook appears in the document window. The *workbook* is the main document used in Excel for storing and manipulating data. A workbook consists of individual worksheets, each of which can contain data. Initially, each new workbook you create contains 3 worksheets, but you can add more worksheets later. In addition to worksheets, you can create charts, macros, and dialog sheets.

Each worksheet is made up of 256 columns and 65,536 rows. The columns are lettered across the top of the document window, beginning with A through Z and continuing with AA through AZ, BA through BZ, and so on through column IV. The rows are numbered from 1 to 65,536 down the left side of the document window.

The intersections of rows and columns form *cells*, which are the basic units for storing data. Each cell takes its name from this intersection and is referred to as a *cell reference*. For example, the address of the cell at the intersection of column C and row 5 is referred to as cell C5.

At the bottom of each worksheet is a series of *sheet tabs*, which enable you to identify each worksheet in the workbook. The tabs initially are labeled Sheet1, Sheet2, and so on, as shown at the bottom of the screen in Figure 12.1.

FIG. 12.1

An Excel workbook is made up of columns, rows, cells, and worksheets.

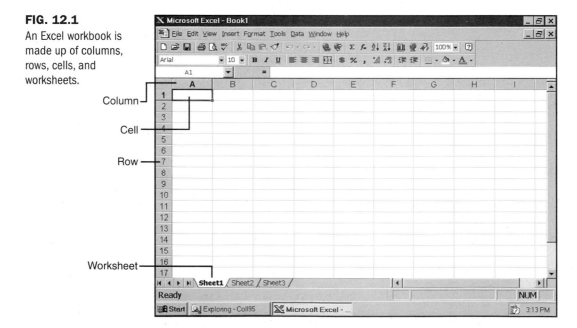

Moving Around in a Worksheet

In a new worksheet, the cell at the intersection of column A and row 1 is highlighted, indicating that cell A1 is the active cell. When you start typing, the data appears in the active cell. To enter data in another cell, first make that cell active by moving the mouse pointer to it, using either the mouse or keyboard. You can also view another area of your worksheet and not move the active cell by using the scroll bars.

With Excel's capability to include up to 65,536 rows per worksheet, learning powerful navigation techniques becomes essential.

Mouse Movements

Using the mouse, you can activate a cell quickly by placing the mouse pointer on the cell and clicking the left mouse button. Figure 12.2 shows the mouse pointer highlighting the active cell.

FIG. 12.2
To activate a cell, place the mouse pointer on that cell and click the mouse.

Mouse pointer

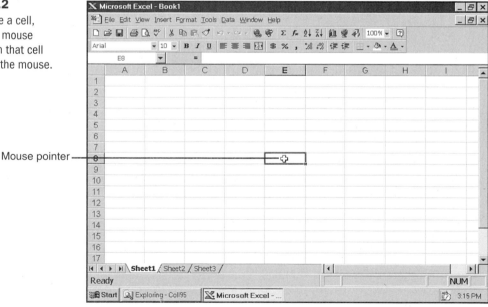

Part
III

Ch
12

Keyboard Movements

You can use the arrow, Page Up, and Page Down keys on your keyboard, or various key combinations, to move to another cell. The keys that you use to move to new locations are listed in Table 12.1.

Table 12.1   Using the Keyboard to Move Among Cells

Keys	Description
←,→,↑,↓	Moves one cell to the left, right, up, or down, respectively
Ctrl+←, →, ↑, ↓ End+←, →, ↑, ↓	Moves to the next nonblank cell
Tab	Moves one cell to the right
Enter	Moves one cell down
Shift+Tab	Moves one cell to the left
Shift+Enter	Moves one cell up
Home	Moves to column A of the active row
Ctrl+Home	Moves to cell A1 of the worksheet
Ctrl+End	Moves to the last cell used in the worksheet
Page Up	Moves up one screen
Page Down	Moves down one screen
Alt+Page Up	Moves one screen width to the left
Alt+Page Down	Moves one screen width to the right
Ctrl+Page Up	Moves to the following worksheet
Ctrl+Page Down	Moves to the preceding worksheet

Use the Go To command to move to a specific cell. Choose Edit, Go To, or press the F5 key to display the Go To dialog box (see Figure 12.3).

FIG. 12.3

The Go To dialog box enables you to move to a specific cell.

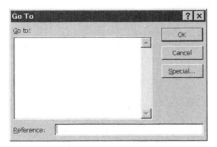

When the Go To dialog box appears, type the reference of the cell you want to move to in the Reference text box, and then press Enter. To move to cell D5, for example, type **D5**

and then press Enter or click the OK button. The mouse pointer moves to cell D5, which now becomes the active cell.

You also can move to a specific cell by using the *name box*, located at the left end of the formula bar. Click the box, type the address of the cell to which you want to move, and then press Enter. (The formula bar is discussed in "Entering Data," below.)

Moving Around by Scrolling

To view another section of the worksheet without moving the active cell, use the vertical and horizontal scroll bars to reposition the screen. Using the mouse, click the up or down scroll arrow to scroll line by line. You also can scroll the screen by dragging the scroll box up and down the scroll bar. If you click the scroll bar above the scroll box, the screen scrolls up one page. If you click the scroll bar below the scroll box, the screen scrolls down one page.

 When you drag the scroll box, the row number or column heading is displayed for your reference.

 To see the active cell when it's not visible in the current window, press Ctrl+Backspace. The window scrolls to display the active cell, and selected ranges remain selected.

To scroll through a worksheet by using the keyboard, press the Scroll Lock key on your keyboard, and use the arrow keys to scroll to the section of the worksheet you want to view. Scrolling moves the screen but does not change the active cell.

 If you're using the IntelliMouse pointing device, you can use the center wheel button to move up and down in the worksheet without using the scroll bars. You can also pan a worksheet by holding down the wheel button and dragging the pointer away from the mark of origin. Dragging away from the mark of origin speeds up scrolling; dragging toward this mark slows it down. This is very useful with large spreadsheets.

Entering Data

After you activate the cell in which you want to enter data, you can type text, numbers, dates, times, or formulas in the cell. As you type, the data appears in the active cell and in the area above the worksheet called the *formula bar* (see Figure 12.4). The active cell displays the *insertion point*, a blinking bar that indicates where the next character you type will appear.

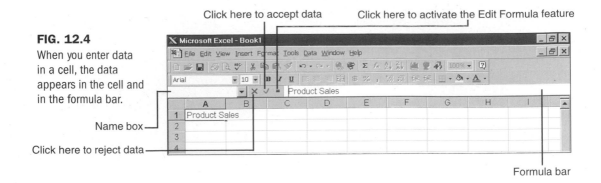

FIG. 12.4
When you enter data in a cell, the data appears in the cell and in the formula bar.

Click here to accept data

Click here to activate the Edit Formula feature

Name box

Click here to reject data

Formula bar

Three small boxes appear between the name box and the insertion point in the formula bar. The first two boxes enable you to reject or accept the data you entered. To reject your entry, click the x box or press Esc. To accept your entry, click the check box or press Enter. The third box in the formula bar activates the Edit Formula feature, which simplifies entering formulas in Excel. See the section "Entering Formulas" for more information on this feature.

Entering Text

Text entries consist of alphanumeric characters such as letters, numbers, and symbols. You can enter up to 32,000 characters in a single cell, although Excel may not be able to display all the characters if the cell is not wide enough and an entry appears in the cell to its right. When you enter text in a cell, Excel stores that entry as text and aligns it to the left edge of the cell.

When you enter data that consists of numbers and text, Excel evaluates the entry to determine its value. If you type an entry such as **1098 Adams Street**, for example, Excel automatically determines that it is a text entry because of the letters.

If you want to enter a number as text, such as a ZIP code, precede the entry with an apostrophe. For example, 46254 would be read as a number, but '46254 would be read as a text entry. You can use the apostrophe when you want to enter a number but do not want Excel to interpret it as a value to be used in calculations.

Entering Numbers

Numeric entries are constant values and consist only of numeric values. You can enter integers (such as **124**), decimal fractions (**14.426**), integer fractions (**1 1/5**), and values in scientific notation (**1.23E+08**).

▶ **See** "Changing Column Width and Row Height," **p. 351**

▶ **See** "Formatting Numbers," **p. 344**

TIP If you enter a long number in a cell and the cell displays as #####, the current column width is too small to display the number in its entirety. To fix this, double-click the right edge of the column to widen it.

Entering Dates and Times

In addition to entering text and numbers, you can enter dates and times in a worksheet cell. When you enter a date or time, Excel converts the entry to a serial date number, so that it can perform calculations based on these dates and times. The information in the cell is displayed in a regular date or time format, however.

 TIP To enter the current date in a cell quickly, press Ctrl+; (semicolon). To enter the current time, press Ctrl+: (colon).

Because Excel converts dates and times to serial numbers, you can perform calculations on these values as you would with any number. For example, you could determine the number of days that have passed between two dates.

You can enter a date using any of these formats:

8/12/96
12-Aug-96
12-Aug
Aug-12

To enter a time, use any of these formats:

14:25
14:25:09
2:25 PM
2:25:09 PM

Entering Formulas

One of the most valuable features of Excel is its capability to calculate values by using formulas. Excel formulas can range from the simple, such as adding a range of values, to the complex, such as calculating the future value of a stream of cash flows.

You can calculate values based on numbers that you type directly into the formula. For example, you can enter the formula **=4+5+7** to add the values 4, 5, and 7. However, the power of Excel's formula capability lies in the fact that formulas also can refer to data in other cells in the worksheet. The formula **=B2+B3+B4**, for example, adds the values in

Part

III

Ch

12

cells B2, B3, and B4. When the values in these cells change, Excel automatically updates and recalculates the formula, using the new data in these cells.

▶ **See** "Creating Formulas," **p. 374**

Excel recognizes a formula in a cell if the entry starts with an equal sign (=) or a plus sign (+) or a minus sign (–). To enter a formula, first type = and then type the formula. The active cell and the formula bar display the formula as you enter it. After the formula is complete, press Enter; the active cell displays the result of the formula (see Figure 12.5). The formula bar continues to show the formula when the cell is the active cell.

FIG. 12.5

When you enter a formula in a cell, Excel displays the result.

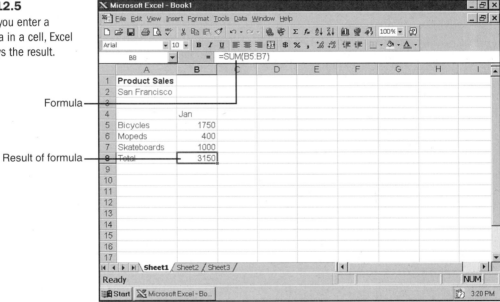

You can also use the Edit Formula feature to assist you in entering a formula. To do so, select the cell where you want to place the formula, then click the Edit Formula button on the formula bar. This activates a drop-down list of available functions to the left of the formula bar (see Figure 12.6). Functions in this list include SUM, AVERAGE, COUNT, and MAX.

Choose More Functions on the drop-down list to open the Paste Function dialog box, where you can create more sophisticated formulas.

▶ **See** "Entering Functions," **p. 393**

Select a function from the drop-down list, which then extends to form a dialog box (see Figure 12.7).

FIG. 12.6
Use the Edit Formula
button to display a
drop-down list of
available functions.

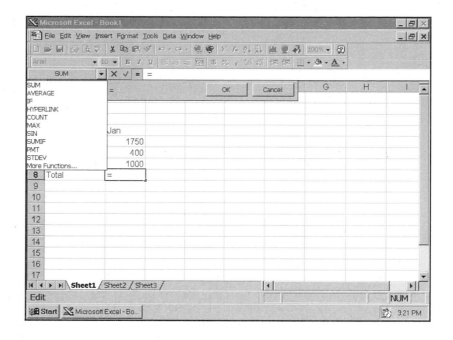

FIG. 12.7
The dialog box
helps you select
cell references for
your formula.

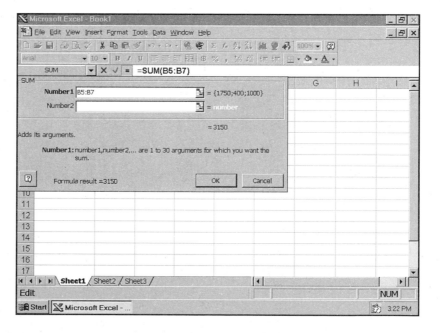

Part
III

Ch
12

Enter the information you want the function to use in the edit boxes that appear.

To use cell references, click the Cell Reference button to return to the Excel worksheet, select the cells, and click the Cell Reference button again to return to the dialog box.

The bottom of the dialog box now displays the formula result. Click OK to close. The formula you created now appears in the formula bar.

TROUBLESHOOTING

A formula used to calculate a range of cells does not calculate properly. Make sure that values in the range have not been entered as text. To do so, highlight each cell in the range and check for the appearance of an apostrophe at the beginning of the entry. If an apostrophe appears, press F2 to enter Edit mode, press the Home key to move to the beginning of the entry, press the Delete key to remove the apostrophe, and press Enter. Continue with these steps until all cell entries have been checked. You can also use the AutoCalculate feature to check the sum, average, or count of a range of data, described in the next section, "Selecting Cells and Ranges."

Excel converted a date to a number. You must enter dates in a format that Excel recognizes—for example, **3/12/96** or **12-Mar-96**. Other characters may not produce a valid date. Sometimes a cell in which you enter a date may already contain a numeric format. Choose Format, Cells to assign a different format.

A formula appears as text in a cell. If you neglect to enter an equal, plus, or minus sign in front of a cell reference, Excel interprets the entry as text. To fix this problem, highlight the cell and press F2. Then press the Home key, type the equal sign, and press Enter.

Selecting Cells and Ranges

Many commands in Excel require that you select a cell or range of cells. You already have learned how to select a single cell. You also can select several cells at the same time. A *range* is a group of cells that can be acted upon with Excel commands.

 Excel makes it easy to determine the active cell or range of cells in your worksheet. It highlights the row and column headings of all selected cells.

N O T E Excel's AutoCalculate feature displays the sum of selected cells in the status bar. This is a useful way to quickly calculate a range. For example, simply selecting cells A1 through A3 shows you the sum of this range. You can also display the average or count of a selected range by right-clicking the status bar at the bottom of the screen (bar that says Ready in the left corner) and choosing either Average or Count from the shortcut menu.

You can use the keyboard or the mouse to select a range. To select a range with the mouse, follow these steps:

1. Click a corner of the range you want to select.

2. Drag the mouse over the range.

3. When you reach the end of the selection range, release the mouse button.

To select a range with the keyboard, follow these steps:

1. Move to a cell at a corner of the range you want to select.

2. Press and hold down the Shift key, and then press the arrow keys to select the range.

Figure 12.8 shows a selected range.

FIG. 12.8

The first cell of the selected range is the active cell and has a white background.

Active cell

Selected range

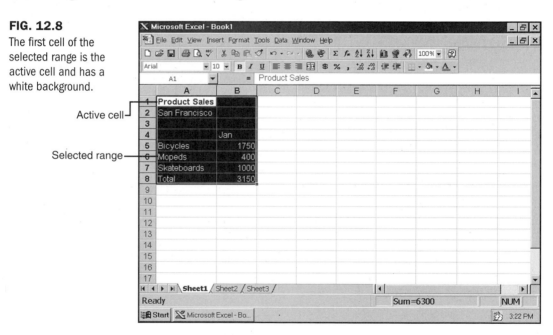

N O T E If you select a range of cells and then move the mouse pointer, the range is deselected. If this happens, just select the range again.

Excel also enables you to select more than one range of cells at a time with the same ease as selecting a single range.

To select multiple ranges with the mouse, follow these steps:

1. Click and drag the mouse over the first range you want to select.

2. Press and hold down the Ctrl key, and continue selecting other ranges.

To select multiple ranges with the keyboard, follow these steps:

1. Press and hold down the Shift key, and use the arrow keys to select the first range.

2. Press Shift+F8. The indicator ADD appears in the status bar at the bottom of the screen indicating that you can extend a selection.

3. Move to a cell at a corner of the next range you want to select.

4. Press Shift and an arrow key to select the range. ADD disappears from the status bar. To add another range, press Shift+F8 to go back to Add mode, and repeat steps 3 and 4.

To select the entire worksheet, click the rectangle directly above the row numbers and to the left of the column headings, or press Ctrl+Shift+spacebar. To deselect a range, click any cell.

> **CAUTION**
>
> When you select an entire worksheet, any command or action you perform affects the worksheet as a whole. If you press Delete while an entire worksheet is selected, for example, you delete all the data in the worksheet.

 T I P   To select nonadjacent columns or rows with the mouse, press and hold down the Ctrl key as you make your selections.

To select an entire row, click the heading of the row you want to select. You also can position the pointer in the row you want to select and press Shift+spacebar. Figure 12.9 shows two ranges selected in a worksheet.

To select an entire column, click the heading of the column you want to select. You also can position the pointer in the column you want to select and press Ctrl+spacebar (see Figure 12.10).

  Excel makes it easy to enter cell and range references in dialog boxes that require them. Clicking the Cell Reference button collapses the dialog box and more fully displays the worksheet so that you can select the appropriate cells. Just click the Cell Reference button again to return to the dialog box.

N O T E   Some Excel commands require a specific action before you can use the command. If you do not cut or copy something to the Clipboard, for example, you cannot choose Edit, Paste (it appears grayed or dimmed). If an object is not selected, the commands that are relevant only to selected objects are dimmed and unavailable. ▪

FIG. 12.9
Two nonadjacent ranges are selected at the same time.

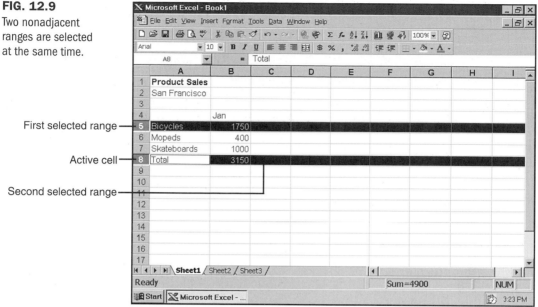

First selected range —
Active cell —
Second selected range —

Click column heading to select entire column

FIG. 12.10
Click a column heading to select an entire column; click a row heading to select an entire row.

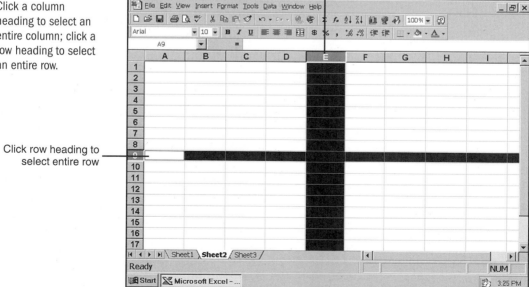

Click row heading to select entire row

Part
III

Ch
12

Entering a Series of Text, Numbers, and Dates

When creating budgets and forecasts, you often need to include a series of dates, numbers, or text. Excel relieves this tedious task by offering the AutoFill feature, which enables you to create a worksheet quickly by filling a range of cells with a sequence of entries. For example, you can fill a range of cells with consecutive dates or create a series of column titles.

You can create a series of entries in two ways:

- Use the mouse to drag the AutoFill handle (the small square at the bottom right corner of the active cell).
- Choose <u>E</u>dit, F<u>i</u>ll, <u>S</u>eries.

Another feature useful in creating a series is AutoComplete. As you enter data in a list, Excel memorizes each entry. If you begin to make an entry that matches a previous entry, Excel automatically completes it for you. You can accept the entry or continue typing new data. For example, if you type **San Francisco** in cell A3 and then begin entering the letter S in cell A4, Excel automatically enters **San Francisco** in A4. This helps cut down on the time it takes to enter data, as well as prevent errors.

You can also choose potential entries from a list of your previous entries, just as you can in the database application Access. To do this, right-click your mouse and choose Pic<u>k</u> From List from the shortcut menu. A list of all your previous entries pops up and you can choose your desired entry from it.

Creating a Series of Text Entries

Excel recognizes common text entries, such as days, months, and quarterly abbreviations.

To fill a range of cells with text entries, follow these steps:

1. Select the first cell that contains the data.
2. Drag the AutoFill handle over the range of adjacent cells that you want to fill (see Figure 12.11).
3. Release the mouse button. Excel fills the range of selected cells with the appropriate text entries (see Figure 12.12).

Excel's AutoFill feature recognizes numbers, dates, times, and keywords, such as days of the week, month names, and quarterly abbreviations. Excel knows how these series run and extends the series to repeat correctly. Table 12.2 shows examples of series that Excel can use with AutoFill.

FIG. 12.11
The AutoFill handle is dragged to the right to create a series of column titles.

AutoFill handle of the cell containing data

Range to fill

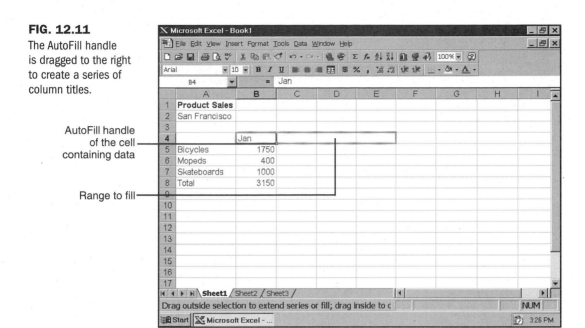

FIG. 12.12
Excel fills the selected range of cells with a series of column titles.

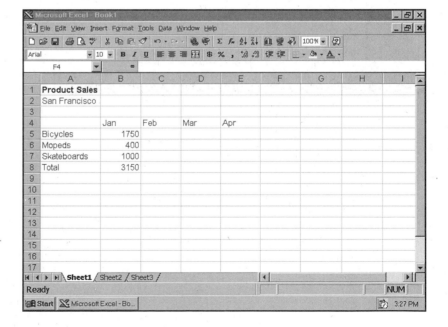

Part
III

Ch
12

Table 12.2   Fill Sequences

Data You Enter	Sequence Returned
10:00	11:00, 12:00
Qtr 1	Qtr 2, Qtr 3, Qtr 4
Product 1	Product 2, Product 3, Product 4
1993	1994, 1995, 1996, 1997
Jan	Feb, Mar, Apr
Jan 93	Jan 94, Jan 95, Jan 96, Jan 97
Jan 96, Apr 96	Jul 96, Oct 96, Jan 97
Mon	Tue, Wed, Thu
North	South, East, West
2, 4	6, 8, 10, ...

Creating a Series of Numbers

You can enter a series of numbers that increment by 1 or that increment by values you specify.

To fill a range of cells with a series of numbers, follow these steps:

1. Enter the starting number in the first cell of the range. If you want to increment the numbers by a value you specify, enter the first two values in adjacent cells.

 Excel uses these two values to determine the amount to increment in each step.

2. Select the range containing the numbers.
3. Drag the fill handle over the range of adjacent cells you want to fill.
4. Release the mouse button. Excel fills the range of selected cells with the appropriate numeric entries (see Figure 12.13).

 To prevent a series from incrementing, hold down the Ctrl key as you drag the AutoFill handle.

To increment by a value other than 1, enter
desired values in the first two cells of the range

FIG. 12.13
The AutoFill handle
creates this series
of numbers in
increments of 100.

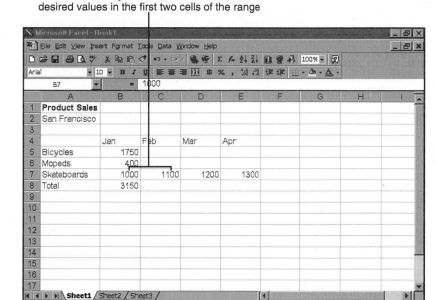

Creating a Series of Dates

You can fill a range of cells with a series of consecutive dates that increment by a specific
value.

To fill a range of cells with dates, follow these steps:

1. Enter the starting date in the first cell in the range. If you want to increment the date
   by a specific value, enter the appropriate date in the next cell in the range.

2. Select the range containing the dates.

3. Drag the AutoFill handle over the range of adjacent cells you want to fill.

4. Release the mouse button. Excel fills the range of selected cells with the appropriate
   dates (see Figure 12.14).

Entering a Series with the Edit Fill Series Command

Choosing Edit, Fill, Series enables you to fill a range of cells with greater precision than
you can with the AutoFill handle. For example, when you choose Edit, Fill, Series, you can
specify a stop value as well as a start value.

Part
III

Ch
12

FIG. 12.14
The AutoFill handle created this series of dates in increments of one day.

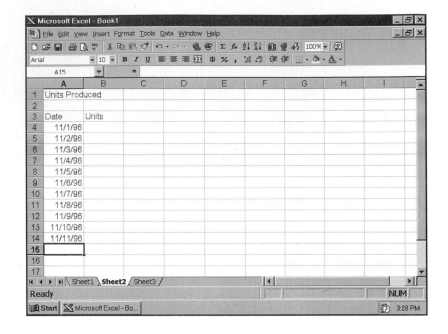

To fill a range of cells by choosing Edit, Fill Series, follow these steps:

1. Enter the starting number or date in the first cell of the range you want to fill.

2. Select the range of cells you want to fill.

3. Choose Edit, Fill, Series. The Series dialog box appears (see Figure 12.15).

FIG. 12.15
In the Series dialog box, select the type of series and the step and stop values.

4. Indicate whether you want to fill your series in Rows or Columns.

5. Specify the Type of series you want to create.

6. If you are creating a series of dates, specify the Date Unit.

7. Enter the Step Value. This value represents the amount by which the series changes from cell to cell.

8. Enter the Stop Value. This value represents the last value in the series.

9. Choose OK.

TROUBLESHOOTING

AutoFill filled the entire range with the same text entered in the first cell of the range. When Excel cannot recognize the correct pattern for entering text, AutoFill copies the selected cells to the entire range. Make sure that the starting text is one that AutoFill can recognize—for example, Qtr 1 or January.

I tried to use AutoFill to extend a series, but numbers were not incremented by the difference of the first two numbers of my series. If the increment in the AutoFill range was 1, you probably did not select the first two cells before using AutoFill. Be sure to select the two cells, because that is what Excel uses to determine the increment; otherwise, it defaults to 1. If the increment was not the difference between your first two cells or 1, you probably selected more than two cells and Excel averaged the difference to determine the increment. Again, be sure to just select two cells.

Repeating and Undoing a Command

 Excel has a built-in safety net that enables you to reverse many commands or actions. The Edit, Undo command reverses the last command you selected or the last action you performed. To undo a command or action, choose Edit, Undo, or press Ctrl+Z.

Undo is not available for all commands. If you choose Edit, Delete Sheet and delete a worksheet from a workbook, for example, the Edit menu shows Can't Undo as a dimmed command. Although Undo can reverse many actions, you still must use certain commands with caution.

 You can undo up to 16 previous actions in Excel. To reverse the Undo command, choose Edit, Undo again or press Ctrl+Z.

Excel also enables you to repeat the last command or action you performed. To repeat a command or action, choose Edit, Repeat, or press Ctrl+Y.

Saving Workbooks

 N O T E If you're saving a copy of a shared workbook, you can merge the contents of other copies of the workbook into it by choosing Tools, Merge Wookbooks and choosing these files in the Select Files to Merge Into Current Workbook dialog box.

▶ **See** "Sharing a Workbook," **p. 1165**

Part

III

Ch

12

When you create a new workbook, Excel assigns to it the name Book1 if it is the first workbook created, Book2 if it is the second, and continues to increment in this pattern. You must save the file to disk to make the workbook permanent. To save a file in Excel, choose File, Save, or press Ctrl+S. Enter a name for the file and specify the location to which the workbook should be saved.

When you have several files open that you need to save when you exit Excel, you can eliminate unnecessary steps by saving all open files at once. To do so, choose File, Exit and then click the Yes to All button in the dialog box that appears.

CAUTION

A macro virus is a virus that's stored in a workbook's macros when you save it. When you open a workbook with a macro virus, the virus is activated and can spread. Excel can display a warning dialog box every time you open a workbook that contains a macro. If you're sure that you want to use the macros in this workbook, you can choose to Enable Macros. If you're not sure about the workbook, choose to Disable Macros so that you can view them, but not activate them. Choose Tools, Options and then check the Macro Virus Protection box in the General tab to use this feature.

In addition to saving new workbooks, you can also save files to other file formats, such as previous versions of Excel or Lotus 1-2-3 or delimited text. Excel also enables you to save workbook settings in a workspace file.

Saving Files to Other File Formats

N O T E   You can also save an Excel worksheet as an HTML file for publishing on the Web by choosing File, Save as HTML, which opens the Internet Assitant Wizard. Excel 97 includes many other exciting new Internet features. You can jump to other files using hyperlinks, access Excel workbooks on your company's intranet, or use the Web toolbar to browse Web files. Refer to Chapter 44, "Navigating and Publishing on the Web with Office 97," for more information. ▪

When you save a file, Excel automatically assigns an extension to the file. If you are saving a workbook, the extension is XLS; the extension for a template is XLT; and the extension for a workspace is XLW.

You can use the Save as Type drop-down list to save an Excel file in another file format. To save an Excel file for use in Lotus 1-2-3, for example, drop down the Save as Type list, and then select the Lotus 1-2-3 file format you want (see Figure 12.16). Excel supports 1-2-3 Releases 1 (WKS), 2 (WK1), 3 (WK3), and 4 (WK4).

If you use a worksheet feature that is not supported by earlier versions of Excel or other spreadsheets, the value result of that feature is calculated and saved with the worksheet.

FIG. 12.16
You can save an
Excel file in a 1-2-3
file format.

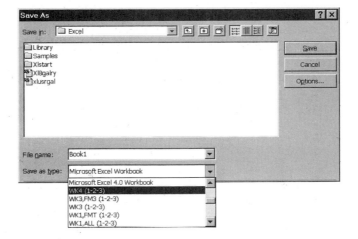

Saving a Workspace File

If you work with the same set of workbooks on a daily basis, Excel enables you to save
information about what workbooks are open and how they are arranged on-screen. The
next time you want to work with these workbooks, you only need to open the workspace
file, and all the workbooks are opened and arranged as they were when you saved the file.

The File, Save Workspace command creates a workspace file that contains the name and
location of each workbook in the workspace and the position of each workbook when the
workspace was saved.

To create a workspace file, follow these steps:

1. Open and arrange the workbooks as you want them to be saved in the workspace.
2. Choose File, Save Workspace. Figure 12.17 shows the Save Workspace dialog box
   that is displayed.
3. Type a name for the workspace file in the File Name text box.
4. Choose OK.

> **CAUTION**
> When you create a workspace file, do not move any of the workbook files to a new location. If you do,
> Excel will not be able to locate the files when you open the workspace file.

Part
III

Ch
12

FIG. 12.17
Type a name for the
workspace file in the
Save Workspace
dialog box.

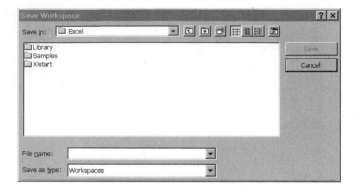

You can open a workspace file just as you would any other Excel file. After you have opened the file, you can save and close the individual workbooks in the workspace as you normally would. When you make changes to a workbook in the workspace, you must save the file by choosing File, Save. The File, Save Workspace command saves only information on which workbooks are open and how they are arranged on-screen.

Saving as an HTML File

You can also save an Excel worksheet as an HTML file for publishing on the World Wide Web by choosing File, Save as HTML, which opens the Internet Assistant Wizard. Excel 97 includes many other exciting new Internet features. You can jump to other files using hyperlinks, access Excel workbooks on your company's intranet, or use the Web toolbar to browse Web files. Refer to Chapter 44, "Navigating and Publishing on the Web with Office 97," for more information.

> **N O T E** Excel 97 includes many exciting new Internet features. You can publish data from Excel workbooks on the Web, jump to other files using hyperlinks, access Excel workbooks on your company's intranet, or use the Web toolbar to browse Web files. ■

▶ **See** "Hyperlinks Between Documents," **p. 1005**
▶ **See** "Navigating and Publishing on the Web with Office 97," **p. 1025**

CHAPTER 13

Editing Worksheets

by Patrice-Anne Rutledge

After creating a worksheet, you will spend the majority of your time editing the work you have done. You may need to move data from one area of the worksheet to another, or you may want to copy a range of data. This chapter presents the basics for editing a worksheet in Excel. ∎

Worksheet data copying

Use the copy and paste, AutoFill, or Format Painter method to copy worksheet data.

Worksheet data movement

In Excel, you can use either the drag-and-drop or cut and paste method to move your worksheet data.

Column, row, and cell insertion and deletion

Excel provides two menu options as well as toolbar buttons to simplify insertion and deletion tasks.

Worksheet insertion and deletion

Excel offers several techniques for inserting, deleting, moving, copying, and renaming worksheets.

Worksheet data find and replace

You can search for and replace data in Excel worksheets by entering exact data or wildcards.

Checking spelling

The Spelling feature enables you to find and correct spelling errors based on a standard or customized dictionary. Excel also automatically corrects many common errors as you type.

Editing Worksheet Data

After you enter data in a cell, you can edit the contents of the cell. You can edit the contents using the formula bar, or you can use the in-cell editing feature of Excel to edit the contents directly in the cell.

N O T E To use the in-cell editing feature of Excel, you must make sure that the feature has been enabled. To double-check, choose Tools, Options, and select the Edit tab. The Edit Directly in Cell option should be selected. If it isn't, click the check box to the left of the option. Choose OK when you finish. ■

Editing an Existing Cell Entry

To edit the contents of a cell, first select the cell you want to edit, and then click the formula bar or press F2. The contents of the cell appear in the formula bar. You can also edit the contents directly in the cell by double-clicking it.

▶ **See** "Formatting Numbers," **p. 344**

To edit the entry, use the left and right arrow keys to reposition the insertion point in the cell, or move the mouse and use the I-beam pointer to reposition the insertion point in the cell. The vertical blinking bar appears where the I-beam is positioned when you click the mouse (see Figure 13.1). Then press Delete or Backspace to delete characters to the right or left of the insertion point, respectively.

When editing a cell, you can reposition the insertion point by using the mouse or the keyboard. Table 13.1 lists the editing keys on the keyboard.

Table 13.1 Editing Keys

Key	Action
←	Moves one character to the left.
→	Moves one character to the right.
Ctrl+→	Moves to the next word.
Ctrl+←	Moves to the preceding word.
End	Moves to the end of the cell entry.
Home	Moves to the beginning of the cell entry.
Delete	Deletes next character to the right.
Backspace	Deletes preceding character.

FIG. 13.1
The insertion point
shows where the next
character you type will
appear.

Insertion point —

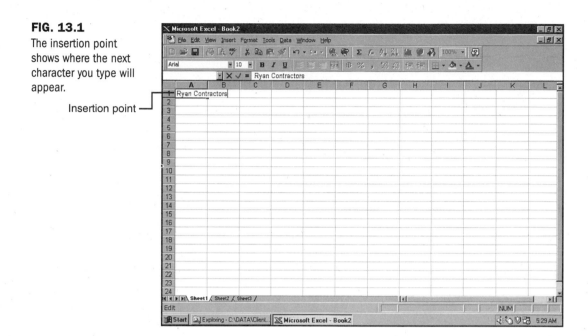

Deleting Worksheet Data

In addition to editing the contents of a cell, you can delete the data in a cell. To replace an existing cell entry, select the cell and type the new entry. When you do, the new entry replaces the current contents of the cell. If you want to delete the contents of a cell or range altogether, the easiest way to do it is to select the cell or range of cells and then press the Delete key. When you do, Excel clears the contents of the cell or range.

Clearing Cell Contents

 T I P To clear the contents of a cell or range quickly, highlight the range, click the right mouse button, and choose Clear Contents from the shortcut menu.

When you use the Delete key to clear a cell, Excel clears all data from the cell, but does not change cell formatting. The Edit, Clear command, on the other hand, enables you to choose what you want to clear from the cell.

To clear the contents of a cell or range, select the cell or range and then choose Edit, Clear. From the Edit Clear submenu, select the command that represents the data you want to clear.

Part
III

Ch

13

Choose All to clear everything from the cell, including cell formatting and cell notes. Choose Formats to clear only cell formatting from the cell. To clear the contents of a cell but leave formatting and cell notes intact, choose Contents. To remove only comments from a selected range of cells, choose Comments.

▶ **See** "Changing Fonts, Sizes, and Styles," **p. 358**

▶ **See** "Annotating Worksheets," **p. 449**

> **CAUTION**
>
> A common error many new users make when clearing cells is selecting the cell and then pressing the space bar. Although the cell may appear to be blank, Excel actually stores the space in the cell. Spaces can cause problems in worksheet calculations. Do not press the space bar to clear a cell. Instead, use the methods outlined in this section.

N O T E Excel's new Track Changes feature enables you to highlight changes you or another user makes to a worksheet. To use this feature, select Tools, Track Changes, Highlight Changes. Select the revised cell; a pop-up box tells you what changes have been made, who made them, and the date they were made. You can also accept or reject these changes later. ■

T I P For more information on the Track Changes feature, please refer to *Special Edition Using Microsoft Excel 97*, also published by Que.

Copying Worksheet Data

The quickest way to copy worksheet data is to use the drag-and-drop method. As its name implies, you simply drag the data you want to copy to another area of the worksheet.

▶ **See** "Copying and Moving Data," **p. 78**

To copy data with drag-and-drop, follow these steps:

1. Select the range of cells you want to copy.

2. Position the mouse pointer on the border of the selected data.

3. Hold down the Ctrl key, and click and drag the selection to the new location.

    As you move the mouse pointer, Excel displays an outline indicating the size and location of the copied data (see Figure 13.2).

4. Release the mouse button to drop the copied data in its new location.

FIG. 13.2
An outline indicates the location where the copied data will be placed.

Selected text to be copied

Location where you want to copy data

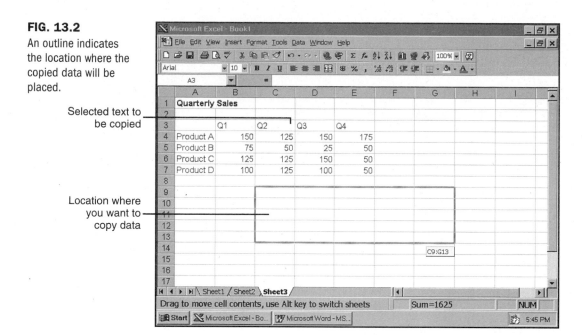

Copying Data with Copy and Paste

When you need to make multiple copies of worksheet data, the easiest way to accomplish this is to use the Edit, Copy and Edit, Paste commands. When you choose Edit, Copy, a copy of the selected data is stored on the Clipboard. You then can paste as many copies in the worksheet as you need.

▶ **See** "Copying and Moving Data," **p. 78**

To copy data by choosing Edit, Copy and Edit, Paste, follow these steps:

1. Select the range of data you want to copy.

2. Choose Edit, Copy, or press Ctrl+C. Alternatively, click the right mouse button and then choose Copy from the resulting shortcut menu.

   A marquee surrounds the selection you copied, and the status bar at the bottom of the screen prompts you to select the location where you want to copy the data (see Figure 13.3).

3. Select the cell in which you want to paste a copy of the data.

4. Choose Edit, Paste, or press Ctrl+V. Alternatively, click the right mouse button and then choose Paste from the resulting shortcut menu. If you want to paste a single copy of the selection, press Enter.

Part
III

Ch
13

FIG. 13.3

A marquee surrounds the copied data.

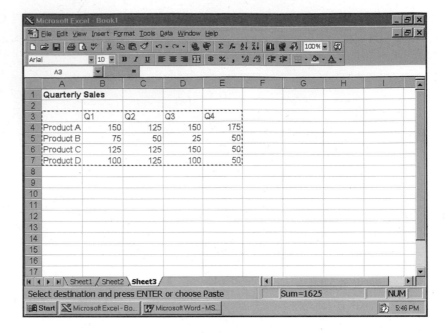

N O T E   As long as the marquee surrounds the copied data, you can continue to choose Edit, Paste to paste copies of the data in the worksheet. If you press Enter to paste a copy of the data in the worksheet, Excel clears the copied data from the Clipboard. ■

Copying Data with AutoFill

The AutoFill command enables you to copy cell contents to adjacent cells quickly. As a bonus, if the entry consists of a date, day of the week, or alphanumeric item such as Product 1, Excel automatically extends the series in the selected cells (see Figure 13.4).

▶ **See** "Entering a Series of Text, Numbers, and Dates," **p. 312**

To use the AutoFill command to copy data, follow these steps:

1. Select the cell that contains the data you want to copy.

2. Position the mouse pointer on the fill handle that appears in the lower right corner of the cell.

3. Drag the fill handle over the adjacent cells in which the copied data will appear, and release the mouse button.

FIG. 13.4
The AutoFill command filled A5..A12 with Product 2 through 12. Product 1 was originally in cell A4.

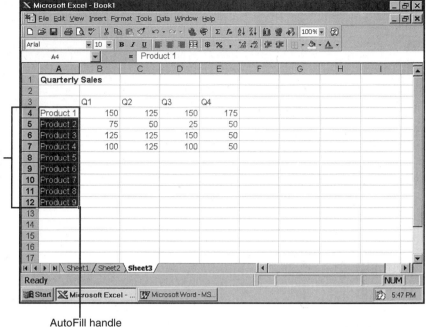

AutoFill extends the series in the selected cells

AutoFill handle

Copying and Applying Formats

Another option for copying data in your worksheet is to copy cell formatting from one range to another. This feature is handy if you want to apply formatting to a range of cells but don't want to create a style.

▶ **See** "Creating and Applying a Style," **p. 363**

To copy formatting from one range to another, follow these steps:

1. Select the range of cells that contains the formatting you want to copy.

2. Click the Format Painter button, or double-click the button if you want to apply the formatting to more than one range. Figure 13.5 shows the result of using the Format Painter.

3. Select the cell or range of cells where you want to apply the formatting. When you release the mouse button, Excel applies the formatting.

4. Continue selecting each additional range of cells. If you double-clicked the Format Painter button, click the button again to turn off the feature or press Esc.

Part

III

Ch

13

TROUBLESHOOTING

I tried to copy data using drag-and-drop, but it wasn't working. Excel would just select the range of cells rather than copy the data. The cell drag-and-drop feature is probably turned off. To check, choose Tools, Options, and select the Edit tab. Make sure that the Allow Cell Drag and Drop check box is selected (if it is, an X appears in the check box). Choose OK.

If the drag-and-drop feature is enabled, remember that you must click the outer edge of the selected range and then drag the selection.

I used the Edit Copy and Edit Paste commands to copy a range of data in my worksheet. I pressed Enter to paste the data into the new location, and it worked without a hitch. But when I tried to choose Edit, Paste to paste another copy, Paste was unavailable. When you choose Edit, Copy to move a range of data, Excel does indeed copy the data to the Clipboard. But when you press Enter to paste the data, Excel clears the contents of the Clipboard. Notice also that the marquee surrounding the data disappears.

If you want to paste multiple copies of the data in the worksheet, do not press the Enter key to paste the data. Instead, continue to choose Edit, Paste to paste the copies in the worksheet.

I tried to copy a range of data by using AutoFill, but I just moved the selected cell when I dragged it. You probably dragged the edge of the cell rather than the AutoFill handle. The AutoFill handle is located on the lower right corner of the cell, and the mouse pointer changes to a solid plus sign (±) instead of an arrow when placed on the AutoFill handle.

FIG. 13.5
The Format Painter button enables you to copy formatting from one range of cells to another.

Format Painter button

Data containing format you want to copy

Selected range to which formats will be copied

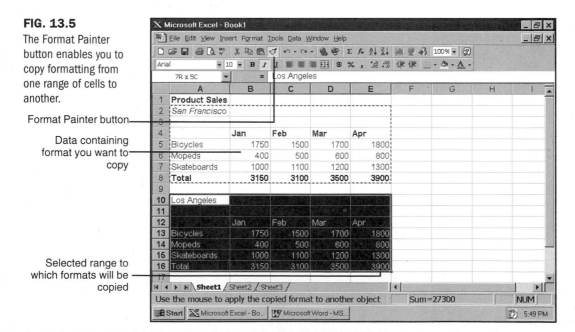

Moving Worksheet Data

As with copying, you can move worksheet data from one area of the worksheet to another. You can use the drag-and-drop method to move a range of data quickly, or you can use the Edit Cut and Edit Paste commands to cut a range of data and paste it in another location.

Moving Data with Drag-and-Drop

When you use the drag-and-drop method to move data, you are physically moving the range of data from one area to another. This is different from copying, which keeps the source data intact.

To move a range of data with drag-and-drop, follow these steps:

1. Select the range that contains the data you want to move.

2. Position the mouse pointer on the border of the selected data.

3. Click and drag the selection to the new location. As you move the mouse, a border appears in the worksheet, indicating the location where the data will appear.

4. Release the mouse button to drop the selected data in the new location.

NOTE Excel does not allow you to overwrite existing data automatically when you use drag-and-drop. A message appears, warning you that you are about to overwrite existing data. Choose Cancel and indicate a new position, or choose OK if you want to overwrite cells.

Moving Data with Cut and Paste

When you choose Edit, Cut (Ctrl+X) to move worksheet data, a copy of the data is stored on the Windows Clipboard. You then can paste the data in another area of the worksheet.

To move data by choosing Edit, Cut, follow these steps:

1. Select the range of data you want to move.

 2. Choose Edit, Cut, or press Ctrl+X. Alternatively, click the right mouse button and then choose Cut from the resulting shortcut menu.

   A marquee surrounds the selection you cut, and the status bar at the bottom of the screen prompts you to select the location where you want to paste the data.

3. Select the cell in which you want the data to appear, and then choose Edit, Paste, or press Ctrl+V. Alternatively, click the right mouse button and choose Paste from the resulting shortcut menu. You also can press Enter.

N O T E   When choosing <u>E</u>dit, <u>P</u>aste to paste data from the Clipboard, indicate a single cell rather than a range of cells in which to paste the data. If you select a range of cells, the range you select must be the same size as the range you placed on the Clipboard. ■

TROUBLESHOOTING

I tried to move a range of data by using drag-and-drop, but the data I was trying to move was instead copied to the range of cells I wanted it to move to. You probably dragged the AutoFill handle rather than the edge of the cell. The AutoFill handle is located on the lower-right corner of the cell and is used to quickly fill a range of cells with the data. When the mouse is positioned on the AutoFill handle, the mouse pointer changes to a solid plus sign (+) instead of an arrow.

To move the data, position the mouse pointer on an edge of the cell, and then drag the mouse to move the data.

When I chose <u>E</u>dit, <u>P</u>aste to move a range of data, Excel pasted only a portion of the data in the selected range. When pasting data, make sure that you select a single cell in which to paste the data. When you do, Excel pastes the entire range. If you select more than one cell and the selected range is smaller than the original range of cells, Excel pastes only the data that will fit in the selected range.

▶ **See** "Referencing Cells in Formulas," **p. 376**

N O T E   When copying and moving formulas, keep in mind that Excel may adjust cell references in the formula to reflect the new location. When you copy a formula, Excel adjusts the cell references. When you move a formula, Excel does not adjust cell references. ■

Inserting and Deleting Columns, Rows, and Cells

Another area of editing you'll perform in Excel is that of inserting and deleting columns, rows, and cells. Sometimes, restructuring a worksheet entails more than moving data to another location. For example, if you add another sales region to your sales tracking worksheet, you can insert a new column to hold the data. Likewise, if you remove a product from your product line, you can delete the rows that contain the data.

Inserting Columns, Rows, and Cells

When you need to insert additional space in your worksheet, you can insert columns, rows, and cells in the middle of existing data. When you insert columns, rows, and cells, existing data shifts to accommodate the insertion.

To insert a column, follow these steps:

1. Position the cell pointer in the column where the new column should appear.
2. Choose Insert, Columns, or click the right mouse button on the column header and then choose Insert from the shortcut menu. Excel inserts a new column, and existing columns shift to the right.

To insert a row, follow these steps:

1. Select a cell in the row below where the new row should appear.
2. Choose Insert, Rows, or click the right mouse button on the row header and then choose Insert from the shortcut menu. Excel inserts a new row, and existing rows move down.

To insert a cell or range, follow these steps:

1. Select the cell or range where the new cells should appear.
2. Choose Insert, Cells, or click the right mouse button and then choose Insert from the shortcut menu. The Insert dialog box appears (see Figure 13.6).

FIG. 13.6

The Insert dialog box prompts you to specify the direction in which the existing cells should move.

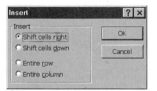

3. Select Shift Cells Right to insert the new cells to the left of the selection. Select Shift Cells Down to insert the new cells above the selection.
4. Choose OK. The selected cells move in the direction you specified.

Deleting Columns, Rows, and Cells

You can delete columns, rows, and cells from your worksheet when they contain data that is no longer needed. When you delete columns, rows, and cells, existing data moves to close the space.

To delete a column, follow these steps:

1. Click the letter of the column you want to delete. To delete multiple columns, highlight each additional column.

2. Choose Edit, Delete, or click the right mouse button in the selection and then choose Delete from the shortcut menu. The selected column is removed from the worksheet, and existing columns move to the left.

To delete a row, follow these steps:

1. Click the number of the row you want to delete. To delete multiple rows, highlight each additional row.

2. Choose Edit, Delete, or click the right mouse button in the selection and then choose Delete from the shortcut menu. The selected row is removed from the worksheet, and existing rows move up.

> **CAUTION**
>
> Use care when choosing Edit, Insert and Delete in your worksheets. When you use these commands, the entire worksheet is affected by your action. If a formula refers to a cell that is deleted, for example, the cell containing the formula returns the #REF! error value. If this occurs, choose Edit, Undo immediately after making a deletion.

To delete a cell or range of cells, follow these steps:

1. Select the range of cells that you want to delete.

2. Choose Edit, Delete, or click the right mouse button in the selection and then choose Delete from the shortcut menu. The Delete dialog box appears (see Figure 13.7).

FIG. 13.7
In the Delete dialog box, specify the direction in which the existing cells should move.

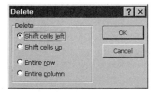

3. Select Shift Cells Left; the existing data moves to the left. Choose Shift Cells Up; the existing data moves up.

4. Choose OK after you make your selection.

Inserting and Deleting Sheets

Excel provides true 3-D functionality, which enables you to create workbooks that contain multiple sheets of data. Each new workbook you create contains 3 worksheets, but you can add additional worksheets, as well as delete worksheets that you no longer need.

Inserting Sheets

 T I P Be sure to position the mouse pointer over the sheet tab before trying to use the shortcut menu (the menu that appears when you right-click the mouse) to insert a new worksheet, or Excel may only provide options for inserting a new row or column. This also applies when using this feature to delete, rename, move, or copy a worksheet.

When you insert a worksheet, Excel inserts the sheet before the current worksheet. To insert a worksheet, select the sheet to the right of where the new worksheet should appear, and choose Insert, Worksheet. Or, position the mouse pointer over an existing sheet tab, right-click the mouse, and choose Insert from the shortcut menu. The Insert dialog box appears (see Figure 13.8); select the Worksheet icon from the General tab and click OK. Excel inserts a sheet and assigns a name to the sheet.

FIG. 13.8
Select the Worksheet icon in the Insert dialog box to add a new worksheet to your workbook.

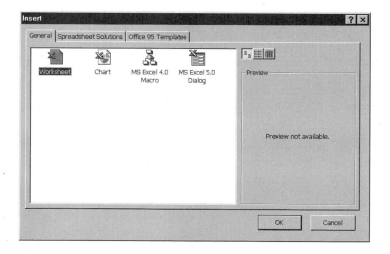

Deleting Sheets

To delete a sheet, move to the sheet you want to delete, and then choose Edit, Delete Sheet. You can also position the mouse pointer over an existing sheet tab, right-click the mouse, and choose Delete from the shortcut menu. Excel deletes the sheet.

Moving Sheets

In addition to inserting and deleting sheets, you can rearrange worksheets in the workbook by moving them to a new location.

Excel employs the drag-and-drop method for moving sheets. To move a sheet, click the tab of the sheet you want to move. Hold down the mouse button, and drag the sheet to the new position in the workbook. When you release the mouse button, the sheet is dropped in its new location.

Alternatively, position the mouse pointer over an existing sheet tab, right-click the mouse, and choose Move or Copy from the shortcut menu. The Move or Copy dialog box appears (see Figure 13.9). Select the book to which you want to move your worksheet in the To Book drop-down list. Choose where to place the worksheet in the Before Sheet drop-down list. You can also select the Create a Copy box to copy your worksheet. Click OK to finish.

FIG. 13.9
Use this dialog box to move or copy Excel worksheets.

Naming Sheets

Initially, Excel names each worksheet in the workbook Sheet1, Sheet2, and continues incrementing. You can, however, easily rename a sheet to reflect the data it contains. In a Monthly Sales worksheet, for example, you can use a separate sheet for each sales region. You then could name each sheet North, South, East, and West. Thereafter, anyone else who uses the worksheet will be able to tell what the worksheet contains just by looking at the name.

To rename a worksheet, double-click the sheet tab of the worksheet you want to rename. Or, position the mouse pointer over an existing sheet tab, right-click the mouse, and choose Rename from the shortcut menu. The worksheet name is highlighted, and you can edit or rename it.

Finding and Replacing Worksheet Data

Excel provides the capability to find and (optionally) replace specific data in your worksheet. You can, for example, search for all occurrences of the value 1995 and replace it with 1996.

Finding Worksheet Data

You can search the entire workbook, or you can search only a selected worksheet range. To search the entire workbook, select a single cell. To search a specified range, select the range that you want to search. Follow these steps to perform a search:

1. Choose Edit, Find, or press Ctrl+F. The Find dialog box appears (see Figure 13.10).

FIG. 13.10
The Find command enables you to locate specific data in your worksheets.

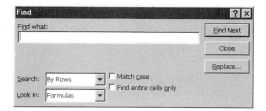

2. In the Find What text box, type the data you want to find. Then specify the search options, described in Table 13.2.

3. Choose Find Next to begin the search. When Excel locates the characters, choose Find Next to find the next occurrence, or choose Replace to access the Replace dialog box (this option is discussed in the next section).

4. Choose Close to end the search and close the dialog box.

TIP If the Find dialog box is obstructing your view of the worksheet, click and drag the title bar of the dialog box until you can see the active cell in the worksheet.

Part
III

Ch

13

Table 13.2   Find Options

Option	Action
Search	Specifies whether to search across rows or down columns.
Look In	Selects the location of the data: cell formulas, cell values, or cell notes.

continues

Table 13.2 Continued

Option	Action
Match Case	Finds only characters that match the case of the characters you specified.
Find Entire Cells Only	Searches for an exact match of the characters you specified. It does not find partial occurrences.
Find Next	Finds the next occurrence of the search string.
Close	Ends the search and returns to the worksheet.
Replace	Opens the Replace dialog box (discussed in the next section).

NOTE If you're not sure of the specific string you are looking for, you can specify wild-card characters in the search string to locate data that contains some or all of the characters. You can use an asterisk (*) to search for any group of characters and a question mark (?) to search for any single character. ▪

Replacing Worksheet Data

The Edit, Replace command (Ctrl+H) is similar to the Find command in that it enables you to locate specific characters in your worksheet. The Replace command then enables you to replace the characters with new data.

To replace worksheet data, follow these steps:

1. To search the entire workbook, select a single cell. To search a specified range, select the range you want to search.

2. Choose Edit, Replace. The Replace dialog box appears (see Figure 13.11).

FIG. 13.11
You can use the Edit Replace command to replace formulas, text, or values.

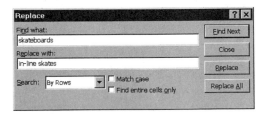

3. In the Find What text box, type the data you want to replace. In the Replace With text box, type the data with which you want to replace the current data.

4. Specify the replace options, as described in Table 13.3.

CAUTION

Make sure that Find Entire Cells Only is activated if you are replacing values or formulas. If it is not selected, Excel replaces characters even if they are inside other strings. For example, replacing 20 with 30 also makes 2,000 become 3,000.

5. Choose Find Next to begin the search. When Excel locates the first occurrence of the characters, choose the appropriate replace option (see Table 13.3).

6. Choose Close to close the dialog box.

Table 13.3   Replace Options

Option	Action
Search	Specifies whether to search across rows or down columns.
Match Case	Finds only characters that match the case of the characters you specified.
Find Entire Cells Only	Searches for an exact match of the characters you specified. It does not find partial occurrences.
Find Next	Finds the next occurrence.
Close	Closes the Replace dialog box.
Replace	Replaces the characters in the active cell with those specified in the Replace With text box.
Replace All	Replaces all occurrences of the characters with those specified in the Replace With text box.

 TIP If you make a mistake when replacing data, close the dialog box, and choose Edit, Undo (Ctrl+Z) immediately to reverse the replacement. Or, save your spreadsheet before replacing and then either save again if everything appears correct, or close without saving if you make a mistake.

Part
III

Ch
13

CAUTION

When replacing data in your worksheet, use Replace All with care, because the results may not be what you expect. Whenever you use Replace, it's a good idea to first locate the data you want to replace to make sure that the data is correct.

Spell Checking the Worksheet

Excel's Spelling command enables you to check worksheets, macro sheets, and charts for misspellings and to correct the errors quickly. The spelling feature offers a standard dictionary and also enables you to create an alternate customized dictionary to store frequently used words not found in the standard dictionary. When you check spelling, Excel looks in the standard dictionary and the custom dictionary for the correct spelling.

In addition to finding spelling errors, Excel finds repeating words and words that might not be properly capitalized. You can check spelling in the entire workbook, a single cell, or a selected range.

 T I P To check the spelling in more than one worksheet, select the tab of each sheet you want to check.

To check the spelling of data in your worksheet, follow these steps:

1. Specify the worksheet range you want to check. To check the entire worksheet, select cell A1. Excel starts checking from the active cell and moves forward to the end of the worksheet. To check a specific word or range, select the cell containing the word, or select the range.

2. Choose <u>T</u>ools, <u>S</u>pelling, or press F7. When Excel finds a spelling error, the Spelling dialog box appears (see Figure 13.12).

FIG. 13.12

The Spelling dialog box appears when Excel finds a spelling error in the worksheet.

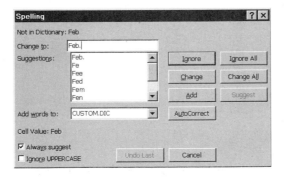

The following options in Table 13.4 are available to correct a spelling error:

Table 13.4	Spelling Dialog Box Options
Option	**Action**
Change To	Types a replacement for the word.
Suggestions	Selects a replacement word from a list of suggested words.
Add Words To	Selects the dictionary to which you want to add words that are spelled correctly but not found in the standard dictionary.
Ignore	Ignores the word and continues the spell check.
Ignore All	Ignores all occurrences of the word.
Change	Changes the selected word to the word displayed in the Change To box.
Change All	Changes all occurrences of the word to the word displayed in the Change To box.
Add	Adds the selected word to the custom dictionary.
AutoCorrect	Adds misspelling and correct entry to AutoCorrect list.
Suggest	Displays a list of additional suggestions based on a selection from the Suggestions list.
Always Suggest	Excel automatically displays a list of proposed suggestions whenever a word is not found in the dictionary.
Ignore UPPERCASE	Skips words that are all uppercase.
Undo Last	Undoes the last spelling change.
Cancel/Close	Closes the dialog box (the Cancel button changes to Close when you change a word or add a word to the dictionary).

▶ **See** "Letting AutoCorrect Do Your Spelling for You," **p. 89**

The AutoCorrect features allows Excel to correct common typing errors as you make them. For example, many people accidentally type two initial capital letters while holding down the Shift key, or routinely transpose letters in certain words such as *adn* for *and*. To set up AutoCorrect, follow these steps:

1. Choose Tools, AutoCorrect. The AutoCorrect dialog box opens, as displayed in Figure 13.13.

CAUTION

Deselecting the Replace Text as You Type box deactivates AutoCorrect.

Part
III

Ch
13

FIG. 13.13
AutoCorrect corrects
your mistakes as soon
as you make them.

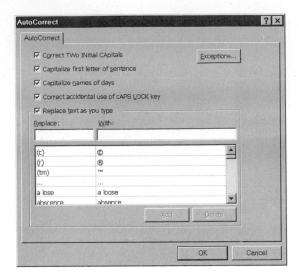

2. Check the appropriate boxes to activate any of the following options: Correct TWo INitial CApitals, Capitalize First Letter of Sentence, Capitalize Names of Days, Correct Accidental Use of cAPS LOCK Key, or Replace Text As You Type.

3. To add a common error to the AutoCorrect list, enter the incorrectly typed word in the Replace box and the correct version in the With box. Then click the Add button to add this entry to AutoCorrect.

4. For more options, click the Exceptions button to open the AutoCorrect Exceptions dialog box (see Figure 13.14).

FIG. 13.14
You can make a
number of exceptions
to AutoCorrect rules.

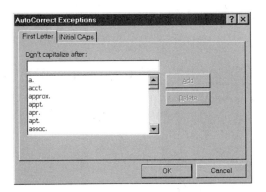

5. In the First Letter tab, you can enter words that you don't want to follow by automatic capitalization. For example, you may not want the word following etc. to be automatically capitalized. Enter the word in the Don't Capitalize After edit box and click the Add button.

6. In the INitial CAps tab, you can enter words for which you don't want Excel to automatically correct a detected initial capitalization problem.

 TIP To remove an AutoCorrect entry, select it and click Delete.

7. Click OK to return to the previous dialog box, then choose OK to return to your worksheet.

Formatting Worksheets

by Patrice-Anne Rutledge

After you create a worksheet, the next step is to change the appearance of data in your worksheet to make it more visually appealing. Excel provides many features and functions that enable you to produce high-quality worksheets. You can include such formatting options as applying different fonts, and you can add graphics, colors, and patterns to worksheet elements. ■

Cell Formatting

Excel provides extensive options for formatting cell data including changing the font, size, style, alignment, pattern, and border.

Numerical Formatting

In Excel, you have many choices for formatting numbers, including the ability to apply formats using either the toolbar or the Style menu.

Column and Row Height Formatting

You can change column and row height with the mouse, with menu commands, or automatically.

Data Alignment

You can align your data in many ways in Excel, including vertically, horizontally, or centered across columns.

Style Creation

Excel enables you to create formatting styles by example and apply them to other cells or ranges of cells.

Graphic Objects

Using the Drawing toolbar, you can create, edit, move, and modify graphic objects including AutoShapes and 3-D images.

Formatting Numbers

When you enter numbers in the worksheet, don't be concerned with the way they look. You can change the appearance of numbers by applying a numeric format.

Excel provides many common numeric formats; you can create your own as well. For example, you can apply a predefined currency format that uses two decimal places or create a currency format that uses an international currency symbol.

To apply a numeric format, follow these steps:

1. Select the cells containing the numbers you want to format.

2. Choose Format, Cells; or press Ctrl+1. Alternatively, click the right mouse button and choose the Format Cells command from the resulting shortcut menu. The Format Cells dialog box appears (see Figure 14.1).

FIG. 14.1

The Format Cells dialog box displays a list of predefined number formats.

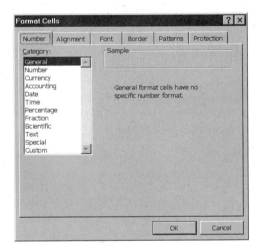

3. Select the type of number format you want to apply from the Category list. A list of sample formats displays in the Type list box for the Date, Time, Fraction, Special, and Custom categories. The Number, Currency, Accounting, Percentage, and Scientific categories include options for setting decimal places, and in some cases, for negative numbers. General and Text categories include no further options.

4. Select the number format you want to use from the choices displayed. A sample of the selected format appears in the Sample area of the dialog box.

5. Choose OK. Excel applies the selected number format to the selected cells in your worksheet.

▶ **See** "Using Toolbars in Microsoft Office Applications," **p. 45**

Applying Number Formats Using the Toolbar

You can quickly apply commonly used number formats—such as Currency, Comma, and Percentage—by using the Formatting toolbar (see Figure 14.2). Use either the number format buttons that appear in the toolbar by default or the Style menu that you manually add to the toolbar.

FIG. 14.2
The Formatting toolbar contains five buttons that enable you to apply common number formats quickly.

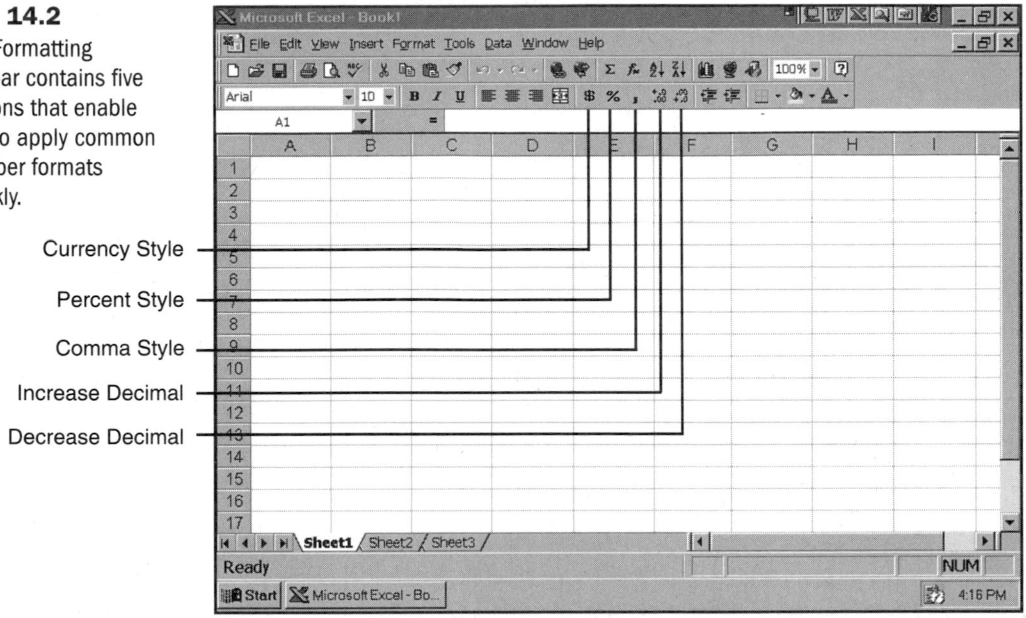

Currency Style
Percent Style
Comma Style
Increase Decimal
Decrease Decimal

To apply a number format by using the Formatting toolbar, select the cells containing the numbers you want to format and then click the appropriate button in the toolbar.

Formatting Numbers Using the Style Menu

You also can format numbers by using styles. To apply one of the predefined number formats listed as a style, select the cells containing the numbers you want to format and choose the Format, Style. The Style dialog box appears (see Figure 14.3). Select the desired style in the Style Name drop-down list, and then choose OK.

Part
III

Ch
14

FIG. 14.3
Format numbers using
the predefined styles
in the Style dialog box.

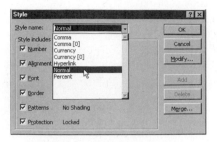

Table 14.1 describes the predefined formatting choices.

Table 14.1   Number Formats Available in the Style Dialog Box

Format	Description
Comma	Adds two decimal places to the number, and adds commas to numbers that contain four or more digits. A number entered as **1000** is formatted as 1,000.00.
Comma (0)	Rounds decimals and adds commas to numbers that contain four or more digits. A number entered as **1000.55** is formatted as 1,001.
Currency	Adds a dollar sign and two decimal places to the number. Also adds a comma to numbers that contain four or more digits. A number entered as **1000** is formatted as $1,000.00.
Currency (0)	Adds a dollar sign to the number and rounds decimals. Also adds a comma to numbers that contain four or more digits. A number entered as **1000.55** is formatted as $1,001.
Hyperlink	Applies blue Arial 10 font and an underline.
Normal	Applies the style that defines normal or default character formatting. A number entered as **1000** is formatted as 1000.
Percent	Multiplies the number by 100 and adds a percentage symbol to the number. A number entered as **.15** is formatted as 15%.

▶ **See** "Customizing Application Toolbars," **p. 949**

N O T E   To add the Styles box to the Formatting toolbar, choose View, Toolbars, and then
choose Customize. Select Format from the Categories list on the Commands tab. In
the Commands section of the dialog box, click and drag the Style button to the Formatting
toolbar, and choose Close. ▓

You also can use the following shortcut keys to format numbers:

Key	Format
Ctrl+Shift+~	General format
Ctrl+Shift+!	Comma format with two decimal places
Ctrl+Shift+$	Currency format with two decimal places
Ctrl+Shift+%	Percent format
Ctrl+Shift+^	Scientific notation format

Creating a Custom Number Format

Although Excel provides most of the common number formats, at times you may need a specific number format that the program does not provide. For example, you may want to create additional numeric formats that use various international currency symbols. Excel enables you to create custom number formats. In most cases, you can base your custom format on one of Excel's predefined formats.

To create a custom number format, follow these steps:

1. Choose Format, Cells; or press Ctrl+1. Alternatively, click the right mouse button and choose Format Cells from the resulting shortcut menu. If necessary, select the Number tab in the Format Cells dialog box.

2. Select Custom in the Category list box. Then select the predefined format in the Type list. Some common symbols used in these formats are listed in Table 14.2. The formatting symbols appear in the Type text box, and a sample appears above the text box (see Figure 14.4).

3. Edit the selected format in the Type text box.

Table 14.2 Numeric Formatting Codes

Code	Description
#	Placeholder for digits.
0	Placeholder for digits. Same as #, except that zeroes on either side of the decimal point force the numbers to match the selected format.
$	Currency symbol is displayed with the number.
,	Placeholder for thousands separator.
.	Placeholder for decimal point.
%	Multiplies number by 100 and displays number with a percent sign.

Part
III

Ch

14

FIG. 14.4
You can define your custom format in the Type text box.

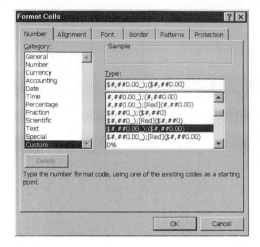

4. Choose OK. The custom format appears at the end of the list.

N O T E You can select and delete custom formats from the list; however, you cannot delete any of Excel's predefined number formats. ▪

Changing Date and Time Formats

Excel recognizes most dates and times entered in a worksheet cell. If you enter **9-1-96** in a cell, for example, Excel assumes that you are entering a date and displays the number in a date format. (The default date format is 9/1/96.) If you enter 9:45, Excel assumes that you are referring to a time and displays the entry in a time format. You can change to another date or time format.

▶ **See** "Entering Dates and Times," **p. 305**

To apply a date or time format, follow these steps:

1. Select the cell or range containing the data you want to format.

2. Choose Format, Cells; or press Ctrl+1. Alternatively, click the right mouse button and choose Format Cells from the resulting shortcut menu.

3. Select Date from the Category list to display the list of date formats (see Figure 14.5). To apply a time format, select Time from the Category list.

4. Select the format you want to use from the Type list box.

5. Choose OK. Excel applies the format to the data.

FIG. 14.5
A list of predefined date formats appears in the Date section of the Format Cells dialog box.

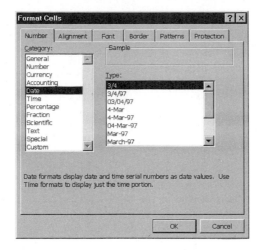

You also can use the following shortcut keys to enter and format the current date and time:

Key	Format
Ctrl+;	Current date (entering)
Ctrl+:	Current time (entering)

Use the same procedure to create custom date and time formats as custom number formats; the only difference is that you use date and time format codes. Table 14.3 lists these codes.

Table 14.3   Date and Time Format Codes

Code	Description
m	Month as a number with no leading zero.
mm	Month as a number with leading zero.
mmm	Month as a three-letter abbreviation.
mmmm	Month as a full name.
d	Day of month with no leading zero.
dd	Day of month with leading zero.
ddd	Day of week as a three-letter abbreviation.
dddd	Day of week as a full name.
yy	Year as a two-digit number.

Part
III

Ch
14

continues

Table 14.3	Continued
Code	**Description**
yyyy	Year as a four-digit number.
h	Hour with no leading zero.
hh	Hour with leading zero.
m	Minute with no leading zero.
mm	Minute with leading zero.
AM/PM	AM or PM indicator.

TROUBLESHOOTING

Excel fills a cell with ##### when I apply a numeric format to a number in my worksheet.
When a cell is not wide enough to accommodate a formatted number, Excel displays the number as #####. To display the complete number in the cell, you must adjust the column width of the cell. When you widen the column sufficiently, Excel displays the fully formatted number in the cell.

A few methods for changing the width of a column are available. You can double-click the right side of the column heading to autofit the column to the data you entered. Or, you can adjust the width to a precise amount, using Format, Column, Width, or you can use the mouse to drag the column border until the column is the appropriate width.

To adjust the width of a column to a precise amount, position the cell pointer in the column and choose Format, Column, Width, or click the right mouse button and choose Column Width from the resulting shortcut menu. In the Column Width dialog box, enter the desired column width; then choose OK. To adjust the width of a column by using the mouse, position the mouse pointer on the right border of the column heading whose width you want to change. The mouse pointer changes to a two-headed horizontal arrow when positioned properly. Drag the arrow to the right or left to increase or decrease the column width. A dotted line in the worksheet indicates the column width. Release the mouse button when the column is the width you want. For more information on changing column widths, see the following section, "Changing Column Width and Row Height."

I want to create a numeric format that uses an international currency symbol. I changed the International setting in the Windows Control Panel to reflect the country I wanted to use, but that changed the symbol for all currency formats. How can I use an international symbol in my custom format without changing the others? To create a custom numeric format with an international currency symbol, choose Format, Cells, and select the Number tab. In the Category list, select Custom; then select the format that closely resembles the format you want to use from the Type list box. Select the Type text box, highlight the currency symbol used by that format, and press Delete to delete the symbol. You then can enter special characters to display the currency symbols. To use the pound symbol (£), press the Num Lock key, hold down the Alt key, and—using the numeric keypad—type **0163**, which is the ANSI character for that symbol. To use the yen symbol (¥), press the Num Lock key if it's not already active, hold down the Alt key and type **0165** in the numeric keypad. The appropriate currency symbols are inserted into the text box when you release the Alt key. Choose OK to save the custom numeric format.

Changing Column Width and Row Height

When you enter data in a cell, the data often appears truncated because the column is not wide enough to display the entire entry. If a cell cannot display an entire number or date, Excel fills the cell with pound signs or displays the value in scientific notation (for example, 4.51E+08). After you adjust the width of the cell, the entire number or date appears.

You can change the column width by using the mouse or menu commands. When you use the mouse to change the column width, you drag the column border to reflect the approximate size of the column. When you choose Format, Column, Width, you can specify an exact column width.

Using the Mouse to Change Column Width

To change the column width by using the mouse, follow these steps:

1. Position the mouse pointer on the right border of the heading of the column whose width you want to change. The mouse pointer changes to a double-headed horizontal arrow when positioned properly. To change the width of multiple columns, select the columns by dragging the mouse over the additional column headings.

2. Drag the arrow to the right or left to increase or decrease the column width, respectively. A dotted line indicates the column width (see Figure 14.6).

3. Release the mouse button when the column is the width you want.

Using the Column Width Command to Change Column Width

To change the column width by using the Column Width command, follow these steps:

1. Click the heading of the column whose width you want to change. To change the width of multiple columns, drag the mouse pointer over each additional column.

2. Choose Format, Column, Width. Alternatively, click the right mouse button, and choose Column Width from the shortcut menu. The Column Width dialog box appears (see Figure 14.7).

Part
III

Ch
14

FIG. 14.6
Drag the double-headed arrow to change the column width.

Double-headed arrow for changing column width

Original column width

New column width

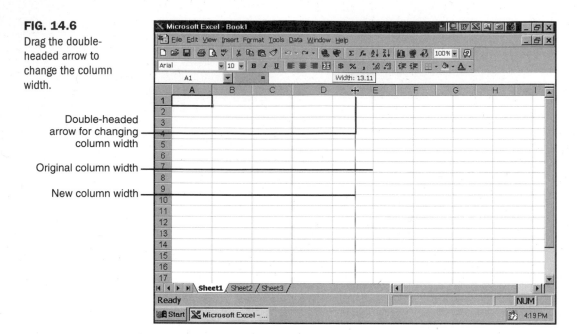

FIG. 14.7
Enter a specific column width in the Column Width dialog box.

3. Enter the column width in the Column Width text box.

4. Choose OK. Excel adjusts the width of the selected columns.

Adjusting Column Width Automatically

In addition to changing column width manually, Excel enables you to adjust the column width to accommodate the widest cell entry in a column.

To adjust the column width to the widest entry, select the cell containing the widest entry, and then choose Format, Column, AutoFit Selection. Excel adjusts the width of the column.

 TIP To quickly change the column width to fit the widest entry, position the mouse pointer on the right border of the column heading and double-click the mouse.

Adjusting the Row Height

Excel automatically adjusts the row height based on the font you are using, but you can change the row height to accommodate additional white space or to minimize the row height in your worksheet. You can use both the mouse and Excel commands to change the row height.

To adjust the row height by using the mouse, follow these steps:

1. Position the mouse pointer on the bottom border of the heading of the row whose height you want to change. The mouse pointer changes to a double-headed vertical arrow when positioned properly. To change the height of multiple rows, drag over the additional row headings.

2. Drag the arrow down or up to increase or decrease the row height, respectively. A dotted line indicates the row height (see Figure 14.8).

3. Release the mouse button when the row is the height you want.

FIG. 14.8
Drag the double-headed arrow to change the row height.

Double-headed arrow for changing row height

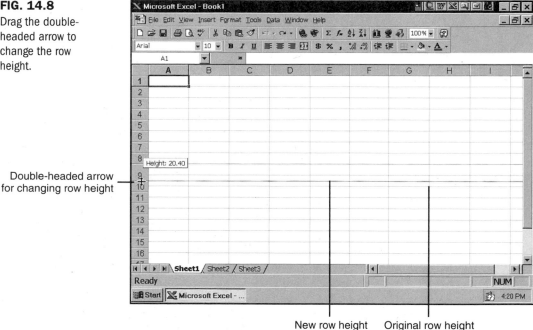

New row height   Original row height

To adjust the row height by using the Row Height command, follow these steps:

1. Click the heading of the row whose height you want to change. To change the width of multiple rows, drag the mouse pointer over each additional row.

Part

III

Ch

14

2. Choose Format, Row, Height. Alternatively, click the right mouse button and choose Row Height from the shortcut menu. The Row Height dialog box appears (see Figure. 14.9).

FIG. 14.9
Enter a specific row height in the Row Height dialog box.

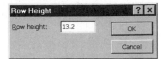

N O T E The row height is measured in points and is based on the size of the default font used in the worksheet. The default font used by Excel is 10-point Arial.

3. Enter the row height in the Row Height text box.

4. Choose OK. Excel adjusts the height of the selected rows.

Aligning Data

Excel provides several formatting options for changing the appearance of data in the worksheet. For example, you can change the alignment of text or numbers within a cell so that they appear left-aligned, right-aligned, or centered. You also can format lengthy text to wrap within a cell, center text across a range of columns, or align text vertically within a cell.

TIP   You can indent data within a cell by selecting the Increase Indent button on the toolbar.

To align data, follow these steps:

1. Select the cell or range that contains the data you want to align.

2. Choose Format, Cells; or press Ctrl+1. Alternatively, click the right mouse button and choose the Format Cells command from the resulting shortcut menu. The Format Cells dialog box appears (see Figure 14.10). Select the Alignment tab.

3. Specify the alignment you want to use in the Horizontal and Vertical drop-down lists. See Table 14.4 for descriptions of alignment options.

4. Choose OK.

TIP Selecting Left (Indent) activates the Indent scroll box where you can specify the exact amount of indentation.

FIG. 14.10
Change the alignment of data in the Alignment tab of the Format Cells dialog box.

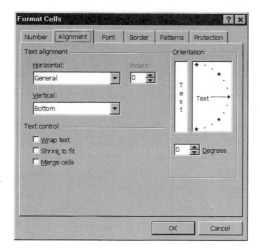

Table 14.4   Alignment Options

Option	Description
General	Aligns text to the left and numbers to the right.
Left(Indent)	Aligns text and numbers to the left edge of the cell.
Center	Centers text and numbers within a cell.
Right	Aligns text and numbers to the right edge of the cell.
Full	Repeats the contents until the cell is full.
Justify	When text is wrapped within a cell, aligns text evenly between the cell borders.
Center Across Selection	Centers text across multiple columns.

Controlling Text

Excel offers several options for controlling text in the Format Cells dialog box Alignment tab. You can align text entries to wrap within a single cell or a range of cells, shrink text to fit within a cell, or merge two or more cells together. If you have data in more than one cell you want to merge, Excel will keep only the data in the upper-leftmost cell.

To use any of these features, select the cell or range of cells containing the entry, and then choose Format, Cells; or press Ctrl+1. You also can click the right mouse button and choose the Format Cells command from the shortcut menu. In the Format Cells dialog box, select the Alignment tab. Then select Wrap Text, Shrink to Fit, or Merge Cells as appropriate and choose OK. Figure 14.11 displays several examples of controlling text.

Part
III

Ch
14

FIG. 14.11

Excel enables you to control text in a variety of ways.

Create one cell by merging the contents of two or more

Excel adjusts row heights for rows with wrapped text in cells

Excel shrinks text to fit the width of the cell

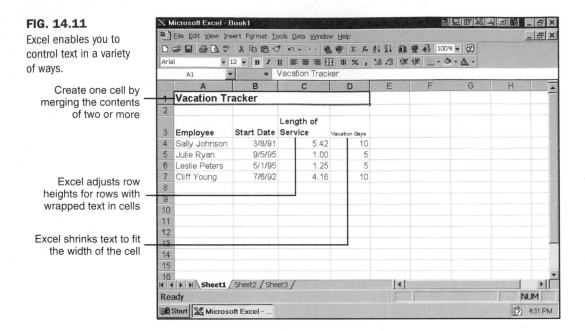

Centering Text Across Columns

 To center text over multiple columns, first select the cell that contains the text and the range of columns across which you want to center the text. Selected cells defining the range of columns must be blank. Choose Format, Cells; or press Ctrl+1. Alternatively, click the right mouse button and choose the Format Cells command from the shortcut menu. The Format Cells dialog box appears. Select the Alignment tab. Then select Center Across Selection from the Horizontal drop-down list and choose OK. Excel centers the text across the specified columns (see Figure 14.12).

Aligning Text Vertically or Horizontally

Excel enables you to align text either vertically or horizontally in a cell. To format text vertically or horizontally, follow these steps:

 TIP When aligning text, use Excel's Format, Column, AutoFit Selection and Format, Row, AutoFit commands to adjust the column width or row height quickly.

FIG. 14.12

Text is centered across the selected columns.

Text centered across columns A-D

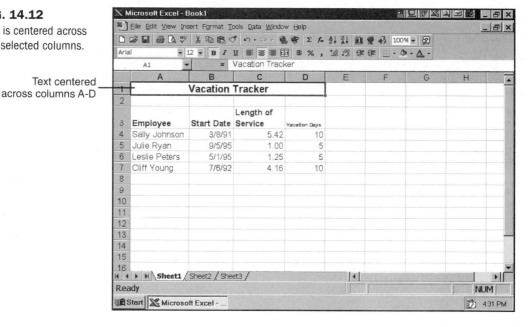

1. Select the cell or range of cells containing the text you want to format.

2. Choose Format, Cells; or press Ctrl+1. Alternatively, click the right mouse button and choose Format Cells from the shortcut menu. The Format Cells dialog box appears. Select the Alignment tab.

3. In the Orientation section, select the vertical or horizontal orientation. If you select a vertical orientation, you also must select a specific vertical alignment (Top, Center, Bottom, or Justify) in the Vertical drop-down list.

4. To rotate text, select the desired degree of rotation in the Degrees scroll box, or click the rotation angle in the horizontal orientation display box.

5. Choose OK. Excel aligns the text (see Figure 14.13).

◆ TROUBLESHOOTING

I used the Center Across Selection command to center a text entry across a range of columns, but the entry would not center. One of the cells in the selection probably contains a space character or some other entry. To remove these characters, select the range of cells (except for the cell containing the entry you want to center) and then press Delete.

After I aligned text vertically in a cell, some of the characters did not display. When a row height is set to the default row height, only a few characters of vertically rotated text display.

Part
III

Ch
14

continues

continued

To display the entire contents, position the mouse pointer on the bottom border of the row and double-click the left mouse button, or click the row heading and choose F̲ormat, R̲ow, A̲utoFit to adjust the height to best fit the row's contents.

FIG. 14.13
Text is aligned vertically in row 4.

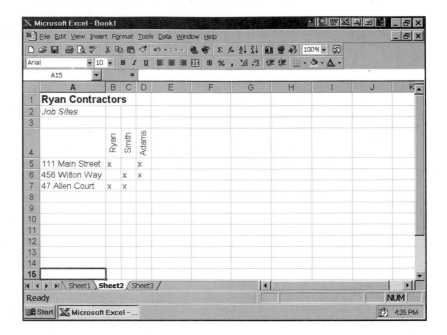

Changing Fonts, Sizes, and Styles

Excel provides several formatting options for changing the appearance of text in your worksheets. You can, for example, choose a different font, change the size of the selected font, and apply a font style to cells in your worksheet.

Changing Fonts

The list of fonts available in the Font dialog box depends on the type of Windows fonts you have installed and the type of printer you are using. You can quickly change the font and font size in the font and font size boxes on the Formatting toolbar. You can also change a font in the Format Cells dialog box. To do so, follow these steps:

1. Select the cell or range of cells that you want to change.

2. Choose F̲ormat, C̲ells; or press Ctrl+1. In the Format Cells dialog box, select the Font tab.

3. In the Font list box, select the font you want to use; to change the text size, select a size in the Size list or type any size in the Size text box (see Figure 14.14).

4. Choose OK.

FIG. 14.14
The Font section of the Format Cells dialog box displays the currently installed Windows and printer fonts.

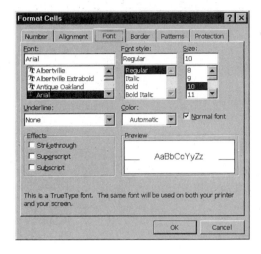

Applying Text Formats

In addition to changing the font and size of data in your worksheets, you can apply text attributes to the data. For example, you can assign such attributes as bold, italic, and underline, and change the color of text.

  To apply one of these formatting attributes, select the bold, italic, underline, or font color buttons on the Formatting toolbar. You can also apply text formats in the Format Cells dialog box by following these steps:

1. Select the cell or range of cells you want to format.

2. Choose Format, Cells; or press Ctrl+1. In the Format Cells dialog box, select the Font tab.

N O T E As you make changes in the dialog box, Excel applies the selections to the text in the Preview box. The changes aren't made to the selected cells until you choose OK. ■

3. Select the style you want to apply in the Font Style list box. Use the Underline dropdown list to select an underline style. To change the color of the data, click the Color drop-down list and select a color. Select Strikethrough, Superscript, or Subscript, if you want.

4. When you finish, choose OK.

Part

III

Ch

14

Formatting Characters in a Cell

You can apply formatting to individual characters in a text entry. For example, you can assign the Bold format to a single character in a cell.

To format characters in a cell, follow these steps:

TIP When formatting characters in a cell, you also can use the buttons in the Formatting toolbar to change the appearance of text.

1. Double-click the cell containing the data you want to format, or select the cell and then press F2.
2. In the cell or formula bar, select the characters you want to format.
3. Choose Format, Cells; or press Ctrl+1. The Font tab displays automatically.
4. Select the attributes you want, and then choose OK.

Applying Patterns and Borders

In addition to formatting numbers or text, you can format cells. For example, you can add a border to a cell or range of cells and fill a cell with a color or pattern.

Applying a Border

Borders enhance a worksheet's appearance by providing visual separations between areas of the worksheet. Borders also improve the appearance of printed reports.

To apply a border, follow these steps:

1. Select the cell or range you want to format.
2. Choose Format, Cells; or press Ctrl+1. Alternatively, click the right mouse button and choose the Format Cells command from the shortcut menu. In the Format Cells dialog box, select the Border tab (see Figure 14.15).

TIP To apply borders quickly, select the cell or range you want to format, and then click the arrow next to the Borders button to display the Border buttons.

3. You can choose one of the preset borders   None(no border), Outline (border around the outside edge of the selected cells), or Inside (border on the inside grid of the selected cells). The preview diagram displays what the border will look like.

FIG. 14.15
In the Format Cells dialog box, select a border to add to a cell.

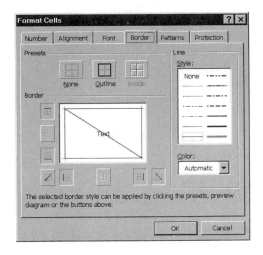

4. Or, you can design your own border with the border buttons that display in the lower half of the dialog box. These buttons provide the option to create top, bottom, left, right, or diagonal borders.

5. Alternatively, click directly on the preview diagram to create borders.

6. In the Style box, select the type of line you want. To change the color of the border, select the color from the Color drop-down list.

7. When you finish, choose OK.

Applying Patterns

You can enhance a cell with patterns and colors. The Format Cells Patterns command enables you to choose foreground and background colors as well as a pattern.

N O T E To apply the same formatting to a different area, select the new area and then click the Repeat button or press F4 immediately after you apply the formatting. ▪

To format a cell with colors and patterns, follow these steps:

1. Select the cell or range you want to format.

2. Choose Format, Cells; or press Ctrl+1. Alternatively, click the right mouse button and choose the Format Cells command from the shortcut menu. In the Format Cells dialog box, select the Patterns tab (see Figure 14.16).

3. Select a background color for the cell in the Color section. The Sample box in the bottom right corner of the dialog box shows you what the color looks like.

Part
III

Ch
14

FIG. 14.16
Apply patterns and colors to a cell with the Format Cells dialog box.

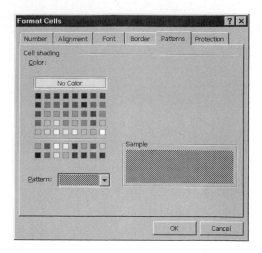

4. Select a pattern in the Pattern drop-down list by clicking the down arrow. To specify a background color for the pattern, select a pattern color from the Pattern drop-down list. If the foreground and background colors are the same, the cell displays a solid color. The Sample box shows you what the formatting looks like.

5. Choose OK.

Using Automatic Range Formatting

If you aren't sure which colors and formats work well together, Excel's AutoFormat feature can eliminate much of the guesswork. AutoFormat enables you to make choices from a list of predefined formatting templates. These formats are a combination of number formats, cell alignments, column widths, row heights, fonts, borders, and other formatting options.

To use the AutoFormat feature, follow these steps:

1. Select the range you want to format.

   ▶ **See** "Using Automatic Formatting," **p. 85**

2. Choose Format, AutoFormat. The AutoFormat dialog box appears (see Figure 14.17).

3. Select one of the format types in the Table Format list box. Excel displays the selected format in the Sample box.

4. Choose OK to apply the format.

FIG. 14.17
The AutoFormat dialog box displays formatting templates.

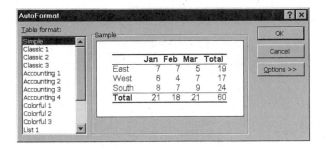

  N O T E To copy the formats from a range of cells to another range in the worksheet, select the range of cells containing the formats and click the Format Painter button in the Standard toolbar. Then, using the mouse, highlight the range of cells to which you want to copy the formats. When you release the mouse button, Excel applies the formats to the selected range. ■

TROUBLESHOOTING

After I changed the color of a cell, the entry was no longer displayed. When the background color of a cell is the same color used by the cell entry, you will not see the entry. To change the color of the cell entry, select the cell and choose Format, Cells. Select the Font tab, select a color from the Color drop-down menu, and choose OK.

After I choose the AutoFormat command, Excel displays an error message, stating that it cannot detect a table around the active cell. You probably selected a single cell before choosing the AutoFormat command. You must select more than one cell for AutoFormat to work.

Creating and Applying a Style

When you find yourself applying the same worksheet formats over and over, you can save yourself some time by saving the formats in a style. Then, when you want to use the formats, you can apply all of them with a single command.

You can create a style based on cell formats that already appear in the worksheet, or you can create a new style by using the options in the Style dialog box.

Creating a Style by Example

You can define a style based on existing formats in your worksheet. When you create a style by example, Excel uses the formats of the selected cell to create the style.

Part
III

Ch
14

To create a style by example, follow these steps:

1. Select the cell that contains the formats you want to name as a style.

2. Choose Format, Style. The Style dialog box appears (see Figure 14.18).

FIG. 14.18
The Style dialog box displays the options you can use to define a style.

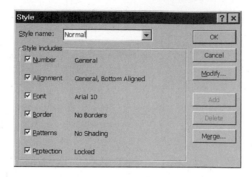

3. Type a name for your new style in the Style Name text box, and then choose Add. The style appears in the Style Name drop-down list.

4. Choose OK.

Defining a Style

To create a new style, follow these steps:

1. Choose Format, Style to display the Style dialog box.

2. Type a name for the style in the Style Name text box. (Normal is the default style.) The current format appears in the Style Includes box.

3. Choose the Modify button. The Format Cells dialog box appears.

4. Select the tab for the attribute you want to change. The dialog box for the selected attribute appears.

5. Enter the changes you want to make. Choose OK to return to the Style dialog box.

6. After you make all the necessary style changes, choose OK. The dialog box closes, and Excel applies the style to any selected cells in the worksheet.

Applying a Style

To apply a style, follow these steps:

1. Select the cell or range to which you want to apply the style.

2. Choose Format, Style to display the Style dialog box.

3. Select the name of the style you want to apply in the Style Name list.

4. Choose OK. Excel applies the style to the selected cell or range.

Creating and Working with Graphic Objects

Excel makes it easy to enhance your worksheets with graphic objects by providing a full set of drawing tools. You can create such objects as circles, squares, and rectangles and add them to your worksheet.

Creating an Object

 To create a drawn object, click the Drawing button in the Standard toolbar to display the Drawing toolbar. Select the Drawing tool that represents the object you want to create.

 N O T E Excel 97 offers several new options on the Drawing toolbar, including the ability to add AutoShapes (automatically define shapes such as connectors, arrows, stars, banners, flowchart symbols, and callouts) as well as convert objects to 3-D images. Excel also refers to basic shapes such as ovals and rectangles as AutoShapes. ■

▶ **See** "Using Drawing Tools," **p. 558**

Position the mouse pointer in the area of the worksheet where you want to start drawing (the mouse pointer changes to a small cross when you position it in the worksheet area). Click and hold down the left mouse button, and drag the mouse until the object is the size you want. Then release the mouse button. Excel adds the drawing to the worksheet (see Figure 14.19).

Selecting, Moving, and Resizing Objects

After placing an object in the worksheet, you can move that object to a new location or resize it.

To Select an Object   Before you can move or resize an object, first select it by placing the mouse pointer next to the object and clicking the left mouse button. The mouse pointer becomes an arrow when positioned on the border of the object. Handles appear around the object, indicating that it is selected (see Figure 14.20).

To Move an Object   Select the object you want to move, and then position the mouse pointer inside the boundaries of the object. When the mouse pointer becomes an arrow, click and hold down the left mouse button, drag the selected object to the desired location, and release the mouse button.

▶ **See** "Moving and Sizing Objects," **p. xx** [ch 21]

Part
III

Ch
14

FIG. 14.19
A rectangle is added to the worksheet.

Rectangle, not a border ——

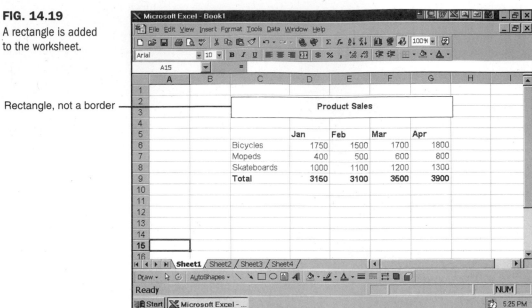

FIG. 14.20
Handles appear around this object, indicating that it is selected and can be moved or resized.

Handles ——

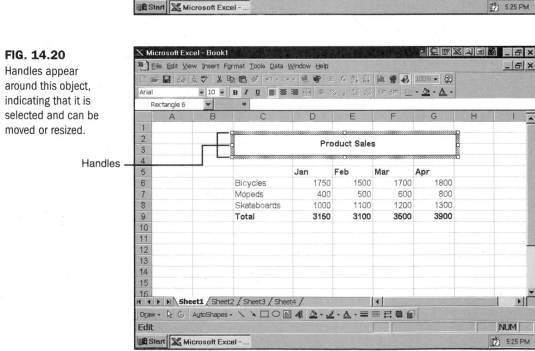

To Resize an Object   Select the object you want to resize. Handles appear around the object; these handles enable you to resize the selected object.

Position the mouse pointer on one of the handles. The mouse pointer changes to a double-headed arrow when properly positioned. To make the object wider or longer, position the mouse pointer on one of the middle handles. To resize the object proportionally, position the mouse pointer on one of the corner handles.

Click and hold down the left mouse button, drag the handle until the object is the size you want (see Figure 14.21), and then release the mouse button.

FIG. 14.21
The rectangular object is resized.

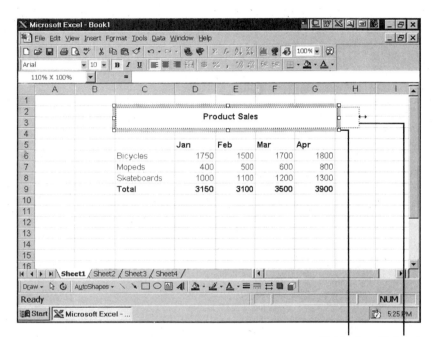

Right edge   Right edge
of original   of resized
rectangle

Formatting Objects

As you can with text, you can add color, patterns, and borders to drawn objects in your worksheet. Use the buttons on the Drawing toolbar to format your objects, by selecting the object and clicking the appropriate button. Pop-up menus appear allowing you to choose the format you prefer. Table 14.5 lists these buttons.

 TIP To format an object quickly, position the mouse pointer on the object you want to format. When the pointer changes to an arrow, double-click the object to display the Format AutoShape dialog box.

Part
III

Ch
14

Table 14.5   Formatting Buttons on the Drawing Toolbar

Button	Description
	Fill Color
	Line Color
	Font Color
	Line Style
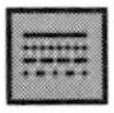	Dash Style
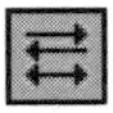	Arrow Style
	Shadow
	3-D

You can also use the Format AutoShapes dialog box to format objects. To do this, follow these steps:

1. Select the object you want to format.
2. Choose Format, AutoShape; or press Ctrl+1. Alternatively, click the right mouse button and choose the Format AutoShape command. The Format AutoShape dialog box appears (see Figure 14.22).
3. Select your desired formatting changes from among the four tabs—Colors and Lines, Size, Protection, and Properties.
4. Choose OK to close the dialog box and apply the selected formats.

Grouping Objects

In creating a graphic or picture, you might draw several separate objects. If you want to work with multiple objects at the same time—for example, if you want to move the object to another area in the worksheet or want to create a copy of the drawing—you can group the objects to form a single object.

FIG. 14.22
Change the appearance of a drawn object with the Format AutoShape dialog box.

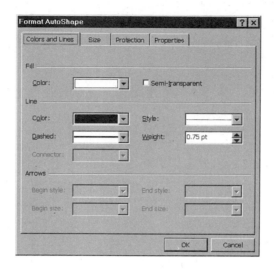

To group objects, first select the objects. (You can use the Select Objects button in the Drawing toolbar or hold down the Shift key as you click each object.) Then, click the Draw button and choose Group from the menu to group the objects together. A single set of selection handles appears around the grouped object (see Figure 14.23).

FIG. 14.23
All selected objects appear as one object, with handles outlining the area of the single grouped object.

Handles

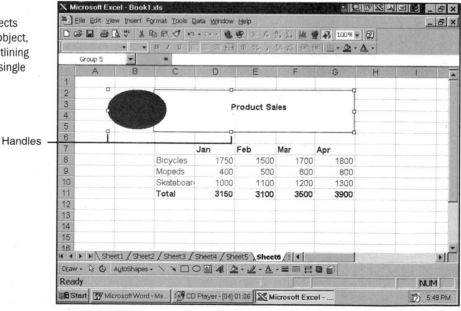

To break a grouped object back into multiple objects, select the grouped object, and then click the Draw button and choose Ungroup from the menu. Individual objects appear, with handles surrounding each object. You can also choose to Regroup previously grouped objects.

Creating a Text Box

Excel enables you to create text boxes in your worksheets for adding paragraphs of text.

 To create a text box, select the Text Box button on the Drawing toolbar and position the mouse pointer in the worksheet (the mouse pointer becomes a small cross). Click the left mouse button, and drag the pointer in the worksheet area. After you release the mouse button, the insertion point appears in the top left corner of the text box, ready to accept the text you type. The text wraps according to the size of the box (see Figure 14.24).

FIG. 14.24

Text wraps within this text box.

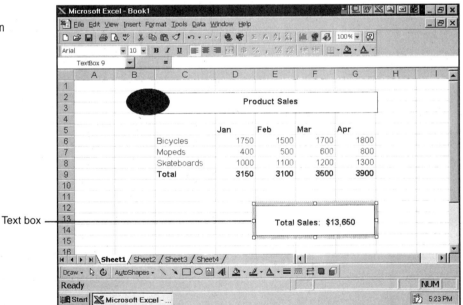

You can format, move, and resize a text box as you can any other object in a worksheet. When you resize a text box, the text automatically wraps to fit the new size of the box. You can apply formats to all the text in the text box or only to individual words. To make the entire text bold, for example, select the text box and click the Bold button in the Formatting toolbar. To make a single word of the text bold, place the mouse pointer inside the text box. The mouse pointer changes to an I-beam. Select the text you want to format by clicking and dragging the I-beam over the text. Then use standard formatting commands, tools, or shortcuts to format the selected text. As long as the insertion point appears inside the text box, you can use normal formatting and editing procedures. For information on formatting, refer to sections "Formatting Numbers," "Aligning Text Vertically or Horizontally," and "Changing Fonts, Sizes, and Styles," earlier in this chapter.

To select and move a text box, position the mouse pointer (arrow) on the border of the text box and then click the left mouse button.

Using Conditional Formatting

Conditional formatting is a new Excel feature that enables you to apply specific formatting to the contents of the cell under certain conditions. If a condition is true, Excel automatically applies that format (such as a certain color) to the cell. Use it to highlight values you want to track or the results of a formula, for example.

To use conditional formatting, follow these steps:

1. Select Format, Conditional Formatting to open the Conditional Formatting dialog box (see Figure 14.25).

FIG. 14.25
With conditional formatting, you specify the conditions under which to apply a format.

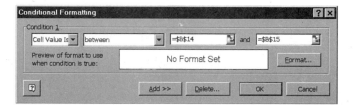

2. In the list below Condition 1, select either Cell Value Is or Formula Is, depending on whether you want to track a cell value or formula.

3. If you choose to track a cell value, select one of the following conditions from the drop-down list: between, not between, equal to, not equal to, greater than, less than, greater than or equal to, less than or equal to.

4. Enter the conditional data in the adjacent edit box, or click the Cell Reference button to return to the worksheet to select the appropriate cell. If you choose a between or not between condition, you must enter data in two edit boxes.

5. Click the Cell Reference button to return to the Conditional Formatting dialog box.

6. Next, select Format to open the Format Cells dialog box. The dialog box only includes the Font, Border, and Pattern tabs when you display it from the Conditional Formatting dialog box.

7. Select your desired formatting and click OK to return to the previous dialog box.

Part
III

Ch
14

8. To include additional conditions, click the Add>> button which adds Condition 2.

9. To delete a condition, select the Delete button which opens the Delete Conditional Format dialog box (see Figure 14.26).

FIG. 14.26
You can easily delete conditional formatting.

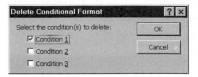

10. Select the condition you want to delete and click OK.

11. When you are done adding conditions, click OK to return to your worksheet.

When you enter data that matches one of your conditions, it formats as you specified. ●

Using Formulas

by Patrice-Anne Rutledge

The greatest benefit in using an electronic spreadsheet program such as Excel, is the program's power to calculate formulas based on values in the worksheet. You can, for example, create a formula that calculates the difference between sales figures on a quarterly basis or that totals the commissions each sales representative has received. Excel includes several tools to simplify creating formulas as well as resolving problems with them. ■

Formula creation

In Excel, you can create formulas by either pointing to or typing data, and also reference either relative or absolute cells.

Formula operators

With Excel's operators, you can perform arithmetic calculations, manipulate text, and perform comparisons as well as refer to several different worksheet ranges.

Debugging formulas

Excel provides several tools for debugging your formulas, including the Edit Go To Special command and Auditing features.

Range names

Range names enable you to refer to ranges of cells by name for easier identification.

Creating Formulas

You can create formulas in Excel in two ways: Type the formula directly in the cell, or point to the cells that you want the formula to compute.

Creating a Formula by Typing

To create a formula by entering the cell addresses and numeric operators in a cell, follow these steps:

▶ **See** "Entering Data," **p. 303**

1. Select the cell in which you want to enter a formula.

2. Type **=** (equal sign) to start the formula.

N O T E You can enter a plus sign (**+**) or minus sign (**–**) to begin a formula; Excel will convert the formula to the appropriate format. If you enter **+B4+B5**, for example, Excel will convert the formula to =+B4+B5. ▪

3. Type the cell references containing the values to be computed, entering the appropriate operator. To find the difference between the two values in cells B5 and B11, for example, enter **=B5–B11** in another cell, for example, cell B14.

4. Press the check box in the formula bar. Excel displays the result of the formula in the active cell, and the formula appears in the formula bar. You can also press Enter to accept a formula entry.

N O T E To display formulas in a worksheet instead of their calculated values, select any cell in the worksheet and press Ctrl+` (accent grave). Press Ctrl+` a second time to display the formula result. ▪

Excel 97 supports natural-language formulas that enable you to enter formula criteria without entering a particular cell reference. You do this by referring to row and column labels in your formula. Say that you have a workbook that tracks financial information for 20 store locations throughout the country. You want to use the sales information for your San Francisco store in a formula, which is located in cell Q127. With a column label of Sales and a row label of San Francisco for that particular cell, you can enter **=Sales San Francisco** in the formula bar instead of Q127. This feature is particularly useful for large workbooks in which locating specific cell references would be time-consuming.

Creating a Formula by Pointing

You can, unfortunately, make errors when typing cell references in a formula. To minimize errors that occur when you use cell references in formulas, build a formula by pointing to cells rather than by typing the cell references.

N O T E After you enter a complicated formula in your worksheet, you may want to protect it to make sure it can't accidentally be erased. To do so, choose Tools, Protection, Protect Sheet to enter a password for your work. To unprotect, choose Tools, Protection, Unprotect Sheet. ■

Pointing to Cells with the Mouse Suppose that you want to enter, in cell B14, a formula that subtracts the total in cell B11 from the total in cell B5. To build a formula by pointing to cells with the mouse, follow these steps:

▶ **See** "Moving Around in a Worksheet," **p. 301**

1. Select the cell in which you want to enter a formula.
2. Type = (equal sign) to start the formula. For this example, type = in cell B14.
3. Click the cell whose reference you want to add to the formula. For this example, click cell B5 to add the cell address in the formula bar.
4. Type – (minus sign).
5. Click the next cell you want to add to the formula. For this example, click cell B11.
6. Click the check box in the formula bar to complete the formula entry. You can also press Enter to accept a formula entry. Figure 15.1 displays another example of a completed formula entry.

 T I P Σ To automatically sum a list of numbers, as in Figure 15.1, you can select the cell where you want to place your summed amount and click the AutoSum button on the toolbar to automatically sum the numbers.

FIG. 15.1
The result of the formula appears in cell B8. The formula appears in the formula bar.

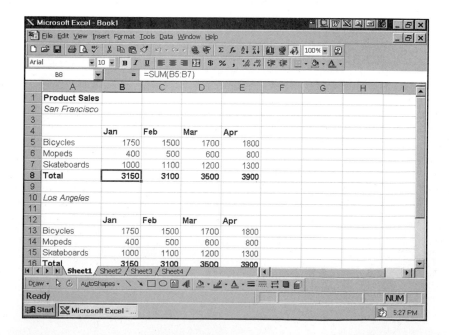

Entering Cell References with the Keyboard   Suppose that in cell D9 you want to build a formula that finds the difference between the totals in cells B9 and C9. To enter cell references with the keyboard, follow these steps:

1. Select the cell in which you want to enter a formula.

2. Type = (equal sign) to start the formula. For this example, type = in cell D9.

3. Use the arrow keys to highlight the cell that contains the data you want to use. For this example, press ← twice to select cell B9. Notice that the marquee is positioned in cell B9. Cell B9 is added to the formula.

4. Type – (minus sign).

5. Use the arrow keys to highlight the next cell you want to use. For this example, press ← to select cell C9. Cell C9 is added to the formula.

6. Press Enter to complete the entry.

Referencing Cells in Formulas

You will often refer to other cells in creating your formulas. Excel provides several options for referring to these cells; you can refer to cells that change for each row or column location, cells that remain absolute in every location, or cells that are located in other worksheets or even other workbooks.

Using Relative References   In most instances, you will want to use a *relative reference* when referring to other cells in a formula. When you copy a formula that contains cell references, the cell references adjust to their new location. For example, if you create a formula based on the data in column A, moving that formula to column B will reference the data in that column, rather than the original data (see Figure 15.2).

Using Absolute References   *Absolute references* are useful when you want your formula to refer to data in a specific cell, rather than allowing the reference to change based on the column or row. For example, say that the current commission rate for your sales staff is displayed in cell A3. Your worksheet also contains columns for sales representative, total sales, and commissions. To calculate the commission each representative receives based on his or her sales, you would divide total sales by the commission rate. The sales figure would change in each row, but the commission rate would remain the same, or absolute. You can make a column, row, or cell reference absolute by placing a dollar sign ($) before the reference. $A$1, $B$7, $AB$8 are all examples of absolute references.

 You can also enter absolute references by entering the appropriate reference manually in the formula bar.

FIG. 15.2

Using relative reference, copying the formula in cell A3 to cell B3 will change the cell references to the data in column B.

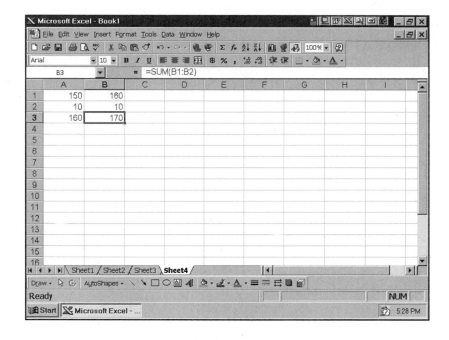

To enter an absolute reference in a formula, follow these steps:

1. In the cell, type the equal sign (=) and the cell you want to make absolute.
2. Press F4 to activate the absolute reference key.
3. Continue pressing F4 until the appropriate combination of letters and dollar signs appears.
4. Enter the remainder of your formula and press Enter.

Figure 15.3 illustrates the use of an absolute reference.

Using Mixed References   You can also combine the use of relative and absolute references into a *mixed reference*. For instance, you may want the column to remain absolute but not the row, or vice versa. Entering **$A1** will allow the row to change if you copy data, but not the column. Use the absolute reference key, F4, to enter the appropriate mixed reference by scrolling through its options.

Editing Absolute and Relative References   To edit an existing reference, place the insertion point on the formula bar within the formula you want to change. Press F4 until the desired change takes place, and then press Enter.

Entering References to Other Sheets   You can also include references to data in other worksheets in your workbook. To do so, enter the name of the sheet, an exclamation mark, and the cell reference. For example, typing **Sheet1!A1** would refer to cell A1 in Sheet1. If you've renamed your sheet, indicate the name you have given it.

FIG. 15.3
The absolute
reference in cell A3
remains the same
when copied to B3.

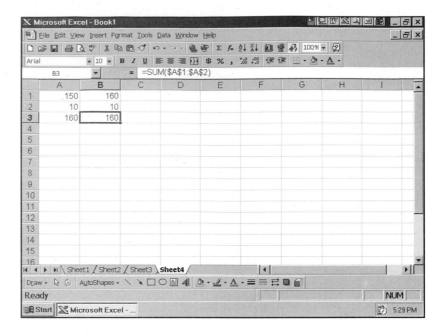

▶ **See** "Linking Data Between Excel Worksheets," **p. 900**

Referencing Other Files   Sometimes you may want to refer to data that is located in another workbook. Suppose you have created separate workbooks containing sales information for each of your company's regions. You may want to refer to data in each of those workbooks when you create a new workbook that summarizes sales information for the entire corporation. To refer to cell C10 in the Sales 1997 sheet in the workbook named "Western," you would enter the following reference:

   ='[WESTERN.XLS]SALES 1997'!$C$10

Using Operators in Formulas

Excel's operators allow you to perform arithmetic calculations with formulas, manipulate text, perform comparisons, and refer to several different ranges in the worksheet with references.

Arithmetic Operators   In addition to using Excel's built-in functions to perform calculations, you can use arithmetic operators to perform a calculation on worksheet data. Following are the arithmetic operators used in basic calculations:

Operator	Purpose
+	Addition
−	Subtraction
*	Multiplication
/	Division
%	Percentage
^	Exponentiation

Text Operators   By using text operators, you can concatenate (or join) text contained in quotation marks or text in other cells. For example, entering the formula ="**Total Sales: "&B4** returns Total Sales: 28 when cell B4 contains the value 28.

Comparative Operators   To compare results, you can create formulas with comparative operators, which return TRUE or FALSE, depending on how the formula evaluates the condition. For example, the formula =**A4>30** returns TRUE if the value in cell A4 is greater than 30; otherwise, it returns FALSE.

Following are the comparative operators you can use in a formula:

Operator	Purpose
=	Equal to
<	Less than
>	Greater than
<=	Less than or equal to
>=	Greater than or equal to
<>	Not equal to

Reference Operators   Reference operators enable you to refer to several different cells in a single formula. For example, entering the formula **SUM(A4:A24)** sums the values located in cells A4 through A24.

Order of Operators   Most formula errors occur when the arithmetic operators are not entered in the proper *order of precedence*—the order in which Excel performs mathematical operations. Following is the order of precedence for arithmetic operations in a formula:

Operator	Purpose
^	Exponentiation
*, /	Multiplication, division
+, −	Addition, subtraction

Exponentiation occurs before multiplication or division in a formula, and multiplication and division occur before addition or subtraction. For example, Excel calculates the formula =4+10*2 by first multiplying 10 by 2 and then adding the product to 4, which returns 24. That order remains constant whether the formula is written as =4+10*2 or 10*2+4.

TIP   If a formula includes arithmetic operators at the same level, the calculations are evaluated sequentially from left to right.

You can change the order of precedence by enclosing segments of the formula in parentheses. Excel first performs all operations within the parentheses and then performs the rest of the operations in the appropriate order. For example, by adding parentheses to the formula =4+10*2 to create =(4+10)*2, you can force Excel first to add 4 and 10 and then multiply the sum by 2 to return 28.

TROUBLESHOOTING

I get an error message when I try to create a formula using parentheses. When creating a long formula, each open parenthesis must be matched by a closed parenthesis, or Excel will not accept the formula. When you use parentheses in a formula, compare the total number of open parentheses with the total number of closed parentheses.

I entered the formula =5+10*2 and received the wrong result, 25 instead of 30. Remember that Excel will always perform multiplication before addition or subtraction. To force Excel to add the first two figures before multiplying, enter the following: **=(5+10)*2**.

Entering Dates and Times in Formulas

You also can create formulas to calculate values by using dates and times. When you use a date or time in a formula, you must enter the date or time in a format that Excel recognizes, and you must enclose the entry in double quotation marks. Excel then converts the entry to its appropriate value. To find the number of days that elapsed between two dates, for example, you would enter a formula such as **="4/2/97"–"3/27/97"**. In this example, Excel returns 6, the number of days between March 27, 1997, and April 2, 1997.

▶ **See** "Entering Dates and Times," **p. 305**

If Excel does not recognize a date or time, it stores the entry as text and displays the #VALUE! error value.

N O T E   You can reduce the time you spend entering repetitive formulas by using arrays. *Arrays* are rectangular ranges of formulas or values that Excel treats as a single group. For more information on using arrays in Excel, see *Special Edition Using Microsoft Excel for Windows 97,* also published by Que. ■

Converting Formulas to Values

In many cases, after you create the formula, you need only the result rather than the formula itself. After you calculate your monthly mortgage payment, for example, you no longer need the formula. In such a situation, you can convert the formula to its actual value.

To convert a single formula to a value, follow these steps:

1. Select the cell that contains the formula.

2. Press the F2 function key, or double-click the cell.

3. Press the F9 function key. Excel replaces the formula with the value.

To convert a range of formulas to values, follow these steps:

1. Select the range that contains the formulas you want to convert.

2. Choose Edit, Copy, or click the right mouse button and choose Copy from the shortcut menu. A marquee surrounds the selected range.

3. Choose Edit, Paste Special. The Paste Special dialog box appears (see Figure 15.4).

FIG. 15.4
Use the Paste Special dialog box to convert formulas to values.

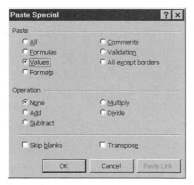

4. Select the Values option.

5. Choose OK. Excel replaces the formulas in the selected range with values.

Solving Problems with Formulas

Excel formulas can be great time-savers, allowing you to quickly create worksheets that include calculations and references to the contents of other cells. On occasion, though, your formulas can produce errors, when you enter them incorrectly or refer to cells that are invalid. Fortunately, Excel offers several ways to locate and solve errors within your formulas.

Debugging Formulas

Several errors can occur when you enter formulas in Excel. In many cases, Excel displays an error value that enables you to debug your formulas based on that value. Following are the error values and their possible causes:

Error	Meaning
#DIV/0!	The formula is trying to divide by zero.
#N/A	The formula refers to a value that is not available.
#NAME?	The formula uses a name that Excel does not recognize.
#NUL!	The formula contains a reference that specifies an invalid intersection of cells.
#NUM!	The formula uses a number incorrectly.
#REF!	The formula refers to a cell that is not valid.
#VALUE!	The formula uses an incorrect argument or operator.

 N O T E When an error value appears in the worksheet, click the Office Assistant button then Tips to see a description of the error value. ▪

Using Edit Go To Special

The Edit Go To Special command provides an easy way to locate cells with errors. To use this feature, follow these steps:

1. Choose Edit, Go To, Special. The Go To Special dialog box appears (see Figure 15.5).

2. Select Formulas, Errors. Be sure all other options are deselected.

3. Choose OK to go to cells that contain errors.

FIG. 15.5
The Go To Special dialog box assists in troubleshooting formula problems.

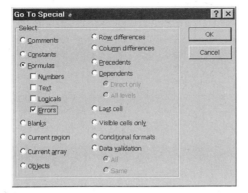

Using Auditing Features

Auditing is another useful feature that helps you trace errors, locate cells that refer to your current cell, and attach comment notes to your cells. You can use auditing to trouble-shoot errors as well as prevent errors by reviewing and commenting on your work.

Definition of Terms   Excel's auditing tools allow you to accomplish four tasks:

- Trace *precedents*
- Trace *dependents*
- Trace errors
- Check for invalid data on worksheets

In a cell that contains a formula, tracing precedents will point to cells included in that formula. Tracing dependents will point to any cells that include a formula reference to the current cell.

For example, if cell A3 refers to the contents of cell A1 plus cell A2, then cell A3 would point to its precedents, cells A1 and A2. Cell A1, however, would point to cell A3 as its dependent. Figure 15.6 illustrates both precedents and dependents.

Choosing from the Menu or Auditing Toolbar   You can access Excel's auditing feature from either the menu or toolbar. To access from the menu, choose Tools, Auditing, and select your option from the menu that displays. Options include Trace Precedents, Trace Dependents, Trace Error, Remove All Arrows, or Show Auditing Toolbar.

To display the Auditing toolbar, choose Tools, Auditing, Show Auditing Toolbar. Table 15.1 illustrates each button on this toolbar.

FIG. 15.6
Arrows trace both
precedents and
dependents in a
worksheet.

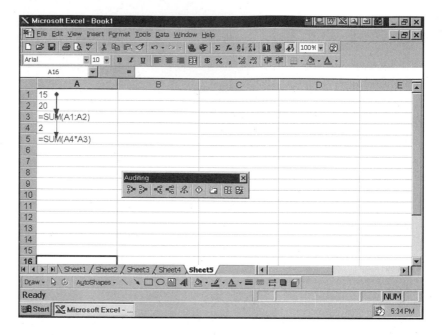

Table 15.1 Auditing Toolbar

Button	Name
	Trace Precedents
	Remove Precedent Arrows
	Trace Dependents
	Remove Dependent Arrows
	Remove All Arrows
	Trace Error
	New Comment
	Circle Invalid Data
	Clear Validation Circles

Auditing an Error

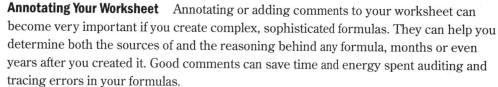

> **CAUTION**
>
> Be sure that the Show All or Show Placeholders option is selected in the View tab of the Options dialog box, or you won't be able to use the auditing features (the toolbar will beep or the menu options will be dimmed). To access this tab, choose Tools, Options.

To audit an error, follow these steps:

1. Select the cell you want to audit.

 2. Click the Trace Error button from the Auditing toolbar, or choose Tools, Auditing, and select Trace Error from the menu.

3. View the precedents of the problem formula to help you determine a solution.

 To locate and identify cells that contain invalid data, choose the Circle Invalid Data button.

Annotating Your Worksheet   Annotating or adding comments to your worksheet can become very important if you create complex, sophisticated formulas. They can help you determine both the sources of and the reasoning behind any formula, months or even years after you created it. Good comments can save time and energy spent auditing and tracing errors in your formulas.

To add a comment, follow these steps:

1. Select the cell you want to annotate.

2. Click the New Comment button on the Auditing toolbar, or choose Insert, Comment.

3. Enter a comment in the box that displays (see Figure 15.7).

4. Click outside the box to close it

After you finish annotating your worksheet, you will notice that all the cells with comments have a small red triangle in the upper right corner. You can position the mouse pointer over any annotated cell to display the contents of the comment. To edit the comment, press Shift+F2. After you create a comment, you can delete it by selecting Edit, Clear, Comments or by right-clicking and choosing Delete Comment from the shortcut menu.

FIG. 15.7
Excel lets you add extensive comments to each cell.

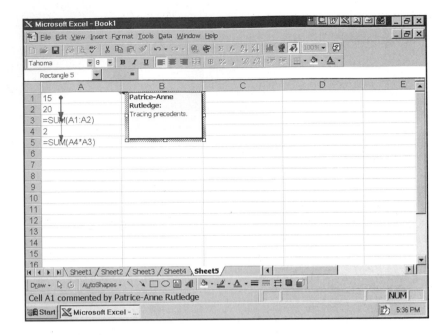

Working with Range Names

As you become more proficient in writing formulas, you will find that cell references are sorely lacking in describing the data that is being calculated. If you saw the formula =B9–C9 in a worksheet, it wouldn't be clear as to which data is being used.

N O T E To display the cells to which a formula refers, select the formula in the worksheet and then click the Trace Precedents button in the Auditing toolbar, as detailed in the previous section, "Using Auditing Features." ■

By assigning a name to a cell or range of cells, you can describe the data in your worksheets. The formula +Total_Sales–Total_Expenses, for example, instantly tells you what data the formula uses.

N O T E If you're editing a formula that includes several ranges, the range finder feature makes it easy to locate these ranges by displaying them with a color border. ■

Creating a Range Name

To create a range name, follow these steps:

1. Select the cell or range of cells you want to name.

2. Click the Name box located at the left end of the formula bar.

3. Enter the name you want to assign to the selected range.

4. Press Enter.

To create a range name using an alternative method, follow these steps:

1. After selecting cells, choose Insert, Name, Define. The Define Name dialog box appears.

2. Type a name in the Names in Workbook text box.

3. Choose OK.

Keep the following rules in mind when choosing a range name:

- The first character of a range name must be either a letter or underline.
- The remaining characters can be letters, numbers, underlines, or periods.
- Spaces aren't allowed in range names.
- Don't name a range like a cell reference (such as B1 or C4, for example).

N O T E You can also create a range name from existing text by selecting the cells to name, and choosing Insert, Name, Create. Define how to create your name in the Create Names dialog box.

 T I P To move to a range quickly, type the range name which you want to go to in the Name box.

To display a list of range names in the active workbook, click the arrow next to the Name box in the formula bar. The drop-down list displays all range names in the workbook (see Figure 15.8).

FIG. 15.8

This drop-down list displays all range names in the workbook.

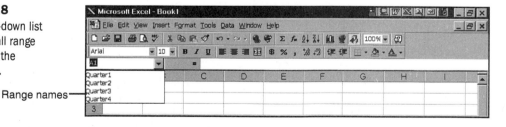

Range names

N O T E You also can use the Name box to insert a name into a formula. Click the drop-down arrow next to the Name box, and select the range name you want to use.

Inserting Names

After you assign a range name, you can refer to that range name the way you refer to cell references.

To insert a name into a formula, follow these steps:

1. To create a formula that uses range names, type = (equal sign) to start the formula.

2. Choose Insert, Name, Paste. The Paste Name dialog box appears (see Figure 15.9).

FIG. 15.9

Insert a name into a formula in the Paste Name dialog box.

3. In the Paste Name drop-down list, select the name you want to insert.

4. Click OK to close the dialog box.

5. Type the rest of the formula, and press Enter or click the check box in the formula bar when you finish (see Figure 15.10).

FIG. 15.10

This formula refers to two range names in the worksheet, Total_Sales and Total_Expenses.

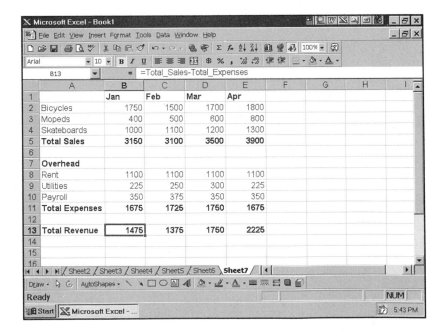

Deleting Range Names

If you change the contents of a range, you may want to delete the range name if it no longer applies. To delete a range name, follow these steps:

1. Choose Insert, Name, Define. The Define Name dialog box appears (see Figure 15.11).

FIG. 15.11
You can delete range names in the Define Name dialog box.

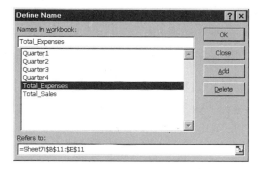

2. In the Names in Workbook drop-down list, select the range name you want to delete.

3. Click the Delete button.

4. Choose OK.

NOTE When you define names in the Define Name dialog box, click the Add and Delete buttons to make multiple changes. Choose OK when you finish making changes. ▪

TROUBLESHOOTING

After I deleted a range name, Excel replaced some of the formulas in the worksheet with the value #NAME?. When you delete a range name, any formula that refers to the range name returns #NAME?. To correct a formula that refers to a deleted range name, replace the #NAME? reference with the appropriate cell address, or choose Insert, Name, Define to re-create the deleted range name.

After I create a formula that uses a name, Excel interprets the formula as a text entry. When you use a range name as the first item in a formula, you must begin the formula with an equal sign (=), as in **=SALES*4.05**. Otherwise, Excel thinks that you are entering a text label.

CHAPTER 16

Using Functions

by Patrice-Anne Rutledge

Excel's functions are built-in calculation tools that perform complex financial, statistical, or analytical calculations; assist in decision-making; and create or manipulate text. Although you can enter many of these functions manually as a formula, using a built-in function can help reduce errors. To make creating a function even easier, Excel offers additional guidance with the Paste Function feature. ■

Creating functions

Excel 97 includes hundreds of predefined functions that enable you to easily create sophisticated calculations.

Paste Function feature

The Paste Function feature guides you step-by-step through using any of Excel's numerous functions.

Understanding Functions

If you could not calculate complex formulas in Excel, creating worksheets would be quite difficult. Fortunately, Excel provides more than 200 built-in *functions*, or predefined formulas, that enable you to create formulas easily for a wide range of applications, including business, scientific, and engineering applications.

Excel comes with a large number of built-in worksheet functions, including mathematical, database, financial, and statistical functions. The program also includes date, time, information, logical, lookup, reference, text, and trigonometric functions.

Using Arguments

Each function consists of the equal sign (=), the function name, and the *argument(s)* (cells used for carrying out the calculation). The SUM function, for example, adds the numbers in a specified range of cells (see Figure 16.1). The addresses of the specified cells make up the argument portion of the function. The active cell shows the result of the function. The most common argument type is numeric, but arguments can also be text, values, dates, times, or arrays.

▶ **See** "Creating a Formula by Typing," **p. 374**

FIG. 16.1
This formula uses the SUM function to total the entries in cells B2, B3, and B4.

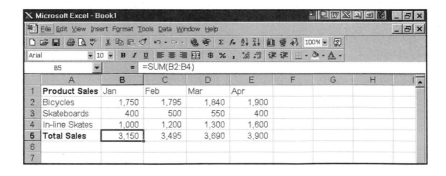

Functions can include both mandatory and optional arguments. Mandatory arguments are indicated in bold italic type; optional arguments are in italic type. For example, the format for the payment function is PMT(**rate,nper,pv**,*fv,type*). This indicates that in order to calculate a payment, you must include the rate, number of periods, and present value, but the future value and type are not required. Functions such as PMT( ) will be explained in more detail later in this chapter.

Observing the Parts of the Screen that Help Create Functions

There are two toolbars that contain buttons or boxes that assist in the creation of functions: the Standard toolbar and the formula bar. The Standard toolbar is the default toolbar; the formula bar appears when you enter data into a cell. Figure 16.2 displays these main areas.

▶ **See** "Using Toolbars in Microsoft Office Applications," **p. 45**

Part
III

Ch
16

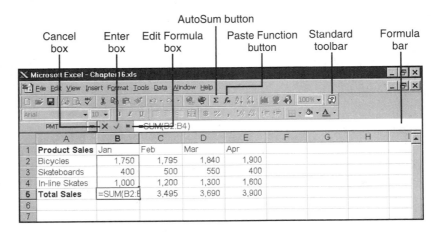

FIG. 16.2
The Standard toolbar and the formula bar contain many features that relate to functions.

When you begin to enter a function into a cell, what you enter will display in the Entry area. To accept the function data, you can press Enter or click the Enter box on the formula toolbar. To cancel your entry, click the Cancel box. The formula bar also shows you the cell reference or name of the active cell in the Name box and the list of named cells or ranges in the Range Name drop-down list. For more automated function creation, you can use the AutoSum button to automatically total a range.

Entering Functions

There are several ways to enter a function in Excel. You can:

- Type the function in yourself.
- Use the AutoSum button to sum ranges of data.
- Use the Paste Function feature to guide you in entering the function you need.

Typing Functions

T I P If you're a Lotus 1-2-3 user, you can enter a 1-2-3 function, such as **@SUM(A1..A4)**, and Excel
will convert it to the appropriate Excel function.

To enter a function in the active cell, type = (equal sign), followed by the function name
(for example, SUM), followed by an open parenthesis. Then, specify the cell or range of
cells you want the function to use, followed by a closed parenthesis. When you press Enter to enter the function in the cell, Excel displays the result of the formula in the cell.

▶ **See** "Entering Data," **p. 303**

N O T E You do not need to enter the last parenthesis if you are creating a formula with Excel's
built-in functions. Excel automatically adds the last parenthesis when you press
Enter. ▮

Using the AutoSum Button to Sum Ranges

  You can use the AutoSum button, located in the Standard toolbar, to sum a range of cells
quickly. You can, for example, use the AutoSum button to total the values in adjacent columns or rows. To do so, select a cell adjacent to the range you want to sum, and then click
the AutoSum button. Excel inserts the SUM function and selects the cells in the column
above the selected cell or in the row to the left of the selected cell.

You also can highlight the range of cells you want to sum. To do so, select the range of
cells (including blank cells) to the right of or below the range, and then click the AutoSum
button. Excel fills in the totals.

Using the Paste Function Feature

If you're not sure how a particular function works, the Paste Function feature can guide
you through the process of entering the function.

  To display the Paste Function dialog box, choose <u>I</u>nsert, <u>F</u>unction (see Figure 16.3).
The Function <u>C</u>ategory list displays Excel's built-in functions, and the Function <u>N</u>ame list
shows an alphabetized list of functions available for the highlighted category. To access
the DATE function, for example, select Date & Time in the Function <u>C</u>ategory list, and
then select DATE in the Function <u>N</u>ame list.

  If you aren't sure which function to use, click the Yes, Please Provide Help button in the
Office Assistant. Then, enter a description of what you want to accomplish in the text box

and click the Search button. Office Assistant responds by providing a list of recommended worksheet functions, with the most likely at the top of the Function Name list. For example, if you enter **I want to create a total**, Office Assistant recommends the SUM function.

After you select the function you want, click OK and the formula palette drops down from the formula bar. The formula palette prompts you to enter the arguments required for the function (see Figure 16.4). An argument can be a single cell reference, a group of cells, a number, or another function. Some functions require a single argument; others require multiple arguments. Function arguments are enclosed in parentheses, and arguments are separated by commas.

Part
III

Ch
16

FIG. 16.3
In the Paste Function dialog box, select the function you want to use.

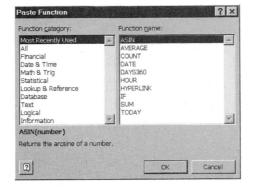

FIG. 16.4
Enter the required arguments for the function in the formula palette.

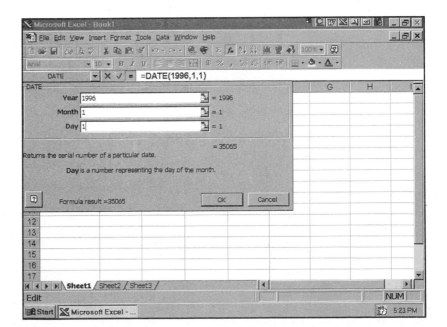

Each argument text box must contain a cell reference or data. If an argument is required, the label to the left of the text box is bold.

To enter argument data, click the mouse or press Tab to position the insertion point in the first argument text box. The formula palette displays a description of the argument in the display area below the text boxes. Enter the values to be used for the arguments or click the Cell Reference button to go to the worksheet to select the cell(s) for the argument. Click the Cell Reference button again to return to the formula palette. The formula result displays at the bottom of the palette.

▶ **See** "Debugging Formulas," **p. 382**

Click OK to enter the function in the cell. The formula palette disappears, and the result of the formula appears in the cell. If the formula contains an error or is incomplete, either an alert box pops up or an error value, such as #NAME? or #NUM!, appears in the cell.

In some cases, Excel highlights the part of the function that contains the error. Edit the function in the formula bar, and when the formula is corrected or complete, click the check box or press Enter.

Editing Functions

After entering a function, you can edit it. You can use the Paste Function feature to edit a function, or you can edit the formula and function directly in the cell.

▶ **See** "Editing Worksheet Data," **p. 322**

To use the Paste Function feature to edit a formula, follow these steps:

1. Select the cell that contains the function you want to edit.

2. Choose Insert, Function. The formula palette appears, displaying the function used in the formula.

3. Change any of the arguments as necessary.

4. Click OK when you complete the function.

To edit a function manually, follow these steps:

1. Select the cell that contains the function you want to edit.

2. Double-click the cell or click the formula bar.

3. Select the argument you want to change.

4. Enter the new argument.

5. Press Enter or click the check-mark button in the formula bar.

Getting Help with Functions

As you are using Excel's functions, you can use Help to get assistance. To access Excel's online help for functions, choose <u>H</u>elp, <u>C</u>ontents & Index and then select the Find tab. Type **functions by category**, and then double-click the topic for the worksheet functions listed by category. This section includes a help topic for each function, with detailed information on the function's syntax, hints, and examples (see Figure 16.5).

▶ **See** "Using Online Help," **p. 133**

FIG. 16.5

Excel's Help feature offers detailed information on many types of worksheet functions.

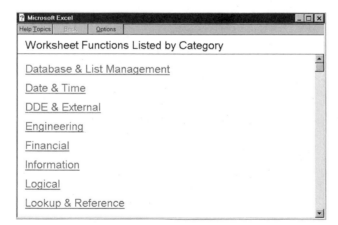

Part III
Ch 16

TROUBLESHOOTING

After I click the AutoSum button, Excel does not produce a total amount. If you click the AutoSum button and there are no surrounding cells with numbers to add, the SUM function does not recognize a range address to sum. Select the range of cells you want to sum; the range address appears within the parentheses. Remember that to use the AutoSum button, you must select a cell adjacent to the values you want to sum, or you must select the range of cells (including any blank cells) and then click the AutoSum button.

After I enter a function, Excel displays the error value #NAME? in the cell. There are two possible causes: you specified a range name that does not exist, or you misspelled the function name. To check, look in the formula bar and double-check the spelling of the function. If this spelling is incorrect, press F2 and correct it. If the function name is spelled correctly, the next step is to make sure that the range to which you referred exists in the worksheet. To do this, click the arrow at the left end of the formula bar, and check the range names in the drop-down list. If the name does not appear in this list, choose Insert, Name, Define to create the range name. When you do, the formula will return the correct result.

CHAPTER 17

Creating and Printing Reports

by Patrice-Anne Rutledge

After you type and format text, formulas, and functions, you'll need to print out your worksheet on paper. Excel provides opportunities for printing all or part of your worksheet, previewing the page, setting margins and page breaks, and creating reports that consist of multiple worksheet areas. ■

Printing in Excel

In Excel, you have many options for defining print areas and page settings as well as previewing and printing worksheet data.

Custom Views

You can define multiple print ranges, with different display and page setup characteristics, in a single worksheet.

Report Manager

Excel enables you to create reports consisting of named views and scenarios.

Printing Worksheet Data

Excel provides many options that enable you to control the printed output of your worksheets. You can use the Print Preview command to preview worksheet data before printing. The Page Setup command enables you to define margin settings and to create headers and footers. Both commands can be found in the File menu.

▶ **See** "Printing All or Part of the Document," **p. 121**

Printing a Particular Area

You can print the entire workbook, a specific worksheet in the workbook, or a selected range of data. By default, Excel automatically selects and prints the current worksheet. You can, however, define a portion of the worksheet to be printed.

Printing a Specific Range   To print a specific range in the worksheet, follow these steps:

1. Select the range to be printed, using the mouse or the keyboard.

2. Choose File, Print, or press Ctrl+P. The Print dialog box appears, as shown in Figure 17.1.

FIG. 17.1
The Print dialog box enables you to specify the data you want to print.

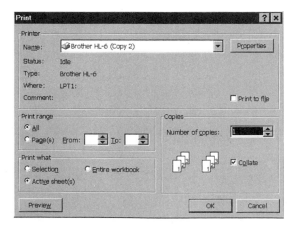

3. In the Print What section of the dialog box, select the Selection option.

4. Choose OK. Excel prints the selected worksheet range.

Defining a Print Area   If you are printing the same range in a worksheet over and over, you can define that range as the print area so that you no longer need to specify the range each time you print the worksheet.

TIP You can also set the print area in the Sheet tab of the Page Setup dialog box (choose File, Page Setup).

To define the print area, follow these steps:

1. Select your specified area, either with the keyboard or the mouse.

2. Choose File, Print Area.

3. Select Set Print Area from the menu.

Removing a Defined Print Area   To remove a defined print area, choose File, Print Area, and select Clear Print Area from the menu. You can also remove a defined print area in the Page Setup dialog box. To do so, choose File, Page Setup, and click the Sheet tab. Delete the reference in the Print Area text box, and then choose OK.

Part

III

Ch

17

Inserting and Removing Page Breaks

When you define a print area, Excel inserts automatic page breaks into the worksheet. Automatic page breaks, which appear as dashed lines in the worksheet, control the data that appears on each printed page. Excel also inserts automatic page breaks when a selected print range cannot fit on a single page. If you aren't satisfied with the location of the automatic page breaks, you can insert manual page breaks.

You can insert two types of page breaks:

■ *Vertical page breaks*. Break the print range at the current column.

■ *Horizontal page breaks*. Break the page at the current row.

Inserting a Vertical Page Break   To insert a vertical page break, follow these steps:

1. Click the heading of the column to the right of where the page break should occur.

2. Choose Insert, Page Break. A dashed line appears in the worksheet, indicating the page break.

Inserting a Horizontal Page Break   To insert a horizontal page break, follow these steps:

1. Click the heading of the row below where the page break should occur.

2. Choose Insert, Page Break. Excel adds the page break.

Excel 97 has a new view for managing page breaks. Choose View, Page Break Preview. Page breaks are indicated by thick blue lines (see Figure 17.2) and page numbers are indicated by a large gray text. To modify the page break, move to a blue line (the mouse pointer changes to a double black arrow) and drag the line to the new position. To return to normal view, choose View, Normal.

FIG. 17.2

Drag a line in Page Break Preview to change page breaks.

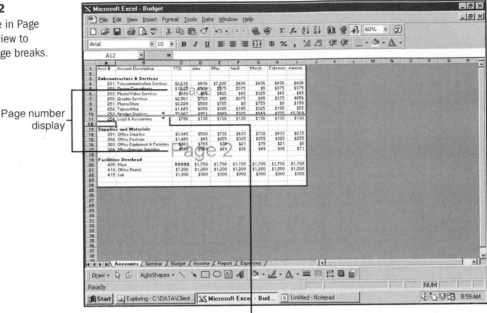

Page number display

Change horizontal page break

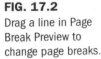 **TIP** To remove all manual page breaks from the worksheet, click the Select All button in the top left corner of the worksheet frame (the rectangular button next to cell A1), and then choose Insert, Reset All Page Breaks.

Removing Page Breaks To remove a page break, position the cell pointer below or to the right of the page-break intersection, and then choose Insert, Remove Page Break.

Fitting the Print Range to a Single Page If the specified print range is a few lines too long to print on a single page, you can fit the worksheet to the page. When you use this method, Excel scales the worksheet so that it fits on a single page.

To fit the print range on a single page, follow these steps:

1. Choose File, Page Setup.

2. If necessary, select the Page tab.

3. Select the Fit To option. By default, the Fit To option is one page wide by one page tall.

4. Choose OK. When you print, Excel scales the worksheet range to a single page.

TROUBLESHOOTING

While attempting to remove a page break, I chose the Insert menu, but the Remove Page Break command was not displayed in the menu. To remove a manual page break, you first must select the cell that contains the manual page break setting. When the cell pointer is correctly positioned, the Remove Page Break command appears in the Insert menu.

After selecting the entire worksheet, I chose Insert, Remove Page Break, but Excel removed only some of the page breaks. A print area must be defined for the worksheet. When you define a print area, Excel automatically inserts page breaks into the worksheet. Although these page breaks appear similar to the manual page breaks that you insert into the document, you cannot use the Remove Page Break command to delete them; instead, you must clear the defined print area.

To clear a defined print area, choose File, Print Area and select Clear Print Area. When you return to the worksheet, the page breaks no longer appear.

Part
III

Ch
17

Modifying the Page Setup

The Page Setup command enables you to define the page settings for the printed output. You can change the orientation of the page, change the margins and text alignment, and set print titles.

TIP To change the worksheet page orientation from the default of *portrait,* select the Landscape option on the Page tab in the Page Setup dialog box.

Changing Worksheet Page Margins   The margins define the distance between the printed output and the edge of the page. Excel enables you to change the top, bottom, left, and right margin settings. In addition, you can specify margins for the headers and footers, as well as center the print range between the margins, either horizontally or vertically.

To change the margins, follow these steps:

1. Choose File, Page Setup.
2. Select the Margins tab.
3. Enter the measurements, in inches, in the appropriate text boxes. You also can click the up and down arrows to change the margin settings by increments. Figure 17.3 shows the margins for the current print range.

FIG. 17.3

Use the Margins tab of the Page Setup dialog box to change the margins and the alignment of data on a page.

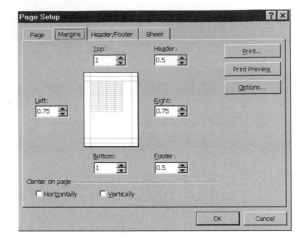

4. To indicate the header and footer margins, specify the measurement in the He<u>a</u>der and <u>F</u>ooter boxes.

 N O T E   You also can change the margins from within print preview by dragging the margin borders. For more information, see "Changing Worksheet Page Margins and Other Settings in Print Preview" later in this chapter.

5. To center the data between the top and bottom margins on the page, select the <u>V</u>ertically option. To center the data between the left and right margins, select the Hori<u>z</u>ontally option. To center the text both horizontally and vertically on the page, select both options.

6. Choose OK.

Setting and Removing Print Titles   When you print large worksheets, you can set print titles so that information such as worksheet titles, column headings, and row headings appears on each page in the printout.

To create print titles, follow these steps:

1. Choose <u>F</u>ile, Page Set<u>u</u>p.

2. Select the Sheet tab, if necessary.

T I P   You can also select the cell reference buttons to the right of the <u>R</u>ows To Repeat At Top or the <u>C</u>olumns To Repeat At Left box to return to the worksheet for cell selection.

3. If you want to define titles across the top of each page, select the <u>R</u>ows To Repeat At Top box. If you want to define titles down the left side of each page, select the <u>C</u>olumns To Repeat At Left box (see Figure 17.4).

FIG. 17.4
In the Page Setup dialog box, define the rows to repeat on every page.

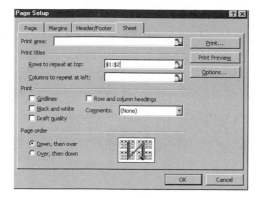

4. If you are defining titles to appear across the top of each page, select the row headings containing the data you want to use as titles, or enter the row references.

   If you are defining titles to appear down the left side of the page, select the column headings containing the data you want to use as titles, or enter the column references.

5. Choose OK.

N O T E When you print a worksheet that contains print titles, do not select the range containing the titles when you define the print area. Otherwise, the titles will appear twice on the first page of the printout. ■

To remove print titles, follow these steps:

1. Choose File, Page Setup.
2. Select the Sheet tab, if necessary.
3. Delete the cell references in the Print Titles section of the dialog box.
4. Choose OK.

Setting Other Print Options

You can define additional print settings in the Page Setup dialog box. You can include the worksheet gridlines in the printout; print notes that have been added to cells; print the data in black and white, even if color has been applied to the worksheet; and include the row and column headings.

▶ **See** "Changing Printing Options," **p. 122**

Choose File, Page Setup, and select the Sheet tab. In the Print section of the dialog box, select or deselect the check box adjacent to the appropriate print option.

Creating Headers and Footers

Headers and footers enable you to add text—such as the current date, page number, and file name—to the top and bottom of the printed page. Excel provides default header and footer information (the name of the current sheet is centered in the header, and the current page number is centered in the footer). You also can select additional options and define your own header and footer information.

Using Predefined Headers and Footers   To select one of Excel's predefined header and footer options, follow these steps:

1. Choose File, Page Setup.

2. Select the Header/Footer tab (see Figure 17.5).

FIG. 17.5
Select the text you want to use in the header and footer area of the printed page.

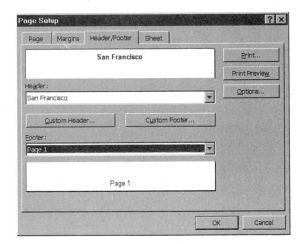

 TIP To remove a header or footer, select None from the appropriate list.

---

3. Click the arrow next to the Header box, and select a header from the drop-down list.

4. Select the data you want to use as a footer from the Footer list.

5. Choose OK.

Creating Custom Headers and Footers   Instead of using a predefined header and footer, you can define your own custom header and footer. Follow these steps:

1. Choose File, Page Setup.

2. Select the Header/Footer tab, if necessary.

3. If appropriate, select an existing header or footer that resembles the header or footer you want to create.

4. Select the Custom Header or Custom Footer option to display a new dialog box. Figure 17.6 shows the Header dialog box.

   Each text box that appears in the dialog box controls the alignment of the text in the header or footer. Data can be left-aligned, centered, or right-aligned. Excel uses codes to create certain types of text in the headers and footers. The Page Number code, for example, is used to insert page numbering. The buttons that appear above the text boxes are used to insert the codes. Table 17.1, which follows these steps, describes the code buttons you can use in the header and footer.

FIG. 17.6

Create custom headers and footers by using the text boxes and buttons that appear in this dialog box.

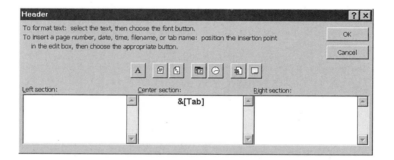

5. Select one of the three text boxes, and then type the header or footer text, or choose a button to enter a header or footer code. To apply text formatting to the header or footer information, click the Font button to display the Font dialog box, and select the appropriate options.

6. Choose OK.

Table 17.1   Header and Footer Codes

Button	Name	Code	Description
A	Font	None	Displays the Font dialog box.
[#]	Page Number	&[Page]	Inserts the page number.
[↕]	Total Pages	&[Pages]	Inserts the total number of pages.

continues

Part
III

Ch
17

Table 17.1   Continued

Button	Name	Code	Description
	Date	&[Date]	Inserts the current date.
	Time	&[Time]	Inserts the current time.
	File Name	&[File]	Inserts the file name.
	Sheet Name	&[Tab]	Inserts the name of the active sheet.

Previewing a Worksheet

You can preview the data before you print the worksheet to make sure that the data appears the way you want. You also can change the margin settings and column widths, if necessary.

▶ **See** "Using Print Preview," **p. 122**

To preview the data, follow these steps:

1. Choose File, Print Preview. Excel switches to Print Preview and displays the print range, as shown in Figure 17.7.

2. Click the Next and Previous buttons to move from page to page. Notice that these buttons appear dimmed if the data you are previewing fits on a single page.

TIP   In Print preview, press Page Up and Page Down to display each page in the document. Press Home to move to the first page; press End to move to the last page.

Zooming In and Out on the Worksheet   For a closer look at data, you can zoom in and view an enlarged display; when you want to see more of the data, you can zoom out.

To zoom in on the worksheet, click the Zoom button, or position the mouse pointer over the section you want to view and click the left mouse button. The mouse pointer changes to a magnifying glass when positioned over the page. To view other areas of the page, use the vertical and horizontal scroll bars. To zoom out, click the Zoom button again, or click the left mouse button.

FIG. 17.7
Print Preview shows what the worksheet will look like when printed.

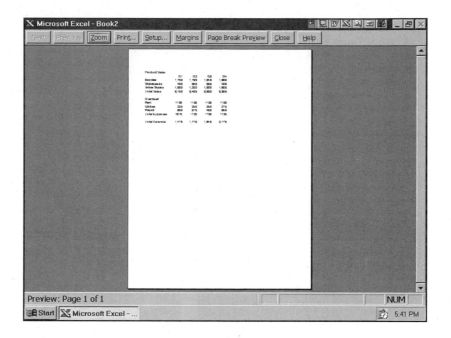

Changing Worksheet Page Margins and Other Settings in Print Preview   If, while previewing the worksheet, you find that the current margins or column widths are not adequate, you can change them in print preview. When you click the Margins button, light-gray boundaries indicating the margins appear around the page. Black handles also appear to indicate the top, bottom, left, and right margins. Square handles appear along the top of the page, with lines indicating the width of each column. Figure 17.8 shows margin and column markers in print preview.

To adjust the margins, click the handle that represents the margin you want to change. When you do, the mouse pointer changes to a crossbar, and the status bar shows the actual margin setting. Drag the handle to the appropriate location. When you release the mouse button, the margin adjusts, and the data is repositioned on the page.

To change a column width, click the square handle that indicates the column width you want to change. The status bar displays the current column width. Drag the marker to increase or decrease the column width. When you release the mouse button, the column width and data adjust to fit the new size.

To adjust page breaks, select Page Break Preview which enables you to click and drag page breaks with the mouse.

▶ **See** "Changing Column Width and Row Height," **p. 351**

See "Changing Column Width and Row Height," **p. 351**

Column marker   Margin markers

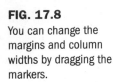

FIG. 17.8
You can change the margins and column widths by dragging the markers.

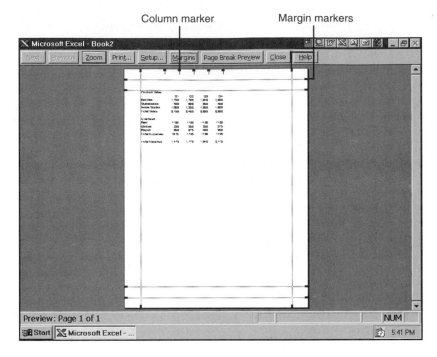

When you're satisfied with the way the data appears, click the Print button to print the worksheet. To return to the worksheet, click the Close button.

Printing the Worksheet

After you define the print settings and preview the data, you're ready to print the worksheet. The File Print command enables you to specify the number of copies you want to print, as well as the number of pages (if the print range spans multiple pages). You also can specify the data you want to print, if you have not already defined a print area.

 TIP Click the Print button in the Standard toolbar to bypass the Print dialog box and send the output directly to the printer with the default print settings.

 To print the worksheet, follow these steps:

1. Choose File, Print, or press Ctrl+P. The Print dialog box appears.

2. If you have not defined a print area, you can specify the data you want to print by selecting options in the Print What section of the dialog box (refer to Figure 17.1).

3. Select the Selection option to print the selected range of cells; select the Active Sheet(s) option to print the selected worksheets in the workbook; or select the Entire Workbook option to print every worksheet in the current workbook.

4. To specify the number of copies to be printed, enter the amount in the Copies box.

5. To specify a specific range of pages to be printed, enter the range in the Print Range section of the dialog box.

6. When you're ready to print, choose OK.

N O T E The Print dialog box also includes a button that enables you to access the Properties box. To change any of these settings, click the Properties button and make the necessary selections. ▨

TROUBLESHOOTING

My data won't fit on the page when I print it. You have several options to get your worksheet data to fit on one page—you can use the Fit to Page option on the Page tab of the Page Setup dialog box, reduce the font size, decrease the margin width, change column widths, or change from portrait to landscape orientation if you haven't already done so.

I created a custom header, and the header overflows onto my data when I print it. To adjust the space between a custom header and your worksheet data, choose File, Page Setup to open the Page Setup dialog box. Select the Margin tab and decrease the size in the Header box (or increase size of Top box). For example, if you reduce the size from .5 (the default) to .25, you will increase the space between the header and your data. You can also adjust the footer in this section as well.

Part
III

Ch
17

Using Views and Reports

Excel provides an add-in that enables you to create and generate printed reports: the Report Manager. This add-in lets you create a report consisting of named views and scenarios.

Installing the Report Manager Add-In

Before you can define a named view or create a report, you must install the Report Manager Add-In. (You must have installed this option during setup.)

To install the Add-In, follow these steps:

1. Choose Tools, Add-Ins. The Add-Ins dialog box appears (see Figure 17.9).

▶ **See** "Creating a Scenario Pivot Table Report," **p. 448**

FIG. 17.9

Use the Add-Ins dialog box to install Excel Add-Ins.

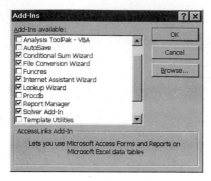

2. Select Report Manager from the Add-Ins Available list.

3. Choose OK. The Report Manager command is added to the View menu.

Creating a View

Choosing View, Custom Views enables you to define multiple print ranges, with different display and page-setup characteristics, in a single worksheet. Normally, every print area of a worksheet must contain the same display characteristics. By using named views, however, you can print multiple ranges with different print settings at the same time.

To create a view, follow these steps:

1. Select the range of cells you want to define as a view.

2. Choose View, Custom Views. The Custom Views dialog box appears (see Figure 17.10).

3. Click the Add button. The Add View dialog box appears (see Figure 17.11).

FIG. 17.10

Create multiple views of worksheet data in the Custom Views dialog box.

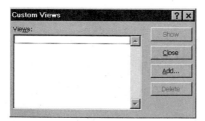

FIG. 17.11
Enter a name for the
view in the Add View
dialog box.

4. Enter a name for the view in the Name text box.
5. Choose OK.

Creating a Report

N O T E   You can also create a report in Access using Excel data (if you have this option
installed). To do so, choose Data, Access Report. To create an Access form with your
data, choose Data, Access Form; to export the data to Access, use the Data, Convert to Access
command. ▮

If your worksheet consists of multiple views of your worksheet, or scenarios of data, you
can print those different views and scenarios as a report.

To create a report, follow these steps:

1. Choose View, Report Manager. The Report Manager dialog box appears.
2. Click the Add button to create the report. The Add Report dialog box appears (see
   Figure 17.12).

FIG. 17.12
Select the views and
scenarios to be added
to the report.

Part
III

Ch
17

3. Enter a name for the report in the Report Name text box.

4. Select the view you want to add to the report from the View drop-down list, and then click Add. The view you added appears in the Sections in This Report list.

5. Select the scenario you want to add to the report from the Scenario drop-down list, and then click Add. The scenario you added appears in the Sections in This Report list.

6. To change the order of the views and scenarios in the Sections in This Report list, select a view or scenario and then choose the Move Up or Move Down button to rearrange the order.

7. Repeat steps 4 through 6 until you finish adding views and scenarios to the report.

8. Select Use Continuous Page Numbers to number the pages consecutively.

9. Choose OK. You return to the Report Manager dialog box.

10. Choose Print to print the report, or Close to close the dialog box without printing the report.

Editing and Printing a Report

If you want to change the contents of a report or print a report, you can use the View Report Manager command to do so.

To edit a report, follow these steps:

1. Choose View, Report Manager. The Report Manager dialog box appears.

2. Select the name of the report you want to edit from the Reports list, and then choose Edit.

3. Change the views and scenarios, as outlined in the preceding section.

4. Choose OK.

To print a report, follow these steps:

1. Choose View, Report Manager. The Report Manager dialog box appears.

2. Select the report you want to print from the Reports list.

3. Click the Print button. The Print dialog box appears.

4. Specify the number of copies to be printed.

5. Choose OK to print the report.

TROUBLESHOOTING

I want to create a report, but the Report Manager command does not appear in the View menu. When the Report Manager command does not appear in the View menu, it means that the Report Manager add-in has not been installed. To install the Report Manager add-in, choose Tools, Add-Ins. In the Add-Ins Available list, check marks appear next to the names of the add-ins that are currently installed. Select Report Manager to add a check mark to the left of the name, and choose OK. The Report Manager command now appears in the View menu.

If the Report Manager is not in the Add-Ins dialog box, launch the Office setup program in the options list, choose Microsoft Excel, Add-Ins, and then check the Report Manager check box.

When I print a report, Excel numbers each page in the report page 1. To use consecutive page numbers in the report, choose View, Report Manager, select the name of the report from the Reports list, and choose Edit. Select the Use Continuous Page Numbers option, and choose OK. The next time you print the report, Excel will number the pages consecutively.

Part

III

Ch

17

CHAPTER 18

Managing Data

by Patrice-Anne Rutledge

With Excel, you can easily manage data by creating a list. After you organize information into a list format, you can find and extract data that meets certain criteria. In addition, you can sort information in a list to put data in a specific order, and you can extract, summarize, and compare data. You also can create a Pivot Table to summarize information in an Excel list. ■

PivotTables

With pivot tables and Excel's PivotTable Wizard, you can quickly and easily summarize and compare data found in a list.

Goal Seeker and Solver

Use these features to determine an answer based on one or more calculations.

Scenario Manager

Excel enables you to generate different answers for what-if analysis with the Scenario Manager.

Advanced Excel features

Excel 97 offers sophisticated data management features, including the use of dialog boxes and functions that help you find data.

Creating and Editing a List

A *list* is information in worksheet cells that contain similar sets of data. When you organize information in a list, you can sort, filter, and summarize data with subtotals. Each *column* in a list represents a category and determines the type of information required for each entry in the list. Each row in a list forms a *record*.

▶ **See** "Using Wizards," **p. 141**

To create a list, enter a column title for each column in the section of the worksheet where you want to start the list. You can create a list in any area of the worksheet. Just make sure that the area below the list is clear of any data so the list can expand without interfering with other data in the worksheet.

You enter data in the rows immediately following the column titles to form a record. Every record must have the same fields, but you do not have to enter data in all fields. Figure 18.1 illustrates a sample list.

FIG. 18.1
In this sample list, product sales are tracked by product, store, region, month, and amount.

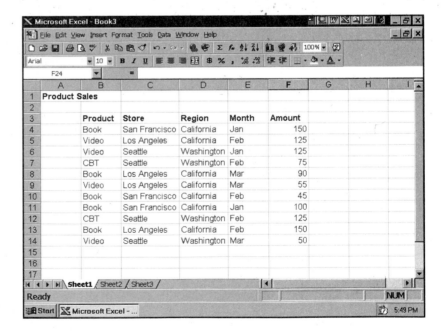

 N O T E Data validation is another feature that facilitates data entry. With it, you can set limits to what data is valid in a certain cell or range of cells. For example, you can validate only numbers less than 100,000 or names you've entered in a list. Choose <u>D</u>ata, Va<u>l</u>idation to set up data validation. ■

To facilitate entering and editing records in a list, Excel provides a *data form* that presents an organized view of the data and makes data entry easier and more accurate. The form displays field names, text boxes for data entry, and buttons for adding, deleting, and finding records. You can enter new records, edit existing records, find records, and delete records using the data form.

N O T E The Template Wizard with Data Tracking is an add-in that creates a template linking selected workbook cells to fields in a database. This feature is useful, for example, in a networked environment where more than one user will enter data into a database. To open this wizard, choose Data, Template Wizard. ■

Adding Records with the Data Form

The data form provides text boxes, using the column titles or the field names from your list. You enter the data for each field in each text box on the form.

To add a record and enter data using the data form, follow these steps:

1. Position the cell pointer in any cell in your list.
2. Choose Data, Form. The Data Form dialog box appears, as shown in Figure 18.2.

FIG. 18.2

The data form displays the field names with a text box to the right of each field name.

3. To add a new record to the list, choose the New button. A new blank form appears.
4. Enter the appropriate data in each text box on the form.

   Press Tab to move forward to the next text box. Press Shift+Tab to move to the previous text box.

N O T E If you type data for a new record in the list and then decide you don't want to add the record, choose the Restore button to erase the entry from the form. You must choose Restore before pressing Enter to save the record. ■

Part

III

Ch

18

5. When you finish entering data for the record, press Enter to add the new record to the list. Another blank form appears, enabling you to enter another new record.

6. Choose the Close button to return to the worksheet.

Viewing Records with the Data Form

You can use the data form to view records in your list. Position the cell pointer in a cell in your list and choose Data, Form.

Use the following procedures to view records in a list:

To	Do this
View the next record	Choose Find Next or press ↓
View the previous record	Choose Find Prev or press ↑
Move to a new record form	Press Page Down
View the first record	Press Page Up

You also can use the scroll bar to view each record in your list.

If you choose the Find Next button to view the next record in the list and Excel beeps, you are viewing the last record in the database. To view the first record in the list, press the Page Up key. As you view each record in the list, the data form displays the current record number in the upper-right corner of the dialog box, as shown in Figure 18.3.

FIG. 18.3
This screen displays the fourth record in a list of 11 records.

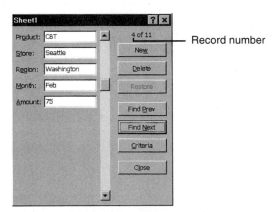

Record number

Deleting Records with the Data Form

You also can use the data form to delete records from your list. When you use the form to delete records, you are able to delete only one record at a time.

To delete a record from the data form, follow these steps:

1. Position the cell pointer in any cell in your list.

2. Choose Data, Form. The data form appears.

3. Choose the Find Next or Find Prev button, or press the up arrow or the down arrow, to move to the record you want to delete.

4. When the record you want to delete appears in the form, choose the Delete button to delete the record.

   The records below the deleted record are renumbered to account for the deleted record. Excel prompts you with the dialog box shown in Figure 18.4 to verify that you want to delete the record.

FIG. 18.4

A message box appears reminding you that the record will be permanently deleted.

5. Choose OK or press Enter to delete the record, or click Cancel to keep the record.

6. Choose the Close button to return to the worksheet.

Finding Records with the Data Form

You can use the data form to find particular records in your database. When you use the data form, you can view only one found record at a time.

To find records with the data form, follow these steps:

1. Select a cell in the list.

2. Choose Data, Form.

3. Choose the Criteria button.

4. Select a text box and enter the criteria or pattern for which you want to search, as shown in Figure 18.5.

5. Choose the Find Next button or press the down arrow after you have entered the criteria. If no matches exist, you hear a beep. Choose the Find Prev button or press the up arrow if you want to search backward through the database to find a match.

6. Choose the Close button to clear the dialog box.

FIG. 18.5
In this example, the search criterion is an amount greater than 100.

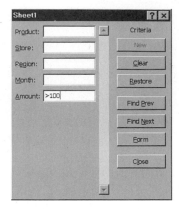

 TIP You can use multiple criteria when searching for records. Just enter the criteria values in the appropriate text boxes.

 TROUBLESHOOTING

After I choose Data, Form, Excel displays an error message stating that no list was found.
Before choosing Data, Form, you must first select any cell within the list you want to modify.

When I choose New to add a new record to the list in the data form, Excel displays the message Cannot extend list or database, and I can't enter a new record. The data form does not allow you to add new records to the list if there are not enough blank rows below the current list range. Choose OK to close the dialog box and then choose Close to close the data form. If any data is below the list range, choose Edit, Cut and Edit, Paste to move the data to a new location. When you create a list, remember to select a location in the worksheet with enough room to expand the list.

Sorting and Filtering Data in a List

An Excel list provides you with flexibility so you can organize data to meet your needs. You can sort the list to display data in a certain order, just as you can sort table data in both Word and Access. You also can filter the list so it displays only certain records.

▶ **See** "Sorting and Filtering Data," **p. 771**

Sorting Data in a List

Excel sorts lists based on fields; it can use any field name you have created in the list as a sort field for reorganizing the list.

N O T E To quickly sort a list, select a cell in the column by which you want to sort, then click the Sort Ascending or the Sort Descending button. ▪

To sort a list, follow these steps:

1. Position the cell pointer in the list you want to sort. Or, if you want to sort only selected records in a list, highlight the records you want to sort.

2. Choose Data, Sort. The Sort dialog box appears, as shown in Figure 18.6.

FIG. 18.6
You can sort a list based on multiple field names.

3. To prevent the column titles from being sorted with the rest of the list, choose Header Row in the My List Has section of the dialog box.

4. The Sort By text box is selected and displays the first field name from the list. Use the drop-down list box to replace the field name in this text box with the field name by which you want to sort. Choose the Ascending or Descending option for the order in which you want to sort the selected records.

5. To sort records using additional fields, press Tab or select the Then By text box and specify the field. Select the next Then By text box if you want to sort by a third field.

6. Choose OK or press Enter. Excel sorts the data in the list, as shown in Figure 18.7.

 T I P If you perform an incorrect sort, choose Edit, Undo Sort or press Ctrl+Z immediately to reverse the sort and return to the original list.

N O T E If you select only certain data in your list, a Sort Warning appears. You can choose to Expand the selection or Continue with the current selection. If you don't expand, remember that only that section will be sorted, and not any of its related columns or rows. ▪

FIG. 18.7
The selected records are sorted according to the options in the Sort dialog box.

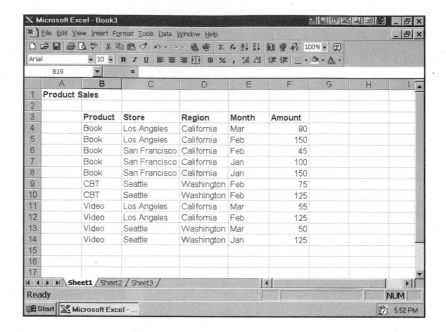

Filtering Data in a List

When you need to work with a subset of data within the list, you can filter the list so only certain records appear. After you have filtered a list, you can modify the records, generate subtotals and grand totals, and copy the data to another area of the worksheet.

When you filter a list, Excel displays only those records that meet the criteria; Excel hides the other records from view. Two methods are available for filtering the records in a list. You can use the AutoFilter command to quickly filter data in a list. Or, to filter data using additional criteria, you can use a custom AutoFilter.

Using AutoFilter to Filter Records

To filter a list with the AutoFilter command, follow these steps:

1. Select a cell in the list you want to filter.

2. Choose <u>D</u>ata, <u>F</u>ilter, Auto<u>F</u>ilter. Excel inserts drop-down arrows next to each column heading in your list, as illustrated in Figure 18.8.

3. Click the drop-down arrow in the column that contains the data you want to display. Excel displays a listing of all the unique items in the column, as shown in Figure 18.9.

FIG. 18.8
Drop-down arrows appear next to each column title.

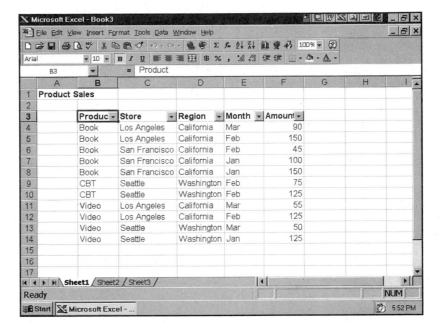

FIG. 18.9
Select the item you want to display from the drop-down list.

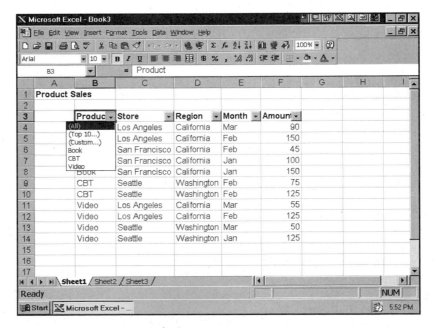

4. Select the item you want to display. If your selection includes blank cells, choose Blanks to display empty cells or NonBlanks to display cells that have value.

5. Repeat steps 3 and 4 for each additional column you want to filter.

Excel displays only those records that meet the filter criteria. Excel displays in a different color the row headings of records that match.

To return the list to its original state, select All from the drop-down list of each column.

 T I P To remove the AutoFilter drop-down arrows from your list, choose <u>D</u>ata, <u>F</u>ilter, Auto<u>F</u>ilter again.

Creating a Custom AutoFilter

You can define a custom AutoFilter when the data you want to filter must meet a specified criteria.

N O T E To automatically filter the top (or bottom) 10 items in your list, select Top 10 from your AutoFilter list to open the Top 10 AutoFilter dialog box. In this dialog box, you can set criteria for filtering a certain number of items. ■

To create a custom AutoFilter, follow these steps:

1. Select a cell in the list you want to filter.

2. Choose <u>D</u>ata, <u>F</u>ilter, Auto<u>F</u>ilter.

3. Click the drop-down arrow in the column that contains the data you want to filter, and choose Custom. Excel displays the Custom AutoFilter dialog box, shown in Figure 18.10.

FIG. 18.10

Define a custom filter in the Custom AutoFilter dialog box.

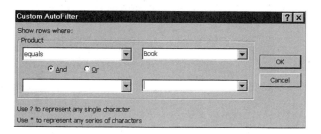

4. Click the arrow in the drop-down list of comparative operators, and select the comparative operator with which you want to compare the data. Enter the data you want to compare in the text box, or click the arrow to display a list of items and select an item.

5. To add a second set of criteria, choose <u>A</u>nd to indicate that the records must meet both sets of criteria. Choose <u>O</u>r to indicate that the records must match either set of criteria. Define the second set of criteria.

6. Choose OK or press Enter. Excel filters the list and displays those records that match the criteria (see Figure 18.11).

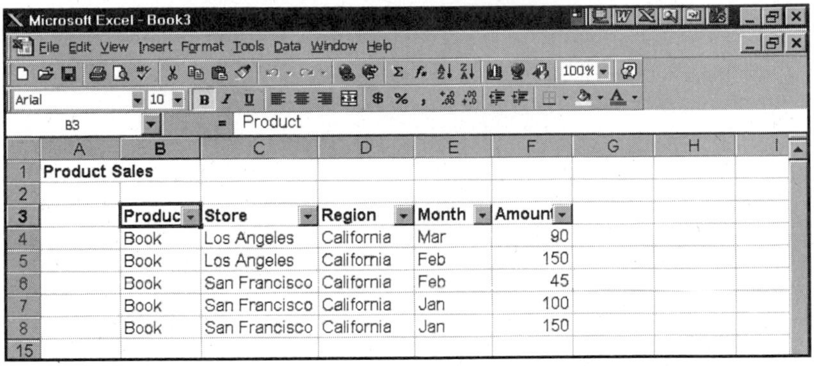

FIG. 18.11

The filtered list displays books only.

	A	B	C	D	E	F	G	H	I
1	Product Sales								
2									
3		Produc ▾	Store ▾	Region ▾	Month ▾	Amount ▾			
4		Book	Los Angeles	California	Mar	90			
5		Book	Los Angeles	California	Feb	150			
6		Book	San Francisco	California	Feb	45			
7		Book	San Francisco	California	Jan	100			
8		Book	San Francisco	California	Jan	150			
15									

TROUBLESHOOTING

After sorting the database, Excel sorts the column titles along with the data in the list.
To prevent the column titles from sorting with the rest of the list, choose Header Row in the My List Has section of the Sort dialog box.

I selected multiple filters, but my list doesn't display any records. Select All from the AutoFilter drop-down list to redisplay the records. When you use multiple filters, each record in the list must contain each of the specified criteria. If a record contains one of the specified criteria but not the other, that record does not display.

Adding and Removing Subtotals

When you sort data in a list, Excel enables you to summarize the data with subtotals. When you summarize a list, Excel calculates subtotals based on subsets of the data and also calculates a grand total.

Creating Subtotals

To add subtotals to a list, follow these steps:

1. Sort the data according to the order in which you want to create subtotals. To generate subtotals based on sales region, for example, first sort the list by Sales Region.

2. Select a cell in the list you want to summarize.

3. Choose Data, Subtotals. The Subtotal dialog box appears, as shown in Figure 18.12.

FIG. 18.12

You can generate subtotals for a list in the Subtotal dialog box.

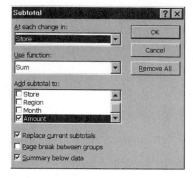

4. Select the group to define the subtotals. To generate automatic subtotals by store, for example, select the Store field from the At Each Change In drop-down list.

5. Select the Subtotal function from the Use Function drop-down list. To create subtotals, make sure that Sum is selected.

6. Choose the data you want to subtotal in the Add Subtotal To box. To subtotal the data found in the Amount field, for example, select Amount.

7. Press Enter or choose OK to add the subtotals to your list, as shown in Figure 18.13.

FIG. 18.13

The Product Sales list shows subtotal lines for each product.

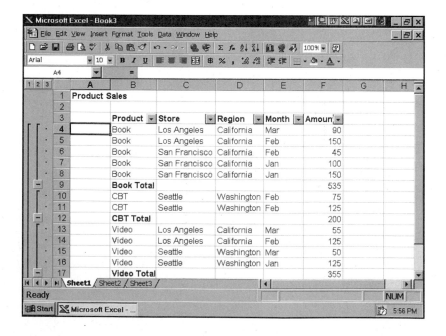

N O T E   If your list is not sorted prior to selecting the Subtotal command, Excel creates a subtotal for each entry in the list. To prevent this occurrence, sort the list before you choose the command. ▪

Hiding and Displaying Data in a Subtotaled List

When you add automatic subtotals to a list, Excel displays the list in Outline view. You can expand and contract the level of detail in the list to display only the subtotals and grand totals of data.

Figure 18.13 showed the list displayed in Outline view. The icons that appear along the left edge of the worksheet window enable you to expand and contract the level of detail.

To hide detail level, select a subtotal cell and click the Hide Detail Level button. Excel contracts the list to display the subtotal detail only (see Figure 18.14).

FIG. 18.14
Click the Hide Detail Level button to hide summary detail.

Level 1, 2, 3 buttons

Show Detail Level button

Hide Detail Level button

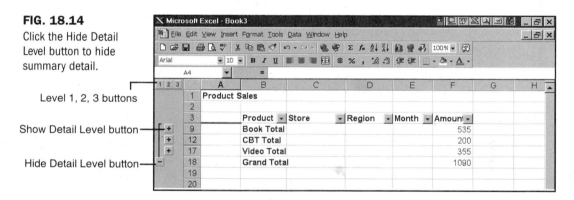

To display a detail level, select a subtotal cell and click the Show Detail Level button. Excel expands the list to show the detail level.

Removing Subtotals from a List

To remove subtotal data from a list, select a cell in the subtotaled list and choose the Data, Subtotals command. Choose the Remove All button from the Subtotals dialog box.

Summarizing Data with Pivot Tables

Excel includes a capability called the *pivot table* that enables you to quickly and easily summarize and compare data found in a list. When you want to summarize your data in another way, you only need to drag and drop fields to create a whole new report, without changing the structure of the data in your worksheets.

Part
III

Ch
18

You use the automated PivotTable Wizard, enhanced for Excel 97, to create pivot tables in Excel. The PivotTable Wizard guides you step-by-step through the process of creating a pivot table. The wizard prompts you to define the pivot table information, using the fields defined in a list.

Creating a Pivot Table with the PivotTable Wizard

When you create a pivot table from a list, the column titles in the list are used as Row, Column, and Page fields. The data in the columns become items in the pivot table. When the data in your list contain numeric items, Excel automatically uses the Sum function to calculate the values in the pivot table. If the data in your list contain text items, Excel uses the Count function to calculate a count of the source items in the pivot table.

 Don't spend too much time deciding where to place the fields. You can always rearrange the fields after you add the pivot table to your worksheet.

To create a pivot table from a list in your worksheet, follow these steps:

1. Choose Data, PivotTable Report. Step 1 of the PivotTable Wizard appears, as shown in Figure 18.15.

FIG. 18.15
Specify the data to use for the pivot table in Step 1 of the PivotTable Wizard.

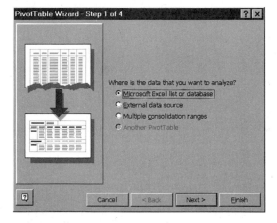

 In addition, you can create Access forms, reports, and databases with your Excel data through AccessLinks. Before you can use AccessLinks, you must first install from setup and load its add-in into memory by using the Tools, Add-Ins command. After loading, the Access Form, Access Report, and Convert to Access commands appear in the Data menu.

N O T E You can retrieve data from other applications, such as Access, by choosing the External Data Source options in Step 1. This allows you to access Microsoft Query, where you choose the exact data you want to analyze in your pivot table. Excel 97 also includes several other powerful new query features—the Query Wizard; report templates; auto-adjust refresh; and sharable, parameterized, and background queries.

2. Specify the data you want to use in the pivot table. Select Microsoft Excel List or Database, and click the Next button. Step 2 of the PivotTable Wizard appears, as shown in Figure 18.16.

FIG. 18.16
Specify the range of data in Step 2 of the PivotTable Wizard.

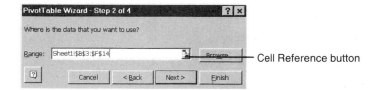

Cell Reference button

N O T E Position the cell pointer in a list in your worksheet prior to choosing the PivotTable command. Excel pastes the range of the list in the Range text box. Click Next if that's the list you want to use.

3. Specify the location of the list in the Range text box (type the range address or click the Cell Reference button to go to the worksheet and highlight the range with the mouse), and then click Next. Step 3 of the PivotTable Wizard appears, as shown in Figure 18.17.

FIG. 18.17
Define the pivot table layout in Step 3 of the PivotTable Wizard.

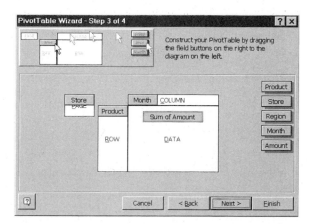

Part
III

Ch
18

4. Define the layout of the pivot table by dragging the field names displayed on the right side of the dialog box to the Data, Row, Column, or Page area. Fields placed in the Row area appear in each row in the pivot table. Fields placed in the Column area appear in each column of the pivot table. Fields placed in the Page area filter the data shown in the pivot table. A field placed in the data area is summarized (totalled, averaged, or other) by grouping of Row, Column, or Page values.

5. Click Next to display the final step in the PivotTable Wizard (see Figure 18.18).

FIG. 18.18

Specify the location of the pivot table in Step 4 of the PivotTable Wizard.

6. Indicate whether you want to place the pivot table in a New Worksheet or an Existing Worksheet. For additional options, choose the Options button.

7. If you choose the Options button, the PivotTable Options dialog box appears (see Figure 18.19). In this dialog box you can enter format and data options, such as using autoformatting and entering grand totals. You also can create a name for your pivot table. Click OK to return to Step 4.

FIG. 18.19

Choose from a variety of formatting and data options in the PivotTable Options dialog box.

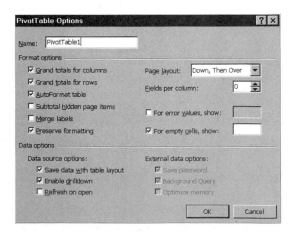

8. Choose Finish. The PivotTable Wizard displays the results in a table on the worksheet (see Figure 18.20).

FIG. 18.20

This pivot table summarizes sales by Product, Store, and Month.

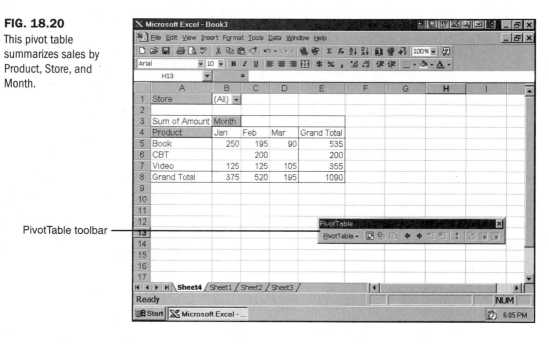

PivotTable toolbar —

When you add a pivot table to the worksheet, Excel automatically displays the PivotTable toolbar. The toolbar contains buttons for the most frequently used pivot table commands (refer to Figure 18.20).

 N O T E To display each page in the data table on a separate worksheet in the workbook, click the Show Pages button on the PivotTable toolbar. ▨

Editing and Updating a Pivot Table

N O T E When you update the data in the source list in your worksheet, you must refresh the pivot table to include the new information. To refresh data in the pivot table, select any cell in the pivot table and choose Data, Refresh Data or click the right mouse button and choose the Refresh Data command from the shortcut menu. ▨

After you have added a pivot table to your worksheet, you can quickly rearrange the fields in the pivot table to display an entirely different view of your data. Each field in the list is represented by a shaded cell in the pivot table. Figure 18.21 shows the fields. You change the view of the data by dragging the fields to other areas in the pivot table.

FIG. 18.21

Change the view in a pivot table by dragging fields to the Row, Column, and Page areas.

Page area field

Column area field

Row area field

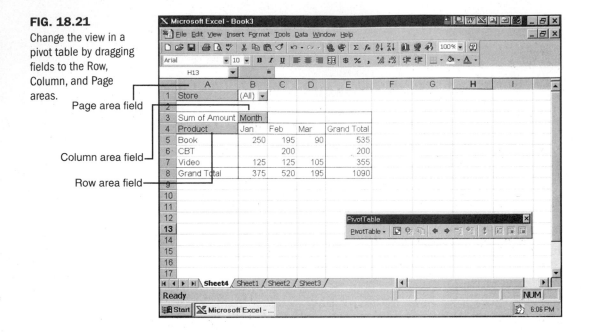

Rearranging a Pivot Table

To change the data displayed on the current page, click the drop-down arrow displayed in the Page area of the pivot table. A list of items for the current field appears. Select an item from the list to filter the data in the pivot table to display data for that item only (see Figure 18.22).

To change the data displayed in the columns of the pivot table, drag a Row or Page field to the Column area of the pivot table. When you do, the pivot table displays a columnar view of the data (see Figure 18.23).

To change the data displayed in the rows of the pivot table, drag a Page or Column field to the Row area of the pivot table. The pivot table displays data in a Row field in each row (see Figure 18.24).

FIG. 18.22
Clicking the Page area drop-down arrow enables you to display data for specific criteria.

Page area drop-down arrow

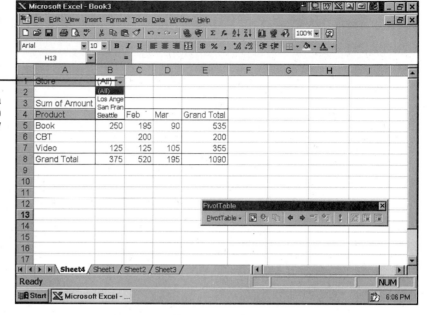

FIG. 18.23
The columns in the pivot table show sales by Month.

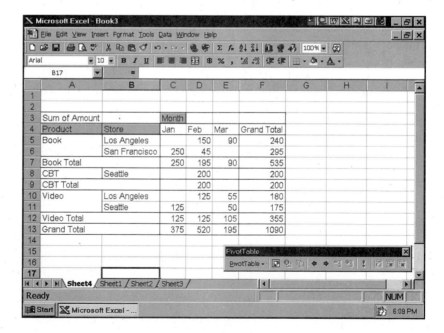

FIG. 18.24
The rows in the pivot
table show sales by
Product and Month.

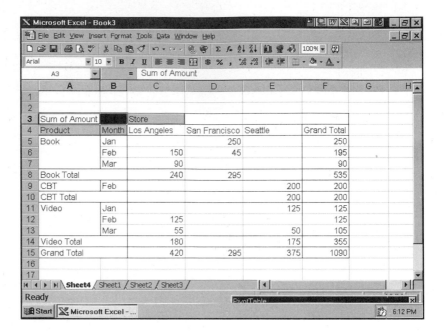

Adding and Removing Fields in a Pivot Table

You can change the data used in a pivot table by adding new fields to the pivot table or by removing fields that you no longer need. When you add a new field to the pivot table or delete an existing field, Excel automatically updates the pivot table.

N O T E   When you add and remove data from a pivot table, the action has no effect on the
source data in the list. ■

  To add a field to the pivot table, follow these steps:

1. Position the cell pointer in the area of the pivot table where you want to add a field. To add a field to the Row area, for example, select a cell in the Row area of the pivot table.

2. Click the right mouse button to display the PivotTable shortcut menu and choose Wizard.

3. Step 3 of the PivotTable Wizard appears. Add the field you want to add and choose Finish.

Figure 18.25 shows the pivot table after adding a field.

FIG. 18.25
The Region field is added to the pivot table layout.

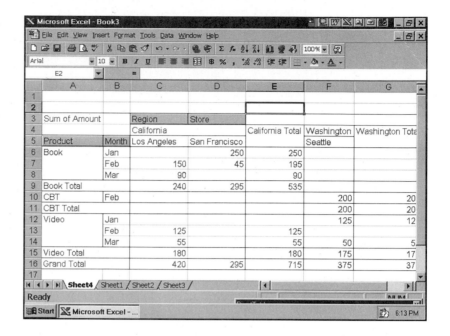

You can remove a pivot table field directly from the pivot table in the worksheet. To remove a field, drag it outside the pivot table area. Excel then removes the data from the table.

Forecasting with the Goal Seeker

Excel's Goal Seek command enables you to perform simple forecasting in your worksheets. You can find a specific value for a defined result by adjusting the value of other cells in the worksheet. For example, you can find out how many houses you need to sell to generate a total sales figure of $1.6 million. The benefit of using the Goal Seek command is that Excel uses the data known—in this case, the total sales amount and the amount per product—and performs the calculation instantaneously, without your having to calculate multiple iterations to come up with the answer.

To use the Goal Seeker, begin by setting up the problem and entering the known variable in the worksheet. The worksheet shown in Figure 18.26 contains the data variable for a sales forecasting worksheet.

FIG. 18.26

Goal Seek adjusts the amount in cell B4 to meet the proposed sales amount.

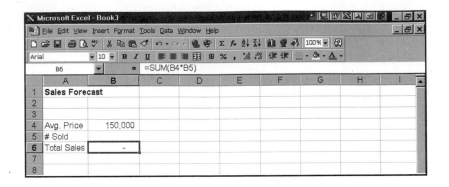

For the Goal Seeker to work, the variable you want to adjust must be a formula, and the formula must refer to the other cells in the worksheet. You specify the cell containing the formula as the Set Cell. Then the formula in the Set Cell refers to the cell to adjust. In the worksheet in Figure 18.26, the Total Sales cell contains the formula =SUM(B4*B5). In this case, you know the average price of a house is $150,000. You want to see how many houses you must sell.

 TIP To proceed through the Goal Seeker one calculation at a time, click the Pause button and then click the Step button until you finish.

To forecast with the Goal Seeker, follow these steps:

1. Choose Tools, Goal Seek. The Goal Seek dialog box appears, as shown in Figure 18.27.

FIG. 18.27

Indicate three input cells in the Goal Seek dialog box: the cell containing the formula, the goal you want to seek, and the cell to adjust.

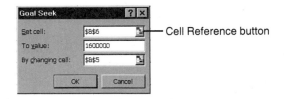

Cell Reference button

2. Specify the cell containing the formula as the Set Cell. Use the Cell Reference button to return to the worksheet to select your data, if you want.

3. In the To Value text box, enter the value the cell must reach.

4. Specify the cell to adjust in the By Changing Cell text box.

5. Choose OK or press Enter after you specify the cells. Figure 18.28 shows the Goal Seek Status dialog box, which informs you of the status of the operation.

FIG. 18.28
The Goal Seek Status dialog box shows the status of the problem.

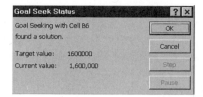

6. Choose OK or press Enter. Excel displays the results in the worksheet cells (see Figure 18.29).

FIG. 18.29
The Goal Seeker returns the result, indicating that 11 houses must be sold to reach a value of $1.6 million in sales.

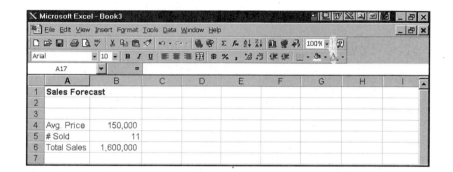

Finding the Best Solution with Solver

The Goal Seek command enables you to generate values based on a single input cell. By contrast, the Solver add-in enables you to calculate the values needed to reach a particular result by adjusting the value of one or more cells. Furthermore, you can define constraints, which Solver must meet when generating the optimum solution.

In the case of the real estate agency determining the number of houses it must sell to meet its annual sales forecast, you must take other considerations into account besides the average price of the house and the goal to meet.

Loading the Solver Add-In

Before you can use the Solver, you must first load the Solver add-in into memory. When you installed Excel, you were given the option of installing the add-ins that ship with Excel. If you chose to install the add-ins, you can use the Tools, Add-Ins command to load Solver into memory. If you did not install the add-ins, you must do so before you can use Solver.

To load Solver into memory, follow these steps:

1. Choose Tools, Add-Ins. Figure 18.30 shows the currently installed add-ins.

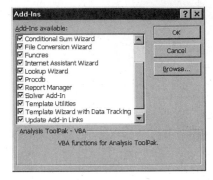

2. From the list of installed add-ins, select Solver Add-In.

3. Choose OK or press Enter. The Solver command appears in the Tools menu.

Setting Up the Problem

To use the Solver in your worksheets, you must first define the problem you need to solve. With Solver, each of the constraint cells is based on formulas. The changing values are the values to which each of the constraint cells refers. Therefore, to set up the problem, determine which of the cells will be used as the constraints and make sure they contain formulas. The worksheet shown in Figure 18.31 illustrates a problem that the Solver will help solve.

Running Solver

After you have set up the worksheet and located the cells to use, follow these steps to run Solver:

1. Choose Tools, Solver to start the Solver add-in. Figure 18.32 displays the Solver Parameters dialog box.

2. Indicate the cell that contains the formula you want to solve in the Set Target Cell text box.

3. Use the Equal To section of the dialog box to indicate the optimum value for the cell: choose the maximum value, minimum value, or a specific value. To meet a specific value, select the Value Of option and type the value in the text box.

4. In the By Changing Cells text box, indicate the cell or range of cells that the Solver will need to adjust to reach the optimum value.

FIG. 18.31
Solver will adjust the data in range B5:D5 until the total sales value in cell E8 equals $1.6 million.

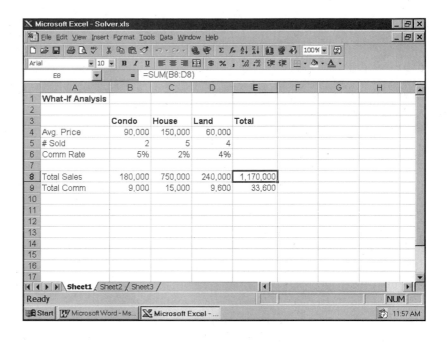

FIG. 18.32
Use the Solver Parameters dialog box to define the optimal cell, the cells to adjust, and the constraints.

5. To specify constraints, choose the <u>A</u>dd button to add each constraint to the problem. Figure 18.33 shows the Change Constraint dialog box.

6. To create a constraint, follow these steps:

- Specify the cell containing the formula on which the constraint is based in the Cell <u>R</u>eference text box.

- Click the drop-down arrow to display the list of constraint operators and select the appropriate operator.

- In the <u>C</u>onstraint text box, type the value the constraint must meet.

- Choose the <u>A</u>dd button to add the current constraint to the problem and create another, or choose OK to add the constraint and return to the Solver Parameters dialog box. The constraints you have defined appear in the Su<u>b</u>ject to the Constraints list box.

7. Choose Solve to start the Solver. The Solver begins calculating the optimal solutions. When Solver finds a solution, the Solver Results dialog box appears, as shown in Figure 18.34.

FIG. 18.33
Specify the constraint to use for the problem in the Change Constraint dialog box.

FIG. 18.34
The Solver Results dialog box gives you options for using the solution that the Solver found.

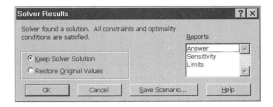

8. Excel adds the solutions to the worksheet. Choose Keep Solver Solution to use the offered solutions. Choose Restore Original Values to return to the original worksheet values. Figure 18.35 shows the worksheet after the Solver found the solutions for the problem.

FIG. 18.35
The results of the Solver show that two condos, eight houses, and five plots of land must be sold to generate $1.68 million in sales and $45,000 of commission.

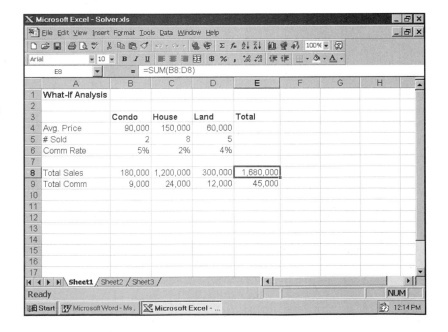

Creating Solver Reports

Solver enables you to generate reports summarizing the results of its solutions. You can create three types of reports:

- *Answer.* Shows the original and final values for the target cell and the adjustable cells, as well as the status of each constraint.
- *Sensitivity.* Shows the sensitivity of each element of the solution to changes in input cells or constraints.
- *Limits.* Shows the upper and lower values of the adjustable cells within the specified constraints.

To create a report, select the report from the list that appears in the Solver Results dialog box (refer to Figure 18.33). Choose OK. Excel creates the report in a separate sheet.

 You can create more than one Solver report by pressing Ctrl while you select the report names.

Performing What-If Analysis with Scenarios

Part
III
Ch
18

For most spreadsheet users, a large portion of analysis involves performing what-if analysis. What effect does changing the average price of home sales have on my forecast? If I sell more condos than houses, will that have a negative impact on total sales?

▶ **See** "Working with Range Names," **p. 386**

The solution to each of these questions requires that input values in the worksheet change. When these values change, however, the original results also change, making it difficult to compare one outcome with another. To account for these changing variables, many users construct multiple data tables to test the outcome of each variable, comparing the original result to the new result.

One of the pitfalls in creating various solution tables is that monitoring the difference between the tables becomes increasingly difficult. When multiple people use the worksheet, keeping track of the ranges proves to be an exercise in frustration. Finally, as you create each additional table to test a scenario, the worksheet grows larger and more unwieldy with each addition.

Excel 97 provides a tool that enables you to track these scenarios with ease. The Scenario Manager feature provides a mechanism that saves each iteration of a problem and then enables you to view one solution at a time.

Creating a Scenario

Before you create a scenario, you must first identify the worksheet range that contains the data, as well as the input cells that will change for each scenario. The worksheet shown in Figure 18.36 illustrates a sales worksheet that enables you to track the change in Total Sales and Total Commission, based on the number of properties sold.

FIG. 18.36

In this sales worksheet, you can perform what-if analysis using the # Sold cells.

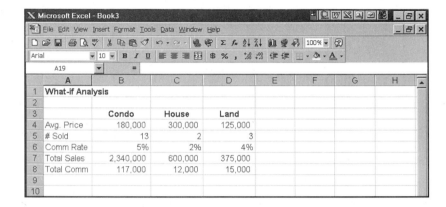

After you have identified the data, follow these steps to create a scenario:

1. Choose Tools, Scenarios. The Scenario Manager dialog box appears, as shown in Figure 18.37.

FIG. 18.37

You use the Scenario Manager dialog box to create scenarios.

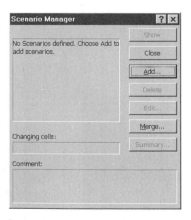

2. Choose the <u>A</u>dd button to display the Add Scenario dialog box, as shown in Figure 18.38.

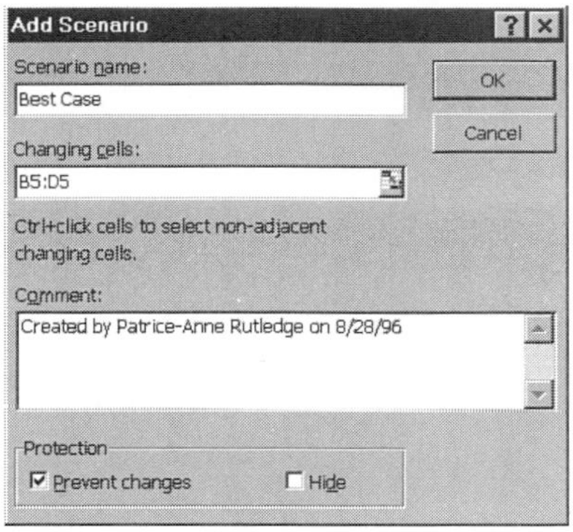

FIG. 18.38
The Add Scenario dialog box enables you to name the scenario and define the cells that will change.

Add Scenario dialog box showing Scenario name "Best Case", Changing cells "B5:D5", Comment "Created by Patrice-Anne Rutledge on 8/28/96", and Protection options with Prevent changes checked.

3. Type a name for the scenario in the Scenario <u>N</u>ame text box.

4. In the Changing <u>C</u>ells text box, indicate the cell or range of cells that will change for each scenario.

5. In the C<u>o</u>mment field, Excel automatically enters your name and the date the scenario was created. Type additional information in the text box as necessary.

6. To prevent changes from being made to the cells in the worksheet, select the <u>P</u>revent Changes option in the Protection section of the dialog box. To hide the cell data from view, select the Hi<u>d</u>e option.

7. Choose OK when you have finished defining the Scenario. Figure 18.39 shows the Scenario Values dialog box, in which you enter the data for each of the cells in the scenario.

   Each displayed text box relates to each specified cell for the scenario. The cell reference of each cell appears for reference.

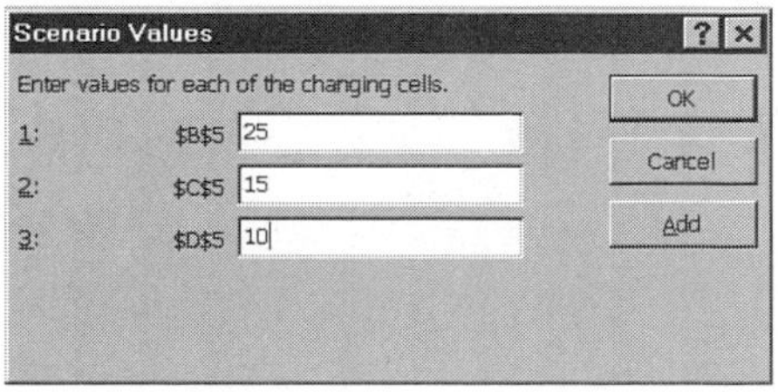

FIG. 18.39
Enter the data for each of the cells in the Scenario Values dialog box.

Scenario Values dialog box showing values for each of the changing cells: 1: $B$5 = 25, 2: $C$5 = 15, 3: $D$5 = 10.

Part

III

Ch

18

N O T E   When creating scenarios, choose Insert, Name, Define to assign a name to each cell in
the scenario. Excel then uses those names in the Scenario Values dialog box and in
scenario reports. ▨

8. Type the data that represents the data to be used for the scenario.

9. When you're finished, choose OK or press Enter. The Scenario Manager dialog box
reappears, as shown in Figure 18.40.

   The name of the newly defined scenario appears in the Scenarios list box. When you
   select a scenario from the list, the Changing Cells field displays the cell addresses of
   the scenario. The Comment field displays the comments you entered to describe or
   annotate the scenario.

FIG. 18.40
The Scenario Manager
dialog box displays
each of the defined
scenarios.

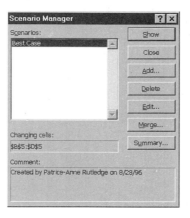

10. To view the scenario, select the scenario name from the list and choose the Show
button. Excel displays the values in each of the cells in the worksheet. If the dialog
box prevents you from seeing the data, click and drag the title bar of the dialog box
to move it out of the way.

11. At this point, you can choose the Add button to define a new range of values as a
scenario, or choose the Edit button to edit the values used by the current scenario.

12. To return to the worksheet, click the Close button. Excel displays the values defined
by the scenario in the worksheet.

Editing and Deleting Scenarios

You can edit an existing scenario or delete a scenario altogether. When you edit a scenario, you can rename the scenario, specify other worksheet cells as the changing cells,
and edit the comment. Furthermore, you can change the values defined by the scenario.

To edit a scenario, follow these steps:

1. Choose Tools, Scenarios to display the Scenario Manager dialog box. Select the scenario you want to edit from the Scenarios list box, and choose the Edit button. Excel displays the Edit Scenario dialog box, shown in Figure 18.41.

FIG. 18.41
Excel automatically adds the modification date to the Comment field.

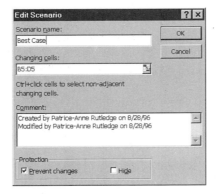

2. Make any modifications necessary to the data shown in the text boxes, and choose OK. The Scenario Values dialog box opens.

3. Enter the new values and choose OK.

To delete a scenario, select the scenario you want to delete in the Scenario Manager dialog box and choose the Delete button. Excel removes the scenario from the Scenario listing.

Summarizing Scenarios with Reports

Excel provides two methods of displaying scenarios in a concise report. The Scenario Summary creates a simple report in table form, showing the data for the changing cells and their effect on the results of formulas in a range. You also can generate a Pivot Table Summary from a multiple scenario set.

Creating a Summary Report   To create a summary report, follow these steps:

1. Choose Tools, Scenarios.

2. Choose the Summary button to display the Scenario Summary dialog box, as shown in Figure 18.42.

Part
III

Ch
18

FIG. 18.42
Choose the type of summary report to create.

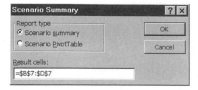

3. Choose Scenario Summary, if it is not already selected, from the Report Type area of the dialog box.

4. In the Result Cells text box, indicate the range of cells that contain formulas based on the input cells.

5. Choose OK. Excel displays a new sheet with a summary table of the scenario inputs and results, as illustrated in Figure 18.43.

FIG. 18.43
This summary report shows current values as well as the Best Case scenario and its results.

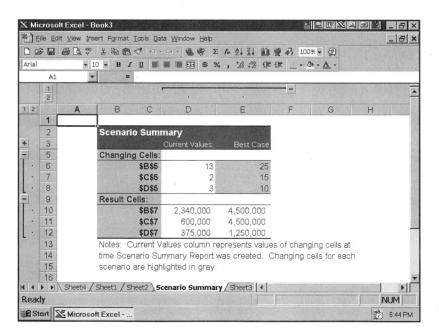

Creating a Scenario Pivot Table Report   To create a pivot table from the scenarios in your worksheet, follow these steps:

1. Choose Tools, Scenarios.

2. Choose the Summary button.

3. In the Scenario Summary dialog box, select the Scenario PivotTable option.

4. In the Result Cells text box, indicate the range of cells that contain formulas based on the input cells.

5. Choose OK. Excel displays a new sheet with a pivot table of the scenario inputs and results, as illustrated in Figure 18.44.

FIG. 18.44

This summary pivot table report shows the Best Case scenario and its results.

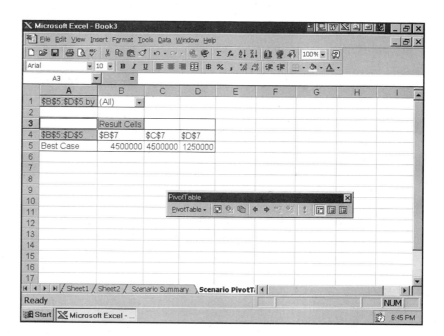

You can manipulate the pivot table summary report as you would any pivot table. If you change a scenario, however, the pivot table is not updated. You must create a new pivot table to account for the changes.

Annotating Worksheets

When you use many formulas and functions for analysis in your worksheets, it can become difficult to remember exactly what each formula is calculating and what data it is using in its calculations. Excel enables you to annotate cells with comments so you can enter descriptive data about a formula. When you share your worksheets with other users, the comments provide a handy mechanism for describing the contents of a cell or for additional information.

▶ **See** "Inserting Comments in Your Work," **p. 272**

Adding and Removing a Comment

To annotate a cell, follow these steps:

1. Select the cell and choose Insert, Comment. The comment box appears, as shown in Figure 18.45.

FIG. 18.45
Annotate formulas and other data in your worksheets with comments.

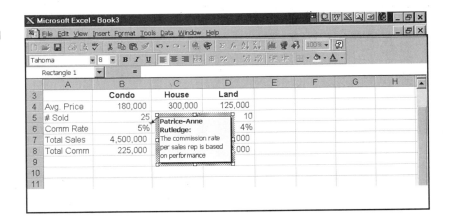

2. Enter the comment in the box that appears.
3. Click outside the box when you're finished.

When a cell in the worksheet has a comment attached to it, a small red triangle appears in the upper-right corner of the cell. To display the contents of the comment, pause the mouse pointer over the cell and the comment will appear in a rectangular box.

N O T E   If the comment indicators do not appear in the worksheet, choose Tools, Options, and select the View tab. In the Comments area you can choose None to display neither comments nor the indicator, the Comment Indicator Only, or Comments & Indicator. ▪

To remove a comment from a worksheet cell, select the cell and choose Edit, Clear, Comments.

Techniques from the Pros

by Conrad Carlberg

Conrad Carlberg is a statistical consultant and a Microsoft MVP. He is the author of several Que books on Excel.

Using Functions to Find Data

It's not immediately apparent, but there's a large variety of ways to use Excel's worksheet functions in combination to make your data management tasks easier.

Suppose that you need to work out a sales commission schedule for your firm's product line. You know how much you want to pay for sales of different products in different quantities, so you have set up the schedule shown in Figure 18.46.

FIG. 18.46

If you know the price of a product and the number of units sold, you can determine the sales commission.

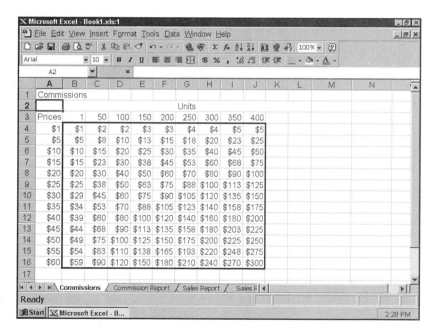

Prices	1	50	100	150	200	250	300	350	400
$1	$1	$2	$2	$3	$3	$4	$4	$5	$5
$5	$5	$8	$10	$13	$15	$18	$20	$23	$25
$10	$10	$15	$20	$25	$30	$35	$40	$45	$50
$15	$15	$23	$30	$38	$45	$53	$60	$68	$75
$20	$20	$30	$40	$50	$60	$70	$80	$90	$100
$25	$25	$38	$50	$63	$75	$88	$100	$113	$125
$30	$29	$45	$60	$75	$90	$105	$120	$135	$150
$35	$34	$53	$70	$88	$105	$123	$140	$158	$175
$40	$39	$60	$80	$100	$120	$140	$160	$180	$200
$45	$44	$68	$90	$113	$135	$158	$180	$203	$225
$50	$49	$75	$100	$125	$150	$175	$200	$225	$250
$55	$54	$83	$110	$138	$165	$193	$220	$248	$275
$60	$59	$90	$120	$150	$180	$210	$240	$270	$300

After setting up the schedule, and for convenience, you name the range that it occupies. You select B4:J16, choose Insert, Name, Define, type **Commissions** in the Name box, and choose OK. It will also be useful to name the range A4:A16 as **Prices** and B3:J3 as **Units**.

Because you want it to be easy to fill in reports, you arrange for each report to show the number of units sold and their price. All that's left is to get Excel to do the necessary research for you (see Figure 18.47).

In Figure 18.47, notice that there's a place to enter the number of units sold and their sales price. The cell that contains the payable commission is empty. Here's the formula that will do the work for you:

```
=INDEX(COMMISSIONS,MATCH(B3,PRICES,1),MATCH(B4,UNITS,1))
```

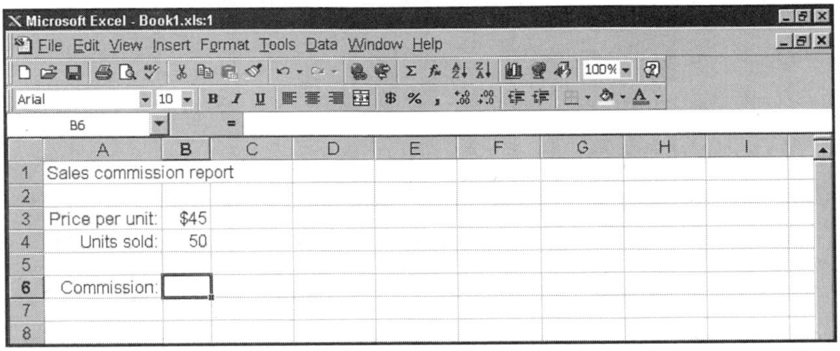

FIG. 18.47
You can arrange things on a report so that it doesn't contain extraneous informa-tion, such as the complete commission schedule.

Does it look intimidating? Perhaps a little, but break it up into fragments.

```
MATCH(B3,PRICES,1)
```

finds a match between the value in cell B3 and a value in the PRICES range that you de-fined earlier. The third argument to the MATCH function (here, 1) causes Excel to find the largest value in PRICES that is *less than or equal to* the value in B3.

The fragment returns the value of 10. In other words, the 10th value in PRICES is less than or equal to $45, the value found in cell B3.

Similarly, this fragment

```
MATCH(B4,UNITS,1)
```

returns 2: the 2nd value in UNITS is less than or equal to 50, the value found in cell B4.

So, if you plug 10 and 2 into the original formula:

```
=INDEX(COMMISSIONS,MATCH(B3,PRICES,1),MATCH(B4,UNITS,1))
```

it simplifies to this:

```
=INDEX(COMMISSIONS,10,2)
```

The INDEX function looks in a range (here, COMMISSIONS) and returns the value found—in this case, in its 10th row and 2nd column. As another example, this formula:

```
=INDEX(COMMISSIONS,2,3)
```

returns the value found in the 2nd row, 3rd column of COMMISSIONS.

Notice that if the COMMISSIONS range begins in cell A1, its 2nd row and 3rd column are the worksheet's 2nd row and 3rd column. But that's just coincidence. COMMISSIONS could begin in worksheet cell H22, and INDEX(COMMISSIONS,2,3) would return the same value as it would if the range began in cell A1. INDEX works on the basis of the *range's* rows and columns, not the worksheet's. Put differently, INDEX's row and column arguments are relative to the upper-left corner of the range, not to that of the worksheet.

Now you're in a position to understand how the overall formula works. Once more, the formula:

```
=INDEX(COMMISSIONS,MATCH(B3,PRICES,1),MATCH(B4,UNITS,1))
```

Now, what the formula does, in words:

1. Match the value in B3 with the values in PRICES. This returns the row number you want in COMMISSIONS.

2. Match the value in B4 with the values in UNITS. This returns the column number you want in COMMISSIONS.

3. Look in the cell defined by the intersection of the row and the column. Return that value, as shown in Figure 18.48.

FIG. 18.48
This is just one way to use the returned value of one function as an argument to another function.

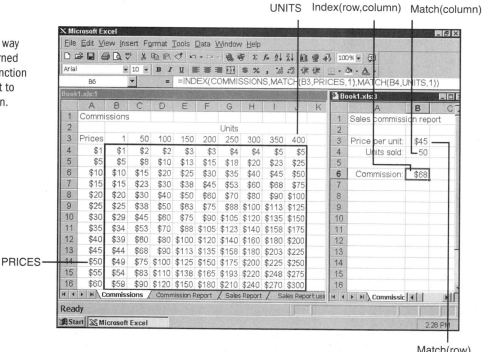

Excel provides a handy way to check your work as you build complex functions. Consider the example that this section has been developing. If you have entered the full formula into a worksheet cell, you can select that cell so that the formula appears in the formula bar.

Now, using your mouse pointer, highlight a segment of the formula in the formula bar by clicking and dragging across it, as shown in Figure 18.49.

FIG. 18.49
This fragment of a formula is highlighted just prior to evaluation by Excel.

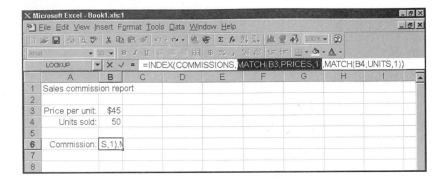

After you have highlighted the portion of the formula that you're interested in, press F9. Excel calculates the portion that you highlighted and displays the result, as part of the formula, in the formula bar (see Figure 18.50).

FIG. 18.50
The fragment is evaluated when you press F9.

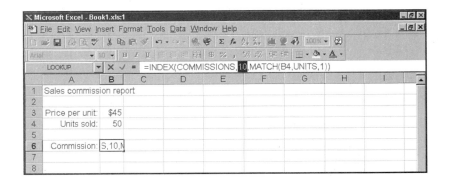

This can be an extremely useful tool when the formula you're creating is at all complicated—it helps keep you straight as to what's happening. It's also a useful way to debug a formula that isn't returning the result that you expect.

N O T E   After you calculate some portion of a formula by using the F9 key, be careful about what you do next. If you press Enter, or otherwise make the change permanent, you will not be able to retrieve the original version except by using Edit, Undo. It's usually best, after you've seen how Excel evaluates a formula's fragment, to abandon the change by clicking the X symbol in the formula bar. ■

Reorienting Worksheet Ranges

It frequently happens that you want to reorient the information in a worksheet range—that is, to put what's in the rows into columns and what's in the columns into rows.

For example, this tends to occur with time-ordered data such as weekly costs or revenues. As you enter new data into the worksheet, it's natural to enter each new week one row below the prior week. Doing it this way is useful for two reasons: a worksheet has 256 times as many rows (65,536) as columns (256), so there's room for more data. And putting each new week's data on a new row enables you to use all the data as a list, where columns are variables and rows are records. So this would be the best way to orient your data for use in, say, a pivot table.

But if you want to display the information in a report, it's the wrong orientation. Most of us are used to seeing time-ordered information laid out so that time proceeds from left to right, not top to bottom.

Excel provides you with two convenient ways to *transpose*, or reorient, worksheet cells: by way of copy-and-paste, and by way of the TRANSPOSE function.

Transposing with Copy and Paste

Using a copy-and-paste operation is usually best if you're confident that your data values will not change after the transposition. Figure 18.51 shows a range of data in A1:C8 and the same data transposed into A12:H14.

Part

III

Ch

18

FIG. 18.51
Notice how the rows and columns have been switched in A12:H14.

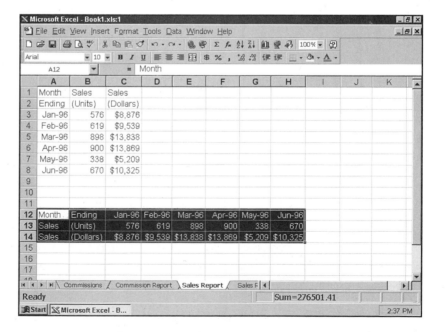

To transpose the range with copy-and-paste, follow these steps:

1. Select A1:C8.

2. Choose Edit, Copy.

3. Select cell A12.

4. Choose Edit, Paste Special. Fill the Transpose box by clicking it (see Figure 18.52).

5. Choose OK.

FIG. 18.52

The Paste Special dialog box provides several useful options for pasting data.

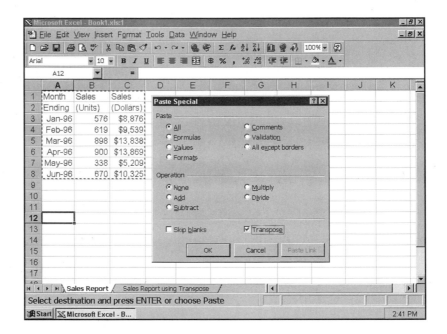

After you choose OK, Excel reorients the data in the new range (refer to Figure 18.51). Notice that not only the values, but their associated formats, have been pasted to the new range.

N O T E If the original range contains formulas rather than values, and if the formulas depend on other cells (for example, =A1), it's usually best also to choose Values in the Paste Special dialog box. Transposing relative reference formulas, instead of values, can cause unanticipated results. However, choosing Values means that neither All nor Formats can be chosen, and therefore, any formatting you have applied will not accompany the transposed values. ▪

Reorienting with the TRANSPOSE Function

An alternative to transposing with copy and paste is the TRANSPOSE worksheet function. TRANSPOSE offers a couple of advantages over the copy-and-paste approach:

- TRANSPOSE works better if you're transposing cells that contain relative reference formulas.

- The transposed information is linked to the original data, so changes in the original values are automatically made to the transposed values.

The use of TRANSPOSE is illustrated in Figure 18.53, which uses the same original information as in Figure 18.51.

FIG. 18.53
The TRANSPOSE function—really a matrix algebra operation—is also useful for reorienting data in reports.

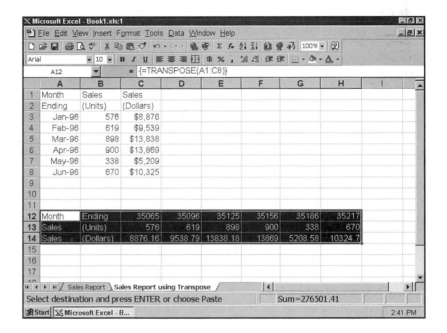

Part
III

Ch
18

Examining Figure 18.53 makes apparent some of the drawbacks to using TRANSPOSE:

- Notice the curly brackets around the formula in the formula bar. These indicate that it must be entered as an array formula (Ctrl+Shift+Enter rather than, more simply, Enter).

- The new, transposed range does not bear the formatting of the original range. It's necessary to format the transposed cells using the Format menu.

■ The entire range to be occupied by the transposed data must be selected prior to entering the array formula. This means that you must carefully count the number of rows and columns in the existing range and mentally transpose them as you select the new range. In contrast, you need select only the upper-left corner of the new range if you use the copy-and-paste approach.

Despite these drawbacks, you will often prefer to use TRANSPOSE because the transposed range is linked by formula to the original data.

To create the transposed range shown in Figure 18.53, take these steps:

1. Select A12:H14.

2. Type this formula:

   =TRANSPOSE(A1:C8)

3. Press Ctrl+Shift+Enter to array-enter the formula.

Any change to a value or formula in the original range that you make will now be reflected in the new, transposed range. This is particularly useful when the two ranges occupy different worksheets—it's easy to make a change in one location and forget to make it in the other.

Using Dialog Boxes in Excel 97

Suppose you have an application for Excel that, to run properly, requires input from the user. The application might need to know where to find worksheet data, for example, or where to write results, or which of several available options to apply. This is where custom dialog boxes, or *UserForms*, enter the picture.

UserForms is the Office 97 designation for what were called custom dialog boxes in earlier versions of Office. The capability is considerably more powerful in Office 97—and it's also much more complex. This section gives you a brief overview of UserForms by stepping you through the creation of a simple dialog box and some associated Visual Basic code.

The earlier Techniques from the Pros section, "Reorienting Worksheet Ranges," discusses the tradeoffs involved in transposing a range by copy-and-paste versus using the TRANSPOSE function. Suppose that you want to eliminate these tradeoffs by automating the process. Then, you could get the best of both worlds: you could transpose a range using formula links, and also use the original range's number formats. Further, you would not have to begin by highlighting the proper dimensions for the new, transposed range.

A UserForm is an ideal means of making this improvement. Here's how you would go about creating this UserForm in the Excel 97 environment.

1. Open a new Excel workbook by choosing File, New from the Excel main menu.

2. Enter the Visual Basic Editor by choosing Tools, Macro, Visual Basic Editor (or, press Alt+F11).

3. Choose Insert, User Form. Your screen now appears as shown in Figure 18.54.

FIG. 18.54
Inserting a UserForm into a Project file provides you with a frame for a dialog box and a toolbox of Controls for the dialog box.

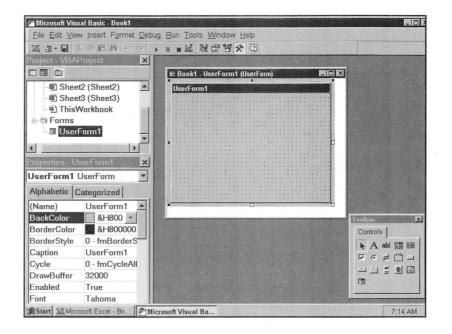

Part
III

Ch
18

TIP To use the same dialog box grid units as were provided in Office 95, choose Tools, Options from the Visual Basic Editor menu. Click the General tab, and set both the Width and Height to 5.

---

4. Click the Label button on the toolbox.

5. Position your mouse pointer in the dialog frame. Hold the mouse button down, and drag in the user form to establish a label. Release the mouse button.

6. In the Properties box (refer to Figure 18.54), drag across the Label1 value in the Caption field to highlight it. Type a new label, **Input Range:**, and press Enter. You could also edit the Label1 value in the label itself on the user form.

7. Click the RefEdit button on the toolbox. Establish a reference edit box on the user form by dragging as you did for the label in step 5. Place it next to the **Input Range:** label. This box will contain the worksheet address of the range that you want to transpose.

8. Repeat steps 4 through 7 to create a label and reference edit box for an output range. The reference edit box will contain the worksheet address of the range that you want to transpose into.

9. Click the Checkbox button on the toolbox. Establish a check box on the user form by dragging. There will be an area for a label to the right of the check box itself. Use **Copy Formats from Input Range** as the label.

10. Click the Command Button button on the toolbox. Create a command button on the user form, and give it the label OK.

11. Repeat step 10 to create a Cancel button on the user form.

You now have a dialog box and the controls needed to automate the transpose operation. It might look something like that shown in Figure 18.55.

FIG. 18.55

A custom user form should always have an OK and a Cancel button, so that the user can choose either to continue or end processing.

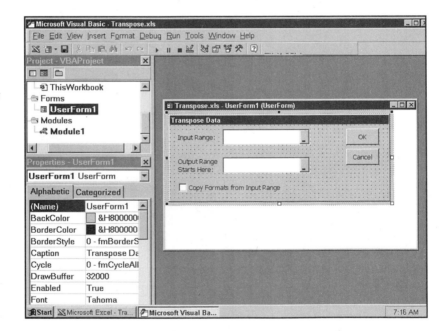

It's necessary now to tell Visual Basic what to do about the information that the user will enter in the dialog box, and what other actions it should perform. Take these steps:

1. Right-click the OK button on the user form. In the shortcut menu, choose View Code. A code module appears as shown in Figure 18.56.

2. Immediately following the subroutine name, `Private Sub CommandButton1_Click()`, type:

UserForm1.Hide

When the user chooses the OK button, you want the dialog box to disappear. In contrast to earlier versions of Visual Basic, you now must explicitly code this behavior.

FIG. 18.56
Code that you enter into a private module, associated with a particular control, executes when the user selects that control.

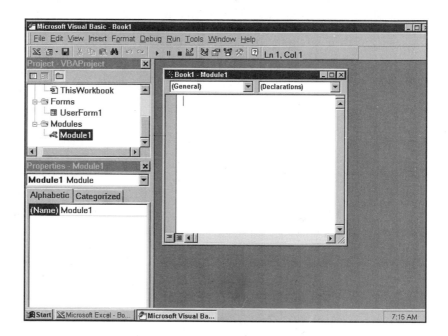

3. Repeat steps 1 and 2 for the Cancel button. However, the code in `Private Sub CommandButton2_Click()` should be:

```
End
```

This will cause Visual Basic to stop executing your program if the user chooses to cancel the operation.

4. Choose Insert, Module from the Visual Basic toolbar. This will provide you with a module in which you can type the following Visual Basic statements:

```
Option Explicit
Sub TransposeData()
Dim InputRange As Range
Dim OutputRange As Range
Dim OutputRows As Integer
Dim OutputColumns As Integer
Dim TransposeFormula As Variant
Dim i as Integer
Dim j as Integer
```

These nine statements take care of some housekeeping matters: requiring that all variables be explicitly declared, identifying the beginning of the subroutine, and actually declaring the names and types of the variables that will be used.

```
With UserForm1
    .RefEdit1.Text = ""
    .RefEdit2.Text = ""
    .CheckBox1 = False
    .Show
    Set InputRange = Range(.RefEdit1.Text)
    Set OutputRange = Range(.RefEdit2.Text)
End With
```

The block of code defined by the With and End With statements initializes the values of the user form's controls: the reference edit boxes are set to blank values and the check box is unchecked. (Using the With structure simply relieves you and Visual Basic of the necessity to repeat the UserForm1 object before the objects and methods that belong to it. Lacking the With, you would have to use UserForm1.RefEdit1.Text, UserForm1.RefEdit2.Text, and so on.) Then, the two Range variables, InputRange and OutputRange, are set to represent whatever the user enters in the reference edit boxes.

The user form is then shown on-screen, and Visual Basic relinquishes control until either the OK or Cancel button is chosen. If the user chooses OK, processing continues; if the user chooses Cancel, processing ends.

Last, two variables that represent worksheet objects are retrieved from the dialog box: a range entered by the user as an input range—this will be transposed—and an output range—the upper-left corner of the range that will contain the transposed information.

```
OutputColumns = InputRange.Rows.Count
OutputRows = InputRange.Columns.Count
```

The variables OutputColumns and OutputRows are needed to determine the dimensions of the output range. They are obtained from the dimensions of the original range. Notice that the number of rows in the input range determines the number of columns in the output range, and the number of input columns becomes the number of output rows.

```
Set OutputRange = OutputRange.Offset(0, 0).Resize(OutputRows, OutputColumns)
```

The dimensions of the output range itself are now set. The Offset method shifts it zero rows and zero columns from the cell identified by the user in the user form—in other words, it doesn't move. The Resize method gives the output range as many rows as the input range has columns and as many columns as the input range has rows. (Compare this with the way that values were assigned to OutputRows and OutputColumns.)

```
TransposeFormula = "=TRANSPOSE(" & UserForm1.RefEdit1.Text & ")"
```

It's now time to start building the formula that will be placed in the output range. Suppose that in the dialog box the user entered A1:C13 as the input range. If so, the initial value of the variable TransposeFormula would be: "=TRANSPOSE($A$1:$C$13)".

When you use Visual Basic to enter a formula on a worksheet, however, it's a requirement that the formula be expressed not in A1 notation but in R1C1 notation. Converting the formula from A1 to R1C1 notation is the purpose of the next statement:

```
TransposeFormula = Application.ConvertFormula _
    (Formula:=TransposeFormula, _
    FromReferenceStyle:=xlA1, _
    ToReferenceStyle:=xlR1C1)
```

Again assuming that the user has entered A1:C13 as the input range, the current value of TransposeFormula is "=TRANSPOSE(R1C1:R13C3)".

```
OutputRange.FormulaArray = TransposeFormula
```

Now that the formula has been built and expressed in the proper notation, it's entered into the output range as an array formula.

There's one last step. The user may have chosen to apply the number formats found in the input range to the output range. If so, the value of CheckBox1 is now True. The next line checks that condition:

```
If UserForm1.CheckBox1 = True Then
```

Part

III

Ch

18

Given that its value is true, the code between the If and the End If statements executes. This code cycles through each cell in the input range, picks up its number format, and assigns it to the corresponding cell in the output range:

```
For i = 1 To OutputRows
    For j = 1 To OutputColumns
        OutputRange(i, j).NumberFormat = InputRange(j, i).NumberFormat
    Next j
Next i
```

Keep in mind that input rows are changed to output columns and input columns are changed to output rows. Therefore, in the loop's assignment statement, the variable *i* identifies a row of the output range and a column of the input range.

```
    End If
End Sub
```

Finally, the If block terminates and the subroutine ends.

To run the subroutine, you activate the sheet that contains the data you want to transpose. Then, choose Tools, Macro, Macros, select TransposeData from the macro name list box, and choose Run.

Figures 18.57 and 18.58 show how the worksheet appears before and after running the subroutine.

FIG. 18.57
The input range has special number formats that you would like to retain in the transposed output range.

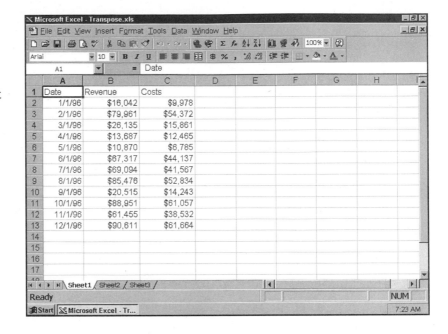

FIG. 18.58
After running the subroutine, the transposed range is linked by formula to the input range, and it has the same number formats as the input range.

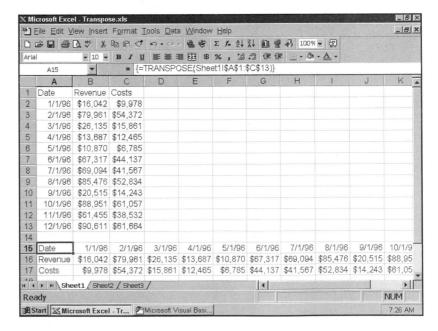

Using Multimedia in Microsoft Office

CHAPTER 19

Using Microsoft Graph

by Rick Winter and Jan Snyder

A graph, or chart, is an effective tool for clearly presenting data in a way that provides instant visual impact. In other words, charts are easier to understand at a glance than are rows and columns of data. Because of the high impact that charts provide, Microsoft Office includes two tools for chart creation—Microsoft Excel's charting capabilities and Microsoft Graph version 97. Chapter 20, "Creating and Printing Excel Charts," describes Excel's charting functions, whereas this chapter is devoted to the use of Microsoft Graph to create charts in PowerPoint presentations, Word documents, and Access forms and reports. ■

Microsoft Graph for charts

Word, PowerPoint, and Access use Microsoft Graph to create charts.

The Datasheet window

Enter and edit data in a Graph's worksheet.

Chart types and chart objects

Choose from many chart types and customizable objects.

Chart colors, patterns, borders, and fonts

Change chart formatting to enhance the chart's appearance.

Existing chart revision

Use Graph to edit an existing chart.

Starting Microsoft Graph

Microsoft Graph is a charting application, separate from PowerPoint, Word, or Access, that is accessible from within PowerPoint, Word, or Access. When you start Graph, a sample chart appears in the current document, and a datasheet appears on top of the chart. The chart appears in the document as an object; the data-sheet appears in a separate window with its own title bar. In Word and PowerPoint the datasheet and chart are displayed on-screen simultaneously and are dependent on each other. When you change data in the datasheet, Graph automatically updates the chart to reflect the new data. With Microsoft Access, you use existing data on a query or table instead of using Microsoft Graph's datasheet.

N O T E In Microsoft Office and other applications, the use of *chart* and *graph* are often interchangeable to mean a graphic depiction of numerical data (such as a pie chart or bar graph). Earlier versions of Microsoft Graph used the term *graph*, but Microsoft Graph 97 and Microsoft Excel generally use the term *chart*. In some cases, people use the term *chart* to include any kind of slide or overhead transparency, whether the slide includes a graph, pictures, or just text. The more general term *graphic* also means any kind of visual object that is not editable text, such as pictures, clip art, and drawings. The word *chart* is used almost exclusively in this book, except when reference is made to the program Microsoft Graph. ▪

Microsoft Graph is not a stand-alone application and is not, therefore, designed to run on its own. Instead, you access Graph from within another application such as Word, PowerPoint, or Access. Before accessing Microsoft Graph, you must be working in another application which supports embedded objects, such as PowerPoint, Word, or Access.

Starting Microsoft Graph in Word

If you are working in Word, follow these steps to start Graph:

1. Position the insertion point at the desired location for the new chart.
2. Choose Insert, Object. In the Create New tab of the Object dialog box, select Microsoft Graph 97 Chart from the Object Type list and click OK.
3. Microsoft Graph will start, and a chart and datasheet will appear.

Starting Microsoft Graph in PowerPoint

If you are working in a PowerPoint presentation, follow these steps to start Graph:

1. Display the slide in which you want to insert a chart, or add a new slide to the presentation. The slide should either be blank or contain a placeholder for a chart.

2. As you learn in Chapter 26, "Creating, Saving, and Opening Presentations," whenever you add a new slide to a presentation, PowerPoint automatically displays the New Slide dialog box, in which you select a slide layout (see Figure 19.1). Three of the 24 available slide layouts include placeholders for charts (indicated by pictures of bar charts on the slide layout). Select a layout that includes a chart placeholder.

FIG. 19.1
The New Slide dialog box includes three layouts that contain chart placeholders.

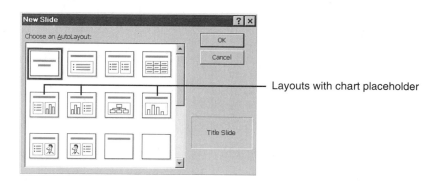

Layouts with chart placeholder

N O T E If you access Microsoft Graph from a slide that contains objects or placeholders other than for a chart, the chart you create appears on top of other objects (such as text or drawn objects). To avoid obscuring other objects with a chart, select a blank slide layout or a slide layout that contains a chart placeholder before you access Microsoft Graph. ▪

PowerPoint displays a slide similar to the one shown in Figure 19.2. A dotted frame defines the boundaries of the chart placeholder. Inside the placeholder is a small picture of a bar chart with the instruction `Double click to add chart`.

3. Starting Microsoft Graph is as easy as the instructions indicate: `Double click to add chart`. After a few seconds, a sample bar chart appears in the chart placeholder in your slide. The datasheet appears on top of the chart in a separate window (see Figure 19.3). The sample data in the datasheet is used to create the sample bar chart.

4. To access Microsoft Graph when your slide is blank or does not contain a graph placeholder, simply click the Insert Chart button in the Standard toolbar, or choose Insert, Chart. The sample chart and Datasheet window appear.

▶ **See** "Creating a Presentation Using a Template," **p. 608**

Part
IV

Ch
19

FIG. 19.2
Chart placeholders
contain a small
picture of a bar chart.

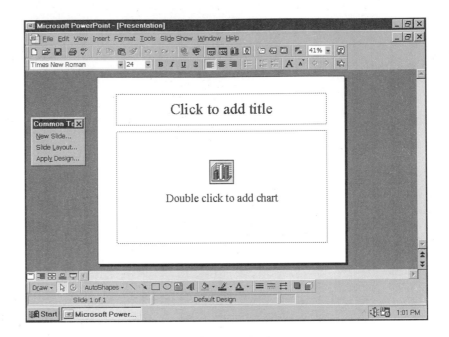

FIG. 19.3
The chart and
datasheet window
appear in PowerPoint.

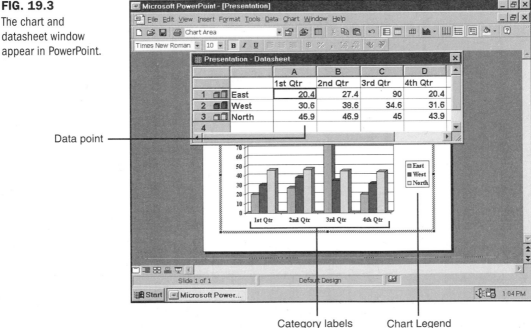

Data point

Category labels   Chart Legend

Starting Microsoft Graph in Access

Using Microsoft Graph in Access is different than in Word or PowerPoint. In Word and PowerPoint you use the Microsoft Graph's datasheet to enter in the values for the chart. In Access, you usually use values from an Access table or query to create the chart. The Microsoft Graph datasheet is irrelevant when creating a graph based on a table or query. When you use Microsoft Graph in Access, you enter a wizard that steps you through the process of creating your chart.

> **N O T E** Although you don't have to use the data in a table or query for a chart in Access, it is most likely that you would. However, if you want to insert a chart using data that you will input in Microsoft Graph's datasheet, go to any OLE data type field in a table, query, or field. Then choose Insert, Object, select Microsoft Graph 97 Chart, and continue as you would in Word or PowerPoint. ▪

If you are working in an Access database, follow these steps to start Graph:

▶ **See** "Exploring Access," **p. 706**

1. Open the table or query with the values you need for your chart.

 2. Click the New Object button and choose Form or Report, as shown in Figure 19.4. The New Form or New Report dialog box opens.

FIG. 19.4
Use Form to create charts you will display on-screen, use Report for charts you will print.

3. In the New Form or New Report dialog box, choose Chart Wizard, as shown in Figure 19.5. Verify that the correct query or table is chosen and click OK.

> **N O T E** If you receive an error message that the Chart Wizard is not installed, you can run Setup to add it. In the setup options for Microsoft Access, check both the Wizards check box and the Advanced Wizards check box to install all of the Wizards for Access. ▪

4. The first dialog box of the Chart Wizard opens, as shown in Figure 19.6. The list of fields from the table or query appears in the Available Fields list box. Double-click a field or select the field and click the > button to put the field in the Fields for Chart list. To put all fields in, click the >> button. Double-click a field in the Fields for Chart list to remove a field, or click the < button.

FIG. 19.5
A chart is only one of the kinds of forms or reports you can create.

FIG. 19.6
Double-click a field in Available Fields to add a field, or in Fields for Chart to remove a field.

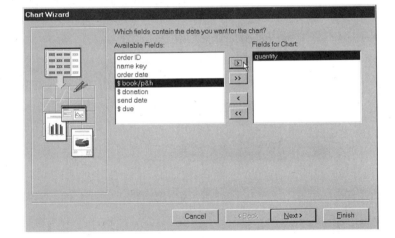

5. When you finish entering the fields, click the Next button at the bottom of the dialog box.

6. On the next step of the Chart Wizard, select the chart type, as shown in Figure 19.7, and click the Next button.

7. The next step of the Chart Wizard asks you how you want to lay out the data on the chart (see Figure 19.8). Drag the field names from the right side of the dialog box to the chart or chart legend area. When you're finished laying out the chart, click the Next button.

FIG. 19.7

The right side of the Chart Wizard dialog box displays hints for choosing each of the chart types.

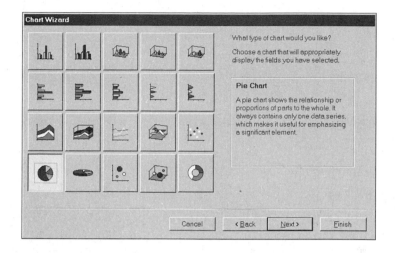

FIG. 19.8

Double-click a field name in the chart area (for example, SumOfquantity) and choose from sum, count, maximum, and so on, to customize how the chart calculates data.

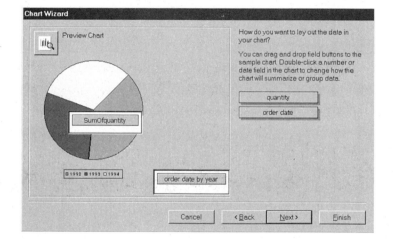

Part
IV

Ch
19

8. On the last step of the Chart Wizard (with the checkered finish flag, as shown in Figure 19.9), type the name you want to appear on the top of your form or report, choose whether you want a legend, and choose Modify the Design Of the Report Or the Chart.

9. Choose Finish. The Chart Wizard window closes. The chart appears temporarily in design view, and then it appears in a print preview window in Access.

10. Choose File, Save and give the form or report a name.

FIG. 19.9
To edit the chart, choose Modify the Design Of the Report Or the Chart. To see the actual values, choose Open the Report With the Chart Displayed On It.

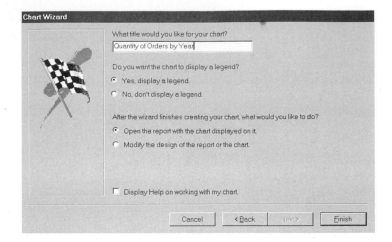

11. Choose OK and then click the Close button on the Print Preview toolbar. The preview closes, revealing a sample chart on the report in design view.

N O T E From the database window to edit the chart and go to Microsoft Graph, display the form or report tab, highlight the name of the form or report, and click the Design button.

To edit the chart within Microsoft Graph, double-click the chart and refer to the rest of this chapter. To display the chart with the actual data, choose File, Exit in the Microsoft Graph window to return to Access and choose View, Form or View, Print Preview (for report). ▩

TROUBLESHOOTING

I don't want to use any of the PowerPoint AutoLayouts that include graphs. How can I add a graph to my slide and arrange other objects on the slide myself? Choose the blank AutoLayout for your slide. When you create a chart using Microsoft Graph, the chart will be centered in the middle of the slide. You can resize the chart object, move it, and add other objects to the slide where you want them.

The datasheet window covers up the chart. How can I see what the chart looks like? The datasheet is contained in its own window, which has standard window controls. You can therefore move and resize the datasheet to make the chart visible.

 I closed the datasheet window in Microsoft Graph before I was finished using it. How can I redisplay it? In Microsoft Graph, choose View, Datasheet, or click the View Datasheet button in the Graph toolbar.

I edited the values in the datasheet window in Microsoft Graph while working on an Access chart and nothing happened to the actual chart. When you use the Chart Wizard to create a chart in Access, Microsoft Graph does not use the values on the Microsoft Graph datasheet window.

Looking at the Microsoft Graph Menus and Toolbar

Notice in Figure 19.3 that the PowerPoint menu and toolbars are replaced by the Graph menu and toolbars when Microsoft Graph is active. This menu and toolbar replacement takes place when Graph is started in Microsoft Word, or when you double-click a chart in design view of an Access form or report. Graph's Standard and Formatting toolbars are displayed.

The buttons in Graph's Standard toolbar greatly simplify working with charts. For example, you can change the color of a set of bars in a bar chart by clicking the Fill Color button. This section emphasizes the use of these buttons, and it also explains menu command techniques. Table 19.1 explains the functions of some of the buttons in the Graph Standard toolbar.

 T I P If you forget the purpose of a toolbar button, position the mouse pointer on the button. A ScreenTip appears with the button's name.

Part
IV

Ch
19

Table 19.1   Microsoft Graph's Standard Toolbar

Button	Button Name	Purpose
Chart Area ▾	Chart Objects	Selects the chart object to which subsequent formatting is applied.
(icon)	Selected [chart object]	Opens a Format dialog box for the selected chart object.
(icon)	Import File	Imports data from another application into the Graph datasheet.
(icon)	View Datasheet	Displays or hides the datasheet for the current chart.
(icon)	Cut	Cuts selected objects.

continues

Table 19.1 Continued

Button	Button Name	Purpose
	Copy	Copies selected objects to the Clipboard.
	Paste	Inserts the contents of the Clipboard.
	Undo	Reverses the last action taken.
	By Row	Causes Graph to use rows of data as data series.
	By Column	Causes Graph to use columns of data as data series.
	Data Table	Displays a grid of data in the chart, based on the charted values.
	Chart Type	Displays a drop-down list of chart types.
	Category Axis Gridlines	Inserts/removes category axis gridlines into the current chart.
	Value Axis Gridlines	Inserts/removes value axis gridlines into the current chart.
	Legend	Turns the chart legend on or off.
	Drawing	Displays or hides a Drawing toolbar for drawing objects in a chart.
	Fill Color	Displays a drop-down fill-color palette.
	Office Assistant	Turns Office Assistant on or off.

Working with the Datasheet

A Microsoft Graph datasheet, made up of rows and columns, is similar to a Microsoft Excel worksheet. Rows are numbered 1, 2, 3 and so on, and columns are labeled A, B, C...

AA, AB, AC, and so on. The intersection of each row and column is a *cell*, in which you enter text or a number. Unlike an Excel worksheet, however, a Microsoft Graph datasheet cannot use formulas.

▶ **See** "Entering Data," **p. 303**

N O T E Don't forget that the Microsoft Graph datasheet is not relevant when working on a chart created with the Chart Wizard in Access. To modify the data, go to the original query or table and change the data. ▨

Understanding How Data Is Plotted

In Figure 19.3, the sample datasheet shows three rows, or *series*, of data: East, West, and North. A *data series* contains individual *data points* that are plotted along the y-axis (vertical axis) of a chart as columns, lines, or pie slices. The first column of the datasheet contains the series names that identify each data series. These headings are translated to the chart's *legend*. The category labels in the first row of the datasheet (the row above row 1) represent *categories* of data. These column headings are translated to the x-axis (horizontal axis) of the chart as category labels. Thus, categories appear as groups in a chart.

Arranging Data by Rows or Columns

By default, Microsoft Graph assumes that data series appear in rows and that categories appear in columns, so Graph plots all charts accordingly. In Figure 19.3, this series-in-rows arrangement emphasizes time spans: 1st Qtr, 2nd Qtr, 3rd Qtr, and 4th Qtr.

If you prefer, however, you can reverse the data series arrangement so that Graph uses columns as data series and rows as categories of data. In Figure 19.10, the series-in-columns arrangement emphasizes regions—East, West, and North—rather than time spans. The arrangement you use depends on personal preference and on the data you want to emphasize. Unless otherwise indicated, the examples in this chapter use the series-in-rows arrangement.

By glancing at the datasheet, you can tell whether rows or columns are represented as data series. When rows are plotted as the data series, miniature graphic representations of the chart type (such as bars or lines) appear next to the row headings. When columns are plotted as the data series, the graphics appear next to the column headings. You can see examples of these miniature graphics in Figures 19.3 and 19.10.

Part

IV

Ch

19

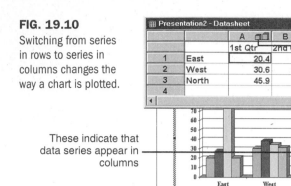

FIG. 19.10
Switching from series in rows to series in columns changes the way a chart is plotted.

These indicate that data series appear in columns

To specify the arrangement of data in a chart, click the By Row or By Column button in the Graph toolbar, or choose Data, Series in Rows or Data, Series in Columns. You can switch back and forth between the two arrangements to decide which one represents your data most effectively.

Entering Data

When you're ready to enter data in the datasheet, type over the existing sample data. You can add more data to the datasheet by filling in blank rows and columns.

▶ **See** "Entering Data," **p. 303**

To highlight a cell in the datasheet, use the arrow keys or click a cell. The *active*, or highlighted, cell is outlined with a bold border. Any entry you type in a cell automatically replaces the current contents of a cell. To complete an entry, press Enter or press any of the arrow keys to move to another cell.

Editing Data

Editing refers to changes that you make in data after it is entered in the datasheet. You change data in a datasheet the same way you do in other spreadsheet programs. Editing includes changing individual entries; cutting, moving, and copying entries; and inserting and deleting rows and columns. Before you can edit cells, however, you must know how to select them.

Selecting Cells, Rows, and Columns

As you enter and edit data in the datasheet, you may want to work with a group of cells rather than just one. You might want to move a group of cells to a new location, for example. In the datasheet, you can select a range of cells, entire rows, or entire columns.

A *range* of cells is any rectangular group of cells. To select a range, click the cell in the top left corner of the range and drag the mouse to the cell in the bottom right corner of the range. The entire range is highlighted.

▶ **See** "Selecting Cells and Ranges," **p. 308**

Selecting an entire row or column is accomplished by clicking the row or column heading. To select all cells in row 3, for example, click the row number 3; to select all cells in column D, click the column label D. You also can select multiple rows or columns by dragging the mouse across row and column headings.

To cancel any selection, whether you have selected a range of cells or a group of columns or rows, press Esc or click any single cell.

Editing an Entry

Editing a cell entry enables you to change only selected characters in an entry. To edit a cell entry, double-click the cell. An insertion point appears in the cell. Use the standard text editing techniques to make the desired changes. When you finish editing, press Enter.

▶ **See** "Editing Worksheet Data," **p. 322**

Clearing Cells

Clearing refers to removing the contents, format, or both from cells. You clear cells to remove unwanted data from a datasheet.

The Clear command gives you the option of clearing the contents of a cell, the format of a cell, or both. *Contents* refers to the data contained in a cell, such as a number or text character. The *format* of the cell refers to a variety of characteristics, including the number format.

N O T E Because you do not print the Microsoft Graph datasheet, the font doesn't matter. Although you can choose Format, Font and change the font, this will change the font for the entire datasheet and not the selected range. The only reason you may want to change the font would be to increase the size so you can more easily see the data. ■

To clear a cell, follow these steps:

1. Select the cell or cells you want to clear.

2. Choose Edit, Clear, or click the right mouse button and choose Clear Contents from the shortcut menu. Select All to clear the contents and formats; Contents to clear the entries but retain the formatting; or Formats to clear the format assigned to the cell, but retain the contents.

Inserting and Deleting Rows and Columns

As you enter your own data into the datasheet, you may find it necessary to insert a new row or column, or to delete an existing row or column.

If you want to insert a row, select the row below the place where you want a new row. To insert a row above row 4, for example, select row 4. If you want to insert a column, select the column to the right of the place where you want the new column. To insert a new column to the left of column D, you would select column D. When you have selected the desired row or column, choose Insert, Cells, or choose Insert from the shortcut menu.

Microsoft Graph enables you to insert several rows or columns at once. Highlight the number of rows or columns you want to insert; then choose Insert, Cells. Microsoft Graph automatically inserts the number of rows or columns you highlighted.

To remove rows or columns from the datasheet, select the appropriate rows or columns; then choose Edit, Delete, or choose Delete from the shortcut menu.

▶ **See** "Inserting and Deleting Columns, Rows, and Cells," **p. 330**

Cutting, Moving, and Copying Data

Microsoft Graph enables you to rearrange data in the datasheet using several standard editing methods. Graph fully supports use of the Clipboard and the associated Edit menu commands Cut, Copy, and Paste.

▶ **See** "Moving Around the Document," **p. 75**
▶ **See** "Copying Worksheet Data," **p. 324**
▶ **See** "Moving Worksheet Data," **p. 329**

Excluding Rows or Columns

Sometimes instead of deleting rows or columns, you simply want to exclude them from a chart. Suppose that your datasheet contains sales figures for 20 departments, but you want to plot the sales performance of only the first five departments. To plot this chart, you need to exclude rows 6 through 20.

To exclude rows or columns from a chart, follow these steps:

1. Select the rows or columns that you want to exclude from a chart.

2. Choose Data, Exclude Row/Col.

 T I P You can also double-click row or column headings to include or exclude rows or columns.

When you exclude cells from a chart, the entries in the cells are grayed, and the buttons for the row or column headings lose their three-dimensional attributes, as shown in Figure 19.11. At the same time, the current chart is updated to reflect the excluded data.

FIG. 19.11
Column D is excluded from this datasheet.

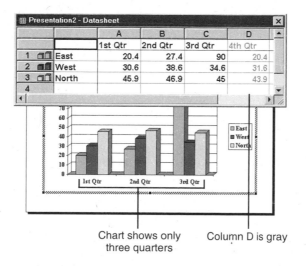

Chart shows only three quarters   Column D is gray

To restore excluded cells to a chart, select the appropriate rows or columns and then choose Data, Include Row/Col. The normal attributes return to the entries in the cells, and the row and column heading buttons.

Choosing a Chart Type

When you start Microsoft Graph, a three-dimensional column chart is created from the sample data in the datasheet. A column chart, however, is not the only type of chart you can create in Microsoft Graph. You can also create the following types of charts, some of which include three-dimensional sub-types:

Area   Pie

Bar   Doughnut

Part
IV

Ch
19

Column	Radar
Line	XY (Scatter)
Surface	Bubble
Stock	Cylinder
Cone	Pyramid

▶ **See** "Changing a Chart Type," **p. 504**

 You may choose any of these chart types by clicking the Chart Type button on the toolbar.

If you need additional charting options, choose Chart, Chart Type to go to the Chart Type dialog box. In the Standard Types page of the dialog box, choose a chart type from the Chart Type list box. Sub-types for the selected type are displayed in the Chart Sub-type group. You can accept the default sub-type, which is highlighted, or choose another sub-type.

Figure 19.12 displays column chart types in the Standard Types page of the Chart Type dialog box.

> **TIP** If you double-click the kind of chart you want in the Chart Type dialog box, you select the default sub-type for the chart and close the dialog box without clicking OK.

For most chart types, Microsoft Graph offers at least one or two variations, or *sub-types*. If you select the column chart type, for example, you then can select one of seven sub-types. Three of these sub-types are 2-D column charts and four of the sub-types are 3-D column charts, as shown in Figure 19.12.

FIG. 19.12

Select the chart type and sub-type in the Chart Type dialog box.

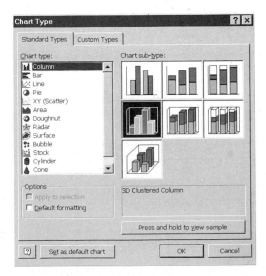

Using Custom Chart Types

Many custom chart types are available, which are accessed by clicking the Custom Types tab in the Chart Types dialog box (see Figure 19.13). Some of these custom chart types are combinations of the standard chart types; others are black-and-white variations or specially colored in gradient tones. Select a custom type in the Chart Type list box to view the chart in the Sample box.

FIG. 19.13
Combination and custom chart types can be selected from the Custom Types page of the Chart Type dialog box.

 TIP You can create your own named chart types by selecting the User-defined option button on the Custom Types tab of the Chart Types dialog box.

Part
IV

Ch

19

Adding Visual Objects to a Chart

Charts often contain additional objects that make the chart easier to read and interpret. For example, you may want to add titles, a legend, axis labels, a data table, data labels, or gridlines. Microsoft Graph 97 has simplified selection of these objects by organizing them in a single dialog box.

▶ **See** "Enhancing a Chart," **p. 507**

Adding Titles

To add a chart title, x-axis title, or y-axis title, choose Chart, Chart Options, which displays the Chart Options dialog box shown in Figure 19.14.

FIG. 19.14

The Chart Options dialog box allows you to add chart objects.

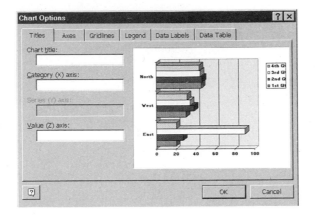

N O T E   The options in the Titles page vary, depending on the type of chart you are using.

To add titles to a chart, follow these steps:

1. Choose Chart, Chart Options, or right-click the chart area and choose Chart Options from the shortcut menu. The Chart Options dialog box appears.
2. If the Titles page is not already displayed, click the Titles tab to display it.
3. In the text boxes, type each title type you want to add to your chart. Each title is displayed on the chart in the sample box as you move the insertion point out of the text box.
4. Click OK. Microsoft Graph adds the titles to the chart.

If you add a title to a chart and then decide you don't want to use it, select the text object in Graph and then choose Edit, Clear, All; choose Clear from the shortcut menu; or press the Delete key.

Adding a Legend

 A *legend* uses color-coded or pattern-coded boxes to identify the data series in a chart. Microsoft Graph automatically adds a legend to every new chart. If you prefer not to include a legend in a chart, you can remove or add the legend to the chart by clicking the Legend button on the toolbar.

To change the position of the legend in the chart, drag it to the desired location, or choose the Legend tab in the Chart Options dialog box and then select an option button in the Placement group.

Adding Data Labels

Data labels mark the exact value or percentage represented by a data point. Data labels are often used in bar or column charts to pinpoint values when data points are close together. These labels also are commonly used in pie charts to identify the exact percentage represented by each pie slice.

To add data labels to a chart, follow these steps:

1. Choose Chart, Chart Options, and then choose the Data Labels tab of the Chart Options dialog box (see Figure 19.15).

2. Select an option.

FIG. 19.15

Add data labels in this dialog box.

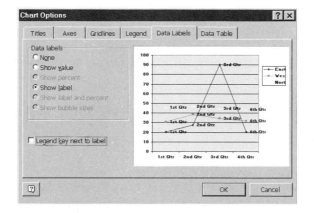

3. If you want the legend key to appear with the data label, check the Legend Key Next to Label check box.

4. Click OK. Data labels are added to the chart.

Adding Gridlines

Gridlines are horizontal and vertical lines that overlay a chart, in all charts except pie and doughnut charts. These lines help you follow a point from the x- or y-axis to identify a data point's exact value. Gridlines are useful in large charts, charts that contain many data points, and charts in which data points are close together. The sample column chart that Microsoft Graph creates includes horizontal gridlines.

To turn gridlines on or off in a chart, follow these steps:

1. Choose Chart, Chart Options, and then choose the Gridlines tab of the Chart Options dialog box, as shown in Figure 19.16.

FIG. 19.16
Use the Gridlines tab to choose gridline options.

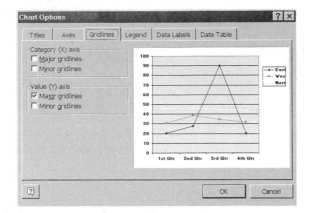

2. For each axis, turn major and minor gridlines on or off. Major gridlines appear at axis labels, and minor gridlines appear between axis labels.

3. Click OK.

  You can also add or delete major gridlines by clicking the Category Axis Gridlines and Value Axis Gridlines buttons on the Standard toolbar.

Adding a Data Table

Microsoft Graph 97 includes a new feature that displays a small data table below your chart. The table is similar to the datasheet and is based on the charted values.

To add a data table to a chart, do the following:

1. Choose Chart, Chart Options, and then choose the Data Table tab of the Chart Options dialog box, as shown in Figure 19.17.

FIG. 19.17
Add a data table to the chart to display the precise charted values.

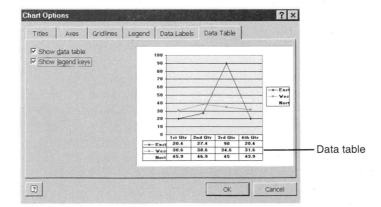

Data table

2. Select the Show Data Table check box. The data table appears below the chart in the sample box.

3. Click OK. The data table is added to the chart.

If the chart appears distorted or crowded after adding a data table, you can resize the chart or the chart window.

 You can also add or remove a data table by clicking the Data Table button on the Standard toolbar.

Specifying Colors, Patterns, Borders, Fonts, and Other Formatting

You can apply colors, patterns, and other formatting to almost any object in a chart. To change a chart object's formatting, follow these steps:

1. Double-click the object you want to change. The Format [*object*] dialog box appears, as shown in Figure 19.18.

 Alternatively, use the new Chart Objects drop-down list on the Standard toolbar to select the object by name and then click the Format [*object*] button, which is located to the right of the drop-down list. Another method of selecting the object to format is to click the object in the chart. The name of the object appears in the Chart Objects text box in the toolbar. Then click the Format [*object*] button to open the Format [*object*] dialog box.

N O T E The name of the Format dialog box varies depending on what *object* you are changing. If you are changing a data series, the [*object*] is Data Series, and the dialog box is titled Format Data Series. ▉

Part **IV**

Ch **19**

T I P   If you make a change to a chart format and don't like the results, you can choose <u>E</u>dit, <u>U</u>ndo or click the Undo button to change it back.

---

2. Choose a tab in the dialog box and then select the desired options.
   ▶ **See** "Enhancing Text," **p. 663**
   ▶ **See** "Working with Colors and Line Styles," **p. 668**

3. Look at the Sample box (if there is one) for a preview of the changes. Repeat steps 3 and 4 to change any additional colors or styles.

4. Click OK. Changes are applied to the chart.

FIG. 19.18
Use the Format
[*object*] dialog box
to change object
attributes.

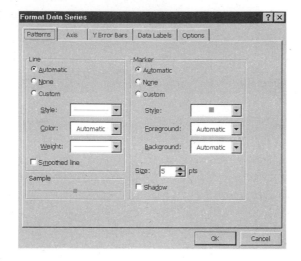

The options available in the Format [*object*] dialog box change depending on the chart *object* you have selected. For example, Figure 19.19 shows the Font page of the Format [*object*] dialog box for a chart axis. Note the variety of formatting tabs available.

FIG. 19.19
The Format [*object*]
dialog box allows
many formatting
options.

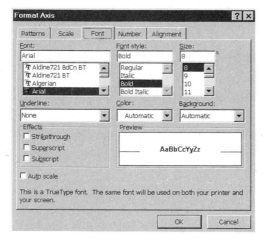

Inserting a Chart into a Document

While you are working in Microsoft Graph and making changes in your chart, the changes you make are updated in your document. As long as you continue working in Graph, the Graph menu bar and toolbars remain active. When you are finished creating your chart and want to return to your document, click any blank area of the document window outside the chart area. The chart becomes an object in the document, and the menus and toolbars of the application from which you launched Microsoft Graph return. In Access, you need to choose File, Exit & Return.

Editing a Chart

To edit an existing Microsoft Graph chart, double-click it in the document in which it appears. This launches Microsoft Graph and enables you to edit any attributes as previously discussed.

▶ **See** "Editing a Chart," **p. 518**

Part
IV

Ch
19

CHAPTER 20

Creating and Printing Excel Charts

by Conrad Carlberg

A chart is a graphic representation of worksheet data. Excel offers 14 types of charts from which to choose, and more than 70 subtypes of these 14 basic types. By selecting from these chart types and subtypes, you can create charts that accurately depict nearly any situation.

You can create charts on an existing worksheet or as a separate sheet within a workbook. If you change data represented by the chart, Excel updates the chart automatically. After creating a chart, you can add elements such as trendlines, and modify existing elements such as titles and gridlines. ■

Create a chart using the ChartWizard

Follow a series of prompts from the ChartWizard that enable you to identify the data, choose a chart type, and set the chart's formatting characteristics.

Arrange a chart's placement

Move and resize a chart on the screen for optimal effect.

Choose the right type of chart for your data

Learn how the nature of different charts' axes, as well as the chart's purpose, dictate the type of chart you should choose.

Revise charts

Modify the nature and appearance of charts after you have created them.

Create a data map

Use the Microsoft Map capability to display your data on a geographic context.

Print a chart

You've set up your chart so that it looks just right on the screen. Choose among Excel's page setup options to make sure that the printed version also looks right.

Creating a Chart with the ChartWizard

The ChartWizard provides an automated, step-by-step approach to creating charts from worksheet data. You can create the chart on the current worksheet, or you can place it on a new sheet in the current workbook. The following sections describe each step in the ChartWizard process.

The first step in creating a chart is to select the data on the worksheet. Although you can select data to be charted before, during, or after the ChartWizard runs, it's typical to select the data first. Use these guidelines when selecting data for a chart:

▇ On the worksheet, the data for the chart must be placed in columns and rows, but need not be in adjacent columns and rows.

▇ Position labels to be used on a chart in the top row and leftmost column of the data range.

▇ Select the labels along with the chart data.

▇ Select nonadjacent cells by holding down the Ctrl key.

Figure 20.1 illustrates sales data for three departments in a layout suitable for charting.

FIG. 20.1
Labels in row 3 and column A are selected along with chart data.

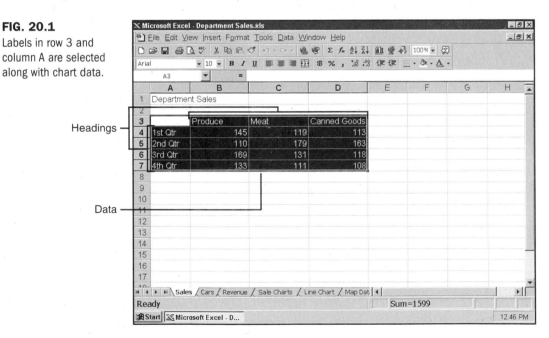

The remainder of this section shows you how to complete the ChartWizard to create a chart. If you want, use the data shown in Figure 20.1 to follow the steps involved.

Step 1: Choose the Chart Type and Subtype

 When you have selected the data, click the ChartWizard button. Step 1 of the ChartWizard is displayed, as shown in Figure 20.2.

N O T E In earlier versions of Excel, you establish the location and size of a chart when the ChartWizard starts. In Excel 97, you locate and size the chart after the ChartWizard has completed.

FIG. 20.2
You can choose from different chart types, both built-in and custom, in Step 1 of the ChartWizard.

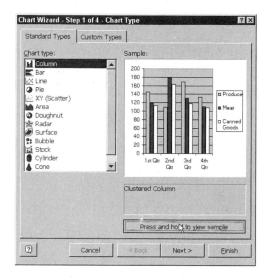

T I P If you selected your data range before starting the ChartWizard, you can preview the chart in Step 1 by using the Press and Hold To View Sample button.

To move from step to step in the ChartWizard, use the action buttons as defined in Table 20.1.

Table 20.1 ChartWizard Buttons

Choose This Button	To Do This
Next	Move to the next step.
Back	Return to the previous step.
Finish	Create a chart using the options chosen so far and exit the ChartWizard.
Cancel	Cancel the ChartWizard and return to the worksheet.

Click the Line chart type from the 14 available chart types and click the Line with Data Markers subtype. Then, click the Next button to go to Step 2 of the ChartWizard.

N O T E The chart is linked to the cell range on the worksheet that contains the data. If data in this cell range changes, the chart is updated automatically. ▨

Step 2: Select or Confirm the Data Range

Step 2 in the ChartWizard gives you another chance to identify the range of cells that the chart will display. The Step 2 dialog box (Data Range tab) is shown in Figure 20.3.

FIG. 20.3

Use this dialog box to select, confirm, or change the range of cells for the chart.

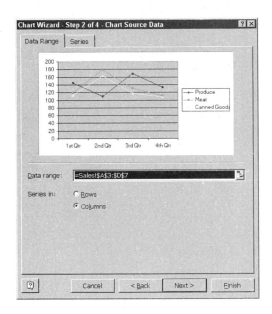

If you're satisfied with the range you selected before starting the ChartWizard, either click the Series tab (to change certain data series options), or click Next.

If you started the ChartWizard before selecting the range that contains your data, use Step 2 to identify the range. The Data Range reference edit box is active when Step 2 appears, so you can drag across the worksheet range that you want to chart. When you drag across the range, the Step 2 dialog box shrinks, leaving only the reference edit box visible. This makes it easy to access the desired worksheet cells.

If you previewed your chart in Step 1, you might have decided to expand or reduce the worksheet selection. Again, in Step 2, you can use the Data Range reference edit box to revise your selection.

Finally, if you have organized your data series in rows rather than columns, as shown in Figure 20.1, choose the Rows option button. The Rows and Columns options allow you to choose the orientation of the chart—that is, whether the data series is entered on the worksheet in rows or in columns.

> **N O T E** A *data series* is the information that's represented on the chart by means of bars, columns, pie slices, lines and data points, and so on. A chart can contain one or more data series.

Figure 20.4 shows two charts: one using the Columns option, and one using the Rows option. Notice that the data series names appear in the legend for each figure.

FIG. 20.4
The chart's data series conform to their orientation on the worksheet.

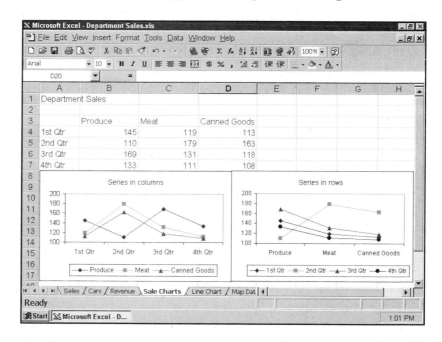

Step 2, Continued: Series Options

Step 2 in the ChartWizard also offers a Series tab, where you can review and modify different options for your chart's data series. A data series contains the data in one column of a column-oriented worksheet range, or in one row of a row-oriented worksheet range.

Step 2's Series tab is shown in Figure 20.5.

Notice in Figure 20.5 that the chart contains three data series: one named Produce, one named Meat, and one named Canned Goods. You can use the Series tab for any of these purposes:

■ *Change the name of a data series.* To do so, click in the <u>N</u>ame box, and then click in a worksheet cell that contains a different label for the data series. Click in any other edit box in the Series tab to see the effect of the change you've made.

■ *Change the worksheet location of a data series' values.* To do this, click in the <u>V</u>alues box, and then drag through a worksheet range to establish a different set of values.

■ *Change the worksheet location of a data series' X axis labels.* To do this, click in the Ca<u>t</u>egory (X) axis labels box, and then drag through a worksheet range that contains different labels.

■ *Remove a data series from the chart.* This is a convenient way to suppress a series that is located between other series on the worksheet. Click the series name in the <u>S</u>eries box, and click <u>R</u>emove.

■ *Add a data series to the chart.* To do this, click <u>A</u>dd, and then fill in the appropriate worksheet ranges for the new series' name, values, and category labels.

When you have finished any customizing that you want to do on the Series tab, click Next.

FIG. 20.5
The references to worksheet ranges are preceded by the name of the worksheet.

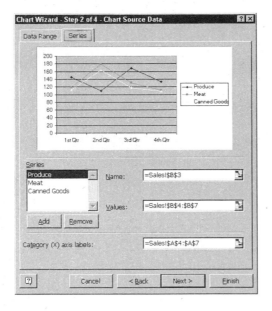

Step 3: Chart Options

Step 3 of the ChartWizard allows you to choose additional charting options. These options are found on six different dialog box tabs:

- The Titles tab allows you to specify a Chart <u>T</u>itle, and labels for the <u>C</u>ategory (X) Axis and for the <u>V</u>alue (Y) Axis. Figure 20.6 displays the Titles tab.

FIG. 20.6

The Titles tab also appears when you format an existing chart. If you have established secondary axes, you can provide them with labels.

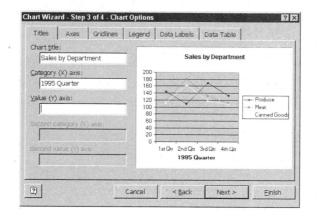

- Use the Axes tab, shown in Figure 20.7, to specify whether you want the chart to display the Y axis, the X axis, or both. Also, use it to choose among X axis formatting options. The Automatic option displays X axis category labels as dates, if they are date formatted on the worksheet. The Category option suppresses date formats, even if the worksheet data is date formatted. The Time-scale option displays date formats, even if the worksheet data is *not* date formatted.

FIG. 20.7

Use the Axes tab to suppress or display X and Y axes on the chart.

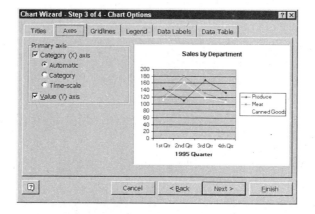

Part

IV

Ch

20

- The Gridlines tab enables you to call for major and minor gridlines on both the X and Y axes, as shown in Figure 20.8.
- On the Legend tab, you can check or clear the <u>S</u>how Legend check box to display or hide a chart legend. The legend associates particular symbols and colors on the chart with the names of the data series. By choosing one of the placement options, you specify the chart location where the legend will appear (see Figure 20.9).

FIG. 20.8

Specifying gridlines on a chart can make it easier to estimate a data series' values, by a reference to the appropriate axis.

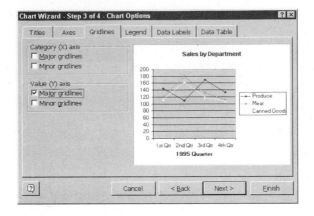

FIG. 20.9

Placing the legend at the top or bottom of the chart helps save space for the plot area.

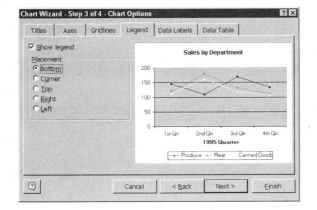

■ At times, it is useful to display the value of a data point next to its symbol on the chart. Using the Data Labels tab, you can choose to display either the point's value or its category label. Notice, in Figure 20.10, that three options are dim, and thus disabled. The Show Percent and the Show Label and Percent options apply to Pie and Doughnut charts only, and the Show Bubble Sizes option applies to Bubble charts only.

 Data labels, whether they show a value or a category, can be edited using the Formula Bar to display any value or label that you want.

FIG. 20.10
If you check the Legend Key Next to Label check box, the colors and patterns associated with each series appear next to each point in the series.

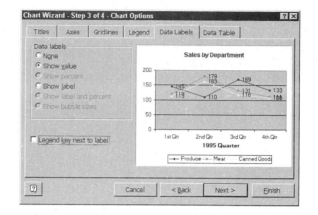

By using the Data Table tab, you can arrange for a table that contains the data used in the chart to appear immediately below the chart area (see Figure 20.11). Check the Show Data Table check box to see the data table.

FIG. 20.11
You are likely to find that including a Data Table in a chart takes up so much of the chart area that the chart itself becomes less legible.

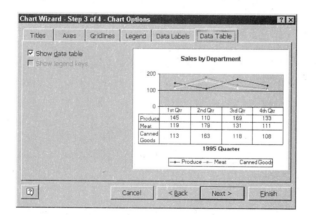

Step 4: Locate the Chart

In the final Step in the ChartWizard, shown in Figure 20.12, you specify whether you want to embed the chart in the worksheet, or create a separate chart sheet.

When you have made your selection in Step 4, click Finish to complete the process. (Notice that you can click Finish in any ChartWizard Step, if you're willing to accept the default options.)

The completed chart and the Chart toolbar are shown in Figure 20.13.

Part
IV

Ch
20

FIG. 20.12

Use the drop-down arrow in the As <u>O</u>bject In edit box to choose to embed the chart in a different worksheet.

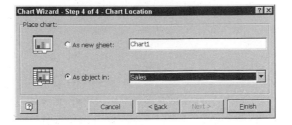

FIG. 20.13

After the ChartWizard has finished, use the Chart toolbar to make changes.

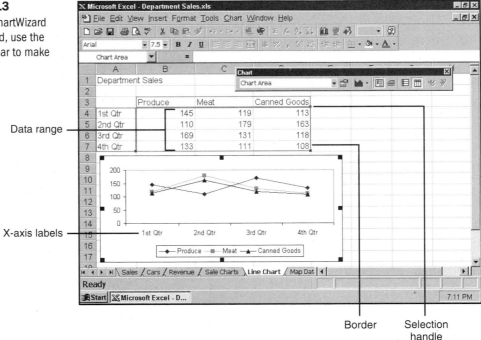

Border   Selection handle

 T I P The Chart toolbar appears automatically when you activate a chart, if it is checked in the submenu that appears when you choose <u>V</u>iew, <u>T</u>oolbars. You also can right-click any toolbar and then choose Chart in the shortcut menu to display the Chart toolbar.

Notice in Figure 20.13 that after the chart is complete, its worksheet data range is surrounded by borders. The borders have selection handles that you can click and drag. This is a convenient way to reduce or expand the range that the chart covers—that is, you can use the handles to add new data to a chart or to remove data from it.

TROUBLESHOOTING

I want to access the chart commands when I embed a chart in my worksheet. To access the chart commands for an embedded chart, you first must activate the chart you want to edit by clicking it. When you do this, Excel adds a Chart menu to the main menu bar. Excel also changes the menu commands in the F_ormat menu to reflect commands for editing charts. When you create and activate a chart in a separate chart sheet, these menu changes are performed automatically.

My chart has only one data series, so I don't want to display the legend with the chart. To remove the legend box from a chart, activate the chart and then click the Legend button in the Chart toolbar. Excel removes the legend box from the chart. Click the Legend button again to reestablish the legend in the chart. You may need to reposition the legend by clicking and dragging it.

Moving and Sizing a Chart Object

After a chart is created, you can make it larger or smaller or move it to a new location on the worksheet.

To size a chart, complete the following steps:

1. Activate the chart by clicking it. Selection handles appear as small black handles around the chart.

2. Position the mouse pointer over a handle. The mouse pointer becomes a double-headed arrow.

3. Click and drag the handle to make the chart larger or smaller. To proportionally size the chart, hold down the Shift key while dragging one of the corner handles.

Figure 20.14 shows the dotted lines that appear so as to indicate the increase or decrease as a chart is being resized. While you are resizing the chart, the pointer changes to a double-headed arrow.

▶ **See** "Selecting, Moving, and Resizing Objects," **p. 365**
▶ **See** "Moving and Copying Objects," **p. 645**
▶ **See** "Resizing and Scaling Objects," **p. 647**

To move a chart to a new location on the worksheet, first click the chart to activate it. Then, click inside the chart boundary (not on one of the handles) and drag the chart to a new position.

Part
IV

Ch
20

FIG. 20.14

The dotted lines show the new size as you drag a handle to resize a chart.

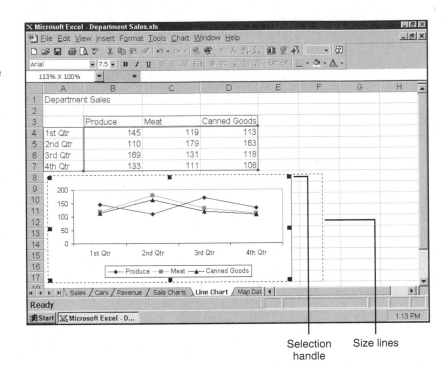

Selection handle   Size lines

 T I P To keep an object aligned with the cell gridlines when moving or resizing, hold down the Alt key. To move an object only horizontally or vertically, hold down the Shift key while dragging.

Choosing a Chart Type

Some chart types work better for particular types of data. For example, a pie chart might be the best choice to view the percentage of total revenue produced by each department in a company. It's often best to base your choice on the nature of the data, because that affects the appearance of the chart axes.

Most Excel chart types have two different kinds of axes: an X-axis and a Y-axis. In Excel terminology, an X-axis is a *category* axis and a Y-axis is a *value* axis. This distinction is extremely important to your choice of chart type.

Suppose that you want to chart revenues for different product lines: Ford, GM, and Chrysler. Each of these product lines represents a category of automobile, and the categories are arbitrary: no category represents more or less of a "car-ness" value than does another. So the product line is best shown on an X, or category axis.

In contrast, the amount of revenue for each product line does represent more or less of a dollar value: $100,000 is more than $50,000, which is more than $25,000, and so on. So a variable such as revenue is best shown on a Y, or value axis.

To chart revenue by product line, a good choice of chart type would be a Bar chart or a Column chart (see Figure 20.15). On the Bar chart, the vertical axis is the X(Category) axis, and the horizontal axis is the Y(Value) axis. Each bar represents a different product line, and its horizontal width indicates the product line's revenue value.

FIG. 20.15

A Bar chart is just a Column chart, rotated 90 degrees.

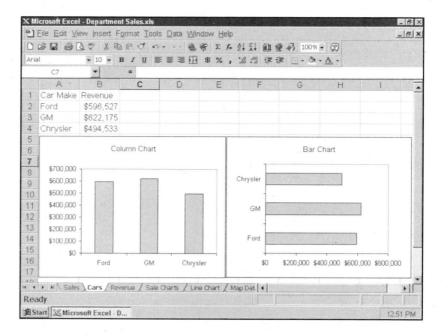

In contrast, a Column chart makes the vertical axis the Y(Value) axis, and makes the horizontal axis the X(Category) axis. Each column represents a different product line, and its vertical height indicates its revenue value.

In both cases, the different products on the X(Category) axis are spaced equally. Their distance from one another says nothing about the relative value of being a Ford versus being a Chrysler, because these arbitrary categories have no relative values.

Now suppose that, instead of automobiles, you're interested in sales at a coffee bar: you want to examine the relationship between the revenues and daily temperature. An XY(Scatter) chart is probably the best choice. This is because an XY(Scatter) chart uses *two* value axes—both the horizontal and vertical axes represent values, not categories. When you look at the relationship between temperature and coffee sales, you are dealing with two continuously valued variables. Neither has categories that are arbitrary. A Line, Bar, or Column chart is not a good choice, because each has one category axis.

Part

IV

Ch

20

Figure 20.16 illustrates the difference between the appearance of a Line chart and an XY(Scatter) chart. Notice that the distance between the temperatures is constant on the Line chart. Each temperature is treated as a separate category, with the same distance between each pair of categories.

But on the XY(Scatter) chart, both axes are value axes. The horizontal axis takes into account the numeric distance between different temperatures and separates them accordingly.

FIG. 20.16

The XY(Scatter) chart's horizontal value axis accurately represents the differences in temperature.

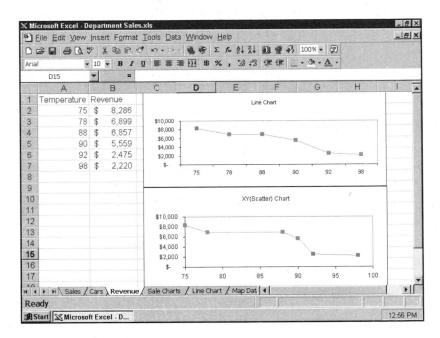

TIP When you want to insert a trendline into a chart, it is best to use an XY(Scatter) chart.

Changing a Chart Type

Excel has options available for displaying data in various chart types, as discussed in the prior section "Choosing a Chart Type." A completed chart of any type can easily be changed to a different chart type at any time.

Complete these steps to change the chart type:

1. Select the chart.

2. Click the arrow next to the Chart Type button on the Chart toolbar.

3. Select the type of chart you want from the displayed palette (see Figure 20.17).

FIG. 20.17
Choose a chart type
from the palette.

Palette

The chart type can also be changed using menu choices. Follow these steps:

1. Click the chart to activate it. The Chart menu becomes available on the menu bar.

TIP To edit a chart, you also can click the right mouse button on the chart and choose from among the available options on the shortcut menu.

2. Choose Chart, Chart Type to display the dialog box shown in Figure 20.18.

FIG. 20.18
Use the Chart Type
dialog box to change
the basic chart
appearance.

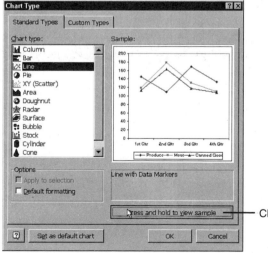

Click here to preview your chart.

Part
IV

Ch
20

3. Select a chart type from the 14 available.

4. Choose a chart subtype within the basic chart type you selected.

5. Click OK.

Chart Type Options

Additional options for chart types are available by selecting the Chart Type, Source Data, Chart Options and Location items in the Chart menu. These menu items correspond to each step in the ChartWizard—that is, choosing one of the menu items displays the same dialog box as a step in the ChartWizard (see Figure 20.19).

FIG. 20.19
You can modify choices you made while the ChartWizard was active with these Chart menu items.

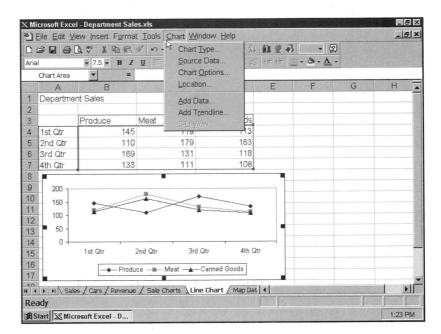

3-D View Options

Most chart types include a subtype with a 3-D format. (The only types that have no 3-D format are XY, Doughnut, Radar, and Stock charts.) When you are working with a 3-D chart type, additional controls for chart appearance are available by choosing Chart, 3-D View. The dialog box shown in Figure 20.20 opens.

Elevation controls the relative level at which the chart is viewed. Enter a value or use the arrow buttons to adjust the value.

Rotation controls the view angle of the chart around the vertical axis. Enter a rotation value in degrees, or click the rotation arrows to change the view angle.

Use the perspective controls to set the amount of depth in the chart view. Select the Right Angle Axes option to remove all perspective from the chart view.

To return to the standard 3-D view, click the Default button.

Elevation controls

FIG. 20.20
Use the Format 3-D
View dialog box to
change the angle,
elevation, and
perspective of the
chart type.

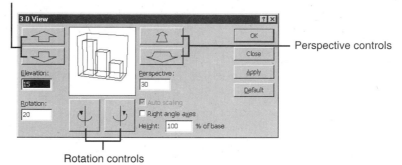

Perspective controls

Rotation controls

Enhancing a Chart

Nearly every part of an Excel chart can be formatted. This flexibility gives you considerable control over the appearance of your chart. Before an individual chart item can be
formatted, it must be selected. Chart items in an active chart can be easily selected with
the mouse. You can also use the Chart Objects button on the Chart toolbar. Table 20.2
lists mouse procedures for selecting various items on an active chart.

▶ **See** "Adding Visual Objects to a Chart," **p. 483**

Table 20.2   Selection Options

To	Do This
Select an item	Click the chart item. Black handles appear around the edges or at the ends of the item.
Select a data series	Click any marker in the chart data series. Handles appear on each marker in the series.
Select a single data marker	Select the entire series, then click again on the desired marker. Handles appear around the edges of the item. The top (larger) handle can be dragged to change the value of a single marker.
Select gridlines	Click a gridline. Make sure the tip of the mouse pointer is exactly on the gridline.
Select an axis	Click the axis or the area containing the axis labels.
Select the legend	Click the legend. Click again to select an individual legend entry or legend key.
Select the entire plot area	Click any area in the plot area not occupied by another item, including gridlines.
Select the entire chart	Click anywhere outside the plot area not containing another item.

Part

IV

Ch

20

N O T E   A *marker* is an object that represents a data point in a chart. Bars, columns, pie
wedges, and symbols are examples of markers.

T I P   It's sometimes easier to select different chart components with the keyboard arrow keys rather
than with the mouse. Click the chart, then cycle through its components using any arrow key.

Each component of an Excel chart can be individually formatted to change its appearance.
To display the formatting options available for a specific chart item, select the chart item
and then press Ctrl+1 or choose Format, Selected [Object] (where [Object] is the name
of the selected item). You can also double-click the desired chart item. Either of these
methods opens a formatting dialog box with options relating to the selected chart item.
Figure 20.21 shows an example of this dialog box. Note the tabs for various formatting
options.

FIG. 20.21

The Format Data
Series dialog box
enables you to change
the appearance of
each data series.

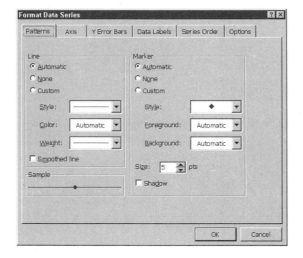

The following sections describe additional enhancement options available for various
chart components.

Using Custom Chart Types

Excel provides several chart types that you can use to enhance your charts. These types
are found on the Custom Types tab of the Chart Type dialog box. In addition, you can
create your own user-defined chart types, based on existing charts that you create.

To apply a custom chart type to a chart, follow these steps:

1. Click the chart you want to modify.

2. Choose Chart, Chart Type or click the chart area with the right mouse button and then choose Chart Type from the shortcut menu. The Chart Type dialog box appears. Click the Custom Types tab (see Figure 20.22).

FIG. 20.22

Choose a built-in custom chart type to apply to a chart.

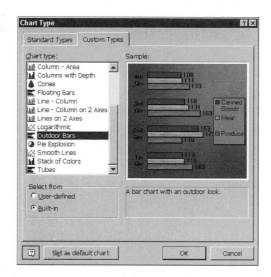

3. Choose the Built-In option to use one of Excel's built-in types.

4. Choose the type of chart you want from the Chart Type list box.

5. Choose OK. Excel applies the chart type to the chart.

To create a custom chart format, follow these steps:

1. Select the chart that contains the formats you want to define as a custom chart format, or activate the chart sheet.

2. Choose Chart, Chart Type, or click the chart area with the right mouse button and then choose Chart Type from the shortcut menu. The Chart Type dialog box appears (refer to Figure 20.22).

3. Select the User-Defined option. After you select that option, the entries in the Chart Type list box change to a list of user-defined types.

4. Choose the Add button. The Add Custom Chart Type dialog box appears (see Figure 20.23).

5. Enter a text name for the chart type in the Name box, and a description of the chart type in the Description box.

6. Click OK. The Chart Type dialog box reappears, as shown in Figure 20.24.

Part

IV

Ch

20

FIG. 20.23
Providing a text description of the new user-defined chart type makes it easier to identify its custom elements.

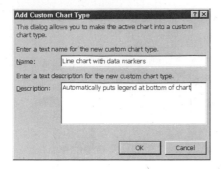

FIG. 20.24
After you have supplied a name for the new chart type, it appears in the Chart Type list box.

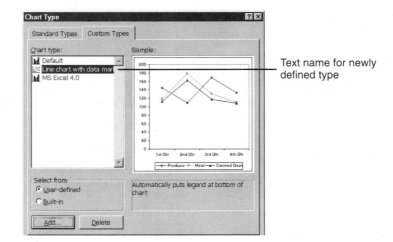

Text name for newly defined type

7. If you want the newly defined chart type to be the default chart type for new charts, click the Set as Default Chart button.

8. Click OK.

To apply a user-defined chart type, follow these steps:

1. Select the chart you want to format, or activate the chart sheet.

2. Choose Chart, Chart Type, or click the chart area with the right mouse button and then choose Chart Type from the shortcut menu. The Chart Type dialog box appears.

3. Click the Custom Types tab, and select the User-Defined option.

4. Choose the chart type you want to use from the Chart Type list.

5. Click OK.

Creating a Data Map

The Data Map is a feature useful for charting geographic data. You can create a map linked to your worksheet data, which provides an effective visual tool for analyzing demographic information. Suppose that you have sales figures for each state in the United States. Instead of comparing data in a simple bar chart, which may not be so simple for 50 states, use a data map to represent ranges of sales data on a color-coded or shaded map of the United States.

Setting Up the Data to Map

Included with Excel is an assortment of statistical data from which you can create maps. The Mapstats workbook contains demographic data that you can illustrate on maps. (Different installation procedures place Mapstats.xls in different folders on your disk. It's best to use Windows Explorer to find it.) You can also embed a map based on data you enter in the worksheet.

A requirement for creating a Data Map is that geographic regions, such as country or state names, must be in one column in the range you select in the worksheet. The geographic data originates from any of the following maps: Australia, Canada, Europe, Mexico, North America, UK Standard Regions, US with AK & HI Insets, United States in North America, and World Countries.

Before you create a map, you need to prepare data in the worksheet by performing the following steps:

1. In a column of your worksheet, enter data that contains names or abbreviations of geographic regions, such as states, countries, or provinces.

   Excel also accepts numeric postal codes, which you should format as text to prevent loss of leading zeros.

N O T E You must use geographic regions that the data map feature recognizes. You can find the correct spelling and abbreviations for the allowable region names in the Mapstats workbook. ▪

▶ **See** "Copying Worksheet Data," **p. 324**

2. In another column, enter numeric values for each geographic region. Figure 20.25 shows sample data for creating a data map. This data was copied from three columns of the USA worksheet in the Mapstats workbook.

3. (Optional) Enter additional columns of numeric data related to each geographic region if you want to represent them on the map.

Part
IV

Ch
20

FIG. 20.25
Geographic regions
and data are prepared
in the worksheet
before creating a map.

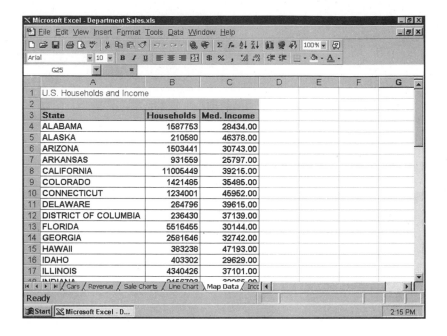

4. (Optional) Enter column headings at the top of each column of data if you want them to be automatically included in the legend on the map.

Plotting the Map

After you prepare the geographic data you want to use in the data map, follow these steps:

1. Select the range of data to map, including the geographic regions, numeric values, and headings.

 2. Choose Insert, Map. Or click the Map button on the Standard toolbar. The mouse pointer turns into a crosshair.

3. Drag on the worksheet where you want the map to appear—from the upper-left corner to the lower-right corner of the map area. The worksheet must be the one that was active when you chose Insert, Map.

You can change the size and position of the map later.

 TIP Create a blank map by selecting only a column of geographic regions.

4. If Excel cannot create the map from the range you selected, a dialog box prompts for more information. For example, if you selected state names, the Multiple Maps Available dialog box appears (see Figure 20.26). Select the map you want and then click OK.

FIG. 20.26

A dialog box appears if Excel needs more information to create the map.

TROUBLESHOOTING

When I try to create the map, I get the Unable to Create Map dialog box. What am I doing wrong? If you have used a geographic name that Excel does not recognize, then Excel does not know which map to create. You can choose a map from the list and click OK, or choose Cancel to return to the worksheet and correct your data. You may also not have the map feature installed. On Office setup, Microsoft Map is an option under Microsoft Excel.

5. The map is displayed on the worksheet. The Data Map toolbar and menu appear, and the Microsoft Map Control dialog box opens. Drag the dialog box (using its title bar) to another location if it is covering the map (see Figure 20.27).

You can drag buttons out of the white box to remove features from the map. The mouse pointer turns into a recycling bin while you are dragging.

6. In the Microsoft Map Control dialog box, drag column buttons and format buttons to the white box. The buttons in the white box determine how data is presented on the map.

When you drag a button, the mouse pointer turns into a hand pulling a handle. In Figure 20.28, the Med. Income column button has been dragged into the white box. The Dot Density format button appears next to it automatically; however, you can drag another format button to replace the Dot Density button.

Table 20.3 shows the format buttons you can choose in the Microsoft Map Control dialog box.

Part

IV

Ch

20

Data Map menu

FIG. 20.27
Microsoft Data Map transforms your Excel menu and toolbar when a map is inserted in the worksheet.

Data Map toolbar

Column buttons

Format buttons

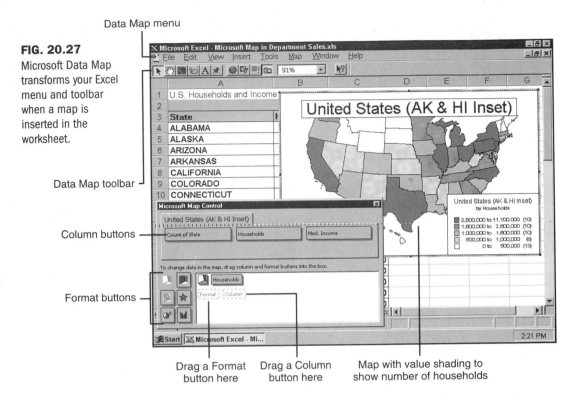

Drag a Format button here

Drag a Column button here

Map with value shading to show number of households

FIG. 20.28
Choose the columns and formats that will appear on the map by dragging them in the Microsoft Map Control dialog box.

The map indicates Median Income by means of the density of the dots

Here, dot density is used to indicate Median Income

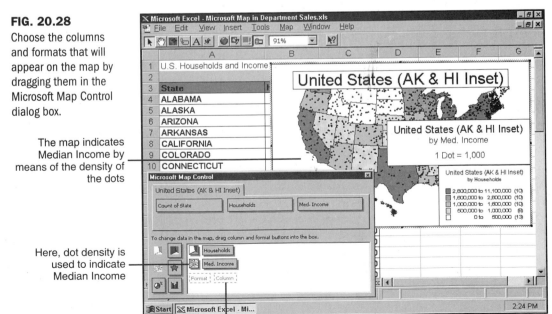

This column button was just dragged into the white box

Table 20.3 Format Buttons for Microsoft Map Control

Choose this Format Button		To Produce this Effect
[icon]	Value Shading	Shades map features according to the numeric values.
[icon]	Category Shading	Colors map features according to their category.
[icon]	Dot Density	Shows numeric data as a quantity of small dots.
[icon]	Graduated Symbol	Shows numeric data as various sizes of symbols.
[icon]	Pie Chart	Displays a pie chart in each map area, which shows data for that area.
[icon]	Column Chart	Displays a column chart in each map area, which shows data for that area.

7. Drag other column and format buttons as needed in the Microsoft Map Control dialog box, and then close the dialog box by clicking its x button.

 To redisplay the Microsoft Map Control dialog box, click the Show/Hide Microsoft Map Control button on the toolbar or choose View, Microsoft Map Control on the Map menu.

After you create a map, you probably will want to make a few changes to it. You do this by using options in the Map menu and toolbar, as described in the following section.

Customizing the Map

Data Map in Excel offers many ways for you to change the appearance of your map. If your map is not activated in Excel, you must double-click it to start Data Map, which displays the Data Map menu and toolbar. An activated map has a hatched border (refer to Figure 20.28).

 The Data Map Help menu offers detailed topics on changing your map. Choose Help, Data Map Help Topics, Contents, How to Use Maps, and then find the feature you want to add, remove, or change.

Following are suggested changes for the map shown in Figure 20.28. Each change is illustrated in Figure 20.29:

■ Stretch the map frame by dragging its selection handles.

Part
IV

Ch
20

■ Change the title by double-clicking it to position the insertion point, and then edit the title. Change the font of the title by right-clicking the title. In the shortcut menu, choose Format Font, and then make selections in the Font dialog box.

■ Edit each legend by double-clicking to display the Format Properties dialog box, and click the Legend Options tab. Clear the Use Compact Format check box to show numeric information in the legend. You also can change the legend title and subtitle.

Click the Edit Legend Entries button if you want to change the numbers in the value ranges.

■ Notice that the legend in Figure 20.29 shows five value ranges. The original map displayed six ranges (six shades on the map) and was changed by choosing Map, Value Shading Options and then changing the Number of Value Ranges. You also can change the Color of the shading in the Value Shading Options dialog box.

FIG. 20.29

You can make few or many changes to improve the readability of your map.

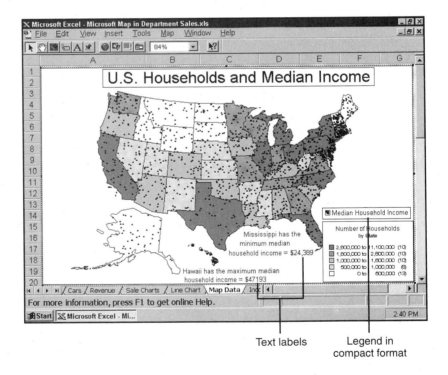

■ Change the number of units represented by each dot by choosing Map, Dot Density Options. In Figure 20.29, the dot density was 1,000.

- Resize a legend by clicking to select and then dragging the selection handles. Move a legend by selecting and then dragging the legend or its border.

- Reposition the map in its frame by clicking the Grabber button in the toolbar. Position the hand-shaped mouse pointer on the map and drag to relocate the map in its frame.

- Add text to the map by clicking the Add Text button on the toolbar. Click anywhere on the map to position the insertion point, and start typing. Press Enter to complete the text, or click elsewhere to type more text.

- Change to the normal mouse pointer by clicking the Select Objects button. Click text to select the text box, and then drag to reposition the text. Or right-click the text and choose Format Font to change its font.

As you can see in Figure 20.29, a few changes can greatly enhance the basic map first created. Other changes you can make on maps are:

- Add map labels by clicking the Map Labels button on the toolbar. In the Map Labels dialog box, choose labels you want to use. To place state names on the map, for example, choose Map Feature Names. Or to put values on the map as labels, choose Values From and select the name of the column that contains the values. After you choose OK, the mouse pointer becomes a crosshair and labels appear as you point to map features. To make the label stick on the map, click where you want to place it. Click the Select Objects button when you finish placing map labels.

- Change the magnification of an area of the map by clicking the Zoom Percentage of Map drop-down list. To return the map to its full display, click the Display Entire button on the toolbar.

- Change the center of the map in its frame by clicking the Center Map button on the toolbar. When you move the mouse point over the map, it becomes a compass rose. By clicking anywhere in the map, you move that location to the center of the frame.

N O T E If you change worksheet data that is represented in the map, the Map Refresh button becomes active. You should refresh the map by clicking the Map Refresh button or by choosing Refresh from the Map menu. ■

- Delete titles, legends, added text, or map labels by selecting them and then pressing Delete.

- Add additional data to the map by choosing Insert Data and specifying the worksheet range to include in the map.

- Add map pins to the map by clicking the Custom Pin Map button on the toolbar. Type a name for the pin map and click OK. Then click the location on the map where you want to place a map pin, type a description, and press Enter.

- Add features such as airports, cities, lakes, and highways, by choosing Map, Add Feature. In the Add Map Feature dialog box, select features and then choose OK.

- Hide map features by choosing Map, Features. Clear the Visible check box next to the feature and then choose OK.

When you finish making changes to the map, click outside the map to close the Data Map program and return to the Excel worksheet. The map is embedded in the worksheet, and the Excel menus and toolbars return. Be sure to save the workbook—the map is saved with the workbook. To edit the map again, you must double-click it to activate it and to turn on Data Map features.

N O T E   Microsoft Data Map was developed by MapInfo Corporation as a subset of the MapInfo desktop mapping software system. You can purchase additional maps and demographic data files from MapInfo Corporation. See the Data Map Help topic, "Purchasing additional maps," for more information. You can create maps in MapInfo and then use the maps with Excel after you first set up the map by running the Data Installer (Datainst.exe). ▪

Editing a Chart

When you use the ChartWizard to create charts, Excel plots the data according to the selected worksheet range. You can use several commands to edit an existing chart. For example, you can delete a data series from a chart, add a new data series to a chart, and change the order in which the data series appear.

To delete a data series from a chart, select the data series you want to remove, and then press the Delete key. Excel removes the data series and redraws the chart to reflect the deletion.

To add a data series, follow these steps:

1. Select the chart to which you want to add new data, or switch to the chart sheet that contains the chart.
2. Choose Chart, Add Data. The Add Data dialog box appears.
3. Enter or select the range in the worksheet that contains the data you want to add.
4. Choose OK. Excel adds the data series to the chart.

To change the order of the data series, follow these steps:

1. Select the chart, and then double-click on any data series. Or, select any data series and choose Format, Selected Data Series.

2. Select the Series Order tab.

3. Select the series you want to change, and then choose the Move Up or Move Down button until the series are listed in the order you want.

4. Choose OK.

▶ **See** "Editing a Chart," **p. 489**

▶ **See** "Editing Objects," **p. 555**

Printing Charts

When you print a worksheet that contains an embedded chart, the chart prints along with the other worksheet data, just as it is displayed on the screen. You can also print the chart only, without other worksheet data.

▶ **See** "Printing Worksheet Data," **p. 400**

Printing charts in Excel is no different from printing any worksheet range. You can specify print options for charts in much the same way that you do for data that appears in the worksheet. You can, for example, specify the size of the chart and the printing quality, and preview the chart before printing.

 TIP To print the chart with the default print settings, click the Print button in the Standard toolbar.

Before you print a chart, you need to specify the chart print settings. Follow these steps:

1. Select the chart you want to print, or move to the chart sheet that contains the chart you want to print.

2. Choose File, Page Setup.

3. Select the Chart tab to view special options for printing charts. Figure 20.30 shows the printing options that are available for a chart.

4. Select the appropriate chart size in the Printed Chart Size area of the dialog box.

5. To print the chart in black and white, select the Print in Black and White option in the Printing Quality area.

6. When you finish specifying the print settings, you can print the chart. Choose Print in the Page Setup dialog box. The Print dialog box appears.

7. Choose OK to accept the print settings and begin printing the chart.

FIG. 20.30
The Chart tab of the
Page Setup dialog box
includes options for
printing charts.

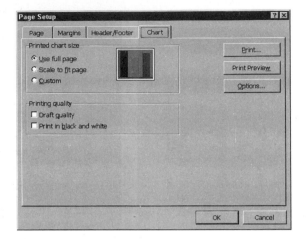

TROUBLESHOOTING

**I want to print a chart that is embedded in a worksheet. But when I select the chart and
choose File, Print, Excel prints the entire worksheet.** To print an embedded chart along with a
selected range of cells, you must highlight the range of worksheet cells that contain the data and
the chart.

Using the New Charting Features

Excel for Office 97 includes several new charting features. This chapter has mentioned a
few of them, such as the Bubble chart type. Here's a brief rundown of the new features for
users of prior versions of Excel:

- *Chart Wizard.* Chart subtypes are now displayed in Step 1, where you select the
  main chart type. You can also preview the chart from Step 1.

- *New chart types.* Types now offered are Bubble, Pie of Pie, Bar Of Pie, Pyramid,
  Cone, and Cylinder.

- *Data points.* Excel charts now permit up to 32,000 data points in a data series, up
  from 4,000 in Excel for Office 95. We know you've been aching for this one.

- *Chart tips.* Positioning your mouse pointer over any chart element now displays
  chart tips, which are much like ScreenTips. You can also display, in the same
  fashion, the values associated with individual data markers. Turn these features on
  and off by choosing Tools, Options, clicking the Chart tab, and filling or clearing
  their check boxes.

- *Time-scaled chart axes.* When the worksheet data are date- or time-formatted, Excel now automatically provides a time-scale axis. The values are displayed in chronological order on the chart, whether or not they have been sorted on the worksheet. If the axis is a category axis, change the unit of measurement shown on the axis by selecting the axis and choosing Format, Selected Axis. Then, click the Scale tab to modify its options.

- *Data tables in charts.* A table containing the charted values can now be placed in a chart (refer to Figure 20.11).

- *Range Finder.* When you create an embedded chart, the charted data range is surrounded by borders so that you can easily expand or reduce the range of charted data (refer to Figure 20.13).

- *Single-click editing.* You no longer need to double-click an embedded chart to open it for editing: one click will do.

- *Additional formatting options.* These include walls and floor, faces of bars, and gradient fills. For specifics, refer to the Help documentation.

Part
IV

Ch
20

CHAPTER 21

Inserting Microsoft Visual Objects

by Jan Snyder

All the applications in the Microsoft Office package allow you to add objects of various types to your documents. You might, for example, add a company logo to a budget created in Excel, or a clip-art image to a newsletter created in Word, or a sales chart to a slide in a PowerPoint presentation. These items, called *visual objects*, can add impact and appeal to your documents. ■

Visual objects

Insert visual objects from menus and toolbars.

Object files

Insert object files into your documents.

Equation and WordArt objects

Create new objects using applications such as Equation and WordArt.

Modifying objects

Move, resize, and manipulate objects that have been inserted into documents.

Getting Started

Visual objects can be inserted in different ways, depending on the application in use and your own personal preferences. The following sections describe some of the methods used to insert visual objects.

Using the Insert Object Command

Primary access to the full range of visual objects is available through the Insert menu in any Office application. Choose Insert, Object to open the dialog box shown in Figure 21.1.

FIG. 21.1

The Object dialog box enables you to choose the type of visual object you want to insert into your document.

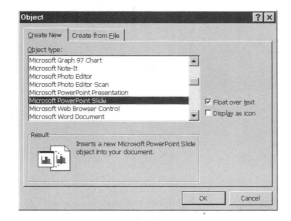

This dialog box has two tabs: Create New and Create from File or options. These represent the two options for adding a visual object to your document. You can create a new object, or use an object already created and saved as an existing file.

The Float Over Text option, which is selected by default, places the object in the drawing layer where you can then position the object in front of or behind text or other objects. Deselect this check box to place the object inline with text. Also note the Display as Icon check box. If you select this option, the actual visual object you insert isn't displayed in your document. Instead, you see an icon representing the visual object type you inserted. If you double-click this icon, the actual object is displayed.

Using the Toolbar Buttons

Some Office applications provide toolbar buttons as an alternative method for inserting particular types of visual objects. Table 21.1 summarizes these buttons.

Table 21.1 Object Insertion Buttons

Button	Application	Function
	Word	Inserts Excel worksheet
	Word	Inserts scanned picture
	Excel	Inserts scanned picture
	PowerPoint	Inserts Word table
	PowerPoint	Inserts Excel worksheet
	PowerPoint	Inserts chart
	PowerPoint	Inserts clip-art image
	PowerPoint	Inserts scanned picture
	Access	Inserts a picture on a form or report
	Access	Inserts an OLE object (a picture, sound, Word document, Excel spreadsheet) on a form or report that remains the same when moving between records
	Access	Inserts an OLE object frame on forms and reports that allows a different object to appear for each record

▶ **See** "Using Toolbars in Microsoft Office Applications," **p. 45**

N O T E The Object dialog box described earlier doesn't appear when you use a toolbar button to insert an object. Instead, you're taken directly to the screen for the object type you're inserting. This might be much faster than using the Insert menu, but you won't have the range of options available in the Object dialog box. ■

Placing an Object

Depending on which Office application you are using, you first indicate the desired location for the visual object:

- In PowerPoint, display the slide into which you want to insert the object.
- In Word, position the insertion point where the object should be inserted.
- In Excel, activate the cell that will be the upper-left corner of the inserted object.
- In an Access record, move to the OLE field in the table, query, or form where you want to insert the object.

Use these methods when steps in this chapter ask you to indicate the desired location for an object.

Inserting an Object from a File

If you want to insert an existing object, such as a company logo created in WordArt, into your document, choose the Create from File tab or option in the Object dialog box. The dialog box changes as shown in Figure 21.2.

FIG. 21.2
The Create from File tab allows you to select the existing object file to insert.

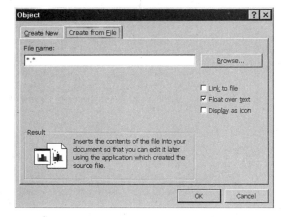

If you know the path and file name for the object you wish to insert, you can type it in the File Name box. If you don't know the path and file name, click the Browse button. The Browse dialog box appears, as shown in Figure 21.3.

Office applications can automatically update documents which contain inserted objects if the original object file is changed. Just click the Link to File check box in the Object dialog box.

▶ **See** "Inserting a New Object into Your Document," **p. 903**

FIG. 21.3
Click the Browse button to open this dialog box. Select the desired file in the file list.

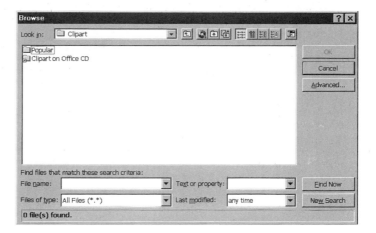

TROUBLESHOOTING

I want to add my company log without looking for the file every time. You can add the logo file as an AutoCorrect entry by selecting the inserted graphic and choosing Tools, AutoCorrect. In the AutoCorrect dialog box, the file name of your selected clip art appears in the With box. Type a text entry, such as **ourlogo** in the Replace box. Click Add to put the entry on the list. Be sure the Replace Text as You Type check box is selected, and then choose OK. Now, when you type **ourlogo**, the text will be replaced by the graphic.

Creating a New Object

The Create New tab or option in the Object dialog box allows you to create a new visual object for insertion into your document. The Object Type list displays all available visual object options. The choices available in this list vary depending on the software installed on your computer. For example, if you don't have Microsoft Excel installed on your system, the options for Microsoft Excel Chart and Microsoft Excel Worksheet won't appear in the Object Type list.

The actual steps used to insert an object vary with the type of object selected for insertion. Some objects, such as clip art, require only a simple selection process to insert. Other object types, such as WordArt and Equation objects, require more complex operations. The following sections describe some of the commonly used visual object types and the steps used to create and insert them.

Using Microsoft Clip Gallery 3.0

One of the best ways to spice up a document is to insert a clip-art drawing. The Clip Gallery contains many drawings that cover a wide range of topics. When you open the Microsoft Clip Gallery 3.0 application window, you can choose from the Clip Art, Pictures, Sounds, and Videos tabs. Figure 21.4 shows the Clip Art tab of Microsoft Clip Gallery 3.0.

> **N O T E** In Office 97, you access clip art by choosing Insert, Picture, Clip Art. You also can open the Clip Gallery window by choosing Insert, Object to display the Object dialog box; then choose Microsoft Clip Gallery in the Object Type list box. ▪

FIG. 21.4

The Clip Gallery window allows you to choose from a variety of clip-art drawings.

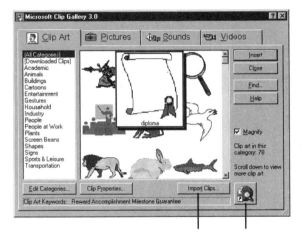

Add additional clips   Connect to Web for additional clips

A list of categories appears at the top of the Clip Gallery window. The box to the right of the category list displays a sample of each clip-art file in the current category. Use the scroll bar, Page Up/Page Down keys, or the arrow keys to see each picture in a category. If you prefer to scroll through the entire selection of clip-art files, select the (All Categories) option in the categories list box.

 TIP In PowerPoint, you can click the Insert Clip Art button on the Standard toolbar to open the Clip Gallery.

 TIP You can enlarge the Microsoft Clip Gallery sample viewing window by dragging the border of the application window. To see an enlarged sample of a selected picture, select the Magnify check box.

To add a clip-art drawing to your document, follow these steps:

1. Indicate the desired location for the clip art object.

N O T E In order to accept clip art and other OLE objects in a field for each record in Access, you must define the field data type to be an OLE Object in table design mode. ▪

In design view of an Access report or form, click the Insert Unbound Object button on the toolbox, click in the report or form, and go to step 3.

2. Choose Insert, Picture, Clip Art. The Microsoft Clip Gallery 3.0 window appears with the Clip Art tab displayed.

 T I P Click the Import Clips button to add pictures. To delete a picture from the Gallery, right-click the picture and choose Delete Clip.

3. Select a category in the list box of categories.

4. Select a picture, and then choose Insert.

The selected picture appears in your document.

▶ **See** "Inserting Clip-Art Pictures," **p. 631**

 ON THE WEB

http://198.105.232.29/ To import clips from Microsoft's Clip Gallery Live on the World Wide Web, click the Connect to Web button in the lower-right corner of the Clip Gallery window. The clip art you select is automatically added to the Clip Gallery.

 TROUBLESHOOTING

I get an error when I try to run Clip Gallery and then the window appears with no categories and no pictures. You haven't properly installed Clip Gallery. Run Office Setup from your original disks or CD to install the program, located in Office Tools.

I want to add clip-art files from other programs to the Clip Gallery. To do this, click the Import Clips button in the Clip Gallery window. Select the clip-art file you want to add in the Add Clip Art to Clip Gallery dialog box. Click Open. When the Clip Properties dialog box appears, enter Keywords that describe the picture, and select a check box in the Categories list. Or choose a New Category. Choose OK to add the picture to the Clip Gallery.

Inserting a Scanned Picture

If you have a scanner connected to your computer, you can insert a scanned picture in Word, Excel, or PowerPoint. To insert a scanned picture, perform these steps:

1. Indicate the desired location for the scanned picture.

2. Choose Insert, Picture, From Scanner. The Microsoft Photo Editor application opens.

3. Scan the picture according to instructions for your scanner. The picture appears in Microsoft Photo Editor.

4. Using Microsoft Photo Editor, edit the picture as desired, including cropping and changes to color, brightness, and contrast.

5. In Photo Editor, choose File, Exit and Return To to close Photo Editor and insert the scanned and edited picture.

T I P You also can insert a scanned picture by selecting Microsoft Photo Editor Scan in the Object dialog box. Refer to Figure 21.1.

N O T E If Microsoft Photo Editor is not installed, a message is displayed indicating that the application cannot be found. You must run Office Setup and choose the Custom installation. Select Microsoft Photo Editor from the Office Tools category in setup. ▪

Using Microsoft Equation 3.0

Microsoft Equation 3.0 is a supplemental application that is a part of Microsoft Office. Equation provides you with typographical capabilities for complex mathematical equations. If you need to incorporate any type of mathematical expression into your documents, Equation provides the tools for creating it.

N O T E Microsoft Equation doesn't *solve* equations. It's designed to allow you to represent equations typographically on a page. ▪

When you choose Microsoft Equation 3.0 in the Object dialog box, the current application's menus and toolbars are temporarily replaced by Equation's menus and toolbar.

You'll use the toolbar for most of your work in Equation. The top row of the toolbar contains individual mathematical symbols, while the bottom row contains templates for common mathematical expressions. Each button on the toolbar opens a palette of options. Figure 21.5 shows Equation's toolbar.

FIG. 21.5

The Microsoft Equation 3.0 toolbar assists you in creating complex equations.

Equation also allows you to type text, numbers, and symbols directly into the expression. Any combination of templates, symbols, and typing can be used to create your mathematical expression.

 TIP Microsoft Equation automatically formats text and numbers you type to match commonly used mathematical conventions. You can change the formatting of selected text, however, by choosing Style, Other.

Using Microsoft Organization Chart 2.0

Microsoft Organization Chart 2.0 is a separate application program bundled with Microsoft Office, specifically designed to create organization charts. The chart is the customary organization tree of a company or department, and can be very basic or branch out with complex relationships. Elements of an organizational chart can be customized with different box and line styles and color fills, and boxes of various kinds can be added with the click of a mouse.

To create an organization chart, follow these steps:

1. Indicate the desired location for the Organization Chart object.

2. Choose Insert, Object, then click MS Organization Chart 2.0 in the Object dialog box. When you click OK, the Microsoft Organization Chart window appears (see Figure 21.6).

   In Excel, you must double-click the inserted object to open the Organization Chart window.

   In PowerPoint, you can create an Organization Chart by choosing Insert, Picture, Organization Chart or by choosing the Organization Chart in Autolayout on a new slide.

3. Click the Chart Title and type a title for your chart. You can press Enter to type more than one centered line.

FIG. 21.6

A basic organization chart appears, ready for editing.

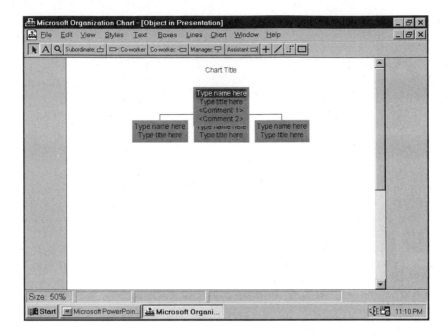

4. Enter text in boxes by clicking the box and typing. The boxes prompt you for a name, title, and comments; however, you can type anything you want to appear in each box.

   Press Esc or click outside of a box to complete it.

5. To create a new box, click the box tool for the type of box you want, and then click the box in the chart where you want to attach the new box.

   The box tools are in the toolbar; each tool illustrates the type of box object it creates (see Figure 21.7).

 T I P Create multiple boxes of the same type by holding down the Shift key when you click the box tool. Click the Selection Arrow tool to deactivate the box tool when you have finished creating boxes.

6. Continue to add boxes and text in the structure you want. You can use the Styles menu to add groups of boxes. Figure 21.7 illustrates some of the organization chart elements.

7. Change the appearance of the text and boxes by selecting the objects and choosing options from the Text and Boxes menus. Change the background color by choosing Background Color in the Chart menu.

FIG. 21.7
The Organization Chart takes the shape of the elements you choose.

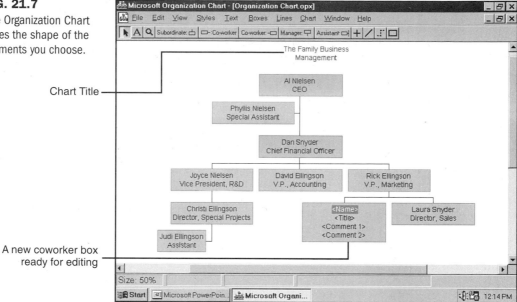

Chart Title

A new coworker box ready for editing

TIP To choose all boxes to apply formatting, choose Edit, Select All, or press Ctrl+A.

---

8. Choose File, Update to update the current organization chart in the document, slide, or worksheet.

9. Choose File, Exit and Return to close the Microsoft Organization Chart window and return to Word, PowerPoint, or Excel.

> ▶ **See** "Inserting an Organization Chart," **p. 636**

Using Microsoft WordArt Gallery

Office comes with a supplementary application called WordArt that allows you to create interesting text effects to enhance newsletters, flyers, brochures, and so on. Using WordArt, you can arrange any TrueType or Adobe Type Manager (ATM) font into a variety of shapes and alignments, add 3-D effects, and more.

To create a special effect with WordArt, complete the following steps:

1. Indicate the desired location for the WordArt object.

   If you are using the Design view of an Access report or form, click the Insert Unbound Object button on the toolbox, click in the report or form, and go to step 3, which follows.

Part
IV

Ch
21

2. Choose Insert, Picture, WordArt, or click the WordArt tool in the Drawing toolbar. The WordArt Gallery dialog box appears (see Figure 21.8).

FIG. 21.8

WordArt presents a gallery of graphic styles.

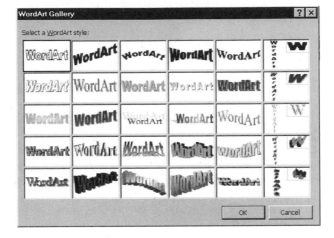

3. Choose a special effect and then click OK. The Edit WordArt Text dialog box appears (see Figure 21.9). If you had preselected text in the document, that text would appear in the Text box in place of Your Text Here.

FIG. 21.9

Type your text and change the font in this dialog box.

4. Type the text you want to apply special effects to in the Text box. Change the Font, Size, and apply bold or italic attributes as needed.

5. Click OK. The styled text appears in the document and the WordArt toolbar is displayed, as shown in Figure 21.10.

6. Choose tools on the WordArt toolbar to further change the appearance of the text. Table 21.2 summarizes WordArt's toolbar buttons.

FIG. 21.10
The WordArt text and
toolbar appear in the
document.

 TIP Various combinations of text effects, fonts, and sizes provide dramatically different results. With
WordArt, you can experiment with many combinations and find exactly what you want. Remember
that you can click Undo to reverse formatting as you work with WordArt.

Table 21.2   Buttons on WordArt's Toolbar

Button	Description
	Creates another WordArt object
Edit Text...	Edits WordArt text; applies font, size, bold, italics
	Changes style using WordArt Gallery
	Formats color, size, position, wrapping
	Changes shape of the WordArt
	Adjusts rotation and angle of text

Part
IV

Ch
21

Button	Description
Aa	Equalizes letter heights
Ab bↄ	Arranges text vertically on the page
≡	Determines text alignment
AV↔	Adjusts spacing between characters

Applying various combinations of the effects available in WordArt can create interesting, attention-getting text to be used in any Office application.

TROUBLESHOOTING

WordArt isn't available on the <u>I</u>nsert, <u>P</u>icture menu. WordArt isn't installed. Install it by running the Office Setup program on your original disks or CD.

How do I get out of WordArt? Just click the page outside the WordArt image or click Cancel from the Edit WordArt Text or WordArt Gallery dialog box.

Manipulating Objects

The previous sections of this chapter described various methods of inserting visual objects into your documents. Once the object has been inserted, you may need to edit, move, size, or position the object.

Editing an Object

All visual objects used in Office are *embedded objects*. This means double-clicking any visual object causes the source application to open, enabling you to edit the object. For example, if you double-click a chart inserted from Microsoft Graph, Microsoft Graph opens. When the source application opens, use that application's tools to modify the object as needed.

Resizing with Handles

To resize any of the objects described in this chapter, first click the object to select it, and then drag any of the resize handles surrounding the object to a new position.

The resize handles on the sides of the selection box resize in one dimension only. For instance, if you click the resize handle at the top of the selection box, you can stretch or shrink the height of an object on its top only; the bottom remains anchored. If you click the right resize handle, you can stretch or shrink the width of an object on its right side only; the left side remains anchored. Release the mouse button when the object is the size you want.

The resize handles at the corners of an object enable you to resize an object in two dimensions at once. If you click the resize handle in the upper-right corner of an object, for instance, you can change the height or width of the object by dragging the handle in any direction. When you drag a corner handle, the handle in the opposite corner remains anchored while you expand or contract the object's height and width.

When you resize in two dimensions at once, you may want to maintain an object's height-to-width ratio. To do so, hold the Shift key as you drag any corner resize handle. The handle in the opposite corner remains anchored while you resize the object.

You might also want to resize in two dimensions at once, from the center of the object outward. Hold down the Ctrl key as you drag any corner handle. By holding both the Shift and Ctrl keys as you drag a corner handle, you can maintain an object's height-to-width ratio *and* resize from the center outward, all in one step.

▶ **See** "Resizing and Scaling Objects," **p. 647**

Using Cut, Copy, and Paste

Visual objects can be moved from place to place within a document, and from one document to another. Follow these steps to move a visual object:

1. Select the visual object you want to move.
2. Choose Edit, Cut, or click the right mouse button and choose Cut from the Shortcut menu. The selected object is removed from its current location and placed on the Clipboard.
3. Select the destination for the object. If necessary, open the desired document. Then, indicate the desired location for the object.
4. Choose Edit, Paste, or click the right mouse button and choose Paste from the Shortcut menu.

Part

IV

Ch

21

To duplicate the selected object rather than move it, choose Copy instead of Cut in step 2.

▶ **See** "Copying and Moving Data," **p. 78**

▶ **See** "Selecting, Moving and Resizing Objects," **p. 365**

▶ **See** "Moving and Copying Objects," **p. 645**

Using Drag-and-Drop

As an alternative to Cut and Paste, you can also move visual objects by using drag-and-drop. To move an object using drag-and-drop, you simply point at the object, hold down the mouse button, and drag the mouse pointer to the new location. Keep these additional points in mind when using drag-and-drop:

▪ Drag-and-drop works within a document, between documents of the same Office application, or between Office applications.

▪ If you want to copy the object rather than move it, hold down the Ctrl key while you drag the object.

▪ If you're dragging from one document to another, the destination location must be visible on your screen before you start dragging.

N O T E   Drag-and-drop *moves* information, even when dragging from one application to
another. Be careful to hold down the Ctrl key if you want to *copy* the information.

Positioning an Object in Word

Visual objects placed in a Word document from any of the sources discussed previously in this chapter can be positioned in the same way. Objects can be centered, and left- or right-aligned with the text using the text alignment tools on the toolbar. When more control over an object's position is necessary, use the Format Object dialog box. To position an object, it's easiest to work in Page Layout view. Switch to Page Layout view if necessary, and complete these steps:

1. Select an object and drag it to the desired position. When you release the mouse button, the graphic moves to its new position.

2. Choose Format, Object.

   Depending on the type of object you selected, the item on the Format menu may be Autoshape, Object, Text Box, Word Art or Picture. Alternatively, you can right-click the object and choose the Format command on the shortcut menu. The Format Object dialog box appears.

3. Choose the Wrapping tab and then choose options in the Wrapping Style and Wrapping To group boxes.

4. Choose OK. Figures 21.11 and 21.12 show an Equation 3.0 object before and after text was wrapped around the object.

▶ **See** "Framing a Picture with a Text Box," **p. 872**

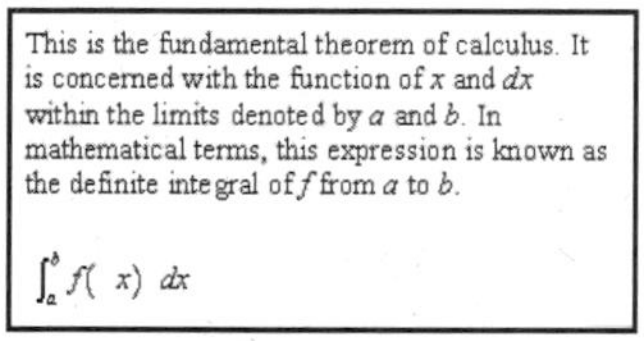

FIG. 21.11
The Equation object in a Word document before repositioning.

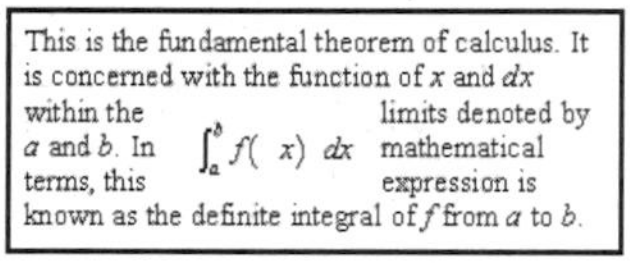

This is the fundamental theorem of calculus. It is concerned with the function of x and dx within the limits denoted by a and b. In mathematical terms, this expression is known as the definite integral of f from a to b.

$$\int_a^b f(\ x)\ dx$$

FIG. 21.12
The object has now been dragged into position with text wrapped around it.

This is the fundamental theorem of calculus. It is concerned with the function of x and dx within the limits denoted by a and b. In $\int_a^b f(\ x)\ dx$ mathematical terms, this expression is known as the definite integral of f from a to b.

CHAPTER 22

Inserting Sound and Motion Pictures

by Jan Snyder

Windows 95 provides full multimedia functionality, supporting devices such as sound cards, CD-ROM drives, audio and video input and output devices, and others. Windows 95 also provides software support for many multimedia features, such as audio CD playback, sound recording, and video clip manipulation. You can use a wide range of Windows multimedia functions in your Microsoft Office applications.

You learned in Chapter 21, "Inserting Microsoft Visual Objects," that you can add many types of objects, such as clip art and organizational charts, to a document created in a Microsoft Office application. This chapter explains how to insert other types of objects, such as sound files, video clips, and PowerPoint presentations. ∎

Media Player sound and video

Use Media Player to insert and control sound and video objects in your documents.

Sound Recorder

Use Sound Recorder to add sound to your documents.

Presentations within documents

Incorporate PowerPoint presentations in Office documents.

Multimedia object manipulation

Move, edit, and resize multimedia objects in your documents.

Understanding Sound and Video in Microsoft Office

Using sound and video objects can add enormous impact to your documents. Sound and video are especially effective for presentations. You can, for example, include a sound or video clip that plays during your PowerPoint presentation. Or, if you have equipment to record sound, add a sound recording to a Word document or Excel worksheet to introduce yourself and explain the contents.

You incorporate sound and video files into a document as objects, much like a simple clip art image. You can set the sound or video object to play the object once or continuously. You also can move and edit the object within the document, just like any other object.

Sound and video files tend to be large in size, adding significantly to the memory and disk space requirements for the file in which they are incorporated. Keep this point in mind as you design your documents. Although it may be fun and impressive to add a video clip to all your word processing documents, this practice may not be efficient. In general, use sound and video when it can enhance the message you are trying to send.

Windows 95 supports a variety of multimedia playback and editing software. One of the most flexible examples of this type of software is Microsoft Media Player, which is included in Windows 95. This application enables you to insert, play, and perform basic editing on sound and video files. By default, Media Player is the application launched when you insert most types of multimedia objects. An exception is audio CD, which starts the new Microsoft CD Player when you insert an audio CD in the CD-ROM drive. For more details on using the Media Player, read the topics on Media Player's Help menu.

Inserting an Object from a File

Multimedia objects are stored in files which you can select for insertion in a document or presentation. These object files are inserted similar to the way you insert visual objects, discussed in Chapter 21, "Inserting Microsoft Visual Objects."

To insert any multimedia object, you use these steps:

1. Choose Insert, Object, which opens the Object dialog box (see Figure 22.1).

N O T E In PowerPoint, the Insert Object dialog box opens, which uses the Create From File option button instead of a tab in the next step. ■

FIG. 22.1
The Object dialog box enables you to choose the type of object you want to insert into your document.

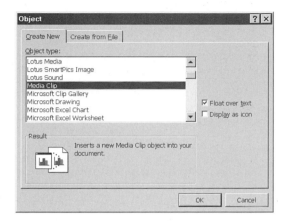

2. If you want to insert an existing video or sound object into your document, choose the Create from File tab in the Object dialog box. A new dialog box appears, enabling you to enter the name of the file to insert.

3. If you know the path and file name for the object, type it in the File Name box. If you do not know the path and file name, click the Browse button to open a dialog box that lists the contents of your folders. Choose the file you want from the list.

4. Microsoft Office applications provide the capability to automatically update documents containing inserted objects if the original object file changes. To use this capability, check the Link To File check box in the Create from File tab of the Object dialog box.

5. Choose OK to close the Object dialog box.

   ▶ **See** "Inserting an Object from a File," **p. 526**

   ▶ **See** "Inserting a New Object into Your Document," **p. 903**

Creating New Objects

You use the Create New tab in the Object dialog box to insert new sound or video objects into your documents (refer to Figure 22.1). As you scroll through the object type list, you see several multimedia object types, including Media Clip, MIDI Sequence, and Video Clip. Select the object type you want to insert and click the OK button. You will find more detailed steps for inserting motion pictures, sound, and PowerPoint presentations later in this chapter.

N O T E You are not actually creating a *new* sound or video file when you use the Create New tab. You are still inserting an existing sound or video file into your document. The advantage of using the Create New tab is that you can exercise more control over the behavior of

continues

continued

the multimedia object, since the application which controls the object file is started. Many options are available through the Create New tab that are not available when you use the Create from File tab. ▪

▶ **See** "Creating a New Object," **p. 527**

▶ **See** "Embedding Information in Your Document," **p. 902**

The following sections provide details on the use of various types of multimedia objects.

Inserting Movies, Animations, and Video Clips

You insert movies, animations, and video clips all in the same way. In fact, you can think of these three types of objects as belonging to the general category of *motion pictures*. Video comes from a few sources: you can put a video-capture board into your computer and hook up a portable video camera or a VCR to it, or you can buy video clips on CD-ROM. Microsoft's Video for Windows is one of several software standards for video.

Inserting Motion Pictures

To insert a motion picture into a document, follow these steps:

1. Indicate where you want the motion picture object by placing the insertion point or by activating the slide or cell.

   ▶ **See** "Placing an Object," **p. 525**

2. Choose the Insert, Object command, and click the Create New tab. In PowerPoint, click the Create New option button in the Insert Object dialog box. In the Object Type list, click Media Clip or Video Clip in the Object dialog box, and then click OK. The Microsoft Media Player menu and tools appear, as shown in Figure 22.2.

FIG. 22.2
The Media Player controls appear when you insert a media clip or video clip.

Media Player menu bar

Media Player controls

Media Player object icon

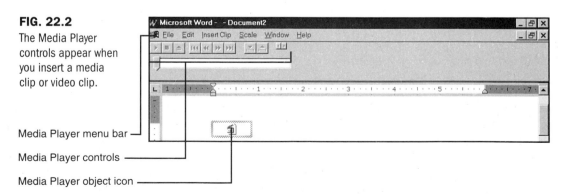

3. Select the Insert Clip, Video for Windows menu option. An Open dialog box appears (see Figure 22.3). Video clips using the Video for Windows file standard have the extension AVI. This extension may not show on-screen, depending on your View, Options settings in Windows Explorer.

4. Select the video file you want in the list box, or type its path and name in the File Name text box. and click the Open button. The Media Clip icon is replaced with the actual video clip you selected, as illustrated in Figure 22.4.

5. Click anywhere in the document outside the video object to return to the original document. The normal application menu bar and toolbars return.

FIG. 22.3
Choose the video file you want from the Open dialog box.

FIG. 22.4
A video clip has been inserted into this Word document.

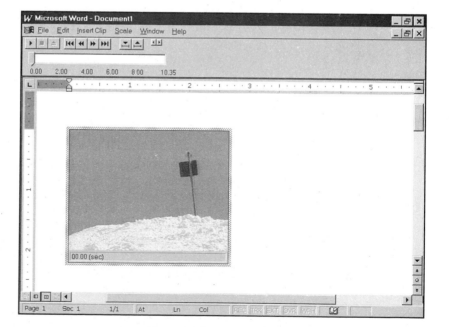

Inserting Movies and Sounds in a PowerPoint Presentation

PowerPoint 97 has additional options on the Insert menu that simplify adding movies and sounds to slide presentations. When you choose Insert, Movies and Sounds, a submenu displays the following choices:

Option	Description
Movie from Gallery	Displays the Clip Gallery Videos
Movie from File	Opens the Insert Movie dialog box
Sound from Gallery	Displays the Clip Gallery Sounds
Sound from File	Opens the Insert Sound dialog box
Play CD Audio Track	Opens the Play Options dialog box
Record Sound	Opens the Record Sound dialog box

The Office 97 CD has several movie and sound files you can access in the Microsoft Clip Gallery 3.0. When you choose Insert, Movies and Sounds, and then Movic from Gallery, the Clip Gallery opens with the Videos tab displayed (see Figure 22.5).

FIG. 22.5
Clip Gallery lets you play the movie before adding it to the slide.

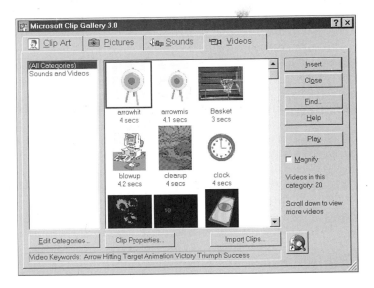

Select a video clip and click Play to preview the movie. Click Insert to insert the movie on the slide. Sound clips are located on the Sounds tab of the Clip Gallery and also can be played before inserting the sound on the slide.

If you have a movie or sound clip that is not in the Clip Gallery, you can add it by choosing the Import Clips button. You also can insert a movie or sound clip by choosing the Movie from File or Sound from File options on the Insert, Movies and Sounds menu.

▶ **See** "Using Microsoft Clip Gallery 3.0," **p. 528**

Playing Motion Pictures in a Document

To play a motion picture in a document, position the mouse pointer over the motion picture object and double-click. The application's normal menus and toolbars disappear, and a control bar appears beneath the motion picture. You can click the Stop and Play buttons on the bar to control playback of the motion picture. Figure 22.6 shows a motion picture during playback.

FIG. 22.6
You control playback of the motion picture using buttons on the control bar.

Stop button

Play button

Setting Motion Picture Options

You can use several settings to control a motion picture's behavior in a document. Access these settings by choosing Edit, Options in the Media Player to open the Options dialog box (see Figure 22.7).

 TIP From the document, you can access Media Player by right-clicking the media object and then choosing Media Clip Object, Edit from the shortcut menu.

FIG. 22.7
Use the Options dialog box to adjust various object settings.

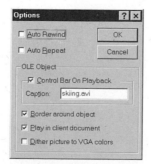

This dialog box provides these options:

- Auto Rewind causes the motion picture to automatically return to the first frame after playback is complete.
- Auto Repeat sets the motion picture to replay continuously until you click the Stop button.
- Control Bar On Playback determines whether the control bar, with the Play and Stop buttons, is visible.
- The Caption box enables you to enter a label for the motion picture. This label appears beneath the motion picture object.
- Border Around Object determines if the object border, including the caption, is visible.
- Play in Client Document enables the motion picture to play without actually launching Media Player.
- Dither Picture to VGA Colors enhances playback on some video systems.

Figure 22.8 shows the motion picture inserted earlier, with the control bar and borders deactivated.

FIG. 22.8
The motion picture has the control bar and borders deactivated.

Media Player provides other controls for enhancing motion pictures in a document. Some of these controls are available as buttons in the Media Player window, as described in Table 22.1.

Table 22.1   The Media Player Controls

Button	Function
▶	Play
■	Stop
⏏	Eject

Button	Function
⏮	Previous Mark
⏪	Rewind
⏩	Fast Forward
⏭	Next Mark
⤓	Start Selection
⤒	End Selection
◂	Scroll Backward
▸	Scroll Forward

Most of the Media Player buttons work the same way as a VCR's controls. The Start Selection and End Selection buttons, however, may be unfamiliar. Use these buttons to select a portion of a motion picture to play in a document. To play just a portion of a motion picture, follow these steps:

1. Move to the beginning of the desired portion of the motion picture. Use the Play, Fast Forward, and Rewind buttons to locate the exact position you want.

 TIP You also can drag the slider to the position you want on the clip.

2. Click the Start Selection button.
3. Move to the end of the desired portion of the motion picture. Use the Play, Fast Forward, and Rewind buttons to locate the exact position you want.
4. Click the End Selection button. The selected portion of the motion picture is highlighted on the time bar as shown in Figure 22.9.

You also can set a specific portion of a motion picture for playback by choosing Edit, Selection when Media Player is active. The Set Selection dialog box opens (see Figure 22.10). You can enter the start and end time in this dialog box.

FIG. 22.9

The highlight indicates a portion of this motion picture is selected for playback.

Selected portion ————

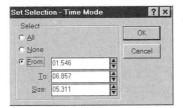

FIG. 22.10

The Set Selection dialog box enables you to enter start and end positions of the motion picture.

TROUBLESHOOTING

My video clip plays continuously and I don't have any control buttons to stop it. You need to change the media player settings for the video clip. Right-click the video clip and select Media Clip Object, Edit. In the Media Player menu, choose Edit, Options. In the Options dialog box, deselect the Auto Repeat check box. If you want controls to show, select the Control Bar On Playback check box. Choose OK.

Inserting Music and Sound

If your computer system has sound capabilities, you can insert sound and music files into your documents. Microsoft Windows includes an application called Sound Recorder that enables you to record and play back sound files. You also can use Media Player to insert sound files, as well as MIDI sequences.

Using Sound Files

Sound files sometimes are called Wave files, because they normally have the extension WAV as part of their file names. Follow these steps to insert sound files into your documents using Sound Recorder:

1. Indicate where you want the sound object.

2. Choose the Insert, Object command and click the Create New tab. In PowerPoint, click the Create New option button in the Insert Object dialog box. In the Object Type list, click Wave Sound in the Object dialog box, then click OK. The Sound Object dialog box appears, as shown in Figure 22.11.

FIG. 22.11
Use Sound Recorder to record and play back sounds.

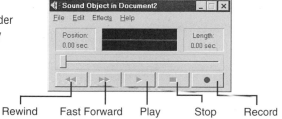

3. If you want to record a new sound, click the Record button, record the sound, and click the Stop button when finished.

 TIP In PowerPoint, you can record a sound by choosing Insert, Movies and Sound, Record Sound.

4. If you want to insert an existing sound, choose Edit, Insert File in the Sound Object dialog box. In the Insert File dialog box, locate the folder where the sound file is stored. Select a file from the list box or type in the File Name text box (see Figure 22.12).

 TIP Click the right mouse button on the audio file icon. The shortcut menu pops up. Choose Wave Sound Object, Edit from the shortcut menu, and the Sound Object dialog box appears, ready for editing.

5. Click Open to choose the file. The Insert File dialog box closes.

FIG. 22.12

The Insert File dialog box enables you to select a sound file for use with Sound Recorder.

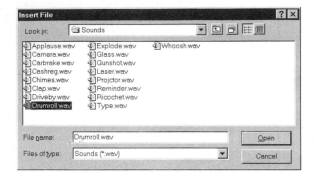

6. Close the Sound Object dialog box. Sound Recorder inserts the sound file as an icon into your document.

7. Double-click the sound file icon to play the sound file.

Using MIDI Sequences

MIDI sequences are digitized musical files created by connecting electronic instruments to a computer. As the musician plays, the music is digitized as a computer file. The musician can then modify the computer file to alter the music. You can insert MIDI sequences into Microsoft Office applications using Media Player. To insert a MIDI sequence, follow these steps:

1. Indicate where you want the MIDI sequence object.

2. Choose Insert, Object and click the Create New tab. (In PowerPoint, click the Create New option button in the Insert Object dialog box.) In the Object Type list, click MIDI Sequence in the Object dialog box, and then click OK. The Media Player menu and controls appear, as shown earlier in Figure 22.2.

3. Choose the Insert Clip, 1 MIDI Sequencer menu option. An Open dialog box appears.

4. Select the folder where your MIDI file is stored. Select a file from the list box and click the Open button. The Media Clip icon appears.

5. Click anywhere in the document outside the video object to return to the original document. The normal application menu and toolbars return.

Media Player enables you to insert existing sound and MIDI files, as well as motion picture files. Sound Recorder enables you to work with sound files only, but you can record new sound files as well as use existing files.

The icons that these two programs produce are:

  Media Player MIDI Sequence sound file

Sound Recorder sound file

Inserting a PowerPoint Presentation

Suppose you have explained in a Word document the agenda for an upcoming meeting, where you plan to include a PowerPoint presentation. You can add an entire PowerPoint presentation to a document created in Word or Excel, allowing the planners of the meeting to read the document and view the inserted presentation at their own workstations.

To use a presentation in a document, follow these steps:

1. Indicate where you want to insert the PowerPoint presentation object.

2. Choose Insert, Object and select the Create from File tab in the Object dialog box. A new dialog box appears, enabling you to enter the name of the file to insert.

3. If you know the path and file name for the PowerPoint presentation, type it in the File Name box. If you do not know the path and file name, click the Browse button to open a dialog box that lists the contents of your folders. Choose the file you want from the list.

4. To link the object to the original presentation, which enables automatic updating of the document when the original file changes, check the Link To File check box in the Create from File tab of the Object dialog box.

5. Choose OK to close the Object dialog box. The PowerPoint presentation is added to your document. The first slide in the presentation is visible, as shown in Figure 22.13.

6. Double-click the slide to start the presentation. PowerPoint launches in Slide Show mode, enabling you to play the presentation by clicking each slide to move to the next slide.

FIG. 22.13
A PowerPoint presentation has been inserted into this Word document.

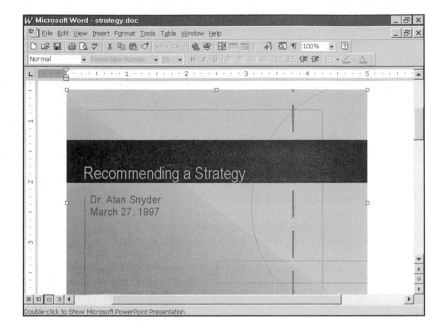

Moving Objects

You can move sound and motion picture objects from place to place within a document, and from one document to another. Follow these steps to move or duplicate a sound or motion picture object:

1. Select the object you want to move.

2. Choose Edit, Cut, or click the right mouse button and choose Cut from the shortcut menu. The selected object is removed from its current location and placed on the Clipboard.

   To duplicate the selected object rather than move it, choose Copy rather than Cut in this step.

3. Select the destination for the object. If necessary, open a different document. Then indicate where you want to insert the object.

 TIP   When you cut and paste multimedia objects that have play settings applied to them, the settings migrate with the objects.

4. Choose Edit, Paste, or click the right mouse button and choose Paste from the shortcut menu.

▶ **See** "Selecting, Moving, and Resizing Objects," **p. 365**

▶ **See** "Moving and Copying Objects," **p. 645**

As an alternative to Cut and Paste, you can move sound and motion picture objects by using Drag and Drop. To move an object using Drag and Drop, you simply point to the object, hold down the mouse button, and drag the mouse pointer to the new location. Keep these additional points in mind when using Drag and Drop:

■ Drag and Drop works within a document, between documents of the same Office application, or between Office applications.

■ If you want to copy the object rather than move it, hold down the Ctrl key while you drag the object.

■ If you are dragging from one document to another, the destination location must be visible on your screen before you start dragging.

N O T E Drag and Drop *moves* information, even when dragging from one application to another. Be careful to hold down the Ctrl key if you want to *copy* the information. ■

Editing Objects

You may want to change some of a sound or motion picture object's properties. To edit an object in a document, follow these steps:

1. Click the sound or motion picture object to select it.

2. Choose Edit, Media Clip Object, Edit.

   Media Player or Sound Recorder opens, depending on the object type you selected. In place of Media Clip Object, you may see Wave Sound Object or MIDI Sequence Object on the Edit menu.

3. Make the changes you want to the object, using the Sound Recorder or Media Player controls and menu options.

4. Click anywhere outside the object to return to the normal application menus and toolbars.

To resize any of the objects described in this chapter, you first click the object to select it and then drag any of the resize handles surrounding the object to a new position.

The resize handles on the sides of the selection box resize in one dimension only. For instance, if you click the resize handle at the top of the selection box, you can stretch or shrink the height of an object on its top only.

The resize handles that appear at the corners of an object enable you to resize an object in two dimensions at once. If you click the resize handle in the upper-right corner of an object, for instance, you can change the height or width of the object by dragging the handle in any direction. The handle in the opposite corner remains anchored.

TIP

To maintain an object's height-to-width ratio, hold down the Shift key as you drag any corner resize handle.

Another option is to resize in two dimensions from the center of the object outward. Hold down the Ctrl key as you drag any corner handle. You can maintain an object's height-to-width ratio *and* resize from the center outward, all in one step, by holding both the Shift and Ctrl keys as you drag a corner handle.

CAUTION

Use caution when resizing motion picture clips. Depending on the recording method used, you may significantly degrade the image by resizing.

▶ **See** "Resizing and Scaling Objects," **p. 647**

CHAPTER 23

Drawing Shapes, Curves, and Lines

by Jan Snyder

One of the easiest and most effective ways to enhance a document is to add a drawn object. In Microsoft Office applications, you can draw common shapes, such as ovals and rectangles, or more unusual shapes, such as stars, arrows, and cubes. You also can draw lines, arcs, and free-form shapes by using various drawing tools. ■

Drawing tools

Use the drawing tools in Office applications.

Shape drawing

Draw various shapes, such as rectangles and ovals, and perfect shapes, such as squares and circles.

Line drawing

Draw lines, arcs, and free-form shapes.

Modifying drawings

Modify shapes after they are drawn.

Using Drawing Tools

Drawing tools are available in Word, Excel, and PowerPoint. To use them, you must first display one or both of the Drawing toolbars. The Drawing toolbar also is available in Microsoft Graph 97.

N O T E   In Access, you can draw lines and rectangles when you are in report or form design. The Line and Rectangle buttons display when you show the Toolbox. To turn the Toolbox on or off, click the toolbox button on the Form or Report Design toolbar. ∎

You may be familiar with the Drawing toolbar in PowerPoint because it is displayed in the PowerPoint window (above the status bar) automatically whenever you start the program.

 The Drawing toolbar is displayed along the bottom of the window in Word by clicking the Drawing button.

To display the Drawing toolbar in Excel, you also can click the Drawing button, or follow these steps:

1. Choose View, Toolbars.
2. In the submenu, click Drawing, as shown in Figure 23.1. The Drawing toolbar appears near the bottom of the application window.

FIG. 23.1

Choose here to display the Drawing toolbar.

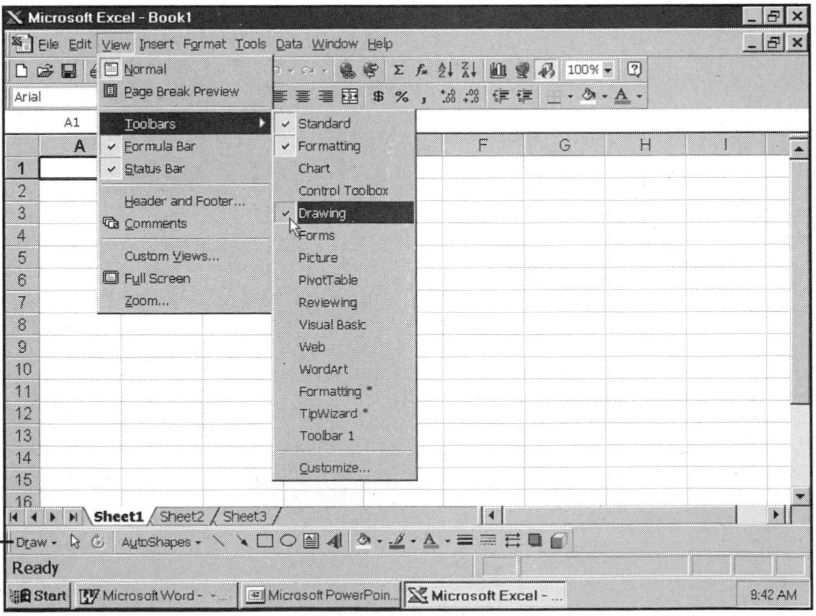

T I P You also can display a toolbar by right-clicking a toolbar and selecting a toolbar name in the shortcut menu.

Notice that the Drawing toolbars in each Office application contain many tools. Table 23.1 illustrates each of these tools and describes its function.

Table 23.1 Drawing Tools

Button	Drawing Tool	Function
Draw ▾	Draw	Opens a pop-up menu with options for grouping and positioning drawings.
▯	Select Objects	Points to select already drawn objects.
⟳	Free Rotate	Rotates the drawing around a point.
AutoShapes ▾	AutoShapes	Opens a pop-up menu with submenus containing many preformed shapes and freeforms.
╲	Line	Draws straight lines in any direction from the point at which you click the mouse.
↘	Arrow	Draws an arrow pointing in the direction you draw it.
▭	Rectangle	Draws rectangles of any dimension.
○	Oval	Draws curved shapes, including ellipses and circles.
▤	Text Box	Draws a box for text entry.
4	WordArt	Presents fancy styles for text you enter.
◇ ▾	Fill Color	Fills selected object(s) with chosen color, texture, or pattern.
✎ ▾	Line Color	Applies color to selected lines.
A ▾	Font Color	Applies color to selected text.
≡	Line Style	Changes thickness of selected lines.

continues

Table 23.1   Continued

Button	Drawing Tool	Function
	Dash Style	Changes selected lines to dashed lines.
	Arrow Style	Changes thickness of arrow lines and shape of arrow heads.
	Shadow	Adds a shadow on various sides of objects.
	3-D	Adds a third dimension to two-dimensional shapes.

To activate a Drawing tool, simply click it. When you click the Line, Arrow, Rectangle, Oval, Text Box, or AutoShapes tools, the mouse pointer changes to a crosshair. To activate any of the remaining tools, you must select an object before you click the tool. (An exception is the WordArt tool, which allows you to type text without pre-selecting it.)

▶ **See** "Using Toolbars in Microsoft Office Applications," **p. 45**

Drawing Shapes

In the context of this chapter, a *shaped object*, or *shape*, is defined as a closed object that you draw using a drawing tool.

To draw a shape, follow these steps:

1. In the Drawing toolbar, click the tool corresponding to the shape you want to draw.

2. Move the mouse pointer to the approximate location on the page where you want to draw the object. The mouse pointer changes to a crosshair.

3. Click and drag the mouse in any direction. As you drag the mouse, a solid outline of the shape appears in the document, worksheet, chart, or slide.

4. When the object is the shape and size you want, release the mouse button.

As you draw, don't feel that you must position your object perfectly the first time; you can relocate, resize, or adjust the object later.

Drawing AutoShapes

 The AutoShapes tool displays a pop-up menu when you click it. The shapes are organized into categories—Lines, Basic Shapes, Block Arrows, Flowchart, Stars and Banners, and

Callouts. PowerPoint also includes Connectors and Action Buttons categories. When you click one of these categories on the AutoShapes menu, a pop-up menu of shapes appears. Figure 23.2 shows the 32 predefined shapes in the Basic Shapes category that you can draw instantly simply by clicking and dragging the mouse. The AutoShapes make it easy for you to draw shapes that you frequently might include in your PowerPoint slides and in other applications.

FIG. 23.2

Add predefined shapes instantly with AutoShapes.

To draw an AutoShape, use the same technique listed previously for other shapes, selecting an AutoShape tool before you begin drawing. Follow these steps:

1. Click the AutoShapes tool in the Drawing toolbar. The AutoShapes menu appears.

2. Click a category and then click an AutoShape to activate it.

3. Place the mouse pointer in the slide, worksheet, or document where you want to draw the object. The mouse pointer changes to a crosshair.

4. Click and drag the mouse in any direction. As you drag, a solid outline of the shape appears.

5. When the object is the shape and size you want, release the mouse button.

Drawing Perfect Shapes

To draw a perfect or *uniform* shape, you follow the same basic steps for drawing a shape, except that you use the Shift key as the "constraint" key. Holding down the Shift key maintains the horizontal and vertical distance from the mouse pointer as you draw, so that you can use the Ellipse tool, for example, to draw a perfect circle. Figure 23.3 shows a perfect circle and a perfect square drawn using the Rectangle tool and the Ellipse tool.

FIG. 23.3
Perfect shapes are drawn by dragging with the Shift key held down.

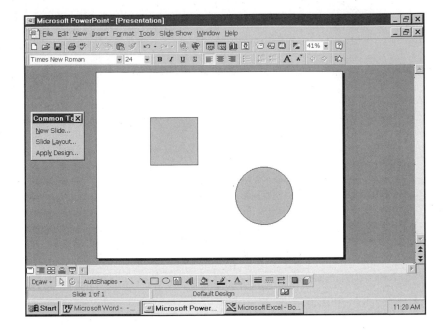

Drawing from the Center Outward

You have learned how to draw a shape by starting at one of the corners and drawing in any direction. Sometimes, you might want to draw a shape from the center outward. To draw an object from the center outward, you use another constraint key: Ctrl. When you press the Ctrl key as you draw a shape, the center of the object remains anchored at the point where you place the crosshair when you begin drawing.

 TIP   You can use the Shift and Ctrl keys together for the combined effect of drawing a perfect circle or square from the center outward.

Drawing Lines and Arcs

The technique for drawing lines and arcs is similar to that used for drawing shapes. The only difference between drawing lines and arcs and drawing other types of shapes is that lines and arcs are not enclosed objects. Lines and arcs have a beginning point and an end point, with resize handles at each of those points. Figure 23.4 shows items drawn with the Line tool and the Arc tool. In Office 97, the Arc tool is located in the Basic Shapes category of the AutoShapes tool instead of directly on the Drawing toolbar.

FIG. 23.4

Draw simple shapes, such as a line or an arc.

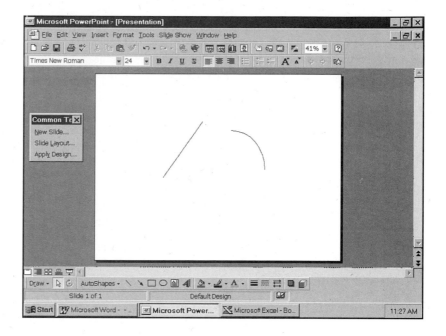

To draw a line or arc, follow these steps:

1. Click the Line or Arc tool in the Drawing toolbar.

2. Place the mouse pointer in the slide area. The mouse pointer changes to a crosshair.

3. Click where you want the line or arc to begin, and then drag the mouse until the line or arc is completed as you want.

N O T E   Used in conjunction with the Line tool, the Shift key enables you to draw vertical lines, horizontal lines, and lines at 15-degree angles.

To draw a vertical line, press and hold down the Shift key, and then drag the mouse vertically from the starting point of the line. To draw a horizontal line, press and hold down the Shift key, and then drag the mouse horizontally from the starting point. To draw a line at a 45-degree angle, press and hold down the Shift key, and then drag the mouse diagonally in the direction you want to draw the line. Experiment with the various angles by holding down the Shift key and moving the mouse in a circle around the beginning point of the line.

When you use the Shift key in conjunction with the Arc tool, you can draw a uniform arc—that is, the shape of the arc you draw (regardless of the size) is always a quarter-circle. A *perfect arc* is one in which two lines drawn perpendicular to the arc's end points form a right angle (90 degrees). ■

Just as you can use the Ctrl key to draw shapes from the center outward, you also can use the Ctrl key to draw lines and arcs from a center point outward. The point at which you place the crosshair in the slide becomes the center point for the line or arc. As you drag the mouse in any direction, this center point remains anchored.

You also can use the Ctrl and Shift keys in conjunction with the Line and Arc tools to draw uniform lines and arcs outward from a center point.

Drawing Free-form Shapes

Using the Freeform tool, you can draw any type of free-form shape or polygon. A *free-form shape* can consist of curved lines, straight lines, or a combination of the two. You might use the Freeform tool to draw a cartoon, create an unusual shape, or write your name. A free-form shape can be *open* (that is, the beginning point and end point don't meet) or *closed* (the beginning point and end point meet to form an object). A closed shape made up of straight lines is called a *polygon*. In Office 97, the Freeform tool is located in the Lines category of the AutoShapes tool (see Figure 23.5) instead of directly on the Drawing toolbar.

To draw a shape (open or closed) consisting of straight lines, click and release the mouse button at each vertex in the shape. A *vertex* is the point at which you click and release the mouse button while drawing a free-form shape. To draw freehand shapes, drag the Freeform tool and then double-click where you want the shape to end. The Freeform tool remains active until you complete the shape you're drawing by double-clicking or by pressing Enter. To create a closed object, click near the beginning point of the shape, which automatically connects the beginning and end points to create an object.

To draw an open or closed shape consisting of straight lines, follow these steps:

1. On the Drawing toolbar, click AutoShapes and then choose the Lines category.
2. Click the Freeform tool.
3. Place the mouse pointer at the point where you want to begin drawing. The mouse pointer changes to a crosshair.
4. Click the mouse button, and then release it.
5. Place the crosshair where you want the first line to end and the second line to begin, and then click and release the mouse button.
6. Repeat step 4, clicking and releasing the mouse button at each vertex.
7. To make the object an open shape, double-click after you draw the last line. To close the shape, place the mouse pointer near the beginning point, and then click the mouse button. A straight line connects the beginning and end points.

To draw an open or closed free-form shape, follow these steps:

1. On the Drawing toolbar, click AutoShapes and then choose the Lines category.
2. Click the Freeform tool.
3. Place the mouse pointer at the point where you want to begin drawing. The mouse pointer changes to a crosshair.
4. Click and drag the mouse in any direction, drawing the shape you want.
5. To create an open object, double-click when you finish drawing, or press Enter. To create a closed shape, double-click near the point where you began drawing, which automatically connects the beginning and end points.

As you draw freehand shapes, you can pause at any point by releasing the mouse button. Before beginning to draw again, place the crosshair where it was located before you paused, and then click and drag to continue drawing. To mix straight and curved lines in the same drawing, alternate between clicking a vertex and dragging the mouse.

Editing Free-form Shapes

When you click a free-form shape to select it, it displays the usual eight resize handles. You can drag any of the resize handles to make a free-form shape larger or smaller. Free-form shapes, unlike other shapes, also contain *control handles* (see Figure 23.5). Control handles enable you to modify the free-form shape in addition to simply resizing it.

FIG. 23.5
A free-form shape
displays control handles.

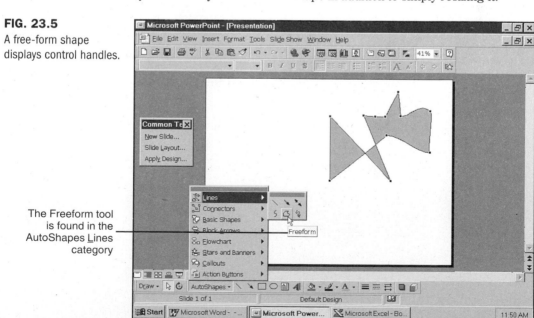

The Freeform tool
is found in the
AutoShapes Lines
category

Part

IV

Ch

23

To display an object's control handles, click the D<u>r</u>aw button on the Drawing toolbar and then choose <u>E</u>dit Points. To move a control handle, position the mouse pointer over the control handle, and then click and drag the handle in any direction. To add a control handle, press and hold down the Shift and Ctrl keys; then click the original line where you want to add the handle. To delete a control handle, press and hold down the Ctrl key; then click the handle.

If you look closely at the control handles of a free-form shape, you can see that the curves of a shape created by dragging the mouse are not actually curves; they are a series of short lines connected to one another.

You can adjust the shape of a free-form object by dragging an existing control handle to a new position, deleting a control handle, or adding a control handle. Curves that you draw slowly often contain more control handles than are necessary; deleting some handles can make working with the curve easier. If an object contains straight lines that you want to convert to gentle curves, add a few control handles so that you can curve the line.

Enhancing a Drawn Shape

After you have created a drawing, you can choose other tools to format the objects. From the Drawing toolbar you can choose the Fill Color, Line Color, Font Color, Line Style, Dash Style, Arrow Style, Shadow, and 3-D tools to change the formatting of the drawing. Alternatively, you can double-click a drawn object to open the Format AutoShapes dialog box, as shown in Figure 23.6.

FIG. 23.6
Change many attributes of the drawn object by using the For-mat AutoShapes dialog box.

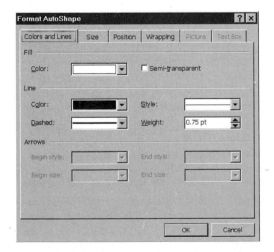

CHAPTER 24

Using Bookshelf

by Conrad Carlberg

Microsoft Office Bookshelf is a reference library for you to use either by itself, or in conjunction with Word or Excel. It provides a way to quickly access information such as a word's definition and pronunciation, a pertinent quotation concerning some concept, or a synonym when you don't know the precise word that you want to use.

Besides the Dictionary, Book of Quotations, and Thesaurus that accompany Bookshelf, other resources—such as an encyclopedia, an almanac, and even an Atlas—are available by subscription. ▪

Navigate through the Book-shelf screen

Use the Book Selector to specify a resource, and choose how to use the resource by means of the action tabs.

Browse and search the sources of information

Look through a resource's contents sequentially, or find a specific topic.

Use the Bookshelf tools to make searches more efficient

Use logical operators and the Advanced Find feature to tailor your information searches.

Integrate Bookshelf with other Office applications

Look up references while you're running Word, Excel, or Power-Point, and copy information from Bookshelf to another document.

Finding Information in Bookshelf

To start Microsoft Bookshelf Basics, click the Microsoft Basics button the Office Shortcut Bar, or in Word or PowerPoint, choose <u>T</u>ools, Loo<u>k</u> Up Reference and choose Microsoft Bookshelf Basics and click OK.

The best way to locate and view information in Bookshelf is through the Contents Panel. This panel consists of the Book Selector and three tabs, shown in Figure 24.1.

FIG. 24.1

Use the Book Selector to specify a book, and use a tab to browse or search through the book.

Action tabs

Book Selector drop-down arrow

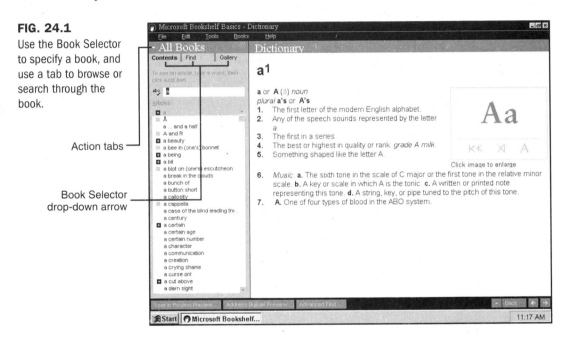

Using the Book Selector

With the Book Selector, you can choose to look at all books or any single book. Clicking the Selector's drop-down arrow displays a list of the books you can choose from, as illustrated in Figure 24.2.

You can hide the entire Contents Panel, and see more of the current entry in the Article Panel. To hide the Contents Panel, click the Hide button on the Book Selector. The result is shown in Figure 24.3.

To return to the normal display, click the Show button.

N O T E   To run Bookshelf, you must first place the Office 97 CD-ROM in its drive. The CD stores the information that you will look up.

FIG. 24.2
Use the Book Selector's drop-down list to restrict the scope of your browse or search.

Hide button

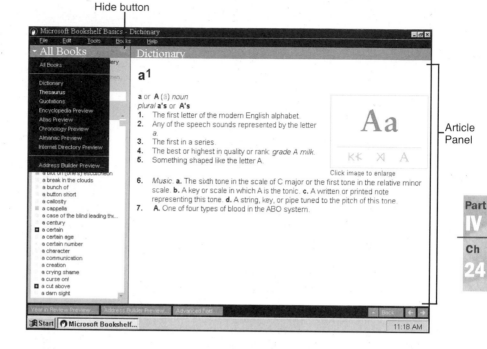

Article Panel

FIG. 24.3
After you click the Hide button, the Bookshelf window has more room to display the current entry.

Show button

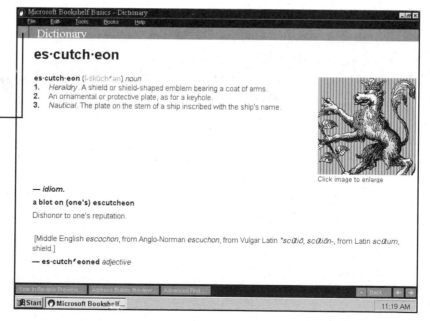

Bookshelf Basics provides you with three primary sources of information:

- *The American Heritage Dictionary of the English Language, Third Edition*
- *The Original Roget's Thesaurus of English Words and Phrases*
- *The Columbia Dictionary of Quotations*

By subscription, you can also obtain these other data sources:

- *The Concise Columbia Encyclopedia*
- *The People's Chronology*
- *The World Almanac® and Book of Facts 1996*
- *Concise Encarta® 96 World Atlas*
- An Address Builder that returns ZIP codes when you supply street, city, and state information.
- *Microsoft Bookshelf Internet Directory 1996-1997*

Previews of the books *not* included in Bookshelf Basics are available from the Book Selector.

Once you have decided which book you want to view, use one of the three tabs on the Contents Panel to select an action.

Using the Contents Tab

When you use the main Bookshelf screen to locate information, you usually employ one of three tabs located beneath the Book Selector bar:

- Use the Contents tab to browse through or to select topics.
- Use the Find tab to locate topics with a keyword.
- Use the Gallery tab to browse topics that contain sound and images.

Figure 24.4 shows how the Contents tab might look.

The appearance of the Contents tab differs according to what information source you have chosen in the Book Selector. On-screen, notice that the bullets to the left of words in the Articles list use different colors when All Books is selected. Position your mouse cursor over a bullet to see a ScreenTip that tells you which book contains the entry.

If you use the Book Selector to identify a specific book such as the Dictionary, all bullets are the same color—unless a topic has more than one entry. If so, its bullet is black with a white cross. This Open List bullet indicates that you can open it to view individual entries, as shown in Figure 24.5. To collapse the list, click the Close List bullet.

FIG. 24.4

Type a word in the Contents tab text box, or use the Articles list scroll bar to locate a word.

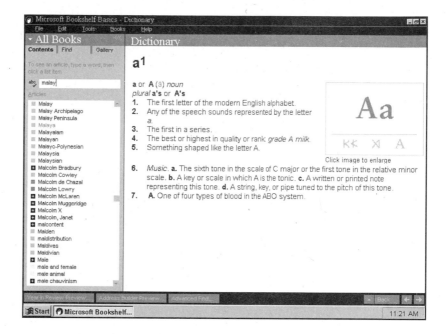

FIG. 24.5

After you click the Open List bullet to view the individual entries in the list, it changes to a Close List bullet.

Using the Find Tab

Suppose that you want to locate a word not only as a main entry, but anywhere in the Bookshelf where it exists. In these cases, use the Find tab.

For example, you might be writing an article on totemism, and cannot recall the name of the author of a book on the topic. From the Find tab, you might type the word **totem** in the text box, and click the Find button (see Figure 24.6).

FIG. 24.6
By using the Find tab, you can locate words *inside* articles.

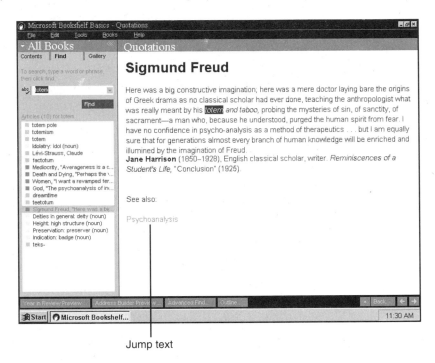

Jump text

Notice in Figure 24.6 that an article on Sigmund Freud was found by searching for *totem* anywhere in the article bodies. Also notice that *Psychoanalysis* is highlighted as jump text. So, should you want to see more on that topic, you can click it to open a window with further information, shown in Figure 24.7.

If you don't care for the colors assigned to jump text links, you can change them. Choose Tools, Options to see the Options dialog box shown in Figure 24.8.

Notice that you can also change the font size of the text in an article from the Options dialog box.

N O T E Clicking a pop-up hotspot shows you an explanation of a term. Pop-ups are shown in colored text and have a dotted underline. ▪

FIG. 24.7
Jump text is a differently-colored link to another article.

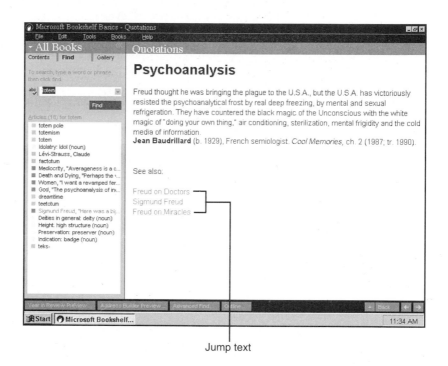

Jump text

FIG. 24.8
From the Options dialog box, you can set your preference for jump text patterns.

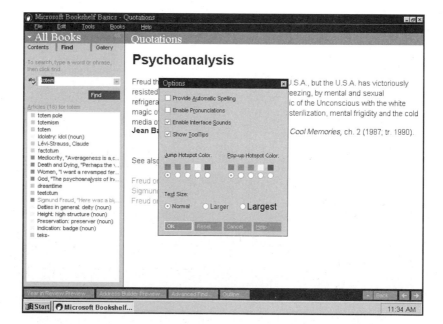

The text box on the Find tab is actually a combination edit/drop-down box. The drop-down contains words that you have previously searched for. Click the drop-down arrow to view these words, and then click a word in the drop-down list to search for it again.

The Find tab (as well as the Contents tab) also has a spell check feature. To verify your spelling, click the Spell Check button. If Bookshelf can't find your spelling in its word list, it displays a list of possible alternative spellings.

For example, suppose that you want to find information about fiddles. If you mistakenly type **fiodle** in the Find tab's text box, and then click the Find button, Bookshelf displays a Spell Check dialog box with suggested alternatives to the misspelled word (see Figure 24.9).

FIG. 24.9
Fiddle and *foible* are the two words that come closest in spelling to *fiodle*.

Spell Check button

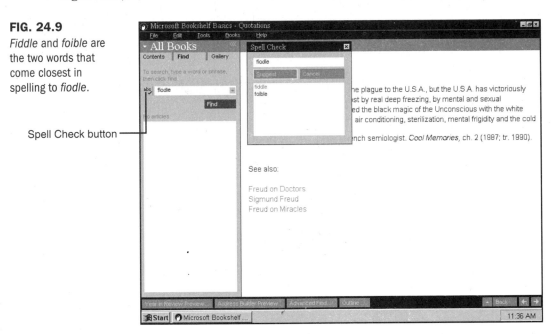

Just click the word *fiddle* in the Spell Check list box to replace your typing of *fiodle*. If you're not a good typist, or if you're using a laptop computer on a bumpy plane flight, the Spell Check button is a good way to replace a misspelled word.

Using the Gallery Tab

The third tab on the Contents panel is the Gallery tab. As shown in Figure 24.10, the Gallery tab is a good way to find Bookshelf contents that have different media attached to them.

FIG. 24.10
Use the option buttons on the Gallery tab to find Bookshelf entries with images.

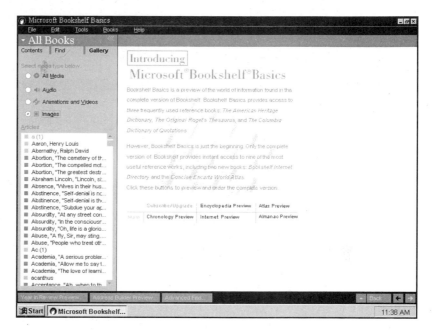

If you want to explore contents that have any of the three media types, choose the All Media option. Otherwise, to narrow your search, you can choose Audio for sound clips, Animation and Videos for motion, and Images for static pictures.

It's best to select All Books from the Book Selector before choosing the Gallery tab. If you have the Thesaurus selected, for example, all options in the Gallery tab are dimmed and unavailable because the Thesaurus has no entries with audio, video, or images.

Figure 24.11 shows a frame of the video for an article on horsemanship.

Click the Play button to start the video. As it moves from left to right, you can click it again to freeze the frame. To start the video over, click the Restart button. And to control the playback manually, click the Manual Frame Advance button and drag it in either direction.

Viewing animations is similar to viewing video clips. Figure 24.12 shows a portion of the animation from the Earthquake article.

N O T E The Bookshelf makes audio available in some video clips, in those entries with sound clips, and by means of the sound icon in Dictionary entries. To hear the audio, your computer must be equipped with a sound card and either speakers or a headset. ▪

FIG. 24.11

Use the play buttons on the video clip to start the video, restart it, stop it, or control its playback manually.

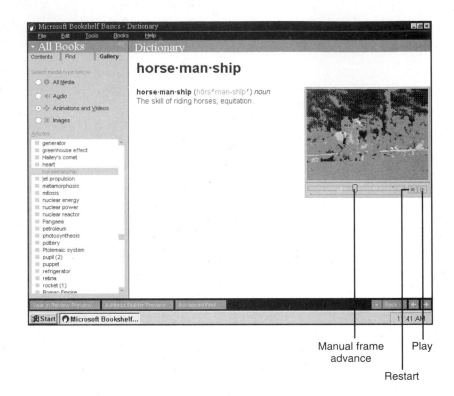

Manual frame
advance

Play

Restart

FIG. 24.12

Animations act the same as videos, but they are drawings rather than captured film or videotape.

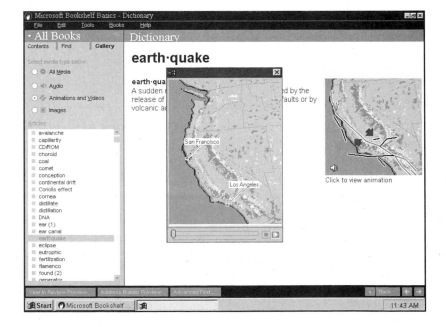

TROUBLESHOOTING

I want to look at a video clip, but the video box says that a file isn't available. If you don't have a video player installed on your computer, the box that normally contains the video appears grayed and hatched, and the video controls are missing. Insert the Windows CD into its drive. From the Windows Start button, choose Settings, Control Panel, and double-click the Add/Remove Programs icon. Select the Windows Setup tab. In the Components list box, choose Multimedia, and then click the Details button. Fill out the check boxes for Media Player and Video Compression, and then choose OK. Choose OK again to leave Windows Setup. Finally, run Bookshelf again to view the video clip.

Using the Feature Bar

The three main parts of the Bookshelf screen are the Contents Panel, the Article Panel, and the Feature Bar. From the Feature Bar, you can return quickly to Bookshelf entries that you've recently seen, and also search a subset of the Bookshelf's contents.

Navigating with the Feature Bar

Besides offering previews of the Year in Review and the Address Builder, the Feature Bar gives you access to some navigational aids. Figure 24.13 shows the Feature Bar.

Suppose that you look up *totem* and then look up *symbol*. A quick way to return to the information on *totem* is to click the Back button.

If you want to jump further back than the most recently viewed article, use the Back List button. This displays several recently viewed articles, and you can go directly to the one you want by clicking it.

You can also use the Browse arrows to go forward and backward in a particular book. For example, you might be using the Dictionary and the article you are currently viewing is on *literate*. Then, clicking the left browse arrow takes you one entry up in the Dictionary to *literary*, and clicking the right browse arrow takes you one entry down to *literately*.

FIG. 24.13

Use the Feature Bar's Back List button to retrace your steps.

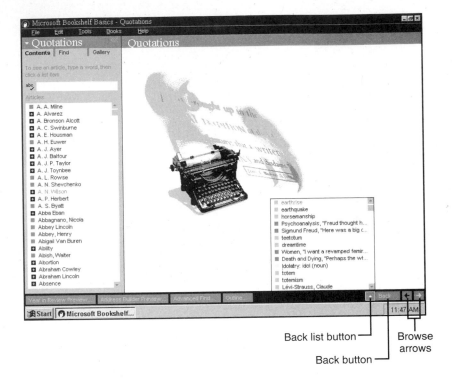

Back list button

Back button

Browse arrows

Using Advanced Find

The Advanced Find feature enables you to be much more specific about topics that you're searching for. By using Advanced Find, you can combine words with logical operators to target a specific concept.

To use Advanced Find, click its button on the Feature Bar (refer to Figure 24.13). The Advanced Find dialog appears, as shown in Figure 24.14.

Suppose that you are interested in finding Bookshelf information about life on the planet Mars. In the text box, you would type **life and mars**, and then click Find. There are a few points about searching on these criteria:

■ The *and* is a logical operator that specifies that Bookshelf is to find articles that contain both *life* and *mars*.

■ You could omit the *and*, like this: **life mars**. Bookshelf assumes that you mean *and* if you type two or more words without any logical operator.

■ The search ignores capitalization. Typing **Mars** is equivalent to typing **mars**.

■ *Mars* is both a noun (the planet) and a verb form ("Graffiti mars a neighborhood"). Because Bookshelf doesn't know which part of speech you have in mind, it searches for all forms: *mar, marred,* and *marring,* for example. This particular search returns entries that contain the phrases "…get to Mars…," "…so mar it now…," and "…sorrow that has marred…," as well as the word *life.*

FIG. 24.14
Use the Advanced Find dialog box to specify both what to search for and where to search for it.

There are several other ways to tailor your search:

■ To find an article that contains one word or the other, but not both, use *or.* If you want to look up information about two cities, Perth and Amboy, but don't want information about Perth Amboy, you can type **perth or amboy**.

■ To avoid articles that deal with unwanted concepts, use *not.* To find information about bridges, but to avoid information about the card game called "contract bridge," you can type **bridge not contract**.

■ To find an exact phrase, enclose it in quotes. **"Contract bridge"** locates articles about the card game, but ignores articles containing phrases such as "a contract to build a bridge."

■ To locate articles with two words that are close together, use *near.* For example, **air condition** returns, among others, an article on inspiration, which includes both words—but they are more than 70 words apart. To restrict the search to something closer to the concept of climate control, type **air near condition**.

 You can also use these logical operators in the Find panel in the Contents section.

Use Advanced Find when you want to search more than one, but not all books. The Book Selector enables you to search all books or to restrict your search to one book. However, it does not enable you to choose to search the Dictionary and Quotations, omitting the

Thesaurus. To do so, use the Advanced Find dialog box and check <u>D</u>ictionary and Thesaurus before clicking <u>F</u>ind.

The Advanced Find feature can be useful when you want to restrict your search to a specific article or articles that you have already found. Suppose that your initial search was for the word *Washington*. That search returns articles about the state, the U.S. Capitol, people named Washington, and so on.

Now, to narrow the search to information about the state, you could enter **state** in the Advanced Find text box and click the La<u>s</u>t Articles Found option button. This restricts the search to only the present set of articles, and you need not repeat the search of the entire Bookshelf contents using *washington and state*.

Finding Topics from Other Office Applications

Suppose that you are searching for a word similar to *pungent*. In Word, one approach is to choose <u>T</u>ools, <u>L</u>anguage, <u>T</u>hesaurus (if you have installed the Thesaurus with Office 97). Although quick and convenient, the Word Thesaurus does not provide as much information as does the Bookshelf Thesaurus: you might find it helpful to get as much information as you can about synonyms for *pungent*.

To look up information in Bookshelf from Word, follow these steps:

1. Make sure that the CD-ROM with the Bookshelf files on it is located in its drive.
2. If you have not yet done so, type the word that's the basis for your search—**pungent**—in your Word document.
3. Click the word you want to search for and choose <u>T</u>ools, Loo<u>k</u> Up Reference.
4. Confirm the word and the reference source in the Look Up Reference dialog box, and choose OK. (This dialog box appears only if you choose <u>T</u>ools, Loo<u>k</u> Up Reference.) The definition appears on your screen as shown in Figure 24.15.

If you follow these steps with the word *pungent*, you'll note that the search begins with the Bookshelf's Dictionary. This is fine if you simply want to verify the meaning of a word. But if you are searching for synonyms, you would prefer to look in the Bookshelf's Thesaurus.

To do so, click the Bookshelf's button on the Windows 95 taskbar. When the Bookshelf screen appears, check to see if Thesaurus is the selected option in the Book Selector. If not, click the Book Selector's drop-down list and choose the Thesaurus from the menu— or, choose <u>B</u>ooks, <u>T</u>hesaurus. The Bookshelf displays the information in the Thesaurus about the word you looked up, and you can now determine whether there is a more appropriate synonym.

FIG. 24.15
The definition box indicates if there is more than one definition of the word you have looked up.

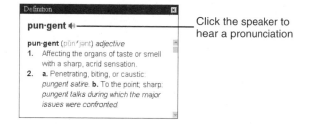

Click the speaker to hear a pronunciation

Copying Information to Other Applications

Often when you look up information in the Bookshelf, it's with the purpose of using it in a Word document. By using common Office commands, you can copy text that you want to cite, a sound object (normally, a pronunciation—perhaps your Word document is intended for a student) that you want a reader to hear, or a static image such as a picture or drawing.

Copying a Complete Article

To copy all the information in an article, including any image in the article, right-click the article in the Article Panel. The shortcut menu displays two options: Copy or Create Shortcut. Choosing Copy places the contents of the article in the Clipboard for subsequent pasting to another application. If you choose Create Shortcut, a shortcut to the article is placed on your Windows desktop.

Copying Videos and Animation

Although copying the complete article copies an image or animation that might be included in the article, when you paste it into another application the medium appears as a picture. Therefore, clicking an animation to view it does not work in the target application.

However, if you want to be able to show an animation or video from another Office document, a workaround is to use a shortcut. Right-click the article and choose Create Shortcut to place a shortcut on your desktop. Then, open your Office document—a Word file, for example, or a PowerPoint presentation—and drag the shortcut into the document. Now, double-clicking the shortcut starts Bookshelf and opens the article with the video or the animation. Play it as you normally would.

Copying Text

Copying text information from Bookshelf to another application such as Word is a familiar process. Just highlight the text that you want to copy by dragging your mouse pointer across it. Then, choose Edit, Copy (or press Ctrl+C). Switch to the target document, position the mouse pointer where you want the text to appear, and choose Edit, Paste (or press Ctrl+V).

When you paste the information to the target document, Bookshelf automatically inserts a footnote that contains copyright information. In Word, you can view the footnote contents by double-clicking the footnote number that's inserted in the text by choosing View, Footnotes, or by moving the mouse pointer over the footnote number to see the footnote as a ScreenTip. In Excel, the copyright information is pasted to a row below the one that contains the information that you copied.

Copying Pronunciations

To copy the audible pronunciation of a word from Bookshelf to another Office application, first make sure that pronunciations are enabled. In Bookshelf, choose Tools, Options and if necessary select the Enable Pronunciations check box (refer to Figure 24.8). With pronunciations enabled, you see a sound icon that looks like a speaker included in the Dictionary entry (refer to Figure 24.15).

Then, select the Dictionary entry whose pronunciation you want to copy. Right-click the sound icon, and choose Copy from the shortcut menu. Return to the target document, and choose Paste. The sound is embedded as a Sound Object in your document.

Copying Pictures

Copying pictures to other applications is very similar to copying sounds. Just right-click the picture and choose Copy from the shortcut menu. Then return to the target application and choose Paste. Or, if you prefer, select the picture by clicking it, and then choose Edit, Copy to put the picture in the Clipboard for later pasting.

Annotating Bookshelf Entries

At times, you might want to add some information to a Bookshelf article. For example, you can add a reminder to yourself to pass along information in the article to a colleague, or to quote from the article in a paper that you are writing. You might even want to add some special fact that you're aware of, but that the article fails to mention.

In cases such as these, add a Note to the article. With the article in view, choose Edit, Note. Bookshelf displays the Note dialog box shown in Figure 24.16.

FIG. 24.16
Whatever you type in the Annotation box is subsequently made available when you choose the relevant article.

Part IV
Ch 24

Click the Add Current Article button to move the article's name into the Articles box. Then, type whatever you want in the Annotation box, and click OK. The note is saved for later retrieval—not, of course, on the CD-ROM that contains the Bookshelf articles, but on your working disk in the folder that contains the Bookshelf program files.

There are two methods to get to your Note. Using either method displays the same dialog box shown in Figure 24.17:

- Open the article to which the note was attached. Click the Note icon in the upper-right corner, as shown in Figure 24.17.

- From any location in Bookshelf, choose Edit, Note. The Note dialog box appears. Click an entry in the Articles box to view its associated Note in the Annotation box.

FIG. 24.17
The Note icon informs you that information has been added to the current article.

Note Icon

Reviewing Front Matter

If you've ever used an unabridged dictionary or thesaurus, you know that it contains a considerable amount of material pertaining to its usage. The Dictionary and Thesaurus in Bookshelf provide this information as Front Matter.

For example, the Dictionary's Front Matter includes the following:

- *Word histories.* An explanation of the difference between terse etymologies and information such as early usage of the word. For example, the word *alligator* has a history that includes the following information: "In The Travailes of an Englishman, published in 1568, Job Hortop says that 'in this river we killed a monstrous Lagarto or Crocodile.' This killing gives rise to the first recorded instance of *alligator* in English."

- *Variants.* Usually variant spellings and how the Dictionary distinguishes among them.

- *Undefined forms.* How to identify closely related words that have different grammatical functions.

- *Inflected forms.* For example, how to determine whether an irregular plural is more common than the regular form.

- *Order of senses.* The order in which the Dictionary lists different meanings of the same word.

And, of course, the Dictionary Front Matter contains the traditional Guide to Indo-European Roots.

In the Thesaurus Front Matter, you can find useful information such as:

- Roget's Plan of Classification, and its rationale

- How words are grouped within articles

■ Recommendations for using the Dictionary in conjunction with the Thesaurus, particularly for non-English speakers

To view the Front Matter for the Dictionary and the Thesaurus, use the Book Selector to select one or the other. Then, choose Help, About the Dictionary or Help, About the Thesaurus.

When you see the Online Help Overview screen, choose Front Matter—Dictionary or Front Matter—Thesaurus. Clicking Front Matter takes you to the appropriate section. ●

Part
IV

Ch
24

Using PowerPoint

CHAPTER 25

Getting Acquainted with PowerPoint

by Nancy Stevenson

PowerPoint is the component of Microsoft Office used to create professional-quality overhead transparency, paper, 35mm slide, photoprint, or on-screen presentations. In addition, this latest version of PowerPoint for Windows 97 allows you to easily publish presentations to the Internet. This chapter familiarizes you with the layout of the PowerPoint window and its tools and capabilities. ◼

Starting and Exiting PowerPoint

PowerPoint offers several options such as Office Assistant, templates, and AutoContent Wizard to get you started on attractive presentations quickly and easily.

Looking at PowerPoint Window Elements

Simple-to-use toolbars and menu commands offer one-touch ease in performing common functions.

Examining Components of PowerPoint Presentations

Use PowerPoint's components to work on slides, organize presentation contents with outlines, and generate speaker notes and audience handouts.

Understanding Masters, Templates, Objects, and Layouts

Several built-in features give you a head start on designing and adding graphic elements to give presentations pizzazz.

Adding visuals to PowerPoint slides

A picture is worth a thousand words, and with PowerPoint you can add anything from a simple drawing to an animated video clip.

Starting and Exiting PowerPoint

Like other applications in Microsoft Office, PowerPoint can be started in more than one way, allowing you to choose the method that is most convenient. The following are ways in which PowerPoint can be started:

■ Click the Start button and choose the PowerPoint shortcut, usually found in the Programs menu.

■ Double-click the PowerPoint icon in the Microsoft Office folder (found in your hard disk window).

 TIP Create a shortcut to PowerPoint by dragging the PowerPoint icon from the PowerPoint folder to the desktop; then double-click the shortcut to open the program.

After a few seconds, the PowerPoint window appears. Like other Microsoft Office applications, PowerPoint displays the Office Assistant, which offers you the most logical options for proceeding at this point. If you don't want to see the Office Assistant each time you start PowerPoint, right click the Office Assistant itself and select Hide Assistant from the shortcut menu that appears.

When you want to exit PowerPoint, choose File, Exit. If the current file is unsaved, PowerPoint displays a dialog box asking if you want to save the changes you made to the current file. Choose Yes if you want to save, No if you don't want to save, or Cancel to return to your file without saving.

Getting Familiar with the PowerPoint Window

PowerPoint automatically displays the dialog box shown in Figure 25.1 when you first open the program. This dialog box lets you choose how you want to create a presentation. PowerPoint offers a variety of methods for creating presentations, including using an existing presentation, opening a blank presentation, using a template, or running the AutoContent Wizard.

▶ **See** "Creating a New Presentation," **p. 608**

Figure 25.2 shows what a typical PowerPoint presentation screen might look like. PowerPoint's standard menu bar, standard toolbar, and formatting toolbar are shown below the window's title bar. The drawing toolbar is displayed along the bottom of the window. In addition, this figure shows a floating menu (which is displayed when you first open a new presentation) called Common Tasks. This menu offers some of the most common functions you'll perform while working on slides including: creating a new slide, modifying the layout of a slide, and applying design elements. The Office Assistant is also displayed near the lower-right corner.

FIG. 25.1
Your first choice is a foundation on which you base your presentation.

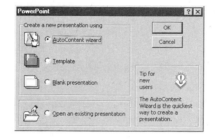

FIG. 25.2
The PowerPoint screen provides tools to help you format text, change views, access other programs, draw on-screen, and much more.

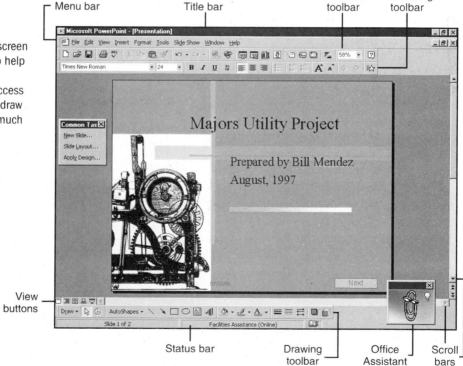

Surrounded by a gray background, each slide in the presentation is displayed on its own page, represented by the white rectangular area in the middle of the screen. These individual "pages" in a presentation that become overheads, 35mm slides, or an on-screen slide show are considered slides. Notice that vertical and horizontal scroll bars are now visible on-screen (compare to Figure 25.1). At the left end of the horizontal scroll bar are view buttons, used for displaying different views of your presentation.

 T I P If your presentation window is smaller than the one in the figure, click the Maximize button to enlarge the window.

N O T E For more information about displaying different views in PowerPoint, see Chapter 26, "Creating, Saving, and Opening Presentations."

Window Elements

The menus in PowerPoint are similar to the menus in other Microsoft Office applications. Menus such as File, Window, and Help are standard across all applications. PowerPoint's menus are most similar to Word's, but the Slide Show menu is unique to PowerPoint. Table 25.1 describes each PowerPoint menu and the types of commands found on them.

Table 25.1   PowerPoint Menus

Menu	Description
File	Contains standard Microsoft Office application File menu and commands specific to PowerPoint, such as Pack and Go and Save as HTML. Additionally, if you're using Outlook, which installs when you load Office 97, an extra section adds Send To mail and routing commands.
Edit	Contains commands for Undo, Cut, Copy, and Paste (including pasting as a hyperlink for online presentations). Duplicate (Ctrl+D) and Delete Slide are also found on this menu, along with commands for creating Links to other files, Find and Replace, and editing an Object.
View	Contains commands to choose the presentation view you want to display on your screen or to display masters. This menu also contains commands for turning on and off the display of toolbars, rulers, and guides. (You learn about rulers and guides in the "Displaying Rulers and Guides" section of this chapter.) Use this menu also to control the zoom percentage used in a particular view or to add Headers or Footers to slides.

Menu	Description
Insert	Contains commands that let you insert a variety of elements in a presentation, from a simple date or time to clip art, graphs, or other objects. You can also insert a new or duplicate slide from here, and establish hyperlinks.
Format	Contains commands for changing all aspects (font, alignment, spacing, color, shadow) of how text and objects look in a presentation. This menu also contains commands for selecting templates, color schemes, and layouts.
Tools	Contains typical Microsoft Office tools (such as Spelling) as well as tools that are unique to PowerPoint. Use the commands on this menu to create transitions between slides, hide slides, or recolor or crop a picture. You also find commands for customizing toolbars and setting PowerPoint options, as well as commands for keeping minutes of meetings and scheduling tasks, interactive settings, and so on.
Slide Show	Contains commands to rehearse a presentation and control animations. You can choose to hide certain slides from a particular presentation, record narration, and set up a variety of special transition effects to occur between slides.
Window	Contains standard Microsoft Office application Window menu, such as New Window and Arrange All, as well as a Fit to Page command.
Help	Contains standard Microsoft Office application Help menu plus a What's This context-specific help pointer and Microsoft on the Web, which connects you to Microsoft assistance on the Internet.

▶ **See** "Creating a New Presentation," **p. 608**

▶ **See** "Enhancing Text," **p. 663**

▶ **See** "Working with Templates," **p. 658**

The PowerPoint Tools menu also contains a feature called PowerPoint Central. If you have an online connection, this feature downloads the latest information from Microsoft on PowerPoint features, articles on how to be a good presenter from Dale Carnegie, and even downloadable media clips. When you select PowerPoint Central from the Tools menu, you are automatically asked if you want PowerPoint to get online and load the latest information.

Along the lower edge of the PowerPoint window is the status bar, which displays the number of the current slide or other element you're working on (Slide Master, Outline Master, Handout Master, or Notes Master) at the left end. The center of the status bar shows the design template currently being used; you can also double-click this area to apply a new presentation template. The last element on the far right of the status bar is a shortcut to check for correct spelling on the currently displayed slide.

Above the status bar is the horizontal scroll bar. At the left end are five view buttons. Each button displays a different view of the current presentation. The group of five view buttons is pointed out in Figure 25.2 and described in the section, "Examining the Components of a PowerPoint Presentation," later in this chapter.

PowerPoint's Standard Toolbar

 T I P Right-click any toolbar to display a list of available toolbars; select a toolbar to display or to hide from the list.

Table 25.2 describes each of the buttons on PowerPoint's Standard toolbar. Each button represents a PowerPoint menu command. You learn how to use most of these buttons while performing common tasks in subsequent chapters. Refer to Chapter 23, "Drawing Shapes, Curves, and Lines," for an explanation of the tools on the Drawing toolbar.

Table 25.2   Buttons on PowerPoint's Standard Toolbar

Button	Description
	Creates a new presentation and displays the New Slide dialog box.
	Displays the Open dialog box, from which you can choose a presentation file to open (or Design Template or Outline).
	Saves the current presentation under the current name and file type. If the presentation has not yet been saved, displays the Save As dialog box.
	Prints the active presentation.
	Checks the spelling in the current presentation. Displays the Spelling dialog box if errors are found.
	Removes the selected text or object from the slide and places it on the Windows Clipboard.
	Places a copy of the selected text or object on the Windows Clipboard, leaving the original text or object unchanged.
	Pastes the contents of the Clipboard into the current slide.

Button	Description
	Copies all attributes (color, font, shadow, pattern, and so on) of the selected object or text selection so that you can apply all those attributes to another object or text selection.
	Reverses the most recent action taken. Note that not all actions (commands) can be reversed.
	Redoes or repeats (depending on the action) the most recent action taken. Not all actions can be redone or repeated.
	Inserts a Hyperlink from the selected text or object on the current slide to a file or URL you specify in the Insert Hyperlink dialog box.
	Displays the Web toolbar which allows you to search the World Wide Web from within PowerPoint.
	Embeds a Microsoft Word table of the size (rows and columns) you specify in your presentation.
	Embeds an Excel worksheet of the size (rows and columns) you specify in your presentation.
	Embeds a chart in your presentation using the data you specify.
	Allows you to insert clip art into your presentation using Microsoft's Clip Gallery.
	Opens the New Slide dialog box from which you can choose an AutoLayout for the new slide.
	Displays the Slide Layout dialog box from which you can change the layout for the current slide.
	Applies a selected design template to the slide show.
	Black and White View switches the display of slides in the current presentation to black and white, and displays a small window with a color version of the presentation. Clicking this again returns the presentation to color display.
69%	Lets you zoom in and out of your presentation.
	Activates Office Assistant which asks you what common task you'd like to perform at this point and offers both Search and Tips features.

continues

Part

V

Ch

25

Table 25.2 Continued

Button	Description
Arial	Shows the current font and displays a drop-down list of available fonts.
24	Shows the current font size and displays a list of available font sizes.
B	Adds or removes boldface to and from selected text (this button toggles on and off with each click).
I	Adds or removes italics to and from selected text (this button toggles on and off with each click).
U	Adds or removes underlining to and from selected text (this button toggles on and off with each click).
S	Adds or removes text shadow to and from selected text (this button toggles on and off with each click).
	Left-aligns selected text.
	Centers selected text.
	Right-aligns selected text.
	Adds bullets to selected text (this button toggles on and off with each click).
	Increases the line spacing between paragraphs for the selected text.
	Decreases the line spacing between paragraphs for the selected text.
A	Increases font size of selected text to the next larger available size.
A	Decreases font size of selected text to the next smaller available size.
	Moves selected text to next higher level in an outline.
	Moves selected text to next lower level in an outline.
	Displays and hides an Animation Effects menu which allows you to add motion to selected text or objects.

Displaying Rulers and Guides

When you work with text documents in Word, it's helpful to display horizontal and vertical rulers in the Word window. Because some slides contain text, rulers can be useful in PowerPoint as well. Rulers give you a reference point within a slide so that you can see at what point on the page (in inches) a text or drawn object appears. They also help you plan the use of space on a slide by providing guides for object and text placement.

To display rulers in the PowerPoint window, choose View, Ruler. Rulers appear in one of two states—*drawing* or *text*—depending on the item currently selected on the slide. In Figure 25.3, rulers are shown in the *drawing state*, which places the zero point at the *center* of each ruler. This allows you to position objects from the center point to the outer edges of a slide. The position of the mouse is indicated on each ruler by a dashed line. In Figure 25.3, the mouse position on each ruler is at approximately 1.5 inches. You also can see that the slide is 10 inches wide and 7.5 inches long.

FIG. 25.3
Rulers and Guides assist in layout and alignment of slide components.

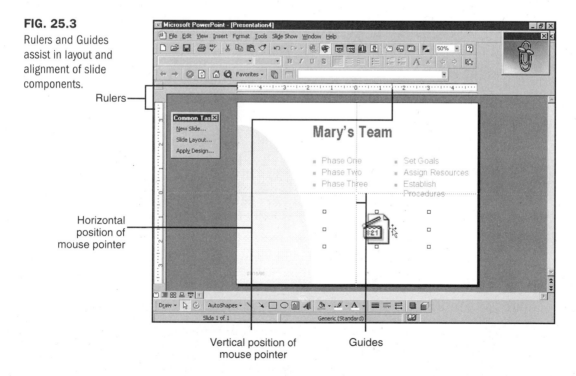

Part

V

Ch

25

When it's important to position slide elements precisely or to align certain elements vertically or horizontally, you can choose View, Guides. This command displays dotted lines which intersect vertically and horizontally through a specific point of a slide. Use the guides to help you visually align elements on a slide. Guides are shown in Figure 25.3.

 TIP You can reposition each of the guide lines by dragging it up and down the page or to the right and left of center.

NOTE Guides do not appear on printed copies of your slide; they only appear on-screen while you are working in PowerPoint. ▨

Examining the Components of a PowerPoint Presentation

At first you might think that PowerPoint is an application used only to create slides for a presentation, but PowerPoint offers much more. It helps you plan, create, and deliver a presentation in a practical way. Think about how a speaker gives a presentation: she might plan the presentation by first creating the outline of its contents; then completing the "look" and content of the slides; and finally printing them. While she speaks, the speaker might refer to printed copies of the slides that contain her own handwritten notes. She might also provide copies of her slides to the audience so that they can follow along or take their own notes.

Key components of a PowerPoint presentation include the following:

- Slides
- Outlines
- Speaker's notes
- Audience handouts

After you create content, you can then use just one component or any combination of the four, depending on your particular requirements. PowerPoint simplifies the task by:

- Automatically generating the slide content in the slide view when you enter text in the outline view

- Automatically generating content in the outline view when you enter text directly on slides
- Automatically generating an audience handout page for each slide when you create a slide, ready for you to add notes that can be used by the speaker

You can view any of the components on-screen or print copies. PowerPoint displays slides, as illustrated earlier in Figure 25.2, by default. Outline pages look like a typical outline, with main headings aligned at the left margin and lower-level headings indented (see Figure 25.4). Note pages contain a reduced version of the slide at the top of the page with space at the bottom of the page for you to add speaker's notes (see Figure 25.5). Audience handouts can contain two, three, or six slides per printed page, as shown in Figure 25.6. Notice that you can't view audience handouts on-screen. When you view the Handout Master, you see dotted frames that outline the location of the slides on the page.

To view slides, the outline, or note pages, choose View, Slide; View, Outline; or View, Notes Page. To view handout pages, choose View, Master; then choose Handout Master from the submenu that appears. After you choose a view, the status bar indicates which view is displayed.

▶ **See** "Outlining a Document," **p. 238**

Part
V

Ch
25

FIG. 25.4
Use Outline view to create a presentation and to organize your slides.

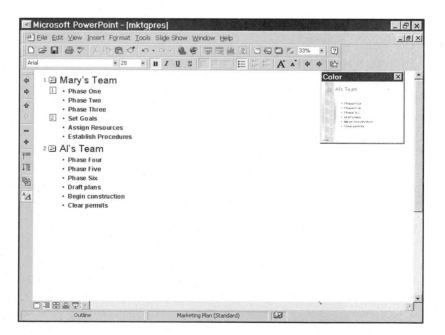

FIG. 25.5
Enter speaker's notes to help you remember important items during your presentation.

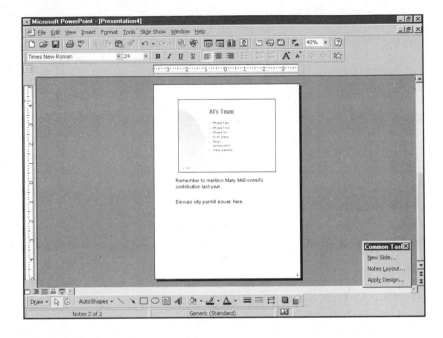

FIG. 25.6
The layout options for audience handout pages are indicated by dotted lines on the Handout Master.

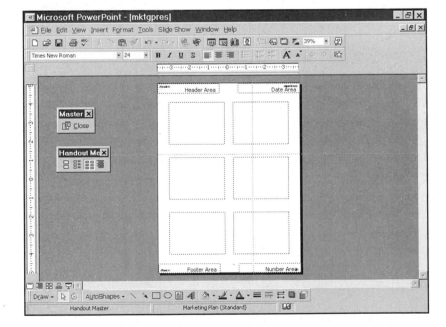

N O T E You can quickly display a presentation component by clicking the view buttons at the left end of the horizontal scroll bar. Click the Slide View, Outline View, or Notes Pages View buttons to display any of these elements. ▪

TROUBLESHOOTING

I clicked on the icon for Slide Show by mistake, and now I've lost my toolbar and menus. How do I get them back? Slide show view displays a slide so that it fills the screen, offering you a way to preview your screen show. However, to show you that full screen display, it removes toolbars, menus, view icons, the title bar, and the status bar from your screen. To get help navigating around while in Slide Show view, press F1 for a list of commands. To get out of the slide show, you can use one of three methods: press the Escape key, press Ctrl+Break, or type the hyphen (-) key on your keyboard. Your regular PowerPoint screen returns with all your tools and menus intact.

Understanding Templates and Masters

Part
V

Ch
25

PowerPoint provides features that help you create attractive, eye-catching slides: Presentation Templates and Masters. Presentation Templates are built-in designs that contain color schemes and design elements that provide a background for a slide. Presentation Templates are also referred to in PowerPoint as designs. A particular design's color scheme employs matching colors for text, lines, background, and so on; design elements are lines, shapes, or pictures added to the background to enhance the text and graphics you add to a slide. A Presentation Template also includes masters with pre-formatted fonts and styles that complement the "look" the template represents; for example, the Company Meeting template looks professional and sophisticated. The use of the Arial font and the square bullet styles add to the clean, corporate look.

The Slide Master allows you to control the global font styles, formatting, and placement of text on a slide. A Slide Master, for example, may place all titles in the top center of each slide and use a 48-point Univers font to represent the titles. The text formatting and placement appears on the Slide Master. You can select one Presentation Template to obtain an overall look for your slides; then you can modify the slide master to change a particular element of that template. For example, you might like to reconfigure where all titles will appear on your slides after you've applied a template.

Using Slide Masters and Presentation Templates creates consistency within a presentation. When you choose a Presentation Template, the color scheme, layout, and formatting are applied to all slides in the presentation. Similarly, the elements and formatting of the Master Slide apply to all slides in the presentation. For added flexibility, PowerPoint enables you to change any of the elements of a Presentation Template: text formatting, color scheme, layout, master elements, and so on. You can even create your own templates and use them again and again.

Using Masters

TIP The Slide Master controls the formatting on all slides except title slides, which are controlled by the Title Master.

For every presentation you create, PowerPoint makes a set of *masters* available: a Slide Master, Title Master, Notes Master, and Handout Master. Masters correspond directly to the slides, speaker's notes, and handout components of a presentation. Masters contain the elements (text or pictures) that you want to appear on every component page. For instance, if you want your company logo to appear on each of your slides, it isn't necessary to insert the logo on individual slides. You add the logo to the Slide Master, and it automatically appears on every slide. Other elements you might add to a master include pictures or clip art, page numbers, the date, the title of the presentation, or reminders such as "Company Confidential."

To display a master, choose View, Master, which displays a submenu. From the submenu, choose Slide Master, Title Master, Handout Master, or Notes Master. Notice that the left end of the status bar indicates which master is currently displayed. The Slide Master shown in Figure 25.7 includes areas for a master title, bulleted text, date, and footer text, included as parts of a master slide. Additionally, the company's logo, a graphic star symbol, has been added to the bottom left corner of the master slide, and therefore to all slides in the presentation.

NOTE You can quickly display a master by using the view buttons at the left end of the horizontal scroll bar. Press and hold down the Shift key; then click the Slide View (for Slide Master), Outline View or Slide Sorter View (for Handout Master), or Notes Pages View (for Notes Master) button. To return to slide, outline, slide sorter, or notes view, choose the appropriate command from the View menu, or click the view button at the lower left corner of the window.

FIG. 25.7
A Slide Master contains all the elements that you might want to appear on each slide.

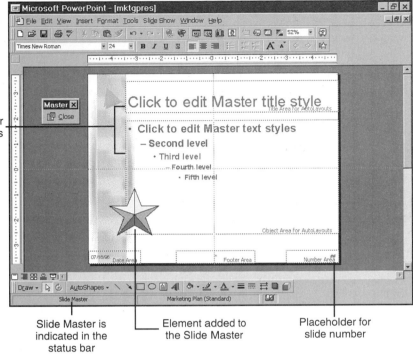

Default master slide elements

Slide Master is indicated in the status bar

Element added to the Slide Master

Placeholder for slide number

Using Presentation Templates

A *presentation template* is a saved presentation file that contains predefined slide and title masters, color schemes, and graphic elements. The presentation templates provided with Microsoft are designed by professional graphic artists who understand the use of color, space, and design. Each template is designed to convey a certain look, feel, or attitude. Figure 25.8 shows how the MARKETING PLAN template looks.

FIG. 25.8
The MARKETING PLAN template conveys a pleasing graphic design.

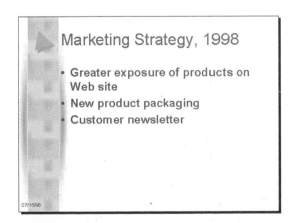

You select a presentation template based on the look you want for your presentation, and then apply the template to your new or existing presentation file. The template applies to all slides in the presentation, and you can apply a new template to a presentation at any time. Keep in mind that if you want selected slides in a presentation to have a look different from the template, you can change any aspect of any slide on an individual basis.

▶ **See** "Working with Templates," **p. 658**

▶ **See** "Working with Color Schemes," **p. 674**

When you create a new "blank" presentation, you use PowerPoint's default template called Default Design. It appears not to be a template at all because it contains no color (except black and white), no graphic elements, and no stylistic formatting. Figure 25.9 illustrates the Default Design template. This is the template you use if you want complete control over your presentation's design, color scheme, and graphic elements, because it lets you start as much "from scratch" as possible. You can, however, modify aspects of *any* template, not just the Default Design template.

FIG. 25.9

A blank Presentation Template and title layout provide a simple look you can use as-is or build on.

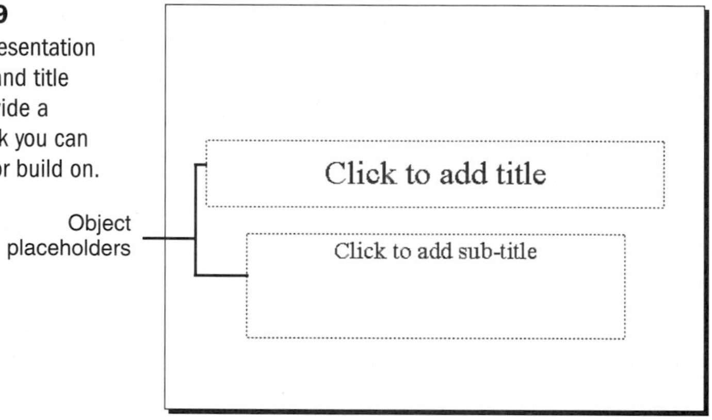

Object placeholders

Click to add title

Click to add sub-title

Understanding Objects and Layouts

PowerPoint slides are made up of *objects*; they are the key elements in any slide. Any time you add text, a graph, a drawing, an organization chart, clip art, a Word table, an Excel spreadsheet, or any other inserted element into a slide, it becomes an object. To work with an object, you select it and then change its content or size, move, copy, or delete it. You also can change *attributes* of an object, such as its color, shadow, border, and so on.

If you don't feel confident positioning or arranging objects on a slide, you can let Power-Point do the work for you by using AutoLayouts. AutoLayouts save you the time and trouble of creating new objects for a new slide, and then arranging, positioning, and aligning them. Each AutoLayout contains placeholders for various kinds of objects such as text, clip art, organization charts, and so on. Placeholders appear as faint dotted lines on the slide and contain identifying text, such as "double-click to add clip art" or "click to add text."

Each AutoLayout contains different object placeholders in different arrangements. For instance, the AutoLayout for a presentation title page contains two text placeholders: one for a slide title and one for a subtitle. The title page AutoLayout was shown earlier in Figure 25.9. The AutoLayout in Figure 25.9 shows these two placeholders: one for a slide title and one for text.

 Whenever you add a new slide to a presentation, PowerPoint automatically displays the New Slide dialog box (see Figure 25.10). Use this dialog box to select the desired AutoLayout. If you want to change the AutoLayout for an existing slide, click the Slide Layout button on the toolbar.

FIG. 25.10
The New Slide dialog box displays a variety of AutoLayouts.

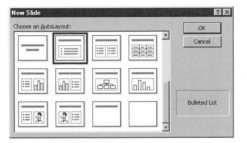

Adding Objects to PowerPoint Slides

There is no reason for a PowerPoint presentation to contain dull slides full of nothing but text. PowerPoint lets you add many different types of objects to your slides to grab an audience's attention, add interest or humor, or to illustrate a particular point. Some objects can be created from within PowerPoint; others can be imported from other applications.

To insert an object from another application into a PowerPoint slide, choose an option on the Insert menu or use one of the buttons on the Standard toolbar. Table 25.3 summarizes the options available on the Insert menu.

N O T E Refer to Chapter 27, "Entering Slide Content," for more information about inserting objects in a presentation. ■

Table 25.3   Insert Menu Commands for Objects You Can Insert in PowerPoint Slides

Object Type	Description
Picture	If you have access to other prepared artwork, such as a bitmap file, you can insert it in a PowerPoint slide. (PowerPoint recognizes many different picture file formats.)
Text Box	You can add an additional placeholder for text to any layout; you need only click the text box to enter text, as with any other standard layout placeholder.
Movies and Sounds	If you have access to movie files, such as Microsoft AVI files or Quicktime for Windows files, you can insert them into a slide. You can similarly insert sound files into any presentation through this menu choice.
Chart	An embedded application that lets you create a chart or graph from tabular data. You create the graph in much the same way as you create a graph from spreadsheet data in Excel.
Object	Gives you access to a wide variety of object types such as clip art, Microsoft Excel spreadsheets and charts, Word documents, Paintbrush pictures, and Microsoft WordArt.

CHAPTER 26

Creating, Saving, and Opening Presentations

by Nancy Stevenson

To work with PowerPoint, you need to understand how to create a new presentation, save a presentation you want to keep, and open an existing presentation when you want to work with it again. PowerPoint provides a variety of methods for starting a presentation. You can create a presentation from a template or wizard, for example. Alternatively, you can start with a blank presentation and add your own colors and graphic elements.

As you work on your presentation, you can choose to view one slide at a time or many slides at once. If you choose to view one slide at a time, you can work on the details of that slide, such as text entry and formatting, adding pictures, changing colors, and so on. When you have several slides completed, you can view them as small pictures, or *thumbnails*, on-screen at the same time so you can organize them.

Finally, you'll want to save your presentation for later editing, printing, or viewing. After saving a presentation, you can open it at any time for modification. ■

Creating a presentation

With predesigned templates and a helpful AutoContent Wizard you can create a new, polished presentation in no time.

Changing your view of a presentation

PowerPoint's different views help you manage the organization of your presentation's content, the overall look of the presentation, and even speakers notes and audience handouts.

Adding, inserting, and deleting slides

The ability to easily add or delete slides makes it simple to edit a presentation to produce one or multiple versions of the same presentation.

Saving a presentation and opening an existing one

After all your hard work, don't forget to save your presentation to the right format for your presentation medium.

Creating a New Presentation

To give you the greatest amount of flexibility, PowerPoint offers a variety of ways to create a new presentation. You can create a "blank" presentation that contains no color or style enhancements; you can copy the appearance of an existing presentation; or you can get step-by-step help in creating a presentation by using a wizard (wizards are described in the following section, "Creating a Presentation Using a Wizard").

When you open the PowerPoint application, the dialog box pictured in Figure 26.1 appears, allowing you to choose the method by which you will create your presentation. The only time you see this dialog box is when you first open PowerPoint.

▶ **See** "Starting and Exiting PowerPoint," **p. 590**

FIG. 26.1
Use this dialog box to choose a method for creating a presentation.

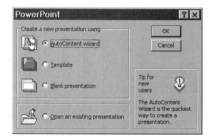

Each of the possible methods is discussed in the following sections.

Creating a Presentation Using a Wizard

In PowerPoint, you can create the framework for a new presentation by responding to questions presented by a wizard.

The AutoContent Wizard asks you questions about the content of the presentation and, based on your answers, the Wizard creates an outline. The Wizard's outline uses each slide's title as the main heading; the heading appears next to a slide number and slide icon. You can then enter body text for the slide—using up to five levels if necessary. The Wizard helps you rearrange points in the outline and even rearrange slides within the outline. Editing is also easy using the Wizard's outline.

Creating a Presentation Using a Template

Sometimes, you want to apply only a design template to a presentation and leave the topics of the presentation for you to complete. In such a case, select the Template option in the New Presentation dialog box.

▶ **See** "Understanding Templates and Masters," **p. 601**

To use a template to create a presentation, you can select Template from the opening dialog box shown in Figure 26.1, or from anywhere else in PowerPoint, follow these steps:

1. Choose File, New. PowerPoint displays the New Presentation dialog box.

2. Select the Presentation Designs tab. PowerPoint displays the dialog box as seen in Figure 26.2. In this figure, the presentation design names are shown in Large Icons view. Other possible views are List and Details. You can select them by clicking the appropriate button in the dialog box, as labeled in the figure.

FIG. 26.2
Choose from among several presentation templates shown in this dialog box.

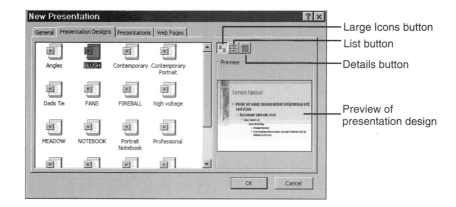

3. Click any presentation template to see a preview of that design in the lower-right corner of the dialog box. You can scroll the window to view more designs.

4. When you have selected a design, click OK to apply it to the presentation.

 TIP Don't forget the additional templates and design elements that come with the ValuPack that loads with Office 97. You can browse through the Overview, which you access through the ValuPack folder, to find other templates that appeal to you.

 N O T E PowerPoint 97 includes both online and standard presentation designs so you can take advantage of Office 97 Web publishing features. Online versions of templates may have buttons and arrows you can use to help online visitors navigate through a presentation using hyperlinks. However, you can use standard templates for Web pages and online templates for slide shows if you want.

Creating a Blank Presentation

When you create a blank presentation, PowerPoint uses the DEFAULT.PPT template. The default template uses no color (black and white only) and includes no styles or enhancements. Creating a blank presentation puts you in complete control of the color scheme,

Part
V

Ch
26

layout, and style characteristics of your slides. You can leave the presentation blank, or you can add a template, colors, and other enhancements selectively at any time by using menu or toolbar commands. Use the blank presentation method when you want the maximum degree of flexibility.

T I P   You can add colors, lines, and objects to a blank presentation and then save it as a Presentation Template file type to create your own template.

▶ **See** "Working with Colors and Line Styles," **p. 668**
▶ **See** "Working with Color Schemes," **p. 674**

To create a blank presentation, follow these steps:

1. Choose <u>B</u>lank Presentation from the choices in the opening dialog box shown in Figure 26.1, or from elsewhere in PowerPoint, select <u>F</u>ile, <u>N</u>ew, or press Ctrl+N. PowerPoint displays the New Presentation dialog box (refer to Figure 26.2).

2. Select the General tab and choose the Blank Presentation icon.

3. Choose OK. PowerPoint displays the New Slide dialog box (see Figure 26.3).

FIG. 26.3
Choose the layout for your first slide in a blank presentation.

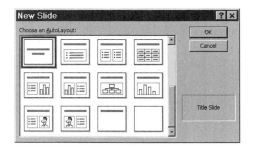

4. Select the layout you want to use for the first slide and then click OK. PowerPoint displays the first slide in your new presentation, using the layout you specify.

N O T E   You can use a template from another presentation, whether the template is one of PowerPoint's or one of your own. (If the template is your own, be sure to save the presentation as a Presentation Template in the Save as <u>T</u>ype list box in the Save As dialog box.) To apply an existing template to a presentation, select the Apply Design tool or choose F<u>o</u>rmat, Apply Design. Choose the folder containing the template and in the Name list, select the template. Click A<u>p</u>ply to close the dialog box and apply the template to the existing presentation. ▓

▶ **See** "Working with Templates," **p. 658**

Moving Through a Presentation

When a presentation contains more than one slide, you must be able to easily display the slide you want. The left end of the status bar displays the number of the current slide. To move from one slide to another in slide view or notes pages view, use the vertical scroll bar. To display the preceding slide, click the Previous Slide button. Click the Next Slide button to display the slide that follows. The Next and Previous Slide buttons are located at the bottom of the vertical scroll bar, and are labeled in Figure 26.4.

FIG. 26.4
Move from slide to slide using the Next Slide and Previous Slide buttons.

Previous Slide button ——

Next Slide button ——

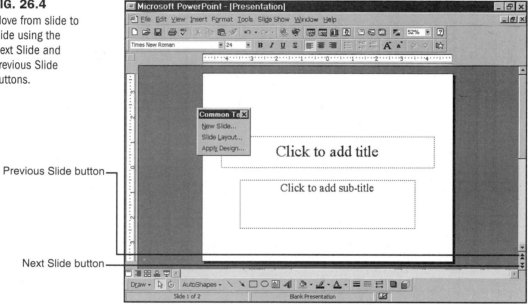

Part
V

Ch
26

T I P If you prefer, you can use the Page Up and Page Down keys to move from one slide to another.

When a presentation contains a large number of slides, the Previous Slide and Next Slide buttons are not efficient for moving from a slide near the beginning to a slide near the end of a presentation. Instead, you can move to a specific slide quickly by dragging the scroll box in the vertical scroll bar. As you drag the box up or down, PowerPoint displays a slide number and if you've entered title text, a title to the left of the scroll bar, as shown in Figure 26.5. When the number of the slide you want to view is displayed, release the mouse button. PowerPoint moves directly to the slide you specify without having to move through each slide in between.

> **N O T E**   Another way to quickly move from slide to slide is to switch to Slide Sorter view, and
> then double-click the slide you want to view. PowerPoint automatically switches back
> to Slide view and displays the slide you select. See the section, "Viewing a Presentation," later
> in this chapter. If you have the Intellimouse, which comes with Office 97, you can also use the
> middle mouse wheel to move from slide to slide. Roll it up or down to go to the previous or next
> slide. This also scrolls the document when you're in Outline or Slide Sorter view. ■

FIG. 26.5
Dragging the scroll box
allows you to move to
a specific slide quickly.

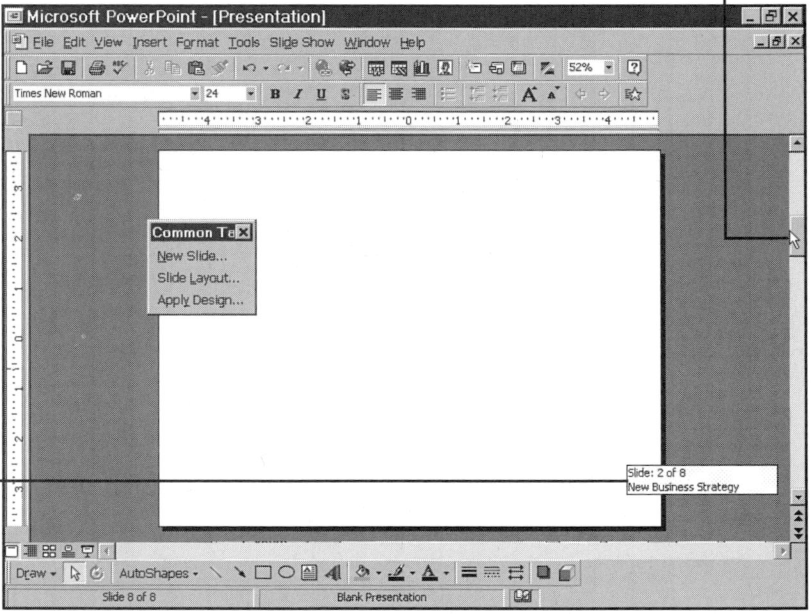

Scroll bar

Slide number and
title displayed

Adding, Inserting, and Deleting Slides

After you create your presentation file, you can add, insert, or delete slides whenever
necessary. To add a slide, follow these steps:

1. Click the Insert New Slide button on the Standard toolbar or the New Slide button
   on the right of the status bar. You can also add a new slide by choosing Insert,
   New Slide or by pressing Ctrl+M. The New Slide dialog box appears (refer to
   Figure 26.3).

CAUTION

To create a new presentation, you use the keystroke combination Ctrl+N, which can easily be mistaken for Ctrl+M to create a new slide. If you make this mistake, simply choose Cancel to close the New Presentation dialog box.

▶ **See** "Inserting Clip-Art Pictures," **p. 631**
▶ **See** "Inserting Other Objects," **p. 637**

2. Choose the AutoLayout for the new slide.

3. Click OK.

T I P If you want to add your own objects and text blocks to a slide, choose the Blank slide AutoLayout in the New Slide dialog box.

The new slide is inserted after the slide currently being displayed in Slide view, or after the selected slide in Slide Sorter view.

 A feature new to this version of PowerPoint is the Slide Finder. Choose Insert, Slides from Files. The Slide Finder dialog box shown in Figure 26.6 allows you to browse through other presentations and select slides you'd like to place in the current set of slides.

FIG. 26.6
You can keep a list of favorite slides, such as a company overview, and insert it easily in every presentation.

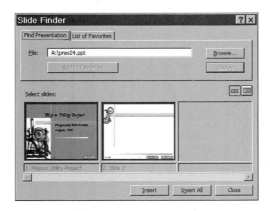

You can delete a slide at any time by displaying the slide you want to delete and choosing Edit, Delete Slide.

N O T E You can also select the slide in Slide Sorter view and press the Delete key to delete a slide. See the following section, "Viewing a Presentation." ■

TROUBLESHOOTING

 I accidentally deleted a slide from my presentation. How can I restore it? In any of the views (Slide, Outline, Slide Sorter, and Notes Pages), you can click the Undo button in the toolbar, choose Edit, Undo, or press Ctrl+Z. Remember that you must use Undo immediately after deleting the slide. If you take any other actions first, the slide may not be able to be restored. To undo the last several actions, you can click the arrow next to the Undo arrow button; drag across as many actions as you want to undo and release your mouse. Each action will be undone in sequence.

I inserted a new slide in the wrong location in my presentation. Can I move it? Yes. It's best to use Slide Sorter view to rearrange slides in a presentation. For specific instructions, see "Using Slide Sorter View" later in this chapter.

Viewing a Presentation

PowerPoint offers several ways to view your presentation. Each view has a particular purpose and advantage. The five views are summarized in Table 26.1 and described in detail in the sections that follow.

Table 26.1   PowerPoint Views

View		Description
▣	Slide	Displays individual slides in full-slide view, which enables you to see the slide in detail.
▤	Outline	Displays the text from all slides in the presentation, giving you an overview of the content of the presentation.
▦	Slide Sorter	Displays a miniature version of every slide in the presentation in proper order; an overview of the look and flow of the presentation.
▣	Notes Page	Displays a miniature version of an individual slide at the top of the screen and a space for speaker's notes below the slide; enables you to review your notes while viewing the slide.
▣	Slide Show	Displays slides as they would appear during an on-screen slide show by using the entire screen area. Press Page Down and Page Up to switch from slide to slide. Press Esc to end Slide Show view.

The quickest way to switch views is to click the view buttons pictured in Table 26.1, which are found in the bottom-left corner of the PowerPoint window. Simply click the button for the view you want to use to change the view of the current presentation.

Zooming In and Out

Regardless of the view you choose, PowerPoint displays your presentation at a preset percentage of its full size. The display percentage is the zoom setting that PowerPoint uses. The percentage PowerPoint uses varies, depending on your video driver, the screen resolution you use, and the size of your monitor.

PowerPoint uses a different zoom percentage in each view. The default percentages are designed to provide an optimized view within the window. If you zoom in closer by setting a higher zoom percentage, you reduce the portion of the page that you are able to view.

 T I P Choose the Zoom Control drop-down list and select Fit to make the slide fit completely on the page.

 To change the zoom percentage in any view, select an option from the Zoom Control drop-down list in the Standard toolbar shown in Figure 26.7, or type a new percentage in the Zoom Percentage box.

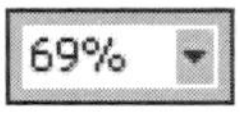

To change the percentage by using a menu command, choose View, Zoom to display the Zoom dialog box. Select a zoom option or type a custom percentage in the Percent box, and then click OK.

Using Slide View

Slide view displays individual slides in the current PowerPoint window. Figure 26.8 shows a presentation displayed in Slide view. This view is the best way to get a detailed picture of each slide. Slide view also is useful when you are entering or changing slide content. To switch from one slide to another, press the Page Up and Page Down keys or use the scroll bar, as described in "Moving Through a Presentation," earlier in this chapter.

Part V

Ch 26

FIG. 26.7
Choose a percentage from the Zoom Control drop-down list, or just type a percentage in the Zoom Control text box.

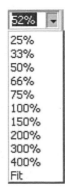

FIG. 26.8
Use Slide view to enter and edit text in individual slides.

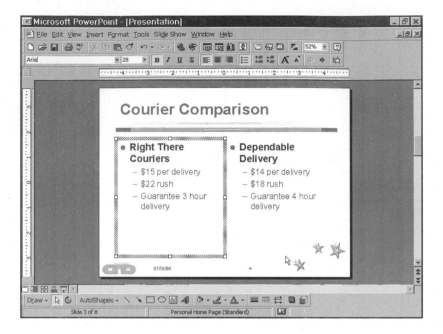

Using Outline View

Outline view displays only the text of multiple slides in outline form, as shown in Figure 26.9. A special set of tools appears to the left of your presentation text in Outline view. A numbered slide icon appears to the left of each slide's title. When a slide contains no pictures or graphics, the slide icon is empty except for a narrow line near the top indicating the title. When a slide contains a picture or other object, the slide icon also contains a graphical representation. This difference helps you identify at a glance which slides contain objects and which slides contain only text.

Also note that a floating window titled Color appears on-screen in the Outline view. If this window doesn't display, choose View, Slide Miniature to turn on. This feature is new to this version of PowerPoint. It displays a miniature view of the slide that relates to where your cursor is resting in the outline. This helps you see how changes to text in this view will appear on your actual slides. The Summary Slide tool, also new to PowerPoint, can automatically generate an agenda slide for your presentation. Highlight the slides you'd like to include in the agenda, and click Summary Slide; a new slide is created with all the selected slide titles in a bulleted list.

  To view only the titles of each slide, click the Collapse All icon; to view all titles and text, click the Expand All icon.

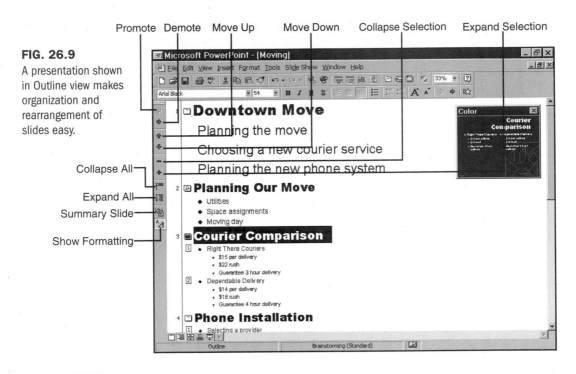

FIG. 26.9
A presentation shown in Outline view makes organization and rearrangement of slides easy.

N O T E You can move slides and their contents around in outline view by clicking and dragging the slide icon to the left of the slide title. To make sure all of a slide's contents move with the title, collapse the outline first. To collapse an outline to just the titles, click the Collapse All icon on the toolbar.

Using Slide Sorter View

Slide Sorter view gives you an overall perspective of your presentation by displaying a miniature version of each slide on a single screen. The number of slides you can view at one time depends on your video card, driver, and monitor, as well as on the zoom percentage used. The lower the zoom percentage, the more slides you can view.

In Slide Sorter view (see Figure 26.10), the slide number appears near the bottom-right corner of each slide. When your presentation output is intended to be a slide show and you've added display durations by rehearsing the presentation, the amount of time each slide is displayed during the slide show appears near the bottom-left corner of each slide.

You can change the order of slides and copy slides in Slide Sorter view. First, you must select a slide.

FIG. 26.10
Notice that the top row of slides in this view has been assigned durations in Rehearse mode.

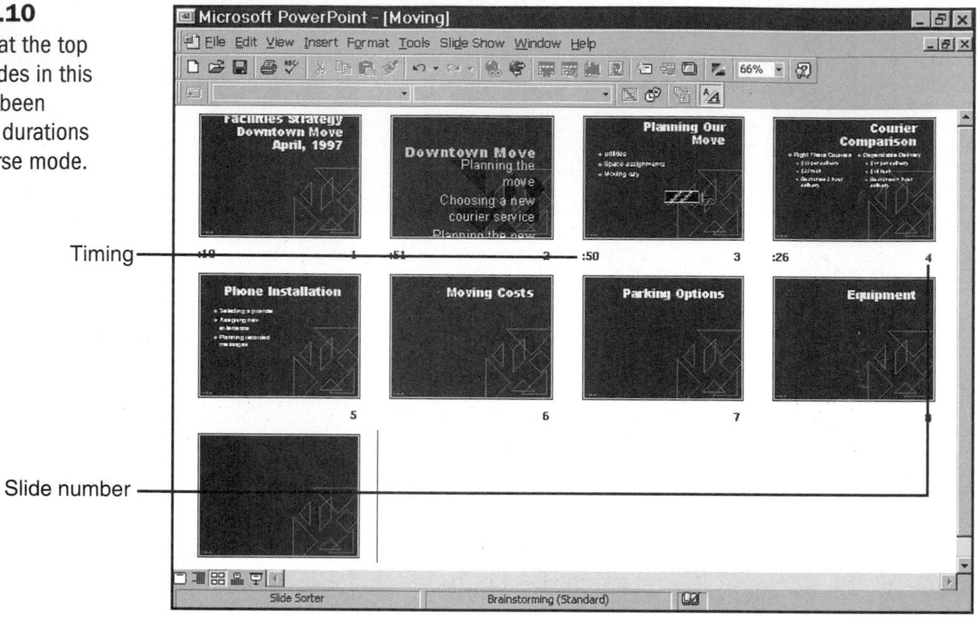

To select a slide in Slide Sorter view, use the arrow keys to highlight a slide, or click the slide you want to select. A bold outline surrounds the selected slide. To select multiple slides, press and hold down the Shift key while clicking all the slides you want to select. Another way to select multiple slides is to click and hold down the left mouse button as you drag an outline around the slides you want to include. To cancel any selection, click any blank area of the Slide Sorter view window.

In Slide Sorter view, rearranging slides is as simple as selecting a slide, and then dragging it to a new location. As you drag the mouse, the mouse pointer changes to a miniature slide with an up arrow. When you move the pointer between two slides, a vertical bar appears to mark the location where the slide will be inserted if you release the mouse button. If you have selected more than one slide, you can move them all at once using this method as well. PowerPoint automatically renumbers the rearranged slides.

Slide Sorter view is the best view to use when copying slides. Select the slide (or slides) you want to copy; then press and hold down the Ctrl key as you drag the slide to the copy location. The mouse pointer changes to a miniature slide with a plus symbol (+), and a vertical bar appears between slides to mark the location where the slide will be inserted.

When you release the mouse button, a copy of the selected slide is inserted in the new location. The slide copy will retain any timing assigned to the original. You can change this by running Rehearse Timings from the Slide Show menu.

TROUBLESHOOTING

I can't select the text on a slide in Slide Sorter view. You cannot edit text or otherwise manipulate individual slide elements when in Slide Sorter view. You can, however, double-click the slide you want to edit to change to Slides view where you can edit.

I can't move slide 2 to slide 1's spot in slide sorter view. To move a slide to another spot, you must click and drag the mouse pointer all the way to the left of the slide until the vertical bar appears. Release the mouse button, and the slide will move.

Using Notes Pages View

PowerPoint provides special notes pages on which you can type notes to be used as you make the presentation. The top half of the page displays a reduced version of the slide; the bottom portion of the page contains a text object in which you can type the text of your notes (see Figure. 26.11).

FIG. 26.11
A slide presentation can be shown in Notes Pages view. To better see the notes on-screen, zoom to 75% or 100%.

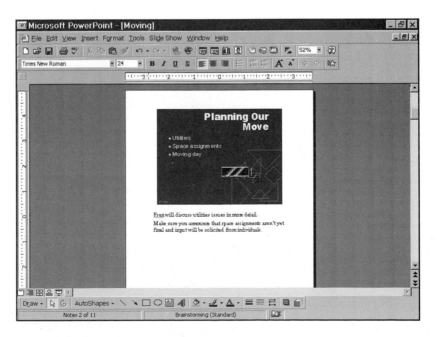

Part
V

Ch
26

At PowerPoint's default zoom percentage, Notes Pages view displays an entire page on-screen. When you are typing or editing speaker's notes, however, it's difficult to read the text at the default percentage. If you use a larger percentage (such as 66 or 75), the text you type is more readable, and you still can view part of the slide content as you type. Another option is to select the text and use the Increase Font Size tool or Font Size drop-down list to make the text more legible.

 To change the view to Notes Pages, click the Notes Pages View icon on the horizontal scroll bar, or choose <u>V</u>iew, <u>N</u>otes Page.

Using Slide Show View

Slide Show view enables you to see each slide in your presentation at maximum size. When you use this view, the PowerPoint window is not visible; each slide occupies the complete screen area, as shown in Figure 26.12. If your final output is intended to be an on-screen slide show, Slide Show view is useful for previewing your slides to see how they will look during the actual slide show.

▶ **See** "Running a Slide Show," **p. 688**

> **N O T E** Slide Show view displays your slides starting with the slide displayed before you switch views. If you want the slide show to begin at slide 1, be sure to select slide 1 before switching to Slide Show view. You can also press Home to move to the first slide, and End to move to the last slide in a presentation. ■

FIG. 26.12
A presentation shown in Slide Show view can be run on-screen for customers to see.

Saving a Presentation

When you save a presentation, PowerPoint saves *all* components of the presentation (slides, outline, speaker's notes, and handout pages) in one file.

 T I P To quickly save changes to an existing file, press Ctrl+S.

 You save a file in PowerPoint the same way you save a file in any other Microsoft Office application. The first time you save a file, PowerPoint displays the Save As dialog box, regardless of whether you choose File, Save, or File, Save As. When you want to save an existing file under a different name, on a different disk or directory, or as a different file type, choose File, Save As. When you want to save changes to an existing file, choose File, Save, or click the Save icon.

You can name the file by using long file names as you would in any other Windows 95 application.

 This latest version of PowerPoint also allows you to make a Web page out of any presentation by saving it in HTML format. To do so, choose File, Save as HTML. The Internet Assistant then appears and walks you through this simple process.

> **N O T E** You can also save your presentation as an animation file and place it as an object in any HTML document. Then, when someone viewing that HMTL document activates your presentation, he or she can watch it as if it were a running animation. Simply save the file in the PowerPoint Show file format; then, from the HTML document, embed that file as you would any animation file. When the viewer of that document clicks on that embedded object, the slide show plays. ■

Part
V
Ch
26

Opening an Existing Presentation

You open a PowerPoint presentation using the same method you use to open any file in any of the Microsoft Office applications.

▶ **See** "Working with Files," **p. 94**

As in many applications, you can open several files at the same time. The active presentation appears on top of the others, and its title bar is highlighted. As with all Windows applications, the names of all open presentation files are listed in the Window menu and appear on the taskbar.

Closing a Presentation

To close an existing presentation, choose File, Close, or double-click the presentation window's Control menu box. If you have made changes in the file since you last saved it, PowerPoint asks whether you want to save those changes. Choose Yes to save the changes, No to ignore the changes, or Cancel to return to the presentation without saving the file. ●

CHAPTER 27

Entering Slide Content

by Rick Winter and Nancy Stevenson

PowerPoint slides can contain much more than just text. You can insert clip art, pictures, tables, worksheets, graphs, organization charts, and many other types of objects into your slides. This chapter begins by teaching you how to choose a slide layout and how to enter and edit slide text. You also learn the steps required for entering information other than text (such as pictures, tables, and graphs). ■

Work with AutoLayout

AutoLayout is a PowerPoint feature that makes arranging the contents of your slides simple.

Enter and edit text

PowerPoint's text formatting facilities will be familiar to you if you've used Word, and are just about as powerful.

Insert clip art, tables, and worksheets

Placing pictures and tables of helpful information on your slides can enhance any PowerPoint presentation, and it's easy to do.

Insert graphs, organization charts, and other objects

With the aid of applets and other Office applications, the possibilities for charts and graphs are practically limitless.

Reviewing AutoLayout

In Chapter 25, "Getting Acquainted with PowerPoint," you were briefly introduced to AutoLayout, a PowerPoint feature that includes 24 prepared slide layouts with different object placeholders and arrangements. Using AutoLayout, you can choose a slide layout that contains the object placeholders you need for your current slide. A title slide, for example, contains two text object placeholders: one for a title and one for a subtitle. After you select a slide layout, you insert the actual content of your presentation—text, pictures, and graphs—into the placeholders on the slide.

 T I P Scroll in the Slide Layout window to display more slide layouts than the first 12 you see on-screen.

Whenever you add a new slide to a presentation, PowerPoint automatically displays the Slide Layout or New Slide dialog box, which contains the 24 AutoLayouts (see Figure 27.1).

FIG. 27.1

Use the Slide Layout/ New Slide dialog box to choose a layout for a slide.

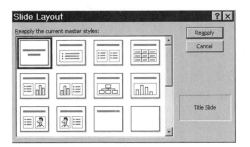

N O T E The dialog box shown in Figure 27.1 is titled Slide Layout or New Slide, depending on the method you use to display it. The contents of the dialog box are always the same, regardless of the name shown in the title bar. To avoid confusion, this chapter refers to this dialog box as the Slide Layout dialog box from here on. ▪

As you select the different AutoLayouts, a description of the highlighted layout appears in the bottom-right corner of the dialog box. This description names the types of objects included in the layout, such as title slide, table, bulleted list, organization chart, and so on.

The solid gray lines at the top of each slide layout represent the slide title; the subtitle on the Title layout is also a solid gray line. Other text in a slide layout is represented by faint gray lines. Text is nearly always formatted with bullets. The placeholders that contain vertical bars represent graphs, and those with pictures represent clip art or pictures.

The empty boxes represent placeholders for other objects, usually imported from other applications, such as Excel. Though not visible in Figure 27.1, if you scroll down in the list of layouts, you'll see a couple of layouts with a small movie slate symbol (a slate is the rectangular panel clicked at the start of a scene when filming a movie). This slate symbol represents some form of media clip.

Highlight the layout you want to use for your new slide and then choose OK, or double-click the layout you want to use. PowerPoint automatically applies the selected layout to the new slide, complete with placeholders for objects. After you choose a layout, you can easily replace the sample in each placeholder with actual text or another object, such as a graph or table.

N O T E Notice that one slide layout in the Slide Layout dialog box is blank; it contains no placeholder. Use this layout when you want to create and place text and the objects in a slide. ▪

 The slide layout can be changed at any time. You can display the Slide Layout dialog box by clicking the Slide Layout button on the Standard toolbar, or by choosing Format, Slide Layout. You can also use the Slide Layout command from the Common Tasks floating toolbar.

> **CAUTION**
> After you enter information in a placeholder, be careful about changing the slide layout. The objects that contain information remain in the slide while the placeholders for the new layout are added. PowerPoint tries to rearrange objects so that all of them will fit, but this isn't always possible. The slide can become cluttered with overlapping objects and placeholders, and sometimes an object will be deleted.

Entering and Editing Text

Virtually every slide in a presentation contains text of some kind, even if it's just a title. Entering and editing text in PowerPoint is similar to entering and editing text in any Office application. The following sections describe how to enter the text content of your slides and how to edit the text when necessary.

▶ **See** "Typing and Editing," **p. 66**

▶ **See** "Using Undo," **p. 74**

Typing the Content for Your Slides

One method of entering slide text involves replacing the sample text in a slide placeholder with your own text. The slide shown in Figure 27.2, for example, includes two placeholders for text: one that contains a sample title and one that contains a bulleted list. The third placeholder is for clip art. A faint dotted line appears around each placeholder.

FIG. 27.2

This slide layout contains two placeholders for text and one placeholder for clip art.

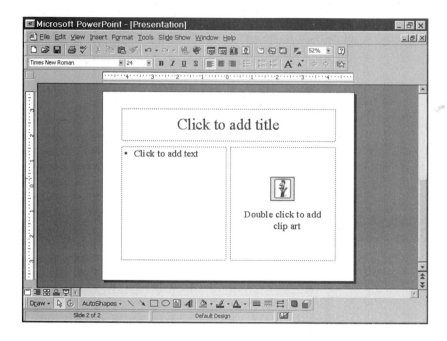

Click anywhere within a placeholder to select it. The faint outline is replaced by a wide, hashed border, shown in Figure 27.3. This border indicates that the current placeholder is selected. The sample text disappears, and an insertion point appears inside the placeholder, indicating that you can enter text. In a title or subtitle placeholder, the insertion point can be centered or left-aligned. In a bulleted-list placeholder, the sample text disappears and the bullet remains, with the insertion point positioned where the text will begin.

Type the actual text for your slide inside the selected placeholder. In the case of titles and subtitles, press Enter only when you want to begin a new centered line of text. In the case of bullets, press Enter only when you want to begin a new bulleted item. If your bulleted text is too long to fit on one line, PowerPoint automatically wraps the text to the next line and aligns the text appropriately.

When you finish entering text, deselect the object by clicking a blank area of the slide or the gray border around the slide. Notice that the object no longer is defined by the faint dotted line (see Figure 27.4). The absence of the dotted line gives you a more realistic idea of how the completed slide will look.

FIG. 27.3
A selected text placeholder is indicated by a wide, hashed border.

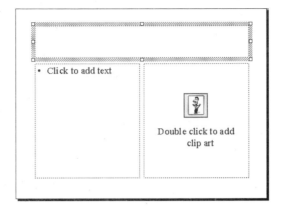

FIG. 27.4
When a text object contains actual text, it is no longer surrounded by a dotted border.

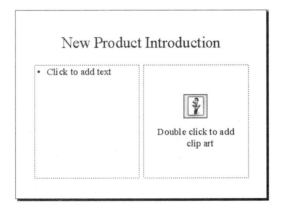

Creating New Text Objects

You may need to add a label or other text that is not part of a placeholder. Suppose that your slide contains a title and a bulleted list like the one shown in Figure 27.5. If you want to add a slogan in the lower-left corner, you could add the note as a separate object and move it around your slide as you like.

To create a text object, follow these steps:

1. Click the Text box button in the Drawing toolbar.
2. Position the pointer where you want the text box to be.
3. Click the mouse button. A text box the size of one character appears. An insertion point is visible in the text box.

T I P You can also click your slide and drag the Text tool to create a rectangle of any size in which the added text will go.

4. Type the desired text. The text box expands to accommodate the text you enter. If you want to type on a new line, press Enter.

FIG. 27.5
Text notes can be added anywhere on a slide.

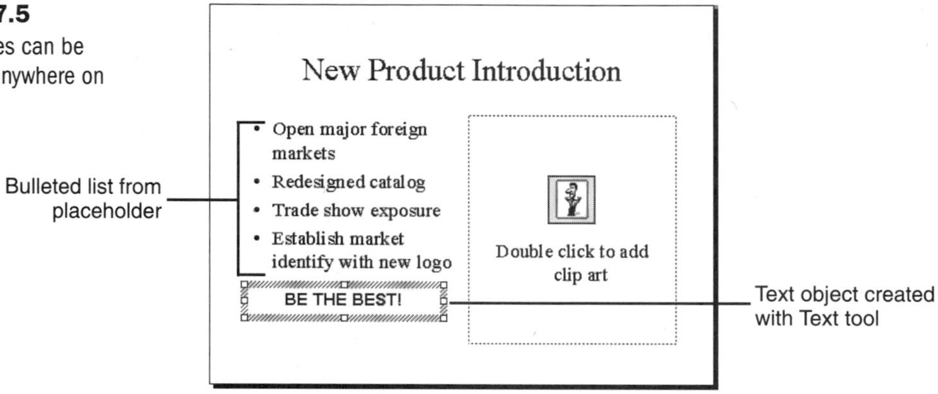

Bulleted list from placeholder

New Product Introduction

- Open major foreign markets
- Redesigned catalog
- Trade show exposure
- Establish market identify with new logo

BE THE BEST!

Double click to add clip art

Text object created with Text tool

TROUBLESHOOTING

I selected an AutoLayout that contains bullets, but I've decided not to use bullets. How do I get rid of them? Click the Bullets button on the Formatting toolbar to add or remove bullets. To change the type of character used for the bullet, choose Format, Bullet, or right-click a bullet item and choose Bullet from the shortcut menu.

Changing Text and Correcting Errors

Text in any text object can be made available for making changes to it by clicking the object. An insertion point appears, indicating that you are able to edit the text. Use standard editing conventions to change text, as summarized in Table 27.1.

▶ **See** "Selecting Text," **p. 73**

Table 27.1 Editing Conventions for Text Objects

Action	Result
Arrow keys	Move the insertion point right, left, up, or down within the text.

Action	Result
Backspace or Delete	Erases characters (to the left and right, respectively) of the insertion point. Also clears selected text from the object without placing it in the Clipboard.
Click and drag the mouse	Selects a string of characters.
Double-click a word	Selects the entire word.
Triple-click a line/paragraph	Selects the entire line (title) or paragraph (bullet item).
Ctrl+A	Selects all text in a selected text object.
Ctrl+*click*	Selects an entire sentence.
Ctrl+X	Cuts selected text and places it in the Clipboard.
Ctrl+C	Copies selected text to the Clipboard.
Ctrl+V	Pastes text from the Clipboard.

In addition to the keyboard shortcuts listed in Table 27.1, you can use the Cut, Copy, Paste, Clear, and Select All commands (on the Edit menu) to edit text. When text is selected on a slide, the Cut, Copy, and Paste commands also appear when you click the right mouse button to display the shortcut menu.

A new feature in this version of PowerPoint, called Expand Slide, allows you to easily break up the points on a single slide into several individual slides. Display a slide with a great deal of text on it, and then choose Tools, Expand Slide. PowerPoint breaks up the text on a busy slide to create several slides. This helps ensure a cleaner, easy-to-read presentation.

You can click the border of a selected text block to reveal handles; drag a corner or side handle to resize the text block. However, any text block will automatically resize itself to accommodate the amount of text you enter.

When you finish editing text in a text box, be sure to click any blank area of the slide or the gray area surrounding the slide to deselect the text box.

If you want to keep track of changes you make to your presentation, you can use Outlook. To do this, you have to display the Reviewing toolbar, and then select Create Microsoft Outlook Task. Tracking changes in Outlook can be especially helpful if more than one person makes changes to a presentation.

▶ **See** "Working with Tasks," **p. 1112**

Checking Your Spelling in PowerPoint

You can set up PowerPoint for automatic spell checking using the Automatic Spell It feature. When a word doesn't match a dictionary entry, it appears on-screen with a wavy red line under it, alerting you to potential misspellings as you type. To turn this feature on, select Tools, Options. On the Spelling tab of the Options dialog box, choose the check box for Check Spelling as You Type section.

The spelling checker in PowerPoint compares all the words in your document with a dictionary file, much the way any Microsoft Office application does. When the spelling checker finds a word that's not in the dictionary file, it highlights the word in your slide and displays the word in the Spelling dialog box, shown in Figure 27.6.

▶ **See** "Checking Spelling," **p. 86**

FIG. 27.6
The Spelling dialog box displays unrecognized words.

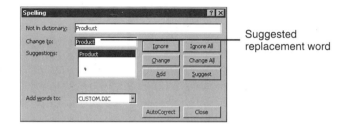

Suggested
replacement word

N O T E   The spelling checker checks text in all objects in a presentation file except those objects that contain text imported from other applications. ▪

The spelling checker moves through your presentation one slide at a time, and then checks the speaker's notes (if any) before closing the Spelling dialog box. You can stop using the spelling checker at any time by clicking the Close button in the Spelling dialog box.

To check the spelling in a presentation file, follow these steps:

1. Choose Tools, Spelling or click the Spelling button on the Standard toolbar to display the Spelling dialog box. The spelling checker highlights the first unrecognized word in the presentation file and displays the word in the Not in Dictionary box.

2. Choose the appropriate command button (Ignore, Ignore All, Change, Change All, or Add). The spelling checker takes the indicated action and then highlights the next unrecognized word.

3. Repeat step 2 until the spelling checker displays a message saying that the entire presentation has been checked.

4. Choose OK.

   ▶ **See** "Letting AutoCorrect Do Your Spelling for You," **p. 89**

N O T E   You can use PowerPoint's AutoCorrect feature (Tools, AutoCorrect) to automatically correct common typing errors. If, for example, you constantly type **wrod** instead of **word**, you can add this to the AutoCorrect list and as you type the wrong letters, PowerPoint automatically corrects your typing.

Inserting Clip-Art Pictures

One of the best ways to spice up a slide show is to insert a clip-art drawing. The Clip Gallery contains many drawings that cover a wide range of topics.

▶ **See** "Using Microsoft Clip Gallery 3.0," **p. 528**

N O T E   You can insert clip art into a slide in several ways. If you have selected a slide layout with a clip-art placeholder, simply double-click the placeholder to choose a clip-art file to insert.

 You can also insert clip art on a slide without a clip-art placeholder by choosing Insert, Picture, then selecting Clip Art from the cascading menu that appears. You can also click the Insert Clip Art button on the Standard toolbar. Regardless of the method used to access clip art, the next step is to select a file in the Clip Gallery 3.0 dialog box.

 T I P   If you want the clip art on every slide in the presentation, insert it on the Slide Master.

To add a clip-art drawing to your slide, follow these steps:

1. Display the slide into which you want to insert clip art.

2. Choose Insert, Picture, Clip Art; click the Clip Art button on the standard toolbar; or, if your slide contains a clip-art placeholder, double-click it. The Microsoft Clip Gallery dialog box appears.

3. Select the Clip Art tab, then choose a category in the category list. If you're not sure of a category, choose All Categories to preview all pictures in the Gallery.

4. Select a picture, and then click OK. PowerPoint closes the Clip Gallery dialog box and inserts the picture into your slide. Figure 27.7 shows a slide with a clip-art picture.

Part

V

Ch

27

FIG. 27.7
Add clip art to a slide to make the presentation more interesting and to make it look more professional.

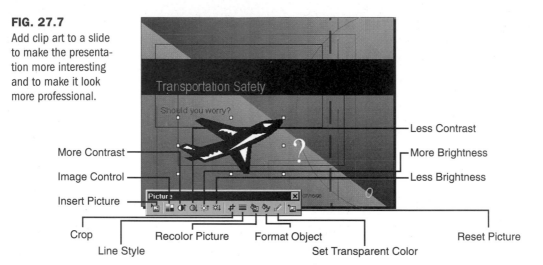

Notice that with a picture inserted and selected, the Picture toolbar may automatically appear on your screen. The names of the tools available here are indicated by callouts in Figure 27.7.

Inserting Other Media

The Clip Gallery contains more than clip art. It's part of a large collection of media called Office Art. You can access the many media files in Office Art by using the Clip Gallery tabs that contain controls for inserting pictures, sounds, and even video animation into your presentation. There is a button on each of these tabs to import media from the World Wide Web. When you select this button, you are connected to Internet Explorer, which you can use to browse an additional page of downloadable images at Microsoft's Web site. If you use any of these clips, they will automatically be added to your Clip Gallery for future use.

▶ **See** "Inserting Movies, Animations, and Video Clips," **p. 544**

The options on these tabs are virtually identical to the options on the Clip Art tab. However, the Sounds and Videos tabs have an additional button called Play. This button allows you to preview sounds and videos before placing these large files in your presentation.

Letting PowerPoint Choose Art for You

Best of 97

You can also have PowerPoint pick the art for your presentation. Follow these steps:

1. Choose Tools, AutoClipArt. PowerPoint will take awhile to analyze your presentation and then go to the AutoClipArt dialog box as shown in Figure 27.8.

FIG. 27.8
Click View Clip Art to
see which clip-art
figures PowerPoint
found that match
words in your
presentation.

2. Select the word from the drop-down list on the left side of the dialog box.

3. To add the art, click the View Clip Art button. Then select one of the objects found in the ClipArt Gallery, and choose the Insert button. If you don't want to insert the picture, choose the Close button.

4. Repeat steps 2 and 3 and choose Cancel or click the Close button when finished.

5. Move or resize the pictures as necessary when you return to the presentation.

T I P PowerPoint may find more than one object that matches a word in your presentation. If there is more than one choice, select the object in the Pictures box and then choose Insert to add the object you want to the slide.

Inserting a Word Table or Excel Worksheet

A table of data can convey useful information on a slide. Although PowerPoint's text-editing tools don't provide the means to create a table, PowerPoint enables you to use Word or Excel to create the tables you need.

To create a worksheet or table, click the Insert Microsoft Excel Worksheet button or the Insert Microsoft Word Table button in the Standard toolbar. A drop-down grid of cells appears. This grid enables you to define the size of your table or worksheet, as shown in Figure 27.9. Click and drag the mouse pointer across the cells in the grid to indicate how many rows or columns you want in your table or worksheet. The cells you select are highlighted, and the dimensions are listed below the grid.

Part
V

Ch
27

Insert Microsoft Word Table button

FIG. 27.9
Use the grid to
choose the number of
rows and columns for
the Word table to be
inserted.

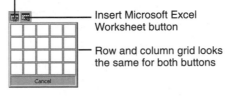

Insert Microsoft Excel
Worksheet button

Row and column grid looks
the same for both buttons

When you release the mouse button, PowerPoint inserts a special object into your slide. In the case of a Microsoft Word table, the object looks like the one shown in Figure 27.10. Notice that PowerPoint's Standard toolbar and menu bar are temporarily replaced by the Word menus and toolbar, so that all Word features and commands are available to you while you create your table. In effect, you are using Word inside a PowerPoint window.

▶ **See** "Working with Tables," **p. 280**

▶ **See** "Editing Worksheet Data," **p. 322**

FIG. 27.10

Inserting a Word table provides Word's formatting flexibility.

Word menu and toolbars

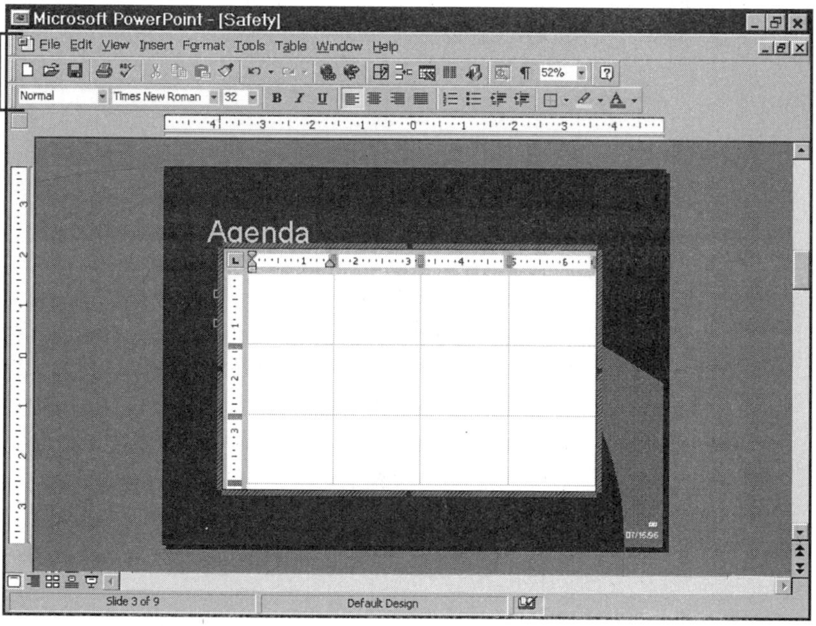

To create the content of your table, click the area in which you want to add text, or press Tab to move the insertion point from left to right across the cells in the table. Press the up- and down-arrow keys to move the insertion point from one row to another. Use standard editing conventions to enter and edit text in the table.

When your table is complete, deselect it by clicking any blank area outside the table or the gray area that surrounds the slide. When the table no longer is the selected object, the PowerPoint menus and toolbar return. You can make changes in the table at any time by double-clicking inside the table. When the table is selected again, the Word menus and toolbar return automatically. Figure 27.11 shows a completed Word table on a PowerPoint slide.

FIG. 27.11
Move a completed
Word table by
selecting it and then
dragging it to a new
position.

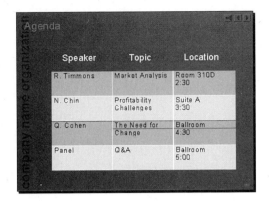

 T I P Resize the table by dragging one of the corner or side handles.

 The same principles that govern Word tables hold true for Excel worksheets: when you
insert a worksheet, you enter, edit, and format the data in Excel and then click outside
of the worksheet to return to PowerPoint. When you click the Insert Excel Worksheet
button in the PowerPoint toolbar, a drop-down grid appears. Click and drag the mouse
pointer across the cells in the grid to indicate the number of rows and columns for your
worksheet. PowerPoint inserts a special worksheet object into your slide, and Power-
Point's standard menus and toolbar are replaced by the Excel menus and toolbar.

T I P Select the text in the table and change the typeface, size, attributes, alignment, and so on, just as
you would any text in Word.

Use Excel's commands and tools to create and edit your worksheet. When the worksheet
is complete, deselect it by clicking any blank area of the slide or the border of the slide;
the standard PowerPoint menus and toolbar return.

▶ **See** "Formatting Text," **p. 172**

▶ **See** "Entering Data," **p. 303**

▶ **See** "Editing Worksheet Data," **p. 322**

▶ **See** "Formatting Numbers," **p. 344**

▶ **See** "Starting Microsoft Graph," **p. 468**

N O T E Graphs, or *charts*, are graphic representations of data in worksheets. In a presentation, a bar, pie, or area chart often can depict data much more clearly than words can.
In PowerPoint, you can insert a graph into a slide by using an application called Microsoft Graph
or by copying a graph from Microsoft Excel. ■

Part
V

Ch
27

Inserting an Organization Chart

Organization charts can be added to PowerPoint presentations. An organization chart can convey information about new management, a group or department reorganization, or people to contact for specific types of information.

▶ **See** "Using Microsoft Organization Chart 2.0," **p. 531**

To insert an organization chart into a PowerPoint slide, you can use a slide layout that includes a placeholder for an organization chart. Choose F<u>o</u>rmat, Slide <u>L</u>ayout, or click the Slide Layout button on the Standard toolbar to display the Slide Layout dialog box (see Figure 27.12).

 You can also add an organization chart by choosing <u>I</u>nsert, <u>O</u>bject, and then choosing MS Organization Chart from the resulting dialog box. To create a new slide that contains an organizational chart, choose the New Slide button on the toolbar and the New Slide dialog box appears, offering identical options to the Slide Layout dialog box.

FIG. 27.12

The Organization Chart layout is selected in the Slide Layout dialog box.

Organizational Chart Slide

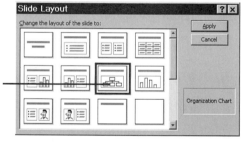

In the dialog box, highlight the layout that includes the organization chart; then click OK. PowerPoint applies the layout to the current slide, inserting an organization-chart placeholder. To access Microsoft Organization Chart, double-click the placeholder. After a few seconds, the Microsoft Organization Chart window appears (see Figure 27.13).

Enter the appropriate information in the sample organization chart, using Microsoft Organization Chart commands. Because Microsoft Organization Chart is a separate application, it contains its own help files. If you are not familiar with this application, select any of the topics listed in the <u>H</u>elp menu or press F1.

 Double-click the chart to open the MS Organization Chart application and edit the chart.

When the organization chart is complete and you're ready to return to your PowerPoint presentation, first choose <u>F</u>ile, <u>U</u>pdate Presentation. Then select <u>F</u>ile, E<u>x</u>it and Return to

Presentation. The organization chart is inserted into the current slide. To deselect the organization chart, click any blank area of the slide or the gray area surrounding the slide.

FIG. 27.13

The MS Organization Chart application enables you to create simple or complex charts for your presentation.

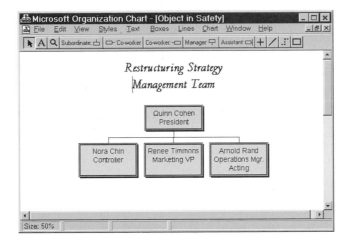

Inserting Other Objects

In this chapter, you have learned how to insert clip art, a Word table, an Excel worksheet, and an organization chart into a PowerPoint slide. You can insert many other types of objects by choosing Insert, Object. This command opens another application on top of your PowerPoint window, enabling you to create a new file or open an existing file within that application. This version of PowerPoint supports more file format versions than ever before, including JPEG, WMP, EPS, PICT, and GIF formats.

▶ **See** "Using the Insert Object Command," **p. 524**

To insert a new file from another application, follow these steps:

1. Display the PowerPoint slide into which you want to insert an object.
2. Choose Insert, Object. PowerPoint displays the Insert Object dialog box (see Figure 27.14). The Object Type list displays all the types of files you can insert into a PowerPoint slide.

Part
V

Ch
27

FIG. 27.14

The Insert Object dialog box lists several types of objects that can be inserted into a slide.

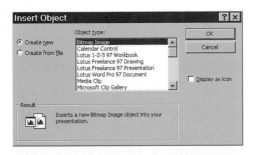

N O T E   Because the Insert Object feature of PowerPoint works by opening another application, you must have that application installed on your computer. ▪

3. Select the Create New option.

4. (Optional) Select the Display As Icon option if you want to display the object as an icon. This merely saves time when working with large graphic object displays on your slides.

5. In the Object Type list, select the object you want to insert; then click OK. The Insert Object dialog box closes, and the window for the appropriate application opens on top of the PowerPoint window.

6. Use the application as you normally would. That is, create a new file if necessary, or simply select an item (such as an equation or a clip-art file). For cases in which you select an item, PowerPoint inserts the item and closes the application. For cases in which you create a new file, return to PowerPoint by choosing the Exit and Return to [*file name*] command from the open application's File menu. The application window closes, and the file you created is inserted into the current PowerPoint slide.

7. Click any blank area of the slide or the gray area surrounding the slide to deselect the object.

▶ **See** "Inserting an Object from a File," **p. 542**

If you want to insert an existing file created in another application into your slide, select the Create From File option in the Insert Object dialog box. When you insert an existing file from another application, the file is inserted into the PowerPoint slide directly; PowerPoint does not open the application that was used to create the file. If you want to modify the file, you must open the application by double-clicking the object after it is inserted into your PowerPoint slide.

To insert an existing file from another application, follow these steps:

1. Display the PowerPoint slide into which you want to insert an object.

2. Choose Insert, Object. PowerPoint displays the Insert Object dialog box.

3. Select the Create From File option. PowerPoint modifies the Insert Object dialog box to match the one shown in Figure 27.15.

4. If you know the name of the file, type the complete path name in the File box. If not, click the Browse button, which displays the Browse dialog box with a directory tree. Select the correct file name, and then click OK. The Browse dialog box closes, and you return to the Insert Object dialog box, where the file name you selected now appears in the File box.

FIG. 27.15

The Insert Object dialog box changes if you choose to create from file instead of creating a new object.

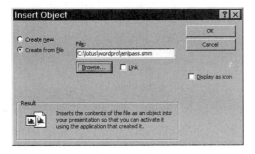

5. (Optional) Select the <u>D</u>isplay As Icon option if you want to display the object as an icon.

6. Click OK in the Insert Object dialog box. The file you specified is inserted into your PowerPoint slide *without* opening the application used to create the file.

7. Click any blank area of the slide or the gray area surrounding the slide to deselect the inserted object.

N O T E You can also use cut and paste or drag and drop functions to move elements contained in another application into a PowerPoint presentation. For example, you could open a Word document, copy a table, then go back into PowerPoint and use the paste function to paste it on a slide. However, the Insert feature streamlines this by opening the other application within the PowerPoint window, and you can edit the inserted object back in its original application just by double-clicking it. You can't edit a pasted object in that same way. ▪

TROUBLESHOOTING

I can't select the text or object on my slide. The text or object is on the slide master. Choose <u>V</u>iew, <u>M</u>aster, and then choose <u>S</u>lide Master or <u>T</u>itle Master. After editing the text or object, choose <u>V</u>iew, <u>S</u>lides.

I inserted a clip-art image and now I can't replace it with another clip-art image by double-clicking the object. If the clip-art gallery doesn't appear when you double-click a clip-art image, you've converted the image to a PowerPoint object. To replace the object, select it, delete it, and then insert a new clip-art object.

CHAPTER 28

Working with Objects

by Nancy Stevenson

You were introduced to objects in Chapter 25, "Getting Acquainted with PowerPoint," and you learned more about entering content in objects in Chapter 27, "Entering Slide Content." Objects are the building blocks of slides that contain primarily text, graphics, or pictures, but also can contain other elements such as tables, spreadsheets, or organization charts. You need to understand how to work with objects because they are the key components of a PowerPoint slide. ■

Select and group objects

Single objects can be grouped together so you can move them, make formatting changes, and even rotate them as a unit.

Move, copy, resize, and delete objects

Being able to duplicate, resize and move objects around your presentation page gives you great flexibility in designing exciting slides.

Align objects

PowerPoint offers several tools to help you arrange objects on your slides, including alignment commands for not only left, right, and center, but also top, middle, and bottom positions.

Use the grid

Another tool to help you position objects is the grid, which offers pinpoint accuracy to place objects on your slide.

Rotate and flip objects

Don't like the arrangement of objects on your slide? Turn them up, down, right, or left till you get just the effect you desire.

Stack objects

PowerPoint allows you to organize objects so that one appears to be behind another, creating a more three-dimensional feel to your images.

Selecting and Grouping Objects

Before you can make any kind of change to an object such as adding color, changing size, moving, or deleting it, you must select the object. Selecting a single object is as simple as clicking it. When you click an object such as a chart, Clip art drawing, or organization chart, *resize handles* surround the object in a rectangular shape. When you click a text object, a gray border appears; click the border to display the handles (see Figure 28.1). Resize handles are small boxes that appear at the four corners and on each of the four sides of the rectangle. Resize handles indicate that an object has been selected. In "Resizing and Scaling Objects" later in this chapter, you'll learn how to use these handles to change the size of an object.

▶ **See** "Drawing Shapes," **p. 560**

▶ **See** "Understanding Objects and Layouts," **p. 604**

FIG. 28.1
An object is selected when its resize handles are visible.

Resize handles

Selecting Multiple Objects

In PowerPoint, you generally select an object to move, copy, or resize it, or to change one or more of its attributes. An *attribute* is any characteristic that is applied to an object, such as color, border, fill, and shadow. Sometimes you may want to select more than one object at a time. Selecting multiple objects can save you the time of applying the same attribute to several objects individually. When you select multiple objects, any attribute you change is applied to *all* selected objects. To change the fill color of several objects to blue, for instance, select all objects and then apply the blue fill color.

To select multiple objects at once, press and hold down the Shift key and then click each object you want to include in the selection. The resize handles appear around each object you select (see Figure 28.2). If you select an object by mistake and want to remove it from your selection, continue holding down the Shift key while you click the object again. PowerPoint removes that object from the selection. Release the Shift key when you have selected all objects.

FIG. 28.2
In a multiple selection, resize handles appear around each selected object.

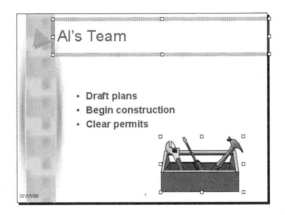

Another way to select multiple objects at once is to use the Selection Tool button on the Drawing toolbar. Click the Selection Tool button, and drag the mouse across all objects you want to include in the selection. As you drag the mouse, PowerPoint draws a dashed rectangle that encloses all selected objects. When you release the mouse button, the rectangle disappears, and the resize handles of each object in the selection are visible.

▶ **See** "Getting Familiar with the PowerPoint Window," **p. 590**

N O T E You must fully enclose all objects within the selection rectangle you draw. If a portion of any object is not enclosed within the rectangle, that object is excluded from the selection. You can add an object to any selection by holding down the Shift key and clicking the object. ■

To quickly select every object on a slide, choose <u>E</u>dit, Select A<u>l</u>l, or press Ctrl+A. PowerPoint immediately displays the selection handles of all objects on the slide.

TROUBLESHOOTING

When I draw a selection box around several objects, some objects are not selected.
Remember that you must fully enclose all objects you want to select in the selection box.
If a portion of an object falls outside the selection box, it isn't selected.

Can I select objects on multiple slides at once? No. The only way to view multiple slides at
once is to use slide sorter view, and you cannot select objects in this view.

I try to select the company logo on my slide, but nothing happens. Why? The logo probably
was inserted into the slide master rather than the individual slide. To select the logo, switch to
Slide Master view (choose View, Master, Slide Master, or press Shift and click the Slide Master
View button in the lower left corner of the window); then select the object. Any changes you make
affect the object on all slides.

▶ **See** "Viewing a Presentation," **p. 614**

Grouping Objects

Grouping objects enables you to treat several objects as a single object. Suppose, for example, that you use PowerPoint's drawing tools to draw a company logo (see Figure 28.3)
made up of more than one object. Each object comprising the logo can be manipulated
independently. Once designed, however, the logo will be used as a single object. Grouping
these objects allows any attributes you choose, such as size, position, or rotation, to be
applied to the grouped object as a whole.

To group several objects, select the objects by using one of the methods you just learned
(by pressing the Shift key or Selection Tool button, or by choosing Edit, Select All). The
resize handles for each object are displayed. Now select the pop-up Draw menu from the
drawing toolbar, and choose Group. The object is now surrounded by an invisible rectangle, indicated by resize handles at the four corners and along each side of the rectangle.
When you select the object in the future, it appears as a single object with one set of resize
handles (see Figure 28.4).

To select an object that's beneath another object, hold the Ctrl key while clicking the top object;
the selection handles indicate which object is selected.

FIG. 28.3
You can use
PowerPoint tools with
drawings comprised
of more than one
object. This logo
contains an oval, an
arrow, and some text.

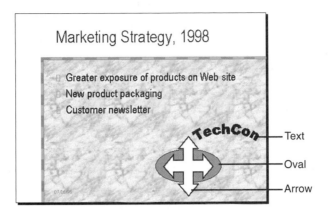

FIG. 28.4
Multiple objects are
grouped as a single
object for easier
editing and
formatting.

Draw ▾ Sometimes you only want to group multiple objects temporarily. Suppose that you have
moved or resized your company logo and now you want to apply different attributes to its
various components. To separate grouped objects, select the grouped object; then choose
Draw, Ungroup. PowerPoint separates the objects, and each object's selection handles are
visible once again on the slide.

Moving and Copying Objects

Moving an object on a slide is as simple as clicking and dragging the object to a new
location. As you drag the mouse to a new location, the object stays in its original location
on the slide while a dotted-line silhouette of the object follows your mouse movements
around the screen. Release the mouse button when the silhouette of the object is positioned correctly. PowerPoint then moves the object to its new location.

Part
V

Ch
28

To move an object from one slide to another or from one presentation to another, choose Edit, Cut and Edit, Paste, or use the keyboard shortcuts Ctrl+X and Ctrl+V, respectively. Follow these steps:

 TIP You can right-click an object to reveal the quick menu and then choose Cut, Copy, or Paste.

1. Select the object to be moved.

 2. Choose Edit, Cut, or press Ctrl+X. The selected object is removed from the current slide and placed on the Clipboard.

3. If you are moving the object to another slide in the same presentation, display that slide. If you are moving the object to another presentation, open the presentation and display the correct slide.

 4. Choose Edit, Paste, or press Ctrl+V. PowerPoint pastes the object on the slide being viewed.

5. Position the object as desired on the slide by clicking and dragging the object.

6. Click any blank area of the slide to deselect the object, or press Esc.

The steps for copying an object are similar to those for moving an object except that you choose Edit, Copy rather than Edit, Cut. As when moving an object, you can also copy an object within a slide, within a presentation, or to another presentation.

To copy an object, follow these steps:

1. Select the object to be copied.

 2. Choose Edit, Copy, or press Ctrl+C. The selected object remains unchanged on the current slide, and a copy is placed on the Clipboard.

3. If you are copying the object to another slide in the same presentation, display that slide. If you are moving the object to another presentation, open the presentation and display the correct slide.

 4. Choose Edit, Paste, or press Ctrl+V. PowerPoint pastes the object on the current slide.

5. Position the object as desired on the slide by clicking and dragging the object.

6. Click any blank area of the slide to deselect the object, or press Esc.

For a true shortcut for both the moving and copying processes between presentations, use the drag-and-drop facility provided among Office products by OLE (object linking and embedding) technology. Display both presentations on-screen and, using the commands in the Window menu, arrange these windows so you can view them side by side. To move an object from one presentation to the other, click the object in the first presentation and drag it to the other presentation. When you release your mouse button, the object will appear in the other presentation. To copy an object, press Ctrl and then click the object and drag it. When you release your mouse button, a copy will appear in the other presentation, and the original object will still be intact in the first presentation.

Resizing and Scaling Objects

Throughout this chapter you have seen several examples of the resize handles that become visible when an object or group of objects is selected. To resize an object, you first click the object to select it, and then drag any resize handle to a new position.

The resize handles that appear on the sides of the selection box resize in one dimension only and do not retain the original proportions of the object. For instance, if you click the resize handle at the top of the selection box, you can stretch or shrink the height of an object on its top only; the bottom remains anchored. If you click the right resize handle, you can stretch or shrink the width of an object on its right side only; the left side remains anchored. Release the mouse button when the object is the size you want.

 When you're resizing an object, position the mouse pointer over a handle until it changes to a double-headed arrow, and then drag the handle.

The resize handles that appear at the corners of an object enable you to resize an object in two dimensions at once. If you click the resize handle in the upper right corner of an object, for instance, you can change the height or width of the object by dragging the handle in any direction. Whenever you drag a corner handle, the handle in the opposite corner remains anchored while you expand or contract the object's height and width.

When you resize in two dimensions at once, you may want to maintain an object's height-to-width ratio. To do so, hold down the Shift key as you drag any corner resize handle. The handle in the opposite corner remains anchored while you resize the object. Or you might want to resize in two dimensions at once, from the center of the object outward. To do so, hold down the Ctrl key as you drag any corner handle. By holding both the Shift and Ctrl keys as you drag a corner handle, you can maintain an object's height-to-width ratio *and* resize from the center outward, all in one step.

Another way to resize an object is to scale it. *Scaling* enables you to specify an object's size by percentage. If you want an object to be half its current size, for example, you scale it by 50 percent. To scale an object, choose Format, AutoShape, which displays the Format AutoShape dialog box. (Note that this Object menu command can change slightly

Part

V

Ch

28

depending on the type of object you've selected. For example, with a WordArt object selected, the menu command is WordArt.) Select the Size tab of this dialog box, shown in Figure 28.5.

FIG. 28.5

Adjust the size of an object using the Size tab of the Format AutoShape dialog box.

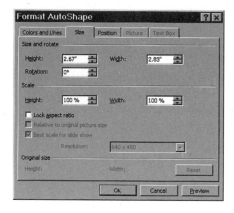

To scale an object, follow these steps:

1. Select the object.

2. Choose Format, Object. The Format Object dialog box appears. Select the Size tab.

3. In the Height and Width boxes, enter a number greater than 100 to enlarge the object; type a number smaller than 100 to reduce the object. You can either type a number or click the up or down arrows to change the setting.

4. To keep the height/width ratio intact, select the Lock Aspect Ratio check box.

5. To preview the object, click Preview. If necessary, use the check boxes and arrow settings to resize the object. When you finish, click OK.

As an alternative to the preceding steps, you can have PowerPoint determine the scale for a picture by selecting the Best Scale for Slide Show option in the Size tab of the Format Object dialog box. This option automatically chooses the best scale for an object to ensure optimal viewing during an on-screen slide show.

Select the Relative to Original Picture Size option to resize the object based on the original size when the object was first inserted or created.

TROUBLESHOOTING

My object is a rectangle one inch wide by two inches high. How can I use the resize handles to add approximately 1/2 inch to the top and bottom of the object uniformly? Hold down the Ctrl key as you drag either the top or bottom resize handle. You also can use the Ctrl key with a side resize handle to add or subtract width uniformly. When used with a corner resize handle, the Ctrl key enables you to resize in two dimensions from the center of the object outward. To help you gauge the measurement of your enlarged object, display rulers on-screen before you resize it.

I entered *100* in the % box to restore an imported picture to its original size, but the picture is still the wrong size, and its dimensions are not correct. When the original dimensions of an imported picture have been altered, choosing 100% scale does not restore them. You must select the Relative To Original Picture Size option as well. This option restores the picture's original height-to-width ratio to the scale you specify (use 100% for the original picture size). If, for example, you select the Relative To Original Picture Size option and enter 200 in the % box for the scale, the original dimensions are restored, and the object is twice its original size.

Aligning Objects

To achieve a neat, professional appearance on your slides, it is helpful to be able to precisely align objects. PowerPoint takes the guesswork out of aligning objects by offering a variety of automatic alignment options. You can use the traditional left, center, or right-alignment styles; or you can align the tops, bottoms, or middles of objects. Each of these alignment options is illustrated in the slide sorter view shown in Figure 28.6.

FIG. 28.6
PowerPoint offers seven automatic alignment styles.

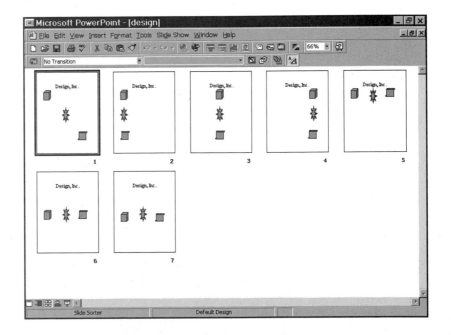

In the figure, slide 1 shows how the objects were originally arranged. Slides 2, 3, and 4 illustrate how the objects are aligned along the left edges of the objects, the horizontal center, and the right edges of the objects, respectively. Slides 5, 6, and 7 show how the objects are aligned at the top, vertical midpoint, and bottom in relationship to each other.

To use any of PowerPoint's alignment options, follow these steps:

1. Select the objects you want to align.

2. Choose <u>D</u>raw, <u>A</u>lign or Distribute. The Align submenu shown in Figure 28.7 appears.

> **CAUTION**
>
> If you do not select two or more objects, the <u>D</u>raw, <u>A</u>lign command will appear dimmed. To select more than one object, hold the Shift key as you click each object.

 TIP   To deselect one object of several, hold the Shift key and click the object you want to deselect.

3. From the submenu shown in Figure 28.7, choose an alignment option. PowerPoint realigns the selected objects.

FIG. 28.7

Choose an alignment from the <u>A</u>lign or Distribute submenu.

 TIP   You cannot apply an alignment to one group of objects but you can align two or more selected groups.

Three more options are offered to you through the Align or Distribute command in the Draw menu. These deal with distributing selected objects across the slide horizontally, vertically, or relative to the slide itself. Here's how each of these works:

- Distribute Horizontally distributes selected objects at an equal distance from each other across the width of the page or equally between the furthest left and right objects.

- Distribute Vertically distributes selected objects at an equal distance from each other across the height of the page or equally between the furthest top and bottom objects.

- To distribute selected objects in relation to the entire slide, select Relative to Slide from the Draw menu. Then, open the menu again and choose any of the alignment or distribute commands. Here's an example of how this works: if you align several objects by the bottoms of the objects, the bottom edges will line up relative to each other. But, if you select Relative to Slide, then Align Bottom, the objects are themselves lined up at the bottom of the slide.

If you have not selected Relative to Slide, which is a function you toggle on and off by selecting it in the Draw menu, you must have at least three objects selected for the Distribute Horizontally and Distribute Vertically commands to be available to you.

Using the Grid

To help you align and position objects on a slide, PowerPoint includes three tools—*guides*, *rulers*, and a *snap* function—that can be toggled on and off with a simple menu command. Guides and rulers are visible markers that appear on a slide to give you a visual reference point.

▶ **See** "Getting Familiar with the PowerPoint Window," **p. 590**

Unlike visible guides and rulers, the snap feature allows you to position objects relative to either a grid or a shape on the grid. A grid is an invisible set of lines that run horizontally and vertically on a slide. The lines (approximately every 1/8 inch) form a grid similar to that of a very fine graph paper.

Using the Snap Feature

When the grid snap feature is turned on, the corners of objects that you draw or move snap into alignment at the nearest intersection of the grid. When you use the To Shape snap feature, you line objects up to grid lines that run through the vertical and horizontal edges of other objects. Using the snap feature helps to make alignment of objects an easier task. The grid is best used when you do not need to align objects more precisely than approximately 1/8 inch.

To turn the snap feature on and off, choose Draw, Snap, then select either To Grid or To Shape. When the grid is turned on, the small button next to the grid or shape command on the side menu appears depressed. (No indicators appear on the main draw menu or in the PowerPoint window.) You also can turn the grid off temporarily by holding down the Alt key as you drag an object to a new location on a slide. If you experiment with pressing the Alt key as you drag an object, you can see for yourself how the snap feature works as you watch the object track smoothly across the screen or snap into place.

 TIP The <u>S</u>nap command is only available in Slides and Notes views.

Nudging Objects

 A feature new to this version of PowerPoint is the <u>N</u>udge command. Use this command when you want to move an object by a small increment in any direction.

To nudge an object, select it, and then choose D<u>r</u>aw, <u>N</u>udge. From the side menu that appears, select a direction: <u>U</u>p, <u>D</u>own, <u>L</u>eft, or <u>R</u>ight. You can also achieve the same effect by selecting an object and using the arrows on the keyboard to designate a direction for the nudge.

Rotating and Flipping Objects

One way to add visual interest to your slides is to rotate or flip an object. *Rotating* refers to turning an object around a 360-degree radius. *Flipping* refers to turning an object over, either horizontally or vertically, to create a mirror image of that object. You can rotate or flip any PowerPoint object.

> **CAUTION**
>
> A PowerPoint object is defined as an object created within PowerPoint using a PowerPoint tool (such as the drawing tools) or an object imported from another program and then converted to a PowerPoint object. To convert an object to a PowerPoint object, you must be able to ungroup its components and then regroup them by choosing <u>D</u>raw, <u>G</u>roup. If you cannot do this, the object cannot be converted to a PowerPoint object and, therefore, cannot be rotated or flipped.

 TIP You cannot flip text objects, although you can rotate text and WordArt objects.

PowerPoint enables you to rotate an object in either of two ways:

■ You can rotate an object to any position in a 360-degree radius.

■ You can rotate an object in 90-degree increments to the left or right, which has the effect of turning the object 1/4 turn.

When you flip an object, you flip it either horizontally or vertically 180 degrees. These choices are illustrated on the Rotate or Flip submenu, shown in Figure 28.8.

FIG. 28.8
Rotation and flipping options are shown in the Rotate or Flip submenu.

To rotate an object by 90 degrees or flip an object 180 degrees, follow these steps:

1. Select the object to rotate.

2. Choose Draw, Rotate or Flip.

3. From the submenu, choose Rotate Left or Rotate Right to rotate the object, or Flip Horizontal or Flip Vertical to flip the object. PowerPoint immediately rotates or flips the object in the direction selected.

4. To rotate the object another 90 degrees, repeat steps 2 and 3.

5. Click any blank area of the slide to deselect the object.

To rotate an object to any angle in a 360-degree radius, use the Free Rotate Tool button on the Drawing toolbar or the Free Rotate command on the Rotate or Flip submenu. The appearance of the mouse pointer changes to reflect which tool is chosen.

To rotate an object to any position on a 360-degree radius, follow these steps:

1. Select the object to rotate.

2. Click the Free Rotate Tool button on the Drawing toolbar, or choose Draw, Rotate or Flip; then choose the Free Rotate command. The mouse pointer changes to a curved arrow that forms a circle with a cursor arrow in the center. In addition, the resize handles of the selected object change to four small circles.

3. Position the mouse pointer on top of any of the object's resize handles. When you have the circular arrow shape centered on a handle, the mouse arrow disappears from the pointer.

4. Click and hold down the left mouse button as you rotate the object either left or right until it is positioned correctly; then release the mouse button.

5. Click any blank area of the slide to deselect the object.

You can rotate or flip several objects at once, and you can rotate or flip grouped objects. When you select multiple objects to rotate or flip, each object rotates or flips independently of the others around its own center point; and each object rotates to the same angle as all others. When you rotate or flip grouped objects, however, the individual objects *do not* rotate or flip independently; they rotate or flip *as a whole*. This difference is illustrated in Figure 28.9.

FIG. 28.9
Multiple objects rotate differently depending on how they are grouped.

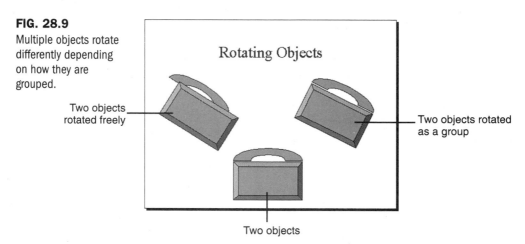

Changing the Stacking Order of Objects

As you add objects to a slide and overlap them, you quickly discover that the object drawn first appears underneath, and the object drawn most recently appears on top of the others. Think of the objects being stacked on the slide as you draw them. The most recently drawn object appears and remains at the top of the stack unless you change the stacking order. In Figure 28.10, the circle was drawn first; then the triangle, and then the star. No matter where you move the objects on the slide, the circle is on the bottom, the triangle in the middle, and the star on top.

FIG. 28.10
Objects overlap each other in the order they are drawn.

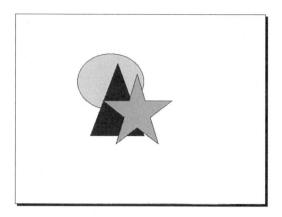

PowerPoint lets you change the stacking order of objects in two ways. The Draw, Order, Bring Forward, and Draw, Order, Send Backward commands let you move an object one step at a time forward or backward through a stack of objects. So, if you have six objects stacked on top of one another and the sixth object is selected, that object becomes the fifth object in the stack if you choose Draw, Order, Bring Forward. If you choose Draw, Order, Send Backward, nothing happens because the selected object is already at the bottom of the stack.

The other way to move objects is by choosing Draw, Order, Bring to Front, and Draw, Order, Send to Back. These commands move a selected object to the top or to the bottom of the entire stack, regardless of its current position or the total number of objects in the stack. In Figure 28.11, the circle was selected and brought to the front.

FIG. 28.11
The circle has been brought to the front of the stack.

T I P Small objects can easily become completely obscured by others. If you cannot find an object to select it, select any object on the slide; then press the Tab key until the object you want is selected. Each time you press the Tab key, a new object on the current slide is selected.

CHAPTER 29

Enhancing a Presentation

by Nancy Stevenson

In this chapter, you see the many different techniques you can use to give your slides a powerful presence. You don't have to be a graphic-arts expert; even the simplest touches can make a world of difference in the appearance and impact of a presentation. ∎

Work with templates

Templates are only a headstart to a great presentation; learning how to add to and customize a template can make a presentation really shine.

Enhance text by changing the font, style, and color

The way you format text can be the key to an attractive presentation.

Work with line spacing, bullets, and alignment of text

PowerPoint offers you tools to easily adjust spacing and alignment, and emphasize points using bullets.

Work with colors, fills, and line styles of objects

With PowerPoint, you can take simple line drawings and add a variety of colors and styles to the lines themselves for greater visual impact.

Add patterns, shading, borders, and shadows to objects

Use a variety of border styles, fill patterns, and shadows to enhance the objects.

Work with color schemes

Create custom color schemes you can use again and again.

Working with Templates

In Chapter 25, "Getting Acquainted with PowerPoint," you learned that templates are saved presentation files for which special graphic elements, colors, font sizes, font styles, slide backgrounds, and other special effects have been defined. PowerPoint includes templates designed for black-and-white overheads, color overheads, and on-screen slide shows.

▶ **See** "Understanding Templates and Masters," **p. 601**

Using a template is the quickest and easiest way to create professional-looking presentations because it takes the guesswork and experimentation out of designing a presentation. PowerPoint templates are designed by graphic-arts professionals who understand the elements required to achieve a certain effect and to convey a particular attitude.

Choosing a Template

To specify a template when you create a new presentation, select the Template option in the PowerPoint dialog box that appears automatically when you start the program.

Figure 29.1 shows a preview of a presentation using Presentation Designs.

FIG. 29.1
Presentation Designs creates a simple design element template.

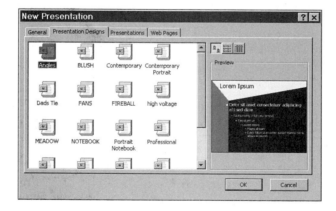

In the New Presentation dialog box, you can choose one of the following tabs:

- *General.* Contains the blank presentation or default format. Using this basic black and white presentation template, you can set your own format by making changes to the master template.

- *Presentation Designs.* Contains professionally designed templates on which you can base a presentation. Each presentation design includes a color scheme, graphics such as lines or art, and a master with complete text formatting.

■ *Presentations.* Contains many specific preset presentation templates (see Figure 29.2) that include color schemes and font formatting, in addition to slide layouts with suggestions for slide content. The Presentations tab also includes the AutoContent Wizard which steps you through the process of creating your own presentation. Select the presentation that best suits your needs.

■ *Web Pages.* Depending on your installation of PowerPoint, you may also have a Web Pages tab to create presentations you can save as Web documents.

FIG. 29.2
Click the Presentations tab to show a list of preset templates with suggested content.

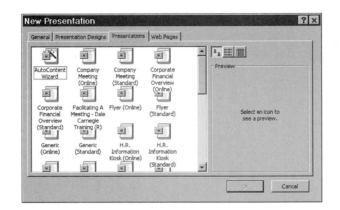

▶ **See** "Reviewing AutoLayout," **p. 624**

If you choose one of the presentation designs—such as Blue Diagonal, Coins, International, and so on—PowerPoint displays the New Slide dialog box from which you choose an AutoLayout. After you choose the layout, PowerPoint applies it to the slide template. Figure 29.3 illustrates the Coins template used with a Title slide.

FIG. 29.3
Use a template when you already have an idea of the content of your presentation.

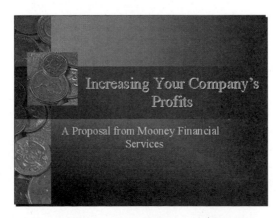

Figure 29.4 illustrates one preset slide presentation available, "Reporting Progress." Notice the second slide suggests you define the subject as a title for the slide, then break the

subject into smaller topics and list them with the bullets. Other slides in this presentation suggest overall status, background information, key issues, and future steps.

FIG. 29.4
PowerPoint's preformatted presentations guide you by suggesting slide content and format.

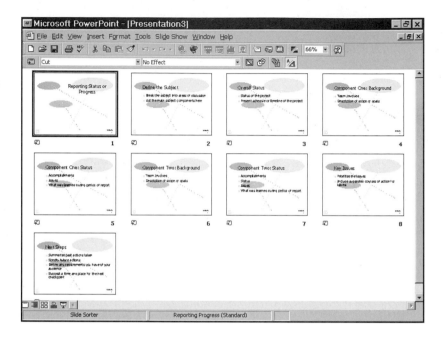

N O T E If your presentation doesn't fit into one of the preset formats in the New Presentation dialog box, choose the Generic presentation for basic formatting and good suggestions for content. ▪

To enter text into any of the Presentation text blocks, click the text block, delete the text, and then enter your own. You also can add new slides, objects, and other enhancements to the presentation.

Altering a Template

 T I P The Slide Master looks very much like a presentation slide, but any changes made here affect all slides in the presentation.

After you select a template for your presentation, you might want to change its characteristics. You might decide to use a different font and larger point size for your slide titles or to add a graphic element to the template. You can choose to change items on just one slide or on all slides. You might change, for example, the font on just one slide's title to set it apart from the other slides. On the other hand, you can make changes to all slides, for consistency, by changing the slide master.

To make changes that affect all slides in the presentation quickly and easily, change the slide master. To access the Slide Master, choose <u>V</u>iew, <u>M</u>aster, and select <u>S</u>lide Master from the resulting menu.

You can change the text in a slide by modifying the font, style, color, and so on. Additionally, you can change fill and line colors of objects, or change entire color schemes. Refer to the sections "Enhancing Text" and "Working with Colors and Line Styles" later in this chapter.

Applying a Different Template

One major change you can make to a slide presentation is to change the template, or presentation design, you're using. When you change the template, you change color schemes, some graphic elements, and the master template. Changing templates does not change "Click here" box contents, added objects such as text blocks, charts, or drawings, slide layouts, or the number of slides in the presentation.

▶ **See** "Understanding Templates and Masters," **p. 601**

> **CAUTION**
>
> Sometimes when changing from one template to another, you may gain an extra "Click here" box or lose a title or subtitle because of individual designs. Check all slides carefully after changing templates to make sure all of your slide contents are there. If you're missing something, you can either go back to the original template or add the missing text.

To change the template of the active presentation, follow these steps:

1. Choose F<u>o</u>rmat, Apply Design or select the Apply Design button on the toolbar to open the dialog box shown in Figure 29.5.

FIG. 29.5

The new Search the Web button allows you to go online to find templates in locations such as Microsoft's home page.

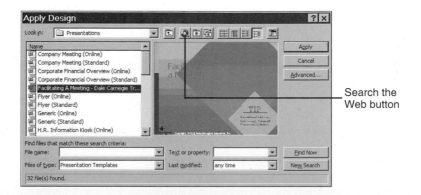

Search the
Web button

2. Choose Presentations in the Look In box, if it is not already selected.

N O T E To preview templates, click each template in the Name list. A sample of the highlighted template appears to the right in the dialog box. ▇

3. Select a template name, click Apply, or press Enter to select the highlighted template. The dialog box closes, and PowerPoint applies the new template to the active presentation.

Figure 29.6 illustrates how a template can create an overall impression for your slide presentation. PowerPoint includes over 50 templates for you to try.

FIG. 29.6
Use a template that best suits the contents of your presentation.

 TROUBLESHOOTING

How can I use more than one template in a presentation? Templates apply to all slides in a presentation; you cannot use more than one template in a single presentation. You can, however, change colors, fonts, shadows, patterns, and other enhancements in individual slides, as described throughout this chapter.

How can I create a custom template so I don't have to alter a PowerPoint template each time I create a new presentation? First, choose the PowerPoint template on which you want to base your custom template. Make the desired changes to the template. When the template looks the way you want it, choose File, Save As. Give the file a unique name, and save it into the appropriate template directory. Be sure to choose Presentation Templates in the Save As Type box.

If I make changes to the slide master in my presentation, how is the PowerPoint template I'm using affected? Any changes you make to a presentation master affect the current presentation only; the PowerPoint template file you are using is not altered.

Enhancing Text

When you enter text in a slide, the font, style (regular, bold, or italic), size, color, and special effects (underline, shadow, and so on) of the text conform to the settings specified in the master assigned to the current template. The International template, for example, uses the 44-point Times New Roman font in gray for slide titles and the 32-point Arial font in white shadowed for slide text. If you want to use a different font, style, size, color, or effect, you can change these settings (collectively called *font settings*) for all slides in a presentation by altering the slide master, or you can change font settings only for selected text objects.

Choosing a Font, Style, and Color for Text

To change font settings, select the text you want to change, then choose F_ormat, F_ont, or the F_ont command on the shortcut menu, to display the Font dialog box (see Figure 29.7). The Font, Font Style, Size, and Color settings are self-explanatory; these options appear in most word processing, spreadsheet, and graphics programs.

▶ **See** "Formatting Documents," **p. 81**

FIG. 29.7

The Font dialog box allows you to choose a font, size, style, color, and text effects.

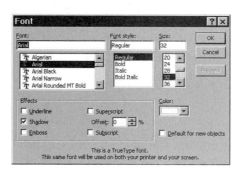

The Effects area, however, contains some options with which you might not be familiar. The Sh_adow option adds a shadow at the bottom and the right side of each character. The E_mboss option gives the text the appearance of raised letters by using a light color for the characters and a faint shadow behind each character. The Su_bscript option drops a selected character slightly below the normal line level, as in H_2O, whereas the Supe_rscript option raises a selected character, as in 10^5. When you choose either of these options, you can specify the Offse_t percentage.

Choose the desired formatting and click OK.

You also can change specific format settings by clicking the following buttons in the Formatting toolbar:

Button	Button Name	Description
`24 ▼`	Font Face	Changes the font of selected text
`Arial ▼`	Font Size	Changes the font size of selected text
A	Increase Font Size	Increases the font size
A	Decrease Font Size	Decreases the font size
B	Bold	Makes selected text bold
I	Italic	Makes selected text italic
U	Underline	Underlines selected text
S	Text Shadow	Adds a drop shadow to selected text
A ▾	Text Color	Changes the color of selected text

Changing Line and Paragraph Spacing

Just as the template defines color schemes, graphics, and other characteristics for a presentation, the master attached to the template defines the line spacing for text in a text object. PowerPoint enables you to set the spacing between lines, as well as the amount of space before and after paragraphs. In most templates, the default spacing is 1 line, the space after paragraphs is 0, and the space before paragraphs is 0.2 or 0.

You might want to change line or paragraph spacing, depending on the content of your slides. To change line and paragraph spacing, follow these steps:

1. Select the text for which you want to adjust line or paragraph spacing, either in the master or on one individual slide.

2. Choose Format, Line Spacing. PowerPoint displays the Line Spacing dialog box, as shown in Figure 29.8.

3. In the Line Spacing, Before Paragraph, and After Paragraph boxes, enter the number of lines or points to be used. If you prefer to use points rather than lines, be sure to choose the Points setting in each drop-down list.

FIG. 29.8
Use the Line Spacing
dialog box to set line
and paragraph
spacing.

4. Click OK. PowerPoint returns to your slide and reformats the selected text.

You also can change the line spacing by clicking the following buttons on the Formatting toolbar:

Button	Button Name	Description
	Increase Paragraph Spacing	Increases the line spacing for the selected text
	Decrease Paragraph Spacing	Decreases the line spacing for the selected text

CAUTION

When setting paragraph spacing, specify a setting for Before Paragraph or After Paragraph, but not both. If you set both options, the actual space between paragraphs will be the sum of the two settings.

Aligning Text

Alignment refers to the horizontal positioning of text within a text object. In presentation slides, text generally is left-aligned for paragraphs or bullets and centered for titles. However, you can also justify or right-align text. Table 29.1 describes the alignment options.

Table 29.1   Alignment Options

Button	Alignment	Result
	Left	Aligns text along the left edge of a text object.
	Right	Aligns text along the right edge.

continues

Table 29.1 Continued		
Button	**Alignment**	**Result**
	Center	Aligns text at the center point of the text object so that an equal number of characters appear to the right and left of the center point.
	Justify	Aligns text along both the right and left edges so that the characters in a line cover the entire width of a text object.

N O T E The Justify button is not available in the default formatting toolbar. If you use this alignment option often, you can customize this toolbar or another toolbar to include this button. Click the right mouse button on any toolbar and choose Customize. On the Commands tab in the Customize dialog box, in the Categories list box choose Format. Scroll down in the Commands list to locate the Justify button. Drag the button to the desired location on any toolbar on your screen. For more information, see Chapter 41, "Customizing the Desktop, Toolbars, and Menus." ▪

Because alignment involves horizontal positioning of text at margins or at the center point of a text object, alignment affects entire paragraphs. In other words, you cannot align a single word or line in a paragraph.

N O T E Use center-aligned or right-aligned text for headings or short lists or phrases. Use left-aligned text for heads, bulleted lists, or paragraphs of text. ▪

T I P Use a bulleted list to show equal importance for each item in the list. Use a numbered list to show some kind of priority or sequence for the items in the list.

You don't have to select any text to align a single paragraph; PowerPoint aligns the entire paragraph in which the insertion point is located. To align several paragraphs, select a portion of text in each paragraph, and then choose an alignment style.

T I P For left, right, or center alignment, you also can use the toolbar buttons shown in Table 29.1.

To change the alignment of text, follow these steps:

1. Select the object that contains the text you want to align.
2. Place the insertion point anywhere in the paragraph you want to align, or select a portion of each paragraph you want to align.

3. Choose Format, Alignment, or choose Alignment from the shortcut menu. The Alignment submenu appears.

4. Choose Left, Right, Center, or Justify. PowerPoint immediately realigns the current paragraph or selected paragraphs.

Adding Bulleted Text

In addition to assigning styles, sizes, and spacing to various fonts you use in your slides, you also can format text to include bullets. In PowerPoint, you can use the default "Click here" bullet lists, or you can create a list in a text block and assign a custom bullet.

 When working with bullets, use the Bullet On/Off icon to show/hide the bullets. You can turn off, for example, bullets for several items on a list or just one item, if you want to skip some text between bulleted items.

▶ **See** "Inserting Other Objects," **p. 637**

To add bullets to text or to customize the bullet used, follow these steps:

1. Select the text to be bulleted or position the insertion point on the first line of text.

2. Choose Format, Bullet. The Bullet dialog box appears (see Figure 29.9).

FIG. 29.9
You can use any available font, such as Symbol or Wingdings, to create a bullet.

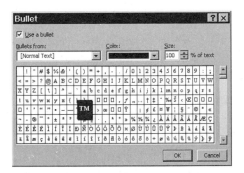

 Click any bullet in the dialog box to display an enlarged view of the bullet. To quickly scan the symbols, hold down your mouse button continuously while moving your cursor over the different symbols; each symbol you pass your mouse over is displayed enlarged.

3. In Bullets From, choose the font you want to use for the bullet.

4. You can use the color assigned in the template (and displayed in the Color box), or you can choose a new color.

5. Size the bullet by changing the percentage in the Size box.

6. Choose OK to apply the bullet to the text.

Working with Colors and Line Styles

All objects that you draw in PowerPoint (except lines) have a fill color, line color, and line style. The *fill color* is the color inside an object; the *line color* is the frame that defines the boundaries of an object; and the *line style* defines the width or style of the object's frame.

For any given object, you can turn off the fill color and line color. In most templates, for example, the line that frames a text object is turned off, because text generally looks better in the slide without a frame. For other objects (such as shapes that you create with the drawing tools), the object's frame usually is visible, and the object has a fill color.

In most templates, an object's line style is a narrow solid line. You can choose any of five wider line styles or any of four double or triple lines. In addition, you can change a solid line to a dashed, dotted, or mixed line by choosing one of the eight dash style options. If an object is a straight line or arc rather than a shape, you can add arrowheads to either end or to both ends of the line or arc.

Choosing Fill and Line Colors and Line Styles

You will use the Colors and Lines dialog box (see Figure 29.10) to set line, fill, and line-style options.

FIG. 29.10
Use the Colors and Lines dialog box to define an object's color and frame style.

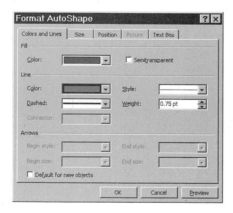

To change an object's fill color, follow these steps:

1. Select the object.

2. Choose Format, Colors and Lines, or choose Colors and Lines from the shortcut menu. The Format AutoShape dialog box appears. Select the Colors and Lines tab to display the current fill color in the Fill Color box.

3. Click the arrow to open the Fill Color drop-down list and display the available fill color options. Then choose from the following options:

- Select the No Fill option to remove the fill color from the object.
- Select one of the colors (derived from the current template).
- Select the More Colors option to open the dialog box shown in Figure 29.11. Select the desired color from the palette on the Standard tab or choose another color on the Custom tab. Choose OK to return to the Colors and Lines dialog box.

FIG. 29.11
The Colors dialog box displays a color palette.

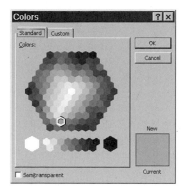

- Select the Fill Effects option to open a Fill Effects dialog box which offers gradient, texture, pattern, and picture effects on four different tabs.

 TIP To make the object show through to the background, choose the Semitransparent check box located next to the Fill Color drop-down palette.

4. Click OK in the Format dialog box. PowerPoint returns to your slide and changes the fill color or pattern of the selected object.

5. Click any blank area of the screen to deselect the object.

To change an object's line color or line style, or to add dashed lines or arrowheads, follow these steps:

1. Select the object.

2. Choose Format, Colors and Lines, or choose Format AutoShape from the shortcut menu. The Format dialog box appears; switch to the Colors and Lines tab to see the current line color in the Line box.

3. Click the arrow to open the Line Color drop-down list and display the available options. Then choose from the options:

- Select the No Line option to remove the object's line color.
- Select one of the colors (derived from the current template).
- Select the More Colors option, which displays the Colors dialog box (refer to Figure 29.11). Select a color from the Standard or Custom tab, and then choose OK.
- Select Patterned Lines to go to the Patterned Lines dialog box, where you can select a pattern to use to fill your line.

4. To select a different line style, highlight a style in the Style list.

5. To use a dashed line, highlight a style in the Dashed list.

6. To add arrowheads to a line or arc, select an option in the Arrows list.

7. Click OK in the Format dialog box. PowerPoint returns to your slide and changes the line color and style for the selected object.

8. Click any blank area of the screen to deselect the object.

A quick way to change an object's fill, line color, line style, dashed lines, or arrowheads is to use the respective tools in the Drawing toolbar. Select the object, and then click any of the tools shown in Table 29.2. In each case, a drop-down list appears, enabling you to select a new color or style.

Table 29.2 Color and Line Tools

Tool	Tool Name
	Fill Color
	Line Color
	Line Style
	Arrow Style
	Dash Style

Using Shading and Patterns

Two effective variations for filled objects are gradient color and two-color pattern. A *gradient* is a dark-to-light or light-to-dark variation of an object's color. This variation can run vertically, horizontally, diagonally, from the center outward, or from any corner. You also can adjust the intensity of the color.

To add a gradient to an object, follow these steps:

1. Select the object you want to shade.

2. Choose Format, Colors and Lines. The Format AutoShape dialog box appears. Select the Colors and Lines tab to see the current fill color in the Fill Color box.

3. Click the down arrow to open the Fill Color drop-down list.

4. Select the Fill Effects option. The Fill Effects dialog box appears, as shown in Figure 29.12. Select the Gradient tab, if it's not already displayed.

FIG. 29.12

Use the options in the Gradient tab of the Fill Effects dialog box to create a gradient fill pattern.

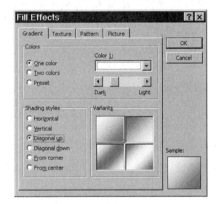

5. Use the Colors option in the Fill Effects dialog box if you want to change the fill color. If you want to blend two colors for the gradient, choose the Two Colors option. Choose the Preset option to display sets of predefined color gradients, such as Nightfall or Sapphire.

6. Select an option in the Shading Styles list.

7. In the Variants box, highlight one variant. The Variants Sample box reflects the choice you make.

8. Click OK in the Fill Effects dialog box. You return to the Format AutoShapes dialog box.

9. Click OK to close the dialog box. PowerPoint applies the gradient to the selected object.

An alternative to shading an object is patterning. A *pattern* is a design (such as lines, dots, bricks, or checkerboard squares) that contains two colors: a foreground color and a background color.

To add a pattern to a filled object, follow these steps:

1. Select the object to which you want to add a pattern.

2. Choose Format, Colors and Lines, or choose Colors and Lines from the shortcut menu. The Format AutoShape dialog box appears. Select the Colors and Lines tab.

3. Click to open the Fill Color drop-down list.

4. Select the Fill Effects option, then display the Pattern tab, shown in Figure 29.13.

FIG. 29.13

Use the Pattern tab of the Fill Effects dialog box to select a fill pattern.

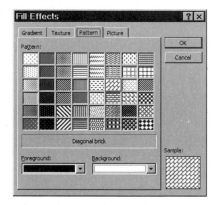

5. In the Pattern box, highlight the pattern you want to use.

6. In the Foreground and Background lists, select the colors for your pattern.

7. When you select a pattern, a preview of it is shown in the Sample box.

8. Click OK to close the Pattern Fill dialog box. You return to the Format AutoShape dialog box.

9. Click OK to close the dialog box. PowerPoint applies the two-color pattern to the selected object.

10. Click any blank area of the screen to deselect the object.

You can also use any of several more complex texturized patterns for your objects. Select the Texture tab rather than the Pattern tab from the Fill Effects dialog box to display the choices shown in Figure 29.14. Choose from several predesigned textured fill patterns in this dialog box.

FIG. 29.14
Predefined fill textures are available in the Textured Fill dialog box.

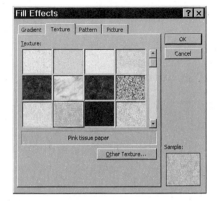

Adding Shadows to Objects

Shadowing can enhance an object's visibility on a slide and make the object more noticeable.

To apply a shadow to an object, follow these steps:

1. Select the object.
2. Click the Shadow button on the Drawing toolbar. From the palette of shadow effects that pops up, you can select from several shadow effects or change Shadow Settings.
3. Select <u>S</u>hadow Settings. The Shadow Settings toolbar appears, as shown in Figure 29.15.

FIG. 29.15
Use the Shadow Settings toolbar to specify shadow color, direction, and offset.

4. To change the color of the shadow, select a color in the Shadow Color drop-down list.
5. To set a vertical shadow offset, select the Nudge Shadow Up or Nudge Shadow Down button. These Nudge Shadow buttons move the shadow offset by one point. If you want to change the shadow offset by 6 points, press Shift+Nudge.
6. To set a horizontal shadow offset, select the Nudge Shadow Right or Nudge Shadow Left button.

7. Close the Shadow toolbar. The changes you made with this toolbar were applied to the object as you made them.

8. Click any blank area of the screen to deselect the object.

 You can add or remove a shadow for an object quickly by clicking the Shadow On/Off tool on the Drawing toolbar.

Copying Attributes from One Object to Another

 Suppose that you have taken care to apply a special color, shade or pattern, line width, line style, and shadow to a particular object. You can apply all these attributes to another object quickly by using the Format Painter button in the Standard toolbar.

To use the Format Painter button, follow these steps:

1. Select the object which contains the desired formatting.

2. Click the Format Painter button. The mouse pointer changes to a paintbrush.

3. Click the object you wish to apply the formatting to. The clicked object will be reformatted to match the original object.

Working with Color Schemes

A *color scheme* is a set of colors that are chosen because they complement one another. Every template has a predefined color scheme that consists of specific colors for the slide background, title text, other text, lines, fills, shadows, and accent colors. You can use the colors defined in a template, choose a different color scheme, or change individual colors in a color scheme.

Changing Individual Colors in a Color Scheme

You can change an individual color in the current color scheme and apply the new color to the current slide or to all of the slides in the presentation. Follow these steps:

1. Choose Format, Slide Color Scheme, or choose Slide Color Scheme from the shortcut menu. The Color Scheme dialog box appears, as shown in Figure 29.16.

2. Click the Custom tab to change the dialog box options to those illustrated in Figure 29.17.

3. Select the item whose color you want to change, and click Change Color.

FIG. 29.16
The Color Scheme dialog box allows you to modify the presentation's colors.

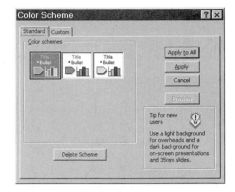

FIG. 29.17
The Custom tab in the Color Scheme dialog box allows you to change individual colors.

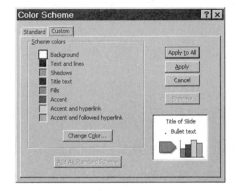

4. A Color dialog box appears, looking similar to the Color palette shown in Figure 29.11. Gradient fill objects will have a slightly different Color dialog box to allow for settings of hue and luminance, like that shown in Figure 29.18. Choose the desired color and click OK.

FIG. 29.18
Color dialog boxes for objects filled with gradients are slightly different from the color palette for a solid fill object.

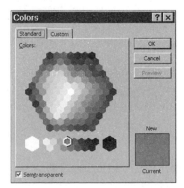

5. Repeat steps 3 and 4 to change other colors in the current color scheme.

6. In the Slide Color Scheme dialog box, click the Apply button to apply the change to the current slide. Click Apply to All to apply the new color to all slides in the current presentation.

N O T E   The number of color schemes you have available in the Color Scheme dialog box (refer to Figure 29.16) depends on which template you are using. To change templates, choose Format, Apply Design Template and select a template (see "Working with Templates" earlier in this chapter). ▪

Choosing a Different Color Scheme

Suppose that a template contains all the graphic elements you want to use, but the color scheme is not appropriate for the topic you are presenting. Rather than change individual colors in the template's color scheme, you can choose a different color scheme for the current template. When you choose a new color scheme, you are choosing a new set of predefined colors. As always, you can change individual colors in the scheme later if you choose.

To choose a color scheme, follow these steps:

1. Choose Format, Slide Color Scheme, or choose Slide Color Scheme from the shortcut menu (when no objects are selected). PowerPoint displays the Color Scheme dialog box (refer to Figure 29.16).

2. Available color scheme options are shown in the Color Schemes section of this dialog box.

3. Select the desired color scheme.

4. Click Apply to apply the new color scheme to the current slide. Click Apply to All to apply the new color scheme to all slides in the current presentation. ●

CHAPTER 30

Printing and Presenting Your Slide Show

by Rick Winter and Nancy Stevenson

As you learned in Chapter 25, "Getting Acquainted with PowerPoint," you can print a variety of components of a PowerPoint presentation, including slides (on paper or overhead transparencies), audience handouts, outlines, and speaker's notes. You can also prepare an on-screen slide show as a special kind of output. ■

Check slides for consistency

When you've done all your entering and formatting of content, Slide Sorter helps you make sure the overall flow of your presentation is consistent in appearance.

Build slide text

Build effects allow you to create visually appealing transition effects as you move from slide to slide in your presentation.

Choose a setup for presentation components

After you've built a presentation, you can output it in a variety of ways such as audience handouts, an outline, or as overhead transparencies.

Set up your printer

PowerPoint presentations can be generated in a variety of media, and printer setup is key to successful output.

Print presentation components

Printing hard copy of a presentation, speaker notes, and audience handouts helps you reinforce your message in a variety of ways.

Create and run an on-screen slide show

Rehearsing the timing and flow of your presentation beforehand can save you mistakes and embarrassment in front of a live audience.

Checking Slides Before the Presentation

Before you output your presentation, you'll want to make sure the presentation is as good as it can be. To do this you can check your slides by running the Style Checker. Style Checker checks for inconsistencies that you set in the Style Checker Options dialog box—inconsistencies such as case, punctuation, and number of fonts used in the presentation.

These kinds of errors can be glaring when projected in front of an audience. When creating a presentation it's easy to place a period at the end of some sentences but not all, or to mistakenly use too many fonts on a page, which makes your text hard to read and your slide look busy. These are the kinds of mistakes that you may miss even on a thorough review, but Style Checker finds them all.

To run the Style Checker, follow these steps:

1. Choose Tools, Style Checker. The Style Checker dialog box appears (see Figure 30.1).

FIG. 30.1

Choose the options you want Style Checker to review in the Style Checker dialog box.

2. Click the Options button to change any of the case, punctuation, or clarity options, as described in Table 30.1 and shown in Figures 30.2 and 30.3.

FIG. 30.2

Define the capitalization and punctuation on the Case and End Punctuation tab of the Style Checker Options dialog box.

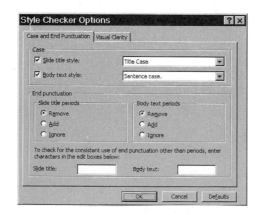

FIG. 30.3
Define information about the fonts and number of bullets on the Visual Clarity tab of the Style Checker Options dialog box.

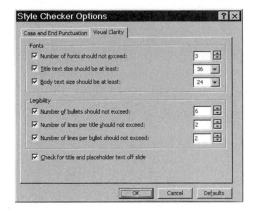

 TIP If you want to revert to the original settings in the Style Checker Options dialog box, click the Defaults button in the dialog box.

Table 30.1   Style Checker Options

Option	Description
Case and End Punctuation Tab	
Case	
Slide Title Style	Choose to apply sentence case, lowercase, uppercase, or title case to the title style throughout your presentation. Choose Toggle Case if you've accidentally typed your titles with Caps Lock on.
Body Text Style	Choose to apply from the same cases you chose for the title style.
End Punctuation	
Slide Title Periods	Choose whether to Remove, Add, or Ignore periods in the slide titles.
Body Text Periods	Choose whether to Remove, Add, or Ignore periods in the body text.
Slide Title text box	Enter any other end punctuation marks you want to check the consistency of in slide titles.
Body Text text box	Enter any other end punctuation marks you want to check the consistency of in the body text.

continues

Table 30.1 Continued

Option	Description
Visual Clarity Tab	
Fonts	
Number of Fonts Should not Exceed	Choose whether to limit the number of fonts used in one presentation, and enter the number to limit to in the text box.
Title Text Size Should Be at Least	Enter the minimum size you want to use for the slide titles.
Body Text Size Should Be at Least	Enter the minimum size you want to use for the body text.
Legibility	
Number of Bullets Should not Exceed	Choose whether to limit the number of bullets used in the body text and if so, enter the number in the text box.
Number of Lines per Title Should not Exceed	Enter the maximum number of lines you want to use for slide titles.
Number of Lines per Bullet Should not Exceed	Enter the maximum number of lines you want to use for bullets.
Check for Title and Placeholder Text off Slide	Choose to see if any text will run off the slide and not be visible.

3. Choose OK to close the Style Checker Options dialog box.

4. Click the Start button. The Style Checker examines the slide presentation and then displays a summary, as shown in Figure 30.4.

N O T E If you've left the Spelling option checked in the Style Checker dialog box, you may get a Spelling Check dialog box at this point offering you the option of making corrections to words not found in Office's dictionary. ■

5. After reading the list of inconsistencies, you can use the various Change and Ignore buttons to make adjustments. Choose OK to close the Summary box.

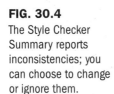

FIG. 30.4
The Style Checker Summary reports inconsistencies; you can choose to change or ignore them.

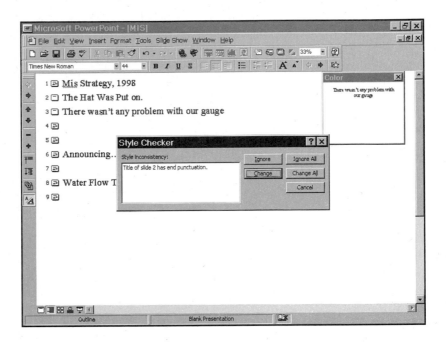

Choosing a Setup for Presentation Components

Before you output a presentation, indicate the type of output in the Page Setup dialog box. You can output a presentation as an on-screen slide show, as 35mm slides, as overheads, or as some other type of printed output. In addition, you can specify other properties of the presentation, and then PowerPoint adjusts the presentation to best suit your selections.

To display the Page Setup dialog box, choose File, Page Setup. Figure 30.5 displays the Page Setup dialog box.

FIG. 30.5
Specify your output and other components for the presentation in the Page Setup dialog box.

The Orientation section of the Page Setup dialog box offers Portrait and Landscape as options. When you choose Portrait, the slide is taller than it is wide. Landscape creates slides that are wider than they are tall. Slides are often printed in landscape orientation, whereas notes, handouts, and outlines are most often printed in portrait orientation. Therefore, PowerPoint offers separate orientation options for slides and notes, handouts, and outlines.

To choose a setup for slides, notes, handouts, and outlines, follow these steps:

1. Open the presentation for which you want to specify a setup.

2. Choose File, Page Setup. The Page Setup dialog box appears (refer to Figure 30.5).

3. Choose the appropriate option in the Slides Sized For drop-down list. Options include:

    - *On-Screen Show.* Uses an area 10 inches wide by 7.5 inches tall so the slides fill the screen.

    - *Letter Paper.* Sets the width to 11 inches and the height to 8.5 inches.

    - *A4 Paper* (210 x 297mm). Sets the width to 10.83 inches and the height to 7.5 inches.

    - *35mm Slides.* Sets the width to 11.25 inches and the height to 7.5 inches so that the content fills the slide area.

    - *Overhead.* Sets the width to 10 inches and the height to 7.5 inches so that the content fills a typical overhead transparency area.

    - *Banner.* Sets the width to 8 inches and height to 1 inch to create a banner effect.

    - *Custom.* Allows you to choose the dimensions you want when you are printing on nonstandard paper. Use the Width and Height arrow key settings to enter a custom size.

4. To begin numbering slides with a number other than 1, enter a number in the Number Slides From box.

5. To change the print orientation for slides, choose either Portrait or Landscape.

6. To change the print orientation for notes, handouts, or an outline, choose either Portrait or Landscape.

7. When all settings are correct, choose OK.

CAUTION

You should complete the page setup before you create a new presentation. If you change the slide setup after your slides are created, you might need to make adjustments to your slides, depending on the setup dimensions you choose.

Printing Presentation Components

Your printer is probably already set up for printing from other Microsoft Office or Windows applications. If you want to use a printer you don't normally use, you can change the printer setup using these steps:

1. Open the presentation you want to print.

2. Choose File, Print. PowerPoint displays the Print dialog box. The current printer is displayed at the top of the dialog box.

3. Click the arrow next to the current Printer Name box to open a list of all installed printing devices.

4. Finish filling out the Print dialog box.

5. Click OK to close the Print dialog box and print the active presentation.

Making Settings in the Print Dialog Box

Once your printer is set up, PowerPoint allows you to print any component of a presentation: slides, notes pages, handouts, and an outline.

To print any component, choose File, Print. The Print dialog box appears, as shown in Figure 30.6. In this dialog box, you choose the component you want to print, the number of copies, the specific pages to print, and other printing options. Table 30.2 describes the options in the Print dialog box.

FIG. 30.6
Use the Print dialog box to choose printing options.

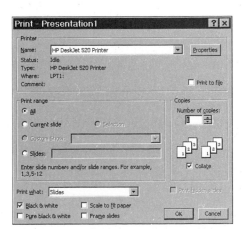

Table 30.2   Options in the Print Dialog Box

Option	Description
Name	Designate the correct printer to send output to by selecting it from this drop-down list.
Properties	Click this button to set properties specific to the printer, such as paper size, orientation, graphics, fonts, and so on.
Print to File	Select this option if you want to print to a named file rather than to a printer. Slides are generally printed to file when they will be produced by a service bureau.
Print Range	This area enables you to print All slides, only the Current Slide, a Selection of slides, or specific ranges of slides you specify. In the Slides box, use a hyphen (as in 5-8) to specify a continuous range. To specify individual pages, use commas (as in 12, 14, 17). For multiple ranges, use a combination of the two (as in 5-8,12,17-21,25). You can also choose to print sets of different pages from a Custom Show you defined through Slide Show, Custom Shows.
Copies	This area enables you to specify the Number Of Copies to print, and to check the Collate radio button if you want to have PowerPoint collate the copies as they print.
Print What	This drop-down box enables you to choose whether to print slides, handouts (2, 3, or 6 slides per page), notes pages, or an outline of the presentation.
Print Hidden Slides	When slides hidden, select this option to include hidden slides in the printing.
Black & White	This option changes all fill colors to white and grayscale and adds a thin black border to all objects that are not bordered or do not contain text.
Pure Black & White	To print in black and white without any grayscale shades, select this option.
Scale to Fit Paper	If you choose a different paper size in the Slide Setup dialog box, this option scales each slide to fit the paper.
Frame Slides	This option adds a frame to the slides when printed.

Printing Different Kinds of Output

The Print What feature of the Print dialog box controls which type of output you want. There are a few variables to keep in mind, depending on whether you've chosen to print slides, an outline, notes or a handout.

■ When you are printing slides, the options in the Print Range area of the Print dialog box give you a number of different printing options. You can print all slides, only the current slide, the slides selected in the presentation, or a range of slides that you specify. Be sure to select the Print <u>H</u>idden Slides check box if your presentation contains slides that are hidden and you want to include them in the printed output.

 T I P To print the current presentation using the default settings in the Print dialog box, click the Print icon.

N O T E The Print <u>H</u>idden Slides option in the Print <u>W</u>hat area appears dimmed, unless you have hidden slides in your presentation. Similarly, the option of printing a <u>S</u>election isn't available unless you have selected objects on a slide. ■

■ If you select Notes in the Print <u>W</u>hat selection of the Print dialog box, you'll print a reduced slide at the top of the page and speaker's notes at the bottom of the page, as shown in Figure 30.7. Since notes pages print one slide per page, you follow the same basic steps for printing notes pages as for printing slides.

FIG. 30.7
A notes page displays a reduced slide at the top of the page and speaker's notes at the bottom.

Slide

Note

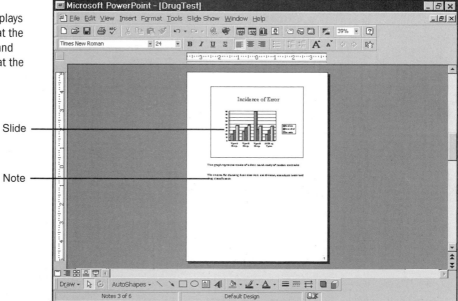

T I P In the Print dialog box, choose Notes Pages in the Print <u>W</u>hat area.

▶ **See** "Viewing a Presentation," **p. 614**

N O T E   When you plan to use speaker's notes, you can choose a layout for the notes and then create your notes in a Word document. Choose <u>F</u>ile, Sen<u>d</u> To and select Microsoft Word. The Write-Up dialog box appears. You can choose to link or embed the notes in the Add Slides to Microsoft Word Document area of the dialog box. When you choose OK, Word opens, ready for you to create your speaker's notes. Update and exit Word using the <u>F</u>ile menu to return to PowerPoint. ▪

 ▪ When you choose to print handouts, PowerPoint lets you print using one of three different layout styles: two, three, or six slides per page. To see how a handout page looks with each of these layout options, display the Handout Master by pressing and holding the Shift key and clicking the Slide Sorter button. Alternatively, choose <u>V</u>iew, <u>M</u>aster; then select the Han<u>d</u>out Master option. You see a handout layout template like the one shown in Figure 30.8. Use the Handout Master toolbar to display a two, three, or six slide layout in this view.

 T I P If you choose to print three slides per page, the slides are printed on the left side of the page; the right side is lined to provide a place for audience members to take notes.

FIG. 30.8
Layout options for handouts include two, three, or six slides per page.

To print handouts, in the Print <u>W</u>hat area of the Print dialog box, choose Handouts (2 Slides Per Page), Handouts (3 Slides Per Page), or Handouts (6 Slides Per Page).

To print selected handout pages, it isn't necessary to determine on which page a slide will print. Just specify the *slide numbers*—set in the Slide Setup dialog box—that you want to print in the Slides box. If, for example, you choose three slides per page and you want to print slides three, four, five, and six, enter **3–6** in the Sl<u>i</u>des text box of the Print dialog box. PowerPoint prints the second handout page.

▶ **See** "Viewing a Presentation," **p. 614**

See "Viewing a Presentation," **p. 614**

When you print a presentation outline, it is printed just as it was last displayed in Outline view. If you click the Collapse All button on the Outlining toolbar to display only titles (no body text), for example, PowerPoint prints only the slide titles. If you change the display scale using the Zoom Control button on the Standard toolbar, the outline prints in the current scale percentage. If you click the Show Formatting button on the Outline toolbar to display the outline text without formatting, the outline is printed exactly as displayed on-screen.

After selecting the Outline View option in the Print <u>W</u>hat section of the Print dialog box enter the slide numbers that you want to include on the outline page. If, for example, you type **1, 4, 5–9**, PowerPoint includes only those slides on the printed outline page.

Setting Up and Running a Slide Show On-Screen

One of the most effective ways to present your slides is to use your computer screen as an output medium. When you use your computer for an on-screen slide show, the entire screen area is used; PowerPoint's title bar, menu, and toolbars are cleared from the screen.

An on-screen slide show offers several advantages over transparencies or 35mm slides. An on-screen slide show:

■ Saves you the expense and time involved in producing slides (or reproducing them if you make any changes to the presentation).

■ Enables you to easily move around the presentation using interesting transition effects.

■ Enables you to utilize multimedia effects such as recorded narration or sounds, and animation and video clips.

- Makes other information available during the presentation; for example you can link to a World Wide Web site or even open another computer program to get additional data.

- Requires no projection equipment.

- Enables you to use your computer's color capability to its fullest extent.

You also can annotate your slides as you give your presentation. (See the later section "Annotating a Slide Show" for more information.)

N O T E You can use PowerPoint's Meeting Minder—Tools, Meeting Minder—to take notes and record items in Slide view or during a presentation. The notes you take are added to your notes pages; recorded action items appear on the last slide of your presentation. ■

You can run a PowerPoint slide show manually (using the mouse or keyboard to advance to the next slide when you're ready); you can set up a slide show to advance slides automatically by recording timings for each slide to be displayed; or you can set up a slide show to run in a continuous "loop" for demonstration purposes, as at a kiosk display.

Running a Slide Show

Several methods exist to run a PowerPoint slide show. To run a slide show from within PowerPoint, use these steps:

1. Open the presentation for which you want to run a slide show.

2. Choose any view.

3. Choose Slide Show, Set Up Show. The Set Up Show dialog box appears, as shown in Figure 30.9.

FIG. 30.9
Use the options in the Set Up Show dialog box to set timing, pen color, and other slide show features.

TIP You can also hold down the Shift key and click the Set Up Show button on the bottom left of the screen to show the Set Up Show dialog box.

4. In the Slides area of the dialog box, select <u>A</u>ll or enter a range of slides to display.

TIP Select Sli<u>d</u>e Show, <u>R</u>ehearse Timings to practice your presentation speech along with each slide.

5. In the Advance Slides area, select <u>M</u>anually or, for automatic slide advance, select <u>U</u>sing Timings, if Present.

6. For a continuously looping presentation—such as you would find at a tradeshow booth—activate the <u>L</u>oop Continuously Until 'Esc' check box.

7. To have your presentation appear filling the entire screen, check either <u>P</u>resented by a Speaker or Browsed at a <u>K</u>iosk.

TIP To view a presentation on two screens so that the presenter sees one and the viewer another, choose Sli<u>d</u>e Show, View on T<u>w</u>o Screens and select which port the presenter will view from.

8. If you've added narration or animations to your presentation and don't wish to use these sound and video files when you run the show, use the Show <u>W</u>ithout Narrations or Show <u>W</u>ithout Animation checkboxes.

N O T E If you choose <u>M</u>anually in step 5, click the mouse, press Enter or press Page Down when you're ready to advance to the next slide. If you choose <u>U</u>sing Timings, the slides advance automatically using the current timings you set by running <u>R</u>ehearse Timings in the Sli<u>d</u>e Show menu. ▨

Table 30.3 lists the methods for controlling your movements through a slide show.

Table 30.3   Methods for Controlling a Slide Show

Function	Method
Show the next slide	Click the left mouse button or press any of the following keys: the space bar, N, right arrow, down arrow, or Page Down.
Show the preceding slide	Press Backspace, P, left arrow, up arrow, or Page Up.
Show a specific slide	Type the slide number and press Enter.
Toggle the mouse pointer on or off	Type **A** or equal sign (=) (Show or Hide).

continues

Table 30.3 Continued

Function	Method
Toggle between a black screen and the current slide	Type **B** or period (.).
Toggle between a white screen and the current slide	Type **W** or comma (,).
End the slide show and return to PowerPoint	Press Esc, hyphen (-), or Ctrl+Break.
Pause and resume an automatic slide show	Type **S** or plus sign (+).

 TIP If you want to see a list of all slides during a presentation, click the right mouse button and choose G̲o, Slide N̲avigator.

N O T E For most of the options in Table 30.3 you can also click the right mouse button in the middle of a presentation and choose items from the shortcut menu. ▪

 Another method for running a slide show is to simply click the Slide Show button along the lower-left side of the PowerPoint window. When you click this button, PowerPoint immediately runs the slide show, beginning with the slide that is currently selected. The slide show runs using current slide timings. If there are no timings set, you must advance each slide manually.

CAUTION

To run a slide show from the beginning using this method, be sure to select the first slide in the presentation before you click the Slide Show button.

N O T E If you have a network with PowerPoint available to other users, you can run your presentation on multiple computers, and the participants can write annotations on the slides. Choose T̲ools, P̲resentation Conference and follow the Presentation Conference Wizard dialog box to set up the presentation.

Another option is to package the presentation on a disk to send to another user. Choose F̲ile, Pac̲k and Go and follow the Pack and Go Wizard to save the file to disk. In this case, the other user does not have to have PowerPoint on his computer to see the presentation. ▪

Setting Transitions and Slide Timings

To add a little more visual interest to your presentation, you can specify a transition style between slides. The transition style determines how one slide is removed from the screen and the next one is presented. These range from one slide simply replacing another, to fancy tiling effects making a new slide seem to rain down onto the screen. When you set up a slide show to automatically advance to the next slide, you can also set the amount of time each slide remains on-screen.

To set transitions and timings, use the Slide Transition dialog box shown in Figure 30.10. From any of PowerPoint's display views, you can display this dialog box by choosing Slide Show, Slide Transition. When using Slide Sorter view, you can display the Slide Transition dialog box by clicking the Transition button at the far left end of the Slide Sorter toolbar. In the Slide Sorter toolbar you can also use the Slide Transition Effects pull-down button to choose from a list of transition effects.

FIG. 30.10
Add transitions to the slide show in the Slide Transition dialog box.

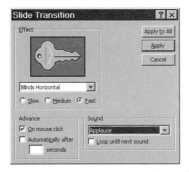

To set timing between slides and specify transitions, follow these steps:

1. Display your presentation in Slide Sorter view.

2. Select the slide for which you want to set timing and transition options. If you want to use the same settings for multiple slides, select those slides as a group.

 3. Click the Transition button at the far left end of the toolbar, choose Slide Show, Slide Transition, or choose Slide Transition from the shortcut menu. PowerPoint displays the Slide Transition dialog box shown in Figure 30.10.

 TIP When you choose an effect, the picture of the dog which appears in the Effect preview when you first open this dialog box changes to a picture of a key using the selected effect.

4. Select a transition style from the Effect drop-down list; when you do, the transition will be previewed in the box above the Effect drop-down list.

5. Select the appropriate speed option.

6. Choose whether you would like to advance the slide with a click of the mouse or automatically at a selected time interval in the Advance area. Add sound to the transition by choosing a sound from the Sound drop-down box. If you'd like to continuously loop the sound until the next preset sound occurs, use the Loop Until Next Sound check box.

7. Click Apply or Apply to All if you'd like these transition effects to apply to all slides in your presentation.

FIG. 30.11

View the timing and transitions for each slide in Slide Sorter view.

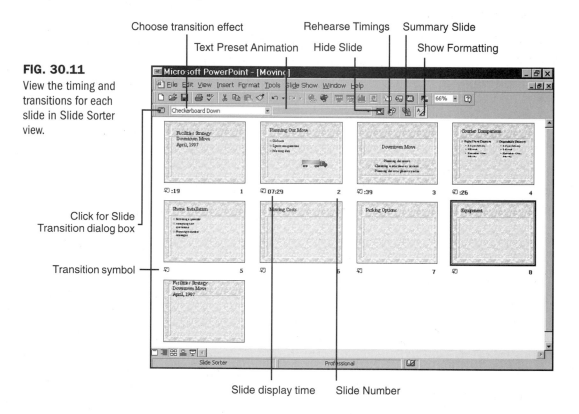

Figure 30.11 shows a transition icon under all the slides and a transition time displayed under the first row of slides in Slide Sorter view indicating that transitions and slide times have been applied. You can click any transition icon to see a demonstration of the transition effect.

You can change transitions or timing at any time by repeating these steps. You also can change slide timing when you rehearse a slide show, as described in the next section.

Automating a Slide Show

As discussed earlier, you can choose to advance to successive slides automatically during your presentation, and you can set slide timings to control advancement to successive slides. You can also set slide timings as you rehearse a presentation by following these steps:

1. From any view, choose Slide Show, Rehearse Timings or from the Slide Sorter view click the Rehearse Timings button. The slide show begins, and a Rehearse Timings dialog box allows you to see the timing as you move among slides.

2. Begin rehearsing your presentation. When you are ready to advance to the next slide, press the arrow on the Rehearse Timings dialog box, click the mouse button, press Enter, or press Page Down.

3. Repeat step 2 until all slides are shown. A message appears telling you the total time for the new slide timings.

   Choose Yes to record the new timings; choose No to ignore the new timings and retain the previous timings.

Part

V

Ch

30

Annotating a Slide Show

When you deliver a presentation using overhead transparencies, you may often circle or underline a specific point, or write notes on the slide in response to audience questions or comments. If you use a dry-erase marker, you can easily wipe off your annotations so that the transparencies are not permanently marked.

When you run an on-screen slide show, PowerPoint gives you the capability to *electronically* annotate your slides in freehand form adding comments using the mouse. For instance, you might want to draw a check mark beside an important point or underline it. As with overhead transparencies and dry-erase markers, electronic comments are not permanent. They are automatically removed when you move to the next slide in a slide show, or you can remove annotations manually as you present your slides.

To add comments to slides during a slide show, follow these steps:

1. Start your slide show.

 To display the pen during a slide show, press Ctrl+P.

2. Press Ctrl+P, click the right mouse button and choose Pen, or click the annotation icon, which appears in the lower-left corner of your screen; choose Pen from the resulting pop-up menu.

   The pointer will turn into a pen.

3. Press and hold the mouse button as you write or draw on-screen by moving the mouse. Release the mouse button to stop drawing or writing.

4. Repeat step 3 to write or draw again on the slide.

5. (Optional) Type **E** to erase all comments on the current slide, so you can circle or check other areas of the slide.

 T I P   You can change from the Pen to the Arrow by pressing Ctrl+A.

6. When you are finished annotating the current slide, press Ctrl+A, click the right mouse button and choose Arrow, or click the annotation icon again; choose the Arrow command from the pop-up menu to restore the mouse pointer.

If you don't type **E** to erase all comments on the current slide (see step 5), PowerPoint erases all comments automatically when you move to the next slide in the slide show.

Building Slide Text

You can apply an interesting animation effect called a build to a slide with a bulleted list or other objects, so that the items on the list appear one at a time. Using build effects makes the show more interesting and keeps the viewers from reading ahead of the speaker.

To add build effects to a presentation, follow these steps:

1. In Slides view, move to the slide you want to apply build effects to and select the bullet list object.

2. Choose Slide Show, Custom Animation. The Custom Animation dialog box appears. Select the Timing tab.

3. Click the object name and select Animate.

4. Choose whether to have animation appear On Mouse Click or Automatically after the number of seconds you enter.

   Now that you've designated on the Timing tab that the object should be animated and how that animation is activated, you can choose which effects to use when it is animated on the Effects tab.

5. Click the Effects tab.

6. Select a style of animation and if you wish a sound effect from the Entry animation and sound section of this tab.

7. If you like you can make settings in the Introduce Text section so that the text can appear letter by letter, word by word or all at once.

> **N O T E** You can also control how charts build on-screen during a presentation by using the Chart Effects tab in the Custom Animation dialog box. Here you can choose whether chart elements come in all at once or one at a time, as well as whether grid and legend elements should be animated.

> **TIP** If you choose to advance the slide show manually, the text builds on-screen each time you click the mouse; otherwise, the build is automatic.

Animating Objects on a Slide

You can also use build and animation effects for any objects (including clip art, slide titles, and other text) on the slide in addition to bullets.

To add an animation effect to art or text on a slide, follow these steps:

1. In Slides view, select the object you want to animate.

2. Click the Animation Effects button on the Formatting toolbar. A group of animation buttons appears.

3. Click one of the animation buttons, described in Table 30.4.

Table 30.4 Animation Buttons

Button	Name	Description (and Sound If Sound Board Installed)	Works with Graphic Objects*
	Animate Title	Title of slide flies from top (turn on or off)	
	Drive-in Effect	Object flies from right with car sound	Yes
	Flying Effect	Object flies from left with whoosh sound	Yes
	Camera Effect	Object starts from center outward with camera sound	Yes

continues

Table 30.4   Continued

Button	Name	Description (and Sound If Sound Board Iinstalled)	Works with Graphic Objects*
	Flash Once	Flashes the object on and then off	Yes
	Laser Text Effect	Drops one letter at a time from top right with laser sound	
	Typewriter Effect	Adds one letter at a time with typewriter sound	
	Reverse Order Build	Quickly builds text from left to right. If bullets selected, reverses order of bullets (builds from bottom to top)	
	Drop-in Text Effect	Drops down one word at a time	
	Animation Order	If multiple objects on slide, chooses order for each animation effect	Yes
	Custom Animation Settings	Opens Animation Settings dialog box, which shows existing settings and gives more options than other buttons on Animation Effects dialog box alone.	Yes

All items in above table work with text. Those indicated with yes in fourth column work with pictures, clip art, and drawn objects.

 T I P To create a movement effect on the slide, select an object and use the Flash Once button. Duplicate the object with Ctrl+D. To leave the last copy of the object on the screen, select the object and display the Custom Animation dialog box (Slide Show, Custom Animation). On the Effects tab choose Don't Dim in the After Animation drop down list.

 If you choose Slide Show, Custom Animation, the Custom Animation dialog box opens as shown in Figure 30.12. The options on the Effects tab of the Custom Animation dialog box are described below.

■ *Introduce Text.* For picture objects you can choose to Build or Don't Build. For text objects you can also build by paragraph level.

- *Grouped By*. You can also choose how each bullet builds (by paragraphs, words, and letters).

- *In Reverse Order*. For bullet items, the slide will build from last bullet item to first bullet item (from bottom to top).

- *Entry Animation and Sound*. With no effects, build item appears immediately at indicated position on slide. With effects, item can appear flying from different positions on the slide or with fades, blinds, flashing or other options. This option gives many more choices than the Animation Effects buttons alone. In the second pull-down button, you can choose a sound that will go with each build.

- *After Animation*. After the build is completed on the object, you can change the color (dim) or hide the object. To keep the object on-screen unchanged, choose Don't Dim.

FIG. 30.12
The Custom Animation dialog box allows you to create special visual and sound effects for objects on your slide.

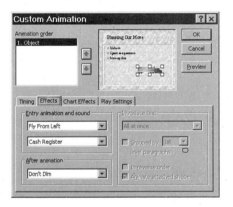

Adding Music and Narration

You can easily add narration or musical background to your presentation. This is especially useful for stand-alone presentations where no live speaker is present. To record a narration, you need a sound card and microphone.

To add narration, simply choose Slide Show, Record Narration. The dialog box that appears offers the option of embedding the narration with your presentation or linking to the narration. If you're going to take your presentation on the road, it's best to embed the narration with the presentation. To start recording, click OK. Your slide show advances as you record. When you reach the last slide, a message will notify you that you have reached the end. You can save the new timings or just save the narration itself at this point. Any slide with narration accompanying it will now have a small sound icon in the lower-right corner.

To add sounds or music to individual slides, you can use the Movies and Sounds command on the Insert menu. However, you might want to explore adding background music to your entire presentation. One way to do that is to add a CD audio track to your presentation. Choose Insert, Movies and Sounds, Play CD Audio Track. You can designate which track of the CD to play and specific stop and start points. Then you can choose to loop the music until the presentation stops, offering you continuous musical background to your slides.

A second option for musical background is the new add-in program available with the ValuPack on your Office CD-ROM called Music Tracks. This program allows you to create custom music and sounds to add to a presentation. Music Tracks lets you indicate the style of music you want and the tempo, and then composes the music you need. You can then use the Insert, Movies and Sounds, Sound From File command to add the file to your presentation.

Interacting with Objects During a Presentation

In addition to build effects you can create for each of the objects on slides, you can have an object react to a mouse click during the presentation. To interact with text and graphic objects on a slide, do the following:

1. Select the object on the slide.
2. Choose Slide Show, Action Settings. The Action Settings dialog box appears as shown in Figure 30.13. This dialog box has two tabs: Mouse Click and Mouse Over. Their settings are identical; the difference is that settings on the Mouse Click tab cause actions when you click an action object; settings on the Mouse Over tab cause actions when you pass the mouse over the action object.
3. Choose one of the following options in the dialog box:
    *   Choose None for no action on a mouse click.
    *   Choose Hyperlink To and select a slide from the pull-down list to go to a specific slide in the presentation. Using this setting, you can create several custom shows from within a single presentation, moving to different slides or to slides in a different order.
    *   To choose a sound when clicking the object in a presentation, choose Play Sound and pick a sound from the pull-down list.
    *   To open an application, choose Run Program and type the name of the application in the text box or look for the program by using the Browse button.

- If you have created a macro using the Visual Basic Editor capability built into all Office products, you can choose to have that macro run when you click or run your mouse over the selected object by choosing Run <u>M</u>acro.

- For an embedded file such as a Word document, Microsoft Graph, Excel spreadsheet, or another PowerPoint presentation, choose Object <u>A</u>ction and select from the options in the pull-down list.

4. Choose OK when finished.

FIG. 30.13

The Action Settings dialog box allows you to choose what kind of action you want to happen when you click the mouse on a slide object.

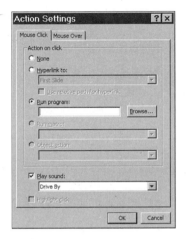

You can also place action buttons on a slide and when you click that button, the designated action will take place. To place an action button, follow these steps:

1. Go to the slide where you'd like to place the action button in Slide view.

2. Select Sli<u>d</u>e Show, Action Butt<u>o</u>ns. The side menu shown in Figure 30.14 appears.

3. Select any of the buttons on this side menu to insert it on your slide.

Once an action button is placed on your slide, you can click it during a presentation to initiate its action. Try this with slide shows run at kiosks so people viewing the show can interact with it by playing a movie or sound.

FIG. 30.14
Any of these action buttons can be dropped onto any slide by selecting them here.

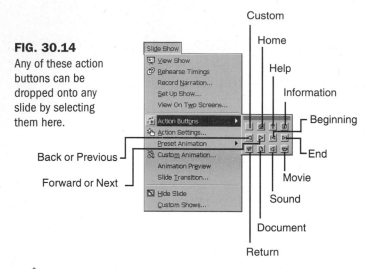

Custom

Home

Help

Information

Beginning

End

Movie

Sound

Document

Return

Back or Previous

Forward or Next

TROUBLESHOOTING

In Slide Sorter view, the Slide Transition Effects and Text Build Effects buttons are blank. How can I use them? The buttons are blank unless a slide is selected. Select the slide you want to apply an effect to and the buttons appear.

N O T E You can take the on-screen slide show with you to show on another computer. The Pack and Go Wizard prepares and copies the presentation for you. To pack and go, choose File, Pack And Go. Follow the directions on-screen to copy the presentation to a disk. ▪

Using Access

Creating a Database

by Rick Winter

Welcome to Microsoft Access 97, the relational database application in Microsoft Office Professional. This chapter is the first of six chapters on Access. If you are new to databases, this chapter provides a basic foundation in database concepts. If you have worked with other database applications, this chapter builds on those experiences while teaching you how to create a database in Access. ■

Defining a database

Learn what a database is and what the different kinds of database management systems are.

Using a database application

Learn the kinds of information that go into a database.

Creating a database

After planning, start a database with and without the Database Wizard.

Maintaining a database

Explore administrative tasks, such as backing up, compacting, converting, encrypting, and repairing a database.

What Is a Database?

Before you explore Access, you need to know what a database is, review some basic database concepts, and identify when to use a database.

A *database* is an organized collection of information. A telephone directory is a good example of a database.

A computerized *database management system* (*DBMS*) is a computer application that helps you store, retrieve, sort, analyze, and print information in a database. In a computerized database, data appears in a *table* that looks very similar to a spreadsheet. The column headings are called *field names* and the columns are called *fields*. The rows of data are called *records*. In Figure 31.1, First Name is a field and Mary Might 345-9977 345-1112 is one of four records in a telephone table.

FIG. 31.1

A telephone database, called a table, consists of rows called records and columns called fields.

First Name	Last Name	Work Phone	Fax Number
Jackie	Joyner	456-2323	456-9988
John	Smith	567-9834	567-4433
Mary	Might	345-9977	345-1112
Carl	Lewis	987-4433	987-2121

Two types of database management systems exist:

- *File management systems.* Sometimes called *flat file databases*, they store data in files without indexing, which means that data is processed sequentially. File management systems lack flexibility in data manipulation. Another drawback of file management systems is the user's tendency toward data redundancy (storing the same data in more than one place) to accomplish common database tasks such as reporting.

- *Relational database management systems.* They enable users to manipulate data in more sophisticated ways—without data redundancy—by defining relationships between sets of data. The *relationship* is a common element, such as a customer's name or Social Security number. The data stored in each set can be retrieved and updated based on data in the other set.

ON THE WEB

Microsoft's Web site has sample files, drivers, and White Papers about many relevant topics to designing a database. For more information on relational design concepts, see *Tech*Ed 95: Fundamentals of Relational Database Design.* For other documents related to this chapter, see *Security White Paper (7.0) Available on MSL, Achieving Optimal Performance Paper, Splitting Applications Paper, Tech*Ed 95: Database Optimization Techniques, Tech*Ed 95: Designing*

Reports. Click this site and choose Download a Driver, Patch, or Sample File, or look at the other options available.

http://www.microsoft.com/MSAccessSupport/

To further illustrate the difference between file management systems and relational database systems, consider the database needs of a video rental store, which needs to maintain information on customers, rentals, and movies in stock. In a file management system, every time a customer rents a movie, the customer's name and phone number must be entered with the movie rented. In a relational database system, the customer's name and phone number would be retrieved automatically from the related (linked) customer list and added to the rental invoice without the need for duplicate data entry and storage.

Knowing When to Use a Database

Think of your computer and computer applications as tools you use each day to accomplish your work. Microsoft Office provides a host of tools you can use to automate daily tasks. Knowing when to use Access, the database tool, is important. The purpose of a database is to store a collection of information. Following are a few common examples of information stored in databases:

- Employee data
- Product inventory
- Customer demographics
- Customer purchases and orders
- Home inventory for insurance purposes
- Exercise/workout log
- Sales contacts
- Suppliers
- Students and classes
- Video collection
- Tracking investments

Notice that the preceding examples emphasize data collection, not calculation. Although you can perform many financial and statistical calculations in a database, database applications do not calculate as quickly as spreadsheet applications do. For example, a database would not be the proper application to automate the calculation of a single loan; a spreadsheet application would be a better choice. However, if you need to track, analyze, and maintain loan data for a number of clients over a period of years, a database application would be more appropriate for that collection of information.

Exploring Access

Microsoft Access is a relational database management system designed for the graphical environment of Windows. With Access, you can perform the following tasks:

- Organize data into manageable related units
- Enter, modify, and locate data
- Extract subsets of data based on specific criteria
- Create custom forms and reports
- Automate common database tasks
- Graph data relationships
- Add clip art to forms and reports
- Create your own turnkey database application, complete with menus, dialog boxes, and command buttons

In this section, you learn how to identify the components of such databases and how to start up Access.

Database Objects

Before you start creating databases in Access, it will help you to understand the components of an Access database. In Access, the term *database* refers to a single file that contains a collection of information. Each Access database consists of the following objects: tables, queries, forms, reports, macros, and modules. Table 31.1 describes the major objects in Access.

Table 31.1 Database Objects

Object	Description
Table	Stores data in row-and-column format, similar to a spreadsheet.
Query	Extracts data from a table based on user-supplied criteria. Queries enable you to view fields from more than one table.
Form	Displays data from a table or query based on a user-defined custom format. Forms enable you to view, edit, and print data. A form can display information from more than one table.

Object	Description
Report	Displays and prints data from a table or query based on a user-defined custom format. You cannot edit data in a report. Reports can contain information from more than one table.
Macro	Automates common database actions based on user-specified commands and events.
Module	Automates complex operations and gives a programmer more control than macros. Modules are procedures written in the Visual Basic for Applications programming language.

N O T E In Access, an *object* is something you can select and manipulate. A table, a field in a table, a form, and a button are examples of objects. ▪

Starting Access

You can start Access by clicking the Windows 95 or Windows NT Start menu and choosing Programs; by using the Microsoft Office Shortcut Bar; or by using the Windows command prompt. Access also has many command-line options for starting Access (for a complete list, search Help for the topic Startup Command Line Options). Command-line options allow you to start Access and automatically have Access perform a task for you. For example, you can have Access run a macro for you or repair a database and then exit Access. In the following example, Access starts opening the Northwind sample database for exclusive access, and then runs the Add Products macro:

```
C:\Access\MSAccess.exe Northwind.mdb/Excl/X Add Products
```

▶ **See** "Using Help and Office Assistant," **p. 127**

▶ **See** "Setting Startup Properties," **p. 720**

Opening a Database

When you launch Access from an icon or menu, the Microsoft Access dialog box appears (see Figure 31.2). By selecting the corresponding option, you can create a new database or open an existing database. Select Blank Database to open a database that doesn't contain database objects such as tables, forms, or reports. When you select Database Wizard, you see a list of over 20 database templates (such as contact management, inventory control, order processing, and video collection) from which to choose. Databases created with the Database Wizard contain predesigned tables, forms, and reports. You can even have the Database Wizard fill in sample data in each database object to help you get started.

FIG. 31.2
The Microsoft Access dialog box allows you to create a new database or open an existing database.

▶ **See** "Saving, Opening, and Closing Files," **p. 97**

Under the Open an Existing Database option button, Access lists the database files you most recently used. The More Files option provides you access to other databases.

 T I P   To open an existing database, double-click the database name.

If you close the Microsoft Access dialog box without making a selection, you are left in the Access application window without any databases open. The menus available at this point include File, Tools, and Help. Other menus, such as Edit, View, and Insert, are visible in Access 97 but most menu items are dimmed. The toolbar provides buttons for creating a new database, opening an existing database, and accessing Help.

To open an existing database from the Access application window, follow these steps:

1. Choose File, Open Database, or press Ctrl+O. The Open dialog box appears (see Figure 31.3).

2. Specify the drive and folder in the Look In text box.

3. Select the desired database file name in the File Name text box.

4. Choose Open.

   ▶ **See** "Finding Files," **p. 105**

 T I P   If you can't find your database, click the Advanced button on the Open dialog box.

FIG. 31.3

The Open dialog box for Access looks and functions the same as it does in any Office 95 application.

 N O T E In a multiuser (networked) environment, opening a database for Exclusive use prevents anyone else from working with that database. ■

 T I P The File menu lists the last few databases you opened. To open one of these databases, click the database name or type the corresponding number.

To close an open database, choose File, Close Database or click Access's Close button (x).

T I P You can open only one database at a time. However, you can run multiple copies of Access if you need to review another database, or copy objects. Keep the second copy of Access open only a short time to prevent system resource problems.

When you create a new database or open an existing database, a database window opens, and more menu and toolbar options become available.

The Database window contains a tab for each type of database object (see Figure 31.4). When you select a tab, such as table, Access lists the existing table names. To open a specific object, double-click the name or select it and click the Open button, which is available only for tables, queries, and forms. The Open button becomes the Preview button for reports; it becomes the Run button for macros and modules. Use the New and Design buttons to create new database objects or modify the design of existing database objects.

FIG. 31.4
When a database is open, the Database window appears by default and provides quick access to the objects in the database.

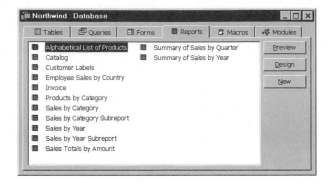

Planning and Designing Your Database

Before you create tables, forms, and reports, you should take the time to plan the database. The time you invest in designing the database will yield productivity gains as you create and maintain the database. Focus your design efforts on the data, the people, and the tasks. The following are some key issues to address as you design your database:

TIP Use the Database Wizard to quickly create a complete database design. Play with your data and modify the design to meet your needs.

- Start by analyzing the existing database (manual or computerized). Review the current forms and reports being used. Determine the source of the data (if computerized, could the data entry be imported or linked?). Meet with the other people who use the database information and discuss their needs. Review the database tasks performed (or to be performed), such as weekly reports, data exports, sorting, and analysis.

- After you identify your data storage and retrieval needs, separate the data into groups of common subjects (for example, separate customer data from invoice data). These groups will become tables.

- Determine the type of information to be stored in each table. (A customer table, for example, might store customer names, addresses, and phone numbers.) These categories of information in a table are called *fields*.

- Look for common elements among the tables. (A customer name might be the common element between the customer table and the invoice table.) This common element is called the *key field*.

- Determine criteria for queries, and determine what questions need to be asked.

- Design forms and reports.

- Consider automating common database tasks, such as opening a form, executing a query, and printing a report.

- Review data-security issues, such as backup policies, data sharing, and network access.

TROUBLESHOOTING

When I start Access, my database does not appear. The Microsoft Access dialog box does not automatically open a database. You can achieve this effect by adding *name* to the icon shortcut properties where *name* is the full directory, folder, and file name of your database.

In designing my database, I find that my tables have too many fields. What can I do? Examine the fields by subject. Do the fields all pertain to the same topic? Consider dividing the large tables into smaller tables based on subtopics. Remember that you can link the separate tables again whenever necessary. "Divide and conquer" is the rule of relational database management.

My database design contains too many tables. I'm afraid the implementation will be overwhelming. Look for unnecessary duplication of fields across tables. Also consider reorganizing the tables into one table with additional fields. For example, if you have separate tables for each week's sales, you might want to create one larger table that has the additional fields WeekBeginDate and WeekEndDate. Then you can use queries to extract weekly data as needed.

Creating a New Database

After you plan your database design, you are ready to create the database. Access provides you with many wizards to help automate the creation of the objects in the database, as well as the entire database itself. You can either use the Database Wizard to create an entire database from templates, or create a blank (empty) database. If you decide to create a blank database, you can populate it later with database objects created from scratch or use an Access Wizard to create each object.

If you are new to Access, use the Database Wizard to generate an entire database. You can always modify the design later.

Using the Database Wizard

The Database Wizard lists over 20 databases complete with tables, defined table relationships, forms, queries, and reports ready for you to use. You can always customize the generic database objects to better meet your needs at a later time. The advantage of the Database Wizard is that you can select a wizard, create a complete database, and get right to work entering data. On the other hand, creating a database from scratch (see the section "Creating a Blank Database" later in this chapter) gives you more flexibility, control over database definition, and a better understanding of your database.

Depending on your installation, the Database Wizard templates may include:

Address Book	Music Collection
Asset Tracking	Order Entry
Book Collection	Picture Library
Contact Management	Recipes
Donations	Resource Scheduling
Event Management	Service Call Management
Expenses	Students & Classes
Household Inventory	Time & Billing
Inventory Control	Video Collection
Ledger	Wine List
Membership	Workout

To create a database using the Database Wizard, follow these steps:

1. From the Microsoft Access dialog box, choose <u>D</u>atabase Wizard. Or, if you already closed the dialog box, choose <u>F</u>ile, <u>N</u>ew Database. The New dialog box appears (see Figure 31.5).

FIG. 31.5
Use the Order Entry database template to create the tables, forms, and reports you need to manage product order data.

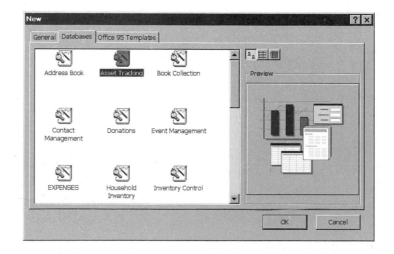

2. Double-click the icon for the kind of database you want to create.

3. When the File New Database dialog box appears, specify a name and location for the database.

4. Click Create to create the new database.

5. Follow the wizard directions to customize the database design to better meet your needs.

Creating a Blank Database

If the Database Wizard templates do not meet your database design needs, create a blank database. Or, if you have experience using Access and want to create the entire database design from scratch, you might prefer creating a blank database. The blank database is empty and doesn't contain any objects, relationships, or sample data.

▶ **See** "Creating a New Table," **p. 724**

▶ **See** "Planning Form Design," **p. 786**

▶ **See** "Creating a New Report," **p. 832**

▶ **See** "Creating a New Query," **p. 815**

To create a new blank database, follow these steps:

1. Choose File, New Database, or choose the File New Database button in the toolbar. The New Database dialog box appears (see Figure 31.6). In the General tab, choose Blank Database and OK.

2. In the Save In list box, select the desired drive and folder.

3. Enter a File Name for the new database file. Access automatically assigns the MDB extension to the new database's file name.

4. Choose OK.

FIG. 31.6
The Database window functions like the Windows 95 Explorer program.

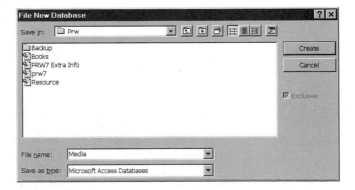

Part
VI
Ch
31

After Access creates the new database, an empty database window opens in the Access window, ready for you to create new objects (see Figure 31.7).

FIG. 31.7
An empty database window appears for the newly created database.

Maintaining an Access Database

As you use your database, you will need to perform various tasks to help protect it and keep it up to date. You should, for example, back up the database regularly. You might want to compact the database files so they run more efficiently and take up less storage space, or encrypt the database to prevent unauthorized persons from accessing the data. You also need to know how to recover damaged database files. Access provides database security features, which provide basic password protection and a more advanced user-level security protection. In addition to security and database management tools, Access allows you to set startup properties for each database. This section discusses each of these procedures and suggests why and when to perform them.

Backing Up Your Database

One of the most important administrative tasks associated with maintaining a database is creating a backup copy of the database. Like all computer data, database backups are important because they protect you against losing critical data. You should back up your database frequently (especially before and after you make major changes to the database).

 TIP To quickly make copies of individual database objects, create a blank database and then import the desired object(s).

Backing up an Access database is easy because all tables, forms, and other objects associated with the database are kept in one file. If you have backup software, simply select your database(s) for backup. Windows 95 comes with Microsoft Backup (you must have specifically installed it using the Custom Windows 95 installation), which you can run by choosing the Start menu, Programs, Accessories, System Tools, Backup.

You can copy the database using the Windows Explorer or My Computer; however, if you are copying to a floppy disk, the database file size might exceed the floppy disk's capacity. By using a backup utility, you avoid this problem—backup utilities prompt you for additional disks as needed.

> **CAUTION**
>
> Make sure the database is closed (across all users on a network) before attempting to copy or backup the database.

Compacting a Database

As you add and delete objects in a database file, the file can become fragmented and inefficient. Compacting the database eliminates the fragmentation and improves performance (speed). Compacting the file also saves storage space. How often you need to compact a database depends on how often the database expands or contracts. For example, a database you use primarily to look up data does not need compacting, but a database in which you enter and delete data each day and view reports each week needs frequent compacting. When you are compacting the database, make sure no other users have the database open.

 T I P Alternatively, in Access 97 you can compact your database with the file open. Choose Tools, Database Utilities, Compact Database.

To compact a database, follow these steps:

1. Close the database (across all users on a network).

2. Choose Tools, Database Utilities, Compact Database. The Database to Compact From dialog box appears (see Figure 31.8).

3. Specify the database file name in the File Name text box and click Compact. The Compact Into dialog box appears (see Figure 31.9).

4. Specify the name, drive, and folder for the compacted database (the name, drive, and folder can be the same as the database being compacted).

5. Choose Save.

6. If you are compacting into a file with the same name as the file you are compacting from, a dialog box asks you to confirm that you want to replace the existing file. Choose Yes to continue compacting.

FIG. 31.8
Compacting databases
saves storage space.

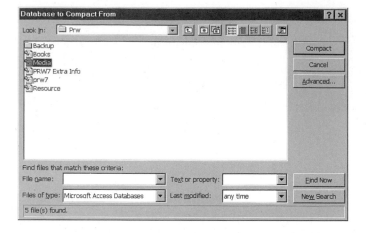

FIG. 31.9
You can save the
compacted database
into the same
database file.

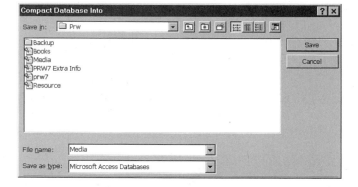

> **CAUTION**
>
> Compacting an Access database from an earlier version will not convert it into the current Compacting an Access format. You must use choose Tools, Database Utilities, Convert Database to do this (see the next section). Don't forget to also maintain backup copies of your database.

Converting a Database

Although you can add and delete data from earlier versions of Access, you can't change the design of objects in that database, create new objects, or take advantage of many of the new features until you convert your database. For each new version of Access from 1.1 to 2.0 to 95 to 97, you need to convert the database to have complete functionality. However, after you convert a database, you can't open that database in a prior version or convert it back. In cases where you have users who can't upgrade to the latest version of

Access, you should maintain installations of the prior versions so you can modify the database design and create new objects. With upgraded versions, make sure you check your licensing agreements.

You can convert a database when you open a database from an older version or by choosing Tools, Database Utilities, Convert Database. Before converting a database, make a backup copy. If the database contains linked (attached) tables, make sure the linked tables are in the referred directory. If Access can't find the linked tables during conversion, you lose the table properties defined in the linking database (Access displays a warning to this effect). After you convert the linking database, you can move the tables and use the Linked Table Manager (by choosing Tools, Add-ins, Linked Table Manager) to relink them.

N O T E   Converting a database that uses linking does not convert the linked tables.

Part
VI
Ch
31

To convert an Access database from an earlier to a later format, follow these steps:

1. Back up the database.
2. Verify that any linked (attached) tables are located in the appropriate drive and folder.
3. Close the database (across all users on a network).
4. Choose Tools, Database Utilities, Convert Database. The Database to Convert From dialog box appears.
5. Specify the database file name and click Convert. The Convert Into dialog box appears.
6. Specify the name, drive, and folder for the compacted database (to keep the same database name, select a different location).
7. Choose Save.

CAUTION

Access 97 is generally compatible with Access version 1.x, 2.0, and 95; however, new features might change the way an object works. For a complete list of differences between the prior Access versions and Access 97, search Help for the topic Conversion and Compatibility Issues.

Encrypting a Database

If you are concerned about the confidentiality of your data, consider using the data encryption feature of Access. Encryption renders a file unreadable by a text editor or utility program—only Access can read your data. This feature can be important if your confidential data travels over phone lines or other unsecured media.

> **CAUTION**
>
> Data encryption alone does not provide complete security. Anyone with a copy of Access could decrypt an encrypted database. For better security, use encryption with password protection (see the next section).

Encrypted databases run about 10 percent slower, but the difference is irrelevant when your main concern is security. You can decrypt a database later if you change your mind.

N O T E Encrypting automatically compacts the database. You do not need to compact the database before or after encrypting/decrypting. ▇

To encrypt or decrypt a database, follow these steps:

1. Close the database (across all users on a network). Back up file for safety.

2. Choose Tools, Security, Encrypt/Decrypt Database. The Encrypt/Decrypt Database dialog box appears.

3. Select or type the name of the database to be encrypted and click OK. The Encrypt/Decrypt Database As dialog box appears.

4. Select or type a database file name (the name can be the same as the database being encrypted or decrypted) in which to store the encrypted database.

5. Choose Save.

6. Confirm the overwrite of the existing file, if applicable.

Securing a Database

Access provides two ways for you to secure a database: passwords and user-level security. The easiest method is to specify a password for each database. Only users who enter the appropriate password can open the database.

▶ **See** "Using Workgroup Security," **p. 1172**

To set up a password, follow these steps:

1. Open the database with the Exclusive option checked on the Open dialog box.

2. Choose Tools, Security, Set Database Password.

3. In the Password text box, type your password. Passwords are case-sensitive.

4. In the Verify text box, confirm your password by typing it again, then click OK.

CAUTION

If you lose or forget your password, you cannot open your database. Keep a list of database passwords in a safe place, and remember that they're case-sensitive.

Also, you can't use password security if you intend to use database replication (Windows 95 Briefcase).

 TIP In a small workgroup or on a single computer, password protection should provide sufficient security.

User-level security allows you to create elaborate and flexible security in and across databases. Each user is assigned a user name and password. The users are organized into groups who share certain rights and privileges. Permission is given to each group and user to regulate what can be done with each object in the database. You control how much each user and group can work with the database objects. For example, you might create a user group called Acctg and allow them to view, edit, and print payroll data, whereas another group, called Sales, can view only employee names and employment status. A complete coverage of user-level security is beyond the scope of this book. Refer to Que's *Special Edition Using Microsoft Access 97* for more information on setting up user-level security.

Part
VI

Ch
31

 ON THE WEB

For downloading software and more information on the *Special Edition Using Access 97* or any other Macmillan titles, go to the SuperLibrary site at

http://www.mcp.com

 TIP In network situations—where many users from various departments have access to a database—consider setting up user-level security.

Repairing a Damaged Database

Power outages and other causes of unexpected computer or network shutdowns can corrupt your database. Data corruption means your data was damaged in some way. When you open a database, Access checks for data corruption and informs you whether the database needs to be repaired. Simply choose OK, and Access repairs the damaged file.

If you suspect data corruption because of lost or damaged data, but Access has not detected a problem, choose Tools, Database Utilities, Repair Database. Specify the name and location of the database you want to repair and click Repair.

> **N O T E** In Access 97 you can repair and compact an open database. Choose Tools, Database
> Utilities and Repair Database or Compact Database. ■

Setting Startup Properties

After you open or create a database, you can control the way in which the database opens in the future. For example, you can specify a form to display, which toolbars and menus to display, and whether to display the status bar. You set startup properties in the Startup dialog box (see Figure 31.10). If you used an AutoExec macro in the prior versions of Access, you might find that the Startup dialog box replaces many of the AutoExec macro commands.

> **N O T E** AutoExec macros run after the Startup options have taken effect. Be careful that your
> AutoExec macro is not undoing or replicating the Startup options you specified. ■

FIG. 31.10

In the Startup dialog box, you can indicate a form to be displayed when the database opens.

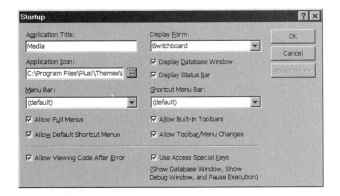

  Use the Startup dialog box to change the application title bar to better describe the database you're working on.

To set Startup properties, follow these steps:

1. Open the desired database.
2. Choose Tools, Startup.
3. Select the desired options and settings.
4. Click OK.

> **N O T E** To bypass the options in the Startup dialog box or the AutoExec macro, hold down
> Shift while opening the database. ■

Optimizing a Database

To optimize the performance of all or selected objects in your database, use the Performance Analyzer. The Performance Analyzer automatically makes changes for you and provides you with a list of other suggested improvements for your consideration.

To run the Performance Analyzer, open the database and choose Tools, Analyze, Performance.

 If you are not going to be modifying forms, reports, or the VBcode of an Access database, you can save the database as an MDE file. This will significantly increase the speed of the database operations. Use of an MDE function would generally be where one person develops and maintains an Access development file and sends out copies to users where the users don't need to make or modify their own reports and forms. To create an MDE file, with a backup of the development database open, choose Tools, Database Utilities, Make MDE File. To open the MDE file, change the Files of Type option in the Open dialog box to MDE files.

Part
VI

Ch
31

Splitting a Database

If you frequently share a database over a network, you might find the Database Splitter feature helpful. Basically, the Database Splitter divides a database into two sections:

- A back end that resides in a shared folder and contains just the tables.
- A front end that resides at end-user computers and contains all other database objects (forms, reports, and queries).

The benefits include faster processing (cuts down on network traffic—only the data moves across the network), and end-users customize to meet specific data entry, analysis, and reporting needs—without affecting everyone using the data.

To split a database, open the database, choose Tools, Add-ins, Database Splitter, and follow the prompts.

Once you split the database, you may need to use the Linked Table Manager if you change the location of linked tables. To start the Linked Table Manager, choose Tools, Add-Ins, Linked Table Manger.

N O T E If you chose the Typical installation of Microsoft Office, you may not have the Linked Table Manager or Database Splitter installed on your computer. Return to Office Setup to include these features. ■

Using the Briefcase Replicator

Windows 95 added a wonderful feature for "road warriors" (computer users who take their work on the road). The Briefcase feature of Windows 95 takes the drudgery—and frustration—out of trying to keep the files on two machines in sync while getting the files you need to take with you transferred to your portable.

Access incorporates the Briefcase feature as the Briefcase Replicator. The Replicator makes a copy of your database (called a *replica*) and places it in your Briefcase. You can make changes to the Briefcase replica while you are away from the office (for example, on your home or laptop computer). When you return to the office, you can use the Update Briefcase commands to merge the changes with any changes made to the replicated copy on the desktop. Access synchronizes the two versions of the same database and keeps both current for you.

To replicate a database, drag the database to the Briefcase icon on the desktop. Or, in Access, choose Tools, Replication, Create Replica. ●

CHAPTER 32

Creating Tables

by Rick Winter

Now that you have planned and created an Access database, the next step is to create the tables that store your data. Tables are the foundation of your database. All other Access database objects, such as forms, queries, and reports, depend on the data in the tables.

If you are new to Access and used the Database Wizard to create tables from predesigned templates, you might want to skip this chapter and proceed to Chapter 33, "Viewing and Editing Data." You can always return to this chapter when you need to create a new table. ■

Create a new table

Microsoft Access stores data in tables rather than queries, forms, or reports.

Modify table design

Table design includes naming fields, determining what kind of information they store, and determining a unique key field.

Set field properties

In order to display data properly or ensure that the correct values are input, use field properties.

Set table properties

Each table can also have a description, rules for data entry, and default display properties.

Set relationships

When you have more than one table in a database, you set relationships to tie tables together.

Creating a New Table

To create a new table, first display the database window. Then select the Table tab and click the New button. Access displays the New Table dialog box (see Figure 32.1). Access provides five methods of table creation:

- Datasheet View
- Design View
- Table Wizard
- Import Table
- Link Table

FIG. 32.1
You can create new tables automatically from your data, by using the Table Wizard or from scratch.

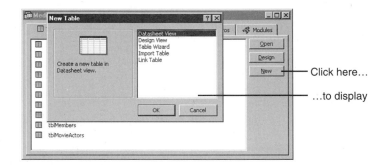

Datasheet view lets you create a table by entering data in a blank datasheet, similar to entering data in a spreadsheet. When you save the datasheet, Access analyzes the data entered and automatically assigns the appropriate field types and formats for you. If you are new to Access and have organized data that you need to start entering immediately, creating tables in Datasheet view is probably the best approach.

Design view allows you to create a table from scratch. In Table Design view you enter the field names, select the field data type, and set field properties such as formats and captions. If you are familiar with database design and Access, you might find that you have more control by creating a table in Design View. For those new to Access and database design, it is important to understand how Design view works so you can customize automatic table creation as needed or change table design in the future.

The *Table Wizard* provides you with a list of common table designs from which you can select and customize to meet your needs. The Table Wizard helps you create tables quickly from numerous personal and business table types, such as mailing lists, invoices, contacts, recipes, and investments. Each predefined table comes with sample fields. Based on your responses, the Table Wizard creates the table you request. If you are new to Access or want to get a quick start by using a table template, creating a new table using the Table Wizard is probably the best approach.

The *Import Table* choice copies data stored in another Access database, or another application format into the currently open Access database and automatically creates an Access table for the data. In cases where the data is stored elsewhere and you intend to maintain the data in Access from now on, importing is the best way to create the new table.

The *Link Table* choice leaves data in its current location and allows you to view and edit the data in Access. In previous versions of Access, linking was called *attaching*. Linking allows you to edit and view the data in Access and in the original application. In cases where the data will continue to be maintained by another application and be used in Access, linking is the best way to create the new table.

▶ **See** "Moving Around in a Worksheet," **p. 301**

▶ **See** "What Is a Database?" **p. 704**

▶ **See** "Creating a New Query," **p. 815**

Creating a Table Using Datasheet View

Part VI
Ch 32

Access allows you to jump right in and start entering data into a datasheet (see Figure 32.2). The datasheet appears and behaves much like an Excel worksheet. After you finish entering data, save the datasheet and Access automatically creates the table for you. The new table has generic field names (such as Field1, Field2, and so on), which you can change to more descriptive names.

FIG. 32.2
You can enter data directly into a datasheet and Access will create the table for you.

Field1	Field2	Field3	Field4	Field5	Field6
Jackie	Joyner	15 Ridge Rd.	Cherry Hill	NJ	08003
Letisha	Johnson	35 Main St.	Haddonfield	NJ	08045
Allen	Krane	909 Elm Ct.	Strafford	NJ	08034
Dean	Linstrom	15 Boulder Ave.	Trenton	NJ	08035
Bonnie	Brown	17 Norwest Dr.	Jersey City	NJ	08002

Record: 6 of 30

Access also looks for a primary key field—a unique tag for a record, such as an ID number. If Access cannot find a primary key field, it asks if you want it to create a primary key for you (see Figure 32.3). If you respond Yes, Access adds an AutoNumber field to the beginning of the table (see Figure 32.4). The AutoNumber field generates a unique number for each record, which Access calls the primary key.

FIG. 32.3

A primary key allows you to find unique records and create relationships between tables.

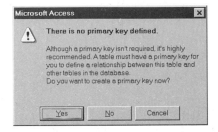

FIG. 32.4

Access assigns data types to each field based on the data entered in Datasheet view when you save the table.

ID	Field1	Field2	Field3	Field4	Field5	Field6
1	Jackie	Joyner	15 Ridge Rd.	Cherry Hill	NJ	8003
2	Letisha	Johnson	35 Main St.	Haddonfield	NJ	8045
3	Allen	Krane	909 Elm Ct.	Strafford	NJ	8034
4	Dean	Linstrom	15 Boulder Ave.	Trenton	NJ	8035
5	Bonnie	Brown	17 Norwest Dr.	Jersey City	NJ	8002
(AutoNumber)						

After you create and save the table, you might want or need to edit the table design. For example, in Figure 32.4 you can see that the Zip Code field lost the leading zero. This is because Access automatically assigned this field a data type of number instead of text. When the data type is number, Access automatically deletes leading zeros. You can easily fix this by entering Table Design view. While in Table Design view, you might want to change the generic field names (Field1, Field2, and so on) to more descriptive names and set other field properties.

TIP When using Datasheet view to create tables, save the table after entering a few rows of data. Look for and fix data type errors before entering more data.

To create a new table by entering data into a datasheet, follow these steps:

1. Open the database window (press F11).

2. Click the New button on the Table tab and double-click Datasheet View.

3. Enter data in each column (field) across the row (record).

4. Continue entering a few rows (records) of data.

5. Save the table.

6. When prompted to create a primary key, choose Yes.

7. Review the data to make sure the field data type Access chose did not alter the data entered.

8. If necessary, enter Design view to change field types or modify the table design.

9. Save the table again.

10. Return to Datasheet view to continue data entry.

> **N O T E**   Access stipulates the following object naming rules, which you should follow when naming objects such as tables, fields, forms, or any object in an Access database:
>
> - Can contain up to 64 characters
> - Characters can be letters, numbers, and spaces
> - Characters can be special characters except for these: period (.), exclamation (!), accent grave(`), or brackets ([ ]).
> - Cannot begin with a space or an ASCII control character from 0 to 31.
>
> In general, avoid names that are too long (cumbersome to type and remember), cryptic names that lack meaning, and names with spaces if you later intend to manipulate the object using Visual Basic for Applications or use them in expressions.

▶ **See** "Understanding VBA," **p. 962**

ON THE WEB

You may want to use a common naming convention such as the Leszynski Naming Convention. In this standard, objects are named with a prefix (tbl for table, qry for query, frm for form, and rpt for report). An example is tblAddresses. You can find the complete convention at

http://www.kwery.com

Creating a Table with the Table Wizard

When you choose Table Wizard in the New Table dialog box, Access displays the Table Wizard dialog box (see Figure 32.5). Sample tables are listed based on the table option you select: Business or Personal. When you select a sample table, the corresponding predefined sample fields appear in the Sample Fields list box. Use the arrow buttons to add fields to or remove fields from your new table definition. You even can edit the field names to make them more meaningful.

FIG. 32.5
The Table Wizard lists sample tables for common business and personal data storage needs.

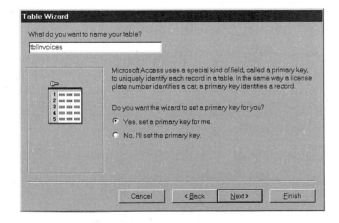

T I P You can use fields from more than one sample table and from Business and Personal tables for your table.

When you select your fields, choose the Next button. Notice that choosing the Finish button at this time closes the Wizard and creates the table based on your selections thus far.

When you choose Next, the next Table Wizard dialog box appears (see Figure 32.6). The text box in this dialog box asks you for the name of your table. The names of objects—such as tables, fields, forms, and reports—can contain up to 64 characters; letters, numbers, and spaces are allowed.

FIG. 32.6
Name the table and decide whether you want Access to generate a primary key for you.

The Table Wizard dialog box also explains that each record (row) in a table needs to have a unique tag called a primary key. The primary key is the unique element that enables you to find records and relate tables of information. The Table Wizard gives you the option of setting the primary key yourself or letting Access set a primary key for you. If you are unsure what field to use as the primary key, let the Table Wizard select one for you. You can change the primary key field at another time, if you want.

N O T E Let Access automatically enter a unique primary key field value for you when you add records. For example, each time you add a new customer record, Access will enter the next sequential number or a random number in the Customer ID field for you. ■

If you decide to set the primary key yourself, the dialog box shown in Figure 32.7 appears. In the What Field Will Hold Data that Is Unique for Each Record drop-down list, select the appropriate field. Then specify the type of data the primary key will contain by clicking one of the option buttons. For more information, see "Setting the Primary Key" later in this chapter.

FIG. 32.7
You can set the primary key field yourself while in the Table Wizard dialog box.

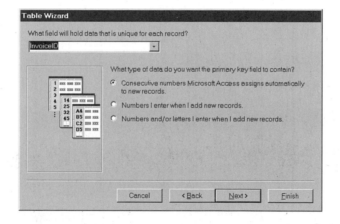

After you choose <u>N</u>ext, Access will ask you if your table is related to other tables. Related tables have records that match based on a primary key from one table to a *foreign key* in a related table. For example, a customer number on an invoice relates the customer to the invoice. The customer number in the customer table would be the primary key. In the invoice table, the customer number would be the foreign key of the relationship. Another field, such as invoice number, would be the primary key of the invoice table. Access lists relationships found between the new table and existing tables (see Figure 32.8). Choose the Relationships button to define additional relationships.

FIG. 32.8

The Table Wizard searches for and creates relationships between the new table and existing tables.

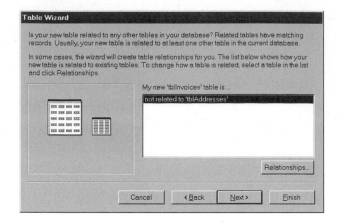

 TIP Use Table Design view to further customize a table you created with the Table Wizard.

When you choose <u>N</u>ext, the last Table Wizard dialog box appears (see Figure 32.9). You can modify the table design, enter data in the table, or enter data in a form the Wizard creates for you. You also can let Help show you how to work with the table. Choose <u>F</u>inish to create the table and display it in the view you selected.

You can view tables in Datasheet or Design view. Datasheet view displays the data in spreadsheet format, ready for data entry and editing. Design view enables you to change the structure or appearance of your table. You cannot enter data in Design view.

FIG. 32.9

After the Table Wizard creates your table, you can enter data, edit the design, or view Table Help.

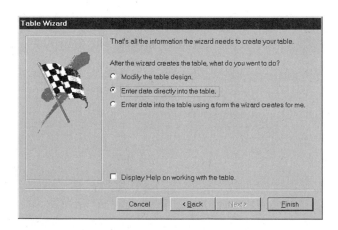

Creating a New Table by Importing

In cases where the data resides in another application format and you need to maintain that data in Access from this point forward, you might prefer using the Import Table option. Access supports the following file types for importing:

- Access (MDB)
- Text (TXT, CSV, TAB, ASC)
- Excel (XLS)
- Lotus 123 (WK*)
- HTML files (Access 97 only)
- Paradox (DB)
- dBASE III, IV, 5 (DBF)
- FoxPro (DBF)
- FoxPro 3 (DBC)
- ODBC Databases

> **TIP** If Access doesn't support the file format you need, try exporting from the original application to a supported file format.

To create a new table using Import Table, follow these steps:

New

1. Open the Database window, select the Tables tab, and select the <u>N</u>ew button.
2. Select Import Table and click OK. The Import dialog box appears (see Figure 32.10).
3. Specify the file format you are importing from in the Files of <u>T</u>ype drop-down list.
4. Specify the location of the file.
5. Select the file name.
6. Choose Import. If the import is successful, the table appears in the Table tab of the Database window. If Access encounters any problems, an error dialog box appears to explain the problem. If you need to define any import options such as spreadsheet range or data width, Access will prompt you with additional Wizard dialog boxes.

> **TIP** You can also Import or Link a table by selecting one of the <u>F</u>ile, Get External <u>D</u>ata options.

Part

VI

Ch

32

FIG. 32.10
When you create a table by importing, edits in Access only affect the new Access table, not the original data file.

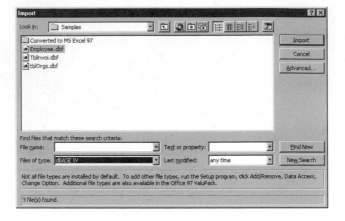

Importing an HTML File

If you find a Web site that has a list or table that you want to add to your database, you can now import the information into Access. You need to save the Web page as an HTML file and then use the Access Import Wizard to bring the information into Access. As with any import, you may need to clean up the table after you import the information.

To import information from a Web page, follow these steps:

1. From within the Web page, save the page as an HTML file. (In Microsoft Internet Explorer choose File, Save As, make sure the Save as Type is HTML, and give the file a location and file name.)

2. As mentioned in the preceding section, choose the New button on the Tables tab of the Database window and double-click Import Table in the New Table dialog box.

3. In the Import dialog box, change the Files of Type to HTML Files and choose the file you saved in step 1.

4. On the first dialog box of the HTML Import Wizard, choose Show HTML Tables or Show HTML Lists. Then pick the appropriate table or list as shown in Figure 32.11 and choose the Next button.

5. In the following dialog boxes, choose whether the first line contains column headings (field names) and whether you want to store the data in a new or existing table. You also choose field options, such as name and data type, and whether to add

a primary key. When prompted, give the name of the table. If you need to clean up the data, choose Text when you come to the data type. Figure 32.12 shows a list of actors imported.

FIG. 32.11

When you import an HTML file, some of the records may not contain the information you need. You will filter those out later.

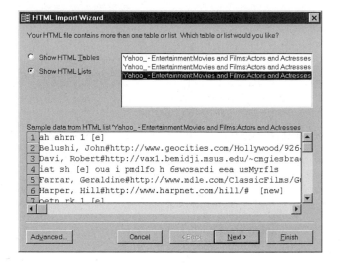

FIG. 32.12

The rows with http as part of the entry will be the ones used in this table.

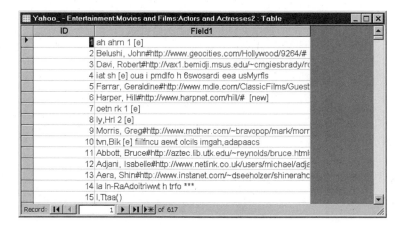

Part

VI

Ch

32

6. If necessary, edit the data and delete any unnecessary rows (see Chapter 33) or create a query to manage the data (see Chapter 35). Figure 32.13 shows the final table.

N O T E In this example, I downloaded the information from the Yahoo, Entertainment, Movies and Films, Actors and Addresses site. Start at **http://www.yahoo.com**.

There were many records that were not useful. One could manually edit the records or use Access to edit the records. The following is an advanced procedure beyond the detailed scope of this book (*see Special Edition Using Microsoft Access 97* for more help). I created a query that used ***http*** in the criteria to filter out all URLs. To separate the HTML from the rest of the text, I created the following new fields in the query:

> **First:InStr$([Field1],"#")**
> **Second:InStr$([First]+1,[Field1,"#")**
> **HTML:Mid$([Field1],[First]+1,[Second]-[First]-1)**
> **Name:Left$([Field1],[First]-1)**

Finally, I changed the table to a make table Query and removed the extra fields leaving the ID, HTML, and Name fields you see in Figure 32.13. ■

FIG. 32.13
This shows the final table example with the table cleaned up of extraneous information.

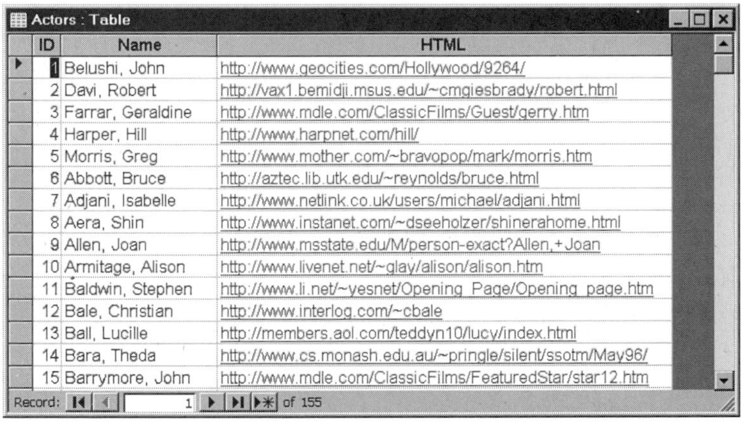

ID	Name	HTML
1	Belushi, John	http://www.geocities.com/Hollywood/9264/
2	Davi, Robert	http://vax1.bemidji.msus.edu/~cmgiesbrady/robert.html
3	Farrar, Geraldine	http://www.mdle.com/ClassicFilms/Guest/gerry.htm
4	Harper, Hill	http://www.harpnet.com/hill/
5	Morris, Greg	http://www.mother.com/~bravopop/mark/morris.htm
6	Abbott, Bruce	http://aztec.lib.utk.edu/~reynolds/bruce.html
7	Adjani, Isabelle	http://www.netlink.co.uk/users/michael/adjani.html
8	Aera, Shin	http://www.instanet.com/~dseeholzer/shinerahome.html
9	Allen, Joan	http://www.msstate.edu/M/person-exact?Allen,+Joan
10	Armitage, Alison	http://www.livenet.net/~glay/alison/alison.htm
11	Baldwin, Stephen	http://www.li.net/~yesnet/Opening Page/Opening_page.htm
12	Bale, Christian	http://www.interlog.com/~cbale
13	Ball, Lucille	http://members.aol.com/teddyn10/lucy/index.html
14	Bara, Theda	http://www.cs.monash.edu.au/~pringle/silent/ssotm/May96/
15	Barrymore, John	http://www.mdle.com/ClassicFilms/FeaturedStar/star12.htm

Record: 1 of 155

Creating a New Table by Linking

When your data resides in another application format and you need to edit and view that data from Access while others edit and view the data in the other application, you might prefer to use the Link Table option to create a new table. Access supports the following file types for linking:

- Access (MDB)
- Text (TXT, CSV, TAB, ASC)
- Excel (XLS)

- HTML Files (Access 97 only). These files would be on an internal Web server.
- Paradox (DB)
- dBASE III, IV, 5 (DBF)
- FoxPro (DBF)
- ODBC Databases

N O T E You cannot link FoxPro 3 (DBC) and Lotus 123 (WK*) files to an Access table. You can import them, however. ■

To create a new table using Link Table, follow these steps:

1. Open the Database window, select the Table tab, and select the New button.
2. Select Link Table and click OK. The Link dialog box appears (see Figure 32.14).

FIG. 32.14
When you create a table by linking, edits made in Access affect the original data file.

Displayed list depends on Files of Type selected

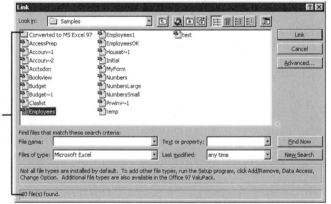

3. Specify the file format you are linking from in the Files of Type drop-down list.
4. Specify the location of the file.
5. Select the file name.
6. Choose Link. If the link is successful, the table appears in the Table tab of the Database window (see Figure 32.15). If Access encounters any problems, an error dialog box appears to explain the problem. If you need to define any link options such as spreadsheet range or data width, Access will prompt you with additional Wizard dialog boxes.

FIG. 32.15
Linked tables appear
in the Database
window with a special
icon.

Paradox Link icon ——

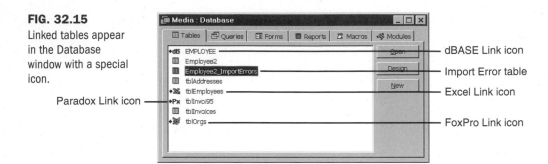

dBASE Link icon

Import Error table

Excel Link icon

FoxPro Link icon

Creating a Blank Table

New

To create a blank table, display the Database window and select the Table tab. Choose the New button to open the New Table dialog box. Choose Design View. Access displays a blank table in Design view (see Figure 32.16). In the top of the Table window, specify the Field Name and Data Type, and provide a Description to appear in the status bar. You use the bottom of the Table window to set field properties, such as format, field size, default value, and validation rules. The following section, "Modifying Table Design," explains how to design and modify the design of a table.

TIP   Use Table Design view to create a custom table from scratch.

◆ **TROUBLESHOOTING**

I need to create a database to manage sales contacts, and I don't know where to begin.
Use the Table Wizard sample table called Contacts as your base table. Modify the table to meet your needs.

I want to change the default field names in the Table Wizard. When you use the Table Wizard to create a new table, you can change the default field names provided by Table Wizards. In the first Table Wizard dialog box, select the sample table and add the desired sample fields to your new table (refer to Figure 32.5). Select the desired field and click Rename Field. Edit the name in the text box and click OK. You can also use Design View to rename fields.

FIG. 32.16
In Table Design view, you can add new fields or edit existing fields.

Field Selector Column —

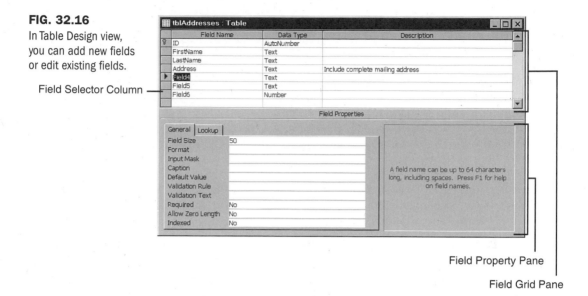

Field Property Pane

Field Grid Pane

Modifying Table Design

You can view a table in Datasheet view or Design view. Datasheet view is where you enter and modify data in your table; Design view is where you add or modify fields. If you created a table using the Table Wizard or any of the other automated table creation features, Access filled out the Table Design view for you. If you selected Design View from the New Table dialog box, Access displayed a blank table in Design view, ready for you to specify the fields to be included. For more information, refer to "Creating a New Table" earlier in this chapter.

To enter Design view for an existing table, follow these steps:

1. Open the database.

2. In the Database window, select the desired table.

3. Choose the Design button.

Alternatively, if you are currently viewing the table in Datasheet view, choose View, Table Design.

Design view contains the following components (refer to Figure 32.16):

- *Table Design toolbar.* Contains various tools that help you design and work with your table.
- *Field Grid pane.* Contains columns that enable you to define field names, data types, and descriptions.
- *Field Properties pane.* Enables you to set various properties for each field.

The next few sections explain how to work with these components.

Working with the Table Design Toolbar

In the Table Design window, the toolbar contains the active buttons listed in Table 32.1.

Table 32.1 The Table Design Toolbar

Button	Button Name	Description
	Datasheet View	Displays the table in Datasheet view.
	Save	Saves the table design.
	Cut	Removes the selected text or object from the Design window to the Clipboard.
	Copy	Copies the selected text or object from the Design window to the Clipboard.
	Paste	Places a copy of the Clipboard contents in the current selection.
	Primary Key	Enables users to select a column or columns as the primary key. Toggles primary key on/off.
	Indexes	Displays the index sheet for the currently selected object.
	Insert Rows	Inserts a row above the current row.
	Delete Rows	Deletes the selected row(s).
	Properties	Opens or closes the property sheet for the currently selected object.
	Build	Helps create an item or property such as a field or input mask property.

Button	Button Name	Description
	Database Window	Displays the Database window.
	New Object	Displays a drop-down list of new objects you can create such as tables, forms, reports, queries, macros, and modules.
	Office Assistant	Runs Office Assistant for help searches or tips.

Working in the Field Grid Pane

The field grid pane enables you to define field names, data types, and descriptions. The grid consists of the field row selector column, the Field Name column, Data Type column, and the Description column (refer to Figure 32.16).

Naming Fields   As is true of most objects in an Access database, field names can contain up to 64 characters (letters, numbers, and spaces). Field names must be unique within the table.

Determining the Data Type   A data type specifies the kind of information you can store in a field. If you define a field as a Date field, for example, Access does not permit you to enter text in that field. When you assign a data type, Access also knows how much storage space is needed. A date value requires eight bytes of storage space, whereas text requires one byte for each character (a 20-character name needs 20 bytes of storage). Based on the data type, Access also determines the types of calculations or other operations available for that field.

Access provides the following basic data types:

- *Text.* Alphanumeric characters, up to 255 bytes (one byte per character).
- *Memo.* Alphanumeric characters, up to 65,535 characters.
- *Number.* Any numeric type; see Table 32.2 for storage sizes and range of values permitted.
- *Date/Time.* Dates and times (eight bytes).
- *Currency.* Rounded numbers that are accurate to 15 digits to the left of the decimal point and to four decimal places.
- *AutoNumber.* Unique sequential (incrementing by one) or random numbering, automatically entered by Access for each record you add.
- *Yes/No.* Logical values (Yes/No, True/False, or On/Off).
- *OLE Object.* OLE objects, graphics, or other binary data.

Part
VI

Ch
32

■ *Hyperlink*. Text and numbers defining a path to a document, Web page, or specific part of a document such as a Word bookmark, Excel range, or database object.

■ *Lookup Wizard*. Walks you through the process to create a field that displays a drop-down list of acceptable values from another table.

Access allows the following range of values for numerical data (identified in the Field Size property), depending on the field and data type you select:

Table 32.2   Numeric Values Permitted for the Number Data Type

Field Size	Storage Size	Range
Byte	1 byte	0 to 255; no fraction
Integer	2 bytes	–32,768 to 32,767; no fractions
Long Integer	4 bytes	–2,147,483,648 to 2,147,483,647; no fractions
Single	4 bytes	Numbers with seven digits of precision: –3.402823E38 to 3.402823E38
Double	8 bytes	Numbers with 15 digits of precision: –1.79769313486231E308 to 1.79769313486231E308
Replication ID	16 bytes	Globally unique identifier (GUID) used for database replication

By default, Access assigns the data type Text to a new field. To assign a different data type, click the down-arrow button and select one from the Data Type drop-down list (see Figure 32.17).

FIG. 32.17

Type the first letter of the data type or select from the drop-down list.

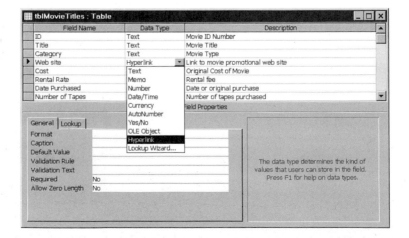

N O T E For numbers containing punctuation (such as hyphens in a Social Security or phone number), you can use the Text data type or change formatting or the input mask, because no punctuation is allowed in a Number data type. ■

CAUTION

Be careful when choosing between the Number and the Currency data type. Entries in Currency fields are rounded, whereas Number fields use floating-point (the decimal point floats as needed) calculation. Currency uses a faster method of fixed-point (predetermined number of decimal places) calculation that prevents rounding errors.

 To speed selection of data types, type the first letter of the data type and press Tab. Access fills in the rest.

Describing Fields   Use the Description column to provide further information about a field. The description is optional, but it does appear in the Status bar when the insertion point is in that field in Datasheet or Form view.

Setting the Primary Key   Although it is not required, every table should have a primary key so that it works efficiently in Access. The primary key identifies a record as being unique. In an Employee database, for example, each employee has a unique Social Security number. The Social Security number field would be the primary key.

The benefits of establishing a primary key include the following:

- ■ *Speed*. Access creates an index based on the primary key, which enables Access to improve processing of queries and other functions.

- ■ *Order*. Access automatically sorts and displays database records in primary-key order.

- ■ *No duplicates*. Access does not permit users to enter data with the same primary key as an existing record.

- ■ *Links*. Access maintains relationships between linked tables based on relating the primary key to a foreign key in another table with the same information as the primary key.

Sometimes, the unique fact about a record is a combination of the information kept in several fields. In an Invoice line item table, for example, the primary key might consist of the invoice number and the line number, because an invoice will probably have more than one item on the invoice. Access enables you to key more than one field in a table to create a *multi-field primary key*. Another name for the multi-field primary key is *composite key*.

To set a primary key, follow these steps:

1. Click the field selector (first column) to select the field you want to use as the primary key. For a multi-field primary key, hold down the Ctrl key and click the field selector for the remaining field(s).

2. Choose Edit, Primary Key. A key icon appears in the field selector column of each primary-key field (see Figure 32.18).

FIG. 32.18
Access displays a key icon in the field selector column to indicate the field(s) that define the primary key.

Table Design toolbar   Click to set Primary key

Select the field row(s)

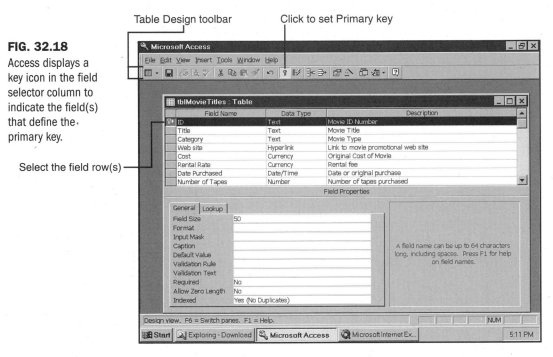

TROUBLESHOOTING

How do I make it so users can enter only Yes or No in a field? You could use data validation, but a more efficient approach is to define the data type as Yes/No.

What would be the proper data type to assign to fields named Client Number, Client Name, Phone, Invoice Total, and Notes? For the Client Number field, use AutoNumber so Access automatically enters consecutive numbers for you. For the Client Name field, use Text. For the Phone field, you could use Number, but Text is easier if you want the phone number field to contain punctuation, such as dashes. For the Invoice Total field, use Currency to get the proper dollars-and-cents format. For the Notes field, use Memo to get more information into the field than a text field allows.

I want to assign a good primary key for the fields in the previous question. What would be the best one? Use Client Number as the unique identifier for each record.

Setting Field Properties

Fields have properties that define the way data is stored and displayed. By setting field properties, you can provide the following:

- A default caption
- A default value
- A format (display layout) for data entry
- Data-entry validation
- An index (for fields that can be indexed)
- Various display qualities, such as field size and formats

The field properties set at the table level are applied automatically to other database objects that use this table, such as forms, reports, and queries. Field properties are organized on two tabs, General and Lookup.

Following is an overview of the General field properties:

- *Field Size*. Limits Text fields to a specific number of characters such as 2 for two characters in a State field; and limits Number fields to a range of values (refer to Table 32.2).
- *New Values*. Specifies how new values for AutoNumber fields should be generated: incremental or random.
- *Format*. Specifies a specific display format for dates and numbers, such as 2/21/96, Monday, February 21, 1996, 1234.5, or $1,234.50.
- *Decimal Places*. Sets the number of decimal places displayed in Number and Currency fields, such as 2.99.
- *Input Mask* (Text and Date data only). Specifies formatting characters, such as dashes in a phone number field, to be filled in automatically during data entry.
- *Caption*. Supplies a label to be used in forms and reports and as header of the datasheet column instead of the field name, such as Movie Tag instead of MovieID.

- *Default Value.* Specifies a default value to be entered automatically in new records, such as the city and state in which a video-rental store is located.
- *Validation Rule.* Restricts data entry to values that meet specific criteria, such as the return date being greater than today's date.
- *Validation Text.* Specifies the error message that appears when data entry violates a validation rule.
- *Required.* Specifies that data be entered in the field, such as the member's ID number.

TIP For help on any property, click the property box and press F1. The help screen displays the property name, a long description, and sometimes includes Examples.

- *Allow Zero Length.* Permits Text and Memo fields to contain zero-length strings (""). By default, Access does not store string values that contain no characters or spaces.
- *Indexed.* Sets up an additional index based on this field. (For more information, see "Setting Index Properties" later in this chapter.)

On the Lookup tab, the properties will change depending on what data type you choose and what the value is for the first Lookup field property, Display Control.

TIP If you use the Lookup Wizard Data Type, Access will help you fill in the Lookup tabs' properties.

- *Display Control.* Specifies the type of control to use to display the field on a form (only for Text, Number, and Y/N fields). The types of controls include Text Box (the default), List Box (shows more than one value at a time with scroll bars), and Combo Box (creates a drop-down list of choices with the result appearing in a text box with a drop-down arrow).
- *Row Source Type.* Specifies whether the values in the List Box or Combo Box come from a table or query, list you type (Value List), or list of fields from a table or query.
- *Row Source.* Name of a table, query, or SQL statement used for the List Box or Combo Box.
- *Bound Column.* The column number shown in the Row Source whose value will be stored in the current table.
- *Column Count.* Number of columns used for the Combo or List Box.
- *Column Heads.* Display the name of the fields from the Row Source.
- *Column Widths.* Width in inches of the drop-down or list box columns separated by semicolons. If you do not want a column displayed, type **0** for the column width.

An example of the Column Widths would be 0;1;1.5 where the first column (this could be the Bound Column such as an ID number) would not display.

TIP For help in entering a validation expression or an input mask, click the Build button in the toolbar while the insertion point is in the field property.

To set field properties in Table Design view, follow these steps:

1. Select the field for which you want to set properties. The bottom part of the window displays the General properties for that field (see Figure 32.19).

2. Click the specific General property you want to set, or press F6 to move to the Field Property pane and tab to the desired property.

3. Enter the property value, or select it from a drop-down list of values (if available).

4. Continue setting other properties for the field.

5. Select the Lookup tab and set properties as needed.

6. Set properties for other fields as needed.

7. When you finish setting properties, save your table.

FIG. 32.19

Each field type has its own list of field properties.

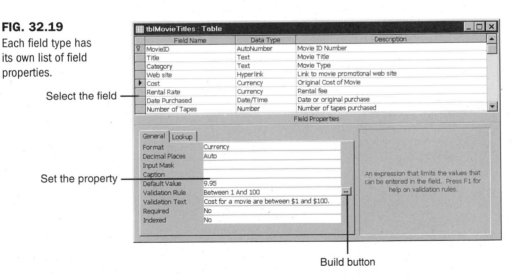

Build button

If the property box is too small for the value you need to enter, press Shift+F2, or click the right mouse button and choose Zoom from the shortcut menu, to display the Zoom dialog box (see Figure 32.20). The Zoom dialog box is available throughout most of Access.

N O T E Right-clicking a field property displays a pop-up shortcut menu containing the Build, Zoom, Cut, Copy, Paste, and Table Properties commands. (Some commands are disabled, depending on the property or data type.)

FIG. 32.20
Use the Zoom box to
see the entire contents
of a field.

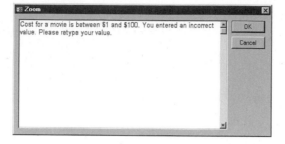

▶ **See** "Creating Formulas," **p. 374**

 The build button on the Table Design toolbar or to the right of the property allows you to
see available functions or examples. Figure 32.21 shows the Expression Builder dialog
box for the Validation Rule property (the same dialog box would be available for the Default Value property). Double-click the yellow folder to open the list of possibilities (Operators in the example). If desired, choose a category in the middle section (<All> is selected
in the example). And double click the value in the third section (Between is selected) to
enter the value in the upper part of the Expression Builder. Then edit the expression as
necessary (replace any bracketed prompts).

FIG. 32.21
Replace any prompts
with actual values in
the Expression Builder.

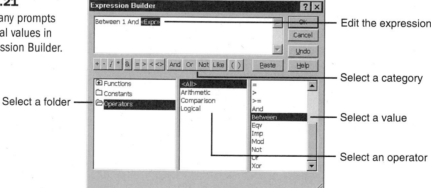

The Builder may also give examples to choose from. If your focus is in a field name, the
Build button will bring up a Field Builder dialog box (see Figure 32.22) where you can
select sample field names from different sample tables. This is the same as one of the
steps of the Table Wizard. When you choose Build for the Input Mask property, Access
will give you a choice of examples that include phone numbers, Social Security numbers,
passwords, and dates.

FIG. 32.22

Choose Business or Personal, the Sample Table, and Sample Field you want.

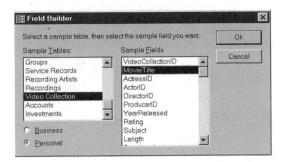

Setting Index Properties

Indexes help Access find values. Access automatically creates and maintains an index for the primary-key fields (see Figure 32.23). You can create additional indexes by setting the field index property.

If you frequently search or sort certain fields (including in queries and reports), you can increase processing speed by creating an index for those fields. You can set up indexes for all field types except OLE, Hyperlink, Memo, and Yes/No.

You can set the following index properties:

- *Yes (Duplicates OK)*. Creates an index that includes duplicate field values.
- *Yes (No Duplicates)*. Creates an index based on unique field values.
- *No*. Has no index.

T I P Set up indexes for fields in which the data varies. Indexing a field that contains the same data throughout the records does not increase search or sort speed.

To set index properties, follow these steps:

1. In the field grid pane, select the field to be indexed.
2. In the field properties pane, select the Indexed property.
3. Select a type of index from the Indexed drop-down list of index property values (see Figure 32.23).

N O T E Although indexes speed searches and sorts, they might slow data processing. Each time a record is added, deleted, or changed, the indexes must be updated. ■

FIG. 32.23
By setting the index
property to Yes, you
speed up searching.

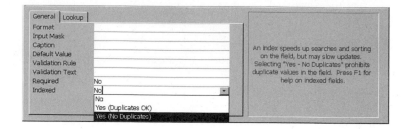

TROUBLESHOOTING

How do I automate data entry at the table level? Set field properties for default values, and use default patterns (input masks) to format data automatically as it is entered.

I want to require data entry in a specific field before allowing a user to move off a record. Set the Required property of the field to Yes, or specify a Validation Rule if the data must meet a certain criterion.

How do I select a display format for dates? Click the Format drop-down list display date formats. Select the desired date format.

I want to eliminate the possibility of someone entering the same title more than once in the table. Set the Indexed property to Yes (No Duplicates).

Setting Table Properties

Like fields, tables have properties. Table properties apply to the entire table and to all the records the table contains. You can set the following properties for a table:

- *Description*. Enter a description of the table and its purpose (for more room, use the Zoom box by pressing Shift+F2). For example, the Movies table could be described as the inventory of movies purchased. If you click the Details button on the Database toolbar, the description as well as date and time appear for the table.

- *Validation Rule*. Restricts data entry to values that meet specific criteria for all records in the table—for example, requiring that category and rental-rate data be entered in all new records.

- *Validation Text*. Displays a message when the record-validation rule is violated—for example, describing why the category and rental-rate data are needed.

- *Filter*. Specifies the filter to be loaded with the table. For example, showing only the movies that are currently in stock.

■ *Order By*. Specifies the order to be loaded with the table. For example, showing movies in descending order of when purchased.

To set table properties in Table Design view, follow these steps:

1. Choose Yiew, Properties. The Table Properties window appears (see Figure 32.24).
2. Enter any desired table properties.
3. Close the Table Properties window.

FIG. 32.24
To apply a validation rule to all records in a table, set the table's Validation Rule property.

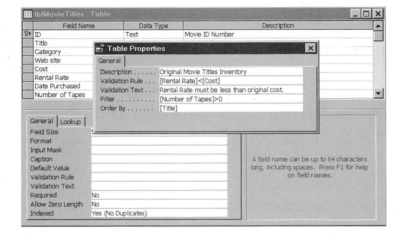

Modifying a Table

Access makes it easy for you to modify your table to meet changing needs. You can add, rename, delete, and move fields. Remember, you should always back up your data before modifying the structure of your table. You should also consider the effects of the following actions on dependent database objects, such as forms, queries, and reports:

■ *Deleting a field*. Fields deleted from tables also must be deleted from forms, queries, and reports.

■ *Renaming a field*. Renamed fields must be renamed in forms, queries, and reports. In addition, you must rename any references to the field in calculations, expressions, macros, and modules.

■ *Changing a data type*. Certain data-type conversions are not allowed, such as converting from any data type to the AutoNumber data type. In other cases, if you convert from a larger data type to a smaller data type, data will be truncated (cut off or lost). For example, changing from a Number data type to a Currency data type truncates values beyond the range allowed for currency, and data will be lost. (For more information, refer to "Determining the Data Type" earlier in this chapter.)

- *Changing the field size.* Changes that truncate numbers with decimals are rounded. If a change makes the value too large for the new field, the data is lost (an error message appears before the data is lost).

To insert a field, follow these steps:

1. Position the insertion point in the row before which you want to insert a row.

 2. Choose <u>I</u>nsert, <u>R</u>ows on the menu or shortcut menu.

Alternatively, click the field selector (first column) to select the row before which you want to insert a new field row, and press Insert to insert a blank row.

To rename a field, follow these steps:

1. Select the field-name cell.

2. Type the new name.

 To delete a field, choose <u>E</u>dit, Delete <u>R</u>ows or click the Delete Row toolbar button. Alternatively, click the field selector (first column) to select the field row you want to delete and press Delete.

To move a field, follow these steps:

1. With the black, right-arrow mouse pointer, click the field selector (first column) to select the field row you want to move.

2. With the white arrow mouse pointer, drag the field row to the new position.

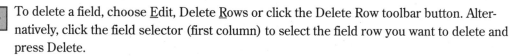

TROUBLESHOOTING

I want to validate data for all records in a table. You can validate data for all records in a table by setting the Properties Validation Rule table property. To set table properties, choose <u>V</u>iew, <u>P</u>roperties and enter the desired validation rule.

 I need to add a new field to the database I just created. If you need to add a field at the end of the table, just start defining the field in a blank row. To insert a field between field rows, position the insertion point in the row before which you want to insert a row and then click the Insert Row button.

Setting Relationships

If you create tables with the Table Wizard, Access will prompt you on how your table will be related to any other tables in the database. Also, if you use the Lookup Wizard as a data type in Table Design, Access may create a relationship for you. If you want to view or edit these relationships or create new ones, choose Tools, Relationships or click the Relationships button on the Database toolbar. If no relationships have been set, you will enter the Show Table dialog box. Add any tables you wish to the relationship window.

You need to create relationships between tables when you have forms and subforms and reports and subreports. When you create relationships in advance, your multiple table queries will also know how tables are related.

Most relationships are a one-to-many type where one record (such as a customer record) is related to many records (such as invoices). The primary key on the one side of the relationship is related to a field (that has information in common) in the related table. This field in the related table is called a foreign key and may or may not be a primary key itself. In the example in Figure 32.25, one movie title can have multiple actors so the MovieID in the tblMovieTitles is the primary key and related to the foreign key MovieID field in the tblMovieActors.

Part
VI

Ch
32

FIG. 32.25
To create the relationship between tblActors and tblMovieActors, drag from ActorID in tblActors to ActorID in tblMovieActors.

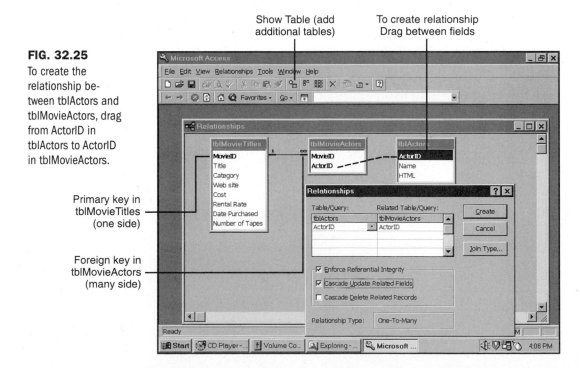

Show Table (add additional tables)

To create relationship Drag between fields

Primary key in tblMovieTitles (one side)

Foreign key in tblMovieActors (many side)

To create a relationship, follow these steps:

1. Choose Tools, Relationships.

2. If necessary, choose Relationships, Show Table and add any other tables.

3. From the Relationship window, drag the primary key field name from one field list (the one side of a relationship) to the related field name in another field list (generally, the many side of a relationship). The Relationships window automatically appears as shown in Figure 32.25.

4. Choose the options in the Relationships window as follow and select the Create button when finished. The relationship will show a line between the two tables connecting the common field.

The following are the options in the Relationship dialog box:

■ *Enforce Referential Integrity.* If this option is checked, if you change or delete the primary key, you will either be prompted that the change is not possible or data in the related table will change.

■ *Cascade Update Related Fields.* If checked, when you change the primary key, the related foreign key will automatically change. If not checked, you are warned that you cannot make a change when you try to edit the primary key.

■ *Cascade Delete Related Fields.* If checked, when you delete the record, any related records that match the primary key are deleted. If not checked, you are warned that you cannot delete the record if there are related records.

■ *Join Type.* The default view for queries. This includes whether you only want to see records that have a common key in both tables or want to see all of one table and any matching records in the other table.

T I P To delete a relationship, click the relationship line and press Delete.

CHAPTER 33

Viewing and Editing Data

by Rick Winter

With your database and table created, you are ready to view and enter data. You can accomplish data entry and display tasks in Datasheet view or Form view. Datasheet view enables you to work in a familiar row-and-column format in which you can see many records at the same time. Form view enables you to focus on one record at a time. This chapter covers the features of Datasheet view. The next chapter shows how to create and use forms for data entry and display tasks. ■

Navigate in Datasheet view

The Datasheet toolbar and navigation keys enable you to quickly accomplish data entry and management tasks.

Perform basic data entry tasks

Adding, editing, and deleting data are the primary tasks associated with getting your information into the database.

Locate, sort, and filter data

After you enter and modify your data, you will need to quickly find and see the data when you need it.

Import and export data

If you have the data in one location, there is no need to type it in more than once if you know how to import and export.

Change the datasheet layout

You can change the font, row, and column size, hide or display columns, and freeze columns.

Navigating in Datasheet View

After you create your table, you are ready to start entering data. To switch from Design to Datasheet view, choose View, Datasheet View or choose the Open button on the database window. Datasheet view enables you to enter and view data in a table (spreadsheet) format of rows and columns. The intersection of a row and a column is referred to as a cell.

Figure 33.1 shows what a new (empty) table looks like.

FIG. 33.1

A new table displayed in Datasheet view contains only a blank record with the insertion point in the first field, ready for input.

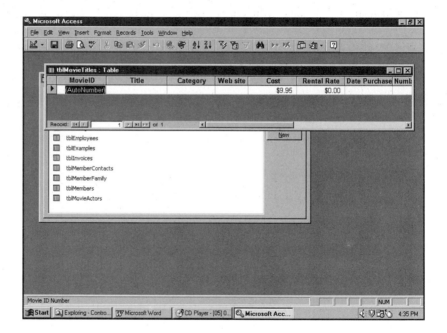

Table 33.1 describes the Active Datasheet toolbar buttons.

Table 33.1   Datasheet Toolbar Buttons

Button	Button Name	Shortcut	Description
	View		Drop-down list of table views: While In Design shows Datasheet view button; while In Datasheet shows Design View button.
	Save	Ctrl+S	Saves the layout of the current table (in Design view, saves the design of the table).
	Print	Ctrl+P	Prints the current table in datasheet format.

Button	Button Name	Shortcut	Description
	Print Preview		Displays the current table in page layout format. Enables you to set up the printer and print the current table in datasheet format.
	Spelling	F7	Spell checks the current table.
	Cut	Ctrl+X	Deletes selected data and copies it to the Clipboard.
	Copy	Ctrl+C	Copies selected data to the Clipboard.
	Paste	Ctrl+V	Inserts Clipboard contents.
	Undo Current Field/Record	Ctrl+Z	Reverses last change to the current field or record.
	Insert Hyperlink		Inserts a link to a Web site or file (Word, Excel, or other Access object).
	Web Toolbar		Turns the Web toolbar on or off.
	Sort Ascending		Sorts data in ascending order.
	Sort Descending		Sorts data in descending order.
	Filter By Selection		Filters data based on selected data.
	Filter By Form		Displays the Filter By Form window (a blank version of the active form or datasheet), so you can enter filter data criteria.
	Apply Filter		Toggles filter on/off.
	Find	Ctrl+F	Searches the current field for user-specified data.
	New Record	Ctrl++	Moves to a new record at the end of a datasheet.
	Delete Record	Ctrl+−	Deletes the selected record.

Part
VI

Ch
33

continues

Table 33.1   Continued

Button	Button Name	Shortcut	Description
	Database Window	F11	Displays the database window.
	New Object		Drop-down list that allows creation of database objects such as forms, queries, and reports.
	Office Assistant	F1	Runs Office Assistant for help searches or tips.

N O T E You can print the contents of a Datasheet view at any time by clicking the Print button in the toolbar or choosing File, Print. To preview the printout on-screen, click the Print Preview button or choose File, Print Preview. ■

Entering and Editing Data

Basic data entry skills include adding, deleting, and editing table records; copying and moving data; and undoing unwanted data changes. Access provides many keyboard shortcuts to speed up data entry and table navigation. Table 33.2 lists the shortcut keys for data entry, and Table 33.3 lists the navigation shortcut keys.

▶ **See** "Typing and Editing," **p. 66**

Entering data in Access is similar to entering data in Excel or a Word table. You type your entry in one cell and press Tab or Enter to go to the next field. When you are in the last field, Tab or Enter automatically takes you to the next record.

Table 33.2   Data-Entry Shortcut Keys

Shortcut Key	Description
Ctrl+;	Inserts the current date.
Ctrl+:	Inserts the current time.
Ctrl+Alt+spacebar	Enters the default field value.
Ctrl+' or Ctrl+"	Enters the value from the same field in the preceding record.
Ctrl+Enter	Inserts a new line in a field, a label, or the zoom box.
Ctrl++	Inserts a new blank record.
Ctrl+−	Deletes the current record.

Shortcut Key	Description
F2	Toggles between edit and navigation mode.
Shift+F2	Displays the zoom box.
Shift+Enter	Saves changes in the current record.
F7	Checks spelling.
Esc	Undoes last change to current record or field.

 TIP To add a new record, press Ctrl++. To copy a field from a previous record, press Ctrl+'.

CAUTION

Unlike Excel and Word, you do not have to choose File, Save to save your work. As soon as you move from the current edited record to another record, the data is saved. Because changes are saved automatically, if you want to do some testing, you should first make a copy of the database.

Access has two modes—edit mode for editing a field in a record and navigation mode for moving between records. Some keys will act differently in the different modes. For example, in edit mode, Home will take you to the beginning of a field. In navigation mode, Home will take you to the beginning of the record. To toggle back and forth between the two modes, press F2.

Table 33.3 Datasheet-Navigation Shortcut Keys

Shortcut Key	Description
F5	Moves insertion point to record number box above the status bar. Type the number of the record you want to go to, and then press Enter.
Enter or Tab	Moves to the following field.
→	Moves to next field when in navigation mode, or moves the insertion point to right within field when in Edit mode.
Shift+Tab	Moves to the preceding field.
←	Moves to previous field when in Navigation mode or moves the insertion point to left within field when in Edit mode.
End	Moves to the last field in the current record when in navigation mode or moves to the end of line in field when in Edit mode.

continues

Part
VI

Ch
33

Table 33.3   Continued

Shortcut Key	Description
Home	Moves to the first field in the current record when in Navigation mode or beginning of line in field when in Edit mode.
Ctrl+End	Moves to the last record's last field when in navigation mode or end of the last line in a field when in Edit mode.
Ctrl+Home	Moves to the first field in the first record when in Navigation mode or beginning of field when in Edit mode.
↑	Moves up one record in the same field.
↓	Move down one record in the same field.
Ctrl+↑	Moves to the current field in the first record.
Ctrl+↓	Moves to the current field in the last record.
Page Up	Moves up one screen.
Page Down	Moves down one screen.
Ctrl+Page Up	Moves left one screen.
Ctrl+Page Down	Moves right one screen.

You also can use the mouse to select fields, edit fields, and move around the table. Click the navigation buttons to move to the first, preceding, following, or last record (see Figure 33.2). The record number box above the status bar displays the current record number; you also can use this box to go to a specific record. (Click the record number box, enter the number of the record to which you want to go, and press Enter.) You can use the scroll bars to scroll across columns or rows that do not appear in the current window.

N O T E   If you have Microsoft IntelliMouse, you can use the middle wheel button to scroll your window. Turn the wheel button to scroll the view up or down one record at a time. Hold down the wheel button and drag to scroll the screen up and down or left and right. ■

Some shortcut keys help you select data within a field, a series of fields, or a series of records. Table 33.4 lists the shortcut keys for selecting data.

Table 33.4   Selection Shortcut Keys

Shortcut Key	Description
Shift	Creates a selection starting from the current point. Use movement keys mentioned in Table 33.2 to expand selection.
Shift+Spacebar	Toggle between selecting field and selecting record when in Navigation mode.

Shortcut Key	Description
Ctrl+Spacebar	Toggle between selecting field and selecting column when in Navigation mode.
Ctrl+A	Select all records.
F8	Extend mode. Press F8 continuously to select word, field, record, all records. After F8 is pressed, using any movement keys will extend highlighted selection (without Shift). Press Esc to turn off.

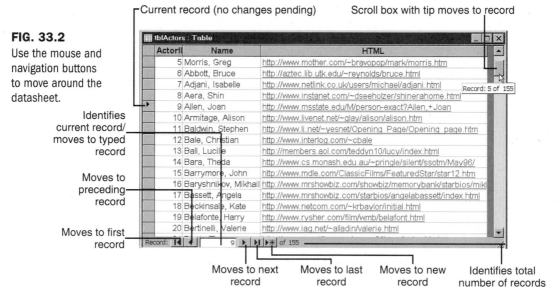

FIG. 33.2
Use the mouse and navigation buttons to move around the datasheet.

Current record (no changes pending) Scroll box with tip moves to record

Identifies current record/ moves to typed record

Moves to preceding record

Moves to first record

Moves to next record   Moves to last record   Moves to new record   Identifies total number of records

Part
VI
Ch
33

Once you have records selected, you can delete them (Delete), copy or cut them to the Clipboard (Ctrl+X or Ctrl+C), or replace selected records with records from the Clipboard (Ctrl+V). You can use the mouse to select one or more records by clicking or dragging the record selectors. To select one or more columns, click or drag the column selectors.

 Click the scroll bar once to scroll one screen at a time. When scrolling through a table, scroll tips tell you what record you're on.

Adding New Records

Access provides two options for adding records: Edit mode and Data Entry mode.

Edit mode enables you to add new records at the end of a table. Whenever you change data or enter new records, Access automatically places you in Edit mode. Data entry mode hides all existing records in the table and displays a blank table, ready for new records. To activate data entry mode, choose Records, Data Entry. To deactivate Data Entry mode, choose Records, Remove Filter/Sort.

In either case, you use the blank record at the bottom of the datasheet to enter new records in a table. You can click in the blank record, press Ctrl++, or click the New Record button on the toolbar or navigation bar to get to the new record. Before you start typing in the new record, any default values show in the record. When you begin to enter data in this row, Access moves the blank record down. When you start typing, if you have an AutoNumber field, the number is automatically entered.

The first column on the left of the datasheet is called the *record selector column* (see Figure 33.3). By clicking this column, you can select the entire row (record).

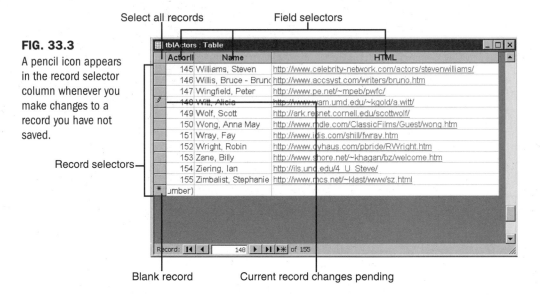

FIG. 33.3
A pencil icon appears in the record selector column whenever you make changes to a record you have not saved.

Access uses the record selector column to display the following record selector symbols:

- The *arrowhead* indicates the current record (no new data entry or edits pending).

- The *asterisk* marks the blank record that Access keeps at the bottom of the table. When you move to this record, the asterisk changes to an arrowhead, which is the current-record indicator.

- The *pencil* indicates that the current record contains data entries or edits you have not yet saved.

■ The *record-locked* symbol indicates that the record is currently being edited by you (on a form or query) or another user in a multiuser environment. This record is read-only to all users except the one who currently is entering data into it.

N O T E You can change the behavior of record locking through the Tools, Options, Advanced tab Default Record Locking section. No Locks allows anybody to make changes to any record. If there is a conflict, the user will be prompted as to which change will take preference, or whether he or she wants to save the changes to the Clipboard. Use All Records to indicate that all records in the table will be locked when one user is editing them. Use Edited Record to lock the current record (and get the record-locked symbol) for the current record (and depending on record size, surrounding records). ■

As you enter data and move from field to field, Access checks data entry for the proper data type and any special properties you set (such as validation). Access notifies you of any invalid entry before you move to the next field or record.

Access automatically saves new records and any changes when you move off a record. You can, however, save changes in the current record at any time by choosing Records, Save Record or pressing Shift+Enter.

N O T E You cannot edit data in AutoNumber fields, because Access automatically enters these fields. Press Tab, Enter, or an arrow key to move past these fields. Access will enter the proper value automatically. ■

To add a new record, follow these steps:

1. If you want to add records without seeing any existing records in the table, choose Records, Data Entry or move to the blank record at the end of the table.
2. Start typing in the record. The record indicator changes to a pencil, and Access appends a blank record. Press Enter or Tab to move to the next field.
3. Continue entering the remaining field data for that record. Access automatically enters data for AutoNumber fields. You can tab past or change any automatically entered values that were entered because of the Default property set in table design.
4. Choose Records, Remove Filter/Sort to view the entire table (new and old records).

 N O T E Entering and displaying dates deserve special mention. You can type **5/5** and Access will automatically enter the current year and display the date in whatever format is defined in the Format Field Property. Access 97 assumes two-digit years entered as 1/1/00 through 12/31/29 are twenty-first century dates (years 2000 through 2029). Dates entered as 1/1/30 through 12/31/99 are assumed to be twentieth century dates (years 1930 through 1999). ■

Editing Data

To edit existing table data, select the field in the record you need to edit. You can select the field by positioning the mouse pointer on the left edge of the cell until the mouse pointer turns to a white plus, and then clicking. Or click the I-beam mouse pointer in the cell and press F2. If no data exists in that cell, simply start typing. To replace the cell contents with new data, start typing. To navigate in the cell, press F2 again and the cursor changes to an insertion point allowing you to edit as you would in Word. For data that exceeds the width of the cell, use the zoom box (Shift+F2).

> **N O T E** To edit data in a field, use your mouse. With one click, you can select the record, select the field, and position the insertion point in the cell. ▪

TROUBLESHOOTING

I can't add new records. You might not have user rights to insert data. Check to see what rights you have by choosing Tools, Security, User and Group Permissions. In the Permissions pane, make sure the Update Data, Insert Data, and Delete Data check boxes are selected. If not, you might not have access rights to the table. If that is the case, ask the database manager to grant you editing rights to the table.

I can't edit the text in a field without retyping the entire cell contents. To edit the data in a cell, click your mouse to insert the insertion point in the data in the cell you want to edit. If you prefer to use the keyboard, move to the desired cell, press F2, and position the insertion point in the data you want to edit.

Undoing Edits

 Access enables you to reverse changes in your data. The Undo button on the toolbar retracts your most recent change. Or, you can choose Edit, Undo to reverse changes. The exact wording of the Edit, Undo command changes to let you know what Access can and cannot undo. Table 33.5 lists the various menu command text and shortcut keys available for each type of undo.

> **CAUTION**
>
> As soon as you begin editing another record, apply or remove a filter, or switch to another window, you cannot use the Undo methods to reverse a change in the last record.

Table 33.5 Edit Menu Undo Commands

Command	Shortcut Key	Description
Undo saved record	Ctrl+Z	Available after saving a record, but before editing another. Reverses all changes in the last saved record.
Undo typing	Ctrl+Z	Available after typing in a field, but before leaving the field. Reverses most recent typed edits without losing other changes to record.
Undo current field/record	Esc	Available after leaving an edited field, but before leaving the record. Reverses all edits to the current record.

TIP Press Esc once to undo typing edits in the current field. Press Esc once more to undo all edits to the current record.

Recent actions that can be undone include the following:

- Last record saved
- Last deletion
- Last cut or paste
- Last characters typed

CAUTION
You cannot undo the most recent paste of a record, a record deletion, or a full replace operation.

 See "Finding and Replacing Text," **p. 90**
 See "Using Action Queries," **p. 829**

Replacing Data

Just as you can in Word, Excel, and PowerPoint, Access has a replace feature to edit records. Choose Edit, Replace (or press Ctrl+H). In the Find What text box, type the text to replace. In the Replace With text box, type the replacement. Use the Find Next button to find and skip entries. Use Replace to replace the currently highlighted find. Use Replace All to replace all occurrences of the Find What text.

Part
VI

Ch
33

Deleting Records

If you need to delete an entire record, click the record selector or use the navigation keys to move to that record, and then choose Edit, Delete Record or press Ctrl+–. Access deletes the current record and the Assistant asks you to confirm or cancel the deletion (see Figure 33.4).

▶ **See** "Asking the Office Assistant for Help," **p. 129**

 T I P To select more than one contiguous record, click the first record selector, and then drag to extend the selection. Then press Delete to delete multiple records.

N O T E You do not need to insert records in a particular place in a table. Access automatically inserts new records where they belong in the table, based on the primary key field. ▪

FIG. 33.4
When you delete a record, the Assistant gives you one last chance to undo the deletion.

Adding Hyperlinks

 If you defined a field's data type as a hyperlink during the design of the table, you can use the field to point to a Web page, Word document, Excel Workbook, PowerPoint presentation, or another Access object (table, form, query, report). You can type or copy the entry in the hyperlink field.

▶ **See** "Enabling Hyperlinks Between Local Documents," **p. 1006**

You enter the hyperlink address with up to four parts (separated by the pound (#) sign):

displaytext#address#subaddress#subsubaddress

Displaytext is optional and is any text you want to see in the field (instead of the address and other information). For example, you may want to see **Macmillan** rather than **http://www.mcp.com**.

Address can be either a unc path or an URL. A *unc path* is a universal naming convention that includes a file server and share names as well as the path to a document. You can include the path of a file name on your computer such as C:\NCAR\FRONT.DOC. You can also point to a file on your network by using the unc notation of \\server\sharename\path\filename (for example, \\FINANCE\DATA\REV97\FORECAST .XLS where FINANCE is the name of the server, DATA is the share name, and REV97 is a folder under DATA).

To access information on the Internet or an intranet, you use an URL (Uniform Resource Locator). Example formats of URLs include:

> **http://www.companyname.com/filename.html**
>
> **fttp://ftp.servername.comanyname/filename.ftp**
>
> **news:groupheading.subheading.subsubheading.**

Subaddress allows you to point to a particular form or report in an Access database, a bookmark in a Word document, a range in Excel (use Sheet!Range), or a slide number in PowerPoint. Examples of different hyperlinks are shown in Figure 33.5.

FIG. 33.5
Use Access to manage other documents and Web pages.

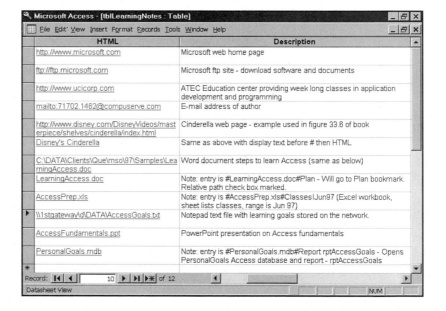

Accessing a Hyperlink When you want to go to the document identified by a hyperlink, click in the field in the datasheet view or on a form. If you want to see or edit the complete address, tab into the field and press F2. On the Internet, it is possible that the site is no longer available, is too busy, or there are other problems. To see any error messages, you need to click the browser button on the task bar.

TIP To see a complete hyperlink address (especially if you have display text) tab into the field, press F2 (edit mode), and if necessary press Shift+F2 (zoom) to see long addresses.

Copying an URL   Because hyperlinks tend to be so long, you can copy a hyperlink reference while you are browsing. To copy a hyperlink from a Web page, follow these steps:

1. Display the Internet or intranet document in your Web browser as shown in Figure 33.6.

2. Select the URL in the location text box. In some browsers, you may need to turn on this text box so you can see the URL.

3. Press Ctrl+C to place the URL in the Clipboard.

4. Go to your Access table or form, and place the cursor in the hyperlink field of the desired record.

5. Press Ctrl+V to paste the URL into the field.

FIG. 33.6
Select the URL and
press Ctrl+C to copy
it to your database.

Select the
URL

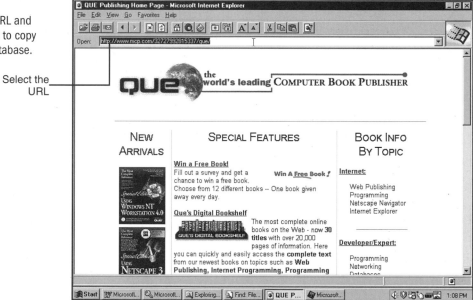

 TIP   Create a simple Access database that keeps track of your Web browsing. Include a hyperlink field for the URL, a description text field (you can usually paste the header as the description), and if desired, a category field.

Browsing to Find a File Hyperlink   You can also use Insert, Hyperlink to browse for a document address. To find a hyperlink, follow these steps:

1. Move to the hyperlink field. If you are editing the field, tab into the field rather than clicking the field to activate the hyperlink.

2. Choose Insert, Hyperlink. The Insert Hyperlink dialog box appears.

FIG. 33.7
Type the URL or click
Browse to add
hyperlink.

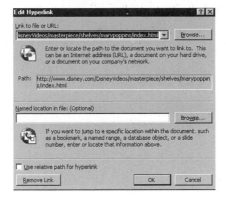

3. Next to the Link to File or URL text box, click the Browse button and use the Link to File dialog box to navigate through your folders on your drive or your server and choose OK on the Link to File dialog box.

4. If there is a location within the file (object within a database for example), click the Browse button and select the entry in the Named Location in File dialog box and choose OK.

5. When finished, choose OK on the Insert Hyperlink dialog box.

Manipulating Data

Moving, copying, locating, and sorting data can be overwhelming tasks, unless you are using Access. Data manipulation is one of the database automation operations at which Access excels.

You can find most of the program's data manipulation features in the toolbar:

Cut

Copy

Paste

Find

Sort Ascending

Part
VI
Ch
33

	Sort Descending
	Filter by Selection
	Filter by Form
	Apply Filter

Cutting, Copying, and Pasting Data

The standard Windows cut, copy, and paste operations work the same way in Access. You can cut, copy, and paste data from one cell to another or from one table to another.

▶ **See** "Copying and Moving Data," **p. 78**

▶ **See** "Moving Data with Cut and Paste," **p. 329**

To cut or copy an entire record, first select the record to be cut or copied. Choose Edit, Cut or Edit, Copy to place the record on the Clipboard. Then, in the target table, select the records to be replaced and choose Edit, Paste or Edit, Paste Append to add the records to the target table.

N O T E To move or copy an entire record to another table, the fields must be the same data types and in the same order in the datasheet. The target datasheet fields must be long enough to receive the data. However, the field names might be different. You cannot paste data into hidden fields.

A paste operation will fail if the data violates a validation property or creates a duplicate primary key (or a duplicate index value for which no duplicates are allowed). Records that cannot be pasted into the target table because of errors (such as validation errors) are placed in the Paste Errors table.

When you paste a record into a table with an AutoNumber field, Access ignores the field in the Clipboard and enters the next number in the AutoNumber sequence. ■

To copy or move records to another datasheet, follow these steps:

1. In the source datasheet, select the record(s) to be copied.

2. Choose Edit, Cut or Edit, Copy.

3. Open the target datasheet. If necessary, rearrange the field order and properties in the target datasheet to match the source datasheet's field order.

4. To replace target datasheet records, select the records to be replaced and then choose Edit, Paste.

5. To add the source records to the target datasheet, choose Edit, Paste Append.

Dragging and Dropping Tables

Access presents users with a handy drag-and-drop feature that's sure to save you time. First, open the desired Word or Excel document and tile or arrange windows as needed (so you can see both applications on screen). To drag and drop an entire table or query, switch to the Access Database window and drag the table or query icon to the Word or Excel document window. To drag and drop a range of cells in a Datasheet window, use the white arrow mouse pointer (point to the left edge of the range) to drag the selected data and drop it in the Word or Excel document (see Figure 33.8).

FIG. 33.8
When you drag and drop selected cells into Word, the formatting is preserved.

First, select cells in Access

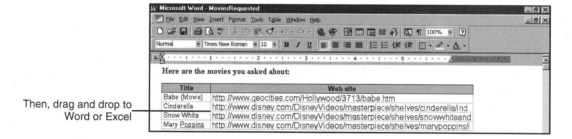

Then, drag and drop to Word or Excel

N O T E To select a range of records and fields in Access, click the first cell, hold down Shift, and click the last cell.

You can also drag and drop an Access object onto the desktop as a shortcut icon. When you double-click the desktop shortcut, Windows opens Access, the database associated with the object, and the object. For example, if you commonly work with a certain table, you could drag and drop it on the desktop. Double-click the table icon and you're ready to start working on the table right away!

▶ **See** "Moving with Drag-and-Drop," **p. 79**

▶ **See** "Launching Programs," **p. 34**

Part
VI

Ch
33

Locating Data

A common database task is finding a record based on a field value. Suppose a customer calls and asks whether you have a certain movie in stock. Using the Find feature of Access, you can locate the movie based on the movie title.

When you choose Edit, Find, the Find in Field dialog box appears, prompting you for the search data (see Figure 33.9). You can instruct Access to search the current field (the default setting) or all fields, to search fields as formatted, and to find exact matches of uppercase and lowercase letters. You also can instruct Access to find matches at the beginning of a field or anywhere in a field, or to find exact matches of the field value. Choose the Find First and Find Next buttons to start and continue your search, respectively.

▶ **See** "Using the Find Command," **p. 90**

▶ **See** "Using Find and Replace," **p. 200**

▶ **See** "Finding Worksheet Data," **p. 335**

FIG. 33.9

The Find feature can help you locate data matching the exact case, if necessary.

To find a record, follow these steps:

1. Choose Edit, Find or press Ctrl+F. The Find in Field dialog box appears.

2. Enter a string to search for in the Find What field.

 TIP You can enter an asterisk in the Find What text box as a wild card for any number of characters. For example, **Sm*th*** will show Smith, Smythe, and Smoothers.

3. Specify the Search direction (All, Up, or Down).

4. Select the Match criteria (Whole Field, Any Part Of Field, or Start Of Field).

TIP If the field is indexed, Access will find the value quicker if you select Whole Field.

5. If desired, select Match Case.

6. If desired, select Search Fields As Formatted (use if you want dates exactly as you type them versus a match independent of format 2/21/59 compared to Feb. 21, 1959).

7. If you want to search only the current field, check the Search Only Current Field check box.

 TIP Select this box to speed up your searches. Doing a find two or three times each on a specific field is much quicker than allowing Access to search all of the fields in a record.

8. Choose Find First to start the search. Access displays the first record that matches your search criteria.

9. Choose Find Next to continue the search and display the next match.

10. To end the search, choose Close.

Sorting and Filtering Data

Access enables you to sort and filter data in Datasheet view. These features can be handy for generating a list of records based on some filtering or sorting criteria. Whereas the Find feature operates on only one criterion, the Filter features enable you to specify criteria in multiple fields.

Access provides the following filtering and sorting features in Datasheet view:

 ■ *Sort Ascending*. Sorts records in ascending order based on the field(s) selected. When the table is saved, Access saves the sort order. For example, sorting on Movie ID number places the records in the order 1, 2, 3, and so on.

 ■ *Sort Descending*. Sorts records in descending order based on the field(s) selected. When the table is saved, Access saves the sort order. For example, sorting on Movie ID number places the records in the order 9, 8, 7, and so on.

 ■ *Filter By Selection*. Searches for records that meet one criteria. You can perform multiple criteria "AND" searches (not "OR") by specifying the criteria one at a time. You cannot enter expressions as criteria.

 ■ *Filter By Form*. Searches for records that meet several criteria. The criteria can be "AND" searches as well as "OR" searches. You can also enter expressions as criteria.

■ *Advanced Filter/Sort*. Combines the power of the sort and filter features into one search engine. You can specify multiple criteria, perform "AND" as well as "OR" searches, enter expressions as criteria, and sort records. The advanced sort feature allows you to sort records in ascending or descending order, or some fields in descending order and others in ascending order.

  TIP Access 97 allows you to right-click in a column and fill in the Filter For text box to filter a column.

N O T E The subset of data created by a filter is a temporary view of your table data. This view does not change the underlying table structure. You can edit, delete, and add records in this view, however. ■

▶ **See** "Exploring Queries," **p. 814**

Sorting in Datasheet View While in Datasheet view, you can sort records in ascending order or descending order. Figure 33.10 shows how the list of movies has been sorted by Category. At any time while in Datasheet view, you can change the sort order or the field to sort on. Access saves the sort order when you save the datasheet. To undo the sort, choose Records, Remove Filter/Sort (if you have also applied a filter, this command removes both the filter and sort).

FIG. 33.10

Use the Sort Ascending and Sort Descending toolbar buttons to quickly re-sort data as needed.

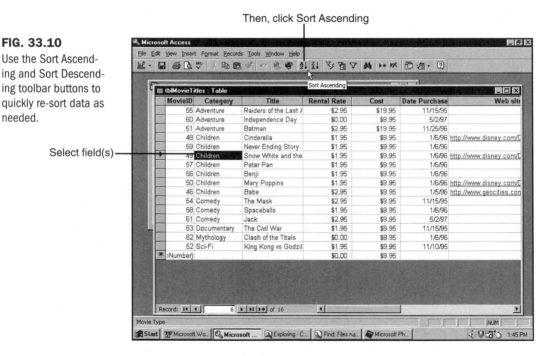

To sort records in Datasheet view, follow these steps:

1. Select the field or contiguous fields you want to sort.

2. To sort in ascending order, choose Records, Sort, Sort Ascending or click the Sort Ascending toolbar button.

3. To sort in descending order, choose Records, Sort, Sort Descending or click the Sort Descending toolbar button.

N O T E In Datasheet view, you can select two or more adjacent fields (columns) at the same time and then sort them in ascending or descending order. Access sorts records starting with the leftmost selected column.

However, in Form view, you can sort on only one field at a time (see Chapter 34, "Creating Forms"). ■

T I P Use the white arrow mouse pointer in the column header to drag and drop non-adjacent columns together in the desired sort order. Then, highlight the multiple columns to sort multiple fields in ascending or descending order.

Filtering by Selection The Filter By Selection feature allows you to select the data you are looking for and view a list of records matching that data value. For example, if you need to see a list of all children's movies, you can just select the words "children" and choose Records, Filter, Filter By Selection (or click the Filter By Selection toolbar button) to view the list (see Figure 33.11). When you want to return to full Table view (see all records), choose Records, Remove Filter/Sort (or click the Remove Filter toolbar button). At any time, you can return to the filtered view by choosing Records, Apply Filter/Sort (or clicking the Apply Filter Button).

Then, click Filter By Selection   Apply/Remove Filter toggle

FIG. 33.11
The Filter By Selection feature shows you a subset of your table, based on the data you selected.

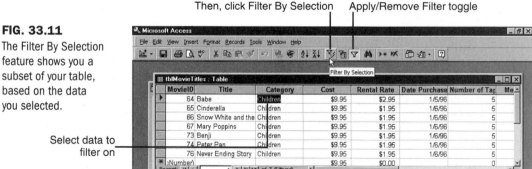

Select data to filter on

N O T E Filter By Selection allows you to select data in more than one field/record. You can do this by selecting contiguous data (hold down the Shift key and select the desired contiguous cells). Or, you can select one item, invoke Filter By Selection, then select another item in the filtered data list and invoke Filter By Selection again. Continue doing this as many times as necessary. ■

Filtering by Form The Filter By Form feature allows you to select the data you are looking for and view a list of records matching that data value. When you choose Records, Filter, Filter By Form, Access displays a blank version of the datasheet. You will notice other screen changes, too. The Format and Records menus are replaced by a new Filter

Part
VI

Ch
33

menu. The Filter menu lists the Filter By Form (currently selected), Advanced Filter/ Sort, Apply Filter/Sort commands. The toolbar changes to include the Load From Query, Save As Query, Close, Clear Grid, and Apply Filter buttons. The File menu lists two new commands. File, Save As Query allows you to save the filter as a Query. File Load from Query lets you use a saved query as a filter.

> **TIP** Use a filter to show all records you want to delete or copy and then select all the records that show when the filter is applied.

In addition, two tabs appear: Look For and Or. The Look For tab is where you begin to define your filter ("AND" search criteria). Use the Or tab to specify alternative values that records can have to be included in the filtered list. Access provides multiple Or tabs for multiple "OR" criteria. When you use the Or tab(s), the filter lists records that have *all* the values in the Look For tab or that match the values in the first Or tab, or the second Or tab, and so on.

> **TIP** For filters you use frequently, choose File, Save As Query to save the filter for future use.

▶ **See** "Exploring Queries," **p. 814**

▶ **See** "Exploring the Query Window," **p. 818**

▶ **See** "Specifying Query Criteria," **p. 825**

In each field for which you want the filter to extract matching records, type the data value or select the data from a drop-down list of table values (see Figure 33.12). When you choose Filter, Apply Filter/Sort, Access searches through the records and displays a list of matching records.

FIG. 33.12
This Filter By Form finds all the records that have comedy in the Category.

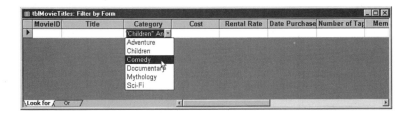

 When you want to return to full Table view (see all records), choose Records, Remove Filter/Sort (or click the Remove Filter toolbar button). At any time, you can return to the filtered view by choosing Records, Apply Filter/Sort (or clicking the Apply Filter button).

N O T E Filter by Form allows you to enter criteria expressions as values in a filter. An expression is a combination of operators, symbols, and values that produce a result. For example, to get a list of all records with a date after 9/1/97, you would enter the following expression in the Date field:

>#9/1/97#

For assistance in entering criteria expressions, right-click in the field, then choose Build from the shortcut menu. ▨

To filter data using Filter By Form, follow these steps:

1. Choose Records, Filter, Filter By Form. The Filter By Form window appears.
2. On the Look For tab, click in the desired field.
3. Type the criteria value or select the value from the drop-down list.
4. Continue specifying the filter criteria in other fields on the Look For tab as needed.
5. If you need to specify alternative criteria values, click the Or tab and fill in any other values to be included in the filtered list. Additional Or tabs appear as needed.

6. To save the filter, choose File, Save As Query.
7. Choose Records, Apply Filter/Sort to view the filter results.

8. To show all records choose Records, Remove Filter/Sort.

T I P To clear the filter criteria, choose Edit, Clear Grid or click the Clear Grid toolbar button.

Performing Advanced Filters and Sorts   The Advanced Filter/Sorts feature provides you with all the power of the filter and sort features through one window. When you choose Records, Filter, Advanced Filter/Sort, the Advanced Filter/Sort window appears (see Figure 33.13). The toolbar and menu options are the same as in the Filter By Form window.

To filter records using the Advanced Filter/Sort window, follow these steps:

1. Choose Records, Filter, Advanced Filter/Sort. The Advanced Filter/Sort window appears.
2. Add to the design grid the field(s) in which you want to specify criteria or sort order.
3. To specify a sort order, click in the Sort cell for a field, and select a sort order from the drop-down list (Ascending, Descending, or Not Sorted).

4. To specify filter criteria, click in a criteria cell for a field and enter the value or expression.

5. To save the filter, choose <u>F</u>ile, Save <u>A</u>s Query.

6. Choose <u>R</u>ecords, <u>A</u>pply Filter/Sort to view the filter results.

7. To show all records choose <u>R</u>ecords, <u>R</u>emove Filter/Sort.

FIG. 33.13

By specifying sort order and criteria in your queries, you can extract specific data in a special order.

Field list box

Field(s) to search

Sort Order

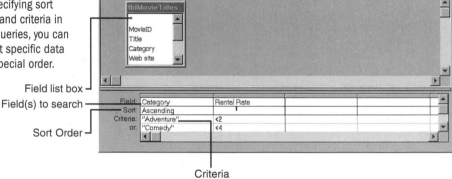

Criteria

T I P If the Filter/Sort feature isn't powerful enough, use a query instead.

▶ **See** "Exploring Queries," **p. 814**

▶ **See** "Creating a New Query," **p. 815**

▶ **See** "Exploring the Query Window," **p. 818**

TROUBLESHOOTING

My filter doesn't list any data. Return to the filter window. Make sure you listed the proper fields and criteria. Check the criteria against the table data to see whether at least one record meets your search criteria. If necessary, enter a test record that meets the criteria. Then test the filter again.

My table data is lost. I have only the subset of data from the filter. Try clicking the Apply/ Remove Filter button. If this does not work, you might have inadvertently saved your filter as a query using the same table name. Revert to the backup copy of the table.

Importing and Exporting Data

You can transfer data in and out of Access. This capability permits you to use data from another computer system or application, such as from a mainframe computer or from a spreadsheet application. Likewise, you can transfer data you store in Access to other computer systems or applications. The Import and Export features allow you to copy data from and to text files, spreadsheets, Access databases, and other database files. The Link Table feature creates a link to a table in another database application so you can work with the data directly. Creating a new table by importing and linking was covered in Chapter 32, so this section discusses importing data to existing tables and exporting data from Access.

▶ **See** "Creating a New Table by Linking," **p. 734**

▶ **See** "Creating a New Table by Importing," **p. 731**

▶ **See** "Creating a New Query," **p. 815**

Table 33.6 lists the application versions and file formats that Access 97 supports for importing, exporting, and linking.

N O T E Depending on your installation of Access, you may need to rerun Access or Office setup to import, export, or link one of the file formats in Table 33.6. ∎

Table 33.6 Import/Export/Link Formats Supported

Application	Version
Access	1.x, 2.x, 95, 97
FoxPro	2.0, 2.5, 2.6, 3.0 (import/export only)
dBASE	III, III+, IV, 5
Paradox	3.x, 4.x, 5
Btrieve	5.1x, 6.0 (requires FILE.DDF, FIELD.DDF, and WBTRCALL.DLL files present)
Excel	3.0, 4.0, 5.0, 95, 97
Lotus 1-2-3	WKS, WK1, and WK3
Delimited text files	MS-DOS or Windows ANSI text format
Fixed-Width text files	MS-DOS or Windows ANSI text format

Part
VI

Ch
33

continues

Table 33.6   Continued

Application	Version
Open Database Connectivity	ODBC formats (ODBC) applications (such as SQL Server, Sybase, Oracle)
HTML and HTX	1.0 (lists) 2.0, 3.x (table or list)

Importing Data to Existing Tables

Sometimes you have an existing table you need to update only with information from another application. The process of adding data to a table is called *appending* data. Unfortunately, Access allows you to append data only to existing tables when importing a spreadsheet or text file. To append data from other sources to an existing table, you must first import the data into a new table and then create an append query to add the records from the new Access table to your existing Access table.

▶ **See** "Using Action Queries," **p. 829**

To import spreadsheet or text data into an existing Access table, follow these steps:

1. Open or switch to the Database window.
2. Choose File, Get External Data, Import.
3. Specify the file format you are importing from in the Files of Type drop-down list.
4. Specify the location of the file.
5. Select the file name.
6. Choose Import.
7. Follow the directions in the Import Wizard dialog boxes. When the wizard asks where you would like to store your data, choose In An Existing Table and select the name of the table (see Figure 33.14).

N O T E   If you are importing to an existing table, the data validation and required properties of the table may cause errors if the imported data doesn't follow the rules. ■

Exporting Data

Often, others in your organization will need to use data you store in Access tables in another application. The Export feature makes it possible for you to provide them with the Access table data in a variety of file formats.

FIG. 33.14
Rather than retype data from a spreadsheet, import the information into your database.

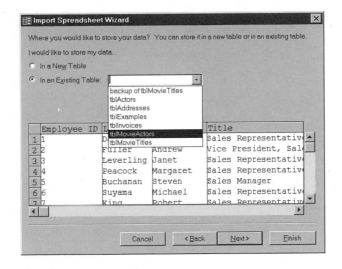

To export data from Access, follow these steps:

1. Open or switch to the Database window.

2. Select the table you want to export.

3. Choose File, Save As/Export. The Save As dialog box appears (see Figure 33.15).

FIG. 33.15
The Save As dialog box allows you to save a table in the current database or to an external file or database.

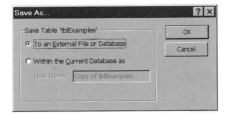

Part
VI

Ch
33

4. Choose the option button To An External File Or Database.

5. Click OK. The Save Table As dialog box appears (see Figure 33.16).

6. In the Save As Type drop-down list, select a file format to export to.

7. Specify the drive, folder, and file name in which to save the exported data.

8. Choose Export.

9. If an Export Wizard dialog box appears, follow the directions.

N O T E If you export to an application with different field naming rules, Access automatically adjusts the names. For example, when exporting to a dBASE table, field names longer than 10 characters are truncated. ■

FIG. 33.16
Select the export file format in the Save As Type text box.

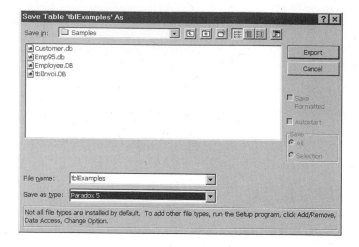

Changing the Datasheet Layout

By modifying the datasheet formatting, you can customize the layout of your table's Datasheet view. Changing the view of the datasheet does not affect the underlying table data. For example, decreasing the width of a column in Datasheet view does not truncate data in the table or change the field width of data.

In Datasheet view, you can use commands in the Format menu to:

- Change font type, style, size, color, underline, and language script
- Change cell appearance such as gridlines, color, and special effects (see Figure 33.17)

FIG. 33.17
Choose Format, Cells to work in the Cell Effects dialog box. Access shows you the cell appearance in the Sample pane.

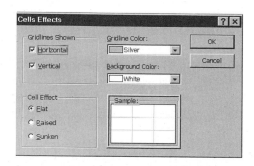

- Change row height and column width

- Hide or display columns

- Freeze or unfreeze columns (columns to the left stay on-screen while you scroll to the right)

You also can perform many of these tasks by selecting the desired column or row and then right-clicking to display the shortcut menu. The shortcut menu changes to reflect the choices available for the selected cell, column, or row (see Figure 33.18).

You can change the width of a column or the row height by dragging the grid line in the header or row selector column to the desired position (see Figure 33.19).

To change the order of columns, select the column and drag it to the new location (see Figure 33.20).

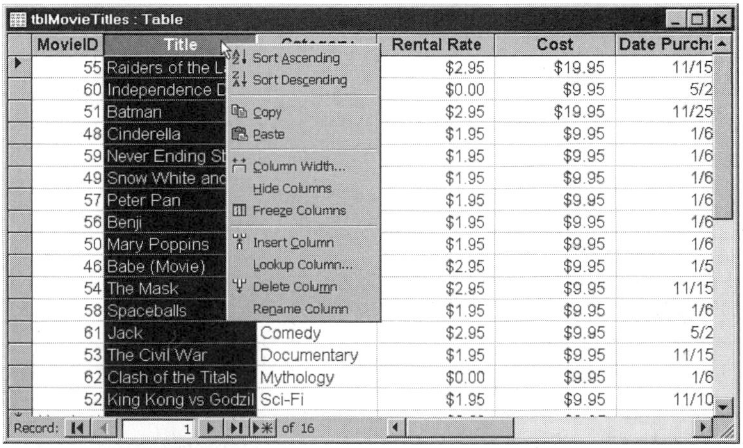

FIG. 33.18
The shortcut menu for a selected column allows you to sort data, find data, and manipulate the column.

FIG. 33.19
You can also double-click the double-headed black arrow to automatically adjust the column to the widest entry.

Column resize arrow

Part
VI

Ch

33

FIG. 33.20

Drag one or more columns to move them in Datasheet view.

White arrow mouse pointer

Thin vertical line indicates where column will move

MovieID	Title	Category	Rental Rate	Cost	Date Purcha
55	Raiders of the Last A	Adventure	$2.95	$19.95	11/15
60	Independence Day	Adventure	$0.00	$9.95	5/2
51	Batman	Adventure	$2.95	$19.95	11/25
48	Cinderella	Children	$1.95	$9.95	1/6
59	Never Ending Story	Children	$1.95	$9.95	1/6
49	Snow White and the	Children	$1.95	$9.95	1/6
57	Peter Pan	Children	$1.95	$9.95	1/6
56	Benji	Children	$1.95	$9.95	1/6
50	Mary Poppins	Children	$1.95	$9.95	1/6
46	Babe (Movie)	Children	$2.95	$9.95	1/5
54	The Mask	Comedy	$2.95	$9.95	11/15
58	Spaceballs	Comedy	$1.95	$9.95	1/6
61	Jack	Comedy	$2.95	$9.95	5/2
53	The Civil War	Documentary	$1.95	$9.95	11/15
62	Clash of the Titals	Mythology	$0.00	$9.95	1/6
52	King Kong vs Godzil	Sci-Fi	$1.95	$9.95	11/10

Record: I◄ ◄ 1 ► ►I ►* of 16

N O T E Access allows you to modify the table design from Datasheet view. You can insert new fields by choosing Insert, Column. To insert a new field using the Lookup Wizard, choose Insert, Lookup Column. To insert a hyperlink column, choose Insert, Hyperlink Column. You can also delete fields (Edit, Delete Column) or rename a field (Format, Rename Column). ■

 When you close the table, Access asks whether you want to save the datasheet layout changes. Choose Yes to save the changes, No to discard the changes, or Cancel to return to the datasheet. To save datasheet layout changes while you work, choose File, Save.

You can change the Datasheet view layout for all datasheets by choosing Tools, Options. When Access displays the Options dialog box, select the Datasheet tab (see Figure 33.21). Notice that you can set the default grid lines, column width, row height, and font for all datasheets.

TROUBLESHOOTING

Every time I export my table to a fixed-width file, I have to redefine the file specifications in the Export Text Wizard. While you are exporting, click the Save As button and save the specification. The next time you need to export the table, launch the Export Text Wizard and click Advanced, then click Specs and select the desired specification file.

My table contains more columns than will fit on-screen. Each time I scroll to the right, I lose track of the client record on which I am working. To keep columns on the left visible as you scroll to the right, choose Format, Freeze Columns.

FIG. 33.21

Use the Datasheet tab of the Options dialog box to customize all newly created datasheets.

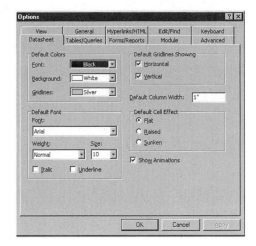

CHAPTER 34

Creating Forms

by Rick Winter

The key to many information systems (manual and computerized) is the *form* used to gather and maintain data. Forms seem to be everywhere we go. Some forms, such as employment applications, simply gather information; others, such as computerized tax forms, also perform calculations. And some forms function as reports (invoices or customer receipts, for example).

Because Access uses the same toolbar buttons and many of the procedures for forms apply to reports as well, some report basics are covered in this chapter. For more information on creating reports, see Chapter 36. ■

Uses of forms and planning a form design

Well-designed forms are usually more efficient than tables for viewing, adding, and editing data.

Use Form Wizards

A Form Wizard often is the quickest way to get started inputting information in a form.

Create a blank form

Creating a blank form allows you more flexibility and understanding of the form design process.

Modify a form design

Once you've designed a form or a report, you may want to move, size, or add items.

Set control and form properties

Properties of forms and reports allow you to fine-tune the display, validate data, and make the form or report easier for the user.

Create additional controls

In addition to text boxes, forms can have drop-down combo boxes, list boxes, command buttons, lines, rectangles and other controls that make input easier.

Planning Form Design

Because forms are just another way to view table data, the first step in designing a form is to create the table(s) or review the design of the table(s). Form problems often can be attributed to an improperly designed table. Remember that table properties and field properties, such as *data validation* and *field type,* help you improve the quality of your data (they are your first line of defense against *GIGO*—garbage in, garbage out).

▶ **See** "Creating a New Table," **p. 724**

▶ **See** "Setting Field Properties," **p. 743**

▶ **See** "Setting Table Properties," **p. 748**

▶ **See** "Modifying a Table," **p. 749**

After you complete the table designs (and you have tested them on end users and data), you are ready to start designing forms. Forms offer several advantages compared to the Datasheet view of your table data:

- Forms can display one complete record at a time, usually in a vertical format.

- Forms allow you to customize the appearance in much more detail than a table with fonts, colors, and graphics.

- Forms can display fields that the user *cannot* edit, as well as fields that the user *can* edit.

- You can design forms to resemble paper forms you currently use.

- Forms enable you to rearrange fields (to make data entry easier and more accurate).

- Forms can contain fields from more than one table (a datasheet shows the data for only one table).

- Forms provide special field display functions, such as drop-down lists, word wrapping in fields, and calculated fields.

- Forms can contain graphs.

- Forms enable you to automate tasks and display custom menus.

A well-designed form is easy to use. You should design forms in ways that facilitate data entry. For example, "busy" forms that contain too many fields crammed into a small screen tend to irritate users and lead to data-entry errors. To prevent these problems, consider using several different forms, spreading data entry over several pages of a single form, or using the Tab control to add tabs to your form.

Following are some general guidelines for designing forms:

- Keep the form simple. Use easy-to-read fonts and colors. Use graphics and other objects to enhance the form, but don't clutter the form with too many objects.

- If your form will be printed on a black-and-white printer, adjust the colors and layout as needed to present a clear printout. Although forms can be printed, it is better to use reports because reports are designed for printing and do a better job.
- Be consistent across forms. For example, use the same design for the Customer data-entry form and the Customer order form.
- Clearly show where data is to be entered and what data should be entered.

N O T E Access allows you to place a graphic (called a *watermark*) in the background of a form. If you have an existing paper form you want to continue using, you can scan the form to convert it to a graphic file. Then, bring the graphic into the background of a new form and drop field controls down where needed on the graphic. For more information, see the "Modifying Form and Report Design" section later in this chapter. ■

Creating New Forms

 You can create new forms via the toolbar or the New Form dialog box. The AutoForm button in the toolbar creates a simple columnar form based on the current table or query and displays the completed form with data in Form view (see Figure 34.1).

T I P The easiest way to create a form is to use AutoForm and then customize the result by deleting and moving fields and labels.

FIG. 34.1
Columnar forms let you focus on one record at a time.

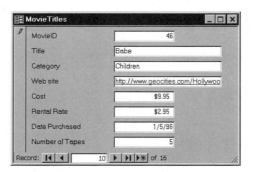

You create all other new forms in the New Form dialog box. To display the New Form dialog box, select the New Form button from the drop-down New Object button on the toolbar. Or, switch to the Database window, select the Forms tab, and click the New button. Either way, the New Form dialog box appears (see Figure 34.2).

Part
VI

Ch
34

FIG. 34.2
The New Form dialog box asks for the table name and enables you to create a variety of new forms.

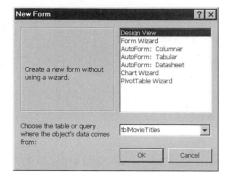

Reviewing the New Form Dialog Box

The New Form dialog box allows you to select the table or query on which you want to base the form and provides the following new form options:

- *Design View.* Allows you to create a custom form design from scratch.

- *Form Wizard.* Assists you in creating a form by asking you questions and using pre-designed form templates (see the next section "Creating a New Form with Form Wizard").

- *AutoForm: Columnar.* Displays one record at a time in a vertical format (each field label value on a separate line, in a single column). The resulting forms are the same as those generated by the AutoForm button on the toolbar (see Figure 34.1).

- *AutoForm: Tabular.* Displays multiple records in a row-and-column format (see Figure 34.3).

FIG. 34.3
Tabular forms allow you to work with multiple records and multiple fields at once.

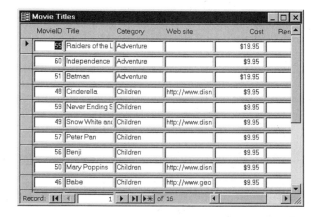

■ *AutoForm: Datasheet.* Displays records and fields in the familiar row and column layout of the Datasheet view (see Figure 34.4). This type of form is often used as a subform within another form.

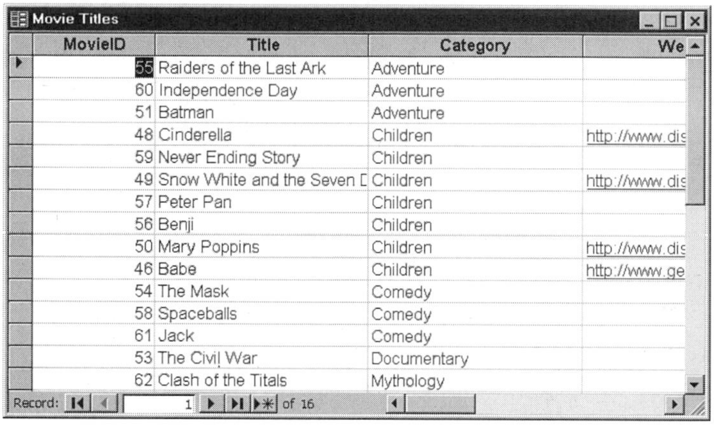

FIG. 34.4
You can even create a Datasheet layout form.

MovieID	Title	Category	We
55	Raiders of the Last Ark	Adventure	
60	Independence Day	Adventure	
51	Batman	Adventure	
48	Cinderella	Children	http://www.dis
59	Never Ending Story	Children	
49	Snow White and the Seven [	Children	http://www.dis
57	Peter Pan	Children	
56	Benji	Children	
50	Mary Poppins	Children	http://www.dis
46	Babe	Children	http://www.ge
54	The Mask	Comedy	
58	Spaceballs	Comedy	
61	Jack	Comedy	
53	The Civil War	Documentary	
62	Clash of the Titals	Mythology	

■ *Chart Wizard.* Displays a form with a graph or chart of the data.

■ *PivotTable Wizard.* Creates a form based on an Excel Pivot Table.

▶ **See** "Creating a Chart with the ChartWizard," **p. 492**

▶ **See** "Summarizing Data with Pivot Tables," **p. 429**

Creating a New Form with Form Wizard

The Form Wizard generates a form design for you, based on your specifications. The Form Wizard asks you a series of questions to determine what table(s) you want to use and what type of form you want to create.

To create a new form using Form Wizard, follow these steps:

1. In the toolbar, click the New Object drop-down button and select the New Form button. The New Form dialog box appears (refer to Figure 34.2).

2. Type or select the name of a table or query in the drop-down list box (Figure 34.2 shows `tblMovieTitles`).

3. Choose Form Wizard and click OK.

4. Select the form type, and then choose OK. The Form Wizard appears (see Figure 34.5).

FIG. 34.5

If you want to create a form based on more than one table or query, choose a second name in the Tables/Queries drop-down list.

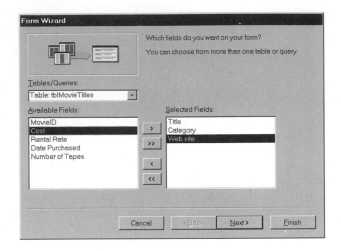

5. In the Tables/Queries drop-down list, select the tables or queries you want to include on the form.

6. In the Available Fields list, select the fields to be included in the form. Choose Next to continue.

N O T E To select fields in the Available Fields list, use the arrow buttons to select individual fields (>) or all fields (>>). To remove fields from the Selected Fields list, use the < arrow key to remove one field or the << arrow button to remove all fields.

When working with more than one table or query on the same form, select the table/query and select the fields, then select the next table/query and select the fields from that table/query, and so on. You may have extra wizard dialog boxes to determine how you want to view your data. ■

7. In the next Form Wizard dialog box, select a layout (Columnar, Tabular, Datasheet, or Justified) and choose Next (see Figure 34.6).

N O T E Columnar, tabular, and datasheet forms are shown earlier in Figures 34.1, 34.3, and 34.4. Justified, a new layout for Access 97, is shown in Figure 34.9. Justified forms show multiple fields on one line. ■

8. In the next Form Wizard dialog box, select a style for the form and choose Next (see Figure 34.7).

FIG. 34.6
You can use the Form Wizard to create columnar, tabular, datasheet, or Justified forms.

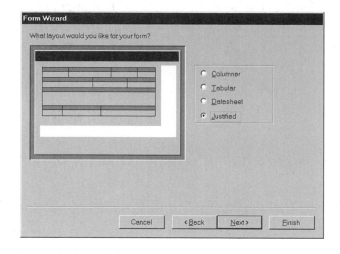

FIG. 34.7
Each form style has a different background and control appearance.

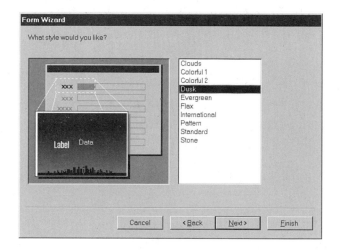

 TIP If you have limited computer memory (RAM) or if your screen takes too long to refresh, you may want to choose the standard style. If you want to change the style after you create the form, choose Format, AutoFormat and select the style.

9. In the next Form Wizard dialog box, enter a title for the form in the Form text box and select the Open the Form To View or Enter Information option or the Modify the Form's Design option (see Figure 34.8).

10. If you want to display Help on working with the form, select that check box.

Part
VI

Ch
34

FIG. 34.8
The last Form Wizard
dialog box completes
the form definition and
creates the form.

11. Choose Finish. Figure 34.9 shows the completed form.

FIG. 34.9
The Form Wizard
creates a more stylish,
polished form than the
AutoForm feature.

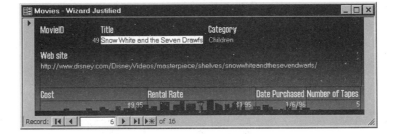

TROUBLESHOOTING

I can't create a form based on two tables. First, check the tables to make sure they have a
relationship (a key field in common). Then launch the Form Wizard. Select the first table and
desired fields from that table to be included on the form. Select the second table and the desired
fields from the second table to be included in the form. The Form Wizard will automatically search
for the common key fields and establish the relationship for you.

**The Form Wizard is asking me to select a form style, but I realize that I forgot to select a
field to be in the form. What do I do?** Click the Back button to move back to the preceding
screen of the Form Wizard dialog box, where you can add the missing field to your form design.

Creating a New Form with Design View

You can use a Design view to create a new custom form that displays data in specific locations, which cannot be achieved by using generic templates in Form Wizard. For example, you might need to create a form that matches a required government form, such as a W-4 form. Or, you might need to create a form that includes pictures in the employee application form. You might also want to create a form that just has labels and command buttons to create a switchboard menu for other forms and reports.

To create a new form using Design view, follow these steps:

1. In the toolbar, click the New Object drop-down and select the New Form button. The New Form dialog box appears.

2. In the drop-down list box, select the table or query for which you want to create a form.

3. Choose Design View and choose OK. Access displays a blank form in Form Design view (see Figure 34.10).

FIG. 34.10
New forms in Design view contain just a Detail section that is the main body of the form.

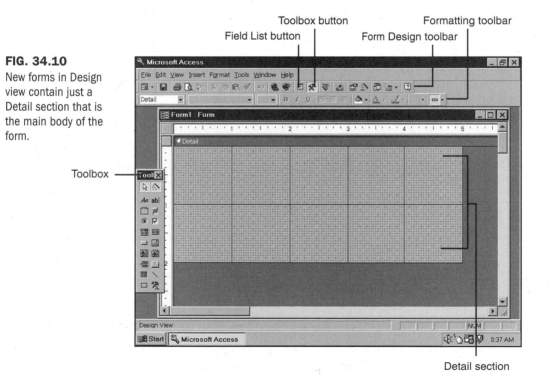

Part
VI

Ch
34

Modifying Form and Report Design

The Design view of Reports and Forms is similar. Both objects have a Design toolbar, Formatting toolbar, a Toolbox, detail sections, page header/footer, and report/form header and footer sections. Because of the similarities, this section discusses both form and report design. More details specific to reports are mentioned in Chapter 36.

▶ **See** "Modifying a Report," **p. 839**

Working with Form and Report Sections

Form and Report Design view is where you can create and modify forms and reports. Although new forms in Design view contain only a detail section, you can add other sections to your form design (see Figure 34.11). To add a header/footer or page header/footer to your form or report, choose View, Form Header/Footer or View, Page Header/Footer.

New reports in Design view automatically contain a Page Header and Footer section. To add a report header and footer, choose View, Report Header/Footer. If desired, you can turn off a Report or Form Header/Footer or Page Header/Footer by selecting the menu item again.

N O T E If you want only a Page Header or Footer, delete any controls you have in the section you want to delete. Then move to the bottom of the section until the mouse pointer changes to a double-headed arrow and drag the section so it has no height. ■

FIG. 34.11
Knowing the sections of a form or report helps you navigate in Form Design view.

Following is an overview of each section that can appear in a form or report:

■ *Form or Report Header.* Appears at the top of the screen. Prints at the top of the first page.

■ *Page Header.* Appears only when printed. Prints at the top of each page.

- *Detail Section.* Displays data.
- *Page Footer.* Appears only when printed. Prints at the bottom of each page.
- *Form or Report Footer.* Appears at the bottom of the screen. Prints at the bottom of the last page.
- *Report grouping headers and footers.* Appear only on reports and organize report into categories.

  ▶ **See** "Sorting and Grouping in Reports," **p. 839**

The Design View Toolbar

Many of the buttons on the Design toolbar are also on the Table Design and Table Datasheet toolbars. The Form and Report Design toolbar provides additional buttons to speed up your form design work. Table 34.1 briefly describes these buttons.

Table 34.1   Design Toolbar Buttons

Button	Button Name	Description
	View	Drop-down list of views: Form view, Design view, or Datasheet view for Forms. Design view, Print Preview, and Layout Preview for Reports.
	Format Painter	Picks up format from the selected object and applies format to next objects selected.
	Field List	Displays a list of the fields linked to the form or report. Drag a field name from the list to place in the form or report.
	Toolbox	Displays or hides the Toolbox, which contains design objects.
	AutoFormat	Applies predesigned styles.
	Code	Displays the Module window (programming statements) for the form or report.
	Properties	Displays the Properties window where you can set characteristics of controls.
	Build	Invokes a Wizard or Builder.

▶ **See** "Working with the Table Design Toolbar," **p. 738**
▶ **See** "Navigating in Datasheet View," **p. 754**

Part
VI

Ch
34

Working with Controls

Changing an existing form or report design, whether it was created with wizards or a blank form or report, is a relatively easy task. In most cases, you just need to click and drag, improve appearance with color, or set some properties.

Objects you place in a form or a report are called *controls*. You move, delete, or change the characteristics of these controls to modify your form or report's design.

Figure 34.12 shows a columnar form created with Form Wizards (in Form view). Although adequate, you can improve the form's appearance. The awkward, extraneous text describing the fields could be modified (or deleted, in some cases). The fields also could be rearranged to fit more on the label (notice the scroll bar indicating more fields). You can use the formatting toolbar buttons to enhance the appearance of the controls.

FIG. 34.12

You can enhance this AutoForm columnar form by rearranging fields, removing unnecessary labels, and adding graphics and other controls.

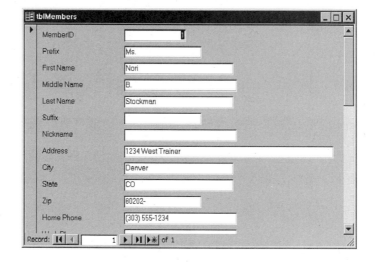

In the next few sections, you learn how to enhance the appearance of this columnar form to produce the enhanced member form shown in Figure 34.13. The second tab of this form with additional formatting is shown later in the chapter in Figure 34.19.

Added company
Logo

Changed window title

Added tabs

FIG. 34.13
The customized
member form shows
the same information
as Figure 34.12, but
in a more familiar
format with some
eye-catching
enhancements.

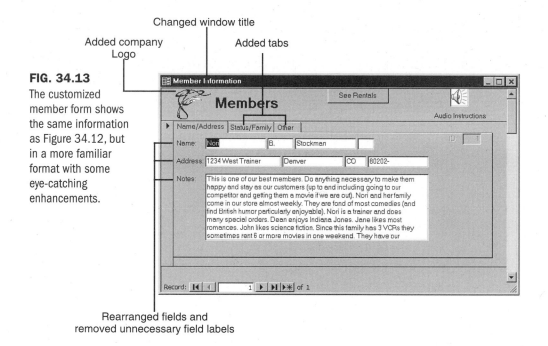

Rearranged fields and
removed unnecessary field labels

Editing a Control

When you click a text control once, you select it. When a control is selected, you can
move it, size it, and change its appearance. If you click inside a control a second time, you
are in Edit mode. You can use Backspace and Delete to delete characters and type new
characters. You will often edit label controls and rarely edit text boxes unless you are
creating calculated expressions.

> **CAUTION**
> Do not edit the name of a field inside a text box unless you are creating a calculated expression. If you
> do edit the name, the text box will no longer know which field to use in the underlying table or query.

Selecting and Adjusting Controls

Before you start modifying controls in your form and setting form properties, you need to
know how to select a control and how to select the form. Figure 34.12 shows the member
form, a single-column form created by Form Wizards, in Form view. As you can see, Form
Wizards creates a label box and a text box for each field. You can select the text-box control (where data is entered and displayed) or the attached label box.

To select a control, click it or select the control name from the Select Object toolbar button. Access displays handles around the control to indicate that it is selected (see Figure 34.14). The smaller black handles are the resizing handles. The larger black handles at the top of the control are called the move handles. Drag the resizing handles (mouse pointer is a double arrow) to change the size of a control. Drag the move handles (mouse pointer is a finger) to move the control to a new location. Drag the border of the control (mouse pointer is a hand) to move both the text box and label controls together.

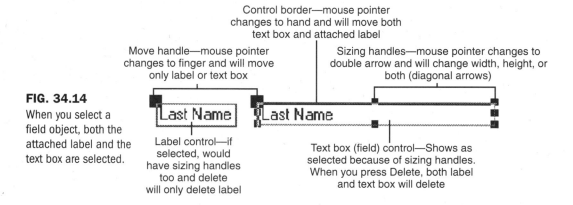

FIG. 34.14
When you select a field object, both the attached label and the text box are selected.

To select more than one control, hold the Shift key down while you click each control. After you select all the controls you want to change, you can drag them to a new location or resize them as necessary.

 TIP You can also use the mouse to draw a box around multiple controls (start outside a control) to select the controls. Additionally, you can click or drag in the horizontal or vertical ruler to select multiple controls.

To select the form or report, click the upper-left corner (see the Form Selector in Figure 33.15) of the form or report, or press Ctrl+R.

After you select one or more controls you can do any of the following:

    To delete selected controls, press Delete. If you have text box controls selected, their attached labels are also deleted. If you accidentally delete the wrong controls, choose Edit, Undo or press Ctrl+Z.

    Drag (when the mouse pointer is a hand) to move all the selected controls at once. In some cases, you can drag the controls to a different section (from Page Header to Form Header, for example). In other cases, you need to choose Edit, Cut and Edit, Paste to move the selected controls.

(One control selected). Take the format of the selected control and apply it to the next control selected. To apply to multiple controls, select the control with formatting to copy, double-click the Format Painter, and then click each of the controls. Click the Format Painter button when you are finished to turn off format copying.

With multiple controls selected, choose Format, Align and then Left, Right, Top, or Bottom to line up the controls with each other. Choose Format, Size and then To Tallest, To Shortest, To Widest, or To Narrowest to make the size uniform. Choose Format, Horizontal Spacing, Make Equal or Vertical Spacing, Make Equal to equalize the space between controls. Once the spaces are equalized, you can choose Format, Horizontal Spacing or Vertical Spacing and then choose Increase or Decrease to change the spacing between the controls.

TIP To make selected controls uniform, choose Format and then one or more of the following menu items: Align, Size, Horizontal Spacing, Vertical Spacing.

Use the features on the Formatting toolbar to change the appearance of the selected control or controls. The features of the Formatting toolbar are described in Table 34.2.

You can change the properties of multiple controls selected at one time. For more information on properties, see the section "Setting Control and Form Properties" later in this chapter.

Using the Formatting Toolbar

Use the Formatting toolbar to enhance the appearance of the form and its contents. You can customize the color of text, background, and border for each control you place in a form.

To use the Formatting toolbar, select an object in the form, a section of the form (Details, Header, or Footer), or select the form itself. You then can change the color of the foreground, background, or border. Use the buttons described in Table 34.2 to add depth to the control (raised, sunken, or etched appearance), set the width of the border or the type of border line (solid, dashed, or dotted). As you click the various formatting buttons, the appearance of the selected object instantly changes to reflect your selections. This way, you can see the effect and decide what appearance you want to give the object.

Part
VI

Ch
34

Table 34.2 Formatting Toolbar

Button	Button Name	Description
CustomerID	Select Object	Drop-down list of all objects on the form or report. Used to select specific objects (can also select objects with mouse).
Arial	Font Name	Changes font of selection with drop-down list of available fonts.
10	Font Size	Changes font size with drop-down list of font sizes.
B	Bold	Boldfaces selection.
I	Italic	Italicizes selection.
U	Underline	Underlines selection.
	Align Left	Aligns selection to the left within control.
	Center	Centers selection within control.
	Align Right	Aligns selection to the right within control.
	Fill/Back Color	Displays palette of colors from which you can select and apply to the background of the selected control(s).
	Font/Fore Color	Displays a palette of colors from which you can select and apply to the text of the selected control(s).
	Line/Border Color	Displays a palette of colors from which you can select and apply to the border of the selected control(s).
	Line/Border Width	Displays a variety of line widths from which you can select and apply to the selected control(s).
	Special Effect	Displays a variety of special effects from which you can select and apply to the selected control(s) such as Raised, Etched, Chiseled, Flat, Sunken, and Shadowed.

Setting Control and Form Properties

Every object in Access has properties. *Properties* determine the appearance and behavior of an object. In Form and Report Design view, you can view and change the properties of controls, sections, and of the form or report itself.

 To display the properties of a control, double-click the control, or select a control and then choose <u>V</u>iew, <u>P</u>roperties. To view the Form or Properties Sheet window, double-click the upper-left corner (Form/Report Selector).

 TIP Right-click a control for quick access to features such as the Properties sheet.

After the Properties window opens, you can select an object and the contents of the window change each time you select a different object.

The Properties window has five tabs. To change formatting and layout properties, choose options on the Format tab. To change the source of data, how the data is organized, or rules for data entry, choose the Data tab. To program what happens when an event happens (a click or change in data for example) to an object, choose the Event tab. For user help and other properties, choose the Other tab. If you don't know where a property is and want to see all properties for the selected object, choose the All tab.

To select the form or report and display the form's or report's properties, double-click the Form/Report Selector (immediately to the left of the horizontal ruler). The Form or Report Properties window appears (see Figure 34.15). You use this window to change the caption at the top of your form or report window (the caption property).

TIP You can copy a form or report that uses a different table or query. In the database window, press Ctrl+C and then Ctrl+V, and type the new name. Go to the new Form or Report's Record Source property and choose an existing table or query from the drop-down list or create a new query with the Build button. For each field with a different name, go to the Control Source property and choose the field name from the drop-down list.

Many property settings are "inherited" from the associated table or query. Some properties are set through the Toolbox and Formatting toolbar, and some properties have no settings.

For more information on a specific property, place the insertion point in that property's field and press F1.

Choose tab for the type of property

FIG. 34.15
By setting form properties, you can customize the appearance and behavior of each form.

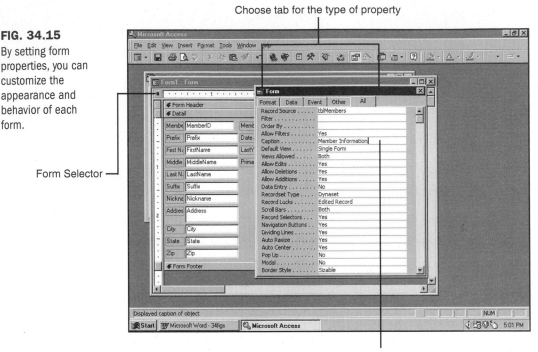

Form Selector

Title bar caption changed

To change a property follow these steps:

1. Right-click the object (control, section, form/report) and choose <u>P</u>roperties.

2. Click in the cell of the property you want to change.

3. Do one of the following: type the new property, choose from the drop-down list of options, double-click to cycle through the list of options, click the Build button to the right of the property or on the Design toolbar, or paste a result from a previously copied property.

  TIP   Double-click Yes/No (or others) properties to alternate between the possible values.

Displaying Help for Users   By default, the status bar in Form view displays the field descriptions you entered in the associated table. You might find, however, that the field name is not enough to direct data entry. Instead of changing the field name, you can override this description and enter new text in the Status Bar Text property for that control (on the Other tab).

Use the ControlTip Text property to display a pop-up message when the user moves the mouse pointer over a control.

Limiting User Input   In addition to security options, you can limit user input through form and control properties. On the form you can change Allow Edits, Allow Deletions, or Allow Additions to No. The Data Entry property is the same as the Records, Data Entry choice in Form and Table Datasheet view. If you want the users to only be able to add records rather than edit them, change the Data Entry property to Yes. For an individual control, you can change the Visible property to No (if you are using the control in a calculation), change the Display When property to only show for printing or for the screen, change the Enabled property to No (unable to get into field), or Locked property to No (unable to change field).

Setting Default Values and Validation Rules   Access enables you to set default field values and validation rules, in both tables and their associated forms. Generally, you should place such data parameters at the table level, but in some cases, the default value or validation rule might apply only to a particular data-entry form. In these cases, you can set default values and validation rules in the property sheet of a control.

 For assistance in writing expressions, click the Expression Builder button next to the property. The Expression Builder helps you write expressions and offers common validation expressions you can use.

Changing Tab Order   *Tab order* refers to the order in which you move from control to control when you press the Tab key. The default tab order of Access forms starts at the upper-left object and moves from left to right, and then from top to bottom. At times, the default tab order might not meet your needs or is changed when you move or add fields. For example, you might be entering data from a source that displays the information in a different order. Rather than rearrange the field controls in your form, you could rearrange the tab order. You also might want to change tab-order properties when your data-entry task starts in the middle of a form. Rather than tab several times to the desired field, you could assign that field a tab-order index of 1.

To change the default tab order in a form, set the Tab Stop and/or Tab Index. A Tab Stop value of Yes enables users to tab to the control; No causes the tab to skip the control. The Tab Index value stipulates the exact numerical tab order (see Figure 34.16).

 To set the tab order for your entire form, choose View, Tab Order. In the Custom Order list, you can drag fields to the desired order. Alternatively, to reset the order to left to right and top to bottom, click the Auto Order button.

You also can set the Auto Tab property. The Auto Tab property controls whether the field automatically tabs to the next field when you type the last allowable character. For example, if a Social Security number field can contain only 11 characters, and the Auto Tab

Part

VI

Ch

34

property is set to Yes, Access automatically tabs to the next field when the user types the 11th character.

FIG. 34.16

Use the Tab Index property of a control or choose View, Tab Order to change the tab order of your form.

Drag field selector to change order of tab

Change Tab Index property on Other tab

Choose Auto Order to reset tab stops to default order

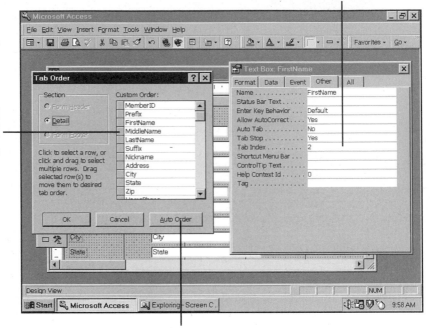

Creating New Controls

If you accidentally deleted a control or you are creating or modifying a form or report, you need to add new controls. The easiest way to add a control is through the Field list. When you drag a field from the Field list (see Figure 34.17), Access creates a default type of control (check box for yes/no data types, Bound Object Frame for OLE data types, list boxes for fields with Lookup properties set, and text box for all other data types). If you want a different kind of control, use the Toolbox described in this section or choose Format, Change To. To turn off or on the Field list, click the Design Toolbar button or choose View, Field List.

To create other controls, select the desired control from the toolbox (described in the upcoming section "Using the Toolbox") and place the control in the form. Alternatively, first select the control from the Toolbox and then drag the field name down from the Field list. There are three categories of controls:

- *Bound controls*, which are linked to a field in a table or query.
- *Unbound controls*, which are not linked to any field in a table or query.
- *Calculated controls*, which are unbound controls that use field data to perform calculations on-screen. The result of the calculation is not stored in any table or query.

N O T E You cannot edit data in calculated fields (a control in a form or report that displays the result of an expression, rather than stored data), because Access enters the appropriate value automatically. Press Tab, Enter, or an arrow key to move past these fields or change their Enabled property or Tab Stop property to No. ■

FIG. 34.17

Drag-and-drop field names from the Field List window onto the form.

Display/Hide Field List

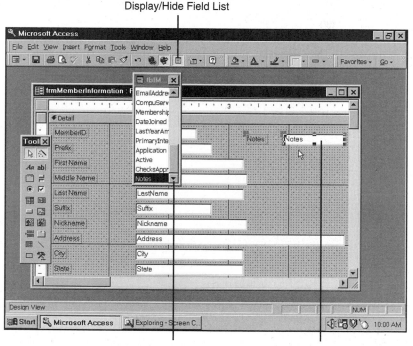

Drag field from Field List...   ...to form

To add a control, follow these steps:

1. Display the toolbox by choosing <u>V</u>iew, <u>T</u>oolbox.

2. Click the desired control tool in the Form Design toolbox.

3. For unbound or calculated controls, position the mouse pointer in the form where you want to add the control. Click to create a default-size control; click and drag to create a custom-size control.

4. For bound controls, display the field list by choosing <u>V</u>iew, Field <u>L</u>ist. Click and drag the desired field name to the appropriate position in the form.

To create a calculated control, follow these steps:

1. Create the unbound Text Box control (one not linked to a field in the table) for the calculated field.

2. Type the expression in the control, or set the control's Control Source property to the expression, as explained in the next section. An example expression is =[Price]*[Quantity], where Price and Quantity are fields in the underlying table (or names of controls) and are multiplied to come up with an extended price. Notice that field names are enclosed in square brackets.

Using the Form Design Toolbox

The toolbox contains design objects (such as fields, text, and boxes) that you can place in a form or report. This section briefly describes each item in the toolbox. Most of the toolbox buttons are used in forms but not all are used in reports. The buttons displaying fields as alternatives to text boxes (option group, drop-down box, list box) would not be likely for reports. Figure 34.18 shows a form that requires many of the tools on the Toolbox to be used. The Form view is shown in Figure 34.19.

The toolbox is a toolbar you can move around and resize just like any other toolbar. To display the toolbox, choose <u>V</u>iew, <u>T</u>oolbox. By default, the Select Objects tool is selected. Use this tool to select the object in your form or report with which you want to work. Access displays handles around the selected object.

To place a new control in the form or report, select the appropriate tool in the toolbox. The mouse pointer changes to a crosshair and displays the tool's icon. If desired, choose a field name from the field list and then move the crosshair to the desired location, and then click and drag the control to the desired size.

The following is a brief description of each tool in the toolbox:

 Select Objects. Selects objects.

 Control Wizards. Turns Control Wizards (help for other tools) on and off. For most users, keep the Control Wizard on to help you through the difficult process of creating option groups, drop-down and list boxes, and subforms or subreports.

 Label. Creates a text control. Use the Label tool to type text in your form or report (such as a title). After you click the form or report and start typing, the label expands to fill the text. Click outside the label and back on the label again to format it. You may need to reformat the label with the Font, Bold, and Font Size text boxes.

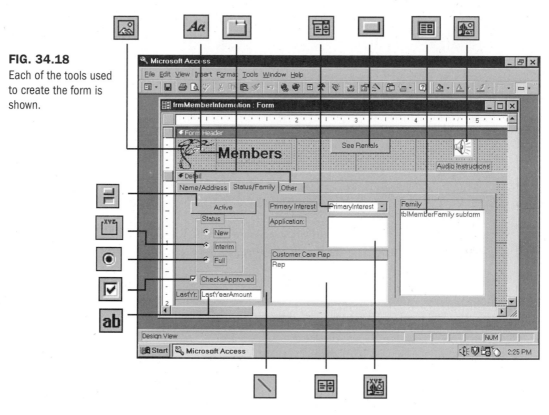

FIG. 34.18
Each of the tools used
to create the form is
shown.

T I P After you change the font of a label, you may need to resize it. Instead of using the resizing
handles, choose Format, Size, To Fit or double-click one of the sizing handles.

 Text Box. Displays field data (label and text box). Because you can just drag a
field from the field list, you won't have to use this option much except for
 calculated controls. To create an expression, type = and the expression.
Alternatively, go to the Control Source property and use the Build button.

If you have a large text box for a memo or large text field, you will probably
want to set the Enter Key Behavior property to New Line in Field, Can Grow
and Can Shrink (When Printed) properties to Yes, and Scroll Bars property
to Vertical.

 N O T E Just like controls and sections of reports and forms, toolbox buttons have properties as
well. For example, the Default Text box has an Auto Label property which automatically
adds a label when you create a text box. There are also Label X, Label Y, and Label Align properties which identify the location and justification of the attached label. To show and edit the
default properties for each of the Toolbox controls, turn on properties and then click the tool in
the toolbox. ■

Part
VI

Ch
34

Option Group. Use the Option Group control when you want to place option buttons or toggle buttons in a group where only one choice is possible within the group. Placing an option group in the form displays the Option Group Wizard, which helps you define the option group and set the desired properties. The option group's Control Source property is usually a field with less than five potential integer number choices. When the wizard asks you, make sure you choose a field from the table in the Store the Values in This Field drop-down choice. Each number possible in this field represents a choice (for example, 1 = Adventure, 2 = Comedy, 3=Children, and so forth).

N O T E Although you can put check boxes within an option group and have option buttons represent yes/no responses for multiple questions, it is better to stick to the standard Windows interface design where option buttons represent a one of many choice and check boxes represent yes/no answers. ▪

Toggle Button. Creates an on/off button, which in the on position, appears depressed. A toggle button can be part of an option group or by itself if the answer is yes or no. If you use toggle buttons, make sure you set the Caption property so you can tell what the button indicates.

Option Button. Usually used as an option within a group. If you use the Option Group tool, option buttons are created for you. If you want to manually add an option button to a group, first create the option group. Then choose the Option Button tool and then click inside the option group (the option group becomes highlighted). Change the label attached to the button to indicate the value. The Option Value property is a number whose value represents one of the choices possible in the field determined by the option group.

Check Box. Creates a check box and a true/false control. You can drag a yes/no field from the field list to create a check box. A check mark indicates yes and a blank indicates no. If you want new records to automatically display yes or no, type **Yes** or **No** in the Default Value property.

Combo Box. Creates a drop-down list of predefined choices, but also enables the user to type values. The combo box and list box are often used when you want to look up values from another table or query. For example, on an orders table you may want to identify an employee. Instead of typing the whole employee's name, create a combo box based on the employee's ID.

When you choose the Combo Box tool, a wizard asks you for the table to use to display the choices and the fields you want to see. The first field you choose should be the one you want to see after the combo box is closed.

You can use any other fields to help identify the employee. For example, you could use Employee Last Name, First Name, Extension, and ID fields for the combo box.

The following properties are important to review if the list box doesn't work:

- *Control Source.* Field in your table where you're storing the answer.
- *Row Source.* Name of table or query used to lookup values. You can click the build button to access the query builder and choose the fields, and sort order of the items that appear in the drop-down list.
- *Column Count.* Number of columns from the row source used for the list.
- *Column Widths.* Display width for each column in the list; 0 will not display column.
- *Bound Column.* Column from the row source that will be placed in the field on the form.
- *List Width.* Width of the entire drop-down list.
- *Limit to List.* This property determines whether you want to limit values to the table/query/list for your combo box or allow the user to type other values as well.

 List Box. Creates a drop-down list of predefined choices, but unlike combo box, does not enable the user to type new values. The list box also is different because you see multiple rows and columns even when the control does not have the focus. Because the list box takes up so much room on a form, it is not used often.

 Command Button. Creates a button that runs a macro or calls an Access procedure when clicked. When you place this tool on a form, the Command Button Wizard steps you through the most used options such as moving to another record, adding and deleting the record, opening a form, and running a report. Access automatically creates a Visual Basic procedure that goes with the button. You could edit the procedure or create a macro to attach to the On Click property of the button.

 Image. Creates a frame to display a static image. When you choose this tool, Access takes you into the Insert Picture dialog box to find the picture file. You may have to change the Size Mode property to display the picture properly.

 Unbound Object Frame. Creates a frame to display pictures, graphs, and OLE objects that are not from the database. Access takes you into the Insert Object dialog box where you can create a new object using one of the registered programs or find the file that contains the object.

Part
VI

Ch
34

Bound Object. Creates a frame to display an OLE object from the database (changes with each record). The Bound Object Frame tool displays pictures, graphs, or other OLE objects stored in an Access database. This type of control is automatically created when you drag an OLE object from the field list. To add a new OLE object into the field for a record, you need to be in the Field in Form view and paste the object from the Clipboard or choose Insert Object.

Page Break. Creates a page break in the form or report. Anything below the control prints on the next page.

Tab Control. Creates a tabbed dialog box effect on the form, allowing user to click a tab for different pages (which are stacked behind each other). Put this control on the form before you add any other controls. Then drag the fields from the field list on to the pages of the control or build the controls from the Toolbox. Change the Caption property of each of the pages on the tab control to identify the pages.

Subform/Subreport. Creates a frame to display an embedded form or report. A common use of the Subform/Subreport tool is to show a one-record-to-many-records relationship between related tables—for example, to show the movie

rentals for each customer. When you want to embed a form in another form, use

the Subform/Subreport tool in the main form. You can save time by using Form Wizards to create both the embedded form and the main form.

The important control properties for the Subform/Subreport control are the Source Object (name of subform or subreport) and the Link Child Fields (name of field on subform/subreport), whose value matches the main form's primary field identified by the Link Master Fields property. In some cases, there is no link. For example, you may want two unrelated summary reports on one page. You can also create subforms or subreports by dragging a form or report from the Database window to the form or report you are building.

Line. Draws a line. Use the Line tool to draw lines and the Rectangle tool to draw boxes that visually group items or draw attention to an item. To draw a straight line, hold Shift down as you drag the mouse. Use the Line/Border Width button to change the thickness of the line.

Rectangle. Draws a rectangle. If you want options within a box, use the Option Group tool instead.

More Controls. Displays a menu of other registered controls which are also called ActiveX Controls. These controls can be accessed by the More Controls button on the Toolbox. These are additional custom controls that are dependent on how you loaded Access, whether you have the Access Developers Toolkit or other programs (such as Visual Basic) that support ActiveX controls. An example is a Calendar Control (that shows a calendar with the date from a date field highlighted). Other examples include scroll bars and spin buttons that are common to the Windows interface.

TROUBLESHOOTING

I can't access the form's property sheet. Choose Edit, Select Form.

One field is not sunken like the others. Use the Format Painter to apply the sunken appearance.

When entering a validation expression into a field control's validation property, I keep running out of room. Press Shift+F2 to open the Zoom box.

 I accidentally deleted a field on my form. How can I get is back? Try to click the Undo toolbar button to get the field back with all formatting and property settings intact. Otherwise, you need to add the field back and apply the format and property settings again. Use the Field List window to quickly add the field, and use the Format Painter to apply formats from a similar field object, if possible.

I only want to see one form on the screen and when I print it. For Form view, change the form's Default View property from Continuous Forms to Single Form. For printing, add a page break control at the bottom of the Detail section.

Navigating Form View

Entering and editing data in Form view is the same as in Datasheet view. All the data-entry shortcuts and tools, such as Find and Filter By Form, are available in Form view. By using the View drop-down toolbar button, you can easily move between Datasheet, Form, and Design view.

Figure 34.19 reviews some of the record navigation features.

▶ **See** "Entering and Editing Data," **p. 756**
▶ **See** "Adding New Records," **p. 759**
▶ **See** "Sorting and Filtering Data," **p. 771**

Part
VI

Ch
34

N O T E If you have Microsoft IntelliMouse, you can use the middle wheel button to scroll through forms. Turn the wheel button down to go to the next form or up to scroll to the previous form.

FIG. 34.19

Navigating on a form is very similar to navigating in Datasheet view.

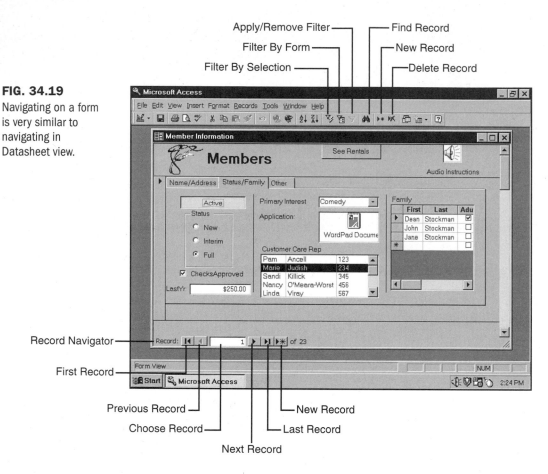

CHAPTER 35

Querying Databases

by Rick Winter

So far, this section of the book has focused on the ways in which you can enter data into your database. Now it's time to explore ways of getting information out of your database. One of the most useful features of modern database applications is the *query,* which provides you a way to "question" your database. The result of a query (the "answer") then can be printed or viewed on-screen. This chapter explains the query features of Access and shows you how to use queries to extract information from your database. ■

Create and save a query

Queries show a subset of your table. You can choose specific fields and records and sort the data display.

Perform query calculations

If you need to add, multiply, or do other calculations, you can add calculated fields. You can also create sums and averages of your data.

Specify query criteria

To limit which records you see, you identify records by criteria.

Modify data with action queries

Instead of individually editing each record, you can create action queries that update, delete, or add many records at one time.

Exploring Queries

A *query* is a statement that tells Access what kind of information you need to extract from one or more tables. A query also can perform an action on the data in the table(s) and summarize data in spreadsheet format.

You can use queries, for example, to accomplish the following tasks:

- Compile a list of employees who live in a certain state.
- Show customer names, demographics, and purchasing information in one report.
- Determine the frequency of movie rentals.
- Calculate the total cost of movies by category.
- Purge the database of customers who have not rented in the past year.
- Add old customer records to a history database.

Queries can be used as a source of information for forms and reports. In such a case, the query enables you to include specific data from more than one table. Access executes the query each time you open the form or report, so you can be sure that the information you see is up to date.

Access enables you to create the following types of queries:

- *Select queries*. Used to extract data from tables based on criteria specified in the query object. This type of query is the most common. A select query could be used to list all customers in New York, for example. You can use select queries to display fields from more than one related table.
- *Action queries*. Used to perform an action on records that meet criteria specified in the query object. This type of query enables you to change or move data, create new tables, or purge records from a table. You could use an action query to purge inactive customer records.
- *Totals queries*. Used to group data with sums, averages, or other summary calculations.
- *Crosstab queries*. Used to summarize data in a spreadsheet format based on criteria specified in the query object. Crosstab queries are often used to calculate data for a graph.
- *Union queries*. Used to combine sets of records from different tables with common fields. For example, you could create a query that combines present and past invoice data.
- *Pass-through queries*. Used to send commands to a Standard Query Language (SQL) database.

■ *Data-definition queries.* Used to perform actions on Access databases with SQL statements.

For each query type, you can specify query parameters that prompt the user to specify query criteria before the query executes. In the video-store application introduced in Chapter 31, for example, you could create a query that lists movies based on each customer's preferences.

▶ **See** "What Is a Database?" **p. 704**

Access places the results of some query or filter operations in a dynaset. A *dynaset* looks and behaves like a table, but it actually provides a dynamic view of the data in one or more tables. You can enter and update data in a dynaset; after you do so, Access automatically updates the data in the associated table or tables. A dynaset is similar to a *snapshot*, which also looks like a table but is not updatable. Crosstab and total queries are examples of snapshots.

N O T E In a multiuser environment, changes made by other users are reflected in the dynaset and its associated tables. ■

CAUTION

Dynasets seem so much like tables that it is hard to remember they really are not. Just keep in mind that the data is stored in the primary tables themselves, not in the dynaset.

Creating a New Query

New Object: Query To create a new query, click the New Object, New Query button in the toolbar, or switch to the Database window, select the Query tab, and then click the <u>N</u>ew button. The New Query dialog box appears (see Figure 35.1). As with tables and forms, Access provides several methods for creating queries.

FIG. 35.1
If you are uncertain of how to create a query, use the Simple Query Wizard.

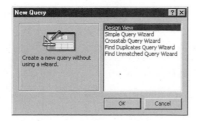

Whichever method you decide to use, it helps to spend some time designing the query before actually creating it. Think about some of the following factors before getting started:

■ Which table(s) contain the information you need

■ Table relationships (are the tables properly keyed?)

■ The type of query you want to perform

■ The field conditions and criteria that the records must meet

■ Calculations, if desired

■ Sort order

■ The name under which you want to save the query

Using the New Query Dialog Box

The New Query dialog box provides five basic types of generic queries (refer to Figure 35.1):

■ *Design View*. Enters Query Design displaying a blank query form for the table(s) you select.

■ *Simple Query Wizard*. Creates a select query from fields you pick.

■ *Crosstab Query Wizard*. Summarizes query data in spreadsheet format.

■ *Find Duplicates Query Wizard*. Locates duplicate records in a table.

■ *Find Unmatched Query Wizard*. Locates records in one table that do not have matching records in a related table.

Each wizard prompts you for specific information needed to create its particular type of query. In each case, you must identify the table(s) or queries on which the new query will be based.

Using Design View

To create a query from scratch, choose Design View in the New Query dialog box. Access displays the Select Query: Query1 window and may open the Show Table dialog box (see Figure 35.2). As you select tables, Access places a field list for the table at the top of the Select Query window.

Before you start the query, highlight the table or query that you want to base the new query on. Then use the New Query button and Access will place the appropriate field list in the query design window. Otherwise, the Show Table dialog box asks you which tables or queries you want to use.

FIG. 35.2
The Show Table dialog box lets you add tables and other queries to your new query design.

To select the table/query you want to add to your query definition, double-click the table/ query name or highlight the table/query name and then choose the Add button. Access adds the table/query to the Select Query: Query1 window; the Show Table dialog box remains open so that you can add more tables, if necessary. Access automatically finds any relationships among multiple tables added to a query definition and shows those relationships by drawing lines between the related fields (see Figure 35.3).

FIG. 35.3
The added tables appear in the top portion of the Query Design view.

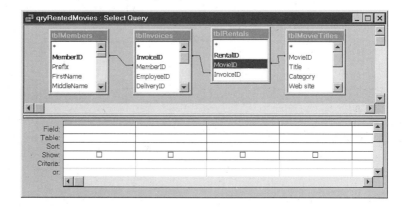

▶ **See** "Setting Relationships," **p. 751**

Access automatically finds table relationships and draws a line between the matching key fields (same field name and field type). These lines are called join lines. *Join lines* apply only to multi-table queries. You can create join lines yourself by dragging and dropping a key field from one table to another.

The bottom half of the window contains the Query-by-Example grid, in which you define the criteria of the query. Query-by-Example (QBE) enables you to define query criteria by providing practical examples of the type of data you need. To find all employees in the state of New Jersey, for example, you would type the example element **NJ**.

Part
VI

Ch
35

After you finish adding tables, choose <u>C</u>lose. To reopen the Show Tables dialog box, click the Show Table button in the toolbar, or choose the <u>Q</u>uery, Show <u>T</u>able command.

 N O T E By default, Access sets the query type to Select Query. You can change the query type by making a different selection from the Query menu or Query Type button on the toolbar. ▪

Exploring the Query Window

 The Query window enables you to see queries in several views (available via the View menu or toolbar):

  Design view. Used to define the query.

  SQL view. Used to view or modify the SQL query-language definition of your query.

  Datasheet view. Used to display the results of your query.

 T I P Remember that in addition to Datasheet view, query results can be used as the basis for a form or a report.

N O T E You can drag and drop queries into Word and Excel. From the Database window in Access, drag a query icon or selected data in Datasheet view to the Word or Excel document (the document must be open). ▪

The Query Design window toolbar provides many buttons that speed your query work. Table 35.1 describes these buttons.

Table 35.1 Query Window Toolbar Buttons

Button	Button Name	Description
	View	Drop-down list of views: Design view, SQL view, or Datasheet view.
	Save	Saves the query design.

Button	Button Name	Description
	Print	Prints the query datasheet (in Datasheet view).
	Print Preview	Displays the query as it appears when printed.
	Spelling	Spell checks the query in Datasheet view.
	Cut	Deletes the selected data or object and copies it to the Clipboard.
	Copy	Copies the selected data or object to the Clipboard.
	Paste	Inserts the Clipboard contents.
	Undo Current Field/Record	Reverses the last change.
	Query Type	Drop-down list of query types: Select, Cross-Tab, Make Table, Update, Append, and Delete.
	Run	Executes the query.
	Show Table	Displays the Show Table dialog box listing available tables and queries for use in the current query design.
	Totals	Displays or hides the totals row in the query grid pane.
	Top Values	Drop-down list of filter values (top 5, 100, 5%, 25%).
	Properties	Displays the Properties window.
	Build	Invokes a Wizard or Builder.
	Database Window	Displays the Database window.
	New Object	Drop-down list that allows creation of database objects such as forms, queries, and reports.
	Office Assistant	Runs Office Assistant for help searches or tips.

Part

VI

Ch

35

Designing a Query

After you start a new query or click the Design button in the Database window for an existing query, Access displays the Query window in Design view. Query Design view (see Figure 35.4) is split into two main sections. The top section contains a field list box for each table being used in the query definition; the bottom section contains the QBE grid, where you define your query. Each column of the QBE grid is a field. For each field, you define the query parameters, such as criteria and sorting, in the rows of the QBE grid.

FIG. 35.4
Define the query in the QBE grid by adding fields and setting query parameters.

Query type and title

Field selector

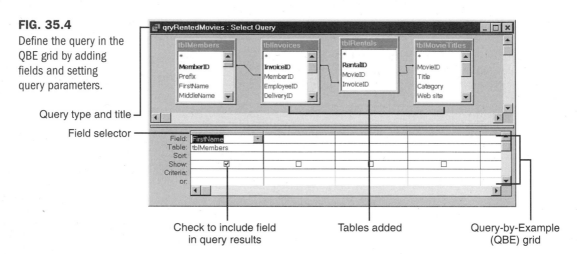

Check to include field in query results

Tables added

Query-by-Example (QBE) grid

Selecting Fields

The QBE grid consists of columns and rows. Each column represents one of the fields used in your query. To add a field to the QBE grid, double-click the field in the field list box, or drag the field name to a column. Access fills in the field name and checks the Show check box. If you want to use the field in sorting or criteria but not display the field in the dynaset, deselect the Show check box.

To select all the fields in a field list box, double-click the Table name and drag the highlighted area to the QBE grid. To remove a field, select the field selector and press Delete, or position the insertion point within the column and choose Edit, Delete Column.

TIP To change the order of the field columns, select a field column by clicking the field selector in the QBE grid and then dragging the column to the new location.

N O T E Suppose that you want a list of your friends' names and phone numbers, but not their addresses and birthdays. Even though all that data is stored in your FRIENDS table, you could get a subset of information by creating a query and selecting only the Name and Phone Number fields.

The QBE grid contains another row that is hidden by default: Totals. To display this row, choose View, Totals. When selected, the Totals row appears below the Field row in the QBE grid.

 N O T E Access also has a Crosstab Query. This summarizes one field by changes in two other fields. When you click the Crosstab Query Type button, two new rows appear in the QBE grid: *Total* and *Crosstab*. The Total row has the same values mentioned later for group calculation queries (Sum, Avg, and so on). Choose this for the value to be summed (usually a numeric data type field) and Value in the Crosstab row. In the other two fields (usually text data types), choose Group By in Total row and Row Heading and Column Heading in the Crosstab row. An example could be Employee (Group By, Row Heading) by Country (Group By, Column Heading) summing Amount (Sum, Value).

TROUBLESHOOTING

I accidentally added too many tables to my design. Click the table titled Field List and press Delete.

My query has way too many records from what I was expecting and it takes an extreme amount of time to run. You probably have not created a join between your tables. Return to Design view and either delete the unnecessary tables or drag a field between tables to create a join.

Adding Calculated Fields

You also can add calculated fields to the QBE grid. Calculated fields are temporary fields created in the dynaset when a query executes; they store the results of calculations on the contents of table fields. You can use a calculated field, for example, to calculate a markup on products or to concatenate text fields.

T I P To change the width of a column, position the mouse pointer above the Field row, on the vertical grid line. The pointer changes to a set of opposing arrows. Drag the grid line to the desired width.

To create a new calculated field, select an empty field-name cell in the QBE grid. You can type the expression (calculation) directly in the cell. Access creates a name for the new field, such as Expr1, which you can change to something more meaningful. Alternatively, you can enter a dynaset field name, followed by a colon (:) and the calculation or concatenation expression. Field names used in the calculation must appear in brackets ([ ]), and spaces must be in quotes, but numeric and arithmetic operators do not require any special notation. The new calculated field name does not need to be entered in brackets. You could create a new field named Total by entering the following:

Total:[Unit Price]*[Quantity]

N O T E When you create calculations or expressions using field names, Access automatically adds square brackets to identify a field when the field is one word. For this reason it is a good idea to keep your field names to one word (FirstName, for example). However, you can always enclose field names in brackets to ensure that Access correctly includes field names in calculations. ▓

 For more help on naming fields, search for the help topic **Renaming a Field in a Query**. For assistance on writing expressions for calculated fields in a query, search for the help topic **Using a Calculated Field in a Query**. You also can click the Build button in the toolbar to launch the Expression Builder, which can help you create the expression. For more information on writing expressions, see Que's *Special Edition Using Access 97*. The following are some calculation examples:

- Increase price by 5%: [Price]*1.05
- 1st five characters of ZIP code: Left([ZipCode],5)
- Name combined: Salesperson: [FirstName] & " " & [LastName]
- Extended price: [Price]*[Quantity]*(1-[Discount])/100)*100
- Year: Format([ShippedDate],"yyyy")
- Month: Format([ShippedDate], "mmm")
- Days between dates: DateDiff("d", [OrderDate], [ShipDate])

Figure 35.5 shows a string concatenation of a member's first and last name and a calculation that computes projected sales based on a price increase of 10 percent.

To create a calculated field, follow these steps:

1. Move to a blank column in the QBE grid.
2. Enter a new calculated field name in the Field row, followed by a colon (:).
3. Continue typing in the field-name cell, and enter the desired calculation expression.
4. Save and execute the query.

FIG. 35.5
Calculated fields allow you to perform calculations in queries and concatenate text fields.

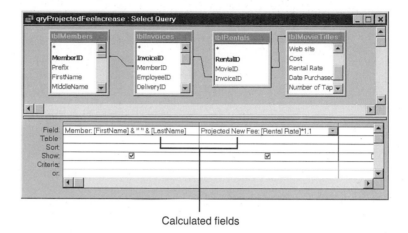

Calculated fields

 T I P To quickly clear the QBE grid pane, choose Edit, Clear Grid.

Adding Group Calculations

Query results sometimes need to perform calculations for groups of records rather than for each record (see Figure 35.6). You might want to see total sales by state, for example, or advertising cost by product. Access enables you to perform sophisticated calculations on groups of records. For example, you could determine the average salary by department or the maximum hours by job order.

FIG. 35.6
Use the Total row to group query results by records and perform group calculations.

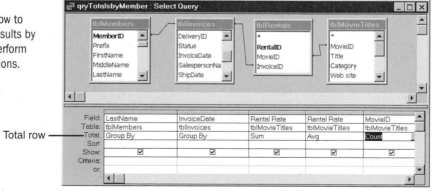

Total row

Part
VI

Ch

35

 T I P Use multiple Group By total types to calculate totals for several groups.

Σ You define groups in the Total row. To display the Total row, choose <u>V</u>iew, <u>T</u>otals. After you add the Total row to your QBE grid, Access automatically adds the words `Group By` in each field. Use Group By to identify the fields (groups) by which you want to perform the calculation. You can change this selection to any of the following types of calculations:

- *Sum.* Totals the field values.
- *Avg.* Computes an average field value.
- *Min.* Finds the minimum field value.
- *Max.* Finds the maximum field value.
- *Count.* Returns the number of values in a field, disregarding null values.
- *StDev.* Computes the standard deviation (square root of the variance) of the field values.
- *Var.* Computes the variance of the field values.
- *First.* Returns the first value in a field.
- *Last.* Returns the last value in a field.
- *Expression.* Enables you to create a calculated field for a group.
- *Where.* Enables you to specify criteria for a field you are not using to define groupings.

N O T E Calculation types—such as Sum, Avg, and Var—that calculate totals can be used only for fields of the following data types: Number, Date/Time, Currency, Counter, and Yes/No. The data type OLE Object also is valid for Count, First, and Last. ▪

To perform group calculations, follow these steps:

1. Create a select query.

Σ 2. In Design view, display the Total row by choosing <u>V</u>iew, <u>T</u>otals.

3. In the Total cell for each field, select a total type.

4. If the totals are for all records, no total cells should be of the type Group By.

5. If the totals are to be calculated by group, set the total cell of the desired fields to Group By.

6. Save the query.

7. Run the query or switch to Datasheet view.

Specifying Query Criteria

The criteria row (see Figure 35.7) of the QBE enables you to include in your query results only records that meet specific conditions. Criteria are conditions used to select records. This query feature probably is used more often than any other.

FIG. 35.7
Limit the records included in your query results by specifying criteria in the Criteria row.

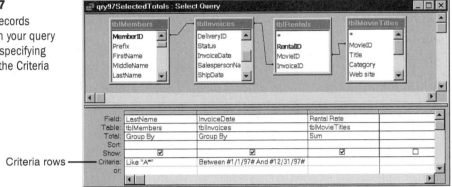

Criteria rows ——

You can select records by entering any of the following conditions:

- *Exact Match.* Use a literal value, such as the text string **NJ** or the currency amount **1000**, which the field value (case-insensitive) must match.

- *Wildcard Pattern Match.* Use a combination of literal characters and wild-card characters (see Table 35.2, which follows this list), such as **N*** or **Like "1###"**, which the field value must match.

- *Elimination Match.* Use the NOT operator to eliminate records that meet the criteria (for example, **not NJ**).

- *Date Match.* Use an exact date or the Date( ) operator, which represents today's date (according to your computer's clock). For example, you could use the criteria **12/1/97** or **Date( )**.

 To find all rentals in 1997, you could enter the criteria ***/*/97** or **Between 1/1/97 and 12/31/97**.

- *Blank Values.* Use the NULL operator to specify that you want to see only blank values. Conversely, use NOT NULL to specify that you do not want blank values in your query results.

 To find all addresses without ZIP Codes (you need to look them up for mailings), use Null in the criteria row for the Zip field.

- *Comparison Operators.* Use any of the comparison operators (see Table 35.3, which follows this list) to compare record data with a specific condition. For example, you could enter **<DATE( )** to see only records with dates before today's date.

- *Yes/No Values.* Use Yes, True, On, or -1 to specify Yes values. Use No, False, Off, or 0 to specify No values.

- *Multiple Criteria.* Use the logic operators (see Table 35.4) to establish multiple criteria within the same field. Use the same criteria row to establish multiple criteria based on multiple fields (where all fields must match). Use different criteria rows (or) where any of the values match.

Table 35.2   Wildcard Operators

Operator	Description
*	Use in place of any number of characters.
?	Use in place of any single character.
#	Use in place of any single digit (for example, **Like "1###"**).
[]	Use to specify characters within the brackets (for example, **N[JY]**).
!	Use to match any character not in the list (for example, **N[!JY]**).
-	Use to match one character in a range of characters (for example, **N[J-Y]**).
LIKE	Use to match any characters (for example, use **LIKE "[A-D]*"** to see a list of members whose names begin with A, B, C, or D). Access often automatically adds the word Like in the grid without you having to type it.

N O T E For more information on operators, refer to online Help (Press Shift+F1 and click the criteria row). ■

Table 35.3   Comparison Operators

Operator	Description
>	Greater than
<	Less than
<=	Less than or equal to
=>	Greater than or equal to
< >	Not equal to
=	Equal to

Table 35.4   Logic Operators

Operator	Description
AND	Requires that all criteria be met
OR	Requires that either criterion be met (either/or)
NOT	Requires that criteria not be met
BETWEEN X and Y	Requires that values be within a specified range
IN	Requires that value be within the same field

N O T E   You can specify multiple rows of criteria for each field. Multiple rows of criteria create an "or" condition. Multiple criteria in the same row create an "and" condition unless the keyword OR is specified. ▦

Sorting Query Results

By default, the results of a query appear unsorted, in the order in which query answers were found. You can specify a sort order to organize the query results into a more meaningful list.

The Sort row of the QBE provides a drop-down list that includes the following sort options:

■ Ascending
■ Descending
■ (not sorted)

By default, no sort order is specified. To specify a sort order, select the field(s) and sort order from the drop-down list.

Specifying Query Properties

 You can view and modify the properties of a query, of the table field lists that a query uses, or of individual fields. To view and modify the properties of any of these objects, choose View, Properties to open the Properties window. Then click the object for which you want to set properties. The contents of the Properties window change to reflect that object's properties.

You might want to specify the format of a calculated field—for example, to specify the number of decimal places to be displayed.

An important query property is the Unique Values property (see Figure 35.8). By default, this property is set to No, indicating that duplicate records, if they exist and meet your criteria, are listed in the dynaset. To exclude duplicate values, set the Unique Values property to **Yes**.

If the goal of your query is to list movie categories and the rental rate by category, by default your query would list duplicates in each category. To list the categories only once, set the Unique Values property to **Yes**.

FIG. 35.8

Set the query property Unique Values to **Yes** to exclude duplicate values from the dynaset.

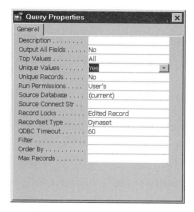

TROUBLESHOOTING

I need to combine the data from two text fields into one field in my query results dynaset. Use a calculated field and string concatenation, as shown in the Member field in Figure 35.5. In an empty field cell, type the new field name, followed by a colon. After the colon, type the field names, enclosed in brackets if necessary. Between the field names, type an ampersand (&). If you want to insert a space or text between the fields, use two quotes and another ampersand:

> **([field1]& " " &[field2])**

The query takes too long to run. Within Access, you can improve the efficiency of queries by using Rushmore Technology. Basically, this technology has you create an index for the fields used in your query. For more information on Rushmore Technology, search for the help topic "Improve Query Performance."

I often need to run queries that depend on uncertain criteria, such as partial spelling of a name. Which query operator should I use? When you are working with uncertain data, the best operator to use is the pattern operator LIKE, which searches for all values that are similar to the value you provide. You also can use the wild-card operator * for situations in which the data is partial (for example, LIKE "Smi*").

Using Action Queries

If you want to update a number of records at one time, Access provides action queries. To create an action query, first create a select query and then modify it to an action query. Table 35.5 shows the different kinds of action queries available. To create an action query, follow these steps:

1. Create a select query first that lists all the fields and necessary criteria.

2. Display the results of the select query in Datasheet view to make sure you are choosing the correct fields and records.

3. Change the query to an Action query by choosing one of the items on the <u>Q</u>uery menu or by clicking the Query Type button (see Table 35.5).

4. If prompted for a table name (Make-Table Query or Append Query), type or choose the table in the Table <u>N</u>ame drop-down list.

5. Choose <u>Q</u>uery, <u>R</u>un or click the Run button.

6. Read any warning messages and reply carefully (see Figure 35.9).

FIG. 35.9
Notice that the dialog prompt says you cannot undo any of the changes and is asking if you are really sure you want to go ahead.

> **CAUTION**
>
> When working with action queries, be extra careful. After you reply to any warning messages, you will not be able to undo your changes and risk deleting or changing the wrong data. Until you are absolutely confident that you won't mess up your data, have a backup copy of the database or a backup copy of any tables affected by the action queries. To make a backup copy of a table, go to the Table tab of the Database window, choose the table, and press Ctrl+C. Press Ctrl+V to paste the new table and give it a name, such as **Backup of Members**.
>
> You can also update your records if you open the query from the Database window. For this reason, if you do not need to save the query, delete it from the Database window to eliminate the possibility of you (or anyone else) running this query by accident.

Part
VI

Ch
35

Table 35.5 shows the different kinds of action queries available. Click the Query Type button and choose the icon shown in the first column. If you save these queries, the query name in the Database window is preceded by the same icon in the first column, with the exclamation point warning you that Access will make major changes to your data if you run the query. Be careful, you will run the query again just by opening it from the database window (choosing <u>O</u>pen or double-clicking the query name).

Table 35.5   Query Types

Icon	Query Name	Description
	Select Query	Use a select query before you create any action queries.
	Make-Table Query	Creates a new table with the fields you identify in your QBE grid. Type in the Table <u>N</u>ame after you click the Query Type button.
	Update Query	Changes the value for the field(s) you identify. After you click the Query Type button, a new row (Update To) appears in the QBE grid. Type the expression in this row. For example, in the Price field column, you could type **[Price]*1.25** to increase the price by 25 percent.
	Append Query	Adds records to the bottom of the table you identify. After you click the Query Type button, choose the name of an existing table. You see a new row, Append To, in the QBE grid. If the field names are different between the two tables, choose the name of the Append To field below the name of the current table's field.
	Delete Query	Deletes any records that match your criteria.

TROUBLESHOOTING

I accidentally ran an action query and didn't mean to. Use your backup copy of the database, or rename your backup copy of the table. If you don't have a backup, you're sunk.

I created a select query, but now realize that I should have created an append query. Rather than re-create the query, you can change the query type in Design view and supply the additional information needed. Open the query in Design view, click the Query Type button, and select Append. Access prompts you for the name of the table to which you want to append data and for the database name.

CHAPTER 36

Creating Reports

by Rick Winter

Whereas forms are primarily for input, reports are only for output. Reports present data in print better than forms or datasheets do. You have more control of the design layout and print output. For example, you can design a report that prints in landscape orientation on legal paper and that subtotals by page or by group. ■

Create a new report

Designing and choosing New Report options are the first steps to creating printed output.

Use Report Wizards

Report Wizards are easier to use than going directly to Design View.

Modify report sections

Report sections allow you to manage how multiple pages of the report will look.

Use groups and totals

In many reports, you will want subtotals by certain categories and a final total for numeric fields.

Insert subreports

Subreports allow you to print unrelated reports on one or more consecutive pages or to show relationships between data that you were unable to display with grouping reports.

Creating a New Report

Before creating a new report, take some time to plan its design. Consider the following items:

- Review the tables, forms, and queries currently used in your database.
- Identify the data components of your report.
- Be sure that all necessary data needed is entered in the appropriate tables.
- Use a form instead of a report if you need to perform any data entry. You cannot enter or modify data in a report.
- Consider creating a query as a preliminary step if your report contains fields from more than one table or if there are derived fields.
- Review existing printed reports, and get feedback from the people who use the reports on outstanding issues or areas that need improvement.

Report creation is very similar to form creation. To create a new report, display the Database window, select the Report tab, and click the New button. The New Report dialog box appears (see Figure 36.1).

▶ **See** "Reviewing the New Form Dialog Box," **p. 788**

FIG. 36.1
The New Report dialog box allows you to choose a Table or Query for your report, and the next step provides related tables and queries if you select Report Wizard.

The following New Report options are listed:

- *Design View.* Enables you to create a custom report from scratch.
- *Report Wizard.* Assists you in creating a form by asking you questions and using predesigned report templates (see "Creating a New Report with Report Wizard").
- *AutoReport: Columnar.* Displays one record at a time in a vertical format (same layout as AutoForm: Columnar).
- *AutoReport: Tabular.* Displays multiple records in a row and column format (same layout as AutoForm: Tabular).

- *Chart Wizard.* Displays a report with a graph or chart of the data.
  ▶ **See** "Creating a Chart with the ChartWizard," **p. 492**

- *Label Wizard.* Creates label reports in a variety of formats.

 N O T E If you have an Access form that resembles your report design, you can save the form as a report. This feature is available as a toolbar button that you can add to any toolbar. First, open the form in Design view and choose View, Toolbars. Click Customize and select the Form & Report Design category on the Commands tab. Drag the Save As Report button to the Form Design toolbar and click Close.

Now you are ready to use the Save As Report Button. Click the Save As Report button and enter a name for the report. Click OK to save the Form as a Report.

To preview the new report, switch to the Report tab of the Database window and double-click the new report name. ▓

Creating a New Report with Report Wizard

When you select a Report Wizard, Access presents a series of dialog boxes that ask you for the report specifications. The Report Wizard functions much the same as the Form Wizard, so many of the dialog boxes will be familiar.

▶ **See** "Creating a New Form with Form Wizard," **p. 789**

To create a new report using the Report Wizard, follow these steps:

1. Click the New Object Report button in the toolbar and select New Report.

2. Type or select the name of the table or query to base the report on.

3. Choose Report Wizard and click OK.

4. Select the fields to be included in the report from the Available Fields pane (they appear in the Selected Fields pane). Then select Next.

5. Specify any desired grouping levels (see Figure 36.2) and select Next (see "Choosing Report Wizard Grouping Options" later in this chapter).

6. Specify any sort order within the groupings and choose Next.

7. Select the desired layout (Vertical, Tabular, or for grouped reports, various step, block, and outline layouts are available) and whether you want Portrait or Landscape orientation.

8. If desired, select to Adjust Field Width to fit on page.

9. Choose Next.

10. Select a style and choose Next (Bold, Casual, Compact, Corporate, Formal, or Soft Gray).

11. Type in the report Title and choose <u>P</u>review the Report or <u>M</u>odify the Report's Design.

12. Select report <u>H</u>elp if desired.

13. Choose <u>F</u>inish. Figure 36.2 shows a finished single table report.

FIG. 36.2
If you choose grouping levels, the Grouping Options button allows you to change intervals for the grouping.

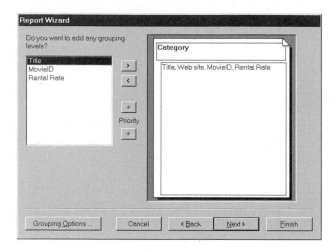

Choosing Report Wizard Grouping Options

If you choose grouping levels in step 5 of the preceding procedure on the Report Wizard, the report breaks into different sections. Each change in the grouping value produces a group header (usually a title) and a group footer (usually subtotals).

The step that asks for grouping has a Grouping <u>O</u>ptions button that opens the Grouping Intervals dialog box (see Figure 36.3). For each text grouping field, you can choose to group on the entire value or the first few characters. For example, if you choose 1st Letter, all the A's are grouped, followed by the B's; instead of a break on every last name.

If the grouping field is numeric, the grouping intervals allow you to group by 10s, 50s, 100s (1–10 can be grouped together, 11–20, and so on).

If the grouping field is date, you can group by Year, Quarter, Month, and other time periods.

On the next step of the Report Wizard, the Summary <u>O</u>ptions button is available if you choose grouping (see Figure 36.4). For each numeric field, you can choose to have subtotals and other subcalculations for each break in the group, and you can create Sum, Avg, Min, and Max calculations. In addition, you can choose between seeing the calculations only (<u>S</u>ummary Only) or seeing the records as well as the calculations (<u>D</u>etail and Summary). You can also obtain percentages by selecting Calculate <u>P</u>ercent of Total for Sums.

FIG. 36.3

This example shows three different kinds of Grouping intervals.

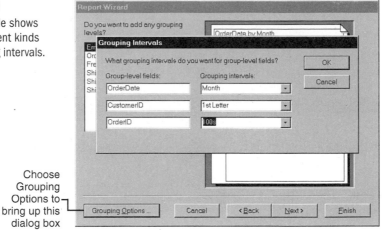

Choose Grouping Options to bring up this dialog box

Do not check numeric ID fields

FIG. 36.4

Choose the Summary Options button to bring up the Summary Options dialog box.

Show no detail and only summary info

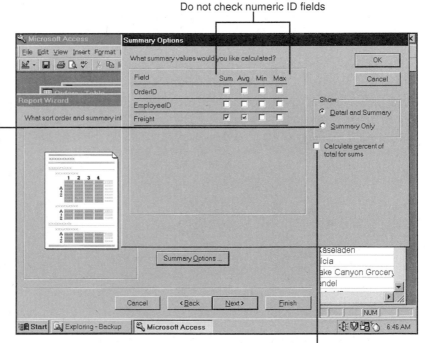

Create percentages

To modify the groups on your report, see the later section, "Sorting and Grouping in Reports."

Creating Mailing Labels

One of the options on the New Report dialog box shows a Label Wizard (refer to Figure 36.1). To create mailing labels, follow these steps:

1. Click the New Object button and choose New Report.

2. On the New Report dialog box, choose Label Wizard and the name of the table or query that contains the addresses (or other fields you want to use) and choose OK.

3. Choose the label size (look on the box your labels come in) and choose Next.

4. If desired, change the text appearance and choose Next.

5. Choose the fields and type text as shown in Figure 36.5 to create your Prototype label, and then choose Next.

6. Choose fields you want to sort the list by (for example, zip) and choose Next.

7. Give your report a name and choose Finish.

FIG. 36.5
Double-click the fields in the Available Fields list to add them to the prototype label.

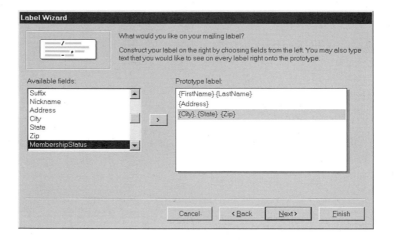

CAUTION

Don't forget commas, spaces, and other punctuation when you create a label. Type these directly in the Prototype Label box (as opposed to clicking the space and comma buttons in version 2 and earlier).

Print Preview

If you selected the Preview the Report option in the last Report Wizard dialog box, Access displays the Print Preview view of the report (see Figure 36.6). Print Preview shows how the printed report will look on-screen. The mouse pointer resembles a magnifying glass. Clicking the report zooms the view in at the location of the mouse magnifying glass. Click again to zoom out.

FIG. 36.6
Click the magnifying glass in the report to zoom in and out.

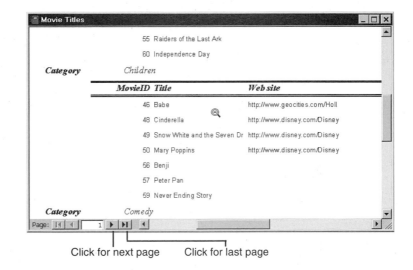

Click for next page   Click for last page

> **N O T E** If you have Microsoft IntelliMouse, you can use the middle wheel button to scroll your window in Print Preview. Hold down the wheel button and drag to scroll the screen up and down or left and right.

▶ **See** "Using Print Preview," **p. 122**

The navigation buttons on the bottom of the screen are similar to those for reports and forms, except now they are used for pages. Choose them to go to the first page, previous page, specific page, next page, or last page.

> **N O T E** You can access Print Preview from the Database window, from Report Design view, and from Report Wizards.

The Print Preview toolbar contains the buttons shown in Table 36.1.

Table 36.1   Buttons in the Print Preview Toolbar

Button	Button Name	Description
View	View	Choose between Design View, Print Preview, and Layout Preview.
Print	Print	Prints the report.
Zoom	Zoom	Toggles zoom in and out.
One Page	One Page	Shows one page at a time.
Two Pages	Two Pages	Shows two pages at a time.
Multiple Pages	Multiple Pages	Click and drag into grid to choose layout of pages to view.
100%	Zoom	Sets the reduction/enlargement percentage for zoom.
Close	Close Window	Closes the Print Preview window.
Office Links	Office Links	Displays a drop-down button list of available Office Links: Publish It with MS Word, Analyze It with MS Excel.
Database Window	Database Window	Switches to the Database window.
New Object: Table	New Object	Displays a drop-down button list that allows you to create various objects such as tables, forms, and reports.
Office Assistant	Office Assistant	Runs Office Assistant for help searches or tips.

Seeing an Example Layout with Layout Preview

 In addition to Print Preview, there is Layout Preview. If you have a lot of data and Access takes a significant amount of time to run Print Preview, choose View, Layout Preview to get an idea of what your report will look like. Click the Last Page navigation button at the bottom of the screen to see how the totals appear in the Report Footer. You will see all sections and sorts, but only for a sample set of data. Make sure that you do not print this view because the totals will be incorrect.

Modifying a Report

If you have not read Chapter 34, "Creating Forms and Report Basics," you may want to now. Working in Design view of forms and reports is almost identical. Chapter 34 talks about working in sections, moving, aligning, and setting properties for controls, using the Design and Formatting toolbars and the Toolbox, and working with expressions. Here is a quick summary of what you need to know for reports:

- Add fields by dragging them from the Field List.
- Select multiple controls with Shift, dragging the mouse, or dragging the mouse in the rulers.
- Delete controls by selecting them and pressing Delete.
- Move controls by dragging them with the hand mouse pointer (both field and label) or the finger mouse pointer.
- Align and size controls with Format menu items.

- If you want additional lines that the Report Wizard did not draw for you, use the Line tool (hold Shift for straight lines).

- Access the properties window by right-clicking the mouse on the object and choosing Properties.

- Create a calculated new field with the Text Box tool by typing = and the formula in the Text Box or the Control Source property.
- Change the appearance of a control with the Formatting toolbar and change the format of a number with the Format and Decimal Places property.
- To hide a section of a report (turn a detail report into a summary report, for example), change the Visible property to No.
- To set page breaks, use the Page Break tool or change the Force New Page or Keep Together properties.
- If text for a field is not large enough to display, change the Can Grow property to Yes so the text will wrap on more than one line.

Sorting and Grouping in Reports

Access enables you to organize report records in a particular sort order or in specified groups. For a mailing-list report, for example, you can print the labels by ZIP code. For a marketing report, you can group customers by state or region.

The grouping feature is available only when you are designing reports (not forms). Grouping divides data into separate groups and sorts records within the groups based on your specifications. In a company phone-list report, for example, you can use the grouping feature to list employees by department. You also can alphabetize the list by department, and alphabetize the names of employees within each department.

You can group on multiple fields. For example, you could use the grouping feature to create a report that lists all employees' names and phone numbers by division, by department within the division, and by position within the department.

 You can add grouping to your report through the Report Wizard (see the preceding section "Choosing Report Wizard Grouping Options") or manually through the Sorting and Grouping window.

To manually add grouping to a report or edit the existing options, choose View, Sorting and Grouping. The Sorting and Grouping dialog box appears (see Figure 36.7). In the top section, select the field on which you want to group, and select either ascending or descending sort order. In the bottom section, set the Group Properties for the grouping (such as whether you want a header or footer and what value starts a new group).

FIG. 36.7
Use the Sorting and Grouping feature to divide and sort records in your report into meaningful sections.

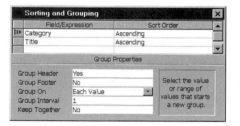

When you use the Report Wizard to create groups, Access automatically adds a group header and group footer. You can turn one or both of these sections on or off in the Sorting and Grouping window.

The Group Property—Group On—is filled out if you choose Group Options during the Report Wizard (refer to Figure 36.3). The Sorting and Grouping window gives you more control over grouping options. The Group On choices correspond to the data type (Prefix characters for text, Interval for numbers, and time intervals for date). The Group Interval property enables you to choose how many prefix characters or how many of the intervals you want to keep together. If you select Group On Year and Group Interval of 5, then your report will have a new group header and footer at every five years.

The Keep Together property enables you to try to fit an entire group on one page (Whole Group) or at least make sure the first line of the detail section prints with the group header (With First Detail).

TIP If you want to exclude the detail section and show only the group headers and footers, change the Visible property of the Detail section to No.

Working with Expressions

Expressions generally are more common in reports than in forms. AutoReport or the Report Wizard will often create subtotals and totals for you. This may even include fields that should not have calculations such as numeric ID fields. To delete unwanted calculations, click the control in the group or report footer section and press Delete.

To create a calculation, choose the Text Box tool and click where you want the calculation to go on the report. Type in the expression or use the Build button in the Control Source property. The placement of the calculation in a section is critical (see Figure 36.8). The following are guidelines for placing calculation controls:

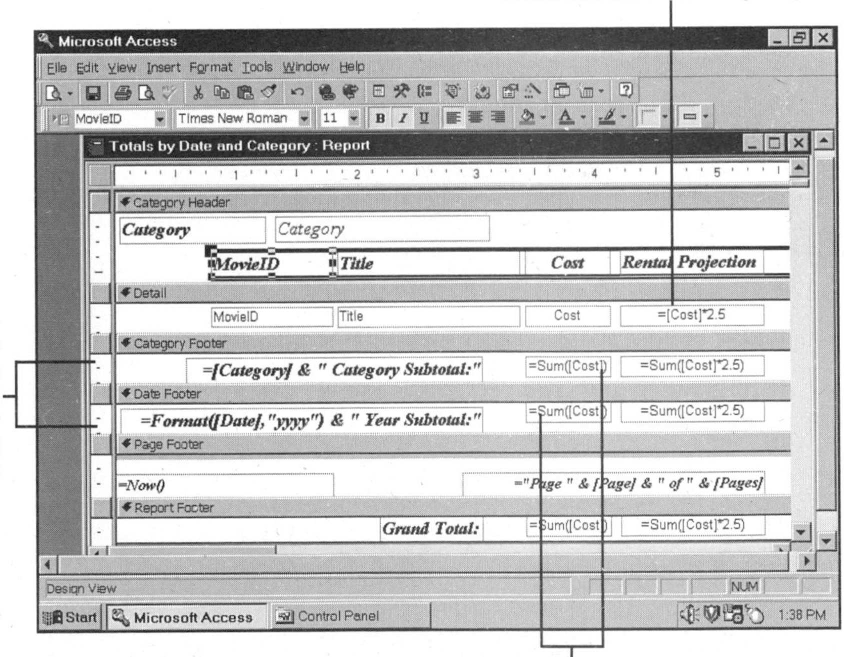

FIG. 36.8
This report has calculated controls in the detail, grouping, and report footer sections.

Detail calculation shows [Cost]*2.5

Labels for category footer, date footer, and page footer have text calculations

Sum of cost in detail, category footer, date footer

- To change the value of a field for every record or create a new calculated field for every record, place the text box in the Detail Section. Common examples include =[FirstName] & " " & [LastName] (name in one field) and =[Quantity]*[Price]

(amount). Use & to combine text data types and the arithmetic operators (+, -, *, and /) for numeric types. The example in Figure 36.8 is =[Cost]*2.5.

■ To have subtotals for a grouping, include the text box in the Group Header or Group Footer section. Common examples include =Sum([Quantity]) and =Avg([Quantity]). The example in Figure 36.8 is =Sum([Cost]). Note that the functions include both parentheses and brackets. If you want to subtotal a calculated field, use the sum function with the calculation: =Sum([Quantity]*[Price]).

■ You can use identical expressions in the different group footers to create subtotals for each grouping and to create grand totals in the report footer section. If you copy the text boxes, make sure the Name properties for each calculated control are not duplicated.

■ If you are grouping on intervals, the group header usually has an expression showing the interval. Examples include =Format$([Date],"yyyy") and =Left$([Name],1). The Format$ expression shows the year (mmm would be three-letter month, mmmm would be full month name, q is the quarter number). The Left$ expression will display the first character from the Name field.

■ Page headers or footers usually have some sort of date reference. For today's date, type **=Now( )** in the text box (or Control Source property) and change the Format property to the desired format—Long Date is the default when created with a Report Wizard.

■ Page headers or footers also usually have page number reference. Use [Page] for the page number and [Pages] for total number of pages. An example is ="Page " & [Page] & " of " & [Pages]. The first page would show Page 1 of 20 in a 20-page report.

■ Do not put summary calculations in page footers; a simple =Sum([Quantity]) formula would not work. Advanced users create a Visual Basic procedure to accomplish the task.

Building Expressions with the Expression Builder

Instead of typing in an expression, you can use the expression builder to help you remember functions, common expressions, and field names. To use the expression builder, follow these instructions:

1. Save the report before you start the expression builder.

2. Create a text box, using the Text Box icon.

3. Choose View, Properties.

4. Move to the Control Source property for the text box.

5. Click the Build button to the right of the Control Source box or on the toolbar.

6. Choose items from the yellow file folders, the operation buttons (+, - , and so on), or type text in the upper part of the Expression Builder (see Table 36.2).

7. When finished building the expression, click the OK button.

Table 36.2   Items in the Expression Builder

Section	Description
Report Name	The first yellow file folder includes the name of the current report. If there are any subreports, they are listed as an indented level under the report name. In the second column, you can choose a name of a control or <Field List>, and the names of the fields in the report are listed in the third column (see Figure 36.9).
Tables, Queries	Shows a list of tables and queries in the database. To refer to a field in a table or query, choose an item in the second column.
Forms, Reports	Shows a list of forms and reports in the database. Choose a control from the second column or <Field List>, and a name of a field from the third column.
Functions	Choose a category in the second column (or keep <All> highlighted and then choose a function in the third column). Any prompts you need to fill (see Figure 36.10) are indicated by <<>>.
Constants	Choose a value such as True or False.
Operators	The third column includes the same operators that appear as buttons in the middle of the Expression Builder. Some additional operators such as Between and >= are included.
Common Expressions	These expressions generally include items that would appear in the report or page header or footer. Choose a page number, date, or user item in the second column and the third column shows the syntax (see Figure 36.11).

FIG. 36.9

The trim function removes any extra spaces before or after the expression in the parentheses.

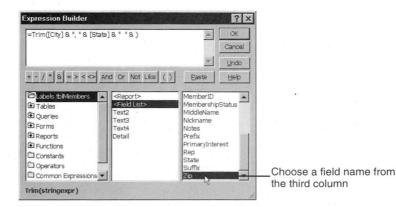

Choose a field name from the third column

Clicking will highlight the <<Falsepart>> and enable
you to replace the prompt with what you type

FIG. 36.10

The Iif expression
with part of the de-
fault input left.

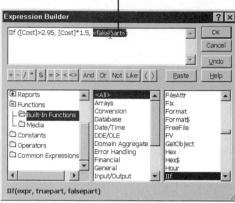

FIG. 36.11

This example of a
common expression
will print the text Page
followed by the page
number.

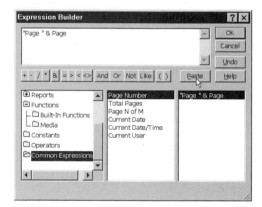

Using Subreports

A report within another report is called a *subreport*. You can use subreports to create a
multitable report in which detailed subreports display records related to the main report's
current record. You also can use subreports to combine two or more unrelated reports in
an unbound main report.

To create a subreport, follow these steps:

1. Create the detailed report that you want to use as the subreport.

2. Display the main report in report design view.

3. Display the Database window.

4. Drag the detailed report object icon to the desired section in the main report.

5. If the subreport records are related to the main report, link them by setting the Link Child Fields and Link Master Fields properties in the subreport's property sheet. The child field is a field on the subreport and the master field is the related field on the main report.

6. Save the report design.

N O T E   You will also want to change the subreport's Can Grow and Can Shrink properties to Yes to expand and contract depending on the amount of data.   ▪

TROUBLESHOOTING

I need to add a paragraph of standard text to my report. Use the Label tool to place a label-box control in the report, and then type your paragraph of text. Use the text-formatting buttons in the toolbar to align the text and select the appropriate font type and size. Use the Formatting toolbar buttons to add color, a border, or depth to your label box.

The grouping report improperly groups my data. The report shows employees by position and then by department. I need to show employees by department and then within department by position. Choose View, Sorting and Grouping. In the top section of the Sorting and Grouping dialog box, make sure that the order of the fields to group by is correct. Access groups based on the order of fields you list in this section.

There is too much white space between records. If necessary, move the controls up to the top of the detail section. Move the mouse pointer to the gray bar at the bottom of the detail section and then use the double-headed mouse pointer and drag to decrease the section height.

Every other page is blank. The width of your report is too long for the page width. Move to the right edge of the report and drag the edge to the left. (You may need to move controls first.) Alternatively, choose File, Page Setup, choose the margin tab, and change the Left and Right margins.

CHAPTER 37

Working with Wizards, Multiple Documents, and Cut, Copy, and Paste

by Rob Tidrow

One of the nicest time-saving features in Microsoft Office is wizards. You can start a new document by selecting the type of document you need to create and work through wizard dialog boxes to set up the document. The benefit of wizards is that you don't need to know *how* to create the document, you just answer the questions in the dialog boxes.

Information within your organization probably is scattered throughout your hard drive and everyone else's. Instead of typing the information over and over, you can use the Cut, Copy, and Paste commands to reuse existing information. This not only saves time but also saves potential errors when retyping information. To start your documents and save time, try the wizards that come with the Office applications. ■

Use wizards to start letters

Because many letters or documents you create include standard information, such as return address, boilerplate text, and other elements, Office provides wizards to help you build letters and documents.

Switch between programs

To reuse data created in one application in another application, you need to learn how to quickly switch between these applications. You learn in this chapter how to perform switching tasks.

Copy text, data, and pictures between programs

One of the strengths of Office applications is the capability to use individual programs to create documents, databases, worksheets, illustrations, and presentations and then copy that information to other applications. This chapter shows you how to use this to create dynamic documents.

Starting a Letter with the Letter Wizard

As mentioned in Chapter 5, "Using Help and Office Assistant," a *wizard* is a subset of templates that walks you through creating a document by asking you a series of questions about what you want to do. Through your answers, the wizard creates a format for your document and adds some text to get you started.

▷ **See** "Using Template Wizards," **p. 256**

To start the Letter Wizard in Word, follow these steps:

1. Choose <u>F</u>ile, <u>N</u>ew. The New dialog box appears, displaying a series of tabs that organize the templates and wizards.

2. Click the Letters & Faxes tab. The tab shows letter and fax templates and the Letter and Fax Wizards, as shown in Figure 37.1.

FIG. 37.1
Letter templates and the Letter Wizard appear in the New dialog box.

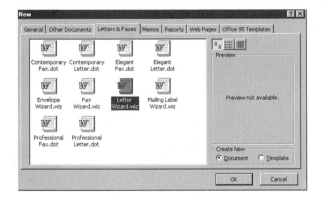

3. Select the Letter Wizard.

4. Choose OK.

N O T E   You can choose the three buttons to the right of the list of templates to see different views of the list:

Large Icons shows large icons.

List shows small icons and a list of file names.

Details shows file details such as name, size, document type, and when the document was last modified. ▪

After you choose OK in the New dialog box, the Office Assistant appears, asking if you want to send one letter or send letters to a mailing list. You also can cancel the operation at this point. Select Send One Letter. The first dialog box of the Letter Wizard appears, shown in Figure 37.2. The dialog box includes four tabs that help you construct your letter. The first tab, the Letter Format tab, includes options that enable you to set the appearance and style of your letter, including the following options:

Part
VII

Ch
37

FIG. 37.2

The first Letter Wizard dialog box enables you to set several settings for your letter.

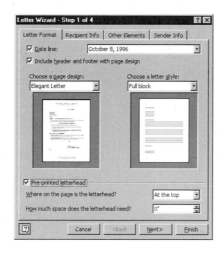

- Date Line places today's date at the top of the letter in one of 11 different date formats. The default date format is Month, Day, Year, such as October 24, 1997. You can select another format by clicking the drop-down list arrow and picking from the list.

- Include Header And Footer With Page Design places a header and footer on your letters, starting with page two of your letter.

- Choose A Page Design includes a drop-down list of templates from which to choose a letterhead style. If a preview picture is available for the letterhead style, you can view it in the preview pane below the drop-down list field.

- Choose A Letter Style includes three types of styles for your letters—Full Block, Modified Block, and Semi-Block. Choose the one that suits your needs and see a preview of it in the preview pane below the drop-down list. Full Block is the default.

- Pre-printed Letterhead is used if you print your letters on company letterhead or stationery. When you choose this option, you can set the following two letterhead options:

- Where on the Page Is the Letterhead? tells Word where your letterhead is pre-printed, including At the Top, At the Bottom, At the Left, and At the Right. If you have letterhead that is preprinted on multiple sides, select the option from the drop-down list where the preprinted information needs the most room. You may need to experiment with this option to get the best results.

- How Much Space Does the Letterhead Need? tells Word how much to reset the margins to avoid printing on top of your letterhead.

After setting the Letter Format tab options, click the Recipient Info tab (see Figure 37.3) to fill out information about the recipient of the letter. This tab includes the following options:

FIG. 37.3

The Recipient Info tab enables you to set options concerning your letter's recipient.

- Click Here To Use Address Book enables you to pull names and addresses from your Outlook contact list to automatically enter the recipient's name and address.

- Recipient's Name includes a space to type in the name of the recipient. If you have used the Letter Wizard in the past, click the drop-down list to see if the recipient's name is already entered and click his or her name to quickly add it to the Recipient's Name field.

- Delivery Address includes space to enter the recipient's address. Use hard returns at the end of each address line to continue entering the address.

- The Salutation area includes options for including salutations at the beginning of the letter. Click one of the four options to the right of the Example field—Informal, Formal, Business, Other—for Word to format the salutation accordingly. If you select Informal, for instance, Word uses the format Dear *First Name*. For more formal or business-oriented salutations, click the Formal or Business options.

The Formal option, for example, formats the name using Dear *First Name Last Name*, such as **Dear Pete Houston**. Click the Example drop-down list for other options.

Copying Information into a Dialog Box

The dialog box shown earlier in Figure 37.3 requests the recipient's name and address. You can type in the information or copy it from somewhere else, if it is available. The recipient's name and address, for instance, may already appear in a Notepad document you created earlier.

▶ **See** "Copying and Moving Data," **p. 78**

To copy information from the Notepad into the Letter Wizard dialog box, follow these steps:

1. Drag the I-beam mouse pointer over the existing information in the Letter wizard (if any exists there already) in the recipient's text box to highlight all the information you will replace.

   ▶ **See** "Switching Between Documents," **p. 124**

2. Switch to the open Notepad document by clicking its button on the taskbar at the bottom of the screen. If a document is not open, you can use the Start button on the taskbar to open programs or documents.

3. In the Notepad window, highlight the information you want to copy (see Figure 37.4).

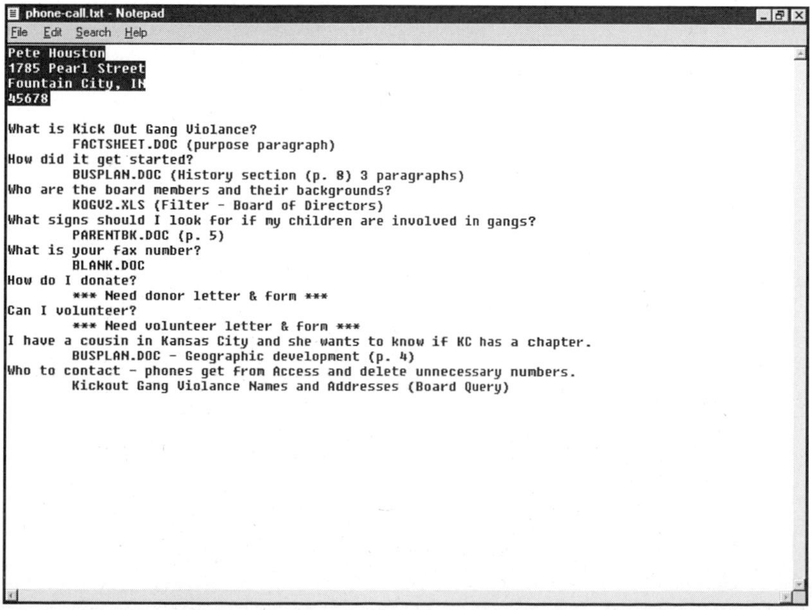

Part
VII

Ch
37

FIG. 37.4

Select the information from the Notepad document you want to copy and paste into the Letter Wizard text box.

```
phone-call.txt - Notepad
File  Edit  Search  Help
Pete Houston
1785 Pearl Street
Fountain City, IN
45678
What is Kick Out Gang Violance?
        FACTSHEET.DOC (purpose paragraph)
How did it get started?
        BUSPLAN.DOC (History section (p. 8) 3 paragraphs)
Who are the board members and their backgrounds?
        KOGV2.XLS (Filter - Board of Directors)
What signs should I look for if my children are involved in gangs?
        PARENTBK.DOC (p. 5)
What is your fax number?
        BLANK.DOC
How do I donate?
        *** Need donor letter & form ***
Can I volunteer?
        *** Need volunteer letter & form ***
I have a cousin in Kansas City and she wants to know if KC has a chapter.
        BUSPLAN.DOC - Geographic development (p. 4)
Who to contact - phones get from Access and delete unnecessary numbers.
        Kickout Gang Violance Names and Addresses (Board Query)
```

4. To copy the highlighted text, choose <u>E</u>dit, <u>C</u>opy, or press Ctrl+C.

▶ **See** "Opening a Document from the Taskbar," **p. 35**

5. Click the Word button on the taskbar to return to the Letter Wizard dialog box in Word.

6. The old entry in the recipient's text box should still be highlighted. Press Ctrl+V to paste the information from the Clipboard to the text box.

N O T E You cannot use the <u>E</u>dit menu or any button in a toolbar while you are in this dialog box. The only way to paste from the Clipboard is to press Ctrl+V or use the shortcut menu by pressing the right mouse button. The same holds true when you are trying to cut or copy from a dialog box. Press Ctrl+X to cut or Ctrl+C to copy highlighted text in a text box, or use the shortcut menu. ▪

Continuing with the Letter Wizard

After you fill in the Recipient Info tab, click the Other Elements tab or the <u>N</u>ext button. This tab (see Figure 37.5) includes letter elements commonly found in formal business correspondence, legal drafts, and other letters that list routing instructions, subjects, and reference information. For many informal and business letters you write, you might elect to leave this tab alone. The options on this tab are as follows:

FIG. 37.5
Use the Other Elements tab to include special elements as part of your letters.

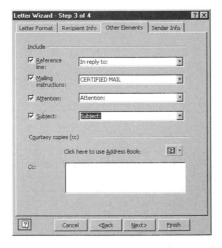

▪ <u>R</u>eference Line includes options enabling you to place a description of what your letter is in response to. Select a standard reference line from the drop-down list, or enter your own.

■ <u>M</u>ailing Instructions enables you to insert directions on how the letter is to be handled en route to its recipient. Select a standard delivery medium, or enter your own.

■ A<u>t</u>tention shows an attention line. Select a standard Attention line, or enter your own.

■ <u>S</u>ubject enables you to include a description of the content of the letter. <u>S</u>ubject lines are common on most business letters. Select the standard Subject option, or enter your own.

■ C<u>o</u>urtesy Copies (cc) includes a field for you to list other recipients who are to receive a copy of the letter. Courtesy copies are also known as *carbon copies*. Click the Address Book icon to select other recipients from your address book.

Part VII
Ch 37

Click the Sender Info tab or the <u>N</u>ext button after you finish with the Other Elements tab. The Sender Info tab (see Figure 37.6) includes information about you or the person sending the letter. In most cases, after you fill in this tab once, you do not have to do so for subsequent letters. The Preview pane shows an example of how the sender information looks. The following are the options on the Sender Info tab:

FIG. 37.6
The Sender Info tab is used to set up the return address and other information regarding the sender of the letter.

■ <u>S</u>ender's Name lists the name of the person sending the letter. You can enter a name, select one from the drop-down list, or click the Address Book icon to automatically enter a name and address from your address book.

■ <u>R</u>eturn Address lists the sender's address.

TIP Click the O<u>m</u>it option if you do not want the sender's address to be included on the letter.

- Complimentary Closing enables you to choose a closing message for your letters, such as Best wishes, Cordially, and so on.

- Job Title lists the title of the sender. For informal letters, this information may not be necessary. For formal letters or business correspondence, including the job title lends professionalism to your letters.

- Company lists the name of the sender's company.

- Writer/Typist Initials includes the typist's initials, in lowercase letters.

- Enclosures lists the number of additional documents or other items included with your letter.

After you fill in the Sender Info tab, click Finish. Word builds the letter and displays a new document with the elements you selected using the Letter Wizard (see Figure 37.7). When the document displays, the Office Assistant asks if you want to create an envelope, a mailing label, or rerun the Letter Wizard to make changes to your new letter. For now, click the Make an Envelope option to create an envelope.

FIG. 37.7

After running the Letter Wizard, your document is ready for you to type in your text, or create other letter elements.

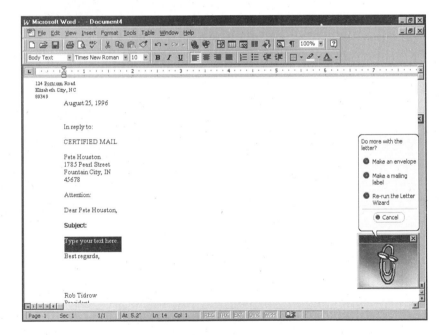

When you select the Make an Envelope option, the Envelopes and Labels dialog box appears (see Figure 37.8). The name of the recipient appears in the Delivery Address text box, and your address appears in the Return Address text box. If necessary, edit these entries in the dialog box. Continue with the following steps:

FIG. 37.8

The Wizard takes you to the Envelopes and Labels dialog box, where you can edit addresses.

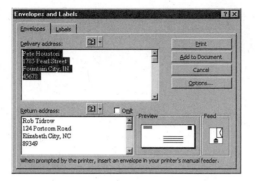

 TIP You also can enter the Envelopes and Labels dialog box by choosing Tools, Envelopes and Labels.

1. Your name and address automatically appear in the Return Address text box. If you have preprinted envelopes, check the Omit check box to remove the return address.

2. To create an envelope, choose the Envelopes tab.

3. To create a label, choose the Labels tab. In the Labels tab, you can specify the label size, which label to print on a label sheet, and whether a bar code prints on the label.

   When the Delivery Address and Return Address appear as you want, you may choose from the following options:

   - Choose Options to display the Envelope Options dialog box from which you can change the envelope size, add or remove a bar code, change the fonts for the delivery or return addresses, or change the placement of the addresses on the envelope. You also can set printing options by clicking the Printing Options tab on the Envelope Options dialog box.

   - Choose Add to Document to add the envelope as a separate page in your document. This option also enables you to preview the envelope before you print it. When you choose this option, you return to the letter document and can continue editing it.

   - Choose Print to print your new envelope directly to the printer.

   - Choose Cancel to exit the Envelopes and Labels dialog box without saving.

Regardless of whether you print an envelope, your letter appears with the current date and the recipient's information. Throughout the letter, information that you need to replace is indicated by brackets or highlighted text, as shown in Figure 37.9. Click the bracketed area or highlighted text and type your replacement text.

FIG. 37.9
Select Type your
text here and type
the body of the letter.

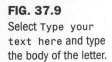

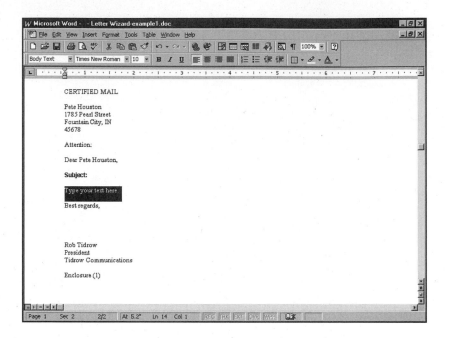

Copying Information from Notepad to Word

You can copy items from a Notepad document into your letter. Click the Notepad button on the taskbar to open the Notepad document. If the program is not open, click the Start button on the taskbar, choose the Programs icon, and then choose the Accessories icon. Click the Notepad icon from the Accessories group and choose File, Open to open your Notepad document.

▶ **See** "Launching Programs," **p. 34**

To place the information in the Clipboard, follow these steps:

1. In the Notepad document, highlight the text you want to copy.

2. Choose Edit, Copy, or press Ctrl+C.

N O T E   To remove the information from the Notepad and place it in the Clipboard, choose Edit, Cut, or press Ctrl+X. ▪

To copy the information from the Clipboard to your Word document, follow these steps:

1. Return to the Word document by clicking the Word button on the taskbar or by pressing Alt+Tab.

2. In your document, position the insertion point where you want to place the copy.

3. Choose Edit, Paste, or press Ctrl+V.

Using the Styles from the Letter Wizard

Part VII

Ch 37

When you use a template or wizard, more than text comes with the document. Styles, AutoText entries, and macros are added to the Normal template entries to give you added flexibility in creating your documents. The first item in the Formatting toolbar shows you the current style for the highlighted text. Figure 37.10 shows that Return Address is the style when the insertion point is in the letter's return address.

▶ **See** "Formatting with Styles," **p. 245**

FIG. 37.10
The Letter Wizard adds a Return Address style and uses it for the return address.

Style box —

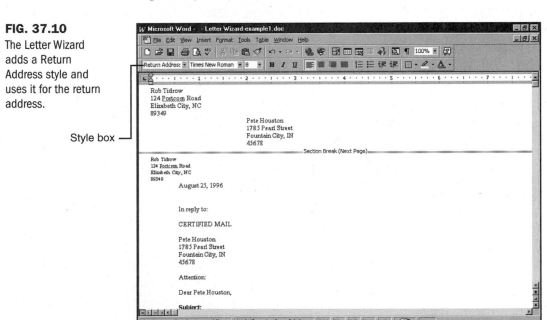

If you display the style area by choosing Tools, Options and increase the size of the style area to .7 or larger, you can then view the different styles applied to each section of the letter. The styles for Pete Houston's address (the recipient address) is Inside Address, and the style for the body of the letter is Body Text. You can apply a style by highlighting the text, clicking the Style box down arrow, and selecting the style from the drop-down list.

Copying Text Between Word Documents

The information for your documents may be scattered throughout existing documents. Learning how to copy text between documents saves valuable time, especially if you want to retype the same text repeatedly.

Opening Word Documents

Part of the process of working with multiple documents in Word is opening those documents. You can open each document separately by choosing File, Open, and you can have more than one document open at a time.

▶ **See** "Working with Files," **p. 94**

To open more than one document, follow these steps:

1. Choose File, Open. The Open dialog box appears.

2. If necessary, select the file location in the Look In drop-down list.

3. Do one of the following:

   - In the file name list, press Ctrl and then click each of the files you want to open, as shown in Figure 37.11.

   - To select contiguous file names, click the first file name, hold down the Shift key, and click the last file name.

   - In the File Name text box, type the names of the files you want to open, separating file names with spaces.

FIG. 37.11
Press Ctrl and click file names to open noncontiguous files.

4. Choose OK. All the selected files open.

Switching Between Documents

When you have several documents open, you need to switch between the documents to copy information between them.

To switch between open documents in Word, do one of the following:

■ Choose one of the documents from the bottom of the Window menu, as shown in Figure 37.12.

■ Press Ctrl+F6 to cycle through the open documents.

FIG. 37.12
To go to the Numbering document, type **2** or click Numbering.doc.

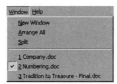

Copying Information from One Word Document to Another

After you open your documents, you can copy information between them. Use the Clipboard method described in this section or the drag-and-drop feature mentioned later in the section "Using Drag-and-Drop to Copy Information Between Documents."

▶ **See** "Copying and Moving Data," **p. 78**

To copy information between documents, follow these steps:

1. Highlight the text you want to copy.

2. Choose <u>E</u>dit, <u>C</u>opy, or press Ctrl+C.

3. Switch to the document that is to receive the copy and position the insertion point where you want to place the copy.

   If you know the target page number, double-click the left portion of the status bar to open the Go To dialog box; type that page number and choose Nex<u>t</u>.

4. Choose <u>E</u>dit, <u>P</u>aste, or press Ctrl+V.

   ▶ **See** "Using Toolbars and Keyboard Shortcuts to Format," **p. 81**

After you copy the text into your document, you may need to reformat the text so that it matches the surrounding text.

Part
VII

Ch
37

N O T E The Format Painter button is handy for copying formats. Position the insertion point within the text that has the format you want; click the Format Painter button. Drag the mouse-pointer paintbrush across the text you want to change. When you release the mouse button, the highlighted text changes the format.

To copy a format multiple times double-click the Format Painter button. ■

N O T E When you use the normal paste procedure in step 4 of the preceding steps, the text retains some formatting from the original document. If you want the text to assume the formatting of the text at the insertion point in your target document, choose Edit, Paste Special. Then select the Unformatted Text option in the As list in the Paste Special dialog box. ■

Arranging Documents

TIP Close or minimize any documents you don't want to view. If you have too many documents open, you can see only a small portion of each document.

If you want to see more than one document at a time, you can display parts of each document window.

To arrange the documents, follow these steps:

1. Open the documents you want to view.

2. Choose Window, Arrange All. The documents are tiled within the window, as shown in Figure 37.13. Use these options to adjust the windows:

   - To change the size or shape of the window, point to a window border and drag the double-headed mouse pointer.

   - To move a window, drag the title bar.

Using Drag-and-Drop to Copy Information Between Documents

When you have more than one document visible, you can drag text between the two documents. To move or copy information with drag-and-drop, follow these steps:

▶ **See** "Moving with Drag-and-Drop," **p. 79**

1. Highlight the text you want to move or copy.

TIP You can use the same drag-and-drop procedure when you move or copy text within the same document.

2. Position the mouse pointer in the middle of the highlighted text.

FIG. 37.13

Two documents, Tradition to Treasure and Company, are open and visible here.

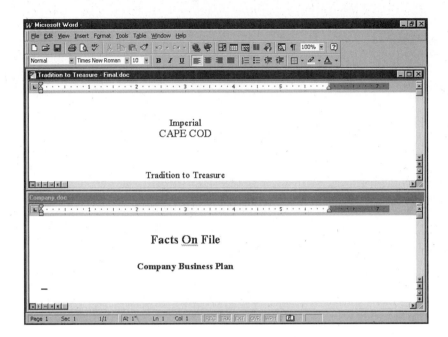

3. To move the text, drag the mouse pointer. The mouse pointer changes to a gray rectangle as you drag, and a gray dashed line indicates where the text will be placed.

   To copy text, hold down the Ctrl key and drag the mouse pointer. A plus sign (+) appears with the mouse pointer (see Figure 37.14).

4. Drag the text into the new window to receive the copy.

5. Release the mouse button to complete the copy procedure.

TROUBLESHOOTING

When I copy information with drag-and-drop, the original document loses its information. You used the move feature instead. Make sure that you hold down the Ctrl key throughout the process. After you drag the information, release the mouse button first and then release the Ctrl key.

My copied text appears in the middle of existing text. Don't forget to watch the gray dashed line that is part of the mouse pointer. This line shows where the copied text will be inserted.

I get a black circle with a slash through it when I try to copy. When it is on the title bar or status bar, the black circle with the slash indicates that you cannot drop as you drag the mouse with a copy. Make sure that you go all the way into the other document before you release the mouse button.

FIG. 37.14
When you copy text, a plus sign (+) appears with the mouse pointer.

Dashed line ——

Mouse pointer (gray rectangle)   Plus sign indicates copy

Copying Spreadsheet Information

The procedure for copying information from an Excel spreadsheet to a Word document is essentially the same as copying between two Word documents. You highlight the area you want to copy and choose Edit, Copy; then move to the location where you want the copy to appear and choose Edit, Paste.

Copying from Excel to Word

To copy information from an Excel worksheet to a Word document, follow these steps:

1. Start Excel by clicking the Start button on the taskbar and choosing Programs, Microsoft Excel.

2. Choose File, Open, or press Ctrl+O.

3. Select the name of the file you want to open and choose OK.

   ▶ **See** "Selecting Cells and Ranges," **p. 308**

4. To highlight the range you want to copy, do one of the following things:

- With the thick, white-cross mouse pointer, drag across the range to copy, as shown in Figure 37.15.
- Hold down the Shift key and use the arrow keys to highlight the range.

FIG. 37.15
In the Excel worksheet, highlight the range you want to copy.

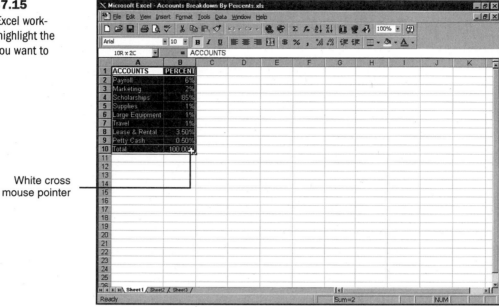

White cross mouse pointer

Part
VII

Ch

37

CAUTION

When you drag the mouse pointer, make sure the pointer is a thick white cross and not the arrow Excel uses for drag-and-drop or the black plus sign used for automatic fill.

---

5. Choose Edit, Copy, or press Ctrl+C. A marquee surrounds the range to be copied.
6. Return to the Word document by clicking the Word button on the taskbar or by pressing Alt+Tab.
7. Position the insertion point where you want the spreadsheet information to appear.

8. Choose Edit, Paste, or press Ctrl+V.

N O T E When you perform a normal paste operation in step 8, the information goes into a table in Word, as shown in Figure 37.16. The light gray grid lines do not print. If you want lines to appear, choose Format, Borders and Shading in Word. To change your columns in Word, drag the column marker. ■

FIG. 37.16

Information from an Excel worksheet appears in Word as a table.

Column marker

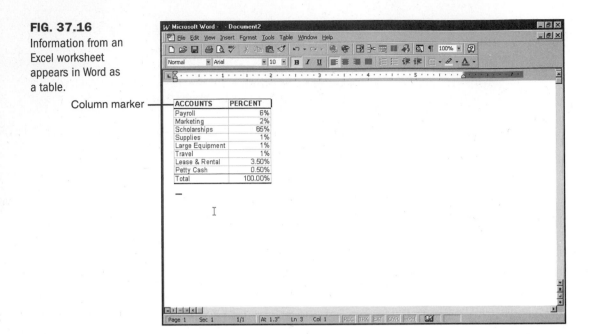

Using Paste Special with a Spreadsheet

If you don't want text to appear in a table in your Word document, you can use the Paste Special option. To use Paste Special with spreadsheet data in the Clipboard, choose Edit, Paste Special. The Paste Special dialog box appears, as shown in Figure 37.17.

▶ **See** "Working with Tables," **p. 280**

FIG. 37.17

Select one of the options in the Paste Special dialog box to format your text.

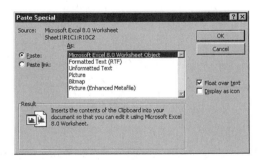

The options in the Paste Special dialog box enable you to link, embed, or specify a format for the spreadsheet. To link information to the spreadsheet, select Paste Link.

In the As list box, select from the following options how you want your Excel worksheet to appear:

- To insert the Excel spreadsheet as an object, select Microsoft Excel Worksheet Object. The Float Over Text option is used when you want to place the inserted object in front of or behind text and objects in the document. To do this, select the Float Over Text option and then use the Draw menu commands to control how the inserted object appears. If you want the inserted object to act as normal text, clear the Float Over Text option box.

- The Display As icon is used when you want to insert an icon in the document instead of the object itself. When viewers want to see the object, they double-click the icon to display the object.

- To insert the spreadsheet as a table in your Word document (the default when you choose Edit, Paste), select the Formatted Text (RTF) option.

- To insert the spreadsheet with tabs separating data that was in columns, as shown in Figure 37.18, select the Unformatted Text option. If you select this option, you probably will need to highlight the data and change the tab stops if you want the information to align.

FIG. 37.18

When you copy information from the spreadsheet by using the Unformatted Text option, set a tab stop to separate the items that were in columns in the worksheet.

New tab stop ──

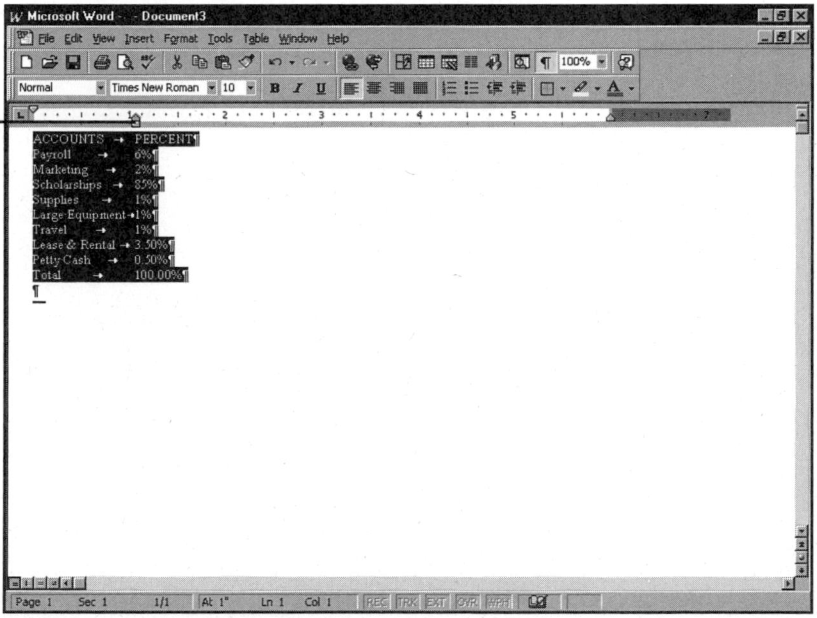

- To insert the spreadsheet as a graphic, as shown in Figure 37.19, select the Picture or Bitmap option in the As list box. Both options insert the spreadsheet as a diagram, but Picture takes up less room in the file and prints faster. You can also insert the graphic as an enhanced metafile, which lets you edit the picture as a metafile.

Part
VII

Ch
37

FIG. 37.19

The top table shows the Bitmap format, and the bottom table shows the Picture format.

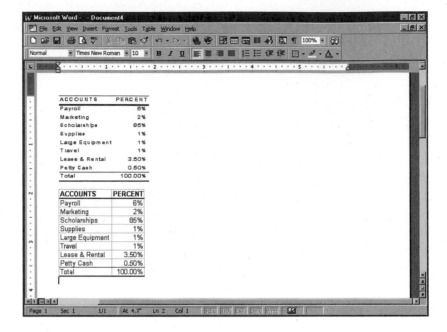

To edit the picture, first select the picture to display the small black handles. To resize the picture, point to one of the handles until the mouse pointer changes to a double-headed black arrow and then drag. To move the picture up or down in the document, drag the drag-and-drop white arrow and rectangle mouse pointer.

TROUBLESHOOTING

I can't see much of my document after I move a table. When you move a table, the right margin of the document may move so that it no longer is visible. To correct the problem, click the horizontal scroll bar after the scroll box and then before the scroll box. This action repositions your document so that you can see both margins. If you still cannot see both margins, you may need to use the Zoom Control (the third item from the right in the Standard toolbar).

Copying Text from a Database

Copying information from an Access database is similar to copying information from a spreadsheet. Because an Access database is organized into many different parts, you first have to select what part of the database you want to copy. In this section, you copy a list of the board members and officers. There is a query with the information you need.

▶ **See** "Exploring Access," **p. 706**

To copy information from a table or query in Access, follow these steps:

1. If necessary to open Access, choose Start, Programs, and select Microsoft Access.

2. If necessary, choose File, Open Database or press Ctrl+O to open the database. The Database window appears as shown in Figure 37.20.

FIG. 37.20
Click the Queries tab
to list queries in the
Database window.

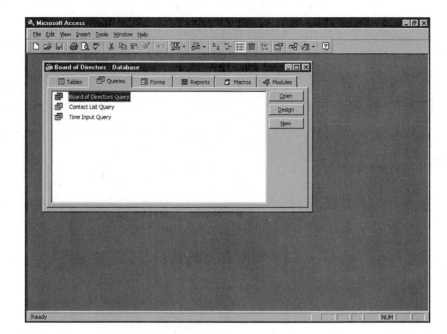

3. Select the Tables or Queries tab in the Database window.

4. Double-click the name in the list of Tables or Queries, or select the name and click Open. The object opens. In this example, the Board of Directors Query opens to a row and column format.

5. Select the items you want to copy. When you move to the field names at the top of the list, the mouse pointer changes to a black down arrow as shown in Figure 37.21. Drag across the field names to select columns. If you position the mouse pointer to the left of the first column, the mouse pointer changes to a black right arrow. Drag the mouse pointer up or down to choose an entire row. You can also select adjacent cells by clicking the first cell, holding down the Shift key, and clicking the last cell.

6. Choose Edit, Copy or press Ctrl+C.

7. Click the Word button on the Windows taskbar and position the insertion point in the Word document to receive the copy.

FIG. 37.21
Drag the black down arrow to select columns to copy.

Black arrow
mouse pointer

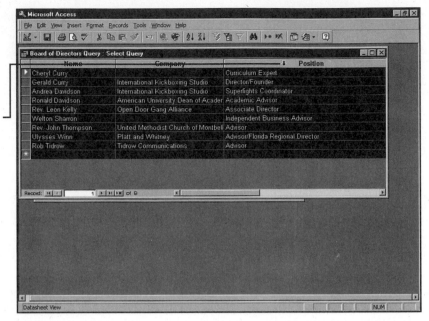

8. Choose <u>E</u>dit, <u>P</u>aste Cell or press Ctrl+V. The Access information appears in a table in Word, as shown in Figure 37.22.

FIG. 37.22
The Access information appears in a formatted table when you paste into Word.

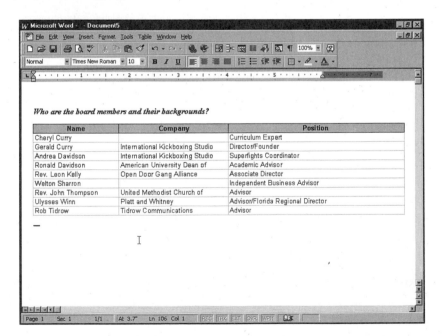

If you use the Edit, Paste Special option with an Access table in the Clipboard, you get two options: Formatted Text (which is the default used for Edit, Paste) and Unformatted Text. When you select Unformatted Text, the table translates to tabs between the columns as shown earlier (in Figure 37.18) for Excel. To align the text, you need to set tabs. You cannot link an Access table or query to your Word document.

Copying Pictures from PowerPoint

In addition to copying text or data, you may want to copy a slide or picture from PowerPoint or a chart from Excel. The procedure is essentially the same: select the object; choose Edit, Copy; then choose Edit, Paste.

To copy a PowerPoint picture, follow these steps:

1. Start PowerPoint by clicking the Start button on the taskbar and choosing Programs, Microsoft PowerPoint.

2. On the initial screen, choose Open an Existing Presentation, and choose the name of the file.

   ▶ **See** "Moving Through a Presentation," **p. 611**

3. Go to the slide, as shown in Figure 37.23, by clicking the Next Slide or Previous Slide buttons (double arrows) in the scroll bar. Or you can use the Slide Sorter View button and double-click the slide you want.

4. Click the object or objects to copy. White handles surround the object to show that it is selected (refer to Figure 37.23).

 5. Choose Edit, Copy, or press Ctrl+C.

6. Return to the position in your Word document where you want to place the copy.

 7. Choose Edit, Paste or press Ctrl+V. The object appears in your Word document.

Choosing Edit, Paste Special does not do anything different from choosing Edit, Paste. You cannot link or embed the object with Paste Special.

To select the picture, click the object. To change the size of the picture in Word, drag a handle. To move the picture vertically in the document, drag it to the new position. To move the picture horizontally or have text wrap around the object, however, you need to frame the picture first, as described in the following section.

FIG. 37.23

You can copy a sample PowerPoint picture into your Word document.

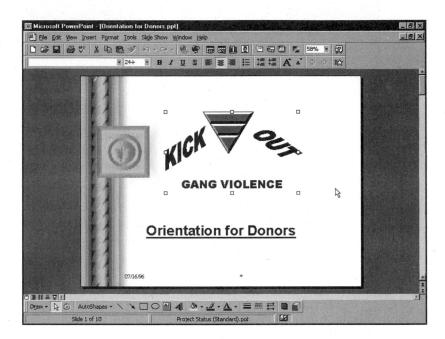

Framing a Picture with a Text Box

When you paste a PowerPoint picture or an Excel chart, or you select Picture or Bitmap in the Paste Special dialog box, the graphic is one object in your Word document. For better control in positioning the object and text around it, you can use text boxes to control the way text flows around the graphic. Figure 37.24 shows an object in page layout view that does not have a text box around it. Text does not wrap around the picture, and you cannot move the picture horizontally on the page.

FIG. 37.24
In this example, the picture had to be made smaller. Notice that the text does not wrap around the picture.

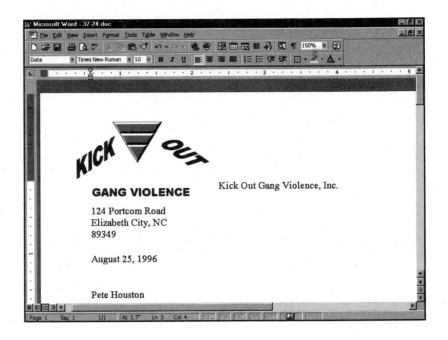

To frame a picture, follow these steps:

1. Select the object.

2. Click the Text Wrapping button on the Picture toolbar. You also can choose Insert, Text Box.

3. Choose Yes if the program prompts you to go to page layout view.

   ▶ **See** "Manipulating Objects," **p. 536**

4. Select from one of the text box choices, including Square, Tight, Through, None, Top and Bottom, or Edit Wrap Points.

When you use a text box around an object, you can flow text around the object. Figures 37.25 and 37.26 show the completed letter.

FIG. 37.25
The first page of a letter is created by using the Letter Wizard command.

Pasted from PowerPoint and inserted into frame

Pasted from Notepad

Pasted from other Word documents

Pasted from an Access database

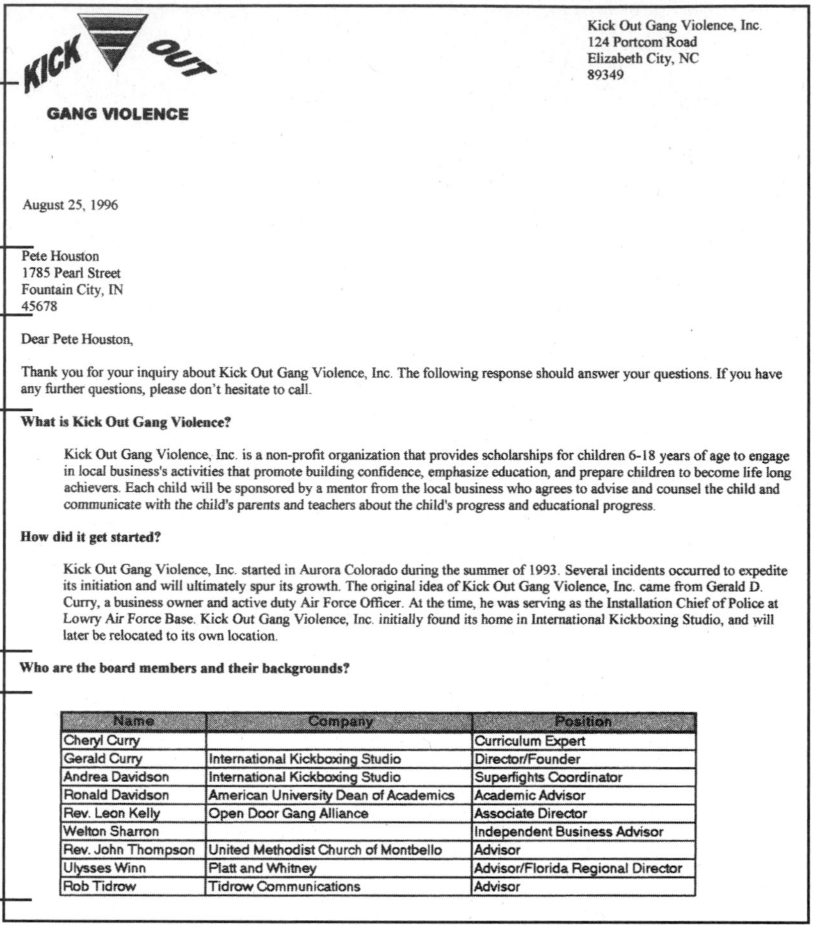

Kick Out Gang Violence, Inc.
124 Portcom Road
Elizabeth City, NC
89349

KICK OUT

GANG VIOLENCE

August 25, 1996

Pete Houston
1785 Pearl Street
Fountain City, IN
45678

Dear Pete Houston,

Thank you for your inquiry about Kick Out Gang Violence, Inc. The following response should answer your questions. If you have any further questions, please don't hesitate to call.

What is Kick Out Gang Violence?

Kick Out Gang Violence, Inc. is a non-profit organization that provides scholarships for children 6-18 years of age to engage in local business's activities that promote building confidence, emphasize education, and prepare children to become life long achievers. Each child will be sponsored by a mentor from the local business who agrees to advise and counsel the child and communicate with the child's parents and teachers about the child's progress and educational progress.

How did it get started?

Kick Out Gang Violence, Inc. started in Aurora Colorado during the summer of 1993. Several incidents occurred to expedite its initiation and will ultimately spur its growth. The original idea of Kick Out Gang Violence, Inc. came from Gerald D. Curry, a business owner and active duty Air Force Officer. At the time, he was serving as the Installation Chief of Police at Lowry Air Force Base. Kick Out Gang Violence, Inc. initially found its home in International Kickboxing Studio, and will later be relocated to its own location.

Who are the board members and their backgrounds?

Name	Company	Position
Cheryl Curry		Curriculum Expert
Gerald Curry	International Kickboxing Studio	Director/Founder
Andrea Davidson	International Kickboxing Studio	Superfights Coordinator
Ronald Davidson	American University Dean of Academics	Academic Advisor
Rev. Leon Kelly	Open Door Gang Alliance	Associate Director
Welton Sharron		Independent Business Advisor
Rev. John Thompson	United Methodist Church of Montbello	Advisor
Ulysses Winn	Platt and Whitney	Advisor/Florida Regional Director
Rob Tidrow	Tidrow Communications	Advisor

FIG. 37.26

The second page of the letter shown in Figure 37.25.

Pasted from other Word document —

Pasted from Excel spreadsheet —

What signs should I look for if my children are involved in gangs?

Be aware if your child:

1. Wants to buy an excessive amount of blue and red for his or her wardrobe.
2. Wears sagging pants on hips or waist.
3. Wears an excessive amount of gold jewelry.
4. Uses excessive amount of gang language.
5. Withdraws from family members.
6. Associates with undesirables.
7. Stays out later than usual.
8. Desires too much privacy.
9. Develops major attitude problems with parents, teachers or those in authority.
10. Starts to use drug and alcohol.
11. Uses hand signs.
12. Receives money or articles without your permission or awareness.
13. Suddenly using racial slurs or hateful comments about other religions.
14. Wants to wear boots, shave his/her head, wear suspenders of a specific color.
15. Lacks identification or has false identification.
16. Wears beepers and begins using cellular phones.

What is your fax number?

555-3317

How do I donate & if I do, where do my funds go?

ACCOUNTS	PERCENT OF DONATION
Payroll	6%
Marketing	2%
Scholarships	85%
Supplies	1%
Large Equipment	1%
Travel	1%
Lease & Rental	3.50%
Petty Cash	0.50%
Total	100.00%

Can I volunteer?

Certainly, we need office workers and volunteers to recruit sponsors, participating organizations, and scholarship candidates. Call us at (303) 555-3646. Thank you for your interest in our organization and for your concern about our children and violence.

Sincerely,

Rob Tidrow

tdt

Enclosure (1)

CHAPTER 38

Sharing Data Between Applications with Linking and Embedding

by Conrad Carlberg and Rick Winter

When you can reuse the same information for different purposes, in different documents, you have the opportunity to save yourself considerable time and effort. Many parts of your existing documents may be useful for information requests and for other reports and documents you might need to create. In a corporation, for example, those who might need the information include prospective customers, business partners, the press, staff, lawyers and accountants, and the board of directors. Trying to provide information to everyone is a huge task. By using Microsoft Office's capabilities to link and embed information, you can streamline the task of supplying information to a diverse audience. ∎

Linking documents

Learn how to place the contents of one document into another, so that the information automatically stays current in both.

Pasting and inserting

Understand the differences between starting the link process from source document and starting from the target document.

Linking documents from different applications

Learn how to get worksheets and charts from Excel, or slides from PowerPoint, into Word documents.

Embedding information

An alternative to linking, embedding lets you keep the source and target separated, yet enables you to edit the document using the source's tools.

Moving Beyond Copy and Paste to Link Information

You may have documents or portions of documents that you need to use over and over. With Microsoft Office applications, you have different options to accomplish the task of reusing the information. The first option is a simple copy and paste. Whenever you need information from one document, open the document, and select and copy the information. Then open the second document and paste the information at the appropriate point.

 TIP To copy and paste information, use your shortcut menu or the keyboard shortcuts—Ctrl+C for copy and Ctrl+V for paste.

▶ **See** "Copying Text Between Word Documents," **p. 860**

Although the copy and paste procedure is the easiest to master, it has two drawbacks. First, if the original information changes, you need to continually repeat the procedure if you want to keep your documents current. The second drawback is that you need to re-member the application that created the information and where you put the files. If you want to edit the data, you may need to return to the original application.

To overcome these drawbacks, you have two additional options for sharing data between files (and applications). One option is to create a link between two files. Whenever the data in the source file changes, the destination file receives the update. The technical term for this is *dynamic data exchange* or DDE.

NOTE This chapter references the *source* application and document as the application and file on disk that supply data. The *destination* or *target* application and document are the application and file on disk that receive the data. ▪

Using Embedding to Connect Documents

Another option is to embed the information into your destination document. When you *embed* the information, you can use the source application's tools to update the information. Depending on the source application, you have two ways to get to the tools (menus and toolbars) of the source application. You can launch the source application from within the destination document, and a separate window appears with the source application showing the information to edit.

A second way to use embedded application tools is called *in-place editing*. When you select the object to edit, your menu and toolbar change to the source application, but you remain in the document and can see the surrounding text or data. The technical term for this kind of sharing is *object linking and embedding* (OLE). Embedding is discussed in more detail in the section "Embedding Information in Your Documents," later in this chapter.

N O T E This chapter mentions objects. An *object* can be text, a chart, table, picture, equation, or any other form of information that you create and edit, usually with an application different from your source application. ■

One difference between linking and embedding is where the information is stored. Linked (DDE) information is stored in the source document. The destination contains only a code that supplies the name and location of the source application, document, and the delineation of the portion of the document. Embedded (OLE) information is stored in the destination document, and the code associated with OLE points to a source application rather than a file.

In some cases, you cannot launch the source application by itself; you need to use your destination application to start the application. These applications are called *applets* (small applications) and include WordArt, ClipArt, Microsoft Graph, and others. You generally launch the source application by choosing Insert, Object.

You may want to look at your existing documents and see whether you will continually use different portions in other documents. Table 38.1 lists examples of some documents that you might use in a business. Suppose that, as an office manager, you use Excel or Access to list the original document and divide the document into parts that may be used repeatedly in other documents. You decide it would be better to create separate documents for each frequently used piece required in multiple documents. You also include a column for the application that may be best for the subdocuments.

Table 38.1   Portions of Documents You Can Link to Other Applications

Portion of Document	Proposed Application	Notes and Where Else Needed
Business Plan Word Document		
Logo	PowerPoint	Use for many documents
Mission Statement	Word	Queries, brochure, many documents
New-franchise procedures	Word	Also instruct new locations

continues

Part

VII

Ch

38

Table 38.1 Continued

Portion of Document	Proposed Application	Notes and Where Else Needed
Business Plan Word Document		
Timeline for development	Word	Goals, manage timeline, board notes
Geographic development	Word	Goals, board notes
Distribution of profits	Excel	Goals, board notes
Benefits to your company	Word	Customer presentation, brochure
History	Word	Queries, press release, brochure
Equipment needed for startup	Excel	Need to update as new numbers, info received
Orgchart	Organization Chart	Will change; board notes
Budget board notes	Excel	Summary, internal management
Board of Directors	Access	Queries, phone list, mailing, board notes
Fact Sheet Word Document		
Logo	PowerPoint	Use for many documents
Purpose	Word	Queries, brochure, many documents
Product feature list	Word	New-franchise notices,
Cost sheet	Excel	New-franchise notices
Price sheet	Excel	Customers, prospects

Using Common Steps to Link Documents

The procedure for linking any kind of document in one application to any other application is essentially the same regardless of the source or destination application. You copy the source into the Clipboard and then use the Paste Link option in the Paste Special dialog box to create the link. In the Paste Special dialog box, you also can specify the type of format in which the information is presented.

TIP Don't forget that you can use the Start button on the taskbar and the Documents icon to locate the files you most recently worked on.

TIP Alt+Tab will cycle through the applications you currently have running. If the target application was running before you opened the source application, Alt+Tab will allow you to fast-switch back to that application.

In some cases, you may not be able to use the Paste Special dialog box to create the link. To link a PowerPoint slide to a Word document, for example, you may need to use the Insert Object dialog box to create the link. This procedure is described in "Linking a PowerPoint Picture to a Word Document" later in this chapter.

To copy an item to the Clipboard and link the item to another document, follow these steps:

1. Select the item in the source document.

2. Choose <u>E</u>dit, <u>C</u>opy or press Ctrl+C.

3. Move to the target application and document. Position the insertion point where you want the link to appear.

4. Choose <u>E</u>dit, Paste <u>S</u>pecial. The Paste Special dialog box appears, as shown in Figure 38.1.

FIG. 38.1
In the Paste Special dialog box, you can choose <u>P</u>aste and Paste <u>l</u>ink.

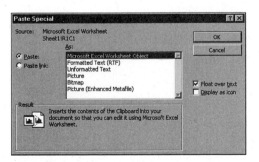

Several format types may be available, depending on the source application. Two options usually are available: <u>P</u>aste and Paste <u>L</u>ink. The Paste <u>L</u>ink option is grayed if you cannot link the source document for the selected format. Choosing <u>P</u>aste moves the item from the Clipboard to the target document, but does not create a link.

A check mark in the <u>D</u>isplay As Icon check box places a small picture symbol in your document.

Part
VII

Ch
38

A check mark in the Float Over Text check box pastes the object into the document in such a way that you can move it over text without disturbing the text's line and character spacing. This option is not available with the text and hyperlink formats.

The Result area gives more detail on what happens with your choices.

5. Select a format option in the As list box as described in the following paragraphs.

6. Choose Paste Link.

7. Choose OK.

The As list box shows different formats. The specific formats that are available change, depending on the source and target applications. Several different formats are available for most links. One of the formats usually is Object. In Figure 38.1, the selected format is Microsoft Excel 8.0 Worksheet Object. When you insert, or embed, an object, you can double-click the object or its icon (if the Display As Icon option is active) and then edit the object with the source application. Embedding is described in the section "Embedding Information in Your Documents" later in this chapter.

Another format option is Formatted Text. This option means that the object appears in your target document with most of the formatting (fonts, borders, and so on) from the source document. This option is different from Unformatted Text, in which the text takes on the format of the target document.

You can also add a picture of the document. The Picture option creates an image of the object. Whether the original document is a picture or text, the link becomes a picture, and you can size and move the picture as one item.

Two additional format options that you may encounter are Bitmap and Hyperlink. A bitmap format is like a picture, but it displays the linked object more precisely on the screen. It also requires more space to store, and it might not print as well as a picture format.

The Hyperlink option allows a user to open the source document (in the source application) by clicking the Hyperlink object. Functionally, this option is very similar to the Object option. In either case, the link takes you to the source document or location. The difference between the Hyperlink and Object options is that the Hyperlink is simply a way to reach the source, while the Object option actually places a view of the source in the active document.

N O T E In order for the hyperlink to take effect when you paste it, it's necessary that the source document has been saved in some location. (Else, the target application would be unable to locate the source when the user clicks it.) ▨

The Object and Hyperlink options are particularly useful when you are pasting summary information. Suppose that you use Word to create an income statement, and that you paste values such as Revenues and Costs from Excel worksheets. A user who wants to examine the underlying information—the specific revenue sources, or the particulars of the operating costs—can open and examine the supporting information in the underlying Excel worksheet.

Apart from the way that the link is stored, the most obvious difference between the Object and Hyperlink options is their appearance on the screen. For example, inserting a hyperlink means that the color of the link changes, depending on whether the user has already used the link to open the source document.

TROUBLESHOOTING

I linked my documents, but the source document isn't there. Where did it go? You may have moved your source document. In Word, check the links by turning on the field codes. Choose Tools, Options, and in the View tab, select Field codes. Then make sure your source file is in the right location. You can use Windows Explorer to find your files.

Linking Two Word Documents

When you want to link two Word documents, you can use Paste Special to create the link, or you can use the Insert, File feature. To insert a portion of a file, use the Paste Special feature, which is helpful if the source information is not a complete file. To insert an entire document, choose Insert, File. In the Insert File dialog box, make sure that you select the Link To File option under the command buttons.

To link two Word documents, follow the steps in the preceding section, "Using Common Steps to Link Documents." Select and copy the text you want to link and then move to your target document and choose Edit, Paste Special. In the Paste Special dialog box, select the Unformatted Text option in the As list box to enable the linked text from the source document to assume the format of the target document.

Table 38.1 shows that a company's mission statement might be mentioned in its business plan, fact sheet, and in most other documents. As office manager for that firm, you may want the changes to be updated in all documents containing the mission statement. Therefore, you might create the separate Word document called Mission.doc, containing a brief statement of the company's aim. Because the text is formatted differently in diverse target documents, you want to link the text using the Unformatted Text option in the As list box of the Paste Special dialog box.

Displaying the Link

When you move within the linked section, as shown in Figure 38.2, the link is highlighted in gray. Although you can edit the linked text, the editing changes disappear when the link is updated (when you open the file again, print the file, or press F9, the Update Field shortcut key). The gray highlight reminds you that your edits will not be permanent.

FIG. 38.2
The linked area in the document is high-lighted in gray.

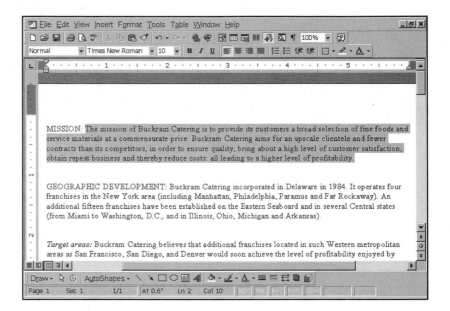

> **N O T E** If the linked text is not highlighted, choose Tools, Options and then select the View tab. In the Field shading drop-down list, select When selected or Always. ▪

To toggle between a selected field code and the display of the text, select the object and press Shift+F9.

TROUBLESHOOTING

I can't see a field code when I press Shift+F9. You probably pasted or paste-linked the object with the Float over Text check box checked. Selecting this option when you paste or paste-link an object prevents the field codes from appearing. Place the object in the document again, but clear the Float over Text check box before choosing OK.

If you used Paste Special to establish a link (rather than Insert, File) and you want to see the name of the source document, you can display the field name codes rather than the actual text. Choose Tools, Options. In the View tab, choose the Field Codes option. (To display the text, deselect Field Codes.) Figure 38.3 shows field codes used in place of text. You can see that the file is linked to Mission.Doc, and Word 8 is the format for the file, so the source application is Word 8. The file also is linked to LOGO.PPT, and PowerPoint is the source application.

FIG. 38.3
Field codes are used in place of text.

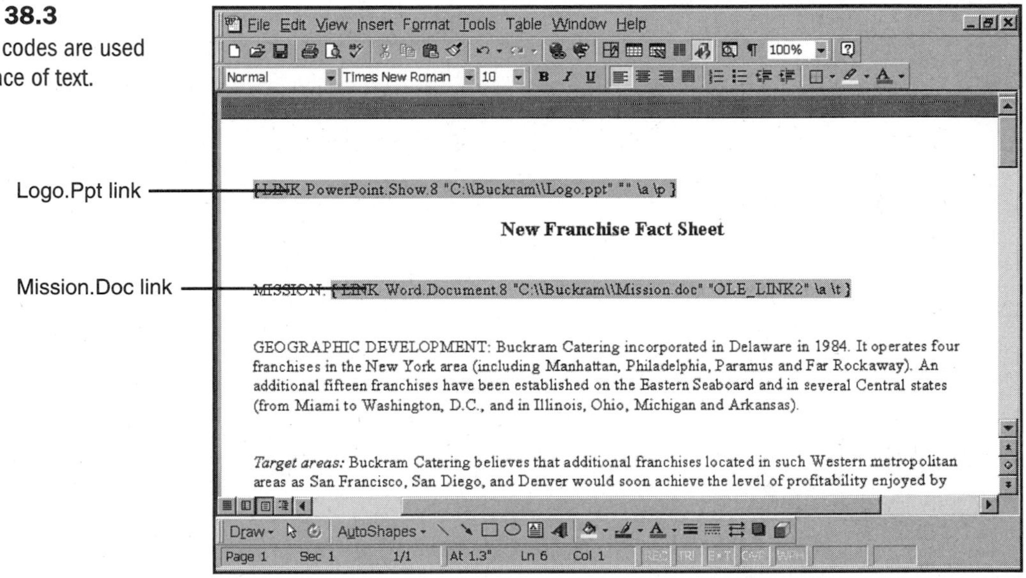

Logo.Ppt link ——
Mission.Doc link ——

{ LINK PowerPoint.Show.8 "C:\\Buckram\\Logo.ppt" "" \a \p }

New Franchise Fact Sheet

MISSION { LINK Word.Document.8 "C:\\Buckram\\Mission.doc" "OLE_LINK2" \a \t }

GEOGRAPHIC DEVELOPMENT: Buckram Catering incorporated in Delaware in 1984. It operates four franchises in the New York area (including Manhattan, Philadelphia, Paramus and Far Rockaway). An additional fifteen franchises have been established on the Eastern Seaboard and in several Central states (from Miami to Washington, D.C., and in Illinois, Ohio, Michigan and Arkansas).

Target areas: Buckram Catering believes that additional franchises located in such Western metropolitan areas as San Francisco, San Diego, and Denver would soon achieve the level of profitability enjoyed by

Part
VII

Ch
38

TIP To go to the previous field code, press Shift+F11.

TROUBLESHOOTING

Changes in my source document aren't reflected in my destination document. The link may be an automatic link or may require manual updating (see the following section, "Editing Links"). You can also do the following:

- To update any manual links, you can go to each field code by pressing F11. To update the code or link, press F9.

- To make sure that your document updates any automatic links when you open the file, choose Tools, Options. In the General tab, make sure that Update Automatic Links at Open is selected.

- To make sure that your document prints with the latest information, choose Tools, Options. In the Print tab, make sure that Update Links is selected.

Editing Links

When you link a document, you must subsequently maintain the source document's name, and keep the source document in the same location (drive and directory) as it was when you created the link. If you rename, delete, or (in most cases) move a document, the link is broken, and you get an error in your destination document. In some cases, you can break the link so that the source document is inserted into the target document without a link; in other cases, you can change the name of the source document.

To change links, follow these steps:

1. Choose <u>E</u>dit, Lin<u>k</u>s. The Links dialog box appears, as shown in Figure 38.4.

FIG. 38.4

The Links dialog box enables you to update, change, or break links.

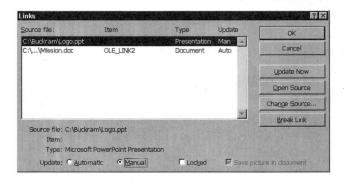

2. Select the file(s) in the <u>S</u>ource file list box.

3. Do one or more of the following things:

   - Choose <u>A</u>utomatic to have the link updated every time the data is available.

   - Choose <u>M</u>anual to require updating through the <u>U</u>pdate Now choice or by selecting the link and pressing F9.

   - Choose Loc<u>k</u>ed to prevent updates to the link. If this choice is selected, <u>A</u>utomatic and <u>M</u>anual choices will not be available, but will be grayed out.

   - Choose the <u>U</u>pdate Now button to update a manual link with any changes from the source file.

 To get out of a dialog box quickly without saving your changes, press Esc.

- Click the Change Source button to change the file name or location of the linked file in the Change Source dialog box.

- Click the Break Link button to insert the object into the document and unlink it. When Word displays a message box asking whether you are sure that you want to break the selected links, choose Yes.

4. Click OK when you finish.

TROUBLESHOOTING

I linked an Excel worksheet to my Word document, but the link won't update. You may have locked the link in the target document, which means you want to prevent updates to the link in your Word document. To unlock the link, choose Edit, Links, choose the link and uncheck the Locked check box, and then update the field by pressing F9.

To unlock a link you can also select the linked text and press Ctrl+Shift+F11.

Part VII Ch 38

Inserting a File into a Document

You also can link documents by using the Insert, File command, which enables you to insert an entire file. You might find this approach more convenient if you want to start the process from the target document, rather than from the source document.

When you use Paste Special to link a file, only the text you select before the Copy command is linked from the target file. If you later go back and insert text before or after the source document selection, the target document does not include the entire text. Insert, File alleviates this problem. The file that you insert can be from the same application or a different application.

To insert a file into a document, follow these steps:

1. Move to the position in the target document where you want to insert the file.

2. Do one of the following:

   ▶ **See** "Using File Dialog Boxes," **p. 94**

   - In Word, choose Insert, File. The Insert File dialog box appears, as shown in Figure 38.5. Keep in mind that with Word's Insert, File command, the file you want to insert must have already been saved to a disk. If you want to create a new file and insert it, use Insert, Object.

FIG. 38.5

The Insert File dialog box enables you to create a link between the files.

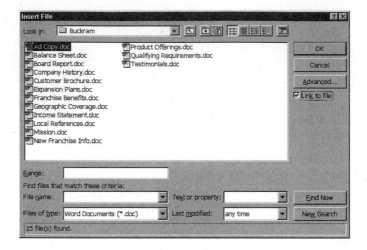

- In Excel, choose Insert, Object. The Object dialog box appears. Choose the Create from File tab; then enter the file name in the File Name text box.

- In PowerPoint, choose Insert, Object. The Insert Object dialog box appears. Choose the Create from File option; then enter the file name in the File text box.

- In Access, move to an OLE data type field on a table, form, or query to insert the file into a field, or go to a form or report design. Choose Insert, Object. The Insert Object dialog box appears. Choose Create from File; then enter the file name in the File text box.

3. Identify the file you want to insert, including the drive and directory if necessary.

4. Choose the Link to File option in Word, the Link to File option in Excel, or the Link option in PowerPoint or Access.

5. Choose OK.

As in the Paste Special example earlier in this chapter, in Word you can display the linked document with a gray highlight or show the field codes. In Figure 38.6, the revised business plan document shows field codes for the linked documents.

N O T E If you want to insert several documents into a single larger document, give your documents a consistent appearance by using the same formats for each one. You also can use templates and styles to help ensure consistency among documents. For more information, see "Formatting with Styles" in Chapter 10, "Working with Large Documents." ■

FIG. 38.6
The field code
INCLUDETEXT
appears for the
Word documents
Mission.doc,
Company
History.doc, Income
Statement.doc, and
Balance Sheet.doc

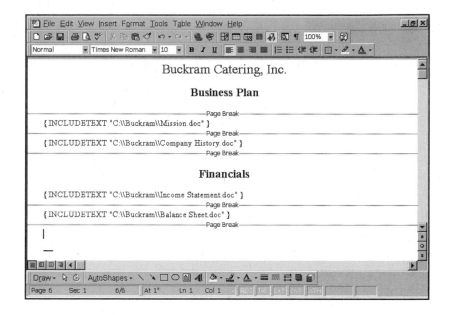

TROUBLESHOOTING

When I make editing changes in my document, why are my changes gone when I open the document again? I know I saved the file. You may be editing a document with a linked file. When you make changes in the linked field, Word will not save them (and Word will not warn you). You need to change the source document to save the changes. To view the field codes, choose Tools, Options and in the View tab select Field codes to view the field codes.

To be able to always see field codes, choose Tools, Options and on the View tab, in the Field shading option, select Always or When selected.

Linking an Excel Worksheet to a Word Document

The procedure for linking a range or an entire Excel worksheet to a Word document is the same as for linking Word documents. You can use either the Paste Special command or choose Insert, File, although formatting a document is easier when you use the Paste Special command. When you use Insert, File, the resulting table sometimes is hard to center on the page because of extra space for the last column or extra cells. In the As list box of the Paste Special dialog box, your formatting choices are different when you Paste Link than when you Paste (see Figure 38.7).

▶ **See** "Copying Text Between Word Documents," **p. 860**

The following list describes the formatting options in the Paste Special dialog box shown in Figure 38.7. The results appear in Figure 38.8.

FIG. 38.7

Choose the Paste Link option to link the worksheet to the Word document.

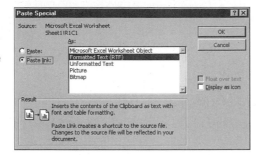

- To insert the Excel worksheet as an object, select Microsoft Excel Worksheet Object. In a Word document, when you double-click the object, you activate the application's tools that created the object. You then can edit the object, using the source application's menus, toolbars, and other commands.

N O T E This is one of the differences between a linked object and an embedded object. When you edit a linked object, you start the source file's application itself. When you edit an embedded object, the target application's menus change to those of the source application. ▪

- To insert the worksheet as a table in your Word document (the default choice when you choose Edit, Paste), select Formatted Text (RTF). You may need to change the column widths for the table to line up properly, as is the case in Figure 38.8.

- To insert the worksheet with tabs separating data, choose Unformatted Text. You may need to highlight the data and change the tabs for the selection if you want the information to align.

- To insert the worksheet as a graphic, select Picture or Bitmap. Both options insert the worksheet as a diagram, but Picture generally takes up less room in the file and prints faster. In Figure 38.8, however, there is almost no discernible difference between Microsoft Excel Worksheet Object, Picture, and Bitmap. In fact, these three options do the same thing. They all insert a picture into the Word document, and you can double-click all three options to go to Excel to edit the object.

▶ **See** "Moving Objects," **p. 554**

FIG. 38.8

You can insert the worksheet as various types of objects.

Unformatted text does not retain formatting ——

Selection handles used for sizing the picture ——

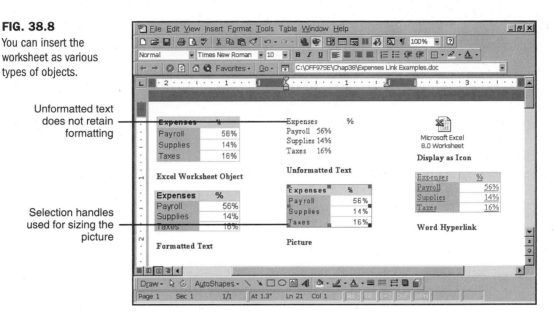

To edit the picture, first select the picture to show the small square selection handles. To resize the picture, point to one of the handles until the mouse pointer changes to a small, double-headed, black arrow; then drag. To move the picture up or down in the document, drag the drag-and-drop white arrow and rectangle mouse pointer. To go to Excel to change the data, double-click the picture.

■ To insert a hyperlink to the worksheet, choose Word Hyperlink. By means of their color, hyperlink formats can help the user determine which links have already been accessed.

■ Put a check mark in the Display as Icon check box on the right side of the dialog box to place a small symbol that represents the program (or any other icon you select).

Suppose that now you need to create a quarterly report that contains text, Excel worksheets, and Excel charts. To do this, you begin by inserting some introductory text at the beginning of the report that includes the purpose and history of the organization. You could link the Mission.Doc and Company History.doc Word documents to the quarterly report file. To report on the sales for the first three months, you probably want to show the amount in a table, a pie chart by type of product sold, and a column chart of sales by month.

Figure 38.9 shows a formatted Excel worksheet. Because the numbers will change, you want to link rather than paste the worksheet and the charts.

FIG. 38.9
Highlight the range in
Excel and choose Edit,
Copy.

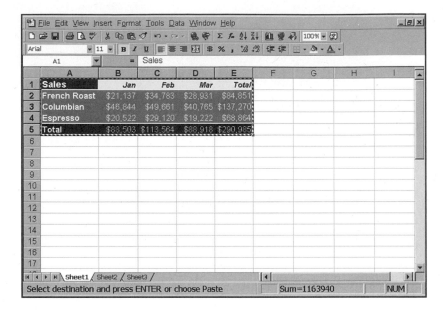

To copy this worksheet into a Word document, follow these steps:

1. In Excel, highlight the range you want to link (A1:E5).

2. Choose Edit, Copy, or press Ctrl+C.

   ▶ **See** "Switching Between Documents," **p. 124**

3. Switch to Word.

4. Choose Edit, Paste Special. The Paste Special dialog box appears.

5. Choose Paste Link, and choose Picture from the As box. Then, choose OK.
   The result appears in Figure 38.10. Notice that the picture is left-justified.

6. If you want to center the worksheet, select the picture and then click the Center
   button.

TROUBLESHOOTING

**We are working in a workgroup, and I know that my coworkers have changed the Excel
document. Why aren't the links updating when I open or print the Word document?** You may
have one of two options turned off. Check Tools, Options, and in the General tab, make sure the
Update automatic Links at Open option is on. In the Print tab, check to make sure the Update
Links option is on.

FIG. 38.10
The worksheet picture appears left-justified in the Word document.

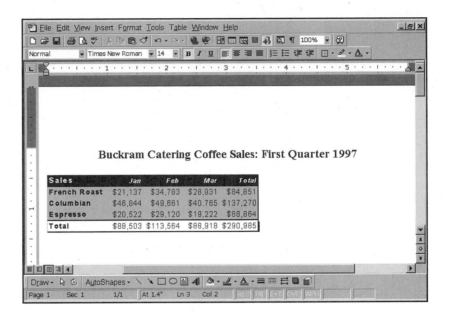

Part
VII

Ch
38

Linking an Excel Chart to a Word Document

Suppose that you want to add a pie chart and column chart to this page in your quarterly report document. You can create charts quickly by clicking the ChartWizard button in Excel's Standard toolbar.

▶ **See** "Creating a Chart with the ChartWizard," **p. 492**

Creating a Pie Chart

To create a pie chart, follow these steps:

1. Drag the white-cross mouse pointer to highlight the titles in A2 to A4 (refer to Figure 38.9).

2. Hold down the Ctrl button and drag to highlight E2 to E4.

 3. Click the ChartWizard button. The ChartWizard dialog box appears, displaying the first of four steps.

4. Select the Pie chart from the Chart Type list box, and the 3D Pie chart in the Chart Sub-type area.

5. Click Next twice to get to the Step 3 ChartWizard dialog box. If necessary, choose the Titles tab. Type **YTD Sales** in the Chart Title text box.

6. Choose the Data Labels tab. Select the Show Label <u>a</u>nd Percent option button.

7. Choose the Legend tab. Fill the <u>S</u>how Legend check box, and choose the Botto<u>m</u> option button.

8. Click <u>F</u>inish. The chart appears on the worksheet the workbook, as shown in Figure 38.11.

FIG. 38.11

The chart appears on the worksheet that contains the data.

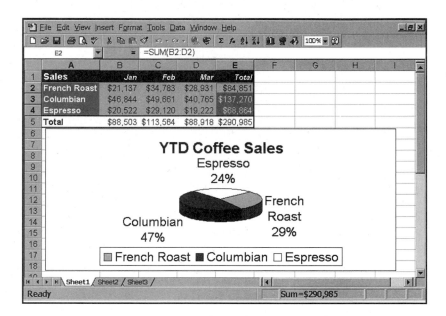

9. You can copy the chart the same way you do a range. If necessary, select the chart, choose <u>E</u>dit, <u>C</u>opy, or press Ctrl+C.

10. Return to the quarterly report document in Word.

11. Choose <u>E</u>dit, Paste <u>S</u>pecial. The Paste Special dialog box appears.

12. Select Microsoft Excel Chart Object, and then choose the Paste <u>L</u>ink option. Click OK. The chart appears in the Word document, surrounded by handles. If the handles do not appear, click the chart.

Creating a Column Chart

To create a column chart in Excel, follow these steps:

1. Drag the white-cross mouse pointer to highlight the range A1 through D4 on the worksheet shown earlier in Figure 38.9.

2. Click the ChartWizard button. Step 1 appears. Select the Column chart type and Clustered Column as the chart sub-type.

3. Click Next twice to reach Step 3 of 4. In the Chart Title text box on the Titles tab, type **Coffee Sales by Month**.

4. Click Next to reach Step 4 of 4, and indicate whether you want to place the chart on the worksheet or on its own sheet. Click Finish.

   The chart appears with selection handles. If, in Step 4, you placed both the Pie and the Column charts on the same sheet, the second chart may appear directly over the first. You can reveal the first chart by dragging the second to the side.

5. With the chart selected, choose Edit, Copy, or press Ctrl+C.

6. Return to the quarterly report document by clicking the Word button in the taskbar.

7. Choose Edit, Paste Special. The Paste Special dialog box appears.

8. In the As list box, select Microsoft Excel Chart Object and choose the Paste Link option. Choose OK. The chart appears in the Word document, with handles.

The data range and charts in the quarterly report are shown in Figure 38.12 and 38.13. When the final numbers come in, simply go to the Excel range and edit them. Figures 38.14 and 38.15 show an updated Word document with the new number for March Espresso sales, and the result of the update is reflected in the charts.

> **N O T E** To remove the border surrounding the charts, change the charts in Excel rather than Word. In Excel, click to select the chart. Choose Format, Selected Chart Area. In the Patterns tab, choose None in the Border section, and then choose OK. ■

Part
VII

Ch
38

FIG. 38.12

The Excel range and column chart appear in the Word document.

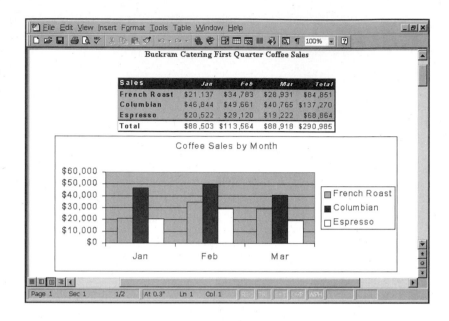

FIG. 38.13

A pie chart is useful for showing differences in *percentages*.

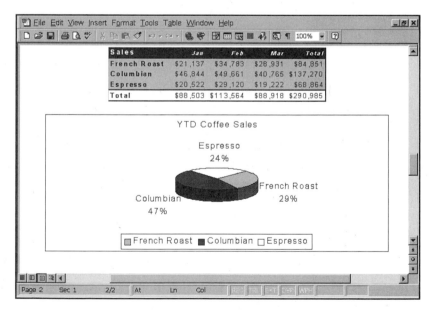

FIG. 38.14
A column chart is useful for showing differences in values.

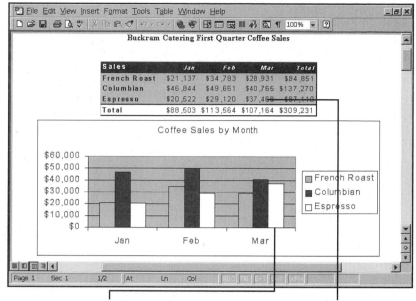

The March espresso column changes height   New number in March

FIG. 38.15
After you update the Excel worksheet, the changes occur in the Word document.

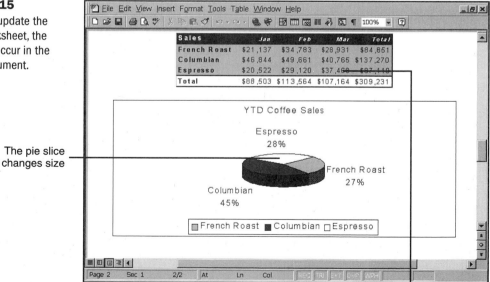

The pie slice changes size

New number in March

Linking a PowerPoint Picture to a Word Document

Suppose that you went through your documents and noticed that the organization logo was on almost every document. If your organization is established, pasting the logo may be appropriate. But you may want to link the logo if the source may change and you want all documents with the logo updated. The Paste Special command, however, does not include PowerPoint as a Paste Link option. Insert, File also does not have a PowerPoint option. To do the link, you need to choose Insert, Object, and the first slide of the presentation must be the picture you want to link.

▶ **See** "Adding, Inserting, and Deleting Slides," **p. 612**

To create your PowerPoint slide, follow these steps:

1. Go to PowerPoint.

2. To insert pictures into your slide, choose Insert, Picture, Clip Art.

 3. To type text, click the Text Box tool. Then click the location in the document where you want to add text, and type.

 4. To create rotated text, click the Free Rotate tool and use the mouse pointer to drag a corner handle of the selected text (see Figure 38.16).

5. Save the document.

FIG. 38.16
Click the Free Rotate Tool and drag a corner handle to change the orientation of the text.

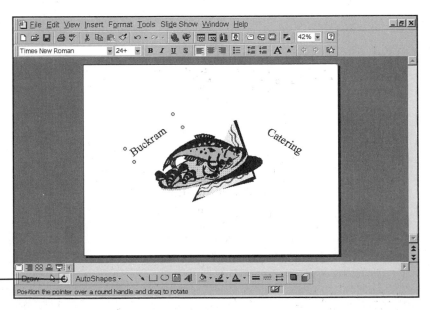

Free Rotate tool ——

To link a PowerPoint slide to Word, follow these steps:

1. Create a PowerPoint slide with a picture and/or text you want to link to your Word document.

2. Save the PowerPoint presentation.

3. Go to the location in your Word document where you want to position the picture.

4. Choose Insert, Object. The Object dialog box appears.

5. Click the Create from File tab and type the File Name or select the file using the Browse button. See Figure 38.17.

FIG. 38.17
Use the Object dialog box to select the type of information you want to insert.

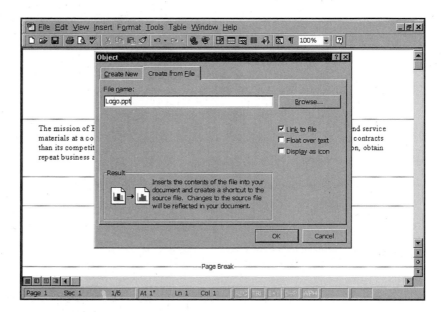

Part
VII

Ch
38

6. Choose the Link to File option and then choose OK.

The picture appears in your Word document. You can resize the picture by selecting the picture and dragging the handles. Figure 38.18 shows the picture in a document.

N O T E You can double-click the PowerPoint picture in Word to launch the PowerPoint presentation. If you launch the presentation, you can play the presentation by clicking each slide to move to the next slide.

Right-click the picture to edit the slide. From the shortcut menu, choose Linked Presentation Object, and choose Edit Link from the cascading menu. PowerPoint appears with your presentation, and you can use its tools to perform any needed editing. Then, save the presentation file and close PowerPoint to return to Word and an updated slide. ■

FIG. 38.18
The PowerPoint slide is inserted into a Word document.

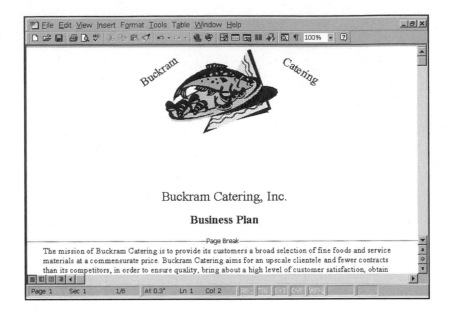

Linking Data Between Excel Worksheets

In some cases, you may want to repeat text or data in an Excel worksheet. For example, you may want to include a summary of actual numbers on a separate sheet of the workbook. You can copy the labels and numbers, or you can create a formula to copy the text and values. If you link through a formula, when the numbers or labels in the source part of the document change, they also change in the target part of the document.

The formula is easy: type an equal sign (=) in the cell to receive the link; move to the source cell you want to link and click the mouse; then press Enter. The source cell you want to link can be in the same sheet, in a different sheet of the same workbook, or in a different workbook file. Figure 38.19 shows an example. The income statement worksheet on the left contains monthly numbers. To see only the categories and the year totals in the target sheet, you can hide columns or create formulas that link to only the totals.

To link the worksheets, follow these steps:

1. Choose File, New to create a blank workbook.

2. Move to cell A2 and type =.

3. Move to the source worksheet (identified as MONTHLY in the example). Click the cell that you want to link.

   ▶ **See** "Referencing Cells in Formulas," **p. 376**

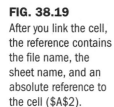

FIG. 38.19
After you link the cell, the reference contains the file name, the sheet name, and an absolute reference to the cell ($A$2).

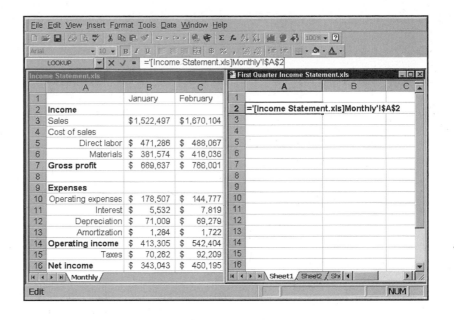

TIP You can remove the dollar sign by selecting the cell with the formula, highlighting the reference in the formula bar, and then pressing F4 three times.

Notice in Figure 38.19 that when you use this method, the reference to the cells includes the file name (Income Statement.xls), the sheet name (Monthly!), and an absolute reference to the cell ($A$2). If you want to copy the information, as in this example, remove the dollar signs to make the reference relative. Then you can copy cell A2 to A3 through A16 to link the other cells. Notice in Figure 38.20 that the cell reference in the SUM formula has no dollar signs (B3:D3).

N O T E To arrange your worksheets side by side, as shown in Figure 38.20, choose <u>W</u>indow, <u>A</u>rrange and then choose the <u>T</u>iled option in the Arrange Window dialog box. You don't need to arrange your worksheets this way, however. You could move to the other worksheet by choosing the document name from the bottom of the <u>W</u>indow menu. ■

▶ **See** "Creating a Formula by Pointing," **p. 374**

The formula automatically contains the file name (if the reference is to a cell in a different workbook), the sheet name (if the reference is to another sheet), and the cell name. The default formula includes dollar signs, which means that if you copy the formula, the reference does not change. Delete the dollar signs so that the copy will work correctly.

Part
VII

Ch
38

FIG. 38.20
To copy the cell information, change the reference so that no dollar signs appear, as shown in the formula bar.

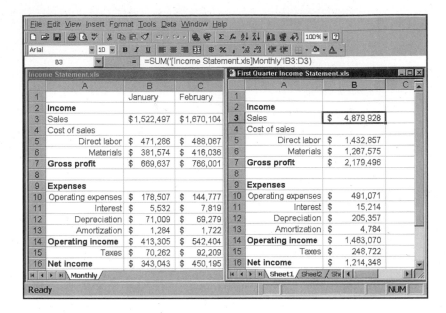

Embedding Information in Your Documents

As mentioned at the beginning of the chapter, in addition to linking information, you can embed information within a document. When you embed an object, the information resides in the destination document, but the source application's tools are available for use in editing.

For example, suppose that you have embedded a Word document in an Excel worksheet. If you now double-click the embedded Word document to edit it, Excel's menus change to Word menus, and you use the available Word commands to edit the embedded document.

You can use any of the following methods to embed information in a document. In each case, to embed the object, choose the Paste option button instead of Paste Link:

- Copy the information to the Clipboard; choose Edit, Paste Special; select an object format. (This method was discussed earlier in the section "Using Common Steps To Link Documents," along with other Paste Special formats.)

  ▶ **See** "Moving with Drag-and-Drop," **p. 79**

- Arrange two windows side by side and use drag-and-drop to copy information between the applications.

- From the target application, choose Insert, Object, choose to Create from File, and open an existing file. (This method was discussed in "Inserting a File into a Document" earlier in this chapter.)

■ From the target application, choose Insert, Object, and Create New object. This section describes this method.

Inserting a New Object into Your Document

If you want to use the features of another application in your document, you can choose Insert, Object and select an application from a list. In addition to the standard Microsoft Office applications, the list contains applets and other Windows applications. Applets are small applications that cannot be run by themselves. When you purchase an application, one or more applets may be available. You may also see other applets when you install other applications such as Lotus SmartSuite.

Following is a list of some of the applets that come with Microsoft Office. If you purchased your applications separately, you may not have all the applets.

Part
VII
Ch
38

Applet	Use
Calendar Control	Inserts a calendar in your document that has drop-down arrows so that you can change the month and year.
Microsoft Clip Gallery	Inserts clip-art pictures
Microsoft Map	Inserts a map showing different levels associated with data
Microsoft Equation 3.0	Creates mathematical expressions
Microsoft Graph 97	Inserts charts from data in a table
MS Organization Chart 2.0	Creates organization charts
Microsoft Word Picture	Inserts a picture and the tools associated with the Word drawing toolbar
Microsoft WordArt	Creates logos and other special text effects

To use the tools from another application or applet within your document to create a new object, follow these steps:

1. Position the insertion point in the destination document.
2. Choose Insert, Object. The Object dialog box appears, as shown in Figure 38.21.
3. In the Create New tab, select an application or applet from the Object type list.
4. If you want to see only an icon for the object, put a check mark in the Display as icon check box. If you want to put the object in the Drawing layer of your document, check the Float over Text check box (but remember that field codes will be unavailable if you do so).
5. When you finish with the Object dialog box, choose OK.

FIG. 38.21

The Object dialog box lists applets as well as Windows applications.

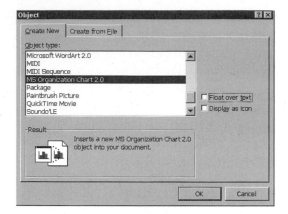

After you complete these steps, one of two things will occur. You may enter a separate window for the application or the applet, as shown in Figure 38.22. The other possibility is that you will remain in your destination document window, but the menu bar and toolbar will change to reflect the source application, as shown in Figure 38.23. For example, when you choose Microsoft Excel Worksheet, the menu bar and toolbar change to Microsoft Excel, enabling you to use Excel features such as the AutoSum button.

FIG. 38.22

When you choose MS Organization Chart, a separate window opens. After you finish with the chart program, choose File, Exit to return to the Word document.

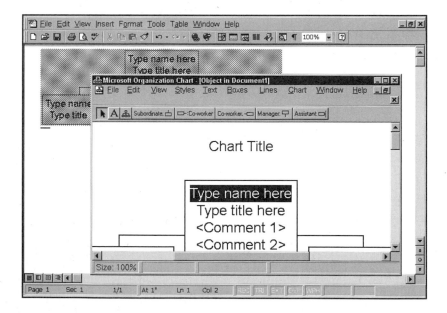

FIG. 38.23
When you choose
Microsoft Excel
Worksheet, in-place
editing enables you to
use Excel features.

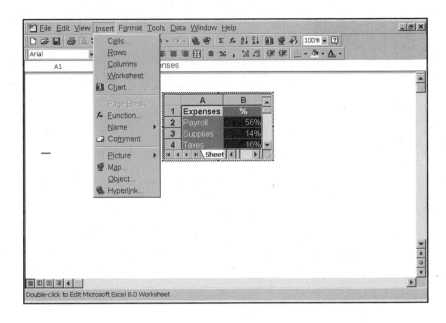

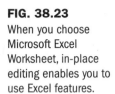

When you finish creating the object, you can exit the object in either of two ways. If you launched a separate window for the application or applet, choose File, Exit. If you stayed in your destination document, click outside the object.

Editing an Embedded Object

Regardless of which of the four methods you use to embed information into your document, you can edit the embedded object with the tools of the source application.

To edit the object, follow these steps:

1. Click the object. Handles appear around the object, and the status bar tells you to double-click the object (see Figure 38.24).

2. Double-click the object. Depending on the source and destination applications, a separate window for the program appears, or the current window's toolbar and menu bar change to those of the source application.

3. Edit the object, using the application's toolbar and menus.

4. When you finish editing the object, exit the object. If you launched a separate window for the application or applet, choose File, Exit. If you stayed in your destination document, click outside the object.

FIG. 38.24

The status bar displays instructions on how to get to the source-application tools.

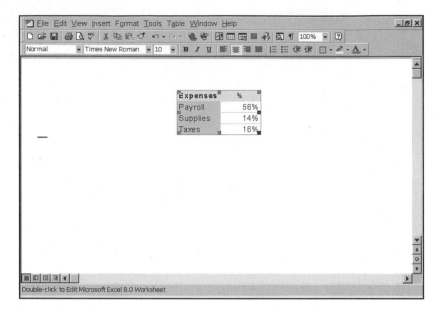

In some cases, you may be prompted if you want to update the object in your destination document. If you want to save the editing changes, choose Yes, otherwise choose No.

TROUBLESHOOTING

Sometimes when I open a Word document with an embedded object, the object returns to its original size instead of staying the size I want. When you embed an object in Word, Word inserts the Embed field code in the document. In the Embed field code, there could be a switch \s which means return the object to its original size. To fix this problem, you need to modify the Embed field code for the object. To view the field code instead of the object, click the object and then press Shift+F9 to switch to the field code. Delete \s at the end of the Embed code.

CHAPTER 39

Using Office Applications to Create Presentations

by Rob Tidrow

The focus of Chapter 38 was integrating Microsoft Office applications through embedding and linking information, mostly into Word documents. This chapter focuses on using Microsoft Office applications to create a presentation. If you need overhead transparencies, 35mm slides, a graphical report, or a computer-driven presentation, you can use PowerPoint to create the presentation. You also can use PowerPoint 97 to help you create World Wide Web pages for publishing Internet or intranet documents. If you have information in other sources, such as Word or Excel, you can copy or link the information from the source application to PowerPoint. ■

Organize a presentation

You can use Word to create and organize your presentation using the Word Outline view. You also can edit, delete, and move text or sections using the Outline view.

Use a Word outline to create slides

After you create an outline in Word, you can place it in PowerPoint, and create a slide presentation. Although you can use PowerPoint to create the initial outline and presentation, Word is sometimes quicker and easier if you already have a document on which you want to base your presentation.

Copy or link information to PowerPoint

If you have an object created in other documents, such as an Excel chart, you can quickly copy it to the Windows Clipboard and insert it into your PowerPoint presentation. By linking the object in the presentation, anytime you change the original object it updates in the presentation automatically.

Embed a presentation in an e-mail message

You can use PowerPoint's built-in messaging features to send a presentation to other department or team members via e-mail.

Organizing the Presentation with a Word Outline

If you are accustomed to using Word, you can create an outline of your presentation in Word and use the outline to create slides in PowerPoint. Suppose that you have to create a presentation for community groups about gangs. You have the basics of the presentation in a Word document. PowerPoint uses Word's heading styles for the title and bullets of slides. Therefore, you first reformat the Word document to include Heading 1 for the planned title of the slide, Heading 2 for each major bullet item, and Heading 3 for each minor bullet item.

▶ **See** "Formatting with Styles," **p. 245**

▶ **See** "Outlining a Document," **p. 238**

If you use Heading 1, Heading 2, and Heading 3 styles, you also can use the Outline feature of Word to organize and view your slides. To change to the Outline view in a Word document, choose View, Outline; alternatively, click the Outline View button in the horizontal scroll bar directly above the status bar. The view changes to show indents for each heading level (see Figure 39.1).

Outlining toolbar

FIG. 39.1

Word's Outline view enables you to organize your presentation.

Heading 1 is the first-level indent

Heading 2 is the second-level indent

Heading 3 is the third-level indent

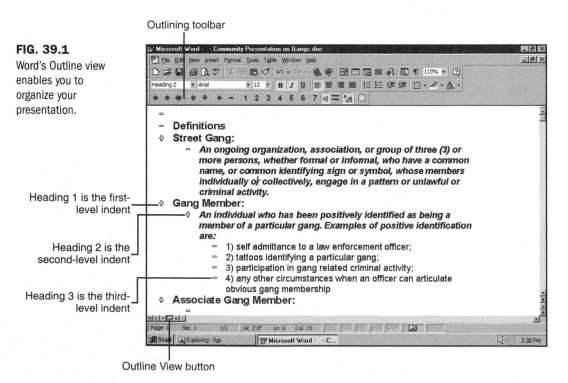

Outline View button

N O T E When you convert to PowerPoint, Heading 1 becomes the slide title. Heading 2 is the second-level indent, which becomes first-level bullets in PowerPoint. Heading 3 is the third-level indent, which becomes second-level bullets in PowerPoint. ■

When you choose <u>V</u>iew, <u>O</u>utline, the document changes to show different levels, and the Outlining toolbar becomes available. You can use the Outlining toolbar to show one or more levels in the outline. In the toolbar, the buttons numbered 1 through 8 enable you to show from one to eight levels of your outline. The 1 button corresponds to Heading 1 style, the 2 button corresponds to Heading 2 style, and so on. When you show Heading 2 styles by clicking the 2 button, Heading 1 styles also appear, and so on. Figure 39.2 shows the outline when you click the Show Heading 1 button. Click the All button to show your entire document. You also can use the Outlining toolbar to promote or demote levels in the outline.

FIG. 39.2

Word's numbered Outlining toolbar buttons enable you to see one or more heading styles.

Text formatted with Heading 1 styles

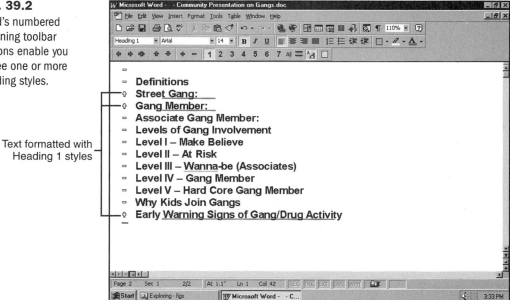

If a Heading 1 contains no supporting text (that is, the heading is followed by no Heading 2), a minus sign appears to the left of the text. If a Heading 1 contains supporting text, a plus sign appears to the left of the text. When you place the mouse pointer over the plus and minus signs, the pointer changes to a four-sided pointer. Double-click the plus sign to show the supporting headings and body text and to select all the text within that level and sublevel. Double-click the plus sign again to collapse the text.

▶ **See** "Moving with Drag-and-Drop," **p. 79**

▶ **See** "Editing a Style," **p. 248**

To move a heading (and all text below the heading), place the mouse pointer on the plus or minus sign in front of the heading you want to move. The mouse pointer changes to a black four-headed arrow (see Figure 39.3). Drag the mouse up or down to where you want to position the selected text. A positioning line appears on-screen at the point at which the new text will be inserted. Make sure that line is in the place you want the new text to appear before releasing the mouse button.

You also can use the Move Up or Move Down button in the Outlining toolbar. The Move Up button moves the selected text up in the outline. The Move Down button moves the selected text down in the outline. To change a level in the outline, use the Promote and Demote buttons in the toolbar, or change the style to a different heading. The Promote button changes the selection to a higher level (for example, from Heading 2 to Heading 1). The Demote button changes the selection to a lower level.

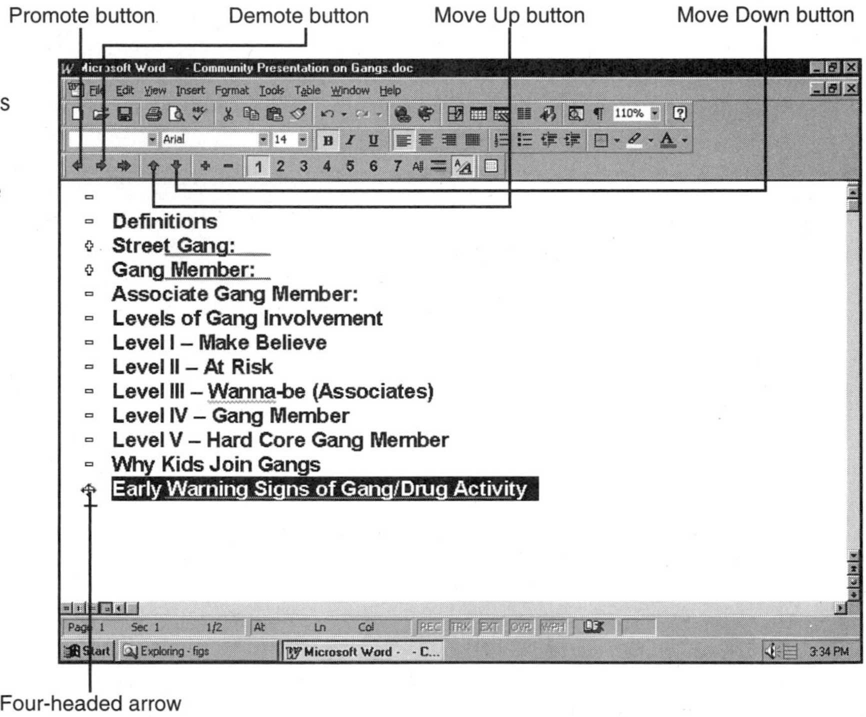

FIG. 39.3
Drag the plus or minus signs, or use buttons in the Outlining toolbar, to change the order of the slides.

When you finish organizing your outline, save and close the document.

Using a Word Outline to Create Slides

When you want to use the Word document in PowerPoint, you can create a new presentation or add to an existing presentation. The Word Heading 1 style becomes the title of each slide. Word's Heading 2 style becomes the first-level bullet for each slide.

To start a new presentation, follow these steps:

1. Within PowerPoint, choose File, Open, press Ctrl+O, or click the Open button on the Standard toolbar. The Open dialog box opens with a list of files or folders.

2. Change the drive and folder, if necessary.

3. If necessary, in the Files of Type drop-down list, select All Outlines to display Word documents.

N O T E You also can use Excel worksheets or HTML files to create slides (the All Outlines file type displays XLS and HTM files as well). ▪

 T I P Instead of doing steps 4 and 5, double-click the desired file name in the list box to open the file.

4. Type the file name in the File Name text box, or click the desired file in the list box to select the file.

5. Choose Open.
   ▶ **See** "Viewing a Presentation," **p. 614**

Figure 39.4 shows the outline view of the presentation in PowerPoint. Slide number 3 (shown in Figure. 39.5) shows the definition of a Gang Member. To switch between views, click the buttons in the bottom-left corner of the presentation window or use the View menu. Compare the slide in Figure 39.5 with Figure 39.1. Notice that the Heading 1 style became the title of the slide, the Heading 2 style became the first bullet, and the Heading 3 style became subpoints of the bullet.

 T I P If you want to add a level or change a level, use the Outlining toolbar in outline view.

▶ **See** "Creating a Presentation Using a Wizard," **p. 608**

After you open a Word file to create a PowerPoint presentation, you can select a more interesting format than simple black text on a white background. To change the format, click the Apply Design button (see Figure 39.6), or choose Format, Apply Design. The

Apply Design dialog box lists the templates available from the Presentation Designs folder and shows a preview of each choice. Figure 39.7 shows the formatted and edited slide from Figure 39.5.

FIG. 39.4
Opening a Word document brings you into a PowerPoint outline.

PowerPoint's Outlining toolbar works the same way as the Outlining toolbar in Word

Microsoft PowerPoint - [Community Presentation on Gangs (from Word).ppt]
File Edit View Insert Format Tools Slide Show Window Help
Arial
32
1 Definitions
2 Street Gang:
An ongoing organization, association, or group of three (3) or more persons, whether formal or informal, who have a common name, or common identifying sign or symbol, whose members individually or collectively, engage in a pattern or unlawful or criminal activity.
3 Gang Member:
An individual who has been positively identified as being a member of a particular gang. Examples of positive identification are:
1) self admittance to a law enforcement officer;
2) tattoos identifying a particular gang;
3) participation in gang related criminal activity;
4) any other circumstances when an officer can articulate obvious gang membership
4 Associate Gang Member:
5 Levels of Gang Involvement
6 Level I Make Believe
7 Level II At Risk
8 Level III Wanna-be (Associates)
9 Level IV Gang Member
Outline
Default Design
Start
Exploring - Icons
Microsoft Word - Comm...
Microsoft PowerPoint...
3:50 PM

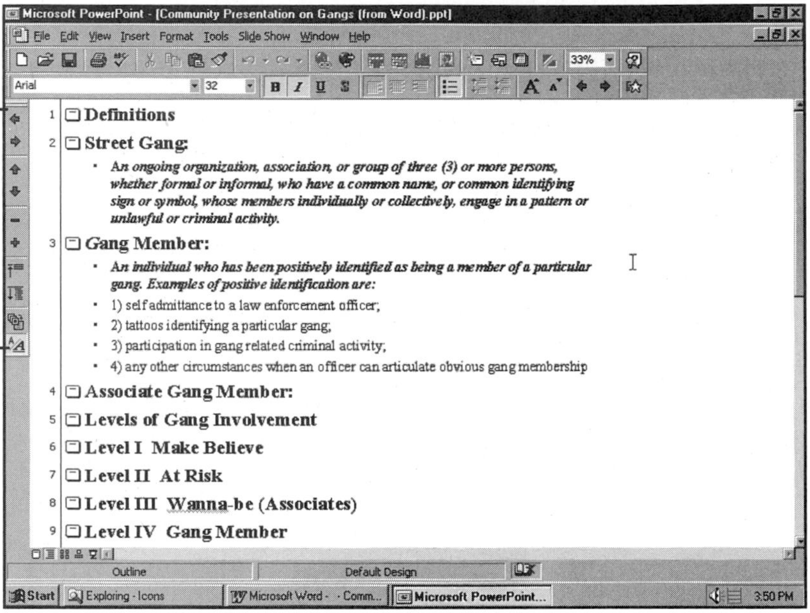

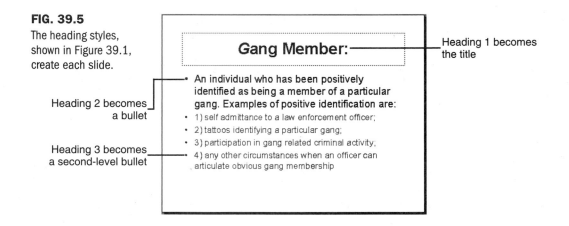

FIG. 39.5
The heading styles, shown in Figure 39.1, create each slide.

Heading 2 becomes a bullet

Heading 3 becomes a second-level bullet

Gang Member:
An individual who has been positively identified as being a member of a particular gang. Examples of positive identification are:
1) self admittance to a law enforcement officer;
2) tattoos identifying a particular gang;
3) participation in gang related criminal activity;
4) any other circumstances when an officer can articulate obvious gang membership

Heading 1 becomes the title

FIG. 39.6
Use the Apply Design
button to change the
formatting of your
presentation.

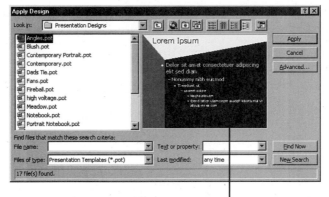

The preview area shows you what the
design of the presentation will look like

FIG. 39.7
The slide shown
originally in Figure
39.5 is formatted
using the Notebook
presentation
template.

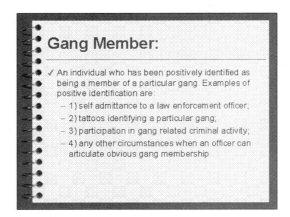

Part
VII

Ch
39

N O T E You can insert the Word outline into an existing presentation. The Word outline
assumes the format of the existing PowerPoint presentation. To insert a file into the
presentation, move to the location in an existing PowerPoint presentation where you want to insert
slides and choose Insert, Slides from Outline and select the file name and location. ■

TROUBLESHOOTING

I can't open or insert my Word Outline file into a PowerPoint presentation. You may not have
closed the Word document before you returned to PowerPoint. Click the Word button on the task
bar. If necessary, choose the Window command in Word and select the document name. Choose
File, Close to close the document. Click the PowerPoint button on the Windows taskbar to return
to PowerPoint.

Summarizing Data in Excel and Linking a Range to PowerPoint

If you have information in Excel that you want to bring to the presentation, you can copy and paste the information or link the information. If you want the data in the presentation to be updated every time the Excel worksheet changes, link the information from Excel.

▶ **See** "Adding, Inserting, and Deleting Slides," **p. 612**

▶ **See** "Inserting a Word Table or Excel Worksheet," **p. 633**

You first must create a new slide to accept the data. To create a new slide that accepts data from Excel, follow these steps:

1. Choose Insert, New Slide, press Ctrl+M, or click the New Slide button.

2. Select the graph layout, and then choose OK (see Figure 39.8). A new slide appears, with instructions on where to add the title and graph.

N O T E   Even though you are selecting the graph slide, you will be inserting a range of cells from Excel. ▦

FIG. 39.8
Select the graph style when you add a new slide to a PowerPoint presentation.

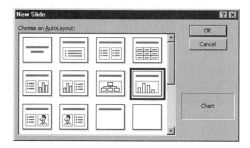

3. Click the middle of the slide once (where the slide tells you to double-click as shown in Figure 39.9), and press the Delete key to remove the graph.

N O T E   If you double-click the graph area, you launch Microsoft Graph. Instead, this procedure uses this layout to keep the area available for Microsoft Excel data (whether it is an Excel worksheet or chart). ▦

▶ **See** "Copying and Moving Data," **p. 78**

▶ **See** "Copying Spreadsheet Information," **p. 864**

FIG. 39.9
Click the graph area
and press Delete to
remove the instruction
to add a graph.

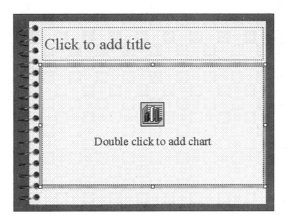

Now you are ready to copy information from Excel into the slide. To copy or link the information from Excel, follow these steps:

1. From the PowerPoint slide in the steps above, choose the Start button on the taskbar, and choose Programs, Microsoft Excel.

2. Open the file containing the information you want to copy or link.

3. Drag the mouse pointer (a white cross) to select the range of data in Excel that you want to place as a graph in PowerPoint (see Figure 39.10).

 4. Choose Edit, Copy, press Ctrl+C, or click the Copy button in Excel's standard toolbar.

5. Click the Microsoft PowerPoint button in the taskbar to return to PowerPoint.

N O T E If both applications are windowed and tiled, just click the slide you want, or use Alt+Tab to switch applications. ▪

6. Choose Edit, Paste Special in PowerPoint. The Paste Special dialog box appears (see Figure 39.11).

7. Do one of the following things:

   - To paste a picture of the Excel worksheet, choose the Paste option button and then select Picture from the As list box.

   - To link the information so that the slide updates when the Excel worksheet updates, choose the Paste Link option button. Select the Microsoft Excel Worksheet Object option in the As list box. When you use this option, you can double-click the worksheet data to enter Excel and edit the worksheet.

Part
VII

Ch
39

FIG. 39.10
Select the range you
want to copy in Excel.

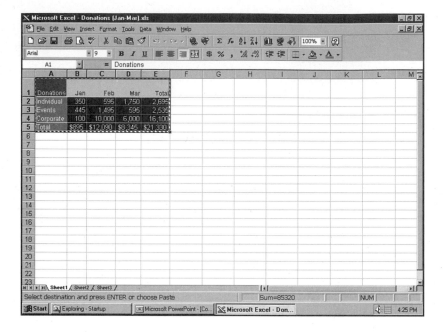

FIG. 39.11
The Paste Special
dialog box enables
you to paste or link
information from Excel.

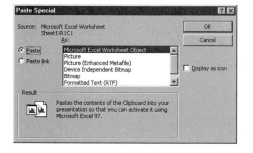

N O T E   If you click the Paste button in the toolbar, choose <u>E</u>dit, <u>P</u>aste, or press Ctrl+V, the
selected data from Excel comes into the slide unformatted. It is better to use the
Paste <u>S</u>pecial options. The Unformatted Text and Formatted Text options bring the information
from the worksheet as text. If the columns do not line up properly in your presentation, you can
reformat the text.

▶ **See** "Entering and Editing Text," **p. 625**

▶ **See** "Resizing and Scaling Objects," **p. 647**

▶ **See** "Sharing Data Between Applications with Linking and Embedding," **p. 877**

8. Choose OK in the Paste Special dialog box. The selected data from Excel appears in
   your slide (see Figure 39.12). Complete the slide as necessary by adding titles and
   sizing and moving the figure.

FIG. 39.12
The selected data from Excel appears in the slide.

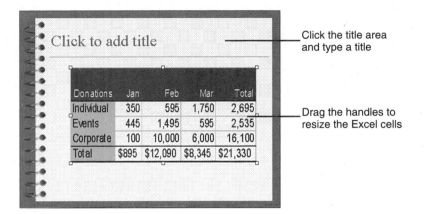

Click the title area
and type a title

Drag the handles to
resize the Excel cells

TROUBLESHOOTING

When I copy to PowerPoint, the data from my Excel spreadsheet is not lined up. Make sure that you select the Picture option in the Paste Special dialog box. Do not choose Edit, Paste, click the Paste button, or press Ctrl+V to bring into PowerPoint the copy of the Excel data.

The Excel worksheet is too big for my PowerPoint slide. Try simplifying the worksheet before you copy it into PowerPoint. You also can change the size of the worksheet in PowerPoint by dragging the picture handles, but remember that your viewers have to be able to read the slide.

Part
VII

Ch
39

Creating Charts in Excel and Copying to PowerPoint

Adding an Excel chart to a PowerPoint presentation is essentially the same as adding a worksheet.

To add an Excel chart to a slide, follow these steps:

1. Click the middle of a chart in an Excel worksheet to display handles on the chart (see Figure 39.13).

2. Choose Edit, Copy, press Ctrl+C, or click the Copy button in Excel's standard toolbar.

3. Click the PowerPoint button on the task bar and go to the PowerPoint slide where you want to copy information.

4. Choose Edit, Paste Special from PowerPoint. The Paste Special dialog box appears (see Figure 39.14). You also can choose Edit, Paste.

FIG. 39.13

Select the Excel chart you want to copy into PowerPoint.

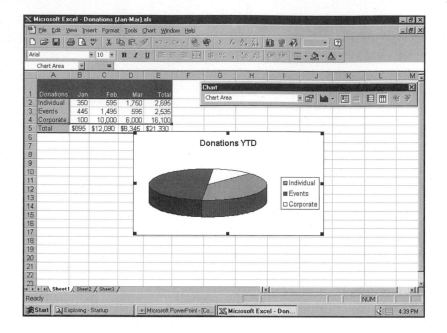

FIG. 39.14

Fill out the Paste Special dialog box to display the chart in the slide. There are less options here than in Figure 39.12 because an Excel chart is being pasted rather than a worksheet selection.

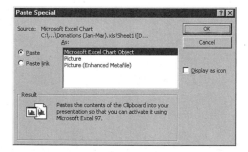

5. Do one of the following things:

   • Choose the <u>P</u>aste option button; from the <u>A</u>s list box, select the Microsoft Excel Chart Object option. This option enables you to double-click the chart to return to Excel and edit the object.

   • Choose the <u>P</u>aste option button; from the <u>A</u>s list box, select the Picture option to see only the chart.

   • Choose the Paste <u>L</u>ink option button; from the <u>A</u>s list box, select the Microsoft Excel Chart Object option to link and embed the slide with the Excel worksheet.

6. Choose OK from the Paste Special dialog box.

FIG. 39.15
The edited slide
appears with the
Excel chart.

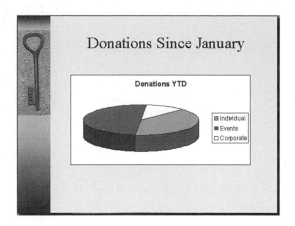

You also may have to resize the chart (drag the handles) and to add a title to the slide. Figure 39.15 shows the completed slide.

N O T E   If you want the Excel chart background to match the existing PowerPoint slide background, make sure you format the chart in Excel before copying the slide to PowerPoint by choosing Format, Selected Chart Area. On the Patterns tab, select None in the Borders area and None in the Area area. ■

Embedding the Presentation in an Electronic Mail Message

As with any document, you should frequently save your presentation so that your updates are protected. When you finish the presentation, make sure that you save it. If you want to send the presentation to others on your network for review, embed the presentation in an electronic mail message.

To create a message that includes the presentation, follow these steps:

1. From PowerPoint with the presentation open, choose File, Send To.

2. Choose Mail Recipient and then choose the profile name for your electronic mail from the Profile Name drop-down list if prompted in the Choose Profile dialog box. Then click OK.

3. Address the message by filling out the To and Cc text boxes.

4. Type a short summary in the Subject text box.

5. Type any message you want in the message area. Your screen should resemble Figure 39.16.

Send button

FIG. 39.16
The PowerPoint presentation appears as an icon in the message text area. Your mail program may look different from this version of WordMail depending on your electronic mail package.

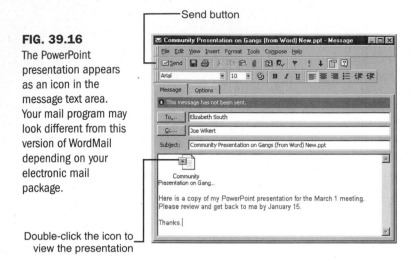

Double-click the icon to view the presentation

When the recipients get the message, they can double-click the PowerPoint icon to see the presentation on their computers. ●

CHAPTER 40

Using Binder

by Rob Tidrow

With the Windows GUI (graphical user interface), you have become familiar with the idea of folders and files. Much like the folder in a standard file cabinet, the computer folder has become a collecting place for all sorts of papers and documents. The trouble is, the more documents and folders you create on your computer, the harder it is to find anything, no matter how neat and tidy you try to be.

By using the Microsoft Office Binder, you can become better organized on the computer. The Binder takes the concept of computer organization one step further than using a folder to store related files. The Binder enables you to organize Microsoft Office documents into a specific order, called *sections*, just like you do with papers in the sections of a real three-ring binder. With Binder, you also can search the World Wide Web using the new Go menu item. ■

Create a Binder and add sections

The Binder includes documents called *sections* that you create with other Office applications. When you select a section in the Binder, that section's application opens in the Binder and displays the specified section.

Rearrange sections

The sections can be arranged to suit your needs or the needs of the project on which you're working.

Remove the section view

You can turn off the section view in Binder to give you more room to edit or read a selected section.

Work in the outside view

The Binder enables you to work outside the Binder in an Office 97 application to update, create, modify, or view a section.

Print options

When you are ready to print sections in the Binder, you can print all of the sections in the open Binder, or print only those you select.

Looking at an Example Binder

The Binder can hold all your files and folders on nearly any subject (see Figure 40.1). The examples in this chapter show you how to use the Binder to put together information for a book on Depression glass for Collector's Loot.

FIG. 40.1

Use Binder to organize your work with sections in the book.

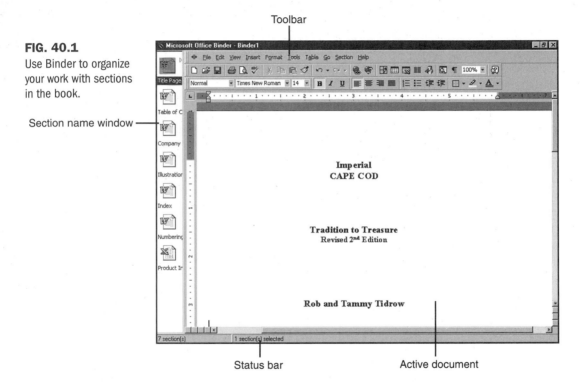

Status bar

Active document

Creating a New Binder

By navigating the taskbar's Start button, you can select Microsoft Binder from the Program group. When Binder opens, it automatically displays a new, blank binder (see Figure 40.2). You also can select New Office Document from the Start menu and choose Blank Binder from the General tab of the New Office Document dialog box to start a new binder.

These areas will be useful to you as you build your binder:

- The *menu bar* contains File, Go, Section, and Help menus.
- The pane on the left contains *section names*. Sections are documents that are added to a binder.

FIG. 40.2

Consider an empty
Binder as another
document type
waiting for you to add
Office documents as
sections.

Show/Hide Left
Pane button

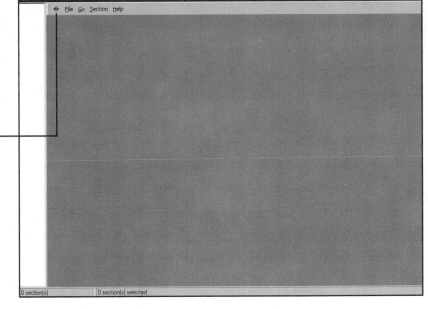

- The pane on the right contains the document of the *active section*.
- The *status bar* shows the number of sections and the number of currently selected sections.

- Hide or display the left window pane by clicking the Show/Hide Left Pane button.

Adding Sections

The Binder opens with no sections in it—you just see an empty binder. Remember, a section can be Office documents from Word, Excel, or PowerPoint. When you are adding a section, the created document is empty. To add a section, follow these steps:

1. Choose Section, Add. You also can right-click the left pane and select Add.

2. Select the correct document type from the Add Section dialog box (see Figure 40.3). For this example, choose Blank Document, which enables you to start a new Microsoft Word document, then click OK.

3. Notice in Figure 40.4 that the section window now looks like Microsoft Word and that the menu bar contains the Word Menu options as well as the binder's Section menu. A section in a binder assumes all the capabilities of the Office application.

FIG. 40.3
Organize your work by placing Office documents in sections of the binder.

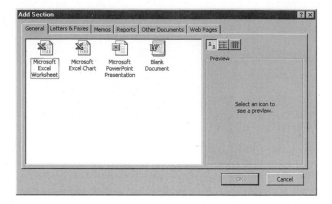

Word icon shows
the type and name
of this section

FIG. 40.4
The active section is now a Word document. All the functionality of Word is available.

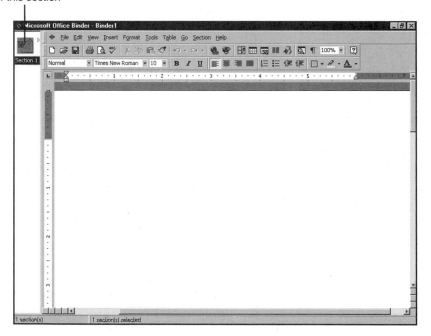

TIP To rename a section, right-click the section's icon and choose Rename, or you can choose Section, Rename.

4. The default section name, Section 1, is not particularly helpful. Fortunately, you can easily rename a section: just click the existing name, Section 1, and the name will be selected (see Figure 40.5).

FIG. 40.5

Edit the section name by clicking the name in the left pane.

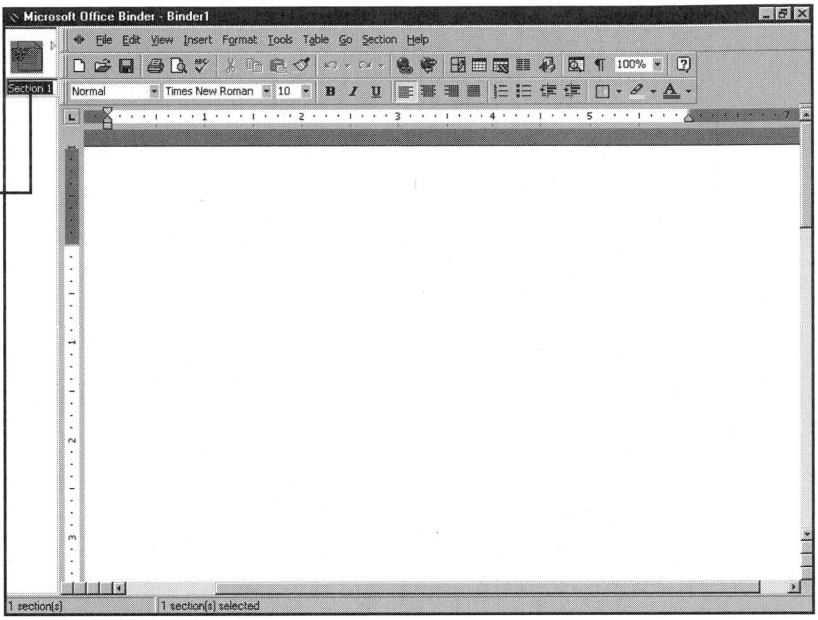

Rename a section by clicking its name

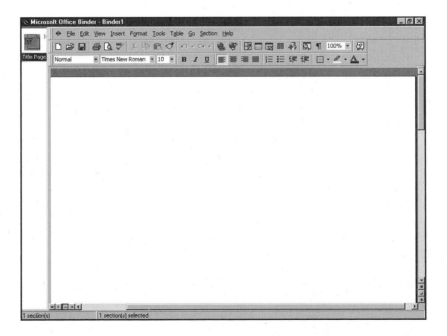

5. Type **Title Page** and press Enter. Your binder should now look like Figure 40.6.

FIG. 40.6

Change the title of the Binder section to label the new document.

Part
VII

Ch
40

Any new document can be added as a section to a Binder. You have all the capabilities of Office available within the Binder. For example, you can cut and paste between sections or link between documents.

Adding Text from Existing Documents

If you already have some Office documents created, you can add them to the Binder. You can add a table of contents to the binder, for example, by following these steps:

1. Choose <u>S</u>ection, Add from <u>F</u>ile to open the Add from File dialog box.

2. The Binder presents a standard Windows File Open dialog box. You can navigate to the correct folder if necessary, and then highlight the file you want to add (see Figure 40.7). You can add the file Table of Contents by selecting the file and clicking OK.

FIG. 40.7
Use the Add From File dialog box to select existing documents to add to a Binder.

N O T E You can use Shift+click or Ctrl+click to select multiple files to add to the binder. When you add files this way, they will appear as sections in the binder in alphabetical order. They will be added to the binder after the active section. Just reorganize them by moving the sections to the desired location. ■

 You can drag documents from the Windows Explorer, My Computer, or from the desktop to the left pane to add sections to a binder.

3. Repeat steps 1 and 2 for each file you want to add to the binder. Figure 40.8 shows a binder with several files added as sections in the binder.

FIG. 40.8

Adding a file does not change the selected section. The last active section remains highlighted.

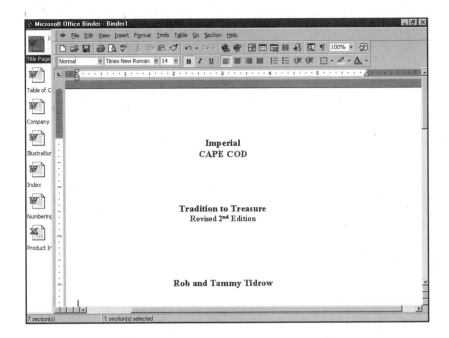

N O T E When you add existing documents to a binder, the documents become part of the binder. Any changes you make to the original document in its host application are not reflected in the binder document (section).

Likewise, changes you make to the document while in the binder are not reflected when you open that document in the host application. If you plan to use the binder to organize your documents, make sure you do all your editing and modifications within Binder. Don't switch between the Binder and the host application to edit your documents, or you will lose modifications you've made to your documents. ▨

Part
VII

Ch
40

Rearranging Sections

As you review your section orders, you may realize that you have a section in the wrong place. (Remember, these sections were just loose in the folder before.) Suppose that you want to rearrange the sections so the Illustration section follows the Numbering section. Follow these steps:

1. Choose Section, Rearrange, to display the Rearrange Sections dialog box (see Figure 40.9). In this dialog box, you can rearrange sections by selecting and then moving them.

FIG. 40.9
Use the Move Up and
Move Down buttons
to rearrange the
placement of sections.

2. Highlight the section you want to move.

 TIP You can quickly rearrange sections by dragging and dropping them in the left pane.

3. Click Move Up or Move Down to move the sections.

4. When you have rearranged the sections as needed, click OK to close the dialog box. The sections appear in the same order as they were listed in the dialog box.

Hiding the Section Window

You may feel a bit crowded working on a document in the binder with the sections showing in the left pane of the Binder window. If you want to make the section full-screen, click the Show/Hide Left Pane button on the menu bar. Figure 40.10 shows the result of hiding the left pane and displaying an Excel worksheet section.

 The Show/Hide Left Pane button works as a toggle. Click the icon again to make the left window pane reappear.

Working in Outside View

In the binder, only the section that is currently active is displayed. You cannot display more than one window by tiling the sections. By choosing Section, View Outside, however, you can reference one document while working on another. Follow these steps:

1. Select the section you want to reference in the left pane. In the example shown here, the Excel worksheet section, Product Info, is selected.

2. Choose Section, View Outside. The current section now becomes a separate window, as in Figure 40.11. You can move the window around the screen like you do any other window.

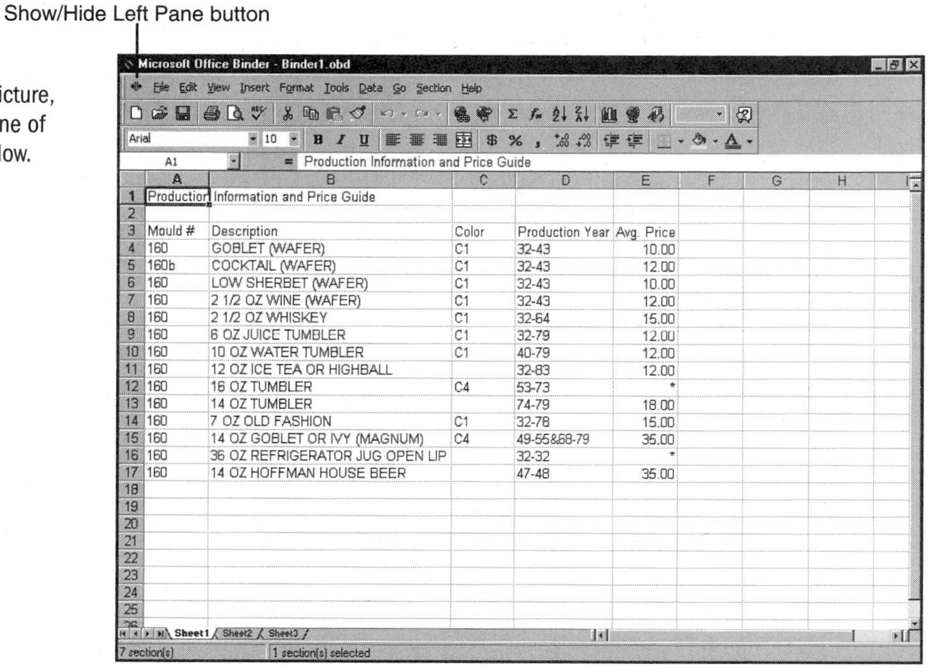

Show/Hide Left Pane button

FIG. 40.10

To get the big picture, hide the left pane of the Binder window.

FIG. 40.11

By viewing a section outside of the binder, you can work on two sections at once.

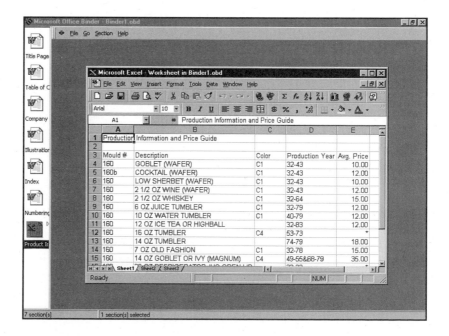

3. Select another section from the left binder pane by clicking its icon. The section opens in the document pane.

4. Arrange the windows as needed so that you can see both documents.

5. To return from Outside view, select File, Close & Return to Binder. You return to the active Binder window. The host application stays open but is minimized on the Windows taskbar.

Printing Options

The Binder gives you three options for printing: you can print the active section, all the sections in the Binder, or a single section.

Printing the Active Section

Printing the active section is similar to printing a document from the normal Office application, except that you find the Print command in the Section menu rather than in the File menu. To print a section, follow these steps:

1. Choose Section, Print.

2. Complete the Print dialog box as needed. (For details about printing, see Chapter 4, "Managing Files and Printing Documents.")

3. Click OK to print.

These steps enable you to print a document as if you were printing from the application itself. You can also print sections from the Print Binder dialog box, as described in the next section.

Printing from the Binder

You can print all binder sections at one time or just print selected sections. To print, follow these steps:

1. To print selected sections, you use normal mouse actions such as click, Shift+click, or Ctrl+click to highlight the sections you want to print.

2. Choose File, Print Binder (or Ctrl+P). The Print Binder dialog box appears (see Figure 40.12).

FIG. 40.12

Choosing the correct options allows you to print the binder the way you want.

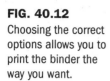

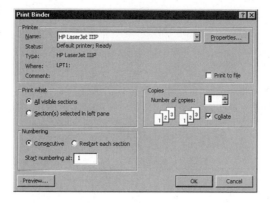

This list contains some of the important print options:

- Use the Print What section to choose <u>A</u>ll Visible Sections or <u>S</u>ection(s) Selected In Left Pane. Selecting <u>A</u>ll Visible Sections enables you to print the entire binder as a complete document in the order of the sections.

- Numbering enables you to select whether each section's page numbers restart or all sections are numbered consecutively. The starting page number is set by entering a value in the Sta<u>r</u>t Numbering At text box.

- Clicking C<u>o</u>llate prints the indicated number of copies in complete sequential sets. If, for example, you have a multiple page document(s) to print several times, a complete copy of the set prints before another set starts printing.

- Preview enables you to view on-screen the selected section(s) as they will print.

3. Fill in the appropriate options, and then click OK to begin printing.

Using the Binder adds a new dimension to Office. You can now organize your document, edit it, and save it as a complete collection of related files. You save a binder just like any other Office document. See Chapter 4, "Managing Files and Printing Documents," for general information on saving.

In Binder 97 you can now have one header or footer appear on different documents. Choose <u>F</u>ile, Binder Page Setup, and fill out th Header/Footer tab.

Creating Binder Templates

A handy feature of the Binder is the capability to create binder templates. *Binder templates* are binders that contain documents you want to use with other projects. You might, for

Part
VII

Ch
40

instance, create a standard scheduling form in Excel that is used to track resources in every project. Instead of re-creating or adding that worksheet to each new binder, create a binder template that includes that worksheet (and other standardized documents).

To create a binder template, use the following steps:

1. Start Binder and select File, New Binder to create a new binder. Select Blank Binder from the New Binder dialog box.

   If you have a binder already created that you want to use as a template, select File, Open Binder and select that binder file in the Open Binder dialog box.

2. Add documents to the binder that you want to include as part of the binder template. You should include only those documents you want to appear every time you use the binder template.

3. Select File, Save Binder As. In the Save Binder As dialog box, name the binder and select Binder Templates (OBT; OBX) from the Save As Type drop-down list.

4. Save the binder template in the TEMPLATES folder. This way, the binder template appears in the New Binder dialog box when you choose File, New Binder.

To use the binder template, choose File, New Binder and select the binder template as you do the Blank Binder template. When the binder template opens, it contains those documents you saved in it in step 2 in the preceding steps.

Sharing Binders with Others

Although you can use the Binder to help you organize and review documents on your own system, the real strength of Binder is not realized until you share binder files with others. You might, for example, work with a team of other users in your department to create memos, update worksheets, modify presentations, and the like. By creating a binder to organize each of the documents for the workgroup, you do not run the risk of individual documents being lost on one person's hard disk or left on the network. You also can make sure the documents incorporate everyone's changes and updates by using the Briefcase application in Windows 95.

The following steps show you how to share binders with others:

1. Create a binder and add documents to it. These can be already existing sections or new sections.

2. Save the binder file to the network server or a shared drive on the network. Binder files have the extension OBD.

3. Have all those included in your workgroup or team drag the shared binder file to the Briefcase application on the Windows 95 desktop (see Figure 40.13).

If Briefcase does not appear, right-click the Windows 95 desktop and select New, Briefcase. If this option does not appear, you must install the Briefcase application using Add/Remove Programs from Control Panel. Refer to Windows 95 online help for more instructions on installing Briefcase.

FIG. 40.13
Members of a workgroup or team can use Briefcase to share and update binder files.

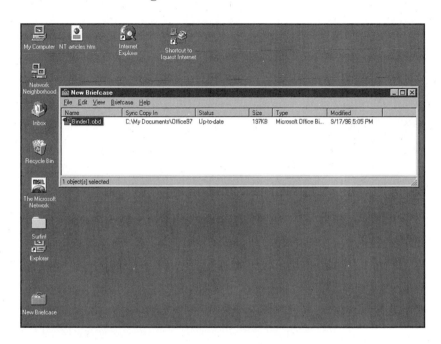

4. To update the binder file in Briefcase, select Briefcase, Update All.

N O T E For information on viewing Binder files on the Internet, see Chapter 44, "Navigating and Publishing on the Web with Office 97." ▪

Part
VII

Ch
40

CHAPTER 41

Customizing the Desktop, Toolbars, and Menus

by Rob Tidrow

Part of the power of Microsoft Office comes from its flexibility; you can change its appearance and structure to fit your work habits. You can create and modify toolbars, buttons, and menus. You can add commands that don't usually appear on the toolbar or menu. You can even assign macros to menu items, tools, and buttons. This flexibility enables you to create your own customized user interface, such as a customized toolbar and menu. And, true to the design goals of Microsoft Office and the "suite" approach, after you learn how to customize one application, you can use that knowledge to customize the other Office applications. ■

Modify the Windows 95 interface

You can modify Windows 95 to work best for you. You can, for example, customize the way in which the taskbar displays, as well as add or remove programs from the Start menu.

Customize the Microsoft Office Shortcut Bar

The Microsoft Office Shortcut Bar displays on your desktop and gives you one-click access to programs, files, and other resources. You can also customize it to display non-Office applications, such as Windows Explorer, Netscape Navigator, and so on.

Add and change toolbar buttons

Microsoft Office 97 makes it easy to add and modify toolbar buttons in Word, Access, Excel, and PowerPoint.

Customize application menus and command bars

New with Office 97 are command bars, which enable you to create customized menus. You also can customize menu commands on standard menus to limit or add commands available on a menu.

Customizing the Windows 95 Interface

The first place you can start customizing your Office installation is the Windows 95 interface. Windows 95 enables you to modify the taskbar, the Start menu, and the icons that appear on the Windows 95 desktop. In Windows 95, you can modify the Start menu program listings, customize the taskbar, and create shortcuts to your favorite Office programs and documents. Figure 41.1 shows a customized Windows 95 Start menu, taskbar, and some shortcut icons on the desktop.

FIG. 41.1
Windows 95 enables you to modify the taskbar, the Start menu, and the desktop.

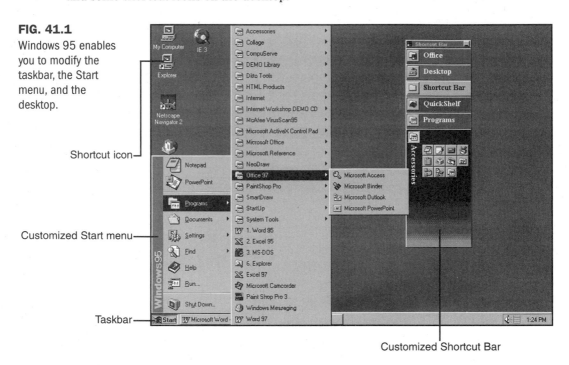

Shortcut icon

Customized Start menu

Taskbar

Customized Shortcut Bar

N O T E For more information on Windows 95, see Que's *Special Edition Using Windows 95* and Que's *Windows 95 Installation and Configuration Handbook*. ▪

Modifying the Windows 95 Taskbar

The Windows 95 taskbar is a handy tool that enables you to start applications and switch between minimized applications with a single-click. In Windows 95, you can change the location and appearance of the taskbar.

To move the taskbar to another location on your screen, drag the taskbar to the location you want (see Figure 41.2). You can drag the taskbar to the top, bottom, right, or left side of your screen.

Taskbar tray

FIG. 41.2
You can move the taskbar on the Windows 95 desktop.

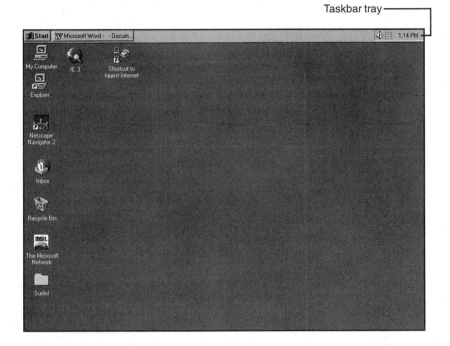

 TIP To view an item on the taskbar tray, double-click its icon. Or you can see a miniature view of the data by pointing to an item in the tray. For instance, to see the day and date, point to the clock to display a pop-up window with the day and data displayed.

TIP If you are hiding the taskbar, be sure to select Always on Top so that you can see the taskbar when running a full-screen program.

Part
VII
Ch
41

To customize the Windows 95 taskbar, follow these steps:

1. Right-click an unused area of the taskbar to display the shortcut menu.
2. Choose Properties to display the Taskbar Properties dialog box.
3. Select the taskbar options you want (see Figure 41.3). Table 41.1 describes the taskbar options you can set to control the appearance of the taskbar.
4. Choose Apply to activate changes immediately and close the sheet.

FIG. 41.3
Using the Taskbar Properties dialog box, you can control the appearance of the taskbar.

Table 41.1 Taskbar Options

Option	Description
Always on Top	Ensures that the taskbar is visible even when running a full-screen program.
Auto Hide	Reduces taskbar to a thin line. To redisplay full taskbar, point to line.
Show Small Icons in Start Menu	Displays smaller icons in Start menu, which reduces the width of the menu.
Show Clock	Displays digital time on taskbar.

Customizing the Start Menu

Clicking the Start button on the taskbar displays a menu, called the Start menu, which lists applications and files you can load. The Start menu is organized into groups called *folders*. (In fact, the Start menu itself is a folder.) For example, the Start menu folder called Programs contains another folder called Accessories that contains a menu item called Calculator, which is a shortcut to the calculator.exe file on your system. You can customize the Start menu by adding your own menu items to the existing folders, by editing the names of existing folders and menu items, or by adding new folders.

To add a new menu item or folder to the Start Menu, follow these steps:

1. Right-click the taskbar to display the shortcut menu.
2. Choose Properties to display the Taskbar Properties dialog box.

TIP You can also choose Start, Settings, Taskbar to display the Taskbar Properties dialog box.

3. Select the Start Menu Programs tab (see Figure 41.4).

FIG. 41.4
Using the Taskbar
Properties sheet,
you can modify the
Start menu.

4. Choose Add. The Create Shortcut dialog box appears (see Figure 41.5).
5. Type the full file path name of the program you want to add to the menu, or choose Browse to select a file. Click Next to continue.

FIG. 41.5
The Create Shortcut
dialog box assists you
in adding a program
to the Start menu.

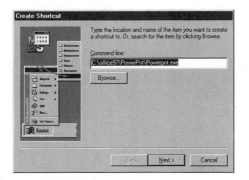

6. Select the program folder in which you want to list the new program (see Figure 41.6). Or choose New Folder to create a new folder in the Start menu. Click Next to continue.
7. Type a name for the new menu choice (see Figure 41.7). Choose Finish to add the new program menu item to the Start menu. The result is shown in Figure 41.8.

 TIP Don't add too many programs to your startup group, only those you really use. Otherwise, you slow down your system and waste resources.

Part
VII

Ch
41

FIG. 41.6
You can place shortcuts in an existing folder or create a new folder on the Start menu.

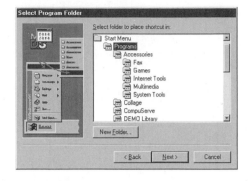

FIG. 41.7
When naming a shortcut, use a brief, but descriptive, name.

FIG. 41.8
You can add new menu items to any folder on the Start Menu, even the Start menu itself.

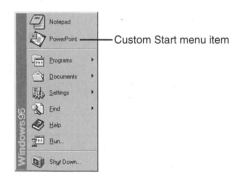

Custom Start menu item

To remove a menu item from the Start Menu, follow these steps:

1. Right-click the taskbar to display the shortcut menu.

2. Choose Properties to display the Taskbar Properties sheet.

3. Select the Start Menu Programs tab.

4. Choose Remove. The Remove Shortcuts/Folders dialog box appears (see Figure 41.9).

FIG. 41.9
Using the Remove Shortcuts/Folders dialog box, you can delete menu items and folders from the Start menu.

5. Select the program folder or program item you want to delete.

6. Choose Remove.

Running Applications on Startup

You can specify that you want Windows 95 to automatically run certain applications when you start up Windows 95. For example, if you use Word and Outlook every day, you may want to instruct Windows 95 to automatically load them for you when Windows 95 first opens. To do this, add the programs to the Startup folder (located in the Programs folder on the Start menu, see Figure 41.10).

FIG. 41.10
Programs listed in the Startup folder of the Start menu automatically load when Windows 95 starts.

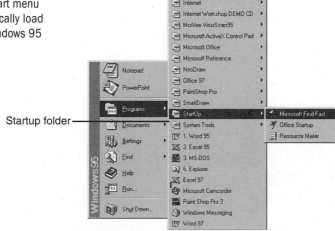

Startup folder

Part
VII

Ch
41

Creating a Shortcut Icon

 TIP You also can drag and drop a program from a browse list onto the desktop to quickly create a shortcut icon.

You can create a shortcut icon to place on your Windows 95 desktop for easy access to a program or document. By default, Windows 95 places several shortcut icons on your desktop such as My Computer, Network Neighborhood, and My Briefcase. Double-clicking the shortcut icon launches the associated program and loads any specified documents. You also can place shortcuts to documents to launch the associated program with the document displayed.

 TIP Remove shortcut icons you rarely use. Add shortcut icons for the documents and programs you use everyday.

To create a shortcut icon, follow these steps:

1. Right-click the desktop to display the shortcut menu.
2. Choose New, Shortcut. The Create Shortcut dialog box appears.
3. Type the full file path name of the program you want to add to the menu, or choose Browse to select a file. Click Next to continue.
4. Type a name for the new shortcut icon and choose Finish. The shortcut icon now appears on your desktop (see Figure 41.11).

FIG. 41.11
You can add new shortcut icons to your desktop to quickly access programs and documents.

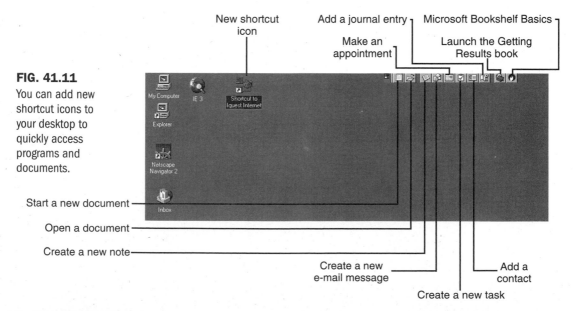

N O T E Shortcut icons you create on the desktop have a small arrow in the bottom-left corner of the icon. ■

Customizing the Office Shortcut Bar

By default, when Office 95 installs, it places the Microsoft Office Shortcut Bar in your Startup folder. The typical installation of Office 97, however, does not include the Shortcut Bar. You have to return to the setup program to install the Shortcut Bar if it is not already installed. Therefore, every time you start Windows 95, the Office Shortcut Bar displays at the top of your screen (refer to Figure 41.11 for a customized Shortcut Bar). The Office Shortcut Bar gives you quick access to common Office tasks such as opening and creating documents. Using the Office Shortcut Bar, you can also add and remove Office programs and control Office settings such as the location of workgroup templates.

▶ **See** "What's New with Office 97," **p. 10**

▶ **See** "Looking at the Microsoft Office Shortcut Bar," **p. 39**

N O T E If you are in a workgroup or have a system administrator who has configured your Office applications, ensure you are authorized to change these toolbar buttons and menu choices before doing so. In many departments, Office 97 is configured to meet the needs of the organization with many customized buttons and other options displayed on specific applications. Nothing irritates managers and administrators more than someone resetting or reconfiguring an application that has customized settings established. ■

You can customize many features of the Office Shortcut Bar to better meet your needs. For example, you can do the following:

- Change the size, location, and appearance of the toolbar
- Change the names and order of buttons on the toolbar
- Hide or display toolbar buttons
- Add a button to the toolbar to load a file or program
- Add more toolbars to the Office Shortcut Bar

Part **VII** Ch **41**

One of the most useful features of the Office Shortcut Bar is that it can display and manage numerous toolbars. As shown in Figure 41.12, the Office Shortcut Bar comes with six default toolbars that you can select to display or hide: Office, Desktop, QuickShelf, Favorites, Programs, and Accessories. You can customize any one of these toolbars or add your own custom toolbars.

Customizing the Office Shortcut Bar is organized into four areas: customizing the view, modifying the buttons, customizing and creating toolbars, and changing settings. The following sections explain how to customize each area of the Office Shortcut Bar.

FIG. 41.12
The Office Shortcut
Bar can display
numerous toolbars.

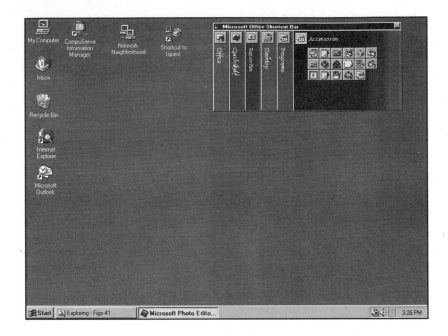

Customizing the View

The View tab of the Customize dialog box enables you to control the color and other display options of the Office Shortcut Bar (see Figure 41.13). For example, by default, the toolbar buttons are set to a small size. You can change the button size to a larger size by clicking the appropriate check box. You can also activate features such as ToolTips, sound, and animation.

FIG. 41.13
Using the View tab of
the Customize dialog
box, you can modify
the display of the
Office Shortcut Bar.

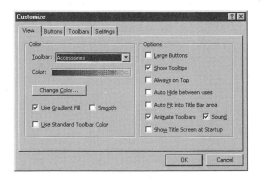

TIP To change the position of the Office Shortcut Bar, drag it to a new location.

To customize the view features of the Office Shortcut Bar, follow these steps:

1. Right-click the Office Shortcut title bar or the background of a toolbar (not the toolbar button, but between the toolbar buttons) to display the shortcut menu.

2. Choose Customize. The Customize dialog box appears with the View tab selected by default (refer to Figure 41.13).

3. Select the desired settings. Table 41.2 describes each of the view settings and options.

4. Click OK when you are done to save changes.

 TIP Dragging the Office Shortcut Bar to the center of your screen helps you better navigate the shortcut menus.

Table 41.2   Options for Customizing Office Shortcut Bar View

Setting	Description
Toolbar	Specifies the toolbar name for which you want to customize the color settings.
Change Color	Displays color palette from which you can select a color.
Use Gradient Fill	Specifies to use gradient coloring.
Smooth	When the Use Gradient Fill option is selected, the Smooth option distributes coloring more evenly.
Use Standard Toolbar Color	Changes color settings back to default colors. When selected, other color options are grayed out. When selected, the Office 97 toolbar takes on the attributes currently set for the desktop. The toolbar color is reflective of the current setting for 3D Objects.
Large Buttons	Specifies to use large buttons and icons on the currently displayed toolbar.
Show Tooltips	Specifies to show ToolTip text that describes what the button does. A ToolTip is the small pop-up message that displays when you move the mouse pointer over the button.
Always on Top	Specifies that the toolbar displays on top of any open windows.
Auto Hide Between Uses	Hides the toolbar when not in use.
Auto Fit into Title Bar Area	Adjusts toolbar size to fit inside the current application's title bar.

continues

Part
VII

Ch
41

Table 41.2   Continued

Setting	Description
Animate Toolbars	Activates any animation features of the toolbar.
Sound	Activates any sound features of the toolbar.
Show Title Screen at Startup	Displays the title screen when first started.

 N O T E To change the position of the Shortcut Bar when the View option Auto Fit into Title Bar is selected, use an editor, such as WordPad, to edit the MSOFFICE.INI file in the Windows folder. In the [OPTIONS] section, change the RightPos = line to a number higher than the default, which varies by the resolution of your display. ■

Customizing the Buttons

The Buttons tab of the Customize dialog box enables you to customize toolbar buttons in the Office Shortcut Bar. You can select which files to display as buttons, arrange the order of buttons, add new files and folders as buttons, delete existing entries, and add spaces between buttons on a toolbar.

TIP Add the MS-DOS prompt button to the Office Shortcut Bar for quick access to the prompt from any application.

To customize the button features of a toolbar in the Office Shortcut Bar, follow these steps:

1. Right-click the Office Shortcut title bar or the background of a toolbar (not the toolbar button, but between the toolbar buttons) to display the shortcut menu.

2. Choose Customize.

3. Select the Buttons tab (see Figure 41.14).

FIG. 41.14

Using the Buttons tab, you can modify the contents and layout of toolbars in the Office Shortcut Bar.

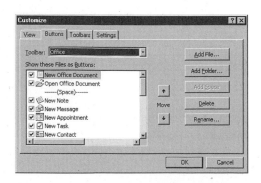

4. Modify and add toolbar buttons as needed. Table 41.3 describes each of the button settings and options on the Buttons tab.

N O T E Buttons are displayed left-to-right in a horizontal Toolbar and top-to-bottom in a vertical Toolbar. In a Toolbar palette, spaces between buttons separate buttons into rows. ■

5. Click OK when you are done to save changes.

Table 41.3   Options for Customizing Office Shortcut Buttons

Setting	Description
Toolbar	Select the toolbar to customize.
Show These Files as Buttons	Select (check) the buttons to include on the toolbar.
Add File	Select a file to add to the toolbar as a button.
Add Folder	Select a folder to add to the toolbar as a button.
Add Space	Insert a space above the currently selected button.
Delete	Delete the selected button or space.
Rename	Rename the selected toolbar.
Move [↑]	Move the selected button up in the toolbar button list (to the left in the toolbar itself).
Move [↓]	Move the selected button down in the toolbar button list (to the right in the toolbar itself).

N O T E By default, a new button displays the icon included in the program's executable file. For files and folders without a defined icon, the Office Shortcut Bar uses the standard file and folder icons. You can change the icon on a button by modifying the button properties: Right-click the button and choose Properties (make sure that the Customize dialog box is closed first). Then, select the Shortcut tab and choose Change Icon, which displays icons available in the SHELL32.DLL file found on your system. Finally, select the icon file name and icon to use, and then click OK. For another collection of icons, click the Browse button and open the MORICONS.DLL file in your Windows folder. ■

Customizing the Toolbars

The Toolbars tab of the Customize dialog box lists the files available to show as toolbars on the Office Shortcut Bar (see Figure 41.15). The checked folders display and the unchecked folders remain hidden. The Toolbars tab also enables you to add your own custom toolbars or remove toolbars.

FIG. 41.15

The Toolbars tab of the Customize dialog box enables you to hide, add, or remove toolbars.

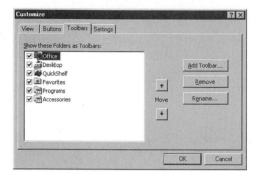

 TIP Create your own toolbar for quick access to frequently used tools such as spreadsheets, documents, or databases.

To add toolbars to the Office Shortcut Bar, follow these steps:

1. Right-click the Office Shortcut title bar or the background of a toolbar (not the toolbar button, but between the toolbar buttons) to display the shortcut menu.

2. Choose Customize.

3. Select the Toolbars tab (refer to Figure 41.15).

4. Select Add Toolbar. The Add Toolbar dialog box appears (see Figure 41.16).

FIG. 41.16

The Add Toolbar dialog box enables you to create new toolbars.

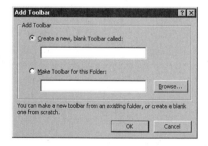

5. To make a toolbar for a folder, type the folder name in the text box labeled Create a New, Blank Toolbar.

   or

   Type a new name in the text box labeled Make a Toolbar for This Folder (or use the Browse button to select a folder).

6. Click OK when you are done to save changes.

N O T E To remove a toolbar from the list of toolbars, select the toolbar name and click the
Remove button. To rename a toolbar, select the toolbar name, click the Rename
button, and fill in a new name in the Rename dialog box. ▪

Customizing Settings

The Settings tab of the Customize dialog box enables you to change Office Shortcut Bar
settings, such as where the user and workgroup templates are stored (see Figure 41.17).
To modify the settings, select the Item you want and choose Modify. A Settings dialog box
prompts you to enter a new file location.

FIG. 41.17
You can change the
location of User and
Workgroup templates
files via the Settings
tab in the Customize
dialog box.

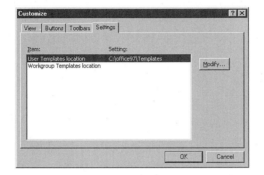

Customizing Application Toolbars

The process of customizing toolbars in Microsoft Office applications is much the same as
customizing the toolbars in the Office Shortcut Bar. In most applications, however, you
have even more options.

Customizing Predefined Toolbars

Each application comes with several built-in toolbars, some of which display automatically.
For example, by default, Microsoft Word displays the Standard, Formatting, and Web
toolbars. In addition to these, you can display a number of predefined toolbars:

- AutoText
- Control Toolbox
- Database
- Drawing
- Forms
- Picture

- Reviewing

- Tables and Borders

- Visual Basic

- WordArt

- Microsoft

- 3-D Settings

- Shadow Settings

- Shortcut Menu

Excel, Access, and PowerPoint also provide sets of predefined toolbars. You can customize any of the built-in toolbars to better meet your needs. (Microsoft Outlook provides you with two toolbars that you can display or turn off to suit your needs.) You could have a toolbar for every type of task you perform (for example, one for mail merges and one for desktop publishing) or for each user of a computer.

N O T E For even more control over your environment, Office 97 includes customizable command bars that enable you to place frequently used menu options on a toolbar. This enables you to quickly access a dialog box without navigating layers of menu options. For more information on how to use this new feature, see "Using Command Bars." ■

To customize a built-in toolbar, follow these steps:

1. Choose View, Toolbars, Customize. (You also can choose Tools, Customize.) The Customize dialog box appears (see Figure 41.18). If you want to select a new toolbar to display, click it on the Toolbars submenu.

FIG. 41.18

The Customize dialog box enables you to customize the view and contents of toolbars.

T I P To quickly customize toolbars, right-click anywhere on any toolbar and select Customize from the shortcut menu. With Office 97, you do not have to be on a blank toolbar area before you press right-click.

2. Select the Commands tab (see Figure 41.19).

FIG. 41.19

The Customize dialog box enables you to drag buttons and other items to or from any toolbar displayed on the desktop.

3. To add items to a built-in toolbar, click the category from the Categories list to display the list of commands available for that category. Then, select a command (button or other item) from the command list. Click the Description button to get a short description of the command button.

   Suppose that you want to add the Mail Recipient command to your toolbar. Click the File category and scroll through the list of options in the Commands list until you locate the Mail Recipient icon.

4. Drag the icon you want from the Commands section to the place on the toolbar you want it to appear.

 T I P If you have too many buttons on your toolbar, adding more buttons to it may push buttons off the right side of the screen.

5. To remove items from the toolbar, drag the buttons or items off the toolbar. The Customize dialog box must be displayed, which can be displayed by selecting Tools, Customize.

6. To move buttons or items, drag them to a new location on the same toolbar or to a different toolbar. The Customize dialog box must be displayed.

7. Click Close to close the Customize dialog box.

Part
VII

Ch
41

Modifying Toolbar Buttons

You can change the way a toolbar button looks, change its name, and make it perform another function by using the Modify Selection button on the Command tab. Some of the toolbar buttons you add may have only text and take up too much space on the toolbar. To minimize their space requirement, you can use a graphic as the toolbar button icon. Office 97 also enables you to attach a macro to a toolbar to make it perform specific actions you program.

To modify toolbar buttons, follow these steps:

1. Choose View, Toolbars, Customize. The Customize dialog box appears.

2. Select the Commands tab.

3. Move the mouse pointer to the toolbar button and click it. A black border appears around the button (see Figure 41.20). The Modify Selection button on the Command tab displays.

FIG. 41.20

The Modify Selection button is dimmed out until you select a toolbar button to modify.

Black border around button to modify

4. Click the Modify Selection button, to display a menu of modification choices (see Figure 41.21). You can also right-click the button to display the same menu.

5. Select a menu command to change the selected toolbar button. Table 41.4 lists and describes each menu command.

FIG. 41.21
Use Modify Selection menu to change a toolbar button.

Table 41.4   Options for Modifying Toolbar Buttons

Command	Description
Reset	Returns the button to its original state.
Delete	Removes the button from the toolbar.
Name	Enables you to rename the button. Use an ampersand (&) character to the left of the character you want to use as the hot key.
Copy Button Image	Places a copy of the button's image in the Windows Clipboard.
Paste Button Image	Inserts the copied image from the Clipboard to the selected button.
Reset Button Image	Returns button image to original image.
Edit Button Image	Displays the Button Editor (see Figure 21.22) so you can create, edit, and add colors to a button image. The Preview area shows the actual size of the image as you create it. Click OK when you finish the image.
Change Button Image	Displays 42 predrawn images you can choose for your button image.
Default Style	Displays the button in the default format for that application. For most buttons, this displays the button as an image only.
Text Only (Always)	Displays the button's command as a text label on the toolbar and in menus (if that command is in a menu).

continues

Part

VII

Ch

41

Table 41.4 Continued

Command	Description
Text Only (in Menus)	Displays the button's command as a text label in menus (if that command is in a menu).
Image and Text	Displays the button's command as an image and text on the toolbar and in menus.
Begin a Group	Places a group divider to the left of the button to enable you to group similar commands together.
Assign Macro	Displays the Assign Macro dialog box, enabling you to assign a macro to the toolbar button. In Excel only.
Properties	Displays the Database Control Properties for button. In Access only.

FIG. 21.22
The Button Editor lets you draw images for toolbar buttons.

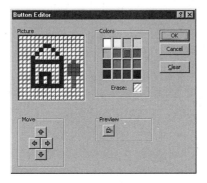

6. Click Close to save your changes.

Setting Toolbar and Menu Options

Office 97 enables you to set display options for toolbar and menus. You can, for instance, set menu animations, which cause menus to appear to unfold or slide across your screen, show toolbar ScreenTips, or display toolbar buttons as large icons.

To set toolbar and menu options, follow these steps:

1. Choose View, Toolbars, Customize. The Customize dialog box appears.

2. Select the Options tab (see Figure 41.23). Table 41.5 summarizes the options you can select on this tab.

Table 41.5   Options for Customizing Toolbars and Menus

Option	Description
Large Icons	Displays toolbar buttons as large icons. Handy for when you use high-resolution displays.
Show ScreenTips on Toolbars	Displays the name of the toolbar button when you move the mouse pointer over the toolbar button.
Show Shortcut keys in ScreenTips	Displays the two- or three-character keyboard shortcuts for each toolbar button and on menus. In Word, Access, and PowerPoint only.
Menu animations	Controls the way menus display when you click them. You can select from None, Random, Unfold, and Slide.
Keyboard button	Displays the Customize Keyboard dialog box to create new keyboard shortcuts. In Word only.

FIG. 41.23
The Options tab enables you to customize toolbar and menu behavior.

Creating a Custom Toolbar

In addition to modifying the default toolbars of Microsoft Office 97 applications, you can create your own custom toolbar. For example, you could have a toolbar for every type of task you do, such as one for mail merge and one for desktop publishing.

For information about each application's Standard toolbar, see Chapter 2, "Getting Started and Identifying Screen Parts," or see the chapters pertaining to the individual applications.

▶ **See** "Formatting with Styles," **p. 245**
▶ **See** "Using AutoFormat," **p. 250**
▶ **See** "Using Template Wizards," **p. 256**

N O T E Although Excel screens are used in this section to illustrate the process of creating custom toolbars, the screens in Word, Access, and PowerPoint are similar. Any exceptions are noted. ▪

To create a custom toolbar, follow these steps:

1. Choose View, Toolbars, Customize to display the Customize dialog box.

2. On the Toolbars tab, click the New button, to display the New Toolbar dialog box (see Figure 41.24).

FIG. 41.24

Use the New Toolbar dialog box to name your new toolbar.

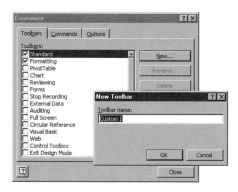

3. Enter a name for the new toolbar in the Toolbar Name text box and click OK. The new toolbar displays, but does not contain any buttons yet. Don't fret if the new toolbar is too small to read its name. It grows as you add buttons to it.

4. In Word, you have the option of naming the document template in which the toolbar is available. Click the Make Toolbar Available To drop-down list to choose a template file.

5. Select the Commands tab on the Customize dialog box.

6. Select the category that contains the buttons or other items you want to add to the new toolbar.

7. Drag the commands from the Commands list to the new toolbar (see Figure 41.25).

8. Repeat steps 5 and 6 until you fill your custom toolbar with the features you want (the toolbar expands to accommodate your selections).

9. Click the Close button to close the Customize dialog box.

FIG. 41.25
The custom toolbar named Finance contains three buttons.

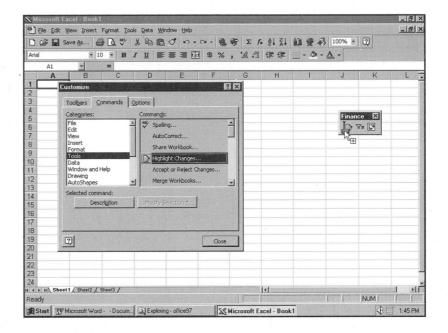

TROUBLESHOOTING

The new toolbar I created contains no buttons. A new toolbar is empty until you add buttons. With the new toolbar visible on-screen, return to the Customize dialog box. Select the category containing the buttons you want to use and drag the button images to your custom toolbar.

Someone customized the default toolbar. I need to get the Standard toolbar back. Choose the View, Toolbars, Customize command, select a toolbar, and choose the Reset button to return to the built-in version of the selected toolbar.

Part
VII

Ch
41

Customizing Application Menus and Command Bars

You can change the organization, position, and content of default Office menus. In addition to modifying the built-in menus, you can add your own custom menus to an Office application's built-in menu bar. This feature is called command bars in Office 97. You could, for example, create a custom menu in Word that lists common tasks you perform such as mail merges, drawing callouts, and applying font changes. The Commands tab of the Customize dialog box provides easy access to this helpful feature.

▶ **See** "Using Template Wizards," **p. 256**

To customize or create menus, follow these steps:

1. Choose the View, Toolbars, Customize command. Alternatively, place the mouse pointer on the toolbar, click the right mouse button, and choose Customize from the shortcut menu. The Customize dialog box appears.

2. Select the Commands tab.

3. Scroll down the list of Categories and click New Menu. The Commands list displays a New Menu item (see Figure 41.26).

FIG. 41.26

Word, as well as other Office 97 applications, enables you to customize its built-in menus.

4. Select the New Menu item in the Commands list and drag and drop it on the menu bar or toolbar where you want the new menu to appear.

5. In the Categories list, click the category that contains the command(s) you want to place on your new menu. Click the Macros category to display a list of macros or VBA routines you have on your system. Click the Save in drop-down list to list macros in different templates.

N O T E Word includes three additional prebuilt menus that do not already appear on the default menu bar—Action, Font, and Work—you can add to your menu bar. PowerPoint includes three additional prebuilt menus that do not already appear on the default menu bar—Custom, Data, and Table—you can add to your menu bar. Excel includes several prebuilt menus you can access from the MenuWell categories. ▪

  T I P If you drop your command next to the New Menu item, that command becomes a new menu instead of a menu item in your new menu.

6. In the Commands list, drag the command you want on the new menu up to the New Menu item. Wait for a small, gray, square box and I-beam to appear (see Figure 41.27) and drop the new command on the box. That command now becomes a menu item in your new menu.

FIG. 41.27

Wait for the small gray box and I-beam to appear before dropping the new menu item.

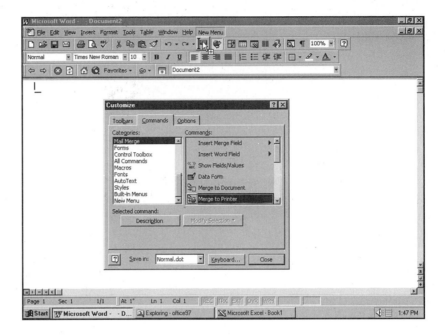

7. Continue adding new menu items until the menu is complete.

8. To assign a command to another menu, select the command from the Commands list and drag and drop it to the place on the menu where you want the command to appear.

9. To change the position of the command in a menu, select the command and drag it up or down to its new position.

10. To change the name, shortcut key, or other property of the menu item, select the command on a menu and click the Modify Selection button on the Customize dialog box. See Table 41.4 for descriptions of each of these commands.

11. To remove a menu item or menu, drag and drop the item or menu from the menu bar to the Customize dialog box.

12. In the Save in drop-down list, select the template in which you want to save the customized menu.

13. Click the Close button when you complete your changes.

Part

VII

Ch

41

TROUBLESHOOTING

I find the default Edit, Links menu command name in Word misleading. I need to change it to something more meaningful. Choose the View, Tools, Customize command and select the Commands tab. Select the Edit menu on the Word menu bar and click the Links command. On the Command tab, click the Modify Selection and change the Name field to your liking. Be sure to place an ampersand (&) in front of the character you want as the shortcut key. Also, make sure your shortcut key is unique for that menu. Click Close.

Someone customized the default menus. I need to get the standard menus back. Choose the Views, Tools, Customize command. Select the Toolbars tab and select the Menu Bar toolbar option in the Toolbars list. Click the Reset button. In Excel, click the Reset button on the Toolbars tab (a Menu Bar toolbar option is not available) and you are prompted whether you want to reset the menu bar.

I pressed Alt+Ctrl+minus sign (–), and I lost a menu item. You pressed a special shortcut-key combination that deletes menu items. Word provides shortcut keys that help you add and delete menu items as you work. Rather than open the Customize dialog box, you can press Alt+Ctrl+minus sign (–) to delete an item from the selected menu, or Alt+Ctrl+equal sign (=) to add a menu item to the selected menu. See the preceding troubleshooting item for directions on resetting the menus.

CHAPTER 42

Using Visual Basic for Applications to Integrate Office

by Paul Sanna

Each Office application can be considered an extremely powerful tool in its own right. Many times, though, you need multiple tools to complete a project. For example, you may need both Access and Word to integrate a large amount of data into a high-quality document. Visual Basic, Applications Edition (Visual Basic for Applications, or VBA) can be the glue that holds multi-component applications together. You can also use VBA to customize the functionality of any application, such as Excel or Word. This chapter shows you how to use VBA to build multi-component, integrated applications. You learn what is possible with Visual Basic for Applications and how to program applications with it. In the "Techniques from the Pros" section at the end of this chapter, you learn how to build a VBA-based and PowerPoint-hosted real-world application. ■

Understand VBA

Explore VBA and get to know what it can do.

Learn about objects

You learn about objects and object-oriented programming.

Work in the VBA Editor

This chapter shows you how to build VBA projects in the VBA Editor, including using the code window, Properties Window, Object Explorer, and Property Editor.

Debug applications

Diagnosing problems in your code and forms is the goal of the debugging tools built into the VBA Editor.

VBA and OLE

Objects and OLE technologies are a major part of VBA. This chapter explains how VBA uses objects and OLE technologies together.

Techniques from the Pros

This section gives you tips on how to build an integrated, multi-application VBA project using PowerPoint as a host.

Understanding VBA

Visual Basic for Applications (VBA) is the standard macro language built into Office 97 applications. In addition, Microsoft has made VBA available via licensing so that other software developers can integrate VBA into their applications. More than just a macro language, however, VBA can be used to significantly customize and extend the functionality of an application that uses VBA. In addition, you can manipulate, retrieve, and/or modify data from other applications that use VBA, such as Visio or AutoCAD.

Comparing Visual Basic to VBA

As you might expect, VBA is closely related to Visual Basic. VBA is a derivative of Visual Basic that has been optimized specifically for use with applications. This point forms an important distinction between the two products: Visual Basic can be used to run applications directly from the Windows 95/NT Desktop; VBA projects can be launched only from inside an application that uses VBA.

There are many similarities between VB and VBA. The language structure is almost identical; you need to learn almost nothing new to code VBA if you already know how to code in Visual Basic.

Comparing Visual Basic Script to VBA

You may have also heard recently of another version of Visual Basic called Visual Basic, Script Edition (VBScript). With the explosion in popularity and use of the Internet and the World Wide Web (WWW), the pace of tools development for building World Wide Web content has also grown dramatically. Microsoft has developed a version of Visual Basic to help WWW developers add interactive content to WWW pages. Using VBScript, you can build small applications integrated directly into Web pages. For more information about VBScript, refer to Que's *Special Edition Using VBScript* and *VBScript by Example.*

Understanding What Is Possible with VBA

When you combine the flexibility and wide range of features provided in the Office 97 suite of applications with VBA, you can develop very powerful applications without using difficult development tools that require many years to master. Here are examples of some of the features and elements you can build into a VBA solution:

- Present the user of your application with a custom, interactive dialog box of your own design.

- Build powerful macros that extend the functionality of the host application.

- Customize the menu structure of an Office 97 application.

- Manipulate the application or data owned by another Office 97 application.

- Integrate data from multiple Office 97 applications.

- Automatically create and/or update Web pages using Office 97.

As a developer of VBA solutions, you're probably interested in the following tools and techniques available to help you build a VBA project:

- Debug applications without having to compile.

- Use services provided by the Win32 API.

- Use SQL and Data Access Objects to manipulate and retrieve data from external data sources, such as Microsoft SQL Server 6.5.

- Easily attach custom code and procedures to events that occur with your VBA project.

Understanding Objects in VBA

VBA makes use of some object-oriented programming (OOP) concepts and techniques. There is the notion of objects and other concepts related to OOP throughout most of VBA. For example, the controls that appear on the forms you build in VBA projects are managed as if they were objects, and the use of objects is the only way to access a foreign application and its data. Later this chapter explores how VBA uses Microsoft's objects. For now, we'll take a look at objects and some object-oriented programming concepts.

Learning About Objects

Before you learn anything about object-oriented programming (OOP), you need to understand the most basic and most important element of OOP: the object. So, what is an object?

An *object* can be anything: a house, a refrigerator, an engine, a table, a seesaw.... Objects can represent real-world things, such as those just listed, or slightly abstract things, like lists or calculations. So, objects are things. What makes them interesting for our purposes is how they are used in programming.

Objects can be used to represent useful things in a program without the programmer having to know much about how the thing is made or its internal workings.

For example, let's say that in your application, you need to access data that appears in a database. Today's top relational database management systems (RDBMS), such as Oracle, Sybase, Microsoft SQL Server, and Red Brick, are incredibly complex applications. A well-designed database object, though, would shield the programmer from those complexities. Rather than make the user specify a number of database-specific options, our well-designed object makes it easy for the programmer to simply retrieve a row of records from some table in the database.

User Interface Objects

In visual programming languages such as VB and VBA, a critical set of objects in your applications are the controls that appear on the forms you build. By *controls* we mean the objects you see in dialog boxes and windows that you use in Windows everyday—lists, buttons, labels, and edit boxes. All the controls on the form and the form itself are objects. These objects are treated no differently from the other objects you use in your applications. You see how to program user-interface objects in the next section of this chapter.

Understanding Classes

Classes are very closely related to objects; a *class* is the blueprint for an object. The class determines what kind of information you can ask of an object and what things you can ask an object to do. So, why are there classes and why are there objects?

To answer the question, let's examine the analogy of a blueprint. With a good blueprint for a house, you could probably build a nice house. You might customize each model of the house you build off the same blueprint, but generally the models will be very similar and will resemble the blueprint. A class acts like a blueprint from which objects are created.

Understanding Instances

Every time you create an object from a class, you create what is known as an *instance* of the class. An instance of a class is known as an object. You can create as many instances of the class as you need. This means that you can create as many objects of the same type as you need. When you create an instance of a class, you have *instantiated* the class.

For example, say that you have a file object. This file object makes it easy to retrieve and save data to some file. If your application needs to read data from a file, process the data, and then store the data in *another* file, you probably will have two instances of the file object: the InputFile and OutputFile.

Creating Instances

So far you've learned about objects, classes, and instances. Let's take a look at some VBA code that demonstrates some of these concepts.

You know that in order to create an object, you must create an instance of the class. To create almost anything in VBA, you must use the Dim statement. The Dim statement tells VBA that you will be using a certain type of data, and that instance of data will have a name. For example, when you "Dim X as Integer", you tell VBA that you will be using *X* to store integer type data. The character *X* is variable, which means it can be used to represent any data you want, as long as, in our example's case, the data is an integer. You also use the Dim statement to declare an object variable:

```
Dim item as item_type
```

As an example, if you create an instance of the File class with the named WorkingFile, your code might appear as follows:

```
Dim WorkingFile as File
```

You can now use the variable you've named WorkingFile in your application, making use of whatever services and characteristics the File class provides. The next few sections take a look at an object's service and tasks.

Understanding Properties

When you create or use objects, you have some interest in these objects beyond the fact that they exist. Generally, the simple existence of an object is not too interesting. What is interesting is the object's characteristics.

Return to the example of the file object. If my application needs to read data from a file, I am probably interested in some aspects of the file, such as where it is located, if it is in the format that I expect, and whether some other user or application is using the file.

The characteristics about an object are known as *properties*. Almost all objects have a set of properties. The information described in the previous paragraph pertaining to the file can be considered *properties* of the file.

In VBA, special syntax is used to refer to an object's properties. The dot character separates an object from its property:

```
object.property
```

Part

VII

Ch

42

Look at some of the properties found in a file object. The following table describes the properties and their functions:

Property	Use
Name	Name of the file
Description	Description of the file
InUse	Tells whether the file has been opened by another application
Length	The length (in bytes) of the file
DateTime	Date and Time the file was last modified

Here is how the properties in the example are associated with the `WorkingFile` instance of the file object.

```
WorkingFile.Name

WorkingFile.Description

WorkingFile.InUse

WorkingFile.DateTime

WorkingFile.Length
```

Retrieving the Value of a Property

Most objects you use in VBA projects have properties. These properties might be ones that you would present to the user of an application, such as the `Date` and `Time` the application was last modified, or properties can be used to help execute an internal procedure. Regardless, properties are useful, and they are easy to identify in VBA code. The following code snippets show how you might retrieve the values of some of the properties in the `WorkingFile` example:

```
MyFileName = WorkingObject.Name

MyFileDescription = WorkingObject.Description

IsTheFileInUse = WorkingObject.InUse

WhenWasFileLastChanged = WorkingObject.DateTime

HowLargeIsMyFile = WorkingObject.Length
```

N O T E   The value of some properties is established the moment the object is created.
For other properties, their value is Null until established either by interaction with the user of the application or by some internal procedure. This is a function, again, of how the class was built originally. ▪

Setting the Value of Properties

In addition to retrieving the value of a property of some object, it's a safe bet that you will need to assign the value to one of the properties of some object. This means that you can tell an object about one of its own characteristics.

The following code snippets show how you might assign the values to some of the properties in the WorkingFile example.

```
WorkingFile.Name = "RESULTS.XLS"

WorkingFile.Description = "Financial Results for the Board Meeting"
```

Understanding Methods

The reason for creating or using objects isn't always to assign or ask about their properties. Most times, you're interested in objects doing work for you. *Methods*, also known as member functions, are the activities or tasks you ask your object to perform.

As with properties, the dot character (.) separates an object from its method:

```
object.method
```

Say that your file object has some methods. This table describes the methods for your example and their use:

Method	Use
Open	Opens the file for use in the application
WriteValue	Writes a data record to the file
Close	Closes the file
Export	Exports some data out of the file using some format
Delete	Deletes the file
RetrieveValue	Retrieves some data record out of the file
Calculate	Performs some calculation on data in the file

Here is how a few of the methods in your example might look in code when associated with the WorkingFile instance of the File object.

```
WorkingFile.Delete

WorkingFile.Close
```

Certain methods may need information in order to be executed. The information you provide to a method is known as arguments or parameters. To pass parameters to a method for an object, do the following:

```
object.method param1, param2,...paramn
```

Part
VII

Ch
42

From the list of example methods, the WriteValue and Export methods probably need more information in order to execute:

- *Export.* Say that the file object supports the extraction of data to comma-delimited files using the Export method. It makes sense that the Export method would need the name of the file to export the data to. In code, then, exporting data to a file named ALLDATA.ASC in the root directory of your C drive might appear as follows:

```
WorkingFile.Export "C:\ALLDATA.ASC"
```

- *WriteValue.* Say that data in the file is organized very rudimentarily by columns and rows. If you needed to write a value to your file, the WriteValue method would expect the number of the row, the number of the column, and the value, in order. In code, then, writing the value 120 to row 2 in column 4 might appear as follows:

```
WorkingFile.WriteValue 2,4, 120
```

N O T E   Again, as with properties, keep in mind that methods are associated with classes. You shouldn't expect a method used with one class to work with an object from another class. Consult any documentation you have for the object you're using in order to determine the method you need. ▪

The next method you'll look at returns a value to the program. Certain methods might execute an action that either returns information describing whether or not the action was successful, or simply returns a piece of data.

When you use a method that returns data, you must supply a variable in which to store the value that returns from the method. Furthermore, the variable must have the same data type as the value that is returned from the method. For example, if a method returns a string, your return variable could not be an integer type.

```
ReturnValue = object.method
```

The last type of method discussed is one that combines aspects of the previous two types looked at: one that requires a parameter(s) and one that returns a value:

```
ReturnValue = object.method param1, param2,...paramn
```

From the list of example methods, the ReturnValue method needs the row and column of the data you want to retrieve, and you need a variable in which to store the data. Say that the data is in row 2 and column 9. Let's also say that you know the data returned will be within the range of possible values defined for an integer data type:

```
Dim MyValue as integer
MyValue = WorkingFile.Calculate(2,9)
```

In this example, the variable MyValue would take on the value of the record in row 2 and column 9.

Working in the VBA Editor

The VBA Editor is an application you use to build VBA projects. While the VBA Editor might appear to be a completely separate application from the products that host VBA (for example, Word, Excel), the VBA Editor runs in the same memory space as the host application and is closely integrated with that application. In this section, you learn about the features of the VBA Editor and how to write code, build forms, and run and test your application.

Starting Your VBA Project

All VBA projects begin at an application that hosts VBA. In the case of Office 97, you can use any of the applications. In the case of other applications, you should consult the documentation supplied with the application.

Choosing the VBA Host Application   If the goal of your VBA project is to customize or automate some process in some application, then its obvious which application to choose as the host for your VBA project. If you are building a multi-application solution with VBA, then you need to carefully choose the host application. Here are two things to consider:

- The VBA host application is where the end user launches the project you build in VBA. So, you must be sure that your end user has installed the application that you choose to host the VBA project.

- Choose as the host application, the one where most of the processing will take place. You will suffer performance degradation if you use one application to drive access objects in another application. For example, if you want to manipulate charts and data on-screen while also presenting some limited textual information, host the application in Excel rather than Word.

 TIP Accessing objects from other applications takes a considerable amount of resources and should be minimized as much as possible.

Part
VII

Ch
42

Creating the VBA Project   There are three ways to create a VBA project and access the VBA Editor:

- *Record a macro and then edit it.* This technique is useful if you want to record a few steps and then enhance the macro in the VBA editor. To do this, record a macro in the host application. Next, choose Tools, Macro, Macros from the menu. Select the macro you recorded and then choose Edit. The VBA editor will open, and your macro code will appear in a minimized code window. Open the code window to see the macro code (see Figure 42.1).

FIG. 42.1

The VBA editor shows you the code created when you record a macro.

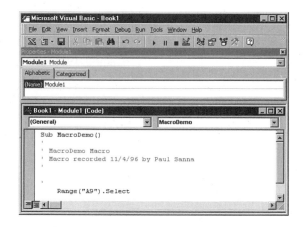

 Recording a macro in the host application is an easy method to help figure out how to code a particular procedure. You can simulate the steps you want to execute by recording them. Then, edit the macro you just recorded and use the code created as a template.

- *Create a macro in the host application and then edit it.* This technique is useful for opening the code window and creating a template for writing your VBA code. To do so, choose Tools, Macro, Macros from the host application menu. Next, enter a name for your macro, and then choose Create. The VBA editor will open and display the code window, set to an empty routine with the name you supplied (see Figure 42.2).

FIG. 42.2

A skeleton function is prepared for you when you create a macro in the host application.

■ *Launch the VBA Editor directly from the host application.* To launch VBA without first creating a macro, choose Tools, Macro, Visual Basic Editor from the host application's menu.

Opening an Existing Project

Associated with any document in a VBA host application may be any number of custom forms, modules, macros, and class modules. A collection of one, some, or all of these make up your VBA project. In fact, you can have a number of VBA solutions in one document. What really defines a project is the collection of forms and code that you use to solve some problem. If there are other forms or code in the document that are unused in your project, who cares? So, to open an existing project, simply access the VBA Editor from the VBA host application and from the document where the VBA code and forms are stored.

Reviewing What You See in the VBA Editor

The VBA Editor employs a number of different on-screen tools to help you build and manage applications. Figure 42.3 shows the tools you'll work with most of the time. The following sections describe how to use these tools.

FIG. 42.3
VBA uses a number of different tools to help you develop applications.

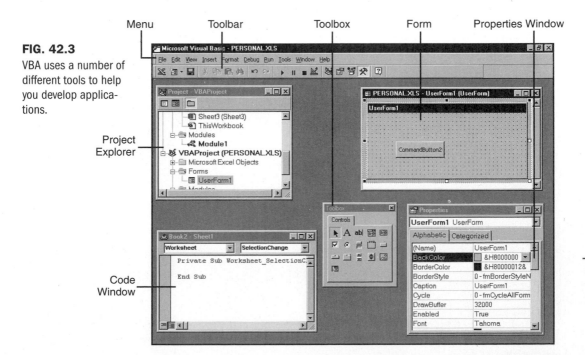

Menu | Toolbar | Toolbox | Form | Properties Window

Project Explorer

Code Window

Part
VII

Ch
42

Using the Project Explorer

The Project Explorer is a special window in the VBA Editor that shows each element of your VBA project. The elements are presented in a tree format, which makes it easy to review the project and select the element you want to work with. The Project Explorer shows the VBA project associated with each document you have open in the host application, so you can easily copy code and forms from one project to another.

Figure 42.4 shows the Project Explorer in Excel and Figure 42.5 shows the Project Explorer in Word.

FIG. 42.4

The Project Explorer in Excel shows elements such as workbooks and worksheets, as well as modules, forms, and class modules.

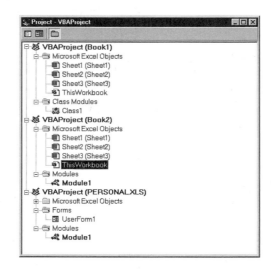

FIG. 42.5

The Project Explorer in Word shows elements such as documents and a template, as well as modules, forms, and class modules.

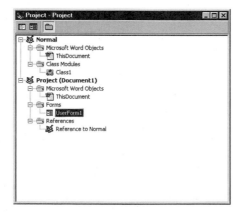

The Project Explorer makes it easy to select the objects you want to work with. After you select an object to edit, the VBA editor opens the appropriate tool. For example, if you select a form, the form appears on-screen with the form toolbox available; if you select a worksheet from Excel, that worksheet becomes active.

There are two ways to select and edit an object that appears in the Project Explorer:

- Double-click the object.
- Choose the object, right-click, and then choose View Object or View Code. The reason for the choice is that some objects (typically the documents for each application—Word document, Excel Workbook, and so on) have both code and user interface elements that you can view.

Using the Properties Window

The Properties window (see Figure 42.6) is used to review and set properties for project objects. For example, you can use the Properties window to set and review properties forms you build, templates in Word projects, and workbooks and worksheets in Excel projects. Only properties relevant to the object appear in the Properties window. The Properties window is divided into two panes: properties associated with the current object appear in the left pane, and the value of the property appears in the right pane.

FIG. 42.6
The Properties window provides a central location for setting properties for most elements of your application.

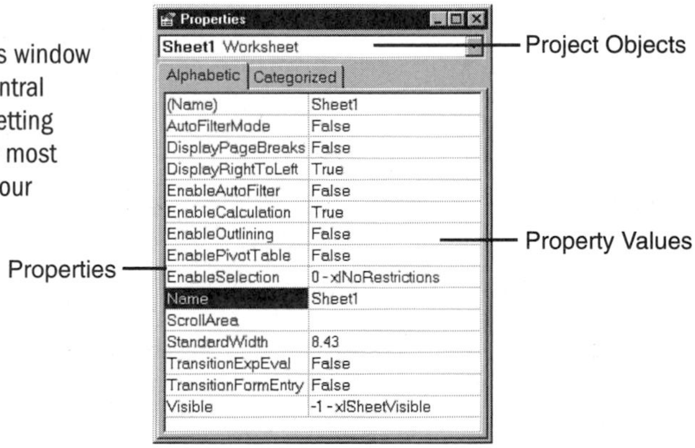

Properties

Project Objects

Property Values

Here are some points to remember about using the Properties window:

- To select an object to work with, either select it from the drop-down list at the top of the Properties window, or select the object from the Project Explorer and then return to the Properties window.

■ To change a property, select the property in the left pane, and then click and edit the value in the right pane. Some property values are limited to a predefined list. In this case, a drop-down list appears in the value column for the property you are setting.

■ To view properties either grouped according to their category or sorted alphabetically, choose the appropriate tab in the Properties window.

Using the Code Window

The code window is where you write any code associated with your VBA project. This includes macro routines, code that responds to user interaction with custom forms you build, and special helper routines you code to support your entire application.

The code window appears when you do any of the following:

■ From the Project Explorer, double-click any code element in your application, such as a module or class module.

■ Double-click any part of the form or controls on the form.

■ Choose View Code from the VBA Editor window. If you want to view the code for a specific project element, such as a worksheet, be sure you select that element first in the Project Explorer.

■ From the host application, edit a macro.

After the code window is displayed, you enter your code directly into the window. Here are some techniques for adding code and navigating through the window:

■ To add a new subroutine or procedure, choose Insert Procedure from the VBA Editor window, supply the name of the procedure, it's type, whether the routine is public or private, and then choose OK.

■ To move quickly to a routine you've written in the module in which you are working, choose (General) from the drop-down list on the left, and then choose the procedure from the drop-down list on the right.

■ To move quickly to an event routine or a method for an on-screen object, choose the name of the object from the drop-down list on the left, and then choose the event or method from the drop-down list on the right.

The code window provides a number of features to help you program productively.

Color Syntax   Different parts of your code can appear with different colors. This helps you identify and review the different elements of your code. For example, comments can be in red, declarations (`dim x as integer`) in blue, and selected text in blue against a pink background. You specify these colors in the Options dialog box under the Editor Format tab. The dialog box appears when you choose <u>T</u>ools, <u>O</u>ptions from the menu.

Help with Objects   The code window can help you when you write code using objects or when you use built-in routines that VBA knows about. When the code window recognizes code you enter, it will display a special message box to help enter the correct syntax.

For example, when you enter

        Dim *variable_name* As

the editor will display a list of all objects and data types it knows about (see Figure 42.7).

FIG. 42.7
The code window will pop up the list of all objects and data types it knows about when you attempt to declare a new variable.

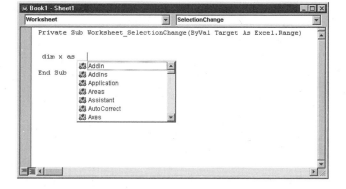

As you'll learn later in the "Working with Application Objects" section, you need to add a reference to another application's set of objects if you plan to reference any of that application's objects in your VBA project. Having done so, VBA will present that application's objects in the list of objects you can use in your code.

Help with Routines   VBA helps you use the routines it provides by presenting you with the proper syntax for the routine when it believes you are using it. When you enter the name of a function or subroutine provided by VBA, a message box appears showing you the parameters required, their data type, and in the correct order. This makes it difficult to introduce problems into your code when using them.

Figure 42.8 shows an example of how VBA helps you code the `MsgBox` (Message Box routine).

FIG. 42.8

The MsgBox routine requires a number of parameters. When you enter M S G B O X into the code window, VBA will pop up a template showing proper coding of the routine.

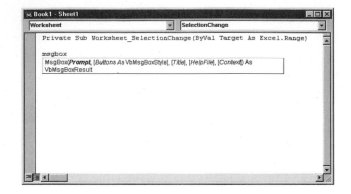

N O T E If you enter the name of a VBA routine into the code window, one or more of the parameters may appear bold. These parameters are required. Any parameters that do not appear bold are optional, such as the *Title* parameter shown in Figure 42.8. Notice that the *Prompt* parameter (the text that appears in the message box) is the only parameter shown bold, hence it is the only required parameter. ▪

Building Forms

It is likely that your VBA project will need a custom form. In VBA, you build forms yourself. You can use these forms to receive or present information to and from the user.

This form can be like any dialog box you've seen or used in any Office application, such as the File Open or Print dialog boxes.

Adding Forms to Your Project   To add a form to your project, follow these steps:

1. If more than one project is opened in VBA, in Project Explorer select the name of the project in which you want to add the form.

2. Choose Insert, User Form from the menu. A blank form and the form Toolbox appear on-screen (see Figure 42.9).

FIG. 42.9

VBA creates a blank form when you request to add a user form to your project.

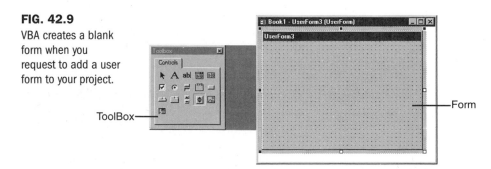

ToolBox

Form

3. From the VBA Editor menu, choose View, Properties Window.

4. Specify properties for your new form, such as Name.

Display the Toolbox VBA provides in the Toolbox a set of controls you can use on your custom forms. If you do not see the Toolbox on-screen, choose View, Toolbox from the menu. Note that the Toolbox disappears when you are working with an object other than a form, such as the Properties window, and it will reappear when you click a form.

Adding Additional Controls to the ToolBox In addition to the controls provided with VBA, a large number of custom controls are available for your use. You may have additional controls already on your system. They may have been by another application, perhaps developed by Microsoft or another software development company. You can find controls advertised for purchase in many magazines with a software development or C++/VB focus.

To see whether additional controls are available and to add them to your project, follow these steps:

1. Select as the active object any form in your project. To do so, you can use the Project Explorer. Display the Explorer and double-click the form name.

2. Choose Tools, Additional Controls from the menu. The Additional Controls dialog box appears (see Figure 42.10).

FIG. 42.10
You choose additional controls to add to your Toolbox from the Additional Controls dialog box. The collections of tools in your Toolbox may differ from that in another Toolbox.

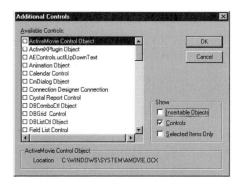

3. Be sure the Insertable Objects and the Selected Items Only check boxes are cleared and the Controls check box is selected. Any additional controls registered with your operating system will appear in the list.

4. Choose the control to add your project by choosing the edit box besides the object's name.

5. Choose OK. The object will appear in the Toolbox.

Part
VII

Ch
42

Placing Controls on the Form   After your Toolbox has all the controls you need, it is time to start adding controls to your form. Just follow these steps:

1. Select the form to which you want to add controls.

2. Click the control you want to add from the Toolbox, and then click anywhere on the form. The control will appear on the form.

3. Click and drag the control to its proper location on the form.

4. Click and drag any border of the control to resize it. You may do the same with the form.

Writing Code for Controls on the Form

You'll provide controls on the form to receive input from the user and to present informa-tion back. Placing controls on the form does nothing more than inform VBA that these items exist on a form in a project. Each user interface object has particular properties and events associated with it. It is up to you to provide the code that runs when events occur, and it is up to you to correctly supply the properties.

Here are examples of occasions when you would want to associate code with a particular event or to set specific properties:

■ Begin processing when the user clicks the OK button.

■ Close the dialog box (and VBA project) when the user clicks the Cancel button.

■ Record the item in a list the user has selected.

■ Disable a particular control if the user selects a specific option that may not be appropriate with all controls and conditions.

Supplying the code associated with a form object is easy. There are two general methods for doing so:

■ Double-click the control on the form. The code window appears, set to the control you double-clicked. Choose the event you want to respond to from the right drop-down list. Enter the code in the subroutine template provided (see Figure 42.11).

■ Click the control once and choose View, Code from the VBA Editor menu. Choose the event you want to respond to from the right drop-down list. Enter the code in the subroutine template provided.

FIG. 42.11
The form shows a button named MyButton with a caption of OK, the Properties window displaying properties for the control, and the code window opened to the button's click event.

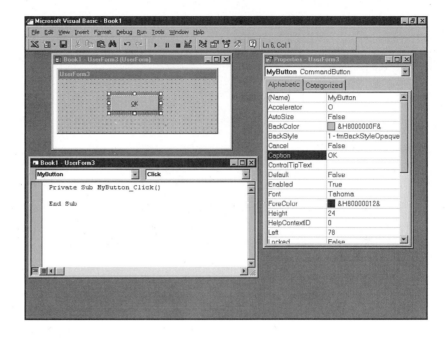

Formatting Your Forms

The VBA editor makes it easy for you to format and generally neaten the appearance of your form. For example, VBA can align controls for you so that your controls do not appear as if they were placed on the form in random positions. Figure 42.12 shows a number of command buttons randomly sized and placed on a form, and Figure 42.13 shows how the form appears after using the Make Same Size Both and Arrange Buttons Right command.

FIG. 42.12
The buttons in this form have been randomly sized and placed on the form.

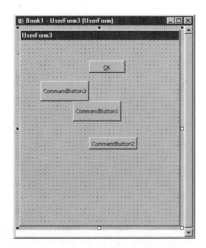

Part
VII

Ch
42

FIG. 42.13
The appearance of the controls on the form has been improved using help from the VBA editor.

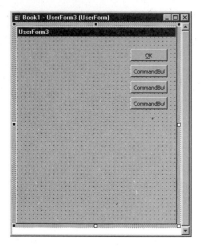

To align controls on your form, select the controls, and then choose the appropriate option from the Fo<u>r</u>mat menu. Formatting your customer forms often requires choosing multiple controls at once. To choose multiple controls, click the first control and then hold the Shift key while you select other controls. As long as you hold the Shift key, you can click an already selected control to deselect it. Also, you can hold the Ctrl key to select multiple random controls.

Adding a Module to Your Project

Depending on the size and design of your project, you might develop a number of helper routines in code that service many parts of your application. You might store these routines separately from the rest of your application. In another scenario, you might organize the code elements of your application into a few code modules that contain related routines. VBA supports this type of work by allowing you to create and code in *modules*.

To add a module to your VBA project, follow these steps:

1. If more than one project is opened in VBA, in Project Explorer select the name of the project in which you want to add the module.

2. From the VBA Editor menu, choose <u>I</u>nsert, <u>M</u>odule. An empty code window appears on-screen.

3. From the Properties window, supply the name of the module.

Adding Class Modules

As you learned earlier in this chapter, objects are instances of a particular class. You also learned that objects can be useful in programming because their use makes your code more readable, more maintainable, and more thoughtfully designed.

VBA provides support for letting you build your own objects. You could create the WorkingFile object used as an example in the "Understanding Objects in VBA" section. You could also create the object's properties and methods.

All of the code used to create an object, its properties, and its methods, is contained in a *class module*. A class module uses as a name the name of the object created in it. For example, the object Webpage would be built in the Webpage class module. All class modules in a project are shown in the Project Explorer under the Class Module heading.

You code class modules as you would other elements of your VBA project. Special syntax, naturally, is used to develop the properties and methods associated with an object. To add a class module to your project, choose Insert, Class Module from the menu. For more information on developing class modules in VBA, please refer to *Special Edition, Using Visual Basic for Applications* by Que.

Switching to the Host Application

While you build your VBA project, you may want to switch to the host application without shutting down your project or the application. Here are a few ways to do this:

- From the Project Explorer, right-click the object you want to view, such as a Word document, and then choose View Object from the menu.
- Choose View, Object from the VBA Editor window.
- Choose View from the VBA Editor menu and then choose the last item, which is usually the name of the host application.

After you switch to the host application, you probably would want to switch back to the VBA project. Here are a few ways to do this:

- Choose Tools, Macros, Visual Basic Editor from the host application menu.
- Choose Visual Basic from the Windows 95/NT Taskbar.

Part

VII

Ch

42

Saving Your Work

Code, forms, and modules you create with VBA are associated with a specific host application and a document associated with the application. For example, if you develop a wizard that executes a special mail-merge when a document is created from a particular Word template, the VBA project is associated with the template in Word. So, saving a VBA project occurs only when you save the host document.

To save a document from VBA, choose File, Save from the menu. This will save any changes you've made to the document, as well as to the VBA project.

N O T E   If you attempt to save from VBA and you have not yet given the host document a name (for example, you start Excel and immediately launch VBA and begin coding), you will be prompted in VBA to provide a name for the host document. ▮

Working with Application Objects

Earlier in this chapter, you learned about objects and how they are used in programming. VBA uses OLE (Object Link and Embedding) technologies to help communicate to and integrate Office 97 applications, as well as other applications that use OLE. You'll make use of OLE in two different ways while building projects:

- VBA and OLE servers
- VBA and OLE automation

VBA and OLE Servers

Yet another element you can integrate into your VBA projects is an *insertable object*. Insertable objects are an implementation of OLE. With insertable objects, your Office 97 documents, such as Excel worksheets or Word documents, can appear embedded in a foreign application's documents. These inserted objects appear to be a normal part of the document in which they are embedded. In fact, when you print a document that contains an inserted object, it is usually impossible to tell from the hard copy that the data in question is an inserted object. The true power of an inserted object, however, becomes apparent when you open the host document in its host application. Having done so, when you click any part of the embedded object, the application associated with the embedded object seems to take over for the host application. The menu structure changes to that of the embedded objects' host application, and you can work with the embedded object as if you were running its host application. When an application is running in another application as an insertable object, the application is known as an OLE Server.

To add an insertable object to your project, follow these steps:

1. Select as the active object any form in your project.

2. Choose Tools, Additional Controls from the menu. The Additional Controls dialog box appears (refer to Figure 42.10).

3. Be sure the Insertable Objects check box is selected and clear the Controls and the Selected Items Only check boxes.

4. Choose the object to add to your project by choosing the edit box beside the object's name.

5. Choose OK. The object appears in the Toolbox.

VBA and OLE Automation

Many applications available today know about and take advantage of OLE. This means that they expose themselves and their data via OLE automation to other applications and development environments. So, how does this work?

When it is installed into Windows 95 or Windows NT, an OLE application registers itself with the operating system. The list of OLE servers installed on a platform is available to any application that wants it. VBA displays the list of applications registered in the References dialog box.

Because a VBA project is hosted by a particular application, a reference to that application's objects is automatically added to any VBA project. For example, if you are building a VBA project from Word, you needn't do anything to use Word objects. If you want to reference objects in Outlook or Excel, you have to add references to those applications.

Doing so makes the host aware of the objects in the other application. The reference is stored in a file known as a *type library* or an *object type library*. The files may end with the extension TLB or OLB. These references may also be stored in a DLL or EXE file.

To add a reference to an OLE automation object in a VBA project, follow these steps:

1. Choose Tools, References from the menu. The References dialog box appears (see Figure 42.14).

2. Scroll through the list to locate the reference you want to add. Choose the reference by clicking the check box.

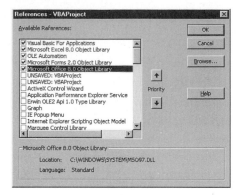

FIG. 42.14
The VBA editor shows you the code created when you record a macro.

3. If you cannot find the reference you're looking for, choose the Browse button. Browse through your system to find the object library that stores the application objects you're interested in (files that have an extension of OLB, TLL, DLL, or EXE). Choose OK.

4. Choose OK from the References dialog box.

Understanding Object Models

As you learned earlier, VBA takes advantage of OLE automation technology. This means you can use objects exposed by other applications in VBA projects you build for *other* applications. For example, in Word 97, you can manipulate Excel 97 and data stored in Excel 97 worksheets by working with Excel's objects. As you might expect, however, the structure and makeup of the objects exposed by Excel will differ significantly from that of other applications, such as PowerPoint or Office Binder. What does this mean? Well, the objects exposed by one application and the way these objects interact with each other differ as much as the actual applications do. For example, an Excel workbook contains worksheets, and each worksheet can be of a few different types (dialog box, worksheet, chart). There is no comparable set of relations in Word, PowerPoint, or Visio, so their object models must differ from that of Excel's. Understanding these object models will help you understand how to manipulate these applications programmatically either from the host application or from another application. Each application that exposes its data and functionality via OLE Automation will provide documentation that describes how the objects work together. This documentation might be in the form of a printed manual, online Help, a sample application, or a combination of each. An example of how these objects are used in code and to develop solutions is provided in the following "Techniques from the Pros" Section.

Techniques from the Pros

by Paul Sanna

Paul Sanna is a Project Manager in the development department of Hyperion Software, Stamford, CT, where he works on the company's line of client/server financial accounting software.

Real World Programming with VBA

Now that you have been introduced to the basics (and more) on VBA, it's time to show you how you can use the tool in real-world situations. This section looks at how you would use VBA to program two different types of applications:

- Microsoft Excel
- The Win32 API

These applications vary such that you will gain an understanding of the different types of solutions you can build and tasks you can complete using VBA. Excel is an extremely feature-rich and complicated application and one of the focal points of the Microsoft Office suite. Learning how to program Excel will serve as a great model for working with the other applications, such as Word and Microsoft Office Command Bars. Using the Win32 API is a great way to add powerful functionality to your VBA solution, so you should definitely benefit from the hints and strategies included here for programming the API. There certainly isn't room enough to exhaustively cover programming Excel and the API, but you definitely should understand what is possible and how to accomplish similar tasks.

N O T E For a complete reference on Visual Basic for Applications, which includes full chapters on Excel, the Win32 API, and a number of other VBA applications, see Que's *Special Edition, Using Visual Basic for Applications.* ■

Programming Microsoft Excel

The Excel object model is large, but well-organized and easy to use. This section walks you through the use of the important objects in the model and shows you how to program and integrate them to create VBA solutions for Excel applications.

Part
VII

Ch
42

Working with the Excel Application Object   The Excel application object gives you access to the top level objects in the Excel class hierarchy. As such, you can control elements of the application via the object, such as display of the status bar, formula bar, behavior of the application after the user presses Enter, as well as information about the Excel installation (path, version).

The following code snippet shows that you can control the Excel application using the object. You'll notice that the first few lines of the snippet create an instance of the Excel application. This is done by using the CreateObject keyword to reference an object class, in this case the class being an Excel application.

```
Dim objExcelApp As Excel.Application
Set objExcelApp = CreateObject("Excel.Application")

objExcelApp.DisplayStatusBar = False
objExcelApp.DisplayFormulaBar = False
objExcelApp.MoveAfterReturn = True
MsgBox objExcelApp.Path
objExcelApp.Visible = True
```

You can use the Application object to launch certain tasks in the application, such as displaying dialog boxes or simply shutting down. In the following code excerpt, an instance of Excel is started, is made visible to the user, the File Open dialog box is displayed, and the application shuts down with no warnings provided to the user:

```
Dim objExcelApp As Excel.Application
Set objExcelApp = Excel.Application

objExcelApp.Visible = True
objExcelApp.FindFile
objExcelApp.DisplayAlerts = False
objExcelApp.Quit
```

Finding a Running Excel Application   The examples in the previous section created an instance of Excel when run. It may be likely, however, that Excel is already running when your user VBA project is launched, either automatically or by the user. If the VBA project is launched by an application other than Excel, then you may need to create an Application object based on the running instance of Excel rather than create a new one. You create an Application object based on a running instance of an application using the GetObject statement. Here is an example:

```
Dim objExcelApp As Excel.Application
Set objExcelApp = GetObject("", "Excel.Application")
```

Using the Workbooks Collection Object   The Workbooks collection object is used to work with all of the workbooks opened in the Excel application. As an example, the following code snippet would print the name of each opened workbook in the current Excel application to the Immediate window:

```
For Each x In Workbooks
    Debug.Print x.Name
Next
```

You can also use the Workbook object to create a new workbook in Excel that the user can see and use:

```
Workbooks.Add
```

Or to open a specific workbook, such as one named "BUDGET.XLS":

```
Workbooks.Open(Filename:="c:\budget.xls")
```

Or to get the total number of workbooks opened in the Excel application:

```
Dim iCount as integer
iCount = Workbooks.Count
```

One of the most important tasks for the Workbooks collection object is to programmatically return a Workbook object that you can use in your VBA code. You'll see how to do that soon, but first you'll see why a Workbook object is so important.

Using a Workbook Object   The Workbook object gives you access to any of the data in the Workbook. This refers to worksheets and charts, as well as the other types of Workbook components allowed in Office 97, namely Excel version 4.0 macros and Excel version 5.0 dialog boxes. Primarily, though, you'll use the Workbook object to do the following:

- Add a worksheet or chart
- Access a specific worksheet or chart
- Delete a specific worksheet or chart

In addition, the Workbook object gives you access to useful methods unrelated to charts and worksheets, such as AddToFavorites, which add the workbook to the list of favorite documents in Windows 95 or Windows NT, some of the document mailing and routing features built into Microsoft Office applications, as well as Save, Save As, and Print functions.

Creating a New Workbook   Your VBA project may require a new workbook to be created. Keep in mind, however, that if all you need is a work area on a spreadsheet, you can create a new worksheet on an existing one. This saves you the overhead of creating a new workbook, which is really a file. If you need a new workbook, however, you create one using the Workbooks collection object. By calling the Add method for the WorkBooks collection, a new empty Workbook object is created:

WorkbookObject = WorkbooksCollectionObject.**Add( )**

Part
VII

Ch
42

Here is how the `Add` method appears in code when used with the WorkBooks collection object:

```
Dim objExcelApp As Excel.Application
Dim wbMyWorkBook As Workbook

Set objExcelApp = Excel.Application
Set wbMyWorkBook = objExcelApp.Workbooks.Add
```

The `Add` method not only creates a new Workbook object for you to work with, but also a new Workbook in the application. If the Application's `Visible` property is `True`, the user will see this workbook appear on-screen.

Opening an Existing Workbook   There may be occasions in your Excel VBA projects that you are required to work with an existing workbook. This workbook may be one that already is loaded into Excel by the user, or it may be stored somewhere on disk. You use the `ActiveWorkBook` property to refer to the current workbook in the current Excel application. Almost any property, method, or event applicable to the Workbook object also is applicable to the `ActiveWorkbook`. The following code demonstrates use of `ActiveWorkbook`. When run, the code adds a new worksheet to the current workbook, names it "Lemon," and then the entire workbook is saved with the name "FRUIT.XLS."

```
ActiveWorkbook.Sheets.Add
ActiveWorkbook.ActiveSheet.Name = "Lemon"
ActiveWorkbook.SaveAs ("C:\FRUIT.XLS")
```

The workbook you need to work with might not already be loaded into Excel. If not, you'll have to open that workbook using the `Open` method. The following code excerpt shows how you might check all of the workbooks in the running instance of Excel for a particular workbook, and if the workbook isn't found, load the workbook into Excel:

```
Public Sub CheckForAndOpen(sFileName as String)
    bFound As Boolean
    If (Right$(sFileName, 4) <> ".XLS") Then
        sFileName = sFileName + ".XLS"
    End If

    bFound = False
    For Each wb In Workbooks
        If wb = sFileName Then
            bFound = True
        End If
    Next

End Sub
```

Working with Existing Worksheets   After you have selected and then have either opened or created an object for a workbook, you'll most likely want to work with a worksheet. The worksheet is probably the most important component of Excel because it is the component you use to work with data. As you probably know, a workbook contains worksheets, so in order to work with a worksheet, you must specify the one you want to use or create a new one.

As with workbooks, there are a number of ways to specify the worksheet you want to work with. The first method we'll look at is using the Worksheets collection object and the index of the worksheet:

Worksheets(*index*)

The index specifies the number of a worksheet. The index also corresponds to the order in which the worksheet names appear at the bottom of the workbook. The following code snippet would specify "Lemon" as the name of the second worksheet in the current workbook:

```
ActiveWorkbook.Worksheets(2).Name = "Lemon"
```

You may also specify a worksheet by name. Because a worksheet name is a string, you must enclose the name of the worksheet in quotes when you refer to it:

```
Worksheets("Fruit")

Worksheets("Nuts")
```

Because the Worksheets object is a collection object, you can easily walk though all the worksheets in a workbook to locate a specific one:

```
For Each x in Worksheets
    If x.name "SALAD" then
    Degug.print "I found my worksheet"
    End If
Next
```

Adding a New Worksheet   You can add a new worksheet from code using the Worksheets collection object and the Add method. You can specify the number of worksheets to add, as well as the position. Here is how the Add method works:

Worksheets.Add([before:=*worksheet***(,)]**
[after:=*worksheet***(,)] [count:=***num_sheets***(,)]**
[type:=*sheet_type***])**

The Before and After parameters specify placement of the new worksheet. You would specify either a number for a worksheet or the worksheet name itself. This is shown later in the example code. If you do not specify either parameter, the new worksheet is added before the active worksheet in the workbook. The Count parameter can be used to specify the number of worksheets to add. The default is one. Last, the Type parameter is used to specify the type of worksheet to be added. Possible values are xlWorksheet, lExcel4MacroSheet, and xlExcel4IntlMacroSheet.

The following example adds a new worksheet before the current sheet:

```
Worksheets.Add
```

The following example adds a new worksheet after a worksheet named "Nuts":

```
Worksheets.Add (after: Worksheets("Nuts"))
```

The following example adds a new worksheet after the last worksheet in the workbook:

```
Worksheets.Add (after: Worksheets.Count)
```

The following example adds three new worksheets before the first worksheet in the workbook:

```
Worksheets.Add count: 3
```

Moving a Worksheet   There may be a situation in which you want to change the order of the worksheets in a workbook. This affects the order in which the worksheet tabs are shown at the bottom of the workbook. You move a Worksheet using the Move method, and you must also use either the After or Before qualifier to specify where you want the worksheet to appear. The following code would move the second worksheet before the first:

```
Worksheets(2).Move (Before:(Worksheets(1))
```

This next example moves the worksheet named "Fruit" after the worksheet named "Nuts":

```
Worksheets("Fruit").Move (After:Worksheets("Nuts"))
```

N O T E   You should understand the difference between the Worksheets collection object and the Sheets collection object. The Worksheets collection returns all the worksheets in a workbook. The Sheets collection, however, returns all the sheets in a workbook, which includes charts as well as worksheets. Use the Sheets collection to work with all the possible types of sheets that may be included in a workbook. ■

Specifying Cells on a Worksheet with the Range Object   Now that you know how to gain access to Excel from code, and how to specify a workbook to work with and then a worksheet, its time to look at how you navigate through the cells on a worksheet to create ranges of cells. Unless you work with only one cell on a worksheet, you will primarily use a Range object. A *Range object* is used to specify one cell, a selection of cells, one row, one column, or all the cells on a worksheet. The Range object takes as a parameter some value that describes the cells on the worksheet that compose the range.

In this example, the Range object points to one cell on the worksheet, specifically its R1C1 reference:

```
Range("B2")
```

As you certainly know, a range can be more than one cell. The following code example shows how a range object specifies a range of 25 cells:

```
Range("A1:E5")
```

Another format for specifying a range of cells using the Range object is with a comma. This allows you to pass in the dimensions of a range without using the R1C1 convention. You can also use an R1C1 reference if you choose. In the following example, say that *x* refers to cell A1 and *y* refers to cell F5. Each use of the Range object refers to the same cell range:

```
Range("A1",F4")
Range("A1:F4")
Range(x,y)
```

In Excel, ranges may have a name that the user specified. You can also specify a name for a range in code. The following code excerpt shows how to specify a named range:

```
Range("BudgetRange")
```

> **N O T E** In the previous few examples, the Range object was used without an object, such as Worksheet(2). Whenever Range is used alone, the active worksheet is used as the context. If you need the Range property to refer to a range on a worksheet other than that which is current, you need to specify the object first, such as
>
> Workbooks(2).Worksheets("Budget").Range("a2").

Specifying Cells on a Worksheet with the Cells Property

Another method for working with cells on a worksheet is with the `Cells` property of the Application object. The `Cells` property takes as parameters the row number of the cell and the column number of the cell.

The following use of the `Cells` property refers to cell A1:

```
Worksheets(1).Cells(1,1)
```

In the following example, cell E5 is returned:

```
Worksheets(1).Cells(5,5)
```

The `Cells` property also can be used to help walk through all of the cells in a range. You saw earlier in this chapter how the `For Each` construct is used to step through all the objects in a collection. In the following example, the `For Each` construct is used to print the value of each cell in a range to the Immediate window.

```
For Each x In Worksheets(1).Range("A1:E5").Cells
    Debug.Print x.Value
Next
```

Working with Cells in a Range   In the previous section, you learned how to move through each cell in a range. You can do so using the `Cells` property or a Range object. As long as you have a reference to each cell in a range, you can do what you like with the cell. For example, in the following code excerpt, each cell in the range is formatted as a decimal value with four places of precision:

```
For Each x In Worksheets(1).Range("A1:E5").Cells
    x.NumberFormat = "0.0000"
Next
```

In fact, almost any task you can execute on a cell manually can be reproduced in code. This includes setting the value of the cell, copying its value, formatting it, or executing a function on it.

Here are a few more examples of specifying values for cell contents.

In the first example, you'll set the value of a cell to 200:

```
Worksheets(3).Range("e3").Value = 200
```

In the next example, you'll enter a value that increments by 1 for each of the 25 cells that value is input to. Also, every other cell in the range will be formatted as Bold:

```
Dim iCounter As Integer
Dim iBoldFlag As Boolean
iCounter = 1
iBoldFlag = True
For Each MyCell In Range("A1:E5")
    MyCell.Value = iCounter
    MyCell.Font.Bold = iBoldFlag
    iCounter = iCounter + 1
    If iBoldFlag Then
        iBoldFlag = False
    Else
        iBoldFlag = True
    End If
Next
```

Last, you'll see how to input a formula into a cell simply by using the `Formula` property of a range object.

```
Worksheets(2).Range("E5").Formula = "-AVERGAE("E1:E4")
```

Understanding Where to Look Next   There certainly is much information to cover if the topic is programming Excel, certainly more than can be presented at the end of a chapter. Hopefully from this section you learned not only how to work with workbooks, worksheets, and ranges, but also understand how application objects work with each other and spawn one another. The interaction you saw between Excel objects is very similar to how Access, Word, Project, and PowerPoint VBA work. No, the objects are not the same, but the idea of creating objects from other objects is consistent.

You'll also find that the object libraries for many VBA applications, including Word, PowerPoint, Project, and Access, expose building block type objects as Excel does with workbooks, worksheets, and ranges, as well as all the bells and whistles you need to extend your VBA projects. The best advice available for working with VBA in other applications is to study the object library. The object hierarchy is usually represented somehow in the application's VBA help file. By understanding how objects are created and what functionality they have, you can build your VBA solution more easily.

Using the Win32 API with VBA

Although VBA includes a wide range of functions and features to help you solve problems in code, VBA cannot match in power or range the functions of the Win32 API. You can enhance the functionality and features in your VBA application by using services provided in the Win32 API. This means you can use in your program the same services and functions that Windows programs, as well as Windows 95 and Windows NT themselves, take advantage of. With this power comes some risk. Using these functions requires special care; it's easy to crash your VBA application or even Windows if you do not properly use the routines provided in the API. We'll take a look in this section at using Win32 API services in your VBA project.

Understanding What the Win32 API Is   One of the key terms to understand in this section is API. The acronym API stands for *a*pplication *p*rogramming *i*nterface. An API is always associated with some application. For example, Microsoft Excel has an API, as does Lotus Organizer and many other applications. Most programs you use today have an API. Software developers do not buy or acquire APIs for their products; they build them while they build their products. An API is used to allow some external program access to the program that provides the API. This means that you can access the functionality in one program from another via the host application's API. By providing an API, a software developer allows other developers the opportunity to use the services and functionality in the program, usually without going through the user interface of the program.

APIs are not used solely by external applications, however. Many large applications use an API to allow one part of the program to communicate with another part. If a suite of serviced or helper functions core to a larger application have been built, it is common to see API developed in order to ease development of the rest of the application. This API might also provide access to external applications.

You've seen how APIs are used, but you still need to understand what exactly an API is. An API is usually nothing more than a set of functions that provide access to some of the operations and services a program can provide. The Win32 API provides access to almost all Windows functionality. The Win32 API is the API that holds Windows 95 and Windows NT together. The Win32 API helps Windows 95 and Windows NT use memory, access devices such as printers, respond when the user clicks the mouse, paint lists and buttons on-screen, and more. The Win32 API is of the type of API described earlier that supports both the application that it rests upon, as well as other applications.

Understanding Dynamic Link Libraries   The Win32 API is presented in the form of dynamic link libraries. These libraries store all the functions and services that Windows NT and Windows 95 make available to other applications. Dynamic link libraries get their name because applications can link to them on-the-fly at runtime, using their services whenever they need to. Dynamic link libraries differ from statically linked libraries, in which the interface to the external libraries some program might use are built into the product when it is compiled. A software developer can build an application that will access a DLL even if no programming has begun on that DLL. As long as the calling program knows the name of the function, the library where the function will live, and the arguments that the function will require, it can build its program to access that dynamic link library.

Dynamic link libraries come in many shapes and sizes. Many dynamic link libraries have an extension of DLL. Others have an extension of EXE. The following files make up the majority of the Win32 API: Comdlg32.dll, Dlllz32.dll, Gdi32.dll, Kernel32.dll, User32.dll, Version.dll.

When you use VBA to program the Win32 API, you work with functions found in these files. You needn't worry about the names of these files or their location for now.

The value of the Win32 API is that it gives you capabilities in your program beyond those of VBA or the application hosting your VBA application. You can use in your VBA project the same services that Windows 95 or Windows NT uses. These services range from managing memory and creating windows to changing the system time. You may find that only 1 percent of all of the functions exposed in the Win32 API would be appropriate for use in your VBA projects, but keep in mind that almost 100 percent of the functions in the API are available to you.

Understanding How to Declare a Routine   Before you can use a Win32 API function or subroutine, you must declare it. Declarations are inserted into the General section of any module. You can create a separate module simply to store your declarations. It may be useful to group all of the declarations, as well as associated data type constructs and constants, in one module.

When you declare a function, you tell VBA the following three pieces of information:

- The DLL in which the function is stored
- The parameters and type that VBA will pass to the function
- The type of value the function call will return to VBA

It is critical that you correctly declare the routine(s) in the API. When you access a routine in a dynamic link library outside the scope of your VBA-host application, you are in a position to modify and use memory that may be used by other applications or by the operating system. Considering this, mistakes can result in a wide range of behavior in your code—from an error message being displayed to crashing your operating system.

The following code snippet shows examples of some Win32 API function declarations:

```
Declare Function GetWindowsDirectory Lib "kernel32" Alias
"GetWindowsDirectoryA" (ByVal lpBuffer As String, ByVal nSize As Long) As
Long

Declare Function GetSystemDirectory Lib "kernel32" Alias
"GetSystemDirectoryA" (ByVal lpBuffer As String, ByVal nSize As Long) As
Long

Declare Function GetTempPath Lib "kernel32" Alias "GetTempPathA" (ByVal
nBufferLength As Long, ByVal lpBuffer As String) As Long

Declare Function SetCurrentDirectory Lib "kernel32" Alias
"SetCurrentDirectoryA" (ByVal lpPathName As String) As Long
```

N O T E You can save yourself much declaration work by acquiring a file named WIN32API.TXT. This file includes declarations for VB for all Win32 API functions. This file is available from many sources, including the shipping version of Visual Basic. It is also included with the Office 97 Resource Kit. This file also includes any data structure or constants that the API functions require. The file is too large to include in its entirety in every VBA project, so you must copy the declaration and any data types or constants you need. ■

Understanding Parts of the Declaration   In order to properly use a declaration in your VBA project, you should understand the different parts of a declaration. Here is a breakdown of a Win32 API declaration:

> **Declare Function|Sub** *name* **Lib** *"library name"* **[Alias** *"aliasname"*] **(arguments) [As** *return_datatype*]

The next few sections look specifically at each section of the procedure declaration.

Understanding Functions and Subroutines   Naturally, the Win32 API includes both functions and subroutines. Depending on the type of routine in the Win32 API you're using, you'll declare either a subroutine or a function. The following code snippet shows two Win32 API procedure declarations, the first for a subroutine, the second for a function.

```
Declare Sub GetSystemTime Lib "kernel32" Alias "GetSystemTime" (lpSystemTime
As SYSTEMTIME)

Declare Function VerLanguageName Lib "kernel32" Alias "VerLanguageNameA"
(ByVal wLang As Long, ByVal szLang As String, ByVal nSize As Long) As Long
```

Notice that the first declaration uses the Sub keyword after the Declare keyword. This means that this function will not return a value.

Notice in the second declaration the word Function used after the Declare keyword. This means that this procedure will return a value. At the end of the second declaration, you should notice the As Long phrase. This means that the function will return a long data type. Every function will specify a return data type, and when you call the function, you should return its value to the appropriate data type.

A critical part of a declaration for a Win32 API routine is specifying the library in which the routine is located. The library is nothing more than the dynamic link library in which the procedure is stored. You usually don't have to guess in which library the function is stored. You specify the library name in quotes following the Lib keyword. You usually do not need to specify the extension of the library name or its location. If you use the WIN32API.TXT file described above, you needn't worry about properly specifying the file.

N O T E When you call a Win32 API function, VBA will look first in the directory where the application is running for the library, and then it will look in the System subdirectory (System32 for Windows NT) of the Windows directory. If VBA cannot find the library in the System/System32 directory, it will look next in the main Windows directory. You won't have to worry about the location of these files, however, unless you move files out of the Windows directory, which certainly is not recommended under any circumstances. ▪

Understanding By Reference and By Value in Arguments The toughest and most critical aspect to declaring calls to a Win32 API function is the argument list. The Win32 API is built for use primarily with the C programming language, and because you are accessing its routines from the Visual Basic language, you need to take care with certain issues. The first area to look at is the difference between declaring variables either by reference or value.

Most of the API procedures you'll call from VBA will require arguments to be passed. By default, VBA passes arguments to DLLs *by reference*. This means that instead of providing to the procedure being called a *copy* of the variable, VBA passes the 32-bit *address in memory* of the variable. With the address of the variable, the procedure can access and/or modify the variable without creating a copy of it. In contrast, because the Win32 API is used primarily with the C language, the API uses the C language convention of functions expecting most parameters to be specified *by value*. This means that, by default, DLL procedures expect the parameter received to be a *value*, not an *address*. This is the case for parameter types except for strings and arrays, which are always passed to DLLs by reference. All this stated, certain API function insist parameters be passed by reference.

The following declaration demonstrates how parameters are passed in different methods:

```
Declare Function ReadFile Lib "kernel32" Alias "ReadFile" (ByVal
hFile As Long, lpBuffer As Any, ByVal nNumberOfBytesToRead As Long,
lpNumberOfBytesRead As Long, lpOverlapped As OVERLAPPED) As Long
```

So what does this mean to you? This means that you must carefully specify in the declaration of any procedure function how each parameter will be passed.

Specifying Strings as Parameters in Declarations

Passing strings as parameters is a bit tricky. As stated earlier, dynamic link libraries expect strings to be passed as reference. This reference points to the address of the first byte in memory of the string. This stated, you still declare the string variable with the ByVal keyword. When VBA passes a string reference to a dynamic link library function, it converts the string into a form that a C function understands—one with a Null character terminating the end of the string. The following code snippet shows a typical Win32 API function with strings as parameters.

```
Declare Function CreateProcess Lib "kernel32" Alias "CreateProcessA"
(ByVal lpApplicationName As String, ByVal lpCommandLine As String,
lpProcessAttributes As SECURITY_ATTRIBUTES, lpThreadAttributes As
SECURITY_ATTRIBUTES, ByVal bInheritHandles As Long, ByVal dwCreationFlags
As Long, lpEnvironment As Any, ByVal lpCurrentDriectory As String,
lpStartupInfo As STARTUPINFO, lpProcessInformation As PROCESS_INFORMATION)
As Long
```

Testing Your Declaration

When you think you have your declaration properly written, you should test it. To test the declaration, you simply run any routine in the module where the declaration is written. Doing so will indicate any problems you might have in the declaration, as well as any constants you may have missed in setting up the declaration. The routine that you run needn't be a completed routine or even one you plan to use in your application. The routine can do as little as setting the value of a variable, as the following code snippet demonstrates. The point of the routine is simply to check the declarations.

```
Public Sub CheckDex()
    X=1
End Sub
```

Part

VII

Ch

42

Calling a Win32 API Routine   After you have added the declarations for the Win32 API routines you want to use, you need to program the call to the routine. Calling a function from the Win32 API is no more complicated than calling a function or subroutine that you have written. The most important considerations you have are:

■ Properly declare variables you'll use in the routine.

■ Properly work with the values returned from the function.

The following listing demonstrates the proper calling of a function:

```
' GetDriveType return values
Public Const DRIVE_REMOVABLE = 2
Public Const DRIVE_FIXED = 3
Public Const DRIVE_REMOTE = 4
Public Const DRIVE_CDROM = 5
Public Const DRIVE_RAMDISK = 6
Declare Function GetDriveType Lib "kernel32" Alias "GetDriveTypeA"
(ByVal nDrive As String) As Long

Public Sub DisplayDriveType()

    Dim sDriveLetter As String
    Dim lDriveType As Long

    sDriveLetter = "F"

    lDriveType = GetDriveType(sDriveLetter)
    Select Case lDriveType
        Case DRIVE_REMOVABLE
            Debug.Print "Drive ", sDriveLetter, " is removable."
        Case DRIVE_FIXED
            Debug.Print "Drive ", sDriveLetter, " is fixed."
        Case DRIVE_REMOTE
            Debug.Print "Drive ", sDriveLetter, " is remote."
        Case DRIVE_CDROM
            Debug.Print "Drive ", sDriveLetter, " is a CD-ROM."
        Case DRIVE_RAMDISK
            Debug.Print "Drive ", sDriveLetter, " is a RAM disk."
        Case Else
            Debug.Print "Problem with function call."
    End Select
End Sub
```

Here are some of the specifics you should understand about this example code:

■ A string is properly passed to the function.

■ A long variable is dimmed to receive the return value from the function.

■ The Select Case construct properly deals with all of the possible return values based on the Constant definitions, including an error condition.

Passing Strings as Return Parameters   One of the most critical areas to understand when you work with the Win32 API is strings. Earlier we discussed how to pass strings as parameters. In a slight variation, many Win32 API functions return a value to a string variable that was passed as an argument to the routine. In these situations, one of the parameters passed to a function is a string variable, and the function itself sets the value of the string variable.

An example of this type of function is the GetTempPath function. This function is used to determine the directory Windows uses for temporary storage of data. All Windows 95 and Windows NT installations require a temporary directory. Here is how the GetTempPath function call looks in code:

```
return = GetTempPath(PathLength, Path)
```

When this function is called, the variable you supply as the path parameter receives as a value the current temporary path. So, when the following code snippet is run, the current path is printed to the Immediate Window:

```
Return = GetTempPath(len(ThePath),ThePath)
Debug.Print ThePath
```

What you haven't seen so far, though, is one of the most critical elements to passing strings to functions that receive a value. It is critical that you define in advance the size of the string that will receive a value from the function. This keeps the function from over-writing another important piece of memory with part of your string. Doing so can result in crashing the application you're running or even the entire operating system. If you predefine the size of the string, the function will write only as much data to that string variable. The following PrintTempPath routine demonstrates how to predefine a variable string length when a function will write a value to it:

```
Public Sub PrintTempPath()
    Dim sThePath as String
    Dim iPathLength as Long
    Dim lResult as Long

    iPathLength = 256
    SthePath = String$(iPathLength,0)
    LResult = GetTempPath(iPathLength,sThePath)
End Sub
```

Understanding Return Values from the Win32 API   Most of the routines in the Win32 API are functions. This means that they return a value. The value returned might be the specific piece of data you require from the function, such as the case with the GetDriveType function shown in the code example that follows. In another case, the function simply returns a value that indicates whether the function executed properly.

Part
VII

Ch
42

An example of this type of function is the SetCurrentDirectory, which establishes the current directory for programming purposes:

```
Dim lReturn as long
LReturn = SetCurrentDirectory(C:\WORK")
```

If the function was able to set C:\QUE\WORK as the current directory, lReturn will have a value other than 0. If the function was unable to set the current directory to C:\WORK, such as if the directory does not exist, then lReturn will have a value of 0.

> **N O T E** Some functions in the Win32 API return a 0 value for success, others return 0 for failure. For an explanation of the possible return values of a Win32 API function, refer to the Win32 SDK documentation. ■

The last type of return value situation you'll look at is with functions that behave similar to both of the situations looked at so far. Some functions will write a value to a parameter you pass in, and will also return valuable information to the return value. An example of this type of function is the GetPrivateProfile function. This function is used to read information out of an INI file, which is used to store configuration information for 16-bit Windows applications:

```
Dim lSize as long
Dim strSize as long
Dim strValue as string
strSize = 256
StrValue = String$(strSize,0)
lSize =
GetPrivateProfileString("CoolApplication","ApplicationPath","",strValue,strSize,
"C:\MYINI.INI")
```

This function call will retrieve the value of the ApplicationPath key in the CoolApplication section and assign its value to the strValue variable, which is passed in as a parameter. At the same time, the lSize variable will receive as a value the length of the string assigned to strVal. If the function runs into an error, however, lSize will receive a Null value.

Working with Handles An element you will get to know well if you work with the Win32 API is the *handle*. A handle is a 32-bit integer value that uniquely identifies certain elements you work with when you program the Win32 API. When you want to work with elements such as dialog boxes, controls in them, windows, bitmaps, brushes used to paint images on-screen, hardware, and more, you usually establish a handle to the items first, and then use the handle to work with the item. You can usually tell where a handle is used in a function because its variable name begins with *h*.

In the following declaration, the second parameter, *hWnd*, is used to specify a handle to a window:

```
Declare Function GetMessage Lib "user32" Alias "GetMessageA" (lpMsg As MSG,
ByVal hwnd As Long, ByVal wMsgFilterMin As Long, ByVal wMsgFilterMax As
Long) As Long
```

And in the first parameter of the following declaration, *hDevice* is used as a handle to a device context:

```
Declare Function DeviceIoControl Lib "kernel32" Alias "DeviceIoControl"
(ByVal hDevice As Long, ByVal dwIoControlCode As Long, lpInBuffer As Any,
ByVal nInBufferSize As Long, lpOutBuffer As Any, ByVal nOutBufferSize As
Long, lpBytesReturned As Long, lpOverlapped As OVERLAPPED) As Long
```

As a VBA programmer, there is nothing special you need to do when working with a handle except remember how one is used: you will typically use one function to return a handle to some item, and then you'll use that handle to work with that object in future functions. ●

Part
VII

Ch
42

P A R T

VIII

Internets, Intranets, and Workgroups

CHAPTER 43

Hyperlinks Between Documents

by Conrad Carlberg

*H*yperlinks. The word conjures Star Trek images of Vulcans melding minds while starships speed across galaxies at Warp Nine and Scottish engineers warn, "She can't take much more, Cap'n!"

If only hyperlinks were that dramatic. Of course, they're much more prosaic. Office hyperlinks are just a way to jump from one document to another, exactly as you would do on the World Wide Web.

Still, hyperlinks are extremely useful. They give you an opportunity to link one document to another in ways that other linking methods do not. They enable you to send messages to other people concerning the document: questions, perhaps, or commentary. They let you tailor the appearance of a document so that a user who is unfamiliar with the Office environment can easily navigate to other files. And they can take you directly to locations such as a Web site or a local area network file. ■

Using hyperlinks

Enable yourself and other users to jump directly from one document to another.

Hyperlinks in combination with Excel functions

Use Excel's new HYPERLINK function to exert more control over a hyperlink's behavior.

Communications by means of hyperlinks

Enable e-mail from inside a document to a specified recipient.

Creating hyperlinks automatically

Cause an Office 97 application to recognize and create hyperlinks on your behalf.

Enabling Hyperlinks Between Local Documents

If you have read Chapter 38, "Sharing Data Between Applications with Linking and Embedding," you are familiar with the concept of linking one document to another. Figure 43.1 shows an example of a Word document with a link to an Excel document.

▶ **See** "Moving Beyond Copy and Paste to Link Information," **p. 878**

FIG. 43.1
A pasted link between the Word document and the Excel document makes it easy to keep the information current.

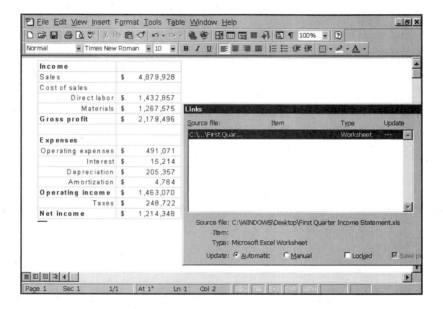

But there's a drawback to using this sort of link. You might not want to actually display the worksheet, either in row-by-column format or in icon format. You might instead find it more useful to display an instruction such as "Click here to view the income statement." Unless the user has an immediate need to see the information in the target file, displaying it can distract attention from the current document.

If clicking the "Click here" instruction in a Word document takes the user to, say, an Excel worksheet, it's termed a *hyperlink*.

It's useful to distinguish the files that are involved in the process. The file that contains the hyperlink is termed the *linked file*, and the file that the hyperlink points to is termed the *destination file*. So, the Word document that contains the hyperlink is the linked file. Clicking the hyperlink takes you to the Excel file—the destination.

Creating a Hyperlink

Suppose that you have saved the income statement shown in Figure 43.1 as INCOME STATEMENT.XLS on the Windows Desktop. To put a hyperlink to that file in a Word document, follow these steps:

1. From the Word document, choose Insert, Hyperlink (or, press Ctrl+K). The Insert Hyperlink dialog box appears, as shown in Figure 43.2.

FIG. 43.2

Use the Insert Hyperlink dialog box to specify the location of the destination file.

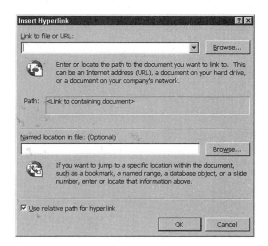

2. Choose Browse. (Be sure to choose the Browse button in the upper-right corner of the dialog box.) The Link to File dialog box appears, as shown in Figure 43.3. Navigate to the Desktop, select INCOME STATEMENT.XLS from the list of available files, and choose OK.

FIG. 43.3

You can use the Link to File dialog box if you prefer not to type the destination file's path and name.

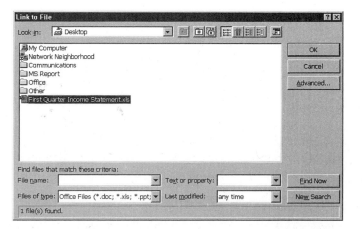

3. You are returned to the Insert Hyperlink dialog box. Choose OK. The hyperlink appears as shown in Figure 43.4.

FIG. 43.4
The hyperlink doesn't look like a standard Office link, but clicking it takes you to the destination file.

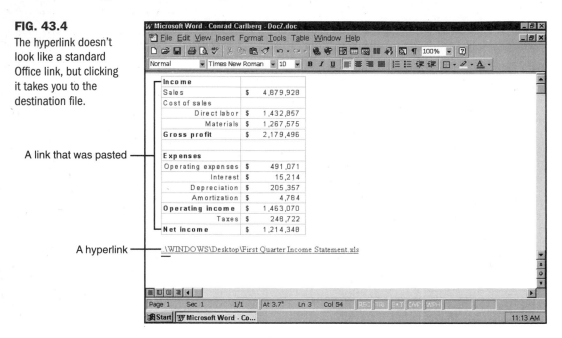

A link that was pasted

A hyperlink

In Word, the appearance of the hyperlink is governed by your choice of hyperlink Style. The default appearance uses a blue, underlined font for a hyperlink that has not yet been followed to its destination. A hyperlink that has been followed to its destination appears, again by default, in a violet, underlined font. You can change these defaults by choosing Format, Style and changing the styles for Hyperlink and Followed Hyperlink.

▶ **See** "Formatting with Styles," **p. 245**

In Word, hyperlinks are inserted as field codes. If, after inserting a hyperlink, it appears as a field code, right-click the hyperlink and choose Toggle Field Codes from the shortcut menu. You will then see the hyperlink itself.

▶ **See** "Linking Two Word Documents," **p. 883**

 You need to save the destination file before you can create a hyperlink to it. It's best also to save the linked file before creating the hyperlink.

When you paste a link to an Excel workbook, you can display the link either as a worksheet object, or as an Excel icon. But when you create a hyperlink, you have other choices:

- You can change the hyperlink text by dragging across it with your mouse pointer and typing some other label—for example, you might type **Click here to view the Income Statement**. (First make sure that the hyperlink text is displayed, not its field code.)

- You can also display the hyperlink as a graphic, as described in the next section.

- In Word, you can display the hyperlink as a cross-reference (see "Creating Hyperlinked Cross-References in Word," later in this chapter).

If you were to change the text of the hyperlink shown in Figure 43.4, the screen might appear as in Figure 43.5.

FIG. 43.5

Move the mouse pointer over the hyperlink to display its destination.

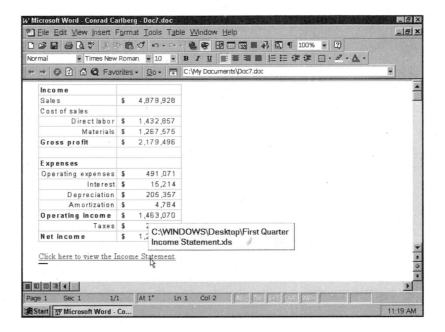

Notice that the user need not know anything about Excel or about opening pasted links in order to use the hyperlink.

When you have arrived at the destination document by clicking the hyperlink, the Office Web toolbar appears in the destination application's window. The toolbar includes a Back and a Forward button, as shown in Figure 43.6, where a hyperlink in an Excel document takes the user to a Word document. Click the Back button to return to the hyperlink; click the Forward button to return to its destination.

FIG. 43.6

The Web toolbar makes it easy to navigate hyperlinks.

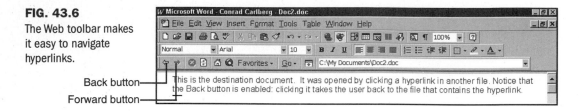

Back button

Forward button

N O T E It's important to understand that a hyperlink does not act in the same way as a pasted link. When you paste a link from one document into another, changes to the information in the source document are replicated in the link itself.

But with a hyperlink, a change made in the destination document has no effect on the hyperlink—neither in its appearance nor in its behavior. Given that the destination document still exists, and that it exists in its original location, clicking the hyperlink still takes you to it. ▪

Using a Graphic as a Hyperlink

You can make your hyperlinks more attractive and intuitive to the user by employing clip art or other graphic images, such as a JPG or GIF file, as the hyperlink. This section explains the process using PowerPoint, but the same technique works, in just the same way, in other Office applications.

Suppose that you are developing a PowerPoint presentation concerning published books. Each slide in your presentation might have information about a different book. You have, on your disk, a JPG graphic with a picture of the book's cover. With PowerPoint running and the slide active, take these steps:

1. Choose Insert, Picture, and select From File in the submenu.

2. Using the Insert Picture dialog box, navigate to the location on your disk that has stored the JPG graphics file, as shown in Figure 43.7.

3. Select the graphics file in the Name box, and choose Insert.

4. The picture appears in your PowerPoint slide. If it does not have handles indicating that it is selected, click it (see Figure 43.8).

5. Choose Insert, Hyperlink. The Insert Hyperlink dialog box appears, enabling you to associate a destination file with the presentation's graphic hyperlink. Typically, the destination document might be a Word file with detailed information about the book's contents, or an Excel file with pricing and discount information for a book retailer.

FIG. 43.7
Use the Files of type
drop-down to specify
the proper extension
for your graphics file.

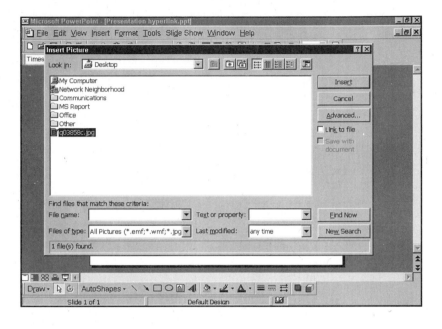

FIG. 43.8
When the picture is
selected, you can
change it to act as a
hyperlink.

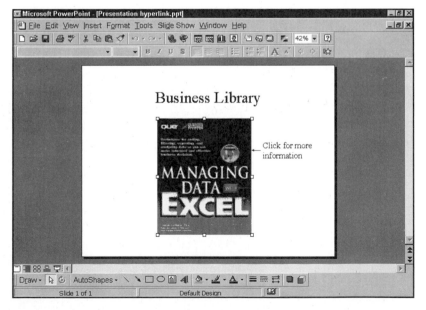

To make sure that the user understands that the graphic image is a hyperlink, you
might want to include on the slide some explanatory text such as "Click here for more
information."

N O T E A graphic used as a hyperlink cannot also be used to execute a macro. ▪

Using Relative Paths

You might have noticed the Use relative path for hyperlink check box in the Insert Hyperlink dialog box (refer to Figure 43.2). This check box is useful if you're still developing the destination document.

Suppose that you eventually plan to place your destination document on your company intranet, or on the Web. (An *intranet* is a network—frequently a local area network—that uses the same protocols such as HTTP and FTP as does the Web.) You can, if you wish, use absolute addresses for your hyperlinks. An absolute address contains the drive designation plus the folder path to the destination document: for example,

> *C:\DestinationFiles\ExcelDocs.*

But when the time comes to move the linked and destination documents onto a Web or intranet server, those absolute addresses might not be accessible. And the server might or might not regard your C: drive as its C: drive. You would have to edit all the hyperlinks to make sure that they link to the proper file locations.

You can save yourself some later headaches by making the addresses relative to some standard location that you can modify later. This standard location is termed a *hyperlink base*. In this example, your hyperlink base might be C:\DestinationFiles. Within the DestinationFiles folder, you might have a subfolder that contains Word destination files, another that contains Excel destination files, and so on.

Later, when you are ready to move the destination documents to a server, you just copy the folder DestinationFiles, its subfolders and their contents, to the server. You then change the hyperlink base to conform to the proper server address, instead of the address on your local drive.

To arrange to use relative paths, follow these steps:

1. If necessary, open your linked document—the one that contains the hyperlinks.
2. Select File, Properties and choose the Summary tab.
3. In the Hyperlink base edit box, type **C:\DestinationFiles** (or whatever location you have decided to use) and choose OK. Then, save the linked document.
4. Using Explorer, place your destination documents in subfolders within C:\DestinationFiles.

5. When you insert a hyperlink in your linked document to one of the destination files, check the Use Relative Path for Hyperlink check box. The Insert Hyperlink dialog box appears (see Figure 43.9).

FIG. 43.9
The hyperlink base appears as the Base, and the path within the base appears as the Path.

When it comes time to move the linked document and the destination document folders onto the server, use File, Properties on the linked document once again to redefine the hyperlink base—then, it might be something such as *F:\DestinationFiles*.

It takes an Office application a little longer to evaluate and open a hyperlink that's based on a relative path. When you're confident that your destination documents' locations will not change, select each of the linked document's hyperlinks in turn, choose Insert, Hyperlink, and clear its Use Relative Path for Hyperlink check box. This will speed up the process slightly.

 In Office applications, *editing* a hyperlink refers to modifying its destination. To edit a hyperlink, do not click it with the left mouse button—that takes you to the destination document. Instead, right-click the hyperlink, choose Hyperlink from the shortcut menu, and then choose Edit Hyperlink from the submenu. You can also drag across it with your mouse pointer and choose Insert, Hyperlink to display the Edit Hyperlink dialog box.

Specifying a Location in the Destination Document

The Insert Hyperlink dialog box has two Browse buttons and associated edit boxes (refer to Figure 43.2). One, Browse, is for the destination file itself. The other, Browse, is for a location within the destination file. In the case of an Excel worksheet, this interior location is a range name.

The destination, if it's an Excel file, is actually a workbook. It would not be unusual for one workbook to contain both an Income Statement and a Balance Sheet. So, you might want to create a different hyperlink for each of those locations. The way to do that is to give them different range names, and then refer to those ranges in the Named Location in File edit box. To do so, follow these steps:

1. From Excel, select the range that contains the income statement figures. Choose Insert, Name, Define and, in the Define Name dialog box, name the range *Income Statement.*

2. Repeat Step 1 for the balance sheet data.

3. Save the Excel file, and open the Word document that will contain the hyperlinks.

4. Choose Insert, Hyperlink. To place the file location in the Link to File or URL edit box, use the Browse button to navigate to the site of the Excel workbook. For the location in the Excel file, type **IncomeStatement** in the Named Location in File edit box.

5. Repeat Step 4 for the hyperlink to the BalanceSheet range. These edit box entries are shown in Figure 43.10.

6. Choose OK.

   ▶ **See** "Working with Range Names," **p. 386**

FIG. 43.10
You can target your hyperlinks even more tightly by specifying a location within a destination file.

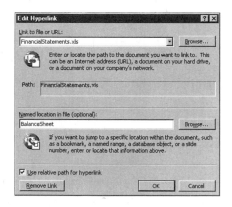

You now have two hyperlinks in the Word document. One takes the user to the Excel range that's named *Income Statement*, and the other takes the user to the range that's named *Balance Sheet*.

N O T E You can also create hyperlinks to applications that are not part of the Office suite. From the Insert Hyperlink dialog box, just navigate to a document that's associated with the application you want to open, and use that file as the hyperlink's destination. ■

Creating Hyperlinked Cross-References in Word

A hyperlink is an ideal way to help a user view a cross-reference. Suppose that you're writing a lengthy document such as a marketing plan. In the product section, you want to draw the reader's attention to a paragraph about the product's target market. You might want the cross-reference to read *See section on Market A*. It's convenient for the reader simply to click the cross-reference in order to get there. It's inconvenient to have to page back and forth looking for the section, or to use <u>E</u>dit, <u>F</u>ind.

To create a cross-reference, you must first outline your document. There are several simple ways to do this:

- By choosing <u>V</u>iew, <u>O</u>utline and increasing or decreasing indents
- By using numbered headings with F<u>o</u>rmat, Bullets and <u>N</u>umbering
- By using F<u>o</u>rmat, <u>A</u>utoFormat

Whichever method you choose, you can insert a hyperlinked cross-reference after the outline is in place. Follow these steps:

1. Select the location where you want to place the cross-reference.
2. Type some introductory text, such as **See** or **Refer to**.
3. Choose <u>I</u>nsert, Cross-<u>r</u>eference. The Cross-reference dialog box shown in Figure 43.11 appears.

FIG. 43.11
The For <u>W</u>hich Heading list box is blank if your document does not contain any instances of the item in the Reference <u>T</u>ype box.

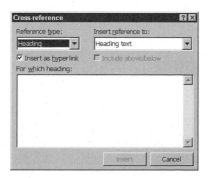

4. Click the Reference <u>T</u>ype drop-down arrow. Your choices appear, as shown in Figure 43.12.

FIG. 43.12
Your choice of reference type determines what you can insert a reference to.

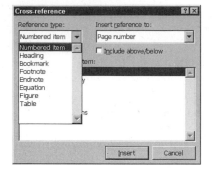

5. Suppose that you chose to number your headings using Format, Bullets and Numbering. You would choose Numbered item in the Reference Type drop-down. When you do so, the appropriate choices appear in the Insert Reference To drop-down. See Figure 43.13.

FIG. 43.13
You can choose to display numbers or text in the cross-reference.

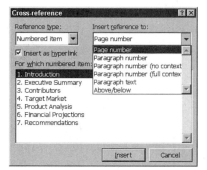

6. Choose an option from the Insert reference to drop-down.

7. Fill the Insert as Hyperlink check box.

8. If you want the cross-reference to show either the direction *above* or *below*, fill the Include Above/Below check box. This is available only if you have chosen a numbered cross-reference, such as Paragraph Number: the result might be *See 2 above*.

9. Choose Insert.

Your cross-reference is now inserted into your document as a hyperlink. Clicking it takes the user to the hyperlink's destination.

The default style for a hyperlink is underlined blue text. However, a hyperlinked cross-reference does not automatically follow that style. To make it more clear to the user that the cross-reference is a clickable hyperlink, select the hyperlink by dragging across it. Then, choose Format, Font, change the cross-reference's font Color to blue, and its Underline to Single.

N O T E Your hyperlinked cross-reference must be to a location in a Word document. If it refers to a location in another Word document, both documents must belong to the same master document. ■

Using Hyperlinks in Excel

Excel offers a special capability for its hyperlinks. This chapter has already shown you that you can insert hyperlinks into Excel worksheets just as you would with another Office document. But you can also use hyperlinks in worksheet formulas.

Particularly when a hyperlink is part of a formula, you need to be careful how you select the cell that contains the hyperlink. It's all too easy to jump to the hyperlink's destination when all you want to do is edit the hyperlink.

This section describes Excel's HYPERLINK function, and how to edit it without making an unintentional jump.

Using the HYPERLINK function

In Office 97, Excel has a new function that gives you additional control over hyperlinks in an Excel workbook. The HYPERLINK function has this syntax:

```
=HYPERLINK(Link location, Friendly name)
```

The first argument, the link location, is just the location and name of the destination file. The second argument, the friendly name, is the value that appears in the cell that contains the HYPERLINK function. See Figure 43.14 for an example.

FIG. 43.14
Use HYPERLINK's second argument to control what the hyperlinked cell displays.

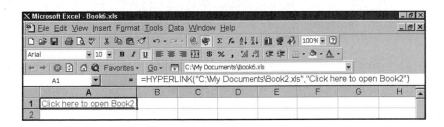

In Figure 43.14, you can see in the formula bar the path to and name of the destination file. Cell A1, where the HYPERLINK formula has been entered, displays the function's second argument—"friendly" text that explains to the user what's going on. You can enter the HYPERLINK function in a cell either by typing it directly, or by using the Function Wizard.

In many cases, you would choose to place a hyperlink in an Excel worksheet by means of Insert, Hyperlink. However, using the worksheet function version extends the hyperlink capabilities: you can use HYPERLINK in conjunction with other tools.

Suppose, for example, that you wanted to make the destination document contingent on a choice made by the user. Figure 43.15 shows an example.

FIG. 43.15
Use the HYPERLINK function to enable the user to control the hyperlink's destination.

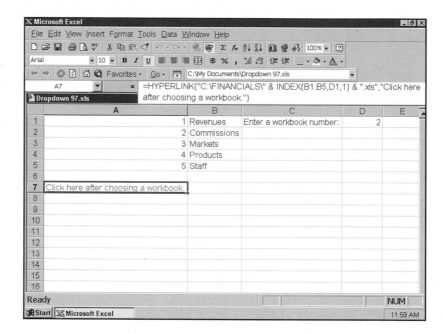

You might decide that a different hyperlink for each one of the available workbooks would clutter up the worksheet too much. So you ask the user to enter the number of the desired workbook in cell D1.

The HYPERLINK function in cell A7, as well as its arguments, appear in the formula bar in Figure 43.15. It is:

```
=HYPERLINK("C:\FINANCIALS\" & INDEX(B1:B5,D1,1) & ".xls","Click here after
    choosing a workbook.")
```

Here, the HYPERLINK function has been combined with the INDEX function to determine which book to open when the user clicks the hyperlink. This fragment:

```
INDEX(B1:B5,D1,1)
```

returns the value in B1:B5 that's identified by the value in cell D1. So, if the user enters the numeral 2 in cell D1, the INDEX function returns the second value in B1:B5, the text value "Commissions".

The formula in cell A7 evaluates the INDEX function. Assuming that the user entered 2 in D1, the formula concatenates the value it returns into the HYPERLINK function, as follows:

```
=HYPERLINK("C:\FINANCIALS\" & "Commissions" & ".XLS","Click here after
    choosing a workbook.")
```

or, equivalently:

```
=HYPERLINK("C:\FINANCIALS\Commissions.XLS","Click here after choosing a
    workbook.")
```

Of course, all the workbooks that are implied by the entries in B1:B5 must exist in the C:\FINANCIALS folder.

You could bulletproof this function a bit more by enclosing it in an IF function that restricted the user's choice to the values 1 through 5. Notice that if the user entered some other number in cell D1, the INDEX function would fail—and, therefore, so would the HYPERLINK function, because it would not receive a valid file name from INDEX.

Here's an example:

```
=IF(AND(D1>0,D1<6),HYPERLINK("C:\FINANCIALS\" & INDEX(B1:B5,D1,1) &
    ".xls","Click here after choosing a workbook."),"D1 must be >0 and <6")
```

The IF invokes the HYPERLINK function only when the user has entered a number greater than 0 and less than 6 in cell D1. Otherwise, the IF function displays D1 must be >0 and <6, as shown in Figure 43.16.

FIG. 43.16
The IF function helps to keep the user from making a mistake.

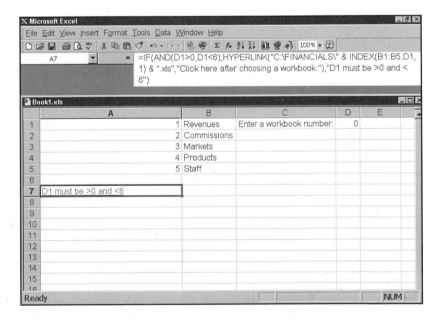

Selecting Hyperlinks in Excel Worksheets

At first, you might find it a little tricky to select a hyperlink in an Excel worksheet. It's natural to simply click the cell that contains the hyperlink—but of course that takes you to the destination document, just as intended.

In Excel, as in all Office applications that offer hyperlink functionality, you can right-click the hyperlink. This action bypasses the jump, and displays a shortcut menu; choosing the Hyperlink menu item displays a submenu, as shown in Figure 43.17.

FIG. 43.17

Right-clicking a hyperlink provides you with a variety of possible actions.

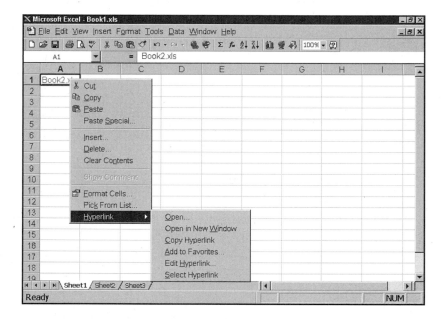

If you want to modify the hyperlink, select Edit Hyperlink from the submenu. This displays the Edit Hyperlink dialog box.

However, if you have used the HYPERLINK function, right-clicking its cell displays a shortcut menu without a Hyperlink menu item. See Figure 43.18.

So, you need another means of selecting the cell with the hyperlink. Old skills are often the best: begin by selecting a cell near the one that contains the hyperlink, and use your keyboard arrows to move to that cell. When you do so, its HYPERLINK function and arguments appear in the formula bar, and you can edit it as you see fit. If you intend simply to edit the HYPERLINK function, you can right-click its cell: so doing displays the formula in the formula bar.

FIG. 43.18
You have fewer and different options if you right-click a cell that contains the HYPERLINK function.

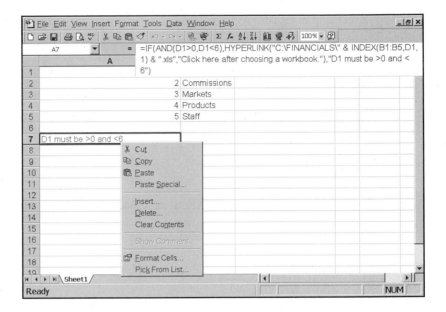

 Selecting the hyperlink in this fashion also enables you to change the text displayed by a hyperlink created with Insert, Hyperlink. When you select the cell that contains the hyperlink, its text appears in the formula bar. Just edit that text to modify what's displayed by the cell.

Sending E-Mail

Suppose that you are responsible for maintaining the information in an Income Statement. While there are generally accepted rules for maintaining the accuracy of the numbers that it reports, you have broad latitude as to the Statement's format. There are many choices available, especially when the Statement is intended to support internal management decisions, as distinct from external reporting.

You would like to provide your users with a means of informing you if they find the Statement useful as a decision-making tool. Office hyperlinks are an ideal way to provide that capability. A hyperlink need not lead simply to another document: clicking it can also invoke an e-mail program that has your e-mail address already provided for the convenience of the user.

In Word, the easiest way to do this is to set the appropriate option:

1. Choose Tools, AutoCorrect. This displays the AutoCorrect dialog box.

2. Select the AutoFormat As You Type tab.

3. Fill the Internet and Network Paths with Hyperlinks check box. This replaces an Internet Protocol address with a hyperlink when you type it.

4. Fill the same check box on the AutoFormat tab. This replaces Internet Protocol addresses with hyperlinks, whenever they are found on an existing document that you open.

Notice that when you set these options, Word will convert anything that looks like a network address, in either an existing or new document, to a hyperlink.

Figure 43.19 shows an example of how the hyperlink appears.

FIG. 43.19
This hyperlink makes it easy for the user to send questions or comments via e-mail.

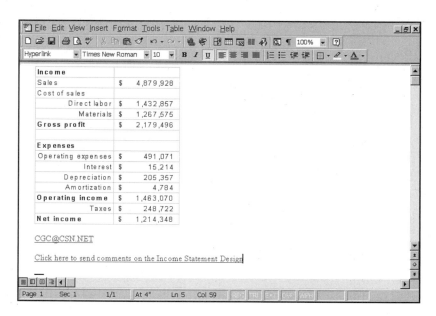

You could also insert the hyperlink yourself as a field code, using Insert, Field and typing the field code into the Field Code text box. An example is:

```
{HYPERLINK mailto:Cgc@csn.net}
```

However you enter it, you just type over the field to replace it with an instruction to the user. In the present example, you might type an instruction such as **Click here to send comments on the Income Statement design**.

If the user has an e-mail program, clicking the hyperlink displays a dialog box with the recipient's address already filled in. For example, if the user has set Microsoft Exchange as the default profile, clicking the hyperlink displays the box shown in Figure 43.20.

FIG. 43.20

All the user needs to do is type the text for the message: the hyperlink and the e-mail program handle the rest.

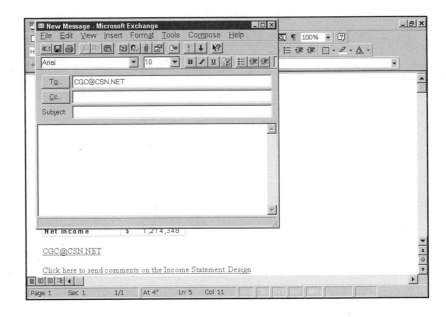

The user types a message and clicks Send. If the user is connected to an e-mail server at this point, the mail is sent. Otherwise, Exchange puts it in its Outbox for later delivery. ●

Navigating and Publishing on the Web with Office 97

by Rob Tidrow

Over the past three years, the World Wide Web has become an essential part of many businesses. Today, the Web is used to locate information, disseminate marketing and sales data, advertise products and services, and deliver software and applications. The Web and its underlying architecture also are making significant inroads in corporate and small business network infrastructure. Intranets, as these internal Webs are termed, enable employees to access company information across networks by using easy-to-use graphical browsers. Moreover, the programming language used to create Web documents (HTML) is relatively easy to learn, enabling employees throughout a company to contribute and update intranet documents.

Office 97 now includes many features that make browsing and publishing on the Web and intranet easy to do. Office 97's Web browsing features enable users to remain in one application (Word, Excel, Access, PowerPoint, or Outlook) to access information from the Web, rather than launch a separate Web browser to

Reviewing Web terminology and connection requirements

New users should get a basic understanding of the World Wide Web and Internet before jumping into these technologies.

Navigating the Web using Office 97 applications

Microsoft has focused much of its development attention on the World Wide Web over the past year, and you can see its effect on Office 97 products. All Office 97 applications have the capability to access and move through the Web.

Publishing Web documents using Office 97 applications

You'll see how easy it is to create a document for the Web using Office 97 programs like Word and PowerPoint. You'll also see how Office 97 applications, such as Excel and Access, can streamline much of the tedious HTML programming you now do to create long tables of data and dynamic data from databases.

Techniques from the Pros: Publishing a corporate policy presentation with PowerPoint

The final section in this chapter shows you how to use PowerPoint to create a corporate policy presentation that you can publish on the Web or an internal intranet.

do the job. Further, users can create Web documents by using the Web publishing features that all Office 97 applications now have. For instance, users can create a PowerPoint presentation and save it as an HTML file to publish directly to the Web or intranet, reducing the time it takes to create content to place on a site. ■

Reviewing Web Terminology and System Requirements

So much has been written about the Internet and the World Wide Web that this chapter concentrates on using Office 97 applications to navigate and publish on the Web. However, some basic terms and system requirements for connecting to the Internet are outlined here to give you an overview of what you need to know before navigating the Web. If you are a seasoned Web navigator, skip to the "Navigating the Web Using Office 97 Applications" section later in this chapter.

A Web Backgrounder

In short, the World Wide Web is part of the Internet. The Internet, which isn't an entity in and of itself, is a collection of computers and networks connected together from all over the world. The following is a list of the various parts of the Internet and short descriptions of each:

■ *World Wide Web* (*WWW or Web*). A graphical hypertext environment that presents users with Web pages from which they can read information, download files, watch videos, listen to audio files, fill out online forms, interact with applications (usually called *applets* or *scripts*), and search for information using keywords and terms. Each Web page has a unique address on the Web, which enables users to locate the page and view it with a Web browser. These addresses are known as Uniform Resource Locators (URLs, pronounced "earls") and begin with an http:// prefix, such as **http://www.microsoft.com**. An example of a Web page is shown in Figure 44.1.

■ *File Transport Protocol* (*FTP*). An Internet service that enables users to transmit (called *downloading* and *uploading*) computer files from one computer to another. Many FTP servers allow only authorized users to access the server, but some allow everyone access using *anonymous* login, which doesn't require users to have a password or login name to access the site.

■ *Gopher.* A hyperlink cataloguing system that helps users locate and download documents and files from the Internet. Gopher offers a more intuitive interface to the arcane and often intimidating interface of FTP, but lacks the browsing and graphical look of the World Wide Web. In practical terms, new Gopher servers are not being developed today.

■ *Electronic mail* (*e-mail*). A messaging service enabling users to transmit text-based messages across the Internet to other users. E-mail is one of the most widely used services on the Internet. Although e-mail messages can comprise only plain ASCII text (that is, without fancy fonts, colors, pictures, and so on), most e-mail applications enable users to send binary files with e-mail messages as attachments. Binary files are word processing documents, Pkzip files, PowerPoint slides, and software applications, and the like. You can use Microsoft Outlook and Windows Messaging to send and receive e-mail messages.

Part **VIII**

Ch

44

FIG. 44.1
Web pages display in a Web browser, such as Microsoft Internet Explorer 3.0.

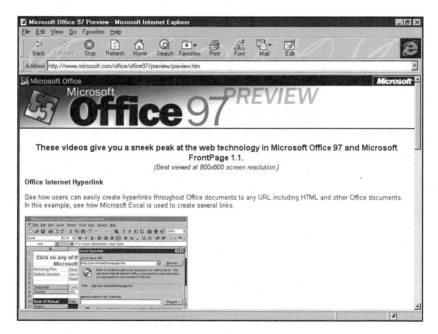

▶ **See** "Sending and Receiving Messages," **p. 1119**

■ *UseNet newsgroups.* An electronic bulletin board system organized by subject areas that enables users to read and post messages about more than 15,000 topics.

■ *Internet Relay Chat* (*IRC or chats*). Service on the Internet that enables users to communicate with another user or a group of users in real time.

A Look at System Requirements

All the software you need to get on and navigate the Web is included with Windows 95 and Office 97. With Windows 95, you get an operating system designed to let you connect to the Internet by a phone line (called a *dial-up connection*), or through a local area network (LAN) you may have at work or school that is in turn connected to the Internet. The following are the software pieces included:

- Dial-up software that enables you to dial an Internet service to connect to the Internet.

- Networking software required by all users to connect to the Internet. Regardless of whether you use a dial-up connection to get online or have a LAN connection, your system needs TCP/IP (Transmission Control Protocol/Internet Protocol) software to connect to the Internet. TCP/IP is a protocol that all computers on the Internet and Web need.

- A Web browser, in the form of Microsoft Internet Explorer (MSIE). Some pre-installed copies of Windows 95 have MSIE included. If it's not already on your computer, Office 97 includes a copy in the \VALUPACK\IEXPLORE folder and displays an icon on your desktop called Setup for Microsoft Internet Explorer 3.0.

Besides the software, you also need an Internet account, a modem (or network card if connecting through a LAN), and a phone line (or network cable).

The instructions for configuring your computer and modem, and for establishing an Internet account, are beyond the scope of this book. For detailed information on setting up your computer, see Que's *Windows 95 Installation and Configuration Handbook*. For online help in Windows 95, see the Help topic "Connecting to the Internet." The following sections assume you have an Internet and Web connection and know how to connect to the Web.

Navigating the Web Using Office 97 Applications

You can use Word, PowerPoint, Excel, and Access to view documents that have hyperlinks in them. These can be documents posted on the World Wide Web, on your computer, or on another computer in your office via an internal network called an intranet. *Hyperlinks* are text or graphics in a document that you click to go to another document, file, location in a document, or a Web page on the World Wide Web.

N O T E You also can use hyperlinks in documents to access other Internet resources, such as Gopher sites, telnet services, newsgroups, and FTP sites. ▪

To access documents on the World Wide Web using Office 97 applications, you first must have access to the Internet as outlined in the preceding section "A Look at System Requirements." The following sections show you how to open a Web document using Word, how to use hyperlinks on a document to access another Web document, and how to store and use previously accessed Web documents using Word. You can use these same steps with Excel, PowerPoint, and Access to access Web documents.

Part
VIII
Ch
44

Opening a Document on the Web

Opening a document on the Web is different from opening one on your hard drive. On your hard drive, you choose File, Open to display the Open dialog box. From this dialog box, you can browse for the file you want to open or enter the name in the File Name field. When you want to open a document located on the Web, you need to be more exact and know the name of the Web document you want to open. The name of a Web document is in the form of an *URL* (Uniform Resource Locator), which is sometimes called a *Web address*. (See "A Web Backgrounder" for more information on URLs.)

To open a document on the Web using Word 97, use the following steps:

1. Display the Web toolbar by selecting View, Toolbars, Web. Figure 44.2 shows the Web toolbar and points out each button.

FIG. 44.2
The Web toolbar is used when you want to access Web documents.

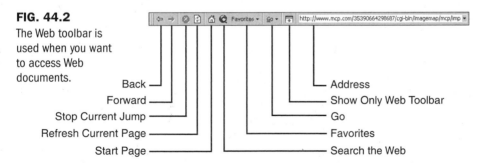

Back

Forward

Stop Current Jump

Refresh Current Page

Start Page

Address

Show Only Web Toolbar

Go

Favorites

Search the Web

2. Type the URL address in the Address box on the Web toolbar. The following example URL links you to the Que Web site:

http://www.mpc.com/que

You must type the URL exactly as shown. If an URL you want to access includes upper- and lowercase characters, be sure to match the spelling so that Word knows where to find the document on the Web.

TIP You also can select File, Open, enter an URL in the File name field, and click OK to open a Web document.

3. Press Enter. Word displays the Web document, such as the one shown in Figure 44.3. The process by which Word displays a document from the Web is called *downloading*. This means that Word receives a copy of the document from the Web by using the connection you have to the Internet, rather than opening a file stored on your local computer.

FIG. 44.3

You can use Word to display documents located on the World Wide Web.

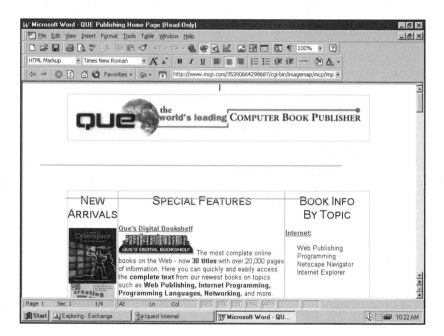

Depending on the speed of your Internet connection, how many other people are downloading the same Web document you are, and the size of the document you are accessing, the speed at which the Web document displays varies. If you connect to the Web using a high-speed connection from work (such as if your local area network is connected directly to the Internet), you should begin seeing the document almost immediately. On the other hand, if you use a modem to access the Internet, you may wait several minutes for the entire document to display. Look at the Word status bar at the bottom left of the screen to watch the status of the document that opens.

If several people download the same document (or are connected to the same Web site as you are), you may need to wait a few minutes to download the entire document. This is because the computer on which the Web document resides is busy handling your request plus the requests (sometimes hundreds or thousands of requests every minute) of other people.

Finally, the size of the Web document affects the download time. If the document contains several pages, has a number of color images, and has multimedia items like sound or animation files, the download time increases. Other special features, like buttons you can click and programming files, also increase the download time.

TIP If you want to halt the download process, click the Stop Current Jump button on the Web toolbar. Click Refresh Current Page to continue the download process or to reload the current document to view any changes made since you downloaded it.

The next section shows what you can do with the Web document in Word.

Jumping to Other Web Documents

You read earlier about how Web documents contain hyperlinks to enable you to go to another document, a location in a document, or to another Internet resource. Hyperlinks are easy to see in documents, because they generally are a different color text (usually blue text) than surrounding text and they almost always are underlined. To use a hyperlink, use the following steps:

1. Move the mouse pointer over to a hyperlink on the Web document and wait for the cursor to change to a hand pointer. For this example, move the pointer to Que's Digital Bookshelf shown earlier in Figure 44.3.

TIP Hold the mouse over the hyperlink for a moment or two to see the URL associated with the hyperlink. This is helpful if you are looking for a particular URL on a document and you are not sure which hyperlink enables you to jump to that URL.

2. Click the left mouse button. The information associated with the hyperlink displays (see Figure 44.4). This is called *jumping*.

3. To return to the original Web document (in this case, the one shown earlier in Figure 44.3), click the Back button on the Web toolbar. You then can click the Forward button to go back to the previous Web document (in this case, the one shown in Figure 44.4).

FIG. 44.4

You can click hyperlinks in Web documents to jump to other resources, such as a document that contains more information about a topic.

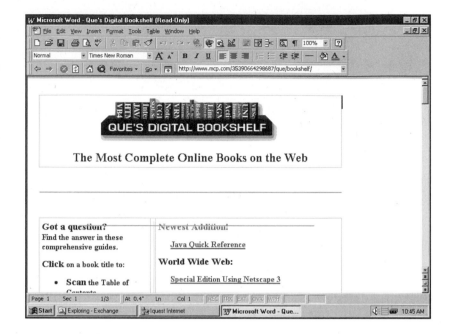

After you click a hyperlink, the color of the text and underline changes (by default it changes to purple) to indicate you've already accessed that resource. You can click that hyperlink again, or click another hyperlink to jump to a new resource.

Images also can be hyperlinked. In some cases, hyperlinked images show a thin, blue box around the image telling the viewer it is hyperlinked. In many cases, however, hyperlinked images are difficult to distinguish from nonhyperlinked images on a Web document because the author of the Web document may not add a blue box around the image. To tell whether an image is hyperlinked, move the mouse pointer on top of an image and see whether the pointer changes to a hand pointer. If it stays an arrow pointer, the image is not hyperlinked; if it changes, you can click the image to jump to another resource.

 Images on a Web document can be saved to your hard drive by right-clicking the image and selecting Hyperlink, Save As from the fly-out menu. Select Save Picture from the Save Options and click OK. If the Connect to the Internet dialog box displays, click Yes if you want to connect to the Internet to save this file (this is in case you are viewing the Web document on your computer when you are not connected to the Internet). The Save As dialog box displays. Select a drive and folder in which to save the image and click Save. You also may want to change the file name in the File Name field before saving the image.

Storing and Retrieving Previously Accessed Web Documents

As you jump from one hyperlink to another, you may find documents or resources you would like to return to in the future. Instead of memorizing or making notes of the URLs of these documents, you can save the URL to a predefined folder Office 97 creates to store URLs, called the Favorites folder. The Favorites folder is like an online address book, storing the path to a document you find on the World Wide Web. You also can store document paths for files on your hard drive or intranet.

N O T E The Favorites folder is the same one used with the Microsoft Internet Explorer 3.0 (MSIE) World Wide Web browser. You can open documents from either MSIE or an Office 97 application using the same URLs stored in the Favorites folder.

The Favorites folder is located in the Windows 95 folder on your system. ■

To add a document URL to the Favorites folder, use these steps:

1. Click the Favorites toolbar button on the Web toolbar.

2. Click <u>A</u>dd to Favorites from the drop-down menu. This displays the Add To Favorites dialog box (see Figure 44.5).

FIG. 44.5

You can save the path to a Web document, a document on your hard drive, or intranet.

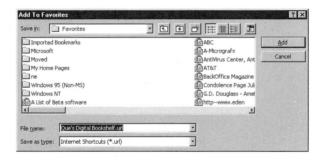

3. Click the <u>A</u>dd button. If you want to change the default name, highlight the text in the File <u>N</u>ame field and enter a new name. Be sure to use an URL extension for a document located on the Web. The name you choose is not the URL for the document, but the name that appears in the title bar when you display the document.

After you save an URL to the Favorites folder, you can access that Web document again without re-entering the URL, as you did earlier in the "Opening a Document on the Web" section. To open a document stored in the Favorites folder, use the following steps:

1. Click the Favorites toolbar button on the Web toolbar.

2. Move the mouse pointer down the list of document names in the drop-down menu and click the document you want to open.

> **N O T E** After you spend some time on the Web, you're likely to save many URLs to the Favorites
> folder. To clean out this folder, click the Favorites toolbar button and select Open
> Favorites to display the Favorites dialog box. Select a file name from the Favorites dialog box and
> press Delete. Click Yes to confirm you want to send the item to the Recycle Bin. ▪

Using the Start Page

When you use a Web browser to navigate the Web, a start page displays when you first
launch the Web browser. A start page can be a page on the Web or a document you store
locally on your hard drive. In Office 97 applications, you can display the start page by
clicking the Start Page toolbar button on the Web toolbar. By default, if you do not have
a Web browser installed on your system, the Office application attempts to display a
document located on the Microsoft Network (MSN) at the URL **http://www.home.
msn.com/**. On the other hand, the start page used by your Web browser opens in the
Office application.

Start pages usually contain a number of links to other resources to help you get started
navigating on the Web. You can create your own start page by following the instructions
on how to create a Web page shown in "Publishing on the Web with Office 97 Applications."

If the default start page doesn't suit your needs, you can change it by following these
steps:

1. Open the document (either a locally stored document or one on the Web) you want
   as your start page.

2. Select Go, Set Start Page from the Web toolbar. The Set Start Page dialog box
   appears (see Figure 44.6).

FIG. 44.6
Word enables you to
customize the start page
to one currently open.

> **N O T E** You can view the URL of your current start page in the Set Start Page dialog box under
> the line that reads `Your Start Page Is Currently`. For documents stored on your
> local hard drive, the syntax `file://C:\`*path* is used. Notice how the URL begins with file://C:\
> to indicate a document stored on your local C: drive. ▪

3. Click Yes, saving the current document as the start page. This new start page is also the start page for your Web browser, if you have one installed.

Microsoft provides some built-in links to sites on the World Wide Web in each Office 97 application. In the Help menu, select Microsoft on the Web to display a fly-out menu with a number of Web sites to help you with Office 97 problems you may encounter, where to find free items from Microsoft, and more. If you need a primer on the World Wide Web, for instance, click the Web Tutorial item. This jumps you to a document on the Web that discusses what the Web is, how to use the Web, and where to find more information about the Web.

Part

VIII

Ch

44

Searching the Web

You learned in the section "Opening a Document on the Web" that you need to know the URL of a document on the Web before you can open it in an Office 97 application. If you don't know the URL of a document, or if you want to search for a document on the Web, use the Search the Web tool. When you use this tool, the Office 97 application downloads a document that displays a number of Internet searching utilities, called search engines.

Search engines enable you to enter search criteria, such as keywords or phrases, for documents you want to locate on the Internet. When the search engine locates a document that contains the keyword or phrase, it displays a list with the name of the document and provides a hyperlink to it. Depending on the search criteria and search engine, this search list (commonly called a *hit* list) may contain zero entries or several hundred.

To perform a search on the Web, use these steps:

1. Click the Search the Web toolbar button on the Web toolbar.

2. Word (or the Office 97 application you are using) displays the Best of the Web Find It Fast Web document (see Figure 44.7).

3. Enter the keyword(s) or phrase you want to search on in the field to the left of the Search button. You might, for instance, be interested in seeing information on tornadoes. If so, enter **tornadoes** in the field.

4. Click in the option button of one of the search engines in the table below the Search button. By default, the WebCrawler item is selected.

5. Click the Search button to begin the search. Again, the speed at which the results display depends on the search engine, number of hits your search criteria generates, and your Internet connection.

6. When the search results display, click a hyperlink of a document that you want to download.

FIG. 44.7
You can use several search engines to locate documents on the Web.

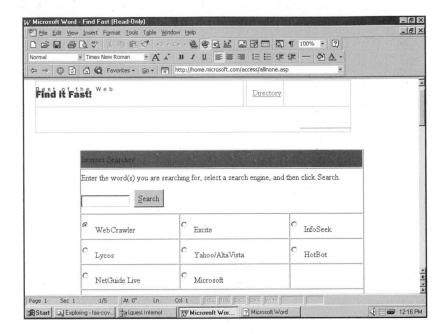

N O T E On the Best of the Web Find It Fast document are links to reference material, news, sports, health, and entertainment information. Scroll to the bottom of the document and click a hyperlink of your choice. You might, for instance, want to look up an e-mail address of a friend or business colleague. To do this, click the E-mail Address and Home Pages link and follow the on-screen instructions. ■

Publishing on the Web with Office 97 Applications

Many organizations already have content they can distribute on the Web or intranet. The problem is that in most cases the documents are in formats other than HTML, such as Word documents, Excel worksheets, and Access databases. The result is that most companies must hire developers to go through the lengthy and often-expensive process of reformatting the content into HTML documents.

Office 97 is designed to get around the problem of creating documents in two formats—one for presentations, distribution lists, memorandums, and so forth, and another for the Web. Microsoft's goal is to have every document, regardless of which application created it, ready to publish on the Web or intranet. For example, users can create a Word document as Normal and then save the file either as a Word document or an HTML file. With the number of companies publishing information on the Web and intranets escalating, the time-sink and expense of converting every document to HTML is reduced to a minimum.

N O T E The following sections show you how to create documents for the Web or intranet using each Office 97 application. Because the goal of the chapter is to describe how to use each application's Web publishing features, very little HTML-specific information is provided here.

If you need more information on HTML or would like to become more fluent in HTML, see Que's *Special Edition Using HTML.* You also can find information on every approved HTML code at the World Wide Web Consortium's Web site at **http://www.w3.org/WWW**. ■

Getting Started

The way each application in the Office 97 suite handles HTML is by including an add-in application to convert its native format to HTML format. In many installations, these add-ins are not added. To make sure the add-in application is installed on your machine, complete the following steps:

N O T E Although Word is shown in the following steps, you can perform the same general steps for the other Office 97 applications. ■

1. Select Tools, Templates and Add-Ins, to display the Templates and Add-ins dialog box. For all other applications, select Tools, Add-Ins.

2. In the list of add-ins, check the HTML.DOT and HTML.WLL items (see Figure 44.8). If these items do not show up here, click the Add button and locate the files on your system or Office 97 setup disk or CD-ROM. They are usually stored in the folder for the application you are working in.

FIG. 44.8

The Templates and Add-ins dialog box enables you to install the HTML add-in.

For applications other than Word, see Table 44.1 for the appropriate add-in.

Table 44.1	**HTML Add-in Files for Office 97 Applications**
Application	**File Name**
Excel	WEBFORM.XLA, HTML.XLA
PowerPoint	PPT2HTML.PPA
Access	Pre-installed
Word	HTML.DOT, HTML.WLL

3. Click OK to install the add-in file. In some applications, the command is Install.

You now return to the main document window and can begin saving your documents to HTML format.

Creating Web Documents in Word

For advanced HTML programmers and Web page designers, the HTML capabilities of Word may seem a bit restrictive. For the beginning Web page designer and those responsible for creating and updating large numbers of documents for a site, Word offers an ideal platform to put together HTML documents.

To begin creating a Web page in Word, you can use a Web page wizard or open a new document and begin adding and formatting content. The following steps show how to use Word's Web Page Wizard to create a professional-looking Web page.

1. In Word, choose File, New.

2. From the New dialog box, click the Web Pages tab and double-click the Web Page Wizard template. The Web Page Wizard dialog box appears (see Figure 44.9).

FIG. 44.9
Word gives you several Web page templates from which to choose.

3. Select Simple Layout and click <u>N</u>ext. The Web Page Wizard dialog box displays with a list of styles from which to choose.

4. Select Elegant and click <u>F</u>inish. As you work through the Web Page Wizard, you can see the template building in the background. If you don't like the design you've chosen, click <u>B</u>ack to return to the previous Web Page Wizard dialog box.

5. You return to the document window with the template open, ready for you to edit (see Figure 44.10). If the Office Assistant displays, turn it off to give you more room to work.

FIG. 44.10
The Web Page Wizard creates a document in which you can replace sample text with your own to create a Web page.

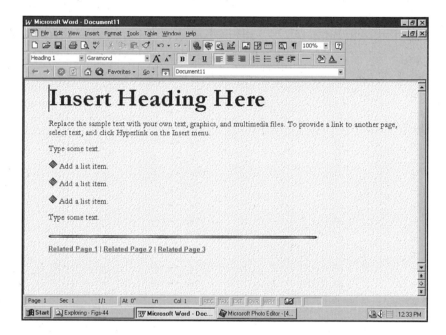

6. Highlight the heading text (Insert Heading Here) and replace it with a title for the page, such as **Welcome To Salisbury Communications Web Page**. For your pages, you may want to include a title describing the content on the page.

7. Move to the first line below the heading and replace the text with the text of your choice.

Creating Hyperlinks in Your Web Pages When you create Web pages, you can link from one page to another using hyperlinks. Although many documents throughout history have been created without the benefit of hyperlinks, not many stand alone without referencing other bodies of work. You should think of this when you create your own pages. Think in terms of how your readers view your document. Look for opportunities to guide the reader to other parts of your document (such as from a table of contents to specific sections). Also, have in mind other documents on your site, whether it's an intranet or Web site, that could benefit by having a link from your page to that document, and vice versa. Finally, if your visitors can access the Web, create hyperlinks to documents on other Web sites that support or complement your discussion.

> **N O T E** If you are on a company intranet, you may not have access to the outside World Wide Web. If this is the case, don't spend time planting hyperlinks to these sites because your visitors won't be able to access them anyway. On the other hand, some companies let users get to the outside and view Web sites. Then it's a good opportunity to take advantage of the abundant resources of the Web.
>
> As you create pages with links, keep in mind that these links don't change even if the document on the other end of the link changes or vanishes. This is equivalent to using an old city map only to constantly turn down dead-end roads that once were state highways. Periodically check your pages to ensure that links still work and the correct document or reference is on the other end. ■

Another way to use hyperlinks is to link to a resource or file area. You might, for instance, create a set of long Word documents or an Access database that is not easily transferred to a Web page. In these cases, a link from your Web page to the DOC file, MDB, or a compressed file (such as Pkzip file) containing the information can be included so that visitors can click the link and download the file(s). This gives you the flexibility to describe the contents of the files, but not require everyone to view or download the files.

To add a link to your Web page, do the following:

1. Insert text you want as the text that appears as the hyperlink to another document or section of a document. Do this by highlighting the first paragraph under the title text and replacing it with the text of your choice. In this case, the words **Salisbury Communications** is used as hyperlink text. This is all the text to be linked in this step, but you can add as much as you want. As a rule, keep anchor text to as few words as possible so that your page doesn't begin looking like one giant hyperlink.

    To follow along with this example, the rest of the paragraph reads as follows:

    > **started designing interactive multimedia learning tools for students beginning in February 1996.**

2. Highlight the words `Salisbury Communications` and click the Insert Hyperlink toolbar button. The Insert Hyperlink dialog box appears (see Figure 44.11).

FIG. 44.11
Use the Insert
Hyperlink dialog box
to specify the
document to which
you want to link.

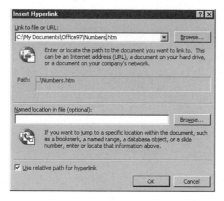

Part

VIII

Ch

44

 Click the drop-down list on the Link to File or URL text box to select frequently referenced links.

3. Enter the URL or file path of the document you want your hyperlink to jump to in the Link to File or URL text box. If you link to a document on the Web, use the format http://*url*, in which *url* is the URL of the document. For documents on your computer or company network, enter the path. Click the Browse button if you don't know the full path by memory. Make sure that you entered the path or URL correctly. Otherwise, your hyperlink will fail. In this example, click the Browse button and select a Word document on your hard drive. This gives you something to link to when you test your document later.

   For hyperlinks that are to go to specific places in a document—such as a bookmark, a specific slide (if you reference a PowerPoint presentation), a named range in an Excel worksheet, or a specific object in an Access database—use the Browse button on the Named Location In File field to specify that location. When you create Web pages using HTML coding, you can place named anchor tags to specify text or a group of text in a document you want to link to specifically. Word's Bookmark feature is identical to named anchor tags. As you create longer Web documents, you may want to insert bookmarks for future hyperlinking.

   N O T E Depending on the document you list in the Link to file or URL, a different dialog box displays when you click the Browse button to specify a named location in a file. ■

4. To finish the Insert Hyperlink dialog box, click Ⓤser Relative Path for Hyperlink if you reference a local file (that is, one on your system or your local Web site) that you do not plan to move to another location. With HTML, you can have two types of links—relative or absolute. The following explains each:

- *Relative links.* These are links to files on the same computer as the document referencing them and are relative to the computer and directory from which the browser originally loaded the Web page. If, for instance, the file you create now is called PAGE1.HTM and is stored in file://C:/WEB-PAGES, the path (or URL as far as the Web browser knows) is file://C:/WEB-PAGES/PAGE1.HTM. If a document you link to is on the same computer (and to make things easier, same folder) and is named PAGE2.HTM, the URL is file://C:/WEB-PAGES/PAGE2.HTM. Using relative references, however, you just have to name PAGE2.HTM for the browser to link to that document.

- *Absolute links.* These are links to documents on other Web sites. Until you start creating your own Web pages, you usually are aware of only absolute links as you navigate the Web, entering long URLs like **http://www.microsoft.com/devonly**.

5. Click OK to place the hyperlink in your Web document. Notice that the green underline is replaced with blue underline to indicate the text is a hyperlink.

6. Select Ⓕile, Ⓢave to save your document. Enter a name for your document. This is the name that appears in the title bar of the Web browser (and Word's title bar) when users load your page.

Adding Lists to Your Web Pages   Continue adding text to your Web page by clicking the field telling you to Click Here to Type Text. This text introduces the bulleted list to follow, and should let the reader know exactly what the bullets refer to. For this example, click the text and change it to read **The following is a list of products Salisbury Communications markets:**.

TIP   Press Enter at the end of the last bulleted item to add another bulleted line of text.

Next, click each bullet point and change them to read the following (see Figure 44.12):

- My Little Schooner
- The Clipper Ship That Could
- An Interactive Guide To Lost Treasures of the Atlantic
- The Rise and Fall of the Titanic: CD-ROM version

FIG. 44.12
Bulleted lists help display your information in short, easily read chunks.

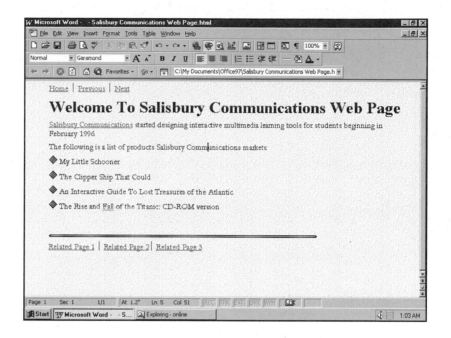

As with regular Word documents, you can change the type of bullets by highlighting the bullet, pressing Delete, and inserting a new bullet. To insert a new bullet, choose Format, Bullets and Numbering and select from the Bulleted tab on the Bullets and Numbering dialog box.

N O T E Because HTML is finicky with the type of bullets displayed in some Web browsers, you may have to experiment to see which ones display the best for the browser you use. In most cases, if your company standardizes on Microsoft Internet Explorer 3.0 (MSIE), you should be able to read many of the bullets from Word in MSIE. ■

One way to get around the problem of using simple bullets in your lists is to use small image files for your bullets. When you do this, you line up your text next to the image file as if the image was a standard bullet. Because all browsers developed today read inline images (see the section "Adding Images to Your Web Pages"), the images you use for bullets will be displayed as you want them to.

N O T E If you plan to create Web documents using HTML, you need to learn about the different types of lists in HTML. These included *unordered* (which are also called bulleted lists), *numbered*, and *glossary lists*. For the most part, unordered and numbered are the two used most frequently and require you to use a few different HTML tags if you want to change the appearance and order of bullets. With Word as your Web page editor, however, you simply click the Bullets or Numbering toolbar buttons to set a line or group of lines to lists. ■

Adding Rules to Your Web Pages   Because the HTML language is not as sophisticated as many word processors, including Word, features such as adding shading, newspaper columns, and dividers are not available. For columns and dividers, you can use tables, which you learn about in "Using Tables in Your Web Pages," but up until recently creating tables in HTML was somewhat time consuming.

One way to break up your page is to use horizontal rules. In the Web page on your screen, a horizontal rule is below the last bulleted list line. You can delete it, move it, center or right-justify it on the page, edit it, or leave it alone.

The following shows how to change the horizontal rule's color and center it on the page:

1. Click the horizontal rule.
2. Right-click and select Edit Picture. This opens the WordArt module, wherein you can modify the rule as a WordArt object.
3. Select the rule. Click the Line Color toolbar button on the WordArt toolbar and change the color to blue.
4. Click Close Picture to return to the Web page.
5. Select the horizontal rule again and click the Center toolbar button. This positions the rule in the center of the page.

To balance the page, you may want to add a horizontal rule below the main heading on the page. To do this, follow these steps:

 Click the Show/Hide ¶ toolbar button to show paragraph marks on your page.

1. Place a paragraph return after the main heading. This places an empty space between the heading `Welcome To Salisbury Communications Web Page` and the first line of text.
2. Select the horizontal rule and click the Copy toolbar button.
3. Move the pointer to the place where you inserted the new paragraph and click the Paste button.
4. Click the Center toolbar button and insert a paragraph return between the horizontal rule and text below it. This gives your page a more balanced look.

To see more of your Web page on-screen, click the Show Only Web Toolbar button to hide the other toolbars on-screen. Figure 44.13 shows you how your page should look now. Click the Show Only Web Toolbar button again to display the other toolbars.

FIG. 44.13
Your Web page with
two horizontal rules
centered on the page.

Shows only Web
toolbar button

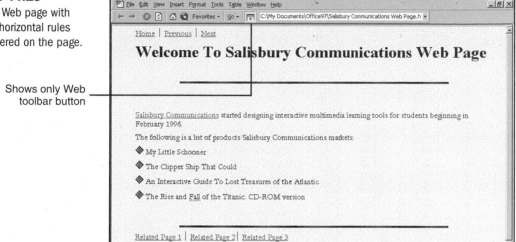

Adding Images to Your Web Pages   If you've spent any time on the Web, you've no doubt
noticed that Web pages are full of images. These images are used for logos, directional
buttons, entertainment, background, advertisements, and whatever else Web authors can
think of. You can insert images in your Web page easily with Word.

N O T E   Most Web browsers display only GIF, JPEG, and XBM image files. (XBM is really a
programming file, but it displays as a picture.) Although Word lets you insert many
different image files, such as PCX, TIF, WPG, and so on, use only GIF or JPEG in your Web pages
to avoid conflicts with browsers.

Also, each image you add to your Web page increases the overall time it takes for users to
download and view your page. Use images sparingly if possible. ■

To insert an image in the Web page, use the following steps:

1. Place a new paragraph return at the top of the document, to the left of the W in
   Welcome. This gives you space between the Home | Previous| Next items and the
   main heading to inset an image, such as a company logo.

2. Move the insertion point to the new paragraph and click the Insert Picture toolbar
   button. The Insert Picture dialog box appears (see Figure 44.14). One option you
   might choose is the Float over Text option. This causes the image to appear on top
   of text, but may not work in all browsers as well as it shows up in Word.

FIG. 44.14
Insert pictures into your Web pages to add color, function, and identification to your pages.

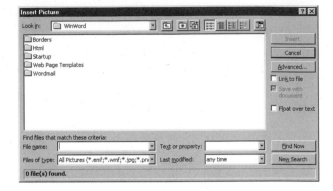

3. Locate the image file to insert in your page and select Insert. The image is inserted into your page at the point you indicated (see Figure 44.15).

FIG. 44.15
Images can be many sizes and shapes and portray a diversity of topics and subjects.

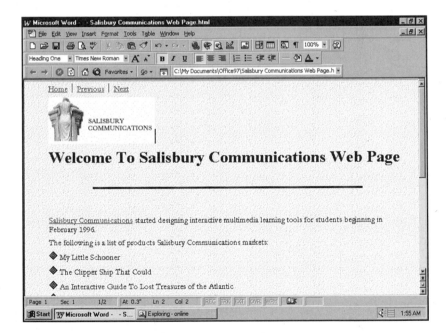

4. If you need to resize the image, click it and drag the resizing handles to meet your needs. As you drag the image, the surrounding text and objects move to accommodate the larger or smaller image. Be sure to save your document often.

5. To position the image next to text, you need to use the Picture dialog box. Right-click the image and select Format Picture.

6. In the Picture dialog box (see Figure 44.16), select the Position tab and click Left or Right to indicate how text is to flow around the image.

   In the Distance from Text area, set the Vertical and Horizontal distances that the image is to be from the text. This is measured in inches.

FIG. 44.16

By default, text does not flow around images, so you need to set how the text should flow.

7. Click the Settings tab (see Figure 44.17). If the image uses an absolute path (such as you insert an image that displays on another page or Web site), click the Use Absolute Path.

   The Picture Placeholder text box is important to fill out. This setting is used to describe or name the image file you inserted. In case the image cannot load or the viewer turns off image display, the placeholder displays on the Web page instead. If the image is used to transfer information or advertise a product or service, the placeholder becomes critical when you want to make sure your visitors get the full impact of your site.

FIG. 44.17

Use the Settings tab on the Picture dialog box to set the path to the selected image and its placeholder text.

8. Click OK to save your settings and return to the Web page.

N O T E To delete an image on your page, click it and press Del. ■

Using Tables in Your Web Pages If you have information that needs to be displayed in columns, such as large lists, a series of images, or columnar data, you must use a table in your Web pages.

Tables are the unsung heroes of many Web sites. On many sites, information is displayed in attractive and even columns, as if a high-end desktop publishing application created the page. Unfortunately, the controls needed to do those layouts are not included in the HTML specifications. You cannot, for instance, instruct the Web browser to display your information in three newspaper columns. The key to using tables without anyone really noticing them is to turn off the display of gridlines.

N O T E Recently, specifications for style sheets, frames, and other layout descriptions have been promoted by the HTML programming community. In fact, Microsoft Internet Explorer 3.0 and Netscape Navigator 3.0 support many of these technologies. However, Word's Web publishing features don't allow for these advancements yet, so tables are used to set up more sophisticated Web page layouts. ■

In this example, tables are used to set up the heading area so that the image and main heading are on the same line.

▶ **See** "Inserting a Table Using the Tables and Borders Button on the Standard Toolbar," **p. 281**

To insert a table in your Web page, follow these steps:

1. Click the Tables and Borders toolbar button to display the Tables and Borders floating toolbar.

2. Click the Draw Table button and drag out the table. You need two columns and one row for the table. Click the Split Cells button to specify the number of columns.

3. Click the image you inserted in your Web page in the section "Adding Images to Your Web Pages" and select the Text Wrapping button on the Picture toolbar. Choose the Through option. This enables you to move the picture inside the table. Now move the image into the left column of the table. Highlight the text of the main heading and move it to the right column of the table.

4. Slide the cell marker to the left closer to the image to give more room for your heading text and to move the text closer to the image (see Figure 44.18).

FIG. 44.18
Word makes creating tables in HTML files a breeze.

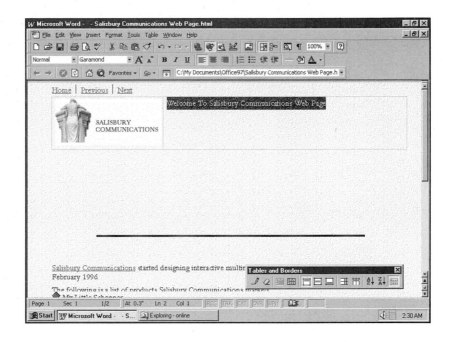

5. If necessary, highlight the heading text, change the point size to a larger size (such as 24), and add boldface to make it easier to see.

6. Turn off the grid lines on the table to hide the table borders.

7. Below the table, delete the extra paragraph returns, if any, to close the gap between the table and the horizontal rule.

N O T E Some of the tricks to using tables in HTML documents is to create tables inside tables to control the layout of page elements even more. To do this in Word, create a different number of columns and rows inside your main table to line up text and images as necessary. You also can use different line widths to make your table more attractive.

Also, think about the content of a table being the same as that of normal text. You can format it, move it, delete it, and even add hyperlinks to it. ■

Adding Controls to Your Web Page   Controls give visitors directions on returning to pages which they've already visited, or continuing with the next page on the site. At the top of the Web page, the following three controls are available:

■ *Home.* Enables the visitor to jump to your company's home page. If the document you are working on is the home page, remove this control.

■ *Previous.* Enables the visitor to return to the page he or she just left.

■ *Next.* Enables the visitor to continue with the next page on the site.

You should make it a habit to provide these controls so that users do not get frustrated as they navigate your site. Plus, you can use controls to direct visitors to strategic or important pages on your site.

Controls are simply text or images hyperlinked to specific pages. You can add hyperlinks to the controls on your Web page now, or wait until you have more pages to see how they relate to this one.

Likewise, the controls on the bottom of the page serve the same purpose as the ones at the top, but are used to link visitors to related Web sites.

Finishing and Testing Your Web Page   To finish, save the document. Although the page shown here was simple, it does give you an idea of how you can create Web pages using Word's built-in features.

 TIP   Use the Spelling and Grammar tool to check your document before sending it out for all the world to see.

The next thing you may want to do is view the HTML code that Word generated for your page. To do so, select View, HTML Source. A view opens showing you the various HTML tags in your Web page. If you are motivated to learn more about HTML, use the File, Print command to print a hard copy of this and use it in conjunction with an HTML guide to see how different options and settings in Word are saved as HTML tags. Click Exit HTML Source toolbar button to return to the normal Word view.

Finally, to see how your Web page looks in a Web browser, select File, Web Page Preview to launch your Web browser and to display your Web page in the browser window. Check to see whether any errors are apparent and test the hyperlinks. If you need to edit text, modify a link, or add to the page, switch to Word, make the changes and save them, and then click File, Web Page Preview.

Creating Web Documents in Excel

In the past, creating HTML files from Excel worksheets was anything but fun. Office 97, however, enables you to quickly create HTML files from worksheet data and charts. You also can take data from worksheets and insert it into Web pages that you've already created. This is handy if you create Web documents containing monthly report summaries using Word's Web-publishing tools and then want to drop in some Excel data or charts. Instead of linking a separate Excel file to the document, converting the data to Word tables, or leaving out the material altogether, you now can drop into Excel and quickly pull out the data you need.

The following are the three tasks you can now do to publish data on the Web using Excel:

- Insert worksheet data or chart data into a Web page
- Compile information using Web forms
- Author a Web page using Excel data

Part

VIII

Ch

44

N O T E Unlike Word's WYSIWYG Web editor interface, which you used in the preceding section, you need to access the HTML source code for some of the following tasks. Although this is not a difficult task, you do need to know how to read HTML tags. To get a great understanding of HTML, see Que's *Special Edition Using HTML*. ■

Using Excel Worksheet and Chart Data in Web Pages Creating Web pages that are continually updated is a common task. With Excel, you can capture data daily or as often as needed and plug the data into your Web pages as necessary. In the time it used to take to copy data from an Excel worksheet over to Word, you can now slide your new data from Excel into the Web page and have it on the site ready to be viewed.

To add worksheet data to a Web page, follow these steps:

1. Open the source code for your Web page in an HTML editor or Windows Notepad.
2. Insert a blank line in the place where you want the Excel data to be inserted.
3. Enter the following text exactly (see Figure 44.19):

```
<!--##Table##-->
```

FIG. 44.19
Create a new line for
the worksheet data
you are adding to
your HTML file.

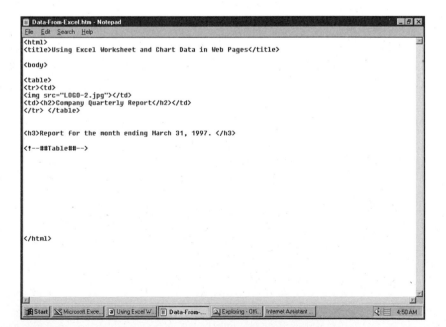

4. Save the HTML file.

5. Return to Excel and highlight the data you want to add to your Web page.

6. Select File, Save as HTML. The Internet Assistant Wizard Excel starts (see Figure 44.20) and converts your data from Excel format to an HTML table that you can add to your Web document.

FIG. 44.20

The Internet Assistant Wizard walks you through adding data to an existing Web document.

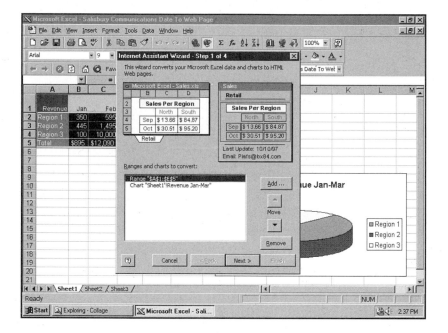

7. Add or remove ranges or charts from the List of Ranges or Charts to Export. Select a range or chart and press Remove to delete it from the list. To add to the list, click Add and fill in the address of the range you want to add, or add the name of the chart to the Internet Assistant Wizard dialog box.

8. Click Next to show step 2 of the wizard (see Figure 44.21). Internet Assistant asks if you want a new HTML document created from the selected data, or do you want to insert a table of Excel data into an existing HTML file. In this case, click the bottom selection.

9. Click Next. You are informed to add a new line to your HTML document, which you already did in step 3. Internet Assistant can open your file based directly on the file's path you enter in the Path of the Existing File text box (see Figure 44.22). Or, if you use Microsoft FrontPage as your HTML editor, Internet Assistant can open the file from the FrontPage Web site. Select the correct choice.

FIG. 44.21
You can choose to create a new Web page from your Excel selection or only a table during step 2 of the Internet Assistant Wizard.

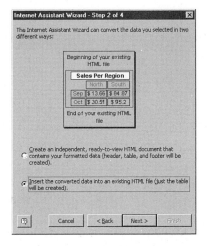

FIG. 44.22
Internet Assistant can add the new Excel data table in a Microsoft FrontPage Web document.

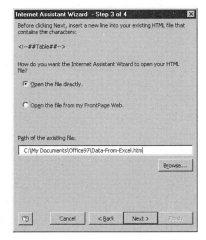

10. Click Next; then choose the way you want Internet Assistant to save the HTML file after the table is inserted. You can pick either to save it as an HTML file or as a FrontPage Web (see Figure 44.23).

11. Click Finish. You see your screen flash a few times and, depending on the size of the table, after a few moments you return to Excel.

12. Switch to your Web browser and open the Web file. The table of data from Excel now displays as HTML data, with much of the same formatting applied as the original (see Figure 44.24).

FIG. 44.23
After the table is inserted in the Web page, it is saved automatically by Internet Assistant.

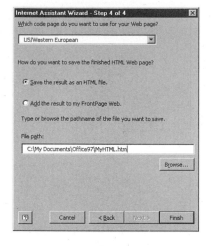

FIG. 44.24
The inserted Excel data and chart, with the chart moved to the side to allow for easier viewing.

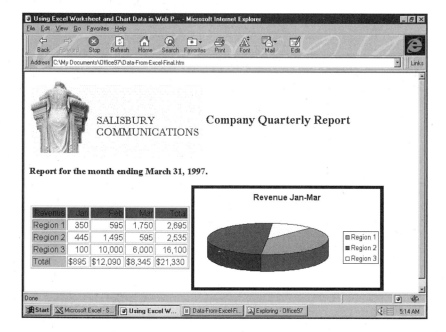

N O T E Internet Assistant converts the Excel data from a worksheet to an HTML table. You can look at the raw HTML code to see all the rows and data values for each item in the table. As for the chart, Internet Assistant simply saves it as a GIF image file and inserts it in the Web page using the `<IMG SRC="CHART.GIF">` tag. ■

If required, you can open the HTML source file and modify the text, colors, table characteristics, or other data in the Excel table.

Creating an HTML File from Excel Data or Charts   The preceding section showed how to take data from your Excel worksheet or chart and plug it into a Web page. If you don't have a Web page created, you can use the Internet Assistant to create the file for you by following these steps:

1. Complete steps 1-7 from the preceding section.

2. When Internet Assistant Wizard - Step 2 displays, leave the top option selected. This lets Internet Assistant create a new Web page based on the Excel data you selected.

3. Click Next. Step 3 of the Wizard lets you customize how the final page looks after the wizard creates it for you (see Figure 44.25). Fill in the information for your new Web page. If you don't specify anything here, you can edit the HTML source code later.

Part

VIII

Ch

44

FIG. 44.25
Use this screen to add some text, your e-mail address, or horizontal rules to your new page.

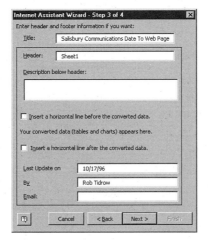

4. Click Next. Specify a file name for the new Web page.

5. Click Finish. Open the new file in your Web browser (see Figure 44.26).

Creating Web Documents in PowerPoint

Microsoft has discovered a natural fit with multimedia content on the Web and PowerPoint. Using the PowerPoint Internet Assistant, users can migrate their highly interactive and rich presentations straight to Web pages, complete with audio, video, full-color graphics, and text. For information on creating Web documents in PowerPoint, see the Techniques from the Pros section "Publishing a Corporate Policy Presentation with PowerPoint" at the end of this chapter.

FIG. 44.26
Without much effort, you get a nice start to a Web page that you can customize for your organization or team.

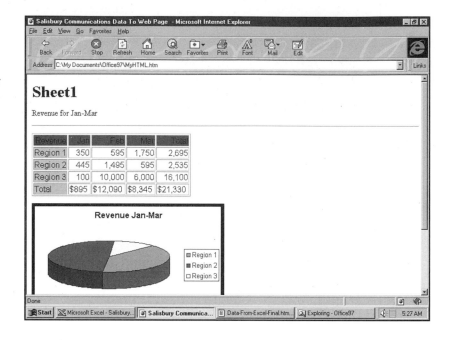

Creating Web Documents in Access

The Access development team has created a couple of different ways you can publish your database information to the Web. You can use the File, Save As/Export command to manually save a report or table to an HTML file. You also can use the Publish to the Web Wizard, which automates the process of creating Web pages from Access data. This section focuses only on using the Publish to the Web Wizard feature.

To use the Publish to the Web feature, follow these steps:

1. Select the item you want to publish, including forms, tables, reports, or queries.

2. Select File, Save to HTML.

3. When the Publish To The Web Wizard screen displays (see Figure 44.27), select Next. If you've already created a publication profile, you can elect to use one from the list at the bottom of the screen by clicking it. A publication profile is an HTML file created from datasheets, queries, tables, forms, and reports.

4. Select what you want to publish on the Web. Click the tabs for each item and then check the box next to the table, query, form, or report you want to publish (see Figure 44.28). You also can click the All Objects tab to view and select all objects in your database.

FIG. 44.27
Use the Publish to the Web Wizard to help you create Web pages using Access data.

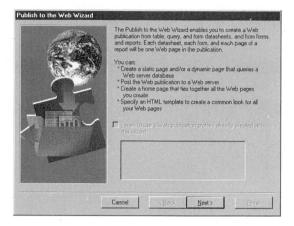

FIG. 44.28
Select the database objects you want to publish.

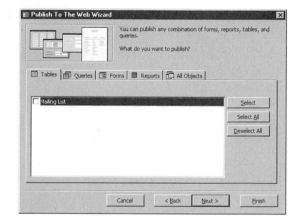

ON THE WEB

You can view and download various templates from **http://www.microsoft.com/msaccess/internet/ia/step.htm**

5. Select <u>N</u>ext. You have the option of selecting a template file to base your published Web files on (see Figure 44.29). You also can select separate templates for each database object you selected in the previous screen.

FIG. 44.29
Specify the templates you want to use for publishing your database objects.

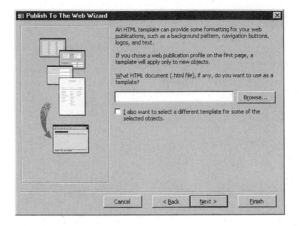

6. Select <u>N</u>ext. Select the type of Web page you want to create (see Figure 44.30). You can, for instance, create dynamic Web pages that are populated by querying your Access database running on IIS or Personal Web Server. Dynamic Web pages take the extension HTX. Another option you can choose is to create static pages that are populated once and then saved. These have HTML extensions. Finally, you can save the publication as a Dynamic ASP file, which is an Internet file created by an ActiveX server. You also can select different types for different database objects.

FIG. 44.30
If you have Web pages on your server that need to be updated constantly, consider using HTX files that get filled by querying Access databases.

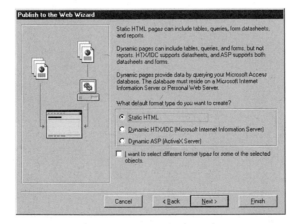

7. Click <u>N</u>ext. Set the folder where you want your Web documents published (see Figure 44.31).

FIG. 44.31
Make sure the folder
you select is
accessible by the
server.

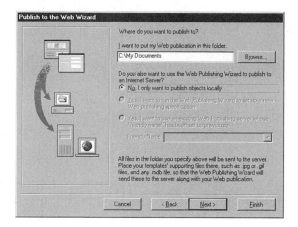

8. Click <u>N</u>ext. Select the <u>Y</u>es, I Want to Create a Home Page option if you want the wizard to set up a home page for you (see Figure 44.32). This home page will keep links of all the published files for your database objects. Place a file name in the text field.

FIG. 44.32
By creating a home
page, you can easily
access links to all the
Web files created for
your selected
database objects.

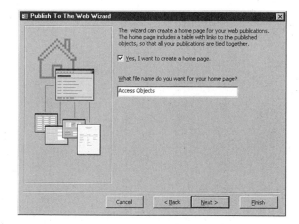

9. Click <u>N</u>ext. Click the check box to save the settings you just established. This eliminates the need to walk through this wizard again to set up a profile for other database objects. Enter a name in the <u>P</u>rofile Name field.

10. Click <u>F</u>inish. The Web Wizard outputs the jobs as you indicate, enabling you to view the Web pages in a Web browser.

Techniques from the Pros

by Rob Tidrow

Rob Tidrow is President of Tidrow Communications, a Windows and Internet consulting company. Rob has been on the Internet and World Wide Web for the past four years and has been creating World Wide Web pages for the past two.

Publishing a Corporate Policy Presentation with PowerPoint

One area in which PowerPoint presentations make great fodder for the Web is in corporate policy plans. Companies investing in intranets can quickly and easily reuse material in different formats (such as HTML documents), which can be delivered to employees at their convenience. Instead of outputting dozens or thousands of hard copy printouts to an organization, the intranet can be used to disseminate information and can be kept up-to-date much more easily. When a change in policy or a new policy emerges, the intranet page can be updated, with pointers to the new material.

Another reason PowerPoint is used to create Web pages is because of its ease of use. Regardless of the types of software available to make HTML coding easy, creating a PowerPoint presentation is much easier and the results are more professional looking.

Putting together a corporate policy presentation for an intranet using PowerPoint involves only a little more time than putting together the PowerPoint presentation itself. Regardless of which medium is used to publish a presentation, the message is much more important than the format. Part V, "Using PowerPoint," explains how to use PowerPoint and how to enhance your presentations with multimedia, graphics, and color schemes. An important facet to remember when placing your PowerPoint presentation on the intranet is your audience. How much time do they have to view your slides? Will they know how to use the Web browser to view the presentation? Are the files too large for those users who must dial in from a remote station and download the files? Keep these considerations in mind as you develop the Web pages and your viewers should be happy.

As you put together documents and projects for an intranet, you need to keep in mind the development stages of creating dynamic Web pages. The next section defines these stages, with the sections that follow showing how to use PowerPoint to put together a corporate policy presentation.

Creating Dynamic Intranet Documents

Whether you create documents for an intranet or the World Wide Web, you need to approach the development cycle with the same discipline. The same fundamentals you applied to designing a Web page should be used for creating a document you place on the intranet. One of the primary differences between the two types of mediums—Web versus intranet—is audience. Information you create for the Web usually is general in nature and is approved for public distribution. For corporate intranets, your audience is internal staff so the documents can focus on a diverse information-set, such as human resource information, team-building exercises, and corporate policy presentations.

When you create an intranet document, there are five stages of development:

- *Define the project.* During this stage, designers should gather the information required for the project, including current paper-based documents that employees may already have. For a corporate policy presentation, the developer may need to update a presentation that was given previously, or create a new one from scratch. In either situation, the developer should meet with the personnel responsible for the policy to outline the presentation. The designer also needs to specify the medium for the presentation. In this case, PowerPoint is used, which will enable the audience (the staff) to view the presentation in HTML format using a Web browser or to view the presentation in PowerPoint.

- *Create navigation and structure.* In this stage, the designer needs to define the types and functions of the information. Do the documents contain required legal information, such as safety and health information (such as OSHA requirements), which must be treated in a serious tone? Or, can the information be presented in a lighter tone, such as policies regarding parking procedures? Is the presentation more useful in a table format, with frames, or should it be in a linear format with a standard table of contents page to help viewers navigate? The designer also should key messages in this stage and establish logical relationships (hyperlinks) between the information. Finally, flow diagrams, storyboards, and thumbnail sketches of images should be created.

- *Design and test the pages.* This is the stage in which the designer puts together the information gathered in stage 1 and designed in stage 2. The look and feel of the presentation is finalized in this stage, with images added, typeface selected, and other Web page elements added. The copy and hyperlinks also are added to the pages at this time. Finally, the pages should be proofed and tested to ensure information is correct, spelling is corrected, and that all hyperlinks work. If something doesn't work, this is the stage where it is fixed.

■ *Publish documents to the server.* The final stage involves publishing the finished presentation to the intranet server. The files that need to be uploaded to the server include the PowerPoint presentation, HTML files of the PowerPoint presentation, images, and any supporting files (such as files users can download from a page). The designer also should include a directory structure showing where each element should be saved on the server, with any new directories that need to be created, so that the intranet administrator (in many cases, this is someone different from the designer of the presentation) knows where to place each file. Finally, an announcement of the new presentation should be sent to all employees who need to review it, emphasizing the URL of the document, why it should be read, and the date by which it should be read.

■ *Maintenance and updates.* This stage focuses on activities after the presentation is published on the intranet. Unlike hard copy presentations or memorandums, which cannot be changed after they are distributed, intranet-based presentations can be updated or changed through the life of the document. If a policy changes, an error is found in the document, or copy needs to be reworded for clarity, this can be done at any time to ensure the document stays current. A good habit to develop is to highlight (with an icon or text label) new information added to a document so that readers can readily know what has changed since the last time they viewed the document. Also, information that is no longer current should be removed immediately and any links to that document should be disabled.

The following sections show you how to use PowerPoint to create a corporate policy presentation by following the preceding five stages.

Defining the Corporate Policy Presentation

When you create a corporate policy presentation, it is more than likely just one of several policies your company has. Most companies publish an employee handbook that includes a number of different sections devoted to specific policies. The following is a table of contents of an example employee handbook that any company may give their employees:

■ Welcome Message

■ Company History

■ What Employees Need To Know

■ Company Benefits Information

■ Special Employee Services

Within each of the preceding sections, specific policies are included to dig deeper into what each employee needs to know. In the third section, for example, there may be policies regarding use of telephones, rest periods, absences reporting, and accident prevention.

The first stage in creating the policy presentation here, therefore, is to identify which policy will be created. In this case, a company training policy is created. The following are the key points to be included in this policy presentation:

Part
VIII

Ch
44

- Create a needs assessment for the employee
- Set objectives for the employee
- Determine the type of employee training
- Select training instructor and/or training company
- Establish the curriculum
- Select the training methods
- Set the training timetable
- Determine training costs and reimbursement plan
- Locate additional training resources

The following section shows how to start putting together the training policy using PowerPoint.

Creating Navigation and Structure of the Training Policy

Both large and small companies can benefit from having a detailed training policy on their intranet. The training policy presentation can link to related policies on the intranet, such as sabbaticals needed for long-term training and advancement possibilities for employees. For companies that have access to the World Wide Web, the training policy can include links to Web sites that offer training courses, white papers on the course the employee wants to take, and other training resources.

To begin designing the navigation and structure of the training policy presentation, you need to know where in the employee handbook this policy fits. Because the training policy is only one of many policies, there needs to be a main page (called a home page) that leads the employee to the training policy. Figure 44.33, for instance, shows the home page for the Salisbury Communications Employee Handbook. Notice the link to the Employee Training Policy Presentation in the Table of Contents section. When users click this link, they are presented with the opening page of the training policy (see Figure 44.34).

FIG. 44.33
The Salisbury
Communications
Employee Handbook
home page.

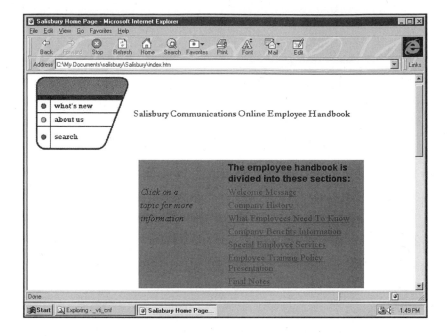

FIG. 44.34
The opening page of
the training policy
presentation.

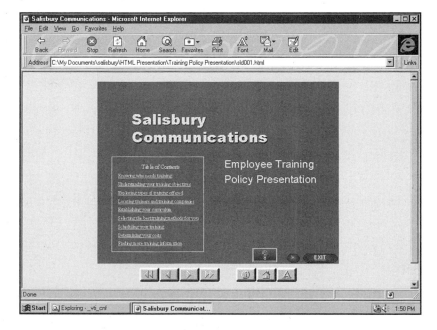

The basic design of the training policy follows the structure of a PowerPoint slide presentation. Each slide presents one of the key points listed in the "Defining the Corporate Policy Presentation" section, with buttons enabling viewers to advance to the previous or next slide. The opening page includes a table of contents of key points to enable users to jump quickly to a specific page. Likewise, each page includes a link back to the opening page. For points that need more information, such as what types of classes are offered, there will be hyperlinks to supplemental slides or to documents created in another application that the user can view.

Designing and Testing the Training Policy Presentation

Now that you have the content for the training policy and the overall flow of how the presentation is to be presented on the intranet, you can begin building it. For the example that follows, it is assumed that the home page for the employee handbook is already created. This section focuses on creating the training policy using PowerPoint.

The general steps for creating the training policy in PowerPoint are as follows:

1. Launch PowerPoint and select a presentation template.
2. Populate the template with the training policy content.
3. Add hyperlinks and action buttons to the presentation.
4. Save the PowerPoint presentation as an HTML file.
5. Run the PowerPoint presentation to test links.

Starting PowerPoint and Selecting a Template   To start PowerPoint and select a template, use the following steps:

1. Start PowerPoint and select the AutoContent Wizard option from the PowerPoint dialog box, and then click OK. The AutoContent Wizard appears (see Figure 44.35).

FIG. 44.35
The AutoContent Wizard walks you through adding some content to your presentation.

2. Click <u>N</u>ext to display the types of template from which you can choose.
3. Click the <u>O</u>perations/HR button (see Figure 44.36) to display presentations associated with operations and human resources.

FIG. 44.36

When you click a presentation category, individual presentation types display on which you can base your policy.

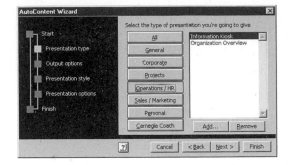

4. Click the Information Kiosk presentation type and click <u>N</u>ext.

5. On the Output options wizard screen, click the <u>I</u>nternet, Kiosks option button. Click <u>N</u>ext.

6. On the Presentation options wizard screen, select the items (see Figure 44.37) you want to appear on the training policy presentation. If you want to include a copyright notice on the page, click the <u>C</u>opyright Notice On Each Page option and fill in the field below it. You may want to include the company name. Click the <u>D</u>ate Last Updated option to include the date you updated the policy. Finally, click the <u>E</u>-Mail Address option and fill in the field below it to add an e-mail address to each page. This e-mail address should be the address of someone who can field questions relating to the policy, or who is responsible for filtering e-mail to the right staff or manager. Click <u>N</u>ext.

FIG. 44.37

You can select different options to add to each page of the training policy presentation.

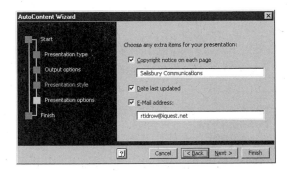

7. Click Finish to instruct PowerPoint to create a presentation based on the choices you made with the AutoContent Wizard. PowerPoint displays an outline similar to the one in Figure 44.38.

You now are ready to add content to the training policy presentation.

FIG. 44.38
PowerPoint creates an outline based on the information you provided the AutoContent Wizard.

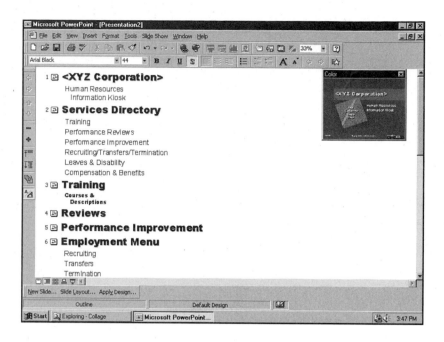

Inserting Content in the Presentation You now can change the content in the outline PowerPoint presents to fit your training policy presentation. The first thing you can do is to reduce the number of slides you need from 12 to 11. This gives you one slide for the opening screen, nine slides for the key points to address, and one slide at the end of the presentation.

> **N O T E** Although you can add any information you want to the slides, the following steps use the information shown earlier in the "Defining the Corporate Policy Presentation" section as the key points in the training policy presentation. You should always keep the audience in mind when you create intranet-based presentations. In step 4 below, notice how the key points are modified slightly to present each directly to the viewer of the presentation. This way, the employee who reads the presentation will understand it is directed at him or her. ■

To add the content to the slides, use the following steps:

1. Highlight the last slide (called Compensation & Benefits) and press Delete to remove that slide. Click OK when asked if it's OK to delete the slide and any notes associated with the slide. You now should have 11 slides in the outline.

2. Change the first slide from <XYZ Corporation> to the name you want to appear on the first slide, such as **Salisbury Communications**.

3. Under the title you just modified, change Human Resource Information Kiosk to the name of the name of the policy presentation, such as **Employee Training Policy Presentation**.

4. Change each of the next nine slides to the key points you want to make in the presentation. In this example, the following items are used. You also can delete the information under each slide heading to make your outline easier to read.

- Knowing Who Needs Training
- Understanding Your Training Objectives
- Exploring Types of Training Offered
- Locating Trainers and Training Companies
- Establishing Your Curriculum
- Selecting the Best Training Methods for You
- Scheduling Your Training
- Determining Your Costs
- Finding More Training Information

5. Change the title of the last slide to show that it is the last slide in the presentation. You might use something like **Exit to Employee Handbook** to enable viewers to return to the employee handbook home page. Figure 44.39 shows how the outline looks at this point.

FIG. 44.39

Fill in key points in the training policy presentation.

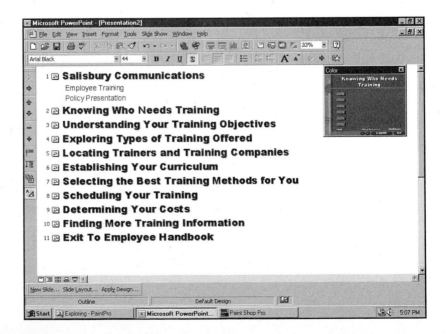

6. Choose <u>F</u>ile, <u>S</u>ave and enter a file name in the Save As dialog box to save the file.

7. Choose <u>V</u>iew, <u>S</u>lide to view the presentation in slide format.

8. Right-click the first slide and select Bac<u>k</u>ground to display the Background dialog box. Click the Omit Background <u>G</u>raphics from Master option and click <u>A</u>pply. This removes the background image on the first slide to give you room to add a table of contents box to that slide.

9. Choose <u>V</u>iew, <u>T</u>oolbars, Drawing to display the Drawing toolbar. Select the AutoShapes button on the Drawing toolbar and choose <u>B</u>asic Shapes. From the context menu, select the rectangle shape (the first shape in the menu).

10. Draw a rectangle under the title on the first slide and to the left of the Employee Training Policy Presentation label. This gives you a box in which to place a table of contents for the presentation.

11. Choose <u>I</u>nsert, Te<u>x</u>t Box from the PowerPoint main menu. Draw a text box inside the rectangle you created in step 10. Add the text **Table of Contents** on the first line and press Enter. Change the font size of this text to 16 points and center the text. Finish the table of contents by adding the title of each slide on a separate line inside the text box. Change the font size of the text of each title to 14 points. The finished table of contents should look similar to the one shown in Figure 44.40.

FIG. 44.40
By adding a Table of Contents to the first slide, users can quickly jump to specific sections of the presentation.

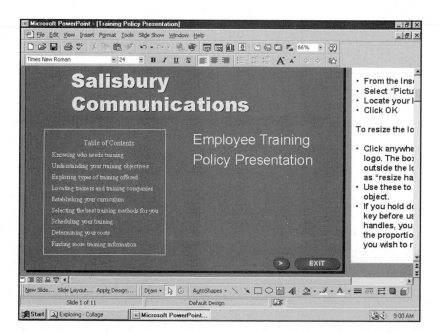

TIP You may want to add bullets at the beginning of each table of contents item to set them apart. You also may want to add a different background color to the table of contents box.

Now that you have the table of contents text added, you need to add hyperlinks to the associated slides in the presentation. The next section shows how to do this.

Adding Hyperlinks to a Presentation   To add hyperlinks to a presentation in PowerPoint, use the following steps:

1. Highlight the text or object you want to add the hyperlink to. In this case, highlight the first item in the table of contents box—Knowing Who Needs Training.

2. Right-click and select Action Settings from the context menu. The Action Settings dialog box appears.

3. On the Mouse Click tab, click the Hyperlink To option button (see Figure 44.41). Select Slide from the drop-down list. From the Hyperlink To Slide dialog box (see Figure 44.42), select the slide to which you want to hyperlink, in this case, 2. Knowing Who Needs Training. Click OK.

FIG. 44.41
When you click the Hyperlink To option button, you can choose the type of hyperlink you want to add.

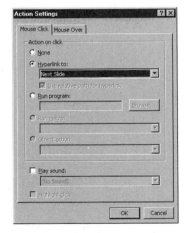

FIG. 44.42
You must select the slide to which you want to hyperlink from the Hyperlink To Slide dialog box.

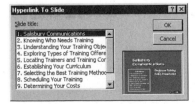

N O T E Although you can select Next Slide in the <u>H</u>yperlink To drop-down list for the first table of contents item, it is better to link to the specific slide as shown. This way, if you add a new slide as the second slide or decide to reorganize slides in the presentation, your hyperlinks point to the correct slide. ▪

4. Click OK to add the hyperlink to the text you selected in step 1. The text now appears in a different color and underlined.

5. Continue by adding hyperlinks to each table of contents item by following steps 1 through 4.

Now that you have the table of contents added, with hyperlinks to each slide, you can add hyperlinks to objects on the slides that help users navigate from one slide to the next. On the first slide, for instance, there is a pre-built navigation arrow object added by the template that you can add a hyperlink to the next slide. In fact, on all the slides here is a navigation object that points to the next slide. Also, for slides 2 through 11, there is a navigation arrow that points to the previous slide, which enables users to jump to the preceding slide in the presentation.

To add a hyperlink to each of these navigation objects, use these steps:

1. Right-click the arrow that points to the next slide and select <u>A</u>ction Settings to display the Action Settings dialog box.

2. Click the <u>H</u>yperlink To option button on the Mouse Click tab. From the <u>H</u>yperlink To drop-down list, select Next Slide.

3. Click OK. This adds a hyperlink to the arrow on the first slide.

4. Press the Page Down key on the keyboard to advance to the next slide. Add a hyperlink to the arrow that points to the next slide by using the same process as shown in steps 1 through 3. Also, right-click the arrow that points to the previous slide and add a hyperlink to the previous slide (you need to select the Previous Slide option from the <u>H</u>yperlink To drop-down list).

5. When you reach the last slide (slide 11 in this case), click the arrow that points to the next slide and press Delete. This deletes the arrow from the slide, which you don't need because there are no other slides after this one.

N O T E On slides 2 through 11 in this example, there is a Main Menu object added. You can link this object back to the first slide in this presentation, or delete the object—whichever situation suits your needs. The steps to do this are similar to the ones shown in the preceding steps, but you add a hyperlink to the first slide. For brevity purposes, those steps are not shown here. ▪

Another way to add a hyperlink to an object in PowerPoint is to point the link to an URL of a page on your intranet. One place you can do this in the training policy presentation is to add a link from the Exit object back to the Employee Handbook page. Because the Exit object is on every slide in the presentation, users can quickly jump from the presentation back to Employee Handbook when they finish reading a slide. If you do not add this flexibility to all your presentations, simply delete the Exit object from the slides.

To add a hyperlink from the policy presentation to a specific URL, use the following steps:

N O T E The following steps assume that an HTML document already exists on the local computer to which to hyperlink. If you do not have an HTML file on your system, open Windows Notepad, insert some dummy text (it doesn't need to be in HTML format), and save the file with an HTM extension. Now when you are asked to provide an URL, simply point to this document on your system. ▪

1. Right-click the Exit object on the first slide and select <u>A</u>ction Settings from the context menu. The Action Settings dialog box appears.

2. Select <u>H</u>yperlink To on the Mouse Click tab and choose URL from the drop-down list. The Hyperlink To URL dialog box appears.

3. Enter the URL of the document to which you want to hyperlink (see Figure 44.43). If the document is on your local hard drive, you must use the format `file:///drive-letter:\path`. For instance, if a document by the name of `EMP-HAND.HTM` is stored in the `SALISBURY` folder on the `C:` drive, the URL you add is as follows:

    `file:///c:\SALISBURY\EMP-HAND.HTM`

FIG. 44.43
When adding an URL, be sure to use precise spelling or your hyperlink will not work.

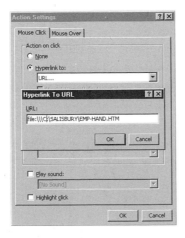

4. Click OK to return to the Action Settings dialog box. Click OK to save the setting to your presentation.

TIP To edit a hyperlink, right-click the object and select <u>H</u>yperlink, Edit <u>H</u>yperlink. In the Edit Hyperlink dialog box, modify the URL as necessary. Click OK when finished.

5. Press Page Down to advance to the next slide and add hyperlinks to the same URL for the Exit object. Perform steps 1-4 for each slide until all Exit objects are set up.

N O T E You now can add an action button to the first slide to link users to a help file. The next section shows how to do this. ▪

Adding PowerPoint Action Buttons PowerPoint 97 includes a number of built-in action buttons you can add to your presentations. Action buttons are 3-D buttons that you can set up to perform various actions, such as Forward, Back, Help, Home, Information, Sound, and Movie. These action buttons are available by choosing Sli<u>d</u>e Show, Action Butt<u>o</u>ns and selecting a button from the context menu. Table 44.2 describes how each of these action buttons can be used.

Part VIII Ch 44

Table 44.2   PowerPoint Action Buttons

Button Name	Description
Custom	Provides a customizable button on which you can add text or graphics.
Home	Provides a button that users click to return to the home or start page of the presentation.
Help	Provides a button that users click to obtain help or instructions.
Information	Provides a button that users click to read general information about the presentation, frequently asked questions (FAQs), or other information.
Back or Previous	Returns user to previous slide or document in the presentation.
Forward or Next	Sends user to next slide or document in the presentation.
Beginning	Sends user to beginning slide of the presentation.
End	Sends user to last slide of the presentation.
Return	Sends user to a previous slide, previous Web page, or another document.
Document	Displays a linked document.
Sound	Plays an audio file.
Movie	Runs a movie clip.

On the first slide of the training policy presentation, you might want to add a Help action button for users to click to receive help on navigating the presentation. You can then link the action button to a text file, HTML document, or presentation that describes how to navigate and use the presentation.

The following steps show how to add an action button to your presentation:

1. Make sure the first slide is displayed and select Slide Show, Action Buttons. From the context menu select the help button, which is the third button on the top row.

2. Drag and draw a help button to the left of the navigation button. The help button you create can be as large as you want it, but you should make it about the same size as the navigation arrow and Exit object. When you release the left mouse button, the Action Settings dialog box appears.

3. Select the Hyperlink To option and select an option from the drop-down list box. If your help file is in another PowerPoint presentation, for instance, select Other PowerPoint Presentation and select the file from the Hyperlink to Other PowerPoint Presentation dialog box that appears. Click OK.

4. Click OK on the Action Settings dialog box to return to the slide presentation.

5. If you want to change the color or other properties of the action button, right-click it and select Format AutoShape. In the Format AutoShape dialog box, change the color settings, size, and position of the action button. Click OK to save these settings. Figure 44.44 shows how your Help action button may look.

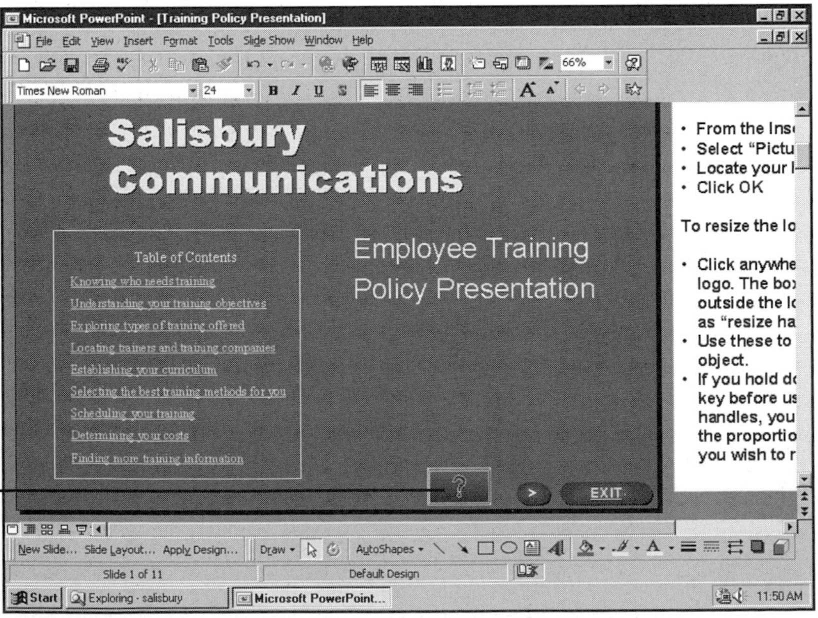

FIG. 44.44
You can add action buttons to your slides to add functionality to your presentations.

Help button

> **N O T E** Another way to use an action button in your presentation is to create a short AVI movie file and link it to your presentation using a Movie action button. ■

You now are ready to finish the presentation.

Finishing and Testing the Presentation   Each slide now contains a title, navigation buttons, and an Exit button. Some slides also contain icons, which are placeholders for launching embedded documents, such as Word documents, Excel worksheets, or another PowerPoint presentation. You can add hyperlinks to these icons by using the procedures shown earlier in the "Adding Hyperlinks to a Presentation" section. You can also delete these icons by selecting them and pressing Delete. You should also delete the text labels that appear beneath the icons to clean up the slide.

To finish the presentation, display each slide and add content related to each heading. For brevity purposes, this chapter does not detail what each slide should have on it. See Part V, "Using PowerPoint," if you have questions regarding how to add content to a PowerPoint slide.

Finally, before preceding to the next section, be sure to run your presentation as a slide show (choose View, Slide Show) and make sure all your hyperlinks work. If one does not work, press Esc to return to Slide view and modify the hyperlink to work.

In the next section, you are shown how to save the presentation as an HTML file.

Saving a Presentation as an HTML File

The finished training policy presentation can be distributed as a regular PowerPoint slide presentation, made available as a download from an intranet or Web document, or converted to an HTML document and stored on the intranet or Web server. You do this by using the Save as HTML wizard.

> **N O T E** PowerPoint enables you to choose between creating a standard HTML document or one that includes frames. The following steps show how to create the standard HTML document. If you want to create one using frames, consult the PowerPoint online help. ■

To save your presentation as an HTML file, follow these steps:

1. Choose File, Save as HTML. The Save as HTML wizard appears (see Figure 44.45).
2. Click Next. Choose a layout from the Load existing layout list, or select Next. By default, the New layout option is selected (see Figure 44.46). As you learn in step 10 later, after you finish using the Save as HTML wizard, the settings you choose can be saved as a layout you can reuse.

FIG. 44.45
The Save as HTML wizard walks you through converting your PowerPoint presentation to an HTML file.

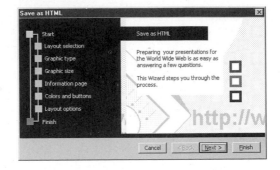

FIG. 44.46
The first time you use the Save as HTML wizard, the Load Existing Layout box is empty.

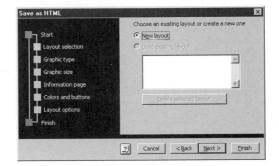

3. Choose a graphic type in which you want to save your presentation slides. By default, the GIF - Graphics Interchange Format is selected. If you want to use a compressed graphics format, select JPG - Compressed File Format and set a compression percentage in the Compression Value field. For HTML files you publish to an intranet server, you usually don't have to worry about compressing graphic files. For HTML files you publish to a WWW server, however, you may want to compress graphics to reduce file size.

4. Click Next. Choose the screen resolution for the graphics created in the HTML file. By default, the 640×480 resolution is selected. You should choose a setting that matches the setting for most users who will view the presentation. From the Width of Graphics drop-down list, select how much screen space you want the graphics to consume. The default is one-half the screen width.

5. Click Next. Fill out the e-mail address to appear on the HTML pages, the URL of your home page, and any other information you want to add to your HTML pages. Choose the Download Original Presentation option if you want your original

PowerPoint presentation to be displayed in the HTML file. If you want to include a hyperlink from the presentation to the Microsoft download area for users to download a copy of Microsoft Internet Explorer Web browser, select the Internet Explorer download button.

6. Click Next. Choose the colors of the text and buttons that appear on each page.

7. Click Next. Select the navigation button style you want to use from the Select Button Style list (see Figure 44.47).

Part

VIII

Ch

44

FIG. 44.47
The type of button that displays on your HTML pages is selected from this wizard screen.

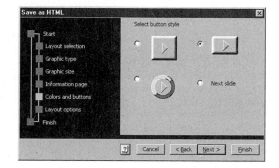

8. Click Next. Select the position where the navigation buttons are to be placed. To include any slide notes with your HTML file, click the Include Slide Notes in Pages option.

9. Click Next. Enter the path where you want to save the new HTML file.

10. Click Next, and then click Finish. In the Save as HTML dialog box, you can enter a name for the layout you just created so that you can reuse it the next time you convert a presentation to HTML format. Click Save after you fill in the layout name. Otherwise, click Don't Save. PowerPoint displays a message box showing you the progress of exporting your presentation as an HTML file.

11. Click OK when the message box displays letting you know the export process is finished.

You can view your presentation as an HTML file by opening it in a Web browser, such as Internet Explorer 3.0. When it displays, click the Click Here to Start Hyperlink to display the first slide of the presentation, as shown in Figure 44.48.

FIG. 44.48
The training policy presentation in HTML format.

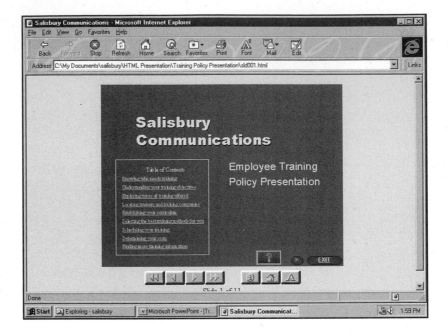

Publishing Your Presentation

To complete the process of creating the training policy presentation, you must publish the presentation to your intranet server. The process for doing this varies from site to site, but the following general steps should be followed:

1. Copy all the files created by PowerPoint during the HTML export process to the intranet server. You can find these files in the folder you specify in step 9 in the previous "Saving a Presentation as an HTML File" section.

2. Copy all supporting files, such as movies, text files, documents, and other objects to the intranet server.

3. Test your presentation using all of the Web browsers available in your company. Click every link in your presentation and download every linked file. If you include movies or audio files, ensure that they are available and work properly.

4. Add a link from the company's home page or other page to link to your presentation. Also, post a message to all users that the presentation is available online and what the URL is.

Consult your system administrator for specific information on how to upload your presentation files to your intranet or Internet server. ●

CHAPTER 45

Using Outlook Desktop Information Manager

by Gordon Padwick

Outlook is a versatile desktop information manager that helps you organize your information, manage your communications with other people, and keep track of activities such as your appointments and tasks. Although you can use Outlook only as a personal information manager (PIM), it has much broader capabilities. You can use it to share e-mail among members of your workgroup or with other people by way of a LAN or WAN. You can also use Outlook to send and receive faxes.

Outlook combines and enhances the facilities previously available in Exchange (supplied with Windows 95 and Windows NT) and Schedule+ (supplied with Office 95). If you don't want to start using Outlook, at least for the present, you can continue to use Exchange and Schedule+ after you have installed Office 97. This chapter deals with using Outlook. See Chapter 46 for information about using Exchange and Schedule+.

There is much more to Outlook than can be covered in one chapter. However, this chapter introduces you to many of Outlook's principal facilities with the intention of getting you started. ■

Getting around in Outlook

Explore the various Outlook windows, information viewers, and dialog boxes you can use to enter, view, and work with various types of information.

Understanding how Outlook organizes information

Learn to use folders and subfolders to organize information—standard folders as well as those you provide.

Using Outlook as a personal information manager (PIM)

Maintain personal information such as appointments and events in a calendar, your to-do list, and information about your contacts.

Maintaining a journal

Keep organized records of your daily activities.

Sending and receiving messages

Interchange e-mail messages with people in your workgroup or who share your LAN or WAN, and people who use Internet e-mail or an e-mail service provided by an information service such as CompuServe. Also send and receive fax messages.

Understanding Outlook's Scope

Outlook's scope is very broad, limited only by your imagination. Perhaps the single most important Outlook feature is its capability to organize and integrate information from many sources. For that reason, Outlook is sometimes referred to as a universal in-box, though this term focuses on only some of Outlook's capabilities. Organizing means providing an easy way to file related information according to its subject, rather than according to its source. For example, if you receive information about a specific topic by workgroup e-mail, from the Internet, from an information service such as CompuServe, or by fax, you can easily place all that information in the same folder. Information you create and send to others about the same topic can be kept in that same folder.

Information is not limited to unformatted text. Because Outlook is compatible with Rich Text Format (RTF), the documents you send and receive can use various fonts in different sizes and colors. (RTF format works only if both the sending and receiving computers support this format.)

Because Outlook is OLE-compatible, the documents you send, receive, and save can include objects created by other OLE-compatible applications. This means that you can work with graphics and sound. You can also attach files to your messages and other items of information.

You can configure Outlook to work with an unlimited number of information sources. Then, Outlook regularly queries these sources automatically, or at your command, to see if information is waiting for you.

Because Outlook's scope is so broad, it can be somewhat confusing. For that reason, this chapter suggests that you start by using Outlook in a very limited way and then, as you gain experience, gradually explore more of its capabilities.

Getting Started with Outlook

The first step in using Outlook is, of course, to install it. As with other components of the Office 97 package, you can install Outlook when you run Setup to install other Office 97 components. If you didn't install Outlook initially, you can use the normal Windows 95 or Windows NT procedure to install Outlook at any time.

After you've installed Outlook, you'll normally have a Microsoft Outlook icon on your Windows 95 or Windows NT Desktop, as shown in Figure 45.1. In addition, buttons on the Office toolbar give you direct access to Outlook facilities.

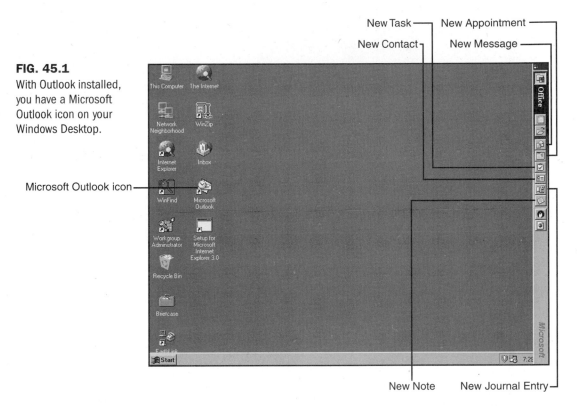

FIG. 45.1
With Outlook installed, you have a Microsoft Outlook icon on your Windows Desktop.

New Task — New Appointment —
New Contact — New Message —

Microsoft Outlook icon —

New Note — New Journal Entry —

The easiest way to start Outlook is to double-click the Microsoft Outlook icon on your Windows Desktop. If, for any reason, the Microsoft Outlook icon is missing, use the following procedure to start Outlook:

1. Click Start in the taskbar to show the Start menu.
2. Point to Programs in the Start menu to show a list of available programs.
3. Click Microsoft Outlook to start Outlook.

N O T E You can also click buttons in the Office toolbar to open individual components of Outlook. ▪

Outlook initially displays the Choose Profile dialog box with the current default profile selected, as shown in Figure 45.2.

N O T E For the present, think of a profile as a definition of how Outlook is used. Initially, you need just one profile. You'll find much more about profiles later in this chapter.

The profile name you see on your screen is probably different from the one shown in this figure. ▪

FIG. 45.2

The Choose Profile dialog box is displayed when you start Outlook. The Profile Name box shows the name of the default profile.

Outlook shares profiles, which are stored in the Windows registry, with Exchange and Schedule+. If you've previously used either of these applications on your computer and, therefore, already have one or more profiles, Outlook recognizes these existing profiles. Under these circumstances, the profile name you see in the Choose Profile dialog box when you start Outlook is the name of the default profile you previously used with Exchange or Schedule+. You can go ahead and, at least initially, use this profile with Outlook.

If your Windows registry contains no profiles, Outlook automatically creates one, naming it Microsoft Outlook Settings. This profile contains the settings you need to start working with Outlook.

N O T E The profile Outlook automatically creates contains two information services: Outlook Address Book and Personal Folders. You'll find out about these services later in this chapter. ▨

Click OK to accept the profile named in the Choose Profile dialog box to continue the startup process. After a few seconds delay, you see the Outlook window with the Inbox Information Viewer displayed, similar to that shown in Figure 45.3.

N O T E The preceding account of what happens when you start Outlook assumes you have just installed Outlook and have not changed any of the default options. You can set Outlook's options so that it opens displaying a window other than the Inbox. If Outlook is configured to connect to e-mail servers, it may automatically connect to those servers to check for e-mail as part of the startup process. Another possibility is that you'll see the Outlook window without first seeing the Choose Profile dialog box. If Outlook behaves in a way you don't expect, check its options as described in the "Setting Outlook Options" section later in this chapter. ▨

Before you can go any further, it's useful to have some understanding of profiles because they control the ways Outlook uses information sources.

FIG. 45.3

The Inbox - Microsoft Outlook window is where you see messages you've received and haven't moved to a folder or deleted. The window shown here is maximized.

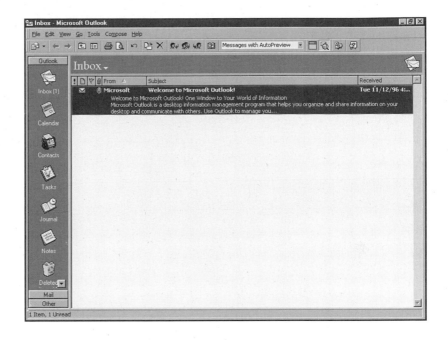

Understanding Profiles

A *profile* is a definition of the information services with which Outlook communicates. For example, if you are part of a Windows workgroup, a profile usually contains information about the postoffice you use to send and receive e-mail within the workgroup. If you try to use a profile that refers to a postoffice, but a postoffice isn't available, the profile will cause an error and Outlook won't start properly.

N O T E Profiles are defined in the Windows registry, so don't expect to find files corresponding to your profiles. ▨

In addition to services that are external to your computer, profiles usually define information services such as address books and personal information folders, which are files on your local hard disk.

After you have Outlook running, you can make changes to profiles from within Outlook. Initially, though, you might have to create or modify a profile outside Outlook. You do this by opening Mail and Fax within the Windows Control Panel.

To start working with a profile, follow these steps:

1. If necessary, start Outlook by double-clicking the Microsoft Outlook icon on the Windows desktop. If the Choose Profile dialog box appears, click OK to choose

the default profile and open the Inbox - Microsoft Outlook window shown previously in Figure 45.3.

2. Click OK in the Welcome to Microsoft Outlook balloon to hide it.

3. Choose Tools, Services to display the Services dialog box (see Figure 45.4).

FIG. 45.4

The Services dialog box is where you can see and change the properties of the profile on which the current Outlook session is based.

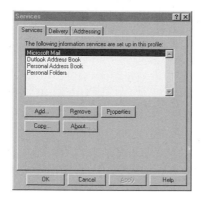

Depending on how you have previously used Exchange or Outlook, the dialog box may be the same as that shown in Figure 45.4, or it may be somewhat different. The dialog box is first displayed with the Services tab selected showing a list of information services defined by the profile. Services are the sources of information available to Outlook. In the example shown here, Outlook has access to Microsoft Mail, Outlook Address Book, Personal Address Book, and Personal Folders. The purposes of these service are:

- *Microsoft Mail* is the information service that provides access to your workgroup postoffice and handles e-mail within the workgroup.

- *Outlook Address Book* is where Outlook stores information about the people with whom you communicate, other than those within your workgroup. There's more information about this in the "Working with Contacts" section later in this chapter.

- *Personal Address Book* is where you can, if you like, keep information about your personal contacts. It also provides facilities for creating mailing lists.

- *Personal Folders* consists of subfolders Outlook uses to store specific types of information. As you'll see in the "Creating and Using Your Own Folders" section later in this chapter, you can create your own subfolders so that you can save information systematically.

You must make sure that each listed service is available. If you are uncertain whether one of the listed services is available, you might want to remove it at this time—you can always put it back later. To remove a service, select its name and then click Remove.

N O T E   The names of most information services are easy to understand. You might, however, be confused if the Microsoft Exchange Server is listed. Microsoft offers two products named Exchange: Exchange Client is the universal in-box that comes with Windows 95 and Windows NT; Exchange Server is available for installation on Windows NT Server. Exchange Server is somewhat like a workgroup postoffice, but provides e-mail services for people connected to a LAN. If you're not connected to a LAN in which the server has Exchange Server installed, you should not list Microsoft Exchange Server as an information service in your profile. ▪

Using the Office Assistant

When Outlook starts, it usually displays the Inbox - Microsoft Office window, over which is superimposed the Welcome to Microsoft Outlook balloon and the dancing paper clip Office Assistant.

If you don't intend to look at the information in the Welcome balloon immediately, click the OK button to remove it—you must do so before you can continue working with Outlook.

 You can leave the Office Assistant on your screen while you're working, or you can hide it by clicking the button marked with an x in its title bar. You can display the Office Assistant at any time while you're working by clicking the Office Assistant button at the right end of the toolbar.

Examining the Inbox

The top section of the Outlook window is similar to that in other Office applications, consisting of a title bar, menu bar, and toolbar. The status bar at the bottom of the window is also similar to other applications.

The column at the left, known as the Outlook Bar, contains shortcut buttons that provide access to the various facilities within Outlook.

The large pane that occupies most of the window is the Information Viewer which, in this case, is where you see the messages you've received. When you select Outlook facilities other than the Inbox, you see different types of information in the Information Viewer.

When the Inbox first appears, it displays any existing messages, as shown previously in Figure 45.3 or, if there are no messages, you see There are no items to show in this view. The first time you run Outlook after you've installed it, the Welcome message you see in the figure is placed automatically in your Inbox.

The number adjacent to the Inbox icon in the Outlook Bar indicates the number of unread messages in your Inbox—this number is present whether or not the Inbox is selected. When Inbox is selected, the status bar at the bottom of the window shows the total number of messages, as well as the number of unread messages, in your Inbox.

 Initially, the title and first three lines of unread messages are shown in the Information Viewer. To show only the titles of messages, click the AutoPreview button in the toolbar. To go back to showing the first three lines of messages, click the AutoPreview button again.

In addition to the title, and possibly the first three lines of messages, icons at the left provide information about each message. These icons are explained in the "Sending and Receiving Messages" section later in this chapter.

But what if you don't see the Inbox, or other unexpected things happen? You need to take a look at some of the Outlook options. If Outlook starts to dial a modem connection, click Cancel as many times as it takes to get back to Outlook.

Setting Outlook Options

If you haven't already done so, click the OK button in the Welcome balloon to remove that balloon from your screen.

You can choose among many Outlook options. As with other Office applications, you access these options by choosing Tools, Options to display the Options dialog box shown in Figure 45.5.

FIG. 45.5

The Options dialog box has 11 tabs, all of which provide numerous choices. The box is shown here with the General tab selected.

While it is beyond the scope of this chapter to describe all the option choices available and how each one affects the ways Outlook behaves, some have such a significant effect that you must know about them. It is strongly recommended that you take a few minutes to open each tab in the dialog box and get a general idea of the choices in each one. Time spent this way is a good way to become aware of many of Outlook's facilities and it will help you solve problems that may arise while you use Outlook. You can click the Help button at the bottom of the dialog box to see detailed information about each option.

Be aware of one important option in the General tab. The Startup Settings panel near the bottom allows you to set startup options. By making choices in this panel, you can have Outline open using a specific profile without showing the Choose Profile dialog box. You can also select a window other than Inbox for Outlook to display when it opens.

The E-mail tab contains more important options. It is here that you select which services Outlook should check for new mail. If one or more of your information services is provided by a telephone connection, you way not want Outlook to call the number automatically. Make sure only those services you want Outlook to check automatically are selected in this dialog box.

If you want to use Word as your e-mail editor, and to have access to Word's spell-checking and other capabilities, you should check the appropriate box near the bottom of the dialog box. If you don't check this box, Outlook uses its own RichEdit editor, which is adequate for most e-mail purposes but doesn't contain spell-checking and other facilities within Word.

After you've finished looking at the options, click OK to save any changes you've made or click Cancel to close the dialog box without saving changes, and return to the Inbox window.

Using the Welcome Information Box

Take the time to look at what's in the Welcome balloon. Unlike the other components in Office 97, most of Outlook's facilities are completely new. It's worth spending an hour or so to explore what's in the Welcome balloon.

To display the Welcome Information balloon, you must close Outlook and then restart it. To close Outlook, choose File, Exit and Log Off to return to the Windows Desktop. Then, double-click Microsoft Outlook and choose a profile. Outlook should open with the Welcome balloon displayed.

N O T E The File menu contains two Exit commands: Exit, and Exit and Log Off. You should usually use Exit and Log Off (not Exit) because that command closes all instances of Outlook and Exchange and also shuts down MAPI. Don't worry if you don't understand the significance of this. Just be aware that you may run into problems if you choose Exit. ∎

For starters, click the first item—See Key Information for Upgraders and New Users. This takes you directly to the Upgrade Help system contents list shown in Figure 45.6.

FIG. 45.6
The Key Information topic provides a wealth of information that will help you migrate from other information and personal information systems you have been using.

The other items in the Welcome balloon provide specific information about things you'll probably want to do quite soon after you start working with Outlook.

When you've finished looking at the information offered, you might want to remove the check mark from the last item in the list so that the Welcome balloon doesn't appear each time you start Outlook. Click OK to remove the Welcome balloon.

Understanding the Microsoft Outlook Window

The top section of the Window is conventional, having a title bar, menu mar, and toolbar. The narrow vertical bar at the left, known as the Outlook Bar, lets you choose what you want to see in the large pane, the Information Viewer, that occupies the remainder of the Window. Initially, the Information Viewer displays the contents of the Inbox, unless you have used the General tab of the Options dialog box to select a different startup folder.

N O T E The Inbox is where Outlook keeps messages you've received but not filed or deleted. ▪

The Outlook Bar at the left of the Microsoft Outlook window is where you select which of Outlook's facilities you want to use. These facilities are available in three groups: Outlook, Mail, and Other. Initially, Inbox in the Outlook group is normally selected.

Using the Inbox Toolbars

The Inbox has a Standard toolbar and a Remote toolbar. By default, the Inbox opens with the Standard toolbar displayed. If the Standard toolbar is not displayed, choose View, Toolbars to display a shortcut menu. In the shortcut menu, choose Standard.

As is the case of other Office applications, the Inbox Standard toolbar shows a full set of buttons when the Inbox is maximized, when the Inbox is displayed in a window that is wide enough to show the complete toolbar, and after you double-click the toolbar to show it in a separate window. The Standard toolbar may show a limited set of buttons if the Inbox is displayed in a window and the toolbar is within that window. The full set of Standard toolbar buttons is listed in Table 45.1. The buttons are listed in the order they appear in the toolbar, from left to right.

Part VIII

Ch 45

Table 45.1 Inbox Standard Toolbar Buttons

Button	Name	Purpose
	New Mail Message	Open the Message dialog box.
	Back	Go back to the previous pane.
	Forward	Go forward to the next pane.
	Up One Level	Go up one level in the folder hierarchy.
	Folder List	Display or hide a list of folders.
	Print	Print the selected message.
	Print Preview	Display a preview of the selected message.
	Undo	Undo your most recent action.
	Move to Folder	Move the selected message to another folder.
	Delete	Delete the selected message.
	Reply	Reply to the sender of the selected message.

continues

Table 45.1   Continued

Button	Name	Purpose
	Reply to All	Reply to all recipients of the selected message.
	Forward	Forward the selected message to another person.
	Address Book	Open an Address Book.
Messages	Current View	Select a different view of messages.
	Group By Box	Change the way messages are grouped.
	AutoPreview	Show or hide the first three lines of unread messages.
	Find Items	Open the Find dialog box.
	Office Assistant	Open the Office Assistant.

While you work with Outlook, you'll see many of these buttons, or similar ones, on other toolbars.

The Remote toolbar, unlike the Standard toolbar, is not displayed by default, and can only be displayed as a floating toolbar. To display the Remote toolbar, choose View, Toolbars to display a shortcut menu. In the shortcut menu, choose Remote. The Remote toolbar buttons are listed in Table 45.2.

N O T E   The buttons on the Remote toolbar provide facilities you use when your computer is connected to others by way of dial-up networking. ■

Table 45.2   Inbox Remote Toolbar Buttons

Button	Name	Purpose
	Connect	Connect to a mail delivery service.
	Disconnect	Disconnect from a mail delivery service.
	Mark to Retrieve	Mark a remote message for retrieval.

Button	Name	Purpose
	Mark to Retrieve a Copy	Mark a remote message to retrieve a copy.
✕	Delete	Delete the selected message.
↰	Unmark	Unmark a previously marked remote message.
↰	Unmark All	Unmark all remote messages.
Close	Close Preview	Close message preview.

Part
VIII
Ch
45

Looking at Folders and Subfolders

Outlook saves items of information in folders and subfolders. For example, the e-mail messages you see in the Inbox Information Viewer are stored in the Inbox subfolder, which is within the Personal Folders folder. Outlook provides an initial set of folders that it uses automatically. You can add your own folders and subfolders.

Click the Folder List button in the toolbar to see the available folders and subfolders (see Figure 45.7). You may see additional folders and subfolders on your screen.

FIG. 45.7
These are the folders and subfolders initially available in Outlook.

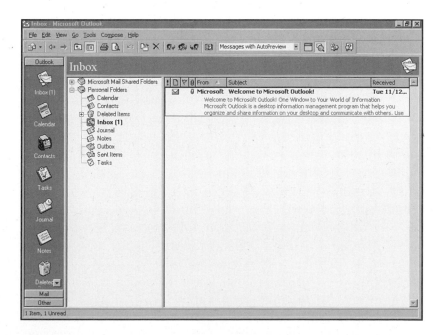

If the folders pane on your screen isn't wide enough to show the folder names completely, you can drag the pane's border to make the pane wider.

After you've looked at the list of folders and subfolders, click the Folder List button in the toolbar again to remove the list.

N O T E   You can also open and close the list of folders and subfolders by clicking the Information Viewer name—Inbox in this case. When you open the list in this way, the list is superimposed over the Information Viewer; some of the functionality described below is not available. ▪

Using Outlook's Standard Folders and Subfolders   You'll usually let Outlook take care of placing items of information in appropriate folders. However, you can easily move items from one folder to another, as described in the "Working with Folders" section later in this chapter.

With the folder list displayed, you can click the name of any folder or subfolder to display its contents in the Information Viewer.

Creating and Using Your Own Folders and Subfolders   One of the most useful features of Outlook is its capability to store items of information in an organized fashion. By default, Outlook stores all e-mail messages you receive in the Inbox subfolder and all messages you send in the Sent Items subfolder. While that may be satisfactory if you don't have many messages, you can organize your messages much better if you create your own subfolders in which you can save messages according to subject.

Suppose that you are involved with three projects; you can easily create separate subfolders for each of those projects. Moreover, suppose that you have several subject areas within each project. You can create subfolders under each of the project subfolders for each of these subject areas. After creating these subfolders, you can file all your messages systematically.

To create your own subfolders, do the following:

1. Click the Folder List button in the toolbar to display the folder list.
2. Right-click Personal Folders to display the shortcut menu shown in Figure 45.8.
3. Choose Create Subfolder to display the Create New Folder dialog box shown in Figure 45.9.

FIG. 45.8
This shortcut menu contains items you can use to work with folders.

FIG. 45.9
Use this dialog box to create a new subfolder.

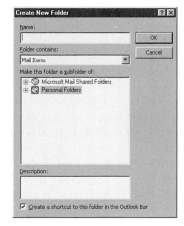

4. Enter a name for the subfolder, select the type of items it will contain, and, optionally, provide a description for the subfolder. Remove the check mark at the bottom of the dialog box unless you want to create a shortcut for the new subfolder.

5. Click OK to create the new subfolder and display its name in the list of folders.

You can create additional subfolders in the same manner.

To create subfolders below an existing subfolder, start by right-clicking the name of a subfolder, then follow the preceding steps. When you've finished, your list of subfolders could look something like the one shown in Figure 45.10.

Later in this chapter, you'll learn how to move and copy items between folders so that you can place your e-mail and other information items in appropriate subfolders.

FIG. 45.10
After you create
your own hierarchy
of subfolders, your
list of folders will
look like this.

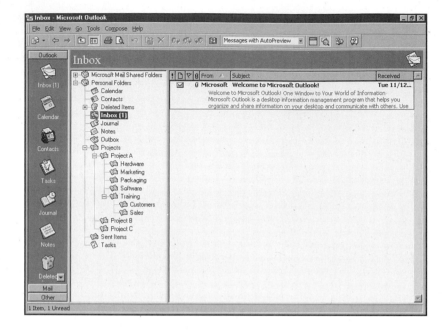

Choosing Another Outlook Facility

To choose another Outlook facility, click its icon in the Outlook Bar. For example, click Calendar to work with your calendar. Several things happen when you do this. The most obvious is that the Information Viewer changes to display a calendar, as shown in Figure 45.11.

Among other things that change are:

- The Windows title bar changes to `Calendar - Microsoft Outlook`.

- The Information Viewer title bar contains the title `Calendar` at the left and the current date at the right.

- The current date is highlighted in the Date Navigator at the top-right of the Information Viewer.

- The menu bar and menu items change to suit the needs of Calendar.

- Some of the buttons in the toolbar change to suit the needs of Calendar.

The Date Navigator may show two complete months' calendars, as in Figure 45.11. If you reduce the size of the window, only one month's calendar is shown. If you drag the vertical border between the left and right sections of the window, you see one, two, three, or even four complete calendars. You can also drag the horizontal border between the Date Navigator and the TaskPad to show additional rows of months in the Date Navigator.

FIG. 45.11

When you choose Calendar, the Information Viewer displays a calendar with the current date highlighted in the Date Navigator.

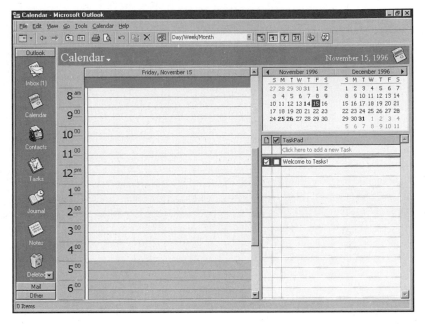

You can learn more about using Calendar in the "Working with the Calendar" section later in this chapter.

To get a first look at more of Outlook's facilities, click each remaining icon in the Outlook section of the Outlook Bar. Table 45.3 summarizes what these buttons show.

Table 45.3 Outlook Bar Icons

Icon	Display and Work with
Inbox	Messages received
Calendar	Calendar, schedule, and to-do list
Contacts	Contact names and other information
Tasks	To-do list
Journal	Record of daily activities
Notes	Miscellaneous notes
Deleted Items	Information you've deleted from folders

After you've taken a quick look at these facilities, click the Mail button near the bottom of the Outlook Bar to see another list of Outlook facilities. You can click any of these facilities to see each one in detail. The list contains the same Inbox and Deleted Items facilities as before, and also Sent Items (e-mail items you have sent by way of an Outlook service) and Outbox (e-mail items you have prepared for sending but have not already sent). Each facility gives you access to items in specific subfolders.

Finally, click Other at the bottom of the Outlook Bar to see the familiar items: My Computer and My Documents (the same items you can choose from your Windows desktop), and also Favorites (the items you can choose from the Internet Explorer menu, if you have Internet Explorer installed).

Now that you've had a preliminary look at Outlook, it's time to start working with it. Probably the best way to get started is to ignore, for the time being, Outlook's communication facilities and use it just as a stand-alone personal information manager. After you're comfortable with that, you can easily start using Outlook's communication facilities.

Before continuing, choose File, Exit and Log Off to close Outlook.

Using Outlook as a Personal Information Manager

A *personal information manager* (PIM) provides facilities you can use to organize information about your friends and business contacts, keep track of your daily activities and commitments, and keep other often-used information at hand. Although you don't need such a sophisticated application as Outlook to do this, using Outlook in this manner is a good way to become familiar with it. Even after you become a skilled Outlook user, you can use it as a PIM when you're traveling with your laptop computer.

Running Outlook as a PIM

If necessary, double-click Microsoft Outlook in your Windows screen to start Outlook based on the default.

Don't be surprised if Outlook opens showing messages in the Inbox, even though your profile doesn't contain any communication services. These messages are present for one or more reasons, such as:

- Outlook automatically places a Welcome message in your Inbox when you first run the application.
- If you previously had Exchange installed as a Windows 95 component and had messages in its Inbox, Outlook sees those messages.

■ If you have previously used Outlook and received messages in its Inbox, you see those messages even though you're running Outlook without communications services.

 T I P The fact that you see Inbox messages while you are running Outlook without communication services suggests how you might use Outlook. Before you run for the plane, download your incoming mail into the Inbox on your laptop computer. While you're on your journey, you can work with your mail and put outgoing messages in the Outbox. As soon as you get to a phone line, you can connect the computer, start Outlook, and send the messages from the Outbox.

While using Outlook as a PIM, you can start becoming familiar with its facilities. We'll start by looking at the Calendar in detail. Much of what you learn as you find your way around the Calendar applies almost identically to other Outlook facilities.

Part

VIII

Ch

45

Working with the Calendar

You use Calendar to keep information about your schedule. Outlook saves this information in the Calendar subfolder, which is within your Personal Folders folder. Your profile must, therefore, contain the Personal Folders information service.

To verify that your current profile does contain the Personal Folders information service, choose Tools, Services to display the Services dialog box. Check that the list of information services includes Personal Folders. If the list does not include Personal Folders, follow these steps:

1. Click Add in the Service dialog box to display the Add Service to Profile dialog box, which lists the services you can add.

2. Select Personal Folders in the list and click OK to display the Create/Open Personal Folders File dialog box.

3. Navigate through the structure of folders on your hard disk to find the place where you want to create the file that will contain Personal Folders. You can, if you prefer, create a new folder for this purpose.

4. Enter a name for the new file. Outlook provides the file name extension PST. This extension is required.

5. Click Open to display the Create Microsoft Personal Folders dialog box, in which the name Personal Folders is suggested for the new folder. You can change this name if you want.

6. Click OK to complete the process of adding the Personal Folders information Service to your profile.

N O T E The profile Outlook (or the previously installed Exchange) automatically uses the name Mailbox.pst for Personal Folders. In the Windows desktop, you can use Start, Find to locate this folder so that you can back it up regularly. ▪

Working with Calendar

Click Calendar in the Outlook Bar to display a calendar similar to that shown earlier in Figure 45.11.

 N O T E Outlook can display a calendar in Day, Week, or Month view. The first time you open the calendar, it appears in Day view. Subsequently, it is displayed in whichever of the three views was displayed previously. If you don't see the Day view, as in Figure 45.11, click the Day button on the Standard toolbar to display the Day view. ▪

The initial calendar window is based on the setting of your computer's internal calendar. However, you can easily display dates for any year and month. The calendar pages in the Date Navigator show the current and next month (or months) with today's date highlighted. The column at the left shows times in the current day with appointments blocked out and events shown as banners. The TaskPad is where you can see information about the current tasks in your to-do list.

N O T E Later in this chapter you'll find more information about appointments, events, and tasks. ▪

Navigating Around the Calendar To change from month to month, click one of the arrows adjacent to the month names in the Date Navigator. If you want to show a date more than a few months before or after the current date, choose <u>G</u>o, Go to Dat<u>e</u> (or press Ctrl+G) to display the Go To Date dialog box shown in Figure 45.12.

FIG. 45.12

You can use the Go To Date dialog box to jump to any date.

In the <u>D</u>ate box, type the date you want to go to. You can use any legitimate Windows format for the date. For example, Outlook understands the following formats:

December 25, 1997

Dec 25, 97

12/25/97

You can also use words and phrases, such as *tomorrow*, *two weeks from now*, *a month ago*, and the names of holidays (only those that occur on the same date every year).

Displaying the Calendar in Different Views   The three buttons near the right end of the toolbar enable you to select alternative views of the calendar, as listed in Table 45.4.

Table 45.4   Calendar Views

Button	View	Description
1	Day view	The column at the left shows hours in the current day. Shown earlier in Figure 45.11.
7	Week view	The column at the left shows days in the current week. Shown in Figure 45.13.
31	Month view	The entire window shows the days in the current month. Shown in Figure 45.14.

N O T E   One or more of these buttons may be missing from the toolbar if the window is not wide enough to show them all. ■

FIG. 45.13
The Week view of the calendar provides a summary of entries for the current week.

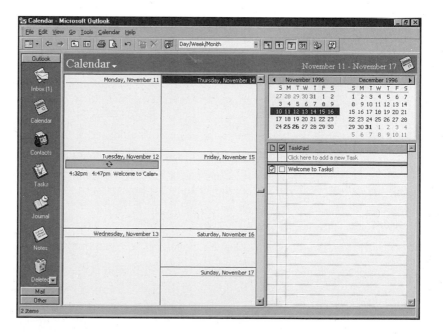

Part

VIII

Ch

45

FIG. 45.14

The Month view of the calendar provides a summary of entries for the current month.

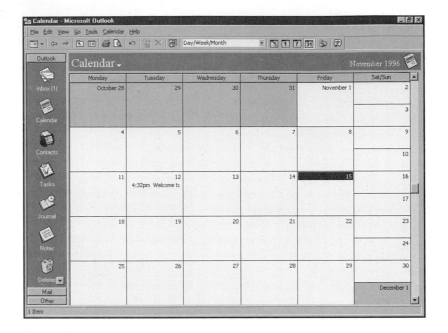

The vertical scroll bar at the right of the hours in the day view lets you scroll through the 24 hours of the day. The vertical scroll bar in the Tasks section lets you scroll through tasks.

The vertical scroll bar at the left of the days in the current week lets you move quickly from week to week.

The vertical scroll bar at the left of the calendar lets you scroll backward and forward from the current date.

Although the Month view doesn't initially show the Date Navigator and TaskPad, you can drag the right border to the left so that they are shown.

To return to the current day (the day set in your computer's internal calendar) click the Go to Today button in the toolbar, or choose Go, Go to Today.

Now that you know how to get around in the Calendar, it's time to add a few appointments.

Adding Appointments and Events to the Calendar You can use Outlook to mark one-time and recurring appointments, meetings, and events to your calendar. Before you do, however, you should clearly understand what appointments, meetings, and events are:

■ *Appointment.* An activity that completely occupies you for a specific period during a day. You can use appointments to block time to meet with other people or to work alone.

■ *Meeting*. Similar to an appointment, but involves you and other people who can interact with your calendar in Outlook.

■ *Event*. Something that occurs during one or more days, but doesn't necessarily occupy any of your time. Birthdays, anniversaries, and trade shows are typical events.

Appointments block time in the calendar. Events are indicated by banners in the calendar without blocking time.

To add a one-time appointment, do the following:

1. In the Day, Week, or Month view, select the date of the appointment by clicking in the Date Navigator.

2. Click the New Appointment button in the toolbar (alternatively, choose Calendar, New Appointment or press Ctrl+N) to open the Appointment dialog box shown in Figure 45.15.

FIG. 45.15
The Appointment dialog box is where you provide details of an appointment.

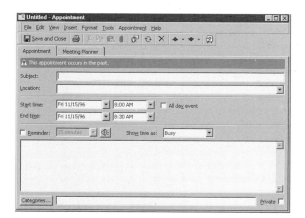

3. Fill in the information about the appointment: the Subject, Location, Start Time, and End Time. You can request a Reminder a certain time before the appointment and add notes about it in the text box at the bottom of the dialog box. The Show Time As box contains Busy by default, but you can choose to mark the time Free, Tentative, Busy, or Out of Office.

4. Click the Categories button and choose one or more categories from the list.

5. If you want, you can check the Private box.

6. Choose Save and Close to save the appointment and return to the Calendar.

N O T E   Reminders appear in message boxes on your screen providing Office is running. You don't necessarily need to have Outlook or any other Office application open to see reminders. ■

When you return to the Calendar, choose the Day view, and maximize the Calendar to see the appointment marked in the hours section at the left side of the Calendar, as shown in Figure 45.16. You can also see the appointment in the Week and Month views, but not with as much detail as in the Day view.

FIG. 45.16
After you create an appointment, the time involved is blocked in the Day view of the calendar.

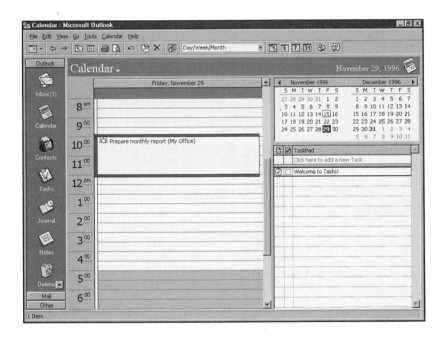

Many more facilities are built into scheduling an appointment than can be described in detail here. Some to be aware of are:

■ Calendar warns you if you attempt to schedule an appointment for a time in the past or at a time that conflicts with an existing appointment or meeting.

■ The Date Navigator calendars show in bold those days on which you have appointments or meetings.

■ Calendar remembers each location you enter in the Location box. After you have entered the names of locations, you can subsequently choose from those locations.

■ You can add, delete, and edit appointment categories by clicking Master Category List in the Categories dialog box.

■ Double-click an appointment in the Day, Week, or Month views of the Calendar to display details in the Appointment dialog box.

■ You can change the start and end times of an appointment by dragging the appointment block in the hours section of the Day view.

■ You can change an appointment from one day to another by dragging the appointment in the Week or Month views.

■ You can open the Current View list box in the toolbar and choose Active Appointments to see a table of all appointments for today and subsequent days.

To create a recurring appointment, do the following:

1. With the Calendar displayed, choose Calendar, New Recurring Appointment to display the Appointment Recurrence dialog box (see Figure 45.17).

FIG. 45.17
Use the Appointment Recurrence dialog box to mark recurring appointments in your calendar.

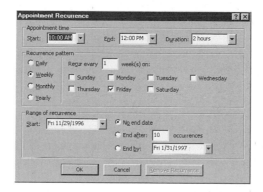

2. Fill in the various boxes in the Appointment Time, Recurrence Pattern, and Range of Recurrence sections of the dialog box, and then click OK to display the Appointment dialog box.

N O T E   In the Recurrence Pattern section of the dialog box, Daily, Weekly, Monthly, and Yearly all provide a variety of choices. ■

3. Provide details of the recurring appointment in the Appointment dialog box, and click Save and Close. The Calendar now shows the recurring appointments.

One useful feature of recurring appointments is that you can double-click a specific occurrence of a recurring appointment in the Day view of the calendar and then change that occurrence. This is useful, for example, if that occurrence is canceled, or you need to make some specific notes about it.

To delete one occurrence of a recurring appointment, right-click that occurrence in any view of the Calendar to display a shortcut menu. In the shortcut menu, click Delete. Your Calendar now contains all the occurrences except the one you've deleted.

You can schedule events and recurring events in a manner similar to appointments and recurring appointments by choosing Calendar, New Event or Calendar, New Recurring Event. After you provide information in the dialog boxes, events and recurring events show in the Calendar in much the same way as appointments. One significant difference, though, is that events don't block out time in the Day view—they merely show as banners at the top of the hours section.

One special class of events is holidays. To add holidays to your calendar, follow these steps:

1. With the Calendar displayed, choose Tools, Options to show the Options dialog box.

2. Click the Add Holidays button at the bottom of the Calendar Tab to display the Add Holidays to Calendar dialog box (see Figure 45.18).

FIG. 45.18

Use the Add Holidays to Calendar dialog box to choose one or more countries whose holidays you want to mark as events on your calendar.

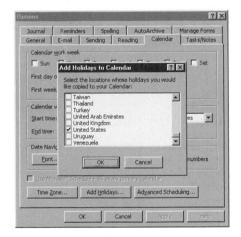

3. Click the check boxes corresponding to those countries for which you want to show holidays in your calendar. Make sure that those countries for which you do not want to show holidays are not checked.

4. Click OK to add the holidays for the selected countries. Outlook copies the appropriate holidays to your calendar. After copying is complete, the Options dialog box is again displayed. Click OK to continue.

N O T E   Outlook adds holidays as one-time events for the period November 1996 through November 2006. ▪

Working with Tasks in the Calendar Information Viewer   Unlike appointments and events, tasks do not occur on a specific date, though they usually have a due date and may have a start date. The TaskPad section of the Calendar shows your current tasks.

While you can add new tasks, delete tasks, edit the names of tasks, and mark a task as completed directly from the TaskPad, it's usually better to work with tasks as a separate item, as described in the "Working with Tasks" section of this chapter. You can move directly to the Task dialog box by double-clicking a task name in the TaskPad.

Working with Contacts

Contacts are the people you are involved with in your personal and business lives. By creating a list of people and always choosing names from the list while you are working with Outlook's various facilities, you make sure that you always refer to a person in exactly the same way. Consequently, when you look for references to that person, you always see all the references to that person. For example, if Kathleen Porter is one of your friends, you or others might sometimes refer to her as Kathleen, Kathy, or Katie with or without the last name. Outlook treats each version of the name as a different person. Avoid this problem by entering one of the names in your list of contacts and always choosing the name from the list.

Entering Contact Information   To start working with Contacts, click Contacts in the Outlook Bar. The first time you do so, you see just your own name listed. Outlook gets your name from the information you provided when you installed Office 97.

 To enter information about a new contact, click the New Contact button in the toolbar (alternatively, choose Contacts, New Contact, or press Ctrl+N) to display the Contact dialog box shown in Figure 45.19.

> **N O T E**   If you already have contacts in your list, you can double-click a contact name to open the Contact dialog box with information about that contact displayed. ■

FIG. 45.19

The Contact dialog box is where you provide information about your contacts.

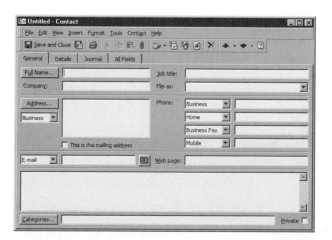

The Contact dialog box lets you enter a great deal of information about each contact, but doing so is very time-consuming. In order to use your time efficiently, it's usually best to enter only the information you expect to need in the future; you can always add more information later. Naturally, the more information you enter, the more useful the contact list will be.

TIP You can import contact information from a database into Outlook. To do so, in any Outlook window, choose File, Import and Export to display the Import and Export dialog box. You will see a list of formats to which you can export and from which you can import. Further information about this is beyond the scope of this chapter, so you'll have to explore this on your own.

Outlook organizes contacts primarily on the basis of people's names, so you start with the Full Name text box in the Contact dialog box. Resist the temptation to enter a person's name directly in the Full Name text box. Instead, click the Full Name button to display the Check Full Name dialog box shown in Figure 45.20.

FIG. 45.20

Use the Check Full Name dialog box to enter a contact's name in the format Outlook can use most effectively.

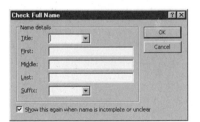

Enter the contact's First name or initial, Middle name or initial, and Last name in the appropriate boxes.

N O T E When you provide only an initial, place a period after the initial if you want the name to appear elsewhere with a period after each initial. Outlook doesn't add the periods for you.

If you want to precede the name with a title, either choose a title from the Title list box or type a title. Similarly, if you want to enter a suffix, choose it from the Suffix list box or type the suffix. Click OK to return to the Contact dialog box, which now shows the name in its conventional form in the Full Name box and in the format in which Outlook proposes to file it in the File As box (see Figure 45.21).

Enter the contact's job title and company affiliation in the appropriate boxes, and then press Tab to move the insertion point to the File As box.

FIG. 45.21

After you've entered a contact's name, the name appears in the File As box in the form Outlook proposes to file it.

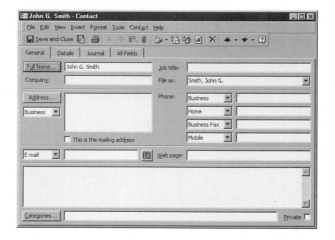

You can open the File As list to look at various ways in which Outlook can file the contact's name, as shown in Figure 45.22. You can choose any way of filing that Outlook suggests or, if you want, you can type another name, a nickname perhaps, by which you want to file the contact. Later in this section, you'll see how Outlook uses the File As name when displaying your contacts.

FIG. 45.22

Outlook can file a contact in various formats as shown in the File As list box.

TIP In order to see File As formats that include the company name, you must provide the company name and then press Tab before you open the File As list box.

You can provide business, home, and other addresses for the contact. Open the list box below the Address button to choose which type of address you want to provide. Then click the Address button to display the Check Address dialog box in which you provide the street address, city, state or province, ZIP or postal code, and country information. After you've entered the information, click OK to display this information in the Contact dialog box. After you've entered one address, you can choose another address type and then provide that address. Outlook saves all three addresses if you choose to provide them. You can specify which is the mailing address by checking the box marked This is the Mailing Address.

Outlook lets you save many different phone numbers for each contact and subsequently use those numbers for automatic dialing. Although the Contact dialog box offers space for only four phone numbers, you can provide many more. When the Contact dialog box first opens, the four Phone boxes are labeled Business, Home, Business Fax, and Mobile. Open any of the phone type list boxes to choose from a list of phone types, and then enter the numbers for those types. You can subsequently change the type for any of the boxes and enter more numbers. Outlook saves all the numbers you enter.

N O T E   If you're going to take advantage of automatic dialing, you must enter phone numbers correctly. Enter phone numbers within your own country in the normal way—Outlook ignores spaces, hyphens, parentheses, and other similar characters, so you can use these or not as you please.

In North America, do not place a 1 before the area code. Your modem's dialing properties should be set to provide the 1 automatically when it's needed.

Always include the area code, even if it's your local area code (which you don't normally need to dial). If your modem's dialing properties are set correctly, Outlook ignores the local area code. With the area code entered, you can use your contact information from a location outside your normal area code.

Enter international phone numbers in the form:

   +021(982)494-4321

where 021 is the country code. The parentheses are optional.

Outlook ignores any notes you place after the phone number. You can enter a phone number such as (805)592-6214 x349 in which the extension number is there as a reminder to you—Outlook ignores it.

You can provide as many as three e-mail addresses for each contact. Simply choose E-mail, E-mail 2, or E-mail 3 from the list and enter the e-mail address. Enter Internet addresses in the standard form, such as esmith@server.com. Enter CompuServe and AOL addresses in the same way you would when sending message by way of the Internet, such as 99999.999@compuserve.com or mailbox@aol.com.

N O T E CompuServe addresses have a comma as a separator between the first and second groups of numbers. If you want to send e-mail to a CompuServe address by way of the Internet, you must replace the comma with a period. ▪

The Contact dialog box also has a provision to enter a Web page address for each contact. After you've entered a Web page address, you can subsequently use Outlook to open that page (providing you have a compatible browser, such as Internet Explorer, installed).

You can assign each contact to a category, using one of the default categories or one you define. Click the Categories button at the bottom of the Contact dialog box to choose from a list of available categories displayed in the Categories dialog box. Check one or more categories in the list, and then click OK to return to the Contact dialog box with the selected category or categories shown in the Categories box. Alternatively, Outlook enables you to enter a category name directly into the Categories box. This is usually not a good practice because you will probably not always be consistent in the way you name categories. Another problem with entering categories in this way is that they do not become part of the Master Category List.

N O T E If you want to add, delete, or edit categories, choose the Master Category List button in the Categories dialog box. ▪

After you've completed supplying all the contact information, choose File, Save, or choose File, Save and New if you want to start supplying information for another contact. Outlook saves your contact information in the Contacts subfolder.

Displaying Contact Information You can display information about your contacts in several views. To do so, open the Current View list box from the toolbar. The views available are listed in Table 45.5.

Table 45.5 Contact View Available

View	Information Displayed
Address Cards	Contact with mailing address, business phone, home phone
Detailed Address Cards	Contact with all addresses, all phone numbers, additional information
Phone List	Contact with company name, home phone number, business phone and fax numbers
By Category	Contact in order of category with company name. business phone and fax number, home phone number

continues

Table 45.5 Continued

View	Information Displayed
By Company	Contact in order of company with job title, company name and department, company phone and fax numbers
By Location	Contact in order of country with company name, state, and country, business and home phone numbers

If you choose Address Cards, you see your contacts in the format shown in Figure 45.23.

FIG. 45.23
After you choose to display Address Cards, you see the principal information about people in your contacts list.

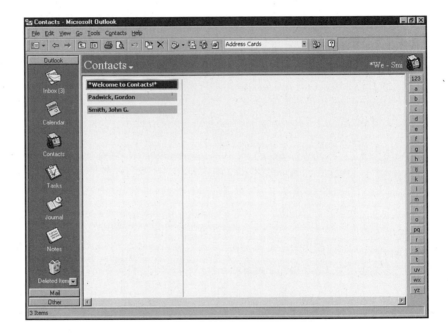

The address cards are listed in alphabetical order, based on the File As name you used when entering contact information in the Contact dialog box, with the first contact in alphabetical order initially selected. The status bar at the bottom of the windows shows the total number of contacts you have listed.

You can use several shortcuts for selecting address cards, as listed in Table 45.6.

Table 45.6 Moving Among Address Cards

Selection	Method
First card	Press Home
Last card	Press End

Selection	Method
Next card	Press the down-arrow key
Previous card	Press the up-arrow key

You can use the selection bar at the right edge of the Information Viewer to choose a section of the list in alphabetical order.

To see complete information about each contact, choose Detailed Address Cards from the Current View list box. With Address Cards displayed in any view, you can double-click anywhere on a card to display the Contact dialog box with all the information for the chosen card available. This provides a fast and easy way to edit information about a contact.

After you've become familiar with one view of your contacts, you should have no trouble finding your way around the other views.

Using Your Contact List to Dial Phone Numbers   If your computer has a modem, you can use your contact list to dial phone numbers automatically.

N O T E   Before you can use automatic dialing, the dialing properties for your modem must be set correctly. To set these properties, open the Windows Control Panel, double-click Modems, choose the modem you're using, click Dialing Properties, and set the properties.

To dial phone numbers automatically, follow these steps:

1. Display any view of your contact list and select the contact whose number you want to call.

2. Point to the AutoDialer button in the Contacts toolbar to display the New Call dialog box (see Figure 45.24).

3. Open the Number list and select the number you want to call.

4. Click Start Call to dial the number.

5. As instructed by the on-screen message, pick up your telephone to use it.

FIG. 45.24
You can use New Call dialog box to automatically dial any phone number in your contact list.

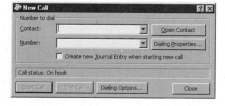

N O T E You can automatically create a Journal entry for a phone call. Before you click Start
Call, click the check box named Create New Journal Entry when Starting Call. For more
information about journals, see "Working with Your Journal" later in this chapter. ■

Working with Tasks

In some ways Tasks, as handled by Outlook, are similar to appointments and events.
Whereas Appointments and Events are scheduled for specific dates (an appointment is for
a specific date and time; an event occurs on a specific date), the only dates that may be
associated with a task are its start and due dates, neither of which is required. A task is
something to be done at any time and on any day provided it is completed by the due date
(if there is a due date).

If you must do something at a particular time on a particular day, it is an appointment (you
can have an appointment with yourself). If you must do something by a particular day, it is
a task.

Outlook can handle one-time tasks and recurring tasks. You can define tasks for yourself
and assign tasks to other people, though this chapter deals only with tasks for yourself.

To start working with tasks, click Tasks in the Outlook Bar to display the Tasks Information Viewer. The first time you display this, it displays the dummy task—Welcome to
Tasks! If you have already entered tasks, they are listed and the status bar shows the
number of tasks entered.

 Creating a New Task   To start creating a new task for yourself, click the New Task
button in the toolbar (alternatively, choose Tasks, New Task or press Ctrl+N) to display
the Task dialog box shown in Figure 45.25.

FIG. 45.25

The Task dialog box is
where you define a
new task for yourself.

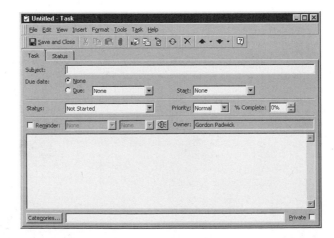

The only box you must complete in this dialog box is Subject because each task must have a name. By default, a new task has no Due date and no Start date. You can enter dates at this time or later. If you do enter a due date, an information bar near the top of the dialog box shows the number of days remaining until the due date.

The middle section of the dialog box contains default entries—Status: Not Started, Priority: Normal; % Complete: 0%. If appropriate, you can change the Priority to Low or High. After you start working on the task, you can reopen this Information Viewer and change the Status to In Progress, and the % Complete to the current percentage.

If you want an automatic reminder about the task, click the Reminder check box. After doing so, you can set a date and time in the two boxes at the right of the Reminder boxes. Subsequently, Outlook flashes a message on-screen when the reminder becomes due or, if your computer is off at that time, the next time you open Office after the reminder becomes due. You can, if you like, set an audible reminder. To do so, click the sound button at the center of the dialog box to display the Reminder Sound dialog box, in which you can specify a sound file.

The text box near the bottom of the dialog box is where you can enter whatever information about the task you think is appropriate.

Just as with Contacts, you should assign a Category that exists in the Master Category List to a task. You can add Categories to the Master Category list.

After you've completed defining the new task, click Save and Close to display the Task list with the new task included. Outlook saves tasks in the Tasks subfolder.

Displaying a Task List   Outlook can display your task list in several views, as shown in Table 45.7.

Table 45.7   Task List Views

View	Information Displayed
Simple List	Minimum task information about
Detailed List	Detailed task information
Active Tasks	Incomplete (including overdue) tasks
Next Seven Days	Tasks due within next seven days
Overdue Tasks	Overdue tasks
By Category	Tasks grouped by category
Assignment	Tasks assigned to others

continues

Table 45.7 Continued

View	Information Displayed
By Person Responsible	Tasks sorted by person responsible
Completed Tasks	Completed tasks
Task TimeLine	Gantt-like chart of tasks

To select a view of your tasks, open the Current View list on the Task toolbar and choose the list you want to see. In any view, you can double-click a task to see the information about that task in the Task dialog box. You can also double-click a task in the Calendar TaskPad to see complete information about that task in the Task dialog box.

There is much more to learn about working with tasks, but that is beyond the scope of this book.

Working with Your Journal

If you're like most people, you're very busy and have many family- and job-related responsibilities. It's impossible to remember when (sometimes if) you did certain things, whom you called and what they said, or when other things happened. Keeping a journal is one way you can simplify your life.

Basically, a journal is a chronological record of things that happen—a diary of sorts. The benefit of keeping a journal on your computer is that it's easy to find information about past happenings. The problem is that a journal is only useful if you are meticulous about keeping it up. Keeping up a journal can be time-consuming, but Outlook helps you solve this problem by automatically recording activities in your journal. The automatic journal entries that Outlook can make include:

- E-mail messages
- Faxes you send and receive
- Meeting requests and responses to meeting requests
- Tasks you assign to others

In addition, Outlook can automatically make journal entries to record documents you create or modify in other Office applications (Access, Excel, Office Binder, PowerPoint, and Word). This capability applies also to applications (from companies other than Microsoft) that satisfy the requirements of the Microsoft Office Compatible program.

N O T E Choose Tools, Options and choose the Journal tab in the Options dialog box to select which items are automatically recorded in your journal.

Microsoft will supply the information other companies need to make their applications compatible with Outlook. ■

Apart from the automatic journal entries Outlook makes, you can manually add whatever journal entries you want. In order to make your journal useful without spending too much time, you must decide how much detail you really need to keep.

Now that you have a general idea of what a Journal is, let's make a short exploration of how it works.

Start using Journal by clicking Journal in the Outlook Bar to display the Journal Information Viewer. What you see at this time depends on what you've done since you installed Office 97. If you've used any of the Office 97 applications, you'll see a banner heading for each application (see Figure 45.26). Later, after you've sent and received e-mail messages, these will also be shown in the Information Viewer. The Journal can also record phone calls you make (and their duration), but not phone calls you receive.

Part VIII
Ch 45

FIG. 45.26
This is a typical Journal view, after you've used several of the Office 97 applications.

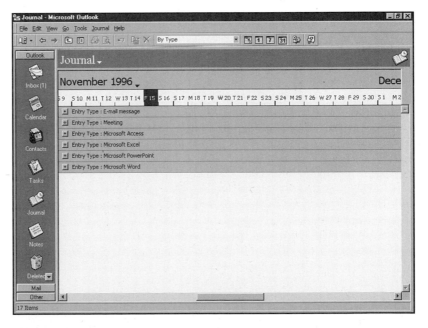

The view you see here is known as a TimeLine because it shows journal entries on a time scale. You can choose a Day, Week, or Month view by clicking buttons in the toolbar.

To show each journal entry separately, choose View, Expand/Collapse Groups, Expand All. Now you see icons in the Information Viewer to indicate each time you worked with a file in each of the applications, as in the example in Figure 45.27.

FIG. 45.27

The expanded Journal TimeLine shows the date on which you worked with various Office applications.

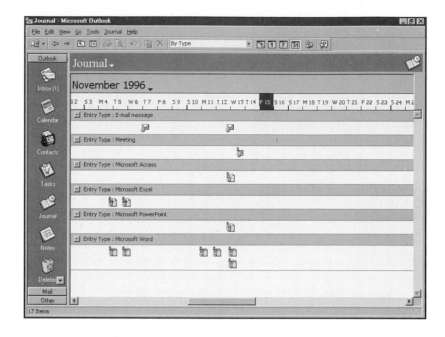

You can move the mouse pointer onto an icon to display the name of the file involved.

N O T E The Journal TimeLine is somewhat like an outline in Word or Excel. You can click the small plus sign at the left of each category to expand that category. When the category is expanded, you can click on the minus sign to collapse it. ▪

You can double-click an icon in the TimeLine to display complete information about an item.

 Making a Journal Entry Manually To start creating a manual Journal entry, click the New Journal button in the toolbar (alternatively, choose Journal, New Journal Entry or press Ctrl+N) to see the Journal Entry dialog box shown in Figure 45.28.

This dialog box automatically shows the current date and time. You can change the date and time if you are recording something that happened previously.

Each entry must have a subject, so make the appropriate entry in the Subject box. Open the Entry Type list box and choose an entry type. If appropriate, you can enter the name of a contact in the Contact box and the name of a company in the Company box, or both. If the contact name already exists in one of your lists, you can choose the name from a list by clicking the button at the right of the Contact box.

If appropriate, you can record the time occupied by the activity in the Duration box.

FIG. 45.28
The Journal Entry dialog box is where you add a journal entry.

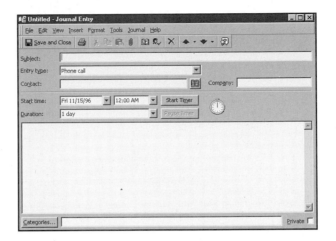

 TIP You can use Journal to keep a record of the time you spend on activities (this is necessary if you bill your time). To do so, open a Journal entry and click the Start Timer when the activity starts. During the activity, you can click Pause Timer if there's an interval during which time should not be recorded, or when the activity is finished. When the timer is running, the Duration box shows the time spent on the activity, starting at the time shown in the Start Time boxes. Outlook saves the duration with the other information about the activity.

You can type any information you like in the text box near the bottom of the dialog box, and you can choose a category by clicking the Categories button.

When you've completed the journal entry, click Save and Close to save the item in the Journal subfolder.

Displaying Journal Entries   Outlook displays journal items somewhat like it displays contacts and tasks. One significant difference is that a TimeLine identifies the time at which you created items.

You can select from six different views of journal items, as listed in Table 45.8.

Table 45.8   Journal Entry Views

View	Information Displayed
By Type	All entries represented by icons on a timeline, grouped by type
By Contact	All entries represented by icons on a timeline, grouped by contact name
By Category	All entries represented by icons on a timeline, grouped by category

continues

Part
VIII

Ch
45

Table 45.8   Continued

View	Information Displayed
Entry List	All entries in a list
Last Seven Days	All entries created within the last seven days, in a list
Phone Calls	Only entries that record phone calls, in a list

With journal entries displayed in any view, you can double-click an entry to return to the Journal Entry dialog box to view or modify that entry.

Working with Notes

Notes are the electronic equivalent of those sticky yellow slips of paper that 3M created by accident and are now so pervasive. You can use notes to jot down reminders to yourself; you can save notes to refer to later; you can leave notes open on the screen while you work; you can drag notes into other Office applications.

To start working with notes, click Notes in the Outlook Bar to open the Notes Information Viewer.

 To create a new note, click the New Note button on the toolbar (alternatively, choose Note, New Note or press Ctrl+N) to see the small, yellow note in the Information Viewer (see Figure 45.29). In the other Information Viewers, Outlook provides an example of a note. You can drag the edges of the note to change its size if necessary. The current date and time are displayed at the bottom of the note and saved with the note.

With the Notes Information Viewer open, type whatever you want in the note. Outlook automatically saves each new note in the Notes subfolder. You can also save the note as a file by clicking the icon at the top-left corner of the note to display a shortcut menu, and then choosing Save As to open the Save As dialog box. You can use this dialog box in the normal way to provide a file name and choose the folder in which you want to save the note.

You can also assign each note to a category. To do so, click the icon at the top-left corner of the note and then, in the menu, choose Categories to display the Categories dialog box. Select the appropriate category from those listed in this dialog box.

By default, notes are yellow but you can change the color to blue, green, pink, or white. You might want to assign a different color to each type of note so that they are easily identified. To change the color of a note, click the icon at the top-left corner of the note and then, in the menu, choose Color to display a list of colors. Choose the color you want from the list.

FIG. 45.29
You can use the Notes Information Viewer to jot down reminders to yourself.

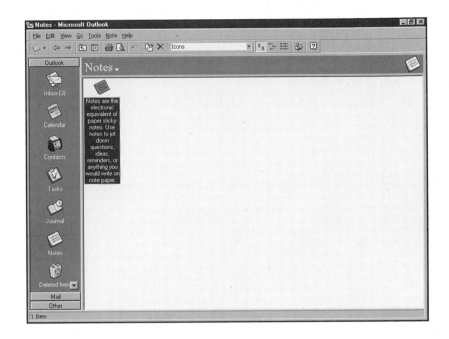

Outlook displays a list of notes in much the same way that it displays contacts, tasks, and so on. You can display notes in various formats by opening the Current View list in the toolbar. You can choose to display notes in the following ways:

- As icons
- Listed with their creation dates
- Created within the last seven days
- By category
- By color

With notes displayed in any format, you can double-click an individual note to see it in the Notes Information Viewer.

N O T E You can drag notes into other documents. For example, you can create a note in Outlook, and then close Outlook with the note remaining on your screen. Subsequently, you can open a Word document, select the note, and drag it into your Word document. ▪

Sending and Receiving Messages

Outlook is intended to be your message center. You can use Outlook to send e-mail messages to, and receive messages from, people in your workgroup, people with accounts on your LAN or WAN, people who have Internet accounts or who use information services such as CompuServe, as well as for sending and receiving facsimile (fax) messages. This chapter deals primarily with sending and receiving messages within a Windows 95 or Windows NT workgroup. After you become familiar with using the workgroup environment, you'll be well prepared to start using Outlook's more extensive e-mail capabilities.

Using the Workgroup Environment

In order to use Outlook to send and receive messages within a workgroup, there are certain essentials to take care of. You must make sure that:

- Your computer is connected to other computers running under Windows for Workgroups, Windows 95, or Windows NT to form a workgroup.

- Someone within the workgroup has set up a workgroup postoffice and that all members of the workgroup are included in the Postoffice Address List.

- You have a profile that includes the Microsoft Mail service.

The following section assumes that you have taken care of the first two points.

Adding Microsoft Mail Service to Your Profile In order to interchange e-mail with members of your workgroup, your profile must contain the Microsoft Mail information service. To check whether you have that information service, choose Tools, Services to open the Service dialog box which shows the services in your profile. If Microsoft Mail is not listed, follow these steps:

1. In the Services dialog box, click Add to see the services you can add to the profile, select Microsoft Mail, and then click OK to display the Microsoft Mail dialog box with the Connection tab selected.

2. Make sure that the path to the postoffice is correct. In most cases, you won't have to be concerned about any other settings in this dialog box. If necessary, enter the path to the postoffice. If you don't know the path to the postoffice, consult your workgroup supervisor.

3. Select the Logon tab and enter the name by which you are listed in the workgroup postoffice and your password. Although you can choose to let Outlook remember your password, you normally shouldn't do so because, if you do, anyone can access your mail.

4. Click OK to accept the Microsoft Mail properties. Read the message about the necessity to log off from Outlook, and then click OK to return to the Services dialog box which now shows Microsoft Mail as one of your services.

5. Click OK to close the dialog box.

6. Choose <u>F</u>ile, Exit and <u>L</u>og Off to close Outlook and return to the Windows Desktop.

7. Double-click the Microsoft Outlook icon on the Desktop to restart Outlook.

8. Choose the profile to which you just added the Microsoft Mail service and click OK. If you didn't choose to let Outlook remember your password (in step 3), you see the Microsoft Mail dialog box which shows the path to your workgroup postoffice, the name by which you are listed in the postoffice, and a blank space for your mailbox password.

9. Type your mailbox password, and then click OK. If you type the password correctly, Outlook opens with the Inbox Information Viewer displayed. If Outlook doesn't recognize your password, you see an error message and you can type the password again (correctly this time).

Part

VIII

Ch

45

N O T E If you run into trouble sending and receiving mail within a workgroup, you may have to return to the Microsoft Mail dialog box and work your way through the many choices available in its tabs.

The preceding steps assume that you have a direct connection to the workgroup postoffice. If you use a dial-up connection, you must provide information in the Remote Connection, Remote Session, and Dial-up Networking tabs of the Microsoft Mail dialog box. ▪

Sending Messages to Workgroup Colleagues   You can choose whether or not to use Word when you are writing and editing e-mail messages. By choosing to use Word, you have access to spell and grammar checking—and other facilities, such as working with tables—that are not available in Outlook's RichText editor. The principal disadvantage of using Word is the delay incurred while Word starts. The information in this session assumes you are using Word as your e-mail editor.

N O T E To use Word as your e-mail editor, choose <u>T</u>ools, <u>O</u>ptions and then open the E-mail tab. Near the bottom of the options dialog box, select the option Use Microsoft Word as the E-mail Editor. ▪

Sending a message is a very simple process. Just follow these steps:

1. Double-click the Microsoft Outlook icon in your Windows screen to start Outlook with the Inbox displayed. Alternatively, if Outlook is already running, choose Inbox in the Outlook Bar.

2. Click the New Mail Message button in the toolbar (alternatively, choose Co<u>m</u>pose, <u>N</u>ew Mail Message or press Ctrl+N) to open the Message dialog box shown in Figure 45.30.

FIG. 45.30

You prepare an e-mail message in the Message dialog box.

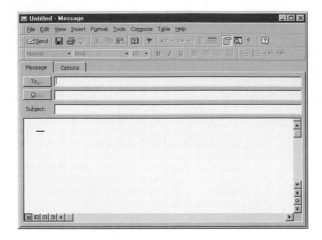

3. Click the To... button to show the Select Names dialog box (see Figure 45.31). The procedure described here assumes you are sending a message to someone whose name is in the Postoffice Address List. If you have a Personal Address List, you can select that list. However, you'll usually find the name of workgroup colleagues in the Postoffice Address List.

FIG. 45.31

The Select Names dialog box shows the names in the Postoffice Address List or in another address list you select.

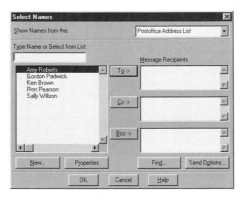

4. Select the name of the person, or several people, to whom you want to send a message, and then click To for the selected name or names to be moved into the Message Recipients box.

5. If you want to send copies or blind copies of the message to other people, select the appropriate name or names and then click the Cc button for copies or Bcc button for blind copies. Click OK to return to the Message dialog box with the recipients names shown.

NOTE Copy (Cc) means that a copy is sent to the designated person and that person's name appears on the messages that all recipients receive so that everyone knows that a copy of the message was sent to that person. Blind copy (Bcc) means that a copy is sent to the designated person but that person's name does not appear on the message other recipients receive; other recipients don't know that a copy of the message was sent to that person. ■

6. Move the insertion point to the Subject box and type a suitable title for the message.

7. Now type the message in the text box in the bottom section of the dialog box.

8. Carefully read your message and make sure that there are no spelling mistakes, grammatical errors, missing words, or other errors.

9. Click the Send button to send the message.

When you click the Send button, the message is immediately sent to the workgroup postoffice. Depending on how other people in the workgroup have set up their computers, they may or may not immediately know that you've sent a message to them. However, your message will be displayed the next time recipients look for mail and open their Inboxes.

You don't have to send a message as soon as you've finished writing it. Sometimes, particularly for important messages, it's a good idea to write a message and think about it for a while before you send it. After you've written a message, instead of immediately sending it, you can place it in the Outbox. To do so, choose File, Move to Folder and from the list of Folders choose Outbox. Later you can open the message in the Outbox, edit it if necessary, and then send it.

Enhancing a Message The preceding account of creating and sending a message covered only the most basic text messages. There are many enhancements you can make to your messages, including:

- Formatting text, using all the facilities within Word
- Attaching files
- Embedding graphics and other objects
- Flagging messages for special attention
- Assigning a level of importance

Receiving Messages You usually don't have to do anything to receive workgroup e-mail messages. With Outlook properly installed on your computer so that either of these applications knows the location of the workgroup postoffice, any messages addressed to you are displayed automatically whenever you open your Inbox.

Part VIII
Ch
45

While you're working, Outlook checks for incoming mail every ten minutes or at some other interval you choose in the Microsoft Mail Properties dialog box. You can also check for mail by displaying the Inbox Information Viewer and then choosing Tools, Check for New Mail On. This displays the Check for New Mail On dialog box, which lists the available mail services. In that dialog box, check one or more mail services and click OK. If any messages are waiting, they are transferred into your Inbox subfolder and displayed in the Information Viewer.

After you've received several messages, your Inbox Information Viewer will be similar to that shown in Figure 45.32.

FIG. 45.32

The Inbox shows all the messages you haven't moved to a folder or deleted.

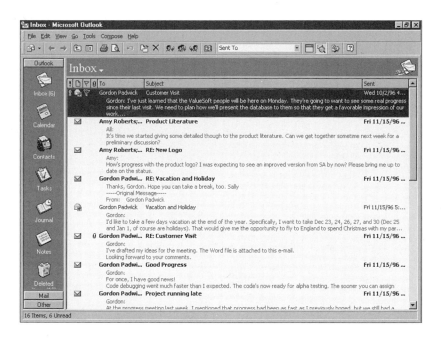

Messages are displayed in two ways: you see the subject line and the first three lines of text of those messages you haven't already read; you see only the subject line of those messages you have read. To read the full text of a message and see any graphics included in the message, just double-click anywhere on the subject line or click anywhere on the first three lines of text if they are displayed.

The four columns at the left of each message indicate the message status, as listed in Table 45.9.

Table 45.9   Message Status Icons

Column	Icon	Message Status
1	None	Normal importance
1	!	High importance
1	↓	Low importance
2	✉	Message unread
2	✉	Message read
3	None	Message not flagged
3	🚩	Message flagged
4	None	No attachment
4	📎	Message has attachment

You can deal with a message in several ways. To do so, right-click anywhere on the message to display a shortcut menu that offers the following items:

- *Open*. Display the entire message
- *Print*. Print the entire message including embedded objects
- *Reply*. Compose a reply to the sender
- *Reply to All*. Compose a reply to the sender and other recipients
- *Forward*. Forward the message to another person
- *View Attachments*. Display attached files
- *Categories*. Assign one or more categories to the message
- *Flag Message*. Mark the message with a flag
- *Mark as Read*. Mark the message as read
- *Find All*. Find related messages of other messages from the same sender
- *Delete*. Delete the message
- *Move to Folder*. Move the message to a specific folder

Instead of selecting from this menu, you can click buttons on the toolbar to select most of these items.

N O T E   View Attachments is available only if the message has attached files. Otherwise, it is not in the shortcut menu.

After you've flagged a message, Flag Message is replaced by Flag Complete (use this when you have taken care of the reason for which you originally flagged the message) and Clear Message Flag (use this if you flagged a message by mistake).

After you've marked a message as read, Mark as Read is replaced by Mark as Unread. ▓

Working with Internet Mail

After you have set up Outlook correctly, sending and receiving Internet messages is as simple as sending and receiving workgroup messages. You must make sure of the following:

- ▓ Your computer is connected to the Internet either directly or by way of an Internet provider.
- ▓ You have a profile that includes the Internet Mail service.
- ▓ Your Outlook Address Book contains the Internet e-mail addresses of the people to whom you want to send messages.

Getting connected to the Internet is beyond the scope of this chapter, so the information that follows is based on the assumption that you already have an Internet connection.

Your profile must include Internet Mail if you are to send and receive e-mail by way of the Internet. Before you begin working with Internet e-mail, do the following, if necessary, to add Internet Mail to your profile:

1. With an Outlook window displayed, choose Tools, Services to display the Services dialog box. This dialog box shows a list of services in your current profile.

2. If Internet Mail is not included among the available services, click Add to see the services you can add to the profile, select Internet Mail, and then click OK to display the Internet Mail dialog box with the General tab selected as shown in Figure 45.33.

3. Enter your name (such as Mary Jones), your Internet e-mail address (such as mjones@company.com), the name of your Internet mail server (such as company.com), your account name (such as mjones), and enter your e-mail password in the appropriate text boxes.

N O T E   If you are uncertain about what information to provide, you should consult a colleague who is already using Internet mail, or consult your Internet provider or LAN administrator. ▓

FIG. 45.33

The General tab of the Internet Mail dialog box is where you provide details about your Internet e-mail account.

4. Open the Connection tab of the Internet Mail dialog box and select whether you connect to the Internet by way of a network or by way of a modem.

5. If you connect to the Internet by way of a modem, open the Dial Using the Following Connection list box and choose your connection name.

6. Click OK to return to the Services dialog box, which now shows Internet Mail available as a service.

7. Click OK to return to an Outlook window.

N O T E If you run into trouble sending and receiving Internet mail, you may have to return to Internet Mail properties and work your way through the many choices available. ▪

After you've added Internet Mail to your profile, you're ready to send and receive Internet e-mail messages.

Communicating with Other Services

The preceding pages have shown you how to send and receive e-mail within your workgroup and by Internet mail. You also can use other information services.

For example, you can install the Microsoft Fax service in a profile, set its properties appropriately, and then use your computer to send and receive faxes.

You can also use Outlook as your message center for e-mail you send and receive by way of an information service such as CompuServe. Subscribers can download the self-extracting file CSMAIL.EXE directly from CompuServe (**GO CISSOFT**).

NOTE At the time this chapter is being written, it is not possible to include AOL e-mail as an information service in a profile. However, AOL has indicated an intention to make the necessary files available before too long. ▪

Working with Folders

In "Looking at Folders" earlier in this chapter, you read about creating subfolders. One of the major facilities in Outlook is the capability to move items of information between folders. You can move items from your Inbox and Sent Items folders to the subject-related subfolders you've created.

Suppose that you want to move an item from your Inbox folder to a subfolder. Follow these steps:

1. In the Inbox Information Viewer, select the item you want to move.
2. Choose <u>E</u>dit, <u>M</u>ove to Folder (or press Ctrl+Shift+V) to open the Move Items dialog box.
3. Choose the folder or subfolder to which you want to move the item, and click OK.

An even simpler method is to display the Folder List and then drag the item from the Information Viewer to a folder or subfolder, just as you do when working with Explorer. ●

CHAPTER 46

Using Exchange and Schedule+ with Office 97

by Gordon Padwick

By upgrading from Office 95 to Office 97 you acquire many enhanced capabilities and quite a few new ones. For the most part, you can gradually learn to take advantage of the enhancements and, one at a time, you can put the new capabilities to good use. Outlook is one exception.

Outlook is a new Office 97 component that didn't exist in Office 95. Outlook provides enhancements to Exchange (a Windows 95 and Windows NT component), enhancements to Schedule+ (an Office 95 component), and also provides additional functionality and improved integration with other Office components. When you start using Office 97, you can choose between adopting Outlook or staying with Exchange and Schedule+. ■

Choosing to Use Exchange and Schedule+

If you haven't previously used Exchange or Schedule+, the choice is clear. Forget that Exchange and Schedule+ ever existed. Go ahead and install Outlook with the rest of the Office 97 components. Then you will be able to take advantage of all Outlook has to offer for your own work, and communicate with other people who use Outlook as well as those who are still using Exchange and Schedule+. If you haven't already done so, read Chapter 45 to gain an insight into Outlook's capabilities.

If you have previously used Exchange, Schedule+, or one of the many competing products that help you manage your information and communications, you should consider whether you want to stay with the applications you currently use or switch to Outlook. If you haven't already done so, take a look at Chapter 45 to get an idea of all that Outlook can do for you. Don't just think about the many separate facilities it offers, consider the value of the way it integrates the processes of organizing information and communicating. You might well come to the conclusion that you should use Outlook.

On the other hand, you might decide that Exchange and Schedule+ serve you well. Even if Outlook offers more, perhaps you can't afford the time or effort involved in switching to Outlook, so you'll stay with Exchange and Schedule+ for the present. If that's the case, this chapter is for you. Be assured that all the work you have already done, and continue to do, with Exchange and Schedule+ won't be wasted; after you make the change to Outlook, you can use all the data you've saved with Exchange and Schedule+.

This chapter tells you how to use Exchange and Schedule+ instead of Outlook and provides a summary of the most important facilities in those applications.

N O T E Before you decide to stay with Exchange and Schedule+, you should understand that Outlook is compatible with almost all the data you may have previously created in Exchange and Schedule+. The many enhanced capabilities in Outlook may well justify the small amount of additional learning necessary to make the switch. ▮

The remainder of this chapter assumes you have made the decision to stay with Exchange and Schedule+.

Exchange is a component of the Windows 95 and Windows NT packages. Its prime purpose is to help you manage your e-mail communications. If you are using Windows 95 and also have Windows Plus, you can use Exchange to manage fax communications. In order to use Exchange, you must include it in your Windows installation.

Schedule+ comes with Office 95 and can also be purchased separately. It's a Personal Information Manager (PIM) whose main purpose is to help you manage your time. To use Schedule+, you must install it under Windows 95 or Windows NT either as part of Office 95 or separately.

NOTE All information about Exchange in this chapter refers to the updated release made available by Microsoft on June 3, 1996, which you can download from Microsoft's Web site. The file to download for use within the United States is named Exupdusa.exe. Versions of this file are also available for use in other geographic areas.

This updated version of Exchange includes several significant performance enhancements. One difference you'll immediately see is that the wording "Microsoft Exchange" has changed to "Windows Messaging" on the splash screen that's displayed while Exchange loads, in the title bars of several dialog boxes, and in some other places. According to Microsoft, this change is intended "to reduce confusion between the Exchange server and the product that ships in the operating system boxes."

This chapter also assumes that you have installed the Internet Jumpstart Kit that's provided with Windows Plus. One component of the Internet Jumpstart Kit provides the ability to use the Internet Mail service with Exchange. If you are using the Internet Mail service, you should install the Internet Mail update, which you can download from the Microsoft Internet site referenced in the following note. The file to download for use within the United States is named Inetmail.exe. Versions of this file are also available for use in other geographic areas.

Later updates for Exchange may be available by the time you read this book.

ON THE WEB

http://www.microsoft.com/windows/software/updates.htm

Some selections you make at the time you install Office 97 affect the availability of Exchange and Schedule+. These are described in the next few paragraphs.

Having Full Access to Exchange and Schedule+

The assumption here is that have previously been using Office 95 with Exchange installed, that you have previously been using Schedule+, and that you are about to install Office 97. If you want to retain full access to Exchange and Schedule+, you should choose Custom installation for Office 97.

Near the beginning of the Office 97 Custom installation, you are shown a list of Office components, one of which is Microsoft Outlook. By default, the Microsoft Outlook check box is gray and checked to indicate that only some of Outlook's components will be installed. At this point, do the following:

1. Select Microsoft Outlook and then click Change Option to show a list of the Outlook components you can install. Almost all of these options are checked.

2. If the Schedule+ 7.0 Group Scheduling option is not checked, select it.

3. Click OK and then continue with the installation process.

Later in the installation process, you will see a dialog box that contains a message telling you that "Many Microsoft Exchange client files aren't used by Microsoft Outlook…". The dialog box offers to delete the unnecessary Exchange files. It's very important to click "No" in this dialog box so that you retain all the Exchange files. After this, continue as normal with the installation process.

> **CAUTION**
> Don't let the Outlook installation process delete any Exchange files.

N O.T E   The reference to "Microsoft Exchange client" in the dialog box refers to the version of Exchange that comes with Windows 95 and Windows NT. This terminology is intended to distinguish that version of Exchange from Microsoft Exchange Server which is a separate product that runs under Windows NT Server. ▪

After you install Office 97 in this manner, your Windows Desktop has the familiar Inbox icon and the new Microsoft Outlook icon.

Click the Inbox icon to start using Exchange. After a few seconds, you'll see the Windows Messaging splash screen which is soon replaced by the Inbox-Windows Messaging window. Now you can use Exchange just as you did before installing Office 97.

N O T E   If you're surprised to see "Windows Messaging" where you previously saw "Microsoft Exchange," refer to the note at the beginning of this chapter about the updated release of Exchange, which you can download from Microsoft's Web site. ▪

Alternatively, you can click the Microsoft Outlook icon to start using Outlook.

To gain access to Schedule+, click the Start button in the Windows Desktop, point to Programs, and then click Microsoft Schedule+ in the list of programs. If you use Schedule+ frequently, you might want to create a shortcut to it on the Windows Desktop.

Installing Office 97 Without Outlook

The preceding section described how to install Office 97 in a way that provides access to Outlook, Exchange, and Schedule+. You might want to do that for the computer you use personally, particularly if you just want to keep using Exchange and Schedule+ for a short while and then switch to Outlook. However, if you are responsible for installing Office 97 on all the computers used by a workgroup, you might come to the conclusion that the best thing to do is to initially install Office 97 without Outlook to avoid the confusion of having some users investigating Outlook while others stick with Exchange and Schedule+.

The normal method of installing Office 97 automatically installs Outlook on your computer. However, if you choose the Custom installation from a list of options offered near the beginning of the installation process, you can choose from a list of Office components, one of which is Microsoft Outlook. Remove the check mark from the check box adjacent to Microsoft Outlook and continue with the installation process. At the completion of installation, you'll have access to all the principal Office 97 components with the exception of Outlook, and you'll still be able to use Exchange and Schedule+.

N O T E If you do install Office 97 without Outlook, you can easily add Outlook to your installation later. ▨

After you install Office 97 components without installing Outlook, the Windows Desktop contains the Inbox icon which you can use to access Exchange.

Replacing Outlook with Exchange

Here's a third scenario that is likely to be all too common in workgroups. Some people install Office 97 in the typical manner. The workgroup decides to stay with using Exchange for a while, at least until everyone has Office 97 and suitable support and training for all its components, including Outlook, is available. The problem is that those who have already installed Office 97 may no longer have access to Exchange.

If you have already installed Office 97 with all its components, you can remove Outlook and replace it with Exchange. You must first remove Outlook and then install Exchange from your original Windows 95 distribution CD-ROM or floppy disks.

The first task is to remove Outlook by following these steps:

1. From the Windows Desktop, open the Control Panel and choose Add/Remove Programs to display the Add/Remove Programs Properties dialog box with the Install/Uninstall tab selected.

2. In the lower part of the dialog box, scroll down the list of installed components, select Microsoft Office 97, and click Add/Remove. Follow the direction to insert your Microsoft Office CD (or floppy disk), and then click OK.

3. Wait while the setup procedure starts. When the Microsoft Office 97 Setup dialog box appears, click Add/Remove to display a list of installed Office components. The list should include Microsoft Outlook with a checked box adjacent to it, indicating that Outlook is currently installed. Remove the check mark, and then click Continue.

4. A message box asks you to confirm that you want to remove components. Click Yes to start the process of removing Outlook. Soon after the process starts, a message box asks you whether you want to remove shared components. Click Remove All. Be patient and wait until you see the Microsoft Office 97 Setup dialog box that tells you Microsoft Office 97 Setup was completed successfully. Click OK to return to the Add/Remove Programs Properties dialog box. Click Cancel to return to the Control Panel.

5. Close the Control Panel to return to the Windows Desktop.

This completes the process of removing Outlook. Now you have to reinstall Exchange which you do by running the Exchange setup program. Here's what you do:

1. From the Windows Desktop, open the Start menu, choose Find, and then choose Files or Folders to display the Find: All Files dialog box.

2. In the Named text box, type Mlset32.exe and click Find Now to find the Exchange setup program. The file should normally be in your C:\Program Files\Microsoft Exchange folder.

3. Double-click the file name Mlset32.exe to start the Inbox Setup Wizard. The first Wizard dialog box asks you to choose the information services you want to connect to. Choose one or more of the services, then click OK. After a short delay, you are asked to insert your Windows 95 CD-ROM (or floppy disk). Insert the disk and click OK to start copying the Exchange files onto your hard disk. During the installation process, you may be asked whether you want to replace files already on your disk with older versions; in each case, choose to keep the later version.

4. After the required files have been copied, a dialog box tells you that you must restart your computer. Choose Yes to do so.

After your computer restarts, the Windows Desktop contains the Inbox icon which gives you access to Exchange. However, the Office toolbar doesn't contain the buttons that give you instant access to appointments, tasks, and contacts in Schedule+. You can use the normal procedure to restore these buttons.

Using Exchange

You have access to the same Exchange capabilities that you had when using Office 95 or, for that matter, without having Office 95 installed because Exchange is part of the Windows 95 and Windows NT packages. The facilities available in Exchange include:

- Sending and receiving e-mail messages to and from members of your workgroup
- Sending and receiving fax messages
- Including files and objects created in other applications in your e-mail and fax messages
- Storing e-mail messages, fax messages, and files in specific folders

The following information about using Exchange is based on the assumption that you have some previous experience with it. If this isn't the case, as an Office 97 user, you should be working with Outlook.

Running Exchange

Double-click the Inbox icon in the Windows Desktop to start Exchange. The Windows Messaging for Windows 95 splash screen is displayed for a few moments; then you see the Inbox-Windows Messaging window that lists the messages in your inbox, as shown in Figure 46.1. The messages you haven't yet read are shown in bold; bold is removed when you read a message. The status bar at the bottom of the window shows the total number of messages, and the number of messages you haven't read.

Part
VIII

Ch
46

FIG. 46.1
The Inbox-Windows Messaging window lists the messages in your inbox.

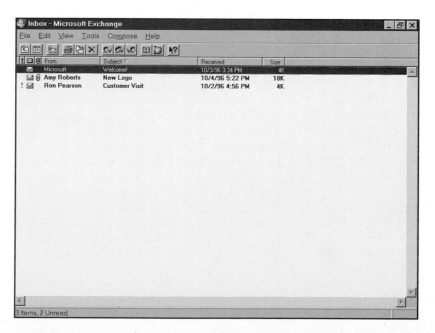

N O T E When you start Exchange, you may see a Choose Profile dialog box. If you do, for the time being accept the proposed profile by clicking OK. The significance of this dialog box is described later in this chapter. Also, there's a possibility that you may see a message box warning you that Exchange has a problem with some aspect of a profile. For the present, ignore this error by clicking OK. ▪

Working with Inbox Messages   The Inbox window contains seven columns. The first three columns contain icons that indicate the priority, status, and presence of attachments. The remaining four columns show the sender's identification, the subject, the date the message was received, and the size of the message. Messages are normally listed in chronological order with the most recent message at the top.

You can double-click any message in the Inbox to see it in detail, as shown in Figure 46.2.

FIG. 46.2

The message shown here is the Welcome message from Microsoft that is automatically placed in your Inbox when you install Exchange.

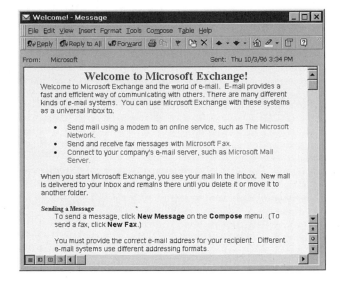

You can click buttons in the toolbar at the top of the Message window to do most common tasks, such as the following:

    Reply to sender

    Reply to sender and other recipients

    Forward the message to another person

Create a new mail message

Print the message

Insert a file into the message (something you might do before forwarding it)

Add a flag to the message

File the message in a specific folder

Delete the message (useful for junk e-mail)

Display the previous message listed in your Inbox

Display the next message listed in your Inbox

Display or hide the message header

If you choose to flag a message, the Flag Message dialog box provides a choice of ten different flags and also the ability to attach a date to the flag. You might, for example, flag the message for follow-up on a specific date. After you have flagged a message, the details of the flag are displayed at the top of the message when you show it in the Message window.

After you finish looking at messages, you can close the Message window in the normal way by clicking the Close icon at the right end of the Title bar to return to the Inbox window.

The Inbox toolbar contains buttons you can use to do many of the tasks also available from the Message window. Specifically, you can reply to and forward messages, create new messages, file messages, and delete messages.

The preceding paragraphs, which provided some introductory information about the Inbox, are based on the assumption that the Inbox contained some messages, if only those automatically provided when you install Exchange. Before going further, you need to understand how messages get into the Inbox and, at the same time, how you can send your own messages.

Understanding Information Services   Exchange, like Outlook, communicates with information services such as your workgroup Postoffice. If your workgroup Postoffice is identified as an information service, Exchange can receive e-mail from other people who share the same Postoffice, and you can send e-mail to those people.

To see what information services you have available, display any Exchange window, open the Tools menu, and choose Services to display the Services dialog box which should be similar to the one shown in Figure 46.3. You may not have all the services shown in the figure, and you may have some that are not shown.

FIG. 46.3

The Services dialog box shows the information services that the Exchange installation on your computer can use.

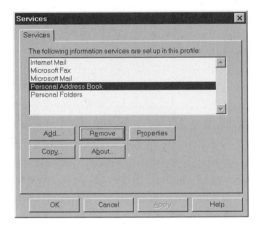

The set of information services, and the settings of those services, available is known as a *profile*. You can have more than one profile available on your computer, and you can choose which profile to use. The profile Exchange automatically selects when it starts is the *default* profile.

A profile may contain two types of services: those that involve communicating with other people and those that provide access to information on your own computer. In the preceding illustration, Internet Mail, Microsoft Fax, and Microsoft Mail are services that communicate with other people; the Personal Address Book and Personal Folders services provide access to information on your own computer's hard drive or other drive to which your computer has access.

The buttons in the Services dialog box allow you to modify a profile, as listed in Table 46.1.

Table 46.1 Services Dialog Box Buttons

Button	Use
Add	Add a service that's already installed on your computer, or a service for which you have the necessary software available on disk
Remove	Remove the selected service from the profile
Properties	View and modify the properties of the selected service
Copy	Copy the selected service to another profile
About	Display information about the selected service

N O T E There's more information about working with profiles in Chapter 45. Although the information there is in the context of Outlook, it applies equally to Exchange.

After you install Exchange, one profile is automatically available. You can create as many additional profiles as you need. If more than one person uses your computer, you will probably need a separate profile for each person. One way to create a profile is to close Exchange, open the Windows Control Panel, and choose Mail and Fax. Another way to create a new profile is to use the Inbox Setup Wizard.

If you have two or more profiles, you need to select which one Exchange is to use. To do so, follow these steps:

1. Start Exchange, open the Tools menu, choose Options, and then select the General tab to display the dialog box shown in Figure 46.4.

Part **VIII**

Ch **46**

FIG. 46.4
The General tab of the Options dialog box lets you choose which profile Exchange uses.

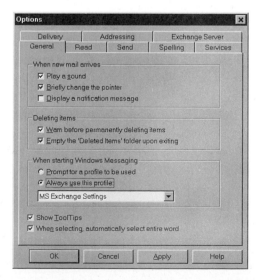

2. If you always want Exchange to open with a specific profile selected, choose Always Use This Profile, open the list of profile names, and select the appropriate one. If you want Exchange to display a dialog box offering a choice of profiles when it opens, choose Prompt for a Profile to be Used.

3. Click OK to accept the changed options.

Subsequently, when you start Exchange, the Choose Profile dialog is displayed and you can use it to choose which profile Exchange uses.

Sending Messages   Once you have Exchange set up, it's very easy to compose and send an e-mail message to someone in your workgroup.

 With the Inbox window displayed, choose the New Message button in the toolbar (alternatively, open the Compose menu and choose New Message, or press Ctrl+N) to open the Message dialog box shown in Figure 46.5.

FIG. 46.5

The Message dialog box is where you compose a new message.

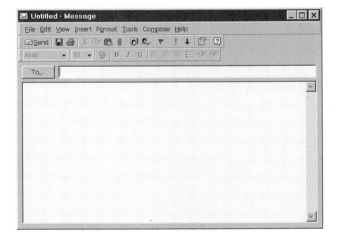

N O T E   The Message dialog box shown here is the one you see if you're using Exchange on a computer on which Outlook is also installed. The dialog box is slightly different if you're using a computer that doesn't have Outlook.

According to how you have previously used Exchange, you may see an expanded header section in the dialog box. ▪

The task of sending an e-mail message has three steps:

1. Identify the recipient or recipients.

2. Type the message.

3. Send the message.

These steps are described in detail as follows:

The first task is to identify the person to whom you are sending the message. If you are part of a small workgroup, you probably know everyone's e-mail address. In that case, all you need to do is type the e-mail address in the To text box. For example, if one of your colleagues is Amy Roberts and her e-mail address is the same as her name, just type **Amy Roberts** in the To text box. (If there are two or more recipients, type all their e-mail names, separating one from the next with a semicolon.) However, if you have many e-mail contacts, you probably don't remember all their e-mail names; in that case, you can use Exchange's address book capability to find people's e-mail names for you. The subject of address books is covered later in this chapter.

N O T E   To send a fax message from Exchange, open the Compose menu and choose New Fax to open the Compose New Fax Wizard. Follow through the steps in the Wizard to compose and send your fax.

To send a message to someone who has an e-mail account on the Internet, type the person's name in the To text box in the format SMTP:aroberts@company.com. Click Send in the toolbar to send the message to the Outbox. Open the Tools menu, choose Deliver Now Using and select Internet Mail to initiate a connection to the Internet. ▪

Part
VIII

Ch
46

The next task is to place the insertion point into the large box that occupies most of the Message dialog box and type your message. Don't forget to read the message carefully and make corrections before you send it.

To send the message, click the Send button in the toolbar (or press Ctrl+Enter). That's all there is to it. The recipients will see your message immediately, within a short while, or the next time they turn on their computers.

Receiving Messages   You really don't have to do anything to receive messages. Each time you open the Inbox window, it contains a complete list of messages received that you haven't yet deleted or filed.

If you're working in the Inbox window and wonder if any messages are waiting, you can open the Tools menu, choose Deliver Now Using, and then select from a list of services. This causes Exchange to query the services you specify and, if messages are waiting, add those messages to your Inbox. To query all message services contained in your profile, press Ctrl+M.

Working with Address Books

Each profile can provide access to information about people in several address books. Most profiles can access a Personal Address Book. Also, if your computer has access to a workgroup Postoffice, profiles can access the Postoffice Address List. You can create and use additional lists.

Using the Postoffice Address List   Only the workgroup Postoffice administrator can add, delete, or change entries in the Postoffice Address List. All members of the workgroup can view entries in the list and use those entries to address their mail. To view entries in the Postoffice Address List:

1. Click the Address Book button in the Inbox toolbar (alternatively, open the Tools menu and choose Address Book, or type Ctrl+Shift+B) to open the Address Book dialog box that shows a list of entries.

2. Open the Show Names From The list box and select Postoffice Address List.

3. Double-click any name to display a Properties dialog box that displays all the information about one person.

You can't change the information in any Postoffice Address List entry (unless you are the Postoffice administrator), but you can copy an entry into your Personal Address Book and make some changes in that copy—but not, of course, the detailed information about a person's Postoffice mailbox.

The information in each Postoffice Address List entry consists of the same fields as those in your Personal Address Book, as described in the next section.

Using Your Personal Address Book   Whereas the Postoffice Address List contains only the names of people who have mailboxes in your workgroup Postoffice and is maintained by the Postoffice administrator, your Personal Address Book can contain information about people in your workgroup, people you communicate with by other types of e-mail, and people to whom you send faxes, and is entirely under your control.

Although it's not required, you may want to copy the entries from the Postoffice Address List to your Personal Address Book so that you have all your contacts' names in one place. To do this, open the Postoffice Address List as described earlier, select the entries one at a time, and click the Add to Personal Address Book button.

N O T E   The disadvantage of copying entries from the Postoffice Address List to your Personal Address Book and then relying entirely on entries in your Personal Address Book is that you won't be aware of any changes that are made to the Postoffice Address List. ▪

To add an entry to your Personal Address Book, use these steps:

1. Click the Address Book button in the Inbox toolbar (alternatively, open the <u>T</u>ools menu and choose <u>A</u>ddress Book, or type Ctrl+Shift+B) to open the Address Book dialog box that shows a list of entries.

2. Open the <u>S</u>how Names From The list box and select Personal Address Book.

3. Click the New Entry button in the toolbar (alternatively, open the <u>F</u>ile menu and choose New <u>E</u>ntry) to display the New Entry dialog box shown in Figure 46.6.

FIG. 46.6
The New Entry dialog box asks you to specify the type of entry you want to make.

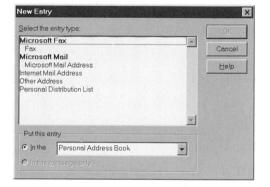

N O T E The list of entry types varies according to the information services specified in the active profile. The lines in bold type are group headings. The lines in normal, unbolded type are those you can choose. ▯

4. Select one of the unbolded entry types in the list, according to which type of entry you want to add. The following steps assume you selected Internet Mail Address. After selecting an entry type, click OK to display a Properties dialog box for that entry type, as shown in Figure 46.7.

5. If you know the person can receive messages in Rich Text Format, click the Always Send Messages in Microsoft Exchange Rich Text Format check box; otherwise, leave it unchecked.

6. Click OK to add the new entry to your Personal Address Book.

Addressing Messages   You can refer to information in the Postoffice Address List and your Personal Address Book (other address books, too, if you have them) when composing messages. The Message dialog box shown earlier in Figure 46.5 contains a To... button adjacent to a text box. You can, if you like, type the recipient's e-mail address in the text box. However, it's usually easier and less likely to cause errors if you choose the e-mail address from a list.

Part
VIII

Ch
46

FIG. 46.7

The New Internet Mail Address Properties dialog box is where you provide information about a new entry in your Personal Address Book for someone who has an Internet mailbox.

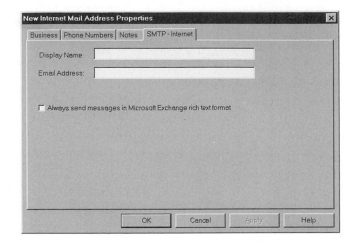

Click the To... button to see the Select Names dialog box shown in Figure 46.8. When this list first appears, it shows a list of names in the Postoffice Address List, your Personal Address Book, or another address book according to which list you have specified to be shown first. To show a different list, open the Show Names From The list box and choose the list you want to see.

N O T E To specify which address list is displayed first, open the Tools menu, choose Options, and select the Addressing tab. Select the list you want to see first from the Show This Address List First list box. ▧

FIG. 46.8

The Select Names dialog box is where you select the recipient for your message. You can also specify who should receive copies and blind copies of the message.

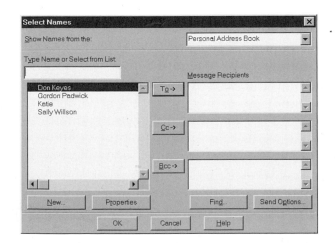

To specify recipients for your message, do the following:

1. Choose a name from the list, then click To to copy the name to the Message Recipients box.

2. Repeat step 1 as many times as necessary if you want to send the message to more than one person.

3. Choose a name and click Cc to name a person who is to receive a copy of the message.

4. Choose a name and click Bcc to name a person who is to receive a blind copy of the message.

5. Click OK to return to the Message dialog box with the recipients' names listed.

Using Schedule+

You have access to the same Schedule+ capabilities that you had when using Office 95. The facilities available in Schedule+ include:

- Keeping track of appointments and events
- Maintaining a to-do list
- Planning meetings
- Recording information about your contacts

To start Schedule+, open the Windows Start menu, choose Programs, and select Microsoft Schedule+.

Understanding Schedule+ Windows

By default, the window you see when you start Schedule+ shows the current schedule for today (determined by your computer's internal calendar), as shown in Figure 46.9.

The pane at the left contains the Appointment Book, which shows appointments and events you've planned for the current day. By default, the Appointment Book divides the day into 30-minute segments, but you can change this by opening the Tools menu, choosing Options, selecting the General tab, and selecting an alternative Appointment Book Time Scale. With the Appointment Book displayed, you can use the vertical scroll bar at the right side of the pane to scroll to hours not initially shown. You can click the small arrows near the top of the pane to move backwards or forwards one day at a time.

Part
VIII

Ch
46

FIG. 46.9

By default, Schedule+ opens with a window that displays a daily schedule.

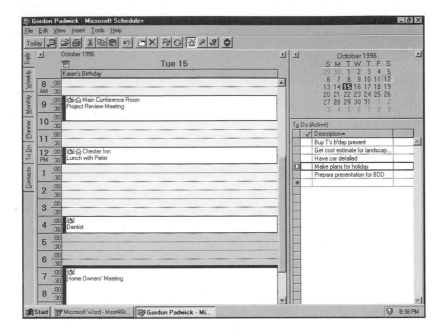

The top-right pane contains the Date Navigator which shows a miniature calendar for the current month with the current day highlighted. Days that have scheduled, non-tentative appointments or meetings are shown in bold. You can move backwards and forwards one month at a time by clicking the small arrows at the top of the pane. You can also click any day in the pane to show the Appointment Book for that day in the pane at the left.

N O T E   The Date Navigator shows the calendar for more than one month if sufficient space is available, as is the case when you maximize the Schedule+ window and drag the boundary of the appointment pane to the left. ■

The pane at the bottom-right shows all the current items in your to-do list.

Selecting Schedule+ Windows

By clicking the tabs at the left side of the window, you can select different views of your calendar as well as views of other information. Initially, the window has the six tabs listed in Table 46.2.

Table 46.2 Default Tabs in Schedule+ Window

Tab	Displays
Daily	Current day's schedule, month calendar, to-do list
Weekly	Current week's schedule
Monthly	Current month
Planner	Two-week planning overview, month calendar, meeting attendees
To Do	Detailed to-do list
Contacts	List of contacts, details of selected contact

You can easily change the tabs at the left side of the Schedule+ window. To do so, open the View menu and choose Tab Gallery to display the Tab Gallery dialog box shown in Figure 46.10. To get an idea of what each tab does, click a tab's name in the Available Tabs list and look at the preview and the description in the bottom part of the dialog box.

FIG. 46.10
In the Tab Gallery dialog box you can choose which tabs are displayed at the left side of the Schedule+ window.

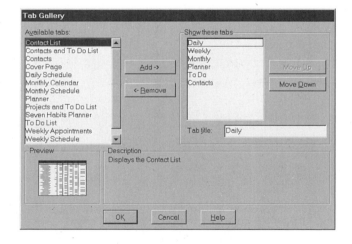

To add a tab, click its name in the Available Tabs list, and then click Add. To remove a tab, click its name in the Show These Tabs list, and then click Remove. Click OK to return to the Schedule+ window.

 With any view of the calendar displayed, you can easily go to another date. Click the Go To Date button in the toolbar (alternatively, open the Edit menu and choose Go To, or press Ctrl+G) to display the Go To dialog box. In that dialog box, select or type the date you want to see. You can also right-click anywhere in the Date Navigator to display a menu from which you can select either Today (to display the current day's Appointment Book) or Go To (to display the Go To dialog box).

Working with Appointments

Schedule+ helps you keep track of one-time and recurring appointments. Schedule+ uses the word "appointment" to refer to an activity that occurs at a particular date and time. When you enter an appointment, Schedule+ blocks time in your Appointment Book to show that you are unavailable for any other activity.

There are two ways to enter appointments into your Appointment Book: by way of the Appointment dialog box or directly into the Appointment Book.

Entering an Appointment by Way of the Appointment Dialog Box   To enter a one-time appointment by way of the Appointment dialog box, do the following:

1. Click the Insert New Appointment button in the toolbar (alternatively, open the Insert menu and choose Appointment, or type Ctrl+N) to display the Appointment dialog box shown in Figure 46.11.

FIG. 46.11
You use the Appointment dialog box to provide information about an appointment.

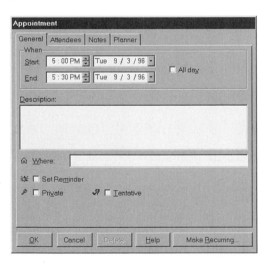

2. In the General tab, enter the Start and End dates and times or, if appropriate, mark the appointment as All Day.
3. Type a Description for the appointment and its location.
4. If you want an automatic reminder, click the Set Reminder check box and then specify the time before the start of the appointment that you want to be reminded.

5. Check the Private and Tentative check boxes, if appropriate.

6. Click OK to block the time for the appointment in your schedule.

After you entered a new appointment, that appointment appears on the daily, weekly, and monthly calendar views. Figure 46.9 showed earlier how the daily calendar view shows time blocked for an appointment. The weekly and monthly views show less detail.

Entering an Appointment Directly into the Appointment Book   To enter an appointment directly into the Appointment Book, do the following:

1. Display the Appointment Book for the appropriate day.

2. Point onto the Appointment Book within the time segment that the appointment starts, press the mouse button, and drag down to select the time you want to set aside for the appointment.

3. Type a description of the appointment. The text you type appears within the blocked region of the Appointment Book.

Modifying an Appointment   After you have placed an appointment in your Appointment Book, you can easily modify it. One way to do this is to double-click the narrow blue region at the left edge of the appointment in the Appointment Book. When you do this, the Appointment dialog box opens with the details of the selected appointment displayed. You can then edit any of the information in any of the dialog box tabs.

You can change the starting time and duration of an appointment by dragging in the Appointment Book. To change the starting time, point onto the top edge of the blocked time and drag; to change the duration, point onto the bottom edge of the blocked time and drag.

To change the appointment to another day, point onto the blue region at the left edge of the blocked time and drag to another day in the Date Navigator.

The examples just described show how to enter and make some changes to a basic appointment. There are many other enhancements you can use, including:

- Creating an appointment that involves other people by using the Attendees tab in the Appointment dialog box

- Adding notes about the meeting by using the Notes tab

- Making the meeting recurring on a daily, weekly, monthly, or yearly schedule by clicking the Make Recurring button

Working with Events

An event, in Schedule+ terms, is something that happens on a specific day (or several days), but does not occupy your time. For example, somebody's birthday is regarded as an event. Events show in your calendar as banners; they do not block time.

To enter a new event, open the Insert menu and choose Event to display the Event dialog box. Use that dialog box to specify the dates the event starts and ends, and to provide a description of the event.

N O T E You can add reminders for events, just as you can for appointments.

If the event is something that occurs on the same day each year, you can make it an annual event by opening the Insert menu and choosing Annual Event.

Working with Tasks

In addition to appointments and events, Schedule+ can also handle tasks. Whereas appointments and events occur on specific dates, tasks are activities that must be done by a specific date. You can think of preparing your income tax forms as a task—you have to do that task by a particular date (or face the consequences). Tasks can be one-time or (unfortunately, like completing income tax forms) recurring.

Entering a New Task   To enter a new task, open the Insert menu and choose Task (or press Ctrl+T) or Recurring Task to display the Task or Task Series dialog box. Enter the appropriate information in the dialog box, and then click OK to save the task information.

The information you provide about a task normally includes an end date (though you can enter tasks without an end date) and a start date that is a certain number of days before the end date. Tasks with or without an end date are listed in the window you see when you click the To Do tab. When you list tasks in this way, you can double-click the column at the extreme left of the list to see the details of the task in the Task dialog box.

After you click the Daily tab at the left side of the Microsoft Schedule+ window, you see tasks in a To Do list at the bottom-right. The tasks shown here are those you entered without an end date and those that should currently be started. Suppose you have a task that must be completed by April 15 and should be started 60 days before that date. If you have the Daily tab selected and the current date is February 13 or earlier, the task doesn't show in the To Do list. However, if the current date is February 14 or later, the task does show in the To Do list. In this view of tasks, you can also double-click the left end of the list of tasks to see the details of a task in the Task dialog box.

Scheduling Time for a Task   In order to get a task finished in time, you need to spend some time working on it. For this reason, it's a good idea to block time in your schedule to work on each task. You do this by making an appointment with yourself and including that appointment in your Appointment book. Here's one way you can block time for a task in your Appointment Book:

1. Select the To Do tab to display the Schedule+ window that shows all your tasks.

2. Select a task by clicking to box at the extreme left end of the row that contains information about that task.

3. Click the Copy button in the toolbar to copy that task to the Clipboard.

4. Select the Daily tab to show your Appointment Book and select the day in which you want to block time for the task.

5. Click the time segment at which you plan to start working on the task.

6. Click the Paste button in the toolbar to block the time segment. The blocked time segment contains the word "Task" followed by the name of the task.

7. Adjust the duration of the blocked time by dragging the bottom edge of the time block in the Appointment Book.

If appropriate, you can convert the appointment to recurring in order to block time on subsequent days.

Keeping Track of Tasks   For all but the shortest tasks, it's useful to be able to keep track of the progress of a task. With Schedule+, you can do this by updating the percentage complete for each task from time to time. When you enter a task, Schedule+ automatically shows the percentage complete as zero. The only way this figure changes is for you to make an estimate of progress and enter an appropriate percentage.

To enter a percentage complete for a task, do the following:

1. Select the To Do tab in the Schedule+ window to display a complete list of tasks.

2. Double-click the box at the extreme left end of the row that defines a task to display the Task dialog box.

3. Open the Status tab as shown in Figure 46.12.

4. Change the Percentage Complete to the appropriate value.

After you've entered a value other than zero for the percentage complete, this value is shown in the To Do tab of the Schedule+ window.

Part
VIII

Ch
46

FIG. 46.12
The Status tab is where you can provide information about the status of a task, as well as other information.

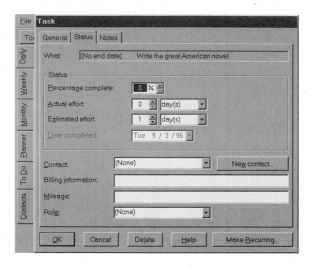

Working with Contacts

The contacts facility within Schedule+ is where you keep your address book.

To add a new contact, open the Insert menu and choose Contact to display the Contact dialog box. The contact dialog box has the four tabs listed in Table 46.3.

Table 46.3	Contact Dialog Box Tabs
Tab	**Displays**
Business	Contact's name, business address, business data, phone numbers
Phone	Phone numbers
Address	Home address, spouse name, birthday and anniversary, phone numbers
Notes	Miscellaneous information

You can provide as much information as you like in the various tabs of this dialog box.

N O T E If you enter a birthday or anniversary for a contact, Schedule+ automatically recognizes those dates as events and shows them as events in your Appointment Book. ■

After you have provided information about your contacts, you can choose the Contacts tab to display a list of contacts and click any name in the list to see details about that person. You can also use the Contacts tab to add contacts to your list.

You can use the contacts list to automatically dial phone numbers providing you have a modem that is properly installed. To do so, choose a name in the contacts list, select the phone number you want to call, then click the Autodialer button.

Other Schedule+ Facilities

The information provided in this chapter is intended to get you started with Schedule+ but is by no means comprehensive. There is much more to Schedule+ that you can discover by looking at the menus and by reading the online help screens. ●

Part
VIII

Ch
46

CHAPTER 47

Using Microsoft Office in Workgroups

by Julie Vigil

In today's business world, connectivity is crucial to the day-to-day tasks you perform. Have you ever decided to leave work early when you found out your network was going to be unavailable that afternoon? What about those times the network fax server took a sabbatical? Your first thought was probably to wait to send your faxes when the server came back up rather than stand in front of the fax machine for a few minutes.

In some ways, you may feel like you're held hostage by your dependence on the connectivity of your computer systems, but you are also empowered by the very same connectivity. The key to enjoying your dependency rather than fighting it lies in your ability to understand the benefits you can obtain via a workgroup environment and to use those benefits to your advantage. ■

Sharing information with other users in your workgroup

Using the Briefcase, public folders, and routing techniques, you can share information with little or no duplicated efforts.

Effectively managing multiple, simultaneous access to your Word and Excel files

Share documents with others on your network and learn to keep track of changes.

Using PowerPoint for remote conferencing

Conferencing enables people from different locations to participate in presentations and discussions.

Using workgroup features with Access

Using an Access database on a network introduces the need for intensified security for users and better database management.

Using Outlook in a group environment

Outlook provides group scheduling and voting capabilities along with standardized electronic mail forms.

Implementing Microsoft Office 97 on a network

Use Office policies and shared resources to ease the daunting task of network administration.

Sharing Information with Others

One of the benefits of using a network is the ability to share files with other people who also use your network. This process can be as simple as storing files in a common area or as complicated as sharing a master/subdocument.

Sharing Directories on a Network

In many cases, a directory is set up on your network or within your workgroup to store common documents meant for company-, department-, or group-wide use. When you save files to these directories, other people can retrieve them and modify them.

Whenever you share files on a network, you open up the possibility for someone to inadvertently harm your file. A user may potentially delete the file, overwrite it, or update it incorrectly. Also, sharing files on a network brings into consideration confidentiality issues. All network operating systems provide the ability to secure files and directories on a user level. However, if you are unsure what security your administrator has set up for a shared directory, you should take precautions to ensure that no one can modify critical files without your permission.

 If you regularly create files that are for public viewing, but not for public editing, ask your network administrator to create a shared directory in which you have the security to update files, but everyone else is limited to viewing only. This step saves you time and eliminates the need to remember a document password.

Using Shared Folders and Public Folders

Shared folders and public folders are two different items. A *shared folder* generally is a folder placed on your Windows 95 or Windows NT 4.0 desktop to which you have granted other users in your workgroup access. Shared folders are extremely useful when your workgroup is small and you have no file server. As an added benefit, you can place security on a shared folder and allow only certain people to perform certain functions. Please refer to Que's *Special Edition Using Microsoft Windows 95* for detailed information on setting up shared folders.

Public folders are folders in Outlook that are available to everyone in your workgroup. You can use public folders as bulletin boards to post information, forums for public debate, or as a repository for commonly used views to locate and organize information. For more information on using Outlook, turn to Chapter 45, "Using Outlook Desktop Information Manager."

N O T E Public folders are available *only* with the postoffices provided through Microsoft Exchange Server for NT or NetWare GroupWise. If you are using Windows Messaging with Windows 95 or with Windows NT Workstation, you can use private folders; you cannot, however, share the information in them with other users. ▪

You create a public folder in the same manner that you create a personal folder, but make it a subfolder of the global public folder:

1. Open Outlook.
2. Choose File, New, Folder (or use the Ctrl+Shift+E shortcut).
3. Enter a name for the new folder in the Name box.
4. Select the public folder from the Make This a Subfolder Of box.
5. Click OK.

After a public folder is set up, you can post documents to that folder just as you can to any other folder.

▶ **See** "Sending and Receiving Messages," **p. 1119**

  N O T E The folder view is not selected by default when you open Outlook. To display folders, click the Folder List button on the toolbar, or click View Folder List from the menu bar. ▪

Using the Briefcase

Part
VIII

Ch
47

The briefcase is a very valuable tool in a workgroup—especially when used with binders. When you store a binder in a shared folder on the file server or host computer, multiple users can copy that binder to their briefcases. When the user selects his or her briefcase and chooses Briefcase, Update All, information in the binder is immediately updated. This method works very well for other documents as well. For more information on binders, see Chapter 40, "Using Binder."

Routing Information

Perhaps you have a file that is for a few eyes only. Posting the file to a public folder or saving it in a shared area provides access to too many people. Consider sending the file as an attachment to an e-mail message. In each Office 97 application is a File, Send To or a File Send command. When you choose this command, you have the option of sending that file to a mail recipient, a routing recipient, a public folder, or a fax.

The difference between a mail recipient and a routing recipient depends on whether you want the document sent back to you after the recipients read it. Routing is the process of sending a document to a person or to several people and getting it back when they are done reading and commenting on it.

A sender can route a document to one person at a time, so that each reviewer can see the previous people's comments, or to many people at once. In addition, the sender can specify what comments, if any, can be added to the document.

▶ **See** "Sending and Receiving Messages," **p. 1119**

In Figure 47.1, Betty is using a routing slip to get feedback from John and Bob on a request for an order change. She has listed Bob second so that he has a chance to see any comments John has made. When Bob is finished with his review, the order change request comes back to Betty so that she can take action on it.

FIG. 47.1
This sequential routing slip is returned to the sender after all recipients have seen it.

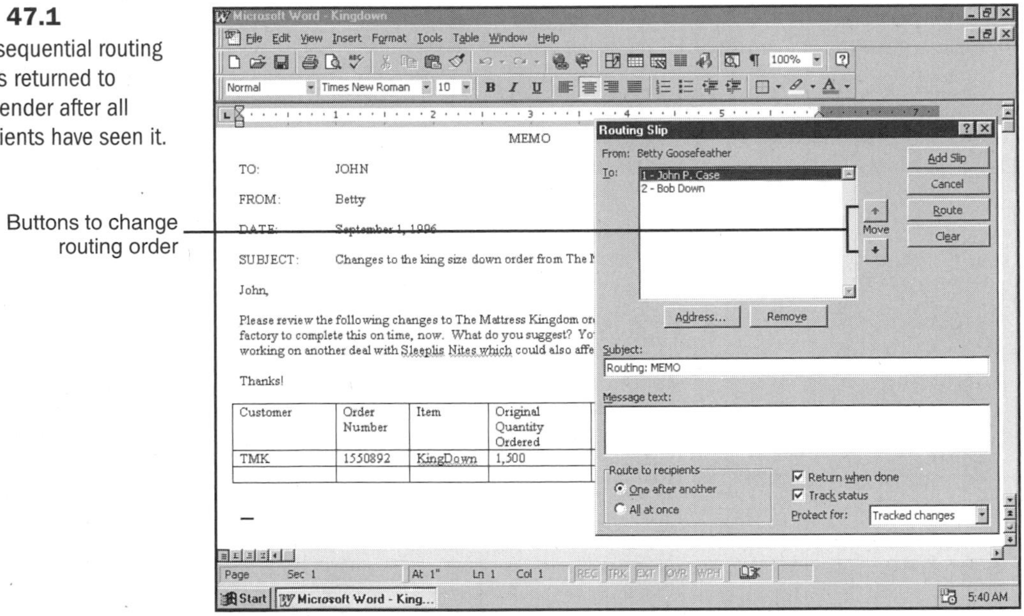

Buttons to change routing order

Using Workgroup Features of Word 97

Sharing documents within a workgroup can entail more than just saving the document to a shared area where others can see it. Microsoft Word 97 offers several options for people to work on a document simultaneously. It also provides security features to protect the author's work when others do work in the same document.

Setting Up a Master Document

A master document is a means of breaking down a large document into smaller docu-ments without losing the cohesiveness of the original document. By setting up a master document and storing it on a network, several people can work on subdocuments within the main document simultaneously. The master document is created in outline form. Subdocuments are created based on the headings of the outline. You could potentially have as many subdocuments as you have headings.

To create a master document, follow these steps:

1. Start with a new file.

2. Choose <u>V</u>iew, <u>M</u>aster Document. The view that you are in is nearly identical to an outline view. The difference is that you now have a Master Document toolbar.

3. Create your master document's outline. Each new subdocument you want to include should have a heading in the master (or main) document. Usually subdocuments start at the level 1 headings and include all text up to the next level 1 heading. You can, however, create subdocuments on second or third level headings as well.

4. Start with the first heading to be its own topic, and highlight the section of the document that you want to divide into subdocuments. Then select the Create Subdocument button from the Master Document toolbar.

5. Use <u>F</u>ile, <u>S</u>ave to save the master document to a network directory so everyone can have access to the document. As Word saves your master document, it also saves each subdocument with a name generated from the heading text.

After you have created subdocuments, they can be collapsed within the master document to display only the file name and path of the subdocument. When a user wants to see the document in its entirety, the subdocuments can be expanded to display their content within the master document. Use the Expand/Collapse Subdocuments button on the Master Document toolbar to toggle between the two views.

By default, subdocuments are automatically locked when they are collapsed and unlocked when they are expanded. This is for the protection of the author. To unlock the document, first expand the master document by clicking the Expand Subdocuments button. Then click the Unlock Subdocument button on the Master Document toolbar. In addition, subdocuments can be locked individually. Simply click within the expanded subdocument that you want to lock, and click the Lock Subdocument button.

In Figures 47.2 and 47.3, you can see a master document that has just been started for a newsletter. Figure 47.2 shows the newsletter's subdocuments expanded. Notice the padlock on "Soft and Fluffy's new web page" subdocument. This subdocument has been manually locked. Figure 47.3 shows the same document with the subdocuments collapsed.

FIG. 47.2
This newsletter is in expanded master document format.

Padlock displaying locked state of subdocument

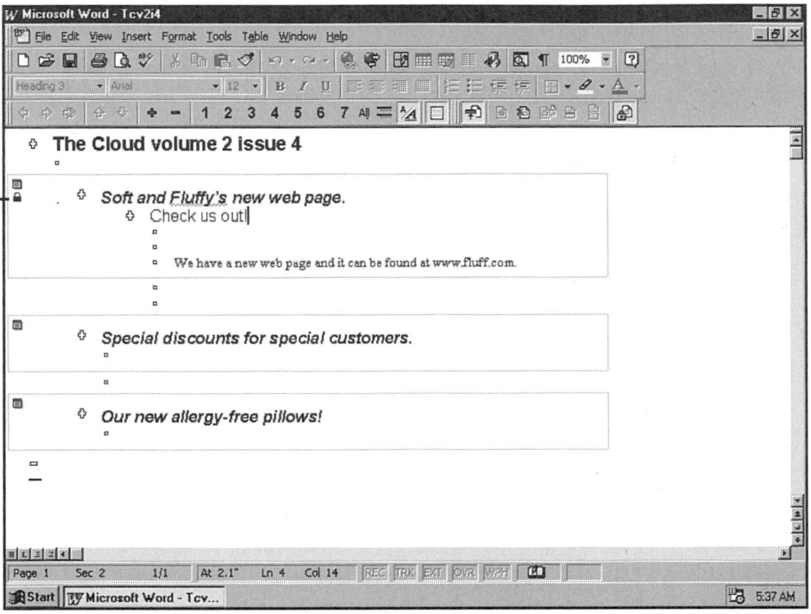

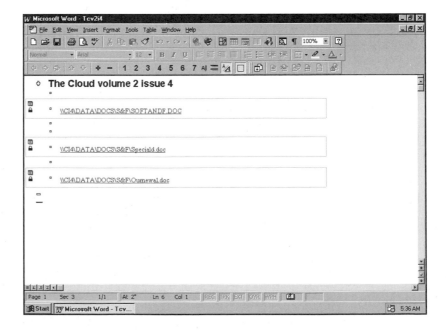

FIG. 47.3
The newsletter is shown in collapsed format.

You can edit subdocuments from within the master document or by opening the sub-document itself. To edit a subdocument from within the master, first expand the master document. To edit the subdocument directly, choose File, Open and enter the name of the subdocument. If you want to change the name of your subdocument from the default, simply choose File, Save As and give it a new name.

Protecting a Document

Word provides several ways to protect your documents. This is an important feature when working on documents that other people can potentially access. Table 47.1 displays several of the choices you have to help you decide where to place protection and to what extent the document is protected. Following the table, each setting is explained in detail.

Table 47.1   Password Protection Options for Word

Protection Choice	Results of Protection
Set password to open a document	Users need to know the password before they can see the document.
Set password to modify a document	Users can open the document but need the password to save any changes.
Set document to read-only	Document opens in read-only mode if a modify password exists and the user doesn't know the password. Otherwise, suggests to others to open the document as a read-only file.
Track changes on routed document	Tracks user, date, and content of changes made to document.
Track comments on routed document	Allows only comments to be added to the document.
Password form fields and sections	Prevents user updates to specific areas of a document.

Part
VIII

Ch
47

You can require passwords for opening or for modifying a document. Assign the pass-words by choosing the Options button in the File, Save As dialog box or in the File, Save dialog box if this is the first time you are saving the document. Type the password or passwords you want to assign in the Password to Open and Password to Modify text boxes under the File Sharing Options section (see Figure 47.4). If you assign a password to modify the document, when someone opens the document he or she will have the option of entering the password or selecting the Read Only button to open the document in read-only mode.

FIG. 47.4

Choose from password protection options.

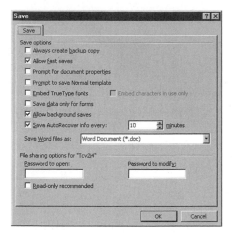

> **CAUTION**
>
> Once a password to open is placed on a form or document, you must use that password to unlock the document. If you forget your password, you have no way of retrieving the information in the document.

Take another look at Figure 47.4. In the same box that you set passwords on a document, you have another choice. You can recommend to others that the document be opened as read-only by selecting Read-Only Recommended. If you select this box and someone else opens your document, the Office Assistant pops up with the statement, `xxx.doc should be opened as read-only unless changes to it need to be saved`. The reader is given the choice to continue and open the document as read-only, continue and open the document as read-write, or cancel the opening altogether. Sometimes just putting up a no-trespassing sign is enough.

You also can assign security when you route a document. Betty enabled tracking on the memo she routed to John and Bob earlier in Figure 47.1. If you want to enable security on your routed document, select the Protect For box on the File, Send To, Routing Recipient dialog box. Choose between tracked changes, comments, or forms. Tracked changes will turn on revision marking so that any changes a reviewer makes within the document are recorded. Comments let reviewers insert comments but not change the contents of the document. Forms allow people to fill in a form, but not change the form itself.

Last of all, you can assign passwords to fields in a form to prohibit data entry into those sections.

Tracking Revisions to Your Shared Document

In Chapter 10, "Working with Large Documents," you learn about tracking revisions to your document. In a workgroup environment it's a good idea to share the document before tracking changes. This way, you can decide which changes to keep and which to discard before they are incorporated into your original document.

Working with Multiple Versions of Microsoft Word

Microsoft Word 97 has a different file format from earlier versions of Word. If your workgroup is using a combination of Word 97, Word 95/7.0, and Word 6.x for Windows, Windows NT, or the Macintosh, your workgroup can exchange documents and templates among these versions.

One way is to save Word 97 documents as earlier versions. Simply choose File, Save As, and select the appropriate type in the Save as type box. Click the Save button to finalize the save.

> **CAUTION**
>
> You must select the Save As Type of Word 2.x if you plan to import the document into Word 2.x, Word 6.x, or Word 95. Do not select the Word 95/6.0 type.

It's easy to open a document from an earlier version of Word. Just open it like you would a Word 97 document. When you save a document that has never been saved as a Word 97 document, Word 97 cautions you that some formatting may not be saved in the earlier version. If you choose to continue with the save, your document will again be saved as the earlier version. If you choose not to continue with the save, a Save As dialog box appears with the file type defaulting to Word Document (Word 97).

Several features in Word 97 are not supported in earlier versions. For a detailed list of these features, use the Office Assistant to search on "File Formats."

> **CAUTION**
>
> Word warns you about saving your document in an earlier format only the *first* time you save the earlier version. The next time you open the document or if you cancel out of the save, Word automatically saves your document in Word 97 format. Choose File, Save As to bypass this potential problem.

Another way to manage multiple versions in your workgroup is to install the Word 97 file conversion tool in the earlier versions of Word. Microsoft is making this tool available for free on its Office 97 CD-ROM.

Part **VIII**
Ch **47**

Using Workgroup Features of Excel 97

Excel has many of the same workgroup features that Word has. Like Word, you can protect workbooks with passwords and you also can share workbooks. This section points out the differences between the workgroup features of Excel and Word. Refer to the previous section, "Using Workgroup Features of Word 97," for more details.

Protecting a Workbook

Excel provides a more detailed approach to security than Word does. With Excel, you can still set a password on the file to read or to modify it. You can also protect the contents of a sheet, the objects in a sheet, the scenarios in a sheet, or the entire sheet. You can even protect the entire workbook if you want. Table 47.2 sums up these options.

As with Word, you assign file password protection when you save the document through File, Save As, Options. You assign the other password protection options through Tools, Protection. Use only the protection that you need and be careful to remember the passwords that you assign.

Table 47.2   Excel Password Protection Options

Password Feature	Results of Protection
Set password to open a workbook	Requires users to know the password before they can see the workbook.
Set password to modify a workbook	Users can open the document but need the password to save any changes.
Set workbook to read-only	Suggests to others to open the document as a read-only file.
Protect worksheet for contents	Prohibits user from making changes to cells, viewing cell formulas, or viewing hidden rows and columns.
Protect worksheet for objects	Prohibits user from making changes to any objects, embedded charts, or maps in the worksheet, or from adding or editing comments.
Protect worksheet for scenarios	Prohibits user from making changes to protected scenarios or viewing hidden scenarios.
Protect workbook for structure	Prohibits user from moving, deleting, renaming, inserting, hiding, or unhiding worksheets and recording new macros.

Password Feature	Results of Protection
Protect workbook for windows	Prohibits user from moving, sizing, or closing windows. User can, however, hide and unhide windows.

N O T E If you write any macros that will be run on a protected worksheet, include the steps necessary to unprotect the sheet prior to performing the rest of the macro. If you don't unprotect the sheet first, the macro will stop running and an error message will occur. ■

Before you embark upon adding passwords to every corner of your worksheet, ask the Office Assistant for complete information on the effects of password protection. Too much protection can make your sheet unmanageable.

Forms such as expense sheets or timesheets created in Excel are good examples of when to use protection. The sheet should be protected, but the data entry areas should be un-protected. This situation reduces calculation errors and enables one person to sum up the expense reports or timesheets much more quickly. Employees fill out the data areas of the reports. (The total fields are protected.) Then they route the sheet to their manager, who in turn routes the sheet to the accounting department or office manager.

Working with Others on a Workbook

Opening a workbook for input from and changes by other people is a great way to allow people to use the data in the workbook for their own purposes without having to re-key the information. It takes either a brave heart or a foolish head to share your workbook without any kind of protection, especially when Excel 97 provides an easy and quick way to track revisions and monitor access.

Sharing a Workbook   A workbook set up to allow more than one person to make changes to it simultaneously is a shared workbook. Without the sharing feature turned on, only the first person to access the workbook can edit it. Anyone else accessing the workbook at the same time can open the file in read-only mode. No users can save their changes until the first person exits the document.

N O T E Only Excel 97 users can make changes to a shared workbook. Earlier versions of Excel do not have this capability. ■

To establish a shared workbook, choose Tools, Share Workbook. Select the check box labeled Allow Changes by More Than One User at the Same Time.

Now that two or more people can edit the workbook simultaneously, save it in a place where other people can get to it, such as a shared network drive.

If you are editing a shared workbook, you can see who else is working on the document by choosing Tools, Share Workbook. Look in the lower box under Who Has the Document Open Now.

Shared workbooks can still maintain that personal touch. Excel 97 keeps track of each user's view filters and print settings in a personal view file. This allows you to maintain your favorite view settings, such as hidden rows or columns and filters, as well as print settings, even if someone else working on the workbook changes the settings to his or her own preference. To create a custom view, follow these steps:

1. Choose View, Custom Views from the menu bar.
2. Click the Add button.
3. Give the view a name that you can identify with the settings you've made.
4. Under Include in view, select the settings you want to save.
5. Click OK.

When you want to view your workbook using the settings you've saved, again choose View, Custom Views, but this time select the saved view from the Views box and click Show.

Resolving Conflicts   If two or more users make conflicting changes to a workbook, Excel 97 gives you two choices of what to do:

- You can have Excel prompt you to view the changes and you can decide, for each conflict, which version wins.
- You can set Excel to save your changes regardless of what the other people have done.

Select the method with which to resolve conflicts by clicking the Advanced Tab under Tools, Share Workbook, Conflicting Changes Between Users.

Tracking Changes   You can track the changes made to a workbook by choosing Tools, Track Changes, Highlight Changes. Then select the box to Track Changes While Editing. If you didn't previously enable workbook sharing and change history, this process does it for you.

Once enabled, you can view the history of all changes made since the last time the document was closed or since the last time you turned on the change history. View the changes individually by placing your cursor over the cell that has been changed. Information on the date, time, and content of the change appears along with the name of the person who made the change. If you want to view all changes at once, choose Tools, Track Changes, Highlight Changes, List changes on a new sheet. Excel will create a history sheet with a database of all changes made since you turned on change history.

N O T E The default in Excel 97 is to display only changes made "Since I last saved." To see the history of changes made since tracking was turned on, change the When option under Tools, Track Changes, Highlight Changes to All. ▪

Removing Shared Access   To remove a user from sharing a workbook while still maintaining the workbook's shared status, choose Tools, Share Workbook. From the Edit tab, select the user to remove and choose the Remove User button.

To remove the workbook's shared status, choose Tools, Share Workbook and deselect the check box labeled Allow Changes Made by More Than One User at the Same Time.

CAUTION

Removing shared access removes the version history permanently. Once shared access is disabled, other users working on the workbook are not able to save it.

Working with Multiple Versions of Microsoft Excel

Excel 95 and Excel 5.0 for Windows shared the same file format; consequently, the files created in either version were interchangeable. Excel 97 has a new format, but it includes a feature that enables you to save a file in a dual format: both Excel 97 and Excel 5.0. When you want to save a document with this dual format, choose File, Save As, and change the Save As Type to Microsoft Excel 97 & 5.0/95 Workbook. When a document that was created in Excel 97 is opened in Excel 5.0 or Excel 95, the document retains all the features embedded with Excel 97 until it is saved in an earlier format.

As with all Microsoft Office 97 products, workbooks created in an earlier version of Excel can be opened into the 97 version without any trouble.

Part
VIII

Ch
47

Using Workgroup Features of PowerPoint 97

One of the most useful tools of PowerPoint is its capability to host online conferences. You can host these conferences over the network or over the Internet.

Using the Meeting Minder

The Meeting Minder is a handy little tool that enables the presenter to take notes and schedule items during an online presentation. The Meeting Minder appears only on the presenter's screen. To use the Meeting Minder, right-click the mouse during the presentation. Then choose Meeting Minder from the shortcut menu.

You can use an Internet PowerPoint presentation for corporate brainstorming. Figures 47.5 and 47.6 display the presenter's Meeting Minder notes and action items that he is recording during the presentation. From the Meeting Minder, the presenter can Export items directly to Microsoft Outlook or Microsoft Word 97 using the Export button. He can also directly access his Outlook calendar to set appointments or schedule meetings by clicking the Schedule button.

FIG. 47.5
Meeting Minder shows presenter's action items during an online conference.

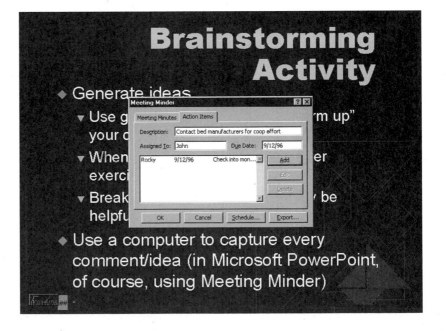

FIG. 47.6
Meeting Minder shows the presenter's notes to himself during the same Goals Planning Conference.

Using the Network for Your Presentations

You can make presentations over a local area network (LAN) or over the Internet. If you want to present your slide show over the LAN or Internet, you need to install the Microsoft TCP/IP -> Dial-Up Adapter for compatibility. Just follow these steps:

1. Double-click the My Computer icon on your desktop.

2. Double-click the Control Panel folder.

3. Double-click the Network icon.

4. If you do not see TCP/IP -> Dial-Up Adapter in The Following Network Components Are Installed box, click the Add button.

5. Click Protocol as the type of network component you want to install, and then click Add.

6. Select Microsoft from the list of Manufacturers.

7. Select TCP/IP from the list of Network Protocols.

8. Click OK, and then click OK again on the next dialog box.

After TPC/IP has been set up, follow these steps to initiate a presentation conference:

1. Choose Tools, Presentation Conference. The Presentation Conference Wizard is initiated. Click Next to continue.

2. Select Presenter and click Next.

3. Verify that the slide show content is accurate and click Next. If the content is not accurate, follow the instructions on-screen to adjust them.

4. If you will be presenting over the Internet, connect to your Internet service provider now. If you are connecting over a LAN, go on to step 5.

5. Click Next.

Part
VIII

Ch
47

6. If you are connecting over the Internet, enter the IP address provided by each user in the Computer name or Internet address dialog box. After each IP address has been entered, click Add.

   If you are connecting over a LAN, enter the computer name provided by each user in the Computer name or Internet address dialog box. After each computer name has been entered, click Add.

7. When you've finished gathering information on the participants, click Next.

8. Now, *wait*! Each participant must click Finish before you do, or the conference won't initiate. When you believe that each participant has had enough time to click Finish, you can click Finish to start the show. If you attempt to start the conference without one of the participants listed, your efforts will be thwarted. In this case, call the person who has not yet joined the conference and ask him or her to click Finish. If a person no longer wants to participate, and you find out prior to the start of the conference, simply remove him or her from the list of particpants. Click Back to return to the list of attendees. Click the name/IP address that you want to disconnect and click Remove.

 T I P After the presentation begins, right-click to access the shortcut menu. Use the Stage Manager tools to control the show.

Participating in a Conference   If you are participating in a conference and not running the show, use a slightly different method to participate:

1. Choose Tools, Presentation Conference. The Presentation Conference Wizard is initiated. Click Next to continue.

2. Select Audience and click Next.

3. Select the type of connection you will use. Click Local Area Network (LAN) or Corporate Network to view a presentation on your internal network. Click Dial-in Internet to view a presentation on the Internet. Then click Next.

4. If you selected Local Area Network in step 3, you will be shown your computer name. If you selected Dial-in Internet in step 3, you will be shown your computer's IP address. Give this name or address to the presenter to add to his list of viewers.

5. Click Finish and wait for the presentation to begin.

N O T E   If you don't click Finish prior to when the presenter clicks Finish, you won't be connected to the conference, so be quick with your click! ▪

After you are connected to the presentation conference, you have the ability to annotate slides while others watch. When you are watching the conference, right-click your mouse and select P<u>e</u>n. In place of your mouse pointer, you now have a pen that is controlled by your mouse. Simply start drawing or writing on the slide to make your annotation.

Understanding Conferencing Limitations   As you build your Internet conference, keep in mind that the PowerPoint conferencing feature has some limitations. Make sure that your presentation does not include any of these limited items:

- The audience cannot see video clips or hear audio clips or sound bites.
- The audience cannot see embedded objects.
- The audience cannot watch you edit any linked or embedded objects.

In addition, presentation conferencing is not supported over Novell NetWare local area networks.

Using Workgroup Features of Access 97

Chapter 31, "Creating a Database," contains a detailed description of Access components. This section emphasizes the items that are important in a workgroup environment.

Understanding Record-Locking Concepts

Record locking prohibits users from editing a record that someone else is already editing. This feature is essential when more than one person will be working in a database at one time. Three types of record locking are available in Access: None, Edited Records, and All Records. Be careful when using the All Records option. This locks the entire form and related datasheet, including any underlying tables until editing is complete, disallowing others from editing other aspects of the form.

You can set record locking through the RecordLocks property on forms, reports, or queries. To enable record locking, choose <u>T</u>ools, <u>O</u>ptions, and click the Advanced tab. Select A<u>l</u>l Records to lock all records in the form or datasheet and any underlying tables that you're editing. Select E<u>d</u>ited Record to lock only the record you are currently editing. <u>N</u>o Locks does not enable record locking. Refer to *Special Edition Using Microsoft Access 97* for detailed information on how to implement record locking.

Part
VIII

Ch
47

Using Workgroup Security

Unlike record locking, which you should apply to databases in any kind of multiuser environment, workgroup security should be applied only in those instances where it is relevant. Workgroup security may be necessary if the Access database is stored on a shared drive that can be accessed by more than just the workgroup users.

Two levels of workgroup security are available: database security and user-level security. Database security requires a password to open the database. Refer to Chapter 31, "Creating a Database," for information on setting a database password.

User-level security limits access to different parts of the database. Security is based on the user who is accessing the database or the groups that the user belongs to. This information is stored in a workgroup information file. With user-level security, users are asked to enter their name and password when opening a database. Use user-level security to control inadvertent changes to the modules and macros that you create in each database.

To set up user-level security, begin by identifying the workgroup for which this security will be established. See your network administrator if you have questions on defining workgroups.

Before you establish user-level security, make sure you complete the following steps:

1. Activate the logon process to avoid having all users signed in as Admin. Do this by changing Admin's password in the workgroup you are targeting. Choose Tools, Security, User and Group Accounts, and select Change Logon Password tab.

2. Create the Administrator's account (in addition to Admin). Select the Users tab from the User and Group Accounts dialog box. Click New and enter the administrator's Name and Personal ID. The Personal ID (PID) is a unique identifier for this workgroup that you create and use whenever you create a new user or group. Click OK to return to the User and Group Accounts dialog box.

3. Assign the new administrator to the Admins group and select the user you just created from the Name box. In the Available Groups box, click Admins, and then click the Add button. Click OK to accept the information and return to the database.

4. Exit Access and log back on as the new administrator.

5. Remove the Admin user from the Admins group. Choose Tools, Security, User and Group Accounts, and select the Users tab. Select the Admin user from the Name box. In the Available Groups box, click Admins, and then click the Remove button. Click OK when you finish to return to the database.

Now that you've done the preliminary steps, you can use the Tools, Security, User-Level Security Wizard to establish the user- and group-level security. The Security Wizard makes a copy of your existing database so you always have one that is not secured (in case you make a mistake). Follow the Security Wizard and set the appropriate security on each table, form, macro, query, report, and module that you want.

After you establish your security through the Security Wizard, you can go back and make changes through the Tools, Security, User and Group Permissions command.

For detailed information on setting security and the privileges granted through each permission, see *Special Edition Using Microsoft Access 97*.

Using Workgroup Features of Outlook 97

Outlook, Microsoft Office's personal information manager, combines many of the features of Microsoft Mail, Exchange, and Schedule+ into one very capable application. Chapter 45, "Using Outlook Desktop Information Manager," contains in-depth information on using Outlook, so this section focuses on the network aspects.

Sharing File Folders with Others

In addition to using public folders, as discussed earlier in this chapter, you may want to share one of your folders with just a few other people. For example, you may want to share a folder with your manager to keep her updated on the issues surrounding a project you are working on. Copy all of your mail messages to the folder. This way, your manager can see all of the problems and issues you are dealing with and be able to take a proactive approach.

N O T E Remember, to share an inbox folder in Outlook, you must be using either the Microsoft Exchange Server, the Microsoft Mail Server, or the Novell Groupwise post office. ■

To share one of your inbox folders with someone else, follow these steps:

1. If you can't see the folders, click the Folder List button on the standard Outlook toolbar, or choose View, Folder List from the menu.
2. Select the folder you want to share and right-click.
3. Click Properties and select the Permissions tab.
4. Click Add.
5. Select the name of the person(s) you want to share with, and then click OK.

Part
VIII

Ch
47

You can assign special permissions or *roles* to the shared user if you don't want them to have full access. You assign roles through the Roles dialog box.

If you are working without a postoffice or with the Exchange postoffice that comes with Windows 95, you can share a file folder on your local drive through Outlook. To share a file, follow these steps:

1. Click the Outlook toolbar and click the Other button.

2. Choose My Computer and open the local drive that contains the folder to be shared. Network drive folders cannot be shared in this manner.

3. Select subsequent folders until you reach the folder you want to share.

4. Right-click the folder and select Sharing, Shared As.

5. Enter the Share Name that your folder will be known as.

6. Select the Add button to pick the users you want to share with.

7. Click the user(s) to add from the Name column.

8. Select the button that will grant them the permissions you want them to have. Read Only allows them to read the contents of the folder but not change anything in it. Full Access gives them the ability to add to, modify, or remove anything in the folder. Custom brings up another dialog box from which you can select a combination of access rights for the person.

9. Click OK to finish.

 TIP After you have shared a folder, create a shortcut to the folder and attach it in a mail message. Send the mail to the people you're sharing the folder with. They just drag the shortcut to their desktop to have easy access to your shared folder.

Using Group Scheduling

Scheduling someone else for a meeting or scheduling a conference room is commonly requested in a workgroup environment. Just think how many times you've been asked in the hall or by phone if you can make a meeting at 1:00 with so and so. Group scheduling enables you to view other people's free and busy times and to request they attend an appointment. Recipients of your request have the option to decline the invitation or to accept it.

To invite a user to an appointment or meeting, do the following:

1. Select the Calendar view from the Outlook toolbar.

2. From the menu bar, choose Calendar, Plan a Meeting or select the Plan a Meeting button on the toolbar.

3. Choose the Invite Others button.

4. Select the names of the people you want to invite.

   Choose Required if you require the person to be there.

   Choose Optional if you would like to have the person there, but attendance is not imperative.

   If the person you want to schedule does not appear in your list of addresses, you may need to open an alternate address book from the Show Names From The drop-down list.

5. Select the Resources button to schedule an inanimate object like a conference room or overhead projector. Your workgroup administrator should have the resources set up in advance.

6. After you've selected all the users, click OK.

7. In the schedule pane at the right side of the window, you can view the times when the other attendees already have commitments.

8. Specify the Meeting start time date, which represents the first day you are open to have the meeting.

9. Specify the Meeting end time date, which represents the last day you are open to have the meeting.

10. If you know precisely what time you want the meeting to be held, use the meeting selection bars in the schedule pane at the right side of the window to select the time or enter the start time and end time for the meeting.

    The difference between the start hour and end hour should indicate the approximate length of the meeting.

TIP Use Autopick to find the next available free time for all of your attendees.

11. Choose Make Meeting.

12. In the Meeting dialog box, you can fill in a Subject line and a Location if you want.

Part
VIII

Ch
47

13. If you want to receive responses to your request, choose Appointment from the Meeting dialog box toolbar. Then select Request Responses.

14. Choose the Send button to issue the request. The meeting shows up on your calendar as a group meeting.

Figure 47.7 shows a meeting that an employee is booking on September 11, 1996, at 10:30 AM. Notice that all three people are available between 10:30 AM and 1:00 PM on 9/11/96.

FIG. 47.7
Scheduling a group meeting for 10:30 AM.

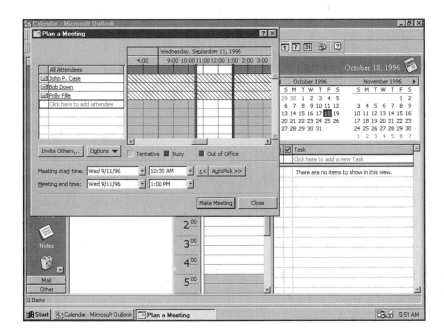

Using Voting Capabilities

Have you ever wanted just a *yes* or *no* answer to a question, or perhaps an answer limited to just certain responses? Voting gives you the ability to provide the recipients of your mail message with a button to click the answer they choose. The method is quick for the recipients, and you get the answers you want.

To send a message with voting buttons, follow these easy steps:

1. Compose a new mail message by choosing File, New, Mail Message from the Outlook Inbox menu bar.

2. Fill in the To..., Subject, and in the open box following Subject, an explanation of the voting buttons you are including.

3. Click the Options tab.

4. Select Use Voting Buttons.

5. Replace the Approve; Reject titles with the text to appear on the buttons—for example, Definitely or No Way. Separate each button title with a semicolon. You can also choose predefined text from the drop-down list on the Use Voting Buttons line.

6. Return to the message tab if you have any further message text to enter.

7. Send the message by clicking the Send button on the toolbar or by choosing File, Send from the menu bar.

At the top of the recipient's mail, the buttons appear. In Figure 47.8, the author of the message is trying to get everyone to narrow down their choices for the company picnic: Willamena's or Leapin' Frog Park. The mail message she sent has the voting choices at the top of the screen under the toolbar.

N O T E   The voting buttons will not appear in a recipient's mail unless the recipient is using Outlook for mail. ■

FIG. 47.8
You have several voting button choices.

Voting buttons—

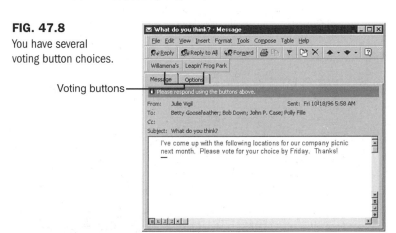

Network Administration Tips

Network administration can be a challenging feat these days. Trying to keep the machines operating at maximum speed while minimizing the desktop management and time investment is not easy. Microsoft Office provides some resources for you harried administrators.

Using Forms

Forms are another great way to minimize redundant work on your network. When you set up a form for items that you commonly e-mail, all the user needs to do is select the appropriate form, fill it in, and send it off. You can create forms in Word, Access, Excel, or Outlook for things like expense reports, time sheets, problem reports, and more. Word and Access are best used when you want to create forms that have embedded objects, drop-down lists, specific data types, and special formatting. Word even has several common forms for you to start with. Use Excel to collect information for use in calculations. Outlook forms are great for customizing mail messages and appointments, and they provide an easy way to distribute and collect information electronically.

Taking Policies into Account

Windows 95 and Windows NT both have a feature called *system policies*. System policies enable you to customize user information to configure network settings, customize the desktop, and control what access to the desktop users have. System policies must be installed through Windows 95 or Windows NT before you can use the policy settings provided by Microsoft Office. Refer to *Platinum Edition Using Windows 95* or *Special Edition Using Windows NT Server 4* for information on setting up policies.

Microsoft Office includes policy templates for Office (OFFICE97.ADM), Access (ACCESS97.ADM), and Outlook (OUTLK97.ADM). The Office policy template includes policies for Word, Excel, PowerPoint, and Office features common to all programs.

There are dozens of settings that can be established via policy templates. Tables 47.3, 47.4, and 47.5 provide a list of some of the workgroup and Internet-related items included in the policy templates.

Table 47.3 Office Policy Template Options

Policy	Default	Notes
User Templates	None	Specifies path to User Templates.
Workgroup Templates	None	Specifies path to Workgroup Templates.
Delete FTP Sites	Do not delete	Can clear first 20 ftp sites before any new sites are added.

Policy	Default	Notes
Add FTP Sites	None	Enter the ftp site names.
Web Search	None	Enter the default HTML or DOC search server address.
Help_Microsoft on the Web	None	Allows you to customize your help screens depending on URL address.
Default Save	None	Default format in which to save Word or Excel files.
Personal Toolbars	None	Provide path to personal custom toolbar in Excel.
File Locations	None	Can set the path to clip-art pictures, user options, autorecover files, tools, and startup.
Web Page Authoring	None	Many features are available under this policy topic.

Table 47.4   Access Policy Template Options

Policy	Default	Notes
Hyperlink Underline	Not underlined	
Hyperlink Address	Don't display address	
Sort Order	None	Specify default sort order for new databases
Record Changes	Don't confirm changes	
Form Template	None	
Report Template	None	
Default Record Locking	None	
Help_Microsoft on the Web	None	Allows you to customize your help screens depending on URL address.
Future File Format Converters	None	Provides an intranet site for future file format converters.

Part
VIII

Ch
47

Table 47.5   Outlook Policy Template Options

Policy	Default	Notes
Synchronize Folders	Not synchronized	Synchronizes all folders upon exiting when online.
Appointment defaults	None	Sets a default duration and reminder time for appointments.
Automatically record these items	None	Automatically enters items such as meeting cancellation, meeting request, meeting response, task request, and task response into the user's calendar.
Help_Microsoft on the Web	None	Allows you to customize your help screens depending on URL address.
Future File Format Converters	None	Provides an intranet site for future file format converters.

Identifying Commonly Shared Resources

Shared resources on your network can be anything from printers to CD-ROMs to folders to conference rooms that you are going to include in your Outlook Resource list. Identifying the components you are going to share can help you plan your network layout. Keep in mind these things when you are planning your implementation of Microsoft Office 97:

- Does your office share templates? Macros? Clip art?

  Consider setting up a network directory that all users can access to hold common files like these. You can point the user's file locations to the shared areas. Then all users have access to the same features that everyone else does.

- Is your company in an industry that has very specific wording (engineering, law, geology, and so on)?

  Perhaps you should add a custom dictionary that resides in a central location that all users can access. Have one person be responsible for updating the dictionary. This practice helps eliminate typos associated with the industry-specific wording.

■ What resources does your company use in the line of meeting rooms, overheads, white boards, VCRs, and so on, that seem to be in constant demand?

Set up these items as resources in Outlook. Then set a corporate policy to schedule all resources through Outlook. This policy eliminates any double bookings.

■ Do people on your network create more shared files than personal files?

If they do, default your users' home directories to shared data areas on the network. This eliminates the need to search for a shared area to store the file or the need to e-mail documents to multiple people.

You probably will encounter many more shared areas as you manage and maintain your network. Keep in mind some of the things this section has discussed, and keep thinking of other ways to improve your network structure. ●

Index

Broaden Your Mind
And Your Business
With Que

The *Special Edition Using* series remains the most-often recommended product line for computer users who want detailed reference information. With thorough explanations, troubleshooting advice, and special expert tips, these books are the perfect all-in-one resource.

Special Edition Using Microsoft Excel 97
- ISBN: 0-7897-0960-0
- $34.99 USA
- Pub Date: 12/96

Special Edition Using Microsoft Word 97
- ISBN: 0-7897-0962-7
- $34.99 USA
- Pub Date: 12/96

Special Edition Using Microsoft Office
- ISBN: 0-7897-0146-4
- $00.00 USA
- Pub Date: 12/96

QUE'S MICROSOFT® OFFICE 97 RESOURCE CENTER

For the most up-to-date information about all the Microsoft Office 97 products, visit Que's Web Resource Center at

http://www.mcp.com/que/msoffice

The web site extends the reach of this Que book by offering you a rich selection of supplementary content.

You'll find information about Que books as well as additional content about these new **Office 97 topics**:

- **Word**
- **Excel**
- **PowerPoint®**
- **Visual Basic® for Applications**
- **Access**
- **Outlook**™
- **FrontPage**™

Visit Que's web site regularly for a variety of new and updated Office 97 information.

The best resources and tips for getting things done with Office 97!

Microsoft® FrontPage™ 97
Web Authoring and Management Tool
with Bonus Pack

Professional Web Site Publishing Without Programming

Microsoft FrontPage 97 with Bonus Pack is the ideal way to get professional-quality Internet or intranet sites up and running fast. It offers all the best new Web technologies, plus powerful tools for all your Web creation and management tasks.

Easy for everyone.

Microsoft FrontPage 97 with Bonus Pack can quickly turn you into a Webmaster. Use more than 30 built-in templates and wizards to build entire Web sites and individual pages easily. And with the WYSIWYG FrontPage Editor, there's no need to know HTML! Insert hyperlinks and add information from Microsoft Office and other sources with drag-and-drop simplicity. And manage your Web sites easily with the graphical tools in the FrontPage Explorer.

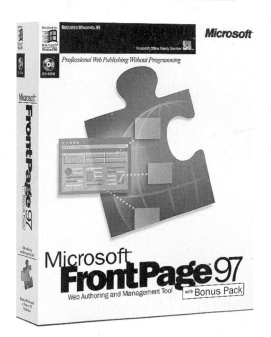

FrontPage 97 with Bonus Pack makes creating professional-quality Web sites effortless with powerful new functionality, support for the latest Web technologies, and seamless integration with Microsoft Office. It's never been easier!

The best of the Web.

The latest Web technologies are at your fingertips. Drop WebBot™ components onto your pages to add such advanced functionality as full-text searching and forms. Customize your Web sites with JavaScript™ and Microsoft Visual Basic®, Scripting Edition, using an intuitive user interface. Or easily connect to databases or add ActiveX™ controls, Java applets™, and Netscape™ plug-ins for interactive, compelling Web pages.

Professional Web site publishing is no longer just for experts!

The complete Web suite.

FrontPage 97 with Bonus Pack gives you powerful tools to create rich content and manage your Web sites effectively. Enliven your Web pages with images designed in Microsoft Image Composer, included in FrontPage 97 with Bonus Pack, or incorporate professional photographs from the Microsoft Image Composer stock photo library. Edit HTML code directly in the FrontPage Editor and preview your Web pages in any browser – without leaving FrontPage. And use advanced tools to remotely author and edit your Web sites.

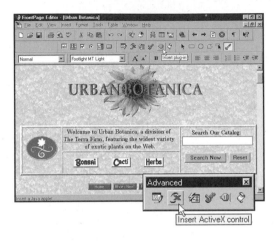

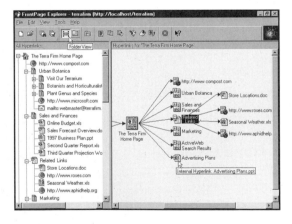

Office integration.

FrontPage 97 with Bonus Pack has a familiar environment that allows you to use any document created with Microsoft Office 97 easily because it works like other Office 97 applications. Use the shared spelling checker, global Find and Replace, and the Microsoft Thesaurus to guarantee your Web sites remain accurate and compelling.

The future of Web publishing is here today! Create and manage your Web sites the fast and easy way with Microsoft FrontPage 97 with Bonus Pack.

Visit the Microsoft Office 97 World Wide Web site at http://www.microsoft.com/office/